# The 20th Century

## 1971-2000

# Great Events from History

# The 20th Century

## 1971-2000

### Volume 5
1990-1997

*Editor*

**Robert F. Gorman**

*Texas State*

SALEM PRESS

Pasadena, California      Hackensack, New Jersey

*Editor in Chief:* Dawn P. Dawson

*Editorial Director:* Christina J. Moose
*Acquisitions Editor:* Mark Rehn
*Research Supervisor:* Jeffry Jensen
*Project Editor:* Judy Selhorst
*Manuscript Editor:* Timothy M. Tiernan
*Production Editor:* Andrea E. Miller

*Design and Graphics:* James Hutson
*Layout and Graphics:* William Zimmerman
*Photo Editor:* Cynthia Breslin Beres
*Research Assistant:* Keli Trousdale
*Editorial Assistant:* Dana Garey

*Cover photos* (pictured clockwise, from top left): Microsoft chairman Bill Gates. (AP/Wide World Photos); Handover of Hong Kong to China, July 1, 1997. (Hulton Archive/Getty Images); Palestinian activist. (AP/Wide World Photos); Russian ballet dancer, Mikhail Baryshnikov. (Andrea Comas/Reuters/Landov); Sojourner rover on Mars. (NASA); Glass pyramid entrance to the Louvre Museum. (Hulton Archive/Getty Images)

Some of the essays in this work originally appeared in the following Salem Press sets: *Chronology of European History: 15,000 B.C. to 1997* (1997, edited by John Powell; associate editors, E. G. Weltin, José M. Sánchez, Thomas P. Neill, and Edward P. Keleher); *Great Events from History: North American Series, Revised Edition* (1997, edited by Frank N. Magill); *Great Events from History II: Science and Technology* (1991, edited by Frank N. Magill); *Great Events from History II: Human Rights* (1992, edited by Frank N. Magill); *Great Events from History II: Arts and Culture* (1993, edited by Frank N. Magill); *Great Events from History II: Business and Commerce* (1994, edited by Frank N. Magill), and *Great Events from History II: Ecology and the Environment* (1995, edited by Frank N. Magill). New material has been added.

**Library of Congress Cataloging-in-Publication Data**

Great events from history. The 20th century, 1971-2000 / editor, Robert F. Gorman.
    p.  cm.
Some of the essays originally appeared in other Salem Press sets. New material has been added.
Includes bibliographical references and index.
    ISBN 978-1-58765-338-4 (set : alk. paper) — ISBN 978-1-58765-339-1 (v. 1 : alk. paper) —
ISBN 978-1-58765-340-7 (v. 2 : alk. paper) — ISBN 978-1-58765-341-4 (v. 3 : alk. paper) — ISBN 978-1-58765-342-1 (v. 4 : alk. paper) — ISBN 978-1-58765-343-8 (v. 5 : alk. paper) — ISBN 978-1-58765-344-5 (v. 6 : alk. paper)
1. Twentieth century. I. Gorman, Robert F. II. Title: 20th century, 1971-2000. III. Title: Twentieth century, 1971-2000.

D421.G6296 2008
909.82′5—dc22

2007051351

First Printing

PRINTED IN THE UNITED STATES OF AMERICA

# CONTENTS

### 1990 *(continued)*

### 1991

## 1992

# CONTENTS

## 1995

CONTENTS

## 1996

## 1997

# KEYWORD LIST OF CONTENTS

# LIST OF MAPS, TABLES, AND SIDEBARS

# AFRICA, 1993

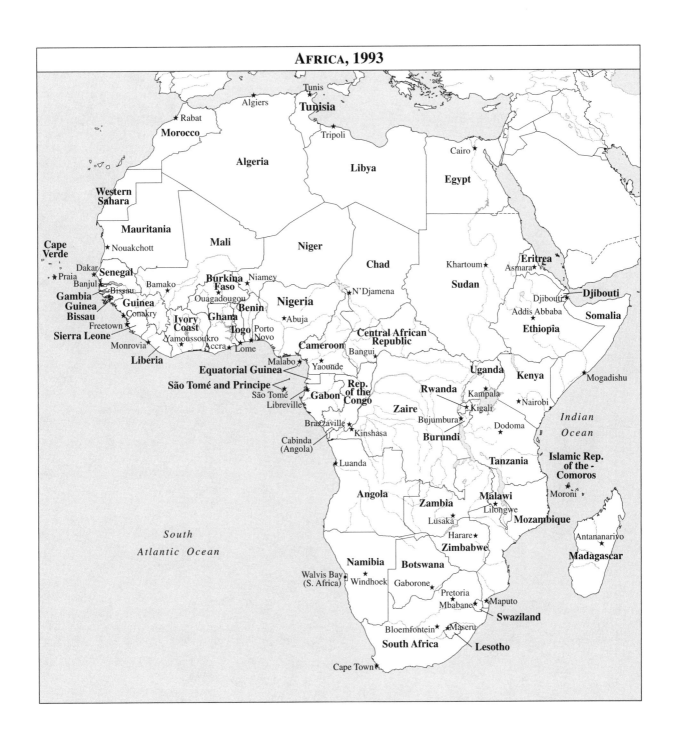

Tunis
Algiers
**Tunisia**
★ Rabat
**Morocco**
Tripoli
**Algeria**
**Libya**
Cairo ★
**Egypt**
**Western Sahara**
**Mauritania**
★ Nouakchott
**Mali**
**Niger**
**Chad**
Khartoum ★
**Sudan**
**Eritrea**
Asmara ★
**Cape Verde**
Dakar ★
★ Praia
**Senegal**
Banjul
Bissau
Bamako ★
**Burkina Faso**
Niamey ★
**Nigeria**
N'Djamena ★
Djibouti ★
**Djibouti**
**Gambia**
**Guinea Bissau**
**Guinea**
★ Conakry
Ouagadougou ★
★ Abuja
Addis Abbaba ★
**Somalia**
**Ethiopia**
Freetown ★
**Ivory Coast**
**Ghana**
**Benin**
**Togo**
Porto Novo
**Sierra Leone**
Yamoussoukro ★
Accra ★ Lome ★
Malabo
**Cameroon**
**Central African Republic**
Bangui ★
Mogadishu ★
Monrovia ★
**Liberia**
**Equatorial Guinea**
Yaounde ★
**Uganda**
**Kenya**
**São Tomé and Principe**
São Tomé
Libreville ★
**Gabon**
**Rep. of the Congo**
**Zaire**
**Rwanda**
Kampala ★
★ Nairobi
**Indian Ocean**
Bujumbura ★
Kigali
Brazzaville ★
Kinshasa ★
**Burundi**
Dodoma ★
Cabinda (Angola)
Luanda ★
**Tanzania**
**Islamic Rep. of the - Comoros**
Moroni ★
**Angola**
**Zambia**
**Malawi**
Lilongwe ★
**South Atlantic Ocean**
Lusaka ★
**Mozambique**
Harare ★
Antananarivo ★
**Zimbabwe**
**Madagascar**
**Namibia**
**Botswana**
Walvis Bay (S. Africa)
Windhoek ★
Gaborone ★
Pretoria ★
Maputo ★
Mbabane ★
**Swaziland**
Bloemfontein ★
★ Maseru
Cape Town ★
**South Africa**
**Lesotho**

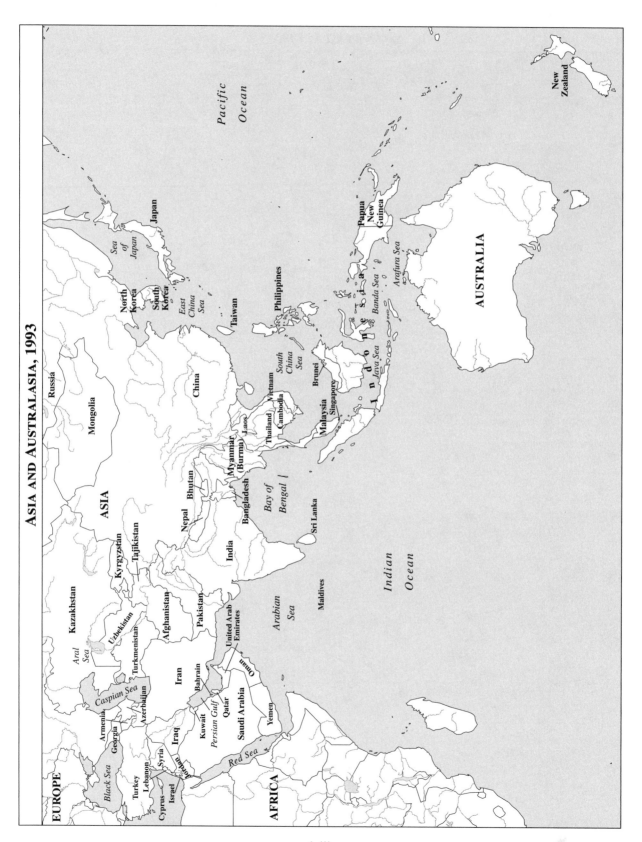

ASIA AND AUSTRALASIA, 1993

EUROPE

AFRICA

ASIA

Russia

Mongolia

Kazakhstan

Kyrgyzstan

Tajikistan

Uzbekistan

Turkmenistan

Afghanistan

Pakistan

Iran

Iraq

Saudi Arabia

Yemen

Oman

United Arab Emirates

Qatar

Bahrain

Kuwait

Persian Gulf

Syria

Lebanon

Israel

Jordan

Cyprus

Turkey

Armenia

Georgia

Azerbaijan

Caspian Sea

Black Sea

Aral Sea

Red Sea

Arabian Sea

Nepal

Bhutan

Bangladesh

India

Sri Lanka

Maldives

Bay of Bengal

Indian Ocean

China

Myanmar (Burma)

Thailand

Laos

Cambodia

Vietnam

Malaysia

Singapore

Brunei

Indonesia

Philippines

Taiwan

South China Sea

Java Sea

Banda Sea

North Korea

South Korea

Japan

Sea of Japan

East China Sea

Pacific Ocean

Papua New Guinea

Arafura Sea

AUSTRALIA

New Zealand

# EUROPE, 1993

# NORTH AND CENTRAL AMERICA, 1993

**Key to Caribbean countries (shown by number on map):**

1. British Virgin Islands
2. United States Virgin Islands
3. St. Martin
4. St. Kitts and Nevis
5. Antigua and Barbuda
6. Montserrat
7. Guadeloupe
8. Dominica
9. Martinique
10. St. Lucia
11. St. Vincent and the Grenadines
12. Grenada
13. Barbados
14. Trinidad and Tobago

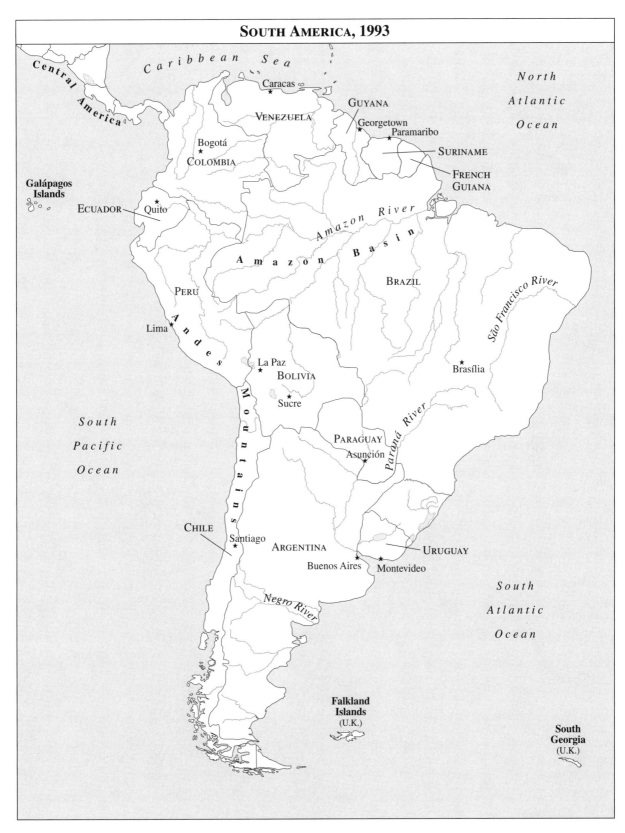

# SOUTH AMERICA, 1993

Central America

Caribbean Sea

North Atlantic Ocean

★ Caracas

GUYANA

VENEZUELA

★ Georgetown

Paramaribo
★

Bogotá
★
COLOMBIA

SURINAME

FRENCH GUIANA

Galápagos Islands

ECUADOR ★ Quito

Amazon River

Amazon Basin

PERU

BRAZIL

São Francisco River

Lima ★

Andes

A n d e s

La Paz
★
BOLIVIA

Brasília
★

Sucre
★

South Pacific Ocean

M o u n t a i n s

PARAGUAY

Asunción
★

Paraná River

CHILE

Santiago
★

ARGENTINA

URUGUAY

Buenos Aires
★

Montevideo
★

Negro River

South Atlantic Ocean

Falkland Islands (U.K.)

South Georgia (U.K.)

# The 20th Century

## 1971-2000

**April 24, 1990**
# NASA LAUNCHES THE HUBBLE SPACE TELESCOPE

*After twenty years of delays, the Hubble Space Telescope was placed in orbit around Earth by the space shuttle* Discovery.

**LOCALE:** Cape Canaveral, Florida
**CATEGORIES:** Science and technology; spaceflight and aviation; astronomy

**KEY FIGURES**
*Charles Robert Odell* (b. 1937), professor of physics and astronomy at Rice University and project scientist for the Hubble Space Telescope, 1972-1974
*Hermann Oberth* (1894-1989), German rocket pioneer

**SUMMARY OF EVENT**
When the Hubble Space Telescope (HST) was succsssfully placed in orbit 612 kilometers above the earth by astronauts aboard the space shuttle *Discovery*, one excited astronomer remarked, "At last we are out of the ocean!" His statement summarized the feelings of astronomers who have had to deal with the frustration of viewing the universe through Earth's atmosphere. No telescope can realize its full potential under 100 kilometers of atmosphere that absorbs much of the visible starlight and particularly the astrophysically important ultraviolet and infrared wavelengths. In 1923, Hermann Oberth, a German rocket pioneer, published *Die Rakete zu den Planetenräumen* (the rocket into interplanetary space), in which he proposed orbiting a telescope as a unique solution to the problem of peering through the distortion and absorption of light by Earth's atmosphere.

In 1962, a Large Space Telescope (LST), 305 centimeters in diameter, was proposed in a report of the National Academy of Sciences titled "The Future of Space Science." Ten years later, the National Aeronautics and Space Administration (NASA) established the LST headquarters at the Marshall Space Flight Center in Huntsville, Alabama, and appointed Charles Robert Odell as lead scientist for the LST project. In 1978, Congress approved the LST project; it later changed the name to the Edwin Powell Hubble Space Telescope (HST) and reduced the mirror diameter to 240 centimeters.

The HST was originally scheduled for launch on December 15, 1983, but political and technical issues resulted in delays, and the launch was rescheduled for August, 1986. Unfortunately, the space shuttle *Chal-*

*lenger* disaster in January, 1986, further delayed the HST's launch while technical problems of the launch vehicle were solved. The HST got as close as the launch pad on March 25, 1990, but again problems prevented a launch. Finally, on April 24, 1990, the hundreds of scientists and engineers associated with the project witnessed the culmination of twenty years of their work as the HST was launched into space.

The Hubble Space Telescope was by far the most ambitious and expensive scientific tool constructed up to that time. Approximately $1.6 billion had been spent on the creation of an instrument whose output was expected to alter the way humankind thinks about the universe. The technical specifications for the optics and supporting hardware pushed industrial standards of precision, innovation, and design beyond previous benchmarks of excellence. Both the technical and the organizational problems posed by building the telescope were complex. For example, scientists and engineers needed to devise a way to keep the telescope (measuring 13.1 meters long and 4.3 meters wide, and weighing approximately 11,600 kilograms, or more than 25,000 pounds) pointing toward one tiny spot in space while orbiting 611 kilometers above the earth at a speed of 27,359 kilometers per hour. Different kinds of problems were how to enlist the support of astronomers and engineers for an untried and unproved long-term project and how to organize them into a coherent team.

The HST was designed to function somewhat like an Earth-based telescope. As the HST orbits Earth, two solar panels point toward the Sun to generate energy for the telescope's scientific instruments. A door at one end of the telescope opens, and light strikes the larger (primary) mirror, which is 94.5 inches in diameter. This mirror reflects light toward the smaller (secondary) mirror, which is 12.2 inches in diameter. From there, the light is again reflected and passes through a hole in the primary mirror. The focused light is converted to an electrical signal, which is transmitted by satellite to White Sands, New Mexico, and then on to the Goddard Space Flight Center and the Space Telescope Science Institute, both of which are in Maryland.

The scientific instruments on the HST help scientists analyze the light that the telescope gathers. The instruments include a wide-field/planetary camera, a faint-object spectrograph, a high-resolution spectrograph, a high-speed photometer, a faint-object camera, and fine-

1990

*A long view of the Hubble Space Telescope flying over Shark Bay, Australia. The photo was taken from the space shuttle* Discovery. *(NASA)*

fied, scientists began planning a mission in which astronauts would repair the HST so that it would focus light as originally planned.

On December 2, 1993, seven astronauts aboard the space shuttle *Endeavour* were launched into a 575-kilometer-high Earth orbit with the mission of repairing the HST. Aboard the shuttle they carried a number of instrument packages to repair and improve the telescope, including new gyroscopes, solar panels for power generation, and two packages containing the corrective mirrors that they would add to the faulty primary mirror to bring the starlight into focus. The astronauts planned to make at least five space walks during the eleven-day mission in order to install the new and corrective devices.

The most important of these devices were the corrective mirrors, which NASA had commissioned to a small firm, Tinsley Laboratories, located behind a shopping mall in the San Francisco suburb of Richmond. Despite its low profile, Tinsley was

guidance sensors. All these instruments are modular in design so that they can be replaced in case of a system failure.

The HST was designed as part of a series of orbiting observatories dedicated to measuring many parts of the electromagnetic spectrum. The instruments on the HST make possible measurements of infrared and ultraviolet radiation as well as visible light. Other orbiting observatories in the series are the Gamma Ray Observatory, the Advanced X-Ray Astrophysics Facility, and the Space Infrared Telescope Facility.

The HST was loaded into the cargo bay of the space shuttle *Discovery* and launched into orbit from Cape Canaveral, Florida, on April 24, 1990. On the following day, astronaut Steven A. Hawley deployed the telescope by using a 50-foot mechanical arm.

Two months after the HST was deployed, astronomers discovered that the telescope's primary mirror—which had been designed at the Perkin-Elmer Corporation in Danbury, Connecticut—had been made slightly too flat, causing starlight to be out of focus; the telescope was producing fuzzy images. Once the defect was identi-

the right choice: Larger corporations such as Kodak, Hughes, and United Technologies had been unable or unwilling to meet NASA's exacting requirements for grinding the mirrors, whereas Tinsley not only ground the mirrors to within a few atoms' length of their specified dimensions but also accomplished this amazing feat well within the twelve-month schedule and at half the cost that NASA had anticipated.

The shuttle was piloted by Colonel Richard O. Covey of the Air Force and Commander Kenneth D. Bowersox of the Navy. Claude Nicollier, a Swiss astrophysicist with the European Space Agency, would be the one to operate the shuttle's mechanical arm, which would reach out to grab the telescope. The remaining four astronauts—F. Story Musgrave, a physician; Jeffrey A. Hoffman, an astrophysicist; Kathryn C. Thornton, a physicist; and Lieutenant Colonel Thomas D. Akers of the Air Force—would perform the space walks necessary to repair the telescope. They would install two new gyroscopes, replace the HST's tracking system (to enable it to point at appropriate celestial objects), replace wobbly solar arrays, and, most important, install the wide-field planetary camera and a set of new instruments—a faint-object camera and two spectrographs.

As the world watched, the spacewalkers performed the intricate maneuvers to place the instruments and make the necessary repairs over the following days. The operations went smoothly, and when the shuttle returned safely to Earth, scientists and astronauts were ecstatic; the great scientific promise of the telescope, which had been delayed for nearly four years since the launching of the HST, now seemed on the verge of being fulfilled. When the telescope began to transmit its first images in January of 1994, the incredibly clear detail astonished astronomers as well as the general public. The HST, according to the mission's chief scientist, Edward Weiler, had been "fixed beyond our wildest expectations," and James Crocker, who had overseen part of the corrective mirror project, stated of the test pictures, "These images are as perfect as engineering can achieve and the laws of physics allow."

## SIGNIFICANCE

The original HST had cost $1.6 billion; the repair mission cost $629 million. In comparison with the Superconducting Super Collider (SSC), another "basic science" project funded with taxpayers' money, these costs were reasonable: The SSC cost $2 billion before its funding was canceled in October, 1993; the Hubble Space Telescope, for about the same cost complete, delivered answers to some of the most fundamental questions about the creation and workings of the universe into the early twenty-first century. Astronomers saw objects 10 to 12 billion light-years away—almost as old as the universe itself. (A light-year is the distance light travels in a vacuum in one year, approximately 5.88 trillion miles, or 9.46 trillion kilometers.) Such sharp "vision" is comparable to seeing a firefly eight thousand miles in the distance.

The HST took pictures of "benchmark" stars that will help scientists to calculate the universe's size and shape. It provided valuable pictures of the globular cluster 47 at Tucanae, 16,000 light-years away, for example, that revealed some previously unknown white dwarf stars; another picture, of the remnants of Supernova 1987A, was extremely sharp and clear.

Some Americans have criticized the spending of federal funds on basic science in view of the nation's overwhelming budget deficit and the need for reform of health care and other basic social systems. When compared with the projected costs of such programs, however, the funds directed to the HST were minimal and

the promised returns unimaginable. The repair mission alone taught scientists and engineers much that was used on future missions that paved the way toward long-term inhabitation of space. Moreover, basic research, far from being useless, has resulted in countless useful technologies, from the lightbulb to computers.

*—Richard C. Jones*

## FURTHER READING

Chien, Philip. "The Launch of HST." *Astronomy* 18 (July, 1990): 30-37. Very readable article recounts the events that took place at the culmination of twenty years of waiting for the launch. Captures the excitement of the first tense moments and the beginning of the HST's fifteen-year mission. Well illustrated with launch and orbit photographs.

Dunkle, Terry. "The Big Glass." *Discover* 7 (July, 1989): 69-72. Presents an exciting, nontechnical account of the construction of the HST's optics. Emphasizes the personalities, skills, and dedication of the people associated with the project.

Field, George, and Donald Goldsmith. *The Space Telescope*. Chicago: Contemporary Books, 1989. Very readable discussion of the HST provides an appropriate starting place for the general reader. Well supported with illustrations, glossary, and suggestions for additional reading.

Leverington, David. *New Cosmic Horizons: Space Astronomy from the V2 to the Hubble Space Telescope*. New York: Cambridge University Press, 2000. Presents the history of space-based astronomy since World War II, devoting the final chapter to discussion of the HST. Includes illustrations, glossary, bibliography, and indexes.

Maran, Stephen P. "The Promise of the Space Telescope." *Astronomy* 18 (January, 1990): 38-43. Presents a well-written account of the main objectives and expected results of the HST.

Petersen, Carolyn Collins, and John C. Brandt. *Hubble Vision: Further Adventures with the Hubble Space Telescope*. 2d ed. New York: Cambridge University Press, 1998. Comprehensive discussion of the astronomical discoveries made possible by the HST. Includes many illustrations, glossary, bibliography, and index.

Smith, Robert W. *The Space Telescope: A Study of NASA, Science, Technology, and Politics*. New York: Cambridge University Press, 1993. Provides a detailed chronological account of the construction of the telescope from its inception to launch preparation.

1990

One of the most complete works available on the subject; includes historical background as well as discussion of the involvement of NASA, industry, and the scientific community.

**SEE ALSO:** July 31, 1973: European Space Agency Is Formed; July 20-Sept. 3, 1976: Viking Spacecraft Send Photographs to Earth from Mars; Aug. 20, 1977-

Oct. 2, 1989: Voyagers 1 and 2 Explore the Outer Planets; 1985: Construction of the Keck Telescope Begins in Hawaii; 1986: Kamiokande Neutrino Telescope Begins Operation; Dec. 2-13, 1993: Astronauts Repair the Hubble Space Telescope; Dec. 2, 1995: NASA Launches the Solar and Heliospheric Observatory; July 23, 1999: NASA Launches the Chandra X-Ray Observatory.

## May 22, 1990
# MERGING OF THE TWO YEMENS

*After extended conflict involving ideological differences and disputes over borders, North Yemen joined with South Yemen to form one nation.*

**LOCALE:** North Yemen and South Yemen (now Yemen)
**CATEGORY:** Government and politics

**KEY FIGURES**
*Ali Abdullah Saleh* (b. 1942), president of North Yemen, 1978-1990, and president of Yemen beginning in 1990
*Ali Nasir Muhammad* (b. 1939), president of South Yemen, 1978 and 1980-1986
*Ali Salim al-Baidh* (b. c. 1940), leader of the troubled South Yemen before the 1990 union

**SUMMARY OF EVENT**
Years of turmoil marked relations between the new Yemen Arab Republic (North Yemen) and the People's Republic of South Yemen following their independence in 1962 and 1967, respectively. Major political differences divided the two countries, even though both espoused leftist-leaning policies.

The Yemen Arab Republic had itself experienced a stormy birth. A civil war began in 1962 that pitted the centuries-old Zaydi imamate against insurrectionary forces led by military officers trained in Egypt with sponsorship from President Gamal Abdel Nasser. The conflict continued until, in the wake of the 1967 Arab-Israeli War (Six-Day War), Nasser decided to drop his military involvement in Yemen's civil war. Soon, a republic was declared with its capital in Sanaa.

Although the nascent Yemen Arab Republic prepared itself for socialist-oriented transformations, it did not adopt an openly ideological position. In contrast, the People's Democratic Republic of Yemen not only

emerged from a very different historical setting but also espoused a radical ideological cause that would contribute to its alignment with the Soviet Union until the final years preceding union with its neighbor.

Until the 1960's, Britain's control over the strategic port of Aden (a colony since 1937) precluded any meaningful political identity either for those living in Aden itself or for the undeveloped hinterland zones of the wider Aden protectorate. Even when measures were taken to join the colony and most of the protectorate to form the Federation of South Arabia in 1962, it was impossible to foresee that, when Britain granted independence to the federation in 1967, serious strife would follow. The first period of South Yemen's independence shifted in June, 1969, when leftist elements of the National Liberation Front carried out a coup, changing the country's name to the People's Democratic Republic of Yemen. Once a single-party system (the Yemeni Socialist Party) was installed, the new regime adopted a clear revolutionary stance.

For a number of years—indeed, off and on until 1986—tensions and military conflict pitted South Yemen against its North Yemen neighbor. Although political feuding was partly the cause for confrontation, there is no doubt that each country was set on staking claims to zones that might offer important economic development possibilities. This was especially true of areas with potential oil and mineral deposits. As early as the 1970's, talks were aimed at possible unification. Although such talks suggested that both parties understood the importance of economic considerations, it was not until a nearly disastrous economic crisis hit South Yemen that serious negotiations set in.

Internal conflicts in South Yemen peaked in 1986 with the defeat of President Ali Nasir Muhammad, who had been the first South Yemen leader to meet personally with North Yemen's president Ali Abdullah Saleh, in 1981, to discuss a possible joint constitution. Factions supporting Ali Salim al-Baidh insisted on Muhammad's exile. Muhammad chose to flee to North Yemen. For a time, his exile only heightened existing tensions, and clashes seemed imminent, not only over claims that Sanaa was arming Muhammad's supporters but also over rival claims to oil exploration rights along the contries' border in the Ma'rib-Shabwah region. Deeper confrontations were averted when, in May of 1988, negotiators agreed to set up a joint oil and mineral exploration authority. The two capitals also reopened talks aimed at reexamining proposals to draft a joint constitution and planning for eventual political union.

Surprisingly, a totally new climate emerged almost overnight, opening the way for a unity agreement that seemed to have come from the top down, solving some of the two countries' political wariness of each other but overlooking many of the basic structural necessities that unification would demand. At a popular level, however, a spirit of cooperation seemed to emerge as the two governments allowed for the first time relatively free passage of their nationals across their border. Joint talks on unification moved rapidly and a plan for legislative approval was produced within two years.

Once the unification decision was ratified by both na-

tional assemblies and announced on May 22, 1990, a very serious task lay ahead: forming institutions that would allow the new government to function effectively. At the highest level, things seemed clear enough. President Saleh was to retain presidential functions over a unified Yemen while the South Yemen president assumed tasks as Saleh's deputy. The two would switch posts after a specified time period. An appointed presidential council was charged with the job of naming a thirty-nine-member cabinet made up of appointees from both Yemens, with necessary attention to avoiding any sense of advantages gained by political groups from either of the two formerly separate countries. Finally, an interim arrangement (pending future elections) provided for joining both existing legislative assemblies into a single Council of Representatives. This body was to be supplemented by the addition of thirty-two appointees to be named by the presidential council.

Most commentators on the union alluded to future difficulties that would arise as issues of political representation took on much more complicated form. They also drew attention to less dramatic but essential factors, including practical issues of joining administrative services and education systems and, very important, forging a sense of one national identity that could incorporate diverse cultural and religious traditions that reflected centuries of distinct historical experiences.

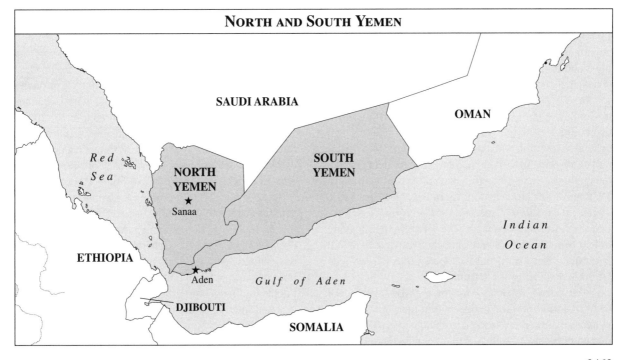

## NORTH AND SOUTH YEMEN

*Sanaa, the capital city of Yemen.* (PhotoDisc)

## SIGNIFICANCE

In many respects the main impulse behind the unity agreement had to do with South Yemen's economic failures, combined with withdrawal of aid that, for two decades, had been forthcoming from its Soviet ally. A major turning point occurred near the end of the 1980's, as the Soviet Union moved toward a policy of glasnost, or openness. This new orientation in the international sphere meant that Moscow would loosen the political and economic aid ties that had linked it to ideologically sympathetic regimes such as that of South Yemen. In 1989 and 1990, Soviet and Eastern Bloc personnel who were sent to South Yemen to assist in military, intelligence, and economic matters were repatriated, leaving only a core of technical units attached to what were still contested, nascent oil fields. As a result of the Soviet Union's distancing itself from Aden, economic conditions worsened, especially for the poorest segments of the population. Several highly placed individuals began to admit that there was a need to change internal policies that had been too closely tied to the Soviet model, which could not fit the particular local conditions of Yemeni society and its economy.

Once union was declared, political obstacles began to loom, hampering agreement concerning the best path to follow in the economic domain. Some of these obstacles stemmed from Yemen's decision to side with Iraq in the 1991 Persian Gulf War. Vital economic aid from the United States and anti-Iraq Arab neighbors, particularly Saudi Arabia, was cut when Yemen most needed it.

Other difficulties emerged as a result of labor strikes in 1991 and 1992, first in the former South Yemen and then in many other regions. Declining economic conditions inevitably led to political splits between the two main parties in the former South Yemen that had lent support to unification in 1990, the General People's Congress and the Yemeni Socialist Party. Political differences blocked important economic and military reform legislation, leaving the regime in a precarious position both internationally and internally, as army loyalties still reflected former northern and southern command structures.

—*Byron D. Cannon*

**FURTHER READING**

Al-Enazy, Askar Halwan. "The International Boundary Treaty Concluded Between the Kingdom of Saudi Arabia and the Yemeni Republic on June 12, 2000." *American Journal of International Law* 96 (January, 2002):161-173. Covers negotiations that finally ended a long historical controversy over disputed territories between the two nations.

Ismael, Tareq, and Jacqueline Ismael. *The People's Democratic Republic of Yemen: The Politics of Socialist Transformation.* Boulder, Colo.: Lynne Rienner, 1986. Political history of South Yemen up to the first unity talks.

Kostiner, Joseph. *Yemen: The Tortuous Quest for Unity,* *1990-1994.* London: Royal Institute of International Affairs, 1996. Very detailed study includes a chapter on the moves toward unification.

Mackintosh-Smith, Tim, and Martin Yeoman. *Yemen: The Unknown Arabia.* Woodstock, N.Y.: Overlook Press, 2000. Combines personal observations of Yemeni traditions with factors that have made the country politically and strategically important in the twenty-first century.

**SEE ALSO:** May 25, 1981: Saudi Arabia Establishes Gulf Cooperation Council; Jan. 17-Feb. 28, 1991: Persian Gulf War; Oct. 12, 2000: Terrorists Attack USS *Cole.*

1990

## June 8-July 8, 1990
# WEST GERMANY WINS A THIRD FIFA WORLD CUP

*The West German team won the 1990 World Cup soccer final against Argentina, a rematch of the 1986 title game. The 1990 final match, however, like the entire tournament that year, was poorly played and laden with fouls.*

**LOCALE:** Rome, Italy
**CATEGORY:** Sports

**KEY FIGURES**

*Diego Maradona* (b. 1960), captain and striker on the Argentine soccer team

*Jürgen Klinsmann* (b. 1964), striker and defender on the German soccer team

*Andreas Brehme* (b. 1960), defender on the German soccer team

*Franz Beckenbauer* (b. 1945), former soccer player who served as the German soccer team's coach

*Claudio Caniggia* (b. 1967), striker on the Argentine soccer team

*Pedro Monzón* (b. 1962), defender on the Argentine soccer team

*Gustavo Dezotti* (b. 1964), striker on the Argentine soccer team

**SUMMARY OF EVENT**

The West German soccer team's victory over Argentina in the 1990 FIFA World Cup final was the most controversial match of what, in summation, seemed to be the poorest played, lowest-scoring tournament in World Cup history. Although no single team or player was held responsible, the Fédération Internationale de Football Association (FIFA), the governing body of international soccer, reviewed its officials and its rules and made changes to both after the tournament, citing the numerous penalties and fouls in the tournament and the thoroughly conservative tactics employed by teams.

West Germany's entry into the final was earned with aggressive offense throughout the tournament. Argentina, however, hampered by injuries, suspensions, and rumors of drug use among players, showed little flair and settled on a defensive showdown with the West Germans. West Germany's victory came in the last five minutes of the match on a controversial penalty kick converted by Andreas Brehme. The rulings on the field, and extreme unsportsmanlike conduct during the tournament as a whole, overshadowed West Germany's third World Cup title, which also signaled the first victory for a European squad against a South American team in a FIFA World Cup final.

Both West Germany and Argentina came into the 1990 tournament as favorites to advance to the final match. They had previously met in Mexico City in the exciting 1986 World Cup final. Argentina's outstanding Diego Maradona commanded the field and set up both his team's 3-2 win and Argentina's second Cup title. Beginning with the 1978 tournament, of which Argentina was the host, Argentine teams were, at least, equal to their powerful neighbors and rivals to the north, Brazil. Observers and commentators expected 1990 to be no different from 1986, but rumors of Maradona's cocaine use

*Rudi Völler of the West German soccer team holds up the FIFA World Cup after his team defeated Argentina 1-0 in the World Cup final on July 8, 1990.* (AP/Wide World Photos)

and the fiery personality he exhibited while a member of club teams in Spain and Italy slightly dampened expectations. As the winners of the previous World Cup, Argentina automatically qualified for the 1990 tournament. Placed in Group B with the Soviet Union, Romania, and Cameroon, Argentina was shocked in its first match, a 1-0 loss to the African newcomers, Cameroon. Argentina recovered to beat the Soviet Union and tie Romania, scoring only three goals in the opening round. Controversy erupted during the Soviet match when Maradona visibly used his hand to knock back a near goal. The Soviets protested in vain, and Argentina won 2-0. On June 24, 1990, Argentina faced South American archrival Brazil for a second-round elimination game and won a close 1-0 match when a Maradona pass into the penalty area was headed in by Claudio Caniggia. The Argentine team advanced to the quarterfinals against Yugoslavia. Again, the match turned into a defensive affair after the dismissal of a Yugoslav player in the thirty-first minute.

Play ended 0-0. However, Argentina advanced by winning the penalty kick shoot-out 3-2. Argentina met the host country, Italy, in the semifinal match on July 3. Italy struck first, but Argentina equalized with a Caniggia goal scored off a Maradona crossing pass. Tied 1-1, the match was decided by penalty kicks, 4-3, and Argentina advanced to its fourth Cup final.

Unlike the Argentine team, West Germany, guided by legendary player-turned-coach Franz Beckenbauer, made headlines only for their skills on the pitch. Second only to the Italians in European national play and tournament victories, the West Germans had consistently fielded excellent squads since their first Cup win in 1954. Placed in Group C with Yugoslavia, Colombia, and the United Arab Emirates (UAE), the West Germans dominated, scoring ten goals in three matches. They met Holland in the second round, a game in which each team had a player dismissed for spitting, then arguing with the referee. The West Germans hung on and won a close match, 2-1, with Jürgen Klinsmann and Brehme providing goals. In the quarterfinal meeting with Czechoslovakia, the West Germans were held to a lone goal by a vigorous Czech defense. Still, they advanced to meet England for the semifinal on July 4. As expected, the match between West Germany and England showcased some of the finest soccer skills and styles. Both teams were aggressive on offense, a change from the previous defense-heavy matches. Brehme pulled the West Germans ahead on a wild, ricocheting free kick, but the English team tied the score at the eighty-minute mark. At 1-1, the match was decided on penalty kicks. The West Germans won 4-3. West Germany advanced to the final. It was West Germany's sixth final appearance in Cup history, and it was the favorite to win against the somewhat lethargic, but lucky, Argentines.

The final, held at Rome's Stadio Olímpico on July 8, was readily anticipated by both the approximately 73,600 spectators at the stadium and the millions of television viewers around the world. It was the sixth time in Cup history that South American and European teams had met for the final, and no European squad had yet defeated a South American team for the FIFA trophy. Four Argentine players, including Caniggia, Argentina's main striking forward, could not play because of yellow cards received in previous matches. Without their main scorer, Argentina fell back into a tight defensive formation, hoping to upset any West German offensive run. As the match progressed toward halftime, it was a stalemate. The aggressive West Germans ran forward, only to be stifled by the Argentine defense. The Argentines put forward no recognizable attack and managed only one shot on goal in the entire match. In the sixty-fourth minute, Argentine defender Pedro Monzón roughly tackled Klinsmann, an obvious foul. However, in a controversial call, the Mexican referee gave Monzón a red card instead of a yellow card, and he was ejected from the match—the first ejection from a final in World Cup history. Argentina played on with ten men. Then in the eighty-fourth minute, because of a rough tackle on a West German player in the penalty area, West Germany was awarded a penalty kick. Argentine players surrounded the referee, unsuccessfully pleading their case. Brehme stepped up and hammered the ball into the net, making the score 1-0 with six minutes left to play. After Brehme's goal, all order seemed lost. Argentine forward Gustavo Dezotti threw his arm around a West German player's neck, pushing him to the ground. Another red card was issued and, in the eighty-seventh minute, Dezotti became the second Argentine player ejected from the match. Argentine players gestured furiously and screamed at the Mexican referee as the West Germans stood back, attempting to regroup for the final minutes. At the final whistle, the West German bench erupted. The final score was 1-0 and West Germany accepted its third Jules Rimet trophy. Argentine players openly wept.

## SIGNIFICANCE

The controversial fouls, penalties, and inconsistent officiating in the final match, and throughout the 1990 World Cup tournament, led FIFA to review refereeing standards and practices, especially concerning tackles and awards for free kicks. After reviewing some matches, there was little doubt that certain players were diving and faking injuries in hopes of forcing the referees to call penalties against opposing squads. In future Cup play, there would be penalties for diving and stricter enforce-

ment of tackling fouls. The referees were also provided safeguards from verbally abusive players and given the power to card offending players according to the severity of their offense. Moreover, rules pertaining to time-delaying tactics, such as kicking the ball back to the goalie, were revised. FIFA declared that if the ball was kicked back to the goalie by his own teammate, the goalie could not pick it up but must use his feet to put the ball back into play. These additional rulings by FIFA, along with other changes, including the fact that goal scoring totals would be factored into advancement into the second round, forced future competitors to be increasingly mindful of offensive tactics. A reunited West and East German team and the Argentine squad both qualified for the 1994 FIFA World Cup in the United States, but there was no third meeting. Both veteran squads were eliminated prior to the semifinals.

—*Tyler T. Crogg*

## FURTHER READING

Crouch, Terry. *The World Cup: A Complete History*. London: Aurum Press, 2002. A complete analysis and record of qualifying and final round play since 1930.

MacDonald, Tom. *The World Encyclopedia of Soccer: A Complete Guide to the Beautiful Game*. New York: Lorenz, 2002. Well-referenced and illustrated guide to the worldwide professional teams and players.

Rollin, Jack. *The World Cup: 1930-1990, Sixty Glorious Years of Soccer's Premiere Event*. New York: Facts On File, 1990. Excellent resource for all matches, scores, photos, national team performances, and the fifty best players since 1930.

**SEE ALSO:** Sept. 15, 1985: Europe Takes the Ryder Cup; Nov. 9, 1989: Fall of the Berlin Wall.

1990

## June 12, 1990
# ALGERIA HOLDS ITS FIRST FREE MULTIPARTY ELECTIONS

*The municipal elections held in Algeria in June, 1990, were the first permitted by the ruling party, the Front for National Liberation, since the nation gained independence from France in 1962.*

LOCALE: Algeria

CATEGORIES: Government and politics; civil rights and liberties

KEY FIGURES

*Abassi Madani* (b. 1931), leader of the Muslim fundamentalist Islamic Salvation Front

*Ali Belhadj* (b. 1956), second in command of the Islamic Salvation Front

*Chadli Bendjedid* (b. 1929), president of Algeria, 1979-1992

SUMMARY OF EVENT

The foundations of modern Algeria were laid by the French, who occupied the country in 1830 and declared it an integral part of France in 1848. French colonists lived mainly along the Mediterranean coast, and the indigenous Muslims—Arabs and Berbers—were largely concentrated in the interior.

In November, 1954, Algerian Muslim nationalists who were organized under the National Liberation Front (known in French as the Front de Libération Nationale, or FLN) launched an armed struggle for independence against French colonialism. After nearly eight years of war that took the lives of more than one million Algerians, the FLN revolutionaries and French president Charles de Gaulle negotiated agreements that led to Algeria's independence under FLN domination in 1962. Ahmed Ben Bella, one of the revolution's leaders, was chosen president and nationalized foreign holdings. In 1965, Ben Bella was overthrown by his defense minister, Colonel Houari Boumédienne, who continued the one-party FLN socialist rule until his death in December, 1978. Boumédienne was succeeded by Colonel Chadli Bendjedid, who was known as a pragmatist and a compromise leader.

Algeria's evolution to secularism, before and after independence in 1962, is largely attributable to French cultural influence. During the colonial era, the French had become a dominant factor in every aspect of Algerian society. As late as 1990, French television and radio programming was widely seen and heard in Algeria, and numerous Algerians traveled freely to France. Nevertheless, despite French secular influence and rapid industrial growth during the 1960's and 1970's, large segments of the population had become disenchanted with the FLN under Bendjedid, with the economic decline, and with the government's sociopolitical policies. In October, 1988, after food shortages led to large-scale riots, the ruling FLN was pressured to surrender its monopoly on power and institute democratic reforms. During the riots, thousands of young protesters had been wounded and at least one hundred were killed. A new Algerian constitution was approved on February 23, 1989, opening the way to a multiparty political system.

On June 12, 1990, the country's first free municipal election took place. Eleven political parties participated in this historic event, chief among which were the FLN; the religious fundamentalist Islamic Salvation Front (in French, Front Islamique du Salut, or FIS), led by Abassi Madani, a professor of philosophy, and his second in command, Ali Belhadj; and the secular Rally for Culture and Democracy (RCD). The results were stunning: The FIS won a majority of the municipal seats in the country's four largest cities—Algiers, Oran, Constantine, and Annaba. The FIS received 65 percent of the popular vote and won 55 percent of fifteen thousand municipal posts throughout Algeria. It won representation in thirty-two of the forty-eight provinces.

In part, support for the FIS was influenced by a growing admiration in the Arab-Muslim world for Islamic fundamentalist leaders in the wake of the revolution in Iran in the late 1970's and the parliamentary victory achieved in 1990 by the Muslim Brotherhood in Jordan, not to mention political gains achieved by such forces in Turkey, Tunisia, and Morocco. Economic factors, however, were equally if not more crucial. When asked what motivated them to support the FIS, numerous voters responded that they backed the Islamists out of revenge against the FLN. *The New York Times* reported on June 25, 1990, that many Algerians used the vote to protest against low salaries, spiraling inflation, and promotions that were given only to those with connections to the FLN. Many contended that the economic choices for young people in Algeria during the 1980's and in 1990 were limited: to remain unemployed and celibate because jobs were unavailable and apartments in short supply, to work in the *trabendos* (black markets) and risk being arrested, to try to emigrate to France to sweep the streets of Paris and Marseilles, or to join the FIS and vote for Islam.

In other words, it should not be ruled out that the vote for the fundamentalists was less a massive support for the FIS than a reaction against what voters regarded as the FLN's record of authoritarian rule and economic mismanagement and corruption. Whether they agreed with the FIS or not, many Algerians, it seems, were content in 1990 with the difference the free ballot had made in their lives. In Algiers, the sense of enthusiasm after the elections was similar to that usually manifested in the wake of a national revolution.

Its electoral successes notwithstanding, the FIS was somewhat vague from the outset about its objectives. It is known, however, that Abassi Madani struck an alliance with local merchants and espoused a free market economy to replace the FLN's state socialism. Both Madani and Belhadj described a woman's primary role as rearing a family and supported limiting women's employment to jobs such as nursing and teaching. The local and provincial municipal councils, which serve five-year terms, have jurisdiction over such matters as renewal of liquor licenses, the types of activities allowed at cultural centers, and the issuance of permits to build mosques. Madani and Belhadj vehemently opposed public drinking, any form of dancing, and secular programming in the media.

Ethnically, the backing of the FIS came from the Arab population, which constituted at least 70 percent of the total Algerian Sunni Muslim population of approximately 25 million. The Berber Muslims, as well as the ethnically mixed Arab-Berber populations, were not necessarily behind the FIS. Both the FLN and FIS had been challenged by the Kabyles, members of the largest, most important Berber tribe. As French colonial rule was drawing to an end during the early 1960's, Kabyle bands carried out the most daring assaults on the French. After 1962, the Kabyles also confronted the Algerian FLN regime in the name of their Berber heritage, demanding political freedom and the kind of administrative autonomy the Kurds in Iraq sought from Saddam Hussein. Their party, the Rally for Culture and Democracy, gained 8 percent of the municipal vote in the June 12, 1990, elections, but the potential for increased electoral support among Berbers was possible once national and parliamentary elections took place. Their attachment to Berber culture and opposition to the advocacy for greater Arabization by the Arab majority threatened to increase political turmoil.

The political headway made by the FIS, Berber cultural and political reaffirmation, and the proliferation of political parties during and immediately following the 1990 elections prompted political observers in Algeria and the Arab world to speculate whether the FLN regime, which still controlled the parliament, the cabinet, the army, and the media, would react to its electoral setbacks by suppressing the freedoms it had granted to the opposition from 1988 to 1990. In fact, when Madani urged the government to permit national and parliamentary elections to take place, the regime in the summer of 1990 did not rule out such a possibility but evinced concern, warning that it would reject attempts to bring Islam back to an era of political opportunism.

### SIGNIFICANCE

The historic event of free elections and their outcome in Algeria hardly evoked enthusiasm in the West and in secular Algerian or other Arab circles. On the contrary, great concern arose regarding the political and social stability of the country. In France, political extremists such as Jean-Marie Le Pen, leader of the French National Front, warned that the French government would have to contend with the integration of many more thousands of Algerians who opposed the FIS and might flee Algeria out of fear that an Islamic regime would emerge there.

Political moderates in Europe also feared that the rise of the FIS would pose a grave population problem for the Mediterranean countries of Western Europe, which in the late 1980's had struggled to absorb an estimated four million legal and illegal North African immigrants. It appeared to Western diplomats and to moderate Middle Eastern and North African regimes that the democratic movement in Algeria produced something radically different from what it had produced in Eastern Europe and Latin America: a brand of anti-Western Muslim fundamentalism. The FIS, the beneficiary of democratic elections, paradoxically did not believe in democracy and freedom.

General parliamentary elections were scheduled for June 27, 1991, one year after the municipal elections had partially reshaped Algerian political life. During that year, more political parties and movements mushroomed in the country, challenging the FLN and the FIS simultaneously. One such party was the Socialist Forces Front (FFS), led by Hocine Ait Ahmad, a hero of the 1954-1962 war of liberation against the French. Many years before, Ahmad had turned against the FLN, leading running battles against the regime. Moreover, as the campaign of strikes and demonstrations led by the FIS intensified in May and early June of 1991, the authorities imposed martial law on June 5, and the elections did not take place as scheduled.

1990

2469

On Sunday, June 30, Madani and Belhadj were arrested after questioning the need for continued martial law and calling for immediate parliamentary elections. The headquarters of the FIS in Algiers was surrounded by the National Guard. Before his arrest, Madani urged his supporters to confront the authorities for having violated the basic political freedoms granted the year before.

*The New York Times* reported on July 2 that upon arresting Madani and Belhadj, the Algerian military charged them with "armed conspiracy against the security of the state" and said they would face trial. Since the beginning of demonstrations and clashes two months earlier, forty people had been killed and more than three hundred wounded. The army had arrested at least seven hundred people in a systematic roundup of political opponents. This was only the beginning of a long period of full-fledged insurgency as the FIS turned to violence against military rule and often against innocent civilians. In the period 1992-1998, which was the active phase of the rebellion, an estimated one hundred thousand people were killed, many in indiscriminate and brutal massacres by FIS extremists.

From 1998 to 2000, the government gradually suppressed the resistance, and the armed branch of the FIS disbanded in January, 2000, although sporadic violence continued. Abdelaziz Bouteflika was installed as president in 1999 after a dubious election, but he won reelection by a wide margin in 2004. Although greater stability had been achieved by then, Algeria still faced serious economic and social problems, an ongoing Berber autonomy movement, and an uncertain future. Even given the uncertainty remaining, however, it is clear that the 1990 municipal elections raised expectations among Algeria's once-dormant political forces.

*—Michael M. Laskier*

## FURTHER READING

Beck, Eldad. "The Kabyle Factor: The 'Kurds of Algeria' Lead Parallel Bids for Berber Rights." *Jerusalem Report Magazine* 2 (June, 1991): 32-33. Presents a concise, informative analysis of the impact of the 1990 elections and their aftermath.

Bennoune, Mahfoud. *The Making of Contemporary Algeria: 1830-1987.* 1988. Reprint. New York: Cambridge University Press, 2002. One of the most comprehensive histories of Algerian political, social, and industrial development available. Provides thorough discussion of the period of French colonial rule and events since independence in 1962 through the Bendjedid era. Includes tables and index.

Entelis, John P. *Algeria: The Revolution Institutionalized.* Boulder, Colo.: Westview Press, 1986. Focuses on the successes achieved, especially by the Boumédienne regime (1965-1978), in promoting economic and industrial expansion as well as a standard of living superior to other Arab nations. Presents an overly optimistic analysis of internal domestic affairs, precluding changes in the status quo.

Gordon, David C. *The Passing of French Algeria.* London: Oxford University Press, 1966. Standard history in English of the Algerian revolution, its aftermath, and FLN rule. Analyzes the internal upheavals of the newly instituted socialist political and economic systems and delves into the major issues faced by the young leadership during the 1960's.

Knauss, Peter R. *The Persistence of Patriarchy: Class, Gender, and Ideology in Twentieth Century Algeria.* New York: Praeger, 1987. Extensive study of Algerian internal affairs and political hierarchies provides general context for understanding of the 1990 elections. Includes bibliography and index.

Martinez, Luis. *The Algerian Civil War, 1990-1998.* Translated by Jonathan Derrick. New York: Columbia University Press, 2000. Presents an interpretive history of the war between Islamic forces and the Algerian military. Includes chronology, map, bibliography, and index.

Quandt, William B. *Revolution and Political Leadership: Algeria, 1954-1968.* Cambridge, Mass.: MIT Press, 1969. One of the best works in English on the Algerian political system under Ahmed Ben Bella and Houari Boumédienne, by one of the world's leading Middle East experts. Includes comprehensive bibliography and index.

Willis, Michael. *The Islamist Challenge in Algeria: A Political History.* New York: New York University Press, 1996. Presents a comprehensive study of the role of Islam in contemporary Algerian politics. Particularly informative concerning the period 1990-1996. Includes glossary, bibliography, and index.

**SEE ALSO:** 1990's: Algeria and Egypt Crack Down on Islamic Militants.

**June 12, 1990**

# LAWSUITS AGAINST MOBIL DRAW ATTENTION TO "GREEN" MARKETING

*When Mobil Corporation was sued for falsely claiming that its Hefty garbage bags were degradable, the lawsuits initiated a trend toward greater accountability in "green" marketing practices.*

**LOCALE:** United States
**CATEGORIES:** Laws, acts, and legal history; marketing and advertising; environmental issues

**KEY FIGURES**

*Hubert H. Humphrey III* (b. 1942), attorney general of Minnesota and director of the State Attorneys General Task Force, which led the action against Mobil Corporation

*Janet D. Steiger* (1940-2004), chair of the Federal Trade Commission

**SUMMARY OF EVENT**

The 1990's may ultimately be designated as the environmental decade. In 1990, the second Earth Day was celebrated by millions of people in the United States and abroad. The early years of the decade also heralded a coming-of-age for environmental groups and a growing recognition by business that the environment is important to most people. Polls conducted by respected organizations revealed not only that people were increasingly interested in and apprehensive about the state of the environment but also that a significant number were willing to put money behind their concerns. For example, a 1990 poll found that 78 percent of consumers were willing to pay 5 percent more for products that were environmentally safe.

Businesses in the United States were not far behind in recognizing the importance of being environmentally aware. They began expressing environmental concern in several important ways, not the least of which was the introduction of new or reshaped products that claim many environmentally responsible characteristics. In 1985, only 0.5 percent of new products introduced by business made environmental or "green" claims. By 1990, the figure had increased to more than 9 percent, and it was reported that in the first half of 1993, the proportion of new products making green claims had increased to nearly 13 percent.

Environmental claims came to be prominently displayed on many commonly purchased household products, such as laundry detergents, paper products, and lightbulbs. A careful look at the shelves of the local gro-

cery store or supermarket, however, reveals differences between the environmental claims of the early 1990's and later claims. After the early 1990's, the packaging claim "Degradable upon exposure to the elements" was replaced by the more carefully worded "Degradable within a short period when disposed of in its customary manner." The 1990 claim of "Recyclable" on a product was adjusted by the mid-1990's to "Recyclable—Check to see if recycling facilities exist in your area." The earlier claim "Ozone-friendly" was replaced by something like "This product is 95 percent less damaging to the ozone layer than past formulations that contained CFCs (chlorofluorocarbons)."

The continued increase in environmental, or green, claims on the part of manufacturers was the result of the sustained conclusion by business executives that what is good for the environment can be good for business. The greater precision in labeling that took place over time is attributable to increased government action on both the state and federal levels, supported by consumers, businesses, and environmental activist groups.

At the national level, the Federal Trade Commission (FTC) is the principal agency charged with restraining deceptive advertising, and most states have deceptive-trade laws modeled after FTC guidelines. Although the agency was established in 1914, it was not until an amendment in 1938 that the FTC was charged with protecting consumers from deceptive advertising. The FTC did little with respect to environmental claims for products before the early 1990's in part because of a lack of scientific agreement about what was bad for the environment and in part because of political circumstances. During the late 1970's, a move toward deregulation of business in the United States was reflected by a noticeable cutback in rule making at the FTC. During the 1980's, the deregulation atmosphere of the late 1970's was heightened by the elections of Ronald Reagan and George H. W. Bush to the presidency. The arrival of these two Republican administrations dampened whatever enthusiasm employees of the FTC might have had for an active policy on environmental marketing assertions.

It was into this vacuum that a group of nine state attorneys general stepped when they formed the State Attorneys General Task Force in late 1989. The task force, headed by Hubert H. Humphrey III (attorney general of

1990

## FTC GUIDANCE ON GREEN MARKETING

*In its "Guides for the Use of Environmental Marketing Claims," first issued in 1992, the Federal Trade Commission includes helpful examples to clarify each of the guidelines presented, as this excerpt illustrates.*

**Overstatement of environmental attribute:** An environmental marketing claim should not be presented in a manner that overstates the environmental attribute or benefit, expressly or by implication. Marketers should avoid implications of significant environmental benefits if the benefit is in fact negligible.

*Example 1:* A package is labeled, "50% more recycled content than before." The manufacturer increased the recycled content of its package from 2 percent recycled material to 3 percent recycled material. Although the claim is technically true, it is likely to convey the false impression that the advertiser has increased significantly the use of recycled material.

*Example 2:* A trash bag is labeled "recyclable" without qualification. Because trash bags will ordinarily not be separated out from other trash at the landfill or incinerator for recycling, they are highly unlikely to be used again for any purpose. Even if the bag is technically capable of being recycled, the claim is deceptive since it asserts an environmental benefit where no significant or meaningful benefit exists.

*Example 3:* A paper grocery sack is labeled "reusable." The sack can be brought back to the store and reused for carrying groceries but will fall apart after two or three reuses, on average. Because reasonable consumers are unlikely to assume that a paper grocery sack is durable, the unqualified claim does not overstate the environmental benefit conveyed to consumers. The claim is not deceptive and does not need to be qualified to indicate the limited reuse of the sack.

*Example 4:* A package of paper coffee filters is labeled "These filters were made with a chlorine-free bleaching process." The filters are bleached with a process that releases into the environment a reduced, but still significant, amount of the same harmful by-products associated with chlorine bleaching. The claim is likely to overstate the product's benefits because it is likely to be interpreted by consumers to mean that the product's manufacture does not cause any of the environmental risks posed by chlorine bleaching. A claim, however, that the filters were "bleached with a process that substantially reduces, but does not eliminate, harmful substances associated with chlorine bleaching" would not, if substantiated, overstate the product's benefits and is unlikely to be deceptive.

original nine), plus Tennessee—issued the Green Report in 1990. This was followed by Green Report II, published in 1991, as the task force grew to include eleven attorneys general (the additional state was Florida). The 1990 Green Report offered an overview of the problem and guidelines for environmental marketing claims. In Green Report II, the task force made some changes in the original recommendations after conducting hearings for comments from industry, environmental groups, and consumers.

Media and public attention was drawn to the State Attorneys General Task Force when seven of the nine original members filed lawsuits in their states against Mobil Corporation on June 12, 1990. The suits challenged Mobil's claim that its Hefty trash bag was degradable even if buried in a landfill. Controversy remains over what initiated the series of suits against one of the nation's largest companies, but there is agreement about some facts. Mobil launched its restaged Hefty degradable product line in the summer of 1989 after being beaten to store shelves by its major competitor, First Brands, the manufacturer of Glad Bags. The introduction of the degradable Hefty bags represented a turnabout in company policy for Mobil, which had for some five years vigorously argued against the potential of degradability as an ecological cure for the plastics industry. This view was promulgated through symposia conducted around the country in the summer of 1988.

Essentially, Mobil took the same position as the U.S. Environmental Protection Agency (EPA), that the solution to the country's problem with solid-waste disposal would best be found in source reduction, recycling, incineration, and selective landfilling rather than in degradability. At one seminar held in Chicago in 1988, Robert Barrett, appointed as Mobil's head of solid-waste management, declared that although degradable plastics would not solve the solid-waste problem, there was public relations value to marketing them. By the fall of 1988, Mobil responded to marketplace pressure and introduced a degradable product.

Minnesota and son of the late senator and vice president), was created to study the trend toward increased green advertising, to learn the extent to which this advertising was deceptive, and to suggest appropriate policy for state and federal governments regarding such advertising.

Shortly after formation of the initial task force, ten states—California, Massachusetts, Minnesota, Missouri, New York, Texas, Utah, Washington, and Wisconsin (the

By 1990, however, there was growing awareness among environmentalist groups that manufacturers' claims of degradability were not justifiable. In late 1989, the Environmental Defense Fund called for a consumer boycott of companies that were making degradability claims for their plastic products. Both Mobil and its principal competitor, First Brands, were on the boycott list. The FTC and the State Attorneys General Task Force asked both companies for substantiation of their claims. By March, 1990, Mobil voluntarily decided to remove all references to degradability from the Hefty packaging. Nevertheless, on June 12, 1990, seven suits against Mobil Corporation were brought by the attorneys general from California, Massachusetts, Minnesota, New York, Texas, Washington, and Wisconsin. The charge was deceptive advertising and consumer fraud concerning Mobil's degradability claims for its Hefty product line.

Mobil settled with Texas later in June, and one year later, Mobil settled with the other states by agreeing to remove the offending claims from its packaging and paying each of the six states $25,000 as a donation to help develop national standards for environmental marketing. On February, 1, 1993, the FTC issued a decision and order notice to Mobil that, among other things, required the company to stop using claims of "degradability" or similar terms in marketing its plastic bags and prohibited the company from making any claims of environmental benefit when such bags are used to dispose of trash in a sanitary landfill.

### SIGNIFICANCE

The Mobil case coincided with the publication of the first Green Report, followed in less than one year by Green Report II and the issuance of the Federal Trade Commission's "Guides for the Use of Environmental Marketing Claims" in July, 1992. The Mobil case helped to focus debate on the issue of environmental advertising by business. At issue was the ability of the unfettered marketplace to respond to the clear call by consumers for products that were less damaging to the environment.

Consumers wanted products that were not only environmentally safe but also priced competitively, with no loss of product quality. Initially, businesses were caught in a dilemma. They needed to respond to consumer demands in order to remain competitive, but the state of scientific understanding of the environmental impacts of many materials and products was debatable. The promise of degradability provided a case in point. Could plastic be altered in a way that would hasten its degradability when exposed to the elements? Mobil thought so and fur-

ther believed that, once the degrading process started, it would continue even when the plastic was disposed of in a sanitized landfill. In the course of little more than one year, the conventional wisdom about the degradability of plastic changed radically.

By 1991, there was a consensus among manufacturers and retailers that a set of national guidelines should be issued under the auspices of the FTC. Business groups joined with the State Attorneys General Task Force in calling for issuance of voluntary guidelines. The problems faced and the issues raised were straightforward. There was the desire to reverse years of environmental neglect. Businesses, through their role as providers of goods and services to the consuming public, and motivated by profit, would modify their production processes to be more environmentally benign once consumers started paying attention to the environmental attributes of the goods and services bought. There existed a wide range of opinion about what was good and what was bad for the environment. For example, are disposable diapers more or less environmentally benign than cloth diapers, once the environmental costs of growing cotton and using energy to deliver and wash diapers are factored in? In the face of scientific uncertainty, the typical consumer is considered to be even less informed.

Lack of information leads to the problem that is created by the ability of a company to sway an uninformed consumer through advertising that is not deceitful but is misleading or irrelevant. The claim of recyclability is often misleading because most products or packages have another use. Most packaging is recyclable in some way, but the cost and labor involved may be prohibitive. In the first years of the 1990's, some paper cups carried the packaging label "Contains no CFCs." The claim was irrelevant, because chlorofluorocarbons are not used in the production of paper cups. Customers must be informed if they are to make appropriate choices. A further issue is the appropriate source of consumer information.

By the mid-1990's, U.S. policy embraced a hybrid approach—both state and federal, both governmental and private—to consumer information. The FTC issued national voluntary guidelines for environmental claims about products. Generally less strict than those published in Green Report II, the FTC guides give broad limits, stating that claims should be "substantiated," "clear," and "not overstated." The guidelines discuss eight commonly used environmental claims and their derivatives, such as "degradability," "recyclable," and "ozone safe," and present numerous examples to illustrate the general

1990

2473

principles as applied to specific cases. States have continued to enforce their particular statutes whether or not these conform to the FTC guides and those contained in Green Report II, but there has been a trend toward increased standardization.

Private organizations have made steps toward environmental certification. Some industrial associations and retail grocery store chains have attempted to develop their own programs for environmental evaluation and promotion. In addition to these industry-specific programs, a more encompassing approach has been taken by two nonprofit organizations operating in the United States. Green Seal, started in 1990, awards a seal to products that meet the group's standards for a number of environmental attributes. Companies awarded the seal pay a license fee based on the cost of certification and monitoring. Scientific Certification Systems (SCS) began operations by verifying manufacturers' claims about single attributes, but since 1991 it has offered an environmental seal based on a product's total environmental impact using a life-cycle analysis model.

Green marketing can have positive effects on the environment if consumers are provided with accurate and meaningful information. Since the beginning of this trend in marketing, observers have increasingly come to believe that such information will be reliably available only with national regulation of claims. More experience with the results of the hybrid approach to environmental claims is likely to initiate a new phase of marketing guidelines that will include greater emphasis on standard setting at the national level and enforcement at both state and federal levels of government, with private organizations playing a large role in the monitoring of environmental claims.

*—Richard R. Bryant*

## FURTHER READING

Coddington, Walter. *Environmental Marketing: Positive Strategies for Reaching the Green Consumer.* New York: McGraw-Hill, 1993. One of the best resources available on the subject. Provides an account of environmental marketing from the perspective of protecting the environment for children. Chapter 4 presents an overview of national, state, and local environmental organizations. Includes informative appendixes.

Lawrence, Jennifer. "The Green Revolution: Mobil." *Advertising Age* 62 (January 29, 1991): 12-13. The article most often cited regarding the story of the 1990 lawsuit against Mobil for deceptive advertising. Em-

phasizes the circumstances that led to the suit and the surrounding controversy.

Ludwig, Dean C., and Judith A. Ludwig. "The Regulation of Green Marketing: Learning Lessons from the Regulation of Health and Nutrition Claims." *Business and Professional Ethics Journal* 11 (Fall, 1993): 73-91. Uses the nutritional marketing of food products in the 1980's as a case study in green marketing. Analyzes regulatory responses of the FTC and the U.S. Food and Drug Administration during the 1980's to suggest directions for regulatory action with respect to green marketing in the 1990's.

O'Reilly, James T. "Environmental Product Certification: The Legal Implications of Green Endorsements." *Journal of Environmental Law and Litigation* 8 (1993): 199-220. Presents a good discussion of the pros and cons of relying on private environmental certification. Expresses pessimism about the long-term effectiveness of private certifiers.

Ottman, Jacquelyn A. *Green Marketing: Opportunity for Innovation.* 2d ed. Lincolnwood, Ill.: NTC Business Books, 1998. Discusses practical options for green marketing and offers two case studies. Includes bibliography and index.

Tarsney, Peter J. "Regulation of Environmental Marketing: Reassessing the Supreme Court's Protection of Commercial Speech." *Notre Dame Law Review* 69, no. 3 (1994): 533-574. Reviews the issue of First Amendment rights as applied to commercial speech and concludes that the Supreme Court in 1993 raised commercial speech to a level of protection that would likely make many state environmental laws unconstitutional. Devotes a special section to analysis of the California law.

Wasik, John F. *Green Marketing and Management: A Global Perspective.* Malden, Mass.: Blackwell, 1996. Presents an enthusiastic view of green marketing's profitability for business. Includes many examples of companies that balance corporate and environmentalist goals. Includes glossary, bibliography, and index.

**SEE ALSO:** 1971: Federal Trade Commission Begins to Endorse Comparative Advertising; May 18, 1971: U.S. Advertising Industry Organizes Self-Regulation; Oct. 1, 1972: Oregon Bans Nonrefillable Bottles; Oct. 21, 1976: Sears Agrees to an FTC Order Banning Bait-and-Switch Tactics; Nov., 1978: FTC Conducts Hearings on Ads Aimed at Children; Mar.-May, 1987: Garbage Barge *Mobro* Cruises U.S. Atlantic and Gulf Coasts.

# June 21, 1990
# MASSIVE QUAKE ROCKS IRAN

*When a deadly earthquake struck northwestern Iran, killing some forty thousand people and destroying hundreds of towns and villages, nations around the world rushed to provide aid, even though Iran's strained relations with some governments made delivering such aid difficult.*

**ALSO KNOWN AS:** Rudbar-Tarom earthquake
**LOCALE:** Provinces of Gīlān and Zanjān, Iran
**CATEGORY:** Disasters

**KEY FIGURE**

*Hashemi Rafsanjani* (b. 1934), president of Iran, 1989-1997

**SUMMARY OF EVENT**

Iran is no stranger to devastating earthquakes; such disasters have occurred far back into the country's history, and a large number took place during the twentieth century. In 1981, the town of Golbaf was destroyed by a quake that killed more than one thousand persons. In February, 1997, about one thousand lives were claimed by an earthquake in northwestern Iran, only to be followed three months later by the loss of more than fifteen hundred lives in a quake in an area of eastern Iran.

The worst earthquake in Iran since one in 1978 that claimed twenty-five thousand lives occurred in the same region, northwest Iran near the Caspian Sea, at 12:30 A.M. on Thursday, June 21, 1990 (about 5:00 P.M. eastern daylight time on Wednesday, June 20, in the United States). The quake registered magnitudes of 7.3 and 7.7, respectively, on the Richter scale in Iran and the United States. It lasted for more than a minute and struck an area of some forty thousand square miles that was populated by Azerbaijani Turks, Gīlānis, Mazandaranis, Kurds, and Persians. The epicenter was identified as being under the Caspian Sea, near the Soviet city of Länkärän. Even in the Iranian capital of Tehran, about 250 miles to the east, there were reports of windows blown out of some buildings.

In the days immediately following the disaster, the earthquake's toll of lives was placed at about twenty-five thousand, with tens of thousands more injured. It became clear that these numbers would rise significantly as relief teams moved in to search for the dead and wounded. The quake had brought down a mountain, destroying hundreds of towns and villages. Aftershocks, mudslides, and flooding precipitated by damaged dams hampered res-

cue efforts. In addition to the dead and the injured, more than half a million people were rendered homeless.

The areas worst affected were the coastal province of Gīlān and the inland province of Zanjān. The region, considered the "breadbasket" of Iran, had a population of about four million. In Rudbar, 90 percent of the town and the surrounding area was leveled; 70 percent of the buildings in the towns of Manjil and Loushan collapsed. According to initial reports, at least fifteen hundred persons were killed and three thousand were injured in Taram-e Oleya in the province of Zanjān. All of the houses in Abbar and Bouin were destroyed, and virtually every resident in these towns was killed or injured. More than seven hundred villages were razed to the ground, and as many as one hundred villages were without drinking water or electricity and were cut off from help. Planes and helicopters were made available to take at least some of the wounded to Tehran. The Islamic equivalent of the Red Cross, the Red Crescent, sent in large supplies of tents, blankets, and food, but relief workers had difficulty reaching some rural areas to distribute the supplies.

As days passed by, the death toll rose to about forty thousand, making the Rudbar-Tarom earthquake the deadliest in Iran up to that time. The death toll might have been even higher had it not been for the fact that when the quake hit, many residents who ordinarily would have already retired for the night were not in bed because they had stayed up to watch the World Cup soccer match between Brazil and Scotland on television. Also, in a number of rural areas, villagers often slept out in the open, away from their houses, on the hot summer nights.

At an emergency meeting of the Iranian cabinet, a special earthquake office was set up, and the government announced that it would accept aid from any source, including countries (except Israel and South Africa) that did not have diplomatic relations with Iran. A three-day period of national mourning was declared.

In addition to messages of sympathy, many nations sent equipment, food, and other supplies to Iran, including the United States, France, Iraq, Switzerland, and Japan. The message from the United States offering condolence as well as humanitarian assistance was delivered by another, unidentified, country, because Iran did not have diplomatic relations with the United States. The European community pledged $1.2 million in addition to other nonmonetary assistance.

By June 25, some religious fundamentalist groups in Iran began urging President Hashemi Rafsanjani to reject foreign helpers, especially Americans. Some French doctors later reported that they had been ordered out of some of the worst-hit areas of the country, where the villagers were pleading for medical help. Editorials in major Iranian newspapers and some government officials took a conciliatory approach, but others accused some of the governments that had sent aid to Iran of doing so to exploit the situation for political purposes. Some pointed out that American earthquake aid would not end years of hostility between the two countries. Rafsanjani himself took a more pragmatic approach, showing gratitude for aid from all groups, with or without diplomatic relations, and Western diplomats in Tehran praised the people of Iran for their admirable attempt to put aside political differences for the good of the country.

As hope began to wane for many survivors in the wake of new tremors, some Islamic clerics who had traveled to the quake region from Tehran moved among the people, promising survivors greater glory for their struggle. One handed out small brochures listing the rewards to be gained from martyrdom. With the large number of dead, Iran's ayatollahs (religious leaders) agreed that, because of the emergency situation, corpses could be buried in mass graves if it was impossible to observe Islamic burial rules.

In the aftermath of the terrible devastation in the area, survivors in at least one town, Rasht, were quoted as saying that there had been unnecessary deaths; they blamed greed, shoddy construction, and governmental indifference for the enormous loss of life. One civil engineer, whose sister and nephews were killed in the earthquake, reflected this feeling; he asserted that, in order to save money and make a larger profit when the seven-story apartment building in which his relatives had lived was sold, builders had used far too little steel in the construction.

## SIGNIFICANCE

Aside from the loss of life, the monetary value of the damage caused by the Rudbar-Tarom earthquake climbed to an estimated $7.2 billion, costing Iran about 7.2 percent of its gross national product. The quake resulted in long-term economic disruption of at least three large provinces, as Iran needed to resettle persons from at least three large cities and more than seven hundred villages. Rebuilding the structures lost while meeting acceptable construction standards would take decades and cost the country a considerable portion of its national budget.

Of all the earthquakes suffered by Iran over its long history, the Rudbar-Tarom quake of 1990 exacted the greatest toll up to that time in terms of loss of life and physical destruction, highlighting the need for increased earthquake education among the Iranian people. This need has been difficult to address in part because of the religious view that such disasters are the will of God and acceptance of such events is virtuous.

The Iranian earthquake of 1990 was also significant in that it showed the extent to which the international community can pull together in times of crisis. Countries that were experiencing strained relationships with Iran were willing not only to pledge large amounts of monetary assistance but also to send hundreds of tons of equipment, medicine, and food as well people to provide hands-on assistance to victims of this horrendous disaster.

*—Victoria Price*

## FURTHER READING

Berberian, M., et al. "The Rudbar-Tarom Earthquake of 20 June 1990 in NW Persia: Preliminary Field and Seismological Observations, and Its Tectonic Significance." *Bulletin of the Seismological Society of America* 82 (August, 1992):1726-1755. Provides a technical explanation of the quake and reveals that the system of surface faults on which it occurred had not been deemed active before, leading to the conclusion that there is a relatively long return period for earthquakes of this type.

Bolt, Bruce A. *Earthquakes*. 5th ed. San Francisco: W. H. Freeman, 2003. Excellent primer on earthquakes for the nonscientist. Includes information on plate tectonics, earthquake magnitude and measurement, and faults.

Gao, Liping, Terry C. Wallace, and James Jackson. "Aftershocks of the June 1990 Rudbar-Tarom Earthquake: Evidence for Slip Partitioning." *Eos, Transactions, American Geophysical Union* 72 (Fall, 1991). Technical article analyzes the nature of the earthquake mechanism and concludes that the rupture was of a complex type, with at least three subevents occurring within the first twenty seconds. Gives examples of the two types of aftershocks involved.

Hough, Susan Elizabeth. *Earthshaking Science: What We Know (and Don't Know) About Earthquakes*. Princeton, N.J.: Princeton University Press, 2002. Good source of basic information about earthquakes. Includes suggestions for further reading and index.

McFadden, Robert D. "Earthquake Kills Thousands in Wide Region of Iran." *The New York Times*, June 23,

1990, p. A10. An example of the coverage of the quake in the American press.

Shenan, Philip. "Iran Debates Accepting Quake Relief from Enemies." *The New York Times*, June 27, 1990, p. A3. Reports on the problems with rescue and relief efforts and the possibility that Iran might refuse offers of help from some nations.

**SEE ALSO:** July 28, 1976: Deadly Earthquake Strikes China; Sept. 19, 1985: Earthquake Devastates Mexico City; Dec. 7, 1988: Armenian Earthquake Leads to Calls for Building Reform; Jan. 17, 1994: Northridge Quake Rocks Los Angeles; Jan. 17, 1995: Kōbe Earthquake Kills Thousands.

## June 22, 1990
# MEECH LAKE ACCORD DIES

*In 1990, Canadian leaders failed in an attempt to reform the Constitution of 1982 by incorporating Quebec.*

**LOCALE:** Canada
**CATEGORY:** Government and politics

**KEY FIGURES**

*Robert Bourassa* (1933-1996), premier of Quebec, 1970-1976 and 1985-1994

*Elijah Harper* (b. 1949), only Native Canadian member of Manitoba's legislature

*Brian Mulroney* (b. 1939), prime minister of Canada, 1984-1993

*Jacques Parizeau* (b. 1930), leader of the sovereignist Parti Québécois

*Pierre Trudeau* (1919-2000), prime minister of Canada, 1968-1979 and 1980-1984

*Clyde K. Wells* (b. 1937), premier of Newfoundland

**SUMMARY OF EVENT**

Constitutionally, much unfinished business faced Canada in the 1980's. The nature of the country's Senate had not been agreed upon. Fueled by sovereignist impulses, Quebec remained outside the 1982 constitution, and the province's leaders demanded that specific conditions be met before Quebec would approve the document. Canadian prime minister Brian Mulroney of the Progressive Conservative Party sought to break the long deadlock on these matters.

On April 30, 1987, following ten hours of intense negotiations at Meech Lake, a resort in Quebec, Mulroney and the ten provincial premiers reached a unanimous agreement designed to bring Quebec into the constitution. Acting in the role of mediator, Mulroney was able to engineer a compromise that would enhance the power of all provinces. The belief that Quebec should be no more than equal to the other provinces was advanced

by the leaders of Nova Scotia, Alberta, Manitoba, and Saskatchewan. Quebec's premier, Robert Bourassa, a Harvard-trained economist and advocate of federalism, eased tensions by indicating a willingness to be flexible. Agreement was made possible when Alberta's premier, Donald Getty, who wanted a powerful, elected Senate representing all the provinces equally, softened his demand that the issue of Senate reform be resolved before the Quebec question.

The key provision of the Meech Lake Accord was the recognition of Quebec as a distinct society within Canada. This was an important concession that would afford certain protections for Quebec's francophone culture. The agreement also included other important provisions. Constitutional changes in federal institutions and provincial boundaries would require the unanimous consent of the federal government and the provinces. The federal government committed itself to addressing the Senate reform issue in the near future. The prime minister and provincial premiers would be required to meet at least twice annually, with one conference devoted to constitutional matters and the other to economic issues. Quebec was guaranteed three judges on the nine-member Canadian Supreme Court—this had been customary but now would be constitutionally entrenched. In most instances, the Parliament in Ottawa would be obligated to choose justices from among candidates proposed by provinces. Within quite broad limitations, any province would be allowed to opt out of federally funded programs under provincial jurisdiction. Quebec would not have to accept immigrants out of proportion to its percentage of the national population.

The Meech Lake Accord was to be final when ratified by Parliament, all ten provincial legislatures, and the premiers at a follow-up conference. A three-year deadline, expiring June 23, 1990, was set for the process.

The pact, characterized as a milestone in federal-provincial relations, was a triumph for Mulroney. Quebec's premier described the pact as "a historic breakthrough for Quebec as a Canadian partner." William Vander Zalm, premier of British Columbia and a leading spokesman for western Canada, stated that the accord "changes the nature of the relationships and responsibilities of our national and provincial governments in a manner that bodes well for our collective future."

Opposition to the Meech Lake Accord surfaced in various quarters. The leaders of the Parti Québécois, a sovereignist political party, accused Bourassa of selling out Quebec. Bourassa's Liberal Party had ousted the Parti Québécois from power in 1985. However, the Quebec public did not appear to share the outrage of the Parti Québécois. René Lévesque—sovereignist, former Quebec premier, and former leader of the Parti Québécois—and former Canadian prime minister Pierre Trudeau, who opposed Quebec's demands, both declined to comment on the accord. Liberal Party leader John Napier Turner commented, "I have the feeling that Mr. Mulroney gave away too much to achieve that deal." He criticized the idea of provinces choosing senators and Supreme Court justices, and he noted that he was worried

*Robert Bourassa.* (AP/Wide World Photos)

about the ability of the federal government to initiate national programs if the provinces were able to opt out. Having not been invited to participate in the conference, Anthony Penikett, leader of the Yukon territorial government, expressed opposition to the agreement because each province would have veto power over the Yukon's aspirations of becoming a full province.

Numerous conferences were convened and studies were initiated to iron out difficulties with the pact, and eight provinces endorsed it. In 1989, however, Newfoundland elected a new premier, Liberal Clyde K. Wells, who had campaigned against the agreement. Under Wells, the Newfoundland House of Assembly voted to rescind its earlier approval of the Meech Lake Accord.

Newfoundland, Manitoba, and New Brunswick argued that the clause declaring Quebec to be a distinct society would give Quebec too much power and enable it to pass laws conflicting with the nation's 1982 Charter of Rights and Freedoms. Those fears were strengthened in 1988, when Quebec overruled a Canadian Supreme Court decision striking down a law restricting the use of any language other than French on public signs. The holdout provinces also objected to what they saw as a failure to address the issues of Senate reform and minority rights. Following the adoption of a compromise designed to address some of these concerns, New Brunswick's legislature voted unanimously to approve the accord. However, opposition remained strong in Manitoba and Newfoundland.

Manitoba, with its large population of indigenous Canadians, had sought the inclusion of a "Canada clause" that would have emphasized the entire nation's multicultural characteristics. The Manitoba legislature's sole Native member, Elijah Harper, sought to block passage of the accord, arguing that it ignored Native concerns. On June 22, Harper refused to give his consent to an extension of the legislature's Meech Lake debate. Because an extension required unanimous approval, Harper's move effectively killed the accord. Harper's action was hailed by other Native Canadian leaders.

In Newfoundland, Wells canceled a scheduled vote on the accord, criticizing what he called the pressure tactics of Mulroney. Wells had been outraged to learn that Mulroney's government had offered a plan to extend the approval deadline in Manitoba but not in Newfoundland. He argued that Mulroney was attempting to make his province a scapegoat for the accord's failure. The Meech Lake Accord died on June 22, 1990, when Newfoundland and Manitoba failed to ratify the agreement.

## SIGNIFICANCE

The defeat of the accord was viewed as a major blow to Mulroney, who had twice been elected on promises to unite the country. Mulroney's popularity plummeted. In a rare televised address, Mulroney acknowledged his disappointment but reaffirmed that "a truly united tolerant Canada endures and will eventually prevail." The Liberal Party accused Mulroney of deliberately fostering a crisis atmosphere in the last days of the debate by delaying talks on a possible compromise in order to create last-minute pressure on the holdout provinces.

The failure of the Meech Lake Accord generated speculation about Quebec's future and prompted a cautious response from Robert Bourassa, who repeatedly stressed that his government would take no action jeopardizing Quebec's economy. Jacques Parizeau, leader of Parti Québécois, jubilantly described the crisis as "the moment of truth." The Parti Québécois had been campaigning to hold a provincial referendum on "sovereignty association" for Quebec, which was generally understood to mean that Quebec would retain economic ties with Canada while gaining political independence. A similar referendum had failed in 1980, but more recent polls had found that nearly 60 percent of Quebecers favored political sovereignty.

Instead of regretting the accord's failure, many Quebecers were elated by the outcome. The failure of the accord had fallen just one day before St. Jean-Baptiste Day, Quebec's national holiday. Expressing their support for an independent Quebec, nationalists celebrated. Nearly 200,000 people turned out for a parade in Montreal, many of them waving Quebec's fleur-de-lis flag and chanting, "Vive le Quebec libre" (Long live free Quebec). This was the first parade of its kind held in twenty years, following the discontinuation of such events after violent demonstrations took place in 1968 and 1969. Many in anglophone Canada also celebrated the failure of the Meech Lake Accord.

In a rare venture into Canadian politics, Great Britain's Queen Elizabeth II pleaded for unity among Canadians as Canada seemed on the verge of plunging headlong into a political crisis. A 1995 referendum for Quebec's sovereignty very narrowly failed to win approval, but the issue remained alive and combustible in Canadian politics into the twenty-first century.

—*Randall Fegley*

## FURTHER READING

Cohen, Andrew. *A Deal Undone*. Vancouver, B.C.: Douglas & McIntyre, 1990. Presents an in-depth look at the negotiations and politics surrounding the making and breaking of the Meech Lake Accord.

Coyne, Deborah. *Roll of the Dice: Working with Clyde Wells During the Meech Lake Negotiations*. Toronto: Lorimer, 1992. Examination of the Meech Lake Accord focuses on Clyde Wells and the politics of Newfoundland.

McMenemy, John. *The Language of Canadian Politics: A Guide to Important Terms and Concepts*. 3d ed. Waterloo, Ont.: Wilfrid Laurier University Press, 2001. Collection of more than five hundred brief essays on a wide range of topics related to the Canadian system of government, Canadian political history, Canadian laws and legal history, and more.

Mathews, Georges. *Quiet Resolution: Quebec's Challenge to Canada*. Toronto: Summerhill, 1990. Presents Robert Bourassa's comments on Quebec, Canadian politics, and Meech Lake.

Milne, David. *The Canadian Constitution*. Toronto: Lorimer, 1990. Reviews Canadian constitutional history through the 1980's.

Monahan, Patrick. *Meech Lake: The Inside Story*. Toronto: University of Toronto Press, 1991. Presents a thorough overview of the accord and the politics that surrounded it.

Newman, Saul. *Ethnoregional Conflict in Democracies: Mostly Ballots, Rarely Bullets*. Westport, Conn.: Greenwood Press, 1996. Examination of ethnoregional movements in democracies includes extensive discussion of the case of Quebec and the Parti Québécois.

Vipond, Robert. *Liberty and Community: Canadian Federalism and the Failure of the Constitution*. Albany: State University of New York Press, 1991. Examines the inability of Canadians to agree on constitutional reforms.

**SEE ALSO:** Apr. 17, 1982: Canada's Constitution Act; Apr. 17, 1982: Canadian Charter of Rights and Freedoms Is Enacted; Sept. 14, 1984: Mulroney Era Begins in Canada; July 25, 1990: Bloc Québécois Forms; Oct. 26, 1992: Defeat of the Charlottetown Accord; Nov. 4, 1993: Chrétien Takes Charge in Canada; June 29, 2000: Canadian Parliament Passes the Clarity Act.

1990

in state laws that allowed the withholding or withdrawing of life support. Posits that the media attention on cases like Cruzan's helped to sway public and political opinion in favor of right-to-die legislation.

Larson, Edward J., and Darrell W. Amundsen. *A Differential Death: Euthanasia in the Christian Tradition.* Downers Grove, Ill.: InterVarsity Press, 1998. Addresses some differences of opinion regarding the history of the Christian perspective on euthanasia, but mainly presents nontheological objections to the right-to-die movement.

Pence, Gregory E. *Classical Cases in Medical Ethics.* New York: McGraw Hill, 2004. Includes a chapter on

the Karen Quinlan and Nancy Cruzan cases, and another on Oregon's assisted suicide law. Examines the legal and ethical controversies surrounding the issue.

**SEE ALSO:** Jan. 22, 1973: U.S. Supreme Court Expands Women's Reproductive Rights; Jan., 1980-Mar., 1983: Presidential Advisory Commission Studies Medical and Research Ethics; Dec. 18, 1982: United Nations Issues Principles of Medical Ethics; July 3, 1989: U.S. Supreme Court Upholds State Restrictions on Abortion; Nov. 8, 1994: Oregon Voters Legalize Physician-Assisted Suicide.

---

## June 29, 1990
# U.N. AGREEMENT PROTECTS OZONE LAYER

*The members of the United Nations took an important step toward protecting the planet when they met to ratify an agreement to phase out substances known to be damaging to the stratosphere's vitally important ozone layer.*

**ALSO KNOWN AS:** Montreal Protocol
**LOCALE:** London, England
**CATEGORIES:** Environmental issues; diplomacy and international relations; United Nations

**KEY FIGURES**

*F. Sherwood Rowland* (b. 1927), professor of chemistry at the University of California, Irvine
*Mario J. Molina* (b. 1943), professor of chemistry at the University of California, Irvine
*Thomas Michael McMillan* (b. 1945), Canadian minister for the environment, 1985-1988, who was highly influential at the 1987 Montreal Protocol meetings
*William Reilly* (b. 1940), administrator of the U.S. Environmental Protection Agency
*Ronald Reagan* (1911-2004), president of the United States, 1981-1989
*Donald Hodel* (b. 1935), U.S. secretary of the interior, 1985-1989

**SUMMARY OF EVENT**

Earth's ozone layer is located in the stratosphere between six and thirty-one miles above the planet's surface. This layer is vitally important to life on Earth because it absorbs ultraviolet (UV) radiation from the Sun. In 1974, F. Sherwood Rowland and Mario J. Molina, scientists at

the University of California, Irvine, published a paper warning of the dangers to the ozone layer of chlorofluorocarbons (CFCs) used in air-conditioning equipment, refrigerators, aerosol spray cans (such as those used for hair sprays and deodorants), industrial solvents, and a wide variety of other manufactured products.

These CFCs were a primary cause of damage being done to the ozone layer. Chlorine atoms from CFCs take one oxygen atom away from the three oxygen atoms that make up an ozone molecule and form chlorine monoxide, which combines with another oxygen atom to form an oxygen molecule and a chlorine atom. The new oxygen molecules thus formed do not block the Sun's UV light, so more of that light reaches Earth's surface. The scientists found that this ozone destruction, caused by human technology, had been going on for years.

When too much UV light falls on the planet's surface, serious damage results. Scientists do not yet understand all the potential harmful impacts of excessive UV light, but many ill effects have been established. It is known that UV light can cause cataracts to develop in the human eye, clouding the lens and resulting in blurred vision and eventual blindness. UV light can also cause skin damage, and increased incidence of skin cancers has been reported in many parts of the world where scientific observers have noted depletion of the ozone layer. UV rays are known to have harmful effects on the human immune system as well, making the body more susceptible to infectious diseases. In addition, UV radiation negatively affects the growth of photoplankton (one-celled animals) and krill (tiny shrimplike animals), which are at the bottom of the ocean food chain. Increased UV radiation is therefore a threat to all the life in the sea, directly or indirectly, and consequently a threat to the lives of human beings who depend on fish for food. UV rays also interfere with photosynthesis in plants and thus pose a potential threat to farm crop yields.

As scientists learned more about the depletion of Earth's ozone layer, citizens of many countries were warned of the growing dangers of exposure to sunlight. They were cautioned to wear hats and protective clothing, to use a broad-spectrum sunscreen with a protection factor of at least 15, to stay out of the sun as much as possible between 10:00 A.M. and 3:00 P.M., and to wear sunglasses treated to absorb UV radiation. Such recommendations became standard throughout the world by the early twenty-first century.

In 1987, representatives of many nations met in Montreal, Quebec, to participate in sessions that produced the Montreal Protocol, which called for the phasing out of substances that harm the ozone layer (a protocol is a preliminary version of a proposed treaty that has yet to be ratified). Some governments were eager to ratify the protocol, but others balked because of the possible expenses and hardships to their nations if they followed the protocol's recommendations, which included phasing out the use of CFCs and converting to harmless substitutes. India and China were two major countries that delayed ratifying the protocol because of the anticipated costs of switching to substitutes for CFCs. Representatives of twenty-four nations, mostly the developed, industrialized nations of the world, signed the agreement in Montreal on September 16, 1987.

The Third World countries that had initially balked at ratifying the protocol were eventually persuaded to do so by the creation of the Montreal Protocol Multilateral Fund. Given that the developed nations had created most of the ozone depletion problem with their heavy commercial use of destructive chemicals, many nations thought it appropriate that the developed nations bear the greatest cost of implementing the protocol's requirements. On June 29, 1990, representatives of ninety-three nations met in London and agreed to ban production of most ozone-destroying chemicals by the end of the twentieth century.

In November, 1992, delegates from all over the world met in Copenhagen, Denmark, to discuss further revisions of the protocol because of alarming new discoveries about the damage being done to the ozone layer. It was agreed to phase out production of CFCs and carbon tetrachloride by January 1, 1996; to ban the production of halons by 1994; to ban production of methyl chloroform by 1996; to control the use of hydrochlorofluorocarbons (HCFSs) and eliminate them completely by 2030; and to increase the Montreal Protocol Multilateral Fund to make it possible for developing nations to accelerate the changeover from machinery and consumer products using ozone-destroying gases to harmless alternatives.

## SIGNIFICANCE

The Montreal Protocol was one of the most important and most successful examples of international cooperation since the formation of the United Nations. The historic agreement served to prove the contention of environmentalists that international peace and cooperation could be achieved through recognition by all the world's people that they are mutually interdependent on the bounty of "Spaceship Earth," a pinpoint of rotating matter that could conceivably be the only home of life in all the vastness of the cosmos.

The publicity attending the various meetings on the Montreal Protocol made the entire world aware of the dangers posed by rampant technological development. Some libertarians and political conservatives argued that the danger of the ozone layer's destruction had been grossly exaggerated and that special interests were using the issue as a scare tactic to promote world government, greater bureaucratic interference in private enterprise, and ultimately universal socialism. Such criticisms were voiced by a minority, however, and did little to impede the world's cooperative efforts to halt ozone damage by banning the use of CFCs and other dangerous chemicals, a goal largely achieved by the end of the 1990's. Thanks to the changes made because of the protocol, ozone depletion had leveled off by the early twenty-first century, leading some scientists to predict that if the trend continued and ozone-depleting substances were eliminated, the ozone layer would naturally regenerate itself by the middle of the twenty-first century.

The Montreal Protocol spurred technological innovation. Scientists, engineers, and manufacturers were motivated to find effective substitutes for CFCs, as there was obviously much money to be made. They also had to invent techniques to replace such potentially dangerous chemicals as those contained in refrigerator coolants without releasing the gases into the atmosphere. The technological responses to the ozone crisis illustrated economist Julian Simon's thesis that, given a free market economy, people are capable of solving any problems they create. It is doubtful that commercial interests would have been motivated to invent substitutes for CFCs without government intervention.

1990

The worldwide attention to the ozone depletion problem made consumers aware of their own important part in environmental damage and their responsibility for environmental protection. The result was a general consciousness-raising that proved beneficial in many ways. Teachers at all grade levels helped by making young people aware of the dangers of ozone destruction, including the dangers of too much exposure to sunlight. As a result of classroom instruction, many young people became more knowledgeable about environmental issues than most of their elders.

The Montreal Protocol proved that rich nations and poor nations—nations with different languages, cultures, religions, and economic interests—could come together to agree on one common program. The complex negotiations conducted over a period of many years provided valuable experience in resolving international problems affecting the global environment. The representatives of the rich and powerful nations learned that they had to understand the problems and aspirations of the world's underprivileged majority, who were only beginning to enjoy the kinds of consumer products that were causing environmental damage.

In the long run, the concern over ozone depletion may prove a boon to humanity because of the lessons learned as governments with conflicting agendas were forced to work together expeditiously for the common good. William Reilly, the administrator of the U.S. Environmental Protection Agency who headed the U.S. delegation to the London conference, accurately described the Montreal Protocol as "a marvelous example of worldwide cooperation really without precedent."

—Bill Delaney

**FURTHER READING**

Benedick, Richard Elliot. *Ozone Diplomacy: New Directions in Safeguarding the Planet.* 2d rev. ed. Cambridge, Mass.: Harvard University Press, 1998. Presents a chronological discussion of the Montreal Protocol meetings and subsequent sessions by the chief U.S. negotiator. Makes technical issues understandable to nonspecialists. Discusses the complex problem of getting many different nations with conflicting interests to agree on a single program.

Clark, Sarah L. *Protecting the Ozone Layer: What You Can Do—A Citizen's Guide to Reducing the Use of Ozone-Depleting Chemicals.* New York: Environmental Information Exchange, Environmental Defense Fund, 1988. Brief volume offers specific guidelines and concrete examples with the aim of involving

consumers in the fight to save the ozone layer from further devastation.

Firor, John. *The Changing Atmosphere: A Global Challenge.* New Haven, Conn.: Yale University Press, 1990. Examines the complex interrelationships among acid rain, climate warming, and depletion of the ozone layer. Provides a good overview of these problems and their possible solutions, with emphasis on the gravity of the situation. Argues that population control is vital to solving the world's atmospheric problems.

Gliedman, John. "Is the Pact Too Little, Too Late?" *The Nation*, October 10, 1987, 376-380. Illustrated article, published shortly after the Montreal Protocol meetings, questions whether the international agreement is comprehensive enough to protect the ozone layer. Suggests that scientists do not have sufficient understanding of the problem.

Gore, Al. *Earth in the Balance: Ecology and the Human Spirit.* 1992. Reprint. Emmaus, Pa.: Rodale Press, 2006. Highly readable book by an environmental crusader who became vice president of the United States in 1993. Presents an overview of the ecological crisis and offers pragmatic suggestions for bringing the earth back into ecological balance. Discusses the Montreal Protocol and the work of Rowland and Molina. Includes excellent bibliography.

Gribbin, John R. *The Hole in the Sky: Man's Threat to the Ozone Layer.* New York: Bantam Books, 1988. Discusses the ozone depletion problem, including a review of the major events and scientific principles, using nontechnical language. Summarizes proposed solutions to the problem.

Klingeman, Henry. "The Twilight Ozone: D. Hodel's Alleged Remarks Concerning the International Protocol on Ozone." *National Review*, August 14, 1987, 40-41. Discusses Interior Secretary Hodel's views on the Montreal Protocol at the time of the initial meetings. Indicates that many important people in government were unimpressed by the scientific data and were instead concerned primarily about the economic effects of banning CFCs.

Lemonick, Michael D. "The Ozone Vanishes." *Time*, February 17, 1992, 60-68. Illustrated cover story warns that the ozone layer is being depleted faster than anyone had previously anticipated and that holes would be opening up above Russia, Scandinavia, Germany, Britain, Canada, and northern New England. Discusses possible technological interventions to save the ozone layer and ways to reduce exposure to UV light.

Molina, M. J., and F. S. Rowland. "Stratospheric Sink for Chlorofluoromethanes: Chlorine Atom-Catalyzed Destruction of Ozone." *Nature* 249 (1974): 810-812. This technical discussion is of great historic importance because it alerted the world to the dangers of ozone depletion and led to the subsequent research, media publicity, consumer activism, political negotiations, and final international accord on the problem.

Parson, Edward A. *Protecting the Ozone Layer: Science and Strategy.* New York: Oxford University Press, 2003. Presents a comprehensive history of international efforts to protect the ozone layer.

**SEE ALSO:** June 5-16, 1972: United Nations Holds an Environmental Conference in Stockholm; Dec., 1973-June, 1974: Rowland and Molina Theorize That Freon Causes Ozone Depletion; Mar. 17, 1978: Chlorofluorocarbons Are Banned in the United States; May 16, 1985: Researchers Discover a Hole in the Ozone Layer; Apr. 27, 1987: *Our Common Future* Is Published; Nov., 1988: United Nations Creates a Panel to Study Climate Change; 1990: "An Anti-Environmentalist Manifesto" Signals a Backlash; June 3-14, 1992: Earth Summit Convenes in Rio de Janeiro.

1990

## July 9-19, 1990
# GENERAL MOTORS SPONSORS A SOLAR-POWERED CAR RACE

*General Motors, the U.S. Department of Energy, and the Society of Automotive Engineers held a race for solar-powered cars in the United States to challenge college engineering students and to show the potential of solar energy and electric vehicles.*

**ALSO KNOWN AS:** GM Sunrayce USA; American Solar Challenge

**LOCALE:** Lake Buena Vista, Florida, to Warren, Michigan

**CATEGORIES:** Energy; engineering; transportation

### KEY FIGURES
*Howard G. Wilson* (fl. late twentieth century), vice president of Hughes Aircraft who led the building of the Sunraycer and proposed holding the first collegiate solar race

*Richard King* (fl. late twentieth century), director of Sunrayce at the U.S. Department of Energy

*Paul B. MacCready* (b. 1925), president of AeroVironment who led teams that built human- and solar-powered aircraft

*Jerry Williams* (1923-1998), program manager of the first Sunrayce who continued as the Sunrayce contact person at General Motors

### SUMMARY OF EVENT
In 1987, Hughes Aircraft, an independently managed subsidiary of General Motors (GM), and AeroVironment, a company in which GM held stock, built a solar automobile called the Sunraycer to compete in the 1,867-mile Pentex World Solar Challenge in Australia. Howard G. Wilson, Paul B. MacCready, Chester R. Kyle, and

their teams combined light weight, aerodynamics, energy efficiency, and reliability in the automobile's design to produce the capacity for an average speed of 41.6 miles per hour. The Sunraycer won the race.

GM could not hope to surpass the tremendous success of the Sunraycer by building another automobile for the next Solar Challenge. Instead, project manager Wilson suggested to GM that U.S. engineering colleges be invited to compete against one another. GM leaders Bob Stempel and Don Atwood recognized the educational potential of solar automobiles, and the idea met with almost instant approval from GM. Other potential backers were contacted. It made sense, according to Richard King of the U.S. Department of Energy (DOE), to encourage future engineers and to stir public interest with a collegiate competition. Accordingly, the DOE and the Society of Automotive Engineers (SAE) joined GM in sponsoring the first collegiate solar automobile competition. The race was named for GM's solar racer: GM Sunrayce USA.

In December, 1988, the three sponsors invited more than one thousand North American colleges and universities offering technology and engineering programs to enter the competition to design and build a solar-powered vehicle. One hundred fifteen colleges responded, and sixty-one colleges completed designs. In April, 1989, twenty-nine entries were selected from U.S. schools, two from Canadian schools, and one from a school in Puerto Rico. The race was the largest such event held up to that time in the United States.

The rules for the race followed those for the 1990 Australian World Solar Challenge. Maximum vehicle

*The University of Michigan's Sunrunner, which won the inaugural General Motors Sunrayce USA in 1990.* (Jim West)

dimensions were 6 meters (19.7 feet) long by 2 meters (6.6 feet) wide by 1.6 meters (5.3 feet) high. Minimum height was 1 meter (3.3 feet). Sunlight was to be the only source of power for the vehicles, and battery storage capacity was limited to five kilowatt-hours. Charging from the automobile's solar array was allowed while the automobile was running the race and for the period two hours before and after each day's racing.

On one-person vehicles, the solar panels could be up to 4 meters long (13.1 feet) by 2 meters wide (6.6 feet) and no more than 1.6 meters high (5.3 feet), or about 8 square meters. Two-person automobiles could be entirely covered with cells. Nevertheless, the entrants were faced with running their cars on less than 1,500 watts, or the power of a hair dryer. Minnesota's Mankato State, for example, found that speeds exceeding twenty-five miles per hour caused energy output to exceed solar energy collection.

Driver compartments were to be enclosed to protect drivers and to ensure that no human power could aid a vehicle's operation. Drivers would be warm and cramped; students would take turns driving to avoid heat exhaus-

tion. Lead weights equalized drivers' weights at 175 pounds minimum. Seat belts, horn, turn signals, taillights, and rear vision system were required.

Beyond these requirements, the focus was on dependability, stability, solar energy collection, storage in batteries, weight reduction, and aerodynamic design. Students were responsible for the design and assembly of every element of their automobiles. Those on the University of Michigan team, for example, voted on everything about their vehicle, even its door color.

Building a solar vehicle from scratch is costly. As an incentive, GM gave each school $5,000, and the DOE added $2,000. Each school had to raise the rest of its budget. The University of Michigan successfully put a team of business students in charge of fund-raising for the project. The schools spent between $30,000 and nearly $1 million to create their solar cars. Furthermore, student time demands ran high. As the race drew near, many teams worked around the clock, seven days a week, to finish their automobiles.

When the entrants from the thirty-two competing colleges and universities brought their completed vehicles to the starting point at EPCOT Center in Orlando, Florida, on July 9, 1990, excitement ran high. The teams saw the work of the other schools for the first time. Many had borrowed ideas from the Sunraycer, but others were more adventurous. Western Washington's vehicle looked like the front of a small airplane. The aerodynamic Sunshine Special, designed by the Florida Institute of Technology, was so low to the ground that the supine driver had to look over his toes to see the road. The automobile even had extra solar cells under the chassis to catch sunlight reflected off the road.

The course followed an eleven-day, 1,625-mile backroad route from Lake Buena Vista, Florida, to the GM Technical Center at Warren, Michigan. The vehicles were timed as they attempted to reach set distances each day, and time bonuses and penalties were awarded. The teams' fortunes varied, depending in large part on communication and teamwork. The competing teams tended to help one another, but sometimes the unexpected happened.

The University of Waterloo's vehicle was in seventeenth place when a local driver in a truck attempted to pass and take a photograph of the unusual vehicle. An oncoming automobile caused all three vehicles to collide, and Waterloo's Midnight Sun left the road looking like a flying saucer. No one was injured, but the Waterloo car was out of the race.

In the end, the University of Michigan's 440-pound Sunrunner finished first with a time of seventy-two hours, fifty minutes. Professor Bill Ribbens was the team's adviser. Susan Fancy was the team captain, and Paula Finnegan, David Noles, and Andrew Swiecki were drivers. Their single-person automobile featured aerospace silicon cells and silver-zinc batteries. Western Washington's two-person car came in second, and the University of Maryland's entry was third. As part of the package, GM sponsored the three automobiles to run in the 1990 World Solar Challenge, a repeat of the race the original Sunraycer had won in 1987.

A second Sunrayce event in 1993 followed a route from Arlington, Texas, to Apple Valley, Minnesota, and in 1995 the route was from Indianapolis to Golden, Colorado. Subsequent races in the series have taken place every two years. The name of the event changed to American Solar Challenge in 2001 and then to North American Solar Challenge in 2005. During the same period, races involving "hybrid" vehicles—vehicles with two power sources, such as an electrical generator and an engine driven by propane, gasoline, or other fuel—began to be sponsored by the SAE, the Ford Motor Company, and Saturn.

## SIGNIFICANCE

The original Sunrayce drew large crowds. People were eager to see if automobiles that were powered by electricity could be more exciting than golf carts, and the idea of using the sun directly was intriguing. Students operating the vehicles were surprised at the public's enthusiasm and felt like celebrities. Grocery stores along the race route sometimes refused payment from race participants, and even some repairs on the solar automobiles were done without charge.

Clearly, automobile manufacturers viewed the race as a window to the future, knowing that they must understand the market as they work to develop vehicles that are friendlier to the environment. Patrick Summers of the DOE noted that Sunrayce was a moving advertisement that automobiles do not have to be powered by gasoline.

Enthusiasm for the engineering project continued at the various schools that competed even after the race was over. The 1991 summer issue of the SAE newsletter, *Student Action in Engineering*, reported that nearly all the Sunrayce schools displayed their vehicles at fairs, career days, automobile shows, and hundreds of regional events. Members of the team from Mankato State University of Minnesota drove their Northern Light to the top of Pikes Peak in Colorado and gained a place in *The Guinness Book of World Records*. Arizona State University competed in the ASHI Solar Car Rally in Japan, where it earned the technology award.

At Auburn University, two students wrote their master's theses on automobile elements. Dartmouth, Worcester Polytech, and Drexel began building new solar automobiles for the 1991 American Tour de Sol. More than 100,000 people saw Iowa State's vehicle. The University of Ottawa presented a paper on solar vehicles at a conference on electric automobiles in Hong Kong and then displayed its automobile in Korea. Waterloo of Canada displayed its vehicle at the Toronto Science Center for three years and made plans for a natural gas-electric hybrid. Rose-Hulman Institute of Technology added a new motor. Stark Technical and Dartmouth reported the establishment of student solar automobile clubs. The hope that participation in the Sunrayce would stimulate the imaginations and energies of U.S. engineering students was clearly met.

College instructors and students saw the contest as an opportunity to build their programs by applying engineering and management principles to a real situation. GM is only one of many U.S. companies that have voiced concern that U.S. industry and competitiveness are being

1990

impaired by a lack of qualified engineering graduates. Events such as Sunrayce stimulate interest in technical education and careers. Realizing this, participating colleges have proudly featured their automobiles in recruitment brochures and videos.

The students who participated in the first Sunrayce recognized it as an extraordinary, life-changing experience. The intensity of the engineering process—how such a project is organized and how results are analyzed in terms of performance—introduced the students to real-life situations faced by engineers.

Richard King, the director of Sunrayce, pointed out that building solar-powered automobiles serves as a research and development test bed for all kinds of vehicles. Research and development under severe power limitations leads to the development of improved efficiency in any type of transportation. Howard Wilson agreed that much can be accomplished through this approach. The development of commercial electric and hybrid vehicles owes much to the lessons provided by competitions such as Sunrayce. A whole new sector of the automobile industry was created as the development of environmentally friendly vehicles proved increasingly feasible. Markets for such vehicles, particularly hybrids, grew substantially as the prices of these vehicles became more competitive and rising gasoline prices made them increasingly attractive to operate.

—*Paul R. Boehlke*

## FURTHER READING

Hampson, Bruce. "Making an Impact on the Electric Car Market: General Motors' High-Tech EV Hits the Streets." *Electric Car* 1 (Winter, 1994): 10-15. Details the development of GM's electric automobile and its marketing strategy. States that GM's interest in electric vehicles was reawakened by the success of the GM Sunraycer in the first Solar Challenge in Australia.

Nadel, Brian. "Sun Racers." *Popular Science* 237 (August, 1990): 49-53, 88. Shows how the various college teams planned and built their vehicles to compete in the GM Sunrayce USA. Offers many details about the various automobiles.

Thacher, Eric F. *A Solar Car Primer*. New York: Nova Science, 2003. Presents comprehensive discussion of all aspects of the design and manufacture of the type of solar cars that take part in the Sunrayce competitions. Includes detailed appendixes and index.

Wilson, Howard G., Paul B. MacCready, and Chester R. Kyle. "Lessons of Sunraycer." *Scientific American* 260 (March, 1989): 90-97. Excellent article points out the problems involved in building electric vehicles. Wilson saw the project as a way to show how Hughes Aircraft and GM could work together. Sunraycer made people think about practical alternatives to gasoline-driven vehicles and caused GM to think about sponsoring its own race.

Zygmont, Jeffrey. "Wheels: Here Comes the Sungo." *Omni* 16 (May, 1994): 20. Describes the experience of riding in a solar automobile and points out the problems of building solar automobiles that can meet U.S. highway safety standards. Notes that the challenges in building these vehicles stem from the weight restrictions attributable to energy constraints.

SEE ALSO: 1974: Automakers Introduce the Catalytic Converter; 1977: Researchers Develop an Integrated Solar Energy System; May 3, 1978: Sun Day Celebration Promotes Solar Energy; May-June, 1981: Bell Labs Improves Solar Cells; Oct. 14, 1988: U.S. Law Mandates Use of Alternative Fuels; Dec., 1999: First Hybrid Car Appears on the U.S. Market.

## July 16, 1990
# GORBACHEV AGREES TO MEMBERSHIP OF A UNITED GERMANY IN NATO

*The two German states achieved political reunification only after Soviet leader Mikhail Gorbachev agreed to permit the new united Germany to remain in the North Atlantic Treaty Organization.*

**LOCALE:** Moscow, Soviet Union (now in Russia)
**CATEGORIES:** Diplomacy and international relations; government and politics

### KEY FIGURES

*Mikhail Gorbachev* (b. 1931), general secretary of the Communist Party of the Soviet Union, 1985-1991, and president of the Soviet Union, 1990-1991
*Helmut Kohl* (b. 1930), chancellor of West Germany, 1982-1990
*Hans-Dietrich Genscher* (b. 1927), foreign minister of West Germany
*Lothar de Maizière* (b. 1940), first non-Communist prime minister of East Germany

### SUMMARY OF EVENT

The division of Germany into two rival states in 1949 was a result of the Cold War between the United States and the Soviet Union. Although the Western democracies created the North Atlantic Treaty Organization (NATO) in 1949, neither German state established a national army until after 1955. The Soviet Union organized the Warsaw Pact only after West Germany was rearmed and admitted to NATO in 1955. East Germany also established an army in early 1956, after having been admitted into the Warsaw Pact. The German armies were integrated into rival military organizations in large part because of a fear of German rearmament held by both Western and Eastern European countries.

The rearmament of the two German states after 1955 solidified the division not only of Germany but also of Europe. Until the fall of the Berlin Wall in 1989, many observers discounted the possibility of German reunification, and many argued that the division of Germany was actually "the cornerstone of a stable Europe." Neither military bloc was willing to give up its German state to the other side. Not until Mikhail Gorbachev gave Germany permission to remain in NATO in July, 1990, was it possible for Germany to complete its political reunification and terminate the special powers exercised by the four major victors of World War II.

The decision to rearm the two Germanies had a dramatic effect on both societies. Rearmament was initially opposed by a majority of Germans in West and East Germany. Although West Germany rearmed in response to American pressures, the West German army was able to fill its ranks with almost equal numbers of draftees and volunteers. In addition, the West German government established a number of guidelines that protected the civil and constitutional rights of soldiers. Everything possible was done to prevent the emergence of a militaristic culture; the emphasis was always placed on the citizen-soldier. By the 1980's, between 10 and 15 percent of West German conscripts opted for alternative service in the military by declaring themselves conscientious objectors. Most West Germans appreciated the more than one-half million foreign troops stationed in their country as valuable allies against potential Soviet aggression. The additional demand on housing and other vital facilities in such a small country, however, was often a source of friction between West Germans and their NATO allies.

In East Germany, rearmament had a much more negative impact on society. The Communist regime did not dare to introduce conscription until 1962, a year after it had built the Berlin Wall to prevent escape from East Germany. There were few safeguards in the East German army that protected civil and religious rights. Although some conscripts were permitted to perform alternative service with military construction units after 1964, the East German army did not officially recognize the status of conscientious objector. Rainer Eppelmann, a Lutheran minister who became defense minister of East Germany after the demise of the Communist government in April, 1990, was imprisoned because he declared that he was a conscientious objector. Furthermore, in 1978 the Communist government introduced compulsory military studies in schools. Almost all East German officers and a majority of noncommissioned officers were members of the official Socialist Unity Party. The presence in East Germany of more than 350,000 Soviet troops ensured that any opposition would be crushed with brutal force.

Both German armies were important to the rival military blocs. The largest Soviet military force in Eastern Europe was located in East Germany, and the commander of that force dominated the East German military establishment. The West German army was crucial to NATO, as it provided half of the ground forces of NATO and 60 percent of the alliance's tank units. Unfortunately for the Germans, they were in the forefront of any potential conflict between NATO and Warsaw Pact forces. Even more disturbing to many Germans was that a conflict between these military alliances would also produce a civil war between Germans.

Although the construction of the Berlin Wall in 1961 violated the human rights of families and friends on both sides of the wall, West German leaders after 1970 decided to establish closer contacts with East Germany. Willy Brandt, the chancellor of West Germany, initiated policies that led to the signing of the Basic Treaty between East and West Germany in 1972. This treaty attempted to establish normal relations between the two German states and, at least in the opinion of West German leaders, permit closer contacts between the two peoples.

By 1979, almost eight million West Germans and West Berliners were able to visit East Germany. Unfortunately for intra-German relations, however, in 1979 the Soviets invaded Afghanistan. Fearing the superiority of Soviet conventional forces, West German chancellor Helmut Schmidt called for the modernization of NATO weapons. By 1983, Pershing II and cruise missiles were being deployed in West Germany. As a result of this NATO decision, significant peace movements emerged in both West and East Germany. Furthermore, Moscow attempted to prevent further German-German détente by preventing Erich Honecker, the leader of East Germany, from visiting Bonn, the West German capital. Not until 1987 was Honecker able to make an official visit to West Germany.

The emergence of Mikhail Gorbachev in 1985 as the leader of the Soviet Union was the most important single event to affect both Eastern European regimes and the relationship between the two German states. Gorbachev called for greater European self-reliance in 1986, and on two different occasions in 1988 he guaranteed Eastern European countries freedom of choice. In effect, he abandoned the Brezhnev Doctrine, which had threatened Soviet military intervention in the case of any East European Communist regime experiencing domestic upheaval. Gorbachev's new policy allowed the Hungarians to remove the fortifications between Hungary and Austria. The opening of the Hungarian border undermined East Germany, as thousands of East Germans fled to the West. East Germans were granted automatic citizenship

in West Germany. By November 9, 1989, the Berlin Wall was opened, and the inevitable process toward German unification was launched by Helmut Kohl, the chancellor of West Germany.

Kohl and the West German foreign minister, Hans-Dietrich Genscher, assured their Western allies that a united Germany would remain in NATO. This decision, however, could never be implemented without the permission of the Soviet Union and the removal of Soviet troops from East Germany. Gorbachev had insisted in 1987 that there were two German states and that any attempt to change this historical reality would be dangerous. As late as December, 1989, in a meeting with U.S. president George H. W. Bush in Malta, Gorbachev insisted on the existence of two Germanies. Only in January, 1990, did Gorbachev change his mind and accept the inevitability of German unification. In February, 1990, he informed Kohl that the Germans could decide on the timing of unification after negotiating with France, Great Britain, the United States, and the Soviet Union. Between January and June, 1990, however, Gorbachev continued to argue that Germany could not join NATO.

The two German states moved closer to unification after the March, 1990, election in East Germany removed the Communist government and established a pro-Western coalition government under Lothar de Maizière. In early July, 1990, the West German mark became the official currency in East Germany. Finally, in order to meet one of Gorbachev's key demands, NATO representatives meeting in London on July 6, 1990, agreed to change the "forward defense theory" and extend a hand of cooperation to Moscow. With this development, Gorbachev could face his domestic opposition and agree with Kohl on July 16, 1990, that a unified Germany would be permitted to remain in NATO.

Kohl agreed that Germany would not acquire nuclear or chemical weapons and that the German army would be reduced to 370,000 soldiers. Furthermore, the Germans would provide massive financial assistance to help the Soviets construct housing facilities for the Soviet troops returning from East Germany. On September 12, 1990, the four powers and the two Germanies accepted this arrangement, and on October 3, 1990, reunited Germany regained its sovereignty.

### SIGNIFICANCE

Gorbachev's decision to permit Germany to remain in NATO, combined with announcements by East European countries that they intended to withdraw from military commitments to the Warsaw Pact, effectively eliminated the confrontation between the two military blocs. This development had long been demanded by peace and human rights movements in Germany. The unification of Germany also resulted in the elimination of the East German army. Only 50,000 former members of the East German army were to be absorbed by the united German army. Although many East German officers who had belonged to the Socialist Unity Party lost their careers, the militarization of East German society and schools was abolished. The former West German army also felt the impact of unification, as the total size of the German armed forces was reduced to 370,000.

The eventual departure of Soviet forces from East Germany and the reduction of foreign troops in West Germany helped to reverse environmental damage and made additional housing and other badly needed facilities available to the Germans. The absence of Soviet protection after 1994 also made it impossible for Moscow to assist, as it did in the case of Honecker, the escape of former East German Communists from German prosecution.

Reunification posed some problems. East Germans suffered from rising unemployment until East German industries became more competitive. The environmental destruction left behind by the departing Soviet troops required attention. Much of the cost of unification was borne by West German taxpayers.

Ironically, with increased political and civil rights, there emerged a virulent and xenophobic nationalism among some East German youths. This hostility was directed against foreigners in general and Jews and Poles in particular. On the other hand, one positive consequence of the agreement between Kohl and Gorbachev in July, 1990, was a treaty between Poland and Germany that guaranteed Poland's border. Although West Germany officially accepted the Oder-Neisse line after 1970, the West German constitution did not permit commitment to a final treaty with Poland until Germany had been reunified. In return, the Poles agreed to end the cultural persecution of and discrimination against ethnic Germans living in the Polish region of Silesia.

German reunification within the NATO alliance reassured neighboring countries that Germany would not represent a threat in the future. With the demise of the Warsaw Pact, Europe was no longer confronted with rival military blocs facing each other along the German borders. That lack of hostility facilitated the expansion of tolerance and human rights on both sides of the old Iron Curtain as Eastern European countries, one after another,

cast aside their Communist pasts and, like East Germany, cast their lot with the hopeful promise of integration into the Western capitalist economy, with its attendant political liberties.

*—Johnpeter Horst Grill*

## FURTHER READING

Adomeit, Hannes. "Gorbachev and German Unification: Revision of Thinking, Realignment of Power." *Problems of Communism* 39 (July/August, 1990): 1-23. Offers one of the best short reviews available of the evolution of Gorbachev's views on the German issue between 1985 and July, 1990. Informative endnotes include citations to articles in the Russian press that reveal Gorbachev's views.

Frey, Eric G. *Division and Détente: The Germanies and Their Alliances*. New York: Praeger, 1987. Remarkable work offers a fine survey of the relationship between the two German states. Includes valuable bibliography.

Herspring, Dale R. "The Soviets, the Warsaw Pact, and the Eastern European Militaries." In *Central and Eastern Europe: The Opening Curtain?*, edited by William E. Griffith. Boulder, Colo.: Westview Press, 1989. Informative chapter questions the reliability of the East European military organizations within the Warsaw Pact.

Kaltenfleiter, Werner. "NATO and Germany." In *NATO After Forty Years*, edited by Lawrence S. Kaplan et al. Wilmington, Del.: Scholarly Resources, 1990. Provides basic information on Germany's role in NATO and offers intelligent interpretations.

Kirchner, Emil J. "Genscher and What Lies Behind 'Genscherism.'" *West European Politics* 13 (April, 1990): 159-177. Reviews Genscher's impact as German foreign minister and argues that Genscher, a native of East Germany, quickly saw the significance of perestroika to German unification.

Macgregor, Douglas. *The Soviet-East German Military Alliance*. New York: Cambridge University Press, 1989. Offers a solid history of the relationship between the Soviet and East German militaries and argues that Moscow would use force to maintain its control of Eastern Europe.

Moreton, Edwina, ed. *Germany Between East and West*. New York: Cambridge University Press, 1987. Interesting collection of essays on the German question from the perspective of the mid-1980's examines in detail the "German plans" of the four major powers and of the two German states.

1990

Stent, Angela E. *Russia and Germany Reborn: Unification, the Soviet Collapse, and the New Europe.* Princeton, N.J.: Princeton University Press, 1999. Remarkable study addresses Russian-German relations following Gorbachev's rise to power.

Tewes, Henning. *Germany, Civilian Power, and the New Europe: Enlarging NATO and the European Union.* New York: Palgrave, 2002. Provides analysis of how Germany's unification affected foreign policy and

how institutions such as NATO and the European Union affected German politics.

**SEE ALSO:** June 21, 1973: East and West Germany Establish Diplomatic Relations; Oct. 1, 1982: Kohl Becomes Chancellor of West Germany; Nov. 9, 1989: Fall of the Berlin Wall; May 27, 1997: NATO and Russia Sign Cooperation Pact; Oct. 27, 1998: Schröder Replaces Kohl as German Chancellor.

## July 23, 1990
# SPOTTED OWL PROMPTS OLD-GROWTH TIMBER CONTROVERSY

*When the northern spotted owl was officially listed as an endangered species, the habitat protection required by the designation forced drastic reductions in the logging of Pacific Northwest old-growth forests.*

**LOCALE:** Pacific Northwest
**CATEGORIES:** Animals and endangered species; natural resources

**KEY FIGURES**
*Eric Forsman* (fl. late twentieth century), student at Oregon State University and wildlife biologist
*Jerry Franklin* (fl. late twentieth century), biologist with the U.S. Forest Service
*Chris Maser* (fl. late twentieth century), biologist with the Bureau of Land Management
*Thomas Zilly* (b. 1935), U.S. district court judge
*William Dwyer* (1929-2002), U.S. district court judge

**SUMMARY OF EVENT**
On June 25, 1990, the cover of *Time* magazine featured an illustration of the northern spotted owl, an indication of the national significance of the controversy swirling around this small bird. The Pacific Northwest timber industry warned that classifying the owl as an endangered species and thus requiring protection of its habitat would cause the loss of tens of thousands of jobs and would make the loggers, millworkers, and rural communities of the region endangered species themselves. At the same time, environmentalists cautioned that the loss of the owl would signal the end of the spectacular, centuries-old forest ecosystem for which the region was famous; the owl's habitat was one of the richest and most productive forests in the world.

The fight over the old-growth forest bubbled to the surface of the U.S. media in the mid-1980's, but the groundwork was laid a decade before. In the early 1970's,

wildlife biologist Eric Forsman, then a student at Oregon State University, became interested in the small, rare owl that would come to have enormous impact on the culture and the economy of the Northwest. The northern spotted owl, which was the object of only twenty-five confirmed sightings before Forsman began his studies, was found almost exclusively in the uncut, old-growth forest. The U.S. Forest Service later declared the bird an indicator species, a representative of the health of the entire old-growth ecosystem.

Also in the 1970's, the scientific community was beginning to develop an interest in the old-growth forest ecosystem itself. Jerry Franklin, a Forest Service biologist, led a team of researchers that produced the 1981 publication *Ecological Characteristics of Old-Growth Douglas-Fir Forests.* This Forest Service document was the first to identify and define the factors that make these forests unique and contradicted the attitude among many forest scientists that old-growth forests are biological deserts made up primarily of dead and dying trees. Chris Maser, a Bureau of Land Management biologist and a coauthor of the report, took the information beyond the scientific community and made public presentations explaining the complex interworkings of old-growth forests. He demonstrated how the interrelationships among the insects, mammals, trees, rotting logs, and even fungus of old-growth systems make these forests irreplaceable.

Environmentalists had long appreciated old-growth forests for their scenic and spiritual values. Many saw the great age of the trees in such forests, from two hundred to as much as one thousand years, as reason enough for protection. Old-growth forests were nevertheless being cut down at alarming rates, and environmentalists' aesthetic arguments carried little weight against the pragmatic economic reasoning of the timber industry and the Forest

Service. Environmentalists seized on the emerging scientific data and, replacing the pejorative term "old-growth forests" with "ancient forests," embarked on a public education and political campaign to reduce logging and preserve as much of the remaining old forests as possible.

The timber industry had a different opinion of old-growth forests. The trees in such forests had grown slowly in dense stands, resulting in tall, straight trunks with few branches near the ground. This growth produced fine-grained lumber with few knots, a product prized by woodworkers the world over. At the same time, the forests often contained standing dead or dying trees, as well as many logs slowly decaying on the ground. The industry saw this as wasteful and lamented the loss of valuable lumber. In addition, the old trees were often beyond the age of mean annual increase; that is, the growth of the trees had slowed, and a particular piece of ground was not producing wood fiber as fast as it could with younger trees. Despite its beauty, old-growth wood, to the loggers and millworkers of the Northwest, was detritus to be cleared off the land; the timber industry argued that this would make the best use of fine wood before it rotted and make way for a second-growth forest of young, faster-growing trees.

The forest-products industry, having cut most of the trees on its privately owned land, had become increasingly dependent for its raw materials on the national forests, public land managed by the Forest Service, an agency of the U.S. Department of Agriculture. Since the end of World War II, the timber companies' annual harvest from the national forests in the Oregon and Washington region had increased fivefold, from 900 million board feet in 1946 to more than 5 billion board feet in 1986.

As the intensity of the controversy about the logging of old-growth forests increased, media attention was drawn to the issue by the activities of radical environmentalist groups such as the loosely organized Earth First! Protesters from Earth First! disabled logging equipment, formed roadblocks, and camped high up in trees that were scheduled for cutting. These techniques rarely did more than delay logging for a few days, but they succeeded in making the clear-cutting of areas such as Millennium Grove, a stand of trees nearly one thousand years old, items on the local television news.

The major national environmental groups worked more quietly, their members pressing the government to reduce the annual harvest in the national forests. In spite of these attempts, the U.S. Congress, at the behest of

The northern spotted owl became an object of national controversy in the 1990's after it was listed as an endangered species, resulting in logging cutbacks of its old-growth forest habitat. (U.S. Fish and Wildlife Service)

senators and representatives from the Pacific Northwest, ordered the Forest Service, through the appropriations process, to cut even more timber than the agency recommended. Then, in 1986, a previously unknown organization based in Massachusetts, GreenWorld, petitioned the U.S. Fish and Wildlife Service to list the northern spotted owl as endangered. The initial report from the Fish and Wildlife Service recommended against listing the bird, but environmentalists protested and then sued, claiming undue pressure from Ronald Reagan's presidential administration. Judge Thomas Zilly of the U.S. district court agreed, forcing the Fish and Wildlife Service to reconsider. Finally, on July 23, 1990, the northern spotted owl was officially listed as an endangered species, triggering major transformations in the management of western forestlands.

## SIGNIFICANCE

After the listing of the northern spotted owl as an endangered species, the Forest Service and the timber industry were left in a quandary. The U.S. Fish and Wildlife Service, contrary to its direction in such matters, failed to designate the critical habitat requirements. The Forest Service moved forward tentatively, allowing limited harvesting and promising to abide by the guidelines for protection of the owl habitat laid down in a report issued by the Interagency Scientific Committee (also known as the Thomas Committee, for its chairman, Jack Ward Thomas). This document, released a few months before the listing of the spotted owl, mapped out 7.7 million acres of old-growth forest that should be off-limits to logging.

In May, 1991, after nearly one year of continued appeals and legal challenges to individual timber sales, Judge William Dwyer of the U.S. district court placed an injunction on all logging in spotted owl habitat in Washington, Oregon, and Northern California. This injunction halted logging in 80 percent of the seventeen national forests in the region and continued in effect until the Forest Service implemented a legal protection plan for the spotted owl, which it was required to do by March, 1992. That same spring, the Fish and Wildlife Service recommended that more than eleven million acres be preserved as habitat for the owl.

One of the immediate reactions to this recommendation was a flurry of bills in Congress attempting to legislate a solution. Proposals varied from environmentalist-supported bills that would create vast ancient-forest reserves to industry-supported bills that would mandate minimum harvest levels and amend the Endangered Species Act to take economic factors into account when species protection was considered. The Endangered Species Committee was also called upon to consider certain tim-

*Old-growth forests in the Pacific Northwest are the only habitat for the famous northern spotted owl as well as a host of other wildlife species.* (PhotoDisc)

ber sales and groups of sales. This committee, made up of highly placed administration officials, had the power to exempt certain projects from Endangered Species Act restrictions and thus was dubbed "the God Squad" for its power over the life and death of species.

The predicted crash in employment in the timber industry, which had been estimated to eliminate up to ninety-three thousand jobs, did not occur immediately, and industry support among the general public was further weakened. Up to three years' worth of timber had already been sold prior to Judge Dwyer's injunction, and harvesting of these sales was allowed to continue, keeping the industry busy in the years following the shutdown of the forests. Economic studies showed that a significant proportion of the job losses in the timber industry during this time resulted from automation, raw log exports, and natural fluctuations of the economy rather than from restrictions on logging in old-growth forests.

Meanwhile, more forest-dependent species were added to the endangered species list. These included the marbled murrelet, a seabird that requires large, old trees for nesting, and several runs of wild salmon that need the clean, clear water provided by unlogged forests.

In the early summer of 1993, when the deadline for the implementation of an owl protection plan had passed, President Bill Clinton convened the Portland Timber Summit in Oregon to consider a solution. This unprecedented conference brought the president, vice president, and leading cabinet officials together with industry, business, environmental, and Native American leaders. From the information gathered at this two-day meeting, the Clinton administration formulated a range of proposals; among these, the administration favored what it called Option 9, a broad-based plan for managing the forests of the Pacific Northwest. Although approved by Judge Dwyer in May, 1994, the plan satisfied neither environmental nor timber interests and was immediately challenged in court, perpetuating the deadlock.

Another sweeping shift that resulted from the furor over the spotted owl was a change in direction of the Forest Service itself. Jack Ward Thomas, the wildlife biologist who headed the Interagency Scientific Committee in 1989, was appointed chief of the Forest Service in 1993, marking the first time that a person other than a career administrator or timber planner had held the post. The appointment of a wildlife biologist to this important position signaled a significant change in Forest Service policy, from primary concern with the production of timber to dedication to managing the broad spectrum of issues related to the public forests.

The timber industry did indeed go through tough times, as the steel industry had before it. Mills were closed and jobs were lost as the industry struggled to adapt to using different sources of timber and smaller trees to process. Much of the private and state land that had been replanted in earlier decades was near harvest age, however, and because much of it was not suitable or designated for owl habitat, it would be available for cutting in a few years. Some experts predicted that cutting levels on all lands could soon reach historic highs.

By the mid-1990's, it appeared that a last-minute bargain with nature had been struck. Although 90 percent of the original old-growth forest had been cut down in the previous 150 years, environmentalists hoped that the last 10 percent could sustain viable stands of natural forest so that the old-growth ecosystem could survive to reveal its values and secrets and teach lessons about interconnection and interdependence. The timber industry continued to provide wood products to the world, although with different methods and materials. The spotted owl would probably survive, with just enough habitat left to hunt, nest, and rear its young as it had for uncounted generations.

—*Joseph W. Hinton*

## Further Reading

Dietrich, William. *The Final Forest: The Battle for the Last Great Trees of the Pacific Northwest*. New York: Simon & Schuster, 1992. Excellent study of the old-growth issue traces the background and consequences of the listing of the spotted owl as an endangered species. Well written, with sensitivity for both the loggers and the forest.

Ervin, Keith. *Fragile Majesty: The Battle for North America's Last Great Forest*. Seattle: Mountaineers, 1989. Focuses on the forest management controversies in Washington State, interspersing chapters on history and technical details with first-person observations of the forest and the environmentalists and timber workers at odds over it.

Gup, Ted. "Owl Versus Man." *Time*, June 25, 1990, 54-64. Presents a concise and informative overview of the issue at the time of the owl's listing as an endangered species.

Kelly, David, and Gary Braasch. *Secrets of the Old Growth Forest*. Salt Lake City, Utah: Gibbs Smith, 1988. First of the popular books about old-growth forests contains many excellent photographs and abundant text to introduce the reader to the intricacies of the ecosystem and the issues surrounding it.

1990

Maser, Chris. *Forest Primeval: The Natural History of an Ancient Forest*. Corvallis: Oregon State University Press, 2001. "Biography" of an old-growth forest traces the development of a fictional stand of trees from its germination after a fire in 988 C.E. to the twentieth century against the background of human history. Clearly explains the biological functioning of the ecosystem.

Siedeman, David. *Showdown at Opal Creek: The Battle for America's Last Wilderness*. New York: Carroll & Graf, 1993. Presents an interesting microcosm of the issue by examining the personalities and the relationship of two good friends who find themselves on opposite sides of the controversy over saving one old-growth forest in Oregon. Puts very human faces on both sides of this contemporary "civil war."

Stout, Benjamin. *The Northern Spotted Owl: An Oregon View, 1975-2002*. Victoria, B.C.: Trafford, 2006. Examines the controversy surrounding the protection of the northern spotted owl and its habitat and the negative effects such protection had on local Oregon communities.

**SEE ALSO:** 1971: Paclitaxel Is Extracted from Pacific Yew Trees; July 23, 1972: Launch of the First Earth Resources Technology Satellite; Aug. 17, 1974: U.S. Congress Revises Resource Management; Oct. 22, 1976: U.S. Congress Limits Forest Clear-Cutting; 1989: Arnold and Gottlieb Publish *The Wise Use Agenda*; Apr. 3, 1993: Clinton Convenes the Forest Summit.

## July 25, 1990
# BLOC QUÉBÉCOIS FORMS

*A new political party was created to contest Canadian general elections on the exclusive issue of sovereignty for the province of Quebec.*

**LOCALE:** Montreal, Quebec, Canada
**CATEGORIES:** Government and politics; organizations and institutions

### KEY FIGURES

*Lucien Bouchard* (b. 1938), leader of the Bloc Québécois
*Robert Bourassa* (1933-1996), premier of Quebec, 1970-1976 and 1985-1994
*Gilles Duceppe* (b. 1947), first Bloc Québécois candidate elected to the Canadian parliament
*Jacques Parizeau* (b. 1930), premier of Quebec, 1994-1995
*Mario Dumont* (b. 1970), leader of the Action Démocratique Party

### SUMMARY OF EVENT

The creation of the Bloc Québécois was a direct result of the constitutional turmoil that gripped Canada in the 1980's. Canada had adopted a new constitution in 1982, but the French-speaking province of Quebec refused to accept the constitution's legitimacy, primarily because the constitution failed to give Quebec adequate powers to protect its French language and unique Québécois culture. In order to secure Quebec's assent, Brian Mulroney, the Canadian prime minister, and all ten provincial lead-

ers met at Meech Lake, Quebec, in 1987, and crafted a series of constitutional amendments favorable to Quebec. However, it became increasingly apparent that not all the provincial legislatures would ratify the Meech Lake Accord by the deadline date of June 23, 1990, no doubt accurately reflecting English-speaking Canada's belief that the accord granted too many concessions to Quebec.

Faced with impending defeat, a number of members of Parliament (MPs) from Quebec, regardless of party affiliation, began to lose hope that the federal government would grant their province enough concessions to justify their remaining within the Canadian federation. If federalism would not work, then full political sovereignty for Quebec was the only plausible alternative. Lucien Bouchard, minister of environment in Mulroney's Conservative government, resigned on May 21, 1990, citing a loss of faith in the way the government had handled the crisis. Other defections, from both the Liberal Party and the Conservative Party, followed. Soon there was talk of forming a bloc of Quebec MPs whose principal task would be to fight for Quebec's sovereignty. Bouchard later claimed that Robert Bourassa, the Liberal premier of Quebec's provincial government, encouraged him to embark on such a project.

On July 25, 1990, the newly formed Bloc Québécois (BQ) announced its manifesto. It stated that the BQ's primary allegiance was to the nation of Quebec and recognized the province's legislature, the National Assembly, as the supreme democratic institution of the Québécois people. The BQ's mission was to defend Quebec's interests in the federal parliament and to promote sovereignty within Quebec. All BQ members would be given a free vote in the Canadian House of Commons; there would be no party discipline, save on the exclusive issue of sovereignty for Quebec. In June, 1991, the BQ transformed itself into a political party at a conference held in Sorel-Tracy. Now sovereignists could be consistent in their voting patterns. On the provincial level, they could vote for the Parti Québécois, a nationalist party established in 1968, and they would vote for the Bloc Québécois in federal elections.

Lucien Bouchard was personally responsible for much of BQ's success. Born in the ultranationalist region of Lac St. Jean in northern Quebec, he was trained as a lawyer and practiced law in Chicoutimi. He voted in favor of the 1980 provincial referendum on the issue of sovereignty, although it was defeated by a decisive margin. After serving on numerous high-profile commissions related to labor relations, Bouchard was appointed as Canada's ambassador to France, in which capacity he served from 1985 to 1988. In 1988, he was elected to Parliament as a Conservative, and the following year he was appointed minister of environment. Handsome, charismatic, and a fine speaker, Bouchard tended to be more intellectual than emotional, although he knew how to tap the impatience and frustrations of the Québécois people. Serving him well was an extraordinary ability to stay in tune with public opinion. From the time the BQ was founded, opinion polls consistently showed him to be by far the most popular politician in Quebec.

## SIGNIFICANCE

The Bloc Québécois experienced a good deal of electoral success in its early years. Shortly after it announced its new manifesto, a federal by-election was held in east Montreal on August 13, 1990. The BQ put up an attractive candidate in Gilles Duceppe, a former labor activist. He captured 66 percent of the vote to become the first sovereignist candidate elected to the Canadian parliament. In 1992, another attempt was made to appease Quebec on the constitutional issue. The Canadian prime minister and the provincial premiers hammered out a series of concessions to Quebec at Charlottetown, Prince Edward Island. Similar in scope to the Meech Lake Accord, these proposals had to be endorsed in referenda held in every province. The Bloc Québécois took the position that the Charlottetown Accord did not go far enough in meeting Quebec's minimum demands and

campaigned against it. The accord was voted down in six out of the ten provinces, and the vote in Quebec was 57 percent against.

When a general election was called for October, 1993, the BQ fielded candidates in all of Quebec's seventy-five constituencies. This was a daunting task, given the fact that the BQ was still a small group, consisting of only eight MPs. In some cases, the BQ encouraged legislative staff from the Parti Québécois to run for office. While the Liberals and Conservatives in Quebec campaigned on the issues of jobs and employment, the BQ was the only party to speak consistently on the sovereignty issue. The BQ won a stunning victory, capturing 49 percent of the vote in Quebec and winning 54 seats. The BQ did very well among former Conservatives, took 60 percent of the French-speaking vote, and had strong appeal among trade unionists and the educated urban elites. Nationwide, the Liberal Party under the leadership of Jean Chrétien won easily, gaining 177 seats, but because of the complete collapse of the Conservative Party vote, the Bloc Québécois emerged as the second-largest party in Parliament and therefore earned the formal status of Official Opposition.

Canadians understandably found it disconcerting that the Official Opposition was a party dedicated to the breaking up of Canada. Compounding the problem was that many MPs of the BQ were new to Parliament and had little interest in pan-Canadian or foreign affairs. Nevertheless, Bouchard had stated he would responsibly fulfill his role as the government's chief critic and act on behalf of all Canadians. So successful was Bouchard that he elicited respect in formerly hostile quarters, and some political analysts suggested that the BQ was more protective of mainstream Canadian values than were some of the more established federal parties. Although the BQ never developed a detailed party program, it emerged as a party that tended to be fiscally conservative and left of center on social welfare issues. It gained popularity by opposing the cuts in popular benefit programs proposed by some economy-minded MPs. Ironically, the electoral success of the BQ and the respect it generated within the House of Commons increased Quebecers' interest in federal affairs.

In 1994, sovereignists in Quebec scored another victory when the Parti Québécois was elected to power in provincial elections. The victory was undoubtedly more a result of the unpopularity of the outgoing Liberal Party than of any dramatic upsurge in sovereignist sentiment. Nevertheless, the new Parti Québécois premier, Jacques Parizeau, promised to hold a referendum on sovereignty

1990

during his term of office. In preparation for the forthcoming referendum, a new sovereignist alliance was forged that included the Parti Québécois, the Bloc Québécois, and the Action Démocratique Party, a small splinter party led by Mario Dumont. On June 12, 1995, they agreed that if the sovereignists won the referendum, there would be a year's time in which to negotiate a new political and economic arrangement with the rest of Canada. If those talks failed, Quebec would issue a unilateral declaration of independence.

The promised referendum was held on October 30, 1995. Prior to the voting, opinion polls showed the sovereignists trailing, but when Bouchard was in effect put in charge of the campaign instead of the heavy-handed Parizeau, there was an upsurge in support. More than 92 percent of Quebec's electorate voted, and those opposed to sovereignty won by a narrow margin of 50.6 percent to 49.4 percent. Fewer than 54,000 votes out of a total of 4,700,000 separated the two sides. On the day after the election, a disappointed Parizeau announced his intention to resign as Quebec's premier, and on January 29, 1996, he was succeeded by Lucien Bouchard. Because Bouchard had to resign his seat in the House of Commons, Michel Gauthier was chosen to be leader of the Bloc Québécois. Although the sovereignists were defeated, their response was one of total defiance; they were confident that the next referendum would finally yield the desired result. The referendum of 1995 thus essentially settled nothing, and both Quebec and Canada faced an uncertain future.

—*David C. Lukowitz*

## FURTHER READING

Bouchard, Lucien. *On the Record*. Translated by Dominique Clift. Toronto: Stoddart, 1994. The leader of the Bloc Québécois discusses his career, the founding of the new party, and the aspirations of the Québécois people.

Dickinson, John, and Brian Young. *A Short History of Quebec*. 3d ed. Montreal: McGill-Queen's University Press, 2003. Concise history provides political, social, cultural, and economic context for the events that took place in Quebec at the end of the twentieth century. Includes tables, illustrations, chronology, bibliography, and index.

Johnson, William. *A Canadian Myth: Québec, Between Canada and the Illusion of Utopia*. Montreal: Robert Davies, 1994. Presents a readable, informative account of Quebec politics in the early 1990's. Marked by a strong anti-Québécois bias.

Noël, Alain. "Distinct in the House of Commons: The Bloc Québécois as Official Opposition." In *Canada: The State of the Federation*, edited by Douglas M. Brown and Janet Hiebert. Kingston, Ont.: Institute of Intergovernmental Relations, 1994. Argues that the Bloc Québécois behaved responsibly during its first year in Parliament and was frequently more in tune with mainstream Canadian values than the more established parties.

Valaskakis, Kimon, and Angéline Fournier. *The Delusion of Sovereignty*. Translated by George Tombs. Montreal: Robert Davies, 1995. Argues that sovereignty would be detrimental to Quebec's economy and culture. Includes bibliography.

Young, Robert. *The Secession of Quebec and the Future of Canada*. Montreal: McGill-Queen's University Press, 1995. Thoughtful and scholarly analysis focuses on the impact that Quebec's secession would have on Canada and Quebec and concludes that it would not be catastrophic for either.

**SEE ALSO:** Apr. 17, 1982: Canada's Constitution Act; Apr. 17, 1982: Canadian Charter of Rights and Freedoms Is Enacted; Sept. 14, 1984: Mulroney Era Begins in Canada; June 22, 1990: Meech Lake Accord Dies; Nov. 4, 1993: Chrétien Takes Charge in Canada; June 29, 2000: Canadian Parliament Passes the Clarity Act.

**July 26, 1990**

# U.S. CONGRESS ENACTS DISABILITY RIGHTS

*Through the passage of the Americans with Disabilities Act, the U.S. Congress extended broad civil rights protections to an estimated forty-three million Americans with disabilities.*

**ALSO KNOWN AS:** Americans with Disabilities Act; U.S. Statutes at Large 104 Stat. 327; Public Law 101-336; U.S. Code 42 § 12101-12213

**LOCALE:** Washington, D.C.

**CATEGORIES:** Laws, acts, and legal history; civil rights and liberties

**KEY FIGURES**

*Tom Harkin* (b. 1939), U.S. senator from Iowa

*Tony Coelho* (b. 1942), U.S. congressman from California

*Steny H. Hoyer* (b. 1939), U.S. congressman from Maryland

*George H. W. Bush* (b. 1924), president of the United States, 1989-1993

**SUMMARY OF EVENT**

In 1991, the U.S. Census Bureau estimated that forty-three million Americans were living with some sort of physical or mental disability. For many years, such Americans were not assured of the basic rights afforded nondisabled people. They often suffered from discrimination when they attempted to do such simple things as get a job, see a movie, go out for dinner with family or friends, or rent an apartment. Frequently, disabled people were relegated to the status of second-class citizens.

Disabled people confront two general types of barriers. The first type is physical, such as the barriers caused for those in wheelchairs by stairs, narrow doorways, and narrow store aisles. The second type of barrier is less visible and includes obstacles such as hiring practices. Many people with disabilities are victims of blatant discrimination in everyday life. In the job market, many disabled individuals face discriminatory evaluations during the application process that focus on the existence of a disability rather than on the ability to perform a job.

Beginning in the 1960's, the U.S. government played an increased role in establishing the rights of disabled individuals. Two acts indirectly provided rights to the disabled. One was the Fair Housing Act of 1968, which required new apartments to be "adaptable" to future disabled tenants, and the other was the 1964 Civil Rights Act, which guaranteed basic rights to women and to members of racial, ethnic, and religious minority groups. The Civil Rights Act did not specifically mention the disabled, however, and thus they were still not guaranteed all the rights accorded nondisabled people in American society.

Other federal government actions focused specifically on the rights of the disabled, including passage of the Rehabilitation Act of 1973, which was the first milestone in this area. Section 504 of the 1973 act prohibited discrimination on the basis of handicap in any program or activity receiving federal funds. This covered, for example, activities in any federal employment, in employment by federal contractors, and in programs and activities receiving federal financial assistance. Any agency that denied access to the disabled risked losing all federal funding.

The Education for All Handicapped Children Act (EAHCA) was another milestone for disability rights. Passed in 1975, the EAHCA established the principle of teaching children with disabilities within the nation's mainstream school systems. The law stated that all children are entitled to a free public education, regardless of disability. As a result of this statute, children with disabilities began to learn alongside nondisabled students, and in the process they became better able to cope with their disabilities. The number of students with disabilities who received a full secondary school education grew dramatically as a direct result of the EAHCA.

The first of the disabled children who attended school under the EAHCA began to enter the labor market in the 1980's. They were well educated and highly motivated, and they had useful work skills. Most important, they wanted to find meaningful employment. Unfortunately, they often found that they faced discrimination both in seeking employment and, if hired, in getting to their job sites. Many Americans with disabilities began to demand the rights afforded to the nondisabled in the workforce.

Groups that advocated for the rights of disabled persons were successful in getting members of Congress to address issues surrounding the rights of the disabled in public places. The many existing organizations that had always focused their work on gaining rights for groups of individuals with particular disabilities—the blind or the deaf, for example—all came together to support the passage of the Americans with Disabilities Act (ADA). One group that brought much public attention to the issue of disabled rights was the National Council on the Handi-

*President George H. W. Bush signs the Americans with Disabilities Act of 1990.* (White House)

capped. Also working to gather support for the ADA was the Leadership Conference on Civil Rights. These groups, along with supporters in Congress, were able to garner great support for the measure.

Tom Harkin, a Democratic senator from Iowa, was the chief sponsor of the ADA in the U.S. Senate. Harkin, who had a brother who was deaf, was keenly aware of the problems faced by individuals with disabilities. He was also a member of the Senate's Labor and Human Resources Committee and chair of the Handicapped Subcommittee, to which the ADA was referred. The ADA had support from the majority of the members of the Senate, and the entire Senate passed the legislation quickly on September 7, 1989.

Tony Coelho, a Democratic representative from California and a person living with epilepsy, first introduced the ADA into the U.S. House of Representatives. When

Coelho was forced to resign his congressional seat in June of 1989 after investigations into his finances raised ethics questions, he asked Steny H. Hoyer, a Democratic representative from Maryland, to act as floor manager for the bill as it progressed through the House. Hoyer had been the original cosponsor of the bill and had worked closely with Coelho in the early stages of the bill.

The bill had to travel through four House committees before it could be introduced to the House for voting. This made for a much longer and more difficult route than in the Senate. The Education and Labor Committee was the only committee to approve the bill in 1989. The other three committees passed the bill in 1990. The Energy and Commerce Committee on March 13, 1990, was the second committee to approve the bill; Public Works and Transportation approved the bill on April 3, 1990; and the Judiciary Committee on May 2, 1990, became the fourth and final House committee to approve the bill. The entire House overwhelmingly passed the bill on May 22, 1990.

Two particular issues slowed the ADA on its path to becoming law. The first had to do with an amendment that would allow employers to transfer workers with contagious diseases out of food-handling jobs, even if such diseases could not be transmitted through food. Lawmakers on both sides of the issue noted that the amendment was aimed at people with acquired immunodeficiency syndrome (AIDS). Proponents of the amendment claimed that restaurant owners needed the flexibility to transfer people out of such jobs because of public perceptions that infected workers would pose a danger. Opponents asserted that the law should not be based on such perceptions, which were exactly the kind of problem the bill was needed to overcome.

The second issue that slowed passage of the ADA had to do with congressional coverage. Members of both chambers of Congress agreed that Congress should be subject to the bill's ban on discrimination but disagreed on how the bill should be enforced. The House version of the bill provided for an internal mechanism; the Senate bill made the provisions applicable to the Congress.

The final bill compromised on both issues. On the AIDS issue, the ADA required the secretary of Health and Human Services to produce a list of communicable diseases that could be transmitted through food. On the congressional coverage issue, the bill provided that the internal mechanism would apply in the House and that the Senate would set up its own internal procedure while also allowing for cases to go to federal court.

The ADA was passed in final form by the House on July 12 and by the Senate on July 13. President George H. W. Bush, who had given strong support to the bill since 1988, when he was vice president, signed it into law at a White House ceremony on July 26, 1990.

### SIGNIFICANCE

The ADA was written much like the 1964 Civil Rights Act, but it was broader in that it included protection for any person with a mental or physical impairment that substantially limited major life activities. The ADA prohibited discrimination against the disabled in employment, public services, and public accommodations and required that telecommunications be made accessible to those with speech and hearing impairments through the use of special relay systems. The law applied to all public facilities, including office buildings, gas stations, airports, hotels, bars, restaurants, lobbies, sports facilities,

libraries, and parks. The ADA was much broader in scope than the 1964 Civil Rights Act in that it increased the accommodations protections to include services ranging from museums, theaters, and sporting events to doctors' offices, hospitals, and pharmacies. Businesses that did not comply with the law might have to give back pay, front pay, attorneys' fees, and job reinstatement to people who had been the victims of discrimination.

Many business interests were opposed to passage of the ADA. Business owners claimed that they would have to spend large amounts of money to comply with the new rules; they would be forced to install wheelchair ramps, elevators, telephone devices for the hearing-impaired, and more. Supporters of the ADA asserted that this was not necessarily true—businesses had only to come up with cheap and creative solutions to allow people with disabilities equal access to their facilities. The federal government also offered a construction tax credit for businesses to help them comply with the law.

The section of the law that affected the greatest number of businesses—the provisions covering hiring practices—would not cost businesses anything. Business owners and managers had to rethink the way they interviewed job applicants to ensure that the questions they asked were relevant and had to examine the essential and nonessential parts of each job. Employers could face lawsuits for turning down applicants who could perform all the essential parts of a job.

Questions remained as to some of the very broad and vague language found in the ADA. For example, the bill required businesses to make "reasonable accommodation" that did not cause "undue hardship" on them. The vagueness of these terms and others troubled business groups, who argued that disagreements over the definitions would lead to a high number of expensive and time-consuming lawsuits.

The ADA also forbade discrimination on public transportation. All new vehicles bought for public transit were required to be accessible to disabled people. Companies that provided intercity transportation were required to make adaptations for wheelchair users. New rail facilities were required to be accessible to persons with disabilities. Also, one car per train in existing rail systems had to be made accessible.

The Department of Justice was assigned the duty of enforcing the ADA and published proposed rules to implement the ADA. The department also established a new office, within the Coordination and Review Section of the Civil Rights Division, expressly to address ADA implementation issues.

On a broad level, sponsors of the ADA hoped the bill would change the way Americans thought about and treated people with disabilities. ADA supporters wanted the bill to be a first step in helping to integrate the disabled into mainstream American society; they looked forward to a day when it would be common to see individuals with disabilities participating in many different activities alongside nondisabled people. The ADA also sent the message to Americans with disabilities that they did not have to be dependent on others and that they could have greater participation in community life.

—*Nancy E. Marion*

## FURTHER READING

Francis, Leslie Pickering, and Anita Silvers, eds. *Americans with Disabilities: Exploring Implications of the Law for Individuals and Institutions.* New York: Routledge, 2000. Collection of essays by experts in many different fields examines the philosophical, legal, and public policy questions surrounding the ADA. Includes an appendix containing the text of related laws and court decisions.

Gearheart, Bill R., Mel W. Weishahn, and Carol J. Gearheart. *The Exceptional Student in the Regular Classroom.* 6th ed. Upper Saddle River, N.J.: Merrill, 1996. Focuses on the challenges of educating students with various kinds of disabilities. Emphasizes that each disabled student has particular needs that the educational system must meet.

Hunsicker, J. Freedley, Jr. "Ready or Not: The ADA." *Personnel Journal* 69 (August, 1990): 81-86. Provides an extremely readable summary of the provisions of the ADA for employers and speculates about the probable effects of the ADA on businesses. Provides legal definitions of some vague terms included in the law.

McKee, Bradford. "Achieving Access for the Disabled." *Nation's Business* 79 (June, 1991): 31-34. Presents a summary of the ADA from the business point of view. Summarizes some controversial aspects of the law and makes predictions regarding the ADA's likely effects on businesses. Notes the effective dates for different parts of the bill.

Rovner, Julie. "Promise, Uncertainties Mark Disability-Rights Measure." *Congressional Quarterly Weekly Report* 48 (May 12, 1990): 1477-1479. Provides a legislative summary of the ADA as well as the proponent and opposing points of view on the proposed bill.

Scotch, Richard K. *From Good Will to Civil Rights: Transforming Federal Disability Policy.* 2d ed. Philadelphia: Temple University Press, 2001. Examines the effects of the ADA as well as the act's failures in the eyes of people with disabilities. Discusses the role of the disability rights movement in passage of the ADA. Includes bibliography and index.

"Sweeping Law for Rights of Disabled." *1990 Congressional Quarterly Almanac* 46 (1990): 447-461. Presents brief background on the bill and describes the path of the bill through Congress. Includes a readable summary of the provisions of the ADA.

SEE ALSO: Sept. 26, 1973: U.S. Congress Responds to Demands of Persons with Disabilities; Nov. 29, 1975: U.S. Law Provides for Public Education of Disabled Children; Dec. 9, 1975: United Nations Adopts a Declaration on Disabled Persons' Rights.

## August, 1990
# GENETICALLY ENGINEERED RABIES VACCINE IS RELEASED

*A vaccinia virus, genetically engineered to contain rabies virus proteins, was released in Virginia to control rabies in raccoons.*

**LOCALE:** Parramore Island, off the coast of Virginia
**CATEGORIES:** Science and technology; health and medicine; genetics

### KEY FIGURES

*Charles E. Rupprecht* (fl. late twentieth century), scientist who developed a live recombinant rabies vaccine

*David A. Espeseth* (fl. late twentieth century), deputy director of veterinary biologics at the U.S. Department of Agriculture

*Edward P. Bruggemann* (fl. late twentieth century), scientist with the National Audubon Society

### SUMMARY OF EVENT

On July 5, 1989, the Virginia Department of Health approved the field testing of baits spiked with a genetically engineered rabies vaccine to control the spread of rabies in raccoons. The initial field test was conducted in 1990 on Parramore Island, off the coast of Virginia, after having been approved by the state and the Nature Conservancy, which owned the island. Both this test and one in Pennsylvania showed the recombinant vaccine to be effective in controlling the spread of rabies in raccoons. Additional tests, using a similar recombinant vaccine, were conducted in Europe to control rabies in foxes. Vaccination programs of this kind, although they undoubtedly helped control the spread of rabies in the wild, were found to be expensive, and it remained unclear whether the technique could be cost-effective when used on a large scale.

After 1977, the number of rabid raccoons reported in the mid-Atlantic states increased dramatically. The initial source of the epidemic was apparently the unknowing transport of rabid raccoons to the border between Virginia and West Virginia by hunting clubs. The epizootic (an epidemic within an animal population) spread slowly up the coast, reaching as far north as southern New Hampshire and parts of upstate New York by late summer, 1993. Although most wild mammals are susceptible to rabies, which is commonly found in many areas throughout the United States, the disease is carried most frequently by skunks, bats, foxes, and raccoons. Foxes, coyotes, and wolves are most susceptible to ra-

bies, followed by raccoons, skunks, bats, and bobcats. Infected wildlife can carry the disease to humans directly or through dogs and cats with which humans come into contact. An effective vaccine to halt the spread of rabies in the wild would help prevent transmission of the disease to humans.

The incidence of rabies in humans in the United States declined considerably after the 1950's, in large part as a result of extensive and successful programs for controlling rabies in pets; few human rabies deaths occur in the United States. In the early twenty-first century, most rabies deaths in humans take place in impoverished countries, where prevention and treatment programs are too expensive to be supported by the local governments. The fatal effects of exposure to known rabid animals can be prevented through cleansing of the wound and timely administration of gamma globulin and an antirabies vaccine.

By the early 1990's, raccoons and animals infected by raccoons accounted for more than 60 percent of all diagnosed cases of rabies in the United States. Although the increased incidence of rabid raccoons after 1970 was not accompanied by an increase in the number of human rabies cases, it led to considerable anxiety.

In the mid-1980's, Charles E. Rupprecht and a team of scientists from the Wistar Institute of Anatomy and Biology in Philadelphia, along with researchers at the Transgène Company in France, created a genetically engineered rabies vaccine that was later manufactured by the French veterinary pharmaceutical company Rhône Mérieux. The vaccine was derived from a weakened strain of vaccinia virus, the virus used for immunizations against smallpox, which causes a mild localized infection. Into that virus Rupprecht inserted the gene that produces the protein found on the surface of the bullet-shaped rabies virus, a sugar-containing protein (or glycoprotein) used by the virus to attach to host cells and against which the host's immune system reacts. In the resultant recombinant, chimeric virus—part vaccinia virus and part rabies virus—the protein produced by the rabies gene finds its way to the surface of the vaccinia virus, where it would be positioned in the rabies virus; a host's immune system would therefore react to the recombinant virus in much the same way as a rabies virus.

A genetically engineered vaccine of this kind has several advantages over traditional rabies vaccines. Unlike other vaccines, it can be administered orally, and it is ef-

1990

fective in raccoons. Moreover, the recombinant vaccine cannot cause rabies because it contains only one of the rabies virus genes and lacks all the genes required to duplicate the virus and cause the disease.

Rupprecht and his team initially sought to test the vaccine in 1989 on Cedar and Murphy islands, off the coast of South Carolina. Island locations were desirable for testing because they would allow the researchers to prevent the possible spread of vaccinated animals to larger, mainland populations. South Carolina state health officials, concerned about the possible danger of the vaccinia virus to humans, suggested that the vaccine should be tested on nonhuman primates. When David A. Espeseth, deputy director of veterinary biologics at the U.S. Department of Agriculture (USDA), disagreed, South Carolina refused to allow the testing. One week later, however, on July 5, 1989, the Virginia Department of Health granted approval to Wistar Institute to carry out the tests on Parramore Island.

Field trials began in August, 1990, and continued for one year. The rabies vaccine was injected into fish that was distributed around the island as bait; uneaten bait was removed after two weeks. The bait, which contained a "marker" substance that allowed scientists to distinguish animals that had eaten it from ones that had not, attracted raccoons but usually not other species. The researchers found that raccoons that ate the vaccine-laced bait produced antibodies against rabies virus, whereas those that did not eat the bait did not produce antibodies.

## SIGNIFICANCE

Humans have feared rabies since antiquity. Left untreated, the rabies virus acquired from the bite of an infected animal proceeds along the host's nerves at a rate of 8 to 20 millimeters per day until it reaches the spinal cord. The virus incubation period can be as short as five days or as long as many years, depending, at least in part, on the distance of the bite from the spinal cord. Once the virus has infected the spinal cord, it is no longer susceptible to the body's immune system and cannot be stopped by immunization. Symptoms then progress rapidly within seven to fourteen days, beginning with spasms of the face and neck, body rigidity, extreme difficulty in swallowing—the disease is sometimes called hydrophobia because even the sight of water causes severe spasms of the throat—hallucinations, disorientation, and high fever. The illness ends with coma and death.

A number of attempts had been made previously to control the spread of rabies in wild mammals. In one method, called culling, the populations suspected of carrying the virus were killed, in the hope that reducing the population size would reduce the likelihood of animal-to-animal virus transmission; this method required the killing of very large numbers of animals to be effective. Another method involved capturing wild animals and vaccinating them with the same vaccine that protects domesticated animals; the percentage of animals captured was never high enough for this method to be effective, however. Several methods of self-vaccination had been tried in the 1960's, but some of the techniques harmed the animals, and it was impossible to ensure that nontarget species were not immunized by mistake. In the mid-1970's, William Winkler, then at the Centers for Disease Control, developed sausage baits containing a plastic drinking straw filled with vaccine to immunize foxes, but because the incidence of fox rabies declined in the United States through natural causes, that method was never field-tested.

Despite the successful results of the Parramore Island tests, a number of scientists believed that raccoon vaccination programs could have little long-term effect on the incidence of rabies. Edward P. Bruggemann, a scientist with the National Audubon Society, declared that rabies vaccination of raccoons would not protect public health because, according to a theoretical model designed by M. J. Coyne, raccoon vaccination reduces the fluctuations in population size that occur as a result of the disease; thus, as the level of vaccination increases, so does the population of raccoons. The percentage of rabid animals would not decrease significantly, however, unless nearly 95 percent of the raccoons were vaccinated. To maintain that level of vaccination, the immunizations would have to be done on a yearly basis. Bruggemann proposed vaccinating an animal species that requires lower rates of immunization to be effective in the population as a whole. Alternatively, a rabies-free area could be maintained through the immunization of animals whose populations are not yet affected.

Bruggemann also questioned the long-term effects of releasing a nonnative virus into the environment. Although vaccinia was used for many years to prevent smallpox, little was known about its host range or its ability to cause disease. The USDA concluded in a 1991 report, however, that laboratory and field tests had shown the genetically engineered rabies vaccine to have had no adverse effects on any species. In the same report, the department approved field testing on the grounds that such tests were safe and posed no significant environmental risk.

Some scientists questioned whether it was possible

for large-scale rabies vaccination of wild mammals such as raccoons to be cost-effective. According to a review in the *New England Journal of Medicine*, 82 percent of expenditures for rabies prevention in the United States is accounted for by the vaccination of pets. Treatment of humans before and after exposure accounts for another 10 percent. The per-capita expense can double, however, when raccoon rabies infects a previously uninfected area, because the cost of oral vaccination of raccoons ranges from $325 to $1,000 per square kilometer of habitat. The cost for protecting an area the size of New Jersey, for example, would be between $6 million and $19 million each year. Expenses for treating humans would not decrease, because there is no way of deducing whether a raccoon that has bitten a human is rabid or not. Once a wild mammal population is known to be largely immune, however, the vaccination of pets would no longer be as imperative.

Although the recombinant rabies vaccine proved biologically successful, it was not successful from an economic point of view. It was thought, however, that the vaccine could eventually replace or become an alternative to the traditional rabies vaccines used in veterinary practice.

*—Linda E. Fisher*

## FURTHER READING

Anderson, Roy M. "Rabies: Immunization in the Field." *Nature* 354 (December 26, 1991): 502-503. Describes the results of field tests in Europe of a recombinant vaccinia virus rabies vaccine. Suitable for general readers. Includes a list of references.

Avise, John C. *The Hope, Hype, and Reality of Genetic Engineering: Remarkable Stories from Agriculture, Industry, Medicine, and the Environment.* New York: Oxford University Press, 2004. Examines the potential of genetic engineering and provides examples of achievements and failures in the field. Includes discussion of the engineering of vaccines.

Bruggemann, Edward P. "Rabies in the Mid-Atlantic States: Should Raccoons Be Vaccinated?" *BioScience* 42 (October, 1992): 694-699. Discusses methods for controlling raccoon rabies in the wild and explains why raccoon vaccination may not be a practical strategy for controlling rabies. Includes illustrations, figures, and an extensive list of references.

Fishbein, Daniel B., and Laura E. Robinson. "Rabies." *New England Journal of Medicine* 329 (November 25, 1993): 1632-1638. Scholarly article presents a thorough review of the biology of rabies and its spread in animals. Discusses the nature and cost of prevention. Includes tables, illustrations, and an extensive list of references.

Petersen, Alan, and Robin Bunton. *The New Genetics and the Public's Health.* New York: Routledge, 2002. Examines the implications of genetic research in general for the public health arena. Includes discussion of the potential impacts of genetically engineered vaccines.

Sun, Marjorie. "South Carolina Blocks Test of Rabies Vaccine." *Science* 244 (June 30, 1989): 1535. Discusses the reasons the first suggested field trial was prevented.

_____. "Virginia OKs Rabies Vaccine Test." *Science* 245 (July 14, 1989): 126. Brief article reports approval for the first field study of the recombinant rabies vaccine in the United States.

Weintraub, Pamela. "Vaccines Go Wild: Once They're Out, Can We Get Them Back?" *Audubon* 95 (January/February, 1993): 16-17. Short report examines the use of recombinant vaccines to prevent the spread of diseases in animals.

Winkler, William G., and Konrad Bögel. "Control of Rabies in Wildlife." *Scientific American* 266 (June, 1992): 86-92. Discusses the methods used to control rabies in wild animals, the recombinant vaccine, and vaccination programs in Europe and the United States. Includes illustrations and references.

**SEE ALSO:** Apr. 7, 1976: Genentech Is Founded; 1980: Berg, Gilbert, and Sanger Develop Techniques for Genetic Engineering; June 16, 1980: U.S. Supreme Court Grants a Patent for a Living Organism; 1981-1982: Geneticists Create Giant Mice; May 14, 1982: Eli Lilly Releases the First Commercial Genetically Engineered Medication; July, 1986: FDA Approves a Genetically Engineered Vaccine for Hepatitis B; Apr. 24, 1987: Genetically Altered Bacteria Are Released into the Environment; May, 1988: Patent Is Granted for Genetically Engineered Mice; May, 1994: Genetically Engineered Food Reaches Supermarkets.

1990

## August 2, 1990
# IRAQI INVASION OF KUWAIT

*On August 2, 1990, Iraq, motivated by a variety of factors, invaded its southern neighbor, Kuwait, thereby initiating a brutal occupation of that country and setting the stage for the Persian Gulf War of 1991.*

**LOCALE:** Kuwait

**CATEGORIES:** Terrorism, atrocities, and war crimes; wars, uprisings, and civil unrest; colonialism and occupation

**KEY FIGURES**

*Saddam Hussein* (1937-2006), president of Iraq, 1979-2003

*George H. W. Bush* (b. 1924), president of the United States, 1989-1993

*Jaber al-Ahmad al-Jaber al-Sabah* (1926-2006), emir of Kuwait, r. 1977-2006

**SUMMARY OF EVENT**

During the early morning hours of August 2, 1990, Iraqi armed forces suddenly invaded neighboring Kuwait, resulting in the looting of that small country and the brutalization of the Kuwaiti people. This act of aggression was the result both of trends that had been developing in the upper Persian Gulf region for several years and of specific problems that, when combined, led to an escalation of Iraqi-Kuwaiti tensions and, ultimately, invasion.

In the broadest sense, three closely interconnected factors contributed to an increasingly explosive situation in the Persian Gulf region. First, throughout the 1980's, Iraqi president Saddam Hussein had systematically and often brutally eliminated all sources of rival political power in Iraq while simultaneously concentrating all power and authority around himself. For example, during the late 1980's, Hussein crushed the Kurdish minority within Iraq, allegedly using chemical weapons to suppress the Kurds and sending more than sixty thousand refugees into Iran and Turkey. Furthermore, the Iraqi authorities forcibly resettled more than half a million Kurds away from the border to secure the frontier areas. Meanwhile, throughout the 1980's, Hussein effectively excluded independent elements of the ruling Ba'th Party from power and increasingly surrounded himself with associates who were disinclined to provide him with independent advice. This served to isolate the Iraqi president, a trend that was particularly dangerous in view of

his lack of personal experience with the Western powers and limited experience even within the Arab world.

Second, in the aftermath of the Iraqi victory over Iran in the lengthy Iran-Iraq War (1980-1988), Iraq emerged as the dominant indigenous military power in the Persian Gulf region. At the conclusion of that war, Iraq's military consisted of more than one million men, including the sizable and well-equipped Republican Guard. In addition, during the Iran-Iraq conflict, the Iraqis had invested heavily in defense industries, particularly in chemical weapons production and the development of missile technology. Following the cessation of hostilities with Iran, the Iraqi authorities continued to emphasize the expansion of Iraq's high-tech armaments industry. In short, as Baghdad entered the 1990's, Iraq's military, backed by the Iraqi defense industrial establishment, placed Saddam Hussein in a strong position to influence Persian Gulf affairs along desired lines.

Third, against the backdrop of his monopolistic consolidation of political power domestically and Iraq's postwar military dominance in the Persian Gulf region, Hussein increasingly aspired to leadership of the entire Arab world. The Iraqi president apparently believed that the collapse of communism in Eastern Europe and the growing internal political, ethnic, and economic chaos within the Soviet Union, combined with other changes in the international power configuration, created an opportunity in which an Iraqi-led coalition of revolutionary Arab states could assert itself and emerge as a more powerful, perhaps regionally dominant, actor in the international arena.

As part of his effort to assert his leadership within the Arab world, Hussein directed his rhetoric against Israel, the traditional adversary of the Arabs. On April 2, 1990, he articulated a new deterrence policy for Iraq under the terms of which, should Israel attack Iraq, as it had in 1981 when the Israelis destroyed the Iraqi Osirak nuclear reactor, Iraq would respond with a chemical attack on Israel. Later, the Iraqi president said that Iraq would extend this deterrent umbrella to any Arab state desiring Iraqi assistance. Simultaneously, Hussein attempted to consolidate additional support for his effort to assert leadership throughout the Arab world by promising Iraqi support for the Palestinian cause. Hussein's bold new military deterrence doctrine directed toward Israel, combined with his encouragement of the Palestinians and other, similar measures designed to appeal to the Arab masses, allowed the Iraqi president to reap a swell of popular support throughout the entire Arab world.

Notwithstanding Iraq's regional military power, along with Hussein's effective concentration of political power within Iraq and his growing prestige as a pan-Arab leader in the aftermath of the Iran-Iraq War, Iraq was confronted by a series of serious problems that threatened to jeopardize Hussein's ambitions for himself and Iraq. The central problem was financial: Iraq emerged from its war with Iran with an estimated debt of eighty billion dollars, thirty to thirty-five billion dollars of which consisted of short-term loans owed to the Western powers, with the remainder owed to the oil-producing Arab states of the Persian Gulf. The debt problem was further compounded by Iraq's postwar policy of continued heavy investment in its high-tech defense industry as well as highly ambitious reconstruction projects in war-damaged areas of Iraq and the importation of consumer goods and food from abroad, all requiring additional hard currency. Finally, Iraq's already high demand for foreign exchange was further amplified by its annual debt service requirements of six to seven billion dollars.

Iraq hoped to meet its financial needs by increasing oil revenues. This hope was predicated on predictions of oil price increases. Unfortunately for the Iraqis, when the price of oil declined from twenty dollars to fourteen dollars per barrel during a six-month period between January and June, 1990, they faced a serious short-term financial shortfall. Many Iraqis blamed the Western powers, arguing that the decline in oil prices was part of a larger Western conspiracy in which the West had manipulated the oil market so as to create financial hardship for Iraq and thereby force Hussein's government to abandon its regional policies and ambitions.

Hussein also accused Kuwait and the United Arab Emirates of "cheating" on OPEC (Organization of Petroleum Exporting Countries) production quotas, thereby further contributing to the decline in oil prices. Tensions between Iraq and Kuwait were further exacerbated by Kuwait's refusal to forgive the debt owed to it by Iraq. In short, rather than recognizing the underlying sources of Iraq's financial instability and adopting effective measures to reorder spending priorities and place Iraq on a sound financial footing, Hussein instead blamed the Western powers, Kuwait, and the United Arab Emirates for Iraq's financial problems.

In addition to its financial differences with Kuwait, Iraq also had a series of territorial disputes with its southern neighbor. Prior to relinquishing claim to all of Kuwaiti territory in 1963, Iraq had made periodic attempts to assert full Iraqi control over the entirety of Kuwait. After 1963, although Iraqi claims against Kuwaiti territory became more limited in scope, such claims remained a topic of contention between the two states. One dimension of the dispute centered on the Khawr Abd Allah estuary, which constitutes the maritime portion of the Iraqi-Kuwaiti border and leads to the Iraqi naval base and port at Umm Qasr. Kuwait applied the midchannel doctrine to divide the estuary, whereas Iraq claimed the entire waterway. Moreover, Iraq sought to obtain control of Būbiyān and Warbah islands from Kuwait, as these islands effectively controlled the estuary's entrance. Kuwait, of course, rejected Iraq's claims, but the Iraqis thought it was vital for Iraq's national security and the success of their political, economic, and military ambitions to obtain full Iraqi control over this important outlet to the Persian Gulf.

In addition to the Khawr Abd Allah waterway dispute, the Iraqis claimed ownership of the entire Rumaila oil field, which lay on both Iraqi and Kuwaiti territory. In addition, Iraq accused Kuwait of pumping from the Rumaila field and selling the oil at considerable profit during the Iran-Iraq War. Hussein's government demanded that the border be revised in accord with Iraq's claims to the entire Rumaila field and that Kuwait pay Iraq two billion dollars for the oil allegedly pumped earlier from the disputed field. Kuwait also rejected these claims, thereby leading to further estrangement between the Kuwaiti and Iraqi governments.

Finally, in the broadest sense, the Iraqi authorities capitalized on popular Arab resentment of the wealthy, conservative monarchies of the Persian Gulf. In this sense, Saddam Hussein was able to frame Iraq's financial and territorial disputes with Kuwait within the larger ideological rivalry between revolutionary pan-Arabism and the conservative monarchies of the Arab world.

Although relations between Iraq and Kuwait had been deteriorating for some time, tensions between the two states began to rise dramatically in late May, 1990. In mid-July, Hussein threatened action if key differences between Iraq and Kuwait were not resolved to his satisfaction. Meanwhile, Iraqi forces concentrated along the Kuwaiti border. Then, suddenly, on August 2, 1990, Iraq invaded Kuwait. Within hours, the entire country was overrun by Iraqi troops. Most of Kuwait's ruling family escaped to Saudi Arabia. Initially, the Iraqis claimed that the Kuwaiti opposition had invited Iraq into Kuwait, but their inability to produce a cooperative Kuwaiti provisional government ultimately led the Iraqi authorities to reassert their old claim to the whole of Kuwait and sim-

1990

ply to annex the entire country. The northern portion of Kuwait was attached to Basra, and the remainder of Kuwait was declared the nineteenth Iraqi province.

## SIGNIFICANCE

The Iraqi invasion of Kuwait had enormous impacts on the Persian Gulf region and the entire Middle East in addition to the effects on Kuwait itself. First, with respect to Kuwait, following the invasion, the Iraqis looted the entire country of any movable items: furniture, autos, Kuwait's gold reserves, industrial equipment, and even treasures from the Kuwaiti museum. Moreover, approximately half of Kuwait's citizenry, along with substantial numbers of Asian and Palestinian workers employed in Kuwait, fled the country. With respect to those who remained, the Iraqis ruthlessly crushed indigenous resistance. Many brutal incidents took place—personal arrests, torture, and executions—and many among Kuwait's male population between the ages of eighteen and forty-five were taken back to Iraq to be held hostage by the Iraqi authorities.

Meanwhile, the international community reacted to the Iraqi aggression against Kuwait. Immediately following the invasion, U.S. president George H. W. Bush ordered an economic embargo of Iraq. The Western European states and Japan also embargoed the Iraqis and, on August 6, 1990, the United Nations Security Council ordered a global economic embargo against the Baghdad regime. The following day, President Bush ordered the deployment of U.S. military forces to Saudi Arabia, thereby commencing Operation Desert Shield. The military deployment was immediately broadened to include representation from a number of Arab powers and members of the international community.

On August 8, Iraqi closed its borders to foreign nationals inside Iraq and Kuwait, thereby preventing thousands of foreigners from leaving either country. On August 25, the U.N. Security Council authorized the use of military force to enforce the embargo against Iraq, and on August 28, the Iraqi government allowed foreign women and children to depart Iraq and Kuwait, but it continued to hold foreign men as hostages.

Throughout the autumn, the crisis mounted as the United States and its Desert Shield coalition partners poured troops and military equipment into Saudi Arabia. On November 29, 1990, the U.N. Security Council established January 15, 1991, as the deadline for Iraq to withdraw from Kuwait and threatened use of military force to drive the Iraqis out if the deadline was not met. Efforts by President Bush to secure an eleventh-hour negotiated

withdrawal and Iraq's December 6, 1990, decision to release the foreign nationals it had been holding since early August failed to secure a peaceful settlement of the crisis. On January 12, 1991, the U.S. Congress authorized President Bush to use military force to drive the Iraqis from Kuwait, thus clearing the way for the commencement of hostilities following the expiration of the January 15 withdrawal deadline.

On January 17, 1991, at 12:50 A.M. (4:50 P.M., January 16, 1991, eastern standard time), with Iraq still in possession of Kuwait, Operation Desert Storm began. Over the next five and one-half weeks, Iraqi military targets were pounded by U.S. and coalition airpower. On February 23, the United States and the other members of the coalition launched ground operations against the Iraqi military forces. Saddam Hussein ordered the withdrawal of Iraqi forces from Kuwait on February 25, and, late the following day, the Kuwaiti resistance declared that it was in control of Kuwait City. On February 27, 1991, President Bush announced the liberation of Kuwait and the defeat of the Iraqi armed forces. He further announced that offensive operations by the United States and its coalition partners would be suspended at midnight.

The war had devastating impacts on Kuwait, Iraq, and the entire region. Extensive damage was done within Kuwait as the result of air and ground operations during the conflict, and the retreating Iraqi forces set fire to Kuwaiti oil wells and also released a significant quantity of oil into the Persian Gulf, thereby creating environmentally disastrous air and water pollution. The oil fires burned for nine months before they were fully extinguished. Moreover, in their haste to withdraw, the Iraqis left within Kuwait a massive number of mines and other explosives that would require years to disarm. In addition, missiles fired by Iraq during the war caused damage in neighboring countries, particularly in Saudi Arabia and in nonbelligerent Israel. Finally, in the aftermath of the war, the weakened but still powerful government of Saddam Hussein brutally crushed Kurdish and other opposition elements that emerged in the wake of Iraq's defeat.

The bitter legacy of Iraq's invasion of Kuwait, the human rights violations that characterized Iraq's occupation of Kuwait and Saddam Hussein's policies toward particular populations within Iraq, and the continued existence of the regime that perpetrated all these horrors left much unfinished business after the Persian Gulf War. The failure of Iraq to live up to numerous U.N. Security Council resolutions in subsequent years continued to generate controversy and ultimately produced a second confrontation with Iraq involving a coalition of more than forty countries, led by U.S. president George W. Bush in 2003, that finally toppled Saddam Hussein's regime. However, a troubled and controversial occupation of Iraq ensued, as elements of Hussein's former supporters continued a bloody insurgency. Nevertheless, in a country that had known only brutal dictatorship for nearly three previous decades, sovereignty was passed to an interim government after one year of occupation, and a new constitution and democratically elected government were fashioned and installed by 2006.

*—Howard M. Hensel*

**FURTHER READING**

Hassan, Hamdi A. *The Iraqi Invasion of Kuwait: Religion, Identity, and Otherness in the Analysis of War and Conflict*. Sterling, Va.: Pluto Press, 1999. Presents a well-balanced analysis of why Iraq invaded Kuwait. Includes bibliography and index.

Lenczowski, George. *The Middle East in World Affairs*. 4th ed. Ithaca, N.Y.: Cornell University Press, 1980. One of the best single sources available concerning the foreign policies of the indigenous and external powers in the Middle East from World War I to the late 1970's. Chapter 7, focusing on Iraqi foreign policy, and chapter 16, assessing the policies of the smaller states of the Persian Gulf, provide important background for understanding the Iraqi invasion of Kuwait.

Makiya, Kanan. *Republic of Fear: The Politics of Modern Iraq*. Updated ed. Berkeley: University of California Press, 1998. Examines Saddam Hussein's motives for invading Kuwait and discusses how the Arab Baʿth Socialist Party changed Iraq from 1968 onward. Includes chronology and index.

Marr, Phebe. "Iraq's Uncertain Future." *Current History* 90 (January, 1991): 1-4, 39-42. Offers one of the best analyses available of the causes of the Iraqi invasion of Kuwait. Provides a valuable framework for analysis of the Gulf War.

_____. *The Modern History of Iraq*. 2d ed. Boulder, Colo.: Westview Press, 2004. Comprehensive history of Iraq provides valuable context for events involving that nation in the late twentieth century. Includes tables, glossary, descriptive list of political personalities, bibliography, and index.

Musallam, Musallam Ali. *The Iraqi Invasion of Kuwait: Saddam Hussein, His State, and International Power Politics*. New York: British Academic Press, 1996. Presents analysis of the roots of the Persian Gulf War and an examination of Saddam Hussein's life. Includes bibliography and index.

**SEE ALSO:** July 16, 1979: Saddam Hussein Takes Power in Iraq; Sept. 22, 1980-Aug. 8, 1988: Iran-Iraq War; June 7, 1981: Israel Destroys Iraqi Nuclear Reactor; Apr., 1987-Sept., 1988: Iraq Uses Poison Gas Against Kurds; Jan. 17-Feb. 28, 1991: Persian Gulf War; Jan. 27-Nov. 7, 1991: Iraq Burns Kuwaiti Oil Wells; Dec. 16-19, 1998: Iraq Disarmament Crisis Climaxes in Air Strikes.

1990

**August 18, 1990**

# U.S. CONGRESS PASSES OIL SPILL LEGISLATION

*In response to the widespread attention to the problem of oil pollution caused by the grounding of the* Exxon Valdez, *the U.S. Congress passed comprehensive environmental legislation in the Oil Pollution Act of 1990.*

**ALSO KNOWN AS:** Oil Pollution Act; U.S. Statutes at Large 104 Stat. 486; Public Law 101-380; U.S. Code 33 § 2701

**LOCALE:** Washington, D.C.

**CATEGORIES:** Laws, acts, and legal history; environmental issues

## KEY FIGURES

*George H. W. Bush* (b. 1924), president of the United States, 1989-1993, who signed the Oil Pollution Act into law

*Walter Jones* (b. 1943), U.S. congressman from North Carolina and chair of the House Merchant Marine Fisheries Committee

*Dan Rostenkowski* (b. 1928), U.S. congressman from Illinois and chair of the House Ways and Means Committee

*Fritz Hollings* (b. 1922), U.S. senator from South Carolina and chair of the Senate Commerce, Science, and Transportation Committee

## SUMMARY OF EVENT

Congress turned its attention to legislation regulating oil spills following the grounding of the oil tanker *Exxon Valdez* in Prince William Sound, Alaska. The oil spill and accompanying damage to the wildlife and its ecosystem were the subject of broadcast news for weeks following the accident and rallied public pressure for action.

To be effective, oil spill legislation had to be at the federal level, because state and local governments could legislate only those terminals and facilities within their jurisdictions. Comprehensive federal legislation had to address not only pollution cleanup problems but also the entire transport system. A number of laws already existed that addressed some of the problems. The earliest of these, the Federal Water Pollution Control Act of 1970, concerned oil spilled into the navigable waters of the United States. The Deepwater Ports Act of 1974 covered spillage in the territorial sea, which extends twelve miles from the U.S. coasts, and the Outer Continental Shelf Lands Act of 1978 covered oil spilled into the waters of

the U.S. exclusive economic zone. In 1980, Congress passed the Comprehensive Environmental Response, Compensation, and Liability Act, which created the first "superfund." The fund was designed to provide the resources needed to clean up an oil spill if a cargo or ship owner was unwilling or unable to pay for it.

The Oil Pollution Act addressed not only the prevention of oil pollution but also oil-pollution response and cleanup. It set standards for crew certification, work hours, and vessel traffic systems. Further, the legislation set new design and life-span requirements for tank vessels and addressed the question of liability for the cleanup of spills and accidents involving tank vessels. Finally, the bill continued provisions for the superfund established by the 1980 act.

The bill had eight sections, each of which added something to the existing body of law. In the first two, Congress significantly increased the liability of the "polluter" and added third-party liability, as well as addressing the new law's relationship with already existing regulations and allowing states to override the federal standards with stricter legislation of their own. The third section addressed the international aspects covered by the act, and the fourth set higher standards for the industry. Issues specifically related to the Prince William Sound situation were covered in the fifth section, in which provisions were made for a technical committee, better oversight of the tanker terminal, and modifications to the navigation aids in that area. The act went on to address miscellaneous issues such as administrative appropriations and a ban on drilling off the North Carolina coast; oil-pollution research and development programs, which included recommendations for the types of equipment required to track and contain oil spills; and liability and pollution issues associated with oil transported by pipeline.

## SIGNIFICANCE

The Oil Pollution Act of 1990 was a far-reaching piece of legislation. Almost immediately, the act had a dramatic impact, not only on the operation of tanker fleets in the United States but also on the operation of international tanker fleets that called at American ports. The act mandated new standards that required both short-term and long-term adaptation on the part of the maritime industry.

The legislation also had a significant impact on the government because it required that a number of agencies, including the Department of Energy, institute the new policies and programs and cooperate in implementing the stricter standards. The U.S. Coast Guard, for example, was made responsible for issues such as crew licensing, vessel inspection, and plans to deal with oil spills and oil transfers.

The act also generated the need for new agencies, such as the Marine Spill Response Corporation, to support oil spill recovery procedures. Vessels specially designed, equipped, and staffed to handle oil spills were stationed around the country, their crews permanently on call to respond to emergencies.

The act affected owners and operators of U.S.-flag tank vessels as well as their crews, who were subject to a new set of certification and licensing standards. The Coast Guard began checking the driving records of all applicants, and periodic renewal became mandatory for a number of endorsements, or jobs, for which crew members were certified. Daily ship operations were also affected by the legislation. To cut down on shipboard fatigue, which often underlies human error, the act limited work hours to no more than twelve per day. That in turn usually required vessels, in order to operate competitively, to hire additional crew.

The act also addressed the issue of vessel obsolescence by requiring that all vessels calling in U.S. ports be double-hulled by the year 2015. Shipyards and ship repair facilities worldwide had to develop plans to meet the new construction standard. Ship terminals, too, were affected by the legislation, which required that they develop and maintain oil spill contingency plans and provide terminal operations manuals to shipboard and shoreside personnel during oil transfers. The law has also had an effect on nonmaritime businesses such as banking and insurance: The act called for minimum insurance coverage and strengthened the government's power to enforce oil-pollution liability.

—*Robert J. Stewart*

## FURTHER READING

Alaska Oil Spill Commission. *Spill: Wreck of the Exxon Valdez.* Juneau: Author, 1990. Report by a govern-ment-appointed state committee discusses in detail the spill as well as the resulting cleanup attempts.

National Research Council, Marine Board, Commission on Engineering and Technical Systems. *Using Oil Spill Dispersants on the Sea.* Washington, D.C.: National Academy Press, 1989. Presents extensive information on the controversial subject of oil dispersants in a fairly readable format. Technical text is supplemented with pictures and graphs, and conclusions are clearly presented.

Smith, Zachary A. *The Environmental Paradox.* 4th ed. Upper Saddle River, N.J.: Prentice Hall, 2003. Provides clear discussion of a complex subject, with examination of both business and environmentalist perspectives concerning petroleum products. Addresses society's reliance on those products and the problems that reliance has created.

Tan, Alan Khee-Jin. *Vessel-Source Marine Pollution: The Law and Politics of International Regulation.* New York: Cambridge University Press, 2005. Examines the history of international oil-pollution regulation and discusses how political, economic, and social forces affect antipollution treaties.

Wardley-Smith, J., ed. *The Control of Oil Pollution.* London: Graham & Trotman, 1983. Collection of essays presents detailed discussion of shipping methods for transportation, loading, and unloading of oil as well as discussion of the environmental effects of oil pollution on birds, fisheries, and plankton. Good resource for the general reader.

SEE ALSO: Dec. 15, 1976: The *Argo Merchant* Spills Oil off the New England Coast; Mar. 16, 1978: The *Amoco Cadiz* Runs Aground; Oct. 17, 1978: U.S. Congress Requires Ships to Safeguard Marine Environment; July 19, 1979: Oil Tankers Collide near Tobago; Mar. 22, 1980: Mexico Controls Huge Leak in Offshore Oil Well; Jan. 2, 1988: Tank Collapse Releases Fuel into the Monongahela River; Mar. 24, 1989: *Exxon Valdez* Oil Spill; Jan. 5, 1993: *Braer* Runs Aground.

1990

## September 23-27, 1990
# *THE CIVIL WAR* RIVETS THE ATTENTION OF THE UNITED STATES

*The broadcast, over five consecutive nights, of Ken Burns's eleven-hour documentary* The Civil War *drew the largest audience in the history of public television to a masterful meditation on national identity.*

**LOCALE:** United States
**CATEGORY:** Radio and television

### KEY FIGURES

*Ken Burns* (b. 1953), producer, director, cowriter, and cocinematographer of *The Civil War*

*Shelby Foote* (1916-2005), historian, novelist, and principal on-camera commentator in *The Civil War*

*Ric Burns* (b. 1955), coproducer and cowriter of *The Civil War*

*Geoffrey C. Ward* (b. 1940), principal writer of *The Civil War*

*David McCullough* (b. 1933), historian and narrator of *The Civil War*

### SUMMARY OF EVENT

For five consecutive nights in September, 1990, an estimated thirty-nine million Americans were mesmerized by a television documentary broadcast by the Public Broadcasting Service (PBS). The project, culled from 150 hours of footage, was a marvel of filmmaking and a triumph of public broadcasting. It took director, coproducer, cowriter, and cocinematographer Ken Burns five years to make *The Civil War*, longer than it took the North and the South to begin and conclude the Civil War itself.

Eleven hours is a sizable investment of time, but no viewer would wish the program one minute shorter. "Our *Iliad* has found its Homer," wrote critic George F. Will of the thirty-six-year-old Burns. Although each had won considerable acclaim, Burns's earlier forays into American history—*Brooklyn Bridge* (1982), *The Shakers: Hands to Work, Hearts to God* (1984), *Huey Long* (1985), *The Statue of Liberty* (1986), *Thomas Hart Benton* (1988), and *The Congress* (1989)—seemed in retrospect but rehearsals for his magisterial survey of and meditation on the most traumatic episode in U.S. history.

More than a million photographs were taken during the Civil War, and rather than rely on specious reenactments, Burns constructed his film almost entirely out of photographs of the era, using not only familiar stills shot by photographer Mathew B. Brady but also thousands of other pictures assembled from archives and

attics. Many, such as a shot of Abraham Lincoln's second inaugural address that was enlarged to reveal the face of John Wilkes Booth in the crowd, astonished even those who thought they knew the period. All lifted the Civil War out of mythic abstraction and into a dense historical moment. Viewers of *The Civil War* observed actual human beings, as though they were gazing at a family album.

The images on the screen—which also included lithographs, newspaper headlines, and newsreel footage of military reunions—were accompanied by voice-over quotations from letters, diaries, and other written testimony. The journals of southern belle Mary Chesnut and New York lawyer George Templeton Strong provided dramatically different vantage points. Burns re-created history from the bottom up, and although he offered engaging, and at times unexpected, portraits of political and military leaders such as Lincoln, Jefferson Davis, Ulysses S. Grant, Robert E. Lee, Frederick Douglass, Nathan Bedford Forrest, and William Tecumseh Sherman, he also followed the fortunes of more obscure figures—in particular, two foot soldiers, one in blue and one in gray. Excerpts from a diary enabled viewers to trace the trajectory of Elisha Hunt Rhodes, who left Rhode Island as a private in 1861 and returned as a colonel in 1865. The memoirs of Sam Watkins, a volunteer in Company H of the First Tennessee, bore witness to every major campaign fought in the western theater.

Burns's choices of voices were especially inspired—not only professional actors Sam Waterston, Julie Harris, Jason Robards, Morgan Freeman, Derek Jacobi, Jeremy Irons, and Colleen Dewhurst, but also such odd but effective speakers as Garrison Keillor, Arthur Miller, Jody Powell, Studs Terkel, Kurt Vonnegut, and George Plimpton. Historian David McCullough provided running narration in a steady, patient, Tiresias-like voice that suggested hard-earned wisdom and inconsolable grief. Historians Shelby Foote, Barbara Fields, Stephen Oates, C. Vann Woodward, and others spoke into the camera and out of knowledge and passion.

*The Civil War* was attentive to the battlefield strategies of commanders who were at times brilliant, audacious, timorous, and stupid. The program, however, was not merely chessboard military history; viewers mingled in the ranks at Antietam, the bloodiest encounter in American history, when twice as many lives were lost as on D day during World War II. The program explored the political collisions that led to continental catastrophe, acknowledging the complexities of the confrontation in the fact that Unionists from every southern state but South Carolina sent regiments to join the North and the fact that the Union cause was bitterly reviled throughout the North—in the New York draft riots of July, 1863, angry mobs attacked and murdered blacks and their sympathizers.

Slavery, even more than sectional pride and prerogatives, was, according to *The Civil War*, central to the conflict. If abolition was not the major objective of the Lincoln administration in 1861, when every seventh American was legal chattel, by 1865, when 10 percent of the Union Army was black, the war had become a struggle over the meaning of freedom. It became, according to Oates, "a testament for the liberation of the human spirit for all time." Its legacy lingered in an incomplete agenda of social justice. This very uncivil war also, as Burns demonstrated, forever altered the role of women in American society.

A lonely cannon set against a radiant sunset was the program's signature image, and period music, performed plaintively on solo fiddle or piano, accompanied the entire experience. For many of the three million soldiers who marched off to defend their cause, the Civil War was, in McCullough's words, "the greatest adventure of their lives." The war inspired acts of transcendent valor, but it also enabled unscrupulous entrepreneurs to enrich themselves through sales of shoddy goods. It was a field of honor but also an occasion for selfish gain; two days after Manassas, a battle that cost five thousand casualties, speculators bought up the real estate as a tourist attraction. *The Civil War* documented wanton atrocities committed by armies from both sides of the Mason-Dixon line.

Although its nine episodes followed a loose chronology from 1861 through 1865, *The Civil War* paused occasionally from the inexorable course of conflict to examine the textures of life in the mid-nineteenth century. Episode 7, for example, addressed such activities as espionage, prostitution, gambling, and profiteering. No viewer could help but gain from the rich experience. "Any understanding of this nation has to be based on an understanding of the Civil War," declared Foote. "It defines us." Not even eleven hours of programming is sufficient for a national definition, but *The Civil War* brought viewers closer to an understanding of American dreams and nightmares than any other television project, except perhaps the ambitious venture that Burns began to work on next: a history of baseball.

## SIGNIFICANCE

Episode 1 of *The Civil War*, which inaugurated the PBS fall season, received a rating of nine and an audience share of thirteen, according to the A. C. Nielsen survey of the thirteen largest American media markets—figures that were records for a PBS broadcast. Episode 2 surpassed even those numbers, and the entire series reached the kind of mass audience expected only of commercial networks. An investment of $2.8 million and five years was rewarded with popular and critical success. *The Civil War*, production of which was underwritten by General Motors, the National Endowment for the Humanities, the Corporation for Public Broadcasting, the Arthur Vining Davis Foundations, and the John D. and Catherine T. MacArthur Foundation, went on to win two Emmy Awards and the affection of millions.

A book—*The Civil War: An Illustrated History*, by Geoffrey C. Ward with Ric Burns and Ken Burns—designed as a companion to the series sold close to a million copies for publisher Alfred A. Knopf, and videocassettes of all nine episodes likewise did brisk business. So, too, did a recording, *Songs of the Civil War*, of music featured in the film.

Union soldier Sullivan Ballou achieved belated, posthumous renown when the letter he wrote to his wife on the eve of the Battle of Bull Run was broadcast at the end of Episode 1; Ballou's letter was reprinted, recorded, and widely quoted. Ken Burns, the series' unprepossessing creator, became an unlikely celebrity and the recipient of eight honorary doctorates. *Empire of the Air*, a televised history of radio that Burns developed while working on his vast documentary about baseball, was eagerly anticipated and, when broadcast on PBS in early 1992, was well received.

The success of *The Civil War* demonstrated the continuing viability of the miniseries, a television form that had been languishing more than a decade after 1977's *Roots* had proved so compelling that audiences sat watching night after night. Burns also attracted uncustomary, if temporary, attention to nonfiction film, a genre largely neglected by programmers and audiences. Nevertheless, PBS remained one of the few institutions hospitable to both the production and exhibition of a work with the magnitude and purpose of *The Civil War*. Even with his post-*Civil War* prominence, Burns continued to work with public broadcasting, where his productions were neither constrained by time and content nor diluted and diverted by commercial breaks.

If PBS was the electronic benefactor of *The Civil War*, the series was a timely boon to public television,

1990

a system that depends financially on contributions from viewers, corporate underwriters, foundation grants, and government allocations. Despite a feeble economy, donations to PBS affiliates increased by 8.4 percent in 1991, and much of the increase could reasonably be attributed to the popularity of *The Civil War*, both in its initial run and in subsequent rebroadcasts. Presentation of the film was a powerful tool for local affiliates during periodic membership drives. WETA, the PBS member station in Washington, D.C., reported that viewers pledged $500,000 during breaks in a rebroadcast of *The Civil War*—the largest sum ever raised by any one program.

As important as the contributions of the broadcast to the fiscal fitness of PBS was the credibility that *The Civil War* provided for the beleaguered network. Two decades after its 1970 founding, PBS was under attack by angry and influential political conservatives who questioned whether, after the proliferation of channels through cable technology, taxpayers needed to be subsidizing any television operation. Conservative critics, moreover, took particular exception to the left-wing political bias and subversion of mainstream American values that they insisted were characteristic of PBS. The attack on PBS was similar to that leveled against the National Endowment for the Humanities (NEH) and the National Endowment for the Arts as alleged patrons of cultural decadence. Congressional defenders of PBS's mission pointed to *The Civil War*, a project admired across the political spectrum, as a powerful—and successful—argument for reauthorization of the Corporation for Public Broadcasting. Likewise, the fact that it had provided partial support for *The Civil War* was an important factor in the victorious battle to sustain the NEH.

*The Civil War* was initially broadcast while the United States was again preparing for military battle. In August, 1990, Saddam Hussein's Iraqi troops had invaded Kuwait, and the United Nations Security Council, meeting in emergency session, had issued an ultimatum insisting on unconditional and complete withdrawal. As an inducement to comply, economic sanctions were imposed against Iraq, and, throughout the fall, while forces were massing in the Middle East, Americans debated the efficacy of the measures and when, or whether, the confrontation should be escalated into open warfare. Burns's study of the causes and costs of organized carnage both reflected and helped shape the mood of America on the eve of the Persian Gulf War.

The U.S. Congress convened an extraordinary session to determine whether to authorize President George H. W. Bush to take military action against Iraq. During the televised debate, during which almost every member of the Senate and the House of Representatives spoke, *The Civil War* was frequently mentioned and quoted, both by those supporting a strike against Iraq and by those opposing one. The United States did go to war in January, 1991, and the memory of another conflict, as interpreted by Burns, was vivid in the minds of those who prosecuted and those who protested the current one. After the shooting stopped, Burns told a reporter that, when he met General H. Norman Schwarzkopf, the commander of Operation Desert Storm, the general had explained the influence *The Civil War* had exerted on him: "I watched the show every night while I was planning the campaign. It made me understand that the arrows on my maps were real human lives."

Newspapers during the Civil War reported a curious phenomenon called "acoustic shadows": Often, the harrowing din of conflict thundered in the ears of listeners many miles away, while in the immediate vicinity of battle an eerie silence reigned. The nation's most traumatic ordeal, a bloody struggle that cost more than 600,000 lives—2 percent of the entire population—cast acoustic shadows over its weary survivors. Some 125 years after Lee's surrender at Appomattox, however, the echoes of it all, broadcast throughout the United States and as far away as Australia, were thunderous.

Although the question is itself evidence of passions lingering from the distant debacle, it is impossible to say whether *The Civil War* was pro-Union or pro-Confederacy. Burns's documentary was, instead, profoundly respectful of the complexities of human entanglement. "Useless, useless" were John Wilkes Booth's dying words. "The greatest mistake of my life," declared Lee in later years, "was taking a military education." Full of sound and fury, and rueful compassion, *The Civil War* provided a military, political, and cultural education that, until the next conflict, seemed to inoculate viewers against future senseless carnage.

*—Steven G. Kellman*

## FURTHER READING

Catton, Bruce. *A Stillness at Appomattox*. Garden City, N.Y.: Doubleday, 1954. A gracefully literary narrative of the Civil War in Virginia, with emphasis on the Army of the Potomac.

Chesnut, Mary Boykin Miller. *Mary Chesnut's Civil War*. Edited by Comer Vann Woodward. New Haven, Conn.: Yale University Press, 1981. A southern aristocrat, Chesnut kept a revealing diary of civilian life during the war and was frequently quoted in the PBS film.

Edgerton, Gary R. *Ken Burns's America*. New York: Palgrave, 2001. Examines Burns's work as a documentary filmmaker from 1982 to the end of the twentieth century. Discusses *The Civil War* and its impacts. Includes videography, bibliography, and indexes.

Foote, Shelby. *The Civil War: A Narrative*. 3 vols. New York: Random House, 1958-1974. A mammoth, magisterial account of the conflict by a principal participant in the PBS project.

Lincoln, Abraham. *Speeches and Writings, 1859-1865*. New York: Literary Classics of the United States, 1989. A central figure in the conflict, Lincoln was also an author of considerable literary grace whose writings were quoted frequently in *The Civil War*.

McPherson, James M. *Ordeal by Fire: The Civil War and Reconstruction*. 3d ed. New York: McGraw-Hill, 2000. Contends that the Civil War produced revolutionary changes in American life and proceeds to ex-

amine how and why. Includes photographs and detailed maps, tables, and bibliographies.

Smith, Page. *Trial by Fire: A People's History of the Civil War and Reconstruction*. New York: McGraw-Hill, 1982. Emphasizes ordinary life over battle scenarios and preoccupation with leaders. Provides an accessible account of how the general population of the Union and the Confederacy experienced the war.

Ward, Geoffrey C., with Ric Burns and Ken Burns. *The Civil War: An Illustrated History*. New York: Alfred A. Knopf, 1991. Sumptuous companion volume to the PBS series is abundantly illustrated with photographs, drawings, maps, and newspaper excerpts. Narrative by Ward and essays by other historians attempt to convey the texture of the past.

**SEE ALSO:** Jan. 17-Feb. 28, 1991: Persian Gulf War; Apr. 14-16, 1994: Alexander Fights to Save the National Endowment for the Arts; Mid-1990's: Cable Television Challenges Network Television.

1990

## October, 1990
# "KILLER BEES" INVADE THE UNITED STATES

*The arrival of Africanized honeybees threatened agriculture, tourism, and the honey industry in the United States.*

**LOCALE:** Southern United States
**CATEGORIES:** Animals and endangered species; health and medicine; agriculture

**KEY FIGURES**

*Warwick Estevam Kerr* (b. 1922), Brazilian geneticist who introduced the African honeybee to South America

*Mark L. Winston* (b. 1950), research professor at Simon Fraser University who studied Africanized bees in both North and South America

*Thomas E. Rinderer* (fl. late twentieth century), insect geneticist at the Honey Bee Breeding, Genetics, and Physiology Laboratory in Baton Rouge, Louisiana

**SUMMARY OF EVENT**

Honeybees originated in tropical regions of Asia and then migrated throughout Europe and into Africa, where they developed a more aggressive nature in response to the threats posed by army ants, honey badgers, anteaters, giant toads, and human beings. Early European settlers

brought the first honeybees to the Western Hemisphere, carrying the relatively docile European variety into the interior, where the bees quickly became an important part of the agricultural economy.

From the early 1980's, scientists, agriculturists, and a curious public followed the progress of migrating swarms of "killer bees" that had terrorized much of Latin America for almost thirty years and were then approaching the United States. In October, 1990, these Africanized bees crossed the Mexican border into southern Texas near Hidalgo. That event significantly affected the lives and jobs of many Americans. In 1993, the first death in the United States attributed to stings of Africanized bees was reported, raising fears among Americans about the potential danger posed by the bees.

In the mid-1950's, the Brazilian government called on geneticist Warwick Estevam Kerr to develop a bee that would be well suited to Brazil's Amazonian climate. Reports of outstanding honey production in Southern Africa convinced Kerr to go there for his breeding stock. He knew that African honeybees are aggressive, but he believed that crossbreeding them with indigenous South American stock would produce a gentler bee capable of greater honey production. In Africa, Kerr collected 173

*Africanized honeybee.* (USDA)

African queen honeybees, less than one-third of which survived the trip back to Brazil. Of those that remained, he chose 35 to use in his breeding program. Headed by African queens, his colonies became some of the most productive ever seen. In 1957, a careless beekeeper allowed 26 of the 35 colonies to escape into the surrounding forest. There is some evidence to suggest that more Africanized queens were reared from the remaining colonies and distributed to Brazilian beekeepers, hastening the rapid spread of Africanized bees.

After 1957, swarms of Africanized honeybees spread at an alarming rate. By 2005, substantial numbers of counties in seven U.S. states (California, Nevada, Arizona, New Mexico, Texas, Oklahoma, and Florida) had reported the presence of Africanized bees, and a few counties in Arkansas and Louisiana had also observed their presence. The bees moved two hundred to three hundred miles each year, migrating through a process known as swarming. When swarming, worker bees first gorge on honey to fuel themselves while the new nest is being established. Next, they go into a frenzy, chasing, biting, and pulling their queen until she is forced out of the nest. Workers and queen then orient themselves to each other by secreting highly attractive chemicals. Finally, scout bees lead the cluster to a new nesting site.

Africanized bees swarm more often, and thus spread more rapidly, than European bees for two principal reasons. European honeybees normally construct large nests and store more honey; this provides them with greater resources but takes up much of the hive's energy. Africanized honeybees build smaller nests and store less honey, reserving more energy to swarm. Africanized bees also tend to swarm at an earlier age. In Africa, this instinct compensates for colonies lost to predators. In Latin America, however, where the bees have fewer natural enemies, colonies proliferate. It was estimated in 1992 that there were one trillion Africanized honeybees in 50 million to 100 million nests throughout the Western Hemisphere.

These estimates, like others required for study, were necessarily difficult to arrive at because there is little physical difference between Africanized and European honeybees. The threat of further migration and its attendant dangers, however, made accurate identification imperative. As a result, Thomas E. Rinderer, an insect geneticist, and his colleagues at the Honey Bee Breeding, Genetics, and Physiology Laboratory in Baton Rouge, Louisiana, developed the Fast African Bee Identification System, which involves measuring bees' wings. The wings of the European honeybees are minutely larger than those of the Africanized bee. Another means of identification, developed around 1990 by entomologist Akey C. Hung, involves the identification of two proteins that are distinct to Africanized honeybees.

Scientists knew that European and Africanized honeybees would meet in a struggle for territory. Because Africanized bees are usually aggressive, they typically win the contest for territory. Sometimes Africanized drones—male bees that live only to mate with new queens—mate with European queens, which lay more Africanized eggs, eventually leading to the conversion of the colony. When swarming, Africanized bees sometimes simply fly in and colonize European hives. At times, when territories overlap, the species interbreed. In these transitional zones, scientists have found gentle Africanized bees and aggressive European bees, although usually the crossbred bees exhibit aggressive traits.

The contest for territory is directly related to the bees' need for flowers from which pollen and nectar are gathered. Nectar, rich in sugars, is the energy source for the hive and is used to make honey. Pollen, which contains proteins, fats, minerals, and vitamins, is used for the growth of larvae and the maintenance of the adults. After pollen is collected, it is moistened with honey, then pressed into compact pellets and stored in special cells inside the nest. Africanized honeybees will fly miles out of their way to locate new sources of flowers for forage, thus challenging their European relatives, which remain in more confined areas.

Many tactics were developed to stop the Africanized honeybees' invasion of the United States. A commission was established in Panama to intercept colonies being transported by ships passing through the Panama Canal. Reports of Africanized bees arriving in California by truck led to the establishment of a quarantine along roads leading out of Mexico. Areas reporting hostile bee activity were flooded with European bees. Traps baited with highly attractive substances (pheromones) were strategically placed in Mexico and the southern United States.

By late 1987, the United States and Mexico had jointly funded and implemented the Bee Regulated Zone, an effort to enforce a biological barrier at the Isthmus of Tehuantepec in southern Mexico. Although this comprehensive plan included quarantines, colony destruction, drone flooding, traps, and educational programs, it had virtually no effect on the advance of Africanized colonies toward the United States. The most effective means of protecting European colonies remained the localized marking of queen bees with acrylic paint, with monthly monitoring to ensure that colonies had not been contaminated. With the failure of international initiatives, American agriculturalists and researchers determined that the Africanized bee had become a permanent part of the natural environment and thus began to focus attention on how to cope with this new member of the insect community.

## SIGNIFICANCE

The United States faces many of the same problems caused by killer bees in Latin America since 1957. First, the threat to humans is significant. The sting of the Africanized honeybee is essentially the same as that of other bees, but the Africanized bees attack in greater numbers, giving off an alarm odor that immediately attracts hundreds of bees to the tagged victim. People who have disturbed Africanized hives have been attacked and followed for more than a mile, and dozens of people have been killed. One of the worst incidents occurred in 1986 in Costa Rica, when Inn Siang Ooi, a botany student from Miami University, died as the result of receiving more than eight thousand stings.

The first death caused by Africanized bees in the United States was reported in 1993, and attacks became more frequent thereafter. On one occasion, four Americans who were hunting near the Texas-Mexico border shot into a rattlesnake hole. Africanized bees immediately attacked David Reddick, who received more than six hundred stings. One of Reddick's friends observed that "he'd pull a handful off his face and they'd be replaced immediately." Such occurrences created a threat to tourism throughout the South, most notably in Texas, which relies heavily on tourism as a source of revenue.

In order to gauge the threat to humans more accurately, Mark L. Winston studied the behavior of Africanized bees in Surinam. Dressed in a veil, heavy gloves, and two layers of clothes under heavy bee overalls, Winston and an apiary owner approached the bees' hives from a distance of five hundred yards. Simply walking toward the nests brought a massive response. Even before the two opened the first hive, bees were stinging through their protective clothing and ferociously slamming into the veils covering their faces. In those few minutes, Winston was stung more than fifty times. Events such as this drove many Latin American beekeepers away from the business, leading to the collapse of the region's honey industry.

The presence of the Africanized bees has also posed a threat to agriculture in the United States. As much as one-third of American food crops rely on annual pollination by honeybees. Apples, berries, cantaloupes, cucumbers, almonds, and melons all require the deliberate transport of more than two million colonies each year. Fear of the Africanized honeybee has the potential to result in huge financial losses to both farmers and beekeepers, which would in turn burden consumers with higher prices.

The presence of Africanized bees also threatens the American beekeeping industry, particularly those beekeepers who rent colonies for the pollination of crops. Almost every acre of crops requires one or two colonies, with up to six in the case of alfalfa seeds; some farmers require four thousand colonies at a time for pollination. Beekeepers, who are paid a set amount for each colony they provide, were badly hurt financially by a quarantine against bee transport that was imposed in parts of Texas to prevent the further spread of Africanized bees.

This quarantine also affected Canadian agriculture. Instead of transporting queens from the south, Canadian beekeepers changed their requeening season to late spring or early summer in order to produce their own. They also started insulating hives and keeping colonies indoors in order to avoid transport to the south for winter. To keep Africanized bees out, Canada closed its borders to bee importation from the United States, buying instead from New Zealand and Australia.

In addition, the quarantine made beekeeping itself more expensive. Beekeepers in the northern part of the

1990

United States traditionally moved their colonies south during the winter, and southern beekeepers moved their colonies north when pollen and nectar were in short supply. Quarantine and fear of Africanization, however, made these practices impossible, costing beekeepers thousands of dollars in lost bees and feeding costs. Beekeepers also faced additional costs in requeening their hives. With 90 percent of queening areas in the southern United States under quarantine, beekeepers found it necessary to purchase queens from other countries at higher prices.

In addition to farmers, beekeepers, and consumers, American taxpayers in general have paid for the entry of the Africanized honeybee into the United States, as the federal government has spent large sums of money on projects to stop or modify the killer bee. In Mexico, at Puerto Escondido on the Pacific coast and at Huatuxco on the Caribbean coast, traps were set to funnel bees flying under three thousand feet into passes, where they are killed. These two projects alone cost the United States and Mexico an estimated $6.3 million. The cost of enforcing quarantines in southern Texas alone during the early 1990's was estimated at more than $1 million.

Although the impact of the Africanized honeybee's arrival has been substantial, the worst fears of early commentators have not been realized. Having learned that the bees cannot be stopped, or the feral population altered, American agriculturalists have instead focused resources on management of the new arrival. With greater resources, decades of experience, better facilities for education, and a widespread agricultural extension program, the United States should be better able to cope with the problem than were Latin American neighbors. Most scientists agree that Africanized bees will not naturally spread north of the thirty-second parallel because of cold temperatures, and this natural barrier serves to assist human efforts. Nevertheless, as much as one-third of the United States may eventually be inhabited by these bees, affecting farmers, beekeepers, and consumers throughout the country.

—*John Powell and Grady Powell*

## FURTHER READING

Borrell, John. "Rising Unease About Killer Bees: But a Surprise Awaits the United States-Bound Invaders in Mexico." *Time*, May 30, 1988, 58. Discusses attempts by the United States and Mexico to destroy Africanized bees before they could cross the Rio Grande. Focuses on funnel traps being built along the Pacific coast, trapping bees in scented bags, and quarantine posts in Mexico. Discusses potential American losses.

Buchmann, Stephen, with Banning Repplier. *Letters from the Hive: An Intimate History of Bees, Honey, and Humankind.* New York: Bantam Books, 2005. Entertaining volume examines the relationship between humans and honeybees throughout human history. Includes index.

Hubbell, Sue. "Maybe the 'Killer' Bee Should be Called the 'Bravo' Instead." *Smithsonian* 22 (September, 1991): 116-126. Downplays the danger posed by Africanized bees and discusses aggressive behavior in American subspecies.

Ocone, Lynn. "Here Come the Dreaded Killer Bees." *Sunset* 192 (February, 1994): 75. Provides a brief history and description of the Africanized honeybees, with helpful advice on how to prevent them from moving into an area and what to do in case of attack.

Seuft, Dennis. "The Africanized Honey Bees." *Agricultural Research* 38 (December, 1990): 4-11. Reviews research findings from the Honey Bee Breeding, Genetics, and Physiology Laboratory in Baton Rouge, Louisiana, involving new means of controlling, repelling, and destroying Africanized colonies moving northward. Includes maps of migration patterns and information on defenses against the bees.

Winston, Mark L. "Honey, They're Here! Learning to Cope with Africanized Bees." *The Sciences*, March/April, 1992, 22-28. Discusses the biology and behavior of the Africanized bee along with the short- and long-term effects of their invasion. Includes pictures of honeycombs constructed by the bees.

_____. *Killer Bees: The Africanized Honey Bee in the Americas.* Cambridge, Mass.: Harvard University Press, 1992. Explains the biology and behavior of the Africanized honeybee for general readers and details the impacts of Africanized honeybees on the United States and Latin America. An excellent starting point for information on the bees.

**SEE ALSO:** Oct. 21, 1972: U.S. Congress Expands Pesticide Regulations; July 10, 1981: Brown Orders Medfly Spraying in California; Nov. 10, 1981: "Yellow Rain" Hearing.

## October 24, 1990
# DEBUT OF BARYSHNIKOV'S WHITE OAK DANCE PROJECT

*Celebrated choreographer Mark Morris provided the repertory for the premiere performance of Mikhail Baryshnikov's White Oak Dance Project, which featured Baryshnikov and other stellar dancers.*

**LOCALE:** Boston, Massachusetts
**CATEGORY:** Dance

**KEY FIGURES**
*Mikhail Baryshnikov* (b. 1948), Russian-born ballet dancer who electrified the Western ballet world in 1974 when he defected from the Kirov Ballet
*Mark Morris* (b. 1956), American dancer and choreographer
*Howard Gilman* (b. 1924), wealthy New York dance enthusiast who provided financial support for the White Oak Dance Project

**SUMMARY OF EVENT**
On October 24, 1990, audience members at the Wang Center for the Performing Arts in Boston, Massachusetts, eagerly awaited the premiere performance of a completely new dance ensemble, the White Oak Dance Project. Nearly thirty-six hundred dance enthusiasts were on hand to see ballet and film star Mikhail Baryshnikov perform the choreography of the world-renowned Mark Morris. Baryshnikov was accompanied onstage by Morris and a superb ensemble of stellar dancers representing a veritable who's who of ballet and modern dance professionals.

Billed as a dance "project" rather than as a company, the White Oak dancers, many of them leading dancers in other companies, were a unique ensemble. Chosen by Baryshnikov and Morris, the dancers included Peggy Baker, Rob Besserer, and Nancy Colahan from the Lar Lubovitch Dance Company; Jamie Bishton and Kathleen Moore from American Ballet Theatre; Kate Johnson, who had recently retired from the Paul Taylor Dance Company; Denise Pons, a soloist with the Boston Ballet; and William Pizzuto, who left the Boston Ballet in 1989.

Noteworthy for its emphasis on mature dancers, many of whom were in their thirties and forties, the ensemble was also unusual in that it made no distinction between ballet dancers and modern dancers; all were viewed first and foremost as dancers, with the primary emphasis on their extraordinary abilities and not on their status as representatives of ballet or modern dance. It was the first time that such disparate and accomplished individuals had combined forces to dance together not as guest soloists from other companies but as an ensemble.

In an interview with *Dance Magazine* writer Nancy Dalva, project manager Barry Alterman made clear the distinction between company and project ensemble members: "A Company is self-perpetuating, with long commitments, and goes on for a long time. *This* might not last beyond this town or might go on to another town. The personnel may change." Indeed, after the Boston premiere, the White Oak Dance Project's personnel did change, as Morris left to resume work in Belgium and dancers such as David Parsons and Donald Mouton briefly joined the touring project.

Created for a single initial tour of seventeen cities in the United States, the White Oak Dance Project took its name from the White Oak Plantation, the estate of philanthropist Howard Gilman. The New York paper manufacturer, ardent balletomane, and supporter of Baryshnikov provided the financial backing for the touring project, offered the use of his estate for rehearsals, and had a state-of-the-art dance studio specially constructed on the property. Located on the St. Marys River near the Florida-Georgia border, the estate became home for the ensemble during July and August, 1990. There the dancers were treated like royalty during the five weeks of preparation: They rehearsed in near-idyllic conditions, and, when not rehearsing, they enjoyed boating, swimming, and other delights of Gilman's paradise. It was, as one dancer involved dubbed it, "the greatest dance camp ever."

When Baryshnikov founded the White Oak Dance Project, he intended it as a temporary vehicle for himself and others. After his tenure as artistic director of American Ballet Theatre, Baryshnikov had no interest in taking on the responsibilities of a permanent company, and he conceived of the White Oak Project as an opportunity to dance in pieces he enjoyed alongside dancers who were his peers in achievement, age, and experience. Baryshnikov chose Morris because of his admiration for Morris's choreographic skills, and he chose the all-Morris repertory for the initial tour because he felt that the dancers would profit by working with the phrasing, style, and demands of a single choreographer at first. A self-proclaimed fan of Morris, Baryshnikov said that he never considered any other choreographer for the White Oak Project.

1990

2519

Baryshnikov's respect for Morris's choreography dated back to 1987, when, as director of American Ballet Theatre, he commissioned Morris to create *Drink to Me Only with Thine Eyes* for the company. After his resignation from American Ballet Theatre in 1989, Baryshnikov surprised the dance world by traveling to Belgium, where he appeared as a guest with Morris's company in *Wonderland* in December of 1989; he repeated the performance during the company's New York season at the Brooklyn Academy of Music. Baryshnikov found the camaraderie he experienced while working with Morris's company a welcome antidote to the tumultuous politics of American Ballet Theatre. "It was such a nice atmosphere," Baryshnikov later recalled. "We thought, 'Why couldn't we find a project to stretch this lovely feeling?'"

Baryshnikov's formation of the White Oak Project may also have had roots in sheer physical reality. At forty-two, Baryshnikov was no longer at the peak of his form; injuries, age, and the demands of a multifaceted career made the continuation of his famous classical roles uncertain. Although both Morris and Baryshnikov denied that Baryshnikov's switch to modern-dance-based choreography was a response to his diminished technical abilities, performing in other than classical roles allowed Baryshnikov greater freedom and evoked fewer unfavorable comparisons to his younger self.

The White Oak Project debut was a benefit preview fund-raiser for the Boston-based Dance Umbrella, an organization that had long supported Morris. The concert included Morris's signature solo *Ten Suggestions*, performed that evening by Baryshnikov; *Pas de poisson*, a trio for Baryshnikov, Kate Johnson, and Morris; and two group works, *Going Away Party* and *Motorcade*.

Although well received by the huge audience drawn by Baryshnikov's name and Morris's choreography, the concert elicited mixed responses from dance critics. In reviewing *Ten Suggestions*, critics were quick to point out the differences between Baryshnikov's fastidious execution of the movements and the vigorous, earthy abandon of Morris, often preferring Morris. *Pas de poisson* drew praise for the sparkling performances of Baryshnikov, Johnson, and Morris but garnered mixed reviews for its choreography. *Going Away Party*, a boisterous, tongue-in-cheek look at love and Americana, was set to the music of Bob Wills and His Texas Playboys. A definite hit, the piece nevertheless prompted performance comparisons between Morris and Baryshnikov as well as between the White Oak dancers and Morris's own troupe. Choreographed specifically for White Oak

dancers, *Motorcade* was emblematic of the strengths of the project: highly technical and virtuosic dancing and alternately humorous, stately, and irreverent choreography.

The Boston debut of "The Mark and Misha Show," as *Time* magazine and others nicknamed the White Oak Dance Project, announced the arrival and immediate departure of a unique enterprise, as it embarked on a seventeen-city tour across the United States. The company that was not a company headed for Minneapolis.

## SIGNIFICANCE

When asked about his rationale for the ensemble, Baryshnikov replied, "In the time I have left, I just want to go onstage and dance for the fun of it. It's really great to go onstage in pieces that people never expected me to be in." The White Oak Dance Project offered Baryshnikov marvelous new performing opportunities, and the experience seemed to be as fulfilling for him as it was financially successful. Because of Baryshnikov's celebrity, the White Oak Project played to full houses at every stop, and by the end of the first tour, plans were under way for subsequent tours.

The White Oak Project further glamorized the reputation of Baryshnikov and extended the recognition of Morris as a major choreographer. The tour's itinerary had snubbed the traditional dance centers of the United States, including New York City, and therefore the impact of the project was oddly minimal in New York. By the spring of 1992, the ensemble had finished four American and European tours without a single performance in New York City. Writing for *The New Yorker*, Alastair Macaulay commented on a London performance of the White Oak Project: "How strange—to watch such dancers . . . all of whom the rest of the world associates with New York, and to know they are appearing in a program that there are as yet no plans to show here."

After the White Oak Project's first three tours, the personnel and repertory of the ensemble changed considerably. Although subsequent tours continued to feature Morris's choreography, the repertory was augmented with works by Paul Taylor, Martha Graham, Lar Lubovitch, and other contemporary choreographers. Works commissioned specifically for the ensemble included Taylor's *Oz*, Lubovitch's *Waiting for the Sunrise*, and David Gordon's *Punch and Judy*. Of the original dancers, only four remained with the ensemble: Baryshnikov, Johnson, Besserer, and Colahan.

How much the success of the project affected Morris is difficult to assess. He was already considered by many the foremost choreographer of his generation, and his reputation was neither significantly enhanced nor diminished by the new works he produced for Baryshnikov's ensemble. Much of the repertory either originated with Morris's own company or was performed by it subsequently, and except for the initial rehearsal process, his contact with the White Oak Project was minimal. In the spring of 1991, Morris's three-year contract as artistic director of the Theatre Royal de la Monnaie in Brussels expired, and Morris and his company returned to the United States. His role with the White Oak Project remained that of guest choreographer, and his primary commitment remained to his company, the Mark Morris Group.

As an entity, the White Oak Project has been such a loosely connected enterprise that its full impact on the dance world is difficult to determine. Certainly, the initial vision of an ensemble of compatible dancers performing choreography they enjoyed without the burden of long-term commitments proved successful. The very ephemerality of the White Oak Project may prove to be an inherently fatal flaw, however: The project's future appears to hinge on the interest and continued participation of Baryshnikov. Without his cachet, it is unlikely that the ensemble could continue to draw audiences or remain financially solvent. Another factor is that the White Oak Project has had no exclusive repertory. It seems unlikely that audiences will sustain a purely repertory company without Baryshnikov if the works are also currently being performed by the choreographers' own companies.

For many reasons, the formation of the White Oak Project was a welcome addition to the dance world. The brilliant and eclectic choreography of Morris offered Baryshnikov and his colleagues the opportunity to shine collectively while at the same time celebrating their individual talents. The White Oak Project also reminded the dance world that excellent dancers should not be classified by genre and style or forced into retirement in their twenties. The rise of the White Oak Project was a luminous occurrence.

— *Cynthia J. Williams*

## FURTHER READING

Alovert, Nina. *Baryshnikov in Russia*. Translated by Irene Huntoon. New York: Holt, Rinehart and Winston, 1984. Written by a Soviet friend of Baryshnikov who defected to the West in 1977. Lavishly illustrated with photographs that had to be smuggled out of the Soviet Union.

*Baryshnikov in Black and White*. New York: Bloomsbury, 2002. Picture book features more than 175 photographs depicting Baryshnikov's work, in both rehearsal and performance, from 1974 to 2000. Includes informative introduction by dance critic Joan Acocella.

France, Charles Engell. *Baryshnikov at Work*. London: Adam and Charles Black, 1977. Beautiful volume features photographs by Martha Swope. Baryshnikov discusses his most famous roles in the Soviet Union, at the New York City Ballet, with American Ballet Theatre, and on Broadway.

Fraser, John. *Private View: Inside Baryshnikov's American Ballet Theatre*. New York: Bantam Books, 1988. Picture book gives a nice feel for the dancers in the company and for Baryshnikov as a person. Features photographs by Eve Arnold.

Morgenroth, Joyce. *Speaking of Dance: Twelve Contemporary Choreographers on Their Craft*. New York: Routledge, 2004. Presents discussion of the differences among the works of the choreographers featured. Individual chapters present personal interviews with the choreographers; chapter 11 is devoted to Mark Morris.

Morris, Mark. "The Hidden Soul of Harmony." In *Dance as a Theatre Art: Source Readings in Dance History from 1581 to the Present*, edited by Selma Jeanne Cohen. 2d ed. Hightstown, N.J.: Princeton Book Company, 1992. Brief essay discusses Morris's choreography, his musicality, and the images used in his masterpiece *L'Allegro, il penseroso ed il moderato*.

Smakov, Gennady. *Baryshnikov: From Russia to the West*. London: Orbis, 1981. Focuses on the early stages of Baryshnikov's career, from his defection from the Soviet Union in 1974 through his acceptance of the directorship of American Ballet Theatre in 1980.

SEE ALSO: Mar. 1, 1973: Tharp Stages *Deuce Coupe* for the Joffrey Ballet; 1980's-early 1990's: Multiculturalism Dominates the Dance World; Fall, 1980: Baryshnikov Becomes Artistic Director of American Ballet Theatre; Oct. 4-10, 1981: New Dance U.S.A. Festival.

1990

## November 5, 1990
# UNITED STATES MAKES POLLUTION PREVENTION A NATIONAL GOAL

*With passage of the Pollution Prevention Act, the United States renewed an old approach to environmental management based on the reduction of pollution at the source.*

**ALSO KNOWN AS:** Pollution Prevention Act; U.S. Statutes at Large 104 Stat. 1388-321; Public Law 101-508; U.S. Code 42 § 13101
**LOCALE:** Washington, D.C.
**CATEGORIES:** Laws, acts, and legal history; environmental issues

**KEY FIGURES**
*Dennis Hertel* (b. 1948), U.S. congressman from Michigan who introduced the bill in the House of Representatives
*John Kerry* (b. 1943), U.S. senator from Massachusetts who introduced the bill in the Senate
*William Reilly* (b. 1940), head of the U.S. Environmental Protection Agency

**SUMMARY OF EVENT**
Until 1990, with the notable exception of the National Environmental Policy Act of 1969 (NEPA), the U.S. government's approach to environmental management was remedial and medium-specific (that is, specifically limited to air, water, or land pollution problems) rather than preventive and comprehensive. This approach failed to address several critical issues in environmental management. First, pollutants do not remain in a single medium, such as air or water; second, there are many thousands of pollutants, with more being created each year; and finally, dealing with pollution at the point of its release to the environment often created new problems. That was the case with efforts to restrict pollutant discharges into surface water, which led to groundwater pollution as generators turned to on-site storage of liquid wastes in unlined ponds. It gradually became clear that a successful approach must attempt to prevent pollutants from being created in the first place, recycle those that are created, and look at the environment in which pollution takes place as an interdependent ecological unit. The result was the major policy shift reflected in the Pollution Prevention Act of 1990.

That Pollution Prevention Act (PPA) established pollution prevention as a "national objective" and declared that pollution can be prevented or reduced at the point of

its creation. The law emphasized that the source-reduction approach to pollution management was "fundamentally different and more desirable" than the approach of the preceding federal laws and regulations, which had focused on the treatment and disposal of pollutants rather than on reduction at the source of their production.

The PPA specified a hierarchical approach to the reduction and prevention of pollution that enters the environment through recycling, treatment, disposal, or unintended escape. The act defined the most desirable approach as reduction at the source, that is, reducing the amounts of hazardous substances before they enter the environment; reduction should occur in such a way as to reduce the health and environmental hazards associated with release. Pollutants that cannot be eliminated at the source should be recycled in an environmentally safe manner. If recycling cannot eliminate all pollutants, those remaining should be treated. Attempts at disposal or other releases of pollutants into the environment should be regarded only as a last resort.

The act mandated three specific programs. The first was the establishment of the Office of Pollution Prevention within the Environmental Protection Agency (EPA) but independent of its "single-medium" programs. The office was made responsible for the development and implementation of a strategy to promote source-reduction practices and reduce hazardous wastes. It was charged with encouraging businesses and other federal agencies to adopt source-reduction techniques, establishing standard methods for measuring source reduction, reviewing regulations to determine their effect on source reduction, determining instances in which the federal procurement process can be used to encourage source reduction, improving public access to data collected under federal environmental laws, and developing a source-reduction clearinghouse, model procedures for auditing source reduction, a training program on opportunities for source reduction, and an annual awards program. This last requirement resulted in the EPA's developing several videos, a speakers bureau, a newsletter, brochures, conferences, courses, and a resource guide to training programs. The EPA also established the Pollution Prevention Information Clearinghouse (PPIC), which offers a telephone hotline for questions related to pollution prevention, an electronic bulletin board, several computerized databases, a reference library, and a document ordering system.

In the second program, the act, in order to encourage businesses to practice source reduction, authorized an $8 million, one- to three-year grant program, with funds allocated to those states that match the federal money. Individual states are responsible for developing their own source-reduction programs.

The third important program established by the act involves facilities that fall under the reporting provisions of the Toxics Release Inventory established by Title III of the Superfund Amendments and Reauthorization Act, or SARA. Commonly known as the Emergency Planning and Community Right-to-Know Act, Title III of SARA requires many businesses and industries to report the amounts of toxic substances released to the air, water, and land each year. These facilities were now additionally required to report their source-reduction practices and changes in production for each facility and each toxic chemical used, including the quantities of each toxic substance emitted, quantities recycled, and the percentage change in these figures from the previous year. The act also required that the EPA report to Congress every other year on the actions needed to implement the source-reduction strategy and that it provide an assessment of the grant and clearinghouse programs.

## SIGNIFICANCE

Since its inception, the PPIC responded to tens of thousands of requests for information. Data from the Toxics Release Inventory showed a 35 percent decline in the total amount of toxic chemicals released to the nation's environment between 1988 and 1992 and a 6 percent decline from 1991 to 1992. In the first four years of the grant program, more than $30 million was awarded to more than one hundred regional, state, and tribal organizations to fund activities aimed at pollution prevention.

The major policy shift legislated with the Pollution Prevention Act was based on the approach taken in the National Environmental Policy Act, which mandated consideration of the cumulative environmental effects of certain activities. NEPA, one of the most successful U.S. environmental laws, radically improved the way these activities were planned, and it withstood many court challenges and was never substantially amended. After NEPA, however, and until the passage of the 1990 Pollution Prevention Act, federal environmental management had taken a very different course. Most of those laws were repeatedly amended, and although billions of dollars were spent, it is questionable whether environmental

quality improved during that time. The greatest significance of the Pollution Prevention Act of 1990 may lie not in its substantive programs but in its indication of a return to the environmental approach of NEPA.

Many of the specific programs defined by the Pollution Prevention Act already existed before 1990. Between the beginning of fiscal year 1988 and May, 1990, the EPA had awarded nearly $10.9 million in multimedia pollution prevention grants to states; in 1989, the agency published a guidance document for industry to use in its efforts to minimize the generation of hazardous waste; and the Office of Pollution Prevention had been established several years before the act's passage. By legislatively sanctioning and strengthening these programs, Congress tried to ensure that their preventive, comprehensive focus would continue to shape federal environmental policy.

In the wake of the Pollution Prevention Act's passage, a number of state offices of pollution prevention were established, most of which received grant funding from the act for special projects. In fact, state involvement and response to industry needs generally increased in response to the act; states adopted their own pollution prevention acts and regulations, and some began to require that companies convicted of violating state laws be environmentally audited. Such increased state activity in turn led to increased industrial compliance.

Local governments also became active in pollution prevention, as reflected in such activities as using waste-disposal companies that offer recycling and sponsorship of household hazardous-waste pickups and educational seminars on waste minimization and conservation. To what extent these changes can be attributed directly to the Pollution Prevention Act is unclear, but the federal government's policy shift toward prevention was undoubtedly an important factor.

*—Elise M. Bright*

## FURTHER READING

Change Management Center. *Applying Industrial Ecology.* Oakland, Calif.: Author, 1993. Provides a comprehensive look at industrial techniques for pollution prevention. Includes an overview of EPA programs and requirements of the Pollution Prevention Act.

Goudie, Andrew. *The Human Impact on the Natural Environment: Past, Present, and Future.* 6th ed. Malden, Mass.: Blackwell, 2006. Excellent general reference on environmental issues, accessible to lay readers. Chapter 7 discusses air pollution. Includes glossary, bibliography, and index.

McGraw, J. "The Denver Airport: Pollution Prevention

1990

mandated warning labels on all containers and products (refrigerators, foam insulation) that enclose CFCs and other ozone-depleting chemicals.

## SIGNIFICANCE

The 1990 Clean Air Act was a notable achievement on several accounts. The law is considered the most comprehensive set of regulations ever developed to reduce air pollution. In this regard, it set up controls for three major pollution problems (CFCs, air toxics, and acid rain) that were not covered by the Clean Air Act of 1970 or the 1977 amendments. The 1990 act clearly limited administrative discretion by specifying the requirements and deadlines for the EPA, states, and regulated industries to come under compliance, and it provided market-like incentives to encourage compliance.

—*Leslie R. Alm*

## FURTHER READING

Bryner, Gary C. *Blue Skies, Green Politics: The Clean Air Act of 1990*. Rev. ed. Washington, D.C.: Congressional Quarterly Press, 1995. Examines what Congress and the executive branch were trying to accomplish in revising the Clean Air Act. Provides an excellent summary of the major titles of the act and the regulatory changes they brought about.

Cohen, Richard E. *Washington at Work: Back Rooms and Clean Air*. 2d ed. Newton, Mass.: Allyn & Bacon, 1994. Presents the story of the passage of the Clean Air Act from the perspective of an insider. Offers a glimpse into the behind-the-scenes operation of Congress.

Doyle, Jack. *Taken for a Ride: Detroit's Big Three and the Politics of Air Pollution*. New York: Four Walls Eight Windows, 2000. Addresses the automobile industry's resistance to environmental regulations.

*Environmental Law* 21, no. 4 (1991). Entire issue provides one of the most comprehensive reviews available of the Clean Air Act of 1990, including a history of air-pollution regulation in the United States and a critique of the major provisions.

Hollander, Jack M. *The Energy-Environment Connection*. Washington, D.C.: Island Press, 1992. Presents an overview of how environmental and energy problems are linked. Several chapters are devoted to the environmental impacts of air pollution and acid rain, with emphasis on how U.S. policy fits in with the policies of the rest of the world's governments.

Rosenbaum, Walter A. *Environmental Politics and Policy*. 6th ed. Washington, D.C.: Congressional Quarterly Press, 2004. Describes the policy and governmental settings that surrounded the passage of the 1990 Clean Air Act. Also discusses the interaction of science and technology with respect to regulatory change.

Switzer, Jacqueline Vaughn. *Environmental Politics: Domestic and Global Dimensions*. 4th ed. Belmont, Calif.: Wadsworth, 2004. Uses the policy process as a framework for reviewing a broad spectrum of environmental problems, including urban air quality and the Los Angeles air-pollution problem.

Vig, Norman J., and Michael E. Kraft. *Environmental Policy in the 1990's*. 2d ed. Washington, D.C.: Congressional Quarterly Press, 1994. Provides a comprehensive look at environmental policy as it developed during the 1980's and 1990's. Includes an excellent chapter on environmental gridlock, especially as it applies to air quality and acid rain.

**SEE ALSO:** 1974: Automakers Introduce the Catalytic Converter; Aug. 7, 1977: Clean Air Act Is Revised; Jan. 1, 1986: U.S. Government Tightens Restrictions on Lead; Nov. 5, 1990: United States Makes Pollution Prevention a National Goal.

# November 28, 1990
# ENVIRONMENTALISTS DEFEAT THE CROSS-FLORIDA BARGE CANAL

*President George H. W. Bush signed a bill that deauthorized the Cross-Florida Barge Canal after environmentalists showed the potential harmful effects that constructing the canal could have on Florida's groundwater supplies.*

**LOCALE:** Florida
**CATEGORIES:** Laws, acts, and legal history; environmental issues

**KEY FIGURES**

*Marjorie H. Carr* (fl. late twentieth century), environmental activist who led the fight against the Cross-Florida Barge Canal
*Franklin D. Roosevelt* (1882-1945), president of the United States, 1933-1945, who started construction of the canal
*Richard M. Nixon* (1913-1994), president of the United States, 1969-1974, who signed legislation stopping further work on the canal
*George H. W. Bush* (b. 1924), president of the United States, 1989-1993, who signed legislation deauthorizing the canal

**SUMMARY OF EVENT**

The idea of digging a canal across the Florida peninsula emerged at least as early as 1829. In that year, Brigadier General Simon Bernard of the U.S. Army presented to Congress the results of several surveys he had made of possible canal routes. Bernard's survey followed a period of canal building in the United States in the first quarter of the nineteenth century. The completion of the Erie Canal in 1825 is an example of efforts to provide waterways to move goods cheaply and safely from farms to major centers of population.

The rationale for building a canal across Florida was simple: Users of such a canal would avoid the risk and expense of sending ships and cargo on the hazardous journey through the Straits of Florida, past Key West, and up the Atlantic coast. Despite many subsequent surveys, however, nothing was done, perhaps because of the generally negative conclusions in the surveyors' reports as to the value of a cross-Florida canal. The reports uniformly stressed the adverse characteristics of the peninsula's underlying limestone, the high cost, and the merely local benefits to be realized. An 1853 report dismissed the canal idea and strongly recommended instead the immediate construction of a railroad across the peninsula. What was preserved from the several surveys was the canal route, which actually was partially completed, from the Withlacoochee River on the Gulf of Mexico eastward to the Oklawaha River near Ocala, then to the St. Johns River, and finally to the Atlantic Ocean.

The canal idea lay dormant for nearly a century, but many people in the Florida business community and in the U.S. Congress remained interested in such a canal. On January 25, 1932, under the provisions of the United States Rivers and Harbor Acts of 1927 and 1930, the chief of engineers (U.S. Army Corps of Engineers) ordered another survey for a canal. On June 3, 1933, the Board of Engineers for Rivers and Harbors, reporting the results of the survey, recommended the canal project as a public necessity that would be both economically sound and of real social value. To support the project, in May, 1933, the state of Florida had created the Ship Canal Authority. Florida sought to have the canal constructed with federal funds under the new federal Public Works Administration (PWA).

The PWA was one of a number of agencies created by President Franklin D. Roosevelt during his first term in office (1933-1937) to combat the effects of the Great Depression. Under the broad rubric of the National Industrial Recovery Act, Roosevelt created agencies and programs to put people to work on government projects. The Cross-Florida Barge Canal seemed a natural for the PWA. It would be mainly pick-and-shovel work, employing large numbers of workers, both skilled artisans and common laborers. Some of the rosy glow surrounding the proposed canal was dimmed in a later report issued by the Army Corps of Engineers, which concluded that a cost-benefit analysis could not support the project. Nevertheless, the canal plan survived.

On August 30, 1935, Roosevelt authorized a sea-level canal across Florida and allocated $5 million toward its construction. In a symbolic stroke, on September 19, 1935, using a telegraph key in the White House, Roosevelt set off a charge of dynamite planted near the city of Ocala to begin excavation for the canal. Approximately fourteen million cubic yards of rock and soil were removed in the first nine months of the project. In addition, office buildings, dormitories for the workers, workshops, and camp facilities were built. The money ran out, however, and in June, 1936, work on the canal stopped.

The canal project had too many friends for it to die. In 1937, a bill was introduced in Congress for the canal's

1990

## PROTECTING HER OWN BACKYARD

*According to the Florida Defenders of the Environment, the organization she founded to fight construction of the Cross-Florida Barge Canal, Marjorie Harris Carr had this to say when asked why she took on the cause:*

Why fight for the Ocklawaha River? The first time I went up the Ocklawaha, I thought it was dreamlike. It was a canopy river. It was spring-fed and swift. I was concerned about the environment worldwide. What could I do about the African plains? What could I do about India? How could I affect things in Alaska or the Grand Canyon? But here, by God, was a piece of Florida. A lovely natural area, right in my backyard, that was being threatened for no good reason.

completion. At hearings before the Congressional Committee on Rivers and Harbors, the Board of Engineers testified that the canal should have a minimum depth of 35 feet and a minimum width of 400 feet to permit the passage of large, oceangoing vessels. Once again, however, the costs greatly outweighed the projected benefits. The chief of the Corps of Engineers recommended a change from plans for a sea-level canal to a canal with locks and revised cost estimates upward. The engineers dismissed fears about the effects of the canal on the groundwater of the state or the possibility of saltwater intrusion. (Florida was and is almost totally dependent on groundwater for its drinking water supplies.)

In 1939 congressional hearings, ship safety was stressed in comparing the proposed 197-mile canal to the 300- to 350-mile trip around the peninsula via Key West. One speaker testified that the canal route would be preferred during hurricanes, for example. These hearings also discussed the different kinds of cargo that might be carried through the canal. Petroleum was expected to constitute 77 percent of the annual volume. The goods would pass down the Mississippi River, along the northeast coast of the Gulf of Mexico, through the canal, and into the Atlantic Ocean at Jacksonville.

The sides were clearly drawn in the 1939 hearings. Supporters of the project included President Roosevelt; the U.S. Departments of Navy, War, and Commerce; the governors of a number of states that abutted the greater Mississippi River system; and numerous elected officials from Florida. Opponents of the canal included the Association of American Railroads, certain railroad workers' organizations, the management of some oil companies, congressmen from southern Florida districts, the Miami Chamber of Commerce, and the Florida Water

Conservation League. Perhaps the greatest support came from Roosevelt and the Navy Department, who saw the canal as of definite value in national defense. Such a waterway would safeguard the movements of shipborne troops as well as military supplies in wartime.

At the conclusion of each of the many congressional hearings, the Corps of Engineers reiterated its position that the canal was vital to the United States and should be completed. A disquieting note had been introduced, however, by Harry Slattery, acting secretary of the U.S. Department of the Interior. Slattery believed that a sea-level canal cut through the Ocala limestone formation would drain the groundwater about forty feet below its natural level. The Senate Committee on Commerce responded that the only water supply of concern was that affecting agricultural crops.

The geopolitical climate of the world was changing, and with the approach of World War II, the canal project was moved to a back burner. The United States emerged from the Great Depression as millions of the unemployed went to work in a variety of industries. The nation, although not officially at war, became the "arsenal of democracy," supplying military and humanitarian supplies to Great Britain and its allies.

Interest in the canal was revived briefly in 1942 when German submarines sank oil tankers that burned within sight of Florida's eastern beaches. In May, at a hearing before the House Committee on Rivers and Harbors, Congressman Joseph J. Mansfield of Texas pointed out that even a twelve-foot-wide channel across Florida would be enough to supply the petroleum requirements of the Atlantic seaboard. Construction of the canal was again authorized in 1942, but no further work was done. In 1958, the Army Corps of Engineers calculated that each dollar spent in construction would return one cent in benefits.

The dormant canal project was revived during the 1960 presidential campaign. Democratic candidate John F. Kennedy was told that the project was popular in Florida and that he could win the state's voters by endorsing it. He took the advice, and, following his inauguration, the U.S. Congress began hearings to authorize the canal's completion. In 1963, Congress voted a token $1 million to restart the canal project. In February, 1964, the Army Corps of Engineers, this time using huge drag-line scoops, began the work. To justify the canal, the Corps of Engineers recalculated costs and benefits to show a profit of seventeen cents for each dollar of cost.

While local business interests in Florida cheered, a growing grassroots campaign of environmentally minded citizens began to look closely at the entire canal project. One source of alarm was what has been termed "the rape of the Oklawaha." The Oklawaha River flows placidly east of Ocala and is supplied in part by water from Silver Springs. The river and its subtropical ecosystem support organisms that are biologically and ecologically unique, an archetypal example of ideal biodiversity. Nearly half the Oklawaha would be obliterated for the canal.

A group of citizens who were opposed to the canal and its environmental impacts organized in the nearby university town of Gainesville. They were appalled at the cavalier attitude of the U.S. government in disregarding the ecology of the area around the canal route. Organizing under the name Florida Defenders of the Environment (FDE) and led by Marjorie H. Carr, they included University of Florida professors from a number of disciplines. They affiliated themselves with the Environmental Defense Fund (EDF), a national organization. Members of the FDE were particularly concerned that the government had not prepared an environmental impact statement as required under the National Environmental Policy Act of 1969 (NEPA).

As prescribed by NEPA, environmental impact statements are to describe a project, why it is needed, what its environmental impacts might be, and what could be done to minimize those impacts. In the absence of an impact statement from the Army Corps of Engineers concerning the canal, the FDE, in March, 1970, published its own statement that specifically emphasized the regional ecosystem of the Oklawaha River. The 115-page document included input from university geologists, hydrologists, ecologists, land-use planners, and economists. The report concluded that the Cross-Florida Barge Canal would be an environmental disaster of major proportions. At greatest risk from the proposed waterway was the groundwater.

The efforts of the FDE seemed to serve as a rallying point for anticanal voices. Articles opposing the project appeared in such diverse popular periodicals as *Reader's Digest*, *Audubon*, and *American Forests*. Newspapers in Florida published editorials blasting the canal, and private citizens badgered their congressional delegations to stop the work.

Outcries against the canal reached the presidential administration of Richard M. Nixon. In his memoirs, John Ehrlichman, who served as Nixon's chief domestic adviser, curiously takes credit for the negative background study on the canal. He states that his staff study found only environmental damage and no positive benefits, and

that he ordered the Army Corps of Engineers to stop work on the canal.

Nixon was outraged at Ehrlichman's action because it displeased Florida business interests. Nixon undoubtedly saw the handwriting on the wall, however, and on January 19, 1971, he issued the order to stop work on the canal. His reason, he wrote, was "to prevent potentially serious environmental damages." He added that the Council on Environmental Quality had recommended an end to the project. Nixon did not mention, however, that only four days earlier, the EDF and FDE had obtained a preliminary injunction in the federal district court in the District of Columbia to force the Army Corps of Engineers to halt the project. In his ruling, the judge noted that the Corps of Engineers had not complied with the requirements of the National Environmental Policy Act.

The canal still was not dead, however; special interests in Florida and sympathetic politicians in Florida's executive and legislative branches, as well as many in Washington, kept the project alive. About one-third of the waterway had been constructed, at a cost of $50 million. Some saw continuation of the work as throwing good money after bad, whereas others saw cessation of the project as a waste of monies already expended. The Florida cabinet supported the Canal Authority of Florida by appropriating $1.13 million for it, plus $38,300 for the Cross-Florida Canal District. In addition, President Gerald R. Ford submitted a budget that included $825,000 for further studies on the canal and $593,000 for maintenance of the completed portions.

In the mid-1970's, major Florida newspapers and television stations published editorials against the canal while the EDF, the FDE, and other environmentalist groups continued their efforts. In a startling turnaround, in 1977 the U.S. Army Corps of Engineers and the Florida cabinet recommended that the canal project be terminated. What followed was classic political maneuvering. In 1979, legislation was filed in the U.S. Congress to deauthorize the canal, but it failed. In 1986, Congress passed a deauthorization bill, but Florida failed to pass the necessary implementing laws. Finally, after tremendous public outcry against the canal, on May 31, 1990, the Florida legislature passed a bill to deauthorize the canal. The bill was signed into law the following June 18 by Governor Robert Martinez. President George H. W. Bush signed corresponding federal legislation on November 28, 1990.

### SIGNIFICANCE
The controversy over the building of the Cross-Florida Barge Canal grew along with the American environmen-

1990

tal movement. Eventually, the raised voices of citizens' groups—including the old-line Audubon Society, the Environmental Defense Fund, and Florida Defenders of the Environment—and a host of concerned individuals succeeded in convincing local and national governments and the courts of the dangers the canal project posed to the environment. The defeat of the canal stands as a high point in the environmental conservation movement in the United States.

The 1990 death of the Cross-Florida Barge Canal project left supporters on both sides of the issue wondering what to do. More than seventy-seven thousand acres of land in six counties had been acquired for the canal, the right-of-way, and support structures. Some land had been bought outright, some was donated, and some was obtained by eminent domain. A few people wanted their land back. Some counties wanted recompense for the taxes they had lost while the land was in federal ownership. One small city, Dunnellon, about twenty miles from the canal's western end, had lost 18 percent of its land to the canal and wanted it back for a wastewater spray field but could not afford to pay for it. Some developers hungrily eyed choice parcels with water access.

The federal government established a system of buy-back under which the state of Florida would have the first opportunity to buy canal land. Any of the land it did not choose to purchase would then be offered to the six counties. The original landowners could choose from what was left, and finally any residue would be sold to the highest bidders.

The state responded with a plan to establish a cross-state park, the Cross Florida Greenbelt State Recreation and Conservation Area. The park would be at least three hundred yards wide, wider where possible. It would include nature trails, campsites, fishing, boating and swimming access, and some supporting amenities. To ensure reasonable development and management of the greenbelt, the state requested a management plan from University of Florida researchers. In addition, a canal lands advisory committee was appointed; its members included FDE founder Marjorie Carr. The successfully reclaimed area was later renamed the Cross Florida Greenway, and in 1998, in honor of Carr's fight to stop the canal, it became the Marjorie Harris Carr Cross Florida Greenway.

—*Albert C. Jensen*

## FURTHER READING

Brooks, Paul. "Oklawaha: The Sweetest Water-Lane in the World." In *The Pursuit of Wilderness*. Boston: Houghton Mifflin, 1971. Lyrical essay describes the natural subtropical beauty of the Oklawaha River before it was engineered for the Cross-Florida Barge Canal. Includes excellent black-and-white photographs of the natural river ecosystem, a map of the canal route and environs, and a photograph of one completed section of the canal.

Ehrlichman, John. *Witness to Power: The Nixon Years*. New York: Pocket Books, 1982. Provides a revealing insightful look at political maneuvering. Briefly describes how the Florida business community sought Nixon's help to push through the Cross-Florida Barge Canal project.

Flippen, J. Brooks. *Nixon and the Environment*. Albuquerque: University of New Mexico Press, 2000. Examines Nixon's reasons for the decisions he made concerning the environment during his presidency. Includes discussion of the Cross-Florida Barge Canal.

Florida Defenders of the Environment. *Environmental Impact of the Cross-Florida Barge Canal with Special Emphasis on the Oklawaha Regional Ecosystem*. Gainesville: Author, 1970. Collection of chapters by University of Florida faculty members examines pertinent ecological and cultural aspects of the canal environs and how they could be greatly damaged by the canal.

Irby, Lee. "A Passion for Wild Things: Marjorie Harris Carr and the Fight to Free a River." In *Making Waves: Female Activists in Twentieth-Century Florida*, edited by Jack E. Davis and Kari Frederickson. Gainesville: University Press of Florida, 2003. Details Carr's role in the fight against the Cross-Florida Barge Canal.

Walsh, John. "Florida: Nixon Halts Canal Project, Cites Environment." *Science* 29 (January, 1971): 357. Detail-packed short article sketches the background of the canal project and the legal actions taken by citizen groups to stop the canal. Also describes some of the justifications used by engineers to support the project.

Wright, Albert Hazen. *The Atlantic-Gulf or Florida Ship Canal*. Ithaca, N.Y.: A. H. Wright, 1937. Includes several historical synopses and the 1829 site survey for a canal route made by General Bernard. Several of the old surveys approximate the route chosen in the 1930's.

**SEE ALSO:** June 29, 1987: Florida Passes the Surface Water Improvement and Management Act; Dec. 11, 2000: U.S. Government Funds Everglades Restoration.

## November 28, 1990
# MAJOR SUCCEEDS THATCHER AS BRITISH PRIME MINISTER

*When it became clear that the Conservative Party could lose the next general election in the United Kingdom under the leadership of Margaret Thatcher, John Major slipped by several other opponents to become the new prime minister and leader of the Conservative Party.*

**LOCALE:** London, England
**CATEGORY:** Government and politics

**KEY FIGURES**

*John Major* (b. 1943), prime minister of the United Kingdom, 1990-1997
*Margaret Thatcher* (b. 1925), prime minister of the United Kingdom, 1979-1990
*Michael Heseltine* (b. 1933), cabinet minister under Margaret Thatcher and later minister for the environment under John Major
*Douglas Hurd* (b. 1930), cabinet minister under Margaret Thatcher and later foreign secretary under John Major

**SUMMARY OF EVENT**

In 1979, the Conservative Party, led by Margaret Thatcher, regained power from the Labour Party in the British parliamentary elections. As leader of the majority party, Thatcher was asked by the queen to form a government and thus became Britain's first woman prime minister. The Conservative Party retained its majority in the next two elections, held in 1983 and 1987, with Thatcher firmly in control.

By 1990, however, opinion polls were beginning to predict a loss for the Conservative Party at the next elections, which were due to be held in two years. Some party members thought that at least part of the public's discontent with the party was related to unhappiness with Thatcher. She had supported a number of rather divisive social policies, some of which were causing continued high unemployment levels; she had pushed through a highly unpopular poll tax to replace the old system of local taxes or rates; and she had demonstrated an increasingly dictatorial style in governing, leading to the resignations of a number of prominent cabinet members, including Michael Heseltine of the Board of Trade in 1986 and Sir Geoffrey Howe, the Chancellor of the Exchequer, in 1990.

In an attempt to make the party more democratic, the Conservatives, also known as Tories, had instituted an-nual leadership elections. For much of Thatcher's tenure, she had been returned as leader unopposed, but first in 1989 and then in 1990, she was opposed. The latter opposition was significant, because it was made by a senior Conservative Party figure, Michael Heseltine, a populist center-right politician who opposed Thatcher's right-wing, patrician leadership. Under party rules, the election could run to three rounds of voting. In the first round, the winner had to have a majority of the votes cast and a clear 15 percent over the next candidate. With 372 members of Parliament eligible to vote, this meant a winner would need up to 214 votes. Otherwise, there would be a second round, and new candidates could enter the race. The winner would need half the eligible votes, in this case, 187. If there was a failure to obtain this number, the best three candidates would go into a third round, which would be decided by a simple majority after a transferable vote from the candidate in third position.

The date for the first round of voting was set for Tuesday, November 20, 1990. Thatcher at once declared her candidacy, saying she still had unfinished business. No other party members put up their names to oppose her apart from Heseltine. Although she won by 204 votes to 152, this was not enough to declare her the outright winner, and there would need to be a second round of voting. At this stage, electioneering became tense, as at first it seemed that Thatcher was willing to head into the second round, even though it was evident she had lost significant party support. Two likely candidates indicated that they would stand for the position of party leader, but only if Thatcher would stand down: John Major, who had replaced Howe as Chancellor of the Exchequer, and Douglas Hurd, the experienced foreign secretary.

At this point, various high-ranking members of the party made it clear to Thatcher that, although she would win the second round, the result would be a divided party almost certain to lose the next election. Within a day, she decided to stand down, giving her preference to John Major, even though he was the youngest and least experienced of all the likely candidates. When nominations closed on Thursday, November 22, there were three candidates: Michael Heseltine, John Major, and Douglas Hurd. Support was growing for Major as the candidate behind whom the party could most easily unite, although at the beginning he had been very much an also-ran. When the second round of voting took place on November 27, Major received 187 votes, Heseltine received

131, and Hurd received 56. Although Major was technically two votes short of what was needed for victory, the two other candidates immediately dropped out of the race, leaving him the undisputed party leader.

Thatcher went to the queen to announce her resignation, whereupon the queen invited John Major to form a new government. He thus became prime minister with immediate effect, even though he had only three years' cabinet experience. Major then brought Heseltine back into the cabinet and retained Hurd, thus unifying the party. He announced that the unpopular poll tax would be reviewed, and that moves toward the United Kingdom's greater integration with the European Union would proceed cautiously.

## SIGNIFICANCE

After Major became prime minister, opinion polls immediately put the Conservative Party back on equal footing with the Labour Party. Major decided not to hold a quick election, however, but to run the full five-year term of Parliament, hoping that the nation's economy would improve and unemployment would come down. Although this did not happen, the Labour Party manifesto at the general election was shown to be the same "spend and tax" program that the electorate had come to associate with past Labour governments. Major managed to persuade the voters that he was a safer pair of hands to manage the economy and guide the nation toward integration with the European Union. In the end, the Conservatives retained power with a small but workable overall majority.

Major's sudden rise to leadership put him at something of a disadvantage, as, in addition to being inexperienced, he had little time to formulate his personal goals and policies. His style was to seek consensus within the cabinet and to hear out his opponents, a style very different from Thatcher's. Major's relative sympathy to the cause of European unity was increasingly opposed by Thatcher, soon to become Lady Thatcher, and many other right-wing Tories. His cause was not helped by the United Kingdom's having to withdraw from the Exchange Rate Mechanism (ERM) of the European Union, an anti-inflationary device that was too much at the mercy of the German economy, now struggling with reunification of the old communist East Germany with West Germany. This "Black Wednesday" of 1992 delayed British economic recovery for several years.

Major's consensus style of leadership became increasingly problematic as opposition to his European stance began to be voiced even within the cabinet. In the end, Major had to resign as leader of the party in 1995,

forcing a leadership contest that he then won comfortably. Division within the party continued, however, to which was added a "sleaze" factor when the press exposed various misdemeanors by Conservative members of Parliament and a number of notorious resignations ensued, even though other accusations were found to be false. In the 1997 elections, the British voters viewed the Conservatives as fatally flawed and the country in need of a change, even though the economy had picked up and unemployment was dropping. The allure of the young Tony Blair's "New Labour" was potent, and John Major's government was defeated in a landslide.

The Major government did, however, produce some solid gains that the new Labour Party was all too eager to retain. The economy had picked up, spending on education and the health service had increased substantially, income taxes had been reduced, and the unpopular poll tax had been replaced by a new council tax. The British currency was doing well despite the United Kingdom's not entering into the single currency of the European Union. Peace initiatives had begun in Northern Ireland, although further terrorist attacks had put these on hold, and in foreign affairs, the British had done well in Iraq by backing President George H. W. Bush in Operation Desert Storm.

—*David Barratt*

## FURTHER READING

Anderson, Bruce. *John Major: The Making of the Prime Minister*. London: Fourth Estate, 1991. Study of Major's early life and development discusses the formation of his beliefs and attitudes.

Major, John. *John Major: The Autobiography*. London: HarperCollins, 1999. Written soon after he left office, Major's personal account deals almost entirely with his years as prime minister.

Seldon, Anthony. *Major: A Political Life*. New York: Weidenfeld & Nicolson, 1997. Biography written before Major's decisive defeat gives a full and detailed account of his political career.

Taylor, Robert. *John Major*. London: Haus, 2006. Provides an accessible introduction to Major and his government for the general reader.

**SEE ALSO:** May 4, 1979: Thatcher Becomes First Woman to Serve as British Prime Minister; Nov. 8, 1988: Bush Is Elected President; Mar. 31, 1990: British Riot over the Poll Tax; Nov. 3, 1992: Clinton Wins the U.S. Presidency; May 1, 1997: Labor Party Wins Majority in British National Elections.

**December 16, 1990**
# Aristide Wins First Democratic Election in Haiti

*After years of autocratic rule under the Duvaliers, Haiti elected Jean-Bertrand Aristide, who won the presidency by democratic vote. His tenure extended from February to September 30, 1991, when he was overthrown in a coup by Raoul Cédras.*

**Locale:** Port-au-Prince, Haiti
**Categories:** Government and politics; diplomacy and international relations

## Key Figures

*Jean-Bertrand Aristide* (b. 1953), president of Haiti, 1991, 1994-1996, and 2001-2004
*René Préval* (b. 1943), prime minister under Aristide and president, 1996-2001
*Raoul Cédras* (b. 1949), military junta leader, 1991-1994, who overthrew Aristide
*Jean-Claude "Baby Doc" Duvalier* (b. 1951), president of Haiti, 1971-1986
*François "Papa Doc" Duvalier* (1907-1971), president of Haiti, 1957-1971
*Prosper Avril* (b. 1937), military dicator of Haiti, 1988-1990

## Summary of Event

For thirty years, Haiti languished under the dictatorial and corrupt rule of the Duvalier family. François "Papa Doc" Duvalier was elected president in 1957 and declared himself "president for life" in 1964. He repressed opposition using a reign of physical terror in the form of his dreaded paramilitary force, the Tontons Macoutes. Leading Voodoo cultists were used to exert psychological terror on dissidents. At Papa Doc's death in 1971, his nineteen-year-old son, Jean-Claude "Baby Doc" Duvalier, continued the presidential dynasty. Under the Duvaliers, Haiti became the poorest nation in the Western Hemisphere while a small number of leading families and the Duvaliers amassed great wealth.

Demonstrations against Baby Doc began in earnest in October, 1985, and did not stop until February, 1986, when Jean-Claude fled to exile in Paris. For the next four years, Haiti was ruled by a number of ineffective provisional governments, mostly of a military caretaker nature. During this period, a constitution for a democratic parliamentary government was drafted. To prevent a recurrence of the Duvalier lifetime presidency, the constitution strictly barred any president from serving two consecutive terms in office. The fact that it was adopted in 1987 by referendum, abolished in 1988 following a military coup, and readopted in 1990 when civilian governance was restored underlined the precarious nature of the transition into democratic government.

Finally, in December, 1990, following concerted pressures by the United Nations, the Organization of American States, and the United States, Haiti's first real democratic election was held under the watchful eyes of a multitude of international observers. Winning over two-thirds of the vote for president was Jean-Bertrand Aristide, a popular Roman Catholic priest who promised major reforms to uplift the poverty-stricken masses. Few could doubt his integrity and sincerity. Many could doubt his ability to survive for long.

Orphaned as an infant, Aristide was raised by the Salesian Order of the Roman Catholic Church, whose mission was to minister to the general needs of the poor, especially those of poor or orphaned children. He was educated in their parochial schools and their seminary before attending the University of Haiti to earn a degree in psychology. As a program director at the Roman Catholic radio station (Radio Cacique) and a newspaper editorialist, Aristide established a reputation as a critique of Baby Doc's government and an advocate of changes to benefit Haiti's poor. His powerful sermons urged the poor to take responsibility for instituting needed changes. His words also earned him death threats from the Tontons Macoutes.

From 1979 to 1985, Aristide studied theology in Israel, Egypt, and Great Britain, ultimately earning a master's degree in theology from the University of Montreal. During this period, he returned only once to Haiti—to receive his ordination as a priest of the Salesian Order in 1982. On his return to Haiti in 1985, he became the parish priest at St. Jean Bosco, one of the poorest parishes in Port-au-Prince. He used his polished oratory skills to help drive Baby Doc from power in 1986. However, his continued emphasis on liberation theology, on priests working with the poor to correct continuing abuses and inequalities, angered the military regimes of Generals Prosper Avril and Henri Namphy that succeeded Baby Doc.

Aristide survived several assassination attempts, the worst being an attack in 1988 by about 100 armed Tontons Macoutes who attacked the congregation at St. Jean Bosco Church during Mass. Aristide barely escaped with his life, but thirteen members of the congregation

1990

2533

lay dead and seventy were badly wounded. The church itself was burned to the ground. To prevent further attacks, Aristide was expelled from the Silesian Order and ordered to Rome, but mass demonstrations at Port-au-Prince blocked any means of sending Aristide abroad. He remained at Port-au-Prince ministering to the needs of street children, opening medical clinics and trade schools.

A few months before the elections in December, 1990, a mass popular movement taking the Creole name of Lavalas (flood) convinced Aristide to run for president against the front-runner, a respected career diplomat named Marc Bazin, several other candidates supported by leading families, and the head of the Tontons Macoutes. Aristide's intent was to send a message about the needs of the poor, and, indeed, his campaign oratory was permeated with this theme. Few realized that since the poor masses would be voting in this free and monitored election, all bets should have been on an Aristide victory. However, the hastily formed Lavalas Party did not realize that Aristide's popularity would not translate into a sweep of the newly formed parliament.

When he took office, Aristide pledged that he would cleanse the civil service of corrupt officials and Duvalier loyalists, fight against drug trafficking, and demolish all remaining vestiges of the Tontons Macoutes. His dedication was underscored when he stated that he would give his entire presidential salary to charity. Clearly, such a man could not be trusted by the former power structure, and on September 30, 1991, a military coup led by General Raoul Cédras took control as Aristide was in New York attending a meeting at the United Nations. Hundreds of Aristide's supporters were killed in the streets while protesting the military's actions, and several thousand more would be killed in the subsequent two years of military rule. More than forty thousand Haitians would become boat people, asylum seekers fleeing oppression in their native land. Most would be returned by the United States to an uncertain fate in Haiti.

In spite of embargoes on Haitian exports and key imports such as oil, the military regime remained entrenched in power. As repression accelerated, Resolution 940 was passed by the U.N. Security Council to use all necessary means to restore the constitutionally elected government to power. After talks between Cédras and Aristide, brokered by the United Nations and the United States under Bill Clinton's presidential administration, failed to produce results, it was obvious that decisive action was needed. Under U.N. mandate, more than twenty thousand U.S. troops prepared, in September, 1994, to launch Operation Restore Democracy. At that time, former president Jimmy Carter was dispatched to Haiti with a small group of negotiators to offer the military junta a last-minute deal. As U.S. troops were airborne, the Cédras military regime agreed to step down and permit Aristide to serve out the remaining twenty-seven months of his presidential term.

**SIGNIFICANCE**

Aristide returned on October 15, 1994, to serve out his term that ended in February, 1996. One of his first acts was to dismantle the troublesome Haitian military and replace it with a civilian police force.

*Future Haitian president Jean-Bertrand Aristide in 1988, when he was gaining a reputation as a Roman Catholic priest unafraid to speak out against the government without the support of his church.* (AP/Wide World Photos)

As promised during his exile, nine state-owned enterprises were privatized, and controls over customs duties and interest rates were lifted. These actions were taken to ease concerns of affluent Haitians. To please his mass support base, the minimum wage was doubled. When parliamentary elections were held in June, 1995, Aristide's Lavalas Party won a sweeping victory. When presidential elections were held on December 17, 1995, Aristide's vice president, René Préval, won 88 percent of the vote. Thus Haiti's first democratic transition took place.

On November 26, 2000, with his Lavalas Family party (formed in 1996 after Aristide broke with Préval) firmly in control of parliament, Aristide registered as a candidate for Haiti's next presidential election. However, claiming major irregularities in the unmonitored parliamentary elections, opposition parties boycotted the presidential elections. Although Aristide received more than 90 percent of the vote, voter turnout was low. For the next four years, both the parliament and the president were viewed by a significant number of Haitians as illegitimate.

Although a coup against Aristide failed in July, 2001, opposition to his rule mounted and violence once again became a daily aspect of Haitian political life. By February 29, 2004, a large rebel force moved toward Port-au-Prince, and Aristide and his wife left Haiti in an American plane escorted by U.S. military and diplomatic personnel. An international peacekeeping force was sent in to try to maintain order. Democracy and stability were elusive as ever in Haiti.

—*Irwin Halfond*

**FURTHER READING**

Dupuy, Alex. *Prophet and Power: Jean-Bertrand Aristide, the International Community, and Haiti.* Lanham, Md.: Rowman & Littlefield, 2006. Analysis of the struggle for democracy in Haiti by a leading scholar on the country. Bibliographic references and index.

Griffiths, Leslie. *Aristide Factor.* New York: Oxford University Press, 1997. A major study and analysis of Aristide's role in Haitian politics. Bibliographic references and index.

Pezzullo, Ralph. *Plunging into Haiti: Clinton, Aristide, and the Defeat of Diplomacy.* Jackson: University of Mississippi Press, 2007. Insider's view of Haitian political struggles and U.S. diplomatic efforts at policy resolution. Bibliographic references and index.

**SEE ALSO:** Apr. 21, 1971: Baby Doc Succeeds Papa Doc in Haiti; July 31, 1994: United Nations Authorizes the Use of Force in Haiti.

1991

---

## 1991-1992

# CAPTIVE-BRED CONDORS AND FERRETS ARE REINTRODUCED INTO THE WILD

*Wildlife conservationists gained valuable knowledge when they sought to increase the wild populations of the endangered California condor and black-footed ferret through captive breeding and reintroduction into the wild.*

**LOCALE:** California; Wyoming
**CATEGORY:** Animals and endangered species

**KEY FIGURES**

*Benjamin B. Beck* (fl. late twentieth century), chair of the Reintroduction Advisory Group of the American Zoo and Aquarium Association and staff member of the National Zoological Park

*E. Tom Thorne* (1941-2004), species coordinator for the black-footed ferret and staff member of the Wyoming Game and Fish Department

*Michael Wallace* (fl. late twentieth century), species coordinator for the California condor and staff member of the Los Angeles Zoo

**SUMMARY OF EVENT**

Introduction, reintroduction, and translocation are old, well-established techniques for managing game and wild animal populations. Introduction involves placing animals in areas where they are not normally found, reintroduction is a means of restocking an area with animals that used to be there, and translocation involves moving animals from one part of their natural range to another. These techniques have traditionally been used for commercial, recreational, and management purposes, such as game ranching, game hunting and fishing, and controlling wild populations. Usually, the animals affected are

*A California condor (identification tags on wings).* (U.S. Fish and Wildlife Service)

wild specimens or semiwild, bred specimens of either game species or large populations of common (that is, nongame) species.

The reintroduction of captive-bred animals to prevent a species from becoming extinct is a technique that developed in the 1980's and 1990's from interdisciplinary studies in conservation management, small population and endangered species population biology, reproductive biology, wildlife veterinary medicine, genetics, and biotechnology. Unlike the older management techniques, this kind of reintroduction depends significantly on interagency cooperation, productive relationships with private landowners affected by the programs, and public support. In the early 1990's, reintroduction of captive-bred animas was used successfully to prevent the California condor (*Gymnogyps californianus*) and the black-footed ferret (*Mustela nigripes*) from becoming extinct.

The California condor, whose nearest relative is the Andean condor of South America, belongs to the family of New World vultures. The bird's habitat is the moun-

tainous terrain surrounding the San Joaquin Valley. Los Angeles is at the southern boundary of the U-shaped range, and the San Francisco Bay Area is at its northern, coastal end. The condor population had decreased steadily since 1840, in part as a result of commercial and Indian ceremonial use of feathers, capture for sport and specimen collecting, wanton shooting and poisoning, and pollution. Primarily, however, the population had decreased as a result of the loss of habitat and food supply. In the early 1900's, the population of California condors was about 150. Between 1920 and 1965, it dropped to 60, and by 1976, to 34.

The California Condor Recovery Plan was initiated in 1974 with the objective of maintaining at least 50 condors in the range they then inhabited. The plan eventually included the use of a captive propagation program begun by the U.S. Fish and Wildlife Service in 1976. Captive propagation of condors is somewhat problematic because the birds have a long period of sexual immaturity (they do not become mature until after the age of eight) and a low reproductive rate of at most one hatchling per year. The birds do well and breed successfully in captivity, however, and they are long-lived, living about twenty years in the wild and thirty-five to forty-five years in captivity. In addition, humans can encourage increased laying in captive birds by removing some of the eggs and hand-rearing the offspring.

It was believed that the wild population of condors had not had the capacity to increase significantly since the beginning of the twentieth century and that the bird was on the brink of extinction by 1974, when the recovery effort began. Despite this effort, the wild population declined further. By 1987, only 14 birds remained in the wild, and it was decided to place them in the captive propagation program, which at that time had 13 young hatchlings from eggs that had been removed from nests in the wild. The 27 birds were held in the San Diego and Los Angeles zoos. By 1990, this captive population had increased to 19 males and 21 females, and in 1991, the numbers had reached 26 males and 26 females. By 1992, an additional 12 juveniles had hatched. These birds began to be released back into the wild as of January, 1992.

The black-footed ferret is a small, nocturnal carnivore that depends on prairie dogs for 90 percent of its diet and shelter. Historically, its range extended throughout the western states, wherever the prairie dog lived. Like the prairie dog, the ferret lives in colonies and uses burrows for shelter. The decline of the black-footed ferret was the direct result of a decline in the prairie dog population, both being results of loss of habitat and of poisoning (the prairie dog was considered a pest and its burrows a hazard to free-ranging cattle). By 1980, the ferret's habitat was so reduced and fragmented that extinction was thought likely to have occurred. When a Wyoming rancher's dog caught a ferret in 1981, a search located a colony of the animals near Meeteetse.

From 1981 to 1984, researchers gathered biological and demographic data on the ferret population. By 1986, funding was obtained and a captive propagation facility established, and from 1985 to 1987, 18 specimens were captured and established at Sybille Wildlife Research Unit in Wyoming. Eventually a number of other organizations—among them Omaha's Henry Doorly Zoo, the National Zoological Park, Louisville Zoological Garden, Cheyenne Mountain Zoological Park, the Phoenix Zoo, and the Metropolitan Toronto Zoo—joined the project.

This program also was successful. In 1987, 8 ferrets were born, of which 7 survived; in 1988, 44 were born, of which 34 survived; and in 1989, 80 were born, of which 58 survived. By 1991, the captive population had increased to 134. Shortly after the program got under way, an epidemic of canine distemper swept through the Meeteetse habitat, and by 1992 the prairie dog population there had declined by 90 percent and the ferret population was totally eradicated. For this reason, the release of captive ferrets, which began in the fall of 1991, was conducted not in Meeteetse but in southeastern Wyoming, near Shirley Basin and Medicine Bow.

## SIGNIFICANCE

The reintroduction programs for the California condor and the black-footed ferret serve as models for bringing other species back from the brink of extinction. From fewer than a couple dozen condors, the population in the wild had risen to about 200 by 2006, as the captive-bred birds had begun to reproduce in the wild. Similarly, the black-footed ferret population in the wild had slowly built up to about 500 by 2005. Although each species has its own requirements, the basic techniques and procedures used for the condor and ferret programs are widely applicable.

Analysis of efforts that fail can also be useful to future programs, as can examination of successful programs for areas where improvements can be made. Evaluations of the condor and ferret programs showed the need for improved cooperation among the organizations involved, better procedures and management programs, and more effective captive breeding programs. Above all else, the evaluations highlighted how crucial it is that the probability of the extinction of a species be determined before the population becomes too small to be able to respond.

With regard to the use of captive-bred specimens in conservation efforts, a number of programs have been established by the American Zoo and Aquarium Association and its member institutions. In addition, a number of studbooks for rare or endangered species have been established, and the U.S. Fish and Wildlife Service has created species recovery teams. The World Zoo Organization has devised a global plan that includes reintroduction of captive-bred animals. The organization's strategy considers the ultimate goal of captive conservation to be the support of species in the wild and field conservation efforts. The organization's philosophy is that reintroductions are of great benefit to natural biological systems and that such efforts are useful if they are carefully planned and well managed. Zoological parks have become involved in many reintroduction projects, and thousands of reintroduced specimens now are born in zoological parks.

One aspect of modern captive propagation that may

1991

prove to be of particular value is the use of biotechnology. Many newly developed reproductive techniques may be used to increase numbers of offspring in endangered species and to improve the success of reproduction. Improvements in knowledge of genetics (both at the individual level and the population level), small population biology, veterinary medicine, and animal management are also expected to contribute to the success of propagation programs.

Continued and improved cooperation among federal and state governments, zoological parks, and the private sector is important to the design, planning, and implementation of effective conservation programs. This is particularly true for reintroduction programs for species that the public may consider dangerous or that private landowners wish to keep off their property. This was certainly the case with the black-footed ferret, which, along with its necessary food supply, the prairie dog, was considered a nuisance. To prevent species from going extinct, human beings must integrate their own interests with the preservation of suitable natural habitat and must use all available biotechnology techniques and biological knowledge.

*—Vernon N. Kisling, Jr.*

## FURTHER READING

Beck, B. B., L. G. Rapaport, M. R. Stanley Price, and A. C. Wilson. "Reintroduction of Captive-Born Animals." In *Creative Conservation: Interactive Management of Wild and Captive Animals*, edited by P. J. S. Olney, G. M. Mace, and A. T. C. Feistner. New York: Chapman & Hall, 1994. Presents a general overview of reintroduction as a conservation strategy and discusses the extent of the use of captive-born specimens in reintroduction programs.

Godbey, Jerry, and Dean Biggins. "Recovery of the Black-Footed Ferret: Looking Back, Looking Forward." *Endangered Species Technical Bulletin* 19, no. 1 (1994): 10, 13. Briefly reviews the effort to save the black-footed ferret.

Nielsen, John. *Condor: To the Brink and Back—The Life and Times of One Giant Bird*. New York: Harper-Collins, 2006. An environmental journalist relates the condor's story. Includes extensive discussion of the at-time controversial captive-breeding program.

Seal, Ulysses S., E. Tom Thorne, Michael A. Bogan, and Stanley H. Anderson, eds. *Conservation Biology and the Black-footed Ferret*. New Haven, Conn.: Yale University Press, 1989. Collection of essays discusses all aspects of the effort to save the black-footed ferret. Also includes several chapters on the captive propagation program.

Snyder, Noel, and Helen Snyder. *The California Condor: A Saga of Natural History and Conservation*. Princeton, N.J.: Princeton University Press, 2000. Comprehensive volume discusses condor biology, nesting characteristics, and breeding behavior as well as conservation efforts and the controversies they have raised. Includes photographs, bibliography, and index.

Thorne, E. Tom, and Bob Oakleaf. "Species Rescue for Captive Breeding: Black-Footed Ferret as an Example." In *Beyond Captive Breeding: Re-introducing Endangered Mammals to the Wild*, edited by J. H. W. Gipps. London: Zoological Society of London, 1991. Reviews the black-footed ferret program as a case study in the development of captive-bred reintroduction programs.

World Zoo Organization et al. *The World Zoo Conservation Strategy: The Role of the Zoos and Aquaria of the World in Global Conservation*. Chicago: Chicago Zoological Society, 1993. A global plan used as a guide for zoological parks, aquariums, wildlife agencies, and conservation organizations. Discusses how zoological parks and aquariums can make contributions to the overall wildlife conservation effort.

**SEE ALSO:** Mar. 3, 1973: International Convention Protects Endangered Species; Dec. 28, 1973: U.S. Congress Protects Endangered Species; 1975: Atlantic Salmon Return to the Connecticut River; July 23, 1990: Spotted Owl Prompts Old-Growth Timber Controversy; June, 1994: Bald Eagle Is No Longer an Endangered Species.

**1991-1993**

# DEVELOPMENT OF HTML

*Hypertext markup language, or HTML, consists of a set of instructions for the creation of display pages on browsers, which made the World Wide Web possible. By the mid-1990's, HTML embedded codes that defined fonts, layouts, graphics, and hypertext links provided a standard protocol that allowed Web page designers to distribute content to any computer.*

**ALSO KNOWN AS:** Hypertext markup language
**LOCALE:** Geneva, Switzerland
**CATEGORIES:** Computers and computer science; inventions; science and technology

## KEY FIGURES

*Tim Berners-Lee* (b. 1955), British physicist who, in 1989, invented what would become the World Wide Web
*Marc Andreessen* (b. 1971), undergraduate student at University of Illinois who developed the early Web browser Mosaic and eventually became cofounder of Netscape
*Robert Cailliau* (b. 1947), codeveloper of the World Wide Web

## SUMMARY OF EVENT

Tim Berners-Lee, while working as a software engineering consultant at the Conseil Européen pour la Recherche Nucléaire (CERN; later known as the Organisation Européen pour la Recherche Nucléaire, or the European Organization for Nuclear Research) in Geneva, Switzerland, was attempting to organize laboratory research documents and statistics from incompatible computer systems submitted by physicists from around the world. In order to pool all of these files for sharing information, Berners-Lee developed a set of formatting codes to work with hypertext protocol by linking text within the files. Hypertext enables the computer user to cross-reference information and link formats together through multiple gateways on the World Wide Web. Each page is provided with a unique location address known as a universal document locator (URL). Robert Cailliau, who worked in the Office Computing Systems, Data Handling Division, at CERN, collaborated with Berners-Lee to get the Web under way. Cailliau's contributions were essential to the development of the Web. He rewrote the original proposal, lobbied administrators for funding, presented papers at conferences, and got programmers to work on the project.

Berners-Lee derived hypertext markup language (HTML) from standard generalized markup language-Standard generalized markup language (SGML), an international standard that emphasizes document structure and textual relationships. However, SGML proved too complex for the average Web page creator, so HTML was developed as a nonproprietary format in order to embed code for text, images, and other files to make them easily accessible through the Web. Berners-Lee's prototype for hypertext was the NeXT computer station, but he encouraged others to program, design, and improve software for displaying HTML documents. In 1993, Marc Andreessen, an undergraduate student at the National Center of Supercomputing Applications (NCSA) at the University of Illinois, designed a Web browser to display HTML documents, called Mosaic, that was widely adopted and accelerated Internet traffic over the following three years.

There are three types of markup language. The first type is procedural, or specific, markup, which provides visual clues for text formatting and indicates printing instructions to the processing system. The second type is descriptive, or generalized, markup, which informs the system of document components and layout, such as headings or paragraph designations. The final type of markup language, content, identifies various portions of the document that specify the speaker or types of speech. Markup codes are not visible when the document is displayed on the browser. HTML unifies elements and attributes using various tags and symbols.

The basic HTML markup statements are tags delimited by pairs of angle brackets. HTML tags contain elements that tell the browser a tag is starting or ending. The head tags indicate to the browser how to display elements of a document, such as font size, color, and title. The body will denote where paragraphs begin or end. The slash mark indicates the end of a section or page. HTML also applies attributes, such as "href," that note a hypertext reference, allowing users to click a link that takes them to another Web site or page. Markup creation had been a tedious process that was prone to human error, but with the advent of HTML editor programs, the insertion of elements, tags, and attributes was made faster and easier. An example of a basic document done in HTML is as follows:

1991

```
<html>
<head>
<title>Hello World!</title>
</head>
<body>
<p>Greetings to everyone viewing this page</p>
</body>
</html>
```

## SIGNIFICANCE

The World Wide Web became a global, economic, and social phenomenon by the end of the 1990's. However, American businesses shied away from the Internet in the early part of the decade, believing that it would be used only for research in the academic environment. In 1994, Berners-Lee, who was now working at the Massachusetts Institute of Technology, founded the World Wide Web Consortium (W3C) to promote guidelines regarding the growth of network infrastructure and strict language syntax with HTML, especially with the emerging browser battles between Netscape and Microsoft Explorer.

HTML promoted interoperability, causing Internet traffic to explode. Search engines had difficulty trying to track all of the pages found on the Web. Companies soon embraced the World Wide Web for commercial ventures, and in response, HTML continued to improve support. Browsers adopted cascading style sheets to improve document appearance. Dynamic HTML added capabilities to respond interactively with JavaScript. Extensible markup language (XML), a relative of HTML, created additional tags to identify structures and relationships within a document. XML had two important features. First, Web page creators had more flexibility to create their own tags. Second, XML separated content from formatting through the use of sophisticated style sheets, ensuring that all data structures and relationships were identified within the XML tags in which they were enclosed. XML made search engines more powerful for cataloging contents, enabling computers to become even more interactive and responsive to user actions.

*—Gayla Koerting*

## FURTHER READING

Bell, Mary Ann, Mary Ann Berry, and James L. Van Roekel. *Internet and Personal Computing Fads*. New York: Haworth Press, 2004. A handbook that defines computer and Internet jargon for a general audience. Lists three to five sources after each term.

Berners-Lee, Tim. *Weaving the Web: The Original De-sign and Ultimate Destiny of the World Wide Web by Its Inventor*. San Francisco: Harper, 1999. A memoir in which the inventor of the World Wide Web explains the philosophy behind, and the development and adoption of, the World Wide Web. Also discusses trends in Internet usage, especially the rise of e-commerce, and predicts the future for this technological revolution.

Cailliau, Robert, and Helen Ashman. "Hypertext in the Web: A History."*ACM Computing Surveys* 31 (December, 1999): 1-6. Provides a historical overview of hypertext and the development of the World Wide Web. The authors also explain the potential of XML in future applications on the Web.

Henderson, Harry. *Encyclopedia of Computer Science and Technology*. New York: Facts On File, 2003. Guide to computer science intended for a general audience. Topics covered include the development of computers, computer architecture, operating systems, programming, and innovations in hardware and software.

Morris, Mary. *HTML for Fun and Profit*. Mountain View, Calif.: SunSoft Press, 1995. Provides a step-by-step tutorial for developing HTML pages for the World Wide Web. Geared toward UNIX, but also addresses PC and Macintosh platforms.

Mowery, David C., and Timothy Simcoe. "Is the Internet a U.S. Invention? An Economic and Technological History of Computer Networking." *Research Policy* 31 (December, 2002): 1369-1387. Traces the history of the Internet and explains why the United States became the source of innovations and development and an adopter of new applications. Key topics addressed include American business organizations, global trade markets, administrative policy, and academic research.

Musciano, Chuck, and Bill Kennedy. *HTML and XHTML: The Definitive Guide*. 4th ed. Sebastopol, Calif.: O'Reilly, 2000. Reference guide intended to help individuals learn HTML 4.0 and XHTML 1.0 for mounting pages on the Web. Examples show how to use style sheets, frames, interactive forms, image and audio files, and JavaScript programs.

Nielsen, Jakob. *Multimedia and Hypertext: The Internet and Beyond*. Mountain View, Calif.: SunSoft, 1995. Explores new applications in HTML, multimedia, and hypertext with Mosaic and Netscape interfaces. Also addresses copyright issues for users and developers.

Ralston, Anthony, Edwin D. Reilly, and David Hemmendinger, eds. *Encyclopedia of Computer Science*. 4th ed. London: Nature Publishing Group, 2000. Comprehensive A-Z reference guide that contains computer science terms about the history of computers, programming languages, and operating systems.

SEE ALSO: 1970's: Retailers Control Inventory Shrinkage with Computer Technology; Nov.-Dec., 1971: Tomlinson Sends the First E-Mail; Nov. 15, 1971: Intel Introduces the First "Computer on a Chip"; Apr. 1, 1976: Jobs and Wozniak Found Apple Computer; Mid-1990's: Rise of the Internet and the World Wide Web; May 23, 1995: Sun Microsystems Introduces Java.

## January 17-February 28, 1991
# PERSIAN GULF WAR

*Kuwait's sovereignty and Western interests were threatened by Iraqi invasion; allied forces, led by the United States, pushed back the invasion and restored Kuwaiti sovereignty. The peace settlement limited Iraq's ability to produce weapons of mass destruction and called for U.N. inspections to verify that such weapons were dismantled. No-fly zones were established in Iraq to protect Kurdish and Shiite populations, requiring an open-ended U.S. military presence in the region.*

ALSO KNOWN AS: Gulf War of 1991; Operation Desert Storm
LOCALE: Kuwait; Iraq; Saudi Arabia
CATEGORY: Wars, uprisings, and civil unrest

### KEY FIGURES

*Saddam Hussein* (1937-2006), president of Iraq, 1979-2003
*Tariq Aziz* (b. 1936), minister of foreign affairs and deputy prime minister of Iraq
*George H. W. Bush* (b. 1924), president of the United States, 1989-1993
*James Baker* (b. 1930), U.S. secretary of state, 1989-1992
*April Glaspie* (b. 1942), U.S. ambassador to Iraq
*Javier Pérez de Cuéllar* (b. 1920), secretary-general of the United Nations, 1982-1991
*Jaber al-Ahmad al-Jaber al-Sabah* (1926-2006), emir of Kuwait, r. 1977-2006

### SUMMARY OF EVENT

In August, 1990, a number of factors contributed to Iraqi president Saddam Hussein's decision to invade and annex neighboring Kuwait. Since Kuwait's independence, in June, 1961, Iraqi leaders had questioned the legitimacy of Kuwait's sovereignty and the border demarcating the two countries. An important oil field straddled the ill-defined frontier, and Kuwait had been tapping it.

Iraq also charged Kuwait with exceeding its oil quota set by the Organization of Petroleum Exporting Countries (OPEC), thereby increasing supplies and depressing prices. The Iraqi government had pressed Kuwait unsuccessfully for the latter to make available to Iraq two islands, Warbah and Būbiyān, strategically located across from Umm Qasr, Iraq's only outlet on the Persian Gulf proper.

Most important, 1990 was a time of acute financial hardship for Iraq because of the great indebtedness the nation had incurred during its murderous eight-year war with Iran, which had concluded in 1988. Iraq had to rebuild its devastated economy, especially its crucial oil industry.

Several factors led Hussein to decide that this was a good time to force Iraq's creditors, especially Kuwait, to relinquish their claims on their wartime "loans": Iranian-Iraqi relations were improving, Iraqi economic problems were becoming more pressing, Hussein had misread the degree of U.S.-Soviet cooperation possible in the post-Cold War era, and he apparently misinterpreted U.S. ambassador April Glaspie's statement to him on July 25, 1990, that the Bush administration was neutral in matters of inter-Arab disputes "like your border disagreement with Kuwait." Hussein also hoped to punish those who had brought down the price of oil through overproduction or had committed other "offenses."

Various meetings of leaders and conferences involving Iraq, Kuwait, and others were fruitless, partly because Kuwait refused to give ground on substantive issues and partly because Hussein seemed to be determined to invade Kuwait. The invasion began at 2:00 A.M. on August 2, 1990. Token resistance by the tiny Kuwaiti army and the escape of most members of Kuwait's ruling family to Saudi Arabia followed within hours. Kuwait was occupied by Iraq and was soon declared to be Iraq's nineteenth province.

Hussein proved to be wrong in his estimate of the re-

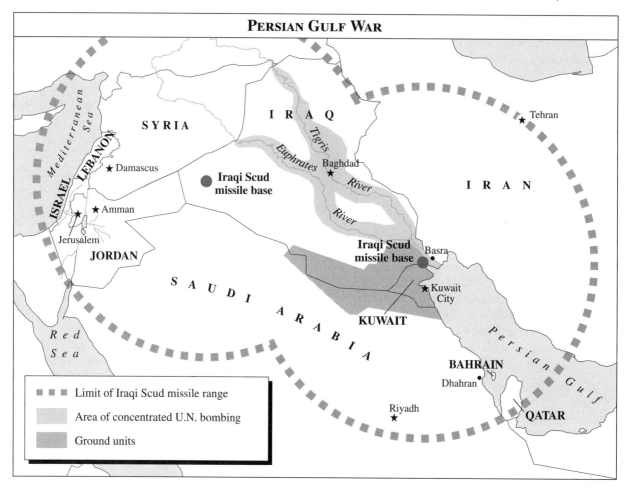

**PERSIAN GULF WAR**

sponse of the international community, which insisted that his invasion of the neighboring country be rolled back. The United States, the Soviet Union, and U.N. Security Council Resolution 660 called for Iraq's immediate withdrawal from Kuwait. Four days later, on August 6, the Security Council imposed mandatory trade sanctions by members of the United Nations, including a ban on Iraqi and Kuwaiti oil (Resolution 661).

Despite Hussein's reassurances to Joseph Wilson, the U.S. chargé d'affaires in Baghdad, President George H. W. Bush ordered the Eighty-second Airborne Division to protect neighboring Saudi Arabia in case Iraq was contemplating monopolizing the bulk of Middle Eastern oil production. Spearheading the emerging international response, Operation Desert Shield became the largest deployment of U.S. troops overseas since the Vietnam War. Iraq's formal annexation of Kuwait brought several Arab and other Muslim countries to side with the U.N.-sponsored, U.S.-led coalition. Westerners in Iraq and

Kuwait were moved as human shields to sites that could become potential coalition targets in Iraq.

On November 29, the U.N. Security Council, acknowledging that its resolution of August 2 ordering Iraq to evacuate Kuwait had not been followed, mandated that all necessary means be used to expel Iraq after January 15, 1991 (Resolution 678). One last meeting between U.S. secretary of state James Baker and Iraqi foreign minister Tariq Aziz in Geneva on January 9, 1991, proved unsuccessful, as Aziz refused to accept Baker's renewed call for Iraq's unconditional withdrawal from Kuwait. Secretary-General Javier Pérez de Cuéllar of the United Nations was also unsuccessful in a visit to Hussein on January 13.

The events surrounding the Persian Gulf War are usually broken down into four stages. Operation Desert Shield covered the period from the invasion of Kuwait on August 2, 1990, to the unleashing of the U.S.-led U.N. coalition's air war on January 17, 1991. The next phase,

Operation Desert Storm, had two components: the air war through February 23 and the ground war from February 24 through February 28. The aftermath following the cease-fire saw the withdrawal of Iraqi forces from Kuwait; the redrawing of the Iraqi-Kuwaiti border by a U.N. commission; the creation of U.N.-sponsored safe zones and no-fly zones in Iraq to protect Kurds and other minorities; U.N. inspection of Iraqi facilities to monitor and force the destruction of any nuclear, biological, or chemical weapons; and the continued imposition of U.N. trade sanctions on Iraq.

The military operations involved more than three-quarters of a million troops on the coalition side (some 541,000 from the United States and about 254,000 from a number of the twenty-nine other countries participating in Desert Storm at its peak) facing some one million Iraqis. The Iraqi numerical advantage was not translated into battlefield successes; the technological edge of the coalition greatly offset other factors. As news reporters from CNN (Cable News Network) broadcast the events

of the air war live, a world audience watched and wondered whether the high-tech advantage of the coalition forces had spawned a new type of "bloodless" war. Such expectations proved illusory: The disproportionate Iraqi casualties not only testified to this fact but also raised the question of a just war among some observers. On March 3, senior military representatives from both sides met to finalize the cease-fire, the terms of which the Iraqis accepted unconditionally.

### SIGNIFICANCE

In the aftermath, a protracted controversy continued over the Bush administration's decision to halt the ground war after a hundred hours, allowing Saddam Hussein and his Baʿth Party regime to remain in power and the Iraqi army to suppress the Kurdish and Shiite uprisings that took place soon after the cease-fire. President Bush was aware that any longer-term entanglement might antagonize his constituency back home, as presidential elections were already on the horizon. He was unable to capitalize on his

1991

*General H. Norman Schwarzkopf visits American troops at the front during the 1991 Persian Gulf War.* (AP/Wide World Photos)

spectacular victory and soaring postwar popularity in the polls, however, because by November, 1992, economic problems had become the electorate's primary concern.

Questions also were raised as to whether enough time had been allowed for the economic embargo to take effect before Operation Desert Storm was initiated. A debate regarding the high cost in Iraqi civilian suffering and lives that the U.N. embargo was exacting also continued. Despite the suspected contraband with its next-door neighbors Jordan and Iran, Iraq, deprived of its major export and foreign currency earner, oil, was becoming impoverished and unable to provide for the needs of the masses. Controversy also continued regarding the degree of encouragement Hussein had taken from the earlier tilt toward Iraq of the administrations of Ronald Reagan and George H. W. Bush and the ambivalent words of Ambassador April Glaspie. U.N. agencies were saddled with additional responsibilities and outlays in their several missions, especially in caring for many internal and external refugees.

As for the overall significance of the Persian Gulf War, there was no consensus either on whether the event was the defining moment of President Bush's "New World Order" to uphold international law or whether it simply reflected oil politics as usual, packaged to appear as a stand for what was right, with a few Arab members in the coalition providing an appropriate cover.

Iraq's failure to live up to numerous U.N. Security Council resolutions in subsequent years continued to generate controversy and ultimately produced a second confrontation with Iraq in 2003. At that time, a coalition of more than forty countries, led by U.S. president George W. Bush, quickly toppled Hussein's regime, and a troubled occupation ensued. Despite the disruptions of a determined insurgency, sovereignty was passed to an interim government after one year of occupation, and a new constitution and democratically elected government were fashioned and installed by 2006.

—*Peter B. Heller*

## FURTHER READING

Clark, Ramsey. *The Fire This Time: U.S. War Crimes in the Gulf.* New York: Thunder's Mouth Press, 1992. Former U.S. attorney general and peace activist presents a spirited indictment of the U.S. role in military operations in the Persian Gulf and in "corrupting" the United Nations to maintain the trade embargo.

Heikal, Mohammed Hassanein. *Illusions of Triumph: An Arab View of the Gulf War.* New York: Harper-Collins, 1992. Interesting account by Egypt's top political observer. Argues that Iraq is only a small part of much deeper Arab problems, many of them of Western origin.

Hilsman, Roger. *George Bush vs. Saddam Hussein: Military Success! Political Failure?* Novato, Calif.: Lyford Books, 1992. Columbia University foreign policy expert critiques what he considers to be the U.S. president's predilection to resort too readily to military force.

Hiro, Dilip. *Desert Shield to Desert Storm: The Second Gulf War.* New York: Routledge, 1992. Comprehensive, well-researched discussion of the Persian Gulf War. Includes maps, bibliography, and index.

Khadduri, Majid, and Edmund Ghareeb. *War in the Gulf, 1990-91: The Iraq-Kuwait Conflict and Its Implications.* New York: Oxford University Press, 1997. Provides in-depth historical context for the Iraqi invasion of Kuwait, discusses the diplomatic efforts that preceded Operation Desert Storm, and examines the aftermath of the war. Includes index.

Marr, Phebe. *The Modern History of Iraq.* 2d ed. Boulder, Colo.: Westview Press, 2004. Comprehensive history of Iraq provides valuable context for events involving that nation in the late twentieth century. Includes tables, glossary, descriptive list of political personalities, bibliography, and index.

Moore, Molly. *A Woman at War: Storming Kuwait with the U.S. Marines.* New York: Charles Scribner's Sons, 1993. The senior military corespondent of *The Washington Post* describes the war and what it meant for a woman to cover it in a conservative Muslim environment.

U.S. News & World Report. *Triumph Without Victory: The Unreported History of the Persian Gulf War.* New York: Times Books, 1992. Includes the texts of all U.N. resolutions from August 2, 1990, through August 15, 1991, as well as the joint congressional resolution of January 12, 1992, authorizing the U.S. president to help implement the U.N. resolutions.

**SEE ALSO:** July 16, 1979: Saddam Hussein Takes Power in Iraq; Sept. 22, 1980-Aug. 8, 1988: Iran-Iraq War; June 7, 1981: Israel Destroys Iraqi Nuclear Reactor; Apr., 1987-Sept., 1988: Iraq Uses Poison Gas Against Kurds; Jan. 27-Nov. 7, 1991: Iraq Burns Kuwaiti Oil Wells; Dec. 16-19, 1998: Iraq Disarmament Crisis Climaxes in Air Strikes.

**January 23, 1991**
# SEINFELD TAKES A REGULAR SLOT ON NBC

*Despite the fact that its early episodes received low ratings and tepid reviews,* Seinfeld, *a situation comedy about a New York stand-up comedian and his eccentric friends, was picked up by NBC for a full season in January of 1991. The show ran for nine seasons and became one of the most popular, acclaimed, and innovative television comedies of all time.*

LOCALE: Los Angeles, California
CATEGORY: Radio and television

KEY FIGURES

*Jerry Seinfeld* (b. 1954), star and cocreator of *Seinfeld*
*Larry David* (b. 1947), cocreator of *Seinfeld*
*Jason Alexander* (b. 1959), actor who played George Costanza on *Seinfeld*
*Julia Louis-Dreyfus* (b. 1961), actor who played Elaine Benes on *Seinfeld*
*Michael Richards* (b. 1949), actor who played Cosmo Kramer on *Seinfeld*
*Rick Ludwin* (b. 1948), senior vice president at NBC
*Brandon Tartikoff* (1949-1997), president of entertainment at NBC

SUMMARY OF EVENT

Stand-up comedian Jerry Seinfeld had garnered a considerable audience in the 1980's through live performances and on television shows, such as *The Tonight Show with Johnny Carson*. He had developed a reputation for observational humor, which focused on the small incongruities and oddities of life, rather than the political or obscenity-fueled comedy that was popular with many of the other 1980's-era stand-up comedians. The programming heads at NBC were suitably impressed with Seinfeld's previous work to offer the comedian his own network comedy special.

Instead of a special, however, Seinfeld and a fellow comedian, Larry David, began to devise a situation comedy (sitcom). David was almost Seinfeld's polar opposite. Whereas Seinfeld's onstage demeanor was sunny and wry, David possessed a dark and sometimes self-loathing sense of humor, which he made no effort to hide from audiences. He often berated crowds for not reacting as he thought they should. As a result, unlike Seinfeld, David was not a very successful stand-up comic. However, other comedians had a great deal of respect for his daring and unwillingness to compromise. David also had experience in television, first as a performer on *Fridays*,

a short-lived imitation of the successful National Broadcasting Company (NBC) show *Saturday Night Live* that aired on the American Broadcasting Company (ABC), and then as a writer for one season on *Saturday Night Live*. During the latter, he later claimed, his work was so poorly received by the executive producer that only one of his sketches was ever performed on the show.

Seinfeld and David decided to create a show that, on the surface, resembled their lives and their friendship. They proposed to the network a show called *The Seinfeld Chronicles*, with Seinfeld essentially playing himself, a stand-up comedian who lived alone in New York City. The show they proposed would focus more on conversation than plot and action. Network president Brandon Tartikoff was unimpressed, but Rick Ludwin, vice president of late night, variety, and specials programming, saw promise in Seinfeld and David's idea and agreed to put up the money for a pilot episode.

With production company Castle Rock Entertainment on board, Seinfeld and David began putting the pilot together. To costar with Seinfeld, character actor Jason Alexander was cast as Seinfeld's friend, George Costanza, who was modeled after David. Michael Richards, who had performed with David on *Fridays*, played Seinfeld's across-the-hall neighbor Kramer, who was based on an eccentric former neighbor of David.

Seinfeld, Alexander, and Richards starred in the pilot for the show, which was then titled *The Seinfeld Chronicles*. The pilot was not well received by test audiences. NBC was also unimpressed with the pilot and initially declined to pick up the show. The episode aired without fanfare on July 5, 1989. However, Ludwin thought the pilot showed promise and urged Tartikoff to give the show another chance. Only four additional episodes of the show, now called *Seinfeld*, were ordered by the network. These episodes aired the following season in May-June, 1990. The network had requested that Seinfeld and David add a woman to the cast. Julia Louis-Dreyfus, a performer on *Saturday Night Live* during David's ill-fated season, was chosen to play Elaine Benes, Seinfeld's ex-girlfriend, with whom he maintained a platonic relationship.

The four episodes were not highly rated, although some critics began to take more notice of the show. It was becoming clear that Seinfeld and David had created a rather unique sitcom. As part of the show, Seinfeld and David interspersed scenes of Seinfeld performing his

1991

*The cast of* Seinfeld *(from left to right): Michael Richards, Jerry Seinfeld, Julia Louis-Dreyfus, and Jason Alexander, backstage at the forty-fifth Emmy Awards in September, 1993. The show won for Outstanding Comedy Series.* (AP/Wide World Photos)

stand-up act. The material he performed was related in some way to the plot of that episode. The idea behind this was to show how incidents from the fictional Seinfeld's life would, in turn, inspire his stand-up comedy routines. The show drew comedy from the little annoyances of life, a method that was rarely seen on television. Even in these early episodes, Seinfeld and Alexander were seen eating in their favorite diner, discussing the minutiae of life. Additionally, the show gave David an outlet for his darker comic sensibilities; the cast was often seen behaving selfishly and cravenly, their schemes usually failing at the episode's end.

Seinfeld and David had also decided to make *Seinfeld*, despite its name, an ensemble show. They realized early that they had four talented, distinct comic performers on hand and could craft the show around all of them. Alexander, who had initially played George as a Woody Allen-type neurotic, began to play the character as desperate and devious, yet still somehow sympathetic. The character of Kramer proved to be an ideal vehicle for Richards's specialization in broad physical humor. Louis-

Dreyfus, with her quirky portrayal of Elaine, showed that she could more than hold her own as the only woman in the cast. Seinfeld, the least experienced actor of the four, had no problem giving a lot of the screen time, and jokes, to his costars.

Also, during the four-episode run, Seinfeld and David had devised a clever device for the show: Each of the four characters would have a separate plot line, with the four plot lines coming together at the end of the show. This was unusual because most sitcom episodes had a primary storyline, the "A" story, and a smaller subplot, the "B" story.

## SIGNIFICANCE

*Seinfeld* would soon gain footing with both critics and the public. By the fourth season, the show was fast becoming one of the most successful and acclaimed sitcoms of its time. It was a regular presence in the top ten of the Nielsen ratings and won several Emmys. *Seinfeld* became a touchstone of popular culture, spawning countless catchphrases that entered parlance. All four cast members became huge stars, especially Seinfeld. The show itself changed the direction of sitcoms; fast-paced shows about single life in urban environments began crowding the airwaves. Many other stand-up comics were lured to network television to try carrying comedy shows. However, very few of the shows that were influenced by *Seinfeld* had the same staying power as the original. Overall, critics cited *Seinfeld* as containing some of the wittiest dialogue and sharpest satire of its time. When, at the end of the ninth season, the show's final episode aired, it was one of the most heavily hyped, and watched, series finales in the history of television.

—*Michael Pelusi*

**FURTHER READING**

Lavery, David, and Sara Lewis Dunne, eds. *Seinfeld, Master of Its Domain: Revisiting Television's Greatest Sitcom*. New York: Continuum, 2006. A collection of essays on the show, written by a number of television scholars and critics. Contains an episode guide, as well as a list of the many catchphrases from the show.

Tracy, Kathleen. *Jerry Seinfeld: The Entire Domain*. Secaucus, N.J.: Birch Lane Press, 1998. A highly readable biography of the comedian that provides a thorough look at the genesis of *Seinfeld*. Contains an episode guide.

Wild, David. *Seinfeld: The Totally Unauthorized Tribute (Not That There's Anything Wrong with That)*. New York: Three Rivers Press, 1998. A lighthearted look at the show, with an episode guide, trivia, and interviews with celebrities. None of the main players are interviewed, but the book concisely sums up the history of the show.

**SEE ALSO:** Jan. 15, 1974-July 12, 1984: *Happy Days* Exemplifies Escapist Television; Jan. 18, 1975-July 23, 1985: *The Jeffersons* Signals Success of Black Situation Comedies; Oct. 11, 1975: *Saturday Night Live* Is First Broadcast; Sept. 20, 1984-Apr. 30, 1992: *The Cosby Show* Makes Television History; Sept. 16, 1993-May 13, 2004: *Frasier* Dominates Television Comedy.

**1991**

## January 27-November 7, 1991
# IRAQ BURNS KUWAITI OIL WELLS

*During their retreat from occupied Kuwait, Iraqi armed forces set fire to nearly seven hundred oil wells, creating the worst oil-field disaster in history.*

**LOCALE:** Kuwait
**CATEGORIES:** Disasters; energy; environmental issues

**KEY FIGURES**

*Saddam Hussein* (1937-2006), president of Iraq, 1979-2003, who launched the 1980-1988 Iran-Iraq War and the 1990 invasion of Kuwait

*H. Norman Schwarzkopf* (b. 1934), American general who commanded coalition forces during the 1991 Persian Gulf War

*George H. W. Bush* (b. 1924), president of the United States, 1989-1993

*Red Adair* (1915-2004), American pioneer in oil well firefighting whose firm extinguished many of the fires in Kuwait

*Jaber al-Ahmad al-Jaber al-Sabah* (1926-2006), emir of Kuwait, r. 1977-2006

*Saad al-Abdullah al-Salem al-Sabah* (b. 1930), crown prince and prime minister of Kuwait, 1978-2003

**SUMMARY OF EVENT**

On August 2, 1990, Iraqi forces invaded the small, oil-rich neighboring nation of Kuwait, triggering the largest military action since World War II. On November 29, 1990, the United Nations voted to permit the use of force to expel the Iraqi invaders from Kuwait. U.S. troops had already been sent to Saudi Arabia to defend against possible Iraqi moves against that nation in Operation Desert Shield. Ultimately, the forces arrayed against Iraq included more than 700,000 troops from a coalition of twenty-eight countries, including 527,000 U.S. troops, 118,000 Saudi Arabian troops, 46,000 British troops, and 40,000 Egyptian troops. On January 16, 1991, coalition forces began air attacks on Iraqi targets. The active combat phase of operations was named Operation Desert Storm.

After six weeks of aerial bombardment, coalition forces launched a ground attack into Kuwait and southern Iraq on February 23, 1991. American and other coalition forces swept into Iraq west of Kuwait. One prong of the offensive thrust north to the Euphrates River, while a second curved east to attack the elite Iraqi Republican Guard, considered the most effective Iraqi fighting force.

U.S. Marines and Arab forces pushed north from Saudi Arabia into Kuwait itself. After one hundred hours of combat, a cease-fire agreement was signed. By that time, Iraqi forces had been driven from Kuwait, some 80,000 Iraqi troops had surrendered, and 30,000 had been killed. (Initial estimates of 100,000 were seriously exaggerated.) During the ground war, Iraqi forces blew up nearly seven hundred Kuwaiti oil wells, setting fire to most of them and creating an unprecedented oil-field disaster.

Oil dominates the politics and military strategy of the Middle East, and it played a key role in the events leading up to the Persian Gulf War. In 1980, Iraq launched an attack on neighboring Iran to gain control of the Shatt-al-Arab, the estuary at the mouth of the Tigris and Euphrates rivers. This waterway between the two nations is Iraq's only outlet to the sea. Most observers expected Iraq to defeat Iran handily, but Iran put up a stubborn resistance, and the war developed into a bloody stalemate that claimed an estimated 600,000 lives before a cease-fire was declared in 1988. Although Iraq has substantial oil reserves of its own (nearly twice those of Kuwait and half those of Saudi Arabia), the war plunged Iraq deeply into debt. Iraq's total debt was $80 billion, including a debt of several billion dollars to Kuwait. In an effort to relieve its debt and increase its revenues, Iraq demanded that Kuwait cancel its debt and yield its portion of the

Rumaila oil field on the Iraq-Kuwait border. Iraq also accused Kuwait of slant drilling—drilling wells that slanted beneath the border to tap oil inside Iraq—and demanded several billion dollars in repayments for oil removed from the field.

Many of the environmental hazards of war in the Persian Gulf had been identified and discussed during the Iran-Iraq War and during the military buildup prior to Desert Storm. The gulf itself is only about one hundred meters deep and is connected to the Indian Ocean only by the fifty-kilometer-wide Strait of Hormuz. Large oil spills in the gulf would endanger valuable commercial fisheries, many threatened species, including dugongs and flamingos, and fragile ecosystems such as coral reefs, mangroves, and delicate tidal flats.

Many of the coastal cities of Saudi Arabia and Kuwait obtain water through desalination of Persian Gulf water; in fact, the largest desalination plants in the world are on the Persian Gulf. Large oil spills would thus also endanger sources of drinking water. A sufficiently large spill might conceivably cover the entire gulf, depriving its waters of oxygen. The restricted circulation in the gulf would slow the dissipation of a large spill. Damage to oil wells on land could cover large areas with oil, and oil could contaminate groundwater, a vital concern in the water-poor Middle East. Large oil fires could generate enough smoke to have large-scale and unpredictable climatic effects.

The materials of war are also of environmental concern. The Iran-Iraq War saw the largest deployment of chemical weapons on the battlefield since World War I. These chemical agents, although they consist of relatively simple molecules, have potential long-term health and ecological effects that are poorly understood. The potential effects of such weapons were of grave concern during the planning of Operation Desert Storm, but chemical weapons were not used during the war, possibly because of unfavorable weather conditions.

Although Iraq announced the annexation of Kuwait as a province of Iraq, the Iraqis' occupation practices seemed to indicate that Iraq did not expect to be able to hold Kuwait. Iraqi troops either looted Kuwaiti technical equipment wholesale and

*When Iraq was forced to withdraw from Kuwait in 1991, it inflicted major damage on Kuwait's oil industry—as well as the Persian Gulf environment—by setting fire to oil wells.* (U.S. Department of Defense Visual Information Center)

removed it to Iraq or sabotaged it to render it unusable. Coalition planners thus took seriously the possibility that Iraq might destroy Kuwait's oil facilities in retaliation for any military action against Iraq. In fact, as early as October, 1990, U.S. intelligence sources reported that Iraq had placed explosive charges on Kuwait's oil wells.

The first act of environmental sabotage came shortly after the start of coalition bombing, when Iraq opened the valves of the Sea Island Oil Terminal on January 23, 1991, releasing about three million barrels of oil into the Persian Gulf (twelve times the amount released by the *Exxon Valdez* tanker accident in Prince William Sound, Alaska, in 1989). The spill would have been far larger had several Kuwaiti refinery workers not sabotaged a valve leading to a group of large storage tanks. The spill was largely halted on January 27, when coalition aircraft bombed the pumping facilities of the terminal and set fire to the oil slick.

By late January, about twenty wells in the Wafra oil field in southern Kuwait were burning, as a result of either deliberate destruction or battle damage. On February 17, as the coalition invasion of Kuwait became imminent, Iraqi forces began detonating explosive charges on the wells. Most wells were ignited, but some merely began spouting oil. Because the oil fields of Kuwait are naturally pressurized by natural gas, the oil kept flowing to the surface to feed the fires and growing lakes of oil on the ground. Bureaucratic problems kept the pace of firefighting slow until early summer, but once those problems were solved, the pace increased dramatically. Most of the oil firefighters in the world were represented in Kuwait, including teams from the United States, Canada, the Soviet Union, and China. Although many published predictions asserted that extinguishing the well fires could take years, the last was extinguished on November 7, 1991, less than nine months after the wells were ignited.

## SIGNIFICANCE

Environmental warfare has been practiced much more often in history than is generally known. Even in premodern times, armies caused tremendous environmental damage. In the thirteenth century, Mongol armies destroyed the irrigation system of Mesopotamia (now Iraq) and so depopulated the region that the system, which had supported agriculture for thousands of years, was never restored. The destruction of the Shenandoah Valley and General William Sherman's March to the Sea, both during the American Civil War, are other famous examples of military destruction of the environment.

The effects of war on the environment can be grouped into four categories. The first is collateral damage inci-

dental to military operations; that is, there is no deliberate intent to cause damage to the environment, but damage occurs as a side effect of military action. Examples of collateral damage include rutting of the land by vehicle traffic, cratering by bombardment, and release of hazardous materials when military storage depots are attacked. A second category is intentional damage—triggering an environmental effect to cause damage to the enemy. For example, during World War I, Italian and Austrian troops in the Alps used artillery fire to trigger avalanches, killing thousands of soldiers.

A third category is modification, generally destruction, of the environment to render military action harder for the enemy or easier for one's own side. In 1938, the Chinese breached the levees of the Yellow River (Huang He) in an attempt to slow the invading Japanese. The resulting floods drowned up to 500,000 civilians. In terms of loss of life, this may have been the worst act of environmental warfare in history. The defoliation of jungle in Vietnam by the United States during the 1960's to deprive Vietnamese guerrilla forces of concealment is another example.

The fourth category, the most modern one, is environmental terrorism: threats to the environment to deter military action or destruction of the environment in retaliation for military action. In environmental terrorism, the targets have no significant military value of their own; rather, they are attacked in the hope that fear of environmental disaster will influence the enemy's decisions or simply to degrade the quality of life for an otherwise victorious enemy. Environmental terrorism is modern for two reasons: The growth of military destructive capability has reached unprecedented levels, and only in recent decades has concern for the environment developed to the point that environmental terrorism stands as a credible weapon. The Sea Island oil spill and the burning of Kuwait's oil wells were not the first, or even the worst, acts of environmental warfare, but they were the worst acts of environmental terrorism up to that time.

The mess created by the destruction of Kuwait's oil wells is difficult to comprehend. Because of the location of Kuwait's oil fields and the prevailing wind directions, Kuwait City was usually free of oil smoke. The town of al-Ahmadi, however, about thirty kilometers south of Kuwait City and situated between two oil fields, lay in nearly total darkness for months. Oil droplets and soot covered every exposed surface, and large areas of desert were plated with a crust of oil residue. About five million barrels of oil burned per day, about one-third of the total oil consumed daily by the United States. The total de-

1991

stroyed was about one-tenth of 1 percent of known world oil reserves.

Contrary to widespread misconception, the greatest problem in controlling a burning oil well is not extinguishing the fire but controlling the flow of oil afterward. Even worse than the burning wells in Kuwait were nonburning wells, which created oil lakes more than one kilometer across and one or more meters deep. Some oil was recovered from the oil lakes and oil spills in the Persian Gulf, and much evaporated, but the heavy residue fraction remained.

The oil smoke was regarded as a test of the "nuclear winter" scenario. In this hypothesis, smoke created by a nuclear war would trap solar heat high in the atmosphere, blocking sunlight and creating subfreezing conditions, even in the summer, for months. Near the fires, the smoke pall was capable of blocking sunlight completely and producing dramatic cooling beneath it, but the smoke pall did not rise high enough to create a true nuclear winter effect over large areas.

The long-term health effects of the smoke are uncertain. Some American troops who served in the Persian Gulf theater later reported puzzling symptoms of fatigue, joint aches, and general malaise. Various causes of these illnesses have been suggested, including exposure to oil smoke, exposure to residues from Iraqi chemical warfare, exposure to uranium used in antitank shells, and experimental immunizations against chemical and biological warfare. Despite widespread acknowledgment that the illnesses are real, and despite a number of epidemiological studies, the causes of the illnesses have proved elusive.

As bad as the environmental effects of the Gulf War were, they could have been far worse. Chemical weapons were a serious threat, but they were not used. Iraqi troops had laid pipelines to fill trenches along the border with oil and create fire obstacles; these also were not used. The oil wells were damaged at the surface; if the Iraqis had lowered explosives down the wells and detonated them below the surface, the oil would have been much harder to contain. Oil would have mixed with and contaminated groundwater, and many wells might have needed to be sealed with concrete and redrilled. Although mines were a hazard around some wells, they were not as numerous or as well hidden as was initially believed. Many of the worst predictions of disaster in the wake of the Persian Gulf War did not come to pass. The smoke pall did not have global or regional climatic effects as feared, and the vast Sea Island oil spill did not extinguish life in the Persian Gulf.

*—Steven I. Dutch*

## FURTHER READING

BBC World Service, comp. *Gulf Crisis Chronology.* Harlow, England: Longman Current Affairs, 1991. Authoritative day-by-day chronology of events during the Persian Gulf War begins with Iraq's invasion of Kuwait and ends with the cease-fire.

Browning, K. A., et al. "Environmental Effects from Burning Oil Wells in Kuwait." *Nature* 351 (May 30, 1991): 363-367. Moderately technical summary concludes that the oil fires had measurable local effects but were unlikely to have significant global effects.

Canby, Thomas Y. "After the Storm." *National Geographic*, August, 1991, 2-35. Presents a nontechnical, dramatically illustrated description of the aftermath of the Gulf War. Offers illustrative anecdotes rather than attempting a comprehensive overview.

Garwin, Richard L., and Henry W. Kendall. "Quenching the Wild Wells of Kuwait." *Nature* 354 (November 7, 1991): 11-14. Provides a simple description of the problems of extinguishing oil fires in Kuwait. Examines a variety of proposed techniques for clearing mines.

Hawley, T. M. *Against the Fires of Hell: The Environmental Disaster of the Gulf War.* Orlando, Fla.: Harcourt Brace Jovanovich, 1992. Presents an assessment of the environmental damage during Operation Desert Storm. Focuses on the efforts of firefighters to extinguish the oil fires, effects of oil spills on the Persian Gulf, and possible health effects of the smoke.

Hobbs, Peter V., and Lawrence F. Radke. "Airborne Studies of the Smoke from the Kuwait Oil Fires." *Science* 256 (March 26, 1993): 987-991. Moderately technical article concludes that climatic effects of the oil fires were less pronounced than predicted in part because efficient combustion produced less soot than some nuclear winter models had assumed.

Horgan, John. "Burning Questions: Scientists Launch Studies of Kuwait's Oil Fires." *Scientific American* 265 (July, 1991): 17-22. Presents a nontechnical summary of some of the results of studies of the Kuwait oil fires. Sidebar discusses allegations that some environmental data had been censored or withheld.

SEE ALSO: July 16, 1979: Saddam Hussein Takes Power in Iraq; May 25, 1981: Saudi Arabia Establishes Gulf Cooperation Council; Apr., 1987-Sept., 1988: Iraq Uses Poison Gas Against Kurds; Aug. 2, 1990: Iraqi Invasion of Kuwait; Jan. 17-Feb. 28, 1991: Persian Gulf War.

## February 1, 1991
# DE KLERK PROMISES TO TOPPLE APARTHEID LEGISLATION

*At the opening session of the South African parliament in 1991, President F. W. de Klerk announced plans to repeal the nation's laws of racial separation.*

**LOCALE:** Cape Town, South Africa
**CATEGORIES:** Civil rights and liberties; government and politics

**KEY FIGURES**
*F. W. de Klerk* (b. 1936), president of South Africa, 1989-1994
*Nelson Mandela* (b. 1918), antiapartheid spokesman released from prison in 1990 and elected president of the African National Congress in 1991
*Mangosuthu Gatsha Buthelezi* (b. 1928), Zulu chief and head of the Inkatha Freedom Party

**SUMMARY OF EVENT**
On February 1, 1991, at the opening session of the racially segregated parliament of South Africa, President F. W. de Klerk delivered a dramatic speech in which he promised to support legislation that would scrap the remaining laws on which the nation's system of apartheid was based. The most important of these laws was the Population Registration Act of 1950, which segregated South Africans into four racial categories: whites, blacks, Indians, and coloreds (people of mixed race). Other legislation included the Native Lands Act (1913) and the Native Land and Trust Act (1936), which reserved 87 percent of the land for the white minority, as well as the Group Areas Act (1950) and related legislation that segregated residential areas.

In addition, de Klerk said that he would submit legislation to allow communities to negotiate a new system of integrated local government based on one tax base for all citizens. Finally, he proposed a multiparty conference to discuss the creation of a new national constitution. These ambitious proposals were outlined in a document titled "Manifesto for the New South Africa." De Klerk declared that these changes in law would mean that "the South African statute book will be devoid, within months, of the remnants of racially discriminatory legislation which have become known as the cornerstones of apartheid."

Because de Klerk was the leader of the National Party, which had a clear majority of votes in the South African parliament, all observers agreed that the proposed legislation would be passed without real difficulty. Previ-

ously, the government's position had been that the Population Registration Act could not be repealed as long as the country was under the triracial constitution of 1983, with its segregated chambers for whites, coloreds, and Indians. On closer inspection, de Klerk explained, legal authorities had concluded that the law could be repealed with temporary transitional measures that anticipated the creation of a new constitution dispensation. Babies born after the repeal would not be classified according to race, but other South Africans would retain their racial classifications until the triracial parliament voted for its own extinction in favor of a new regime.

In his address, de Klerk failed to mention three homeland laws: the Bantu Self-Government Act (1959), the Bantu Homelands Citizenship Act (1970), and the Status Acts. The first two laws had transferred limited powers of self-government to ten tribal "homelands" and had conferred all blacks with citizenship in one of these ethnic homelands. The Status Acts had recognized the "independence" of four of the homelands (Transkei, Ciskei, Bophuthatswana, and Venda), requiring that their citizens forfeit their South African nationality. A series of coups in the four homelands in the period 1987-1990 had marked the collapse of the homeland system, but a final settlement of the issue would be reached only under a new constitution.

Reaction to de Klerk's speech was predictable. Rightist Afrikaner legislators were horrified, and during the speech they shouted, "Traitor to the nation!" and "Hangman of the Afrikaner!" Andries Truernicht and the forty other representatives of the Conservative Party angrily marched out of parliament. In contrast, South Africa's Democratic Party, which opposed apartheid, welcomed the proposals. In the United States, the administration of President George H. W. Bush saw de Klerk's speech as evidence that the American antiapartheid policy was working. One State Department official stated, "It's the equivalent of the fall of the Berlin Wall."

As expected, de Klerk's program did not go far enough to please black organizations in South Africa, especially the African National Congress (ANC). Nelson Mandela and other ANC leaders denounced the fact that de Klerk had rejected an ANC proposal to elect a constituent assembly to draft a new constitution, meaning that the de Klerk government was determined that whites would retain disproportionate influence in negotiations over the constitution. Likewise, the ANC leaders were unhappy

2551

that there were no specific plans to repatriate forty thousand political refugees, to release political prisoners in the "independent" homelands, or to repeal the security laws that gave the police sweeping powers to detain political suspects. "We still do not have the vote," declared ANC leader Walter Sisulu, "and this is what our people demand today, to vote for a constituent assembly." Throughout the country, hundreds of thousands of blacks marched to demand additional changes.

Three days before de Klerk's speech, Mandela and his major black rival, Zulu chief Mangosuthu Gatsha Buthelezi, had met for the first time in twenty-eight years. Following an eight-hour discussion, they had announced a peace pact for Natal province, where violent fighting between ANC supporters and Buthelezi's Inkatha Freedom Party had claimed four thousand lives in five years. Despite this announcement, however, factional violence in the townships resumed within two days and continued

throughout the summer and early fall of 1991. Another difficulty for the ANC was the trial and conviction of Nelson Mandela's wife, Winnie, in May. While her husband had been in prison, Winnie Mandela had assembled some bodyguards known as the Mandela United Football Club. They were accused of abducting and beating four youths suspected of collaboration with opponents of the ANC, killing one of the four. When Winnie Mandela was sentenced to six years in prison, many ANC supporters feared that the "Winnie problem" would damage the prestige of the organization.

As the South African parliament prepared to pass the promised legislation, many leaders of other African nations showed evidence of a desire to reestablish ties with South Africa. At the annual summit of the Organization of African Unity (OAU), held June 3-5, 1991, the organization, after a long debate, issued a statement promising to lift sanctions if South Africa adopted measures dem-

*Nelson Mandela and F. W. de Klerk accepting UNESCO's Félix Houphouët-Boigny Peace Prize in Paris in February, 1992, for their contributions to ending apartheid in South Africa. (AP/Wide World Photos)*

onstrating "profound and irreversible change toward the abolition of apartheid." In fact, a number of countries, such as Zimbabwe, were already increasing their trade with South Africa, and just after the OAU conference, Kenya and Madagascar announced that they were restoring trade and transportation ties with the country.

The same day the OAU ended its summit, the South African parliament voted to repeal the Land Acts of 1913 and 1936 and the Group Areas Act. South Africans were thus given the legal right to buy property and live where they pleased. Even more significant, on June 17, the Population Registration Act was repealed, with the white House of Assembly voting 129 to 38, with 11 abstentions. This meant that citizens would no longer be registered into racial categories at birth, although the existing racial register would be maintained until a nonracial constitution was approved. The ANC issued a statement that noted that the average black citizen was no better off than before the reforms had been enacted. The document stated that discriminatory treatment in areas such as education, employment, and state pensions continued as before and asserted, "As long as such blatantly racist practices continue, the Population Registration Act will have been removed in name only."

President Bush and other Western leaders were more impressed with the reforms. Early in July, the U.S. State Department informed Bush that South Africa had fulfilled the five conditions contained in the Comprehensive Anti-Apartheid Act of 1986, and on July 10 the president formally lifted U.S. trade and investment sanctions. Bush spoke of the "profound transformation" in South Africa and expressed the opinion that "this progress is irreversible." Mandela and antiapartheid groups throughout the world criticized Bush's decision as premature; in contrast, Chief Buthelezi, who had long opposed sanctions, welcomed the action. Several countries, including Finland and Japan, soon announced that they were following the American example, and the International Olympic Committee lifted its twenty-one-year boycott of South Africa after judging that the nation had made significant advances in ending racial discrimination in sports.

## ENDING APARTHEID

*The "Manifesto for the New South Africa," which President F. W. de Klerk issued on February 1, 1991, included the following statement of commitment to a "free and democratic political system":*

We commit ourselves to the creation of a free and democratic political system in South Africa, in which:

All people shall be free in this, their country of birth;

All the people of our land shall participate fully at all levels of government on the basis of universal adult franchise;

The government of the country shall at all times be based upon the consent of the governed;

All people shall be equal before the law, and shall enjoy equal rights regardless of race, colour, sex or creed;

The rights of all individuals and minorities defined on a non-racial basis shall be adequately protected in the constitution and in a constitutionally guaranteed and justiciable Bill of Rights;

Freedom of expression, within the generally recognised bounds of responsibility, shall be the right of all people;

Freedom of movement and of association shall be guaranteed to all.

1991

### SIGNIFICANCE

The changes that took place in South Africa in 1990 and 1991 were indeed spectacular. For decades, the apartheid system had been the most flagrant example of injustice and oppression anywhere in the world. By the summer of 1991, the legal foundations for this system had come to an end. Certainly, the South African problem was far from settled, and extremely difficult negotiations were necessary before South Africans would arrive at a consensus for a new constitution. Even after a new constitution was established, socioeconomic inequalities between blacks and whites would continue to be an issue, and there did not appear to be any easy solutions to ending the ethnic violence in the townships. Nevertheless, just a few years earlier, when President Pieter W. Botha had stubbornly resisted fundamental reforms, few observers expected that the foundations of apartheid would be abrogated by the summer of 1991.

In the short term, the most important issue involved the negotiations for a new constitution. It appeared that the constitution had to be completed before 1994, the deadline for the calling of parliamentary elections. The National Party, with its popularity uncertain, had no intention of conducting another whites-only election under the old constitution. This meant that de Klerk had to operate under severe time limitations in preparing a new constitution. The ANC was determined that the new constitution should provide for majority rule based on the principle of "one person, one vote." In contrast, de Klerk and the National Party were determined to have a constitution that would include a veto and disproportionate influence for the white minority.

In September, 1991, de Klerk proposed a blueprint for a constitution that would replace the presidency with an executive council made up of members of the three largest parties in Parliament's lower house and would assign more powers to regional and local governments. Mandela, who had recently been elected president of the ANC, strongly denounced such an arrangement. White voters approved of de Klerk's efforts in a referendum on March 17, 1992. Almost 90 percent of eligible voters cast ballots, and two-thirds of them stated approval of de Klerk's efforts to end apartheid.

Although nobody expected future negotiations to be easy, the two sides did agree on many basics, including support for a two-house legislature, the right of each citizen to have one vote, a guarantee of individual liberties, an independent judiciary, and the end of the black homelands. The ANC was less insistent on nationalizing key industries and in seeking massive redistribution of wealth, questions of major concern to white South Africans.

Most experts believed that economic sanctions had been one of the major influences leading de Klerk's government to agree to the reforms of 1991, and continuing economic difficulties added to the urgency for seeking a political settlement as soon as possible. In 1991, black unemployment in South Africa was estimated at more than 35 percent, and simply to remain at this unsatisfactory level would require an economic growth rate of 5 percent per year. During the years of the sanctions, South Africa's gross national product had grown by less than 1 percent per year, and it actually shrank by 1 percent in 1990.

With its resources and infrastructure, however, South Africa had the potential to become one of the most prosperous countries in the world, if only it could resolve its political problems. To a very substantial extent, by the end of the century it had done just that. After arduous but determined and respectful negotiations, de Klerk, Mandela, and many others steered the country toward its first fully participatory elections in April, 1994. Mandela and the ANC, not unsurprisingly, won the elections by a substantial majority but agreed to form a national unity government that included the National Party and the Zulu-based Inkatha Freedom Party as the country moved in peaceful fashion from minority to majority

rule. For their work in making this change, which many considered a miracle, de Klerk and Mandela were jointly awarded the Nobel Peace Prize in 1993, even before the historic elections took place.

*—Thomas Tandy Lewis*

## FURTHER READING

Baker, Pauline. "South Africa: Old Myths and New Realities." *Current History* 90 (May, 1991): 197-200. Presents excellent analysis of the crumbling of apartheid, with a useful chart of major laws. Argues that sanctions had been effective, that the right wing was not a major threat, that blacks did not want a Marxist state, and that there were good reasons to hope for a peaceful settlement.

De Klerk, F. W. "South Africa and Apartheid." *Vital Speeches* 57 (March 1, 1991): 294-300. The complete text of de Klerk's important speech before Parliament on February 1, presenting his program for the end of legal apartheid as well as other issues of South African politics.

Guelke, Adrian. *Rethinking the Rise and Fall of Apartheid: South Africa and World Politics.* New York: Palgrave Macmillan, 2005. Discusses the nature and significance of South African apartheid and the reasons the apartheid system ended, with particular attention paid to the international antiapartheid movement.

Johnson, Shaun, ed. *South Africa: No Turning Back.* Bloomington: Indiana University Press, 1989. Scholarly essays written just before de Klerk came to power address topics such as South African politics since 1976, internal resistance to apartheid, the police in South Africa, the Afrikaner establishment, and the history of the Inkatha Freedom Party.

Laurence, Patrick. "Repealing the Race Laws." *Africa Report* 36 (March/April, 1991): 34-37. Presents clear analysis of de Klerk's parliamentary speech of February 1. Written from a pro-ANC perspective and emphasizes the limitations of de Klerk's policies, especially the issues of the constituent assembly and the homelands.

Lemon, Anthony. *Apartheid in Transition.* Boulder, Colo.: Westview Press, 1987. Provides a useful history of apartheid as well as a sociological analysis of the situation in the late 1980's, with much information about the ethnic groups of South Africa. Written before de Klerk's election; concludes that apartheid was being dismantled and that the logical result would be for whites to have a minority share of power.

Mandela, Nelson. *The Struggle Is My Life*. New York: Pathfinder Press, 1986. Brief autobiography explains Mandela's political beliefs and his goals for South Africa.

Mufson, Steven. "South Africa 1990." *Foreign Affairs* 70 (1991): 120-142. Provides excellent analysis of de Klerk's policies as well as those of Inkatha and the ANC. Written just before the reforms of 1991 and emphasizes the uncertainty of the government's goals as well as the uncertainty of the outcome of negotiations.

Thompson, Leonard. *A History of South Africa*. 3d ed. New Haven, Conn.: Yale University Press, 2000. Covers South African history from precolonial times to the end of the twentieth century. Includes excellent discussion of the rise and fall of apartheid in the post-1948 period.

Thörn, Håkan. *Anti-apartheid and the Emergence of a Global Civil Society*. New York: Palgrave Macmillan, 2006. Sociological study examines the power of collective action and places the antiapartheid movement within the context of global politics.

**SEE ALSO:** Nov. 30, 1973: United Nations Sanctions South Africa for Apartheid; June 16, 1976: South African Government Suppresses Soweto Student Rebellion; Sept., 1977: South African Government Kills Biko; Nov. 4, 1977: United Nations Imposes an Arms Embargo on South Africa; May, 1979: U.N. Declaration Condemns Apartheid; 1987: South African Black Workers Strike; Feb. 11, 1990: Mandela Is Freed; 1995: South Africa Establishes a Truth and Reconciliation Commission.

## February 12, 1991
# MONGOLIA SHEDS COMMUNISM

*Despite its isolation, the political changes of 1989 in other Soviet bloc countries quickly reverberated in Mongolia. Following the pattern set in several Eastern European nations, street protests were followed by democratic elections in July, 1990, leading up to the proclamation of a revamped constitution in the following year.*

**LOCALE:** Mongolia
**CATEGORY:** Government and politics

**KEY FIGURES**
*Jambyn Batmönkh* (1926-1997), leader of the Mongolian People's Revolutionary Party, 1984-1990

*Punsalmaagiyn Ochirbat* (b. 1942), Mongolia's first democratically elected president, 1990-1997, and a member of the Mongolian People's Revolutionary Party

*Mikhail Gorbachev* (b. 1931), general secretary of the Communist Party of the Soviet Union, 1985-1991, and president of the Soviet Union, 1990-1991

*Dashiyn Byambasüren* (b. 1942), Mongolia's first democratic prime minister, 1990-1992

*Büdragchaagiyn Dashyondon* (b. 1946), former Communist who became chairman of the Mongolian People's Revolutionary Party, 1991-1992

*Davaadorjiyn Ganbold* (b. 1957), young economist whose policies eased Mongolia's transition to a market economy

*Erdeniyn Bat-Üül* (b. 1957), scientist who functioned as an intermediary between the Mongolian government and democratic activists

**SUMMARY OF EVENT**
When Jambyn Batmönkh came to power in Mongolia in 1984, he was seen as somewhat of a breath of fresh air after the stagnant and monolithic rule of Yumjaagiin Tsedenbal as leader of the Mongolian People's Revolutionary Party (MPRP), the Communist party of Mongolia. Tsedenbal's notoriety stemmed from his nearly absolute subservience to the Soviet Union and the way he flaunted his wealth in Mongolia's capital, Ulaanbaatar. Batmönkh, a former academic, was a comparative reformer, but he proceeded very slowly, and Mongolia remained a regressive, one-party Communist state throughout the 1980's, although, it is important to note, the nation established diplomatic relations with the United States in 1987.

Although an underground Mongolian democratic movement had existed for years, it took until late 1989, with the combination of Soviet leader Mikhail Gorbachev's liberalization within the Soviet Union itself and the upheaval in Eastern Europe, culminating in the fall of the Berlin Wall in November, 1989, to occasion widespread demonstrations in Mongolia. On December 10, 1989, the Mongolian Democratic Union (MDU) was formed, largely by intellectuals in Ulaanbaatar. In January, Batmönkh stated that he would negotiate with the opposition. A scientist and academic with strong MPRP connections, Erdeniyn Bat-Üül, was sent to meet with some of the opposition leaders about possible negotiations. Talk ensued, accelerated by huge demonstrations on March 4. These prompted Batmönkh to announce, on March 12, that he was resigning. That day, Punsalmaagiyn Ochirbat, a man of a younger generation, was selected as chair of the Mongolian parliament, the Great People's Hural. On May 14, it was announced that free elections for the Hural would be held on July 25.

These elections saw the MPRP win 86 percent of the seats. Although the MDU claimed that the process was biased against opposition parties, Mongolians in general reveled in their country's first-ever free election. The newly elected Great People's Hural constituted the Baga Hural (small Hural) as a provisional government. Ochirbat was named president, and Dashiyn Byambasüren was appointed as prime minister. Büdragchaagiyn Dashyondon, an experienced Communist who was yet not seen as a Batmönkh loyalist, became head of the MPRP. Byambasüren visited Moscow that same month, obtaining a new friendship treaty that affirmed a relationship of equals and disposed of the old patron-satellite relationship. Meanwhile, a young economic minister, Davaadorjiyn Ganbold, began to preside over a process of privatization, though exceptions were made for natural resources and central financial and transportation holdings, which remained under government control. Ganbold was praised for the decisiveness of his privatization policies. However, because of the severe shock administered to the Mongolian economy by the collapse of its major Soviet trading partner, economic conditions in Mongolia were unstable throughout the transition period.

Bat-Üül, Byambasüren, and Ganbold all possessed some non-Mongolian ancestry, whether Russian, Chinese, or Buryat. Their ethnicities were comparatively uncontroversial at the time of the transition, but accusations of their being insufficiently pure in ethnicity were to undermine any future leadership role for these men in the Mongolian polity, although Bat-Üül still harbored national ambitions as of 2006.

On February 12, 1991, a new constitution heralded an irreversible change in Mongolian politics. On one level, a total revolution had not occurred in Mongolia; the Communist Party simply reformed itself from within. On another level, the consultative and deliberative nature of the process augured well for an opposition party coming to power, as indeed occurred in 1996. The gradual quality of the Mongolian transition was also seen in the names given to cities and the society's treatment of its own historical tradition. Though new attention was paid to old, pre-Communist heroes such as Genghis Khan, the capital, Ulaanbaatar, kept its name (in honor of the 1920's Communist hero Damdin Sükhbaatar). The Mongolian People's Republic had been consigned to history, but the new Mongolia retained substantial continuity with it.

**SIGNIFICANCE**

Mongolia was one of the world's least-known nations in 1990. Some, confusing the "Outer Mongolia" that is Mongolia outside of China with the "Inner Mongolia" within China, thought the country was part of China. Others, conscious of the Soviet Union's strong political control over Communist Mongolia, assumed the country was an integral part of the Soviet Union in the manner of Central Asian nations such as the Kazakh, Kyrgyz, and Uzbek Soviet Socialist Republics. Mongolia's methodical and orderly democratic transition brought the country to wider international notice and respect than had occurred within recent memory.

Although the world's eyes were focused on other aspects of the Soviet implosion in 1990-1991, most notably the impending reunification of Germany and its effect on the North Atlantic Treaty Organization (NATO) and European integration, Mongolia's democratic transition was not without its own geopolitical implications. Possessing a long border with China, Mongolia had traditionally served as a buffer state between Russian and Chinese aspirations in inner Asia. Given that China had recently experienced the upheaval of the Tiananmen Square student protests and their harsh repression in 1989, any spasms in Mongolia could well have reverberated across the border. This did not happen; nor was Mongolian democracy driven off course by the implosion of its northern neighbor, the Soviet Union. Mongolia neither affected these outside developments nor was particularly affected by them.

Mongolian democracy acquired another significance by the late 1990's. Taking note of the economic successes of mainland China, Singapore, and Malaysia with social systems that were imperfect or undemocratic, some analysts spoke of an Asian model where free markets were not necessarily accompanied by freedom of speech. In 1998, Mongolian prime minister Tsakhiagiyn

Elbegdorj cited his own country's experience as a refutation of the assertion that Asian culture and electoral democracy did not mix. Once a virtually unknown adjunct to Soviet power, Mongolia had become a regional exemplar.

At the end of the Cold War, Mongolia was seen as one of the most pliant and obscure Soviet satellites. In the 1990's, Mongolia surprised most outside observers by quickly shifting to a stable, multiparty democracy in which two major parties peaceably competed, occupying office when the people elected them to do so. Mongolia made a smoother and more effective transition to democracy than many nations formerly part of the Soviet Union and by the end of the 1990's was touted as an example of how democracy could flourish in an Asian country with an authoritarian past.

*—Nicholas Birns*

## FURTHER READING

Fish, M. Steven. "Mongolia: Democracy Without Prerequisites." *Journal of Democracy* 9, no. 3 (1998): 127-141. Scholarly essay provides a lucid overview of the striking rapidity of Mongolia's democratic evolution. Gives concrete details of the growth of political pluralism, multiparty cooperation, and a strong civil society. Attributes the unusually tranquil progress of Mongolia toward democracy less to cultural factors than to Mongolian politicians' avoiding concentrating too much power in the hands of one leader.

Kaplonski, Christopher. *Mongolia: Democracy on the Steppe.* New York: Routledge, 2004. One of the leading historians of post-Communist Mongolia mounts a comprehensive survey of the country's recent history, examining both the mechanics of the transition itself and some of the nonstate actors (such as nongovernmental organizations) who played as pivotal a role as did the politicians in government.

_____. *Truth, History, and Politics in Mongolia: Memory of Heroes.* New York: Routledge, 2004. Examines the struggles of the Mongolian People's Revolutionary Party to dissociate itself from the people's memory of repressive Communist persecutions of the predemocracy period.

Rossabi, Morris. *Modern Mongolia: From Khans to Commissars to Capitalists.* Berkeley: University of California Press, 2005. Famous for his biography of Genghis Khan and his work on earlier Mongolian history, Rossabi here turns to a survey of recent Mongolian history. Focuses more on economic issues than on political issues, but provides a sense of overall background that makes the relatively seamless nature of the transition more explicable to the casual observer. Excellent overview is ideal for the beginning student of the subject.

Sanders, Alan. *Historical Dictionary of Mongolia.* Lanham, Md.: Scarecrow Press, 1996. This handy reference, part of an invaluable and much-consulted series, was published well in time to take account of the democratic transition. Provides crucial basic data about prominent Mongolian political personalities of the era as well as a thumbnail sketch of twentieth century Mongolian history.

1991

**SEE ALSO:** Mar. 11, 1985: Gorbachev Initiates a Policy of Glasnost; Feb. 4, 1989: Soviet Farmers Gain Control of Land and Crop Selection; June 4, 1989: China Crushes Prodemocracy Demonstration in Tiananmen Square; Dec., 1991: Dissolution of the Soviet Union.

**March, 1991**

# MEDICAL RESEARCHERS TEST PROMISING DRUGS FOR THE TREATMENT OF AIDS

*In 1991, medical researchers at Merck Laboratories announced the first clinically promising protease inhibitor for the treatment of patients infected with HIV. This and similar compounds formed the basis for highly active antiretroviral therapy, which dramatically improved the life expectancy of persons with HIV/AIDS.*

**LOCALE:** Whitehouse Station, New Jersey
**CATEGORIES:** Health and medicine; science and technology

**KEY FIGURES**
*Joseph P. Vacca* (fl. late twentieth century), research biochemist with Merck Laboratories
*David A. Kessler* (b. 1951), commissioner of the U.S. Food and Drug Administration
*Robert Gallo* (b. 1937), virologist at the National Institute for Cancer Research

**SUMMARY OF EVENT**
By the time acquired immunodeficiency syndrome (AIDS) became recognized as a major public health problem in the mid-1980's, the science of molecular genetics had progressed to levels at which gene sequencing of a virus and complete characterization, at the molecular level, of all the steps involved in pathogenesis had become almost routine. Once Robert Gallo and other virologists had isolated the virus that causes AIDS, grown it in cell culture, and determined both the molecular structure of key enzymes and the underlying gene sequence coding for them, research biochemists employed by pharmaceutical companies were able to predict, synthesize, and test compounds capable of pinpointing virus replication without disrupting critical aspects of human metabolism.

Human immunodeficiency virus (HIV) consists of a single strand of ribonucleic acid (RNA) surrounded by a protein coat. It is a retrovirus, meaning that the viral RNA serves as a template for assembling deoxyribonucleic acid (DNA), which then attaches itself to the genome of a host cell, a reversal of the process in which host-cell DNA codes for RNA, which in turn serves as a template for the proteins forming the building blocks of cells. During retrovirus replication, DNA generated by the virus, now inserted into a host chromosome, produces multiple copies of viral RNA particles. These in turn synthesize their own protein coats.

The first drug designed specifically for HIV-1 infection, AZT (azidothymidine) is a reverse transcriptase inhibitor that blocks synthesis of DNA from RNA. It has no effect on virus production by an infected cell. Approved by the U.S. Food and Drug Administration (FDA) in 1987, AZT therapy alone resulted in an increased survivorship following diagnosis of clinical AIDS of less than four months—hardly a miracle cure. Addition of specific therapeutic agents for important secondary infections in 1990 initially boosted average survivorship by another three months; this figure increased substantially in 1994, as many of those treated survived to benefit from highly active antiretroviral therapy (HAART) involving the new protease inhibitors.

The search for a more effective therapeutic agent proceeded simultaneously in the research laboratories of a number of pharmaceutical firms—notably Merck, Hoffmann-La Roche, and Eli Lilly—and focused on a different phase of the viral cycle: the production of a protein coat, without which the virus is not infective. Coat production requires a specific enzyme, HIV protease. Its chemical structure is somewhat similar to human renin, an enzyme involved in hypertension. Several drug companies had already synthesized and tested renin inhibitors, which proved clinically disappointing; this aborted research effort was now directed toward development of an HIV protease inhibitor.

The research programs involved synthesizing literally hundreds of extremely complex organic chemicals in sufficient quantities for testing their antiviral activity against HIV in cell culture. In late 1990, a team at Hoffmann-La Roche reported and obtained a patent for saquinavir (trade name Invirase), the first such compound to be later approved for clinical use. This was followed shortly by Merck's announcement of indinavir (trade name Crixivan) in March, 1991. Other companies followed suit.

Between identification of a potential therapeutic agent in the laboratory and its release on the open market lies a long and costly road of animal testing, controlled clinical testing, testing to determine the best way to administer the drug, and development of a manufacturing process to ensure the quantities needed. In the early 1990's there was widespread sentiment on the part of the drug companies, the medical community, and advocates for persons with HIV/AIDS that the situation at the time demanded some means of shortening this process. In response to this pressure and recommendations from David A. Kessler, commissioner of the FDA, the U.S. Congress authorized an accelerated approval process for drugs used to treat life-threatening diseases. Drug companies were required to continue clinical trials following FDA approval. Some years later, when the multiple side effects of protease inhibitors began surfacing, AIDS advocates accused the pharmaceutical companies of failing to provide adequate follow-up testing.

As a result of the accelerated approval process, the first protease inhibitor, Merck's Crixivan, developed by biochemist Joseph P. Vacca and his colleagues, became available on a limited basis in mid-1995. Because demand far exceeded initial supplies, Merck conducted a lottery to determine who would receive the drug. For another year, the company closely controlled access to Crixivan through a single supplier. Saquinavir gained approval in January, 1996, and other compounds followed in rapid succession.

The problem of resistant strains of HIV-1 surfaced almost at the outset. The AIDS virus has a high mutation rate, and because neither AZT nor protease inhibitors completely eliminate the virus from an infected person, emergence of a strain resistant to a particular drug is virtually inevitable, especially if a patient ceases taking prescribed medication for a period of time and then resumes it. This was one reason for Merck's limiting access to a defined number of patients for whom adequate stocks were available. Combining lower doses of several protease inhibitors reduces the chance that viral resistance to any one of them will develop. The spread of Crixivan-resistant strains of HIV-1 in the United States and Europe led to disuse of this agent in the developed world; this helped convince Merck to allow indinavir's release as a generic in Africa and Asia, although Merck's patent remained in force.

## SIGNIFICANCE

HAART combining HIV protease inhibitors, AZT, and prophylaxis for secondary infections is credited with transforming HIV/AIDS from a sentence of death into a chronic, manageable condition. When administered late in pregnancy, HAART greatly reduces the chance of intergenerational HIV infection during childbirth. Such therapy is not a cure, however, and it carries high physical, social, and monetary costs.

Protease inhibitors exact a heavy toll in side effects, some of them potentially lethal in their own right. The oral medications must be taken at precisely timed inter-

vals, because the compounds are rapidly metabolized once ingested. Although considerable improvements in delivery were made in the years after the drugs were introduced in 1995, in the early twenty-first century HAART remains a time-consuming occupation requiring a great deal of self-discipline on the part of the patient. Consequently, many HIV/AIDS patients fail to adhere to their treatment regimens and relapse, facilitating the spread of drug-resistant viral strains.

The annual cost of drugs alone for an HIV-positive patient on HAART in the United States exceeds twenty thousand dollars. Since passage of the Ryan White Comprehensive AIDS Resources Emergency Act of 1990, the U.S. government has underwritten this cost for those without insurance. Regardless of whether the source of funding is public or private, HAART represents a major drain on the health care dollar. Inefficiencies of the American health care delivery system and excessive profits for the pharmaceutical industry are somewhat to blame, but even if these were addressed, providing state-of-the art HIV/AIDS therapy for 1.5 million Americans would produce a staggering bill.

The development and adoption of protease inhibitors as standard therapy for HIV/AIDS illustrated the mismatch between science and technology on one hand and social reality on the other. If a molecular knowledge of a biological process affecting human health and the tools required to use that knowledge to synthesize an agent for regulating that process were all that were required to combat a scourge such as AIDS, the outlook for human happiness would be rosy indeed. In reality, the main benefit of HAART has been to prolong the useful lives of HIV patients who, unless an actual cure is developed, will eventually succumb to AIDS. Moreover, to the extent that infected people who fail to adhere to treatment protocols also engage in risky behavior and uninfected people use the availability of therapy as an excuse for not taking precautions against exposure (both of which are known to occur), HAART has actually served to amplify the AIDS epidemic.

—*Martha A. Sherwood*

## FURTHER READING

Dutta, A. S., ed. *Small Peptides: Chemistry, Biology, and Clinical Studies.* New York: Elsevier, 1993. Includes two chapters on inhibitors of aspartyl proteases, with an overview and structures of HIV protease inhibitors being developed.

Feldman, Douglas A., and Julia Wang Miller, eds. *The AIDS Crisis: A Documentary History.* Westport,

Conn.: Greenwood Press, 1998. Collection of essays on the AIDS crisis includes source documents on drug development and the logistical and financial barriers to drug therapy.

Roberts, Noel A., J. Charles Craig, and Jonathan Sheldon. "Resistance and Cross-Resistance with Saquinavir and Other HIV Protease Inhibitors: Theory and Practice." *AIDS* 12 (March 26, 1998): 453-460. Provides a good account of efforts to prevent emergence of drug-resistant HIV strains.

Vacca, Joseph P. "Design of Tight-Binding Human Im-

munodeficiency Virus Type-1 Protease Inhibitors." In *Retroviral Proteases*, edited by Lawrence C. Kuo and Jules M. Shafer. San Diego, Calif.: Academic Press, 1994. Presents a comprehensive, highly technical description of the development of anti-AIDS drugs and the functioning of these drugs at the molecular level.

**SEE ALSO:** June 5, 1981: U.S. Centers for Disease Control Recognizes AIDS; 1998: AIDS Devastates Africa.

## March, 1991
# SUPREME SOVIET DECLARES THE ARAL SEA A DISASTER AREA

*Massive development of irrigated agriculture in Soviet Central Asia between 1950 and 1990 caused drying up and salinization of the Aral Sea, degrading the environment and creating a public health crisis. Acknowledged by the Soviets shortly before the breakup of the Soviet Union, the Aral crisis became the responsibility of independent Central Asian republics that were ill equipped to handle it.*

**LOCALE:** Central Asia, between Kazakhstan and Uzbekistan

**CATEGORIES:** Disasters; environmental issues

**KEY FIGURES**

*A. S. Monin* (b. 1921), Russian oceanographer and environmental activist

*Nikita S. Khrushchev* (1894-1971), general secretary of the Communist Party of the Soviet Union, 1958-1964

*Leonid Brezhnev* (1906-1982), general secretary of the Communist Party of the Soviet Union, 1966-1982

**SUMMARY OF EVENT**

In 1960, the Aral Sea was a landlocked, brackish lake 66,000 square kilometers in extent, bounded by the Soviet republics of Uzbekistan and Kazakhstan. Constantly renewed by the Amu Dar'ya and Syr Dar'ya rivers, it supported a thriving fishery. Forests and wetlands in the river deltas harbored a wealth of wildlife and sheltered migratory waterfowl. The rivers and sea formed the basis of an extensive, diverse, and renewable system of agriculture dating back to antiquity.

Beginning with Nikita S. Khrushchev's "virgin lands" program in the early 1960's, the Soviet Union embarked on an ambitious program of economic expansion in Cen-

tral Asia. This program was based on a philosophy, later termed "ecoperestroika," that saw restructuring of the environment for human development, without regard for environmental consequences, as part of socialist destiny. Ignoring early signs that diverting river water for hydroelectric power and irrigation was damaging regional ecology, central planners encouraged wholesale expansion of cotton cultivation, from 4.6 million hectares in 1960 to 7 million hectares in 1990. Shifting from diversified agriculture to cotton monoculture had many adverse environmental consequences. Cotton is a thirsty crop and quickly exhausts the soil. Marginal lands required huge inputs of fertilizer and pesticides. Irrigated land became progressively more saline, increasing water demand in a vicious cycle ultimately leading to abandonment. In an effort to reduce downstream pollution, irrigation runoff was diverted into evaporation reservoirs, creating poisoned human-made lakes. By the late 1970's, river flow to the sea had almost ceased.

Begun in 1954, completed in 1988, and extended in 1993, the 1,350-kilometer Karakum Canal in Turkmenistan epitomizes poor construction and planning. Open and unlined for most of its length, the canal, which diverts nearly 20 percent of the total flow of the Amu Dar'ya River, loses more than half of its water through evaporation and seepage into nonagricultural land. Much of the land so hopefully brought into cultivation has since been abandoned.

Signs of deterioration first became evident in the mid-1960's, when a new phase of hydrotechnological construction coincided with a drought. Responding to a documented decline in fisheries, the Soviet Council of Ministers recommended an integrated approach to resource management in the region, but no action was taken. By 1975, the level of the lake had dropped more than 4 meters, and its salinity had increased noticeably. A 1975 commission concluded that at current irrigation levels, the sea would eventually be reduced to a small hypersaline reservoir. Projecting to 1990, it predicted a sea level of 46.3 meters and a salinity of 1.8 percent, based on improvements in irrigation efficiency that were not implemented. The actual figures in 1990 were 38 and 3 percent, respectively.

In the early 1980's, Soviet planners seriously entertained the possibility of diverting water from the Ob' and Irtysh rivers in western Siberia to expand irrigated acreage in Kazakhstan. Abandoned in 1986 as economically unfeasible, this effort might have slowed desertification in the Aral basin but would not have reversed it. Diversion of Siberian rivers to replenish the Aral Sea was again suggested in 1990. It has become a political as well as economic impossibility since the breakup of the Soviet Union in 1991.

By 1990, total surface had shrunk by 40 percent, and volume by 60 percent. The sea had completely lost its productive fisheries. Retreating waters left behind expanses of wind-swept salt flats producing dust storms that spread salt and pollutants on surrounding agricul-

tural land. Deprived of the moderating influence of the sea, the area became drier and subject to temperature extremes. The Karakalpaks, the indigenous ethnic group inhabiting the Amu Dar'ya delta region, exhibited high rates of respiratory disease, infant mortality, and birth defects.

The nuclear meltdown at Chernobyl in 1986, coming at the beginning of Mikhail Gorbachev's policy of glasnost, led to more open discussion of environmental problems in the Soviet Union. A. S. Monin, a corresponding member of the Soviet Academy of Sciences, published a series of articles in *Novy Mir* in 1987 documenting the extent of the Aral Sea disaster and criticizing agencies that should have taken action. In 1988, *Novy Mir* collaborated with several newly founded environmental groups to send a fact-finding expedition to the Aral Sea. For the first time, scientists from the West traveled to the affected region, closed to outsiders for decades. In October, an International Symposium on the Aral Crisis brought scientists and environmental policy makers from the Central Asian republics, Russia, Europe, and the United States to Nukus, Uzbekistan. This body addressed a resolution to the Supreme Soviet recommending that the Aral Sea basin be declared a disaster area.

On paper, the Soviet government was committed to

1991

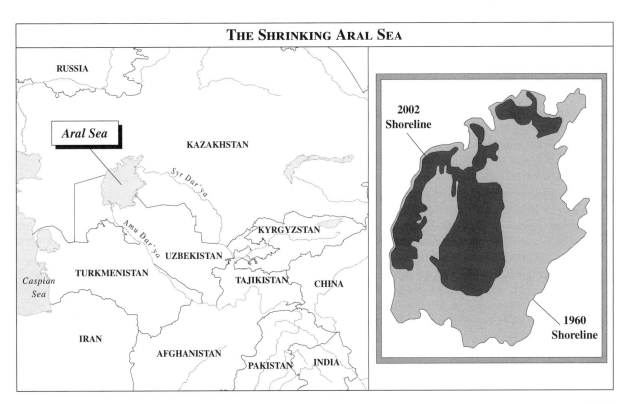

**THE SHRINKING ARAL SEA**

RUSSIA

Aral Sea

KAZAKHSTAN

Syr Dar'ya

Amu Dar'ya

KYRGYZSTAN

UZBEKISTAN

Caspian Sea

TURKMENISTAN

TAJIKISTAN

CHINA

IRAN

AFGHANISTAN

PAKISTAN   INDIA

2002 Shoreline

1960 Shoreline

addressing the problem. The Central Committee and Council of Ministers passed a resolution titled "On Measures for a Fundamental Improvement of the Ecological and Sanitary Conditions in the Aral Sea Region" in September, 1988. Unfortunately, the Soviet economy was then in the process of unraveling. The same agencies and individuals that had created the crisis controlled the little funding available for environmental amelioration.

On June 23, 1990, the presidents of Kazakhstan, Uzbekistan, Turkmenistan, Tajikistan, and Kyrgyzstan presented a joint resolution calling for the Supreme Soviet to declare the Aral Sea basin a region of national calamity and to provide real help. In March, 1991, the Supreme Soviet finally responded by declaring the region a disaster area. By that time, any response requiring funding was out of the question. In December, the Soviet Union ceased to exist, and the task of amelioration fell to five newly independent republics, each with its own suite of social, environmental, and political problems.

## Significance

The degradation of the Aral Sea basin ranks as one of the most egregious examples of creeping environmental problems being allowed to accumulate, despite repeated warnings, until they reach a level where restoring the original ecosystem is impossible and simply preventing further damage is prohibitively expensive.

Under the premiership of Leonid Brezhnev, a climate existed in which individual agencies responsible for monitoring environmental problems produced high-quality research but were unable to communicate with each other or the public. Decision makers who saw increasing cotton production as an economic panacea in Central Asia did not have access to data documenting environmental deterioration. The Karakalpaks, who initially bore the brunt of mismanagement, are a minority group in Uzbekistan, one of the poorest of the Soviet republics. Had local people had the ear of the central government in the Brezhnev era, steps could have been taken to arrest desertification.

In 1998, the World Bank, in collaboration with the United Nations Development Program, initiated a major effort to help restore the Aral region. By that time, the sea had lost 80 percent of its volume, and had split in two. Increasing irrigation efficiency in Kazakhstan and better regulation of hydroelectric resources in Kyrgyzstan restored flow in the Syr Dar'ya to a level where the North Aral, now separated from the larger southern portion by a

dike, is refilling rapidly and supports a healthy introduced fish population. The ecological situation in the South Aral continues to deteriorate. Turkmenistan still relies on the Karakum Canal, with increasingly poorer efficiency. With a cotton-based economy and a skyrocketing population, Uzbekistan is poorly situated to introduce conservation measures. Afghanistan increasingly removes irrigation water from the Amu Dar'ya. In common with other arid regions, Central Asia will probably experience increasing evapotranspiration and water-supply problems associated with global warming.

The Aral Sea crisis holds lessons for the rest of the world on the importance of close monitoring of regional ecology and early intervention, even at the expense of economic development, to forestall irreversible environmental collapse. Analogous conditions exist in the Western United States, where environmental warnings, although openly disseminated and discussed, too frequently fail to translate into national policy.

—*Martha A. Sherwood*

## Further Reading

Glantz, Michael H., ed. *Creeping Environmental Problems and Sustainable Development in the Aral Sea Basin*. New York: Cambridge University Press, 1999. Collection of authoritative scholarly papers, including two on health issues and one on the Karakum Canal.

Glantz, Michael H., Alvin Z. Rubenstein, and Igor Zonin. "Tragedy in the Aral Sea Basin: Looking Back to Plan Ahead." In *Central Asia: Its Strategic Importance and Future Prospects*, edited by Halik Malez. New York: St. Martin's Press, 1994. Good for facts and a detailed chronology including the political background.

Micklin, Philip. "The Aral Sea Crisis and Its Future: An Assessment in 2006." *Eurasian Geography and Economics* 47, no. 5 (2006): 546-567. Good for an update on the political situation and reclamation efforts.

Stone, Richard. "Coming to Grips with the Aral Sea's Grim Legacy." *Science* 284, no. 5411 (1999): 30-33. Gives a chronological account and outlines the World Bank's proposals for restoration.

**See also:** June 24, 1980: Soviet Union Passes Environmental Legislation; Mar. 11, 1985: Gorbachev Initiates a Policy of Glasnost; Apr. 26, 1986: Soviet Chernobyl Nuclear Plant Undergoes Meltdown.

**March 26, 1991**

# BIRTH OF THE SOUTHERN COMMON MARKET

*Four countries in South America's Southern Cone—Brazil, Argentina, Uruguay, and Paraguay—established MERCOSUR, a trade organization intended to increase economic cooperation among the member nations.*

**ALSO KNOWN AS:** Mercado Común del Sur (MERCOSUR); Mercado Comum do Sul (MERCOSUL)

**LOCALE:** Asunción, Paraguay

**CATEGORIES:** Diplomacy and international relations; trade and commerce; organizations and institutions

**KEY FIGURES**

*Raúl Alfonsín* (b. 1926), president of Argentina, 1983-1989

*José Sarney* (b. 1930), president of Brazil, 1985-1990

*Hugo Chávez* (b. 1954), president of Venezuela, 1999-April 11, 2002, and beginning again April 13, 2002

**SUMMARY OF EVENT**

Throughout the decades of the 1970's and 1980's, the economies of the world's major industrial countries became increasingly subject to the pressures of globalization. The concept of free trade, the unrestricted movement of goods across national borders, came to be regarded as a positive economic goal to be pursued.

In 1991, four countries of South America's Southern Cone—Brazil, Argentina, Uruguay, and Paraguay—initiated a treaty designed to increase economic cooperation and to expedite trade among members of the group. This goal was to be accomplished through the reduction of tariffs on the imports and exports levied on the goods of the member nations as they passed among these nations. The agreement would act as a positive influence on trade and permit the four countries to be more competitive internationally with such industrial giants as the United States and the European Union.

In 1985, José Sarney, Brazil's first civilian president in twenty-one years, joined with Argentina's president, Raúl Alfonsín, in the planning of the treaty that would establish the Southern Common Market, or Mercado Común del Sur (MERCOSUR; in Portuguese, Mercado Comum do Sul, or MERCOSUL). Brazil was plagued by inflation, an enormous foreign debt, and internal corruption when Sarney assumed the presidency, and he believed that an economic treaty among South America's southern countries could do much to reduce the boom-and-bust pattern of the area's economies. Alfonsín was interested in such a treaty because he thought it would help to control Argentina's continuing problems with inflation.

The treaty that established MERCOSUR was signed in Asunción, Paraguay, on March 26, 1991. It called for the formation of a number of groups to administer the operation of the member nations' goals. The primary unit of MERCOSUR is the Common Market Council, which is charged with setting policy and ensuring member nations' compliance with the goals of the treaty. The Common Market Group is MERCOSUR's executive body, representing all member countries through their respective Ministries of Foreign Affairs, and the Administrative Office and Socioeconomic Advisory Forum serves as the record-keeping and communications facility of MERCOSUR. A number of work subgroups conduct surveys and submit recommendations to the Common Market Council regarding a wide range of specific issues involving MERCOSUR's continuing operations.

In the years after MERCOSUR's founding, a number of additional South American countries became associate members of the organization: Bolivia, Chile, Colombia, Ecuador, and Peru. Ultimately, MERCOSUR announced, its goal is to incorporate all Central and South American countries into MERCOSUR membership. In July, 2006, Venezuela became the fifth nation with full membership in MERCOSUR.

The anticipated trading potential of MERCOSUR proved to be correct. The volume of business among the member countries increased markedly after the inauguration of the Treaty of Asunción, and the addition of Venezuela in 2006 further improved matters for these South American nations. Although the MERCOSUR member nations compete in the production of some exports, the overall trade balances among them produce a positive flow of commerce.

**SIGNIFICANCE**

Although MERCOSUR's economic program led to substantial increases in both imports and exports among the organization's member nations, the internal economic problems of Argentina and Brazil complicated the relationships between these two countries as well as the relations between them and the smaller participants in MERCOSUR. The political leadership within the member countries found that they had to respond to domestic

1991

considerations before the could acquiesce to the recommendations of MERCOSUR's governors.

Although MERCOSUR is not designed to be a political instrument, undoubtedly the organization has fostered good political relationships among its members. The original four member nations have held to democratic formats in terms of the operations of their respective governments, where once, in most, military dictatorships had dominated. In contrast, Hugo Chávez, the president of the newest MERCOSUR member, Venezuela, has seized increasingly dictatorial powers for his government. Moreover, Chávez has been bitterly critical of the United States and has sought to rally opposition to U.S. involvement in Latin American affairs. Chávez has dispersed millions of dollars to a number of Latin American countries from Venezuela's lucrative petroleum profits to undermine relationships between the United States and its Latin American neighbors.

*—Carl Henry Marcoux*

## FURTHER READING

Behar, Jaime. *Cooperation and Competition in a Common Market: Studies on the Formation of MERCOSUR.* New York: Physica-Verlag, 2000. Examines the establishment of MERCOSUR and includes discussion of the association's progress through 1996. Includes methodological and statistical appendixes, bibliographic references, and index.

Grimson, Alejandro, and Gabriel Kessler. *On Argentina and the Southern Cone: Neoliberalsim and National Imaginations.* New York: Taylor & Francis, 2005. Provides an in-depth analysis of Argentina's history and the nation's adaptation to the political and economic challenges it has faced in recent decades.

Heymann, Daniel. *Regional Interdependencies and Macroeconomic Crises: Notes on MERCOSUR.* Buenos Aires, Argentina: United Nations, 2001. Takes a critical look at the actual progress of the members of MERCOSUR in reaching macroeconomic stability.

Machinea, José Luis, and Guillermo Rozenwurcel. *Macroeconomic Coordination in Latin America: Does It Have a Future?* Santiago, Chile: United Nations, 2005. Brief work offers presents negative evaluation of MERCOSUR's accomplishments up to 2005.

Roett, Riordan, ed. *MERCOSUR: Regional Integration, World Markets.* Boulder, Colo.: Lynne Rienner, 1999. Collection of essays includes discussion of the immense effects Brazil has had on its relationships with the other members of MERCOSUR, especially Argentina.

Weintraub, Sidney. *Development and Democracy in the Southern Cone: Imperatives for U.S. Policy in South America.* Washington, D.C.: Center for Strategic and International Studies, 2000. Examines the effects that Brazil's and Argentina's domestic economic problems have had on internal MERCOSUR operations.

SEE ALSO: Mar. 15, 1985: Democracy Returns to Brazil; Dec. 9, 1985: Argentine Leaders Are Convicted of Human Rights Violations; Oct. 12, 1988: Brazilian President Announces Plans to Protect Rain Forests; July 23, 1989: Mexico Renegotiates Debt to U.S. Banks.

March 28, 1991
# U.S. COURTS RESTRICT RIGHTS TO PHOTOCOPY ANTHOLOGIES

*The court ruling in the case of* Basic Books, Inc. v. Kinko's Graphics Corp. *greatly restricted the commercial creation of photocopied "course packs" by requiring copy shops to obtain permissions in advance.*

**ALSO KNOWN AS:** *Basic Books, Inc. v. Kinko's Graphics Corp.*, 758 F.Supp. 1522
**LOCALE:** New York, New York
**CATEGORIES:** Laws, acts, and legal history; publishing and journalism; trade and commerce

**KEY FIGURES**
*Constance Baker Motley* (1921-2005), U.S. district court judge for the Southern District of New York
*Kurt Koenig* (fl. late twentieth century), vice president and general counsel for Kinko's Graphics
*Carol Risher* (fl. late twentieth century), director of copyright and new technology for the Association of American Publishers

**SUMMARY OF EVENT**
Kinko's Graphics Corporation (later FedEx Kinko's) operates photocopy shops, customarily situated near colleges and universities, around the United States. In the 1980's, Kinko's started a service it called "Professor Publishing" in which it assembled custom-made anthologies by photocopying preexisting materials, usually excerpts from books. These anthologies were created at the request of professors and sold to professors' students as supplements to, and sometimes in place of, other course materials.

Kinko's profited handsomely from this endeavor, in part because the company often neglected to obtain, or even seek, permission from copyright holders to copy the published material that went into its course packs. In May, 1989, some of these copyright holders sued Kinko's in federal court for copyright violation, claiming that the photocopy chain had illegally reproduced "substantial portions" of their works. The efforts of these plaintiffs, eight publishing houses, were orchestrated by the Association of American Publishers. Their suit was aimed at two New York City Kinko's stores, one serving professors and students at Columbia University and the other serving those at New York University and the New School for Social Research.

The case was decided by Judge Constance Baker Motley, who ruled against Kinko's on March 28, 1991,

in the U.S. Federal Court for the Southern District of New York. Finding for the publishers, Judge Motley ruled that Kinko's was guilty of copyright infringement and ordered the chain to pay $510,000 in damages in addition to the publishers' legal fees. She also prohibited Kinko's from selling copies of any copyrighted material—including that from nonexistent works that, on creation, would automatically be covered by copyright—without first obtaining permissions from the copyright holders and paying any required royalties.

Judge Motley rejected the defense offered by Kinko's that its practice of producing customized course anthologies was protected by the doctrine of fair use. Fair use is an exception to the limited monopoly granted to copyright holders, authorizing reproduction, within limits, of copyrighted works without permission for such purposes as criticism, research, and teaching. Judge Motley distinguished for-profit copy shops from nonprofit educational institutions, saying that photocopied course packs do not become educational until they are in students' hands. In the hands of copy shop operators, she said, the purpose of such anthologies is clearly commercial.

In her written opinion, Judge Motley refused to state unequivocally that the act of compiling course packs without prior permission from copyright holders is per se illegal. In the opinion, she referred frequently to the "Agreement on Guidelines in Not-for-Profit Educational Institutions," part of the legislative history of the Copyright Act of 1976, which first codified the fair use doctrine. That act, together with advances in photocopying technology, arguably gave rise to parallel publishing industries such as Kinko's. The classroom guidelines clearly state that copying shall not be used to create or to replace or substitute for anthologies, compilations, or collective works. In addition, copying shall not substitute for the purchase of books, publishers' reprints, or periodicals. Finally, no charge was to be made to students beyond the actual cost of photocopying.

Judge Motley's opinion indicated that although Kinko's violated these mandates, other assemblers of photocopied customized anthologies might be able to survive a fair use analysis balancing the interests of copyright users against those of copyright holders. The difficulty with this loophole is that although the 1976 Copyright Act codifies fair use, it does not define the doctrine, which was evolved through the accretion of generations of judicial decisions, each of them weighing different sets of facts. Section 107 of the 1976 Copyright Act, devoted to fair use, provides only a list of nonexclusive factors to be balanced in reaching a determination of whether a secondary use of copyrighted material is permissible. These factors include the purpose and character of the use (such as whether the use is of a commercial nature or is for nonprofit educational purposes), the nature of the copyrighted work, the amount and substantiality of the portion used in relation to the copyrighted work as a whole, and the effect of the use on the potential market for or value of the copyrighted work.

Judge Motley devoted five and one-half pages of her opinion to analyses of these and other factors. Few copy shops can devote the time and resources needed to make such refined analyses with regard to each of the copyrighted works they use. As the judge herself acknowledged, the anthology form of the course packs militates against a finding of fair use, in that it implies a period of planning that could also accommodate the process of seeking permissions.

Judge Motley found that only one of the fair use factors, the nature of the copyrighted work, weighed in favor of Kinko's. The books infringed in the suit were factual in nature, and the scope of fair use is greater with regard to factual works. With regard to other factors, however, the judge's opinion was damning. Not only was the use of copyrighted materials by Kinko's unquestionably commercial, the chain made no transformative use of—no changes to—the materials it copied. Kinko's also copied substantial portions of the copyrighted works, almost always entire chapters meant to stand alone as complete representations of the concepts they explored. This extensive unauthorized copying clearly diminished the market for the works excerpted in the course packs.

The effect of the copying was especially detrimental to out-of-print works. Judge Motley rejected the argument that as these books were no longer available, there was no market for them, finding instead that the damage to out-of-print works was pronounced precisely because permissions fees might provide the only income for the holders of copyrights for these works.

Finally, Judge Motley discarded the "fair use by reason by necessity" argument offered by Kinko's—that is, the argument that following permissions procedures would inhibit the educational process. Although the costliness of texts and rapid changes in course subject matter were good rationales for the use of customized course anthologies, Kinko's was unable to produce even one witness who could testify that he or she would be unable to

teach effectively if Kinko's had to seek and pay for permissions in order to produce class packets.

## SIGNIFICANCE

Kinko's first reacted to the decision against it by initiating a program called "Partners in Education," which was intended to permit the continuation of its course-pack business by providing a more efficient method of clearing permissions. "Partners in Education" was, however, dependent on publishers' willingness to sign blanket permissions agreements that would allow Kinko's to reproduce their works at will. Understandably, publishers balked at granting such open-ended licenses, and they were supported by the stance of the American Association of Publishers, which insisted that its members need to protect their right to object to copying.

Ultimately, Kinko's announced that it was discontinuing its course-pack service, choosing instead to focus on the needs of the commercial nonacademic market, such as photo and document transfer and electronic publishing services. The continuing demand for customized course anthologies did not, however, go unmet. The decision in *Basic Books v. Kinko's* essentially deprived commercial copy shops of the fair use exemption, and many such operations ceased after 1991. Meanwhile, however, increasing numbers of campus bookstores—seeking to take advantage of the loophole left open by Judge Motley—stepped up their own course-pack services, and some have reportedly been highly lucrative. In addition, publishers themselves became involved in the business of creating their own customized anthologies.

An underground market for course packs also developed. The Copyright Clearance Center, which acts as the agent for numerous publishers in processing permissions requests, has estimated that 60 percent of the course packs produced commercially do not conform to the requirements set out in Judge Motley's decision. Some professors get around the *Kinko's* ruling by handing out a limited number of master copies of course anthologies to students, who then copy them on their own. In another variation on this technique, professors place course materials on reserve in college libraries, resulting in increased profits to companies licensing copying machines to such institutions. In all such cases, publishers never see the permissions fees to which they are legally entitled.

*Basic Books v. Kinko's* was the first case involving the relationship between education and electronic copying to go to trial since the new copyright law went into effect in January, 1978, but it was not the first case brought. In

1983, New York University settled a similar copyright infringement case out of court. It appears that even the decision in *Kinko's*, however, did not put an end to such litigation. In 1993, three publishers filed suit in U.S. district court in Michigan against James M. Smith, owner of Michigan Document Services, which operated five photocopying stores that produced course packs. After concluding that the permissions process was too expensive and cumbersome and that royalty rates were too high, Smith began charging an arbitrary royalty fee of one cent per page and forwarding those payments to publishers.

Smith's tactics point up some of the difficulties that developed in the wake of *Basic Books v. Kinko's*. One of the case's primary effects was to increase the number of permissions requests dramatically, to the point where some publishers became so inundated that they were unable to process requests in a timely fashion. In addition, the costs of processing such requests sometimes outstripped publishers' royalty revenues. As a result, many publishers signed on with the Copyright Clearance Center, which established an Academic Permissions Service to cope with the profusion of requests created by the *Kinko's* decision.

In an effort to alleviate the permissions bottleneck, which persisted both at individual publishing houses and at the Copyright Clearance Center, some copyright users turned to computer technology. Xerox Corporation began work on a system called Docutech, which would hold textbooks and other materials in electronic memory until an individual student ordered a customized course pack. PUBNET Permissions, an electronic copyright request system, became available to college bookstores in September, 1991.

Systems such as PUBNET are designed to make the permissions process not only faster but also cheaper. Royalty rates directly charged by publishers can vary widely, from nothing to exorbitant amounts per page. Rates charged by the Copyright Clearance Center can be even higher, because the center charges copyright holders a percentage of all the payments it collects, in addition to registration and annual fees. Kurt Koenig, vice president and general counsel for Kinko's, suggested that a licensing arrangement similar to that employed by the American Society of Composers, Authors, and Publishers (ASCAP) might provide a salutary alternative to the high administrative costs charged by the Copyright Clearance Center.

Regardless of the development of new alternatives, the need for affordable, flexible-format course packs remains, prompting both producers and consumers of these products to agitate for changes in the copyright laws. According to course-pack advocates, these changes should acknowledge the special nature of these products and permit the repeated use of copyrighted materials in customized class anthologies in exchange for reasonable royalties. In addition, they should eliminate the need for judicial determination of what constitutes fair use. As numerous commentators have pointed out, technological developments in such areas as electronic publishing have only intensified the need for rules that clearly designate the use of copyrighted materials as educational throughout the process of producing course packs.

*—Lisa Paddock*

**FURTHER READING**

Crews, Kenneth D. "Federal Court's Ruling Against Photocopying Chain Will Not Destroy 'Fair Use.'" *Chronicle of Higher Education* 37 (April 17, 1991): A48. Analyzes Judge Motley's opinion and argues that it allows fair use to continue to exist in academic environments. Also makes the case that the ruling may stimulate innovation in academic text delivery.

Kozak, Ellen M. *Every Writer's Guide to Copyright and Publishing Law*. 3d ed. New York: Henry Holt, 2004. Handbook designed for writers provides clear background information on U.S. copyright law and revisions in the law over time. Includes index.

Magner, Denise K. "Copy Shops, Publishers Still Seek Common Ground on Permissions Process." *Chronicle of Higher Education* 39 (June 16, 1993): A15-A16. Details the lawsuit against James M. Smith as well as other reactions to and difficulties associated with the *Kinko's* decision.

Orfalea, Paul, and Ann Marsh. *Copy This! Lessons from a Hyperactive Dyslexic Who Turned a Bright Idea into One of America's Best Companies*. New York: Workman, 2005. Kinko's founder Orfalea mixes memoir with business advice in this interesting work. Includes some discussion of the copyright-related lawsuits faced by the company.

Reid, Calvin. "Kinko's Solicits Publishers to Sign Blanket Agreements for Copying." *Publishers Weekly* 238 (May 17, 1991): 8-9. Explores Kinko's reactions in the marketplace to the ramifications of the decision against the copying company.

Reuter, Madalynne. "Judge Rules Kinko's Infringes Copyrights." *Publishers Weekly* 238 (April 12, 1991): 10. Brief but well-written news item sets forth the facts of the case with clarity.

1991

Strong, William S. *The Copyright Book: A Practical Guide*. 4th ed. Cambridge, Mass.: MIT Press, 1998. Provides a straightforward presentation of the rights and responsibilities connected with copyright law, addressed to the average citizen. In addition to being revised every few years (this is the third update of the fourth edition), the work is supplemented more frequently by unbound updates.

Tackett, Raymond. "Copyright Law Needs to Include 'Fair Use' for Course Materials." *Chronicle of Higher Education* 38 (February 12, 1992): B3-B40. Opinion piece chronicles the author's difficulties in obtaining permissions in the wake of the *Kinko's* decision and argues for modification of the definition of fair use to accommodate the need for course packets.

Turner, Judith Axler. "Eight Publishers Charge Copyright Violation, Sue Copying Chain." *Chronicle of Higher Education* 35 (May 3, 1989): A1, A21. Early story lays out the initial positions of the antagonists in the case.

**SEE ALSO:** Oct. 19, 1976: Expanded Copyright Law Reflects New Technology; Oct. 27, 1998: Reform of the Copyright Act; June 1, 1999: Napster Is Released.

## May 5, 1991
# SWISS BANKS END SECRET ACCOUNTS

*In a move aimed at repairing the reputation of Swiss financial institutions, the Swiss Federal Banking Commission announced a plan to eliminate secret Swiss bank accounts by September, 1992.*

**LOCALE:** Zurich, Switzerland
**CATEGORY:** Banking and finance

**KEY FIGURES**
*Elisabeth Kopp* (b. 1936), first female justice minister of Switzerland
*Markus Lusser* (1931-1998), member of the board of governors of the Swiss National Bank
*Dick Marty* (b. 1945), Swiss federal prosecutor whose investigation of Sharkarchi Trading contributed to the scandal involving Elisabeth Kopp

**SUMMARY OF EVENT**
As part of a long campaign designed to rescue the tarnished image of the nation's financial institutions, Switzerland, deservedly known as the financial capital of the world, on May 5, 1991, announced that it was abolishing the most secret "Form B" bank accounts. Secrecy-loving depositors had long used these accounts to keep their identities hidden by using other agents as fronts.

According to a rule of the Swiss Federal Banking Commission, after June 30, 1991, Swiss banks would not accept any more Form B or "anonymous" accounts. A few exceptions to this ban were allowed. The preexisting thirty thousand account holders were given until September 30, 1992, to divulge their identities or close their accounts. Numbered accounts that keep the owner's name separate from all other records would still be allowed, provided that the account holder's name is known by at least two bank officers.

The widely hailed demise of secret accounts came about primarily as a result of concerted international pressures directed against the Swiss haven for financial hideaways. The Swiss authorities gradually responded to these external pressures. In 1986, the Swiss government froze assets of dictators Ferdinand Marcos of the Philippines and Jean-Claude "Baby Doc" Duvalier of Haiti. During the same year, to cooperate with a U.S. investigation, Bank Leu of Switzerland turned over files to U.S. officials for use in the Dennis Levine insider trading case. Insider trading was declared a crime in Switzerland in 1988. In 1990, the Swiss government froze Iraqi assets and made money laundering a crime. Swiss banks were directed to make customers certify that their deposits are not linked with any criminal activities. Then came the abolition of secret bank accounts.

For more than half a century, unpopular dictators of many developing countries secretly amassed wealth, often in violation of their domestic laws. They needed a financial haven such as that offered by Switzerland to protect their treasures, in secret, from instability in their countries as well from the insecurity of their regimes. International networks of drug lords and terrorists also needed financial conduits that permitted anonymous, secret accounts to facilitate their schemes. Secret accounts were no less valuable to wealthy tax evaders, particularly those from European countries with especially high taxes. These accounts were also instrumental for regimes with ambitious military programs that faced international sanctions. The elimination of Form B accounts was expected to curb undesirable financial activities, particularly those related to drug trafficking, terrorism, and international sanction-violating actions.

The tough antilaundering stance of the Swiss authorities was prompted by the international chastening Swiss banks had received after disclosures that their accounts were being widely used by global money-laundering operations, which attempted to hide sources of cash by routing the money through legitimate outlets. The Swiss banking system, renowned for its secrecy, for many years attracted the wealth of dictators and tax-evading wealthy people. In the 1970's and 1980's, illegal drug operations found the time-honored Swiss tradition of secrecy very convenient. Until the mid-1980's, it was a well-founded speculation that drug operations were using the Swiss banking system for their highly lucrative schemes. Hard and concrete evidence started to surface when, in 1987, Los Angeles narcotics officers seized three Zurich-bound suitcases stuffed with $2 million in currency.

Although the entire Swiss financial and banking system was accused of being a haven for dirty money, Switzerland's Federal Banking Commission, in a twenty-eight-page report published in mid-1989, faulted Credit Suisse in particular. Credit Suisse handled the bulk of the money in that billion-dollar scheme involving the laundering of drug money and was disciplined for inadequately supervising its accounts.

The Swiss government also faced domestic scandals, one of which involved Hans Kopp, a prominent Zurich lawyer and the husband of the nation's first female justice minister, Elisabeth Kopp. A money-laundering case at the time involved Sharkarchi Trading, a Zurich-based firm dealing in currency. Elisabeth Kopp tipped off her husband, a director and vice chairman of Sharkarchi Trading at that time, shortly before publication of the prosecutor's report. News of the tipoff resulted in a high-level scandal and the justice minister's resignation. This incident and others tarnished the image of the Swiss government as well as that of the country's banking system. This was particularly damaging because Switzerland was considering becoming a member of the European Community (EC) and was working toward conformity with the rules and regulations of that organization.

Reforms of the Swiss banking system reflected Swiss authorities' response to the changing world around them and their effort to adjust and redefine Switzerland's role as a leading financial center. The number of dictators trying to hide money was gradually decreasing. The powerful nations of the world were showing their concerns about money laundering, particularly that related to the drug trade. European competition in the international financial industry became increasingly intense. In this context, when the Swiss government announced its plan, and then took steps, to abolish the Form B accounts and pledged broader reform of the Swiss financial system, the news drew global attention.

Earlier Swiss legislation outlawing money laundering that went into effect on August 1, 1990, added teeth to the regulations. That legislation, with a provision of maximum penalties of five years in prison and one million Swiss francs (at that time the equivalent of US $734,200) in fines, covered accountants, lawyers, and portfolio managers who could be linked to any accounts related to money-laundering schemes.

## SIGNIFICANCE

The most important impact of the Swiss abolition of secret accounts was symbolic. Switzerland, the long-standing financial capital of the world, recognized and poised itself to adjust to ongoing changes in the world in general and in Europe in particular.

As a result of outlawing money laundering and insider trading and of abolishing secret accounts, some loss of existing as well prospective deposits was inevitable. The postreform impact on deposits was less than it might have been, however, because several Switzerland-based institutions, including Bank Julius Baer and Credit Suisse, had anticipated the change and stopped accepting Form B accounts as early as 1989.

Some other countries with extensive offshore banking, such as Austria, Luxembourg, Hungary, and the Bahamas, were expected to attract some of the secrecy-cherishing foreign depositors away from Swiss banks. None of these countries, however, had large-scale global financial institutions similar to those of Switzerland, and their strength, efficiency, and capacity to absorb and utilize deposits were no match for their Swiss counterparts. Furthermore, as the international momentum to eliminate money laundering continued, these countries increasingly came into the spotlight and were pressured to tighten their banking laws. Most began adjusting to the changing global conditions by introducing new regulations.

Private Swiss bankers expressed mixed feelings about the reforms. Many believed that the loss of deposits would be compensated for by improved image. The political stability of Switzerland, the discretion among private bankers, the abundance of sound institutions, the absence of foreign-exchange controls, tax avoidance, and

1991

secrecy were some of the factors, they argued, that would help them retain clients and continue to attract new ones. Swiss bankers were aware that Switzerland's charms, as the grandfather of all offshore investment centers, with 70 percent of total bank deposits belonging to foreigners, were quite faded. The Swiss franc, renowned for its stability, had experienced serious turbulence. The Swiss inflation rate, at about 5 percent, was no longer the lowest in Western Europe. Efforts by the Swiss National Bank to tighten monetary policy were not sure to restore the Swiss franc's once legendary financial health.

The Swiss reformed their banking system less for domestic reasons than for international ones. With the domestic market cooling, Switzerland had embarked on a large-scale global expansion of investment. The leading Swiss banks owned large brokerage houses in London and New York and managed hundreds of billions of dollars in corporate pension funds worldwide. The Swiss concluded that hiding dirty cash might prove risky and costly for them in the future. They understood their long-term interests in maintaining an image of providing reputable financial services to the world.

In an increasingly globalized economy, Switzerland faced stiff European competition. Frankfurt and Paris as well as London bid for bigger slices of the action in the international financial market. Many European depositors, traditionally concerned about socialism in their own countries, found their domestic banks preferable as socialist tendencies declined worldwide. Tax evasion remained an attractive feature of Swiss banks because it was not yet illegal in Switzerland. Declining top tax rates made tax evasion less worthwhile, however. Switzerland's share of offshore asset management was two-fifths of the world's total in 1991, and the nation's financial services, most of them driven by non-Swiss money, accounted for more than 10 percent of gross national product, employing 120,000 people and adding US$6.5 billion a year to Swiss tax revenue. Swiss stakes in this competition, therefore, were very high.

Switzerland also aggressively sought its share in the international stock market. It lagged behind London and Frankfurt in stock market operations, and the lack of a unified trading mechanism, high trading costs, poor liquidity, inadequate regulation, and lack of dealing transparency handicapped the growth of the Swiss stock market. Proposed reforms to augment the stock market, including the opening of share registers, were intended to attract more foreign vestment and push up undervalued share prices, which were depressed by restricted ownership. Once Switzerland joined the European Commu-

nity, the big Swiss banks would be well positioned, particularly with their subsidiaries or branches in EC countries. A strong deposit base at home and steady inflows of foreign capital would still be critical for overseas ambitions, particularly as half of Switzerland's 630 banks and near banks faced the prospect of merger or shutdown in the mid-1990's.

In the context of this global scenario, improving the tarnished image of its financial institutions was critical to Switzerland. The issue of secrecy, apparently at the core of reform, may have been misunderstood by many. To say that anonymous or numbered accounts were completely secret from the Swiss authorities before this change is incorrect; therefore, the steps to eliminate secret accounts and reform the system to bring everything into the open cannot be taken at face value.

The elimination of Form B accounts, the most secret Swiss accounts, may not have ended secrecy itself, but it did end a myth about such secrecy. The implied secrecy simply never existed. Anonymous numbered or secret accounts were governed by the Due Diligence Convention of the Swiss banks. The convention, a codified standard of ethics of the Swiss banking community first issued in 1977, remained in effect until September 30, 1992. To comply with the convention, banks were required to identify their clients and maintain records of their identities.

For an account representing a legal person (such as an offshore company) opened by a member of an association affiliated with the Swiss Institute of Auditing Firms and Certified Accountants or by a "person bound by professional confidentiality" (in most cases a Swiss lawyer), a bank could shift the burden of due diligence to such an agent. The bank could rely on a written statement made by the agent, using a standard account-opening form (Form B), that the beneficial owner had been identified by the agent and that the identified client was not abusing bank secrecy. Practically, the signing of Form B shifted the bank's obligation of due diligence to the Swiss lawyer or accountant.

Even before the reform, the identity of the secret owner of an account could be ascertained by a Swiss judge in criminal proceedings, whether initiated in Switzerland or abroad. In the case of criminal prosecution requested by a foreign country, assistance from Swiss banks was required (and bank secrecy possibly lifted) only in compliance with Swiss laws, particularly in the case of acts defined as crimes under the laws of both the requesting country and Switzerland. This created a loophole for cases involving tax evasion or violations of exchange control regulations, neither of which was illegal in Switzerland.

The immediate consequence of the new regulations was that the burden of due diligence was shifted back to banks, which would have to know their clients' identities systematically. The legal situation of account holders (or beneficial owners), as far as bank secrecy and the criminal sanctions provided for in case of its violation were concerned, would not be affected.

In sum, the abolition of Form B accounts did not change Swiss banking to any great degree. Swiss lawyers are still entitled to serve their clients and to be protected by Swiss professional secrecy as long as such activity takes place in the course of their "typical activity." The legendary Swiss bank secrecy and legal privilege thus continued unabated, although the myth of the truly anonymous or secret Swiss bank account came to an end.

It is not surprising that Swiss bankers insisted that privacy and discretion would remain key features of Swiss private banking. To minimize the possible impacts of the perceived end of bank secrecy, the Swiss Bankers Association assured the world, in a press release shortly after Form B accounts were abolished, that the decision "has not in any way changed the contents and significance of Swiss banking secrecy." The reforms did close many of the loopholes used in money laundering by drug lords, terrorist networks, unpopular and militarily ambitious dictators, and tax evaders, thus promoting a global environment for business and commerce that is more conducive to emerging international legal frameworks and norms.

—*Mohammad O. Farooq*

## FURTHER READING

Block, Alan A., and Constance A. Weaver. *All Is Clouded by Desire: Global Banking, Money Laundering, and International Organized Crime.* Westport, Conn.: Praeger, 2004. Examines the role of international banking in money laundering for organized crime. Focuses on a scandal featuring the Bank of New York, but provides information on Swiss banking practices as well.

Braitman, Ellen. "Swiss Expect to Weather Curbs on Account Secrecy." *American Banker* 156 (May 15, 1991): 6. Brief article intended for a general audience

discusses the views of Swiss bankers about the potential effects on their business of eliminating secret accounts.

Dunant, Olivier, and Michele Wassmer. "Swiss Bank Secrecy: Its Limits Under Swiss and International Laws." *Case Western Reserve Journal of International Law* 20 (Summer, 1988): 541-575. Article written before the reforms provides a thorough legal analysis of banking secrecy in Switzerland.

Gautier, Horace. "Anonymous Swiss Bank Accounts: The End of a Myth?" *International Financial Law Review*, July, 1991, 9-10. Presents an excellent nontechnical review of the implications of abolishing Form B accounts.

Kochan, Nick. "Service or Sophistication?" *Euromoney* (July, 1992): 84-86. Analyzes Swiss bankers' perspectives on how they can succeed in international competition after the reforms.

Lombardini, Carlo. "Swiss Keep It Secret." *International Financial Law Review*, July, 1991, 35-37. Discusses the legal implications behind the 1987 agreement between the Swiss Bankers Association and its members on the observance of care in accepting funds and on the practice of banking secrecy.

Ramasastry, Anita. "Secrets and Lies? Swiss Banks and International Human Rights." *Vanderbilt Journal of Transnational Law* 31, no. 2 (1998): 325-456. Discusses the uses of Swiss bank accounts by dictators and criminals, which contributed to the Swiss decision to end the practice of bank secrecy.

Swary, Itzhak, and Barry Topf. *Global Financial Deregulation: Commercial Banking at the Crossroads.* Cambridge, Mass.: Basil Blackwell, 1992. Survey of commercial banking in seven major industrial countries, including Switzerland, examines and analyzes the development, organization, regulatory environment, domestic and foreign competition, relationship to economic activity, and performance of commercial banks. Also reviews effects of various factors on the future role and functioning of commercial banks.

**SEE ALSO:** Mar. 31, 1980, and Oct. 15, 1982: U.S. Congress Deregulates Banks and Savings and Loans; 1998: Reparations Funds for Holocaust Victims Are Established.

1991

at state and federal levels. All of the legislation and policies at federal, state, and local levels were influenced by the public's demands for a reduction in the risk of developing lung cancer as a result of breathing secondhand smoke.

From the late 1960's onward, evidence on the health risks of involuntary smoking was increasingly accompanied by social action designed to protect individuals from exposure to sidestream smoke by regulating the circumstances in which smoking was permitted. Initially, state and local governments took legislative action that dealt with nonsmokers' rights to smoke-free workplaces. In the late 1970's, the private sector began to adopt policies aimed at protecting the health of nonsmokers: Restaurants adopted nonsmoking areas, hospitals restricted smoking, and hotels and motels offered nonsmoking rooms. This trend was the result of growing evidence about the health effects of both voluntary and involuntary smoking, but it also reflected changing public attitudes toward smoking. Since 1964, when the U.S. surgeon general's report on cigarette smoking first called widespread attention to health hazards, public smoking has declined and public support has increased for the right of nonsmokers to breathe smoke-free air.

Most legislation restricting smoking has been enacted at the state level. Cigarette smoking, for nearly a century, had been the subject of restrictive legislation intended to protect the public from fire and other safety hazards. The early legislation also stemmed from a moral crusade against cigarettes similar to the one against alcohol; this movement lost momentum when the enforcement of regulations proved controversial and difficult.

During the 1960's, as the health risks of smoking became more recognized, public policy on smoking began to focus on encouraging smokers to quit. Legislation began to employ more restrictive language to promote the safety and comfort of nonsmokers. Three federal agencies—the General Services Administration, the Department of Defense, and the Postal Service—administered 90 percent of federal office space. More than two million civilian and federal workers and two million military personnel were affected by the policies of these agencies, which drastically revised their policies on smoking to provide more protection to nonsmokers by prohibiting smoking in all federal buildings.

After the mid-1980's, many states and communities also passed laws regulating smoking in workplaces. Two provisions were common to many of the state laws: restricting smoking to designated areas and requiring signs to define smoking and nonsmoking areas. After 1991, smoking was banned on state-owned premises. Smoking policies in the private sector were revised in accordance with the federal and state policies. Many companies had banned smoking in their workplaces, whereas others allowed smoking but only in specially designated areas. Smoking on interstate transport vehicles such as buses, trains, and airplanes was regulated by federal agencies and often banned completely.

State and local legislation prohibited smoking in retail and department stores, and proprietors and trade associations supported these restrictions because of the cost of damage to facilities and merchandise from cigarette burns. Smoking regulations in restaurants developed through both private initiatives and public mandate. In 1974, the state of Connecticut was the first to require restaurants to have nonsmoking sections. Soon, the other states followed suit. Smoking restrictions in hotels and motels came mainly in response to customer demands, although later state and local regulations were put in place.

State legislation, state and local school board regulations, and individual school policies initially regulated smoking by students in schools, but eventually smoking was banned within school buildings and allowed only in designated areas outside the school building. Restrictions on smoking in health care facilities were considered particularly important, because many patients in those facilities have conditions that could be worsened by exposure to tobacco smoke. Smoking was eventually banned completely in all health care facilities across the United States.

*—Palaniappa Krishnan*

## FURTHER READING

Douville, Judith A. *Active and Passive Smoking Hazards in the Workplace*. New York: Van Nostrand Reinhold, 1990. Presents excellent discussion of the dangers posed by smoking in the workplace for both smokers and nonsmokers. Somewhat technical, but accessible to general readers.

Jenkins, R. A., M. R. Guerin, and B. A. Tomkins. *The Chemistry of Environmental Tobacco Smoke: Composition and Measurement*. 2d ed. Boca Raton, Fla.: Lewis, 2000. Technical study provides ample data and references useful for the consideration of ETS as a public health issue.

Lee, P. N. *Environmental Tobacco Smoke and Mortality*. Basel, Switzerland: Karger, 1992. Gives a detailed review of epidemiological evidence for environmental tobacco smoke as a cause of cancer, heart disease, and other illnesses in nonsmoking adults. Intended for scientists, but includes several sections accessible to nonscientists.

U.S. Department of Health and Human Services. *Smoking, Tobacco, and Health: A Fact Book.* Atlanta, Ga.: Author, 1987. Presents a discussion of smoking and its health effects in lay terms.

U.S. Environmental Protection Agency. *Respiratory Health Effects of Passive Smoking: Lung Cancer and Other Disorders.* Washington, D.C.: Author, 1992. Discusses the respiratory health effects of passive smoking, with particular focus on lung cancer. Scientific in presentation, but each chapter is summarized, and many sections are accessible to nonscientists.

Watson, Ronald R., and Mark Witten, eds. *Environmental Tobacco Smoke.* Boca Raton, Fla.: CRC Press, 2001. Collection of technical essays describes the health effects of exposure to ETS among pregnant women, young people, the elderly, and other groups.

**SEE ALSO:** June, 1988: Canada Passes the Tobacco Products Control Act; June 13, 1988: First Monetary Damages Are Awarded to the Estate of a Cigarette Smoker; 1989: U.S. Surgeon General Reports on Tobacco and Health; July 3, 1997: Mississippi Settles Lawsuit with Cigarette Makers.

## June 12-15, 1991
# ERUPTION OF MOUNT PINATUBO

*The eruption of Mount Pinatubo resulted in the deaths of more than seven hundred people locally, and aerosols injected into the stratosphere affected both the earth's ozone layer and global temperatures.*

**LOCALE:** Mount Pinatubo, Luzon, Philippines
**CATEGORIES:** Disasters; environmental issues

### KEY FIGURES
*James E. Hansen* (b. 1941), director of Goddard Institute for Space Studies
*S. Fred Singer* (b. 1924), director of the Science and Environmental Policy Project
*John R. Christy* (fl. late twentieth century), scientist with the Earth System Science Laboratory at the University of Alabama
*Charles D. Keeling* (1928-2005), American climate scientist at Mauna Loa Observatory

### SUMMARY OF EVENT
Mount Pinatubo lies 100 kilometers northwest of Manila in the Philippine Islands. Pinatubo erupted in about 1356, sending flows of hot ash down its slopes and growing to a height of 1,743 meters. By the time the Spanish conquistadores arrived in the islands, the volcano had been inactive for two centuries. To these early explorers, Mount Pinatubo was but one of two hundred dormant volcanos that dotted the land. Then, some 635 years after its last eruption, Mount Pinatubo began rumbling as lava rose beneath it.

Scientists set up a monitoring network and watched as the volcano's internal pressures mounted. They used tiltmeters to detect bulging of the mountainside, seismometers to measure the small earthquakes caused by magma (molten rock) thrusting its way toward the surface, and gas detectors to measure the types and amounts of volcanic gases being released. Pinatubo thus became an important instructional tool concerning events that precede a major eruption. Further measurements made during and after the volcano's eruption in 1991 have played an important role in the continuing debate over mathematical climate models, which predict greenhouse warming.

On April 2, 1991, an explosion within Mount Pinatubo blew open a geothermal area leaving a one-kilometer-long line of new fumaroles—holes that emit volcanic fumes and steam. Various minor quakes and explosions occurred with growing intensity and frequency, causing the local authorities to evacuate ever-larger regions. The U.S. government evacuated the dependents of military personnel from Clark Air Force Base, which lies approximately 20 kilometers east of Pinatubo's summit.

More than two thousand minor quakes were recorded on June 7, as magma worked its way to the surface. Two days later, Pinatubo erupted, spewing forth lava and volcanic gases. By June 11, a large lava dome appeared near the summit, generally a sign that a large explosion is imminent. Three tremendous explosions rocked the volcano the next day. The first occurred early in the morning and lasted for fifteen minutes. The second, more powerful, blast occurred later that morning and sent a tephra (volcanic ash) column thundering 20 kilometers into the sky. The third blast occurred slightly before noon. Grapefruit-sized pumice stones peppered the countryside, including the Clark air base. Ash fell everywhere; it

1991

2575

so thick in the air that day turned to night, and people had to cover their faces with cloth or plastic to keep the ash from getting into their eyes and noses.

Pyroclastic flows—flows of hot gases, steam, and incandescent ash—cascaded down the volcano's slopes. Riding on a cushion of entrapped air, one pyroclastic flow traveled 15 kilometers from the vent; some flows would eventually reach twice that distance. Such flows can reach speeds of 120 kilometers per hour, and at temperatures of thousands of degrees Celsius, they kill any living thing they touch. In contrast, lava flows so slowly that it destroys only things that cannot move out of its way, such as trees and buildings.

Another major eruption occurred at Pinatubo on June 13, and by June 14, fifty-five thousand people had been evacuated from the villages within a 20-kilometer radius of the volcano. The volcanic activity then appeared to have subsided, but that afternoon the quiet was shattered by the largest eruption yet. A heavy rain was easily brushed aside by the ash plume, which shot upward at twice the speed of sound to a height of 30 kilometers. Pyroclastic flows again snaked down the mountain's flanks, destroying villages and vegetation.

The next morning brought Pinatubo's biggest eruption. On June 15, 1991, a gigantic explosion ripped the top from the mountain and thrust a plume of ash an astounding 40 kilometers into the sky. Ash darkened the sky in regions as far away as Manila, where it fell so thickly that drivers had to stop from time to time to brush it from their windshields. Earthquakes rocked the region as subterranean caverns, newly emptied of lava, collapsed. The eruption thundered on for fifteen hours. The situation was judged to be so dangerous at the Clark air base that an additional fifteen thousand Americans were evacuated. Ash collected on roofs and became heavy with water from the monsoon rains. Unable to bear the weight, buildings collapsed.

Pinatubo erupted intermittently throughout June and into July. Lahars—mudflows of volcanic ash and water—posed a great danger both during the eruptions and for years afterward. Because of the added weight of the ash, a lahar can be much more destructive than water alone. It is estimated that Mount Pinatubo produced more than 8 cubic kilometers of volcanic ash, enough to cover all of Washington, D.C., with a layer of ash nearly fifty meters thick. Much of this ash fell on Pinatubo's slopes, leaving it poised to strike the countryside below. Whenever ash is saturated with rain, it becomes fluidized and can flow downslope with very little friction to slow it. During the monsoon rains, lahars rampaged across the countryside for up to 80 kilometers, generally following riverways, destroying bridges, roads, houses, and even entire towns. For example, on August 20, lahars five meters high flowed down ten rivers, damaging more than nine thousand homes and killing thirty-one people. Lahars covered farmland with ash layers one meter or more thick, making cultivation of the fields impossible. They filled river channels with mud so that the rivers either no longer flowed or flooded over their banks.

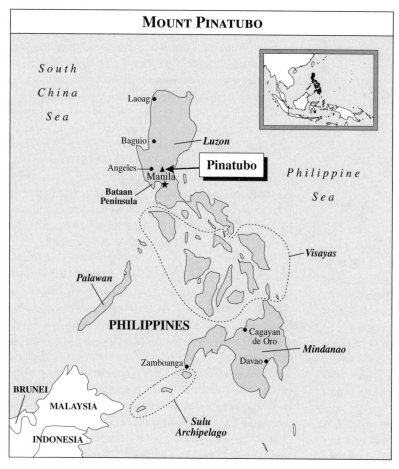

**MOUNT PINATUBO**

South China Sea

Laoag

Baguio

Luzon

Angeles
Manila
**Pinatubo**

Bataan
Peninsula

Philippine Sea

Palawan

Visayas

**PHILIPPINES**

Cagayan de Oro

Zamboanga

Davao

Mindanao

BRUNEI

MALAYSIA

Sulu Archipelago

INDONESIA

---

## IMPORTANT WORLDWIDE VOLCANIC EVENTS

| | |
|---|---|
| 5000 B.C.E. | The volcano now known as Crater Lake, in Oregon, erupts, sending pyroclastic flows as far as 37 miles from the vent; 25 cubic miles of material are erupted as a caldera forms from the collapse of the mountaintop. |
| August 24, 79 C.E. | Vesuvius erupts, burying Pompeii and Herculaneum, two cities in what is now the Italian region of Campania. |
| June 8, 1783-February 7, 1784 | The Laki fissure eruption in Iceland produces the largest lava flow in historic time, with major climatic effects. |
| April 5, 1815 | The dramatic explosion of Tambora, approximately 250 miles east of Java, the largest volcanic event in modern history, produces atmospheric and climatic effects for the next two years. Frosts occur every month in New England during 1816, the Year Without a Summer. |
| August 26, 1883 | A cataclysmic eruption of Krakatau, an island volcano in Indonesia, is heard 2,968 miles away. Many die as pyroclastic flows race over pumice rafts floating on the surface of the sea; many more die in the tsunamis that follow the eruption. |
| May 8, 1902 | Mount Pelée, on the northern end of the island of Martinique in the Caribbean, sends violent pyroclastic flows into the city of Saint-Pierre, killing all but 2 of approximately 30,000 inhabitants. |
| June 6, 1912 | Katmai erupts in Alaska, producing an ash flow that creates the Valley of Ten Thousand Smokes. |
| February 20, 1943 | Paricutín comes into existence in a cultivated field in Mexico. The eruption of this volcano continues for nine years. |
| March 30, 1956 | Bezymianny, in Russia, erupts with a violent lateral blast, stripping trees of their bark more than 18 miles away. |
| May 18, 1980 | Mount St. Helens, in Washington State, erupts with a directed blast to the north, moving pyroclastic flows at velocities up to more than 900 feet per second. |
| November 13, 1985 | Mudflows from the eruption of Nevado del Ruiz, in Colombia, kill at least 23,000 people. |
| August 21, 1986 | At Lake Nyos, in Cameroon, carbon dioxide built up from volcanic emanations escapes and kills more than 1,700 people and some 8,000 head of livestock. |
| June 12-15, 1991 | Mount Pinatubo, in the Philippines, erupts after having been dormant for four hundred years, killing more than 700 people and injecting aerosols into the stratosphere that have long-term effects on both Earth's ozone layer and global temperatures. |
| September-November, 1996 | Eruption of lava beneath a glacier in the Grimsvötn Caldera, Iceland, melts huge quantities of ice, producing major flooding. |

1991

---

### SIGNIFICANCE

The region immediately surrounding Mount Pinatubo became a vast wasteland. Damage estimates were in the billions of dollars. Hundreds of square kilometers of cropland were destroyed. More than 108,000 houses were partially damaged or destroyed, leaving more than 200,000 people homeless. At least 722 people were killed: 281 in the initial eruption, 83 in lahars, and 358 as a result of exposure to diseases such as measles and pneumonia in the evacuation camps. Clark Air Force Base was ruined. Ironically, the U.S. and Philippine governments were engaged in negotiations over the future of the air base when the eruption of Pinatubo intervened and left little to negotiate. For those living near Mount Pinatubo, the eruption was a tragedy of the first magnitude.

The eruption of Pinatubo also had global physical consequences. Every eruption injected tremendous amounts of dust, water vapor, carbon dioxide, sulfur dioxide, and hydrochloric acid into the atmosphere. Each of these substances might be expected to affect climate locally or globally. The modern-day study of the effects of volcanoes on climate goes back to Benjamin Franklin, who described a peculiar fog that hung over northern Europe in 1783 and made the sun's rays so faint that the summer was cooler than normal. Franklin suggested that this fog might be attributable to the volcanic eruption at Laki, Iceland. Franklin had no way to verify his conjecture, but Pinatubo's investigators were able to monitor the dust cloud produced by the volcano from space. Dust can remain in the stratosphere for up to two years, and, by tracing its progress, scientists gained a better understanding of the dynamics of the stratosphere.

One of the most important challenges in environmental science is to predict the effects that human beings have on climate. In order to do this, scientists use mathematical models—that is, sets of physical laws expressed as mathematical equations. Herein lies the most important impact of Pinatubo's eruption: It provided scientists with a way to see if any of the existing climate models were good enough to predict what actually happened.

This study is more than a matter of mere academic interest because of its significance in the understanding of the greenhouse effect. This effect is so named because sunlight shines in through the windows of a greenhouse with the result that the inside of the greenhouse becomes hotter than the air outside. Although the physical mechanisms at work are different, a similar thing happens with the earth's atmosphere, in that sunlight shines in through the atmosphere and heats the ground, but certain gases (called greenhouse gases) in the atmosphere trap some of the heat and keep it from being radiated back into space. This trapping keeps the surface of the earth warmer than it would be without the greenhouse gases. Three of the most important greenhouse gases are water vapor, carbon dioxide, and methane. Human beings increase the amount of carbon dioxide in the atmosphere chiefly through the burning of fossil fuels, and climate models predict that this should lead to a global temperature increase.

James E. Hansen, the director of the Goddard Institute for Space Studies, galvanized the scientific and political community when he testified before the U.S. Congress in 1988 that global warming as a result of an increase in carbon dioxide released by human beings was already occurring. Jeremy Leggett, the director of science in Greenpeace International's Atmosphere and Energy Campaign, agreed. He acknowledged the uncertainties in the climate models but added that, as in the case of military defense, action is needed to prevent the occurrence

of the worst-case scenario, in which coastal cities may be flooded as polar ice melts and drought-induced famines become widespread. S. Fred Singer, the director of the Science and Environmental Policy Project (SEPP), pointed out that, so far, global climate models had not been accurate enough to reproduce the past climate, let alone to predict the future climate.

What has been learned from the Pinatubo eruption that might clarify the issue of global warming? Although some results are encouraging, climate models are not yet good enough to forecast climate changes accurately. John R. Christy and his colleagues with the Earth System Science Laboratory at the University of Alabama began using satellites to monitor microwave emissions from the earth. With this information, they were able to obtain a truly global average of the temperature of the lower few kilometers of the atmosphere. Some climate models predicted that Pinatubo's eruption would cool the earth by about 0.5 degrees Celsius for one or two years and that increased greenhouse gases would warm the earth about 0.4 degrees Celsius over ten years. Christy and his group found that Pinatubo cooled the earth by 0.65 degrees Celsius, in reasonable agreement with the prediction. Using fifteen years of data, however, they found little or no evidence for any increased greenhouse warming.

Even though Pinatubo released large amounts of carbon dioxide, the amount of carbon dioxide in the air actually decreased after the eruption, according to Charles D. Keeling, who operated the gas analyzer at Mauna Loa in Hawaii. It was speculated that the slight cooling of the earth caused by Pinatubo allowed more carbon dioxide to dissolve in the ocean.

Satellite observation showed that Pinatubo released twenty times more sulfur dioxide than would have been expected based on an analysis of the cooled lava using traditional techniques. The sulfur dioxide was ejected high into the stratosphere along with water vapor, where the two combined to form tiny droplets of sulfuric acid. A suspension of tiny particles in a gas is called an aerosol. The estimated 30 megatons, or 30 million metric tons, of sulfuric acid aerosol produced by Pinatubo played three important roles. First, it formed a haze in the stratosphere, which joined the volcanic dust in blocking sunlight to produce global cooling. Second, it eventually drifted down to the upper troposphere, where the sulfuric acid droplets acted as nucleation sites around which water droplets formed. This produced high cirrus clouds that again blocked sunlight and contributed to global cooling. Third, the sulfuric acid made the chlorine already in the stratosphere more active in destroying ozone.

It is estimated that this caused an additional 20 percent loss in ozone over the poles. Apparently, the four megatons of hydrochloric acid produced by the volcano itself did not rise to the stratosphere but instead were quickly washed from the volcanic cloud by rain.

Scientists have learned a great deal by carefully monitoring the effects of the eruption of Mount Pinatubo. The better understanding of nature that such studies can achieve is expected to lead in turn to a better understanding of human effects on the environment.

—*Charles W. Rogers*

## FURTHER READING

Abrahamson, Dean Edwin, ed. *The Challenge of Global Warming*. Washington, D.C.: Island Press, 1989. Collection of essays written for the layperson provides an overview of global warming, its causes, and its effects. Contributors are scientists writing in their areas of expertise. Includes an interesting chapter about possible actions to take and an extensive recommended reading list.

Anderegg, C. R. *The Ash Warriors*. Washington, D.C.: U.S. Government Printing Office, 2005. Presents an account of Mount Pinatubo's eruption and the heroic evacuation of Clark Air Force Base.

Castro, Eddee Rh. *Pinatubo: The Eruption of the Century*. Quezon City, Philippines: Phoenix, 1991. Provides brief, accurate treatments of the eruption and its global effects as well as its local effects on the land and people. Includes more than one hundred photographs.

Leggett, Jeremy. "Global Warming: The Worst Case." *Bulletin of the Atomic Scientists* 48 (June, 1992): 28-33. Presents an overview of the problem and the worst-case consequences. Argues against taking speculative action.

Seitz, Stefan. *The Aeta at the Mt. Pinatubo, Philippines: A Minority Group Coping with Disaster*. Translated by Michael Bletzer. Quezon City, Philippines: New Day, 2004. Details the evacuation of the aboriginal people of Mount Pinatubo, the group hardest hit by the eruption.

Shimizu, Hiromu. *The Orphans of Pinatubo*. Manila: Solidaridad, 2001. Presents stories from the Aeta of the eruption and life following the event.

Simkin, Tom, and Richard S. Fiske, eds. *Krakatau 1883: The Volcanic Eruption and Its Effects*. Washington, D.C.: Smithsonian Institution Press, 1983. Contains eyewitness accounts and various studies of the eruption and its climatic and other effects. Features Benjamin Franklin's comments on the climatic effects of an Icelandic volcano. Includes pictures, maps, figures, bibliography, and index.

Singer, S. Fred. "Warming Theories Need Warning Label." *Bulletin of the Atomic Scientists* 48 (June, 1992): 34-39. Discusses the great uncertainties involved in predictions of global warming and recommends further study of the issue.

_____, ed. *Global Climate Change: Human and Natural Influences*. New York: Paragon House, 1989. Collection of essays by twenty-one scientists addresses many topics related to climate change, including the atmosphere, the oceans, nuclear winter, asteroid impacts, and volcanoes. More cautious and optimistic than many other works about global warming. Intended for readers with at least some background in the physical sciences.

1991

**SEE ALSO:** May 18, 1980: Mount St. Helens Erupts; May 16, 1985: Researchers Discover a Hole in the Ozone Layer; Aug. 21, 1986: African Lake Emits Toxic Gas; Nov., 1988: United Nations Creates a Panel to Study Climate Change; June 29, 1990: U.N. Agreement Protects Ozone Layer; June 3-14, 1992: Earth Summit Convenes in Rio de Janeiro.

## June 25, 1991
# CIVIL WAR BEGINS IN YUGOSLAVIA

*Civil war in Yugoslavia unleashed ethnic violence and resulted in the atomization of Yugoslavia into separate republics.*

**LOCALE:** Yugoslavia (now Croatia, Slovenia, Bosnia and Herzegovina, Serbia and Montenegro, and Macedonia)

**CATEGORIES:** Government and politics; wars, uprisings, and civil unrest

### KEY FIGURES

*Alija Izetbegović* (1925-2003), president of Bosnia and Herzegovina, 1990-1996

*Radovan Karadžić* (b. 1945), Bosnian Serb leader

*Stjepan Kljuić* (b. 1939), Bosnian Croat leader

*Slobodan Milošević* (b. 1941), president of Serbia, 1989-1997

*Ratko Mladić* (b. 1943), commander of the Bosnian Serb army

*Franjo Tudjman* (1922-1999), president of Croatia, 1990-1999

### SUMMARY OF EVENT

Ever since the seventh century, when three Slavic tribes—Serbs, Croats, and Slovenes—migrated from Russia to the Balkans, the groups had maintained their separate existence, until the formation of the Kingdom of the Serbs, Croats, and Slovenes by King Alexander I on December 1, 1918. This separate existence has been the outcome of fundamental historical and cultural differences among the groups. Although Croats, Slovenes, Serbs, and Bosnians speak basically the same language, Serbs and Bosnians write with the Eastern or Cyrillic alphabet, whereas Croats and Slovenes use the Western or Roman alphabet. In addition, Croatians are Catholics, Serbs are Orthodox Christians, and a substantial proportion of the population of Bosnia and Herzegovina are Kosovo Muslims.

Hostilities between Serbs and Croats date back to the Schism of 1054, and those between Serbs and Muslims may be traced to the invasion of the region by the Ottoman Turks in 1463. The feeling of "otherness" between Serbs and Croats was further fueled by the fact that the latter belonged to the Austro-Hungarian Empire and the former belonged to the Ottoman Empire. The rivers Sava and Danube, serving as borders between Croatia and Serbia, once demarcated the two imperial regions. Serbo-

Croatian antagonism also colored the relationship of both Serbs and Croats with the Bosnian Muslims. Croats have appeared to be less hostile toward the Muslims, viewing them as heretics but redeemable through baptism. Serbs have viewed the Muslims as both heretics and traitors. A great number of Bosnian Muslim converts were adherents of a heretical Christian sect called Bogomils (meaning "pleasing to God") who had in fact invited the Turks with a view to protecting themselves against invasion by the Hungarian army.

In 1929, Alexander I founded the state of Yugoslavia ("land of the South Slavs") by reorganizing the kingdom into six republics—Slovenia, Croatia, Bosnia-Herzegovina, Serbia, Montenegro, and Macedonia—and the two autonomous provinces of Vojvodina and Kosovo. The concept of Yugoslavism was problematic because it implied, essentially, the unification of culturally and ethnically diverse southern Slavs under Serbian hegemony. Following World War II, however, all ethnic and religious groups of Yugoslavia remained united under the leadership of Tito's slogan of "Brotherhood and Unity"; the Socialist Federal People's Republic of Yugoslavia was a Communist state but free from Soviet control. Tito's one-party state, however, while depriving the national communities of their democratic rights, deliberately devised a constitution in 1974 to keep Serbia relatively weak while according a position of primacy to the Serbs in the bureaucracy, the secret police, and the army and making Belgrade the national capital. Naturally, Serbs controlled the economic system.

The different levels of development among the various nationalities in Yugoslavia have paralleled ethnocultural differences. Economically, Slovenia and Croatia became more developed than the other republics, whereas the less-developed ones were more populous, and Serbia and Montenegro, in particular, became politically stronger. In general, however, the Yugoslav economic system was regimented by the state apparatus manned mostly by Serbs.

Although the constitution of 1974 divided economic enterprises into Basic Organizations of Associated Labor and fostered a semblance of market system and private ownership, economic policies were not based on rational market criteria; rather, they were administrative and arbitrary. The performance of the Yugoslav economy during 1953-1989 revealed the negative outcome of a nonmarket and centralized economic system. Prime

Minister Ante Marković's attempted reforms of 1990-1991 provided for a "heavy" convertible currency, balanced budget, restrictive monetary policy, wage freeze, selective relaxation of price controls, and, above all, private enterprises. These reforms were subverted by the basic flaw of the top-heavy economic system, which did not allow any scope for republics to take independent action at a time when the unity of the Yugoslav market collapsed because of ethnonationalist movements that seized the Balkan world following the breakup of the Soviet Union and the demise of Communism in Eastern Europe in 1989-1990.

Yugoslavia's political disintegration was initiated by the abortive "Croatian Spring," a separatist movement of 1970-1971 that called for the establishment of a sovereign Croatian state. This crisis prompted Serbia, led by the Socialist Party of President Slobodan Milošević, to

be especially watchful of Albanian nationalist upheaval in Kosovo, considered Serbia's "mythical heart." The Kosovars agitated against Serb control in 1989-1990, and Kosovo's example was followed by Croatian and Slovenian secession on June 25, 1991, under the leadership of Franjo Tudjman and Milan Kučan, respectively. The secession of these two republics led the Serbs to realize that a Greater Serbia would be the best possible guarantee for the Serbs in diaspora (17 percent in Croatia, 34 percent in Bosnia-Herzegovina, 55 percent in Vojvodina, 10 percent in Kosovo).

Hours after the Croatian-Slovenian declaration of independence, the Serb-dominated Yugoslav army moved into Slovenia. By the time the European Community endorsed United Nations sanctions against this action, Serbia controlled 30 percent of Croatian territory and had revoked the autonomy of Kosovo (thus alarming the Al-

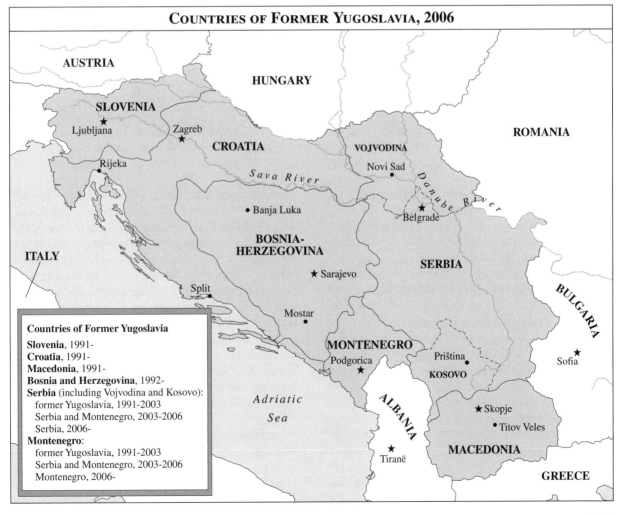

**COUNTRIES OF FORMER YUGOSLAVIA, 2006**

**Countries of Former Yugoslavia**

**Slovenia**, 1991-
**Croatia**, 1991-
**Macedonia**, 1991-
**Bosnia and Herzegovina**, 1992-
**Serbia** (including Vojvodina and Kosovo):
　　former Yugoslavia, 1991-2003
　　Serbia and Montenegro, 2003-2006
　　Serbia, 2006-
**Montenegro**:
　　former Yugoslavia, 1991-2003
　　Serbia and Montenegro, 2003-2006
　　Montenegro, 2006-

*Serb troops and civilians walk by a body in the fallen city of Vukovar, Croatia.* (AP/Wide World Photos)

banian majority there) and Vojvodina (thereby making the adjacent Hungarians nervous).

The Serbo-Croatian developments affected Bosnia-Herzegovina most strongly. Since 1971, this republic had been granted the status of "three constituent nations"—Muslims (Serbs and Croats whose ancestors had converted under Ottoman rule, constituting 43 percent of the population), Serbs, and Croats (17 percent)—who had to agree on any act of secession. The German recognition of Croatia in January, 1992, forced Bosnia's hand. Bosnia's Muslim president, Alija Izetbegović, was forced into choosing between joining the truncated Serbian Yugoslavia—something none of his people would have accepted—or declaring independence.

A plebiscite held February 28 and March 1, 1992, that showed a joint Croat-Muslim majority in Bosnia met with the European Community criteria of referendum validating independence but violated the 1971 principle of three constituent nations. The Bosnian proclamation of independence on March 1 was thus opposed by the

Bosnian Serbs. On March 18, Izetbegović, Radovan Karadžić (leader of the Bosnian Serbs), and Stjepan Kljuić (leader of the Bosnian Croats) met in Lisbon, Portugal, and agreed on an ethnically based canton system for Bosnia and Herzegovina. Upon his return home, however, Izetbegović was persuaded by his own hard-liners to renege on the Lisbon agreement. On April 6, the weekend of formal recognition of independent Bosnia and Herzegovina by the European Community, the battle of Sarajevo began, initially between Serbs and Croats, with Croats being aided by Bosnian Muslims. By the late spring of 1992, Serbian forces joined by the Yugoslav National Army seized Sarajevo, which was inhabited mostly by Muslims.

### SIGNIFICANCE

The European Community and a U.N.-sponsored trade embargo against Serbia could not prevent the de facto proclamation of Republika Srpska (or Serb Republic) by Karadžić's Serb nationalists commanded by General

Ratko Mladić. Bosnia and Herzegovina subsequently witnessed massive "ethnic cleansing." The U.N. sanctions against Serbia and Montenegro on June 1, 1992, failed to stop the massacre. Indeed, the sanctions tended to favor the better-armed Serbs.

In time, North Atlantic Treaty Organization (NATO) forces intervened and the tide was turning against the Serbs in 1995, disposing them to accept American demands that they negotiate a peace agreement with Bosnia and Croatia. The Dayton Accords of that year produced an agreement that ironically recognized what Bosnian Serbs had demanded all along, an autonomous Serb Republic within Bosnia. The follow-up to the Dayton Accords in subsequent years saw the repatriation of displaced persons and refugees, new elections, and the restoration of peace and stability, even as war crimes trials brought numerous Serbs, including Mladić, as well as Croats and Bosnian Muslims to account for the crimes committed on all sides against innocent populations.

—*Narasingha P. Sil*

## FURTHER READING

Danopoulos, Constantine, and Kostas Messas, eds. *Crisis in the Balkans: Views from the Participants*. Boulder, Colo.: Westview Press, 1996. Collection of essays provides historical background on each region of the Balkans as well as discussion of contemporary concerns. Written from the perspectives of regional and international participants in the Balkan crisis and divided into discreet chapters on each region of Yugoslavia as well as the Balkans.

Djordjevic, Dimitrije. "The Yugoslav Phenomenon." In *The Columbia History of Eastern Europe in the Twentieth Century*, edited by Joseph Held. New York: Columbia University Press, 1992. Presents excellent analysis of the historical background of the civil war.

Glenny, Misha. *The Fall of Yugoslavia: The Third Balkan War*. 3d rev. ed. New York: Penguin Books, 1996. Journalist and scholar with linguistic competence and intimate knowledge of Eastern Europe and the Balkans provides a reliable guide to the complicated issues and developments of the civil war.

Pinson, Mark, ed. *The Muslims of Bosnia-Herzegovina*. 2d ed. Cambridge, Mass.: Harvard University Press, 1996. Anthology contains five excellent articles that are helpful for anyone trying to understand the history of the Muslims of Yugoslavia from the Middle Ages down to the civil war. Ivo Banac's "Bosnian Muslims: From Religious Community to Socialist Nationhood and Post-Communist Statehood, 1918-1992" is especially highly recommended.

Ramet, Sabrina Petra, and Ljubisa Adamovich, eds. *Beyond Yugoslavia: Politics, Economics, and Culture in a Shattered Community*. Boulder, Colo.: Westview Press, 1995. Collaborative enterprise among American, Croatian, and Serbian scholars provides an excellent analysis of the multiple issues plaguing a polyglot state.

Rieff, David. *Slaughterhouse: Bosnia and the Failure of the West*. New York: Simon & Schuster, 1996. Provocative and passionate study of the carnage in Bosnia and Herzegovina provides an account of the escalation of the civil war.

Thompson, Mark. *A Paper House: The Ending of Yugoslavia*. New York: Pantheon Books, 1992. Insightful, scholarly, and eminently readable and dependable travelogue and firsthand account of the civil war by the London correspondent for the Slovenian periodical *Mladina*.

**SEE ALSO:** May 4, 1980: Death of Tito; July-Nov., 1988: Ethnic Violence Erupts in Yugoslavian Provinces; Oct.-Nov., 1991: Yugoslav Army Shells Dubrovnik; Feb. 21, 1992: United Nations Authorizes Troop Deployment to the Balkans; Feb. 13, 1995: Serbs Face Charges at the International Criminal Tribunal for Yugoslavia; Nov. 21, 1995: Dayton Negotiations Produce Bosnian Peace Accord; Jan. 14, 2000: Hague Court Convicts Bosnian Croats of 1993 Massacre.

1991

# July 1, 1991
# BUSH NOMINATES SECOND AFRICAN AMERICAN TO THE SUPREME COURT

*When Thurgood Marshall, the nation's first African American Supreme Court justice, retired in 1991, President George H. W. Bush nominated another black judge, Clarence Thomas, to replace Marshall. Thomas's confirmation hearings, contentious from the start, became truly sensational when Thomas was accused of sexual harassment by Anita Hill, a law professor who had previously worked for Thomas.*

**LOCALE:** Washington, D.C.
**CATEGORIES:** Organizations and institutions; government and politics

**KEY FIGURES**
*Clarence Thomas* (b. 1948), associate justice of the United States beginning in 1991
*George H. W. Bush* (b. 1924), president of the United States, 1989-1993
*Thurgood Marshall* (1908-1993), first African American to serve as associate justice of the United States, 1967-1991
*Anita Hill* (b. 1956), law professor who worked for Clarence Thomas at the Equal Employment Opportunity Commission

**SUMMARY OF EVENT**
Thurgood Marshall was the first African American to serve as a justice on the U.S. Supreme Court. At the time of his appointment in 1967, he was a renowned advocate for civil rights. As counsel for the National Association for the Advancement of Colored People (NAACP), Marshall had argued thirty-two civil rights cases before the Supreme Court, winning twenty-nine, including the landmark school desegregation case, *Brown v. Board of Education of Topeka, Kansas* (1954). He had been a federal appeals court judge and U.S. solicitor general. He was known for his concern for racial equality and the rights of the criminally accused. When Marshall retired from the Supreme Court in 1991, President George H. W. Bush, a Republican, was under intense political pressure to replace Marshall with another African American. On July 1, 1991, President Bush nominated Clarence Thomas, an African American, for Marshall's seat on the Court. Thomas was as conservative as Marshall had been liberal.

In 1987, President Ronald Reagan had nominated Robert H. Bork to the Supreme Court. Bork, like Thomas,

was known to have a conservative judicial philosophy. Acrimonious hearings before the Senate Judiciary Committee culminated in the Senate's rejection of Bork's nomination by a vote of fifty-eight to forty-two. The approach taken by Bork's opponents to attack him personally led to the coining of the term "to bork," which is defined in the *Oxford English Dictionary* as follows: "To defame or vilify (a person) systematically, esp. in the mass media, usually with the aim of preventing his or her appointment to public office." Four years later, abortion rights activists and other liberal interest groups mobilized for the "borking" of Clarence Thomas. They attacked on two fronts, emphasizing Thomas's purported lack of qualifications and his ultraconservative judicial philosophy.

Announcing the appointment, President Bush called Thomas "the best person for this position." Critics of the nomination pointed out Thomas's slight judicial experience, only a year and four months on the U.S. Court of Appeals for the District of Columbia Circuit. His other experience included eight years as chairman of the Equal Employment Opportunity Commission (EEOC). Thurgood Marshall, by comparison, had authored ninety-eight majority decisions in his four years on the U.S. Court of Appeals for the Second Circuit. Thomas's supporters countered that many Supreme Court justices had little or no judicial experience before they were named to the Court, including such highly esteemed justices as Joseph Story, Earl Warren, William H. Rehnquist, Felix Frankfurter, and Louis D. Brandeis. At the heart of the confirmation controversy, however, were Thomas's views on such contentious issues as abortion rights, affirmative action, and the constitutional role of the Supreme Court vis-à-vis the legislative and executive branches of the U.S. government.

Clarence Thomas was born in 1948 in the small town of Pin Point, Georgia. He was raised by his grandparents, attended Catholic schools, and graduated from Holy Cross College in 1971 and Yale Law School in 1974. During his confirmation hearings, Thomas explained how the values imparted to him by his grandparents and the nuns who taught him led him to believe that hard work and the overcoming of obstacles, rather than preferential treatment based on race, would lead to a better life for black Americans. He expressed his beliefs that affirmative action had been of greatest benefit to middle-class rather than poor blacks and that government entitlements create a cycle of dependence and poverty, ultimately doing more harm than good for the poor. Thomas's detractors saw him as a beneficiary of affirmative action who was hypocritically attempting to deny the same help to others.

Thomas's confirmation hearings before the Senate Judiciary Committee began on September 10, 1991. The first attack on Thomas targeted his affinity for "natural law." Some senators worried that such a belief might lead Thomas to subordinate constitutional principles to principles of dubious provenance, such as the notion that an unborn child has the rights of persons, a position that could lead to the overturning of abortion rights. Thomas explained that he viewed certain principles of natural law—such as equality and limited government with the consent of the governed—as guides for how properly to interpret the U.S. Constitution, so as to guard against both run-amok majorities and run-amok judges.

Thomas was asked numerous times for his views on abortion, which he resisted providing. He claimed that he had never "debated" the 1973 abortion case *Roe v. Wade*. This response was met with skepticism, and Thomas lost some credibility that he would need when the hearings soon took a dramatic turn.

The Judiciary Committee sent the nomination to the full Senate without a recommendation for confirmation. The Senate vote was originally scheduled for October 8, but on October 6, the existence of sensational allegations of sexual impropriety against the nominee were leaked to the press. Thomas requested a delay so that the Judiciary Committee would have time to investigate the charges before the Senate voted. On October 11, the hearings reopened, with the public's attention firmly riveted by the sensational allegations.

The accuser was Anita Hill, a law professor at the University of Oklahoma who had worked for Thomas in the past, first at the U.S. Department of Education and later at the EEOC, when Thomas became the commission's chair. Thomas testified first, making a statement in which he categori-

cally denied Hill's allegations. Hill then testified. She related that when she and Thomas worked together at the Department of Education, Thomas had repeatedly asked her out on dates; she further stated that in workplace conversations he had described acts he had seen in pornographic films and that he had bragged about his sexual prowess. Hill admitted that when Thomas left the Department of Education to take the EEOC job, she agreed to go with him. That admission cost Hill some credibility, as many observers wondered why someone who had been treated so shabbily would agree to accompany her harasser to another job.

Later that day, Thomas gave a second, highly emotional and dramatic statement in which he described the

1991

## JUDGE THOMAS RESPONDS

*At the evening session of the hearing of the Senate Judiciary Committee on the nomination of Clarence Thomas to the U.S. Supreme Court on October 11, 1991, Thomas lashed out after testimony was presented against him by Anita Hill, a former employee:*

Senator, I would like to start by saying unequivocally, uncategorically, that I deny each and every single allegation against me today that suggested in any way that I had conversations of a sexual nature or about pornographic material with Anita Hill, that I ever attempted to date her, that I ever had any personal sexual interest in her, or that I in any way ever harassed her.

A second, and I think more important point, I think that this today is a travesty. I think that it is disgusting. I think that this hearing should never occur in America. This is a case in which this sleaze, this dirt, was searched for by staffers of members of this committee, was then leaked to the media, and this committee and this body validated it and displayed it at prime time over our entire nation. How would any member on this committee, any person in this room, or any person in this country, would like sleaze said about him or her in this fashion? Or this dirt dredged up and this gossip and these lies displayed in this manner? How would any person like it?

The Supreme Court is not worth it. No job is worth it. I'm not here for that. I'm here for my name, my family, my life and my integrity. I think something is dreadfully wrong with this country when any person, any person in this free country would be subjected to this.

This is not a closed room. There was an FBI investigation. This is not an opportunity to talk about difficult matters privately or in a closed environment. This is a circus. It's a national disgrace. And from my standpoint as a black American, as far as I'm concerned, it is a high-tech lynching for uppity blacks who in any way deign to think for themselves, to do for themselves, to have different ideas, and it is a message that unless you kowtow to an old order, this is what will happen to you. You will be lynched, destroyed, caricatured by a committee of the U.S. Senate rather than hung from a tree.

*Justice Byron White (right) swears in Clarence Thomas as associate justice of the United States during a ceremony at the White House on October 18, 1991.* (AP/Wide World Photos)

proceedings as a "high-tech lynching for uppity blacks who in any way deign to think for themselves." Witnesses were then brought in to corroborate both Thomas's and Hill's testimony, but ultimately the Judiciary Committee concluded its hearings without making a determination on the charges. On October 15, 1991, the Senate voted to confirm Thomas as an associate justice of the United States by a vote of fifty-two to forty-eight, the slimmest margin in history.

### SIGNIFICANCE

Public opinion at the time of Thomas's confirmation hearings was as closely divided as the Senate vote, and debates about who was telling the truth continued for years afterward. Some observers vilified Thomas as an Uncle Tom, a race traitor who served his (conservative) white masters. Some were embarrassed that Thomas had been portrayed in the mass media as the negative stereotype of the black man who could not control his sexual appetites. Thomas's defenders saw him as a latter-day Booker T. Washington, a man who had pulled himself up out of poverty by his own bootstraps and who believed that progress for blacks would come from hard work and the self-esteem that one earns by overcoming obstacles,

rather than from special treatment or government handouts.

Some saw Anita Hill as a feminist heroine who struck a blow against the sexual harassment of women. Others saw her as a liar who was simply determined to destroy Clarence Thomas for personal reasons or who, for political reasons, was a conspirator in the borking of a conservative nominee who happened to be black.

The Thomas hearings served to increase public awareness of the problem of sexual harassment in the workplace, and in subsequent years, additional scandals arose involving accusations of unwanted sexual advances by public figures. Senator Robert Packwood of Oregon was forced to resign in 1995 following complaints from several female employees, and President Bill Clinton was accused of sexual impropriety by Paula Jones and others.

Before Hill's accusations added high drama to the proceedings, Thomas's confirmation hearings had already been contentious. After the Thomas nomination battle, it appeared that presidents had learned that their Supreme Court nominees would be more likely to be confirmed if the nominees were not perceived as ideologically extreme. Nominees appeared to have learned, following the examples of Bork and Thomas, that their confirmation would be more likely if they could avoid giving any indication of how they might vote on controversial issues.

—*Howard C. Ellis*

**FURTHER READING**

Foskett, Ken. *Judging Thomas: The Life and Times of Clarence Thomas*. New York: HarperCollins, 2004. Biography draws on extensive interviews with Thomas himself as well as with his family members, friends, and colleagues.

Gerber, Scott Douglas. *First Principles: The Jurisprudence of Clarence Thomas*. New York: New York University Press, 1999. Provides a balanced review of Thomas's first five years on the U.S. Supreme Court, gleaning his judicial philosophy from his opinions, public speeches, and scholarly writings.

Hill, Anita Faye, and Emma Coleman Jordan, eds. *Race, Gender, and Power in America: The Legacy of the Hill-Thomas Hearings*. New York: Oxford University Press, 1995. Collection of essays discusses the legal, political, and social aftermath of Thomas's confirmation hearings from the perspective of issues of race and gender.

Mayer, Jane, and Jill Abramson. *Strange Justice: The Selling of Clarence Thomas*. New York: Houghton Mifflin, 1994. Work by two investigative reporters concludes that Thomas lied at his confirmation hearing in his response to Hill's accusations as well as about his judicial philosophy. Asserts that Hill was the victim of a Bush administration smear campaign.

Thomas, Andrew Peyton. *Clarence Thomas: A Biography*. San Francisco: Encounter Books, 2001. Sympathetic biography focuses on Thomas's life before his appointment to the U.S. Supreme Court. Takes a dim view of Anita Hill and Thomas's opponents in his confirmation battle.

Thomas, Clarence. *My Grandfather's Son: A Memoir*. New York: HarperCollins, 2007. Thomas provides an account of his life, from his childhood in poverty to his first days as a member of the U.S. Supreme Court. Includes discussion of the contentious confirmation hearings.

**SEE ALSO:** Sept. 25, 1981: O'Connor Is the First Woman to Serve as Supreme Court Justice; Nov. 3, 1983: Jackson Becomes the First Major Black Candidate for U.S. President; Nov. 7, 1989: Wilder Becomes the First Elected Black Governor; June 29, 1992: U.S. Supreme Court Restricts Abortion Rights; June 12, 1995: U.S. Supreme Court Limits Racial Preferences in Awarding Government Contracts; June 26, 1995: U.S. Supreme Court Rules on Random Drug Testing in Schools; May 20, 1996: U.S. Supreme Court Strikes Down Colorado Antigay Law; June 25, 1998: U.S. Supreme Court Rules That "Decency" Can Be Required for Federal Arts Grants; June 25, 1998: U.S. Supreme Court Strikes Down the Line-Item Veto; June 28, 2000: U.S. Supreme Court Protects Restrictions on Membership in Private Groups.

1991

# July 1, 1991
# DISSOLUTION OF THE WARSAW PACT

*The Warsaw Pact, a Cold War institution, dissolved as the Soviet Union and former communist countries of Eastern Europe turned to the West for security and assistance in hopes of achieving greater prosperity.*

**ALSO KNOWN AS:** Treaty of Friendship, Cooperation, and Mutual Assistance; Warsaw Treaty Organization

**LOCALE:** Prague, Czechoslovakia (now in the Czech Republic)

**CATEGORY:** Diplomacy and international relations

**KEY FIGURES**

*Mikhail Gorbachev* (b. 1931), general secretary of the Communist Party of the Soviet Union, 1985-1991, and president of the Soviet Union, 1990-1991

*Ronald Reagan* (1911-2004), president of the United States, 1981-1989

*George H. W. Bush* (b. 1924), president of the United States, 1989-1993

**SUMMARY OF EVENT**

The end of the Soviet era came in 1991, following a cascading series of external and domestic catastrophes that led to the dissolution of the Soviet Union. Prior to the official end of the Soviet Union, the entire system of Eastern European communist satellite nations collapsed and was replaced by independent nations with electoral democracies. The communist satellite system had begun as an outgrowth of the success of Soviet arms in World War II; the Soviet Union's hegemony was founded on its victory over the invading Wehrmacht, which left the Red Army in complete control of all the territory up to and including the eastern portions of Austria and Germany. However, these territorial gains were made at an unspeakable cost in blood and treasure (as many as thirty million killed), and the trauma of those losses to the national psyche shaped the Soviet vision of the postwar order and the nation's strategic objectives.

Having been invaded twice through the Polish Corridor within two generations, the Soviet Union determined that no such threat would face future generations, and so the prime postwar goal of Soviet leaders was the construction of a security buffer zone in the countries under their control in Eastern Europe. Further, they felt that a permanently weakened Germany was key to the fulfillment of this strategic objective, and this became the focal point for the breakdown in relations among the members of the wartime "Grand Alliance." When the United States, France, and Great Britain included the Federal Republic of Germany (West Germany) in the North Atlantic Treaty Organization (NATO), the Soviets responded by formalizing the existing network of bilateral treaties under the rubric of a multilateral agreement, the Treaty of Friendship, Cooperation, and Mutual Assistance, commonly known as the Warsaw Pact.

On one hand, the Soviets sought security, socialist economic development, and political influence on the world stage in the context of a sphere of influence based on wartime successes. On the other hand, the United States and its Western allies wanted containment of Soviet expansionism, open markets, and limitations on the role played by the Soviet Union in global institutions. This fundamental strategic divide, along with the moderating influence of the existence of nuclear arsenals on both sides, shaped the basic nature of the chronic state of conflict known as the Cold War.

The Warsaw Pact's initial signatories (Albania, Bulgaria, Czechoslovakia, Hungary, Poland, Romania, and the Soviet Union) agreed to an arrangement whereby Soviet troops would remain within the territories of the allied nations, and all would come to the defense of all in the event of external aggression. The treaty established a unified political and military structure (the Political Consultative Committee and Joint Command) for the coordination of allied military policies and to guarantee consistency with Soviet strategic objectives. Although the treaty functioned primarily as an instrument of control in its early years, the evolution of the system was in the direction of greater autonomy for the satellite nations and something approaching genuine consulta-

tion among equal and sovereign states in decision making. By the 1970's, serious debates were heard concerning the Soviet domination of the alliance, the appropriate apportionment of costs among the allies, and the unequal sharing of risks in the event of war.

The period of détente coincided, paradoxically, with an increasingly offensive alliance policy with respect to NATO, along with the development of assorted intra-alliance coalitions designed to oppose and obstruct Soviet intentions. The 1980's witnessed the rise of the Polish union movement Solidarity; unlike earlier challenges to Kremlin authority, this did not result in direct intervention by Warsaw Pact forces to suppress the movement.

The ascendancy to the leadership of Soviet Union by Mikhail Gorbachev in 1985 came at a time when cohesion among Warsaw Pact members was at a historic low ebb. Gorbachev's response was to increase the degree of autonomy available to allied governments, increase the scope for allied input into policy making, and shift the strategic posture of the alliance to a purely defensive one. Meanwhile, Gorbachev engaged in summitry with U.S. president Ronald Reagan at Geneva, Reykjavik, and Moscow, with the purpose of pursuing nuclear disarmament.

Gorbachev, along with the young reformers who rose to power along with him, felt that the twin burdens of an arms race and the continual flow of aid and subsidies to the satellite nations of Central and Eastern Europe were incompatible with successful political and economic reform (glasnost and perestroika). This dual approach—employing diplomacy with the West while reorienting the Soviet economy toward greater satisfaction of consumer needs—meant that it was no longer feasible for the Soviet Union to attempt to assert centralized control over the other Warsaw Pact nations. This set the stage for the events of 1989, the "Autumn of Nations," throughout eastern Europe.

Lacking the support of the Soviet government, and with Soviet troops remaining in their barracks, Eastern European nations held democratic elections that led to the replacement of communist regimes by liberal democracies. The Berlin Wall was breached, and Germany reunified as a member of NATO; Nicolae Ceauşescu's regime in Romania was overthrown by a popular uprising. Gorbachev met with U.S. president George H. W. Bush in December, 1989, at Malta and declared his intention to restructure the Warsaw Pact so as to make it an instrument of diplomatic communications; this essentially ended the Cold War. The new governments in Eastern Europe were no longer beholden to the Soviets, and they felt no need to support their former alliance partner. By the end of 1990, all of the former satellites had announced their withdrawal of support from the alliance, effective no later than June 30, 1991. All that remained was for the final meeting of Warsaw Pact ministers (held in Prague, Czechoslovakia) to conclude with the official announcement of the alliance's demise on July 1, 1991.

## SIGNIFICANCE

The dissolution of the Warsaw Pact marked a historic shift in Soviet strategic thinking in two respects: First, it indicated that the Soviet leaders recognized that the chief security concerns they faced were internal rather than external; and second, it showed that they understood that national security is more a function of economic capabilities than of the capacity for organized violence. This realization led to a reevaluation of the practice of spending a quarter or more of the nation's gross domestic product on a system of military alliances that made Soviet security dependent on the armed forces of Bulgaria. Furthermore, the reduction in subsidies to satellite governments implicit in this reevaluation contributed to the eventual demise of communist systems of governance in Eastern Europe. This wave of democratic change could hardly be stopped at the borders of the Soviet Union, and so the abandonment of communist governments abroad accelerated the end of the political system of "Soviet Socialist Republics" at home.

The end of the Warsaw Pact also necessitated a wholesale reorientation of the world system of political, economic, and security institutions that had existed primarily because of the opposition of the two great postwar superpowers, the United States and the Soviet Union. The role of NATO was no longer clear in a unipolar world system, and the task of cultivating military alliances through economic means now fell to the only remaining superpower, the United States.

*—Ivan Weinel*

## FURTHER READING

Gaddis, John Lewis. *The Cold War: A New History.* New York: Penguin Books, 2005. Concise and accessible overview by a leading Cold War scholar. Organized thematically to capture the most significant features without in-depth treatments of places and personalities. Includes maps, bibliography, and index.

Mastny, Vojtech, and Malcolm Byrne, eds. *A Cardboard Castle? An Inside History of the Warsaw Pact, 1955-1991.* Budapest: Central European University Press, 2005. Work of the Parallel History Project on NATO and the Warsaw Pact presents newly available materials from the Warsaw Pact archives along with commentary. Shows previously unsuspected weaknesses of the alliance as well as its relatively fractious internal relations. Includes chronology, bibliography, and index.

Powaski, Ronald E. *The Cold War: The United States and the Soviet Union, 1917-1991.* New York: Oxford University Press, 1997. Provides a thorough introductory treatment from the orthodox perspective of the historical backdrop and political contexts surrounding U.S.-Soviet relations. Includes maps, bibliography, and index.

**SEE ALSO:** May 26, 1973-Dec. 26, 1991: Détente with the Soviet Union; Dec. 8, 1987: Intermediate-Range Nuclear Forces Treaty; 1990-1994: United Nations Admits Many New Members; Feb. 26, 1990: Soviet Troops Withdraw from Czechoslovakia; July 16, 1990: Gorbachev Agrees to Membership of a United Germany in NATO; Sept. 27, 1991: Bush Announces Nuclear Arms Reductions; Dec., 1991: Dissolution of the Soviet Union; May 27, 1997: NATO and Russia Sign Cooperation Pact.

1991

## July 1, 1991
# SWEDEN APPLIES FOR MEMBERSHIP IN THE EUROPEAN COMMUNITY

*With its application for membership in the European Community in the wake of German reunification, Sweden indicated that it had overcome the view that such membership would be incompatible with the nation's traditional policy of neutrality.*

**LOCALE:** Sweden
**CATEGORIES:** Diplomacy and international relations; economics; government and politics

**KEY FIGURES**
*Östen Undén* (1886-1974), Swedish foreign minister, 1924-1926 and 1945-1962
*Olof Palme* (1927-1986), prime minister of Sweden, 1969-1976 and 1982-1986
*Ingvar Carlsson* (b. 1934), prime minister of Sweden, 1986-1991
*Carl Bildt* (b. 1949), prime minister of Sweden and leader of the Conservative Party, 1991-1994

**SUMMARY OF EVENT**
The road to Sweden's application for membership in the European Community was a long one. Sweden formed its attitude toward Europe and the rest of the world immediately following World War II, under the leadership of Foreign Minister Östen Undén. Guarding his country's traditional neutrality, which had served it well during two world wars, Undén set Sweden on a course of well-armed nonalignment between the two hostile superpowers, the North Atlantic Treaty Organization (NATO) and the Soviet bloc. He also advocated free trade, a policy in the best interest of Sweden's export-oriented economy. Finally, while eager to see Sweden play an active role in the United Nations, Undén would not countenance any surrender of sovereignty to a supranational entity. The dominant view among the country's political elite was one of Sweden in a Europe of sovereign states trading freely with one another.

At odds with this Swedish view of Europe was the gathering of nations that eventually became the European Community (later the European Union). From its inception in 1951 as the European Coal and Steel Community, the institution was supranational in certain key economic and political matters. These issues were defined fundamentally in the Treaty of Rome of 1957, which joined France, the German Federal Republic, Italy, Belgium, the Netherlands, and Luxembourg in the European Economic Community (EEC). It called for the

elimination of barriers to trade within the community and a common tariff policy toward the outside.

In 1960, several European nations outside the EEC that shared Sweden's point of view on free trade and national sovereignty formed the European Free Trade Area (EFTA). They included, in addition to Sweden, the United Kingdom, Norway, Denmark, Switzerland, and Portugal, and later Iceland and Finland. In contrast to the EEC, EFTA always had a loose, temporary character.

Throughout the 1960's, a minority in Sweden argued for Swedish membership in the EEC because the country traded much more within the EEC than within EFTA. The prevailing point of view, put forward by the governing Social Democratic Party and shared by the agrarian Center Party, was that Swedish neutrality ruled out the nation's joining the EEC, which appeared to overlap NATO too much. Moreover, Sweden appeared economically strong enough to need nothing more than friendly trade agreements with the EEC. It was also widely felt that membership in the EEC would threaten Swedish "identity." The EEC seemed too Catholic, too capitalist, and too conservative.

The question of Sweden's membership grew more urgent in the early 1970's, as EFTA virtually disintegrated. In 1973, after two earlier failed attempts, the United Kingdom entered the European Community (EC), as the organization had been known since 1970, together with Denmark and the Irish Republic. Sweden's Social Democratic prime minister, Olof Palme, inclined toward a Swedish application for full membership but bowed to opposition from within his party. In 1972, Palme's government negotiated a free trade agreement between Sweden and the EC that covered mainly industrial products.

During the 1970's, as Sweden's trade with the EC grew ever more significant, the country also was reminded that its policy of armed neutrality had certain limitations. Military expenses had to be cut during the recession that weakened Sweden's economy in the mid-1970's. At the same time, Leonid Brezhnev's regime in the Soviet Union heated up the Cold War. It became clear that Swedish national security increasingly depended on indirect support from NATO.

With the death of Brezhnev in 1982 and the thaw in the Cold War that followed, the basic assumptions of Sweden's foreign policy changed. In 1985, Mikhail Gorbachev came to power in the Soviet Union and initiated reforms in 1987, such as glasnost and perestroika, that promised the end of dictatorship in that nation. In 1989, the Berlin Wall came down, the Cold War ended, and Sweden could rethink the Undén doctrine of neutrality. Simultaneously, the EC became a more attractive option for Sweden. By the mid-1980's, it had expanded to include Greece, Spain, and Portugal. Austria, a nonaligned country like Sweden, applied for membership in the EC in 1989.

In 1984, virtual free trade in industrial products having been achieved, the EC and EFTA reached an agreement in Luxembourg to expand cooperation in a common European Economic Area (EEA). In 1987, realizing that Europe was being restructured in accord with EC plans and that Swedish industry was being tempted to move to EC countries, the Swedish government declared its wish to join the EC single market. In 1990, as EEA negotiations began in Brussels, Sweden announced its goal of securing EC membership.

During that year, the question of membership became a major domestic issue, pressed by Carl Bildt on behalf of an alliance of Conservatives and Liberals. Influenced by a strong showing of popular support for membership—about 60 percent for, 20 percent against, and 20 percent undecided—the Social Democratic government led by Ingvar Carlsson laid the matter before the Riksdag, the Swedish parliament. On December 2, 1990, the Riksdag voted overwhelmingly to apply under the condition of preserving Sweden's neutrality. Opposition came only from members of the Communist and Environment parties.

In the following months, the Riksdag's foreign affairs committee examined specific conditions for the application. Of particular concern was whether the EC might eventually impose a compulsory defense obligation on its members and, if so, whether Sweden could comply. The committee took the view that in the short run, such an obstacle was unlikely, and if such an obligation arose, Sweden's membership in the EC would allow Sweden to be involved in shaping future policy. On July 1, 1991, Prime Minister Carlsson submitted Sweden's application, without qualifications, to the EC in Brussels.

## SIGNIFICANCE

Swift changes in world affairs had swept Sweden's leaders into the application too quickly for the Swedish public to examine what membership might mean to the country's special interests, and a genuine national consensus in favor of membership had not yet formed. Popular support for membership peaked at 60 percent in October, 1991, shortly after the general election that brought Bildt

to power at the head of a coalition of middle-class parties. Thereafter, opponents of EC membership exploited fears of its possible negative impact. The Bildt government's austerity program, linked in the public's mind with the need to adapt Sweden to the structures of the EC, drew popular resentment to the application. The EC became identified with Sweden's problems rather than with its opportunities. EC membership also appeared to jeopardize Swedish identity, raising fears that foreigners would overrun the country and faceless bureaucrats in Brussels would govern it.

During December, 1991, at Maastricht in the Netherlands, the EC's members agreed to prepare themselves by 1999 for a common monetary system and other far-reaching measures of unification. In November of 1993, the European Community became known as the European Union. Negotiations with Sweden had begun in February, 1993; in March of the following year, an agreement was reached. Much of the work on this agreement had already been done when the EEA treaty was signed in 1992. Sweden's membership was approved, pending results of a national referendum. Prime Minister Bildt signed the accession treaty for Sweden at a European Union summit meeting held in the summer of 1994.

In the debate leading up to the referendum, Swedish public opinion remained evenly divided. Finally, it shifted in favor of the treaty, influenced by what seemed favorable to Sweden's long-term interest and appeared inevitable. On November 13, 1994, 52.3 percent voted in favor of membership in the European Union, 46.8 percent voted against, and 0.9 percent turned in blank ballots. The turnout was high: 83.3 percent of eligible voters. The Riksdag ratified the results on December 15, 1994, and Sweden became a full European Union member on January 1, 1995.

*—Charles H. O'Brien*

## FURTHER READING

Gstöhl, Sieglinde. *Reluctant Europeans: Norway, Sweden, and Switzerland in the Process of Integration.* Boulder, Colo.: Lynne Rienner, 2002. Examines why the three nations discussed chose for so long to remain outside the European Community and explains their eventual integration.

Hill, Richard, and David Haworth. *The New Comers: Austria, Finland, and Sweden.* Brussels, Belgium: Europublications, 1995. Popular survey offers useful insights into the national characteristics that impeded the entry of Sweden as well as Finland and Austria into the European Union.

1991

Huldt, Bo. "Sweden and European Community-Building, 1945-92." In *Neutral States and the European Community*, edited by Sheila Harden. New York: Macmillan, 1994. Offers well-balanced, detailed historical analysis and discusses the forces pulling Sweden away from its traditional stance of neutrality toward full membership in the European Union.

Milward, Alan S., ed. *The Frontier of National Sovereignty: History and Theory, 1945-1992*. New York: Routledge, 1993. Collection of essays by Milward and four other expert contributors argues that interrelated economic, social, and political changes in the postwar period motivated Sweden and other Western European states to integrate.

Pedersen, Thomas. *European Union and the EFTA Countries: Enlargement and Integration*. London: Pinter, 1994. Discussion of the integration of the European Union includes succinct analysis of Sweden's reasons for abandoning EFTA.

Scott, Franklin D. *Sweden: The Nation's History*. 2d ed. Carbondale: Southern Illinois University Press, 1988. Standard English-language survey of Swedish history offers a sound understanding of the growth of a national identity in Sweden marked by democratic social cohesion at home and neutrality in foreign affairs.

**SEE ALSO:** Jan. 1, 1986: Portugal and Spain Enter the European Community; Feb. 28, 1986: European Economic Community Adopts the Single European Act; Nov. 1, 1993: Unification of the European Market.

## July 3, 1991
# IBM AND APPLE AGREE TO MAKE COMPATIBLE COMPUTERS

*After years of rivalry, IBM and Apple agreed to work together to create a new processor and a common hardware reference platform that would enable their computers to use the same software.*

**ALSO KNOWN AS:** AIM alliance
**LOCALE:** Cupertino, California; Armonk, New York
**CATEGORIES:** Computers and computer science; trade and commerce; business and labor

**KEY FIGURES**
*John Sculley* (b. 1939), chief executive officer of Apple Computer, Inc.
*John Akers* (b. 1934), chief executive officer of International Business Machines

**SUMMARY OF EVENT**
Almost from the beginning, incompatible hardware and software had been the bane of the microcomputer industry. In its early days, there were dozens of companies, each with its own proprietary architecture. Changing computers often required one to laboriously retype all of one's existing data. The introduction of the International Business Machines (IBM) personal computer (PC) in 1981 and the subsequent development of IBM compatibles, or "clones," created a de facto standard throughout much of the computer industry. However, when Apple introduced the Macintosh in 1984, it chose to develop a completely different standard.

By the 1990's, the field had settled down to a rivalry between the Windows-based descendants of the IBM PC on one side and the Apple Macintosh on the other. However, IBM itself was rapidly losing market share in the microcomputer business, particularly to such firms as Compaq, Dell, and Gateway 2000. Thus IBM became increasingly interested in the possibility of a joint venture with Apple that would eliminate the seemingly unbridgeable gap between the two parts of the microcomputer world.

The idea was to create a new hardware platform based on a new microprocessor architecture and an advanced new operating system (OS) that would take advantage of the new chip's particular strengths. All microprocessors up to that time were based on the complex instruction set computing (CISC) paradigm. However, Apple and IBM engineers were becoming increasingly convinced that CISC was ultimately a dead-end technology, and the future lay with a new theory known as RISC, or reduced instruction set computing. While a CISC microprocessor would have a large number of instructions, one for each possible task it might be asked to perform, a RISC microprocessor would be based on a few basic instructions that could be put together to build the equivalents of the specialized instructions of a CISC chip.

Because each instruction in a RISC chip has the same number of steps, it would also make the transition to a superscalar architecture easier. With a superscalar architecture, the processor has more than one data pipeline and is able to process more than one instruction during each clock cycle. If instructions require a number of steps to complete, it would be more difficult to keep the data pipelines synchronized. Periods in which one side was waiting for the other to finish an instruction represented processor power wasted. By contrast, the basic "building block" instructions of a RISC chip would always stay neatly in step with one another.

Along with this revolutionary new microprocessor design, IBM and Apple set forth ideas for the computers that would run them. The Common Hardware Reference Platform (CHRP) would be a standard architecture that would ensure that hardware worked in predictable ways and programmers would no longer have to rewrite their software completely with every change of basic hardware.

In order to realize these visions, Apple and IBM brought chip manufacturer Motorola on board, forming an organization called the AIM alliance. Motorola had been having trouble with the 88000 chip, the RISC-based successor to the old standby 68000 series of chips, which had been the brains of Apple computers to date. Thus Motorola gained access to IBM's established POWER (Performance Optimization With Enhanced RISC) architecture, which had proven its worth in mainframes. Apple and IBM created two joint-venture companies, Taligent and Kaleida, to create a new operating system and a powerful new object-oriented scripting language for developers. Both were intended to concentrate on fully utilizing the potential of this powerful new platform.

## SIGNIFICANCE

The long-term success of the AIM alliance was mixed. On one hand, the PowerPC chip became the basis for all of Apple's computers for more than a decade, giving them the name of Power Macintosh. On the other hand, most of the other initiatives faced various problems.

IBM designed a new line of PowerPC-based computers, but problems getting an operating system that would run on them delayed its release. Originally they were planned to run Windows, but Microsoft failed to roll out a compatible version of its popular OS in time. IBM then fell back on its own OS/2 operating system, but rewriting it to work on the PowerPC chip consumed valuable time. By the time IBM's programmers had the new version of OS/2 ready, the critical moment had already passed for the hardware, and only a few machines were ever sold. IBM ended up returning to the Intel fold and ultimately sold its microcomputer division to an Asian firm, Lenovo, in order to concentrate on its real bread and butter, mainframe computers such as the RS/6000 and its descendants.

Apple got around the operating system bottleneck by rewriting its existing System 7 to run on the PowerPC chip and by creating a 68K emulator to handle a few pieces of seldom-used code. However, Apple's efforts to create a next-generation operating system became sidetracked into a multiplicity of approaches, and both OS 8 and OS 9 proved to be little more than updates of an operating system that dated back to the early days of the Macintosh. Finally, in danger of failing altogether, Apple brought back cofounder Steve Jobs and thus gained access to his powerful NEXTSTEP, a UNIX-based operating system that would become the basis of OS X.

The much-vaunted CHRP, later renamed PReP (PowerPC Reference Platform), ultimately went out with a whimper. Although a few machines based on it were shipped in the late 1990's and it attained some currency among users of various flavors of UNIX, there simply was not enough advantage to the CHRP/PReP hardware over comparable Intel-based machines to allow them to compete. The BeBox, a machine designed to run the innovative BeOS, incorporated PReP hardware but was not completely compatible with the design. The machine never gained enough market share to be more than a curiosity. (However, before Jobs brought NEXTSTEP to Apple, there were some negotiations toward buying or licensing BeOS as the foundation of a replacement for the old Macintosh operating system.) The iMac, which has often been credited with saving Apple in 1998, incorporated some CHRP hardware ideas but did not stick rigorously to the CHRP standard.

By 2005, even the PowerPC chip was losing ground. Apple was becoming increasingly disappointed with Motorola's inability to produce a PowerPC G5 chip that would reliably run at 3 gigahertz. Also, Motorola's plans for future chip development did not match Apple's plans for computer development. In January, 2006, Jobs made a shocking announcement: Henceforth, Apple would be using Intel's Core and Core Duo chips as the brains of their computers. Many die-hard Apple loyalists decried the decision as selling out to the "Wintel" world, but as it became clear that the new Macintosh Pro line ran OS X just as well as the old PowerMacs, resistance subsided.

*—Leigh Husband Kimmel*

## FURTHER READING

Carlton, Jim. *Apple: The Inside Story of Intrigue, Egomania, and Business Blunders.* New York: Random House, 1997. Corporate history of Apple, with some material on the AIM initiative.

1991

Duntemann, Jeff, and Ron Pronk. *Inside the PowerPC Revolution: The Inside Story Behind the Chips, Software, and Machines That Are Changing the Computer Industry.* Scottsdale, Ariz.: Coriolis Group Books, 1994. Specifically examines the history of the PowerPC chip.

Levy, Steven. *Insanely Great: The Life and Times of Macintosh, the Computer That Changed Everything.* New York: Viking Penguin, 1994. Published on the tenth anniversary of the Macintosh, the book came out just as the AIM alliance was bearing fruit, and thus shows the enthusiasm of those heady days.

Malone, Michael S. *Infinite Loop: How Apple, the World's Most Insanely Great Computer Company,* *Went Insane.* New York: Doubleday, 1999. Examines some of Apple's corporate politics related to the development and implementation of the PowerPC chip.

Riordan, Michael, and Lillian Hoddeson. *Crystal Fire: The Birth of the Information Age.* New York: W. W. Norton, 1997. Helps place the microchip in the larger context of the convergence of information technology.

**SEE ALSO:** Nov. 15, 1971: Intel Introduces the First "Computer on a Chip"; Aug. 12, 1981: IBM Introduces Its Personal Computer; Jan. 24, 1984: Introduction of the Apple Macintosh; Nov. 20, 1985: Microsoft Releases the Windows Operating System.

## July 14, 1991
# PESTICIDES ARE RELEASED INTO THE SACRAMENTO RIVER

*When a railroad accident six miles north of Dunsmuir, California, spilled thirteen thousand gallons of the pesticide metam sodium into the Sacramento River, aquatic life was destroyed in more than forty miles of the river.*

**LOCALE:** Sacramento River, Northern California
**CATEGORIES:** Disasters; environmental issues; animals and endangered species

### KEY FIGURES
*D. Mike Mohan* (fl. late twentieth century), president and chief executive officer of the Southern Pacific Railroad
*William Reilly* (b. 1940), director of the Environmental Protection Agency
*Dick May* (fl. late twentieth century), president of California Trout, Incorporated
*Leo Cronin* (d. 1995), western regional vice president of Trout Unlimited

### SUMMARY OF EVENT
On July 14, 1991, a railroad car containing 19,500 gallons of the pesticide metam sodium derailed, and the pesticide leaked into the upper Sacramento River six miles north of Dunsmuir, California. The pesticide killed all aquatic life in the river for a distance of forty-five miles downstream to Lake Shasta, a huge impoundment that supplied irrigation and drinking water to most of Northern California.

The accident occurred on the main rail line of the Southern Pacific Railroad at a curve known as Cantara Loop, where the railroad crosses the Sacramento River. The train was made up of ninety-seven cars with a combined weight of 4,290 tons and four locomotives pulling the train from the front. Trains weighing more than 4,500 tons require the use of a pusher locomotive at the rear, to maintain traction when ascending mountain bases as well as to relieve the lateral strain around the 180-degree curve of Cantara Loop. On the night of the accident, the locomotives lost traction rounding Cantara Loop, then regained traction and yanked the train forward. A locomotive and seven cars were pulled off the rails. The tank car carrying the metam sodium fell from the curved bridge into the Sacramento River. A hole was torn in the car's single-walled tank, and most of the contents leaked into the river.

Railroad crews following standard procedure immediately rushed in and pumped the diesel fuel that had begun to leak from the derailed locomotive but did nothing about the pesticide leaking from the ruptured tank car. The Environmental Protection Agency (EPA) and the U.S. Department of Transportation do not consider metam sodium a hazardous material; therefore, the train manifests listed the contents of the tank car simply as a weed killer, with no special precautions noted for handling the contents in case of accident or spillage.

Metam sodium is a popular pesticide in part because it effectively kills a wide range of both plant and animal life. It is used as a soil fumigant. When mixed into soil, it reacts with water in the soil to produce two deadly chemicals, methyl isothiocyanate and hydrogen sulfide gas.

When the metam sodium leaked into the river, the river flow carried it downstream more than forty miles, until the mass of pesticide reached Lake Shasta, the huge impoundment that supplies water to much of Northern California. On its trip down the river to Lake Shasta, the pesticide killed every organism in the river, from ducks and trout (which supplied the region with its economic base as a sportfishing destination) through the insects and smaller fish that make up the trouts' diet, down to the algae. Several days after the spill, even the trees along the riverbank began to die. The death of the river also affected the myriad animals—including beavers, eagles, bears, and otters—that depended on the river as a major food source.

In addition to the devastating effects on the environment, the spill also affected the residents and the economy of the area. Sixty miles of Interstate Highway 5, the main road that shares the valley with the Sacramento River and the railroad line, were closed. Hundreds of residents were evacuated from the area. Boating and fishing were banned at the northern end of Lake Shasta, where the flow of poisoned water entered the lake. The area's economy is based on recreation, sportfishing in particular, so the death of the river was expected to have long-term economic impacts.

Thirteen thousand gallons of the poisonous metam sodium eventually leaked from the tank car and made its way into the northern end of Lake Shasta, where it floated as a huge green mass near the surface of the lake. To clean up the lake, authorities implemented a newly developed process of spraying the toxin-containing water into the air under a water canopy.

Lake Shasta is the largest artificial reservoir in California, supplying both drinking water and agricultural water for much of Northern California. Because of the lake's enormous water capacity—550 billion gallons—officials declared that the spill would pose no danger to humans and that the water supplied by the lake would be safe to drink.

Officials at the Southern Pacific Railroad quickly changed the company's policy to lower to 3,600 tons the maximum weight that a train can pull without the use of a pusher engine at the rear of the train. Had a pusher engine been in use on the ill-fated train, it likely would not have lost traction, and the accident that caused the spill could have been averted. Railroad officials also promised to pay compensation for the environmental damage caused by the spill and urged restocking of the river with hatchery trout as soon as possible to minimize the economic damage to the region.

If the death of the Sacramento River was a frightening reminder of how the modern industrial world can destroy an ecosystem in a moment, the rebirth of the river was a reminder of the resilience of nature. Within five months of the disaster, diatoms—tiny single-celled plants—were collecting on rocks in the river, and fly larvae were found at the bottom of the river. Full recovery, however, took much longer; some aspects were still ongoing in the early years of the twenty-first century.

The Sacramento River's recovery from this disaster sparked immediate debate about the extent to which human intervention should be used to accelerate the recovery and ultimately how possible modes of intervention would affect the ecosystem of the river. Among the interventions considered were the use of various methods of stocking trout and the option of not stocking trout at all. Leo Cronin, western regional vice president of Trout Unlimited, a nonprofit organization concerned with trout conservation, proposed not stocking any trout in the Sacramento River. Trout fry from the spring spawning were still in the smaller tributaries of the Sacramento River, where they were unaffected by the chemical spill. Cronin argued that if the trout were allowed to repopulate the river naturally, the trout population would remain genetically the same as the wild trout population before the spill, although it would take years to restore the trout population to its level before the spill.

Dick May, the president of California Trout, Incorporated, a leading lobbying group, proposed taking some of the wild trout upstream of the spill site, breeding them in hatcheries, and replacing the trout one generation at a time with hatchery-raised trout genetically equivalent to the wild trout existing in the river before the spill. This scenario would maintain the genetic integrity of the trout population while hastening the recovery of the river and the return to an economically viable sportfishing industry. Cronin rejected this idea on the grounds that hatchery-raised trout do not possess the same self-preservation skills that wild trout do, as only the fittest of the wild trout survive to adulthood.

The most expedient method, proposed by the Southern Pacific Railroad and many local businesses, would be to stock the river with hatchery-bred and hatchery-raised rainbow trout; this option would provide the most rapid return to an economically viable fishery. Both Cronin and May rejected this idea, arguing that stocked hatchery trout would eat the remaining wild trout fry, thus eliminating the native strain of trout in the Sacramento River.

Another dimension to the issue of restoring trout to

1991

the river concerned other wildlife. Not only was sport-fishing affected by the death of the trout, but the eagles that populated the valley also lost their primary food supply. If hatchery trout were released into the river, they would provide food for the eagles and could provide prey for sportfishing. Trout, however, are relatively high on the food chain. Because there would be no other source of food for stocked trout until the lower organisms on the food chain reestablished their populations, the trout would eat any food that migrated into the area, including the young trout migrating into the river from the tributaries, or would move downstream until they found a suitable food source. This could both eliminate the source of native trout existing as fry in the tributaries and leave the river without fish as the stocked fish migrated downstream into Lake Shasta in search of food.

The compromise solution that was finally reached was a novel one. Hatchery trout were placed in pens in the river to provide for the eagles, and the river was closed to fishing while the native trout population was allowed to recover.

## SIGNIFICANCE

The Sacramento River metam sodium spill had important short-term impacts: the disruption of an ecosystem and the disruption of the lives of people living in the area who were dependent, perhaps more than they realized, on the river. These impacts were met by short-term solutions directed at particular problems; these included the initial cleanup of the chemical spill and efforts to restore and monitor the river.

The Southern Pacific Railroad quickly provided $2 million for cleanup operations. The EPA, along with the Department of Agriculture and the Department of the Interior, ultimately sued the Southern Pacific Railroad and other companies implicated in the disaster for $40 million.

When a disaster occurs and the short-term remedies have been executed, the next step is to determine how the disaster happened and how it could have been prevented, then to develop long-term strategies both for dealing with a similar disaster in the future and for preventing the occurrence of future disasters. In 1990, more than 1.5 million railroad carloads of pesticides, solvents, and hazardous materials were hauled in the United States, and 1,254 spills of toxic materials occurred from railroad operations that year, but none was as devastating as the Sacramento River spill.

Metam sodium was not classified as a hazardous chemical by either the EPA or the U.S. Department of Transportation. The Sacramento River spill focused attention on the shortcomings of the federal laws and regulations dealing with hazardous chemicals, in particular the issue of what constitutes a hazard. The Toxic Substances Control Act of 1976 specifically excluded pesticides from its jurisdiction. The Federal Insecticide, Fungicide, and Rodenticide Act of 1972 required the EPA to register the more than fifty thousand pesticides in use in the United States and to limit severely or ban the most dangerous pesticides. Metam sodium was listed by the EPA, but the agency still did not consider the substance dangerous. In the aftermath of the accident, however, it was revealed that the EPA had overlooked warnings on at least ten chemicals, including metam sodium.

The Hazardous Materials Transportation Act of 1975 established minimum safety standards for the transport of hazardous material, but metam sodium was not considered hazardous under the guidelines of the act. The regulations that classified chemical hazards were written primarily in regard to human populations and were based on flammability, explosion hazard, and toxicity to humans; environmental risks were not generally considered. After the metam sodium spill, critics noted that the train manifest listed the contents of the tank car simply as a weed killer, without any hazard warnings or spill procedures; the tank car was not even required to display a placard identifying its contents. Had the contents of the tank car, and the dangers of metam sodium, been known at the accident site, the spill's effects might have been minimized.

The pesticide spill in the Sacramento River also raised concerns about the technology of the tank cars that carry potentially dangerous materials. The tank car that spilled the metam sodium had a typical single-walled tank that ruptured relatively easily as a result of the derailment. The accident opened debate on the technology and operating practices used by the rail transportation industry in transporting hazardous materials.

—*Robert E. Haag*

## FURTHER READING

Carson, Rachel. *Silent Spring*. 1962. Reprint. Boston: Mariner Books, 2002. The book that first popularized environmental concerns, in particular the dangers of pesticides.

Dorn, Dick. "The Other Side of Cantara." *Trains Magazine* 53 (May, 1992): 27. Argues that public officials overreacted to the spill and that the news media treated the story in a sensationalist manner.

Elmer-Dewitt, Philip. "Death of a River: An Ecological

Catastrophe in California Points to the Need for New Rules on the Transport of Toxic Compounds." *Time*, July 29, 1991, 24. Argues that the spill demonstrated the need for new regulations for the transport of materials that may be hazardous to the environment but are not considered hazardous to humans.

Powell, Mark R. *Science at EPA: Information in the Regulatory Process*. Washington, D.C.: Resources for the Future, 1999. In-depth examination of the EPA includes discussion of how the agency acquires and uses science for policy making.

Rosenbaum, Walter A. *Environmental Politics and Policy*. 6th ed. Washington, D.C.: Congressional Quarterly Press, 2004. Good resource provides background that clarifies how politics can produce policies that allow a material such as metam sodium to destroy an ecosystem and yet not be considered hazardous.

Thomas, David. "Sacramento River Killed: Nearly Fifty Miles of Blue Ribbon Water Destroyed by Chemical Spill." *Fly Fisherman* 23 (December, 1991): 10-16. Presents an excellent overview of the accident and the controversy surrounding the restocking of the river with trout.

Van Strum, Carol. *A Bitter Fog: Herbicides and Human Rights*. San Francisco: Sierra Club Books, 1983. Discusses the use of herbicides from an environmentalist viewpoint. Includes an interesting chapter titled "Poisons: Innocent Until Proved Guilty" that deals with the process and ramifications of the EPA's actions in determining the safety of a pesticide.

**SEE ALSO:** 1970's: Growth of Organic Farming; Oct. 21, 1972: U.S. Congress Expands Pesticide Regulations; Dec. 31, 1972: U.S. Government Bans DDT; Dec. 16, 1974: U.S. Congress Requires Safe Drinking Water; Nov. 1, 1986: Swiss Warehouse Fire Causes Toxic Spill into the Rhine; Jan. 2, 1988: Tank Collapse Releases Fuel into the Monongahela River.

1991

## August, 1991
# AFRICAN COUNTRIES BEGIN TO REVIVE DEMOCRATIZATION

*A number of African countries—including Zambia, the Republic of the Congo, Madagascar, Mali, Ghana, Guinea-Bissau, Mozambique, and the Central African Republic—established democratic governments, setting the example for other African governments to follow suit.*

**LOCALE:** Malawi; Zambia; Madagascar; Republic of the Congo; Ghana; Central African Republic; Mali; Mozambique; Guinea-Bissau

**CATEGORY:** Government and politics

**KEY FIGURES**

*Hastings Kamuzu Banda* (c. 1898-1997), president of Malawi, 1966-1994

*Kenneth Kaunda* (b. 1924), president of Zambia, 1964-1991

*Didier Ratsiraka* (b. 1936), president-dictator of the Democratic Republic of Madagascar, 1975-1993 and 1997-2002

*Albert Zafy* (b. 1927), president of the Democratic Republic of Madagascar, 1993-1996

*Denis Sassou Nguesso* (b. 1943), president-dictator of the Republic of the Congo, 1979-1992 and 1997

*Jerry John Rawlings* (b. 1947), president-dictator of Ghana, 1979 and 1981-2001

*André Kolingba* (b. 1935), dictator of the Central African Republic, 1981-1993

*Moussa Traoré* (b. 1936), president of Mali, 1968-1991

*Bernardo Vieira* (b. 1939), president of Guinea-Bissau, 1980-1984, 1984-1999, and again beginning in 2005

*Joaquim Chissano* (b. 1939), president of Mozambique, 1986-2005

**SUMMARY OF EVENT**

The exhilaration of freedom from European colonial rule and the initial hopes for a prosperous, harmonious, and democratic future in sub-Saharan Africa proved to be short-lived, crumbling under the realities of military coups, one-party dominance, authoritarianism, and lingering internal enmity among various ethnic groups. This resulted in impoverishment in nearly every region of the continent.

As Africa became increasingly involved in global Cold War politics, strong-armed despots who claimed to be anti-Communist secured money, arms, and even military support from the United States and Western democracies because Western nations feared that strategic areas would fall under Soviet influence. Other tyrants—notably those in Guinea and the Republic of the Congo—

chose to play on self-proclaimed Marxist and Socialist credentials to secure Soviet support to retain power. The disintegration of the Soviet Union and the end of the Cold War by the early 1990's had a triple effect: Western governments were no longer inclined to prop up repressive regimes, assistance to Soviet client states gradually dried up as the Soviet Union weakened, and—inspired by the downfall of the Eastern European one-party states—dissident groups in Africa were emboldened to greater militancy in their demands for more freedom. While most international observers focused on the liberation struggle in South Africa as it developed during the years following Nelson Mandela's release from prison and the subsequent dismantling of apartheid, less-publicized democratization movements taking place in other parts of Africa achieved varying levels of success.

In Ghana, the first sub-Saharan state to achieve independence from colonial rule, the Provisional National Defense Council, under the leadership of Jerry John Rawlings, wielded absolute power beginning in 1981. In 1992, a largely peaceful but persistent campaign by Adu Boahen provoked a constitutional transition to a multiparty system. The stage was set for a presidential election between Boahen's newly legalized New Patriotic Party (NPP) and Rawlings's political apparatus, which was now called the National Democratic Congress (NDC). Rawlings, a charismatic and reasonably likable personality, retained enough popular appeal to prevail in the voting to remain president for another nine years.

In contrast, one of the more violently repressive regimes in Africa, that in Mali—which had held sway since a military coup on November 19, 1968—was led by former army Lieutenant Moussa Traoré. His Democratic Union of the Malian People (UDPM) was the only sanctioned political party. By 1990, the National Committee of Democratic Initiative (CNID) had been formed to challenge the UDPM's stranglehold on power. A demonstration in the capital city of Bamako, organized by the CNID and student activists, culminated in an uprising that raged through the streets from March 25 to March 29, 1991. Although the military ultimately crushed the insurgency, Traoré was arrested and deposed. A temporary government striving for national conciliation drafted a constitution in August of 1991. It established a multiparty electoral system. On April 26, 1992, Alpha Oumar Konaré was elected president of Mali.

The government of Guinea-Bissau, formerly known as Portuguese Guinea, had been monopolized by Bernardo Vieira and the African Party for the Independence of Guinea and Cape Verde (PAIGC) since 1973. Multi-

party politics were allowed in May of 1991. It was not until July 3, 1994, that free elections were held, however, with Vieira the clear victor. In contrast, Benin's unpopular dictator Mathieu Kérékou triggered strident protests and was repudiated emphatically at the polls in 1991, in favor of Nicéphore Soglo.

In the Central African Republic, the military strongman André Kolingba clung obstinately to power initially, but then was forced by the French government—which had previously bankrolled his regime—to hold elections. In October, 1993, Kolingba was decisively defeated by longtime opposition leader Ange-Félix Patassé. The neighboring Republic of the Congo was a Marxist-Socialist state that had become unviable by 1991. Again, the French were instrumental in compelling the dictator, Denis Sassou Nguesso, to hold democratic elections. In July of 1992, Pascal Lissouba won a runoff presidential vote.

The oldest dictator in Africa was Hastings Kamuzu Banda of Malawi, who, by 1992, was approximately ninety-four years old and had ruled in an increasingly iron-fisted manner for twenty-eight years. Although his physical vigor and grasp of reality had markedly declined, he adamantly resisted change until strikes, riots, and foreign condemnation made him set up elections. In 1994, Banda was voted out in favor of Bakili Muluzi.

Kenneth Kaunda came to power in Zambia at the same time as Banda had in Malawi and assumed similarly notorious status. Kaunda had assumed the presidential office immediately following his country's independence from Britain and, from 1964 to 1972, Zambia operated under a multiparty system. However, Kaunda and his United National Independence Party (UNIP) systematically intimidated and legally obstructed all opposition factions until Kaunda proclaimed a one-party dictatorship in 1972.

By 1990, discontent arising from Kaunda's increasingly repressive methods, and the country's economic malaise that resulted from Kaunda's semisocialist policies, brought about the illegal formation of the Movement for Multiparty Democracy (MMP). After food-price riots and a nearly successful military coup, Kaunda acquiesced to holding elections. In October, 1991, MMD leader Frederick Chiluba was elected overwhelmingly to the presidency.

In 1992, Mozambique ended a lengthy civil war between the warring FRELIMO (Frente de Libertação de Moçambique, or Mozambique Liberation Front) and RENAMO (Resistência Nacional Moçambicana, or Mozambique National Resistance) factions. The subsequent elections of October 27-29, 1994, resulted in a victory for FRELIMO and its leader Joachim Chissano, who continued to serve in the presidential seat he had held since 1986.

In Madagascar, former Lieutenant-Commander Didier Ratsiraka's military regime had control. In 1989, a rigged election ignited riots and an international outcry for change. A transitional government planned and held elections in February, 1993. Albert Zafy assumed the presidency after winning by a substantial margin.

Democratization was also implemented with relative ease and minimal resistance in Burkina Faso, Cape Verde, São Tomé and Príncipe, Mauritania, Niger, Chad, Guinea, Cameroon, Gabon, Burundi, Angola, and Kenya. Similarly, from February, 1990, to March, 1992, these countries agreed that new constitutions, establishing multiparty systems with reformed—in some cases, monitored—electoral procedures were to be included and set into operation. Even in the autocratic state of Equatorial Guinea, a liberalized constitution and free contested elections were promised.

## SIGNIFICANCE

The impact of the democratization revival of the early 1990's varied from one nation to another. In some instances, it appeared that little lasting effect was achieved: Vieira in Guinea-Bissau, Sassou Nguesso in the Congo, and Ratsiraka in Madagascar all eventually returned to power. By 2007, Guinea, Chad, Niger, and Mauritania had reverted to authoritarianism. Kenya's reforms proved merely cosmetic. Equatorial Guinea's democratic vision never progressed beyond lip service, and oppression remained the norm.

Democratization struck deeper roots in Ghana, Benin, and Mali. The ultimate success or failure of the early 1990's movements that instituted multiparty civilian governments in Africa remained ambivalent.

—*Raymond Pierre Hylton*

## FURTHER READING

Allen, Philip M. *Madagascar: Conflicts of Authority on the Great Island*. Boulder, Colo.: Westview Press, 1995. Clear, concise summary of the political disturbances in an enigmatic and little-known land.

Gocking, Roger. *The History of Ghana*. Westport, Conn.: Greenwood Press, 2005. Jerry Rawlings is credited with influencing the direction of Ghanian democratization.

Meredith, Martin. *The Fate of Africa: From the Hopes of Freedom to the Heart of Despair: A History of Fifty Years of Independence*. New York: Public Affairs, 2005. Provides excellent analysis of postcolonial Africa. Directly links the colonial legacy with the problems experienced in establishing democracy.

Shillington, Kevin. *A History of Africa*. New York: Palgrave Macmillan, 2005. Presents a summary of the rise of authoritarianism and the counteractive democratic surge of the 1990's.

Smith, Malinda S., ed. *Globalizing Africa*. Trenton, N.J.: Africa World Press, 2003. Expresses a more pessimistic view than most sources and depicts the democracy movement as a long-term failure.

**SEE ALSO:** June, 1981: Organization of African Unity Adopts the African Charter on Human and Peoples' Rights; Nov. 6, 1986: Chissano Succeeds Machel in Mozambique; Dec. 8, 1996: Rawlings Wins Reelection to Ghana's Presidency; May 29, 1999: Democracy Returns to Nigeria.

1991

## September, 1991-November, 1992
# IMMIGRANTS IN GERMANY BECOME TARGETS OF VIOLENCE

*Protests and violence against immigrants in Germany in the wake of the nation's reunification were followed by brutal murders of ethnic minorities in November that shocked the world, forcing the German government to address the problem of neofascism in German society.*

LOCALE: Germany

CATEGORIES: Government and politics; immigration, emigration, and relocation; wars, uprisings, and civil unrest

KEY FIGURES

*Helmut Kohl* (b. 1930), chancellor of Germany, 1990-1998

*Volker Rühe* (b. 1942), general secretary of the Christian Democratic Union

*Rudolf Seiters* (b. 1937), German interior minister

*Alexander von Stahl* (b. 1938), German chief prosecutor

*Hans-Ludwig Zächert* (b. 1937), head of the Bundesdriminalamt

SUMMARY OF EVENT

After the reunification of Germany in October of 1990, the nation experienced an unanticipated dramatic increase in acts of violence against foreigners by the indigenous German population. The victims included recruited foreign laborers and their families as well as refugees who had been granted political asylum in Germany. Although discrepancies are found in the data provided by various government agencies, the situation was appalling by all accounts. Estimates of the numbers of xenophobic and racist attacks that took place in Germany in 1991 range from 1,255 to 2,426; in 1992, they range from 2,285 to 4,587. Estimates of deaths from these attacks in 1992 range from 17 to 26. Hans-Ludwig Zächert, head of the Bundeskriminalamt (BKA), the German national police, stated that in October of 1992 alone, 904 such attacks took place, including more than 150 involving firebombs.

There is no way to know how many individual acts of racially motivated violence were not included in these statistics. The apparent pattern of escalation, however, and the large scale of the incidents indicated that a violent sociopolitical movement was gaining momentum and was becoming increasingly well organized. The first highly publicized mass attack took place in September, 1991, in Hoyerswerda, a town of approximately 70,000 people. A mob of neo-Nazis and hundreds of local residents assaulted foreigners with baseball bats and bicycle chains and destroyed their homes. Police did nothing to stop the violence, which went on for six days. In the end, all 230 foreign-born residents of Hoyerswerda were forced to leave town. Representatives of the federal government, in effect, blamed the victims, saying that they were opportunists who falsely claimed they were fleeing political persecution in order to live off German social welfare.

The events in Hoyerswerda sparked a dramatic upsurge in xenophobic violence in Germany, and attacks continued to escalate in 1992. The victims were predominantly foreigners, but they also included Jews, homeless persons, homosexuals, and even the physically challenged.

In August, 1992, in the Baltic city of Rostock, a mob burned a refugee hostel and the adjoining guest-worker housing. More than one hundred Vietnamese men, women, and children barely escaped being incinerated. The neofascist rioters and their supporters numbered in the thousands. As in Hoyerswerda, the police did not intervene, the foreigners were relocated, and the government responded with only qualified condemnation of the perpetrators. Some politicians even expressed their sympathy for the rioters.

Because of the success that the xenophobic mobs achieved in eliminating the foreign populations of Hoyerswerda and Rostock, the same kind of violence erupted in Wismar and Quedlinburg in September of 1992, with identical results. Political refugees were attacked and their quarters were destroyed, and the German government responded by relocating the foreigners.

After the September incidents, the racist violence continued until, in Mölln, in November of 1992, a Turkish family was murdered in a firebomb attack by perpetrators who shouted, "Heil Hitler!" The incident drew horrified responses from governments around the world, international human rights organizations, and a majority of the German public.

Most observers acknowledge that a majority of German citizens disapproved of the vicious assaults and murders of foreigners that had been taking place. However, it may be that the ethnic nationalism and anti-foreigner sentiment that formed the backdrop for those acts was much more widespread. Some have asserted that the answers to questions relating to why the purveyors of xenophobic violence were repeatedly able to apply a strategy for creating "foreigner-free cities" with little federal or local government opposition and only qualified condemnation can be found in Germany's traditions and laws regarding citizenship and immigration, and in the partisan political dynamics of the time.

The constitution and laws of modern Germany are based on the historical concept that Germany is an ethnically defined country—a nation-state based on one culture. Full rights of citizenship are constitutionally guaranteed only to ethnic Germans. This legal fact is the basis for laws dealing with people who enter from foreign countries. German policies on foreign residents distinguish rights and access to citizenship based on ethnicity.

Upon entering Germany, an individual is classed as an ethnic German, a recruited foreign worker, or a refugee. The concept of the ethnically defined nation means that there is an institutionalized legal structure of differential treatment of these groups. Ethnic Germans residing in the countries that were annexed by the Third Reich as of December 31, 1937, and their descendants, are considered to be eligible for German citizenship upon entering the country, as are the descendants of ethnic Germans who were scattered throughout Europe during World War II. This is not considered an immigration policy; rather, it is seen as the repatriation of true Germans.

Because the government's policy is that Germany is "not an immigration country," refugees and recruited workers are not eligible for citizenship, have significantly limited rights, and are viewed as temporary residents in spite of the fact that some "guest-worker" families have been in the country for three generations. In 1990, legislation was passed that made it possible for second- and third-generation foreign-born residents to apply for German citizenship under certain conditions, but these are still exceptions to the rule of the ethnic state. Some observers have asserted that the laws pertaining to citizenship and differential rights based on ethnicity created a segmentation of German society, with foreigners being designated a less desirable group. This in turn fostered an atmosphere in which a significant proportion of the German population felt that strong antiforeigner sentiment was socially acceptable and justified.

## SIGNIFICANCE

The lack of a decisive government response to the violence throughout 1991 and most of 1992 was related to the political struggles of Chancellor Helmut Kohl's Christian Democratic Union (CDU) with several right-wing parties, the most prominent being Die Republikaner (REP). Before East and West German reunification seemed probable, the REP had been gaining some political support with calls for a restoration of Germany's 1937 borders and drastic reductions in the foreign population. The CDU had long advocated the reunification of East and West Germany, and when the Berlin Wall fell with little warning in November of 1989, the party was able to preempt the REP's position by making reunification a reality in less than one year.

Kohl, however, had promised that taxes would not be raised in the West as a result of reunification, and it soon became apparent that the enormous cost of shoring up the economy of the former East Germany would require just that. In the face of growing public opposition to increased taxes and reductions in public spending in the West, the CDU opened, during the summer of 1991, what was called the "Asylum Debate," through which the party hoped to eliminate Article 16 of the German constitution, which guaranteed asylum to foreigners fleeing political persecution. The main thrust of this event was the idea that Germany's economic problems could be alleviated through the elimination of the cost of providing for refugees; repeated references were made to "fake asylum seekers," and it was asserted that many refugees were really "economic migrants."

Some observers have asserted that the CDU's determination to eliminate or amend Article 16 was the reason for the government's conditional criticism and lack of strong action following the mob violence against foreigners in 1991 and 1992, and this may have encouraged neo-Nazis to escalate the level of xenophobic violence. After the Hoyerswerda incident, for example, national-level politicians—including the federal interior minister, Rudolf Seiters, and the general secretary of the CDU, Volker Rühe—issued statements to the effect that the violence was understandable given the strain caused by the large numbers of refugees in Germany as the result of large-scale abuse of asylum laws.

The level of xenophobic violence reached in November, 1992, forced the German government at last to take a number of actions. Alexander von Stahl, chief prosecutor, directed law-enforcement agencies to arrest members of four neo-Nazi organizations that were responsible for much of the violence, and a government ban on those organizations followed. In addition, Article 16 was amended to limit the admissions of those seeking asylum in Germany.

*—Jack Carter*

1991

## FURTHER READING

Betz, Hans-Georg. *Radical Right-Wing Populism in Western Europe.* New York: St. Martin's Press, 1994. Provides an examination of the political movements in Western Europe that provide the backdrop for extremist violence. Includes tables, bibliography, and index.

Björgo, Tore, and Rob Witte, eds. *Racist Violence in Europe.* New York: St. Martin's Press, 1993. Collection of essays includes two chapters that focus on racist violence in Germany during the 1980's and 1990's.

Fekete, Liz, and Frances Webber. *Inside Racist Europe.* London: Institute of Race Relations, 1994. Provides concise description of racist and xenophobic acts in Europe and explores the role played by various European governments, including Germany, in discouraging, encouraging, or even participating in such acts.

Fenner, Angelica, and Eric D. Weitz, eds. *Fascism and Neofascism: Critical Writings on the Radical Right in Europe.* New York: Palgrave Macmillan, 2004. Collection of essays addresses both historical fascism and contemporary neofascism throughout Europe. Several chapters discuss Germany. Includes index.

Kemper, Franz-Josef. "New Trends in Mass Migration in Germany." In *Mass Migration in Europe: The Legacy and the Future*, edited by Russell King. London: Belhaven Press, 1993. Discusses the impacts of recent increases in the foreign population in a society with a long tradition as an "ethnic state."

Kurthen, Hermann, Werner Bergmann, and Rainer Erb, eds. *Antisemitism and Xenophobia in Germany After Unification.* New York: Oxford University Press, 1997. Collection of essays discusses many aspects of the violence that followed unification in Germany. Contributors include American and German scholars in political science, mass communication, history, and sociology.

Solomos, John, and John Wrench, eds. *Racism and Migration in Western Europe.* Providence, R.I.: Berg, 1993. Collection of essays examines racist and xenophobic responses to large-scale population redistribution all over Europe. Includes a chapter focused on contemporary Germany.

**SEE ALSO:** Nov. 23, 1973: West Germany Bans Immigration of Workers from Outside the EEC; Oct. 1, 1982: Kohl Becomes Chancellor of West Germany; Nov. 9, 1989: Fall of the Berlin Wall; July 16, 1990: Gorbachev Agrees to Membership of a United Germany in NATO.

## September 3, 1991
# NORTH CAROLINA FIRE POINTS TO WORKPLACE HAZARDS

*Workplace safety standards gained national attention when twenty-five employees of a food-processing plant died as the result of being trapped by a fast-moving fire in a structure with inadequate exit facilities.*

**LOCALE:** Hamlet, North Carolina
**CATEGORIES:** Disasters; business and labor

## KEY FIGURES

*Emmett Roe* (fl. late twentieth century), owner of the Imperial Food Products Company
*James N. Hair* (fl. late twentieth century), plant manager of the Imperial Food Products Company
*Brad Roe* (fl. late twentieth century), son of Emmett Roe and plant operations manager of the Imperial Food Products Company
*David Fuller* (fl. late twentieth century), fire chief of Hamlet, North Carolina
*Gerard F. Scannell* (b. 1934), administrator of the U.S. Occupational Safety and Health Administration who investigated the plant after the fire for compliance with workplace fire safety
*Charles Dunn* (fl. late twentieth century), deputy director of the North Carolina State Bureau of Investigation
*Charles Jeffress* (fl. late twentieth century), assistant labor commissioner for North Carolina

## SUMMARY OF EVENT

On September 3, 1991, a fire at the Imperial Food Products processing plant in Hamlet, North Carolina, took the lives of more than two dozen of the plant's workers. Subsequent investigation of the site revealed that illegally locked and blocked exit doors had been a major contributor to the tragedy. Hamlet was a community of fewer than seven thousand residents, and the town had limited firefighting resources. Although the fire department's response was prompt, the fire had already gained such headway by the time firefighters arrived that they could do little to save the people inside the building.

Fires that kill large numbers of people usually occur in hotels or places of entertainment such as theaters and nightclubs rather than in workplaces. The fire in Hamlet was reminiscent of New York City's Triangle Shirtwaist Factory fire of 1911, in which approximately 146 people died because the factory's exit doors were locked to keep employees in the building.

The building where the North Carolina fire occurred was a one-story, windowless structure in which poultry was processed, trimmed, cooked, packaged, and refrigerated before shipment. During a normal shift, about ninety people worked in the trimming, marinating, and cutting rooms and in the large processing and cooking area. The building also included storage areas where the finished product awaited shipment to restaurants in the eastern part of the United States. The structure had no built-in systems to protect the building or employees in case of fire, such as sprinklers or alarm systems. In addition, the employees had never received any training in what to do in case of fire.

The Imperial Food building was rectangular, about one hundred by three hundred feet. The fire began in the center of the building near a large gas-fired cooker when a hydraulic oil line in the processing room, which was being repaired, burst under increased pressure and the hose separated from its coupling. The oil spewing from the hose at high pressure was ignited by the gas flame.

The fire intensified rapidly, cutting off escape for many of the employees, who had just begun their work shift. About forty workers were in the trimming room as the fire started. Unable to reach the front doors, their normal path out of the building, they attempted to use an alternate exit but found it inoperable; another nearby door was blocked by a large truck. Many employees found their way out, and some retreated to a cooler room to avoid the acrid smoke, but eleven of the twenty-five fatalities were found in that room, suffocated by smoke. Another eleven people died in the processing room where the fire had started, on a loading dock, and in a freezer room. When the firefighters arrived, they found several other fatalities outside the building.

Following the fire, the North Carolina State Bureau of Investigation found that the building was deficient in the number and arrangement of exits available. The National Fire Protection Association (NFPA), a private organization dedicated to furthering fire safety, also investigated the fire and concluded that the inadequate exits were a significant factor in the high number of fatalities.

The NFPA's analysis pointed out the importance of built-in protections such as fire sprinklers and detectors;

the presence of such systems would have led to a very different outcome in the Hamlet fire. The NFPA also suggested that it might have been helpful if employees had been trained in the correct use of fire extinguishers, but the association also acknowledged that the rapid spread of this fire might have precluded the use of extinguishers. The NFPA stressed that the presence and operability of exits from a building are essential for workplace safety, as is a workable fire plan, practiced periodically, that trains employees to react properly in an emergency.

The U.S. Department of Labor's Occupational Safety and Health Administration (OSHA) concurred that the lack of exits contributed to the large loss of life in the Hamlet fire and noted that the Imperial Food Products building was in violation of nationally recognized standards. Upon investigation, OSHA discovered similar fire hazards at other workplaces around the country. As a result, the agency sent fact sheets providing basic information on fire prevention to state agencies and fire chiefs in major metropolitan areas. OSHA also established a toll-free telephone number that employees could call to report suspected fire hazards or other dangers, such as the presence of toxic wastes, in their workplaces.

In the aftermath of the North Carolina fire, it became clear that failure to provide the number of exits required by code was a prevalent practice in industrial settings; managers often limited the number of exits to minimize pilfering by employees. Further, owners often made modifications to their buildings without considering the effects the changes would have on emergency exits. In addition to the main entrance, the Imperial Food Products plant had only two exits from which people could leave the building rapidly, and one of those was blocked at the time of the fire.

**SIGNIFICANCE**

The violations found after the Imperial Food Products fire were so blatant and the results so tragic that Emmett Roe, the owner of the business, was convicted of twenty-five counts of involuntary manslaughter. The North Carolina Labor Department also imposed a fine on the company of $800,000. News of the fire was a shock to many Americans, who were puzzled by conditions so unsafe that twenty-five people died in a one-story building. Those familiar with occupational fire safety were not surprised, however. Conditions such as those at Imperial Food Products—an almost complete lack of fire protection in the building, the absence of a training program or emergency plan for employees in case of fire, and the locked exit doors—could be documented in at least one-fourth of all businesses.

After the 1911 Triangle Shirtwaist Factory fire in New York, legislation was passed to protect the rights of employees against business owners who kept their workplace doors locked to keep employees inside. The Cocoanut Grove nightclub fire in Boston in 1942 resulted in laws to improve fire safety in dining and drinking establishments. The Beverly Hills Supper Club Fire in Kentucky thirty-five years later showed that what was needed was adequate enforcement of existing statutes, not more statutes.

Experts disagreed as to whether government or private industry should provide the driving force behind efforts to improve fire prevention and safety standards. Some claimed that because fires are counterproductive to profits, the business world would itself try to minimize the incidence of fires for economic reasons. Employees, on the other hand, often claimed that managers tried to push production ever higher at the expense of workplace safety.

Many laws in the United States regulate business for the greater good of employees and the public, and such regulations operate at every level of government. The federal Occupational Safety and Health Act of 1970 set standards for workplace safety, but it was left to the states whether they wished to enforce the law themselves or allow the federal government to do so. North Carolina had opted to enforce OSHA regulations itself. The OSHA regulations, as well as most federal, state, and local fire safety regulations, were based on codes set by the NFPA, but enforcement of the regulations remained a problem in many cases. Like many other states, North Carolina had not taken adequate measures to enforce its fire safety laws. One state investigator admitted shortly after the fire in Hamlet that the state did not inspect plants such as the Imperial Food facility as frequently or thoroughly as was mandated by law.

The enforcement of fire codes at the county and city levels also varied widely in the United States. Although some small jurisdictions were conscientious in this regard, small fire departments normally did not enforce regulations aggressively. Lack of personnel was a primary reason for this, as was a basic lack of understanding of the fire codes. Large fire departments had their own impediments to effective enforcement, but they generally performed more effectively than smaller departments. The fire in North Carolina brought increased attention to the inadequacy of fire safety enforcement in many jurisdictions, at least in the short term.

—*William A. Greene*

**FURTHER READING**

Aulette, Judy Root, and Raymond Michalowski. "Fire in Hamlet: A Case Study of State-Corporate Crime." In *Political Crime in Contemporary America: A Critical Approach*, edited by Kenneth D. Tunnell. New York: Garland, 1993. Examines the fire as a crime committed by a corporation with the tacit collusion of state authorities.

Kerr, Mary Lee, and Bob Hall. "Chickens Come Home to Roost." *Progressive* 56 (January, 1992): 29. Describes the poultry industry's long history of abusive practices toward employees.

_____. "N.C. Chicken Plant Fire Kills 25." *Facts On File* 51 (September 5, 1991): 659. Discusses the cause of the fire at the Imperial Food Products plant, the fact that some doors were locked at the facility, and that North Carolina officials acknowledged a serious lack of human resources to enforce state OSHA requirements.

Klem, Thomas J. "Twenty-Five Die in Food Plant Fire." *NFPA Journal* 86 (January/February, 1992): 29-35. Definitive investigative document of this disaster by the National Fire Protection Association, which is respected for its investigative impartiality and thoroughness.

**SEE ALSO:** July 10, 1976: Italian Factory Explosion Releases Dioxin; Nov. 1, 1986: Swiss Warehouse Fire Causes Toxic Spill into the Rhine; Oct. 26-Nov. 3, 1993: Fires Devastate Southern California; Mar. 24-26, 1999: Fire Disaster Closes Mont Blanc Tunnel.

## September 27, 1991
# BUSH ANNOUNCES NUCLEAR ARMS REDUCTIONS

*Evidencing improved relations between the United States and the Soviet Union, President George H. W. Bush announced plans for the unilateral reduction of U.S. nuclear armaments and level of military readiness.*

**LOCALE:** Washington, D.C.
**CATEGORY:** Diplomacy and international relations

**KEY FIGURES**

*George H. W. Bush* (b. 1924), president of the United States, 1989-1993
*Mikhail Gorbachev* (b. 1931), general secretary of the Communist Party of the Soviet Union, 1985-1991, and president of the Soviet Union, 1990-1991

**SUMMARY OF EVENT**

After four decades of Cold War suspicion and periodic confrontations between the United States and the Soviet Union, an era of significantly improved relations between the two nuclear superpowers developed after 1985. A major foreign and military policy speech by President George H. W. Bush on September 27, 1991, marked the efforts of both nations to reduce their nuclear armaments and lessen the dangers of nuclear confrontation and possible war. What was especially striking about the president's policy statement was that the reductions he announced were not the result of specific negotiations with the Soviet government, but were taken unilaterally by the United States.

Since atomic weapons first appeared in 1945, the designs, destructive power, and possible uses of nuclear weapons had expanded greatly. By the 1970's, both superpowers possessed large numbers of these destructive devices. Initial negotiations to limit the rate of growth of certain types of nuclear weapons earlier had resulted in two groundbreaking agreements stemming from the Strategic Arms Limitation Talks of 1972 (SALT I) and 1979 (SALT II), and U.S.-Soviet negotiations continued sporadically during the 1980's, culminating in a 1987 treaty to eliminate intermediate-range nuclear missile systems located in Europe.

The greatest danger to both nations, in size and destructive power, involved powerful intercontinental ballistic missiles (ICBMs), which possessed the necessary range to reach each other's territory. Negotiations to limit this class of strategic weapons continued between the U.S. and Soviet governments for several years, lead-ing to an agreement in July, 1991. Soviet leader Mikhail Gorbachev and President Bush signed the first treaty of the Strategic Arms Reduction Talks (START I) in Moscow as the first step to beginning the numerical reduction of these powerful strategic missiles (the treaty was ratified in early 1992). This atmosphere for greater cooperation, building on prior arms control efforts, provided the background for the president's dramatic announcement in September.

Other favorable conditions in 1990 and 1991 also signaled an improved relationship between the two Cold War rivals. Soviet military intervention in neighboring Afghanistan had ended in 1989; Communist governments in Central and Eastern Europe had fallen from power in 1989 with minimal violence, the nations of East and West Germany had united in 1990, and growing economic ties between the Soviet Union and the West promised more cooperation. A significant agreement to limit military forces and nonnuclear weapons in Europe was adopted in November, 1990, by the Warsaw Pact (the Soviet Union and its European Communist allies) and the North Atlantic Treaty Organization (NATO), of which the United States was a member. The following year, the Warsaw Pact itself ended.

The Soviet Union's cooperation with the United Nations and the West during the Persian Gulf War against Iraq in early 1991 also showed willingness to work together in common purpose. When the leaders of the world's most economically powerful nations, known as the Group of Seven (G7), held their annual meeting in London in July, 1991, Gorbachev was invited to attend as an eighth participant. A few days later, Bush flew to Moscow to sign the START agreement. The conditions were thus favorable for additional proposals from each side to continue the trend to reduce the threshold of nuclear danger.

In a televised address to the nation on September 27, 1991, President Bush discussed a broad range of nuclear weapons systems and outlined the changes in military policies the United States would unilaterally adopt. He first described changes in the Cold War environment and the growing cooperation between the superpowers and asserted that the possibility of a Soviet attack on Western Europe was no longer likely. Essentially, Bush declared that the Cold War was over and said that the two nations could work together in the future. This opportunity to improve the relationship now required both sides to under-

1991

take additional steps toward increased cooperation and peace.

Building on previous arms control agreements, the president specified steps he intended to adopt for the U.S. military. Some decisions were immediate and unilateral, falling under Bush's authority as U.S. commander in chief. For example, approximately twenty-one hundred U.S. nuclear artillery shells and short-range nuclear missiles located in Europe, originally designed for tactical battlefield use in case of war with the Soviet Union and its Warsaw Pact allies, were ordered withdrawn and destroyed. More than eight hundred nuclear weapons were removed from U.S. surface warships and naval aircraft.

Bush also gave orders for the U.S. long-range bomber force to end its twenty-four-hour alert status. This policy, in place since the 1950's, had required warplanes with nuclear weapons to be kept in continual readiness in case of crisis and possible nuclear war. A category of ICBMs scheduled to be eliminated under the START agreement,

450 Minuteman IIs, would be dismantled immediately rather than during the longer period specified in START. Further development of several new types of nuclear missiles, including the controversial MX missile with ten nuclear warheads, was canceled.

In the speech, Bush further identified several long-term objectives requiring future negotiations with the Soviet government. He proposed joint talks to seek the eventual elimination of all land-based multiwarhead nuclear missiles as well as to improve procedures for the future supervision and dismantling of nuclear weapons of both nations. He recommended consideration of joint efforts to develop antiballistic missile defense systems for each nation.

**SIGNIFICANCE**
President Bush's dramatic announcement of September 27, 1991, caught the world by surprise because of its sweeping provisions and important implications for

*U.S. president George H. W. Bush (center left) and Soviet president Mikhail Gorbachev (center right) sign the first treaty of the Strategic Arms Reduction Talks in the Kremlin in Moscow, Soviet Union, on July 31, 1991. (NARA)*

the future. Western military analysts interpreted the president's overture as having several purposes. In addition to the arms cuts and other steps, the United States hoped to support Gorbachev, who faced the imminent collapse of the Soviet Union. If that occurred, it would be even more difficult to negotiate the control and elimination of the former nation's nuclear armaments.

Prior to making his public speech, the president had privately communicated its contents to major world leaders, including Gorbachev. The Soviet response was considered to be the most significant. On September 28, Gorbachev gave cautious support to the U.S. proposals and reiterated the Soviet interest in reducing nuclear weapons. He noted his regret that the U.S. president had not gone further, however, such as suspending U.S. underground nuclear testing. The Soviet leader promised careful consideration of the U.S. declaration, and the Moscow government indicated that it would present its own proposals.

On October 5, the Gorbachev government announced a comparable set of reciprocal policies and unilateral cuts in Soviet military forces. Several steps paralleled Bush's orders, including removal of the Soviet strategic bomber force from ready-alert status, removal and destruction of tactical battlefield nuclear armaments, and a promise to dismantle more than five hundred ICBMs. Several missile projects also were canceled. Additional Soviet proposals even went beyond Bush's September announcement, including adoption of a one-year moratorium on Soviet nuclear weapons testing.

The two governments, within a two-week period, had announced substantial reductions in nuclear weapons systems and the general level of military preparedness. The extent of the decisions and the rapidity of their implementation signified continued cooperation between the two superpowers. The decisions announced by both leaders in their September 27 and October 5 statements provided the basis for further advances in shrinking the arms race and resolving the potential dangers of nuclear conflict, including the signing of the more ambitious START II agreement in January, 1993, by Bush and Russia's new president, Boris Yeltsin.

*—Taylor Stults*

---

## MAKING THE WORLD A LESS DANGEROUS PLACE

*President George H. W. Bush began his address to the nation on September 27, 1991, by reminding the American people of the changes that had recently taken place in the Soviet Union and in Eastern Europe:*

Tonight I'd like to speak with you about our future and the future of the generations to come.

The world has changed at a fantastic pace, with each day writing a fresh page of history before yesterday's ink has even dried. And most recently, we've seen the peoples of the Soviet Union turn to democracy and freedom, and discard a system of government based on oppression and fear.

Like the East Europeans before them, they face the daunting challenge of building fresh political structures, based on human rights, democratic principles, and market economies. Their task is far from easy and far from over. They will need our help, and they will get it.

But these dramatic changes challenge our Nation as well. Our country has always stood for freedom and democracy. And when the newly elected leaders of Eastern Europe grappled with forming their new governments, they looked to the United States. They looked to American democratic principles in building their own free societies. Even the leaders of the U.S.S.R. Republics are reading the Federalist Papers, written by America's founders, to find new ideas and inspiration.

Today, America must lead again, as it always has, as only it can. And we will. We must also provide the inspiration for lasting peace. And we will do that, too. We can now take steps in response to these dramatic developments, steps that can help the Soviet peoples in their quest for peace and prosperity. More importantly, we can now take steps to make the world a less dangerous place than ever before in the nuclear age.

1991

---

### FURTHER READING

"Arms Control: U.S. and Soviet Announcements and Proposals of Major Reductions on Nuclear Weapons." *Foreign Policy Bulletin* 2, no. 2 (September/October, 1991): 47-51. Comprises the complete texts of three documents: Bush's September 27 speech, a September 27 "White House Summary of U.S. Initiatives on Nuclear Arms," and Gorbachev's October 5 response.

Beschloss, Michael R., and Strobe Talbott. *At the Highest Levels: The Inside Story of the End of the Cold War.* Boston: Little, Brown, 1993. Assesses the major leaders involved and describes the events that took place between the United States and the Soviet Union in the period 1989-1991.

Crockatt, Richard. *The Fifty Years War: The United States and the Soviet Union in World Politics, 1941-1991.* New York: Routledge, 1995. Shows the shift from confrontation to cooperation in agreements on nuclear weapons and other issues.

Gaddis, John Lewis. *The United States and the End of the Cold War: Implications, Reconsiderations, Provocations*. New York: Oxford University Press, 1992. Presents a broad interpretation of the changing Cold War relationships by the 1990's.

Oberdorfer, Don. *The Turn: From the Cold War to a New Era—The United States and the Soviet Union, 1983-1990*. New York: Poseidon Press, 1991. Covers the period of improved U.S.-Soviet Union relations under Reagan and Gorbachev.

Powaski, Ronald E. *Return to Armageddon: The United States and the Nuclear Arms Race, 1981-1999*. New York: Oxford University Press, 2000. Discussion of the arms race includes extensive attention to disarmament talks. Addresses the importance of the role of each of the U.S. presidents during the period discussed.

Rotblat, Joseph, ed. *Nuclear Weapons: The Road to Zero*. Boulder, Colo.: Westview Press, 1998. Collection of essays covers a wide range of issues related to international nuclear disarmament.

**SEE ALSO:** May 26, 1973-Dec. 26, 1991: Détente with the Soviet Union; June 18, 1979: SALT II Is Signed; Dec. 8, 1987: Intermediate-Range Nuclear Forces Treaty; Jan. 3, 1993: United States and Russia Reach Nuclear Arms Reduction Agreement.

## October, 1991
# IIJIMA REPORTS THE PRODUCTION OF MULTIWALL CARBON NANOTUBES

*Sumio Iijima's production of multiwall tubes of interconnected carbon atoms many nanometers in diameter, which he later named carbon nanotubes, heralded the birth of electronic nanoscience.*

**LOCALE:** Tsukuba, Honshū, Japan
**CATEGORIES:** Science and technology; chemistry; physics

### KEY FIGURES
*Sumio Iijima* (b. 1939), Japanese crystallographer and electron microscopist
*Donald S. Bethune* (b. 1949), American materials research scientist
*Robert F. Curl* (b. 1933), American research chemist
*Harold W. Kroto* (b. 1939), English research chemist
*Richard E. Smalley* (1943-2005), American research physicist and laser spectroscopist
*L. V. Radushkevich* (fl. late twentieth century), Russian research chemist
*V. M. Lukyanovich* (fl late twentieth century), Russian research chemist

### SUMMARY OF EVENT
Sumio Iijima's interest in carbon nanostructures began during the 1970's while he was a research crystallographer at Arizona State University. After developing an improved electron microscope, Iijima used the instrument to examine closely the crystals of many substances. During the course of this work, he observed sooty,
nanoscale, onionlike spheroids of graphite, and he published his observations in 1980. (Nanoscale objects are extremely small, measurable in nanometers; a nanometer is equal to one-billionth of a meter.) He did not explore the significance of these spheroids further until the subsequent laboratory production and structural documentation of graphitic fullerenes.

In 1985, Richard E. Smalley and Robert F. Curl of Rice University in Houston, Texas, along with Harold W. Kroto of the University of Sussex in the United Kingdom, found small quantities of nanoscale carbon 60 ($C_{60}$) after they vaporized graphite in their laboratory with a laser. Along with amorphous soot, $C_{60}$ was latently deposited on the wall of their experimental containment vessel. The molecules were shaped like soccer balls, with each closed, hollow orb comprising sixty hexagonally interconnected carbon atoms. Because the molecule structurally resembled the geodesic architecture of R. Buckminster Fuller, it was named Buckminsterfullerene, shortened to fullerene for verbal ease. Reported in the widely read scientific journal *Nature*, Smalley and his colleagues' investigations initiated a frenzy of solid-state carbon research, especially of graphite, one of two naturally occurring structural forms of pure carbon (the other being diamond). These three researchers subsequently shared the 1996 Nobel Prize in Chemistry for their discovery of fullerenes.

Although carbon nanostructures occur in nature, they became apparent to scientists only after the development of X-ray diffraction and invention of the transmission electron microscope in the 1930's. In October, 1991, during a scientific conference at Richmond, Virginia, Iijima, who by that time was working as an industrial scientist with Japan's NEC Corporation, reported producing nanoscale, multiwall tubes of graphitic carbon at his research laboratory in Tsukuba, Honshū, Japan, while microscopically searching for fullerenes. The carbon nanotubes formed a soot that had been deposited serendipitously on the positive graphitic electrode or cathode of an electric arc lamp.

The imaged carbon nanotubes strikingly appeared as elongated, tubular fullerenes, closed at each end, with variable diameters comprising multiple layers of rolled graphite. Each multiwall carbon nanotube resembled a large roll of chicken wire with an inside hollow diameter. Each hexagonal ring within the crystal lattice of the rolled carbon nanotube displayed even smaller individual, interconnected atoms, each measuring approximately one angstrom (an angstrom is equal to one ten-billionth of a meter).

After the Richmond conference, Iijima published his findings in *Nature*, and his announcement initiated a second enthusiastic wave of applied research regarding graphitic carbon. Like most scientists, Iijima was unaware that his report represented at least the third independent documentation of carbon nanotubes. These structures, and possibly fullerenes, were first definitively discovered and photomicrographed in 1952 by two Russian scientists, L. V. Radushkevich and V. M. Lukyanovich, after they thermally decomposed carbon monoxide in the presence of catalytic iron particles. Unfortunately, little information was recorded in the former Soviet Union about these two resourceful investigators, although their published report has remained readily available.

Carbon has the extraordinary property of being capable of bonding not only with itself but also with the atoms of many other elements in chains, rings, and combinations of these two structures, producing an incredible diversity of natural and human-made substances. Like fullerenes and nanotubes, graphite and diamond are composed solely of interconnected carbon atoms—that is, they contain no atoms of other elements. The significant qualitative differences between diamond and graphite are a consequence of their different physical arrangements and crystal lattices. The atoms of lamellar graphite are cyclically bound to three adjacent carbon atoms of the same planar sheet. Not directly connected, the individual, slippery sheets of graphite are easily separated,

making the erasable substance found to be useful in pencils. Cubic diamonds, in contrast, contain carbon atoms densely connected to four other carbon atoms. Much softer than diamond but more tensile, graphite looks and behaves like a metal. A graphitic derivative, carbon nanotubes share graphite's conductive properties and lamellar, polycyclical crystalline structure with electrons freely circumnavigating individual sheets.

## SIGNIFICANCE

As a scientist with NEC, Iijima comprehended the commercial significance of nanoscale graphitic carbon structures. Founded in 1899 as Nippon Electric Company, NEC had become a multinational conglomerate of affiliated companies specializing in electronic components, including semiconductors and video displays. Unlike diamonds, graphitic carbon nanotubes were found to conduct electricity even better than copper; thus they lent themselves well to electronic applications.

Iijima's published research reached a broad scientific audience that also understood the potential applications for carbon nanotubes. Before the rapid advances that were made in the electronics industry in the late twentieth century, other discoveries concerning multiwall carbon nanotubes had been reported to very limited audiences. Nevertheless, the substantial international examinations of solid-state carbon prior to the discovery of fullerenes and single-wall carbon nanotubes prepared a strong foundation for the groundbreaking research of the 1980's and 1990's.

Not surprisingly, carbon nanotubes drew the interest of industrial researchers at another international electronic giant, International Business Machines (IBM) Corporation. Like Iijima, the IBM scientists foresaw industrial possibilities for carbon nanotubes, including in the manufacture of electronic circuitry and storage tubes. Remarkably, Iijima and Donald S. Bethune of IBM announced their independent, coincidental discoveries of metalocatalyzed, single-wall carbon nanotubes in the same 1993 issue of *Nature*. One nanometer or more in cross-section and capped at each end, a single-wall carbon nanotube is a seamless, single-layered, hollow cylinder of graphene, generally several millimeters in length. In 2002, both scientists were acknowledged by the American Physical Society as codiscoverers of single-wall carbon nanotubes.

Historically, carbon nanotubes were productively deposited after different methods of high temperature graphite, hydrocarbon, or carbon oxide decomposition in the absence of free oxygen. These processes prevented the reactive production of carbon dioxide, a gaseous compound physically more stable than either graphite or diamond. Although these processes were cost-effective, by 1999 manufacturing focused on catalytically controlling the structural quality, electrical conductivity, and tensility of carbon nanotubes. One of the strongest known materials, carbon nanotubes reportedly exhibited a tensile strength approximately fifty times greater than steel. Soon after their discovery, carbon nanotubes were combined with other industrially manufactured composite materials, such as concrete, to enhance the structural integrity of those materials.

By the beginning of the twenty-first century, IBM and NEC researchers had announced significant progress toward the mass production and use of carbon nanotubes as fuel cell electrodes to power electronic devices efficiently and as potential nanowiring and switches in efficient, low-voltage electrical circuits. Hoping to exploit carbon nanotubes as storage vessels, in 2004, scientists at the Argonne National Laboratory in Illinois successfully drew water into a single-wall carbon nanotube.

*—Hayes K. Galitski*

## FURTHER READING

Bethune, Donald S., et al. "Cobalt-Catalysed Growth of Carbon Nanotubes with Single-Atomic-Layer Walls." *Nature* 363 (1993): 605-607. Documents the production of single-wall carbon nanotubes at IBM's research laboratories in Almaden, California. Includes micrographic illustrations.

Harris, Peter J. F. *Carbon Nanotubes and Related Structures. New Materials for the Twenty-First Century.* New York: Cambridge University Press, 1999. Presents a thorough examination of the history, science, manufacturing, and potential applications of carbon nanotubes. Introductory chapter describes the beginnings of nanotube research. Includes illustrations and indexes.

Iijima, Sumio. "Helical Microtubules of Graphitic Carbon." *Nature* 354 (1991): 56-58. Outlines the serendipitous 1991 production of multiwalled, graphitic carbon nanotubes at NEC's research laboratory in Japan. Includes micrographic illustrations.

_____. "High Resolution Microscopy of Some Carbonaceous Materials." *Journal of Microscopy* 119 (1980): 99-111. Iijima's earliest documentation of sooty, nano-sized, graphitic carbon particles as elaborated through his electron microscopy at Arizona State University.

Iijima, Sumio, and Takehashi Ichihashi. "Single-Shell Carbon Nanotubes of 1-nm Diameter." *Nature* 363 (1993): 603-605. Documents the 1993 discovery at NEC of single-wall carbon tubes having diameters of 1 to 4 nanometers. Includes micrographic illustrations.

Kroto, Harold W., Richard E. Smalley, and Robert F. Curl. "$C_{60}$: Buckminsterfullerene." *Nature* 318 (1985): 162-163. Highlights the laboratory production of carbon-60, or fullerenes, at Rice University by these collaborative researchers.

Monthioux, Marc, and Vladimir L. Kuznetzov. "Who Should Be Given the Credit for the Discovery of Carbon Nanotubes?" *Carbon* 44 (2006): 1621. Clarifies the confusion regarding the time line of discovery for both multiwall and single-wall carbon nanotubes.

Oberlin, A., M. Endo, and T. Koyama. "Filamentous Growth of Carbon Through Benzene Decomposition." *Journal of Crystal Growth* 32 (1976): 335-349. Details the independent 1970's production of multiwall carbon nanotubes through controlled laboratory decomposition of liquid benzene. Includes micrographic illustrations.

Radushkevich, L. V., and V. M. Lukyanovich. "O strukture ugleroda, obrazujucegosja pri termiceskom razlozenii okisi ugleroda na zeleznom kontakte." *Russian Journal of Physical Chemistry* 26 (1952): 88-95. Earliest known report photodocumenting the discovery of metalocatalyzed multiwall carbon nanotubes (the title translates as "Carbon structures formed during thermal decomposition of carbon oxide on an iron contact"). General global knowledge of this report was hampered by the Cold War and limited readership for this Russian journal.

**SEE ALSO:** Aug. 12, 1981: IBM Introduces Its Personal Computer.

## October-November, 1991
# YUGOSLAV ARMY SHELLS DUBROVNIK

*During the autumn of 1991, the city of Dubrovnik in Croatia was bombarded by Yugoslav federal forces, an assault that resulted in numerous casualties as well as significant damage to medieval structures in and around the city.*

LOCALE: Dubrovnik, Croatia
CATEGORIES: Terrorism, atrocities, and war crimes; wars, uprisings, and civil unrest

KEY FIGURES

*Ante Marković* (b. 1924), prime minister of Yugoslavia, 1989-1991
*Stipe Mesić* (b. 1934), Croat who became president of Yugoslavia, 1991
*Franjo Tudjman* (1922-1999), president of Croatia, 1990-1999
*Slobodan Milošević* (1941-2006), president of Serbia, 1989-1997
*Tito* (Josip Broz; 1892-1980), post-World War II Yugoslav leader

SUMMARY OF EVENT

The city of Dubrovnik, situated on the Dalmatian coast on the eastern side of the Adriatic Sea, traces its history to the end of the seventh century C.E. The city, originally called Ragusium and subsequently known as Ragusa, was founded by displaced Roman settlers from the Greek city of Epidaurus (located immediately to the southeast) after Epidaurus had been seized by Slavs. Eventually, as the Slavic and Latin communities became integrated, Dubrovnik came under the autonomous control of the Byzantine Empire.

Between 1205 and 1358, Dubrovnik was controlled autonomously by Venice. Between 1358 and 1526, it fell under Hungarian protection. Subsequently, Dubrovnik came under the protection of the Ottoman Empire but retained a large measure of independence. Dubrovnik was a leading center of maritime commercial activity in the fifteenth through eighteenth centuries, second in the Adriatic only to Venice. Dubrovnik also emerged as an important intellectual center in the development of Balkan culture. Indeed, throughout its history the city has retained a strong cosmopolitan flavor that has blended Mediterranean influences with the diverse cultural characteristics of the Balkan region.

Beginning in 1272 and continuing through the seventeenth century, the city erected an elaborate series of for-

tifications. Dubrovnik's main city wall, approximately six thousand feet in circumference, between thirteen and twenty feet thick on the land side, five to ten feet thick on the sea side, and about eighty feet high, surrounded what has become known as the old city. Punctuating the walls are five bastions, two corner towers, twelve square towers, three round towers, and the citadel of Fort St. John (Sveti Ivan), a formidable defensive structure guarding the old harbor. Dubrovnik's medieval character has been preserved within the old city, with many of the buildings dating back to the fourteenth and fifteenth centuries. The physical characteristics of medieval Dubrovnik, combined with its rich cultural and artistic attractions, made the city Yugoslavia's principal historical tourist site, with thousands of visitors flocking to the city annually. In recognition of Dubrovnik's unique historical value, the city was placed on the United Nations World Heritage List in 1979 as a site whose safety and preservation are said to be humankind's collective responsibility.

In 1808, Dubrovnik was taken by Napoleon, but in the settlement at the Congress of Vienna in 1815, the city was awarded to Austria. It remained under Vienna's control until the defeat of the Austro-Hungarian Empire in World War I. After 1918, Dubrovnik was attached to Croatia, within the framework of the newly created state of Yugoslavia, which was dominated by Serbs. Historically, Croatia and Serbia represented two different aspects of their common Balkan heritage. Whereas the Serbs were Orthodox in religious persuasion, the Croats were predominantly Catholic. Linguistically, the Serbs used the Cyrillic alphabet, and the Croats used the Latin alphabet. Eastern Ottoman Turkish influences remained strong in Serbia, whereas Croatia followed the lead of Central Europe.

During the interwar period, tensions mounted among the Serbs, the Croats, and the other nationalities within Yugoslavia. These tensions were manifested during World War II, when, under Nazi sponsorship, Yugoslavia was broken up and an independent Croatia was established. Nazi atrocities, combined with traditional Balkan hatreds, led to persecutions and massacres that left postwar Yugoslavia deeply scarred. In the wake of the collapse of Nazi Germany in 1945, Yugoslavia was reestablished, this time under the leadership of the Communist Party, guided by the partisan leader Marshal Tito. Tito managed to suppress the national hostilities, but af-

1991

ter his death in 1980, these hostilities gradually resurfaced.

The collapse of communism in Eastern Europe at the end of the 1980's created the context for the disintegration of postwar Yugoslavia. Croatia and Slovenia elected governments pledged to assert independence from the Yugoslav state. On June 25, 1991, the Slovenes and Croatians declared their independence from Yugoslavia. Slovenia moved immediately to secure its borders. Following a brief series of clashes with the Yugoslav federal army that left fifty people dead, the fighting subsided and attention shifted southward to Croatia.

Approximately 600,000 of Croatia's 4.5 million citizens were ethnic Serbs. They contended that they did not wish to become an ethnic minority within an independent Croatian state. Serbian leaders outside Croatia supported these claims, asserting that Serbs left within an independent Croatia would be persecuted by the Croatian majority. Consequently, even prior to Croatia's formal declaration of independence, and with Serbian support, the Serbs within Croatia began to prepare for an armed insurgency.

Following Croatia's declaration of independence, the Serbian-dominated Yugoslav federal army began operations against the rebellious Croats. Simultaneously, the federal army gradually began to coordinate its activities with the Serbian insurgents. Although the Yugoslav federal army cited a variety of goals to justify its military operations against Croatia, ranging from protecting the Serbian minority in Croatia to defending and restoring Yugoslavia, the Croatians contended that Serbia was using the federal army and the ethnic Serbs in Croatia as instruments to dismember Croatia and create a Greater Serbia. In any case, by autumn, 1991, the Yugoslav federal army and the Serbian insurgents had captured approximately one-third of Croatian territory. By that time, an estimated 3,000 to 5,000 people had been killed in the intensifying Yugoslav civil war, with as many as 10,000 wounded and more than 300,000 displaced from their homes.

By the beginning of October, 1991, fighting between Croatian forces and units of the Yugoslav federal army had spread to the area around Dubrovnik. On October 1, the Yugoslav army surrounded the city, laying siege to it and its 60,000 inhabitants, 90 percent of whom were Croats. Dubrovnik's citizens, joined by refugees from outlying areas, were deprived of electric power, telephone communications, and fresh water. By late October, rationing had been introduced. Families were allocated 1.3 gallons of fresh water daily, with very small supplements sometimes collected from Dubrovnik's cisterns. People were reduced to washing and flushing toilets with water from the Adriatic Sea. Food was also rationed, with a family's weekly portion consisting of one quart of cooking oil, one pint of milk, one pound of potatoes, one pound of bread, two tins of fish, and two tins of meat. The people of Dubrovnik were concerned particularly with the prospect of disease that might result from untreated sewage and a shortage of medicine. Tensions among the population increased with the duration of the siege, as people spent long hours in basement shelters or in chambers within the walls of the old city.

By mid-October, planes from the Yugoslav federal air force had bombed the marina, and federal artillery had shelled the city, although at that point the old city remained undamaged. By October 23, units of the Yugoslav federal army had moved to positions within three miles of the old city, and the danger to Dubrovnik increased daily. As the Serbian-dominated Yugoslav military continued to increase its pressure on Dubrovnik, international efforts to prevent the situation from further deteriorating also continued. Representatives from the European Community and the United Nations, in addition to their efforts to secure a comprehensive cease-fire in the Yugoslav civil war, appealed to both Serbs and Croats to honor the U.N. convention protecting historic sites and to spare Dubrovnik from further destruction. The United States condemned the Yugoslav federal army's attack on Dubrovnik as an irresponsible assault on a civilian center that was devoid of military value. For their part, Yugoslav military authorities denied that their forces had attacked the old city and pledged to keep them from doing so.

In late October, Croatian and Yugoslav army leaders agreed on a partial evacuation of Dubrovnik under the supervision of European Community monitors and the Red Cross. Males between the ages of eighteen and sixty, however, would not be allowed to leave the city unless they were joined by ill or elderly relatives. By the end of October, Dubrovnik's population had decreased only marginally, because refugees from outlying areas continued to arrive. The old city had sustained only light damage up to that time. As of October 28, the Red Cross reported that fifty-two people had been killed and slightly more than two hundred had been wounded in the fighting in and around the city.

In early November, 1991, Dubrovnik was subjected to its heaviest artillery and gunboat bombardment. Yugoslav federal shells hit targets inside and immediately around the old city. On November 9, the Yugoslav military intensified its joint bombardment of the old city, the surrounding tourist hotels, and adjacent civilian targets.

## SIGNIFICANCE

The bombardment of Dubrovnik in early November caused significant damage to the old city and adjacent areas. Approximately fifty people reportedly were killed, and many more were wounded in the land, air, and naval bombardment, which continued until November 13. Several of Dubrovnik's tourist hotels were seriously damaged or destroyed as Croatian defenders attempted to halt the advance of the Yugoslav federal forces. Federal planes attacked Croatian positions in the Napoleonic-era fort, constructed in 1808 on Brdo Srdj (Mount Sergius), which rises above Dubrovnik. Fort St. John, as well as many of the towers along the city walls, was damaged, as were a number of sites within the medieval city itself. Both the fourteenth century Dominican friary and the Franciscan friary at the opposite side of the old city were damaged, as was the seventeenth century Jesuit church. Elsewhere in the old city, such medieval architectural treasures as Dubrovnik's clock tower were hit during the shelling.

Even after considering the physical damage to Dubrovnik and the suffering of the city's people, Croatia's new leaders vowed to defend the city against the Yugoslav federal military attacks. From their perspective, Dubrovnik had become a symbol of Croatian independence and resistance to Serbian domination.

On November 13, the Yugoslav federal shelling tapered off, and in the afternoon, a relief ship was allowed to enter Dubrovnik's harbor. Food, medical supplies, and fresh water were unloaded, and on the following day, more than two thousand refugees were evacuated from the city. This set the stage for subsequent relief efforts. Eventually, a spokesperson for the Yugoslav federal army apologized for the shelling of Dubrovnik, attributing the action to local forces that allegedly acted without permission from the central authorities.

In eastern Croatia, the eighty-six-day siege of the city of Vukovar ended on November 17 with the city's capture by Yugoslav federal troops and Serbian insurgents. Like Dubrovnik, Vukovar had become a symbol of Croatian resistance to Serbian efforts to suppress Croatia's spirit of independence. Unlike Dubrovnik, Vukovar was reduced to ruins, and extremely heavy civilian casualties were sustained as Serbian forces bombarded the city into submission.

At the end of 1991, as Germany led members of the European Community in formal recognition of Croatia and Slovenia, the Croatian government remained com-

mitted to recapturing those territories it had lost at the outset of its war for independence. An internationally brokered cease-fire among the belligerents had been put in place at year's end.

Although it had been damaged significantly, Dubrovnik had escaped the level of destruction visited on Vukovar. The fact that the priceless treasures of this historic medieval city were damaged at all, combined with the tragic loss of human life and the wounding of a large number of Dubrovnik's citizens, amplified the need for a common commitment by all nations to honor U.N. agreements governing the protection of the irreplaceable relics of humankind's global heritage.

The Balkans as a whole continued in bloody warfare that spread into Bosnia and Herzegovina, as that province also sued for independence. Not until the Dayton Accords of 1995 was a degree of order and peace restored to the troubled region.

—*Howard M. Hensel*

## FURTHER READING

Binder, David. "Dubrovnik Diary." *The New York Times*, November 16, 1991, p. 4. Vital account provides a firsthand description of the shelling of Dubrovnik from November 10 to November 14, 1991. Should be read in conjunction with the author's other articles published in *The New York Times* on November 9, 1991 (pp. 1, 4), November 10, 1991 (p. 8), and November 15, 1991 (p. 3).

Djukić, Slavoljub. *Milošević and Marković: A Lust for Power*. Translated by Alex Dubinsky. Montreal: McGill-Queen's University Press, 2001. Presents an account of Milošević's political career, including discussion of his wife's influence, and a close examination of his regime.

Nelson, Daniel N. *Balkan Imbroglio: Politics and Security in Southeastern Europe*. Boulder, Colo.: Westview Press, 1991. Informative volume focuses on contemporary problems of the Balkans. Includes a chapter devoted to the problems of Yugoslavia.

Sell, Louis. *Slobodan Milošević and the Destruction of Yugoslavia*. Durham, N.C.: Duke University Press, 2002. Presents a comprehensive examination of the political life of Milošević and how his policies led to the breakup of Yugoslavia.

Shoup, Paul. *Communism and the Yugoslav National Question*. New York: Columbia University Press, 1968. Key background study provides context necessary to an understanding of the complexities of the Yugoslav nationality question.

1991

Tanner, Marcus. *Croatia: A Nation Forged in War.* 2d ed. New Haven, Conn.: Yale University Press, 1997. Presents a thorough account of Croatia's history.

Wolff, Robert L. *The Balkans in Our Time.* New York: W. W. Norton, 1967. Classic work focuses primarily on the development of the Balkans during the first half of the twentieth century.

**SEE ALSO:** May 4, 1980: Death of Tito; July-Nov., 1988: Ethnic Violence Erupts in Yugoslavian Provinces; June 25, 1991: Civil War Begins in Yugoslavia; Feb. 21, 1992: United Nations Authorizes Troop Deployment to the Balkans; Feb. 13, 1995: Serbs Face Charges at the International Criminal Tribunal for Yugoslavia.

## November 7, 1991
# U.S. CONGRESS STRENGTHENS EQUAL OPPORTUNITY LAWS

*With passage of the Civil Rights Act of 1991, Congress restored equal opportunity law to its status before 1989, the year in which several U.S. Supreme Court decisions weakened two decades of legal precedents.*

**ALSO KNOWN AS:** Civil Rights Act of 1991; U.S. Statutes at Large 105 Stat. 1071; Public Law 102-166

**LOCALE:** Washington, D.C.

**CATEGORIES:** Civil rights and liberties; laws, acts, and legal history

### KEY FIGURES

*George H. W. Bush* (b. 1924), president of the United States, 1989-1993

*John Danforth* (b. 1936), U.S. senator from Missouri

*Ted Kennedy* (b. 1932), U.S. senator from Massachusetts

### SUMMARY OF EVENT

The Civil Rights Act of 1991 has been described as among the most sweeping civil rights laws to be passed by Congress. In response to several adverse decisions by the U.S. Supreme Court, Senators Ted Kennedy, a Democrat, and John Danforth, a Republican, jointly sponsored the Civil Rights Act of 1991, which was drafted with the objective of overturning these decisions. President George H. W. Bush, who had vetoed a similar bill in 1990, signed the bill into law in 1991.

Through congressional hearings, Congress concluded that additional remedies under federal law were needed to deter unlawful harassment and intentional discrimination in the workplace; decisions of the U.S. Supreme Court had weakened the effectiveness of federal civil rights protection; and legislation was necessary to provide additional protection against unlawful discrimination in employment. The expressed purpose of the Civil Rights Act of 1991 was to restore the state of discrimination law to what it had been before 1989, the year in

which a conservative Supreme Court issued several decisions that seriously threatened the enforceability of equal opportunity laws. The act further expanded the scope of coverage of relevant civil rights statutes to include individuals or plaintiffs who sued under the Age Discrimination Act (ADA) or the Rehabilitation Act of 1973, and granted coverage to federal employees of Congress and employees of U.S. companies located in foreign countries.

Title VII of the Civil Rights Act of 1964 had made it unlawful to discriminate in employment because of race, ethnicity, color, sex, or religion. The primary issue facing judicial bodies empowered to adjudicate claims of discrimination was to define what employment practices violated Title VII and other antidiscrimination laws. Traditionally, employers screened potential employees by the use of general intelligence and aptitude tests, word-of-mouth recruiting, and other subjective criteria that disproportionately excluded minorities from employment and promotion or had disparate impacts on their possibilities of employment or promotion.

In *Griggs v. Duke Power Company* (1971), which is considered the most important decision in the evolution of equal employment opportunity law, the Supreme Court had articulated the major principle that invalidated general intelligence tests and other criteria that had the effect of excluding minorities, regardless of the intent of the employer. The Court stated that if any criteria had a disparate impact on the protected group, the criteria were unlawful and could be sustained only if they were related to the job and necessary for business. The burden of proof to rebut the claim shifted to the employer once the possibility of discrimination had been shown through statistical or other evidence.

In 1989, the Supreme Court issued several decisions that reversed the *Griggs* burden-of-proof standard and several other major legal principles governing unlawful discrimination. In *Wards Cove Packing Company v. Atonio*, the Supreme Court changed the *Griggs* standard by holding that employees not only must show that they were disparately and discriminatorily affected but also must prove that the employer could have employed alternate ways with less disparate impact. In *Price Waterhouse v. Hopkins*, the Court held that even after the employer has been found guilty of unlawful discrimination, it could still escape liability by showing that the employee would have been dismissed or treated differently for another nondiscriminatory reason. These changes made it significantly more difficult for plaintiffs to prevail in suits.

## SIGNIFICANCE

The Civil Rights Act of 1991 restored the *Griggs* principle. It also reversed the *Price Waterhouse* decision, stipulating that an unlawful practice is established when the complaining party demonstrates that race, color, religion, or national origin was a motivating factor for any employment practice, even though other factors also motivated the decision.

In *Patterson v. McLean Credit Union* (1989) the Supreme Court severely limited section 1981 of the Civil Rights Act of 1866 when it held that the act covered only unlawful discrimination with regard to race and national origin at the time of hiring. Acts of discrimination that occurred after hiring were no longer illegal under the Civil Rights Act of 1866. The Civil Rights Act of 1991 reversed this decision by prohibiting pre- and postemployment discrimination.

In *Lorance v. AT&T Technologies* (1989) the Supreme Court upheld the dismissal of discrimination charges by female employees who charged that the implementation of a new seniority system discriminated against them. This decision established the principle that although women had been adversely affected by a new seniority policy, their complaint was barred because the statute of limitations had expired. The Supreme Court ruled that the timing began at the time of the policy change and not when the women became aware of the discriminatory effects of the policy. This reasoning was criticized on the grounds that an individual often may not know the discriminatory impact of the policy change until long after the statute of limitations for filing has passed. The Civil Rights Act of 1991 restored the legal principle that the statute of limitations begins when the individual becomes aware of the discrimination.

Many municipalities have entered into consent decrees that grant relief to minority employees to avoid lengthy and costly litigations. Such consent decrees may adversely affect the interests of white male employees. However, all parties affected by the decree are notified and given an opportunity to intervene to protect the interests of their members. Once the consent decree has been approved by the court, it cannot be challenged in the future. In *Martin v. Wilks* (1989) the Supreme Court established a new principle. It allowed new white firefighters who were not a party to the original consent decree and judgment to reopen the decision. Had this new principle been allowed to stand, it would have threatened the validity of hundreds of consent decrees in the United States. The Civil Rights Act of 1991 reversed this decision. The act precluded any later challenge by a present employee, former employee, or applicant to a consent decree granting affirmative rights to minority employees.

Several major differences existed between section 1981 of the Civil Rights Act of 1866 and other equal opportunity laws with respect to remedies available to plaintiffs. Whereas a plaintiff had a right to a jury trial and compensatory and punitive damages under section 1981 of the 1866 act, plaintiffs who sued under Title VII, the ADA, and the Rehabilitation Act had no right to a jury trial and could only seek compensatory damages. The Civil Rights Acts of 1991 expanded these rights accorded to plaintiffs under section 1981 to plaintiffs who were subjected to intentional discrimination under Title VII, the ADA, and the Rehabilitation Act.

Another notable limitation in the equal opportunity law was the absence of protection from discrimination for federal employees and U.S. citizens working in U.S. firms overseas. The Civil Rights Act of 1991 extended the right to sue to federal employees in the legislative and executive branches under Title VII, ADA, and the Rehabilitation Act. One exception was made to the definition of unlawful practices: that party affiliation and political compatibility may not be attacked as unfair employment practices. Furthermore, the act extended coverage to U.S. employees employed in foreign lands by U.S. firms.

Civil service examinations are required for most jobs and promotions in the public sector. Applicants are supposed to be chosen based on competitive scores earned. It has been charged, however, that these tests are biased in favor of white men in particular and white applicants and employees in general. Generally, a higher proportion of whites will score higher than members of minority groups. To ensure that a larger number of minorities will be hired and promoted, the scores are adjusted for minorities such that some minorities with lower scores occasionally may be selected over whites with higher scores.

1991

This adjustment of test scores, which is referred to as race norming, emerged as a contentious issue in the United States. The Civil Rights Act of 1991 expressly prohibits compensatory adjustments to test scores in employment based upon race or other protected characteristics.

*—Richard Hudson*

**FURTHER READING**

Anderson, Terry H. *The Pursuit of Fairness: A History of Affirmative Action.* New York: Oxford University Press, 2004. Addresses all aspects of the history of affirmative action and equal employment opportunity law and practice in the United States. Includes discussion of the Civil Rights Acts of 1964 and 1991.

Kmiec, D. W., et al. "The Civil Rights Act of 1991: Theory and Practice—A Symposium." *Notre Dame Law Review* 68 (1993): 911-1164. Presents six critical articles on different aspects of the act.

Practising Law Institute. *The Civil Rights Act of 1991: Its Impact on Employment Discrimination Litigation.* New York: Author, 1992. Manual written for lawyers and other legal professionals offers an analysis of the Civil Rights Act of 1991.

*Rutgers Law Review* 45, no. 4 (Summer, 1993): 887- 1087. Contains eight critical articles on different aspects of the act. All were previously delivered at a symposium titled "The Civil Rights Act of 1991: Unraveling the Controversy."

U.S. Equal Employment Opportunity Commission. *EEOC Compliance Manual.* Chicago: Commerce Clearing House, 1995. Provides clear, comprehensive descriptions of unlawful practices, types of proofs and evidence that establish discrimination, and procedures to pursue claims of unlawful discrimination.

**SEE ALSO:** Mar. 8, 1971: U.S. Supreme Court Bans Discrimination in Hiring; Mar. 22, 1972-June 30, 1982: ERA Passes Congress but Falls Short of Ratification; Mar. 24, 1972: U.S. Congress Mandates Equal Employment Opportunity; Aug. 6, 1975: U.S. Congress Bans Literacy Tests for Voting; June 27, 1979: U.S. Supreme Court Rules on Affirmative Action Programs; June 12, 1984: U.S. Supreme Court Upholds Seniority Systems; 1986: U.S. Supreme Court Upholds Goals, Not Quotas, to Remedy Discrimination; Mar. 22, 1988: U.S. Congress Mandates Nondiscriminatory Practices by Recipients of Public Funds; July 26, 1990: U.S. Congress Enacts Disability Rights.

---

# December, 1991
# DISSOLUTION OF THE SOVIET UNION

*During late 1991, disastrous economic conditions, worsening quality of material life, growing nationalist separatism, and a coup attempt destroyed confidence in the central government of the Soviet Union and led to the creation of the Commonwealth of Independent States.*

**LOCALE:** Soviet Union
**CATEGORIES:** Government and politics; diplomacy and international relations

**KEY FIGURES**

*Mikhail Gorbachev* (b. 1931), general secretary of the Communist Party of the Soviet Union, 1985-1991, and last president of the Soviet Union, 1990-1991

*Boris Yeltsin* (1931-2007), president of the Russian Soviet Federated Socialist Republic, 1991-1999

*Gennady Yanayev* (b. 1937), vice president of the Soviet Union, December, 1990-August, 1991

*Leonid Kravchuk* (b. 1934), president of the Ukraine and one of three creators of the Commonwealth of Independent States

*Stanislav Shushkevich* (b. 1934), chairman of the Belorussian Supreme Soviet and one of three creators of the Commonwealth of Independent States

**SUMMARY OF EVENT**

According to the 1936 constitution of the Union of Soviet Socialist Republics, or Soviet Union, citizens of that nation possessed freedom of speech, press, assembly, and demonstration, as well as equality of rights, irrespective of nationality or race. The constitution also guaranteed to member republics the right of secession. The history of the Soviet Union, however, shows evidence of ongoing disregard for these rights. The social and economic consequences of that disregard prompted the Soviet Union's dissolution.

The year after the Bolshevik Revolution in 1917, Vladimir Ilich Lenin established the Soviet Republic of Russia. At first, the government declared that all land, housing, and large factories were public property, to be managed by the central government. In 1921, however,

**CAUCASUS AND FORMER SOVIET REPUBLICS OF CENTRAL ASIA**

Lenin combined privatized small industries and retail trade with state-controlled large industry, banking, and foreign trade. When the Union of Soviet Socialist Republics was founded in 1922, however, its agricultural, industrial, and other economic resources already were exhausted.

Joseph Stalin took over the Communist Party of the Soviet Union in 1924 and inaugurated highly centralized economic planning. He created collective farms and launched his country into rapid industrial development. Unfortunately, the Soviet people suffered from a neglect of both agriculture and production of consumer goods, declining living standards, and increasing political coercion. In the 1930's, Stalin eliminated political opposition with mass arrests, forced labor, and executions. He also extended Soviet domination in Europe, beginning with annexation of the Baltic States on the eve of World

War II and continuing with the establishment of the Iron Curtain in the postwar period. In the mid-1950's, the Soviet Union's economic growth began to slow, worker productivity fell, and consumption of goods declined.

Nikita S. Khrushchev, who emerged as the new Communist Party leader in 1953 and became premier in 1958, eased Stalinist restrictions, but his attempts to reform the Soviet economy were unsuccessful. When his farm program collapsed in 1964, Khrushchev was forced into retirement.

Leonid Brezhnev, who succeeded Khrushchev as party leader and later became president of the Soviet Union, stifled political reform. As economic growth slowed further in the 1960's and 1970's, Brezhnev continued to use central economic planning and attempted to improve living conditions. With gains in agricultural production barely matching population growth, food importation became necessary. After 1979, Soviet productivity declined dramatically, living standards fell, and shortages of goods and services became severe.

In 1986, Mikhail Gorbachev (general secretary of the Communist Party since 1985) launched a radical economic reform program known as perestroika (restructuring), accompanied by a policy of glasnost (openness) in Soviet society. In a general loosening of central economic control, in 1987 Gorbachev removed industrial subsidies and moved industry into partial free market operation. He decentralized economic management, allowed individual farmers to work private plots and sell produce on a free market basis, and ordered payment of workers according to productivity. Gorbachev also restructured prices, generally upward, to ease consumer

shortages. An obstructionist bureaucracy, however, implemented these reforms slowly.

Many Soviets initially supported the 1987 reforms, but by late 1989 most considered the economic situation to be deteriorating and blamed the deterioration on Gorbachev's reforms. Because of the reforms, workers had to work longer, harder, and often for lower wages. They faced higher prices in state stores, where goods were increasingly difficult to find. Supplies were more plentiful in privatized markets and on the black market, but prices there were even higher. Perestroika had resulted in frustration, erosion of support for Gorbachev, party defection, and work stoppages.

In 1988, Gorbachev began restructuring the Soviet government, and in 1989 his democratic reforms resulted in the first free, multicandidate election in the Soviet Union since 1917. With the economy and living standards worsening, however, the Communist Party spiraled into decline. Soviet satellite states swept away their Communist regimes, and Soviet republics declared sovereignty (Azerbaijan in 1989) and independence (Lithuania in 1990). Having legalized opposition parties early in 1990, the Communist Party relinquished formal control over the Soviet Union. Separatist sentiments and activity increased in the Soviet republics. In May, 1990, anti-Communist nationalist Zviad Gamsakhurdia of Georgia and radical populist reformer Boris Yeltsin of Russia won the presidencies of their republics in popular elections.

In mid-1991, Gorbachev formulated a treaty to transform the Union of Soviet Socialist Republics into a confederated "Union of Sovereign Soviet Republics." The proposed treaty called for a new constitution that would allow national elections and diminish the power of the Communist Party and the Soviet central government. The signing of the treaty was scheduled for August 20, 1991.

Instead, on Sunday, August 18, 1991, a coup d'état began with Gorbachev's arrest. Involving all but two

**FORMER SOVIET EUROPEAN NATIONS**

of Gorbachev's own ministers, the coup sought to overthrow Gorbachev, prevent the signing of the treaty, and return the Soviet Union to strong centralized Communist Party rule. On Monday, August 19, Vice President Gennady Yanayev was proclaimed acting president of the Soviet Union, and an emergency committee assumed power. The Soviet military commander in the Baltics took control of the three secessionist Baltic republics, Lithuania, Latvia, and Estonia. In Moscow, Yeltsin persuaded a unit of Soviet tanks to protect the Russian government. He called for nationwide resistance, the return of Gorbachev as Soviet president, and a general strike.

On August 20, Soviet tanks moved to within one mile of Yeltsin's headquarters. Fearing attack, tens of thousands of resisters erected barricades to protect Yeltsin and his democratically elected government. Strong protests against the coup and other scattered Soviet military activity erupted in Moldova (formerly Moldavia), the Ukraine, and Kazakhstan. Shaken by intense, widespread anticoup sentiments, three members of the emergency committee resigned, and the coup began to fall apart.

On August 21, coup opponents gained ground. Soviet tanks withdrew from Moscow, and in the Baltics, Soviet troops began returning to their bases. In Moscow, the Communist Party denounced the coup, the Congress of People's Deputies demanded Gorbachev's reinstatement, and crowds celebrated outside the Russian parliament. Latvia and Estonia, where military crackdowns had been severe, declared immediate independence. Gorbachev returned to Moscow on August 22. With most coup leaders under arrest, Gorbachev and his ally, Yeltsin, began rebuilding the Soviet government. Even as Gorbachev proclaimed his devotion to socialism and the Communist Party, the Lithuanian government banned the party and confiscated its property.

The August, 1991, coup attempt had several effects. It elevated Yeltsin to the forefront of Soviet and world affairs, where he became a symbol of Western democracy. Defeat of the coup also removed high-level obstructions to Gorbachev's reforms, the very reforms the coup's instigators had tried to prevent. The coup also fanned republican independence movements and precipitated the dissolution of both the Communist Party and the Soviet Union.

While Gorbachev set Soviet political and economic reforms in motion on August 23, Yeltsin began chipping away at Soviet authority. Latvia banned the Communist Party, and republican governments seized party property. Across the Soviet Union, citizens turned on party

bosses and organizations, and crowds vandalized statues of Communist heroes.

Gorbachev's proposed new union grew shakier. Late in August, more Soviet republics declared independence, ignoring Gorbachev's exhortations to preserve a modified union. On August 26, leaders of the breakaway republics firmly declared central authority to be dead. Three days later, the Communist Party ceased to exist. On September 5, the Congress of People's Deputies transferred power to the republics. The next day, the Baltic States' independence was approved.

As central power crumbled, republican leaders took political and economic control. On December 7, 1991, Yeltsin, Ukrainian president Leonid Kravchuk, and Belorussian chairman Stanislav Shushkevich met to discuss a trade agreement. Deciding that it was impossible to reform the economy within the Soviet structure, the three leaders formed the Commonwealth of Independent States on December 8 and proclaimed the Soviet Union's end. According to their agreement, Commonwealth republics would launch coordinated economic reforms and jointly move toward free market prices, beginning on January 2, 1992. Other articles of the agreement concerned liquidating nuclear arms, respecting the territorial integrity of other republics, and guaranteeing all citizens equal rights and freedoms.

On December 17, 1991, Gorbachev agreed to dissolve the Soviet Union. Five days later, Russia, Ukraine, Armenia, Belorussia, Kazakhstan, Kyrgyzstan, Moldova, Turkmenistan, Azerbaijan, Tajikistan, and Uzbekistan approved the Commonwealth pact and sealed the fate of the Soviet Union. On December 25, 1991, Gorbachev formally resigned as president, the first Soviet leader ever to leave office voluntarily. Six days later, the Soviet Union, the world's first communist state, officially ceased to exist. In its place was the ill-defined but diplomatically useful Commonwealth of Independent States.

### SIGNIFICANCE

The Soviet Union collapsed as a result of poor economic conditions, worsening quality of life, growing nationalist separatism, and a bankrupt ideology. The political and economic health of its successor, the Commonwealth, was very poor at its beginning. One political result of the dissolution of the Soviet Union was increased potential for ethnic and nationalist ferment. After the dissolution, fears that the new republics would follow the course that Romania and Yugoslavia had taken after their break from the Soviet Union were borne out. Georgia came close to civil war within weeks, and within one week eth-

1991

nic strife led to violence in Armenia and Azerbaijan. Fears also arose that political upheaval might come at the hands of ill-provisioned and disgruntled Soviet military personnel.

Popular uncertainty about the future also increased following the dissolution. The example of Eastern Europe was not encouraging. When Communist Party control in the Soviet bloc collapsed in 1989, many people suffered. Following the implementation of free market economic reforms, unemployment rose, production decreased, shortages became more common, and inflation raged at rates as high as 700 percent per year. Consumer goods became too expensive for purchase by many potential buyers. In Albania, starvation loomed as a threat. Although economists in the Soviet Union predicted that within months the cost of goods would stabilize and more products would become available, in the Russian Republic families prepared for the worst, stockpiling food in preparation for famine.

That the disintegration of the Soviet Union freed the former Soviet republics to move toward economic reform was most apparent in Russia. After the dissolution, President Yeltsin quickly began privatization of state-owned property, agriculture, and industry. He also introduced new monetary and fiscal policies, the most important of which was the elimination of price controls early in January, 1992. The prices of basic commodities (bread and gasoline, for example) remained controlled, but all other prices were set free for the first time in more than seventy years. The hope was that this would stimulate manufacturing, yield the production of more goods, bring supply in line with consumer demand, and thus moderate inflation.

The early effects of these reforms on the economy and on material conditions of life were worse than the Russian populace expected. Unemployment soared, and more was likely to come as the huge Soviet bureaucracy and military were disassembled. In addition, the ruble lost value. In Russia at the time prices were freed, 100 rubles were worth 63 American dollars. Two weeks later, 110 rubles brought one dollar. By late February, however, the Russian government had moved to stabilize the ruble, and its value appeared to be rising. Even so, at that time the Ukraine, Belarus (the former Belorussia), Moldova, and Kazakhstan planned to begin printing their own currency.

Hand in hand with the devaluation of the ruble, inflation soared. In the first month without price controls, Russian prices increased an average of 200 percent. In St. Petersburg, food costs soared to ten times their previous level, while salaries remained the same. There were no significant increases in available supplies of goods. During the winter of 1992, St. Petersburg faced real hunger. Supplies there had become scarce at the end of the summer, after the neighboring Baltic States had lifted price controls and Baltic shoppers had flooded into Russia, where goods were cheaper, to buy supplies. Rationing was begun in St. Petersburg in the fall of 1991, but when Yeltsin freed prices, almost everything disappeared from the store shelves.

Standing out among the immediate effects of the disintegration of the Soviet Union was popular discontent in both political and economic realms. Within months of the formation of the Commonwealth of Independent States, ethnic and nationalist violence erupted. In the face of shortages of crucial foodstuffs and supplies, there was fear that bread riots, another coup, or the dissolution of the Commonwealth might be on the horizon. Ultimately, however, the Commonwealth was not a truly unified body or even a confederation; rather, it was more a diplomatic means of making the collapse of the Soviet Union more collaborative and civilized. It continued in existence into the twenty-first century, even though its members increasingly faced very different political and economic trajectories. It persisted because of the promise of closer trade and economic ties and because of its utility as a forum where the member states could address security issues, control cross-border criminal activity, promote degrees of democratization, and seek humanitarian cooperation.

*—Martha Ellen Webb*

## FURTHER READING

Church, George J. "Postmortem: Anatomy of a Coup." *Time*, September 2, 1991, 32-34. Well-written article presents a detailed, play-by-play account of the coup, its major players, and their motivations.

Goldman, Marshall I. "The Consumer." In *The Soviet Union Today: An Interpretive Guide*, edited by James Cracraft. 2d ed. Chicago: University of Chicago Press, 1988. Provides a broad look at agriculture, housing, and the availability of consumer goods in the Soviet Union from the 1940's to the 1980's. Alludes to increasing popular discontent.

Gorbachev, Mikhail. *Gorbachev: On My Country and the World*. Translated by George Shriver. New York: Columbia University Press, 2000. Gorbachev reflects on the Soviet experiment from the October Revolution to the Cold War. Discusses leaders such as Joseph Stalin and Boris Yeltsin and examines the twenty-first century challenges facing Russia and the world.

Johnson, D. Gale. "Agriculture." In *The Soviet Union Today: An Interpretive Guide*, edited by James Cracraft. 2d ed. Chicago: University of Chicago Press, 1988. Gives a brief but detailed overview of Soviet agricultural production from the 1950's to 1985, compares it with U.S. production, and explains factors that led to the Soviet Union's poor agricultural performance and increasing costs.

Kenez, Peter. *A History of the Soviet Union from the Beginning to the End.* 2d ed. New York: Cambridge University Press, 2006. Concise work covering the Soviet Union's life span focuses on economics and also provides sociocultural context for events. Includes chronology.

Matthews, Mervyn. *Patterns of Deprivation in the Soviet Union Under Brezhnev and Gorbachev.* Stanford, Calif.: Hoover Institution Press, 1989. Discusses the results of sociological surveys done in the Soviet Union from the 1960's to the mid-1980's. Heavy on statistics, but also presents detailed information on food, clothing, and household goods; public desires to obtain consumer goods; and the popular assessment of living conditions in 1985.

Millar, James R. "An Overview." In *The Soviet Union Today: An Interpretive Guide*, edited by James Cracraft. 2d ed. Chicago: University of Chicago Press, 1988. Surveys the Soviet economy and presents information on its consumer impact. Also analyzes the potential of various reforms.

Shelton, Judy. *The Coming Soviet Crash: Gorbachev's Desperate Pursuit of Credit in Western Financial Markets.* New York: Free Press, 1989. Macroanalysis of the Soviet economy and East-West relations as of 1988 includes informative sections on consumer conditions in the Soviet Union in chapter 2. Chapter 3 details Gorbachev's plans for economic reform. Unlike several other authors cited here, Shelton predicted an economic crash in the Soviet Union.

Smith, Gordon B. *Soviet Politics: Struggling with Change.* 2d ed. New York: St. Martin's Press, 1992. Indispensable source of information on the Soviet Union immediately prior to its disintegration. Chapter 10 treats the Soviet economic system, and chapter 11 outlines social policy and problems.

**See also:** May 26, 1973-Dec. 26, 1991: Détente with the Soviet Union; Mar. 11, 1985: Gorbachev Initiates a Policy of Glasnost; Nov. 19-21, 1985: U.S.-Soviet Summit; Apr. 26, 1986: Soviet Chernobyl Nuclear Plant Undergoes Meltdown; Feb. 4, 1989: Soviet Farmers Gain Control of Land and Crop Selection; Mar. 6, 1990: Soviet Parliament Allows Private Ownership; Mar. 11, 1990: Lithuania Declares Independence from the Soviet Union.

1991

## December, 1991-1992
# Muslim Refugees Flee Persecution in Myanmar

*An estimated 250,000 to 280,000 Muslims fled to Bangladesh from the primarily Buddhist nation of Myanmar from the end of 1991 through the spring of 1992 after apparent oppression and denial of basic human rights by the Myanmar military.*

**Locale:** Myanmar; Bangladesh
**Categories:** Immigration, emigration, and relocation; human rights

**Key Figures**
*Begum Khaleda Zia* (b. 1945), prime minister of Bangladesh, 1991-1996 and 2001-2006
*U Thaung Tun* (fl. late twentieth century), deputy minister of the Myanmar mission to the United Nations
*Boutros Boutros-Ghali* (b. 1922), secretary-general of the United Nations, 1992-1996

**Summary of Event**

Myanmar, the nation formerly known as Burma, has strong historical connections to Buddhism, and the overwhelming majority of its people are Buddhists. Close to 70 percent of the people in Myanmar are of the ethnicity known as Burman, and the dominant Burmans hold political power. Continual conflicts with ethnic and religious minorities, particularly with tribal groups in the northeast, have contributed to keeping Myanmar under repressive military rule for much of its history.

The largest concentration of Muslims in this primarily Buddhist country is in the west, near the border with Bangladesh. At the end of the twentieth century, there were one to two million Muslims living in the region of Myanmar commonly known by the older name of Arakan Province, renamed Rakhine Province by Myanmar's military government. These Arakanese Muslims, who refer to themselves as Rohingyas, outnumbered the Buddhist Arakanese in several districts of the province.

Myanmar's Buddhist authorities have long been suspicious of the Muslims. In addition to the Muslims' different religious belief, the Muslims' movement back and forth across the border has often raised questions in the minds of government officials about the citizenship and loyalties of the Muslims. In 1971, the eastern portion of Pakistan broke away and established the nation of Bangladesh. Although Burma was one of the first states in Asia to recognize Bangladesh, problems soon developed between the two countries over illegal immigration and the smuggling of goods. In 1977 and 1978, the Tatmadaw, the national army of Burma, conducted a massive crackdown on suspected illegal immigrants, and more than 200,000 Rohingyas fled into Bangladesh. Following mediation on the part of the United Nations, Burma and Bangladesh signed an agreement for repatriation of the refugees in July, 1979. Although most returned, a substantial number remained in Bangladesh.

In 1982, Burma passed a citizenship law that appeared to be designed to deny citizenship rights to many of the nation's ethnic minority groups, particularly the Muslims in the west of the country. Under this law, to qualify for full citizenship individuals in Burma had to prove that their ancestors had lived in the country in 1823. That date was one year before the British colonial government had made Arakan part of Burma, so few Rohingyas could obtain the basic rights of citizenship under the new law.

Burma's military government became even more repressive in 1988. After popular demonstrations in Yangon (formerly known as Rangoon), the Burmese leader Ne Win resigned, a civilian government was elected, and the Burmese military staged a coup. A shadowy military junta known as the State Law and Order Restoration Council (SLORC) seized control. This junta, which changed the name of the country to Myanmar in 1989, acted primarily on the belief that the nation was falling apart and that therefore unity had to be imposed and maintained through force.

One of the actions of the new military government that was especially oppressive for the Muslims was the issuing of identity cards. To travel in the country, to obtain a job in the civil service, or to enroll a child in school, each citizen of what was now Myanmar had to show an identity card that included a photograph of the individual and statements of his or her ethnicity, religion, and place of residence.

During the last two weeks of 1991, Myanmar's new military government undertook Operation Pyatya in Arakan. The government maintained that this was another check for illegal immigrants. According to Muslims, however, Muslim men were being taken away from home for forced labor, and soldiers were raping Muslim women. On January 10, 1992, the newspaper *Sangbad* in Dhaka, Bangladesh, reported claims of Muslim refugees that the Myanmar government had issued arrest warrants for ten thousand Muslims under suspicion of participating in an antigovernment insurgency. The newspaper also reported that the soldiers had imprisoned about twenty-eight hundred Muslims in Myanmar and that seven hundred of these detainees had died in crowded warehouses.

From January through February, an estimated forty-five thousand to sixty thousand Muslims fled across the Naf River into Bangladesh. In early March, the Office of the United Nations High Commissioner for Refugees (UNHCR) issued an official statement in Geneva that called the situation along the border of the Southeast Asian nations a serious crisis in which five thousand to seven thousand people were fleeing to Bangladesh every day. This was particularly worrisome because Bangladesh, as one of the world's poorest nations, was ill equipped to help the newcomers. Nevertheless, Bangladeshis and refugees from the 1978 exodus did form some organizations, such as the Rohingya Muslim Welfare Association, to help the refugees. Rabita, a relief organization for Muslims from Mecca in Saudi Arabia, also provided some assistance. The United Nations became involved also, airlifting blankets and plastic sheets to the desperate Rohingyas and establishing refugee camps in Bangladesh.

The Myanmar government rejected criticism of its actions. U Thaung Tun, deputy director of the Myanmar mission to the United Nations in New York, declared that there was no religious discrimination in his country. The problem, he stated, was one of illegal immigration; his government's Immigration and Manpower Department had simply carried out routine citizenship checks, and these checks had resulted in the return to Bangladesh of about three thousand illegal immigrants from that country. This version of the events was not widely accepted by representatives of other governments.

In the middle of March, Prime Minister Begum Khaleda Zia of Bangladesh visited the United States and complained that her country could not take care of so many refugees. President George H. W. Bush promised the prime minister that the United States would provide $3 million to help settle the refugees. The secretary-general of the United Nations, Boutros Boutros-Ghali, met with the Bangladeshi prime minister the day after she met with President Bush and told her that the United Nations would help solve the problem.

In April, the government of Bangladesh came to an agreement with the government of Myanmar. Under this agreement, Bangladesh would force the refugees to return. After about five thousand refugees were pushed back across the border, the UNHCR threatened to close the camps and withdraw its assistance. At the end of 1992, under pressure from the UNHCR, Bangladesh temporarily stopped forcibly repatriating people to Myanmar. In May, 1993, the UNHCR and Bangladesh entered into a formal agreement that Bangladesh would not force Muslim refugees across the border. However, Bangladesh still saw the Rohingyas as uninvited guests that it could not afford. According to some reports, by November, 1993, as many as fifty thousand refugees had been forced to return to Myanmar.

## SIGNIFICANCE

One of the few positive outcomes of the 1992 refugee crisis was that agents of the United Nations were allowed into Myanmar to oversee the resettlement and condition of Muslims in western Myanmar. In late 1993, the UNHCR was able to place a small staff of officials in Arakan to contribute to the peaceful return of people from Bangladesh. This was a marked accomplishment for the United Nations, as the government of Myanmar was usually reluctant to allow any outsiders into the country. Nevertheless, this did not solve the problems of the Rohingyas or end the problem of flight across the border. Under the agreement between the UNHCR and Myanmar, all refugees were to have been returned to their homeland by December, 1995. By that date, however, as many as thirty-five thousand Rohingyas were still reportedly in Bangladesh, and many of those who had returned home had done so unwillingly.

Bangladesh grew increasingly impatient with its refugee burden, and the refugees themselves appeared unwilling to return to Myanmar. In 1996, the government of Bangladesh told officials of voluntary agencies working in the refugee camps that all the agencies would have to leave by March, 1997, and that Bangladesh would take over and resolve the refugee situation without outside assistance. The deadline was extended, however, and voluntary agencies continued to work in the camps. By the end of the 1990's, most of the refugees had returned to Myanmar, but several thousand remained in Bangladesh. Moreover, the opposite movement across the border continued—during the first half of 1997, for example, as

many as fifteen thousand Rohingyas were reported to have fled into Bangladesh.

Those who had gone back to Myanmar found that their situation had not greatly improved. Newly arrived refugees in Bangladesh reported that despite the presence of U.N. representatives in Myanmar, the army continued to demand forced labor, to impose heavy taxes, and, in some cases, to rape women. Many Muslims were also unable to return to their former homes. In Myanmar, the government is considered the owner of all land, and citizens are regarded as tenants who are given permission to live on government land. Because most Muslim residents are not considered citizens, they have no right to live on any land in Myanmar, even if their families have lived on it and farmed it for generations. As a part of the military government's efforts to control Myanmar society, the army has forced many Muslims to relocate to towns and has created "model villages" on land that formerly belonged to the Muslims. Buddhists are then moved into the model villages, giving the army greater power over civilian social structure.

Government ownership of land in Myanmar has also subjected the Muslims to heavy taxation. Farmers must hand over a certain percentage of their harvests of rice and other crops to the government at low fixed prices. The government calculates this percentage on the basis of acreage of land, rather than on the basis of the crops yielded by the land. Because the Muslims farm the poorest and least productive plots, they pay relatively higher taxes than non-Muslims. All families in a province must also pay a chili tax by selling the government chilis at fixed prices, whether or not these families actually grow chilis. The Rohingyas thus are frequently forced to buy chilis in local markets and sell them to the government at a loss. According to officials of the organization Human Rights Watch, Muslims in Myanmar are forced to pay taxes for fishing, for going to the market, and for almost all other necessary activities of daily life.

Although the 1992 refugee crisis received some international attention, the situation of the Muslims of Myanmar has had relatively little media coverage. They make up one of the smaller minority groups in a country known for massive abuses of human rights and for violent ethnic struggles in many parts of the country.

*—Carl L. Bankston III*

## FURTHER READING

Becka, Jan. *Historical Dictionary of Myanmar*. Metuchen, N.J.: Scarecrow Press, 1995. Presents brief entries, arranged alphabetically, on a wide variety of

1991

historical events in Myanmar and other topics related to the country's history. Useful as a general reference source.

Fink, Christina. *Living Silence: Burma Under Military Rule*. New York: Zed Books, 2001. Examines changes in how people live in Myanmar since the military took control of the country in 1988. Includes maps, bibliography, and index.

Steinberg, David I. *Burma: The State of Myanmar*. Wash-

ington, D.C.: Georgetown University Press, 2001. Discusses social, economic, and political events in Myanmar since the military takeover in 1988. Contains some information on the 1992 refugee crisis. Includes maps, glossary, and index.

**SEE ALSO:** Aug. 8, 1988: Auspicious Day of 8/8/88 Turns Deadly in Rangoon; Jan.-Mar., 1997: Karen Refugee Crisis.

## December 10, 1991
# GORDIMER RECEIVES THE NOBEL PRIZE IN LITERATURE

*Nadine Gordimer, whose fiction depicts South Africa's racial turmoil, was awarded the Nobel Prize for her achievement as an artist and as a humanitarian.*

**LOCALE:** Stockholm, Sweden
**CATEGORY:** Literature

**KEY FIGURES**
*Nadine Gordimer* (b. 1923), South African novelist
*Sture Allen* (b. 1928), literature professor and member of the Nobel Academy

**SUMMARY OF EVENT**

After being passed over several times because of disagreement among Nobel Academy members, Nadine Gordimer was named on October 3, 1991, as the year's recipient of the Nobel Prize in Literature. Interviewed in New York City on the day of the announcement, Gordimer commented, "I had been a possible candidate for so long that I had given up hope." As is the custom of the academy, the nature of the disagreement that delayed Gordimer's being honored will remain secret for fifty years. Gordimer was presented with the award, which carried a stipend of approximately $985,000, in a ceremony in Stockholm on December 10, 1991.

The academy may have taken several years to name Gordimer, but her international audience greeted the announcement with immediate approval and genuine enthusiasm, considering the Nobel Prize an honor long overdue. News reports stressed that Gordimer was the first woman in twenty-five years to receive the literature award and only the seventh woman selected in the literature prize's ninety-year history. Although such statistics are revealing, they in no way reflect the thrust of Gordimer's writing. Never considering herself a feminist

writer and sometime even castigated by feminist critics, Gordimer has created a world of women and men—lovers, parents, children, husbands, wives, friends—who struggle most often to establish relationships in what the Nobel Academy called, in its statement on her work, "an insupportable society."

This "insupportable society" has always been South Africa, where Gordimer was born, the daughter of immigrant Jewish parents from Europe. That Gordimer received the Nobel Prize during the dismantling of South Africa's infamous apartheid system led some observers to call the award politically motivated. Sture Allen, the Nobel Academy member who announced Gordimer's selection, pointed out that the Nobel Peace Prize is given for outstanding political contributions. (South African Bishop Desmond Tutu had received the Nobel Peace Prize in 1984.) Gordimer's award, Allen stressed, was "literary," adding that "her works have a political basis, but her writing is different."

What makes Gordimer's writing "different" may be explained in two ways: first, through its structure and style; second, through its universal concerns in spite of the specific time and place. During a period when many writers were experimenting with postmodern techniques such as unreliable narrators and unexplained shifts in time, ignoring the line that divides fantasy and realism, and taking language to sometimes incomprehensible limits, Gordimer has remained a traditional novelist, more similar to the great British and European writers of the nineteenth and early twentieth centuries than to many of her contemporaries. Gordimer's major works, such as *A Guest of Honour* (1970), *The Conservationist* (1974), *Burger's Daughter* (1979), and *A Sport of Nature* (1987), are all big novels, big in that they fully and faithfully realize the basic elements of fiction: plot, character, and setting. This realization comes about through a distinctive style, yet one that is in itself traditional.

The style bears resemblance to the diamonds for which South Africa is famous. Like them, it is tempered and durable, admirable in its clarity, varied in its facets. Again, like a diamond, the style draws no attention for its flashiness, but gains notice for its inexplicable beauty and perfection. At times the prose turns bright and lyrical in description of the landscape; at other points, it takes on a harsh, dark quality when depicting human cruelty in graphic detail or when describing the ugliness of poverty-striken South African townships. The style is also purely African in the way it makes use of nature—animals, sounds, plants, trees, the texture of the soil, the shape of rocks, the sky's colors. The integration of these natural elements into the narrative not only establishes setting but also serves to formulate metaphors delineating the human condition.

The other aspect that makes Gordimer's fiction "different" from purely political writing lies in the way it handles the polarity created by a social system based on racial separation. Neither didactic nor outwardly censuring, Gordimer's short stories and novels pit individuals against an ideology that intrudes on their lives—apartheid. Human relationships are ultimately what matter in the fiction, however—relationships between white and white, black and black, black and white, male and female, young and old.

Gordimer's work records how the political ideology that controlled South Africa for almost half a century affected those who lived it, but to label the work a mere history of what life was like during the apartheid era would be to limit its moral vision. Gordimer's fellow South African Nobel laureate, Archbishop Tutu, commented when he learned of her award, "She's an outstanding artist . . . but more than anything else she has had this tremendous commitment and caring about people, caring about jus-

*South African writer and Nobel laureate Nadine Gordimer.* (AP/Wide World Photos)

## GORDIMER ON WRITING AND BEING

*In her Nobel lecture, delivered on December 7, 1991, Nadine Gordimer discussed the relationship between writing and human understanding of being:*

Perhaps there is no other way of reaching some understanding of being than through art? Writers themselves don't analyze what they do; to analyze would be to look down while crossing a canyon on a tightrope. To say this is not to mystify the process of writing but to make an image out of the intense inner concentration the writer must have to cross the chasms of the aleatory and make them the word's own, as an explorer plants a flag. Yeats' inner "lonely impulse of delight" in the pilot's solitary flight, and his "terrible beauty" born of mass uprising, both opposed and conjoined; E. M. Forster's modest "only connect"; Joyce's chosen, wily "silence, cunning and exile"; more contemporary, Gabriel García Márquez's labyrinth in which power over others, in the person of Simon Bolivar, is led to the thrall of the only unassailable power, death—these are some examples of the writer's endlessly varied ways of approaching the state of being through the word. Any writer of any worth at all hopes to play only a pocket-torch of light—and rarely, through genius, a sudden flambeau—into the bloody yet beautiful labyrinth of human experience, of being.

*Source: Nobel Lectures, Literature 1991-1995*, edited by Sture Allen (Singapore: World Scientific Publishing, 1997).

tice." Those are the qualities that imbue Gordimer's fiction and will continue to do so long after the policies of apartheid become mere historical notes.

### SIGNIFICANCE

Unlike some of those who received the Nobel Prize in Literature before her, Gordimer had established an international reputation before she was honored with the Nobel. Therefore, although the prize certainly enhanced her standing, it seemed likely to have a greater impact on other writers. In particular, the award's prestige carried over into the field generally called international literature in English—that is, writing from countries other than Great Britain and the United States. English-language literature coming from such places as the West Indies, Africa, Australia, India, Canada, and New Zealand had for some time been considered a minor appendage to the long-established literatures of Great Britain and the United States. This attitude changed in the late twentieth century, as the literary world began to look with greater interest and respect beyond traditional boundaries. The publicity surrounding Gordimer's Nobel Prize definitely served to heighten awareness of such literature.

This prestigious award brings recognition first to the

writer, then to his or her country, and then to the literature represented. When two other writers of international literature in English were so honored, Patrick White from Australia in 1973 and Wole Soyinka from Nigeria in 1986, other writers from White's and Soyinka's countries, as well as those from the regions that once made up the British Commonwealth, probably gained far more than did the Nobel laureates themselves. White placed the money that accompanied the Nobel honor into a trust fund that provides from its earnings a sizable cash award given each year to an Australian writer. Gordimer planned to carry out a similar project with part of her Nobel stipend by assisting the Congress of South African Writers, a predominantly black organization. She explained that most of these black authors write in English, the imposed language of the colonizer, but she hoped that they could be encouraged to make use of African languages as well.

The establishment of a black literature in South Africa, whether in English or in native tongues, is long overdue. Many of the African countries that gained their independence after World War II built indigenous literary traditions both in English and in African languages, but the political climate of South Africa was not conducive to such development. Publishing opportunities for black writers were either scant or nonexistent; in fact, government oppression and censorship often prevented black writers from even speaking to their fellow South Africans. A major figure such as Alex La Guma, for example, spent most of his life in exile, and his work was never published in South Africa.

Given the restrictive conditions of South African life from 1948 to 1994, it is surprising that a literature of protest developed at all, but books critical of the system did appear—by white authors. The first such novel to receive international recognition was Alan Paton's *Cry, the Beloved Country* (1948). The novels of André Brink and J. M. Coetzee and the plays of Athol Fugard also found audiences overseas. Much of this work, along with Gordimer's, was long banned by the South African government, but its white authors were not jailed or exiled, perhaps because the government feared the diplomatic consequences of persecuting white writers with reputations abroad. Some observers concluded that books inveighing against the regime in truth did little good, as the works were not generally available in South Africa. Nevertheless, the Nobel citation called Gordimer "the doyenne of South African letters" and praised her for a "continual involvement on behalf of literature and free speech in a police state where censorship and persecution of books and people exist."

In a country with a small population, the emergence of one writer who overshadows all the others creates both bad and good effects, no matter how generous the major writer may be with time, attention, and money. This was certainly the case with Patrick White and Australia; even though White died in 1990 and his Nobel award is long in the past, younger Australian writers still feel their work is too often judged in the light of his brilliant achievement. Soyinka has been both lionized and denigrated in Nigeria, called the voice of Africa in one breath and in the next called a panderer to the literary tastes of the white world overseas. On a more positive note, the attention accorded Gordimer may help to validate her country's literature in the eyes of the rest of the world. From that validation, her contemporaries and successors, black and white, cannot help but gain.

—*Robert L. Ross*

**FURTHER READING**

Clingman, Stephen. *The Novels of Nadine Gordimer: History from the Inside*. 2d ed. Amherst: University of Massachusetts Press, 1986. Covers Gordimer's work through *July's People* (1981). Focuses for the most part on the way Gordimer creates a historical chronicle of South Africa in her novels. Emphasizes the relationship between the fiction and political events. Provides valuable background on the political and legal events that help to shape the outward form of the fiction. Includes extensive bibliography.

Cooke, John. *The Novels of Nadine Gordimer: Private Lives/Public Landscapes*. Baton Rouge: Louisiana University Press, 1985. Close readings of the texts emphasize how all the novels are essentially about the private concerns of individuals who live their lives in the shadow of a "public landscape" formed by political oppression and social injustice. Also addresses the recurrent theme of a daughter rebelling against an overbearing mother. Includes extensive bibliography.

Gordimer, Nadine. *Conversations with Nadine Gordimer*. Edited by Nancy Topping Bazin and Marilyn Dallman Seymour. Jackson: University Press of Mississippi, 1990. Collection of reprints of selected interviews with Gordimer over two decades provides insights into Gordimer's work through her comments on South African politics, the place of the writer in society, and her own theory of writing. Includes extensive bibliography.

Roberts, Ronald Suresh. *No Cold Kitchen: A Biography of Nadine Gordimer*. Johannesburg: STE, 2005. Biography provides some context for Gordimer's works over the course of her lifetime and also offers interpretations of those works. Includes bibliography and index.

Smith, Rowland. "Truth, Irony, and Commitment." In *International Literature in English: Essays on the Major Writers*, edited by Robert L. Ross. New York: Garland, 1991. Examines how Gordimer's work constantly scrutinizes the peculiar role of whites in South Africa. Shows how Gordimer has always been truthful and committed in her fiction while stressing the irony of white South African life.

_____, ed. *Critical Essays on Nadine Gordimer*. Boston: G. K. Hall, 1990. Collection of previously published material on Gordimer's work includes some pieces not otherwise easily available. Offers a variety of approaches and a wide span of critical appraisal from 1953 to 1988. Provides discussions of Gordimer's novels and short stories through *A Sport of Nature*. Includes extensive bibliography.

Yelen, Louise. *From the Margins of Empire: Christina Stead, Doris Lessing, Nadine Gordimer*. Ithaca, N.Y.: Cornell University Press, 1998. Focuses on the issue of national identity in the writings of these three women, all of whom were born or grew up in British colonies or former colonies. Includes bibliography and index.

**SEE ALSO:** Dec. 10, 1978: Singer Is Awarded the Nobel Prize in Literature; Dec. 10, 1986: Soyinka Receives the Nobel Prize in Literature; Dec. 10, 1988: Mahfouz Receives the Nobel Prize in Literature; Dec. 10, 1994: Ōe Receives the Nobel Prize in Literature; Dec. 10, 1995: Heaney Receives the Nobel Prize in Literature; Dec. 10, 1996: Szymborska Receives the Nobel Prize in Literature.

1991

## 1992

# AUDUBON SOCIETY OPENS ENVIRONMENTALLY RESPONSIBLE HEADQUARTERS

*"Green" architecture and design gained public interest when the National Audubon Society purchased and renovated a one hundred-year-old office building using nontoxic, recycled materials and energy-conserving systems.*

**ALSO KNOWN AS:** Audubon House
**LOCALE:** New York, New York
**CATEGORIES:** Architecture; organizations and institutions; environmental issues

**KEY FIGURES**

*Peter A. A. Berle* (fl. late twentieth century), president of the National Audubon Society who headed the renovation of Audubon House

*Jan Beyea* (fl. late twentieth century), chief scientist for the National Audubon Society and the leading environmental consultant for Audubon House

*Kirsten Childs* (fl. late twentieth century), chief interior designer for Audubon House and an expert in environmentally sensitive interior design

*Randolph R. Croxton* (fl. late twentieth century), chief architect for Audubon House and an expert in environmental and sustainable building design

*Peter Flack* (fl. late twentieth century), chief of engineering design for Audubon House and an expert in the design of energy-efficient, cost-effective buildings

**SUMMARY OF EVENT**

Between 1989 and 1992, the National Audubon Society built an environmentally responsible national headquarters that became internationally celebrated as a working model of energy conservation, resource recycling, indoor air quality, and cost efficiency in office-building design. Developers, architects, engineers, and interior designers from around the world have toured Audubon House to gather ideas for environmentally sound building design.

In 1987, the Audubon Society was leasing four floors of a thirty-story skyscraper in midtown Manhattan. Rent was increasing steadily, the organization needed additional space, and employees frequently complained of headaches, fatigue, and respiratory discomfort as a result of the building's poor air quality. The society needed a new location. In 1989, it purchased the eight-story, century-old Schermerhorn Building, located at 700

Broadway in a lively lower Manhattan neighborhood. At the time of purchase, all but the ground floor of the building had been unoccupied for at least ten years. Designed by renowned architect George Browne Post in the 1890's, the building was structurally sound. Its elegant old exterior was in good condition, but its interior was dilapidated.

Vast amounts of natural resources and energy go into the construction, maintenance, and operation of office buildings; such consumption has led to the destruction of habitats and has had negative impacts on the earth's natural systems. Annually, energy production alone for office buildings produces hundreds of thousands of metric tons of air pollutants that contribute to acid rain, global warming, and depletion of the ozone layer. In Audubon House, the Audubon Society was determined to meld its need for new offices with the organization's environmental missions to protect and restore vital habitats for wildlife and to promote sustainable development to ensure a healthy environment for all beings. Sustainable development uses natural resources frugally, in a nonexhaustive way, and minimizes or eliminates impacts on natural systems.

The Audubon Society staff selected architects, engineers, and interior designers who were committed to the environmental goals of the project and who had previous experience in environmentally sound design. These professionals worked together as a team, integrating their efforts to achieve the "greenest" possible building.

In renovating the building, the designers recycled discarded materials from the old interior; used nontoxic materials and furnishings with recycled content to create the new interior; installed energy-efficient lighting, cooling, and heating systems; and created an internal recycling system for office waste. All material gutted from the building's interior, except window glass and heating oil, was recycled. Iron, tin, and steel were sold as scrap metal, wood was sold for use as landscaping material, and concrete and masonry were crushed for roadbed fill.

In selecting materials and furnishings for the new interior, the Audubon Society's environmental consultant considered the entire life cycle of the product: Was it made from sustainable rather than dwindling resources? Did it contain recycled content? Did the extraction of raw materials for the product or its manufacture damage natural habitats or the atmosphere? Would the product emit

2628

gases or particles toxic to building inhabitants or to the environment? How would the product's eventual disposal affect the environment?

The designers minimized the use of adhesives and pressed woods in the new interior because of these materials' tendency to emit formaldehyde and volatile organic compounds. Recycled newsprint bound with a low-toxicity bonding agent was used for subflooring instead of plywood. The drywall used contained a partially recycled gypsum core and outer layers of 100 percent recycled paper. Studs contained recycled steel.

An odorless, nontoxic paint was selected, and synthetic carpets and pads—sources of formaldehyde and other toxins—were avoided. An undyed, 100 percent wool carpet was installed over a nontoxic jute-hair pad that was tacked down to minimize the use of adhesives.

The building's new bathroom countertops were made with plastic recycled from detergent bottles. Floor tiles in the ground-floor lobby and elevator vestibules contained recycled waste glass from the manufacture of lightbulbs. To support sustainable rain-forest industries, the Audubon Society purchased furnishings certified to be constructed from sustainable rain-forest resources.

*Headquarters of the Audubon Society in New York.* (Geographer/GFDL)

To convince the business community that environmental design could be practical for office buildings and could be achieved at a reasonable cost, the society made the decision that materials, furnishings, and systems for the new headquarters had to be purchased "off the shelf" and had to have been on the market for at least one year. Novel uses were found for traditional products, but no experimental items were used. Simple, no-cost or low-cost design solutions were employed in tandem with advanced technologies to achieve desired levels of performance.

The Audubon Society reduced its lighting needs by more than 75 percent by using natural light, adapting light level to need, and integrating high-performance lighting components. Workstations in an open floor plan were oriented to receive the natural light flooding through the floor-to-ceiling windows of the building's southern and western exposures. Ceiling and workstation partitions were stepped to admit as much light as possible. Offices along the west wall had large clerestories in their inward-facing walls. Venetian blinds with perforated slats were installed to admit diffused light while reducing glare. The light paint colors used on walls, floors, and ceilings maximized the reflection of natural light.

Artificial ambient (background) light levels were reduced by one-half, and task lighting used high-efficiency fluorescent lamps fired by electronic ballasts and coated so that the light they produced resembled natural light as closely as possible. Occupancy sensors turned lights off when no motion was detected in an area for six minutes, and daylight dimming sensors adjusted the level of artificial light as natural light fluctuated.

The building's outer walls and roof were insulated far in excess of what was required under New York State code. A foam made of magnesium and dolomite was used instead of traditional foam insulation, which is often manufactured with chlorofluorocarbons (CFCs), the leading cause of stratospheric ozone depletion. The designers also installed energy-efficient windows and skylights that deflected the sun's radiant heat outward in summer and building heat inward in winter.

Insulation, energy-efficient windows, and reduced levels of artificial light enabled the Audubon Society to downsize its heating, ventilation, and cooling system by nearly one-half. The system was selected for its energy efficiency and low environmental impact. Unlike conventional systems, it emitted no CFCs and no sulfur oxides, a major source of acid rain; emissions of nitrogen oxides, also a source of acid rain, were reduced by 60 percent. The system, fueled by natural gas, placed no demand on the region's electrical power supply, which was generated by burning fossil fuels, the source of vast amounts of carbon dioxide, a major element in global warming. In addition, electricity demand in the region was driving the development of hydroelectric power in Quebec's James Bay region, with the potential of destroying vast areas of Subarctic habitat.

Another major objective the Audubon Society had in creating Audubon House was to demonstrate that a healthy, human-oriented work environment is compatible with both energy efficiency and cost efficiency. Audubon House's ventilation system provided six air exchanges per hour and exchanged 30 percent more outside air than conventional systems. Employees could control the temperature in their work areas. Windows could be opened. The carefully selected furnishings were aesthetically pleasing and nontoxic, and natural light was abundant.

The Audubon House planners installed an internal recycling system for office waste. Four twenty-inch steel chutes, accessible from each floor, emptied into collection bins in the subbasement. Each chute was designated for a specific material: white and computer paper, mixed paper, aluminum cans and plastic bottles, or food wastes. Newspapers, magazines, and coated papers were recycled. Food wastes and soft paper were composted and spread on potted plants on the building's roof. Other materials were sold to recyclers.

## SIGNIFICANCE

The stereotype of the environmentally responsive, or green, building is that of a small, futuristic prototype that utilizes expensive, experimental technology to achieve energy efficiency and minimize environmental impact—perhaps a model home on exhibit or a private home, owned and occupied by individuals who place environmental objectives above cost. Audubon House demonstrated that an eight-story office building with 170 employees in the center of New York City could be environmentally responsible and affordable.

Prior to completion of Audubon House, those in the development sector believed it was too expensive to construct office buildings that could be cost-effective, energy-efficient, resource-conserving, relatively nonpolluting, and safe for employees. Consequently, the project's success created quite a stir. Audubon House was featured on television, in national publications such as *Newsweek* and *The New Yorker*, and in every major periodical devoted to architecture and interior design. It was often cited as a case study in discussions regarding the feasibility of making building codes more stringent.

The success of the Audubon Society's effort spurred worldwide interest in green architecture. The organization's public relations department received thousands of inquiries regarding the building, and many visitors toured it to see for themselves what Audubon House designers had accomplished.

Audubon House demonstrated that environmentally sound design can enhance cost efficiency. Its basic renovation and redesign costs were kept within the market rate for an equivalent, code-compliant project. Simple design solutions and the use of advanced technology enabled Audubon House to consume 62 percent less energy than an equivalent code-compliant building. This reduced the society's operating costs by $100,000 per year, allowing the society to apply the savings to its environmental programs.

The fact that the Audubon Society was able to reduce its use of electricity for lighting by 75 percent demonstrated the inefficiency of most lighting systems used in office buildings. The society estimated that if all new office buildings built between 1994 and 2020 were to use the Audubon House approach to conserving electricity, 100,000 megawatts per day would be saved, eliminating the need to construct additional power-generating sources equivalent to fifty nuclear power plants.

Audubon House demonstrated that it is possible to insulate and air-condition a large structure without releasing ozone-destroying CFCs into the atmosphere. The

Audubon Society estimated in 1994 that if every building in the United States were to reduce direct and indirect output of CFCs to zero, total emissions would be cut by 25 percent, significantly reducing the assault on the stratospheric ozone layer.

Audubon House also demonstrated that it was profitable for organizations to revitalize the inner city by renovating existing structures. In the early 1990's, many organizations were moving to the suburbs, destroying natural habitats and consuming thousands of tons of natural resources in order to build new structures. The Audubon Society paid only $10 million for the Schermerhorn Building—essentially the cost of the land on which it sat—and then spent an additional $14 million to renovate the structure. The cost to purchase the Schermerhorn, demolish it, and replace it with an equivalent structure would have exceeded $30 million. Retention of the old structure preserved 300 tons of steel, 9,000 tons of masonry, and 560 tons of concrete, in addition to the energy and materials that would have been required to erect a new building.

In addition, the recycling of the materials gutted from the old interior of the Schermerhorn demonstrated a significant method for reducing the solid-waste burden on landfills, which were reaching capacity in many parts of the country by the end of the twentieth century. In 1994, construction and demolition waste constituted from 23 to 33 percent of municipal solid wastes. The Audubon Society also discovered that recycling of office waste was less expensive than garbage hauling. By recycling 80 percent of the 59,000 pounds of office waste generated each year at Audubon House, the society reduced its fees for waste disposal by $12,000.

—*Linda Sims Anderson*

## FURTHER READING

Cagin, Seth, and Philip Dray. *Between Earth and Sky: How CFCs Changed Our World and Endangered the Ozone Layer*. New York: Pantheon Books, 1993. Presents a thorough account of the discovery and restriction of CFCs and examines the social, political, scientific, and economic factors behind the long battle to ban them.

Crosbie, Michael J. "Practicing What They Preach: The Natural Resource Defense Council's Humane and Environmentally Responsive Headquarters." *Progressive Architecture* 74 (March, 1993): 84-89. Discusses the Natural Resource Defense Council's 1989 energy-efficient office renovation, a project on a smaller scale than the Audubon Society's but sharing some features. Includes photographs and diagrams illustrating energy-saving systems.

Gissen, David, ed. *Big and Green: Toward Sustainable Architecture in the Twenty-First Century*. New York: Princeton Architectural Press, 2002. Collection of essays focuses on skyscrapers in discussing all aspects of "green architecture." Includes glossary, bibliography, and index.

McDonough, William, and Michael Braungart. *Cradle to Cradle: Remaking the Way We Make Things*. New York: North Point Press, 2002. Interesting discussion of green design by an architect and a chemist who are partners in a design firm that specializes in environmentally sound buildings, products, and equipment.

National Audubon Society and Croxton Collaborative, Architects. *Audubon House: Building the Environmentally Responsible, Energy-Efficient Office*. New York: John Wiley & Sons, 1994. Presents a detailed, comprehensive account of the renovation of Audubon House. Discusses the philosophical basis for the project and the impact of office buildings on the environment.

National Trust for Historic Preservation. *All About Old Buildings*. Edited by Diane Maddex. Washington, D.C.: Preservation Press, 1985. Focuses on the advantages of renovating rather than removing and replacing old buildings that are historically or architecturally significant. Discusses methodologies for preservation and renovation. Includes wonderful photographs and lists of supportive organizations.

Nesmith, Lynn. "Ready or Not, Construction Recycling Is on the Way." *Architectural Record* 181 (December, 1993): 18-23. Provides an overview of the growing trend in the construction industry to recycle construction and demolition wastes and to use construction materials with recycled content. Informative chart shows the recycled content, disassembly, reuse, and disposal of common components.

Wann, David. *Biologic: Designing with Nature to Protect the Environment*. Rev. ed. Boulder, Colo.: Johnson Books, 1994. Suggests that designers study natural systems to find efficient, sustainable ways of organizing energy use, food production, housing, transportation, and recycling of wastes. Surveys a variety of designs in use or being developed that do this.

Young, Louise B. "A Bitter Wind Blowing." In *Sowing the Wind: Reflections on the Earth's Atmosphere*. New York: Prentice Hall, 1990. Presents excellent discussion of acid rain and its causes and effects.

_____. "Hothouse Earth?" In *Sowing the Wind: Reflections on the Earth's Atmosphere*. New York:

1992

Prentice Hall, 1990. Offers a thought-provoking, balanced discussion of the greenhouse effect that separates fact from conjecture.

**SEE ALSO:** Dec., 1973-June, 1974: Rowland and Molina Theorize That Freon Causes Ozone Depletion; 1974-

1980: Sick Building Syndrome Is Recognized; Oct. 11, 1976: EPA Is Charged with Regulating Toxic Chemicals; Mar. 17, 1978: Chlorofluorocarbons Are Banned in the United States; May 3, 1978: Sun Day Celebration Promotes Solar Energy; 1980's: Radon Is Recognized as an Indoor Air Hazard.

## January 13, 1992
# JAPAN ADMITS TO SEX SLAVERY DURING WORLD WAR II

*During World War II, the Japanese army held men and women as sex slaves, a practice that was kept secret until 1990 allegations by former Korean "comfort women" were confirmed by Japanese government documents in 1992.*

**LOCALE:** Burma, China, Indonesia (Dutch East Indies), Japan, Korea, Philippines, Singapore, Taiwan, Thailand

**CATEGORIES:** Terrorism, atrocities, and war crimes; colonialism and occupation; military history; women's issues; World War II

### KEY FIGURES
*Hak-soon Kim* (1925-1997), first person to admit publicly that she was a sex slave for Japanese soldiers during World War II
*Yoshimi Yoshiaki* (b. 1946), professor of modern Japanese history, Chuo University, Tokyo
*Kiichi Miyazawa* (1919-2007), prime minister of Japan, 1991-1993
*Tomiichi Murayama* (b. 1924), prime minister of Japan, 1994-1996

### SUMMARY OF EVENT
The Convention with Respect to the Laws and Customs of War on Land, as adopted in 1899 and reiterated in subsequent treaties, obligated armies engaging in military occupation of other countries to respect the liberties of those under occupation. Nevertheless, Japan's army in continental Asia during World War II violated the accepted terms of wartime propriety by utilizing men and women for sex. Because serving as a prostitute is a humiliation that Asians find difficult to admit, and because Japanese culture frowns on bringing up negative matters, the issue of sex slavery was ignored for forty-five years.

During World War II, the Japanese army's leaders believed that morale among the troops would be improved if "comfort women" who were known to be free of sexually transmitted diseases were available to soldiers. Ac-

cordingly, some 80,000 to 200,000 persons in Japan and in areas of Asia occupied by Japanese military forces served as sex objects. Most of the sex slaves were held at about two thousand "comfort stations" in China, Korea, and Taiwan. Some were brought to Japan for the benefit of soldiers on rotation or in training. All of the sex slaves were held at Japanese military bases or encampments. Most of them were women, although some males and cross-dressers were forcibly raped.

In Japan, authorities attended to the health of the comfort workers and often provided lavish accommodations and income. However, elsewhere in Asia the sex workers were treated with less dignity. Accordingly, a dispute arose between those who stressed the horrors of Japan's system of sex slavery and those who pointed out the economic advantages of serving as comfort women.

Early in the war, Japan offered monetary inducements to secure willing prostitutes. Existing prostitutes applied, while some poor families sold their teenage children. Later, Japanese troops kidnapped women and forced them to engage in nonconsensual sex. Some of the women developed medical problems, notably genital injuries. Others were beaten and tortured into complying with their forced assignments. Virgins were supplied to officers. Pregnant women underwent forced abortions and sometimes died during these operations.

Less than 30 percent of those forced into sexual slavery survived the ordeal, which involved submitting to sex an average of ten times daily and, in some cases, as many as forty times a day. Although the Charter of the International Military Tribunal for the Far East, adopted in 1946, cited rape as a war crime, because of taboos about sexual behavior nothing was said about the practice for forty-five years after the war. Additionally, the American military extended the Japanese practice of sex slavery by utilizing comfort women during the occupation of Japan from 1945 to 1951.

In 1948, in Jakarta, Indonesia, the Netherlands held

the only military tribunal concerning the sexual abuse of comfort women. Several Japanese military officers were convicted of forcing thirty-five Dutch women into comfort stations. However, there were no trials in which native Indonesians or women of other ethnic backgrounds were plaintiffs.

In 1990, the Korean Council for Women Drafted for Military Sexual Slavery was formed and filed suit in Japan, demanding an official apology and compensation for forced prostitution during World War II. In 1991, Hak-soon Kim, a Korean woman, made a public admission that she was a victim of Japanese sexual slavery during World War II. Lawsuits were filed by other women who made similar public admissions. The Japanese courts, however, dismissed the cases. During 1991-1992, a major newspaper in Japan, *Asahi Shimbun*, ran a series of articles on comfort women, thereby raising consciousness about the issue. At first, the Japanese government refused to offer any apology or compensation.

In 1992, historian Yoshimi Yoshiaki's discovery of incriminating documents in the archives of Japan's National Defense Agency forced the government to admit that the Japanese military was directly involved in the use of sex slaves throughout Asia during World War II. The article was published five days prior to a visit to South Korea by Japanese prime minister Kiichi Miyazawa, who made a formal apology during that visit. In 1992, North Korea also published a report about sex slaves during the Japanese occupation.

In 1995, the Japanese government, having admitted moral but not legal responsibility since prostitution was legal in Japan, assisted in setting up the nongovernmental Asia Women's Fund to provide surviving comfort women with compensation and an unofficial, signed apology from the prime minister. In announcing the establishment of the fund, Prime Minister Tomiichi Murayama issued a "profound apology."

Because of the unofficial nature of the fund, many comfort women rejected these payments and continued to seek an official apology, along with compensation. However, in 2005, the Japanese Supreme Court turned down a bid by some victims for compensation. Another case, involving a Chinese woman, was dismissed by a lower court in Japan in 2006.

In American courts, several cases, including 2003's *Joo v. Japan*, were pursued against the Japanese regarding their conduct during World War II, only to be rejected on the basis that the Japanese/American peace treaty of 1951 settled all such claims. Although some members of Congress sought to reinterpret the peace treaty through

proposed new legislation, the threat of a presidential veto, on the grounds that new litigation against Japan might adversely affect cooperation with Tokyo on matters of terrorism, ensured that the proposed law did not pass. South Korea regarded the issue of comfort women settled because of the 1965 peace treaty with Japan, which compensated South Korea with $800 million for Japan's colonial rule, which lasted from 1910 to 1945.

### SIGNIFICANCE

The practice of maintaining thousands of sex slaves was part of the larger use of forced labor throughout Asia by Japanese private corporations under contract with the government to produce goods needed for the war. Rape as a technique of military conquest has occurred over the centuries, but it was not specifically considered a war crime until 1946, under the terms of the Tokyo War Crimes Trials.

Rape is an actionable offense in accordance with the statutes of the International Criminal Tribunal for the former Yugoslavia and the International Criminal Tribunal for Rwanda, as adopted in 1994. The Rome Statute for the International Criminal Court, as adopted in 1998, identifies rape as a war crime, though legal proof is often difficult to obtain in the midst of battle.

—*Michael Haas*

### FURTHER READING

Hicks, George L. *The Comfort Women: Japan's Brutal Regime of Enforced Prostitution in the Second World War*. St. Leonards, N.S.W.: Allen & Unwin, 1995. Based in part on stories of comfort women. Tends to be overly sensationalistic.

Schellstede, Sangmie Choi. *Comfort Women Speak: Testimony by Sex Slaves of the Japanese Military*. New York: Holmes & Meier, 2000. Presents firsthand accounts of former sex slaves. Includes bibliographic references.

Stetz, Margaret, and Bonnie Oh, eds. *The Legacies of the Comfort Women of World War II*. Armonk, N.Y.: M. E. Sharpe, 2001. Presents personal reports by survivors of the Japanese sex slavery. Includes bibliographic references and index.

Tanaka, Yuki. *Japan's Comfort Women: Sexual Slavery and Prostitution During World War II and the U.S. Occupation*. London: Routledge, 2002. Presents a balanced account of the issue. Includes tables, figures, photographs, and index.

Yoshiaki, Yoshimi. *Comfort Women: Sexual Slavery in the Japanese Military During World War II*. Trans-

1992

lated by Suzanne O'Brien. New York: Columbia University Press, 2000. Scholarly account is based on the documentary record. Includes bibliography and index.

**SEE ALSO:** May 15, 1972: United States Hands Okinawa to Japan; June 19-July 2, 1975: World Conference on Women Sets an International Agenda; Oct. 10, 1975: Tokyo Declaration Forbids Medical Abuses and Torture; Dec. 9, 1975: United Nations Issues a Declaration Against Torture; Aug. 10, 1988: U.S. Congress Formally Apologizes to Japanese Internees; June 14-25, 1993: World Conference on Human Rights.

## February, 1992
# PEQUOTS OPEN GAMING FACILITY

*One of the first successful Indian gaming ventures, the Pequots' Foxwoods Resort Casino highlights the issue of Indian gaming in general, which provoked controversy on three fronts: philosophical, geographical, and political. The success of Foxwoods and similar ventures also attests to Native Americans' self-reliance.*

**ALSO KNOWN AS:** Foxwoods Resort Casino
**LOCALE:** Mashantucket, Connecticut
**CATEGORIES:** Indigenous peoples' rights; trade and commerce; social issues and reform; travel and recreation

**KEY FIGURES**
*Elizabeth George Plouffe* (d. 1973), Pequot activist
*Skip Hayward* (b. 1948), Foxwoods founder and chair of Mashantucket Pequot Tribal Nation, 1975-2002
*Lowell P. Weicker, Jr.* (b. 1931), governor of Connecticut, 1991-1995
*Michael Thomas* (b. 1965), chair of the Mashantucket Pequot Tribal Nation beginning in 2003

**SUMMARY OF EVENT**
In the early 1970's, the Mashantucket Pequot Indian Tribe seemed on its way to extinction for the third time, but twenty years later, it was the richest tribe in the country, owner of the largest gaming casino in the world. Proceeds from the Foxwoods Resort Casino, which opened in February, 1992, would provide money, housing, college tuitions, health care, and other needs of the nearly six hundred tribal members, as well as contributing more than $200 million annually to the state of Connecticut, giving grants to area groups, and enabling the tribe to contribute heavily to political parties.

In 1986, the tribal nation opened its original 40,000-square-foot, high-stakes bingo hall on its reservation in southeastern Connecticut, featuring 125 tables and three eating facilities. By 2006, the facility would grow to 1.5 million square feet, including gaming space in six distinct casinos, more than thirty-five food and beverage outlets, conference facilities, a shopping mall, a conference center, and 1,416 guest rooms in three hotels. In a nearby but separate location, the $150 million Museum of the American Indian, billed as the largest Native American center in the country, was opened in 1998.

Casinos operated by Native American nations were and still are, in general, popular but controversial. The controversy surrounding the Pequots was, like their casino and wealth, writ large. Their enterprise is both the most famous and the most criticized of the Native American rags-to-riches stories of the 1970's and 1980's.

Once a nation of 8,000 people, the Pequots, like other indigenous peoples, were decimated by wars and disease after the arrival in the early seventeenth century of European settlers of North America. The 600 remaining Pequots were divided between the Mohegans and the Narragansetts. Pequot sachem Robin Cassacinamon negotiated for 3,000 acres in Mashantucket, but in 1761 Connecticut reduced it to 989 acres for the some 150 members remaining. By 1856, illegal land sales by the state had reduced the reservation to 213 acres. A 1935 report lists 42 on the reservation, but in 1970 only 2 remained.

One of them was Elizabeth George Plouffe, who with her husband had written a tribal constitution in the late 1960's and now convinced her grandson, Skip Hayward, to live on the reservation. Before Plouffe died in 1973, they started to locate and bring back other Pequots scattered from New England to New Mexico. Hayward was elected the first tribal chairman. A new constitution was written. The tribe subsisted on funds from the sale of cordwood, maple syrup, garden vegetables, a swine project, and a hydroponic greenhouse. Hayward enlisted the aid of the Native American Rights Fund and the Indian Rights Association. From 1976 to 1983, he and attorney Tom Tureen skillfully manipulated laws, court decisions, and political connections to persuade Congress and President Ronald Reagan to recognize those living on the reservation as Pequots, enabling the tribe to purchase 1,250 acres and put that land in trust under the Settlement Act passed by Congress.

That same year, 1983, the tribal council agreed to finance an on-reservation bingo facility. The state of Connecticut threatened to prosecute. The Pequots sued, on the basis of a 1976 U.S. Supreme Court ruling in *Bryan v. Itasca County*, that states do not have regulatory jurisdiction over Native American tribal lands, and in 1986 they won. With title to the land, a loan of $4 million was obtained and paid off in two years. Timing, location, plentiful funds, and skillful political maneuvering swiftly advanced the bingo project.

In 1988, Congress passed the Indian Gaming Regulatory Act (IGRA), which divided gaming activities on tribal land into three categories. Class I gaming included social games solely for prizes of minimal value or traditional forms of Indian gaming engaged in by individuals as part of tribal ceremonies or celebrations. These were to be regulated by the tribe itself. Class II gaming (bingo, pulltabs, and certain card games), were legal if the state allowed "gaming by any person for any purpose." In Connecticut, nonprofit organizations were allowed to run bingo games, although prize amounts were limited by law. Because native tribes are considered sovereign nations, the state could not limit their prizes. The tribe renamed its facility Foxwoods High Stakes Bingo and Casino, added roulette, and became the only East Coast facility offering poker. It lacked only slot machines.

Under the 1988 act, Class III gaming—involving all manner of gaming, including slot machines—required negotiation between the tribe and the state, approval by the secretary of the interior, and a gaming ordinance approved by the new Indian Gaming Regulatory Commission (IGRC). The tribe started work on this venture, and eventually agreement was reached. The tribe and Governor Lowell P. Weicker, Jr., signed a compact under which Foxwoods would pay the state 25 percent of its slot machine take, or $100 million annually, whichever was larger.

## SIGNIFICANCE

In fiscal year 2007, Connecticut received more than $200 million as its share of slot machine proceeds. The National Indian Gaming Commission (NIGC) is composed of three members, at least two of whom must be enrolled members of a federally recognized Indian tribe. Its mission statement is threefold: to shield tribes from organized crime, to ensure that tribes are the primary beneficiaries of gaming profits, and to assure that gaming is conducted fairly and honestly.

In 2007, there were 557 tribes in the United States, and more than 200 of them were conducting some form of gaming. However, only 22 had Class III licenses. Indian gaming brought in more than twice as much money as private casinos in Nevada and Atlantic City, and had grown from $5 billion in 1995 to $22.6 billion in 2005. Profits from gaming gave Native Americans money to use for political purposes and made the richest tribes strong players in their states and in the nation's capital. Gaming has also spawned a corps of consultants eager to help in economic development ventures and to become investment counselors to these tribes.

In contrast, tribes that are not participating in gaming, because of either their geographical location or their philosophy, still depend on government funds and suffer from poverty and an average of more than 25 percent unemployment.

The story of Foxwoods illustrates a dramatic reversal of the way native peoples have been historically treated by the U.S. government. Accounts abound about the broken treaties, cavalier treatment, and continued paternalism that kept native tribes in poverty. With skill and determination, the Pequots used the political system to their advantage and amassed virtually unlimited amounts of money, which not only benefited tribal members but also ensured their continued influence in the U.S. political system, in which they are now important players rather than poor petitioners.

—*Erika E. Pilver*

1992

## FURTHER READING

Benedict, Jeff. *Without Reservation: The Making of America's Most Powerful Indian Tribe and Foxwoods, the World's Largest Casino.* New York: HarperCollins, 2000. Narrative account of the Maine Passamaquoddys' and Penobscots' and the Connecticut Pequots' battle with Congress. Asserts that in the case of the Pequots, recognition standards maintained by the Bureau of Indian Affairs were not followed. Features discussion of then tribal chief Skip Hayward and attorney Tom Tureen.

Eisler, Kim Isaac. *Revenge of the Pequots: How a Small Native American Tribe Created the World's Most Profitable Casino.* New York: Simon & Schuster, 2001. Also centers on the character and actions of tribal chairman Richard "Skip" Hayward and attorney Tom Tureen. Includes an account involving members of Congress and Donald Trump in political machinations and heavy campaign contributions to both the Democratic and Republican parties.

Frantz, Klaus. *Indian Reservations in the United States: Territory, Sovereignty, and Socioeconomic Change.* Chicago: University of Chicago Press, 1999. Starting with a two-hundred-year historical perspective, the book compares the socioeconomic status and value systems of Native Americans with other racial groups. Treats conflicts with the states and with other tribes on issues of mining, manufacturing, services, agriculture, and forestry on reservation lands.

Light, Steven Andrew, and Kathryn R. L. Rand. *Indian Gaming and Tribal Sovereignty: The Casino Compromise.* Lawrence: University Press of Kansas, 2005. A short (162-page), heavily annotated (63 pages) volume of clear, readable history, legal standing, and wide-ranging examples of tribal experience. Authors advocate for a change in the way the federal government, the states, and the tribes interact, urging that they find common ground rather than continue their adversarial relationship.

Mason, W. Dale. *Indian Gaming: Tribal Sovereignty and American Politics.* Norman: University of Okla-

homa Press, 2000. Views history, legal action, and federal-state-tribal relations through the lens of political science theory.

Mullis, Angela, and David Kamper, eds. *Indian Gaming: Who Wins?* Los Angeles: UCLA American Indian Studies Center, 2000. Opposing essays by sixteen tribal leaders, lawyers, public policy makers, consultants, and academics who participated in a 1997 conference at UCLA, based on the assumption that economic self-determination and legal sovereignty create a paradox.

Williams, Mary E., ed. *Legalized Gambling.* San Diego, Calif.: Greenhaven Press, 1999. From the Opposing Viewpoints series, the volume includes positive and negative perspectives on the social costs and benefits of gambling in terms of individuals, families, governments, and native tribes.

**SEE ALSO:** 1971: New York State Allows Offtrack Betting; Nov. 2, 1976: Atlantic City Legalizes Casino Gambling; Oct. 17, 1988: U.S. Law Supports Indian Gaming.

## February, 1992
# YANKEE ROWE NUCLEAR PLANT IS SHUT DOWN

*Deeming the cost of safety tests too high, the Yankee Atomic Electric Company decided to shut down its nuclear power plant permanently.*

**LOCALE:** Rowe, Massachusetts
**CATEGORIES:** Energy; environmental issues

### KEY FIGURES

*Ivan Selin* (fl. late twentieth century), chairman of the Nuclear Regulatory Commission, 1991-1995
*Robert D. Pollard* (fl. late twentieth century), senior nuclear safety engineer with the Union of Concerned Scientists

### SUMMARY OF EVENT

In February, 1992, Andrew C. Kadak, president of the company that had operated the Yankee Rowe nuclear power plant for thirty-two years, announced that the plant would be closed permanently. The plant had been shut down since September of the previous year, because the Nuclear Regulatory Commission (NRC) had ordered the company to conduct tests of the reactor container to

determine whether radiation embrittlement of its steel and its welds was advanced enough to lead to rupture under emergency conditions. When estimates for the testing and possible repair or replacement of the reactor container parts came to nearly $23 million, the company realized that it could not recoup such an expenditure in the foreseeable future and elected to close down the plant.

Yankee Rowe is situated in the northwestern Massachusetts town of Rowe, about four miles south of the Vermont-Massachusetts border. It was the first nuclear reactor commissioned by the NRC's predecessor, the Atomic Energy Commission. It was also the smallest reactor in use at the time, producing some 175 megawatts of power, or about 1 percent of the power fed into the Massachusetts grid. Yankee Rowe had a reasonably good safety record, with shutdowns averaging one per year. Most of the shutdowns were for the purpose of routine maintenance and refueling. The plant was operated by Yankee Atomic Electric Company, which was owned by a consortium of ten Massachusetts power companies.

Electricity industry officials hoped to use Yankee Rowe as a test case to demonstrate that nuclear plants could operate safely for sixty years.

When the difficulties that led to the closing began, Yankee Atomic was preparing to submit a request to the NRC for a twenty-year renewal of its original forty-year operating license, which would expire in the year 2000. As the company was making its preparations, a group of engineers and safety specialists from the Union of Concerned Scientists (UCS) were analyzing government documents, including periodic reports by Yankee Atomic to the NRC. These reports showed that the steel reactor vessel (a cylinder thirty-three feet high with a diameter of ten feet and eight-inch walls) and, in particular, the copper-containing weld at its waist were probably beyond the level of radiation-induced brittleness at which NRC regulations required intensive study of the situation. In June, 1991, the UCS filed a petition with the NRC, asking that the plant be shut down immediately and that the necessary tests be conducted. The commission turned down the petition and announced that the tests would be conducted in April, 1992, when the plant was scheduled for refueling.

The UCS's concerns stemmed from the fact that the reactor at Yankee Rowe was of the pressurized-water design that normally operates at about 500 degrees Fahrenheit. Under emergency circumstances, the vessel is flooded with cold water (under 100 degrees) while full pressure is maintained to prevent boiling at the fuel-rod bundles. This thermal shock, together with the continued pressure, could cause a very brittle vessel to crack like a hot drinking glass when cold water is poured into it. This cracking would have disastrous effects in Yankee Rowe, because although the plant had the usual double-system safety design external to the reactor, there was no backup containment for the vessel itself. A rupture would mean unmanageable loss of coolant, overheating of the fuel elements, and meltdown.

At the time that the NRC turned down the UCS's petition, it was also at work developing rules for relicensing, which Yankee Atomic's impending application made necessary. The outgoing chairman of the NRC, Kenneth Carr, was called "an advocate for the industry" by Peter Kostmayer, chairman of the Interior Subcommittee on Energy and Environment of the U.S. House of Representatives. Carr insisted on adoption of broad relicensing rules rather than specific rules because he wanted the rule-making task completed before his five-year term expired. Relicensing rules must address many complex questions, not simply questions related to aging equip-

ment, such as whether tighter standards established for later plants should be applied to the old plants in relicensing or whether those standards should be waived. Broad relicensing rules threatened to oversimplify the relicensing issue.

Carr was replaced as NRC chair by Ivan Selin on July 1, 1991. Selin immediately displayed a skeptical view of both the relicensing rules and Yankee Rowe. He persuaded the commission to do a thorough job of rewriting the rules before their final adoption. He toured the Yankee Rowe plant with various members of Congress and with UCS nuclear safety engineer Robert D. Pollard, and he announced that Yankee Rowe was "the most current issue we have." In August, the NRC reaffirmed its June decision to allow the plant to remain in operation but continued to study the matter, asking for further information from Rowe.

In October, the NRC, citing a computer-modeling study done by its staff that cast doubt on the plant's safety beyond those expressed in the earlier UCS petition, prepared to notify Yankee Atomic that shutdown would be required. The company forestalled formal action by shutting down voluntarily, maintaining that it expected the plant to be back online as soon as the NRC could be convinced that the reactor was indeed safe. In the meantime, Yankee Atomic dropped its relicensing efforts, because engineering time had been monopolized by concerns with safety matters.

By the end of October, Yankee Atomic announced that it would not try to reopen the plant early but would wait until the scheduled inspection in March. Over the next few months, the company obtained bids for the requisite safety testing and found the $23 million estimate for repairs too high. Company officials announced at the end of February, 1992, that the plant would close permanently and would be decommissioned.

## SIGNIFICANCE

The closing of the Yankee Rowe plant was both encouraging and educational. The performance of the NRC under the leadership of Selin was exemplary during the process of the plant's closure, and the methods and costs of closing nuclear power plants were more clearly understood after the experience at Yankee Rowe.

Selin gave credit to citizen groups for urging his commission to act cautiously in the case of the Yankee Rowe plant. He even suggested that it might be appropriate for such groups to receive public funding. Selin, holder of a Yale University Ph.D. in electrical engineering who possessed the technical background that his

1992

two predecessors had lacked, was acutely aware of the design and safety problems in the nuclear power industry. He noted at the outset of his tenure at the NRC that, with its 111 reactors of eighty different designs, the industry was difficult to manage and difficult to regulate. The goals of his five-year term involved the establishment of a small number of standardized designs and sound procedures for relicensing old plants as well as an effort to make the licensing of new plants quicker and more efficient.

Under Selin's leadership, the NRC more quickly identified problem nuclear plants, although, as Pollard pointed out in a 1993 article in the UCS's quarterly, *Nucleus*, the NRC was still slow to demand corrections. In general, however, the experience of Yankee Rowe and the 1993 closing of the Trojan nuclear plant in Oregon showed that the NRC had become more responsive to problems.

Yankee Rowe's closing set in motion the decommissioning and dismantling of nuclear plants that were no longer operable. The matter of permanent shutdown is very complex and has economic, technological, and political repercussions.

In 1993, Yankee Atomic awarded a contract for decommissioning of the Rowe plant to the engineering firm of Stone and Webster. The firm's bid was a staggering $247 million, and no detailed plans accompanied the bid. One year later, the estimate was increased to $370 million. Yankee Atomic had only about one-fifth of this amount set aside for closing costs in its original planning for decommission. The early closing of the plant was expected to save some $116 million in expenses, but even combined, these figures totaled a little more than one-half of the increased estimate. Additional monies were expected to be garnered by electricity rate increases on future sales by members of the consortium that owned Yankee Atomic. A grim irony is at work in these cost figures. Yankee Rowe cost only $39 million to construct in 1962. Even allowing for massive inflation in its thirty-year lifetime, shutdown costs exceeded start-up costs, and consumers ultimately paid the difference.

The technological problems that had to be solved in the dismantling of the Yankee Rowe power plant were not insurmountable, but they were problems that no electric power company had ever had to address before. The problems had to do principally with the induced radioactivity in many of the core components of the plant. The classic demolition method of controlled explosion followed by bulldozer clearing cannot be employed in such

a situation. Even standard practices such as using cutting torches to reduce large metal components to the size of pieces that fit on a truck could be used only under rigorously controlled conditions. The volatile nature of the materials that required dismantling meant that the decommissioning cost estimates were staggering.

The last, and possibly the greatest, difficulty in the closing and razing of Yankee Rowe was deciding what to do with all the radioactive waste materials, both fuel and components, from the dismantling operation. At the time of shutdown, it was arranged that the Commonwealth of Massachusetts would dispose of the low-level radioactive waste and the federal government would handle the high-level waste, principally fuel rods. Neither agreement was fulfilled, however. Officials in Massachusetts could not agree on a site for low-level waste, and all the materials were stored at the plant in Rowe. Most of the induced radioactivity in the low-level wastes had a relatively short half-life, so it could be left to cool down and could then be disposed of as ordinary toxic or hazardous waste. Nevertheless, the time span involved in the cooldown period would be a matter of decades.

After many efforts to solve the problem of where to dispose of the radioactive wastes from Yankee Rowe, it was decided to transfer them from wet to dry cask storage. This was completed by June, 2003, allowing for the structural demolition of the plant two years later, as further grading of the former plant site continued with a view to restoration of the land. Storage of the wastes at the site will continue under Nuclear Regulatory Commission license arrangements until the U.S. Department of Energy transfers the wastes to a suitable final location at some unspecified future date.

*—Robert M. Hawthorne, Jr.*

## FURTHER READING

Beauchamp, Marc. "Caution: This Corpse Is Radioactive." *Forbes*, March 7, 1988, 117-119. Brief but very informative article discusses the technological and financial difficulties of decommissioning and closing nuclear plants.

Breen, Bill, and Ethan Seidman. "Dismantling Nuclear Power Plants." *Garbage: The Practical Journal for the Environment* 4, no. 2 (1992): 40-47. Discusses the waste-disposal problem in detail.

Kotval, Zenia, and John Robert Mullin. "The Closing of the Yankee Rowe Nuclear Power Plant: The Impact on a New England Community." *Journal of the American Planning Association* 63, no. 4 (1997): 454-468. Focuses on the societal effects of nuclear plant closure on the surrounding communities and argues that these effects are rarely considered when closure decisions are made.

Pollard, Robert D. "See No Evil." *Nucleus: The Magazine of the Union of Concerned Scientists* 15 (Winter, 1993/1994): 1-3, 12. One of the principals in the Yankee Rowe case presents a general discussion of NRC safety regulations and their enforcement.

Pollock, Cynthia. *Decommissioning: Nuclear Power's Missing Link.* Washington, D.C.: Worldwatch Institute, 1986. Provides thorough discussion of all aspects of nuclear power plant closure.

_____. "Radioactive Headache." *The Futurist* 20 (March/April, 1986): 47-48. Presents a useful summary of the material explored at more length in Pollock's book, cited above.

Ramsey, Charles B., and Mohammad Modarres. *Commercial Nuclear Power: Assuring Safety for the Future.* New York: John Wiley & Sons, 1998. Compre-

hensive volume covers all aspects of nuclear power production and takes a positive view of the potential such production has for meeting the world's energy needs.

Shulman, Seth. "Nuclear Reactors: The High Cost of Early Retirement." *Technology Review*, January 20, 1994, 20-21. Focuses on the closed Trojan reactor in Oregon, giving a compact picture of the costs of its closing.

Weissman, Robert. "A Nuclear Tombstone." *Multinational Monitor* 13 (April, 1992): 7-8. Briefly describes Yankee Rowe's closing and discusses the safety aspects of its continuing operations.

**SEE ALSO:** Mar. 28, 1979: Three Mile Island Accident; Dec., 1985: European Nations Open Superphénix; Apr. 26, 1986: Soviet Chernobyl Nuclear Plant Undergoes Meltdown; Jan. 4, 1993: Trojan Nuclear Plant Is Retired.

# February 20, 1992
# PEROT MOUNTS A THIRD-PARTY BID FOR THE U.S. PRESIDENCY

*Despite a somewhat eccentric campaign, Texas billionaire Ross Perot set a third-party record when he ran for the U.S. presidency, winning 19 percent of the vote. Perot's candidacy showed that many Americans could relate to a "radical center" movement emphasizing economic nationalism.*

**LOCALE:** United States
**CATEGORY:** Government and politics

**KEY FIGURES**

*H. Ross Perot* (b. 1930), independent U.S. presidential candidate in 1992

*George H. W. Bush* (b. 1924), president of the United States, 1989-1993, and Republican presidential candidate in 1992

*Bill Clinton* (b. 1946), Democratic presidential candidate in 1992 and president of the United States, 1993-2001

**SUMMARY OF EVENT**

The American electorate's mood in the presidential election year 1992 was weary and wary. After the breakup of the Soviet bloc in 1989, American voters felt free to turn to domestic issues that were affecting their own lives, and many did not like what they saw. George H. W. Bush, the sitting president, had focused on international

affairs. His popularity peaked during the Persian Gulf War of 1991 but plummeted afterward as a recession set in. Bush's pragmatic approach to taxes and the federal deficit had alienated Republican conservatives, members of the president's own party. Many Americans doubted that Bush understood their problems, but many were also unsure whether the Democrats could make things better. At the beginning of 1992, the Democratic Party had no front-runner for the presidential nomination and had not put forward any comprehensive plan to deal with the nation's ills.

The time was ripe for an unconventional and forceful "outsider" to join the race, and H. Ross Perot, with his "United We Stand America" movement, stepped forward. Perot, a colorful Texan entrepreneur, had made a fortune by recognizing the profit potential in electronic data processing. His company, Electronic Data Systems (EDS), processed Medicare claims and data in the 1960's; Perot later sold EDS to General Motors and started other successful enterprises. Perot's interests were not limited to business, however. During President Richard M. Nixon's administration, Perot set up a group to support American prisoners of war held in North Vietnam (this was the original United We Stand organization); he continued to agitate on behalf of the prisoners

1992

after hostilities ended. He also arranged for the daring rescue of two EDS executives from an Iranian prison in 1979. Perot had worked closely enough with high government officials to irritate them and to form his own ideas about what the country needed. Although he had always considered himself a Republican, by the time of George H. W. Bush's presidency he was at odds with both Bush himself and the president's policies.

In 1991, Perot spent a considerable amount of time on the television talk-show circuit, criticizing the Gulf War and the growing federal deficit, and arguing that ordinary citizens needed to take back the U.S. government. On February 20, 1992, in an interview on the Cable News Network (CNN) program *Larry King Live*, Perot stated that if volunteers could get his name on the presidential ballot in all fifty states, he would run for president. The idea electrified part of the show's large audience, and their excitement spread to other citizens. Thousands of spontaneous calls of support poured in to Perot's office over the next week. Across the country, volunteers and Perot staffers joined in setting up the basics for his broad-based third-party candidacy. Although Perot had already laid some groundwork for a campaign, it is unlikely that anything would have come of it without this early outpouring of support.

Perot had little intention of running a conventional campaign. He was willing to spend some of his considerable fortune to run for the presidency, but he saw no reason to pay for television ads when he could get free airtime by making talk-show appearances, and he proceeded to do just that during the spring and early summer of 1992. He often presented charts and other visual aids during his talk-show interviews to illustrate his points about the U.S. economy. Among the issues he discussed were the problem of the growing federal deficit, the dangers for the United States of enacting the proposed North American Free Trade Agreement (NAFTA), and the insulation of current officeholders from the worries of ordinary Americans.

Perot was not the only candidate focusing on these issues. Republican pundit Pat Buchanan made an unexpectedly good showing in the New Hampshire primary by highlighting President Bush's ignorance of paycheck realities, and former U.S. senator Paul E. Tsongas won the Democrats' New Hampshire primary by calling for fiscal sobriety. As Arkansan Bill Clinton racked up delegates and won the Democratic Party's nomination, "It's the economy, stupid," remained his campaign's watchword.

*President George H. W. Bush (front), Independent candidate H. Ross Perot (center), and Democratic candidate Bill Clinton (back) during the second presidential debate at the University of Richmond on October 15, 1992.* (AP/Wide World Photos)

Perot, however, pulled these strands together in a package that appealed especially to people who had become wary of both major parties. Despite Perot's wealth, his folksy and plainspoken manner convinced alienated voters that he shared their values and concerns.

Perot had to be talked into employing professional campaign staff. After he hired two experienced operatives—Democrat Hamilton Jordan and Republican Ed Rollins—he clashed with them constantly over strategy. Perot continued to schedule his own television appearances, and when the questions he faced in interviews predictably grew tougher, he blamed his consultants. Soon, Perot's political staff started to leave the campaign. By July, when Perot had hoped to roll out a series of television ads, most of the staff had quit or been fired, and it was rumored that the campaign was falling apart. Perot himself thought so, and in mid-July, he announced that he was abandoning his presidential run. His stated reasons—concern for his children's privacy and threats to disrupt his daughter's wedding—seemed bizarre and added to the growing impression among many Americans that Perot was a "flake" with an explosive temper.

Actually, the campaign was suspended rather than completely closed down. State groups that were still seeking Perot's inclusion on the ballot were told to continue, and Perot said he was "still in the stadium" if not in the game. In retrospect, it appears that Perot used the withdrawal to buy himself some time. He thus dodged increasingly critical press scrutiny and confounded political players' expectations. On the day he qualified for the ballot in Arizona, the fiftieth state to include him, he invited Democratic and Republican delegations to meet with him, supposedly to help him decide which party he might support in the election. Instead, on October 1, 1992, he announced he was reentering the race.

From Perot's standpoint, it was an optimal time to make this move. With no consultants, he now ran the campaign his way. He reentered the contest in time to participate in the three candidate debates. With his wry humor and plain speaking, he was easily the star of these, and his performance boosted the spirits of flagging supporters. On election day, Perot polled an average of 19 percent of all voters—the best showing for a third-party candidate since Teddy Roosevelt's Bull Moose Party run in 1912 and the most total votes up to that time for a third-party presidential candidate.

Perot's very weaknesses accounted in part for his strong showing. In an era when political "spin" and double-talk had been honed to a fine art, many Americans found it refreshing when a candidate talked "off the top of his head" (or at least appeared to). Moreover, unlike most American third-party movements, which have built their appeal on minority ideological stances (such as Libertarians and Greens) or regional issues (such as the Dixiecrats), Perot claimed the broad middle ground of "sensible" positions: fiscal responsibility and economic nationalism. The major parties seemed to honor these in name only, while their policies tilted in other directions.

Perot wisely avoided taking on the era's radioactive "cultural issues" (such as abortion and gay rights), and as a result he drew followers from both Democratic and Republican camps in approximately equal numbers. In addition, the anger among Americans that he helped to legitimate proved a powerful tool for energizing previously unaligned voters. Studies of those who voted for Perot have shown that a large proportion of them had weak ties, or no ties at all, to the other parties; this was the only way they differed markedly from other voters.

## SIGNIFICANCE

Perot was not done with politics after 1992. He was soon back in the public eye, speaking at rallies against NAFTA and debating Vice President Al Gore about the issue in November, 1993 (a debate that Gore "won"). In 1995, Perot set up the apparatus for another presidential run by organizing the Reform Party, and in the 1996 election he won 9 percent of the vote as that party's candidate. Although the result was a disappointment to Perot, this percentage of the vote qualified the party for federal matching funds in 2000. Pat Buchanan secured the Reform Party's 2000 nomination and came in a distant fourth in the general election. The party did have one electoral success when former professional wrestler Jesse Ventura won the Minnesota governorship in 1998 on a Reform Party ticket.

American third parties have traditionally brought new issues into the mainstream, forcing major-party politicians to deal with those issues. Perot's campaign served this function with the federal deficit, enabling President Bill Clinton to make deficit reduction a high priority and the cornerstone of U.S. prosperity in the late 1990's. Perot's campaign also showed how a third-party candidate can gain credibility by combining effective media appearances with the work of an army of enthusiastic volunteers.

—*Emily Alward*

## FURTHER READING

Asher, Herb. "The Perot Campaign." In *Democracy's Feast: Elections in America*, edited by Herbert F.

1992

Weisberg. Chatham, N.J.: Chatham House, 1995. Examines data on Perot supporters and the campaign's dynamics to explain Perot's success.

Germond, Jack W., and Jules Witcover. *Mad as Hell: Revolt at the Ballot Box, 1992*. New York: Warner Books, 1993. Readable history of the entire 1992 presidential campaign by two veteran political reporters.

Jelen, Ted G., ed. *Ross for Boss: The Perot Phenomenon and Beyond*. Albany: State University of New York Press, 2001. Collection of scholarly studies examines various aspects of Perot's run and discusses the campaign's impacts on independent and third-party candidacies in general.

Rapoport, Ronald. *Three's a Crowd: The Dynamic of Third Parties*. Ann Arbor: University of Michigan Press, 2005. Presents a well-argued theory that Republican victories in 1994 and after owe a debt to Perot voters and their "issue awareness."

**SEE ALSO:** Nov. 2, 1976: Carter Is Elected President; Nov. 4, 1980: Reagan Is Elected President; Nov. 3, 1983: Jackson Becomes the First Major Black Candidate for U.S. President; Nov. 8, 1988: Bush Is Elected President; Nov. 3, 1992: Clinton Wins the U.S. Presidency; Aug. 19, 1996: Green Party Nominates Nader for President.

## February 21, 1992
# UNITED NATIONS AUTHORIZES TROOP DEPLOYMENT TO THE BALKANS

*As chaos spread in the former Yugoslavia in the early 1990's, the United Nations sought to minimize casualties by creating safe havens and deploying a lightly armed protection force in that violently disintegrating country.*

**LOCALE:** Yugoslavia (now Bosnia and Herzegovina; Croatia, Macedonia; Serbia and Montenegro, and Slovenia)

**CATEGORIES:** United Nations; diplomacy and international relations; wars, uprisings, and civil unrest

**KEY FIGURES**

*Slobodan Milošević* (1941-2006), president of Serbia, 1989-1997, and president of Yugoslavia, 1997-2000

*Franjo Tudjman* (1922-1999), president of Croatia, 1990-1999

*Boutros Boutros-Ghali* (b. 1922), secretary-general of the United Nations, 1992-1996, and a leading advocate of inserting U.N. peacekeepers between the warring communities in Yugoslavia

*Satish Nambiar* (b. 1936), commander of the first U.N. peacekeeping force deployed in the Yugoslav civil war and subsequently a harsh critic of the limitations imposed on the force's operations

**SUMMARY OF EVENT**

By the time the Security Council of the United Nations authorized the formation of the first U.N. Protection Force (UNPROFOR I) for deployment in the former Yu-

goslavia on February 21, 1992, political circumstances had been deteriorating there for years and warfare had been sweeping across the nation's westernmost corner for more than six months. Indeed, with the exception of its years under Tito's rule, Yugoslavia had been troubled by communal conflict in general, and the tension between its Serbian and Croatian communities in particular, from its earliest days. Even its post-World War I creation in 1918 as the Kingdom of the Serbs, Croats, and Slovenes had less to do with the contracting parties' strong desire for union than with Croatian fears that if the state was not quickly finalized they would find themselves facing alone an Italy that was already attacking Croatia's Dalmatian coastline. Thereafter, matters worsened.

To Serbian nationalists, the new state was a means of achieving a Greater Serbia, which would unite all of the Balkans' Serbs (including the sizable Serbian minority in Croatia) under Belgrade's centralized rule. In contrast, the country's minority communities (Slovenes, Montenegrins, Bosnian Muslims, Kosovo Albanians, Macedonians, Montenegrins, and, in particular, the Croats) wanted maximum regional and/or local autonomy in any union. During the interwar period, Serbian objectives generally prevailed, although at a cost. In 1929, for example, the kingdom's Serbian ruler, Alexander I, reacted to minority demands for federalism by assuming essentially dictatorial powers over the state even as he renamed it Yugoslavia (land of the Slavs), only to be slain five years later himself by an assassin with ties to Croatian nationalists.

Even the country's occupation by German forces during World War II exacerbated Croat-Serbian antagonisms when the occupiers established puppet regimes in Croatia and in Serbia's heavily Muslim Kosovo province in order to control Yugoslavia more easily. With German approval, these rump governments soon set about settling scores against their former Serbian rulers. In turn, they soon also became the targets of the anti-German underground led by Tito (née Josip Broz, a Croat by birth) that is estimated to have killed at least 200,000 (mostly Croat) collaborators before the war ended.

It was only during the era of Tito's rule (1945-1980) that Yugoslavia at last achieved a measure of unity and such an appearance of stability that when the 1984 Winter Olympic Games were held in Sarajevo, the host city was held out to the world as a symbol of interethnic harmony. In reality, even then the fissures separating Yugoslavia's communities were again widening. Tito had been a major unifying element in his own right—a Yugoslav wartime hero who had offered Yugoslavia's principal minorities substantial federal autonomy within the framework of the country's (mostly Serb-dominated) Communist Party. With his death in 1980, old rivalries and resentments quickly resurfaced, and the Communist Party of Yugoslavia began to disintegrate into ethno-regional wings.

By the late 1980's, the country's survival depended precariously on the long-standing shared fear of its various communities that a disintegrating Yugoslavia might easily fall into the Soviet Union's Central European empire. Thus, when the Soviet Union itself began to disintegrate in 1989-90, that unifying element, too, dissolved, and—often with Western European encouragement—in June of 1991, Croatia and Slovenia seceded despite Belgrade's threat of military reprisals.

Belgrade was soon true to its word, and the summer of 1991 witnessed a brief war in Slovenia before the Yugoslav military conceded the independence of that barely (3 percent) Serbian republic and applied its full weight to crushing Croatia's attempt at secession. By December, the world's twenty-four-hour cable television news networks were carrying to their Western audiences grim live coverage of the heavy fighting in Croatia. The United Nations acted shortly thereafter, diplomatically recognizing the independence of Croatia and Slovenia on January 15, 1992, and—at approximately the same time that Bosnia was voting to secede from Yugoslavia despite the overwhelming opposition to separatism of its plurality Serbian community—on February 21 authorizing the creation of a U.N. military presence in Cro-

atia to establish and maintain a cease-fire and safe havens there.

## SIGNIFICANCE

Debate has long lingered over the value of and the lessons to be drawn from the deployment of UNPROFOR I and its companion peacekeeping force, UNPROFOR II, which was established with similar charges in Bosnia when that republic seceded and the Yugoslav civil war spread to Bosnia and remained concentrated there until November, 1995, when the official conclusion of the war was negotiated at Dayton, Ohio. On the positive side of the ledger, the diplomatic intervention of the United Nations in the war in Croatia did produce the desired cease-fire between Belgrade's forces and those of the Croatian government as well as the withdrawal of the Yugoslav army from Croatia. Similarly, the "safe" areas designated by the United Nations, first in Croatia and later in Bosnia, did provide a sanctuary and, much of the time, safety for those displaced civilians who were able to make it to them. In addition, the lightly armed peacekeeping force deployed in Macedonia in December of 1992 may have played a small part in preventing the warfare from spreading to that breakaway republic.

Nonetheless, the consensus is that the UNPROFOR missions were, on balance, failures—so systemically flawed that future peacekeeping missions of their design should probably be avoided. At its inception, UNPROFOR was meant to be a middle-ground form of military intervention located between the traditional U.N. peacekeeping missions, which were normally deployed in areas where there was a peace to be kept (a cease-fire line or treaty provisions to be policed, for example), and the type of large-scale military operation that would have been required to end the fighting in the former Yugoslavia (that is, "peace-making" forces). Hence, except where cease-fire lines were temporarily arranged while diplomatic efforts were being pursued to end the fighting, military operations continued despite UNPROFOR presence both throughout Bosnia and around such areas in Croatia as the self-proclaimed (and short-lived) independent Serbian Republic of Krajina.

Moreover, as the fighting increasingly came to involve the extremist, paramilitary organizations of each community, ethnic cleansing and other war crimes at times escalated even in those theaters where the U.N. units were present but too lightly armed to provide the protection they were suppose to offer noncombatants. Sometimes UNPROFOR personnel were themselves taken hostage and bartered by their captors for goods that

1992

allowed the paramilitaries to pursue their belligerent ways more effectively. Sometimes the outcome was tragic, as in the "safe" city of Srebrenica, where on July 11, 1995, thousands of Muslims were massacred by Serbian forces almost before the eyes of the few hundred Dutch peacekeepers deployed there when the Serbs seized control of the city.

Ultimately, it was the brazen and ultraviolent nature of the attack on Srebrenica that, combined with the subsequent Serbian shelling of two other U.N.-designated safe havens (Tuzla and Sarajevo), prompted the North Atlantic Treaty Organization (NATO) to undertake the aggressive military action that finally led the protagonists to seek a diplomatic solution to the conflicts in Croatia and Bosnia. The end of the Yugoslav civil wars, however, left still unanswered the basic questions raised when UNPROFOR I was authorized. If there is neither a peace to keep nor the will to undertake costly peace-making operations, is there an effective means of protecting noncombatants available to the international community when civil warfare occurs, or must outsiders accommodate themselves to watching the casualties mount?

—*Joseph R. Rudolph, Jr.*

**FURTHER READING**

Biermann, Wolfgang, and Martin Vadset, eds. *U.N. Peacekeeping in Trouble: Lessons Learned from the Former Yugoslavia*. Brookfield, Vt.: Ashgate, 1998. Presents a critical analysis of the U.N. peacekeeping operations in Croatia and Bosnia, drawing heavily on the experiences of those involved in the operations.

Esman, Milton J., and Shibley Telhami. *International Organizations and Ethnic Conflict*. Ithaca, N.Y.: Cornell University Press, 1995. Discusses the general challenges facing peacekeeping forces in civil war zones. Includes several chapters on U.N. peacekeeping in Yugoslavia.

Ramet, Sabrina P. *Balkan Babel: The Disintegration of Yugoslavia from the Death of Tito to the Fall of Milošević*. 4th ed. Boulder, Colo.: Westview Press, 2002. Outstanding work helps readers to understand the context and consequences of the U.N. decision to deploy a peacekeeping force in war-torn Yugoslavia. Includes maps, bibliography, and index.

Silber, Laura, and Allan Little. *Yugoslavia: Death of a Nation*. New York: Penguin Books, 1997. One of the most informative and widely available short accounts of Yugoslavia's final days.

Thakur, Ramesh, and Carlyle A. Thayer, eds. *A Crisis of Expectations: U.N. Peacekeeping in the 1990's*. Boulder, Colo.: Westview Press, 1995. Collection presents interesting essays on both the U.N. protection forces in Yugoslavia and the general problems that confront peacekeeping operations in civil war zones.

**SEE ALSO:** May 4, 1980: Death of Tito; July-Nov., 1988: Ethnic Violence Erupts in Yugoslavian Provinces; June 25, 1991: Civil War Begins in Yugoslavia; Oct.-Nov., 1991: Yugoslav Army Shells Dubrovnik; Feb. 13, 1995: Serbs Face Charges at the International Criminal Tribunal for Yugoslavia; Nov. 21, 1995: Dayton Negotiations Produce Bosnian Peace Accord; Jan. 14, 2000: Hague Court Convicts Bosnian Croats of 1993 Massacre.

# March 17, 1992, and July 18, 1994
# TERRORISTS ATTACK ISRAELI EMBASSY AND JEWISH CENTER IN ARGENTINA

*In 1992, a suicide bomber drove a truck loaded with explosives into the Israeli embassy in Buenos Aires, killing twenty-nine and wounding more than two hundred. A group called Islamic Jihad, an affiliate of Hezbollah, claimed responsibility. In 1994, again in Buenos Aires, a bomb destroyed a building where several Israeli Argentine associations were headquartered. More than ten years after the attacks, both cases remained unsolved.*

**LOCALE:** Buenos Aires, Argentina
**CATEGORY:** Terrorism, atrocities, and war crimes

**KEY FIGURES**

*Carlos Saúl Menem* (b. 1930), president of Argentina, 1989-1999
*Monzer al-Kassar* (b. 1945), a Syrian believed to be a drugs and arms trafficker
*Mohsen Rabbani* (b. 1952), former cultural attaché of the Iranian embassy in Argentina
*Hafez al-Assad* (1930-2000), president of Syria, 1971-2000
*Ibrahim Hussein Berro* (1973-1994), Lebanese Hezbollah militant and alleged suicide bomber

**SUMMARY OF EVENT**

On March 17, 1992, a suicide bomber drove a Ford F-100 pickup truck loaded with explosives into the Israeli embassy in Buenos Aires, Argentina. Besides the embassy, a Catholic church and a school were destroyed. Twenty-nine people were killed and more than two hundred wounded. Some were Israelis, but most were Argentine, the majority of whom were children. Iran and Hezbollah were accused. A group called Islamic Jihad, an affiliate of Hezbollah, claimed responsibility.

On July 18, 1994, again in Buenos Aires, a bomb destroyed the seven-story building housing the Asociación Mutual Israelita Argentina (AMIA, the Argentine Israelite Mutual Association), and the Delegation of Argentine Israelite Associations (DAIA). A group called Ansarollah claimed responsibility. There were eighty-five fatalities, while more than 150 were injured. The identity of the group or groups responsible for both attacks remained disputed years after the incidents.

In both Buenos Aires attacks, the target was the Jewish population of Argentina; numbering 300,000, it was the largest Jewish population in Latin America. The first

bombing was allegedly a counterattack after the killing of the secretary-general of Hezbollah (party of God), ʿAbbas al-Musawi, and his wife and child in Lebanon on February 16, 1992, for which Hezbollah had vowed revenge. Although Hezbollah had denied any involvement in the second attack, Argentine investigators officially explained it as the organization's way of expressing its resentment of Argentina's inclination toward North American politics.

Evidence pointed toward Iranian-Syrian complicity in both Buenos Aires bomb attacks. The truck in the first bombing was hired for twenty-one thousand dollars by someone using a false identity. The rental fee was traced to a currency-exchange bureau in Biblos, Lebanon, which was a subsidiary of a larger exchange bureau, Society for Change in Beirut, owned by a Syrian, Monzer al-Kassar. He was believed to be a drugs and arms trafficker and a key player in the world of terrorism.

Hezbollah also had serious ties to the Syrian government. The probability of Syria's culpability was strengthened in the light of events leading to the election of Argentine president Carlos Saúl Menem. He and relatives of his first wife were originally from Syria. A presidential aspirant when he visited Syria in 1988, Menem met with top officials of the Syrian government, including Vice President ʿAbd al-Halim Khaddam and President Hafez al-Assad's brother, Rifaat al-Assad. During this time, Menem made the acquaintance of al-Kassar and Alfredo Yabrán, both of whom originated from the same town in Syria as Menem. On that trip, they promised political funding to Menem in return for nuclear and missile technology that had originally been promised to Iraq, traditionally a mutual enemy of Iran and Syria.

In the early 1980's, Argentina was pioneering nuclear technology in Latin America with the development of the Condor II missile. Former president Raúl Alfonsín had signed an agreement with Egypt and Iraq in January, 1984, to build this missile, which was to be superior to America's Pershing II. Syrian officials invested millions of dollars in the development of the Condor II missile, believing it to be far superior to the Scud and Badr 2000 missiles.

However, after the widely condemned Iraqi invasion of Kuwait, Menem, who assumed the presidency in 1989, believed that partnership with Iraq would no lon-

1992

2645

ger be gainful. Argentina had suspended the installation of its nuclear reactor in Syria in 1991. It also dismantled the Condor II because of pressure from America and Israel. This breach of contract forced Syria to purchase an inferior missile from China, a decision that did not go down well with investors. There were also unconfirmed reports that Iran had purchased Scud missiles from North Korea.

The Buenos Aires bombings left few Argentines in doubt that the attacks were retaliation from the aggrieved parties of the unfulfilled missiles contract. However, the Argentine government placed blame on Iran, ignoring any possible involvement by Syria. This was perceived by some parties to be a cover-up on the part of the Argentine government, what some called "Menemism." Official exposure of its dealings with Syria would not augur well for President Menem's government. In May, 1998, the Argentine government announced to the world that it had proof of Iranian complicity in the 1994 attack, and seven Iranian diplomats were expelled from Argentina.

*Argentine president Carlos Saúl Menem speaking at a Latin American economic conference in Miami, Florida, in early 1998.* (AP/Wide World Photos)

Notwithstanding, the investigative and judicial process was fraught with irregularities. A Brazilian named Wilson Dos Santos reportedly informed the Argentine consulate in Milan that the group responsible for the 1992 attack was planning another. Dos Santos claimed to have obtained this information from his Iranian girlfriend, Nasrim Mokhtari, who worked with the group of terrorists, and he unwittingly became involved in their activities.

Dos Santos's warnings were acknowledged only after the 1994 attack, when the Federal Bureau of Investigation discovered how accurate his initial testimony had been. The activities of the unnamed terrorist group were found to have been coordinated by Mohsen Rabbani while he was cultural attaché of the Iranian embassy in Argentina. According to investigators, most of the terrorists had entered Argentina through the Argentine-Brazilian-Paraguayan border. Rabbani was also cited in connection with the 1994 bombing in the testimony of a former Ira-

nian intelligence officer who had been under German protection since 1996. The officer's testimony also established a "local connection," in which members of the Argentine police force and civil employees were either bribed or coerced into joining the plot. However, in September, 2004, four former police officers and an alleged car thief were acquitted because of lack of evidence.

Evidence from Spanish intelligence showed that al-Kassar had transported the explosive Semtex, part of the composition of the 1992 bomb, from Spain into Argentina via Damascus. Ownership of the company that carried the Semtex to Argentina, Cenrex Trading Corporation of Varsovia, was traced to al-Kassar, who had flown to Argentina from Spain on Iberia Airlines Flight 6940 at the time of the attack.

In January, 2003, a report by Secretaría de Inteligencia de Estado, Argentina's intelligence agency, was handed to federal judge Juan José Galeano, who refused to issue arrest warrants for some individuals indicted in the report. Most of the individuals named would remain free; al-Kassar was even granted Argentine citizenship.

In August, 2005, Galeano was impeached for his mishandling of the investigation.

While links among Iran, Syria, and Hezbollah were first established by the Central Intelligence Agency in Argentina, Syria later faded from suspicion, partly because of the Menem government's cover-up efforts. At the same time, Syria was considered a veritable tool in peace negotiations in the Middle East. Thus Argentine Jews, believing that Israel's position in the Middle East peace process could be strengthened, were not enthusiastic about pursuing the theory of Syrian involvement in the Buenos Aires bombings, especially the investigations of al-Kassar's activities.

## SIGNIFICANCE

The Buenos Aires bombings of 1992 and 1994 were the worst attacks up to that time on Argentina and the largest attacks on Jews since the Holocaust. Both cases remained unsolved into the twenty-first century; no one had been convicted. In October, 2006, Argentine prosecutors charged Iran and Hezbollah with the 1994 bombing. According to chief prosecutor Alberto Nisman, the bombing was carried out by Hezbollah and ordered by Iran. Nisman's report indentified Ibrahim Hussein Berro, a Hezbollah militant, as the suicide bomber in that attack. Argentina, the United States, and Israel accused Iran of involvement, which the Iranian government denied. It was argued that Hezbollah did not have a motive to attack and that the organization had never carried out an attack outside the Middle East.

Some claimed that Syria was the lead party in the attacks, but that the planning and execution were carried out by Iran. Accusations of cover-ups and mishandling of the cases continued for years after the incidents.

—*Oyekemi Oyelakin*

## FURTHER READING

Barsky, Yehudit. *Terrorism Briefing: Hezbollah*. New York: American Jewish Community, 2003. Discusses the evolution of Hezbollah and its obligations to the philosophies of terrorism and anti-Semitism. Analyzes its networking with other terrorist groups in the Middle East and its role in the Argentine attacks.

Escudé, Carlos, and Gurevich Beatriz. "Limits to Governability, Corruption, and Transnational Terrorism: The Case of the 1992 and 1994 Attacks in Buenos Aires." *Estudios Interdisciplinarios de America, Latina y el Caribe*, July-December, 2003. Provides a detailed description of events, an examination of the local politics of the investigative process, and an analysis of the Syrian-Iranian connection.

Quillen, Chris. "Mass Casualty Bombings Chronology." *Studies in Conflict and Terrorism* 25 (September/October, 2002): 293-302. Examines descriptive forms of terrorism. Mass terrorism—an attack involving more than twenty-five fatalities—is the modern form of terrorism.

**SEE ALSO:** Fall, 1982: Pro-Iran Radicals Form Hezbollah; Feb. 23, 1998: Osama Bin Laden Declares Jihad Against "Jews and Crusaders"; Aug. 7, 1998: Terrorists Bomb U.S. Embassies in East Africa; Oct. 12, 2000: Terrorists Attack USS *Cole*.

1992

## April 12, 1992
# EURO DISNEYLAND OPENS

*The opening of Euro Disneyland near Paris, France, continued the spread of American culture to France and was expected to improve France's economy.*

**LOCALE:** Marne-la-Vallée, France
**CATEGORIES:** Trade and commerce; travel and recreation

**KEY FIGURES**
*Michael Eisner* (b. 1942), chief executive officer of the Walt Disney Company
*Frank Wells* (1932-1994), president and chief operating officer of the Walt Disney Company
*Robert John Fitzpatrick* (b. 1941), chairman of Euro Disneyland

**SUMMARY OF EVENT**
On April 12, 1992, the Walt Disney Company opened its fourth major theme park in Marne-la-Vallée, on the Marne River about twenty miles east of Paris, France. This was Disney's second theme park outside the United States; Tokyo Disneyland opened in 1983. Disneyland in Anaheim, California, and Walt Disney World in Orlando, Florida, began the string of Disney theme parks.

The entire complex known as Euro Disney Resort occupied forty-eight hundred acres of what used to be farmland. It included the Euro Disneyland theme park, six hotels with a total of fifty-two hundred rooms, dozens of restaurants, a twenty-seven-hole golf course, a 139-acre campground called Camp Davy Crockett, and a 10-acre artificial lake. Eleven million people were expected to visit the resort in the first year of operation; each was expected to purchase an average of $33 worth of items as well as paying admission and accommodation costs.

Marne-la-Vallée was chosen for this project out of two hundred possible locations in Western Europe, even though it has cold weather in the winter months and Euro Disneyland would stay open all year. Tokyo has similar weather, and Tokyo Disneyland had been successful in the winter, so planners were sure that cold winters would not pose a problem. Much of Euro Disneyland would be covered, so visitors could spend as much as 80 percent of their time indoors. Factors favoring Marne-la-Vallée were the large, flat tract of land available and its proximity to Paris, Europe's largest tourist draw. Seventeen million people can drive to Euro Disneyland in two hours or less, another 109 million can drive there within six hours, and 310 million people are within two hours by air. This potential market was larger than the markets available at any of the other proposed sites.

Euro Disney's financial structure was unlike those of the other three Disney resorts. Euro Disney was the first to be a public company, with 51 percent of its stock owned by European individuals and institutions and 49 percent owned by Disney. France does not allow foreign enterprises to have majority ownership. About half of the European investors were French. Original agreements called for the Walt Disney Company to receive 10 percent of all ticket sales, 5 percent of all merchandise sales, a management fee of 3 percent of gross revenues (until 1997, when the fee increased to 6 percent), and incentive management fees of up to 50 percent of pretax cash flow. This was anticipated to amount to as much as 57 percent of Euro Disney's profits by 1997. Pretax profits were expected to be 227 million French francs in 1994 and as high as 3 billion francs by 2001.

A master agreement between Disney and the French government was to be signed on June 18, 1986, but the signing was postponed because thirty to forty issues remained to be resolved. The parties finally signed an agreement in March, 1987, that gave Disney loans of up to 4.8 billion French francs at an interest rate of 7.85 percent, much less than the going rate at that time of 9.25 percent. Euro Disney also was permitted to write off construction costs against taxes at rates higher than those allowed for other companies.

In addition, the French government agreed to pay for and build metro and road links into Paris at a cost of more than $350 million. The agreement also required that Euro Disney put maximum effort into hiring French people, a major concern of the French government at a time of 9 percent unemployment in France. At the time the resort opened, about 60 percent of the employees were French. Disney was allowed to buy the forty-eight hundred acres of land on which the resort was set at 1971 agricultural prices. The average cost was 11.1 French francs per square meter, a small fraction of the cost of land in other Paris suburbs.

The project initially provoked considerable opposition in France. Prior to the beginning of the Euro Disney project, Jack Lang, France's minister of culture, had been opposed to importing American culture into France. Many French intellectuals called Euro Disney a "cultural Chernobyl" and expressed concerns about such elements as the resort's architecture, saying it was too American.

In 1989, when Disney executives visited Paris, they were met by demonstrators protesting the Euro Disney project. French citizens held demonstrations protesting the spending of $350 million by the French government on the project; they wanted the money to be spent on other projects, such as building schools. Some of this opposition dissipated, however, as the French people began to appreciate the prospect of increased employment opportunities.

In January, 1992, sixteen French contractors claimed that Euro Disney owed them $150 million for construction. A bitter public battle ensued, threatening the opening of the resort, and an arbitrator had to be called in to settle the issue.

## SIGNIFICANCE

Euro Disney was expected to have a large influence on the economy of the surrounding area of France as well as on the growth of the Walt Disney Company. Many analysts believed that the "boom" years of Disney in the United States were over, and to continue to grow, the company had to extend its operations into other countries. Robert John Fitzpatrick, chairman of Euro Disney, indicated that the resort would be Disney's big project for the 1990's. Disney executives believed that by the time the project was finished, Paris would be only a "side trip" for visitors to that part of the world; Euro Disneyland and other parts of the resort would be the main attractions.

The Euro Disney Resort initially employed approximately ten thousand people; by 2005, the resort, now known as Disneyland Resort Paris, employed some forty thousand. Finding housing for employees posed problems at the beginning, so Disney constructed eight hundred units of new housing of various types, including singles, dormitories, and family quarters. The company also looked for other housing opportunities in the area and as far away as Paris, reserving apartments and single rooms for employees of Euro Disney. The demand for housing in the area benefited the construction industry in a time of recession and increased occupancy rates for many landlords. A few problems also arose because of housing issues: Some people were evicted after illegally camping out on local farmland, and some villagers in the area surrounding Euro Disney were fined for triple-renting rooms, or renting rooms in eight-hour shifts, to Disney employees.

Not everything at Euro Disney went according to plan at first. Disney had projected that eleven million people would visit the resort in the first year of operation. In the first five months of operation, about six million visited Euro Disneyland, or an average of forty-one thousand per day. Attendance reached seven million by October,

1992, but daily attendance fell during the winter months, and the first year's projections were not met.

The continuing recession in Europe meant that many families were unable to afford the high cost of visiting Euro Disney. Hotel occupancy rates at the resort did not reach projected levels: August of 1992 saw nearly complete occupancy of the fifty-two hundred hotel rooms, but other months saw lower occupancy, especially the winter months. In October, 1992, the Newport Bay Club, the largest of the six hotels at the resort and one of the largest in Europe, shut down its eleven hundred rooms until spring, even though it had originally planned to stay open through the winter. Two other hotels cut their rates up to 25 percent, and some of the resort's restaurants offered meals at reduced prices.

Profits did not live up to expectations in the resort's rugged early years, but Disney responded by adding new attractions and making some changes. In 2002, another theme park, the Walt Disney Studios Park, was added to Disneyland Resort Paris, and by 2005 the resort was consistently recording twelve million visitors per year, surpassing any other Parisian tourist attraction.

*—Brenda Carlyle*

## FURTHER READING

"Anything but a 'Mickey Mouse' Project." *International Business* 44 (January, 1989): 5. Contains information about the financial arrangements involved in the Euro Disneyland project but offers few details.

"Disney Gears up for Fairy-Tale Opening." *International Management* 47 (March, 1992): 16. Explains some of the problems Euro Disneyland faced as projections for attendance failed to be realized in the first year of operation.

Dunlop, Beth. *Building a Dream: The Art of Disney Architecture.* New York: Harry N. Abrams, 1996. Uncritical, enthusiastic presentation of the architecture of Disney from the original Disneyland forward. Includes discussion of the Euro Disney buildings and their architects. Features photographs and architectural drawings.

Gooding, Judson. "Of Mice and Men." *Across the Board* 29 (March, 1992): 40-44. Addresses the impact that Euro Disneyland had on farmers whose land was taken for the project as well as impacts on other businesses in and around Paris. Also discusses the housing problem faced by employees.

Kobliner, Beth. "Next Stop Eurodisney." *Money* 21 (March, 1992): 155-156, 158. Explains the scope of the initial development project and facilities that were

1992

a part of the first phase of Euro Disneyland. Also gives a limited cost comparison between Euro Disneyland and Walt Disney World in Florida.

Lainsbury, Andrew. *Once upon an American Dream: The Story of Euro Disneyland*. Lawrence: University Press of Kansas, 2000. Former employee of Euro Disney draws on company archives and interviews to examine the history of Euro Disneyland and Europeans' love/hate relationship with the park and with American culture. Includes bibliography and index.

"Mickey Goes to the Bank." *Economist* 312 (September 16, 1989): 78-79. Very informative article describes the master agreement signed by the French government and Walt Disney Company and discusses many of the very favorable terms given to Disney and how Disney opened Euro Disneyland as a public corporation.

"The Not-so-Magic Kingdom." *Economist* 324 (September 26, 1992): 87-88. Describes projections for attendance at Euro Disneyland, hotel occupancy, and profits and examines why these projections were not realized in the first year of operation.

Toy, Stewart. "Mouse Fever Is About to Strike Europe." *BusinessWeek*, March 30, 1992, 32. Provides some examples of the opposition that Disney faced in opening Euro Disneyland.

_____. "The Mouse Isn't Roaring." *BusinessWeek*, August 24, 1992, 38. Very informative article discusses Euro Disneyland's failure to meet projections. Compares the cost of visiting Euro Disneyland with that of visiting Walt Disney World in Florida.

**SEE ALSO:** Oct. 1, 1982: EPCOT Center Opens; 1990's: Disney Emerges as an Architectural Patron.

## April 29-May 1, 1992
# LOS ANGELES RIOTS

*Verdicts of not guilty in the trial of four police officers accused of police brutality revealed the wide gap between African Americans' and Euro-Americans' views of the criminal justice system and sparked the worst rioting the city of Los Angeles had experienced up to that time.*

**LOCALE:** Los Angeles, California
**CATEGORY:** Wars, uprisings, and civil unrest

**KEY FIGURES**
*Rodney King* (b. 1965), African American who was the subject of a videotaped beating by Los Angeles police
*Stacey Koon* (b. 1950), Los Angeles police sergeant involved in the beating of Rodney King
*Daryl F. Gates* (b. 1926), chief of the Los Angeles Police Department
*Reginald Denny* (b. 1953), white truck driver severely beaten by African Americans during the early hours of the riots
*Damian Williams* (b. 1973), African American charged with participating in the beating of Reginald Denny

**SUMMARY OF EVENT**
Before the Rodney King beating on March 3, 1991, many in the Los Angeles community believed that the Los Angeles Police Department (LAPD) had demonstrated a pattern of excessive force, particularly against members

of minority groups. One significant example was Operation Hammer, begun in 1989, during which the LAPD allegedly rounded up African Americans and Hispanics without any reasonable suspicion that they had committed any crime, simply because of the way the suspects looked and because the police wanted to avert the threat of gang violence. As a result, the chief of the LAPD, Daryl F. Gates, was despised by many in the African American community. The videotape of Rodney King's beating by members of the LAPD, therefore, came as no surprise to the African American community of Los Angeles. It merely confirmed what they already thought: that police use of excessive force against minorities was a common practice.

The videotape of King's beating, recorded by private citizen George Holliday in the morning hours of March 3, 1991, was eighty-one seconds in duration. The footage from the tape that was seen throughout the United States on television news programs showed King, a six-foot, three-inch African American weighing 225 pounds, prone on the ground, sustaining blows to his head, neck, kidney area, and legs from four policemen, who were kicking and smashing at him with their truncheons. Also present, but not in full view on the videotape, were nineteen other police officers surrounding the four who were administering the beating. In addition, onlookers—not seen on the tape—were pleading that the beating stop. The police paid no attention to them. As a result of the beating, King sustained eleven fractures to his skull, a crushed cheekbone, a broken ankle, internal injuries, a burn on his chest, and some brain damage.

Television viewers also did not see what preceded the beating. During the evening, King had consumed the equivalent of a case of beer (it was later determined that his blood alcohol level was twice the legal limit for operation of a vehicle). He was on parole at the time, and he ran the risk of landing back in jail if caught speeding. The police, led by Stacey Koon, started to pursue King because his car was seen to be exceeding the speed limit. The chase through the streets of Los Angeles escalated to one hundred miles per hour at one point, before the police were able to stop King and force him out of his car. Television viewers did not see King fighting with the police at that point, even standing up after being stunned twice with a Taser (electroshock weapon). Those who saw the videotape saw only the prone body of an African American man being assaulted repeatedly by white police officers.

The four officers seen delivering the blows to King on the videotape, including Koon, were charged with the beating at the end of March, 1991, in Los Angeles. Their attorneys moved for a change of venue for the trial, which was granted, and in the spring of 1992 the trial took place in Simi Valley, a suburban town an hour's drive north of Los Angeles. The town was home to a large proportion of LAPD officers and retirees and was dominated by law-and-order conservatives. Six men and six women, none of whom was African American, made up the jury.

According to those who were present, the prosecution presented a weak and diffuse case. The defense, however, was strong. Defense attorneys played the videotape in slow motion over and over until its effects became trivialized. The defense also emphasized how King presented a threat to the police. Koon testified about King's "Hulk-like strength and how he groaned like a wounded animal," conjuring up for the jury the image of police representing the "thin blue line" that protects the forces of civilization from the savagery represented by King. Among the jurors, many of whom had likely settled in Simi Valley to get away from the alleged evils and crime of the inner city, the message resonated. After thirty-two hours of deliberation, the jury acquitted

*A fire rages near Vermont Avenue in Los Angeles during the riots caused by the acquittals of four police officers in the beating of African American Rodney King.* (AP/Wide World Photos)

1992

the four officers on April 29, 1992. The verdicts were announced on television at 2:50 P.M.

At 4:00 that afternoon, in South Central Los Angeles, five African American gang members went to get some malt liquor at the Payless Liquor Store near the intersection of Florence and Normandie avenues. They started to take it without paying, and the store owner's son tried to stop them. One of the gang members smashed the son on the head with a bottle and allegedly said, "This is for Rodney King." The other gang members hurled the bottles they held through the store windows while the owner pressed the alarm for the police. By the time two officers arrived in response, the suspects were gone.

At 5:30 P.M., at the corner of Florence and Normandie, eight black men wielding baseball bats started breaking the car windows of passing motorists. Eighteen police cars and thirty-five officers from the LAPD sped to the area. They arrested three suspects and then left at 5:45. In the next hour, the crowd attacking cars grew to some two hundred people. One of the victims was Reginald Denny, a white truck driver, who was pulled from his truck and beaten by African Americans, including Damian Williams, with a fire extinguisher. The police did not return. Chief Gates had left police headquarters at 6:30 to attend a fund-raising event in the affluent suburb of Brentwood.

By 7:30, the crowd at Florence and Normandie had started lighting fires. An hour later, the LAPD finally returned to the area and began trying to disperse the crowd. By that time, the fires, rioting, and looting had spread to other parts of the city. As the riots continued for two more days, local television news crews flooded the airwaves with helicopter views of hundreds of fires throughout the city and normally law-abiding citizens looting stores. On Friday, May 1, 1992, Rodney King appeared on television to appeal for calm with the plea, "Can we all get along?" By the end of that day, the violence was over.

## SIGNIFICANCE

The acquital of the four officers charged with assaulting Rodney King reinforced the perceptions of many that the American criminal justice system treats whites and African Americans differently. Some observers, however, have argued that the riots were less the result of racial tensions than of persistent localized disparities between economic and social classes.

By the time the riots ended in Los Angeles on May 1, 1992, fifty-eight people had died, more than twelve thousand people had been arrested, and property damage was estimated to be as high as $1 billion. In addition, similar uprisings had started in Atlanta, Las Vegas, Minneapolis, New York, Omaha, and Seattle. The 1992 riots in Los Angeles caused more damage and spread across a wider area than did any incidents of urban unrest in the city during the 1960's.

In part as a result of the criticism he received for his handling of the riots and his role in fostering the police culture that had contributed to them, Gates resigned from the LAPD in late 1992. He was replaced by an African American chief of police, Willie L. Williams. Koon and one of the other officers originally charged with beating King, Laurence Powell, were tried and convicted in federal court of violating King's civil rights. King won a civil suit against the city of Los Angeles and was awarded $3.8 million.

—*Jennifer Eastman*

## FURTHER READING

Abelmann, Nancy, and John Lie. *Blue Dreams: Korean Americans and the Los Angeles Riots*. Cambridge, Mass.: Harvard University Press, 1995. Examines the relationship between African Americans and Koreans in Los Angeles and discusses the impacts of the riots on the Korean community there after Korean businesses were targeted during the unrest.

Cannon, Lou. *Official Negligence: How Rodney King and the Riots Changed Los Angeles and the LAPD*. New York: Random House, 1997. Journalist's account places blame for the riots primarily on the political, judicial, and police leadership of Los Angeles.

"Los Angeles, April 29, 1992, and Beyond: The Law, Issues, and Perspectives." *Southern California Law Review* 66 (May 1993). Presents a panoply of views on the trial and the riots, from why the videotape did not guarantee a guilty verdict to the role the federal government should play in monitoring police brutality. One of the most comprehensive discussions of the issues available.

"Symposium on Criminal Law, Criminal Justice, and Race." *Tulane Law Review* 67 (June, 1993). Discusses the use of racist imagery in the acquittal of the police officers and the view that there are two systems of justice in the United States, "one black, one white—separate and unequal."

*Time* 139, May 11, 1992. Much of this issue is devoted to discussion of the riots. The articles "The Fire This Time" and "Anatomy of an Acquittal" provide good overviews of the events of April 29, 1992, and what followed.

"The Urban Crisis: The Kerner Commission Report Revisited." *North Carolina Law Review* 71 (June, 1993). Symposium contributors discuss how the riots of 1992 differed from those of the 1960's in terms of the minority groups involved and the areas affected.

Whitman, David. "The Untold Story of the L.A. Riot." *U.S. News & World Report*, May 31, 1993, 34-39. Provides an objective account of the events that led to the beginning of the riots at Florence and Normandie avenues and the escalation of the violence from that point on.

**SEE ALSO:** May 17-19, 1980: Rioters Protest Miami Police Brutality.

## May, 1992
# HARIRI BEGINS RECONSTRUCTION OF LEBANON

*Self-made billionaire Rafik Hariri assumed the office of prime minister of Lebanon, beginning the first of two interrupted terms in that capacity. He was widely credited both for his political moderation and for his commitment of personal wealth to the reconstruction of Lebanon.*

**LOCALE:** Beirut, Lebanon
**CATEGORIES:** Government and politics; urban planning

**KEY FIGURES**

*Rafik Hariri* (1944-2005), prime minister of Lebanon, 1992-1998 and 2000-2004
*Émile Lahoud* (b. 1936), president of Lebanon beginning in 1998
*Bashar al-Assad* (b. 1965), president of the Syrian Arab Republic beginning in 2000
*Fahd* (1922/1923-2005), king of Saudi Arabia, r. 1982-2005

**SUMMARY OF EVENT**

Lebanon, particularly its capital, Beirut, was devastated by the 1975-1990 Lebanese Civil War. The city was divided among Maronite Christians, Shiite Muslims, Sunni Muslims, and Orthodox Christians. While the 1943 National Pact had established terms under which those factions could coexist, the Christians had lost their majority as Palestinian refugees moved into Lebanon and Christians emigrated to the west. This demographic change caused Muslims to rankle at Christian control of the government. Some Muslims advocated union with Syria. The Palestine Liberation Organization (PLO) would base operations out of Lebanon, leading to attacks by Israel. All these tensions were at work in the fifteen-year war.

Rafik Hariri was a Sunni Muslim from Lebanon who had gone to Saudi Arabia as a teacher in 1965, built a fortune in construction and other ventures, and became one of the world's richest men. During the Lebanese Civil War, he acted behind the scenes to help bring an end to the conflict. Even as the conflict raged during the early 1980's, he sent his company's trucks to Beirut to begin rebuilding.

Granted Saudi citizenship, Hariri acted as King Fahd's emissary to Lebanon during the civil war. He coordinated conferences in Geneva and Lausanne, Switzerland, in 1983 and 1984. As Syria was one of the major international influences on the civil war, Hariri worked to build relations with the Syrian government. Generally, Hariri favored Syrian occupation of Lebanon, and he tried to negotiate to that end, even offering to pay off the leaders of the other factions.

In a 1989 "national reconciliation" conference in Taif, Saudi Arabia, Hariri won over the parliament's support for Syrian occupation. Syria assumed control in 1990, installing its own government. The new government granted the reconstruction contracts to Hariri's company. Hariri's "donations" to various government officials led to his colleagues' receiving prominent appointments. He offered to subsidize the country's national debt, and he bought control of several television and radio stations, newspapers, and magazines.

In 1991, Syria ordered Hezbollah (a paramilitary organization of Lebanese Shiites) to attack Israeli forces in southern Lebanon. The international backlash caused the Lebanese economy to collapse. Despite their many ties, Syria had been reluctant to give Hariri direct power, but the economic collapse forced action. A staged parliamentary election was held in 1992, and Hariri was appointed prime minister.

Hariri was widely popular. Syria granted him autonomy in most matters of government while maintaining control in matters of security. Hariri's status as an international businessman won him support from the United States, Europe, and other Arab nations. The economy began to improve as a result of his election.

Hariri sought to return Beirut to its former status as a regional center for international trade, what he frequently called the Singapore of the Middle East. His plan, Horizon 2000, involved extensive reconstruction of the city of Beirut but seemed to ignore national infrastructure outside the capital. Hariri asserted that the focus on Beirut was attributable to population density. He cut corporate taxes to a flat 10 percent and appointed the executives of his company as the ministers in his cabinet. These moves led to a soaring national debt.

Hariri was the major shareholder in Solidere, the company in charge of redeveloping Beirut's Central District following the civil war. The company bought most of the property in Beirut's business district, purchasing the land with corporate stocks that were worth a fraction of the land itself. Contracts that were not given to Hariri's own companies were granted to the companies owned by other members of the government or their relatives.

Hariri came to be Lebanon's largest landowner, purchasing many prominent buildings and historical landmarks, most of which he converted into headquarters for his companies.

While there was some improvement in the nation's economy, most of the benefits were felt by the elites. Hariri cut social programs and the salaries of lower-level government employees and began to suppress opposition voices. Pro-Syrian elites were given control over all media.

Bashar al-Assad, the heir of Syria's dictator, began to see Hariri as a threat and had him deposed in 1998. Hariri was replaced as prime minister by Selim al-Hoss. While al-Hoss and president Émile Lahoud took power as the "anticorruption" government, public support for their policies dwindled and the country fell into recession.

Hariri was reelected in 2000. During his second administration, he helped revitalize his nation's tourist industry. He resigned in 2004 over Syrian policy and was assassinated in 2005.

## SIGNIFICANCE

Hariri's reconstruction of Beirut was arguably the fastest such effort to rebuild a war-torn city. However, it occurred without much concern for social infrastructure. During his second term in office, Hariri worked more toward building than social infrastructure and getting Syria out of Lebanon. He did achieve his dream of returning Beirut to its prewar status as an economic center. After he resigned in 2004, it was expected that he would try to force Syria out of Lebanon and increase Western influence.

However, Hariri's assassination on February 14, 2005, became a source of international controversy. Some charged the Syrian government with ordering the assassination, and a U.N. investigation into the circumstances was ordered. As a result, Syria withdrew from Lebanon in April, 2005, and fully democratic elections were held.

Whatever Hariri may have done to bring Lebanon's economic infrastructure back to pre-civil-war levels, he did not do much effectively to create greater social cohesion among the factions. The fundamental tensions that had caused the civil war remained present, and without healing the divisions between the sects, no government could last.

—*John C. Hathaway*

*Rafik Hariri attends a meeting at the Pentagon in April, 2001.*
(Helene C. Stikkel/Department of Defense)

## FURTHER READING

Iskander, Marwan. *Rafiq Hariri and the Fate of Lebanon*. San Francisco: Saqi Books, 2006. Characterized as "essential reading" by Lebanese prime minister Fuad Siniora, this study by a distinguished economist examines the Hariri years in Lebanon.

"Lebanon: The Return (?) of Rafiq al-Hariri." *Estimate* 12, no. 18 (September 8, 2000). Discusses the then-upcoming elections that would ultimately return Hariri to power. Examines his previous administration, its strengths and defects.

Picard, Elizabeth. *Lebanon: A Shattered Country*. Rev. ed. London: Holmes & Meier, 2002. Deals with the recovery and national reconciliation process in the 1990's and how it was impeded by continued sectarian hostilities.

**SEE ALSO:** Mar. 14, 1978: Israel Invades Southern Lebanon; Sept. 16-18, 1982: Palestinians Are Massacred in West Beirut.

## May 1, 1992
# ASIAN PACIFIC AMERICAN LABOR ALLIANCE IS ESTABLISHED

*The Asian Pacific American Labor Alliance, a labor-activist organization, was formed to address the needs of a growing Asian and Pacific Islander community in the United States.*

**LOCALE:** Washington, D.C.
**CATEGORIES:** Organizations and institutions; business and labor

**KEY FIGURES**

*Art Takei* (1922-1997), founder and president of the Alliance of Asian Pacific Labor

*Kent Wong* (b. 1956), national president of Asian Pacific American Labor Alliance

*Joseph Lane Kirkland* (1922-1999), president of the AFL-CIO

*Jay Mazur* (b. 1932), chair of Asian Pacific American Labor Committee, 1991-1992

*Philip Villamin Vera Cruz* (1904-1994), vice president of the United Farm Workers during the 1930's

*Ah Quon McElrath* (b. 1915), organizer of the Longshore Workers Union in Hawaii

**SUMMARY OF EVENT**

On May 1, 1992, the Asian Pacific American Labor Alliance (APALA) held its founding convention in Washington, D.C. The gathering drew five hundred Asian American and Pacific Islander unionists and laborers from around the United States, including garment factory workers from New York City, hotel and restaurant workers from Honolulu, longshoremen from Seattle, nurses from San Francisco, and supermarket workers from Los Angeles. The establishment of APALA was the culmination of several decades of Asian American unionization activity.

Since the mid-1970's, Asian American labor activists in California had worked to strengthen unionization attempts by holding organizational meetings in the large Asian American communities within San Francisco and Los Angeles. Through the efforts of such neighborhood-based organizations as the Alliance of Asian Pacific Labor (AAPL), stronger ties between labor and the community were forged, and Asian union staff members were united more closely with rank-and-file labor leaders. Those localized efforts of the AAPL, however, failed to organize significant numbers of Asian American workers. In order to begin unionizing on the national level, AAPL administrators, led by Art Takei, solicited organi-

zational aid from the AFL-CIO, a key U.S. labor collective.

At the invitation of the AFL-CIO executive board, AAPL vice president Kent Wong attended the 1989 national AFL-CIO convention in Washington, D.C., to lobby for the establishment of a national labor organization for Americans of Asian and Pacific Island descent. In addressing Wong's request, AFL-CIO president Joseph Lane Kirkland acknowledged the local accomplishments of the AAPL in California and recognized the organizing potential of the growing Asian American workforce. In 1991, Kirkland appointed the national Asian Pacific American Labor Committee, which was headed by Jay Mazur. This group of thirty-seven Asian and American labor activists met for more than a year to create the Asian Pacific American Labor Alliance.

In planning for the 1992 convention, the committee put out a nationwide invitation for Asian American and Pacific Islander unionists, labor activists, and workers to gather in Washington, D.C., to take on the responsibility for bridging the gap between the national labor movement and the Asian American and Pacific Islander community. The response exceeded the committee's expectations. At the May 1, 1992, convention, more than five hundred delegates participated in adopting a constitution for APALA and in setting up a governmental structure for the organization, with a national headquarters in Washington, D.C., and local chapters throughout the United States. Organized in this manner, APALA could receive recognition and control from a national administration guided by the AFL-CIO while still using its powerful techniques of community organization at the local level.

During the convention, APALA organizers and delegates also recognized and honored Asian Pacific American labor pioneers whose achievements had melded national and local unionization efforts successfully. Among these was Philip Villamin Vera Cruz, the eighty-seven-year-old former vice president of the United Farm Workers of America. Vera Cruz, a Filipino American, had worked since the 1930's to create local unions for farmworkers in the southwestern United States and continuously lobbied for national support of farmworkers' unionization. Other honorees included those who had made significant contributions toward heightening the recognition of Asian American laborers, such as Ah Quon McElrath of the Hawaiian Longshore Workers

1992

Union. As a result of McElrath's efforts throughout the 1950's, sugar and pineapple plantation workers in Hawaii achieved greater workplace and community status.

In addition to recognizing the history of Asian American labor activism and honoring the achievements of Asian Americans and Pacific Islanders, the newly created APALA looked ahead toward its role in continuing activism and achievement. The organization drafted a document titled "Commitment to Organizing, to Civil Rights, and to Economic Justice," which called for empowerment of all Asian and Pacific American workers through unionization on a national level; it also called for the provision of national support for individual, local unionization efforts.

APALA also promoted the formation of AFL-CIO legislation that would create jobs, ensure national health insurance, reform labor law, and channel financial resources toward education and job training for Asian and Pacific Island immigrants. Toward that end, the organization called for a revision of U.S. government policies toward immigration. APALA's commitment document supported immigration legislation that would promote family unification and provide improved access to health, education, and social services for immigrants. The document also stated APALA's support for national government action to prevent workplace discrimination against immigrant laborers and vigorous prosecution for perpetrators of racially motivated crimes.

To solidify their commitment, delegates at the founding convention of APALA passed several resolutions that they then forwarded to the AFL-CIO leadership. These decried the exploitative employment practices and civil rights violations alleged against several specific U.S. companies. Convention delegates also participated in workshops that focused on APALA members' individual roles in facilitating multicultural harmony and solidarity, enhancing Asian American participation in unions, and advancing a national agenda to support more broadly based civil rights legislation and improved immigration policies and procedures.

From the workshops held at the first APALA convention, two national campaigns were launched. The first involved working with the AFL-CIO Organizing Institute to recruit a new generation of Asian Pacific American organizers at both national and local levels. The second

---

## APALA'S AIMS AND OBJECTIVES

*The constitution of the Asian Pacific American Labor Alliance states that the "primary aims and objectives of this organization . . . shall be" to do the following:*

- Educate Asian Pacific American Workers and their communities about Labor Unions and the principles of Trade Unionism, as well as to provide a vehicle for the particular concerns of Asian Pacific American Workers.
- Promote, support and assist the organizing of Asian Pacific American Workers into Unions.
- Promote political education and voter registration programs among Asian Pacific American Workers.
- Promote the training, empowerment and leadership of Asian Pacific Americans within the Labor Movement and the Asian Pacific American Communities.
- Defend and advocate for the civil and human rights of Asian Pacific Americans, immigrants and all other people of color.
- Develop ties with international Labor Organizations, especially with Labor Unions in Asia and the Pacific, and seek steps to promote world peace.

---

campaign involved building a civil and immigration rights agenda for Asian Pacific American workers based on APALA's commitment document and convention resolutions.

### SIGNIFICANCE

Through the legislative statement of its goals and in lobbying for the substantive societal implementation of those goals, the Asian Pacific American Labor Alliance was the first Asian American labor organization to achieve both national and local success. Although by the time of the 1992 APALA convention Asian Americans had been engaged in various forms of unionization activity for more than 150 years, establishment of APALA within the ranks of the AFL-CIO provided Asian American and Pacific Islander workers with more powerful organizational techniques. APALA was able to unite Asian Pacific workers solidly while simultaneously integrating them into the larger U.S. labor movement.

*—Thomas Jay Edward Walker and*
*Cynthia Gwynne Yaudes*

### FURTHER READING

Aguilar-San Juan, Karin, ed. *The State of Asian America: Activism and Resistance in the 1990's*. Boston: South End Press, 1994. Collection of essays explores the connections among race, identity, and empowerment within the workplace and the community. Compares European American, African American, and Asian American cultures. Includes bibliographic references and index.

Chang, Edward, and Eui-Young Yu, eds. *Multiethnic Coalition Building in Los Angeles*. Los Angeles: California State University Press, 1995. Papers from a two-day symposium suggest ways to build multicultural harmony within the community and the workplace. Contributors discuss labor union organization among African Americans, Chicanos, and Asian Americans in California. Includes bibliographic references.

Friday, Chris. *Organizing Asian American Labor: The Pacific Coast Canned-Salmon Industry, 1870-1942*. Philadelphia: Temple University Press, 1994. Analyzes the positive impact of Asian Pacific immigration on the formation of industries on the West Coast and in the Pacific Northwest in the period discussed. Includes maps, bibliographic references, and index.

Omatsu, Glenn, and Edna Bonacich. "Asian Pacific American Workers: Contemporary Issues in the Labor Movement." *Amerasia Journal* 8, no. 1 (1992). Discusses the advance in status achieved by Asian American workers in the late twentieth century and summarizes the remaining political, economic, and social issues impeding their progress.

Rosier, Sharolyn. "Solidarity Starts Cycle for APALA." *AFL-CIO News* 37 (May 11, 1992): 11. Summarizes the AFL-CIO conference report on the establishment of APALA.

Wong, Kent. "Building Unions in Asian Pacific Communities." *Amerasia Journal* 18, no. 3 (1992): 149-154. Assesses the difficulties of Asian American unionization and gives suggestions for overcoming those problems.

**SEE ALSO:** 1972: AFL-CIO Recognizes the United Farm Workers; Aug. 10, 1988: U.S. Congress Formally Apologizes to Japanese Internees.

---

## June 3-14, 1992
# EARTH SUMMIT CONVENES IN RIO DE JANEIRO

*Representatives from 172 nations met in Rio de Janeiro to make recommendations for the preservation of the environment in a rapidly developing world. The assembled leaders signed the Convention on Climate Change and the Convention on Biological Diversity, endorsed the Rio Declaration and the Forest Principles, and adopted Agenda 21, a three-hundred-page plan for achieving sustainable development in the twenty-first century.*

**ALSO KNOWN AS:** United Nations Conference on Environment and Development
**LOCALE:** Rio de Janeiro, Brazil
**CATEGORIES:** Diplomacy and international relations; environmental issues; trade and commerce

**KEY FIGURES**
*Maurice F. Strong* (b. 1929), secretary-general of the Stockholm and Rio U.N. conferences on the environment and member of the World Commission on Environment and Development
*Gro Harlem Brundtland* (b. 1939), Norwegian minister of environmental affairs, 1974-1979, and chair of the World Commission on Environment and Development

*George H. W. Bush* (b. 1924), president of the United States, 1989-1993

**SUMMARY OF EVENT**
On June 3, 1992, the United Nations Conference on Environment and Development, also known as the Earth Summit, convened in Rio de Janeiro, Brazil. The summit attracted some ten thousand delegates from 172 countries along with twenty thousand other participants interested in discussing environmental issues of global concern.

The Rio conference had its roots in the 1972 United Nations Stockholm Conference on the Human Environment and in the work of the World Commission on Environment and Development (WCED), an organization created in 1983. The WCED, chaired by Gro Harlem Brundtland (a Norwegian parliamentary leader who would later become prime minister of Norway), in 1987 published *Our Common Future*, also known as the Brundtland Report, which defined major global environmental problems. This document became an important basis for the discussions that culminated in the 1992 Earth Summit. Maurice F. Strong, a Canadian businessman and environmentalist who had served as secretary-general of the 1972 Stockholm Conference, provided

1992

continuity by also acting as secretary-general of the Rio conference.

The central concern of those who planned the 1992 meeting was how to promote "sustainable development"—that is, how to encourage progress and economic growth without causing irremediable damage to the environment. The environmental costs of the industrialization of the world's developed nations had proven to be quite high. The probable consequences of the continuing destruction of natural resources worried many observers in the developed world, as the world's developing nations seemed embarked on a similar course. Delegates in Rio thus had to consider how to repair the damage already wrought by industrialization and, furthermore, how to encourage the developing nations of the Southern Hemisphere to avoid the course of action

undertaken by the richer nations to the north.

Apprehension about the fate of the global environment had escalated with evidence of dramatic increases in atmospheric pollution. During the 1980's, levels of atmospheric carbon dioxide had grown at an alarming rate. With the acceleration of automobile production and the growth of other heavy industries in the Third World, factory emissions and exhaust from ever-greater numbers of automobiles caused severe pollution in and around such cities as Rio de Janeiro, São Paulo, and Mexico City, at times reaching crisis proportions.

As "progress" in the developing world fueled pollution, the role of tropical rain forests in the global environment became ever more important. Through the process of photosynthesis, trees absorb carbon dioxide and, in its place, release oxygen into the atmosphere, helping to

*Representatives from more than 170 nations stand for a moment of silence during a 1997 meeting at the United Nations. The special session was called to review progress on environmental issues since the 1992 Earth Summit in Brazil.* (AP/Wide World Photos)

mitigate the atmospheric effects of air pollution. The 1980's, however, also witnessed the accelerated deforestation of the world's tropical areas. Countless trees were cut down; moreover, people who cleared forestland often burned tree stumps, releasing additional carbon monoxide and carbon dioxide into an already heavily polluted environment.

The possibility that damage to the atmosphere could cause global warming heightened public concern. Many observers predicted that the combination of industrialization and deforestation might result in the melting of polar ice caps and a consequent rise in sea levels that would flood many of the earth's coastal regions. Inhabitants of the industrialized nations of the Northern Hemisphere, in particular, insisted that measures needed to be taken to protect the future of the planet. Environmentalists in general believed that only resolutions made on a global level could ensure common survival.

There was a different emphasis, however, among the developing nations, overwhelmingly situated south of the equator, which had embarked on a process of industrialization modeled on that undergone by the nations of the North decades earlier. In the South, progress was inextricably linked to competitive industrialization. Environmental measures, which were often tied to expensive technologies to control industrial emissions as well as to the protection of forested regions, seemed likely to slow the economies of developing countries.

The delegates to the Rio conference were thus naturally divided between representatives of the North and representatives of the South, between those concerned with assuring continued industrial development and those intent on preserving the environment. Representatives of developing nations argued that they needed assurances that developed nations would help to pay the costs of promoting environmentally friendly development. Developing nations called for richer countries to increase their foreign aid expenditures to 0.07 percent of their economic output by the year 2000, nearly double the approximately 0.04 percent level of 1992. The northern nations, however, hesitated to make promises to meet any specific target for overall aid in a recessionary environment.

The delegation from the United States, furthermore, resisted targets, claiming that the large ballpark figures did not sufficiently take into account the developing nations' abilities to absorb the aid. U.S. delegates also argued that increased aid would make developing countries less interested in courting foreign investment, thereby limiting potential for economic growth. The

---

### FROM THE PREAMBLE TO AGENDA 21

*Agenda 21, the plan for achieving sustainable development that came out of the Earth Summit, begins with this statement of purpose:*

Humanity stands at a defining moment in history. We are confronted with a perpetuation of disparities between and within nations, a worsening of poverty, hunger, ill health and illiteracy, and the continuing deterioration of the ecosystems on which we depend for our well-being. However, integration of environment and development concerns and greater attention to them will lead to the fulfillment of basic needs, improved living standards for all, better protected and managed ecosystems and a safer, more prosperous future. No nation can achieve this on its own; but together we can—in a global partnership for sustainable development.

---

United States came to be viewed as the most recalcitrant of the northern nations in acknowledging the need to promote sustainable development in the South; among developed nations, Japan led the way in promising to increase its aid from $800 million per year in 1992 to $1.4 billion per year by the end of the decade.

The possibility of hostile standoffs concerned participants and observers alike. Although delegates agreed regarding the need to develop a multibillion-dollar aid package to promote environmentally sustainable development in the poorer South, leaders of northern powers worried about locking themselves into commitments to increase aid while their own economies were plagued by recession. Leaders in the South were concerned that efforts to monitor spending of aid money might interfere with their national sovereignty. On a more positive side, participants were hopeful that agreements made in Rio would mark the beginning of an environmental revolution as significant as the agricultural and industrial revolutions.

Three key issues dominated the discussions: the global climate, the preservation of endangered species, and the repair of an already damaged environment. The nations of the North supported measures to restrict the emissions of heat-trapping gases, especially by tightening standards on automobile exhaust. At the conclusion of the conference, a climate agreement was signed that set vague targets for bringing dangerous emissions under control. The agreement on biodiversity proved more problematic. The U.S. delegation refused to sign the con-

1992

vention, arguing that the agreement threatened to hinder developments in biotechnology by not fully protecting patent rights. Before adjourning on June 14, 1992, delegates approved a massive global cleanup plan called Agenda 21; the plan comprised a series of recommendations on nearly every known environmental issue.

The Earth Summit thus focused global attention on worldwide environmental concerns and on environmental problems caused by development. In the months and years that followed the meeting, however, the implementation of the agreements and recommendations reached collectively became the responsibility of individuals and governments around the world, and their compliance with the guidelines and goals set at the Earth Summit was at best mixed.

## SIGNIFICANCE

The agreements signed at the 1992 Earth Summit represented remarkable achievements in bringing together almost the entire world community, but the conference nevertheless generated intense controversy. The underlying assumption of those who supported the need for the Earth Summit was that all of humanity is part of a global community in which local damage to the environment affects the whole. Individuals, therefore, must work toward the global good; in other words, they must "think globally and act locally." The conference, however, demonstrated that the globe is seriously divided, not only between developed and developing nations but also between those who believe that governments and supragovernmental organizations should enforce sustainable development and those who believe that individuals should be allowed to make their own decisions without such intervention.

In the wake of the summit, the concern grew that environmental globalism might mask a new kind of colonialism. Some posited that the enforcement of environmental standards imposed by the already industrialized nations of the North on the industrializing nations of the South meant that the North would continue to dictate the kind (and speed) of development in the South. Advocates for the developing nations insisted that the North should not be allowed to impose tough standards on the South simply because the developed nations had destroyed their own resources first. It soon became clear that compromises on environmental issues would have to be worked out carefully and slowly.

The Earth Summit also highlighted the intensely political nature of environmentalism, locally as well as internationally. The recalcitrance of the United States, for example, had much to do with the fact that the country's delegates had been selected by the administration of President George H. W. Bush, a Republican, during a presidential election year. Many U.S. Democrats, including vice presidential candidate Al Gore, strongly supported tougher environmental standards; in contrast, Bush ardently courted more conservative Republican voters, many of whom insisted that the role of government needed to shrink. In such a context, it was not surprising that the United States did not assume a leadership role in Rio.

The case of Brazil also illustrated the precarious political nature of environmentalism. When the summit met, President Fernando Collor de Mello had already demonstrated his own commitment to improving Brazil's record in combating deforestation and pollution. Collor had appointed his country's first minister of the environment and had given him the support necessary to curb burnings in the Amazon and Atlantic rain forests. Collor's government created extractive reserves to protect the livelihood of rubber tappers in Amazonia and also formalized the demarcation of lands belonging to the Yanomami Indians along Brazil's northern border. Little more than one year after the Rio conference, however, Collor was impeached for corruption and removed from office. As the attention of Brazilians shifted to their pressing political problems, environmental concerns receded into the background.

The impacts of the Earth Summit thus proved to be mixed. On one hand, it opened, on a grand scale, international discussion of issues critical to the future of the planet; on the other, it demonstrated that finding global solutions to environmental problems requires respect for individual freedoms as well as generous diplomatic skills and ability to compromise. If nothing else, the summit generated a heated debate on the nature of the world's environmental ills. At the very least, the exchange enriched understanding of worldwide environmental problems and strengthened hopes that lasting solutions might be found. It was succeeded by ongoing U.N. meetings and conferences to discuss unresolved concerns in subsequent years.

—*Joan E. Meznar*

## FURTHER READING

Brown, Lester R., Christopher Flavin, and Sandra Postel. *Saving the Planet: How to Shape an Environmentally Sustainable Global Economy.* New York: W. W. Norton, 1991. Written shortly before the Earth Summit. Urges delegates to the conference to view the

1990's as a pivotal decade and argues that governments need to begin actively shaping environmentally healthy societies. Provides practical definitions of environmentally sustainable economies and societies and describes ways to achieve them.

Coleman, Daniel A. *Ecopolitics: Building a Green Society*. New Brunswick, N.J.: Rutgers University Press, 1994. Begins with a brief history of environmental problems and a look at what might lie ahead. Concludes that personal and social responsibility, translated into "green politics," can ensure changes necessary to protect the environment.

Goodstein, Eban S. *Economics and the Environment*. 4th ed. New York: John Wiley & Sons, 2005. Presents in-depth, balanced analyses of environmental policy debates. Includes author and subject indexes.

Middleton, Neil, Phil O'Keefe, and Sam Moyo. *The Tears of the Crocodile: From Rio to Reality in the Developing World*. Boulder, Colo.: Pluto Press, 1993. Discusses some of the major issues addressed at the Rio conference. Contends that the interests of the North won out over those of the South at the Earth Summit and displays pessimism that much substantive change would take place in the aftermath of the conference.

Rogers, Peter, Kazi F. Jalal, and John A. Boyd. *An Introduction to Sustainable Development*. Cambridge, Mass.: Harvard Division of Continuing Education, 2006. Accessible introductory-level textbook includes discussion of the impacts of multinational corporations and globalization on the world environment.

Sachs, Wolfgang, ed. *Global Ecology: A New Arena of Political Conflict*. London: Zed Books, 1993. Collection of essays stresses the conflict between North and South in the Earth Summit deliberations, pointing to the pitfalls of relying on solutions that emphasize globalism.

Sitarz, Daniel, ed. *Agenda 21: The Earth Summit Strategy to Save Our Planet*. Boulder, Colo.: Earth Press, 1993. Abridged version of the final official text of Agenda 21, as adopted at the U.N. Conference on Environment and Development. Organized somewhat like a long-range planning document but serves as a good attempt to educate lay readers on steps that are needed to protect the environment.

World Commission on Environment and Development. *Our Common Future*. New York: Oxford University Press, 1987. Discusses environmental issues common to the global community, including food supply, population pressure, energy sources, and biodiversity. Contains a global agenda for changes recommended to enable the achievement of sustainable development. Throughout, the emphasis is on multilateral action.

**SEE ALSO:** 1971: Earthwatch Is Founded; Apr., 1972: Ward and Dubos Publish *Only One Earth*; June 5-16, 1972: United Nations Holds an Environmental Conference in Stockholm; 1975: U.N. Global Environment Monitoring System Is Inaugurated; 1985-1987: Rainforest Action Network Boycotts Burger King; Oct. 12, 1988: Brazilian President Announces Plans to Protect Rain Forests.

1992

# June 24, 1992
# TAILHOOK SCANDAL

*Inappropriate behavior during the convention of an organization for naval aviators revealed the hostile environment that existed for women in the U.S. military and resulted in the resignation of the secretary of the Navy.*

**LOCALE:** Washington, D.C.; Las Vegas, Nevada
**CATEGORIES:** Women's issues; crime and scandal; military history

## KEY FIGURES

*Paula Coughlin* (b. 1963), U.S. Navy lieutenant and Tailhook whistle-blower

*John W. Snyder, Jr.* (fl. late twentieth century), commanding officer at the Naval Air Test Center, Patuxent River

*H. Lawrence Garrett* (b. 1939), secretary of the U.S. Navy

*Frank B. Kelso II* (b. 1933), chief of naval operations and later acting secretary of the U.S. Navy

## SUMMARY OF EVENT

Tailhook, the annual convention for members of the Tailhook Association, a naval aviators' organization (named for the arresting device that helps stop a Navy jet landing on an aircraft carrier at sea), was a well-known bacchanal. At these yearly meetings of the U.S. Navy's elite "top guns," drunkenness, pranks, and lewd behavior were de rigueur. Tailhook celebrated aviator "machismo" and skill. As the September, 1991, Tailhook convention approached, aviators expected the meeting, to be held at the Las Vegas Hilton, to be the bawdiest yet—a reward for their heroism in the recent Persian Gulf War.

Two incidents occurred at Tailhook in 1991 that reflected women's status in the U.S. military. At a panel discussion that provided a forum for aviators to question admirals, a female aviator asked when women would be allowed to fly tactical or combat operations. The mostly male audience of aviators laughed and heckled the questioner, Lieutenant Monica Rivadeneira, and the panel of admirals responded minimally without admonishing the audience. Women in the military and those who have studied women's integration in the armed forces maintain that only when women are permitted to serve in combat will their male peers treat them with due respect. One indication of the disrespect accorded to women in the military during the 1990's was the sexual harassment that many endured. Sexual harassment of women in the

armed forces has a long history, and Tailhook was only one in a series of events that drew nationwide attention to the issue in the early 1990's.

On the evening of September 7, 1991, Lieutenant Paula Coughlin, an aide to Rear Admiral John W. Snyder, Jr., went to the third floor of the Las Vegas Hilton. What Coughlin saw and experienced there became the first part of the Tailhook scandal. Immediately after Coughlin exited the elevator, she saw fellow officers lining either side of the thirty-foot-long hotel corridor in the Tailhook formation known as the gauntlet. Aviators closed in on her, preventing her escape. Coughlin was shoved down the hall, fondled by her assaulters as she passed them. Calls of "admiral's aide" preceded her, demonstrating that her assailants knew her identity and her rank. The aviators ignored her pleas for help, her angry shouts, and her attempts to fight back.

When Coughlin emerged from the gauntlet—bruised, covered with beer, and with her clothes disheveled and torn—she fled. The next day, she reported her experience to her commanding officer, noting that she had feared gang rape. Her complaint was dismissed with an offhand comment that one had to expect such things at Tailhook. After repeated attempts to get action from Snyder, Coughlin decided to go over his head.

Upon learning of the assaults, the secretary of the Navy, H. Lawrence Garrett, denounced the convention and ordered an investigation; he seemed to be intent on applying the Navy's policy of "zero tolerance" for sexual harassment. In June of 1992, when Garrett responded to the report on Tailhook by the Naval Investigative Service (NIS) with a call for complete accountability of squadron commanders at the Tailhook convention, NIS released a supplemental report that was Garrett's undoing: It placed Garrett at Tailhook and said he had turned a blind eye to the sexual antics and violations of junior officers. After the Navy's internal investigation failed to uncover any culprits and called into question the ability of the Navy to police itself, Garrett called on the Office of the Inspector General of the Department of Defense (DOD) to do its own probe of Tailhook.

On June 24, 1992, Paula Coughlin went public, taking her story to the national media. Frustrated by the Navy's failure to punish the perpetrators nine months after the event, Coughlin hoped to spur on the investigation by coming forward. Two days later, Garrett resigned, taking full responsibility for the Tailhook scandal. This was the

Navy's first real step toward accountability for Tailhook.

The DOD report of April, 1993, detailed the second scandalous revelation of Tailhook, the cover-up. The investigators found that eighty-three women (revised upward from the original NIS figure of twenty-six) had been involved and that excesses at Tailhook 1991 extended beyond the gauntlet. The hospitality suites on the third floor of the hotel had been the sites of further exploits, including indecent exposure and pornographic movies. The DOD report also disclosed that the sexual misconduct occurred with the knowledge of Navy higher-ups. The efforts at damage control and cover-up, in which naval officers closed ranks to protect those at all levels within the Navy and the Navy itself, made a mockery of the policy of zero tolerance for sexual harassment and demonstrated the pervasiveness of the attitudes toward women that were behind the Tailhook abuse.

## SIGNIFICANCE

Although the events that took place at the 1991 Tailhook convention stemmed in part from a masculine military culture that viewed sexual exploits as just rewards for the risks Navy fliers take on a daily basis, there was more to them than that. The U.S. military in the early 1990's was at a crossroads, and the Tailhook episode was an example of deep resistance to changes in the gender composition of the armed forces. By 1991, many well-trained female pilots had hit the "glass ceiling" in the military, a limitation upheld by the Combat Exclusion Act of 1948. Military women were exerting steady pressure through various channels to overturn the law that banned women from combat and, by extension, from promotion and equal treatment.

In 1991, in the Persian Gulf War, women in the military again had served bravely and with valor, and in greater numbers and in greater danger than ever before. As a result, the topic of gender and military service was on the nation's mind. In addition, the Department of Defense was reducing the size of the armed forces, shaping a national defense in line with the post-Cold War world. Men and

## THE SECRETARY OF THE NAVY EXPRESSES OUTRAGE

*On October 29, 1991, Secretary of the Navy H. Lawrence Garrett wrote the following letter to the president of the Tailhook Association, Captain F. G. Ludwig, Jr. Although Garrett claimed to be angered by the events that took place at the 1991 Tailhook convention, it was later revealed that Garrett had attended the convention, and he was forced to resign his position.*

Dear Captain Ludwig,

I am writing to you, and through you to your organization, to express my absolute outrage over the conduct reported to have taken place at the Tailhook Association symposium in September. . . .

Besides my anger, I am more than personally disappointed. The Tailhook Association has been, in the past, a source of great professionalism and esprit, an organization where productive dialogues and seminars have had a home. In particular, Tailhook '91 provided me with a superb forum to air some of the most serious issues that Naval Aviation has ever faced. But none of those attributes can make up for the personal abuses, behavioral excesses, and quite possibly criminal conduct that took place at Tailhook '91 and have now been reported to me.

There are certain categories of behavior and attitudes that I unequivocally will not tolerate. You know the phrase: "Not in my Navy, not on my watch." Tailhook '91 is a gross example of exactly what cannot be permitted by the civilian or uniformed leadership of the Navy, at any level. No man who holds a commission in this Navy will ever subject a woman to the kind of abuse in evidence at Tailhook '91 with impunity. And no organization which makes possible this behavior is in any way worthy of a naval leadership or advisory role.

Admiral Frank Kelso, our Chief of Naval Operations, and I have discussed this matter and, based upon his recommendation and with his full support, I am terminating, effective immediately, all Navy support in any manner whatsoever, direct or indirect, for the Tailhook Association.

Last April I sent a message to every command in the Navy about the progress of our women officers and sailors. I said then that I would reinforce a position of zero tolerance of sexual harassment, and I meant it. That policy was not new in April, nor when I became Secretary—but obviously it was as necessary then as it is now to reiterate just how strongly I feel about this matter. Also in April, with my strong concurrence, Admiral Kelso made specifically clear in a parallel message that a Navy free from sexual harassment or intimidation is a leadership issue. Together we made certain that the whole Navy knew: "Each of you, from the most junior sailor to the most senior officer, has a responsibility to build working and living spaces free from unprofessional conduct, fear, and prejudice." The Tailhook Association most certainly did not live up to that responsibility.

Very Truly Yours,

H. Lawrence Garrett III
Secretary of the Navy

women in all branches of the service wondered where they would fit in the new downsized military. With fewer positions available at all levels, many military men viewed their female counterparts as unwelcome competitors.

Tailhook therefore called attention to the plight of women in the military. As a result of the scandal, the Navy ended its support of the Tailhook Association after thirty-five years, and the congressional Armed Services Committee held a hearing on gender discrimination in the military. Garrett created the Standing Committee on Women in the Navy and Marine Corps in June, 1992. In January, 1993, the Navy revised its policy on sexual harassment and made any violation of the code a punitive offense. The Navy established a definition of sexual harassment along the guidelines used in civilian society, noting both "sex for promotion" and "hostile environment" components. On April 28, 1993, the Navy opened competition for combat assignments, excluding ground fighting. Although 40 percent of the jobs were still closed to women, flying combat missions and going to sea—the most important aspects of naval service—were finally open to women.

Only one aviator was formally censured for his behavior at Tailhook. Rear Admiral Snyder was removed from command in 1991 for not responding to Coughlin's complaint. Several of the most zealous participants at Tailhook benefited from the investigator general's frustration with aviator stonewalling. In return for immunity, they testified, but they did not provide enough evidence against their peers to result in courts-martial. Admiral Frank B. Kelso II, acting secretary of the Navy, retired early because of his presence at Tailhook but kept his stars. Paula Coughlin resigned from the Navy when she found it impossible to do her job in a climate of ongoing hostility. She filed a civil suit against Hilton Hotels and won.

*—Jessica Weiss*

## FURTHER READING

Chema, J. Richard. "Arresting 'Tailhook': The Prosecution of Sexual Harassment in the Military." *Military Law Review* 140 (Spring, 1993): 1-64. Argues that existing naval codes, if enforced, cover sexual harassment, and that no new guidelines are required.

Ebbert, Jean, and Marie-Beth Hall. *Crossed Currents: Navy Women in a Century of Change.* 3d ed. Washington, D.C.: Batsford Brassey, 1999. Comprehensive history of women's participation in the U.S. Navy includes discussion of the first women clerks during World War I, the WAVES of World War II, and the women of the 1990's who fought for the right to fly combat missions and serve at sea. Chapter 14 deals specifically with the Tailhook scandal.

Holm, Jeanne. *Women in the Military: An Unfinished Revolution.* Rev. ed. Novato, Calif.: Presidio Press, 1992. Provides a thorough account of the integration of women into the U.S. military, from the founding of the country through the Persian Gulf War. Includes bibliography and informative appendixes.

McMichael, William H. *The Mother of All Hooks: The Story of the U.S. Navy's Tailhook Scandal.* New Brunswick, N.J.: Transaction, 1997. Journalist's account of the scandal and its aftermath includes discussion of the culture of the military that contributed to the events and the failure to punish those responsible.

Office of the Inspector General. *The Tailhook Report: The Official Inquiry into the Events of Tailhook '91.* 1993. Reprint. New York: St. Martin's Press, 2003. Presents the findings of the DOD's own investigation of the 1991 Tailhook convention and the events that followed.

Zimmerman, Jean. *Tailspin: Women at War in the Wake of Tailhook.* New York: Doubleday, 1995. Places Tailhook in the context of the changes within the military in the 1980's and 1990's. Discusses the changing role of women in combat operations and post-Cold War downsizing.

**SEE ALSO:** 1970's: Women's Military Roles Expand; Oct. 8, 1975: U.S. Congress Admits Women to Armed Services Academies; Oct. 24, 1988: BRAC Commission Is Established to Close U.S. Military Bases; Jan. 17-Feb. 28, 1991: Persian Gulf War.

**June 29, 1992**

# U.S. SUPREME COURT RESTRICTS ABORTION RIGHTS

*Changes in the U.S. Supreme Court's composition in
the 1980's and early 1990's led abortion opponents to
believe that a majority of justices might eliminate
women's constitutionally protected right of choice.
Instead, a majority of justices continued to endorse a
right of choice, but the Court's jointly authored
majority opinion in the case of* Planned Parenthood of
Southeastern Pennsylvania v. Casey *expanded
opportunities for states to impose regulations that
affect abortion.*

**ALSO KNOWN AS:** *Planned Parenthood of Southeastern Pennsylvania v. Casey*, 505 U.S. 833
**LOCALE:** Washington, D.C.
**CATEGORIES:** Laws, acts, and legal history; women's
issues

**KEY FIGURES**

*Sandra Day O'Connor* (b. 1930), associate justice of
the United States, 1981-2006
*David Souter* (b. 1939), associate justice of the United
States beginning in 1990
*Anthony Kennedy* (b. 1936), associate justice of the
United States beginning in 1988
*Antonin Scalia* (b. 1936), associate justice of the
United States beginning in 1986
*Clarence Thomas* (b. 1948), associate justice of the
United States beginning in 1991
*Robert P. Casey* (1932-2000), governor of
Pennsylvania, 1987-1995
*George H. W. Bush* (b. 1924), president of the United
States, 1989-1993
*Ronald Reagan* (1911-2004), president of the United
States, 1981-1989
*Harry A. Blackmun* (1908-1999), associate justice of
the United States, 1970-1994
*William H. Rehnquist* (1924-2005), associate justice of
the United States, 1972-1986, and chief justice,
1986-2005
*Byron White* (1917-2002), associate justice of the
United States, 1962-1993

**SUMMARY OF EVENT**

The U.S. Supreme Court's decision in *Roe v. Wade*
(1973), establishing women's constitutional right to obtain abortions during the first six months of pregnancy,
unleashed years of political maneuvering by and conflict
between politicians and interest groups on both sides of

the abortion issue. Governors and state legislatures created new laws intended to restrict access to abortions in
the hope that, as the U.S. Supreme Court's composition
changed over the years, new appointees would endorse
the restrictions and thereby either diminish or eliminate
the right of choice established in *Roe v. Wade*.

Throughout the 1980's, whenever a Supreme Court
justice retired, President Ronald Reagan sought to appoint a replacement who would vote to overturn *Roe v.
Wade* and thereby eliminate American women's right to
obtain abortions. When the Court examined new restrictions that the state of Missouri sought to impose on the
availability of abortions in 1989, all three of Reagan's
appointees, Justices Sandra Day O'Connor, Antonin
Scalia, and Anthony Kennedy, joined the two dissenters
from the original *Roe v. Wade* decision, Chief Justice
William H. Rehnquist and Justice Byron White, to approve the restrictions (*Webster v. Reproductive Health
Services*, 492 U.S. 490). Justice Scalia openly advocated
overturning *Roe v. Wade*, and Justices Kennedy and
White joined an opinion by Chief Justice Rehnquist that
presented many arguments for eliminating the right to
obtain abortions. Justice O'Connor, however, said that
the Missouri law did not directly challenge the original
decision in *Roe v. Wade*, so there was no reason to examine whether the right of choice should be eliminated. The
opponents of abortion thus still lacked the needed fifth
vote to form a new majority against women's right of
choice on the nine-member Supreme Court.

By 1992, only one justice, Harry A. Blackmun, remained on the Supreme Court from the original seven-
member majority that established the right of choice in
*Roe v. Wade*. President George H. W. Bush followed
President Reagan's lead in promising to appoint new justices who would oppose the right of choice. However,
neither of Bush's appointees in the early 1990's, Justices
David Souter and Clarence Thomas, had demonstrated a
clear position on the abortion issue prior to joining the
Supreme Court. Because Souter and Thomas replaced
two members of the original seven-member majority in
*Roe v. Wade*, it was widely assumed that the right to obtain abortions might be eliminated in the Supreme Court's
next case considering the issue. Based on the Court's decision in *Webster v. Reproductive Health Services*, if any
one justice from among O'Connor, Souter, and Thomas
voted to overturn *Roe v. Wade*, that would provide the
fifth vote to eliminate the right of choice.

1992

*Activists for and against abortion rights face off outside the Supreme Court building shortly after the Court upheld restrictions on abortion set forth in a Pennsylvania law.* (AP/Wide World Photos)

In 1992, the Supreme Court heard arguments in *Planned Parenthood of Southeastern Pennsylvania v. Casey*. Governor Robert P. Casey of Pennsylvania had successfully advocated the passage of new laws to regulate abortions in his state. Among the provisions in the state law was a requirement that at least twenty-four hours before performing an abortion, the physician must inform the woman about the health risks of abortion, probable gestational age of the fetus, and the availability of printed material about adoption services as alternatives to abortion. Another provision required a married woman seeking an abortion to verify that she had informed her husband about the planned abortion unless certain specified exceptional circumstances existed. An additional provision required a minor female to obtain the consent of one of her parents or a judge before obtaining an abortion. Five abortion clinics and one physician filed a legal action alleging that these laws violated women's right of choice as established in *Roe v. Wade*.

Although Supreme Court opinions are usually written by a single justice, in the case of *Planned Parenthood of Southeastern Pennsylvania v. Casey*, the Court issued an extraordinary majority opinion jointly authored by three justices, Sandra Day O'Connor, David Souter, and Anthony Kennedy. These three justices formed the core of a five-member majority that preserved *Roe v. Wade* and

women's right of choice with respect to abortion. However, the opinion also softened the Court's analysis of states' abortion regulations by replacing the original analysis in *Roe v. Wade* with an "undue burden" test. Under this test, state laws regulating abortion are permissible as long as they do not impose an undue burden on a woman's right of choice.

Previously, under the standards of *Roe v. Wade*, states were barred from regulating abortion during the first three months of pregnancy and could impose in the second three-month period only regulations that were necessary to protect the health of the mother. After the decision in *Planned Parenthood of Southeastern Pennsylvania v. Casey*, states could create a variety of regulations affecting abortions throughout the term of a pregnancy, as long as those regulations did not impose an undue burden on women's opportunity to choose to have an abortion. In applying the new test to Pennsylvania's laws, the three-justice majority opinion approved the provisions except for the spousal notification requirement, which the justices feared could lead to domestic violence in some situations.

Supporters of a right of choice for abortion were relieved that a narrow five-member majority on the Supreme Court declined to overturn *Roe v. Wade* and thereby preserved women's opportunities to choose to terminate their pregnancies. The survival of the *Roe* precedent depended on Justice Kennedy's parting company with the critics of abortion with whom he had joined in *Webster v. Reproductive Health Services*. Justice O'Connor, who had previously declined to rule on the continuing validity of *Roe v. Wade*, and newcomer Justice Souter, who had never stated a position on abortion, both made it clear that they supported a continuation of the right of choice.

**SIGNIFICANCE**

Although the Supreme Court's decision in *Planned Parenthood of Southeastern Pennsylvania v. Casey* preserved the right of choice, it simultaneously made it much easier for state legislatures to impose regulations on abortion providers, including regulations that could affect certain aspects of abortion counseling and other matters affecting women seeking to terminate early-stage pregnancies. The Supreme Court had previously looked closely at a variety of abortion-related laws enacted by state legislatures and city councils. Under the new test focusing only on laws that created an undue burden on the right of choice, the Supreme Court effectively announced that it would no longer give close scrutiny to all legislative activity affecting abortion providers and women seeking to terminate pregnancies. Women still possessed the right of choice, but they faced the possibility of brief, mandated waiting periods, counseling that included information intended to discourage abortions, and other regulations designed by legislators who were seeking to reduce the numbers of women who would ultimately choose to have abortions.

Legal analysts saw the Supreme Court's decision as weakening the right of choice by permitting various regulations that would previously have been impermissible under the standards originally established in *Roe v. Wade*. The decision also illuminated the deep divisions among the Court's nine justices and thereby encouraged abortion opponents to push for the subsequent appointment of additional new justices who might tip the balance in favor of eliminating the right of choice.

—*Christopher E. Smith*

## FURTHER READING

Biskupic, Joan. *Sandra Day O'Connor: How the First Woman on the Supreme Court Became Its Most Influential Justice*. New York: Ecco Press, 2005. Comprehensive biography draws on interviews with O'Connor and other justices. Includes detailed coverage of *Planned Parenthood of Southeastern Pennsylvania v.*

*Casey*, for which many analysts believe O'Connor was the lead author in the three-justice opinion.

Craig, Barbara Hinkson, and David M. O'Brien. *Abortion and American Politics*. Chatham, N.J.: Chatham House, 1993. Presents detailed analysis of the historical development of judicial decisions and statutes affecting abortion rights, concluding with coverage of the Supreme Court's decision in *Planned Parenthood of Southeastern Pennsylvania v. Casey*. Illuminates the political context in which states created abortion regulations that were challenged in the Supreme Court.

Greenhouse, Linda. *Becoming Justice Blackmun: Harry Blackmun's Supreme Court Journey*. New York: Times Books, 2005. Uses Justice Blackmun's papers to show the inside story of the Supreme Court's development of decisions on abortion, including the justices' behind-the-scenes interactions in developing their decision in *Planned Parenthood of Southeastern Pennsylvania v. Casey*.

Yarbrough, Tinsley E. *David Hackett Souter: Traditional Republican on the Rehnquist Court*. New York: Oxford University Press, 2005. Discusses Souter's role on the Supreme Court, including his involvement in the development of the three-justice majority opinion in *Planned Parenthood of Southeastern Pennsylvania v. Casey*.

**SEE ALSO:** Jan. 22, 1973: U.S. Supreme Court Expands Women's Reproductive Rights; May 22, 1978: Italy Legalizes Abortion; 1982: Baulieu Develops a Pill That Induces Abortion; Apr. 9, 1989: NOW Sponsors a March for Abortion Rights; July 3, 1989: U.S. Supreme Court Upholds State Restrictions on Abortion.

1992

## August 24, 1992
# HURRICANE ANDREW DEVASTATES SOUTHERN FLORIDA

*Hurricane Andrew was the costliest and most damaging hurricane to hit the United States in the twentieth century and resulted in the deaths of sixty-five people. The storm's record winds included gusts nearing speeds of two hundred miles per hour. Government response to the vast destruction and chaos revealed bureaucratic confusion and incompetence and miscommunication at local, state, and federal levels.*

**LOCALE:** Southern Florida; Louisiana; Bahamas
**CATEGORY:** Disasters

**KEY FIGURES**

*Lawton M. Chiles, Jr.* (1930-1998), governor of
    Florida, 1991-1998
*Edwin Edwards* (b. 1927), governor of Louisiana,
    1972-1980, 1984-1988, and 1992-1996
*George H. W. Bush* (b. 1924), president of the United
    States, 1989-1993
*Robert C. Sheets* (b. 1937), director of the National
    Hurricane Center, 1987-1995
*Wallace Stickney* (b. 1934), director of the Federal
    Emergency Management Agency, 1990-1993
*Andrew Card* (b. 1947), U.S. secretary of
    transportation, 1992-1993
*John C. Heldstab* (b. 1940), U.S.
    Army director of military
    disaster relief
*Kate Hale* (b. 1951), director of
    Dade County Office of
    Emergency Management

**SUMMARY OF EVENT**
For almost three decades, no severe hurricanes had struck southern Florida until August, 1992. Two days after a tropical wave formed off western Africa on August 14, the National Hurricane Center (NHC) in Coral Gables, Florida, said that the wave had become a tropical depression. On August 17, the NHC designated that depression the tropical storm Andrew. Moving west across the Atlantic, the storm grew into Hurricane Andrew, which would become the costliest hurricane in U.S. history until Hurricane Katrina struck the Gulf coast in 2005.

Several weather systems shaped Hurricane Andrew's strength and path, and it reached the northwestern islands of the Bahamas before evening on August 23. The storm's 120-mile-per-hour winds caused a surge to rise twenty-three feet, engulfing coastal areas on Eleuthera Island, damaging buildings, eroding beaches, and resulting in the drowning of four people. Heading west through the Florida Straits, the hurricane intensified to a category 4 before making landfall.

At the NHC, meteorologists monitored the storm during the night, recommending an evacuation of people from the southeastern Florida coast. NHC director Robert C. Sheets appeared on television, warning south Floridians to leave, and newspaper, radio, and television reporters stressed the urgency of the impending hurricane. Governor Lawton M. Chiles, Jr., declared a state of emergency for Florida.

Before dawn on August 24, Hurricane Andrew moved through Elliott Key, Florida, and reached shore near Homestead in Dade County, approximately thirty miles south of Miami. Meteorologists measured the storm's central barometric pressure at 922 millibars (27.23 inches) and its winds at 145 miles per hour. Winds accelerated to 175 miles per hour, gusting to 190 miles per

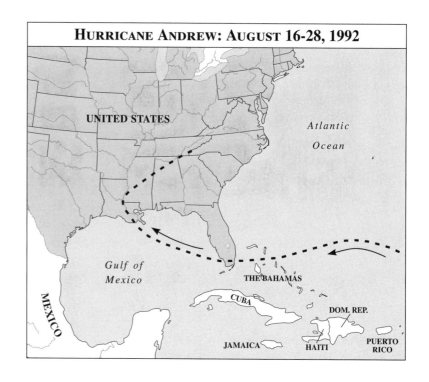

**HURRICANE ANDREW: AUGUST 16-28, 1992**

hour, and the surge neared seventeen feet. Pouring rain, gusts, and mini-swirls, which resembled tornadoes, sheared trees, flooded transportation routes, and severed electrical cables. The Everglades suffered significant losses of mangroves, wildlife, and habitats.

Because most television stations lost broadcasting equipment, only two stations aired during the hurricane. Meteorologist Brian Norcross of station WTVJ broadcast via television and radio from a storage room, comforting listeners throughout the storm. Reconnaissance airplanes observed the hurricane, and satellite and radar images documented its movement. Hurricane Andrew's winds destroyed measuring instruments and the radar dish at the NHC.

By August 25, Hurricane Andrew had entered the Gulf of Mexico. The warm temperatures of the gulf's waters intensified the hurricane's energy as it moved northwest, arcing toward Louisiana. Because NHC personnel projected Hurricane Andrew and its accompanying surge might hit near New Orleans, approximately 1.2 million residents evacuated areas vulnerable to flooding.

On the next morning, Hurricane Andrew's winds struck Louisiana ninety miles west of New Orleans near Lafayette and New Iberia at a speed of 115 miles per hour, with gusts as high as 160 miles per hour, severely damaging structures and disrupting utilities. Lafayette and Marsh Island were hardest hit. Two people died when a tornado from the hurricane hit La Place. By nightfall on August 26, Hurricane Andrew, designated a tropical storm earlier at noon, headed northeast, losing wind speed. Tornadoes caused damage as the hurricane's remnants moved through Mississippi toward the mid-Atlantic coast.

National Weather Service Disaster Survey Team crews flew above damaged areas in helicopters. Although statistics on the hurricane damage vary, according to the National Oceanic and Atmospheric Administration U.S. damages totaled $26.5 billion, with $1 billion in damages in Louisiana and the rest in southern Florida. At the time, Andrew was the costliest natural disaster in U.S. history. Approximately $250 million in damages occurred in the Bahamas. About 250,000 Floridians lost their homes. Damages included U.S. Air Force property at the Homestead military base, and 22,000 homes were damaged in Louisiana. The hurricane was responsible for twenty-three deaths in the United States and three in the Bahamas, with the storm indirectly causing thirty-nine deaths.

President George H. W. Bush arrived in Florida twelve hours after the hurricane left the area. Kate Hale, director

*The category 4 winds of Hurricane Andrew embedded this plank in the trunk of a royal palm.* (National Oceanic and Atmospheric Administration)

1992

of the Dade County Emergency Management Agency, met him, Governor Chiles, and Federal Emergency Management Agency (FEMA) director Wallace Stickney at the airport. The president declared South Florida a disaster area and visited his son's home, which had sustained some damage. Two days later, President Bush designated hurricane-damaged areas in Louisiana as federally recognized disaster sites when he met with Governor Edwin Edwards. Despite the president's declarations, relief did not immediately arrive.

Major General John C. Heldstab, Army director of military disaster relief, had tracked Hurricane Andrew's path in the Atlantic Ocean and prepared at the Pentagon for relief work but was frustrated that he could not deliver those services, because there was no effective communication and coordination between state and FEMA officials. Secretary of Transportation Andrew Card talked with Chiles and state legislators regarding the aid impasse, explaining that unless the state asked for help formally, none would be issued. Chiles did not understand that President Bush's declaration of disaster sites had not automatically deployed military and FEMA aid.

In Florida, three days after Hurricane Andrew had hit, Dade County leaders worried their communities, lacking electricity and experiencing water and food shortages, would escalate into violence. Emergency aid providers were poorly prepared to help the hurricane's victims. Local and state relief efforts were insufficient.

Furious about the lack of relief, Hale spoke out on national news programs, stressing the urgent need for federal assistance. Soon after this, President Bush arranged for twenty thousand soldiers, and ships with several hundred tons of food and supplies, to be deployed to the disaster areas. The U.S. Army sent personnel to erect tents for those left homeless by the hurricane. More than three thousand National Guard troops assisted people and protected them from looters.

## SIGNIFICANCE

Meteorologists declared Hurricane Andrew the third-strongest hurricane in U.S. history. (It was moved to fourth when Hurricane Katrina took its place in 2005.) Hurricane Andrew caused overwhelming physical and socioeconomic devastation, leveling entire neighborhoods and communities. Florida's agriculture suffered more than $1 billion in damages. Fifty percent of Louisiana's agriculture, worth $350 million, was destroyed. Approximately 86,000 Floridians lost jobs as a result of the hurricane when businesses were wiped out physically or financially.

Victims filed insurance claims for damaged properties. Some insurance agencies went bankrupt, because policyholders filed as many as 700,000 claims, which paid $18.5 billion. Unfortunately, some property owners had not paid for complete coverage of losses and could not afford to rebuild. Post-Andrew insurance premiums increased to offset hurricane losses, and policies distinguished between wind and water damages, limiting owners' options to protect investments in hurricane zones.

The hurricane severely wounded the environment. Scientists detected damaged reefs seventy-five feet deep. Surges and winds impacted natural gas and oil reserves and released toxic materials. The U.S. Army Corps of Engineers cleaned up 12.7 million cubic yards of debris. The National Park Service oversaw the restoration of damaged sites that had natural resources and archaeological value.

As a result of the devastating hurricane, scientists strived to develop better forecasting methods. Many government relief agencies, including FEMA, were criticized for their mishandling of the disaster, and their shortcomings would be revealed again when Hurricane Katrina struck in 2005. Chiles encouraged Florida legislators to improve disaster preparation and response. He promoted the Emergency Management Assistance Compact, in which states assist others if governors declare emergency situations.

In 2002, Hurricane Andrew survivors remembered the impact of that storm when a plaque commemorating the tenth anniversary was placed at Biscayne National Park.

—*Elizabeth D. Schafer*

## FURTHER READING

Lyskowski, Roman, and Steve Rice, eds. *The Big One: Hurricane Andrew*. Kansas City, Mo.: Andrews McMeel, 1992. Photographs and text from the *Miami Herald* and *El Nuevo Herald* presented chronologically. Includes people's accounts of the disaster.

Peacock, Walter Gillis, Betty Hearn Morrow, and Hugh Gladwin, eds. *Hurricane Andrew: Ethnicity, Gender, and the Sociology of Disasters*. New York: Routledge, 1997. Focuses on socioeconomic and racial aspects of Hurricane Andrew relief policies.

Provenzo, Eugene F., Jr., and Sandra H. Fradd. *Hurricane Andrew, the Public Schools, and the Rebuilding of Community*. Albany: State University of New York Press, 1995. Examines Hurricane Andrew's damage to schools and how education provides continuity during relief and recovery.

Provenzo, Eugene F., Jr., and Asterie Baker Provenzo. *In the Eye of Hurricane Andrew*. Gainesville: University Press of Florida, 2002. Interviews with people who experienced the storm firsthand.

Tuckwood, Jan, ed. *Hurricane Andrew: Images from the Killer Storm*. Marietta, Ga.: Longstreet Press, 1992. Includes articles, images, and maps from the *Palm Beach Post* thoroughly documenting diverse aspects of Hurricane Andrew experiences and relief work.

**SEE ALSO:** Apr.-Oct., 1993: Mississippi and Missouri Flooding Brings Misery to Middle America; Oct. 29-Nov. 3, 1998: Hurricane Mitch Floods Central America.

**October 6, 1992**

# U.S. GOVERNMENT FACILITIES MUST COMPLY WITH ENVIRONMENTAL STANDARDS

*The Federal Facility Compliance Act required all agencies of the federal government to comply with environmental laws of the United States.*

**ALSO KNOWN AS:** Federal Facility Compliance Act; U.S. Statutes at Large 106 Stat. 1505; Public Law 102-386

**LOCALE:** Washington, D.C.

**CATEGORIES:** Laws, acts, and legal history; environmental issues

## KEY FIGURES

*George H. W. Bush* (b. 1924), president of the United States, 1989-1993

*George Mitchell* (b. 1933), Democratic senator from Maine who sponsored the Federal Facility Compliance Act in the Senate

*Dennis Eckart* (b. 1950), Democratic congressman from Ohio who sponsored the Federal Facility Compliance Act in the House of Representatives

## SUMMARY OF EVENT

On October 6, 1992, President George H. W. Bush signed into law the Federal Facility Compliance Act (FFCA), which authorized states to impose civil fines on federal facilities operating within their jurisdictions for violations of the Resource Conservation and Recovery Act of 1976 (RCRA). The FFCA eliminated federal facilities' sovereign immunity and allowed states to impose fines on federal facilities for noncompliance. Other important provisions of the act included a two-year moratorium on enforcement of rules concerning hazardous and radioactive wastes, provisions for new Environmental Protection Agency (EPA) rules on when munitions and explosive wastes become RCRA waste, a measure to place sewage systems at federal facilities under rules similar to those for municipal systems, and provisions to give the EPA broader enforcement authority at federal facilities.

The FFCA represented an abdication by Congress of federal responsibility for federal compliance with federally mandated environmental standards. By eliminating federal facilities' sovereign immunity, Congress allowed the states to become part of the enforcement mechanism to pressure federal facilities into compliance.

The RCRA of 1976, as amended, was the toughest U.S. environmental law passed up until that time. The act regulated the ongoing disposal of hazardous and solid wastes. Toxic substances released into the environment do not necessarily remain at the point of release. By migrating through the soil, pollutants can infiltrate groundwater and underground aquifers and contaminate them. This contamination may cause severe health problems, depending on the amounts and types of substances released. Given that no federal statute directly regulates groundwater pollution, RCRA compliance can be viewed as essential to protecting groundwater and aquifer quality. Provisions within the RCRA also help to prevent polluted rainwater runoff from disposal sites from flowing into surface waters such as streams, rivers, and lakes.

Federal facilities often failed to comply with the RCRA, however. By the early 1990's, the EPA regulated about 350 federal treatment, storage, and disposal facilities; of these, only about 40 percent were in overall compliance with the RCRA. Those not in compliance violated the RCRA by, for example, failing to report releases of hazardous wastes into the environment or failing to conduct adequate groundwater monitoring to document the extent of existing contamination. One examination found 116 federal facilities under the Departments of Defense, Transportation, Energy, and the Interior, along with facilities of the Small Business Administration, that were so contaminated with dangerous wastes that they were listed as national priority sites to be cleaned up under the 1980 Superfund law, the Comprehensive Environmental Response, Compensation, and Liability Act, which requires that polluters pay to clean up the nation's worst toxic-waste problems.

Although the majority of attention has focused on the Department of Defense (DOD) and the Department of Energy (DOE), the two largest federal generators of hazardous waste and the most blatant violators of federal environmental laws, the DOD and DOE have not been the only offenders. Many federal agencies conduct activities that subject them to RCRA provisions. In addition, many civilian agencies do not report, or conduct surveys to determine, the extent of environmental contamination on lands under their jurisdictions. In 1989, only six of sixteen federal departments required by Congress to file environmental audits did so. Many federal agencies, moreover, are responsible for the generation of hazardous

1992

wastes. Serious environmental hazards may be involved; for example, Bureau of Land Management lands in the early 1990's contained an estimated 450 active and 1,000 inactive landfills, and the Department of the Interior surveyed many of the 250,000 mining sites in Interior lands to identify the locations of mining waste.

Individual states have sought to exercise control over federal polluters in order to force compliance with RCRA standards. The initial efforts focused on the courts and on the use of fines on noncompliant federal agencies. The U.S. Supreme Court hampered many of these efforts through a narrow interpretation of waivers of federal sovereign immunity in the RCRA. The FFCA can thus be understood in part as a congressional response to these narrow judicial interpretations and an attempt by Congress to overrule the courts and explicitly waive sovereign immunity.

The narrow judicial interpretation of sovereign immunity frustrated state attempts to regulate federal facilities in relation to environmental laws from the time of the passage of the Clean Air Act (CAA) in 1970. The sovereign immunity doctrine, which was introduced into federal common law by the Supreme Court in *McCulloch v. Maryland* in 1819, prevents any entity, state or private, from suing the federal government without its permission. Without a statutory waiver, the federal government need not comply with state or federal laws, and its noncompliance cannot be punished.

The first legal confrontation between federal agencies and states over federal facility environmental compliance involved the permitting requirements of the CAA and the Clean Water Act (CWA). In 1970 and 1972, Congress inserted compliance mechanisms into the CAA and the CWA, respectively, mandating that federal agencies comply with federal, state, interstate, and local requirements with respect to control and cleanup of pollution. Some states interpreted "requirement" in this language to include permitting. The EPA contended that the statutes should be read more narrowly to require compliance only with substantive standards, not with procedural standards or enforcement mechanisms such as state emission permits.

The U.S. Supreme Court agreed with the federal government. In 1975, the Court held, in *Hancock v. Train*, that Congress had not waived sovereign immunity for permitting requirements in the CWA and, in the companion case of *EPA v. California ex. rel. State Water Resources Control Board*, held that a waiver had not occurred in the CAA. In *Hancock*, the Court emphasized the rule that waivers of sovereign immunity had to be

clear and unambiguous and were to be construed narrowly. The *Hancock* decision was a message to Congress that waivers of sovereign immunity in environmental statutes had to be drafted clearly and expressly.

In 1977, Congress responded to *Hancock* by amending the CAA to waive immunity for both permits and state-imposed civil penalties. Federal agencies interpreted this language as giving states power to fine agencies for CAA violations and never challenged state impositions of fines. In 1978, the comptroller general issued an opinion holding the National Oceanic and Atmospheric Administration liable to the Puget Sound Air Pollution Control Agency for administrative fines issued in response to a violation of local air-quality standards.

Congress also revised the CWA in an attempt to waive sovereign immunity, but federal agencies once again fought the applicability of the waiver to state-imposed civil fines. Lower federal courts split on the immunity issue. In the 1986 case of *McClellan Ecological Seepage Situation (MESS) v. Weinberger*, a federal district court considered two alternative readings of the statute. First, it held that civil penalties could be applied under a state or local court provision or under a state or local ordinance that is an exact duplicate of the CWA; these same fines could, however, be imposed under the CWA itself. Second, the issue of which court had jurisdiction over such petitions was unclear. Because of the ambiguity in the language of the statute, the court refused to find a waiver of sovereign immunity.

In *U.S. Department of Energy v. Ohio*, the Sixth Circuit Court reached the opposite conclusion. The court found that the language of the CWA waiving all requirements and sanctions must be read to allow state-imposed civil penalties. The court explained that federal agencies' sovereign immunity applied only to those penalties imposed under state water-pollution programs not approved by the EPA.

The Supreme Court, however, reversed the circuit court's ruling in *DOE v. Ohio* (1992). The Court supported its holding with a comprehensive analysis of the meaning of the word "sanction," holding that "sanction(s)" in reference to the CWA meant only penalties associated with judicial or administrative judgments. The Court noted that the CWA suggested a waiver of sovereign immunity, but the justices held that the statute's language was too ambiguous to create such a waiver.

Congress passed the RCRA three months after the Supreme Court's companion decisions in *Hancock* and *EPA v. California ex. rel. State Water Resources Board* and before it amended the CAA and CWA. The legislative history of the RCRA was unclear on the subject of state-imposed civil penalties.

The Sixth Circuit Court, interpreting the provision in *DOE v. Ohio*, ruled that although Congress had intended to waive sovereign immunity for civil penalties, it had not done so clearly enough to satisfy the standard articulated in *Hancock v. Train*. The circuit court based its opinion on a comparison of the CWA waiver and the RCRA waiver. The court asserted that the CWA waived immunity for both requirements and sanctions, suggesting that sanctions are not included in requirements. The RCRA waived immunity only for requirements. The court also stated that there was no language in the RCRA that protected agencies from the imposition of state civil fines for violations of state waste-management laws not approved by the EPA. It also pointed out that the statute's explicitness in regard to court-imposed penalties, combined with its lack of civil penalties, suggested that sovereign immunity had not been waived as to the latter. The Supreme Court upheld the circuit court's decision that the RCRA did not waive sovereign immunity for civil penalties.

### SIGNIFICANCE

In late 1991, Congress overwhelmingly passed the FFCA. The law contained two major provisions. First, it amended the RCRA to permit states to impose civil penalties on federal facilities for RCRA violations. Second, it overruled a policy of the executive branch that had previously prevented the EPA from imposing administrative fines on noncompliant federal agencies. All federal facilities thus lost their claim to sovereign immunity in regard to environmental legislation and were required to comply with state or federal fines imposed for noncompliance.

The law also contained two major exemptions. First, as long as the DOE issues and complies with plans for waste treatment and storage and cannot be fined for RCRA violations for its storage plans, it cannot be fined for RCRA violations for its storage of mixed hazardous and radioactive wastes. The DOE was granted this waiver because no technology existed for the proper storage or disposal of these types of wastes. Second, federal employees are granted immunity from civil liability authorized by the FFCA.

The FFCA was intended to ensure greater compliance by federal facilities with requirements of the RCRA for management, treatment, storage, and disposal of hazardous and solid wastes. Supporters of the law believed that civil fines assessed by the states would have the same ef-

fect on compliance for the RCRA as for the CWA and the CAA. In regard to the CAA and the CWA, federal compliance was 98 percent and 89 percent, respectively, as assessed in the early 1990's by the EPA's Office of Federal Facility Enforcement. Supporters of the FFCA thus believed that state fines would close the compliance gap in the RCRA.

Civil fines imposed under the FFCA were expected to improve compliance rates in two ways. First, because civil penalties accrue from the date a violation occurs and continue until the violation is remedied, the fines would encourage compliance by reducing the incentive to delay through litigation. Fines would have to be paid out of operating funds, so agencies should comply as quickly as possible to maximize the use of appropriated funds and to avoid diverting them for fines. Second, agencies might fear political backlash from Congress if appropriations are diverted to pay state fines for noncompliance with environmental regulations.

Other factors could hamper RCRA compliance under the FFCA. First, many federal agencies cannot comply with the RCRA because they have no means by which to dispose of the waste they create. The RCRA prohibits both the land disposal of hazardous wastes and the storage of such wastes aboveground for more than one year. The DOD and the DOE annually generate nearly twenty million tons of hazardous wastes and mixed waste. Additionally, about 80 percent of the biomedical waste produced by the National Institutes of Health and the Veterans Administration is radioactive and thus also is mixed waste. Treatment technologies to handle mixed wastes, however, have not been developed. It is thus inevitable that these wastes will be stored aboveground for more than one year, in violation of the RCRA. Congress responded to the dilemma by exempting the DOE from this provision of the RCRA.

Second, if federal facilities have the technology to deal with their wastes, institutional impediments may prevent their compliance. In 1991, for example, the DOD proposed eleven amendments to the House version of the FFCA to exempt certain defense activities from RCRA regulations. DOD officials argued that, without amendments, the FFCA would prevent them from performing their primary mission. Mission activities thus take precedence over environmental compliance in the view of DOD administrators. Fines alone are not likely to alter such perceptions.

Third, the congressional appropriations process may prevent federal agencies from receiving the funds needed to obtain compliance even in the presence of civil

1992

fines. In a political climate that favors cutting budgets, it is more difficult for federal agencies to obtain necessary funding increases to gain compliance. This is an institutional problem that is not addressed by the FFCA.

Fourth, federal agencies do not have any monetary incentive to seek compliance. Unlike private entities, federal agencies do not need to fear bankruptcy as a result of compliance fines. Without reform of agencies' perceptions of their missions, federal agencies may be less likely than private entities to comply with environmental regulations before violations are discovered. After discovery, adverse publicity may be more effective as a threat than the fines imposed by the state. A system of state-imposed fines thus may do little to improve federal facility compliance unless additional measures are taken to change the manner in which agencies comprehend problems and seek solutions.

Fifth, federal agencies have an incentive to engage in litigation over fines instead of paying them. The availability of federal agency litigation budgets may encourage legal challenges in circumstances in which a private entity would be forced to comply in the interest of cost-effectiveness. Federal agencies' fines are paid out of a separate federal judgments fund known as the Tucker fund, not out of the agencies' operating budgets. Agencies therefore have some incentive to litigate fines before acknowledging liability.

*—Kevin B. Vichcales*

**FURTHER READING**

Axline, Michael D., et al. "Stone for David's Sling: Civil Penalties in Citizen Suits Against Polluting Federal Facilities." *Journal of Environmental Law and Litigation* 2 (1990): 20-21. Argues that the courts should consider congressional purpose, rather than the judicial doctrines of sovereign immunity and narrow construction, when making environmental decisions.

Cheng, Elizabeth. "Lawmaker as Lawbreaker: Assessing Civil Penalties Against Federal Facilities Under RCRA." *University of Chicago Law Review* 57 (1990): 845-854. Examines the contradiction inherent in the federal government's capacity as both the issuer of environmental requirements and the largest generator of hazardous wastes and subsequent polluter of the environment.

Gross, Andrea. "A Critique of the Federal Facilities Compliance Act of 1992." *Virginia Environmental Law Journal* 12 (Summer, 1993): 691-712. Lucid, scholarly article presents a valuable legal critique of the act. Provides a strong overview of the act and the problems of federal facility compliance with earlier environmental legislation.

Hourcle, L. R., and W. J. McGowan. "Federal Facility Compliance Act of 1992: Its Provisions and Consequences." *Federal Facility Environmental Journal* 3 (1993): 359-382. Discusses all provisions of the new act relevant to federal facilities and addresses some of the act's implications, such as funding for penalties.

Lazarus, Richard J. "Fairness in Environmental Law." *Environmental Law* 27, no. 3 (1997): 705-739. Looks at the history of environmental law in the United States from the standpoint of fairness. Includes discussion of the FFCA and RCRA.

Millan, Stan. "Federal Facilities and Environmental Compliance: Toward a Solution." *Loyola Law Review* 36 (1990): 319-323. Provides an overview of federal facilities and their lack of environmental compliance. Argues that the elimination of sovereign immunity is the means of achieving greater compliance.

Schroeder, Mark C., et al. "Regulation of Nuclear Materials: Should National Defense and Other National Policies Override State Standards?" *Environmental Law Report* 22 (January, 1992): 10014-10015. Argues that adherence to state environmental standards might jeopardize Department of Energy missions involving national defense.

Wolverton, J. B. "Sovereign Immunity and National Priorities: Enforcing Federal Facilities Compliance with Environmental Statutes." *Harvard Environmental Law Review* 15 (1991): 565-568. Addresses the issue of sovereign immunity in relation to the enforcement of federally mandated environmental laws on federal facilities.

**SEE ALSO:** Mar. 1, 1972: U.S. Congress Updates Water Pollution Law; Oct. 21, 1972: U.S. Congress Expands Pesticide Regulations; Oct. 27, 1972: U.S. Government Regulates Noise Pollution; Dec. 31, 1972: U.S. Government Bans DDT; Dec. 16, 1974: U.S. Congress Requires Safe Drinking Water; Jan. 3, 1975: U.S. Congress Protects Public Against Hazardous Waste in Transit; Oct. 11, 1976: EPA Is Charged with Regulating Toxic Chemicals; Oct. 21, 1976: "Cradle-to-Grave" Legislation Covers Hazardous Wastes; Aug. 7, 1977: Clean Air Act Is Revised; Mar. 17, 1978: Chlorofluorocarbons Are Banned in the United States; Dec. 22, 1980: U.S. Congress Addresses "Low-Level" Nuclear Waste.

## October 12, 1992
# COLUMBUS DAY DEBATES REFLECT CULTURAL DIVERSITY

*The five hundredth anniversary of Christopher Columbus's first voyage to America was celebrated and condemned as scholars, educators, ethnic groups, and the public attempted to interpret the world-altering events of 1492 with historical objectivity and multicultural sensitivity.*

**LOCALE:** United States
**CATEGORIES:** Arts; literature; publishing and journalism

**KEY FIGURES**

*Christopher Columbus* (1451-1506), explorer who made the first important contact between Europe and the Americas

*Carlos Fuentes* (b. 1928), Mexican novelist who interpreted Columbus's significance in a television special and a book

*Jay Levenson* (fl. late twentieth century), chief curator of a major exhibit of Columbus-era art

*Kirkpatrick Sale* (b. 1937), author of the celebrated and controversial revisionist text *The Conquest of Paradise*

*Joaquín Balaguer* (1906-2002), president of the Dominican Republic, 1960-1962, 1966-1978, and 1986-1996, who oversaw the creation of a costly Columbus memorial

**SUMMARY OF EVENT**

On October 12, 1492, Christopher Columbus stepped off his ship and onto an island in the Caribbean. This encounter between Europe and the Americas launched a chain of events that literally remade the world. October 12, 1992, marked the five hundredth anniversary, or quincentennial, of Columbus's landing, and the event was commemorated with speeches, parades, protests, and mourning. Columbus was both praised and vilified.

Continuing tradition, many cities in the United States held parades, mock ship landings, and fireworks displays to mark the Columbus quincentennial. The Smithsonian Institution's National Museum of Natural History in Washington, D.C., sponsored an exhibition titled *Seeds of Change*, which focused on five "seeds" that had been critical to the evolution of the New World: sugar, corn, the potato, the horse, and disease. In New York City, the New-York Historical Society held an exhibit of European art depicting the New World as seen by the Old World. The Intrepid Sea Air Space Museum told the story of Columbus and other early explorers through displays and reenactments.

Perhaps the most ambitious of the Columbus-related exhibitions was *Circa 1492: Art in the Age of Exploration*, a mammoth show mounted by the National Gallery of Art in Washington, D.C. The show's chief curator, Jay Levenson, had spent more than three years assembling a massive collection of art from around the world, including works from fifteenth century Japan, China, India, Africa, the Middle East, and South America. Some critics alleged that the vast scope of the show revealed an ill-conceived effort to avoid charges of Eurocentrism; in broadening the exhibit's focus to include art from so many cultures, it was argued, the National had lost sight of the reason for mounting a 1492-centered show in the first place. The renowned Harvard University historian Simon Schama, for example, criticized *Circa 1492* for its "refusal to consider head-on the phenomenon of Columbus himself and the historical experience of his four voyages." Schama characterized the exhibit as "the blockbuster that lost its nerve" in choosing to act with "a sense of preemptive prudence."

Other exhibits unequivocally adopted the viewpoint of the conquered. The Caribbean Cultural Center in New York City sponsored events highlighting pre-Columbian cultures. In Virginia, an exhibition at the historic Jamestown settlement portrayed the many "discoverers" of America, including the Paleo-Indians who crossed the Bering Strait.

Many Native Americans mourn on Columbus Day, as contact between Europe and the American continent spelled disaster for their cultures. Diseases such as smallpox decimated Indian populations, and European invaders killed, enslaved, or dispossessed countless indigenous Americans. American Indians thus used the Columbus quincentennial to call attention to past crimes and present inequalities. A group of Choctaws hiked the five-hundred-mile Trail of Tears first walked by the tribe during its forced resettlement from Mississippi to Oklahoma in the 1830's. In California, the International Indian Treaty Council held a "Five Hundred Years of Indigenous Resistance" concert in San Francisco, and the neighboring city of Berkeley officially changed the holiday's name to Indigenous Peoples Day. In Pasadena, California, the naming of a Columbus descendant as grand marshal of the city's famous New Year's Day Rose Parade touched off a dispute that was settled only when an American Indian was named as a co-grand marshal.

1992

Throughout Latin America and the Caribbean, Columbus Day, 1992, was marked by official silence and increased security around Spanish embassies. Many peaceful protests took place, but demonstrators in Mexico City, San Salvador, and Santo Domingo attacked statues, burned tires, and clashed with police. The Pan-American Highway in Ecuador and Colombia was blocked in some places by sit-ins and was closed at one location by a dynamite blast.

Santo Domingo, the capital of the Dominican Republic, had intended to hold an elaborate celebration, including a worldwide television extravaganza hosted by Bob Hope. The plans fizzled, however, in the wake of the controversy caused by President Joaquín Balaguer's white elephant of a Columbus memorial. The Faro a Colón (Columbus's Lighthouse) is ten stories tall and nearly half a mile long. Fifty thousand people were evicted from their homes to make way for the structure, which cost about $70 million to build. A high wall surrounds the Faro, shielding visitors from the sight of an adjacent slum. The lighthouse is designed to project 138 laser beams into the sky in the shape of a cross—in a city that suffers frequent blackouts.

Numerous other Columbus-centered projects were received with varying degrees of controversy. Two major Hollywood films, *1492: Conquest of Paradise* and *Christopher Columbus: The Discovery*, received generally poor reviews; despite the fact that neither was idolatrous, the works were decried by anti-Columbians. (Marlon Brando, who portrayed the notorious inquisitor Tomás de Torquemada in the latter film, insisted that his name be removed from the credits because the finished picture did not depict Columbus as "the true villain he was.") A public television special narrated by author Carlos Fuentes also stirred controversy; a revival of *Cristoforo Colombo*, an opera composed for the 1892 anniversary, proved less inflammatory.

The Columbus issue had become such a hot potato that the explorer was, ironically, largely ignored at the 1992 World's Fair held in Seville, Spain. In concert with the 1992 Olympic Games in Barcelona, the fair was the centerpiece of the "Year of Spain," a celebration of the country and its history planned to coincide with the five hundredth anniversary of Columbus's voyage. October 12 had even been chosen as the fair's closing date, but by then nervous organizers decided to downplay the Columbus connection. One reviewer wrote, "In the end he was an unwanted guest. . . . Whatever his merits, Spain concluded, Columbus should not be allowed to spoil the party."

## SIGNIFICANCE

The commemoration of a historic event often tells more about the people doing the commemorating than it does about the event itself. The Columbus quincentennial was characterized by increased historical awareness and multicultural sensitivity. What about Columbus Day celebrations of the past? How did Columbus attain the hero status that is now widely believed to be so undeserved?

In the United States, patriotic businessmen were largely responsible for Columbus's traditional image as a praiseworthy American hero. On October 12, 1792, the Tammany Society, a New York fraternal organization, held the first Columbian commemorative dinner. A symbolic monument representing Columbus's achievements was placed in the society's museum. Inspired by the festivities in New York, the Massachusetts Historical Society of Boston honored Columbus with a procession and a poem on October 23. The press praised these events, encouraging other towns to organize celebrations.

Enthusiasm for Columbus as a symbol of progress reached a peak in 1893, when the World's Columbian Exposition opened in Chicago. Bigger than any previous World's Fair, the exposition honored American technology, resources, power, and general superiority. Reigning over it all was a noble statue of Columbus, armored and bearing an upraised sword.

In 1934, President Franklin D. Roosevelt proclaimed October 12 the official Columbus Day and called on the public to observe the day with ceremonies in schools and churches. Columbus Day, the anniversary of the "discovery" of America, had become a symbol of nationalism and progress and a firmly entrenched American tradition.

The Columbus quincentennial countercelebrations and pluralistic exhibits reflected a changing sensibility in the United States. As the twentieth century drew to a close, ethnic pride and multicultural awareness began to gain ground on Eurocentric domination of U.S. culture. As scholars attempted to paint a more realistic picture of the past, many educators fought to implement programs designed to support, rather than conflict with, minority students' sense of self. Debate raged between advocates of multicultural curricula and defenders of educational orthodoxy. Hollywood, too, produced a number of high-profile projects about minority groups, including such films as *Dances with Wolves* (1990) and *The Last of the Mohicans* (1992). African American filmmakers such as Spike Lee and John Singleton emerged as among the film industry's most popular.

When did American society begin to heed the ethnic voice? Columbus's portrayal over the past century is a benchmark of popular opinion, evidence of a notable shift in attitude over the years. In 1892, Columbus was popularly believed to have been a great hero who had brought civilization to a virgin land. The indigenous people he "discovered" were alternately thought to have been immoral cannibals or noble savages, with childlike minds suitable for Christian conversion. This viewpoint had been espoused by Washington Irving's *A History of the Life and Voyages of Christopher Columbus* (1828), a romanticized version of the explorer's life that was the first full-length biography of Columbus published in English. Irving portrayed the explorer as courageous, wise, and enterprising, the archetype of an early American hero. This image endured and was accepted even by Native Americans and African Americans.

During the 1892 celebration of Columbus in New York, Indian students marched in the parade and were praised for their "civilized" regimentation. Others rode on horseback wearing war paint and feathers. The prevailing attitude was that Indians had benefited from their "discovery." The value of indigenous cultures was measured by the contributions of those cultures to the society of their European conquerors.

At the time of the four hundredth anniversary of Columbus's first voyage, moreover, legal slavery had been abolished for less than thirty years. Even so, black citizens were enthusiastic about the World's Columbian Exposition in Chicago. Their efforts to be included, to portray African American accomplishments as part of the greatness of the United States, were, however, dismissed at every turn.

By 1992, ethnic groups in the United States had completely rejected the idea that they were entitled to recognition only by riding on Euro-Caucasian coattails. Newspapers and magazines of the day were filled with protestations condemning both Columbus's cruelties toward the indigenous population and the continued crimes and inequalities perpetrated against American minorities in succeeding centuries. Columbus was charged with everything from genocide to ecological devastation.

The public mudslinging was aided and abetted by revisionist historians who rewrote the past to suit the modern environment. The quincentennial evoked a flood of books that historian Arthur Schlesinger, Jr., claimed reflected the "end of European domination of the planet . . . the bad conscience of the West and the consequent reexamination of the Western impact on the rest of humanity." Among the most celebrated—and contro-

versial—of these publications was Kirkpatrick Sale's *The Conquest of Paradise* (1990). Sale portrayed the pre-Columbian continent as an "Eden of astonishing plenitude" where people lived in "balanced and fruitful harmony" with nature and with one another. Other scholars criticized Sale's and similar books as exercises in mythmaking that ignored historical realities of pre-Columbian America, such as the institutionalized slavery and ritual murder practiced by the Aztecs and other indigenous peoples.

Although Christopher Columbus did not "discover" the American continent, his arrival there certainly spurred monumental changes. Controversy concerning the impact of Columbus's landings will doubtless persist far beyond their five hundredth anniversary. The Columbus quincentennial reinvigorated debates concerning the rights and contributions of indigenous peoples and minority groups, both on the American continent and elsewhere. As the twentieth century drew to a close, the renewed interest in non-European cultures seemed likely to bring greater diversity into popular culture for years to come.

*—Susan Frischer*

## FURTHER READING

Bushman, Claudia L. *America Discovers Columbus: How an Italian Explorer Became an American Hero.* Hanover, N.H.: University Press of New England, 1992. History of American commemoration of Columbus emphasizes the effect that a popular image can have on the shaping of public consciousness. Includes reproductions of many paintings of Columbus, none of which resembles any other.

Davidson, Miles H. *Columbus Then and Now: A Life Reexamined.* Norman: University of Oklahoma Press, 1997. Biography of the explorer also examines the changes in perceptions of Columbus over the last decades of the twentieth century. Includes maps, bibliography, and index.

Fuentes, Carlos. *The Buried Mirror: Reflections on Spain and the New World.* New York: Houghton Mifflin, 1992. Presents a wide-ranging discourse on the significance of Columbus's journey and its implications for the New World. Published as an outgrowth of the author's public television series.

Harjo, Suzan Shown. "I Won't Be Celebrating Columbus Day." *Newsweek* (special issue), Fall/Winter, 1991, 32. A call to arms by the national coordinator of the 1992 Alliance, a coalition of Native American groups. Demands that both church and state act to

1992

make restitution for the past and resolutions for the future.

Krauthammer, Charles. "Hail Columbus, Dead White Male." *Time*, May 27, 1991, 74. Presents a cool-headed attack on the politically correct opinions that Columbus was a villain and the indigenous people were noble savages. Briefly describes the totalitarian Incan civilization and justifies its destruction by stating that humankind is better off in the late twentieth century.

Levenson, Jay A., ed. *Circa 1492: Art in the Age of Exploration*. New Haven, Conn.: Yale University Press, 1991. Scholarly, impressive catalog produced for the massive exhibit of Columbus-era art presented at the National Gallery.

Schama, Simon. "They All Laughed at Christopher Columbus: Circus 1492—Who the Admiral Was, and Who He Wasn't." *The New Republic*, January 6, 1992, 30-40. Penetrating review of the National Gallery's massive exhibit of Columbus-era art provides a masterful overview of the cultural and artistic debates inspired by the quincentennial.

Schlesinger, Arthur M., Jr. "Was America a Mistake? Reflections on the Long History of Efforts to De-

bunk Columbus and His Discovery." *The Atlantic Monthly*, September, 1992, 16-30. Comprehensive article by a noted historian debunks the nineteenth century Columbus myth and criticizes twentieth century revisionist overkill. Describes the cruelties of pre-Columbian America and concludes that the Mexican and European civilizations of 1492 were not essentially different in moral terms.

Summerhill, Stephen J., and John Alexander Williams. *Sinking Columbus: Contested History, Cultural Politics, and Mythmaking During the Quincentenary*. Gainesville: University Press of Florida, 2000. Two of the organizers of an intended quincentennial celebration of Columbus examine the failure of that effort and discuss the critique of the explorer's legacy that took place, especially in the United States, Latin America, Spain, and Italy. Includes bibliography and index.

**SEE ALSO:** 1970's: Spanish Art Thrives After Years of Suppression; May, 1987: National Museum of Women in the Arts Opens Amid Controversy.

---

## October 26, 1992
# DEFEAT OF THE CHARLOTTETOWN ACCORD

*Canada's constitutional crisis deepened when the electorate rejected an intensely negotiated package of reforms.*

**LOCALE:** Canada
**CATEGORY:** Government and politics

**KEY FIGURES**
*Brian Mulroney* (b. 1939), prime minister of Canada, 1984-1993
*Robert Bourassa* (1933-1996), premier of Quebec, 1970-1976 and 1985-1994
*Pierre Trudeau* (1919-2000), prime minister of Canada, 1968-1979 and 1980-1984
*Joe Clark* (b. 1939), Canadian constitutional affairs minister and prime minister of Canada, 1979-1980
*Jacques Parizeau* (b. 1930), leader of the sovereignist Parti Québécois

**SUMMARY OF EVENT**
The 1990 failure of the Meech Lake Accord plunged Canada into a serious constitutional crisis. Political par-

ties saw a great deal of turmoil. A Quebec-based reform party, the Bloc Québécois, was formed by defectors from the Progressive Conservative and Liberal parties. The leaders of western Canada forged links to face off against both Quebec and the federal government in Ottawa.

On November 1, 1990, Prime Minister Brian Mulroney created a national commission to study the future of Canada. This move was criticized by Native Canadians, who were in the midst of a dispute with the government, and by Quebecers, who had established their own panel to examine the future. The leaders of French-speaking Quebec remained cool to federal efforts to proceed on constitutional and trade issues. Quebec premier Robert Bourassa introduced a Liberal Party plan for radical decentralization of the country. Meanwhile, Mulroney pleaded for unity. On September 24, 1991, Mulroney unveiled a series of constitutional reforms under the collective name of Shaping Canada's Future Together. These proposals came under immediate criticism, not only by the usual Quebecers and Native critics but also by those from the Canadian West who felt the reforms weakened their provinces' economies.

Attitudes hardened throughout 1992, with Alberta premier Donald Getty opposing policies of bilingualism while he and Newfoundland's Clyde K. Wells pressed for a strong Senate based on provincial equality. Five conferences on constitutional reform attempted to hammer out the differences among provinces. Numerous plans were debated in a nationwide discussion on Canada's future, and criticism arose throughout the country from Quebecers, Native Canadians, residents of the western provinces, and feminists who feared an undermining of the Canadian Bill of Rights. Hopes rose and fell as detailed debates revolved around such highly theoretical concepts as "asymmetrical federalism," senatorial equality, and the exact nature of Quebec's distinct society.

On August 27, 1992, Mulroney, the provincial premiers, territorial leaders, and representatives from four Native Canadian associations finally agreed unanimously on a constitutional reform package known as the Charlottetown Accord, named for the capital of Prince Edward Island, where it was signed. The accord's provisions included the Canada Clause, a statement of principles on which the country was founded, which was to serve as a guide for the courts to interpret the constitution. It decreed that Quebec constituted "within Canada a distinct society," with a French-speaking majority, a unique culture, and a civil-law tradition (in contrast to the common-law tradition prevailing elsewhere in Canada). The federal and provincial governments would be committed to the development of minority-language communities. The nation would be committed to respecting individual and collective human rights and freedoms. In the words of the document, "Canadians confirm the principle of the equality of the provinces at the same time as recognizing their diverse characteristics."

An elected Senate with expanded powers was to be created to replace the appointed body that had been convened since 1982. Each province would be equally represented with six senators, and the territories would each have one senator. Additional seats were to be apportioned to indigenous peoples. The House of Commons, Canada's lower house, would be expanded to reflect population distribution more closely. Ontario, Quebec, British Columbia, and Alberta would gain seats. In recognition of its distinctiveness, Quebec would be guaranteed at least 25 percent of the seats.

The nine Supreme Court justices would be named by the federal government from lists submitted by the prov-

inces, as opposed to the practice of being appointed at the sole discretion of the federal government. Three would always be from Quebec.

The accord provided constitutional recognition that indigenous peoples had "the inherent right of self-government within Canada." Although there was no agreement on what that concept meant, it did not include the notion of separate sovereignty for indigenous peoples, who were to negotiate the details of the concept with federal and provincial governments. If the Native Canadians' rights had not been defined after five years, the courts could issue a final determination.

The federal government would retain control of national entities, such as the Canadian Broadcasting Corporation and unemployment insurance. Provincial governments would have exclusive jurisdiction over culture and job retraining programs. The federal government would withdraw completely, whenever provincial authorities requested, from forestry, mining, tourism, recreation, housing, and municipal and urban affairs. Provinces could negotiate administrative agreements with the federal government for increased control over immigration and regional development.

The accord's opponents were numerous. Former prime minister Pierre Trudeau denounced what he saw as Quebec's unduly large role. Even more scathing in their criticisms, western Canadians tended to oppose the accord because they did not favor concessions to Quebec, whereas Quebecers opposed the accord because they thought it did not deliver them enough concessions. Native Canadians, women's groups, and others also had their doubts.

On October 26, 1992, Canadian voters overwhelmingly defeated the accord. Ending an often divisive national campaign, a majority of voters in the provinces of Quebec, Nova Scotia, Alberta, British Columbia, Saskatchewan, Manitoba, and the Yukon Territory voted no to the question, "Do you agree that the Constitution of Canada should be renewed on the basis of the agreement reached on August 28, 1992?" The yes side won in Ontario, New Brunswick, Newfoundland, Prince Edward Island, and the Northwest Territories. Nationwide, the no side outpolled the yes side 54.4 percent to 44.6 percent, with a 74.9 percent turnout of eligible voters. The referendum was technically a nonbinding guide for the ten provincial assemblies, all of which needed to grant approval for formal ratification of the accord. A no vote in any one province had been widely viewed as all that would be necessary to kill the accord.

1992

## SIGNIFICANCE

Constitutional Affairs Minister Joe Clark offered a bleak assessment of what the no vote meant: "We thought after two decades of failure, the failure of six rounds of constitutional discussions, we had found in the Charlottetown Accord a way to resolve these deep and dividing problems in Canada, or begin their resolution. . . . It's clear tonight that that solution has not been accepted. What's not clear tonight is what solution might be available to us." A few hours after the rejection of the accord had become evident, Prime Minister Mulroney declared, "The Charlottetown agreement is history." Canadians and their governments should now set aside the constitutional issue, he said, and concentrate on fostering "strong and durable economic renewal."

On October 26, Jacques Parizeau, leader of the sovereignist Parti Québécois, told supporters in Montreal that Quebec's rejection of the accord "said what we didn't want—the next time we will say what we want. Québécois are a people, they are a nation, and very soon they will be a country." Parizeau had made clear during the referendum campaign that if the Parti Québécois won the next provincial election in Quebec, he would call for a referendum on independence. He argued that the nationwide no vote on the accord had effectively been a plea to abandon efforts to revise the constitution. He insisted that the only options remaining for Quebec were sovereignty or a vastly revised federal arrangement.

The leader of the Bloc Québécois, Lucien Bouchard, offered a different appraisal of the options facing Quebec. Bouchard reasoned, "There were two roads for Québécois before the referendum—profoundly renewed federalism and sovereignty. These two options must now find a convergence." Robert Bourassa, Quebec's Liberal premier who had led the yes campaign in that province, pointed to the results of two polls indicating that most Quebecers preferred to remain part of the Canadian confederation and reiterated his party's goal to "build Quebec within Canada," saying that federalism would "advance the cause of Quebec."

Many Canadians voted no on the Charlottetown Accord to vent their anger against the political and business establishment in general and the Progressive Conservative Party and Mulroney in particular. The most significant victim of the accord's failure was Brian Mulroney. Facing growing pressure to step down, given the implicit "no confidence" nature of the referendum, he resigned as the leader of the Progressive Conservative Party and as prime minister on February 24, 1993, after a frustrating decade-long campaign for Canadian unity, during which the country's worst recession raged.

*—Randall Fegley*

## FURTHER READING

Hurley, James Ross. *The Canadian Constitutional Debate: Fron the Death of the Meech Lake Accord of 1987 to the 1992 Referendum*. Ottawa: Privy Council Office, 1994. Presents a thorough examination of Canadian constitutional history during the period covered.

McMenemy, John. *The Language of Canadian Politics: A Guide to Important Terms and Concepts*. 3d ed. Waterloo, Ont.: Wilfrid Laurier University Press, 2001. Collection of more than five hundred brief essays on a wide range of topics related to the Canadian system of government, Canadian political history, Canadian laws and legal history, and more.

McRoberts, Kenneth, and Patrick Monahan, eds. *The Charlottetown Accord, the Referendum, and the Future of Canada*. Toronto: University of Toronto Press, 1993. Collection of papers presented at a conference provides an excellent examination of the negotiations and politics surrounding the Charlottetown Accord and its subsequent failure to be approved by the Canadian electorate.

Smith, David E., Peter MacKinnon, and John C. Courtney, eds. *After Meech Lake: Lessons for the Future*. Saskatoon, Sask.: Fifth House, 1991. Collection of essays examines the possibilities facing Canada following the 1990 failure of the Meech Lake Accord.

Sutherland, Kate. *Referendum Round-Table*. Edmonton, Alta.: Centre for Constitutional Studies, 1992. Informative monograph provides analysis of the Charlottetown Accord.

Vipond, Robert. *Liberty and Community: Canadian Federalism and the Failure of the Constitution*. Albany: State University of New York Press, 1991. Examines the inability of Canadians to agree on constitutional reforms.

**SEE ALSO:** Apr. 17, 1982: Canada's Constitution Act; Apr. 17, 1982: Canadian Charter of Rights and Freedoms Is Enacted; Sept. 14, 1984: Mulroney Era Begins in Canada; June 22, 1990: Meech Lake Accord Dies; July 25, 1990: Bloc Québécois Forms; Nov. 4, 1993: Chrétien Takes Charge in Canada; June 29, 2000: Canadian Parliament Passes the Clarity Act.

**November 3, 1992**

# CLINTON WINS THE U.S. PRESIDENCY

*Bill Clinton promised change and met with intense congressional resistance when he became the first Democrat to capture the White House in a decade.*

**LOCALE:** Washington, D.C.
**CATEGORY:** Government and politics

**KEY FIGURES**

*Bill Clinton* (b. 1946), president of the United States, 1993-2001

*George H. W. Bush* (b. 1924), president of the United States, 1989-1993

*H. Ross Perot* (b. 1930), independent candidate for president

*Newt Gingrich* (b. 1943), Republican leader in the U.S. House of Representatives

**SUMMARY OF EVENT**

On January 20, 1993, Bill Clinton was sworn in as the forty-second president of the United States. In a three-cornered race, he had won a substantial electoral victory on November 3, 1992, over the incumbent Republican president, George H. W. Bush, and independent candidate H. Ross Perot, a Texas billionaire. Clinton's victory can be traced to events in the late 1960's that reshaped both major U.S. political parties. Since the Great Depression, the Democratic Party had been the country's dominant political force, forming a coalition of southern white politicians and northern urban and labor leaders. The Democrats could rely on votes from large cities, minorities, unionized workers, southerners, Catholics, and Jews. The Republicans were led by northeastern and midwestern Protestants. They could usually count on support from the business community and middle- and upper-class suburban voters.

Two powerful political struggles of the 1960's brought about a reconstruction of both national party coalitions. Opposition to the war in Vietnam induced many liberal Democrats to attack and ultimately weaken or destroy the big-city Democratic machines and labor leaders. Liberal activists for a variety of other causes began to support special-interest groups rather than the party itself. The Civil Rights movement weakened Democratic strength in the South. Although liberals controlled many congressional districts, the party's strength in presidential campaigns was diminished. For thirty years, the pattern of Republican presidents and Democratic Congresses was established; before Clinton's election to the presidency,

only Jimmy Carter had been able to overcome the trend.

During the first days of his administration, Clinton seemed to be well positioned to produce new programs and initiatives. Not only had the election ended twelve years of Republican control of the executive branch, but the Democrats also were in control of both houses of Congress. Many observers believed that the coalition assembled by President Ronald Reagan—right-wing Republicans together with Republican and Democratic centrists—finally had come unraveled as a result of the somewhat weakened U.S. economy. Clinton's campaign promises had included restoration of economic health, deficit reduction, health care reform, campaign spending reform, and support for the North American Free Trade Agreement (NAFTA). Taken as a whole, the elements of Clinton's program seemed to be well calculated to expand or restore the power of the Democratic Party in national politics.

However, the president found within a few months that there were severe limits on what he could accomplish. Solid Republican opposition to his proposals, coupled with the defection of many Democrats whose interests were adversely affected by Clinton's program, prevented him from achieving much in the early days of his administration. His efforts to find compromises acceptable to Congress often made him appear to vacillate, further weakening his political influence. Moreover, he had invested a great deal of political capital to persuade the armed forces to accept the presence of homosexuals in the military. Clinton found the going tough on this issue and was forced to accept a compromise that satisfied neither side in the dispute.

By the end of his first two years in office, Clinton had achieved only two major legislative victories: passage of his budget and approval of NAFTA. The president's budget was a success, resulting in a real reduction in the projected budget deficit and a real reduction in the number of federal employees. The unemployment rate dropped substantially, as many new jobs were created. In the case of NAFTA, Clinton found it necessary to appeal to Republicans for additional legislative support. The treaty passed, but its results were not immediately clear, and controversy continued over its impact on U.S. workers (although in the long run NAFTA proved beneficial to the U.S. economy).

President Clinton failed to persuade Congress to pass an elaborate health care reform plan, which had been his

1992

## CLINTON'S INAUGURAL ADDRESS

*In his inaugural address, delivered on January 20, 1993, President Bill Clinton emphasized themes of renewal and change:*

My fellow citizens, today we celebrate the mystery of American renewal. This ceremony is held in the depth of winter, but by the words we speak and the faces we show the world, we force the spring, a spring reborn in the world's oldest democracy that brings forth the vision and courage to reinvent America. When our Founders boldly declared America's independence to the world and our purposes to the Almighty, they knew that America, to endure, would have to change; not change for change's sake but change to preserve America's ideals: life, liberty, the pursuit of happiness. Though we march to the music of our time, our mission is timeless. Each generation of Americans must define what it means to be an American. . . .

Today, a generation raised in the shadows of the Cold War assumes new responsibilities in a world warmed by the sunshine of freedom but threatened still by ancient hatreds and new plagues. Raised in unrivaled prosperity, we inherit an economy that is still the world's strongest but is weakened by business failures, stagnant wages, increasing inequality, and deep divisions among our own people.

When George Washington first took the oath I have just sworn to uphold, news traveled slowly across the land by horseback and across the ocean by boat. Now, the sights and sounds of this ceremony are broadcast instantaneously to billions around the world. Communications and commerce are global. Investment is mobile. Technology is almost magical. And ambition for a better life is now universal.

We earn our livelihood in America today in peaceful competition with people all across the Earth. Profound and powerful forces are shaking and remaking our world. And the urgent question of our time is whether we can make change our friend and not our enemy. This new world has already enriched the lives of millions of Americans who are able to compete and win in it. But when most people are working harder for less; when others cannot work at all; when the cost of health care devastates families and threatens to bankrupt our enterprises, great and small; when the fear of crime robs law-abiding citizens of their freedom; and when millions of poor children cannot even imagine the lives we are calling them to lead, we have not made change our friend.

We know we have to face hard truths and take strong steps, but we have not done so; instead, we have drifted. And that drifting has eroded our resources, fractured our economy, and shaken our confidence. Though our challenges are fearsome, so are our strengths. Americans have ever been a restless, questing, hopeful people. And we must bring to our task today the vision and will of those who came before us. From our Revolution to the Civil War, to the Great Depression, to the civil rights movement, our people have always mustered the determination to construct from these crises the pillars of our history. Thomas Jefferson believed that to preserve the very foundations of our Nation, we would need dramatic change from time to time. Well, my fellow Americans, this is our time. Let us embrace it.

highest and most publicly visible priority. So many interests had been consulted in the formation of the plan and so many compromises had been made that the proposal lost clarity and focus; public support waned, and the president and his wife, Hillary Rodham Clinton, who had assumed a large role in orchestrating the plan, had to accept defeat.

Both before and after the election, Clinton's greatest political challenge had come from opponents who made a variety of charges. The president and the First Lady were accused of conflicts of interest and financial improprieties in connection with the Whitewater real estate development in Arkansas years before Clinton's presidency. After the senior staff of the White House Travel Office were dismissed and replaced with people known to the Clintons, Mrs. Clinton was charged with cronyism in what became known as "Travelgate." In 1993, President Clinton was charged with propositioning and sexually harassing a former Arkansas state employee, Paula Jones. Jones, with the financial support of conservative groups opposed to the president, filed a suit against him in spite of his denials. In the meantime, Mrs. Clinton—having been attacked for her groundbreaking role in the health care reform effort and for impropriety in the Travelgate and Whitewater matters—was forced to redefine her role as First Lady in a more traditional way, and her participation in the affairs of government became less visible.

President Clinton also faced strong factional opposition among Democrats. He had campaigned for office as a centrist "new Democrat," but in order to prevail with Congress and the bureaucracy, he found it necessary to adopt a much more liberal stance as president than he had presented as a candidate. His new positions on rights for homosexuals, abortion rights, and minority representation were not generally popular with the public. They also made the president appear to be waffling on a variety of campaign promises. The administration's abandonment of a promised middle-class tax cut and welfare reform were particularly damaging.

Clinton's apparent inability to prevail in

the legislative process or to become popular enough to silence the critics of his personal behavior made him appear weak and vacillating. In the midterm elections of 1994, the Democrats suffered a stunning reversal, losing control of both houses of Congress for the first time in more than forty years. After that election, President Clinton moved back toward the political center. This second major turnabout did little at first to reestablish his reputation for principled and steadfast political leadership. By late 1995 and early 1996, however, the president had rebounded. He vetoed Republican measures—part of the 1995-1996 budget bill—that would have shifted the administration of welfare and Medicare programs from the national to the state governments, and the Republicans did not have enough votes in Congress to override the veto.

In welfare policy itself, Clinton had Republican support for ending the controversial and counterproductive Aid to Families with Dependent Children (AFDC) program. AFDC was eliminated at the federal level, with funds going in block grants to the states for distribution to recipients who faced a new five-year limit on the time they could receive welfare. Although many Democrats stood in opposition, Clinton had substantial Republican support to make these changes. In the long run, the new policy was widely credited with having reduced the problem of intergenerational poverty. Clinton's success in the public relations battle over the budget and in the successful passage of welfare reform did much to restore his political standing.

Although the crucial decisions of the second half of Clinton's 1992 term were legislative rather than administrative, the president also had some very visible foreign policy and administrative successes. He successfully withdrew the troops sent to Somalia by President Bush in 1992, and U.S. military intervention in Haiti proved successful, bringing about peaceful elections and a peaceful presidential transition for the first time in that country's history. Clinton's administration also established a coalition to intervene militarily to end the savage war between Bosnia and Serbia in the former Yugoslavia.

The political situation after 1994, with a Democratic

*President Bill Clinton takes the oath of office.* (Library of Congress)

1992

2683

president and a Republican Congress, had been practically unknown in the United States since before the Great Depression. Unusually sharp administrative and policy differences existed between the Clinton administration and the Republican majorities in Congress. The Republicans in the House of Representatives, under the leadership of Speaker Newt Gingrich of Georgia, were as a group both highly ideological and highly disciplined. The fierce struggle between President Clinton and the congressional Republicans established the critical and defining nature of the 1996 election to the future of U.S. politics.

Reelected in 1996, Clinton served a second term marked by few successes and a tendency to focus on less important policy matters. By the last two years of his second term, Clinton was embroiled in a scandal involving White House intern Monica Lewinsky, which resulted in his impeachment for alleged perjury before a grand jury. He successfully weathered the impeachment trial, but his final two years in office were dogged by controversy.

## SIGNIFICANCE

Although Clinton struggled early in his presidency with the appearance of inconsistent political ideals, delays in cabinet appointments, inexperienced staff, and debacles such as Travelgate and the Whitewater affair, in the long run he made progress in lowering a mushrooming federal budget deficit, in bringing health care reform to the Congress as a serious issue, and in working with a midterm Republican Congress toward welfare and other social reforms.

During Clinton's presidency the U.S. economy did very well, and the American public gave Clinton substantial credit for that as well as for the balanced budgets that the economic prosperity engendered through major increases in federal tax revenue. However, even this legacy was tarnished as the NASDAQ collapsed in March, 2000, owing to what later was described as the technical sector bubble. The economy slowed in that year, giving some ammunition to the Republican presidential contender, George W. Bush, who defeated Democrat Al Gore, Clinton's vice president, in the controversial November, 2000, presidential election. When Bill Clinton left office, both houses of Congress and the White House were in Republican hands—a situation that did not reflect a strong public endorsement of his years as president.

—*Robert Jacobs*

## FURTHER READING

Campbell, Colin, and Bert A. Rockman, eds. *The Clinton Presidency: First Appraisals*. Chatham, N.J.: Chatham House, 1995. Collection of excellent essays on the Clinton presidency by political scientists. Harold Stanley's "The Parties, the President, and the 1994 Midterm Elections" is particularly insightful.

Clinton, Bill. *My Life*. New York: Alfred A. Knopf, 2004. Exhaustive memoir offers Clinton's own perspective on the events of his campaigns and his presidency.

Cohen, Richard E. *Changing Course in Washington: Clinton and the New Congress*. New York: Macmillan, 1994. Documents Clinton's shift toward the conservative side of the Democratic Party.

Denton, Robert E., Jr., and Rachel L. Holloway, eds. *The Clinton Presidency: Images, Issues, and Communications Strategies*. Westport, Conn.: Praeger, 1996. Collection of essays focuses on communications aspects of Clinton's presidency. Offers expert analysis of the images, issues, and rhetoric used by Clinton during and after the 1992 presidential campaign.

Drew, Elizabeth. *On the Edge: The Clinton Presidency*. New York: Simon & Schuster, 1994. Recounts the internal policy struggles of the Clinton administration during its first two years.

Greenberg, Stanley B. *Middle Class Dreams: The Politics and Power of the New American Majority*. Rev. ed. New Haven, Conn.: Yale University Press, 1996. Provides thoughtful analysis of the central trends in U.S. public opinion. Suggests that the electorate is becoming more conservative.

Hohenberg, John. *The Bill Clinton Story: Winning the Presidency*. Syracuse, N.Y.: Syracuse University Press, 1994. Presents scholarly analysis of Clinton's 1992 campaign strategy.

SEE ALSO: Nov. 2, 1976: Carter Is Elected President; Nov. 4, 1980: Reagan Is Elected President; Nov. 8, 1988: Bush Is Elected President; Apr. 3, 1993: Clinton Convenes the Forest Summit; Oct. 12, 1996: Clinton Signs Legislation to Help Restore the Everglades; Mar. 4, 1997: Clinton Rejects Federal Support for Human Cloning; June 25, 1998: U.S. Supreme Court Strikes Down the Line-Item Veto; Oct. 15-23, 1998: Wye River Accords; Dec. 19, 1998: Clinton Is Impeached.

December 9, 1992

# U.S. MARINES ENTER SOMALIA

*Under the auspices of the United Nations, U.S. forces entered a nation in anarchy to secure humanitarian operations.*

**LOCALE:** Somalia

**CATEGORIES:** Diplomacy and international relations; wars, uprisings, and civil unrest; United Nations

### KEY FIGURES

*Muhammad Farah Aydid* (c. 1930-1996), prominent Somali military leader

*George H. W. Bush* (b. 1924), president of the United States, 1989-1993

*Boutros Boutros-Ghali* (b. 1922), secretary-general of the United Nations, 1992-1996

*Bill Clinton* (b. 1946), president of the United States, 1993-2001

*Ali Mahdi Mahammad* (b. 1939), prominent leader in the Hawiye clan

*Robert B. Oakley* (b. 1931), U.S. special envoy to Somalia

*Muhammad Siad Barre* (1910-1995), president of Somalia, 1969-1991

### SUMMARY OF EVENT

President George H. W. Bush announced on December 4, 1992, that U.S. forces would be sent to Somalia to provide security for the provision of emergency humanitarian assistance. This announcement followed months of civil war and famine in Somalia and many months of international debate about how other nations could best address that country's deteriorating situation.

On December 3, 1992, the United Nations Security Council authorized a member state to intervene in Somalia, where anarchy reigned. The intervening power was authorized to use all necessary means to provide security for humanitarian relief. The Bush administration, which had been preparing for this eventuality, took formal steps to mount a peacekeeping operation, called Operation Restore Hope, under U.S. command. The first troops landed in Mogadishu, Somalia's capital and largest city, in the early hours of December 9. U.S. forces remained in Somalia until March 31, 1994, when President Bill Clinton formally called for the withdrawal of all but a handful of U.S. troops in the face of ongoing civil strife and discord. Although the operation failed to produce a political resolution to the Somali civil war, it did restore considerable order to the Somali countryside and ended the famine.

Although Somalia is a largely homogeneous country in terms of ethnicity, religion, and language, its people are divided into six major clans and numerous subclans. The majority of Somalis are fiercely independent nomads with strong loyalty to family and clan. Traditionally, Somali clans and subclans have engaged in disputes over pasture and water resources, but significant interclan marriage has muted such conflict, as has the mediating authority of clan elders. This traditional capacity for conflict resolution was weakened during the 1980's, as President Muhammad Siad Barre, who had seized power in a coup in 1969, nine years after Somalia's independence, sought to manipulate the clan system to maintain his increasingly unpopular regime.

Most Somalis welcomed Siad Barre's policies of reform in his early years. After Siad Barre failed in an attempt to capture the predominantly Somali-inhabited Ogaden region in Ethiopia, however, his regime gradually became more authoritarian and increasingly brutal. As opposition to Siad Barre grew, he responded by rewarding fellow Marehan clan members with positions of power. Other clans responded with determined resistance, and the northwestern part of Somalia fell into open rebellion in May, 1988. Siad Barre responded ruthlessly with aerial bombings of Hargeisa, the regional capital, and hundreds of thousands of Isaq Somali took refuge in nearby Ethiopia.

The civil war in the north continued for three years, culminating in a declaration of independence on May 17, 1991, and the formation of Somaliland Republic. During the late months of 1990, civil war had spread throughout southern Somalia. Awash in arms from years of military assistance received during the Cold War, opposition groups flourished. Muhammad Farah Aydid's well-armed Somali National Army (SNA) gradually gained the upper hand against Siad Barre's forces, which had been reduced by defections to Marehan clan units. Aydid's forces captured Mogadishu in late January, 1991, as Siad Barre fled from the capital city after plundering it and retreated into the southern countryside, where his troops fought pitched battles with Aydid's forces in fertile agricultural areas, interrupting local farming and precipitating famine.

If Siad Barre's opposition had been united, Somalia might not have devolved into anarchy. However, disputes over who should govern the country developed immediately after Siad Barre's flight, the principal contest being between Aydid and Ali Mahdi Mahammad, a

## BUSH ADDRESSES THE NATION ON SOMALIA

*On December 4, 1992, President George H. W. Bush announced in a televised speech that the United States would send troops to Somalia to provide security for humanitarian efforts there. He began by explaining the situation:*

I want to talk to you today about the tragedy in Somalia and about a mission that can ease suffering and save lives. Every American has seen the shocking images from Somalia. The scope of suffering there is hard to imagine. Already, over a quarter-million people, as many people as live in Buffalo, New York, have died in the Somali famine. . . .

For many months now, the United States has been actively engaged in the massive international relief effort to ease Somalia's suffering. All told, America has sent Somalia 200,000 tons of food, more than half the world total. This summer, the distribution system broke down. Truck convoys from Somalia's ports were blocked. Sufficient food failed to reach the starving in the interior of Somalia. . . .

. . . In many cases, food from relief flights is being looted upon landing; food convoys have been hijacked; aid workers assaulted; ships with food have been subject to artillery attacks that prevented them from docking. There is no government in Somalia. Law and order have broken down. Anarchy prevails.

One image tells the story. Imagine 7,000 tons of food aid literally bursting out of a warehouse on a dock in Mogadishu, while Somalis starve less than a kilometer away because relief workers cannot run the gauntlet of armed gangs roving the city. Confronted with these conditions, relief groups called for outside troops to provide security so they could feed people. It's now clear that military support is necessary to ensure the safe delivery of the food Somalis need to survive.

It was this situation which led us to tell the United Nations that the United States would be willing to provide more help to enable relief to be delivered. Last night the United Nations Security Council, by unanimous vote and after the tireless efforts of Secretary-General Boutros-Ghali, welcomed the United States offer to lead a coalition to get the food through.

After consulting with my advisers, with world leaders, and the congressional leadership, I have today told Secretary-General Boutros-Ghali that America will answer the call. . . . As I speak, a Marine amphibious ready group, which we maintain at sea, is offshore Mogadishu. . . . These and other American forces will assist in Operation Restore Hope. They are America's finest. They will perform this mission with courage and compassion, and they will succeed.

The people of Somalia, especially the children of Somalia, need our help. We're able to ease their suffering. We must help them live. We must give them hope. America must act.

Mogadishu businessman. Both men were members of the Hawiye clan of the United Somali Congress (USC), but they hailed from different subclans. Ali Mahdi Mahammad had considerable political support, especially among his Agbal subclan, but Aydid had a more effective fighting force. In late 1991, the two sides clashed for several months in the streets of Mogadishu. International relief organizations of the United Nations withdrew from the country because of the complete lack of security, leaving only the International Committee of the Red Cross and some private agencies to cope with the growing famine. Regional diplomatic efforts failed.

In February, 1992, a cease-fire was agreed upon and a special coordinator was appointed to reinitiate a U.N. presence. These efforts failed, however, and Secretary-General Boutros Boutros-Ghali of the United Nations called for a more concerted international effort. The U.N. Security Council responded by creating the United Nations Operation in Somalia (UNOSOM, later known as UNOSOM I), which was directed by Mohamed Sahnoun. This ill-fated effort was underfunded and met with strong Somali resistance. The famine deepened during 1992, and relief supplies could not be delivered because of the ongoing civil war. Boutros-Ghali and Sahnoun clashed over how the United Nations should respond, and the latter resigned in September, just before a planned national reconciliation conference.

Matters deteriorated further as death rates from starvation and disease skyrocketed. Facing this grim humanitarian situation, the Bush administration, in its waning months in office, offered to deploy U.S. troops to provide security for relief supplies. Bush dispatched special envoy Robert B. Oakley to negotiate smooth entry for U.S. forces with Somali factional leaders, and U.S. forces, designated the Unified Task Force (UNITAF), were on the ground by December 9, 1992, with assistance from military units of Canada, France, Italy, Belgium, and Morocco.

The troops initially received a hero's welcome from the Somali people and cautious acquiescence from the Somali factions. Within a month, Mogadishu and key regional cities had been secured, relief supplies were reaching famine-stricken areas, and the emergency situation had been greatly stabilized—but the political situation remained tenuous. Diplomatic efforts to restore the local elders' influence, to establish an interim police force, and quietly to impound the large caches of weapons were initiated.

Public support for Operation Restore Hope was strong among Americans in the beginning. Most U.S. citizens perceived the operation as being consistent with American humanitarian policies, even though the United States paid for three-fourths of the UNITAF expenses. The problems came after the United States handed over authority to a reconstituted UNOSOM, known as UNOSOM II. President Clinton, a newcomer to foreign policy, was eager to reduce the U.S. presence in the region and for the United Nations to take overall operational control. Oakley, the American special envoy, finished his assignment in March, 1993. Later in the same month, UNITAF functions were transferred formally to UNOSOM II, and the U.S. Marines began to withdraw from Somalia, leaving a much smaller U.S. contingent of four thousand to join UNOSOM II.

## SIGNIFICANCE

With the United Nations taking a more direct role, Aydid's forces became bolder in resistance to UNOSOM II. Aydid greatly resented Secretary-General Boutros-Ghali and took an early opportunity to challenge him. SNA forces attacked a Pakistani patrol in early June, 1993, killing many. Boutros-Ghali called the action a war crime and Aydid a criminal. U.N. forces began a cat-and-mouse effort to capture Aydid, and UNOSOM II became increasingly unpopular among Somalis.

In early October, 1993, U.S. units of UNOSOM II engaged in a running gun battle with Aydid's forces and suffered more than ninety casualties, including eighteen dead. This event stirred outrage in the United States and sparked calls for complete U.S. withdrawal. Bowing to political pressure, the Clinton administration agreed to withdraw all U.S. forces by March 31, 1994.

The vast majority of U.S. forces were withdrawn from Somalia by the summer of 1994, although several thousand U.S. troops were deployed in 1995 to provide security for the complete withdrawal of U.N. forces, leaving Somalis to work out a political solution for themselves, a task that continued to elude almost all efforts by the badly divided political forces in the country.

Southern Somalia remained in a state of continual instability following the withdrawal of international forces despite several efforts to establish transitional governments. The Somaliland Republic, by contrast, proved to be an island of stability and increasingly of democratic politics; despite these remarkable successes, however, the international community stubbornly resisted recognizing that nation.

In northeastern Somalia, Puntland declared autonomy in 1998 from the conflict-ridden south, indicating that future reunification would depend on the restoration of order. Jubaland also proclaimed autonomy in 1998, although it was absorbed by Southwestern Somalia, which was proclaimed an autonomous state in 2002. This area's leaders moved toward union with Somalia's transitional government in 2005.

—*Robert F. Gorman*

## FURTHER READING

Clarke, Walter, and Jeffrey Herbst, eds. *Learning from Somalia: The Lessons of Armed Humanitarian Intervention.* Boulder, Colo.: Westview Press, 1997. Collection of essays by observers and, in some cases, participants in the U.S. intervention sheds light on various aspects of the actions taken in Somalia.

Ghalib, Jama Mohammed. *The Cost of Dictatorship: The Somali Experience.* New York: Lilian Barber, 1995. A fascinating autobiographical account of life under the Siad Barre regime.

Hirsch, John L., and Robert B. Oakley. *Somalia and Operation Restore Hope: Reflections on Peacemaking and Peacekeeping.* Washington, D.C.: U.S. Institute for Peace, 1995. An informative account of Operation Restore Hope by two men with practical experience.

Makinda, Samuel M. *Seeking Peace from Chaos: Humanitarian Intervention in Somalia.* Boulder, Colo.: Lynne Rienner, 1993. A brief analysis of the Somalia civil war and the early phases of Operation Restore Hope.

Sahnoun, Mohamed. *Somalia: The Missed Opportunities.* Washington, D.C.: U.S. Institute for Peace, 1994. A somewhat biased critique of the U.N. handling of the Somali humanitarian crisis, written by the U.N. diplomat responsible for implementation of UNOSOM I.

Samatar, Ahmed I., ed. *The Somali Challenge: From Catastrophe to Renewal?* Boulder, Colo.: Lynne Rienner, 1994. A collection of perceptive essays that assess why Somalia collapsed and how it might restore itself.

SEE ALSO: July 23, 1977-Mar. 15, 1978: Ogaden War Between Somalia and Ethiopia; Feb. 21, 1992: United Nations Authorizes Troop Deployment to the Balkans; Dec. 16, 1992: U.N. Security Council Brokers Peace in Mozambique; July 31, 1994: United Nations Authorizes the Use of Force in Haiti.

1992

## December 16, 1992
# U.N. SECURITY COUNCIL BROKERS PEACE IN MOZAMBIQUE

*The United Nations Operation in Mozambique pacified that nation after nearly two decades of civil war. Peacekeeping troops, police, and civil administrators demobilized the contending national and international forces in the country, organized a reconstituted national defense force, and organized a national electoral process to sustain the peaceful, constitutional transfer of political power.*

**ALSO KNOWN AS:** United Nations Operation in Mozambique

**LOCALE:** Mozambique

**CATEGORIES:** Diplomacy and international relations; United Nations; government and politics

### KEY FIGURES

*Samora Machel* (1933-1986), head of FRELIMO and first president of Mozambique, 1975-1986

*Joaquim Chissano* (b. 1939), second president of Mozambique, 1986-2005

*Afonso Dhlakama* (b. 1953), head of RENAMO

### SUMMARY OF EVENT

On December 16, 1992, the United Nations Security Council established the United Nations Operation in Mozambique, known as ONUMOZ (from its name in French, Opération des Nations Unies au Mozambique). The agency was given extraordinary responsibility. Its duties were to demobilize the country after nearly two decades of civil war and supervise elections that would support its transition to a multiparty democracy. The basis for the mandate of ONUMOZ was the peace agreement signed in Rome on October 4, 1992, between the two contenders in the civil war, Frente de Libertação de Moçambique (the Mozambique Liberation Front, or FRELIMO) and the Resistência Nacional Moçambicana (the Mozambican National Resistance, or RENAMO). The former was headed by Joaquim Chissano, the president of Mozambique; the latter was led by Afonso Dhlakama.

In 1974, the authoritarian regime that had governed Portugal for nearly half a century was overthrown. The new Portuguese regime granted independence to the country's colonies, most of which were in Africa. Among these was Mozambique, on the southeast coast of Africa. To the north of Mozambique lay Tanzania; to the northwest, Malawi and Zambia; to the west, Rhodesia (later Zimbabwe); and to the south, Swaziland and South Af-

rica. The country was of strategic geopolitical and economic importance. Its location made it a crucial center for controlling access both to the Indian Ocean and the interior of Southern Africa. The Zambezi River, the fourth-longest river in Africa, penetrated the interior of the country, which was rich in strategic minerals. The rival interests of Mozambique's neighboring countries and of international powers provoked a prolonged series of conflicts that continued for much of the final part of the twentieth century, producing the bloodiest warfare in the modern history of the region.

FRELIMO had emerged in the decade of the 1960's as an anticolonialist, armed independence movement. It was supported by Tanzania, a newly independent former British colony created from the union of Tanganyika and Zanzibar. FRELIMO thus concentrated its combat efforts in the north of Mozambique. With the achievement of Angolan independence in 1975, FRELIMO became the government of the new country. Initially, it was under the Marxist leadership of Samora Machel, the first president of Mozambique, who was supported internationally by the Soviet Union. After his death in an airplane crash in 1986, party leadership and the presidency of the country passed to Joaquim Chissano, who led the country away from its Marxist orientation.

Just as Mozambique had received support for independence from Tanzania, so the new country supported the opposition movements to the white-dominated governments of Rhodesia and South Africa. Rhodesia, therefore, sought to destabilize the Mozambique government. It supported the foundation of RENAMO under the leadership of the anti-Communist guerrilla fighter Afonso Dhlakama and provided RENAMO with arms, funding, and a safe haven. However, the white-dominated regime of Rhodesia collapsed, and in 1980 the victors renamed the country Zimbabwe. South Africa and the United States thereby became the principal supporters of RENAMO.

During the decade of the 1980's, an unprecedented crescendo of violence grew in Mozambique as neighboring countries and regional and international powers fought there. Beyond the conflict between FRELIMO and RENAMO, there was the alliance known as Front Line States (those countries bordering South Africa) backing Mozambique under FRELIMO and South Africa backing RENAMO and its counterrevolution effort. Furthermore, FRELIMO had the international support of the Soviet Union and China; RENAMO had the support of the United States.

The intensity of conflict and a scourge of drought in Mozambique produced nearly six million displaced persons and refugees, approximately one-third of the country's population. Hundreds of thousands were killed or died of starvation in what was among the largest human-made and natural disasters in modern African history. Land mines planted throughout the country caused many fatalities and injuries.

The conflict abated toward the end of the 1980's, and a peace process that was begun in 1992 managed to make some progress. The clergy of the country, particularly the Catholic hierarchy, became increasingly active in efforts to quell the violence. Moreover, the support of the Soviet Union ended as Communism collapsed there. Furthermore, the force of South Africa withered as its white-dominated regime came to an end. FRELIMO relinquished its Marxist orientation and agreed to establish a multiparty system, and RENAMO agreed to transform itself from a guerrilla movement into a political party.

After a series of negotiations in Rome, the Mozambique government and RENAMO signed a peace agreement on October 4, 1992, and on December 16, 1992, the United Nations Security Council authorized ONUMOZ. Its duties were to supervise a cease-fire, demobilize the contending parties, and reconstitute the country's armed forces. For this purpose, ONUMOZ installed seventy-five hundred peacekeepers in the country; the force comprised troops, police, and civil administrators. Beyond these immediate tasks, ONUMOZ had to organize and supervise national elections that would put into place a framework for a functioning democracy. The Rome peace agreement called for elections to be scheduled for October 27-28, 1994. By that date, a National Elections Commission had been established, and it successfully conducted the elections under the supervision of more than two thousand international observers. ONUMOZ also progressively disarmed RENAMO forces and established the new Mozambican Defense Force.

## SIGNIFICANCE
ONUMOZ effectively achieved most of its objectives during its two-year mission. It disarmed rebel forces, reorganized national defense, and established an electoral framework that incorporated dissidents into a peaceful political process. In the national elections of 1994 and 1999, Chissano defeated Dhlakama for the presidency. The latter claimed that electoral fraud had taken place, and some violence resulted, but the electoral process remained a stable framework for political change. In 2004, the FRELIMO successor to Chissano, Armando Guebuza, defeated Dhlakama for the presidency.

Several factors contributed to the success of ONUMOZ. FRELIMO had adopted a position favorable to market economics and liberal democracy. Moreover, the outside forces that had intervened in the country, the white regime of South Africa and the Communist government of the Soviet Union, had disappeared by the early 1990's. In addition, numerous countries and international agencies provided financial support in amounts totaling more than one billion dollars to rebuild the country. The overwhelming desire of the Mozambican people was for the conflict to end, as it had devastated the lives of almost everyone in the country. In this regard, therefore, all

---

## THE ONUMOZ MANDATE

*The United Nations Operation in Mozambique (ONUMOZ) was established by Resolution 797 of December 16, 1992, to help implement the General Peace Agreement, signed on October 4, 1992, by the president of Mozambique, Joaquim Chissano, and the leader of Mozambican National Resistance (RENAMO), Afonso Dhlakama. ONUMOZ's mandate formally came to an end at midnight on December 9, 1994, and the mission was liquidated at the end of January, 1995. The ONUMOZ mandate was as follows:*

- To monitor and verify the ceasefire, the separation and concentration of forces, their demobilization and the collection, storage and destruction of weapons
- To monitor and verify the complete withdrawal of foreign forces and to provide security in the transport corridors
- To monitor and verify the disbanding of private and irregular armed groups
- To authorize security arrangements for vital infrastructures and to provide security for United Nations and other international activities in support of the peace process
- To provide technical assistance and monitor the entire electoral process
- To coordinate and monitor humanitarian assistance operations, in particular those relating to refugees, internally displaced persons, demobilized military personnel and the affected local population

substantial political sentiment and force favored the peacekeeping efforts of the United Nations.

Commitment by all parties to the maintenance of some form of consolidated and effective national government became fundamental. Mozambique experienced torrential floods during the early years of the twenty-first century after the droughts of the previous decades. The floods devastated the nation's agriculture, its export sector, and its rural and urban populations. Hidden land mines that had been put in place during the conflict continued to cause fatalities and injuries, and the spread of acquired immunodeficiency syndrome (AIDS) reached epidemic proportions. Following the ONUMOZ peacekeeping project, FRELIMO remained in power into the early years of the twenty-first century. The ultimate test of Mozambique's democratic resilience will be the continued existence of an opposition party and the peaceful transfer of power between parties through fair elections.

—*Edward A. Riedinger*

**FURTHER READING**

Cabrita, João M. *Mozambique: The Tortuous Road to Democracy*. New York: St. Martin's Press, 2000. A Mozambican journalist living in exile presents a critical analysis of the historical development, policies, and actions of FRELIMO. Includes maps, tables, and bibliography.

Chan, Stephen, and Moisés Venâncio. *War and Peace in Mozambique*. New York: St. Martin's Press, 1998. Discusses the background and the conclusion of the Mozambique conflict. Includes text of the peace agreement, election data and analysis of election results, and bibliography.

Finnegan, William. *A Complicated War: The Harrowing of Mozambique*. Berkeley: University of California Press, 1992. Presents accounts of the experiences of Mozambican refugees and civil war survivors gathered by the author in field research in his role as a writer for *The New Yorker*.

Synge, Richard. *Mozambique: U.N. Peacekeeping in Action, 1992-94*. Washington, D.C.: U.S. Institute of Peace Press, 1997. Provides detailed analysis of accomplishments and frustrations of the ONUMOZ mission, based on research in U.N. documentation and interviews with key personnel. Includes maps and bibliography.

United Nations. *The United Nations and Mozambique, 1992-1995*. New York: Author, 1995. Presents an official overview of ONUMOZ operations with compilation of relevant documents.

**SEE ALSO:** Mar. 16, 1984: South Africa and Mozambique Sign Nkomati Accord; Nov. 6, 1986: Chissano Succeeds Machel in Mozambique; Aug., 1991: African Countries Begin to Revive Democratization.

---

## December 31, 1992
# UNITED NATIONS BANS THE USE OF DRIFT NETS

*In a controversial action, the United Nations banned the extremely damaging fishing technique of using drift nets.*

**LOCALE:** New York, New York
**CATEGORIES:** Diplomacy and international relations; United Nations; animals and endangered species

**KEY FIGURES**

*Curtis Bolen* (fl. late twentieth century), assistant U.S. secretary of state for oceans and international, environmental, and scientific affairs, who actively lobbied for the U.N. drift-net ban

*William T. Burke* (fl. late twentieth century), law professor from the University of Washington who actively fought the U.N. ban on drift-net fishing

*Jolene Unsoeld* (b. 1931), U.S. congresswoman from Washington who led the fight to ban drift nets worldwide

*Frank H. Murkowski* (b. 1933), U.S. senator from Alaska who, with Unsoeld, coauthored the U.S. High Seas Driftnet Fisheries Enforcement Act

*Yannis Paleokrassas* (fl. late twentieth century), chair of the European Parliament Committee on Fisheries who lobbied strongly for the U.N. ban on drift-net fishing

**SUMMARY OF EVENT**

Drift nets, or gill nets, have been used for thousands of years in the commercial fishing industry. Fish attempt to swim through the net, become entangled in its mesh, and are caught. Such a capture technique is not selective; many types of animals, not only target commercial species, are caught when they encounter the net. In addition to fish, many birds and sea mammals, such as dolphins and whales, are indiscriminately destroyed when fishers use drift nets. During the 1989-1990 fishing season, it was estimated that from 300,000 to 1 million dolphins drowned in drift nets. It was this incidental catch that caused critics to label drift nets "curtains of death."

Between 1950 and 1990, there was a 400 percent increase in the harvest of marine fishes; more than ninety million tons of these animals were harvested in 1989. The United States, Japan, the Soviet Union and its fragments, South Korea, and Taiwan accounted for nearly 90 percent of the world's fishing effort. Between 20 percent and 50 percent of the protein ingested in many Asian and African countries comes from fish. Worldwide, some 200 million people were engaged in fishing in the 1990's. Annually, approximately $124 billion was spent to harvest about $70 billion worth of fish; government subsidies made up the difference.

Catch levels from drift-net use rose dramatically in the 1980's, and the fish harvest increased some 33 percent. Five species of fish made up most of this increased harvest: Alaskan pollack, Chilean jack mackerel, Peruvian anchovies, and Japanese and South American pilchards. This increase in the annual catch resulted primarily from the use of new technology. Sonar and radar were used to locate fish, winches and motors were developed to haul up drift nets holding forty thousand pounds or more of fish. In addition, nets became longer, and nylon replaced cotton fibers in the nets. The nylon required fewer repairs, did not deteriorate in salt water as rapidly as cotton, and was stronger than cotton, so nylon nets could catch and hold more fish. Ironically, the United Nations promoted and popularized drift-net fishing technology in the 1970's as a means to provide protein to feed rapidly increasing human populations in developing countries.

In 1982, passage of the Law of the Sea Treaty repealed the twelve-mile offshore legal boundary for coastal countries and moved this national border to two hundred miles offshore. By 1990, three-fourths of the world's fish were found in waters controlled by individual nations. Some three million or more vessels actively fished these waters. Overfishing was responsible, at least in part, for the dramatic decline in the abundance of fish in many areas of the marine ecosystem. Fish that migrate long distances and move in and out of the two-hundred-mile limits, such as tuna and swordfish, create serious management problems.

In the late 1980's, it was estimated that some $22 million worth of nontarget fish species captured by drift nets

were wasted each year. These fish were killed in the nets but then discarded by commercial fishers. Shrimp fishing was estimated to waste twenty kilograms of fish for every kilogram of shrimp caught.

In 1989, the United Nations passed a resolution restricting drift-net use in international waters and called for a global moratorium on the use of this modern technology. The administration of U.S. president George H. W. Bush lobbied hard for this moratorium and greatly aided its passage. The international moratorium on the use of drift nets grew out of activities by groups such as Greenpeace, the Bering Sea Fishermen's Association, the American Oceans Campaign, and Defenders of Wildlife. The South Pacific Forum banned the use of drift nets more than 2.5 kilometers (more than 1.5 miles) in length in the territorial waters of its member nations, which covered most of the Pacific. The United Nations stated its worldwide drift-net moratorium in General Assembly Resolution 46/215, passed on December 20, 1991; the ban became effective December 31, 1992.

## SIGNIFICANCE

U.N. General Assembly resolutions do not in themselves constitute binding obligations on U.N. member states; they are only recommendations. To enforce the terms of U.N. resolutions, member states must take action within their own domestic jurisdictions. The initiation of the recommended ban on drift nets was met with varying degrees of compliance by different governments and fishers. One year after the U.N. resolution, most nations honored the ban, but it remained a controversial subject.

Some countries were still allowing the use of drift nets many miles long. Russia, Japan, Canada, and the United States had essentially ceased using drift nets in the northern Pacific Ocean. These nations formed the North Pacific Anadromous Fish Commission to address issues facing proper management of fisheries in these northern waters. Drift nets of many miles in length all but disappeared from the North Pacific, and drift-net use essentially ceased in the South Pacific. In 1991, Japan, South Korea, and Taiwan agreed to stop deploying thirty- to forty-mile-long drift nets in the Pacific Ocean.

In response to some countries' failure to observe the U.N. ban on drift-net fishing, the U.S. Congress passed the High Seas Driftnet Fisheries Enforcement Act in 1992. This gave the U.S. Department of Commerce the power to impose sanctions, deny port privileges, or take other measures against nations that violate the U.N. ban. Early in May, 1993, the U.S. Coast Guard boarded two Chinese vessels using drift nets eight hundred miles

1992

south of Alaska and ordered both ships to return home. This was the first documented instance of violation of the U.N. resolution banning drift-net fishing. The Republic of China had promised to end drift-net use on the high seas by June, 1992.

Most of the resistance to the drift-net ban came from the European Union. On December 21, 1993, the United Nations again called for all nations to abide by the total ban on drift-net use. The European Parliament Committee on Fisheries was created to address the problems facing fishers of the European countries. Overfishing of waters bordering Europe had depleted fish stocks there, and violent incidents had occurred between fishers competing for resources. Fishers from Spain, the United Kingdom, and France battled in 1993, and in 1994 thirty violent conflicts between fishers were reported to authorities.

Within the European Union, for some time only Greece and Spain supported a total ban on drift-net fishing. After continued debate, however, in 1998 the European Union stated that by 2002 it would no longer allow the use and possession of drift nets by European vessels fishing in European waters.

—*David L. Chesemore*

## FURTHER READING

Barrett, Scott. *Environment and Statecraft: The Strategy of Environmental Treaty-Making.* New York: Oxford University Press, 2003. Scholarly work examines the difficulties involved in establishing cooperation among nations for the sake of protecting the environment. Includes discussion of overfishing and the use of drift nets.

Baum, Julian. "Nets Across the Strait: Driftnet Fishing Thrives Under Chinese Flag." *Far Eastern Economic Review*, July 8, 1993, 22. Discusses the possibility that Taiwanese boats were avoiding Taiwan's ban on drift nets by flying the Chinese flag and using Chinese ports as bases. Taiwanese fishing companies have argued that the U.N. ban on drift nets does not apply to them because Taiwan is not a member of the United Nations.

"Japan to Ban Driftnets!" *Earth Island Journal* 7 (Winter, 1992): 8. Describes plans by the Japanese government to phase out drift-net use. Discusses the criticism of drift-net use by the United Nations.

Patel, Tara. "France Thumbs Its Nose at Drift-Net Ban." *New Scientist* 142 (April 30, 1994): 8. Notes the violations of European fishing agreements by France regarding the use of drift nets that came in the wake of a proposed ban on drift nets by the European Commission. Discusses the effects of continued use of drift nets.

Rothwell, Donald R. "The General Assembly Ban on Driftnet Fishing." In *Commitment and Compliance: The Role of Non-binding Norms in the International Legal System*, edited by Dinah Shelton. New York: Oxford University Press, 2000. Discusses the U.N. ban as an illustration of the impacts of nonbinding international norms on state behavior.

"U.N. Conference on Environment and Development: Earth Summit Puts Future of Rich and Poor Alike 'in Our Hands.'" *U.N. Chronicle* 29 (March, 1992): 81. Discusses plans for the U.N. Conference on Environment and Development, known more popularly as the Earth Summit, which examined various worldwide environmental issues, including the use of drift nets.

Wehrfritz, George. "Gone Fishing: Rogue Trawlers May Be Dodging Official Driftnet Ban." *Far Eastern Economic Review*, February 25, 1993. Reveals doubts that Taiwan complied with the U.N. ban on drift nets.

SEE ALSO: 1971: Canadian Activists Found Greenpeace; Jan.-Mar., 1971: Animal Welfare Institute Launches the "Save the Whales" Campaign; Jan., 1973: Cousteau Society Is Founded; Aug., 1977: Watson Founds the Sea Shepherd Conservation Society; Jan. 1, 1986: International Whaling Ban Goes into Effect; 1993: Norway Resumes Whaling in Defiance of International Ban.

## 1993
# NORWAY RESUMES WHALING IN DEFIANCE OF INTERNATIONAL BAN

*Despite the International Whaling Commission's ban on commercial whaling, Norway resumed the practice in 1993, arguing that evidence pointed to an abundance of minke whales in the North Atlantic.*

**LOCALE:** Northeastern Atlantic Ocean

**CATEGORIES:** Diplomacy and international relations; animals and endangered species; trade and commerce

### KEY FIGURES

*Luis Fleischer* (fl. late twentieth century), chairman of the International Whaling Commission, 1991-1994

*Peter Bridgewater* (fl. late twentieth century), vice chairman of the International Whaling Commission, 1991-1994

*Philip Hammond* (fl. late twentieth century), population biologist and chair of the Scientific Committee of the International Whaling Commission in the early 1990's

*Gro Harlem Brundtland* (b. 1939), prime minister of Norway, 1981, 1986-1989, and 1990-1996, who supported Norwegian whaling despite her position as a leading environmentalist

*Lars Walløe* (b. 1938), physiologist and Norwegian representative to the International Whaling Commission who strongly supported Norwegian whaling

### SUMMARY OF EVENT

Norway has a rich and venerable whaling tradition. Four-thousand-year-old Norwegian rocks are etched with pictures of men killing whales and dolphins. Subsistence whaling in the North Atlantic was probably developed and spread by the Norse. Although the Basques around the Bay of Biscay in Spain and France are generally credited with the invention of commercial whaling, they probably learned whaling techniques from the Norwegians. Modern whaling technology is also based on Norwegian ingenuity. The harpoon gun, the explosive harpoon, and the factory ship are all Norwegian inventions.

Norway also pioneered accountability and management in the whaling industry. In the 1920's, Norway set up the Bureau of International Whaling Statistics to publish reports on the numbers of whales taken each season. In 1946, Norway was instrumental in establishing the International Whaling Commission (IWC) to oversee whaling in such a way that whales would be conserved

and the future of whaling ensured. Norway contributed significantly to whaling and to its management; along with other whaling nations and the IWC, however, Norway was slow to recognize the effect of the commercial practice on whale populations. As a result, many species were reduced to population sizes dangerously near extinction.

Early in its history, the IWC was essentially a "whalers' club." Despite the organization's dual mission—to protect whale populations and to support the whaling industry—the conservation of whales always took a backseat to the whaling nations' desire to hunt whales. Catch limits were always set far above the limits suggested by the admittedly meager scientific information. In some years, the limits were set so high that the whalers were unable to reach them. Even this warning was ignored by whalers and the IWC.

The IWC gradually became primarily a whale conservation organization, however, as the world's environmental consciousness grew; as studies on whale brain size, songs, and other sounds sometimes interpreted as languages suggested that the animals had substantial intellectual abilities; and, perhaps most important, as some member countries ceased whaling because of declining whale populations. This shift occurred in the late 1960's and throughout the 1970's. Some IWC member nations, Norway among them, resisted the shift. Because of the low limits the IWC wanted to set for the 1959-1960 whaling season, Norway and the Netherlands withdrew from the commission and set their own limits for that season. The IWC set no limits for the next two seasons (1960-1961 and 1961-1962) in the hope that Norway and the Netherlands would rejoin the commission. In the three whaling seasons from 1959 to 1962, the catch in Antarctic waters fell far short of quotas. Norway rejoined the commission in 1960, and the Netherlands rejoined in 1962.

Despite the whalers' inability to reach their self-imposed quotas, and despite much lower quotas recommended by the IWC's Scientific Committee, which had been set up in 1961, the 1962-1963 IWC quota for Antarctic whales was set only a little lower than the unfilled quotas of the preceding years. Again, the actual catch fell far short of the quota. As a result, Norway and some other nations began to reduce their Antarctic whaling efforts. Quotas were subsequently reduced dramatically to reflect the estimates of the Scientific Committee. Over the next decade, the commission's emphasis shifted to con-

1993

servation of whale stocks, culminating in a 1982 moratorium on whaling. The moratorium became fully functional in 1986 and allowed exceptions only for scientific research and for indigenous cultures for which whaling was an aboriginal activity.

Although collecting information on whale populations and predicting sustainable yields for a stock was more an art than a science, most whale observers believed that stocks grew appreciably after the cessation of whaling. In 1992, the IWC's Scientific Committee suggested that minke whale populations in the Antarctic and in the North Atlantic had grown large enough to sustain some whaling. The IWC refused to follow the suggestion, however, continuing its policy of disregarding science in decisions relating to whaling (although in this case reversing the direction of discrimination). The commission also refused to declare a quota under a revised management procedure set up by the Scientific Committee.

In response, Iceland withdrew from the commission and announced its intent to renew whaling activities. Japan continued to carry out research whaling, which many observers considered to be a cover for commercial whaling. Norway also remained involved in scientific whaling and produced its own quota for minke whales in the North Atlantic. At the 1993 meeting of the IWC, Norway declared its intention to resume hunting minke whales, setting a quota of 296 whales for that year. International response was intensely negative. Members of the Sea Shepherd Conservation Society attempted to block Norway's whaling by placing their boats (and bodies) between the whalers and their prey. Many groups, including Greenpeace (which had invented the Sea Shepherd tactic), encouraged trade sanctions against Norway. Norway nevertheless took 226 whales in 1993 and set a quota of 301 for 1994.

## SIGNIFICANCE

Many considered the struggle for the conservation of whale populations to be a model for resource conservation in general. The IWC ban and Norway's resistance highlighted three factors that often restrict the making of optimal conservation decisions: First, scientific evidence usually does not suggest irrefutable conclusions; second, moral and ethical considerations enter into the decision-making process and make reaching a consensus even more difficult; and third, given economic and political constraints, international (and national) organizations are often not free to act on even the strongest scientific and ethical evidence.

Norway calculated the sustainable yield for its minke whale hunt (the number of whales that could be killed in a given whaling season and replaced by whale reproduction before the next season) using methods developed by the IWC Scientific Committee. Some whale experts believed, however, that the Norwegians failed to make corrections for whales that had been counted more than once and thus overestimated the whale population, which led them to allow an unsustainable harvest. The Norwegian calculation arrived at an estimate of sustainable yield of nearly three hundred minke whales for 1993; critics contended that correct calculations would have indicated a sustainable yield of one minke whale. The inaccuracy of the whale count made it impossible to determine which, if either, yield calculation was correct.

Poor understanding of interactions between the different whale species and their resources further complicated the scientific picture. The Japanese pointed out that, in the Antarctic, the minke whale populations were higher than they were thought to have been before whaling began. They interpreted this as evidence both that minke populations were kept down by competition with other whale species and that high minke populations might slow the recovery of other whales. Skeptics pointed out that evidence for competition between the minke and other whales was not convincing; the minke whale, for example, is known to take more fish and more kinds of crustaceans than the blue whale, suggesting minimal competition between the two. These and many other considerations made the determination of appropriate conservation strategies exceptionally complex.

That determination, however, is simple compared to the moral and ethical questions involved. In the context of any animal conservation, the most basic question is, Do humans have a right to kill other species? Whales are among the most charismatic of organisms. The large size, mysterious lives, haunting songs and calls, large brains, and imputed intelligence of whales have led some people to place them at the pinnacle of the animal world. To these people, the killing of whales is criminal. Studies have suggested, however, that whales' intelligence is probably not superior to that of many other mammals, given that whales' brains are not especially large for their bodies (brain size compared to body size is a better measure of intellect than is absolute brain size).

Whales certainly use songs and calls to communicate, but these are probably no more sophisticated than the songs and calls of many other mammals. Presumed demonstrations of whales' superior emotional and ethical capacities, such as instances of their pushing drowning swimmers to shore, are probably outnumbered by instances in which they were not so helpful and pushed swimmers away from shore. In short, most scientists see whales as no more intellectual or sentient than other mammals. Nevertheless, the conviction that all animals have greater reasoning and emotional capacities than previously believed has continued to grow among scientists and the general public, generating questions about the human right to kill animals.

Even some people who believe that humans do have the right to kill and use animals have questioned the cruelty of whaling. The issue of whether whalers' means of killing are any more cruel than other hunting methods, or than methods for killing domesticated animals, has been debated extensively. Norway's defiance of the IWC's ban on whaling also raised the question of whether humans, with their presumed superior moral and ethical codes, should kill only with demonstrably humane techniques.

Ultimately, the Norwegian position on whaling emphasized the inability of national and international conservation organizations to act on the basis of either scientific evidence or moral-ethical principles. Instead, decisions are often made according to political expediency. Early in its history, the IWC repeatedly acted against strong evidence that whaling harvests were too high to be sustained and set quotas that allowed such harvests. After the shift in public opinion in the 1970's— and despite evidence that harvests of minke whales, at least in the Antarctic, could be sustained and might even be necessary to allow rapid recovery of other species— the IWC continued to deny whalers access to the resource. A second example bore more directly on the Norwegian situation. The IWC allowed Arctic Natives of North America to hunt the bowhead whale, which was far more endangered than the minke. The reasoning behind the discrepancy, although complex, was essentially political. Certainly, the inconsistency did nothing to advance conservation goals.

At the 1994 meeting of the IWC, most of the world's oceans south of 40 degrees south latitude were declared a whale sanctuary, off-limits to commercial whaling for at least ten years. This action and the whaling moratorium of 1982 were likely made possible only by the whales' charisma. Norway's challenge to the moratorium emphasized how important it was for the IWC to develop a consistent position with regard to regulation of whaling. The controversy also demonstrated that conservation and governmental organizations, national and international, needed to achieve and maintain consistent and effective positions regarding the conservation of resources at all levels and of all types.

In the years since the IWC's 1994 meeting, pro-whaling forces have grown in the commission and have challenged the moratorium on whaling, which has been preserved by only the barest of majorities. The IWC has granted the expansion of whaling for scientific purposes, and in its 2006 St. Kitts and Nevis Declaration, the IWC for the first time in many years expressed support for a return to regulated commercial whaling, suggesting erosion of the more conservation-minded bent of earlier decades.

*—Carl W. Hoagstrom*

## FURTHER READING

Birnie, Patricia, ed. *International Regulation of Whaling: From Conservation of Whaling to Conservation of Whales and Regulation of Whale Watching*. Dobbs Ferry, N.Y.: Oceana, 1985. Considers the conversion of the IWC from an organization dedicated to the continuation of whaling to one attempting to ensure the protection of whales. Includes bibliography.

Butterworth, Douglas S. "Science and Sentimentality." *Nature* 357 (June 18, 1992): 532-534. Argues the pros and cons of the scientific, as opposed to sentimental, approach to whaling regulation. In May, June, or July of each year (depending on the time of the IWC meetings), this periodical's "News" section reports on the IWC proceedings.

Day, David. *The Whale War*. San Francisco: Sierra Club Books, 1987. Presents an interesting description of the struggle to save the whales, written from the environmentalist perspective. Includes illustrations and index.

Freeman, Milton M. R. "The International Whaling Commission, Small-Type Whaling, and Coming to Terms with Subsistence." *Human Organization* 52 (Fall, 1993): 243-251. Thoughtfully compares subsistence whaling, which is allowed by the IWC, and small, traditional whaling operations such as Norway's, which are not allowed. Includes bibliographic references.

Friedheim, Robert L., ed. *Toward a Sustainable Whaling Regime*. Seattle: University of Washington Press, 2001. Collection of essays explores the possibilities for establishing viable international cooperation in the management of whales and whaling.

Horwood, Joseph. *Biology and Exploitation of the Minke Whale*. Boca Raton, Fla.: Chemical Rubber Company Press, 1990. Provides a thorough and well-written description of the minke whale's biology and the history

1993

of its exploitation. Includes illustrations, bibliography, and index.

McHugh, J. L. "The Role and History of the International Whaling Commission." In *The Whale Problem: A Status Report*, edited by William E. Schevill. Cambridge, Mass.: Harvard University Press, 1974. Historically interesting because it was written during the time of transition of the IWC from "whalers' club" to whale conservation organization. Considers Norway's pioneering efforts in whaling and in regulating whaling.

MacKenzie, Debora. "Whales Win Southern Sanctuary." *New Scientist*, June 4, 1994. Report on the 1994 IWC meeting includes an explanation of Norway's purported calculation error. This general weekly science magazine follows whaling issues, and in May, June, or July each year (depending when the IWC meetings are held), the section titled "This Week" reports on the IWC proceedings.

Plutte, Will. "The Whaling Imperative: Why Norway Whales." *Oceans*, March, 1984, 24-26. Attempts to explain the reluctance of Norwegians to give up whaling. Another article in the issue explores the transformation of the IWC from a whalers' organization into a whale-conservation organization. Includes illustrations.

Victor, David G., Kal Raustiala, and Eugene B. Skolnikoff, eds. *The Implementation and Effectiveness of International Environmental Commitments: Theory and Practice*. Cambridge, Mass.: MIT Press, 1998. Collection of essays examines how environmental policies are put into practice on an international level. Includes numerous case studies and some discussion of Norway's whaling regime.

**SEE ALSO:** 1971: Canadian Activists Found Greenpeace; Jan.-Mar., 1971: Animal Welfare Institute Launches the "Save the Whales" Campaign; Jan., 1973: Cousteau Society Is Founded; Aug., 1977: Watson Founds the Sea Shepherd Conservation Society; Jan. 1, 1986: International Whaling Ban Goes into Effect; Dec. 31, 1992: United Nations Bans the Use of Drift Nets.

# January 1, 1993
# CZECHOSLOVAKIA SPLITS INTO TWO REPUBLICS

*The splitting of Czechoslovakia into two republics—in a peaceful process that came to be known as the Velvet Divorce—offered a sharp contrast to the violent breakup of Yugoslavia at roughly the same time.*

**ALSO KNOWN AS:** Velvet Divorce

**LOCALE:** Czechoslovakia (now Czech Republic and Slovakia)

**CATEGORIES:** Government and politics; diplomacy and international relations

**KEY FIGURES**

*Václav Havel* (b. 1936), president of Czechoslovakia, 1989-1992, and president of the Czech Republic, 1993-2003

*Václav Klaus* (b. 1941), prime minister of the Czech Republic, 1993-1997

*Vladimír Mečiar* (b. 1942), leader of the Movement for a Democratic Slovakia and prime minister of Slovakia intermittently beginning in June, 1990

**SUMMARY OF EVENT**

The victors of World War I created Czechoslovakia, along with a number of other countries, out of territories that had belonged to the defeated Austro-Hungarian Empire. The new Czechoslovakian state drew together the "Czech lands" of Bohemia and Moravia with the northern Hungarian territory of Slovakia. Czechoslovakia's population thus largely comprised two western Slavic peoples, the Czechs and the Slovaks. Soon after the creation of the country, leaders of these national groups argued over the structure of the government and the relative autonomy of the two peoples. The Czechs tended to prefer a more unified state, which the Slovaks feared would be a vehicle for Czech political, economic, and cultural domination.

Czechoslovakia was taken over and dismembered by Nazi Germany in 1938; it was resurrected when the war ended in 1945. A Soviet-sponsored coup d'état in 1948 imposed a highly centralized Communist regime. After a short-lived popular rebellion in 1968 known as the Prague Spring, the Soviets reimposed strict Communist control. This time, however, Czechoslovakia was structured as a federation, consisting of separate Czech and Slovak republics. For the next two decades, dissident movements maintained pressure against the Soviet-backed regime, demanding democratic and political reforms and an end to human rights violations. The 1975

Helsinki Accords provided these groups with a link to the international community. One of the most popular and powerful of the post-Helsinki groups was Charter 77, founded in February, 1977, by several hundred Czech citizens. One of Charter 77's leaders was Václav Havel, a playwright by profession; Havel was repeatedly jailed for his activities and writings.

In 1989, Czechoslovakia decisively overthrew its Soviet-sponsored government in what has come to be known as the Velvet Revolution. The Velvet Revolution, which occurred near the end of the series of Eastern European revolutions that took place in the fall of 1989, was notable for its breathtaking speed and lack of bloodshed. Havel and other Charter 77 leaders had formed a new movement, Civic Forum, which placed unrelenting pressure on the Soviet-backed regime. Abandoned by his Soviet patrons, the Czechoslovak president, Gustáv Husák, resigned on December 9. Havel was unanimously elected president by the Federal Assembly (parliament), which itself was soon replaced through free elections.

No sooner had Czechoslovakia become free of Soviet domination, however, than the issues of state unity and Slovakian autonomy reemerged. Slovakians had always felt dominated within the federation by the more populous and wealthy Czechs. From the time of Czechoslovakia's creation, Slovakia was less industrialized, less connected with the West, and less tied to Western capital investment. After the fall of the socialist regime, Slovakians feared that the economic reform policies pursued by the new central government would be too jarring for their more agrarian and isolated economy. The calls for Slovakian autonomy were meant to address the perceived inequality between the constituent peoples of Czechoslovakia. They also gave voice to a growing nationalist movement among Slovakians.

In an initial, symbolic move to placate Slovakian separatism, the Federal Assembly changed the country's name to the Czech and Slovak Federal Republic in early

1990. This gesture, however, only whetted Slovakians' appetites for further redress of the perceived injustices against them. In countrywide elections in June, 1990—the first truly free elections since the country was drawn into the Soviet bloc—parties advocating Slovakian autonomy gained considerable support. This affected the cohesiveness of the national government, and not only in the legislative branch. As president of Czechoslovakia, Havel had initially enjoyed popular support based on his political reputation as a leader of the Velvet Revolution. He was a Czech, however, and before long Slovakians began to perceive him as another manifestation of the Czechs' domination of the country.

The Slovakian republican government, based in Bratislava, demanded greater decentralization of economic policy making. Sometimes the federal government in Prague relented, and sometimes it insisted on maintain-

1993

2697

*Slovak prime minister Vladimír Mečiar (left) and Czech prime minister Václav Klaus in Piešťany, Slovakia, in 1997, before they began their first talks since the split of Czechoslovakia.* (AP/Wide World Photos)

ing national unity. All the while, Bratislava increasingly postured as an independent government. In the fall of 1990, for example, it established its own "Ministry for International Relations," implying that it developed its own foreign policies.

There was some disagreement among the Slovakian parties as to their ultimate goals. Some promoted a looser federation, some confederation, and still others outright secession. Over time, however, the more nationalistic, separatist groups solidified power. A turning point occurred on June 5-6, 1992, when new legislative strength shifted from the parties associated with Civic Forum and the Velvet Revolution to more nationalistic parties from both republics. As a result, Vladimír Mečiar, a man firmly committed to Slovakian independence (although perhaps not secession), was elected prime minister of Slovakia. At the same time, Slovakian opposition in the

Federal Assembly foiled Havel's reelection bid. A breakup of the country seemed almost certain. On July 17, 1992, the Slovak National Council declared Slovakia an "independent country." It was unclear what this declaration meant as a practical matter.

On the other side of the federation, Czech nationalism also was growing, largely as a reaction to perceived Slovakian insolence. In the fall of 1991, the Czech National Council passed a resolution declaring any Slovakian assertion of sovereignty unconstitutional. After Slovakia's declaration of independence in July, 1992, however, Czech leaders formally agreed to negotiate a dissolution of the federation. Most Slovakians were taken by surprise, and not a few were somewhat worried that their brinkmanship had gone too far.

On July 23, 1992, Mečiar and Czech prime minister Václav Klaus established procedures to hammer out a "divorce" between the two republics. Subsequent discussions expanded in scope to cover the most minute details, such as the division of file cabinets owned by the federal government. By the late fall of 1992, the two sides had arrived at an agreement. The Federal Assembly approved the separation plans in November, and several dozen agreements were signed to formalize the country's division and to establish relations between the successor states. Czechoslovakia officially dissolved into its constituent republics on January 1, 1993.

## SIGNIFICANCE

The two new states, the Czech Republic and Slovakia, or the Slovak Republic, were immediately recognized by the other countries of Europe as well as by nations around the world and received membership in the United Nations. Both later became members of the European Union. The manner in which the split played out—in a peaceful process that came to be known as the Velvet Divorce—offered a sharp contrast to the violent breakup of Yugoslavia at roughly the same time, along with some optimism concerning the aftermath of Soviet dissolution and its impact on geopolitics.

*—Steve D. Boilard*

## FURTHER READING

Bugajski, Janusz. "Central European Disputes." In *Nations in Turmoil: Conflict and Cooperation in Eastern Europe.* 2d ed. Boulder, Colo.: Westview Press, 1995. Presents an overview of political conflicts among different national groups in central Europe in the twentieth century, with particular emphasis on the immediate post-Cold War years. Includes notes and illustrations.

Innes, Abby. *Czechoslovakia: The Short Goodbye.* New Haven, Conn.: Yale University Press, 2001. Presents an in-depth analysis of the causes and consequences of the breakup of Czechoslovakia, placing the events within the context of the history of the Czechoslovak state. Includes photographs, bibliography, and index.

Leff, Carol Skalnik. *National Conflict in Czechoslovakia: The Making and Remaking of a State, 1918-1987.* Princeton, N.J.: Princeton University Press, 1988.

Written scarcely a year before the revolutionary process liberated and divided Czechoslovakia, this sweeping historical account suffers from bad timing, but its detailed exploration of the nationalism that pulled at the Czechoslovakian state throughout its seventy-five years makes it indispensable for fully understanding the Velvet Divorce.

Rosenberg, Tina. *The Haunted Land: Facing Europe's Ghosts After Communism.* New York: Random House, 1995. The first section of this volume presents an engaging narrative that explores the demise of Communism in Czechoslovakia and the problems that subsequently arose. Includes discussion of the Velvet Revolution. Features glossary of names and selected bibliography.

Stokes, Gale. *The Walls Came Tumbling Down: The Collapse of Communism in Eastern Europe.* New York: Oxford University Press, 1993. Although written before the formal division of Czechoslovakia, provides critical background leading up to the Velvet Divorce. Chapter 5 examines the revolutions of 1989, including Czechoslovakia's Velvet Revolution. Chapter 6 explores the revolutions' aftermath, including the growing split between Czechs and Slovakians.

Svec, Milan. "Czechoslovakia's Velvet Divorce." *Current History* 91 (November, 1992): 376-380. Briefly summarizes the events leading up to the Velvet Revolution, with particular emphasis on economic matters. Written several months before the formal division of the country, this article concludes that Czechoslovakia's breakup "seems all but certain."

Whipple, Tim D., ed. *After the Velvet Revolution: Václav Havel and the New Leaders of Czechoslovakia Speak Out.* New York: Freedom House, 1991. Although compiled before the Velvet Divorce, this collection of speeches and writings by the architects of the Velvet Revolution conveys a sense of the political problems that confronted post-Cold War Czechoslovakia.

**SEE ALSO:** Nov. 17-Dec. 29, 1989: Velvet Revolution in Czechoslovakia; Feb. 26, 1990: Soviet Troops Withdraw from Czechoslovakia.

1993

**January 3, 1993**

# UNITED STATES AND RUSSIA REACH NUCLEAR ARMS REDUCTION AGREEMENT

*The United States and Russia commited to deep reductions in their nuclear arsenals and inaugurated a post-Cold War environment of reduced superpower threats with the second treaty to come out of the Strategic Arms Reduction Talks.*

**ALSO KNOWN AS:** START II
**LOCALE:** Moscow, Russia
**CATEGORY:** Diplomacy and international relations

**KEY FIGURES**

*George H. W. Bush* (b. 1924), president of the United States, 1989-1993
*Boris Yeltsin* (1931-2007), president of the Russian Soviet Federated Socialist Republic, 1991-1999
*James Baker* (b. 1930), U.S. secretary of state, 1989-1992
*Lawrence Eagleburger* (b. 1930), U.S. secretary of state, December, 1992-January, 1993
*Andrei Kozyrev* (b. 1951), foreign minister of the Russian Federation

**SUMMARY OF EVENT**

For decades after the end of World War II, the United States and the Soviet Union amassed ever-increasing numbers of weapons. For most of that time, arms control agreements were elusive. The continuous improvement in East-West relations in the late 1980's paved the way for unprecedented agreements to reverse the arms race in Europe, including the treaty to eliminate intermediate-range nuclear forces (INF) in 1987 and to cut conventional forces in Europe (CFE) significantly in 1990. A year later, culminating almost a decade of arms control talks initiated by President Ronald Reagan, the United States and the Soviet Union signed an agreement to reduce strategic nuclear weapons, which by definition threatened the territory of the superpowers themselves. Only months after the first treaty of the Strategic Arms Reduction Talks, or START, was signed, however, the Soviet Union dissolved into fifteen sovereign countries.

The United States and the former Soviet republics—particularly Russia—set about to restructure their relationships in the post-Soviet, post-Cold War world. In terms of nuclear arms, two issues were paramount. First, how could START be implemented when one of its signatories no longer existed? It was agreed at a meeting in Lisbon, Portugal, on May 23, 1992, that all the former

Soviet republics would be bound by the treaty, that Russia would possess the remaining, permitted nuclear weapons, and that the other former Soviet republics would commit to forgo the acquisition of any nuclear arms. The second issue was how the nuclear reductions called for in START could be extended, acknowledging that the Cold War's nuclear legacy posed an unacceptable threat that must be reduced even more severely. Accordingly, the United States and Russia began work on the treaty that would be known as START II.

The president of the Russian Federation, Boris Yeltsin, was absorbed by numerous issues during his country's first year as a sovereign state. Russia was threatened by ethnic and national tensions, economic collapse, burgeoning crime, societal instability, tense relations with its newly independent neighbors, and a variety of other problems. Yeltsin, like Soviet president Mikhail Gorbachev before him, sought above all else to stabilize relations with the West, particularly the United States. Western cooperation, technical assistance, and financial aid would be critical to Yeltsin's efforts to address his country's problems. The United States, as the world's sole superpower, clearly approached the START II talks from a position of strength.

In a Washington, D.C., summit on June 17, 1992, scarcely six months after the collapse of the Soviet Union, the United States and Russia signed a joint understanding to reduce their strategic nuclear arsenals by two-thirds. In Moscow, six months later, on January 3, 1993, Yeltsin and President George H. W. Bush signed the Treaty Between the United States of America and the Russian Federation on Further Reduction and Limitation of Strategic Offensive Arms, commonly known as START II.

**SIGNIFICANCE**

One of the key features of START II was that it called for the complete elimination of heavy intercontinental ballistic missiles (ICBMs) and all ICBMs with multiple warheads. These land-based ICBMs are considered particularly threatening to international stability because they are effective offensive weapons and are relatively vulnerable to destruction by a preemptive strike. As a result, logic compels leaders in charge of these weapons to favor using them in a time of heightened international tensions. Therefore, eliminating these weapons can be expected to enhance stability in crisis situations. Because the Soviet Union, and thus Russia, traditionally had placed a large proportion of their nuclear warheads on heavy ICBMs, this provision of START II was seen to be of greater benefit to the United States.

---

## START II AND A NEW WORLD OF HOPE

*At the Moscow press conference held by Russian president Boris Yeltsin and U.S. president George H. W. Bush on the occasion of the signing of the START II agreement on January 3, 1993, President Bush spoke of the significance of the treaty:*

We meet at the beginning of a new year, at a moment that is also a new era for our two nations and for the world. For half of this century, the Soviet Union and the United States stood locked in a nuclear standoff. For our two nations and for the world, cold war, hot words, and the constant threat of war seemed imminent, indeed, at times inevitable. The time that we might meet as friends and the time that we might meet in freedom seemed distant, indeed a dream.

Today, the Cold War is over, and for the first time in history an American President has set foot in a democratic Russia. And together we're now embarked on what must be the noblest mission of all: to turn an adversarial relationship into one of friendship and partnership.

We stand together today in this great city at the threshold of a new world of hope, a widening circle of freedom for us and for our children. This historic opportunity would simply not have been possible without our combined common effort. . . .

We seek a new relationship of trust between our military forces. They once confronted each other across Europe's great divide, and let them now come together in the cause of peace. We seek full cooperation to employ our collective capabilities to help resolve crises around the world. We seek a new cooperation between the U.S. and Russia and among all states to prevent the spread of nuclear weapons and other weapons of mass destruction.

The world looks to us to consign the Cold War to history, to ratify our new relationship by reducing the weapons that concentrate the most destructive power known to man. The treaty we signed today builds on the strong beginning we made with START I, and, together, these treaties will reduce by more than two-thirds the strategic arsenals in place today. And just as important, START II will bring much better stability to remaining forces.

This agreement represents a common effort to overcome the contentious differences and complexities that surround nuclear weapons. In the face of many who doubted Russia and America's intentions and our energy, it vindicates our insistence that arms control must do more than simply freeze the arms race in place. . . .

In closing, let me tell you what this treaty means, not for Presidents or Premiers, not for historians or heads of state, but for parents and for their children: It means a future far more free from fear.

---

Although START II was to eliminate the most destabilizing ICBMs, single-warhead ICBMs were still permitted. So were nuclear weapons deployed on aircraft and on submarines. The Central Limits provision of START II placed ceilings on the total number of strategic nuclear weapons, irrespective of deployment. The first phase of this provision, to be completed seven years after implementation of the first START treaty (now known as START I), required that Russia and the United States reduce their number of deployed strategic warheads to 3,800 and 4,250, respectively. (START I had set a limit of 6,000 for each country.) The second phase of START II, which was to be concluded by January 1, 2003, requires a further reduction to 3,000 for Russia and 3,500 for the United States. By this date, all heavy and multiwarhead ICBMs must be eliminated. Unlike its predecessor, START II required that certain classes of decommissioned missiles be destroyed. In general, START I allowed undeployed, decommissioned missiles to be stored or converted.

START II could not be implemented until START I was ratified by the respective legislatures and entered into force. In many ways, START II built upon and complemented START I. Specific sublimits placed on submarine- and plane-deployed warheads by START I remain in effect under START II. START I's ceiling of sixteen hundred total strategic nuclear delivery vehicles (such as missiles and bombers, as opposed to the warheads deployed on them) also remains in effect. START II did, however, change the way that bombers are counted. Under START I, each bomber would count toward the country's nuclear ceilings as one warhead, regardless of how many warheads were actually on board. START II counts the actual number of warheads on board.

Compliance with the provisions of START II was to be ensured by a series of highly intrusive verification measures. U.S. and Russian representatives would be permitted to observe the removal, conversion, and destruction of missiles.

Heavy bombers could be inspected to confirm weapon loads. Various other remaining weapons systems must be exhibited to confirm their compliance with the treaty's provisions. The verification regime of START II built substantially upon that of START I.

Although START II was signed by the Russian and U.S. presidents, ratification of the treaty was not assured. Several factors interacted to complicate the situation. The first START treaty, a precondition for START II, had not gone into force at the time START II was signed. In addition, the Republican Bush administration was replaced by the Democratic administration of Bill Clinton only weeks after the Moscow summit. Although Yeltsin remained president of Russia, his policies and international agreements, including START II, were seen as too hasty and pro-Western by the new, independent Russian parliament—a far cry from the compliant Soviet-era legislature. Finally, the legal questions arising from the disintegration of the Soviet Union complicated the question of precisely who was bound by START. For these reasons, the Clinton administration withdrew the treaty from Senate consideration until a more opportune political environment could be achieved. The December, 1998, bombing of Iraq by the United States and the Kosovo conflict in March, 1999, played a large part in the delay.

START I finally went into force on December 5, 1994. Controlled by the new Republican majority, Senate hearings on START II resumed in early 1995, and in January the Senate ratified the treaty. The Russian parliament also was considering the treaty, and on April 14, 2000, the Duma, the lower house, ratified START II, opening the door to negotiations on START III, which was designed to make even greater arms reductions.

—*Steve D. Boilard, updated by Christina J. Moose*

## FURTHER READING

Arbotov, Alexei. "START II, Red Ink, and Boris Yeltsin." *Bulletin of the Atomic Scientists* 49 (April, 1993): 16-21. Suggests that the treaty is biased in favor of the United States.

Mendelsohn, Jack. "Next Steps in Nuclear Arms Control." *Issues in Science and Technology* 9 (Spring, 1993): 28-34. Places START II in the broader context of world politics and nuclear stability.

Powaski, Ronald E. *Return to Armageddon: The United States and the Nuclear Arms Race, 1981-1999.* New York: Oxford University Press, 2000. Discussion of the arms race includes extensive attention to disarmament and the START I and II agreements.

Quester, George H., and Victor A. Utgoff. "Toward an International Nuclear Security Policy." *Washington Quarterly* 17, no. 4 (Autumn, 1994): 5-19. One of the first comprehensive articles on the role of the United States in stopping nuclear arms proliferation after the signing of START II. Posits that the disintegration of the Soviet Union probably will not create new nuclear states, but identifies new and continuing nuclear threats.

Rotblat, Joseph, ed. *Nuclear Weapons: The Road to Zero.* Boulder, Colo.: Westview Press, 1998. Collection of essays covers a wide range of issues related to international nuclear disarmament. Includes discussion of START II.

"START II Treaty Approval Urged." *U.S. Department of State Dispatch* 4, no. 20 (May 17, 1993): 345-347. Transcript of Secretary of State Warren Christopher's speech calling on the U.S. Senate to approve ratification of the treaty.

"START II: Treaty Between the United States of America and the Russian Federation on the Further Reduction and Limitation of Strategic Offense Arms." *Arms Control Today* 23, no. 1 (January-February, 1990): S5-S8. Supplemental section presents the treaty language. The issue also includes a variety of articles concerning the treaty.

Winkler, Allan M. "Keep Pressing for Arms Control." *Chronicle of Higher Education* 39, no. 37 (May 19, 1993): B1-B4. Assesses arms control efforts in the post-Cold War era. Suggests that START II provides significant progress toward an arms control regime, but notes that it does not address several important nuclear threats.

**SEE ALSO:** May 26, 1972: SALT I Is Signed; June 18, 1979: SALT II Is Signed; Nov. 19-21, 1985: U.S.-Soviet Summit; Dec. 8, 1987: Intermediate-Range Nuclear Forces Treaty; Sept. 27, 1991: Bush Announces Nuclear Arms Reductions; May 27, 1997: NATO and Russia Sign Cooperation Pact.

# January 4, 1993
# TROJAN NUCLEAR PLANT IS RETIRED

*The Trojan nuclear power plant was retired after seventeen years of service because the safety of its deteriorating steam generators was questioned and the generators were too expensive to replace.*

**LOCALE:** Rainier, Oregon
**CATEGORIES:** Energy; environmental issues

**KEY FIGURES**

*Lloyd Marbet* (fl. late twentieth century), spokesman for the Don't Waste Oregon Council

*Robert D. Pollard* (fl. late twentieth century), member of the Union of Concerned Scientists

*Joram Hopenfeld* (fl. late twentieth century), scientist with the Nuclear Regulatory Commission's Reactor and Plant Safety Issues branch

*Ken Harrison* (fl. late twentieth century), chairman and chief executive officer of Portland General Electric Company

**SUMMARY OF EVENT**

On January 4, 1993, the Trojan nuclear power plant, which had been licensed to operate until 2011, was shut down permanently. Portland General Electric Company (PGE) closed the seventeen-year-old plant because of rising repair costs and regulatory uncertainty at both the state and federal levels concerning the safety of Trojan's deteriorating steam generator tubes. Located forty miles north of Portland, Oregon, on the Columbia River, the 1.13 million-kilowatt plant began producing electricity in 1976. It operated at an average annual capacity of 52 percent, supplying 10 to 15 percent of Oregon's electricity and 25 percent of PGE's customer demand.

The Trojan plant was a pressurized water reactor (PWR). In a PWR, uranium fuel in the reactor's core undergoes fission, producing tremendous heat. This heat flashes water to steam, which drives turbines and a generator to produce electricity. The uranium fuel rods in the reactor core of a PWR must be constantly covered with water to prevent them from overheating, melting down, and possibly releasing radioactive material into the environment. At Trojan, 88,500 gallons of water per minute circulated through the reactor coolant system, absorbing heat and radioactivity from the core and being warmed to 617 degrees Fahrenheit. A constant pressure of 2,250 pounds per square inch within the system prevented the water from boiling. From the core, this water flowed into four steam generators, filling thousands of tall, U-shaped

tubes in each. Water from the steam system within each generator, maintained at a pressure of 900 pounds per square inch, flowed over the outsides of the tubes and was flashed to steam by the heat of the water inside.

The condition of steam generator tube walls is critical to safe operation of a nuclear power plant, because the walls form the barrier that keeps the radioactively contaminated water in the reactor coolant system. Over time, the higher pressure within the tubes, the water chemistry, and operational vibration can cause cracking and pitting of tube walls. The pressure differential between the reactor coolant system and the steam system will drive contaminated water into the steam system through any cracks that penetrate the walls. If the pressure differential between the two systems increases suddenly—for example, when a main steam line breaks—new cracks may develop and existing cracks may leak copiously or even rupture. If enough water escapes to deplete seriously the reactor cooling system and its emergency backup system, the core will melt down, releasing quantities of radioactive material into the steam system, from which it may escape into the environment.

The Nuclear Regulatory Commission (NRC) regulates the operation of nuclear power plants in the United States. According to NRC-established criteria, steam generator tubes must be inspected periodically, and tubes with even microscopic cracks more than 40 percent deep must be plugged or strengthened by insertion of a sleeve.

For the last ten years of its operation, Trojan was increasingly plagued by deterioration of its steam generator tubes. In spring, 1991, inspection during the plant's annual refueling and maintenance outage revealed thousands of tubes that required attention. By the end of the year, 20 percent of Trojan's tubes had been plugged, and many others had been sleeved. In addition, 428 tubes had microcracks of varying depths where they passed through the tube support plates.

On December 15, 1991, PGE submitted a license-change application to the NRC, asking that the Trojan plant be allowed to return to service for a one-year cycle without repairing the 428 tubes, stating that the three-quarter-inch-thick support plates surrounding the microcracking would prevent leakage or rupture. In return, PGE would agree to a reduction in the NRC-allowed leakage from the reactor coolant system, making it easier to detect the emergence of small leaks from microcracks and to take corrective action in time. The license-change amendment was issued on February 5, 1992, and Trojan returned to service on February 29, 1992, after being down for nearly one year.

Since the plant's construction, Trojan had been the target of organized opposition by residents of the surrounding area who believed that the plant was unsafe. State referenda in 1986 and 1990 to close the plant had failed. The Don't Waste Oregon Council (DWOC), sponsor of the 1990 referendum, repeatedly petitioned the Oregon Public Utilities Commission (OPUC) in 1990 and 1991 to include the cost of steam generator replacements in its consideration of the cost of electricity generated by Trojan. PGE was required, under the least-cost planning process imposed on Oregon utilities in 1989, to produce electrical power at the lowest cost consistent with the public's long-range good. Replacement of the two most deteriorated generators at $100 million each would have forced closure of Trojan because alternative energy sources would have cost less. These petitions were denied.

In December, 1991, the DWOC petitioned the Oregon Department of Energy's (ODOE) Energy Facilities Siting Council, which could revoke Trojan's site certificate, to hold a hearing to investigate fully the degradation of Trojan's steam generator tubes. This petition was denied.

Two more state referenda to close Trojan immediately were planned for the November, 1992, election. On August 10, 1992, PGE announced that, as a result of its most recent least-cost analysis, which had included the cost of replacing two generators, it would phase out Trojan by 1996. PGE believed that it could continue to operate profitably and safely until then at 60 percent capacity, allowing the company time to find substitute resources for Trojan. Both referenda failed. One week after the election, on November 9, 1992, Trojan went off-line again when monitors detected radioactive gas emissions. PGE attributed the leak to a faulty sleeve weld in a steam generator tube.

On November 23, 1992, internal NRC memoranda were leaked to Robert D. Pollard, a nuclear safety engineer for the Union of Concerned Scientists (UCS), who released them to the media. These memoranda increased concerns about the safety of Trojan among the public and state regulators of the plant in Oregon. The first memorandum, submitted in December, 1991, and augmented in March, 1992, by Joram Hopenfeld of the NRC Reactor and Plant Safety Issues branch, addressed the license-change amendment allowing Trojan to operate with 428 unrepaired tubes. The safety analysis submitted by PGE in support of its request for this amendment concluded that tubes with microcracks at support plates would not rupture at pressures typical of those in the break of a main steam line. Hopenfeld believed that depletion of reactor-cooling water leading to a meltdown could occur if enough tubes only leaked and that the likelihood of such a situation developing was far greater than had been expressed in PGE's report.

The other memorandum, submitted in March, 1992, by Joseph Muscara, the research program manager for the NRC's eleven-year steam generator tube integrity program, did not allude to Trojan but addressed a relevant issue. It expressed Muscara's concern about the apparent movement of the NRC away from its long-standing policy of prohibiting plants with unrepaired steam generator tubes from operating. Muscara believed, based on years of research on steam generator tubes, that it was not possible to predict with accuracy how cracks in tube walls would develop during an operating cycle. It was therefore not possible to guarantee that a plant could operate safely with unrepaired tubes.

On December 1, 1992, NRC officials met with PGE officials to consider PGE's request to return Trojan to service without additional analysis of other steam generator tubes. Antinuclear activists, opposed to Trojan's being restarted without a public hearing that included testimony by Hopenfeld and Muscara, blocked the gate to the plant on both December 1 and December 3. A number of the activists were arrested, jailed, and charged with trespassing.

Shortly thereafter, PGE withdrew its request to restart Trojan and announced that it would conduct additional inspections of the tubes. As a result, on December 9, the ODOE, charged under state law with preventing Trojan from operating if clear evidence of an immediate danger to the public existed, urged the NRC to participate in a public hearing in Oregon regarding safety issues at Trojan.

On January 4, 1993, PGE closed Trojan permanently, stating that it was confident that Trojan could operate safely but was no longer certain that it could operate profitably because of probable future downtime for regulatory hearings and repairs. PGE had also determined that abundant replacement power resources would be available in the Northwest for the next few years. Shutting Trojan down immediately rather than operating it until 1996 had become the least-cost option.

## SIGNIFICANCE
Trojan's closing eliminated the threat of a core meltdown but posed new environmental issues related to the stor-

age of spent nuclear fuel, plant decommissioning, and replacement of the power previously generated by the plant. In January, 1993, the 193 partially used fuel assemblies were transferred from Trojan's reactor to its spent-fuel pool. The pool housed 781 fuel assemblies—every fuel assembly used at Trojan since it began operation in 1976—or approximately 450 tons of spent fuel. Originally designed to hold one year's worth of spent fuel until it could be reprocessed, the pool was reracked to hold more when reprocessing was made illegal in the 1970's under Jimmy Carter's presidential administration.

The Nuclear Waste Policy Act of 1982 and its amendment in 1987 required nuclear power plants to store their spent fuel on-site until January, 1998, when the federal government would assume responsibility for it. By then, the United States would have forty thousand metric tons of spent fuel—high-level radioactive waste—stored at some seventy sites awaiting disposal. The U.S. Department of Energy (DOE) predicted, however, that its proposed permanent repository for high-level radioactive waste, Nevada's Yucca Mountain, would not be ready to accept waste until at least 2010. The DOE was not developing a temporary facility for storing waste in the interim. On June 20, 1994, PGE and thirteen other utility companies filed suit against the federal government to force it to begin providing storage for spent reactor fuel.

Did the storage of spent fuel at Trojan after closure pose an environmental risk? In the 1980's, geologists demonstrated the potential of a severe earthquake in the Pacific Northwest. Both the NRC and the ODOE concluded that Trojan's used-fuel storage facility could withstand the largest credible earthquake for the region. Others were less certain, however. A seismic fault line lies beneath the Columbia River near the plant, and there are fractures in the base rock under the plant. One fracture passes under the spent-fuel pool. If an earthquake were to rupture the pool and the water level dropped, the fuel assemblies could ignite and burn, releasing radioactive material.

Early in 1994, at the Dresden nuclear plant in Illinois (retired in 1978), a pipe ruptured during freezing weather, and fifty-five thousand gallons of water leaked from the spent-fuel pool. Consequently, the NRC required a safety inspection of Trojan's pool in April, 1994, and began developing an inspection program focused on spent-fuel pools at retired plants.

Do staff cutbacks at closed plants pose an environmental safety issue? The NRC granted a possession-only license to PGE on March 24, 1994, enabling it to reduce its staff at Trojan from 1,100 employees to approximately 150 employees. In June, 1993, the NRC cited PGE for allowing equipment removed from the containment building to accumulate near the spent-fuel pool, stating that the equipment might fall into the pool during an earthquake and rupture a fuel assembly. The NRC attributed the accumulation of equipment around the pool to extensive staff cutbacks at Trojan.

Decommissioning of a nuclear power plant is the process of safely removing the plant from service and decontaminating it so that the site can be released for unrestricted use. Contaminated equipment and facilities may be decontaminated and left at the site or may be transported to low-level waste depositories, depending on plans for the site's future use. Utilities are required by law to decommission closed plants.

PGE filed its decommissioning plan for Trojan in January, 1995. Decommissioning of Trojan was to begin in 1998 and was estimated to cost $500 million. In addition to high-level radioactive waste, there is a considerable amount of low-level radioactive waste in a plant the size of Trojan—enough waste to cover a football field to a depth of about five feet. This waste must be disposed of or decontaminated. In 1994, only two low-level waste-disposal sites were operating in the United States; PGE had access to one of these, U.S. Ecology, near Richland, Washington.

In July, 1994, PGE filed with the ODOE's Energy Facilities Siting Council to move the four steam generators (four stories high and 330 tons each) and a pressurizing unit to U.S. Ecology in the fall, stating that it could save $4.5 million by disposing of these components before disposal rates increased in 1995. PGE planned to fill them with concrete and barge them 270 miles up the Columbia River. The DWOC sued to prevent this from occurring before Trojan's decommissioning plan was reviewed by the public and approved by the siting council, citing the threat to the spent-fuel pool, workers, nearby residents, and the Columbia River of moving these large, radioactive components before their radioactivity had had a period of years in which to diminish.

Financing decommissioning has environmental implications. As part of its decommissioning regulations, the NRC expects utilities to collect, over the projected lifetimes of their plants, adequate funds to decommission in a safe and timely manner. If funding is inadequate, plant sites, facilities, and equipment may not be safely or completely decontaminated; equipment may not be disposed of at licensed facilities. Trojan's decommissioning fund was planned to be collected from ratepayers

1993

been inadvertently run over by a camera crew covering the spill. The potential *Braer* catastrophe simply failed to materialize.

## SIGNIFICANCE

The wreck of the *Braer* underscores the numerous problems that exist with the shipping of vast quantities of petroleum to meet the world's demand for energy and fuel. Multinational corporations, intent on preserving profits, may skimp on training and maintenance in order to maximize returns. International regulations are difficult to negotiate and to enforce because national interests often supersede international concerns. The fears of scientists and environmentalists, although based in reality, are often at odds with the cost-containment policies of govern-

ments and corporations, resulting in distrust and suspicion on the part of all. Despite all this, on occasion, nature still surprises with its ability to withstand and to deal with humankind's abuses of the environment.

The economics of large ships is simple: Giant tankers save money; the larger the tanker, the more money saved. Sizes of 400,000 deadweight (dwt) are currently common, with the largest being above 600,000 dwt. The *Braer* itself was small as modern supertankers go; still, the problems with supertankers can be seen clearly in the wreck of the *Braer*. Despite constant improvements in ships and equipment, accidents still happen; when massive oil spills follow, environmental disaster can occur.

Compounding the problem of size is the difficulty of assignment of responsibility for such oil spills. The *Braer*'s captain was Greek; the ship's crew was a multinational mix of Greeks, Filipinos, and Poles; the ship sailed under a Liberian registry and was operated by Bergval and Hudner Ship Management of Stamford, Connecticut; and it had been chartered by a Canadian firm. Such multinational practices make adherence to professional standards, ship maintenance, and crew training haphazard, at best.

Early analyses of the wreck focused on those very problems. Some observers criticized Captain Gelis for having left the *Braer* so quickly. It was theorized that had someone remained on board, a line could have been fired from the *Braer* to a salvage tug, thereby permitting an opportunity to tow the tanker away from danger. Given the weather conditions and the dangers of shipwreck, however, the captain and his crew could hardly be faulted for leaving when they did. On the other hand, underpaid and poorly trained crews do pose problems. Working without gloves, in tennis shoes, in subzero temperatures, as had been observed on other supertankers, is simply not conducive either to high ship morale or to a smoothly functioning crew. Ship maintenance suffers when working conditions such as these occur. Moreover, communication on multinational crews can be difficult, particularly in an emergency such as that of engine failure.

It was also suggested that specific problems indigenous to that particular type of ship, and complicated by the nature of the crew, may have led to the shipwreck. A twin of the *Braer*, the *Celtic*, had had similar problems with its en-

**BRAER DISASTER SITE**

SHETLAND ISLANDS

Norwegian Sea

Unst

Yell

Fetlar

Papa Stour

Mainland

Whalsay

Bressay

*North Sea*

Foula

Lerwick

Garths Ness

Sumburgh Head

*Quendale Bay*

Fair Isle

gine, also in January. On the *Celtic*, ice had been allowed to build up around the ship engine's cooling system, causing the engine to overheat. A similar problem could possibly have caused the *Braer*'s engine to shut down.

The investigation also revealed that, in 1992, the *Braer* had undergone extensive repairs to its engine and pumps. The *Braer* was eighteen years old, and an extensive overhaul was probably overdue. When a ship is being overhauled, however, it is not making money, so overhauls are postponed until absolutely necessary. It is possible that the engine might well have failed as a result of maintenance left incomplete to get the *Braer* back to sea quickly. The failure may have resulted from seawater fouling fuel because of the storm. This, too, could have been the result of improper training and procedures. In any event, once the *Braer*'s engine hit Garths Ness, there was no way to tell with absolute certainty what caused it to stop; the damage done in the collision destroyed any useful evidence.

International and national policies make the enactment of laws dealing meaningfully with the above-noted problems difficult, if not impossible. Nations can enact and enforce their own maritime laws. The United States has many laws dealing with water pollution. The Oil Pollution Act, enacted in 1990 following the *Exxon Valdez* disaster, provides for strict regulations and penalties within U.S. territorial waters. Internationally, the Intergovernmental Marine Consultative Organization has sought to tighten international regulations, establishing significant agreements in 1954, 1962, 1975, 1982, and 1988. Unfortunately, international laws govern only certain areas and then only deliberate acts. National governments are loath to transfer their own power and control to international agencies.

Dangers clearly exist because of the tremendous size of oil tankers. The supertankers *Atlantic Empress* and *Aegean Captain* collided in 1979, spilling 300,000 tons; the 250,000 dwt *Castillo de Bellver* sank off Capetown, South Africa, in 1983; and the 223,000 dwt *Amoco Cadiz* ran aground off the Breton coast in 1978. The 1989 *Exxon Valdez* spill of eleven million gallons (37,415 tons) ranked only thirty-first in tanker oil spills by 1995. These spills are dwarfed when compared with oil well blowouts such as one that occurred off the Yucatán Peninsula in 1979, spilling 600,000 tons of oil.

Tragically, oil spills at sea can be so massive and the need for cleanup so immediate that speed and efficiency are often more important than safety and biodegradability. Oil cleanup tactics include skimming, sinking, absorbing, burning, and emulsifying. Skimming is

least harmful, but high seas often make this impractical. Sinking through the use of an adhesive agent such as powered chalk hides the mess but usually devastates marine life close to shore. Absorbing oil with straw and sawdust results in massive amounts of debris to be collected and destroyed. Burning works only when the spill is compact and only when wave and wind action are low. Emulsifying is usually the solution of choice, but its use near or on shore is a disaster. As an example, the *Exxon Valdez* cleanup left clean but biologically dead beaches and rocks.

In the case of the *Braer*, nature cleaned up the mess before humans had the opportunity to make things worse. One marine biologist noted, "I don't think anyone would have thought the oil would disappear so quickly. After two weeks even the press left." Still, it is important to remember that less than 10 percent of oil spilled into waters comes from disasters such as that of the *Braer*. Most comes from deliberate dumping, the only cure for which is improved enforcement of regulations. As for major oil spills, virtually every study and report issued after an oil disaster concludes that nothing really works well. The only cure is prevention.

—*William S. Brockington, Jr.*

## FURTHER READING

Burger, Joanna. *Oil Spills*. New Brunswick, N.J.: Rutgers University Press, 1997. Comprehensive volume includes an overview of the history of oil spills as well as discussion of their impacts—legal, economic, social, and ecological. Also examines the efficacy of cleanup efforts.

Graham, Frank, Jr. "Oilspeak, Common Sense, and Soft Science." *Audubon* 91 (September, 1989): 102-111. Surveys the impact of oil spills on the environment and the oil industry's public relations responses. Notes the differences in findings released by oil companies and those released by scientists.

National Research Council. *Oil in the Sea III: Inputs, Fates, and Effects*. Washington, D.C.: National Academies Press, 2003. Summarizes scientific investigations of major oil spills and counters the contention by oil industries that ocean oil spills have minimal environmental impact.

Robert J. Meyers and Associates, Research Planning Institute, Inc. *Oil Spill Response Guide*. Park Ridge, N.J.: Noyes Data, 1989. Describes equipment and methods used in dealing with oil spills. Focuses primarily on the 1989 *Exxon Valdez* Alaskan oil spill.

Spyrou, Andrew G. *From T-2 to Supertanker: Develop-*

1993

*ment of the Oil Tanker, 1940-2000.* Lincoln, Nebr.: iUniverse, 2006. Describes the efforts of the oil tanker industry to improve these vessels' safety and efficiency over time.

**SEE ALSO:** Dec. 15, 1976: The *Argo Merchant* Spills Oil off the New England Coast; Mar. 16, 1978: The *Amoco Cadiz* Runs Aground; Oct. 17, 1978: U.S.

Congress Requires Ships to Safeguard Marine Environment; July 19, 1979: Oil Tankers Collide near Tobago; Mar. 22, 1980: Mexico Controls Huge Leak in Offshore Oil Well; Jan. 2, 1988: Tank Collapse Releases Fuel into the Monongahela River; Mar. 24, 1989: *Exxon Valdez* Oil Spill; Aug. 18, 1990: U.S. Congress Passes Oil Spill Legislation.

---

**February 5, 1993**

# U.S. CONGRESS GUARANTEES JOB SECURITY DURING FAMILY EMERGENCIES

*American workers gained greater job security with the passage of the federal Family and Medical Leave Act, which guaranteed adequate leave time for employees in times of family and medical emergency.*

**ALSO KNOWN AS:** Family and Medical Leave Act; U.S. Statutes at Large 107 Stat. 6; Public Law 103-3; U.S. Code 29 § 2601
**LOCALE:** Washington, D.C.
**CATEGORIES:** Laws, acts, and legal history; social issues and reform; business and labor

**KEY FIGURES**

*George H. W. Bush* (b. 1924), president of the United States, 1989-1993
*Bill Clinton* (b. 1946), president of the United States, 1993-2001
*Christopher John Dodd* (b. 1944), Democratic senator from Connecticut who cosponsored the act
*Pat Schroeder* (b. 1940), Democratic congresswoman from Colorado who was a major proponent of the act

**SUMMARY OF EVENT**

On February 3, 1993, the U.S. Congress passed the Family and Medical Leave Act of 1993, a comprehensive plan to ensure job security and leave opportunities for U.S. employees in times of family and medical need or crisis. President Bill Clinton signed the act into law on February 5, and it took full effect on August 6, 1993.

Through much of the twentieth century, the paradigm for families in North America was clearly defined: Husbands worked in the marketplace and provided financial support, and wives stayed home managing domestic life and child care. Women looked after children or ailing family members. Husbands tended to be "company men," so employers were not likely to accommo-

date family crises. Extended families were concentrated; there was often a grandparent, cousin, or other relative nearby who could help with family caretaking.

Shifts in lifestyles, demographics, and work patterns had rendered this paradigm virtually meaningless by the 1980's. The number of women in the workforce increased dramatically during the wartime 1940's, declined temporarily after the war's end, but then grew again. Economic realities engendered double-income families, and the women's movement encouraged women to establish their own careers. Only 19 percent of women in the United States worked outside the home in 1900, but by the early 1990's, that figure was as high as 74 percent. With increased rates of divorce and unmarried parenthood, single-parent families became common, especially in inner-city, impoverished, and minority communities. In 1988, 27 percent of families had a single parent, twice the percentage of 1970.

Another change was the increase in life expectancies as a result of advances in medical technology, both in general and in the treatment of serious illnesses. People lived longer, and the U.S. population as a whole had aged dramatically. In 1993, the thirty-two million citizens over the age of sixty-five constituted 12 percent of the populace and was its fastest-growing segment. Home care of the elderly often was viewed as preferable to institutionalization, and many serious illnesses could be treated without hospitalization. According to the National Council on Aging, at least 20 percent of the workforce had some caregiving responsibilities.

As a result of these factors, a vast majority of American workers potentially faced difficult choices between work and family. A 1990 study by the Southport Institute for Policy Analysis estimated that 11 percent of caregivers were forced to quit their jobs to care for relatives. The U.S. Small Business Administration estimated that 150,000 workers were losing their jobs annually because they could not take medical leave. Others found their jobs less than secure when they were ready to return from leave. In the absence of a national policy, even sympathetic employers could change policy without notice. The employee had little true protection.

The Civil Rights Act of 1964 and the Pregnancy Discrimination Act of 1978 provided certain guarantees, but comprehensive federal legislation was needed. Prior to the Family and Medical Leave Act of 1993, the United States was the only industrialized nation in the world without such a law; Japan provided twelve weeks of pregnancy leave with partial pay, and Canadian women were given forty-one weeks. Sweden offered eighteen months of family leave for use at the time of birth and when a child entered school. Norway, Austria, France, England, and Luxembourg had laws that provided leave for the care of an elderly parent.

Family and medical leave legislation was proposed several times during the 1980's, only to meet congressional gridlock and presidential vetoes. Earlier versions of the act were very strong, offering up to twenty-six weeks of leave. Conservatives of both parties feared that such legislation would weigh heavily on businesses and strongly opposed any federally mandated employee policies. President George H. W. Bush vetoed a watered-down 1992 bill, offering instead his own plan based on refundable tax credits for employers. Even the 1993 measure was almost blocked by Senate Republicans with an extraneous amendment reaffirming the ban on homosexuals in the military. However, in the opening weeks of the Clinton administration, the 1993 act was passed by bipartisan margins in both houses.

The Family and Medical Leave Act required U.S. employers to offer limited unpaid leave in four circumstances: upon the birth of an employee's child; upon the arrival of an adopted child; in cases in which the employee is needed to provide care for a spouse, child, or parent with a serious health condition; or in cases in which the employee is afflicted with a debilitating health condition. The act also provided definitions and restrictions to balance employers' and employees' interests. It ensured that employees returning from leave be given the

---

## PROTECTING AMERICAN WORKERS

*In the "findings and purposes" section of the Family and Medical Leave Act, Congress laid out the reasons such a law was needed:*

Congress finds that—
1. the number of single-parent households and two-parent households in which the single parent or both parents work is increasing significantly;
2. it is important for the development of children and the family unit that fathers and mothers be able to participate in early childrearing and the care of family members who have serious health conditions;
3. the lack of employment policies to accommodate working parents can force individuals to choose between job security and parenting;
4. there is inadequate job security for employees who have serious health conditions that prevent them from working for temporary periods;
5. due to the nature of the roles of men and women in our society, the primary responsibility for family caretaking often falls on women, and such responsibility affects the working lives of women more than it affects the working lives of men; and
6. employment standards that apply to one gender only have serious potential for encouraging employers to discriminate against employees and applicants for employment who are of that gender.

---

same or a comparable position and salary with full benefits reinstated. The act exempted businesses with fewer than fifty employees, which could be seriously impaired by the loss of essential employees, and established employee eligibility according to length of employment. It also dealt with issues such as the substitution of available paid leave, advance notification of leave-taking, and formal certification of debilitating health conditions. The act established the bipartisan, sixteen-member Commission on Leave and gave the secretary of labor investigative authority for enforcement. It also opened the door for employees to initiate civil actions to remedy alleged violations.

### SIGNIFICANCE

Many viewed the act as a halfway measure that achieved more by its mere existence than by its specific guarantees. The national policy stopped short of numerous state laws and countless corporate policies already in effect. Conversely, an estimated 50 percent of U.S. workers did not work enough hours or for large enough companies to be covered. The cost to the employee of unpaid time off remained too high for many workers to afford to leave to take care of family problems.

1993

In 1992, the Family and Work Institute released a three-year study of a thousand companies in Rhode Island, Oregon, Minnesota, and Wisconsin regarding compliance with state leave laws. The researchers found that 91 percent reported no trouble adapting to state rules, 94 percent of leave takers had returned to their positions, and 75 percent of supervisors reported a positive effect on company business. It was estimated to be two to five times as expensive to replace an employee permanently as to grant temporary leave. A large number of companies with established leave policies, including such giants as Du Pont, AT&T, and Aetna, reported limited problems and favorable results—including cost-effectiveness—from their family leave programs.

The Family and Medical Leave Act of 1993 established important guarantees without a major overall effect on either the nation's economic health or its business practices. It helped to standardize those practices and relieve family leave policy making of the pressures of business competitiveness. Since the act has taken effect, hundreds of lawsuits and complaints have been brought to the courts and the Department of Labor. In 1995, new rules were issued to clarify the situations covered by the act and the procedures required of both employees and employers in requesting and granting leave.

*—Barry Mann*

## FURTHER READING

Bauer, Gary L. "Leaving Families Out." *National Review*, March 29, 1993, 58-60. Argues that the Family and Medical Leave Act is a betrayal of conservative approaches to strengthening the family.

"Family and Medical Leave Legislation." *Congressional Digest* 72, no. 1 (January, 1993): 2-32. Provides an overview of family and medical leave legislative history and prospects as of the start of the 103rd Congress. Presents arguments for and against the policy by thirteen lawmakers, including President George H. W. Bush and Senators Bob Dole and Ted Kennedy.

Jasper, Margaret C. *Your Rights Under the Family and Medical Leave Act*. Dobbs Ferry, N.Y.: Oceana, 2005. Brief work explains the provisions of the law in lay terms.

Maynard, Roberta. "Meet the New Law on Family Leave." *Nation's Business* 81, no. 4 (April, 1993): 26. Explains the act in lay terms and explores the problems it might pose for employers.

Murray, Marjorie. "Family Leave: Read This Before You Take (or Give) It." *Working Woman* 20, no. 5 (May, 1995): 15. Presents an update on the law and explains the clarifying rules issued two years after its passage. Emphasizes the limits of the act and the confusion it has engendered in a variety of situations.

Saltzman, Amy. "Time Off Without Pain." *U.S. News & World Report*, August 2, 1993, 52-55. Offers a practical discussion on the new law, including anecdotes about several workers who experienced the types of difficulties the law was intended to address.

**SEE ALSO:** Mar. 8, 1971: U.S. Supreme Court Bans Discrimination in Hiring; Mar. 24, 1972: U.S. Congress Mandates Equal Employment Opportunity; Sept. 2, 1974: U.S. Congress Protects Employee Benefits; Oct. 31, 1978: U.S. Congress Protects Pregnant Employees; June 12, 1984: U.S. Supreme Court Upholds Seniority Systems.

**February 26, 1993**
# WORLD TRADE CENTER BOMBING

*The bombing of the World Trade Center in New York City proved to Americans that the United States is not immune to international terrorism.*

**LOCALE:** New York, New York
**CATEGORY:** Terrorism, atrocities, and war crimes

## KEY FIGURES
*Mahmoud Abouhalima* (b. 1960), West Bank Palestinian who was a coconspirator in the bombing
*Ahmad M. Ajaj* (b. 1967), West Bank Palestinian who was a coconspirator in the bombing
*Nidal A. Ayyad* (b. 1968), West Bank Palestinian who was a coconspirator in the bombing
*Mohammed A. Salameh* (b. 1968), West Bank Palestinian who was a coconspirator in the bombing
*Kevin Thomas Duffy* (b. 1933), U.S. federal district court judge
*Eyad Ismail* (b. 1971), West Bank Palestinian who drove the van that carried the explosives
*Omar Abdel Rahman* (b. 1938), Egyptian Muslim fundamentalist cleric and spiritual leader
*Abdul Rahman Yasin* (b. 1960), American of Iraqi heritage who was a suspect but remained at large
*Ramzi Yousef* (b. 1968), Kuwaiti who was thought to be the mastermind behind the plot

## SUMMARY OF EVENT
At 12:17 P.M. on February 26, 1993, a yellow rental van loaded with some twelve hundred pounds of nitrate explosives blew up in the garage of the World Trade Center's North Building, in lower Manhattan Island, New York City. The van, driven by Eyad Ismail, had a twelve-minute fuse located between the front seats. Once the fuse was lit, Ismail and his passenger, Ramzi Yousef, a friend with whom he had grown up in Kuwait, jumped into another car driven by a third companion.

The 110-story tower, like its twin, was part of a seven-structure complex where some fifty thousand people were employed; the complex also hosted some eighty thousand visitors per day. The blast created a huge crater and tore through four levels of the multilayered basement. The maelstrom of smoke, darkness, and chaos left six individuals dead and more than a thousand injured—mostly from smoke inhalation, debris, and psychological trauma. The explosion, which was felt several miles away, knocked out the twin towers' generators, ripped doors off elevators, silenced radio and television sta-

tions, and nearly damaged the wall that held back the waters of New York Harbor.

It took some of the occupants of the higher floors as long as five hours to climb down the quarter mile of stairways, much of it in pitch darkness. Some smashed windows to get relief from the smoke, which had risen through elevator and ventilation shafts. Emergency crews responded quickly in helping the occupants out of the building, plucking some from the roof by helicopter.

Four days after the bombing, *The New York Times* received a letter from a group calling itself the Liberation Army Fifth Battalion. Although the group was unknown to law-enforcement agencies, the letter was authenticated by the Federal Bureau of Investigation (FBI) as originating with a West Bank Palestinian named Nidal A. Ayyad. The message stated that the attack was "in response to the American political, economical, and military support to Israel, the state of terrorism, and to the rest of the dictator countries in the region." It continued: "The American people are responsible for the actions of their government and they must question all of the crimes that their government is committing against other people. Or they—Americans—will be the targets of our operations that could diminish them."

Four Arab Muslim militants were eventually arrested. All had been influenced by blind Egyptian cleric Sheikh Omar Abdel Rahman, who earlier had been charged in his native country with involvement in the assassination of former president Anwar al-Sadat but later was released. Authorities made the first arrest, of Mohammed A. Salameh, by tracing the person who had rented the van and then asked for his $400 deposit back because, he claimed, the vehicle had been stolen. Arrests of three other alleged conspirators—Nidal A. Ayyad, Mahmoud Abouhalima, and Ahmad M. Ajaj—followed. Abdul Rahman Yasin, also named as a suspect in the case, remained a fugitive.

The five-month trial of the accused began in October, 1993. On March 4, 1994, the four were found guilty on all thirty-eight counts of conspiracy to blow up the building, explosive destruction of property, and interstate transport of explosives. Some ten thousand pages of testimony from 207 witnesses were collected. Each of the men was sentenced to 240 years in prison without parole by Judge Kevin Thomas Duffy of the U.S. federal district court in Manhattan. Because there were no eyewitnesses, the convictions hinged mostly on forensic evidence ex-

1993

## CLINTON SPEAKS ABOUT THE WORLD TRADE CENTER BOMBING

*In a radio address on February 27, 1993, President Bill Clinton spoke about the terrorist bombing of the World Trade Center before moving on to economic concerns:*

I want to say a word to the good people of New York City and to all Americans who have been so deeply affected by the tragedy that struck Manhattan yesterday. A number of innocent people lost their lives, hundreds were injured, and thousands were struck with fear in their hearts when an explosion rocked the basement of the World Trade Center.

To their families, you are in the thoughts and prayers of my family. And in the synagogues and churches last night, today, and to-morrow you will be remembered and thought of again and again. My thoughts are also with the police, the firefighters, the emergency response teams, and the citizens whose countless acts of bravery averted even more bloodshed. Their reaction and their valor reminds us of how often Americans are at their best when we face the worst. I thank all the people who reached out to the injured and the frightened amid the tumult that shook lower Manhattan.

Following the explosion I spoke with New York's Governor Mario Cuomo and New York City Mayor David Dinkins to assure them that the full measure of Federal law enforcement resources will be brought to bear on this investigation. Just this morning I spoke with FBI Director Sessions, who assured me that the FBI and the Treasury Department are working closely with the New York City police and fire departments. Working together we'll find out who was involved and why this happened. Americans should know we'll do everything in our power to keep them safe in their streets, their offices, and their homes. Feeling safe is an essential part of being secure, and that's important to all of us.

tricated from the rubble, such as shards of the van, along with telephone and bank records and other documentary evidence. Most of the conspirators had connections with El Sayyid A. Nosair, an Egyptian convicted of assault and weapons charges for a shooting at the time of the assassination of militant Rabbi Meir Kahane in 1990.

Long after the bombing, fugitives and additional suspects were apprehended, extradited, and eventually tried. Ramzi Yousef, who was believed to be the mastermind of the bombing, was located in Pakistan and returned to New York in February, 1995. He was considered to be a trained professional terrorist, unlike those he recruited, entering countries under different aliases, with false papers, cash, and connections. Eyad Ismail was traced to Jordan and returned to New York in July, 1995.

## SIGNIFICANCE

After the blast, the tower and other areas in the World Trade Center complex were closed for varying lengths of time as the federal government made low-interest loans available to many small businesses to offset their forgone earnings. The hundreds of millions of dollars' worth of structural damage to property was covered, in part, by insurance carriers and federal assistance. Repair work to the extensively damaged area provided reconstruction and renovation work for local contractors. The psychological trauma—both to many individuals at the blast site and, more generally, to the collective American psyche—was much longer-lasting. The attack on a symbol of American commerce had largely destroyed the previous sense among many in the United States that they were immune from foreign terrorism on home territory.

In addition, there continued to be lurking suspicion that some fundamental questions had not been fully answered. Who was behind the conspiracy? Who had transferred $8,500 from Europe to some of the defendants? Why was the bombing carried out? Were the eleven persons accused in 1995 of plotting to bomb the headquarters of the United Nations in New York, the FBI office in Washington, two Hudson River tunnels, and a bridge across the river part of this larger montage?

As the authorities pondered these fundamental questions, the more practical and immediate concerns of securing possible future targets from terrorists also were addressed. Although previous procedures—such as checking identities and parcels, restricting the use of space, and exchanging information among law-enforcement agencies—could be intensified, and possibly done better, there was clearly no fail-safe system against terrorism, any more than against other forms of crime. For one thing, terrorists were using advanced technology in their operations; for another, a number were sufficiently motivated to undertake suicide attacks.

Because terrorism is often the result of deep, long-nursed grievances whose solutions lie in difficult political remedies, angry and determined individuals and groups continue to exist. Furthermore, in an open society such as that of the United States, eager media looking for the newsworthy often have been too willing to publicize such groups' causes and air their grudges. Following the 1993 World Trade Center bombing, most American citizens simply resigned themselves to living with the hope that they would not meet the fate of Steven Knapp, William Macko, Robert Kirkpatrick, Monica Smith, John DiGiovanni, and Wilfredo Mercado, the six who died at the complex on that fateful winter day.

In a few short years, however, the entire world would be shocked by the September 11, 2001, attacks in which terrorists destroyed the World Trade Center by crashing commercial jets into the two towers. The resultant horror and loss of life dwarfed the 1993 incident, prompted a complete reconsideration of American intelligence operations, and provoked a determined counterattack against the al-Qaeda terrorist organization led by Osama Bin Laden. This included American and international intervention into Afghanistan, where the Taliban government had given Bin Laden's organization free reign to train and plot terrorist attacks. Reorganization of the security-related functions of the federal government and its ties to state and local governments took place with the establishment of the Department of Homeland Security, and a new "intelligence czar" was appointed to overcome the separation between domestic and foreign intelligence agencies that had developed and deepened in the post-Vietnam era, to the detriment of overall national security.

—*Peter B. Heller*

**FURTHER READING**

Behar, Richard. "The Secret Life of Mahmud the Red." *Time*, October 4, 1993, 54-61. Describes the role of defendant Mahmoud Abouhalima in the World Trade Center bombing.

Gauch, Sarah. "Terror on the Nile." *Africa Report* 38, no. 3 (May, 1993): 32-35. Connects the World Trade Center bombing in New York and terrorist attacks in Cairo, Egypt, focusing attention on the rise of Islamic radicalism.

MacDonald, Eileen. *Shoot the Women First*. New York: Random House, 1991. Provides insight into the role of women in terrorist groups around the world, including Palestinian groups.

Nacos, Brigitte L. *Mass-Mediated Terrorism: The Central Role of the Media in Terrorism and Counterterrorism*. Lanham, Md.: Rowman & Littlefield, 2002.

1993

*Emergency vehicles fill the street near the World Trade Center in New York City after the 1993 explosion in the underground parking garage.* (AP/Wide World Photos)

practice of keeping bugs a secret to all but a few large and valued customers. Not only was Intel pressured into publishing a complete list of known bugs in its flagship processor, but also rivals such as Motorola and IBM found it impossible to resist the pressure to do likewise. As a result, the nontechnical public became increasingly aware of the complexity of modern microprocessors and the sheer impossibility of producing one completely free of all bugs.

Subsequent generations of the Pentium chip, including the Pentium Pro and Pentium III, steadily increased in computing power. Later additions to the Pentium family moved away from that name, instead using such name as Xeon, Core, and Duo Core, but they continued to use the X86 instruction set. These chips proved so successful that even longtime holdout Apple began to use Intel chips on models of the Macintosh computer.

—*Leigh Husband Kimmel*

**FURTHER READING**

Jackson, Tim. *Inside Intel: Andy Grove and the Rise of the World's Most Powerful Chip Company*. New York: Dutton, 1997. Solid corporate history. Focuses on the Grove years, including the Pentium.

Reid, T. R. *The Chip: How Two Americans Invented the Microchip and Launched a Revolution*. New York: Random House, 2001. A basic history of the development of the microchip and the founding of Intel.

Riordan, Michael, and Lillian Hoddeson. *Crystal Fire: The Birth of the Information Age*. New York: W. W. Norton, 1997. Good background. Helps place the microchip in the larger context of the convergence of information technology.

Seitz, Frederick, and Norman G. Einspruch. *Electronic Genie: The Tangled History of Silicon*. Urbana: University of Illinois Press, 1998. Includes information on Grove's role in Intel's leadership.

Yu, Albert. *Creating the Digital Future: The Secrets of Consistent Innovation at Intel*. New York: Free Press, 1998. Concerns the development of the Pentium in the context of Intel's role as industry leader.

**SEE ALSO:** Nov. 15, 1971: Intel Introduces the First "Computer on a Chip"; July 3, 1991: IBM and Apple Agree to Make Compatible Computers; Dec. 15, 1994: Release of Netscape Navigator 1.0; Mid-1990's: Rise of the Internet and the World Wide Web; May 23, 1995: Sun Microsystems Introduces Java.

---

## April-October, 1993
# MISSISSIPPI AND MISSOURI FLOODING BRINGS MISERY TO MIDDLE AMERICA

*Heavy rains and an unusually high snowmelt caused rivers throughout the Midwest to begin rising in the spring of 1993, and unremitting rainfall throughout the summer led to record flooding on the Missouri and Mississippi Rivers, as well as many major tributaries, breaching or overtopping levees and causing major damage to agricultural regions and several urban areas over a six-month period.*

**LOCALE:** Midwestern United States
**CATEGORIES:** Disasters; environmental issues

**KEY FIGURES**

*Bill Clinton* (b. 1946), president of the United States, 1993-2001
*Mike Espy* (b. 1953), U.S. secretary of agriculture, 1993-1994
*Mel Carnahan* (1934-2000), governor of Missouri, 1993-2000
*Jim Edgar* (b. 1946), governor of Illinois, 1991-1999

*Terry E. Branstad* (b. 1946), governor of Iowa, 1983-1999
*James Lee Witt* (b. 1944), director of the Federal Emergency Management Agency, 1993-2001

**SUMMARY OF EVENT**

A confluence of weather-related events beginning in the autumn of 1992 initiated a chain reaction that produced one of the greatest natural disasters to befall the United States in the twentieth century. Unusually heavy fall rains followed by considerable winter snowfalls combined to create higher-than-average spring runoff into rivers and streams in the upper Midwest, swelling tributaries that fed into the country's major midwestern rivers, the Missouri and Mississippi. Heavy spring rains throughout the region added to the problem. Unfortunately, although forecasters realized that rivers might rise to higher-than-normal levels, few predicted the magnitude of the floods that would cripple the nation's midsection for nearly six months.

By May, 1993, the Redwood River in Minnesota, the Arkansas River in Kansas, the Mississippi River, and the Missouri River were at flood stages in several areas. Officials in Kansas City and St. Louis were already expressing concern for the safety of individuals and businesses in those metropolitan areas. Constant rains continued to swell tributary rivers in South Dakota, Wisconsin, Minnesota, and Iowa, and as the crests along these rivers moved downstream, the waters in the Missouri and Mississippi rivers continued to rise. Many communities were forced to mobilize emergency efforts to sandbag levees in an attempt to prevent major flooding. Nevertheless, by June levees were beginning to break, and those living in areas immediately adjacent to the rivers were forced to begin evacuations.

As waters rose throughout the region, the economy began to suffer as well. As water swept downstream, levees were topped or breached, and land became flooded. River traffic was halted as major port cities along the Missouri and Mississippi began to feel the effects of rising water that swamped docks, breached levees, and flooded areas along the rivers' banks. Highways and railways adjacent to the rivers became impassable, and bridges over key waterways were washed out. Crops could not be planted; as a result, costs for staples such as corn and soybeans rose significantly.

Many small towns were completely underwater, and even larger cities had to conduct evacuations. Limited evacuation occurred in St. Louis as well, where the water remained above flood stage for nearly three months. Several cities, including Des Moines, Iowa, were without potable water for weeks. An even more sinister tragedy struck Quincy, Illinois, where someone intentionally damaged the levee along the Mississippi, causing the entire city to become submerged.

The strain on state governments was significant. Governors Jim Edgar of Illinois, Mel Carnahan of Missouri, and Terry E. Branstad of Iowa were forced to call out National Guard troops, mobilize community emergency-preparedness units, and plead with federal officials for emergency assistance. They spent considerable time as well lobbying their own legislatures for funds to provide

1993

*Two bridges over the Mississippi River were washed out during the 1993 flood.* (FEMA)

temporary shelter for those displaced by rising waters and to pay for resources needed by agencies fighting the floods. These governors, as well as those in other states, including Wisconsin, South Dakota, and Minnesota, which also suffered flood damage, were visible presences in the areas most damaged, as were federal officials, who, after some initial reluctance to recognize the seriousness of the problem, eventually mobilized the resources of the U.S. government to assist in combating the disaster.

Among national leaders who responded aggressively to the calamity was President Bill Clinton, whose administration was facing its first major natural disaster. Although initially slow to recognize the severity of the situation, the Clinton administration made the disaster a national priority once it became apparent that the floods would have significant impact on the country's economy. Clinton made several trips to the region, including one on July 4 to give national visibility to the scope of the disaster. In Washington, members of the president's cabinet worked with leaders in the House of Representatives and the Senate to pass legislation providing emergency funding to those whose lives were being disrupted.

Secretary of Agriculture Mike Espy was also a frequent visitor to the affected states and led the federal drive to provide accurate estimates regarding damages to the annual harvest in the region typically thought of as the breadbasket of America. Although late in responding, the Federal Emergency Management Agency (FEMA), under the capable leadership of director James Lee Witt, worked tirelessly throughout the summer to get relief supplies and other resources to stricken areas during the height of the flooding.

Government efforts had only limited impact, however, as nothing could be done to alter the weather. Fueled by continuing rain falling on ground that was already saturated, rivers remained at record flood stages throughout the summer and into the fall. From March to September, record flooding occurred along more than eighteen hundred miles of river in nine midwestern states, while another thirteen hundred miles were subjected to significant flood damage. When the waters finally subsided in September and October, thousands of individuals displaced by the floods returned to find homes and businesses that could not be repaired. Many were forced to rebuild farther away from rivers; in fact, in some locations entire communities were relocated on higher ground to prevent them from being wiped out again in future floods. In the aftermath of the flooding, state and federal officials estimated that damages throughout the region exceeded fifteen billion dollars, and more than fifty lives were lost.

## SIGNIFICANCE

The short-term effect of the flooding was serious in all nine states in which rivers overflowed their banks. Farmers lost a season of planting, manufacturing industries were temporarily prevented from turning out goods, and many service industries suffered loss of business. The federal government was required to provide billions of dollars in emergency assistance to supplement funds made available by state governments Nevertheless, many affected by the disaster were dissatisfied with what they saw as slow and sometimes inadequate responses to obvious needs. The U.S. Army Corps of Engineers was required to conduct extensive repair work on levees breached by numerous rivers. A thorough review by federal and state authorities conducted in the months following the flooding uncovered numerous deficiencies in weather forecasting, flood prevention, and emergency preparedness. At the federal level, FEMA revised its procedures for dealing with disasters in the hope of being able to be more responsive to future crises.

The long-term effects on some individuals and communities hit hardest by the flood were decidedly more negative. Because the Missouri and Mississippi rivers had wreaked such havoc on areas in their natural floodplains despite the presence of levees designed to protect these areas, significant arguments over the wisdom of reconstructing homes and businesses in the rivers' natural floodplains led many officials to recommend that funds for rebuilding in these areas be withheld. Congress reexamined its program for providing flood insurance and made significant changes that virtually prohibited those living in flood-prone areas from purchasing coverage. Although some communities eventually managed to rebuild on their original sites, several others were not so fortunate. For example, residents of the town of Valmeyer, Illinois, reluctantly voted to reconstruct their entire town on higher ground in the hope that they could avoid a repeat of the disaster that wiped out businesses and homes that had been in some families for generations.

*—Laurence W. Mazzeno*

## FURTHER READING

Chagnon, Stanley A., ed. *The Great Flood of 1993: Causes, Impacts, and Responses.* Boulder, Colo.: Westview Press, 1996. Collection of essays discusses many aspects of the flood, including climatology, hy-

drology, economic impact, and political fallout. Includes an annotated chronology explaining the events
that occurred during the six months that floodwaters
covered parts of the midwestern states.

Mathur, Anuradha, and Dilip da Cunha. *Mississippi
Floods: Designing a Shifting Landscape*. New Haven, Conn.: Yale University Press, 2001. Presents
photographs of the Mississippi River supplemented
by commentary outlining the influence of the river on
the landscape and the people who live within its
floodplain. Includes discussion of the impact of various floods, including the 1993 flood.

Miller, E. Willard, and Ruby M. Miller. *Natural Disasters: Floods*. Santa Barbara, Calif.: ABC-CLIO, 2000.
Handbook on the causes and consequences of floods

provides information on government attempts to prevent and control flooding. Includes extensive bibliography.

Wegner, Michael, Lyle Boone, and Tim Cochran, eds.
*Iowa's Lost Summer: The Flood of 1993*. Ames: Iowa
State University Press, 1993. Presents an exceptionally detailed record of the impact of the 1993 flood on
the people and economy of Iowa, one of the states
hardest hit by the disaster.

**SEE ALSO:** Aug. 20-21, 1971: Heavy Rains Flood the
Red River Delta; Aug. 24, 1992: Hurricane Andrew
Devastates Southern Florida; Aug. 7, 1998: Chang
River Breaks Through Its Main Bank.

## April 3, 1993
# CLINTON CONVENES THE FOREST SUMMIT

*President Bill Clinton's administration held the
Portland Timber Summit in an effort to find new
directions for the management of federally owned
forestlands in the Pacific Northwest.*

**ALSO KNOWN AS:** Portland Timber Summit
**LOCALE:** Portland, Oregon
**CATEGORIES:** Environmental issues; government and
politics; natural resources

**KEY FIGURES**
*Bill Clinton* (b. 1946), president of the United States,
1993-2001
*Al Gore* (b. 1948), vice president of the United States,
1993-2001

**SUMMARY OF EVENT**
The Portland Timber Summit was designed to bring together disputing parties in the conflict between loggers
and supporters of the northern spotted owl to present
their perspectives and to identify mutually acceptable
new directions in American forest management. In 1972,
the U.S. Forest Service adopted the northern spotted owl
as a symbol of vulnerability of old-growth forests. In
June, 1990, the U.S. Fish and Wildlife Service declared
the northern spotted owl to be an endangered species. In
May, 1991, U.S. District Judge William Dwyer ruled that
President George H. W. Bush's administration was deliberately violating the Endangered Species Act by failing to develop an adequate plan to protect the owl from

extinction. The judge placed an injunction against logging on approximately three million acres of federally
owned old-growth forestland in Northern California, Oregon, and Washington until an acceptable plan was developed. This ruling effectively meant that the forests
were being managed by the federal courts rather than by
the U.S. Forest Service.

Fulfilling a campaign promise to put the full power of
the presidency into solving this dispute, President Bill
Clinton held the daylong Portland Timber Summit with
Vice President Al Gore. Participants included the secretaries of the interior, agriculture, labor, and commerce;
the administration of the Environmental Protection
Agency (EPA); the deputy budget director; and the president's science and technology adviser. The president
hoped that the casual town-meeting approach of the conference would be effective in resolving the dispute. Clinton believed that people in the Northwest wanted a truce
in the timber wars and that they were disconcerted by the
federal government's disjointed policy in regard to the
dispute and its resolution. He framed the government's
mission as "a heavy, almost moral, imperative." He saw
the government's role as one based on the vision of the
economic and ecological future of the residents of the
Northwest. Clinton recognized the difficulties of resolving the dispute in a way that was fair to the people and
their livelihoods as well as fair to the environment.

Prior to the Portland Timber Summit, environmental,
timber, industry, and logger groups made a number of ef-

1993

2721

forts to "sell" their perspectives on the logging situation to administration officials. On the day before the conference, representatives of these groups took officials on helicopter, airplane, and four-wheel-drive vehicle tours of the forests. Employees of all the timber mills in Oregon were given the day off and were bused to Portland to demonstrate at the conference hall, carrying signs proclaiming the need to save jobs and protect families. Fifty thousand people attended a free outdoor concert supporting the preservation of old-growth forests on the night preceding the summit. National environmental groups invited federal officials to a "forest feast" dinner at which they could dine on Northwest venison, salmon, fiddlehead ferns, mushrooms, and hazelnut biscotti. Local radio stations broadcast numerous paid announcements concerning the issues at stake.

The conference was expressly designed as a forum for participants to present their perspectives on the conflict in their own words. The loggers tended to focus on the negative effects of the logging ban on individuals, families, and logging communities. In these presentations, loggers were often depicted as environmentalists with a vested interest in a healthy forest ecology and as modern-day Paul Bunyans unable to pass on their culture to the next generation. Logging company officials often focused on the economic difficulties they faced in competitive international markets and the country's need for housing lumber and other wood products. Small logging companies that had successfully adapted to changes in timber supplies and markets and innovations in technology and forest management were also represented.

Native Americans described the traditional and continuing significance of the forest in their lives. Environmentalists acknowledged the economic plight of the logging communities but argued that these communities' economic problems were not a result of the restriction of cutting on federal lands; rather, the problems were a consequence of general economic conditions, such as the low number of housing starts in the United States and a general decline in the logging industry. Environmentalists claimed that the loggers' desire for federal old-growth timber was a result of mismanagement of old growth on private lands. Environmentalists also asserted that logging-related jobs in the United States could be saved through the reduction of log exports to foreign countries.

## SIGNIFICANCE

Despite the differences in perspectives reflected in the presentations at the Portland Timber Summit, at the end

of the day many participants expressed a new optimism about finding solutions to the conflict. A common theme in these reactions was relief that the federal government and the opposing sides had met to share their views and to begin thinking of mutually acceptable solutions. The optimism, however, was short-lived.

Following the summit, the task of developing a management plan was turned over to thirty-seven physical scientists, economists, and sociologists working in three teams meeting in Portland, Oregon. The teams developed ten options, ranging from option 1, the "save it all" option, which allowed 190 million board feet to be cut and would have saved all the federally owned old-growth forests, to option 10, which permitted the cutting of 1.84 billion board feet. (One board foot of wood measures one foot square by one inch thick. An average American home requires about ten thousand board feet of lumber.)

In June, 1994, a committee of senior federal officials began considering the options and prepared decision memoranda for the president. Clinton selected option 9, which set annual harvests at 1.2 billion board feet. This level of harvest was about one-fourth of that in the 1980's but more than twice the level of harvest since the northern spotted owl was declared an endangered species. This option was known as the "efficiency option" because it focused on watersheds as the basic building blocks of the ecosystem. It therefore included actions likely to protect dwindling salmon stocks. Salmon are considered to be the next endangered species if old-growth forests are lost. Managing watershed ecosystems was believed to be more efficient than waiting to deal with salmon as a separate issue.

The management plan also called for the provision of $270 million for 1994 and $1.2 billion over five years to offset economic losses from logging. The plan eliminated 6,000 jobs in 1994 but created more than 8,000, retaining an additional 5,400 jobs. The option also established ten adaptive management areas in which local community and government groups would work together to allow logging and protect wildlife. Salvage logging, the cutting of fire- and insect-damaged trees, and thinning would be permitted in some sections of old-growth forest if an interagency team determined that these practices would not be detrimental to the northern spotted owl's habitat.

Clinton introduced his timber management plan for federal lands in the Pacific Northwest with the prophetic words, "Not everyone is going to like this plan. . . . Maybe no one will." Although many observers judged the plan to be a fair solution, none of the parties directly involved publicly expressed satisfaction with it. Loggers did not believe they could trust the promise of economic aid, especially at a time when the federal government was attempting to balance the budget through spending cuts. They further concluded that the plan was unfair because it contained few provisions for meeting their main concern of preserving logging jobs and the logging-based economies of their small towns. Retraining funds were offered for the purpose of equipping loggers with the skills to be employed in other jobs. Timber industry leaders believed that the plan was based on faulty assumptions about forest productivity and that it unduly restricted logging.

Environmentalists believed that the plan was unfair because it provided for more cutting than was previously permitted under the court injunction and it allowed loopholes that the timber industry would use to conduct even more logging. They believed that the provision to allow salvage logging would be used to cut green trees, as definitions of salvage logging had been stretched in the past. Whistle-blowers within the U.S. Forest Service had leaked a memorandum that explicitly directed employees to allow green cutting to happen. Workers in the Inspector General's Office of the U.S. Department of Agriculture had also found documents indicating that Forest Service officials may have in the past made questionable agreements with logging company officials prior to timber sales. Environmentalists also believed that expected large cuts in the number of Forest Service staff would make policing of the plan difficult.

Representatives of all sides in the dispute stated that they were considering bringing lawsuits against the plan. One basis for such a lawsuit was the lack of public participation in and review of the plan's development. Although the Portland Timber Summit was a putative effort to bring the sides together and to discover mutually agreeable solutions, the alternative management options were developed by experts working in seclusion after the summit had concluded. The summit gave participants voice by allowing them to articulate their ideas, but the participants did not have the power to determine the specifics of the selected management plan.

On June 6, 1994, Judge Dwyer ruled that the option 9 management plan satisfactorily addressed the concerns about protection of the northern spotted owl that had prompted the original injunction. Despite the continued threat of lawsuits, U.S. Forest Service officials stated that, as a result of the lifting of the injunctions against logging, they would proceed with plans to sell timber in the disputed areas.

In another ruling with significant implications for the northern spotted owl and other endangered species, a three-judge panel of the U.S. Court of Appeals for the District of Columbia Circuit concluded in April, 1994, that the Endangered Species Act does not define destruction of a species' habitat as a prohibited activity. The ruling was made in a lawsuit brought by a Sweet Home, Oregon, logging group, which claimed that the U.S. Fish and Wildlife Service had incorrectly decided that the logging of forests containing endangered species or other habitat modifications constitute harmful activities as defined by the act.

—*George Cvetkovich and Timothy C. Earle*

## FURTHER READING

Clinton, Bill, and Al Gore. *Putting People First: How We Can All Change America*. New York: Times Books, 1992. Collection of speeches by Clinton and Gore includes presentations of their views on citizen participation in public discourse.

Dietrich, William. *The Final Forest: The Battle for the Last Great Trees of the Pacific Northwest*. New York: Simon & Schuster, 1992. Provides an illuminating look at the old-growth controversy. Focuses on the logging town of Forks, Washington, in examining how such communities have been affected by the debate.

Ervin, Keith. *Fragile Majesty: The Battle for North America's Last Great Forest*. Seattle: Mountaineers, 1989. Presents a history of Washington State forest management controversies. Includes bibliography and index.

Forest Ecosystem Management Assessment Team. *Forest Ecosystem Management: An Ecological, Economic, and Social Assessment*. Washington, D.C.: U.S. Government Printing Office, 1993. Presents descriptions of the forest management options developed following the Portland Timber Summit. Includes detailed reference to supporting materials and a content summary of presentations at the conference.

Gore, Al. *Earth in the Balance: Ecology and the Human Spirit*. 1992. Reprint. Emmaus, Pa.: Rodale Press, 2006. Highly readable book by an environmental crusader who became vice president of the United States in 1993. Details human effects on the physical environment, including the effects of deforestation. Includes excellent bibliography.

Stout, Benjamin B. *The Northern Spotted Owl: An Oregon View, 1975-2002*. Victoria, B.C.: Trafford, 2006. Examines the controversy surrounding the protection

1993

of the northern spotted owl and the negative impacts of that protection on local timber-dependent communities.

SEE ALSO: 1971: Paclitaxel Is Extracted from Pacific Yew Trees; July 23, 1972: Launch of the First Earth Resources Technology Satellite; Aug. 17, 1974: U.S. Congress Revises Resource Management; Oct. 22, 1976: U.S. Congress Limits Forest Clear-Cutting; 1989: Arnold and Gottlieb Publish *The Wise Use Agenda*; July 23, 1990: Spotted Owl Prompts Old-Growth Timber Controversy.

## April 19, 1993
# BRANCH DAVIDIANS' COMPOUND BURNS

*When the Federal Bureau of Investigation carried out a raid on the Branch Davidian religious cult, the action resulted in the deaths of more than eighty persons, led to an investigation of the government agencies involved, and became a rallying point for antigovernment sentiment.*

LOCALE: Waco, Texas

CATEGORIES: Religion, theology, and ethics; wars, uprisings, and civil unrest

KEY FIGURES

*David Koresh* (Vernon Wayne Howell; 1959-1993), leader of the Branch Davidian cult

*Janet Reno* (b. 1938), attorney general of the United States

*William Sessions* (b. 1930), director of the Federal Bureau of Investigation

SUMMARY OF EVENT

On April 19, 1993, more than eighty members of the Branch Davidians, a religious sect, died during a government raid on the group's compound in Waco, Texas. The fiery battle was exactly what cult leader David Koresh had predicted, and the loss of life fulfilled Attorney General Janet Reno's greatest fear.

The tragedy occurred at Mt. Carmel, called Ranch Apocalypse, in the wake of a decision by the Federal Bureau of Investigation (FBI) to end a fifty-one-day standoff with force. The decision had been a difficult one, and the results convinced the U.S. attorney general, Janet Reno, that it had been the wrong one. The Mt. Carmel residents were members of the Branch Davidian cult, an offshoot of the Seventh-day Adventist Church. The group had lived peacefully in Waco since 1935, with only one flare-up of unrest—when Vernon Wayne Howell (later known as David Koresh) challenged George Roden's leadership during the 1980's. When Roden was incarcerated on murder charges, Howell took over the Davidians, and peace seemed to reign. Eventually, however, dis-

turbing reports began to surface. Neighbors complained of hearing machine-gun fire, and it was reported that children in the compound were being sexually abused. A delivery man informed authorities about shipments of grenades. Finally, the U.S. Bureau of Alcohol, Tobacco, and Firearms (ATF) began to investigate.

The ATF leadership became alarmed when they substantiated reports that the cult had amassed nearly $200,000 worth of guns and other weapons. On February 28, 1993, the agency moved to take control of Mt. Carmel. The attempt failed, and a shootout ensued in which four agents and six Davidians died. It was uncertain who had fired first, but the ATF received great criticism for its show of force. Because Koresh was often seen in the community, many people questioned why the authorities had not arrested him in town instead of attempting to take the compound. Some critics accused the ATF of tipping off the media in order to gain publicity and protect the agency from budget cuts. Others believed that ATF leaders knew they had lost the element of surprise, yet sent their agents into a seeming death trap. Whatever the truth behind the failed raid, the result was a nerve-wracking standoff.

In the weeks that followed, the FBI surrounded the compound and attempted to persuade the Davidians to surrender. First, the agency gave Koresh whatever he requested, including broadcast of a rambling, fifty-eight-minute speech. In exchange, Koresh allowed thirty-seven Branch Davidians, including twenty-one children, to leave the compound. When conciliation yielded no more results, the FBI began to flood the compound with annoying bright lights and loud sounds. The agents even attempted to smuggle listening devices into Mt. Carmel to gather intelligence that would enable agents to devise better strategies. Koresh and the remaining cult members held their ground.

A ninth-grade dropout and disappointed rock musician, Koresh had become convinced that he was God incarnate. He claimed that he was a sinful Jesus whom God had sent to earth to experience the vices of man—training that would prepare Koresh to stand in judgment of the sinners of the world on the final Judgment Day. True to his convictions, Koresh denied himself nothing. He enjoyed beer, fast cars, and promiscuous sex but denied them to his followers. He isolated the men and took every female he desired as a wife—even girls as young as eleven years of age—claiming he was the only one holy enough to sire children. His followers gave in to these demands, surrendered their possessions, and submitted themselves to hours of rambling sermons. Koresh maintained his control over the adults by withholding food. To ensure the proper behavior of children, Koresh established a spanking room.

During the siege, the FBI consulted psychological experts who became increasingly alarmed at Koresh's behavior. They told the agency that Koresh saw himself as invincible, and they predicted that he would never allow the remaining Branch Davidians to leave the compound. The FBI searched for a plan to bring the standoff to a conclusion. It was rumored that the entire compound was booby-trapped, so any attack had to proceed cautiously. The ATF had proof that the Davidians possessed powerful weapons and night-vision scopes. Sentries appeared to guard the windows at all times and held children up to the windows whenever agents approached. Strategists considered attacking with a water cannon, but they were worried that the force of the blow could cause the building to collapse on the children. FBI director William Sessions and his top deputies put together a plan based on the use of gas to cause confusion; they then approached Attorney General Reno for approval of the plan.

Reno questioned the FBI about the danger of exposing people to any form of noxious gas. She was concerned that an anesthetic gas might be too strong for the children and might cause their deaths. The FBI brought in an expert who persuaded Reno that tear gas would not be carcinogenic or otherwise inflict permanent harm. Reno

---

## THE WHITE HOUSE BACKS RENO

*On April 20, 1993, President Bill Clinton held a press conference to address the events that took place in Waco the day before. Before taking questions, he made a statement:*

On February the 28th, four federal agents were killed in the line of duty trying to enforce the law against the Branch Davidian compound, which had illegally stockpiled weaponry and ammunition, and placed innocent children at risk. Because the BATF operation had failed to meet its objective, a 51-day standoff ensued.

The Federal Bureau of Investigation then made every reasonable effort to bring this perilous situation to an end without bloodshed and further loss of life. The Bureau's efforts were ultimately unavailing because the individual with whom they were dealing, David Koresh, was dangerous, irrational, and probably insane.

He engaged in numerous activities which violated both federal law and common standards of decency. He was, moreover, responsible for the deaths and injuries which occurred during the action against the compound in February. Given his inclination towards violence and in an effort to protect his young hostages, no provocative actions were taken for more than seven weeks by federal agents against the compound.

This weekend I was briefed by Attorney General Reno on an operation prepared by the FBI, designed to increase pressure on Koresh and persuade those in the compound to surrender peacefully. The plan included a decision to withhold the use of ammunition, even in the face of fire, and instead to use tear gas that would not cause permanent harm to health, but would, it was hoped, force the people in the compound to come outside and to surrender.

I was informed of the plan to end the siege. I discussed it with Attorney General Reno. I asked the questions I thought it was appropriate for me to ask. I then told her to do what she thought was right, and I take full responsibility for the implementation of the decision.

Yesterday's action ended in a horrible human tragedy. Mr. Koresh's response to the demands for his surrender by federal agents was to destroy himself and murder the children who were his captives, as well as all the other people who were there who did not survive. He killed those he controlled, and he bears ultimate responsibility for the carnage that ensued.

---

also wanted to know how Koresh would react to this type of pressure. No one could say for sure if he would lead his followers to death. Negotiators had questioned Koresh about his plans for suicide more than once, and each time he denied such plans. However, a warning concerning Davidians in Australia had been received the year before, predicting they would never be taken alive. Reno weighed the evidence and demanded that the FBI restate its justification. Finally, she contacted President Bill Clinton and made her recommendation to approve the attack.

At 6:00 A.M., April 19, the barrage began. Two armored combat engineer vehicles (CEVs) began moving

*Fire consumes the Branch Davidian compound in Waco, Texas, on April 19, 1993.* (AP/Wide World Photos)

toward the compound as loudspeaker announcements urged the cult members to surrender. Koresh ordered his followers to don gas masks. Then the shooting began. The CEVs began breaking holes in the compound's walls, and gas was pumped throughout the building. The women and children gathered in the center of the second floor, where there was no exit. Around noon, the announcements urging surrender were repeated. The gas was so thick, the agents urged the people in the compound to walk toward the sound of the loudspeaker. Then explosions shook the area—the ammunition stores had exploded.

Winds began gusting to thirty miles per hour, and the building—which had been constructed of flimsy, flammable materials—was engulfed in fire. The flames were further fueled by bales of hay that had been placed against windows for warmth and by a propane tank that had been used to block the door. As the agents watched helplessly, several people suddenly remembered hearing about a school bus that had been buried on the grounds for use as a bunker. They investigated to see if the chil-

dren had been hidden there, but it was empty. By the time the blaze was out, nothing was left but ashes and bodies.

**SIGNIFICANCE**

Later that day, Reno addressed the media and took full responsibility for the decision that had precipitated the Waco disaster. Many people thought she was committing political suicide, but she stood firm. She noted that she deeply regretted the loss of life, and she insisted that the decision had been hers alone. Some analysts held that Reno could not be considered completely to blame; many speculated that Koresh had planned to set the fires from the beginning. His few surviving disciples, however, denied any plans of mass suicide. One young man who had lived in the compound for a year asserted that the residents had intended to evacuate—that many of them were near the front of the building when a CEV caused it to collapse, starting a fire that filled the area with black smoke, making it impossible for anyone to see any escape routes. Children and adults fled for the interior areas, but the fire spread too quickly and they were trapped. Another survivor told of trying to get to the children but finding the way blocked with debris caused by government vehicles.

The FBI agents on the scene insisted that their CEVs did not start the blaze. They contended that the fire began in several locations at the same moment; they believed that Koresh deliberately murdered his followers to fulfill his prophecy. Some experts who have been trained to deal with terrorists, however, remained critical of the FBI's handling of the Branch Davidians, contending that the use of gas was a mistake and suggesting that the FBI never considered seriously the possibility of the cult members' willingness to die for Koresh. Some theologians, moreover, argued that the federal agents neglected any opportunity to use the cult's religious leanings to approach a peaceful resolution. Regardless of who was at fault, or whether (as seems likely) both Koresh and the FBI agents contributed to the events that resulted in the deaths, the Waco debacle soon assumed symbolic importance among certain antigovernment groups. Along with similar incidents at Ruby Ridge, Idaho, and, in the spring of 1996, near Jordan, Montana, the events at Waco reinforced the sentiments of some Americans that the federal government was taking too much control of the lives of U.S. citizens.

—*Suzanne Riffle Boyce*

## FURTHER READING

Breault, Marc. *Inside the Cult: A Member's Exclusive Chilling Account of Madness and Depravity in David Koresh*. New York: Dutton, 1993. Account published soon after the events at Waco by a former recruiter for the Branch Davidians provides some background information. Includes photographs.

Gibbs, Nancy, et al. "Oh My God, They're Killing Themselves!" *Time*, May 3, 1993, 26-42. Much of this issue is devoted to a series of articles providing background and accounts of the events at Waco.

Gotschal, Mary G. "A Marriage Made in Hell." *National Review*, April 4, 1994, 57-60. Discusses the legal background of the Branch Davidians' clash with government agencies.

Reavis, Dick J. *The Ashes of Waco: An Investigation*. New York: Simon & Schuster, 1995. Journalistic account examines the events at Waco from the perspectives of both the federal agencies involved and the followers of David Koresh. Draws on interviews with Branch Davidian survivors, trial transcripts, published accounts, and other sources. Includes bibliography.

Tabor, James D., and Eugene V. Gallagher. *Why Waco? Cults and the Battle for Religious Freedom in America*. Berkeley: University of California Press, 1995. Discusses the Branch Davidians as an unconventional religious group and examines American reactions to such groups. Includes illustrations and index.

Wright, Stuart A., ed. *Armageddon in Waco: Critical Perspectives on the Branch Davidian Conflict*. Chicago: University of Chicago Press, 1995. Collection of essays by scholars in history, law, sociology, and religion provides background on the Branch Davidians and their leader as well as wide-ranging analysis of the events that took place in Waco. Includes index.

**SEE ALSO:** Nov. 18, 1978: People's Temple Members Commit Mass Suicide; Mar. 20, 1995: Terrorists Use Sarin Gas in Tokyo Subway Attack; Mar. 23-25, 1997: Heaven's Gate Cult Members Commit Mass Suicide.

1993

## April 22, 1993
# UNITED STATES HOLOCAUST MEMORIAL MUSEUM OPENS

*The 1993 opening of the United States Holocaust Memorial Museum, the nation's preeminent institution for the study of the Holocaust and for commemorating its victims, marked the culmination of a fifteen-year effort to preserve the memory of one of the most horrifying events of the modern era.*

**LOCALE:** Washington, D.C.
**CATEGORIES:** Organizations and institutions; terrorism, atrocities, and war crimes

**KEY FIGURES**

*Michael Berenbaum* (b. 1945), deputy director of the President's Commission on the Holocaust, 1978-1980, and project director of the United States Holocaust Memorial Museum, 1988-1993
*Elie Wiesel* (b. 1928), chair of the President's Commission on the Holocaust
*James Ingo Freed* (1930-2005), architect of the United States Holocaust Memorial Museum
*Ralph Applebaum* (fl. late twentieth century), exhibition designer for the United States Holocaust Memorial Museum's Permanent Exhibit

**SUMMARY OF EVENT**

In November, 1978, President Jimmy Carter created the President's Commission on the Holocaust to suggest ways in which the United States might best commemorate the victims of the Holocaust. Chaired by Elie Wiesel, a Holocaust survivor, acclaimed writer, and Nobel Peace Prize winner, the thirty-four-member commission delivered its recommendations in 1979. The group called for the creation of a "living memorial" that incorporated a museum, a foundation to advance education on the Holocaust, and a "Committee on Consciousness" to raise public awareness of acts of genocide. The commission's ideas were enacted by a sixty-eight-member United States Holocaust Memorial Council, which Congress established in 1980.

Fifteen years later, on April 22, 1993, President Bill Clinton presided over the official dedication of the United States Holocaust Memorial Museum. Approximately ten thousand people stood in a cold rain expectantly awaiting the museum's opening. The crowd contained Holocaust survivors, veterans of World War II, heads of state, and representatives from twenty different countries. The dedication ceremony featured speeches by President Clinton; Chaim Herzog, the sixth president

of Israel; Harvey Meyerhoff, chairman of the U.S. Holocaust Memorial Council; and Wiesel. Wiesel delivered a powerful keynote address in which he shared the poignant story of his mother, a victim of the Holocaust. He also reminded his audience of society's responsibility to learn from, and prevent the recurrence of, such atrocities. The opening ceremony was the highlight of a week-long series of events in Washington, D.C., that included a "Days of Remembrance" ceremony, worship services, a concert, and tributes to those who rescued Holocaust survivors and liberated the concentration camps. On April 26, 1993, the museum opened to the general public. Its first visitor was the Dalai Lama, Tibet's exiled political and spiritual leader.

The United States Holocaust Memorial Museum is located one block from the National Mall and within site of the Washington Monument and the Jefferson Memorial. It rests on a 1.9-acre site that was donated by the federal government. More than $168 million in private donations funded the museum's construction. The museum has a threefold mission: to educate visitors about the history of the Holocaust, to memorialize the millions of Holocaust victims, and to promote reflection on the lessons that can be learned from the Holocaust.

The museum building was designed by James Ingo Freed, senior partner of the New York firm Pei, Cobb, Freed & Partners. Freed was a Jewish refugee who escaped from Germany as a child, in 1939. He spent several months researching the Holocaust and visiting concentration camps. Profoundly affected by his experiences at these camps, he created a highly compelling building that is freighted with meaning.

Freed's award-winning, 285,000-square-foot structure is built primarily of brick, limestone, steel, and glass. The exterior is neoclassical in design, much like other federal buildings found in Washington, D.C. The museum's interior architecture, however, is designed to transport visitors emotionally into a much different world, one that disturbs their senses. The experience begins in the Hall of Witness, an immense, four-story atrium that functions as the museum's entrance hall. The girders that support the ceiling of skylights are twisted and cast odd shadows across the floor. The steel braces and arches in the brick walls suggest the crematoria found in the concentration camps. Catwalks span the hall, creating the sensation that visitors are being watched. A tapering staircase bears an eerie resemblance to the railroad tracks that led to the arched gate of the Birkenau concentration camp.

The museum's second major component is the 36,000-square-foot Permanent Exhibit conceived by Ralph Applebaum, an acclaimed designer and founder of Ralph Applebaum Associates. Unlike many museums, this three-floor space is organized in a narrative fashion. It tells the story of the Holocaust by engaging visitors in an emotional fashion. It does so largely through multimedia displays and artifacts. Many of the artifacts incorporated into the exhibit were donated by Holocaust survivors and countries in which the Holocaust took place. Some objects represent the victims: passports, shoes, suitcases, eating utensils, toys, clothing, and family photographs. Other objects represent the machinery of the Holocaust: a section of a camp barracks; prisoner uniforms; canisters of Zyclon B, the gas used to kill many prisoners; and a railway car like those used to transport prisoners to the camps.

The narrative begins in the elevator that transports visitors from the Hall of Witness to the fourth floor, the top floor of the Permanent Exhibit. In the elevator, visitors watch a video about the liberation of the concentration camps. When visitors exit the elevator, they face a wall-sized photograph of American soldiers liberating a concentration camp. The horrific scene in this photograph prompts visitors to contemplate how such an unspeakable atrocity could occur. From there, the exhibit space winds down to the second floor. This area chronicles the post-World War I rise of the National Socialist German Workers' (Nazi) Party and Adolf Hitler, the oppression experienced by those under Nazi rule, the enactment of Hitler's "final solution," the liberation of the camps at the end of World War II, and the Nuremberg Trials. The narrative concludes with a film in which Holocaust survivors relate their experiences.

Upon exiting the Permanent Exhibit, visitors encounter the Hall of Remembrance. This hexagonal area is the

*An exterior view of the United States Holocaust Memorial Museum in Washington, D.C.* (Raul654/GFDL)

1993

museum's formal memorial. Illuminated chiefly by a domed skylight, this solemn area promotes reflection. The hall features an eternal flame to honor the memory of those who died in the Holocaust. Buried under the flame is dirt from Holocaust locations, including the concentration camps.

The remainder of the United States Holocaust Memorial Museum contains a variety of spaces, including two auditoriums, two galleries for temporary exhibits, and an expansive library and archive. In addition, the museum contains an interactive, computer-based learning facility, a research institute, an exhibit especially designed for children, and classrooms.

## SIGNIFICANCE

According to Michael Berenbaum, noted Holocaust scholar and project director of the museum, the United States Holocaust Memorial Museum represents the "Americanization" of the Holocaust. That is, the museum adopts an American perspective, enabling American audiences to identify with its narrative.

The museum's popularity as a site for learning suggests that it has accomplished this end. Beginning in 1993, the museum has attracted approximately two million visitors per year. Despite early concerns that the museum would interest only Jewish visitors, approximately 90 percent of its guests are non-Jewish. The museum's highly compelling narrative has viscerally awakened visitors to the enormity of the crimes committed against humanity during the Holocaust. This educational mission has become increasingly important as the body of Holocaust deniers grows. As a national institution, the United States Holocaust Memorial Museum also guides the country in conducting an annual civic commemoration of the Holocaust's victims. It holds annual "Days of Remembrance" observances and provides resources to others who wish to do so.

Finally, the museum's significance is apparent in its attempts to marshal the Holocaust's memory to prevent such atrocities in the future. For example, the museum campaigned to raise public consciousness about similar acts of genocide in Bosnia, Rwanda, and Darfur. In October, 2000, President Clinton approved a law that gave the United States Holocaust Memorial Museum permanent standing. This "living memorial" will thus continue to serve as a powerful example for other museums that similarly seek to merge education with commemoration and protest.

*—Beth A. Messner*

## FURTHER READING

Berenbaum, Michael. *The World Must Know: The History of the Holocaust as Told in the United States Holocaust Memorial Museum.* 2d ed. Baltimore: The Johns Hopkins University Press, 2006. Exceptional exploration of the Holocaust narrative as it is imparted by the museum's Permanent Exhibit. Contains historical photographs and testimony from Holocaust victims and witnesses.

Kernan, Michael. "A National Memorial Bears Witness to the Tragedy of the Holocaust." *Smithsonian* 28 (April, 1993): 50-65. Follows the author's personal tour of, and thoughtful response to, the museum. Highlights some of the museum's history and key features.

Linenthal, Edward T. *Preserving Memory: The Struggle to Create America's Holocaust Museum.* 2d ed. New York: Columbia University Press, 2001. An insider's insightful chronicle of the tensions arising from the difficult decision making that influenced the museum's focus, mission, and architectural and exhibition design.

Weinberg, Jeshajahu, and Rina Elieli. *The Holocaust Museum in Washington.* New York: Rizzoli International Publications, 1995. Details the museum's creation, the principles that guided that process, and the activities promoted by the museum. Provides outstanding photographs of the museum's architecture and exhibits.

SEE ALSO: Jan., 1971-Apr., 1979: Amin Regime Terrorizes Uganda; May-Aug., 1972: Burundi Commits Genocide of Hutu Majority; Apr. 17, 1975: Khmer Rouge Comes to Power in Cambodia; May 11, 1987: Barbie Is Tried for Nazi War Crimes; Apr. 18, 1988: Israel Convicts Demjanjuk of Nazi War Crimes; Apr. 6-July, 1994: Rwandan Genocide; 1998: Reparations Funds for Holocaust Victims Are Established; Sept., 1998: U.N. Tribunal Convicts Rwandans of Genocide.

## May 4 and November 23, 1993
# KUSHNER'S *ANGELS IN AMERICA* PREMIERES ON BROADWAY

*With its rich variety of characters and its determination to address social problems and the AIDS crisis, Tony Kushner's two-part play* Angels in America *was widely hailed as the most original work on Broadway in the 1990's.*

**LOCALE:** New York, New York
**CATEGORY:** Theater

**KEY FIGURES**

*Tony Kushner* (b. 1956), American dramatist
*Roy M. Cohn* (1927-1986), American lawyer and political insider who achieved fame in the prosecution of Julius and Ethel Rosenberg and in the Army-McCarthy hearings in the 1950's
*Ethel Rosenberg* (1915-1953), American housewife who, with her husband Julius, was convicted of espionage and executed

**SUMMARY OF EVENT**

With its subtitle *A Gay Fantasia on National Themes*, Tony Kushner's *Angels in America* announces its aspirations to supernatural, sexual, and political commentary. For that portion of the Broadway audience in the early 1990's that hungered for serious nonmusical plays, the two parts of *Angels in America* provided a serious meditation on social upheaval at the end of the millennium, the struggles of an unlikely coalition of minorities (gays, Jews, and Mormons) to preserve their dignity and identity, the consequences of the acquired immunodeficiency syndrome (AIDS) crisis, the abuse of justice in American society, and the need for acceptance—of AIDS victims and gays, of sharp political differences, and of human mortality. Even more startlingly, in a commercial theater not known for its sensitive treatment of religious issues, *Angels in America* explored the transcendental meaning of human suffering and the possibility of divine intervention, in the form of angelic messages from heaven and ghostly appearances, and pondered the sobering notion of God's disappearance.

The play interweaves a rich collection of fictional characters, including an AIDS victim who is given a prophetic role by an angel and a gay Mormon Republican lawyer who is torn by conflicting values, with vivid historical characters: Roy M. Cohn, the American lawyer and power broker, and, with a deft Shakespearean touch, the ghost of Ethel Rosenberg, the American housewife who was tried and executed for passing nuclear bomb se-

crets to the Soviets at the height of the Cold War. Like William Shakespeare's Richard III, the dying Cohn is visited by an otherworldly nemesis: Rosenberg comes to haunt Cohn for sending her to the electric chair but stays to say the Kaddish, the Hebrew prayer for the dead, for Cohn when he is in the last stages of his deathbed agony.

*Angels in America* was originally commissioned by the Eureka Theatre Company, and the two parts were performed in San Francisco, Los Angeles, and London before settling in on Broadway. Part one of *Angels in America*, titled *Millennium Approaches* (pr. 1991), opened on Broadway on May 4, 1993, and then was joined, in repertory, by part two, *Perestroika* (pr. 1992), on November 23, 1993. With the success of *Millennium Approaches* on Broadway, Kushner persisted in revisions of *Perestroika* until its opening a half year later. Nothing is resolved in *Millennium Approaches*, which elaborately sets up the exposition for *Perestroika*; the promised angelic intervention occurs in *Millennium Approaches* only as the curtain falls and is revealed in full in the second play. *Perestroika* contains the three richest scenes in the two parts but retains signs of hasty revision and ends on an ambivalent note of cosmic optimism.

*Angels in America* contains four main plots. Two of these show the deterioration of a pair of relationships: In the first, a gay couple, Prior Walter and Louis Ironson, separate when Ironson is frightened by the onslaught of AIDS in Walter; in the second, a Mormon married couple, Joe Pitt and his wife, Harper, are broken apart by Joe's neglect of his wife, his slow recognition of his homosexuality, and Harper's subsequent dependence on drugs and escape into a fantasy life. The third plot deals with Cohn's refusal to accept his diagnosis of AIDS and his own physical deterioration and disbarment after a notorious career as a lawyer. The fourth plot deals with a series of supernatural interventions, including the angel who appoints Walter as a prophet, the fantasy figure ("Mr. Lies") who visits Harper in her drug-induced euphoria, and the ghost of Rosenberg.

*Millennium Approaches* sets up the exposition, and *Perestroika* impressively pulls together the various plots. The first part ends with the arrival of the long-promised supernatural intervention; the second ends with the hope of eventual healing. Cohn is gone, but Walter has survived five years after the onset of AIDS, and there is a hint that he and Ironson may be reconciled. Various other characters, such as Joe Pitt's pious Mormon mother,

1993

*Tony Kushner.* (Columbia University/Courtesy Jay Thompson)

Hannah, and a male nurse and drag queen, Belize, help to connect the main plots.

It was audacious of Kushner to link the AIDS crisis in the gay community of the 1980's with the anxieties and expectations concerning the millennium in the 1990's. His decision to include the historical figure of Roy Cohn among a set of invented characters created some controversy, but the choice pays off with the emergence of a great comic villain. Because the main plot follows Ironson's inability to deal with the advent of AIDS in his lover, it makes good dramatic sense to add a character such as Cohn, who seems historically to have denied to the end that he was gay and that he had AIDS. One of Cohn's biographers, Nicholas von Hoffman, quotes him as saying, "There would be no reason to stick around and live if I had AIDS, so I don't."

Cohn is largely remembered among liberals as a bogey figure, famous as a prosecutor for winning the convictions of Julius and Ethel Rosenberg and for his role as chief counsel to Senator Joseph McCarthy during the Army-McCarthy hearings. Cohn had a deep hatred for Ethel Rosenberg, even though most legal scholars now

see her role in the case as secondary, and he is widely suspected of using illegal influence over the judge in his effort to secure the executions of both Rosenbergs. As a gay Jewish playwright living in an age more sympathetic to, but still uneasy about, homosexuality, Kushner grasped the dramatic potential of a contradictory figure such as Cohn.

The complex sources of the play include biographies of Cohn, the Book of Mormon, the poetry of Walt Whitman, and the angelic visions of the Swedish mystic Emanuel Swedenborg. The play favors the overwrought emotions and improbable coincidences of nineteenth century melodrama, and the vivid characterization of Cohn resembles both the villains of melodrama and the "trickster" character in folk literature. When Walter, at the urging of Joe Pitt's mother, wrestles with the angel who has come to invest him with prophetic powers, the playwright taps into the Old Testament story (in Genesis 32) of Jacob wrestling with the angel: "So Jacob was left alone, and a man wrestled with him there till daybreak.... The man said, 'Let me go, for day is breaking,' but Jacob replied, 'I will not let you go unless you bless me.'" Walter demands of the angel, "Bless me anyway. I want more life." The blessing is playfully inverted in the scene where Cohn, on his deathbed, tricks the ghost of Rosenberg into providing him with the blessing on the dying, the Kaddish.

## SIGNIFICANCE

Even before its premiere on Broadway, *Angels in America* was widely praised for its richness, complexity, and vivid theatricality, and enthusiastic reports from the National Theatre production in London created high expectations for the Broadway production. Audiences enjoyed the vivid characterizations and the flair of George C. Wolfe's direction. Theater critics were generally highly enthusiastic about the play, praising it for its willingness to confront American problems and anxieties on the edge of the next millennium. The reviewer for *The New York Times* called *Millennium Approaches* "the most thrilling American play in years" and argued that *Perestroika* serves as "a stunning resolution" of the issues raised in the first part. The Broadway production won several Tony Awards, and *Millennium Approaches* earned for Kushner a Pulitzer Prize in 1993.

*Angels in America* reawakened hopes that Broadway, which had witnessed the great plays of Eugene O'Neill and Tennessee Williams, would once again stage plays of complex ideas and cosmic scope. *Angels in America* is especially unusual in breaking with the predominant form of spoken plays since the 1930's, the realistic middle-class drama, for which playwrights such as Williams and Arthur Miller had set a high standard in the 1940's. In some ways, *Angels in America* is closer to older historical plays such as Robert E. Sherwood's *Abe Lincoln in Illinois* (pr. 1938) than to the more narrowly focused domestic plays of Miller and Williams.

*Angels in America* rejects the psychological credibility of "method acting," dominant on Broadway since the 1940's, in favor of a broadly comic and melodramatic style of acting. In his flamboyant villainy, the play's Cohn seems closer to Shakespeare's wicked kings or Charles Dickens's villains than to the more familiar tormented introverts of Williams, Miller, and Edward Albee. The angels, meeting in heaven, speak in a kind of Whitmanesque discourse, while the earthly characters speak in a rich polyglot, including the pious Mormon platitudes of Hannah Pitt, the Yiddishisms of Ironson and the rabbi who officiates at the funeral of his grandmother, the "girl talk" of Belize, the anguished moral confusion of Joe Pitt (who mixes pious Mormon talk with the bromides of Reaganite conservatism), and the boisterous profanity of Cohn.

The three most theatrically effective scenes in *Angels in America* come in *Perestroika*. The first is a flashback in which Walter explains to Belize how the angel crashed through his ceiling (the moment shown as the climax of *Millennium Approaches*) to charge him with his prophetic commission to reveal that the "Great Work" has begun. The second takes place in the Mormon Visitor's Center in New York, where Hannah Pitt and Walter (who is there to investigate angels) join the delusional Harper Pitt in watching the diorama of the Mormon pioneers' trek across America. To their surprise, the roles of the mechanical pioneers are usurped by Joe Pitt and Ironson. The scene links the plot elements of the abandoned wife and gay lover with the themes of Mormon rectitude and the possibility of supernatural intervention.

The third notably effective scene, that of Cohn's death, successfully mixes pathos and comedy. The ghost of Rosenberg tells the dying Cohn of his disbarment and offers to forgive him for sending her to the electric chair. In his delusion, Cohn calls Rosenberg "Ma" and asks her to sing. Rosenberg provides a Yiddish lullaby and thinks Cohn is dead, but in the tradition of the folk trickster, Cohn pops up and says, "I fooled you Ethel, I knew who you were all along. . . . I just wanted to see if I could finally, finally make Ethel Rosenberg sing!" Only then, after this heroic burst of energy, does Cohn fall back and die. The scene is so startling that the play's final act,

which ties up a number of loose plot elements, runs the danger of being anticlimactic.

Audiences generally responded enthusiastically to the play's epic grandeur and buoyant engagement of such widely disparate topics as the AIDS epidemic and angelic intervention. Some of the mainstream Broadway audience found the play "too gay," but others understood that Kushner was adding to the efforts of gay playwrights such as Larry Kramer, Harvey Fierstein, and Terrence McNally in bringing gay culture into the mainstream in Broadway plays. Others took exception to the play's apparent Mormon bashing, to the simulated episodes of gay sex, and to the relentless obscenity of Roy Cohn's language.

The weaknesses of the play include the sprawling and diffuse plot, which relies heavily on coincidence: For example, one of Walter's earlier lovers, Belize, improbably turns up as the nurse for the dying Cohn. The play's opposing moral poles, the prophetic Walter and the demonic Cohn, are never shown together. The play's depiction of heaven is unpersuasive, and it seems a remarkable admission of defeat that Kushner lists as optional three scenes set in heaven in the final act of *Perestroika*.

*Angels in America*, which had undergone a long period of gestation in productions before arriving on Broadway, reminds audiences jaded by high-tech movie special effects of the power of theater when it is willing to entrust the discussion of great contemporary themes to vivid characters who use distinctive styles of speech. The play has a frank dependence on melodramatic devices but also a willingness to contemplate the possibility of divine interaction with human affairs. What reporter and AIDS activist Randy Shilts said of the AIDS crisis of the 1980's was true of *Angels in America* in the 1990's: "The AIDS epidemic is, ultimately, a tale of courage as well as cowardice . . . and redemption as well as despair." Kushner's epic play helped to advance tolerance of homosexuality, compassion for AIDS victims, and awareness of the need for understanding, forgiveness, and "more life."

—*Byron Nelson*

## FURTHER READING

Berkowitz, Gerald M. *American Drama of the Twentieth Century*. London: Longman, 1992. Provides an excellent overview of the work of U.S. playwrights just prior to the emergence of Kushner. Stresses American drama's long dependence on realism and domestic issues and suggests the need for more experimental approaches.

1993

Cohn, Roy. *The Autobiography of Roy Cohn.* Edited by Sidney Zion. Secaucus, N.J.: Lyle Stuart, 1988. Cohn's life story in his own words. Zion labels Cohn "one of the most fascinating characters imaginable."

Kushner, Tony. *Angels in America: A Gay Fantasia on National Themes. Part One: Millennium Approaches. Part Two: Perestroika.* 1993/1994. Reprint. New York: Theatre Communications Group, 2003. Both parts of Kushner's sprawling work available in this single volume. Includes photographs from productions.

Radosh, Ronald, and Joyce Milton. *The Rosenberg File.* 2d ed. New Haven, Conn.: Yale University Press, 1997. Presents an exhaustive study of the evidence against the Rosenbergs. Asserts that Julius Rosenberg was "the coordinator of an extensive espionage operation" and that Ethel almost certainly "acted as an accessory," but nonetheless concludes that the government was guilty of "a grave miscarriage of justice."

Sharlitt, Joseph H. *Fatal Error: The Miscarriage of Justice That Sealed the Rosenbergs' Fate.* New York: Scribner's, 1989. Ponders the "gross miscarriage of justice" that sent the Rosenbergs to their execution.

Shilts, Randy. *And the Band Played On: Politics, People, and the AIDS Epidemic.* New York: St. Martin's Press, 1987. Famous indictment of the American government's early indifference to AIDS as merely a gay issue helped to galvanize public support for AIDS research.

Von Hoffman, Nicholas. *Citizen Cohn.* New York: Doubleday, 1988. Acerbic look at Cohn from a liberal perspective stresses the deep contradictions in Cohn's character: Jewish man, homosexual, lawyer, conservative power broker, and sincere anticommunist.

Wilmer, S. E. *Theatre, Society, and the Nation: Staging American Identities.* New York: Cambridge University Press, 2002. Examines how theater in the United States has reflected political and social change since the time of the American Revolution. Chapter 7 includes discussion of *Angels in America.*

**SEE ALSO:** Feb. 10, 1971: Guare's *The House of Blue Leaves* Joins Naturalistic and Nonrepresentational Theater; June 27, 1978-1979: Shepard's *Buried Child* Promotes Off-Broadway Theater; June 5, 1981: U.S. Centers for Disease Control Recognizes AIDS; June 10, 1982: Fierstein's *Torch Song Trilogy* Meets with Unexpected Success; June, 1986: Akalaitis's *Green Card* Confronts Audiences with Harsh Realities; Mar., 1991: Medical Researchers Test Promising Drugs for the Treatment of AIDS.

## May 9, 1993
# PARAGUAY EMBRACES DEMOCRACY

*Paraguay's May, 1993, presidential election was a watershed event in the country's transition to democracy. In the subsequent years, Paraguayans won many civil liberties, and free and fair elections became the norm.*

**LOCALE:** Asunción, Paraguay
**CATEGORIES:** Civil rights and liberties; government and politics

**KEY FIGURES**
*Juan Carlos Wasmosy* (b. 1938), president of Paraguay, 1993-1998
*Alfredo Stroessner* (1912-2006), authoritarian dictator of Paraguay, 1954-1989
*Andrés Rodríguez* (1923-1997), leader of a coup d'état against Stroessner who succeeded him as president, 1989-1993
*Lino César Oviedo* (b. 1937), leader of an attempted coup d'état against Wasmosy in 1996

**SUMMARY OF EVENT**
On May 9, 1993, Juan Carlos Wasmosy was elected president of Paraguay, an event that ushered in democracy after decades of dictatorial rule. The seeds of democracy in Paraguay had been planted several years earlier, however, during the administration of President Andrés Rodríguez. He came to power following a military coup d'état that brought an end to the thirty-four-year dictatorship of Alfredo Stroessner. Although not strongly committed to democracy, Rodríguez took actions that enabled democracy to flourish later. Among the most important of these was the institution of multiparty elections—the first in several decades—held on May 1, 1989, in which Rodríguez won the presidency as the Colorado Party candidate. This action established an important precedent for future elections. He also facilitated the development of a new constitution, which took effect on June 20, 1992, that provided the foundation for a democratic Paraguay.

When Wasmosy was inaugurated as president of Paraguay on August 15, 1993, he faced a number of almost insurmountable obstacles. His support among the political elite and the Paraguayan population was minimal. There was strong evidence that he had won the Colorado Party nomination through fraud, which considerably diminished his support within the party.

Although the 1993 presidential general election was generally considered fair, and Wasmosy received more votes than any of his competitors, his ability to assert presidential authority was diminished because he received less than 40 percent of the popular vote. Beyond these limiting considerations, he was a political novice who possessed no broad political support even within the Colorado Party. In fact, his strongest opposition came from factions within his own party. Moreover, opposition parties controlled both houses of the congress, the Senate and the Chamber of Deputies. Thus Wasmosy's legislative support was virtually nil. Wasmosy's strongest support came from President Rodríguez and the military hierarchy, a factor that contributed to his alienation from several factions of the Colorado Party who strongly distrusted the military. Finally, his credentials as a democratic reformer were considered dubious by most Paraguayans. In short, Wasmosy's mandate to govern was exceptionally weak.

Among the major issues that confronted President Wasmosy during his five-year term were those related to the status of the military and its role in government and society in Paraguay. During the decades that Stroessner governed Paraguay, an alliance among the Colorado Party, military leaders, and the government dominated every facet of Paraguayan life. The result was an exceedingly repressive and, at times, brutal authoritarian regime that was the antithesis of democracy. In 1993, the military remained a potent force; it was feared by large segments of society and continued to be a grave threat to democracy. The dilemma for Wasmosy was that he was indebted to the military for its support during the primary and general elections. Early in Wasmosy's term, the Paraguayan congress initiated efforts to curtail the influence of the military in government and society. These efforts were largely opposed by Wasmosy. Eventually, the congress was successful in restricting the power of the military. The most important restriction, approved by the congress in May, 1994, made political party affiliation unlawful for members of the armed forces.

Perhaps the most serious crisis faced by President Wasmosy occurred in 1996 and involved civilian control of the military. This crisis was precipitated by the overt political activities of charismatic army commander General Lino César Oviedo, who had been a political ally of Wasmosy at the outset of his term. Oviedo was strongly opposed to limitations imposed by Paraguay's congress on the political activities of military officers and continued to participate openly in such activities. On April 22, 1996, Wasmosy was forced to dismiss Oviedo as leader of the army. Oviedo refused to accept the dismissal and tried to seize power through a coup d'état, which was quickly aborted. Following his forced retirement as army commander, Oviedo became a candidate for president in 1997. Wasmosy responded by having Oviedo arrested and charged with insubordination, based on the events of April, 1996. He was convicted by a military tribunal in March of 1998, and sentenced to ten years in prison. This series of events undoubtedly served notice to the Paraguayan military leadership that political activity and insubordination to civilian authority would not be tolerated. These events also contributed to the advancement of democracy.

Another major issue confronting President Wasmosy in his accession to power was the status of the legal system and its role in a democratic Paraguay. Under the Stroessner and Rodríguez regimes, judgeships were the exclusive domain of the Colorado Party, and appointments to these coveted positions were made by the president. A fundamental requirement for participation in the judiciary at virtually any level—from the supreme court to the lower courts—was membership in the Colorado Party. In 1993, there were compelling reasons to reform the legal system, such as widespread abuse and corruption. Wasmosy, however, was indebted to the Colorado Party, which strongly opposed any reforms that would alter the status quo. Consequently, efforts to reform the legal system were initiated by the congress.

In November, 1993, the Senate enacted legislation assigning responsibility to the congress for appointing supreme court judges. There was immediate conflict and much political wrangling between the executive and legislative branches over this issue. Eventually, in August, 1994, a compromise was reached by which a judicial council would appoint supreme court judges. Finally, in March, 1995, the judicial council appointed a new, nine-member supreme court, whose membership included only four members of the Colorado Party. This action significantly reduced that party's influence and power. Over the long run, these events resulted in a more independent judiciary and facilitated the transition to democracy.

Although some efforts to institute democratic reforms

1993

were successful, others largely failed, most notably efforts to eliminate or reduce corruption within the government, which had been a holdover from the Stroessner era. Paraguay continued to be one of the world's most corrupt nations. In a region where high-level corruption is the norm, institutionalized corruption in Paraguay remained pervasive. Much of the corruption was tied to smuggling and narcotics trafficking whose primary beneficiaries were government officials. Paraguay's informal economic sector, including smuggling and the illicit drug trade, was thought to have exceeded the formal sector, a situation found in few, if any, other nations. There remained scarcely a single government agency in which corruption was not rampant. Significant evidence indicates that endemic and systemic corruption extended to the highest levels of government. The three former presidents who served in succession beginning in August, 1993, were charged with corruption, tried, convicted, and sentenced to prison, including Juan Carlos Wasmosy, who was found guilty of bank fraud and sentenced to four years in prison.

## SIGNIFICANCE

Although the transition to democracy in Paraguay was not smooth, the free and fair election of Juan Carlos Wasmosy and the eventual completion of his five-year presidential term were especially significant because this period allowed the nascent democracy to become better established. Not only did several democratic institutions become stronger but, in some cases, they flourished as well. After the election of Wasmosy, there were three attempted military coups, all of which ultimately failed. The last two attempted coups, in 1999 and 2000, failed, at least in part, because of the precedents established by President Wasmosy during the 1996 Oviedo coup d'état attempt.

Beyond these achievements, this fragile democracy appeared to make credible advancements in a number of other areas, especially in the development of a strong and active civil society. On both the local and national stages, frequent and often passionate debate raged over funda-

mental democratic issues and the methods needed to resolve long-standing problems. Such discussions were unheard of in the four decades before 1993. Moreover, as a new generation of political leaders emerged, democratic ideals and values continued to be embraced. Many of these leaders were intolerant of the status quo and a political system that failed the nation for generations. The post-Wasmosy generation of leaders made new demands on an archaic political system and compelled Paraguay to continue to respond to democratic principles.

—*Robert R. McKay*

## FURTHER READING

Lambert, Peter. "A Decade of Electoral Democracy: Continuity, Change and Crisis in Paraguay." *Bulletin of Latin American Research* 19 (July, 2000): 379-396. Traces the evolution of democracy in Paraguay by examining political conflict and change in the 1990's.

Lambert, Peter, and Andrew Nickson, eds. *The Transition to Democracy in Paraguay*. New York: St. Martin's Press, 1997. Collection of articles that examines the roles of institutions, organizations, and individuals as democracy took root in Paraguay.

Repucci, Sarah, and Christopher Walker, eds. *Countries at the Crossroads: A Survey of Democratic Governance*. Lanham, Md.: Rowman & Littlefield, 2005. A discussion of the transition to democracy in Paraguay in relation to other democratic movements.

Valenzuela, Arturo. "The Coup That Didn't Happen." *Journal of Democracy* 8 (January, 1997): 43-55. Detailed account of the mid-1990's constitutional crisis created by General Lino César Oviedo, including an examination of the roles of Paraguayan institutions, civil society, and international entities during the crisis.

SEE ALSO: Aug. 18, 1971: Bánzer Seizes Power in Bolivian Coup; June 15, 1977: Spain Holds Its First Free Elections Since the Civil War; June 30, 1980: Paraguayan Torturer Is Convicted of Violating the Law of Nations; Mar. 15, 1985: Democracy Returns to Brazil.

## May 24, 1993
# ERITREA SECEDES FROM ETHIOPIA

*After thirty years of active civil war, Eritrea gained independence from Ethiopia after the assumption of power by the Eritrean People's Liberation Front.*

**LOCALE:** Eritrea
**CATEGORIES:** Independence movements; wars, uprisings, and civil unrest; government and politics

**KEY FIGURES**
*Haile Selassie I* (1892-1975), emperor of Ethiopia, 1930-1974
*Abdelaziz Bouteflika* (b. 1937), president of Algeria beginning in 1999
*Isaias Afewerki* (b. 1945), president of Eritrea beginning in 1993
*Kofi Annan* (b. 1938), secretary-general of the United Nations, 1997-2006
*Mohamed Sahnoun* (fl. late twentieth century), United Nations special envoy to Ethiopia and Eritrea, 1998-1999

**SUMMARY OF EVENT**
Eritrea, which is located on the western coast of the Red Sea, fulfilled its long struggle for independence from Ethiopia on May 24, 1993. Eritrea's liberation struggle began in 1961, when Emperor Haile Selassie I of Ethiopia masterminded the abrogation of its federation with Ethiopia. However, the groundwork for the country's independence was prepared as early as February 5, 1941, when the British ended fifty years of Italian colonial rule and administered Eritrea for ten years. As soon as the British liberated Eritrea from Italy, they were mandated by the United Nations to administer the territory and prepare the population for a transition to independence.

The proclamation of the British Military Administration (BMA) of Eritrea envisioned a democratic political system for the country. It allowed free press, freedom of association, and due process of law for all Eritreans for the first time in their modern history. At the end of British rule, when the United States, Great Britain, the Soviet Union, and France could not agree on the Eritrean question, the General Assembly of the United Nations looked into the status of Eritrea. In 1950, the U.N. General Assembly made a recommendation that Eritrea be federated with Ethiopia on September 15, 1952. The United Nations also designated a special commissioner for Eritrea to find out the preference of the Eritrean people once federation was implemented. The commissioner had a man-

date to consult with the population and prepare a constitution.

On October 17, 1951, the commissioner completed his consultation. Immediately, the BMA issued Proclamation No. 121, setting ground rules for an Eritrean representative assembly. On March 26, 1953, polling was conducted for the sixty-eight seats of the assembly. The result was split between thirty-four Christian and thirty-four Muslim representatives.

On July 10, 1952, the Eritrean constitution was adopted by the assembly. Two months later, on September 11, Emperor Haile Selassie ratified the constitution, formally completing the federation process. The British departed on September 15.

The federation was a transitional phase meant to last for ten years and to prepare the Eritrean people for a 1962 referendum on union with Ethiopia versus complete independence. During this transitional period, Emperor Haile Selassie instructed his representative in Eritrea to emphasize Ethiopia's right to the country, and to campaign on the benefits of Eritrea's union with Ethiopia.

The emperor lobbied individual members of the Eritrean assembly, and when independent-minded members would not comply with Ethiopian demands, they were forced to resign or face violence. On November 14, 1962, the assembly was forced to meet and dissolve both itself and the federation. The anticipated democratic transition to independence was aborted, triggering a thirty-year war for liberation.

As early as 1958, an underground organization known as the Eritrean Liberation Movement was agitating against Ethiopian interference in Eritrea. By 1962, it came out in the open, calling itself the Eritrean Liberation Front (ELF). ELF fighters were a resourceful political and military force when they began their struggle. Their clandestine operations and guerrilla tactics presented a formidable challenge to the Ethiopian army.

As time progressed, ELF lost its focus. It lacked discipline, a cohesive political program, and committed leadership. In 1969, Marxist-leaning elements within ELF's ranks split and formed the Eritrean People's Liberation Front (EPLF). Between 1970 and 1980, ELF and EPLF fought against each other while simultaneously fighting Ethiopian troops. By 1980, EPLF gained the upper hand because of a large influx of new recruits, mainly young people escaping Ethiopian atrocities in the cities.

In 1980, ELF was driven out of the Eritrean battle-

1993

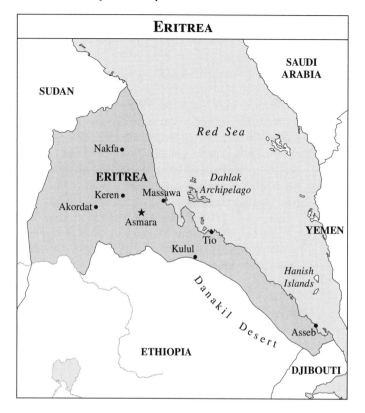

**ERITREA**

SAUDI ARABIA

SUDAN

*Red Sea*

Nakfa

ERITREA

*Dahlak Archipelago*

Keren    Massawa

Akordat

Asmara

Tio

YEMEN

Kulul

*Hanish Islands*

*Danakil Desert*

Asseb

ETHIOPIA

DJIBOUTI

field, its fighters seeking refuge in Sudan. EPLF, under the leadership of Isaias Afewerki, increased in strength and discipline. It scored successive victories in guerrilla ambushes against the Ethiopian army. One of its decisive victories occurred in 1987 at the battle of Afabet, where one-third of the Ethiopian army was defeated. The entire lowland of Eritrea was liberated as Ethiopian troops abandoned their positions and garrisoned themselves in the cities of Asmara, Keren, Massawa, and Dekemhare.

In 1990, the ancient Eritrean seaport of Massawa was liberated, a development that exposed the Decamare and the Asmara garrisons to attack by the EPLF. Ethiopian troops outnumbered the Eritreans by five to one, but they were dispirited over their poor leadership. When Eritrean fighters mounted the last offensive in 1991, against Decamare and Asmara, Ethiopian troops retreated and scattered in confusion.

On May 24, 1991, the Eritrean capital of Asmara was liberated. Eritrean liberation, anticipated as early as 1941 but circumvented in 1962, had finally been achieved. The EPLF called for the implementation of the referendum that was derailed by Haile Selassie in 1962. A referendum was held in 1993, under the supervision of the United Nations. The overwhelming majority of Eritreans voted for the complete independence of Eritrea. Ethiopia, under a new, pragmatic regime, was the first country to recognize Eritrea's independence, declared on May 24, 1993.

For a brief period, it looked as if sovereign Eritrea and Ethiopia were opening up a new chapter of peace and good-neighborliness. This apparent friendliness between the countries was deceptive. A series of economic and political disputes escalated into border war on May 13, 1998, when the Ethiopian parliament declared war on Eritrea over a border skirmish around the small village of Badme.

At first, the war appeared to be heading toward stalemate. However, given Ethiopia's ample manpower and Eritrea's critical shortage of troops, it was a matter of time before Ethiopian forces breached Eritrean defenses. The destruction of Eritrean defense positions occurred on February 26, 1999, when all Eritrean borders were overrun and Asmara was exposed to Ethiopian artillery. A day later, Eritrea accepted a peace plan mediated by the Organization of African Unity (OAU) that called for a cease-fire and withdrawal of Eritrean forces to their pre-crisis positions.

Eritrea sought frantically for a peaceful resolution of the crisis, but Ethiopia refused and escalated the war. Secretary-General Kofi Annan of the United Nations appointed Mohamed Sahnoun as his special envoy to mediate peace between the warring parties. President Bill Clinton's administration appointed Anthony Lake, former U.S. national security adviser, as a special envoy from the United States. The chairman of the OAU, President Abdelaziz Bouteflika of Algeria, appointed former Algerian prime minister Ahmed Ouyahia as a special OAU envoy.

All parties worked tirelessly for two years, until they were able to secure and sign the Cessation of Hostilities Agreement on June 18, 2000. The two countries were represented by their foreign ministers, Haile Woldetensae of Eritrea and Seyoum Mesfin of Ethiopia.

On July 31, 2000, the United Nations Security Council passed Resolution 1312 establishing the United Nations Mission to Eritrea and Ethiopia (UNMEE). Under UNMEE authorization, the United Nations stationed more than four thousand peacekeepers in the temporary security zone between Eritrea and Ethiopia.

On December 12, 2000, the two sides signed the Comprehensive Peace Agreement, which established the

Boundary Commission and the Claims Commission. The latter was charged with determining culpability for the initiation of the war.

## SIGNIFICANCE

On May 24, 1993, Eritrea joined the family of nations as a sovereign state with internationally recognized boundaries. However, its 1998 war with Ethiopia was as much a reminder of its fragile existence as it was confirmation of its sovereignty. The war demonstrated that smaller states on the global stage risk their sovereignty and security unless they surrender to the demands of larger neighbors. At the same time, Ethiopia's rejection of the OAU-brokered peace plan in favor of prolonging the war increased its casualties.

Even after the signing of the Comprehensive Peace Agreement, ethnic conflict between Eritrea and Ethiopia continued, along with reports of human rights violations from both sides. A December 19, 2005, decision by the Claims Commission in the Hague found Eritrea guilty of triggering the war with Ethiopia in 1998, ruling that it should not have resorted to force over its claims to the village of Badme.

—*Tseggai Isaac*

## FURTHER READING

Gebre-Medhin, Jordan. *Peasants and Nationalism in Eritrea: A Critique of Ethiopian Studies*. Trenton, N.J.: Red Sea Press, 1989. Condemns the argument for a "Greater Ethiopia" as a new form of African imperialism advanced by Western apologists for Ethiopian elites.

Longrigg, Stephen H. *A Short History of Eritrea*. Oxford: Clarendon Press, 1945. The first book on modern Eritrea contending that its historical, political, and economic conditions make it unviable for sovereignty.

Negash, Tekeste. *Eritrea and Ethiopia: The Federal Experience*. Uppsala, Sweden: Nordic Africa Institute, 1997. Offers analysis of the political drama that resulted in the union of Eritrea with Ethiopia, with a pro-Ethiopia slant.

Pateman, Roy. *Eritrea: Even the Stones Are Burning*. Trenton, N.J.: Red Sea Press, 1989. Presents a catalog of Eritrean war casualties during the mid-1980's.

Trevaskis, G. K. N. *Eritrea: A Colony in Transition, 1941-1953*. London: Oxford University Press, 1960. Analysis of Eritrean history and political affairs during British administrative rule.

Wrong, Michela. *"I Didn't Do It for You": How the World Betrayed a Small African Nation*. New York: HarperCollins, 2005. A journalistic analysis of Eritrea's struggle for global attention.

SEE ALSO: 1974: Portugal Grants Independence to Its African Colonies; Feb., 1974: Military Junta Comes to Power in Ethiopia; Nov. 6-13, 1975: Dispute over the Western Sahara Erupts in the Green March; July 23, 1977-Mar. 15, 1978: Ogaden War Between Somalia and Ethiopia; June, 1981: Organization of African Unity Adopts the African Charter on Human and Peoples' Rights; Oct., 1984: Ethiopia Resettles Famine Victims from the North to Southern Ethiopia; Dec. 22, 1988: Namibia Is Liberated from South African Control; Aug., 1991: African Countries Begin to Revive Democratization; Dec. 16, 1992: U.N. Security Council Brokers Peace in Mozambique; May 6, 1998-Dec. 12, 2000: Eritrean-Ethiopian War; July 10, 1999: Six African Nations Sign the Lusaka Peace Accord; July 11, 2000: Organization of African Unity Moves to Establish the African Union.

1993

## May 27, 1993
# BOMB DAMAGES THE UFFIZI GALLERY

*When a car bomb destroyed part of the Uffizi Gallery, the Mafia was suspected of perpetrating the attack in response to the Italian government's crackdown on organized crime.*

**LOCALE:** Florence, Italy
**CATEGORIES:** Arts; crime and scandal; terrorism, atrocities, and war crimes

**KEY FIGURES**
*John Paul II* (Karol Józef Wojtyła; 1920-2005), Roman Catholic pope, 1978-2005
*Giovanni Falcone* (1939-1992), chief prosecutor of Mafia figures in Italy
*Salvatore Riina* (b. 1930), boss of all bosses of the Sicilian Mafia

**SUMMARY OF EVENT**

Just after 1:00 A.M. on May 27, 1993, a five-hundred-pound bomb concealed in a stolen Fiat exploded, gravely damaging the west wing of the Galleria degli Uffizi (the Gallery of Offices) in Florence, Italy. The bomb killed five people, destroyed a part of the five-hundred-year-old structure, damaged the Corridoio Vasariano (Vasari Corridor), and weakened the Buontalenti staircase, the gallery's old exit. The fireball destroyed the newly completed catalog of the Uffizi Gallery collection as well as the world's oldest assembly of agricultural research documents, which had been housed in the Academia dei Georgiofili. Four of the dead were from a single family, the caretakers and inhabitants of the Torre Della Pulci, a medieval tower behind the Uffizi.

The Uffizi Gallery is Florence's principal museum. It houses the world's finest collection of Italian paintings created from the thirteenth through the eighteenth centuries. Aside from the loss of life, perhaps the greatest tragedy of the bombing was the permanent loss of three paintings by seventeenth century followers of Caravaggio: *Giocatori di Carte* (*Men Playing Cards*) and *Concerto* (*Concert*) by Bartolomeo Manfredi and *L'Adorazione dei Pastori* (*Adoration of the Shepherds*) by Gherardo delle Notti.

The damage to other artwork was extensive and varied. Sculptures were broken. Some thirty paintings had pigment blasted from their surfaces, others were slightly damaged, and still others were shredded by flying glass. The original estimate at the time of the attack was that thirty paintings were in need of repair. Nearly one year later, closer examination had revealed that the total number of damaged works was nearly one hundred. In nearby rooms, bulletproof glass that had been installed to protect against vandalism protected the paintings of Titian, Raphael, Paolo Veronese, Caravaggio, and Michelangelo from flying debris. More than two hundred works had to be removed from their galleries because the blast had blown out skylights, exposing the works to the weather.

Also, as the Uffizi Gallery is a sixteenth century building, the structure itself is considered a work of art. Although it would have been faster, simpler, and most likely less expensive to demolish and rebuild the damaged areas, restoration of the building proceeded with the same care and attention as the restoration of the damaged works of art.

No party was immediately prosecuted for the blast, but authorities strongly suspected Mafia involvement. The plastic explosives used in the attack were identical to those used in an attack in Rome against an anti-Mafia journalist just two weeks earlier. The bombings were viewed as responses to a police investigation in Milan that had resulted in the roundup of hundreds of alleged Mafia gangsters and bosses. These terrorist acts were intended as blows against government attempts to diminish the power and control of the Mafia; they were perpetrated to draw attention away from political corruption trials and to break the growing popular will for reform. The Mafia targeted a world-famous museum to underscore the vulnerability of Italy's thirty-five hundred museums and hundreds of thousands of public monuments and, by extension, the foreign tourists visiting the treasures of Italian history. The day after the explosion, more than twenty thousand people marched through the streets of Florence in mourning and in anger, as a demonstration against armed intimidation.

The Uffizi Gallery is one of the world's greatest repositories of Italian art. The building was designed by Giorgio Vasari to house the government offices of the Tuscan state. Vasari also built the so-called Corridoio Vasariano, which stretches from the Uffizi across the Arno River, via the Ponte Vecchio, to the Pitti Palace. The corridor, which is nearly half a mile long, now serves as a gallery for the world's largest collection of self-portraits. After Vasari's death, Bernardo Buontalenti carried on the work. The resultant structure consists of an elongated-U-shaped three-story building that borders the Arno River on one side and is within sight of the Piazza della Signoria on the other. The Uffizi became a public museum in 1859 after Tuscany joined the Italian state.

In 1991, Milanese authorities had uncovered a vast network of corruption involving business executives and politicians who exchanged huge bribes for public works contracts. Nearly twenty-five hundred politicians and corporate leaders were implicated. Later, two leading businessmen associated with the scandal committed suicide. The Mafia retaliated by bombing cultural sites and assassinating government and church officials. In May, 1992, Italy's chief prosecutor of Mafia figures, Giovanni Falcone, was murdered. Two months later, another judge was killed. Salvatore Riina, the boss of all Mafia bosses, was believed to be involved and was arrested. It was also in May of 1992 that Pope John Paul II, during a visit to Sicily, made the Catholic Church a Mafia target when he urged people to resist the crime lords. In September, Giuseppe Puglisi, a Palermo priest who was an outspoken critic of the Mafia, was murdered.

The Uffizi attack was one of five car bombings that took place from May through August of 1993 in Rome, Florence, and Milan. The attacks left ten people dead and dozens wounded. Cultural sites, journalists who opposed the Mafia's efforts to destabilize the government, church figures, and church properties all were among the targets. Two venerable Roman churches were bombed. The first was San Giovanni in Laterano, a seventeenth century baroque masterpiece by Francesco Borromini and the church where the pope serves as bishop. The second was San Giorgio in Velabro, one of Rome's oldest churches and the site where Romulus and Remus are said to have founded Rome. It was surmised that the churches were targeted because of the pope's call for resistance to organized crime. In the minds of Mafia members, that statement abrogated the Church's unwritten hands-off policy toward their activities.

Nearly a year after the Uffizi bombing, Italian investigators confirmed original suspicions when they officially declared that the Mafia was behind the 1993 bomb attack. Four suspects with ties to organized crime were named, but in the years following the attack, no individuals were indicted.

## SIGNIFICANCE

The Uffizi bombing and others like it were designed to terrorize by destroying irreplaceable items of cultural heritage. The attacks had little effect on tourism and served to galvanize Florentine resistance, however. The bombings led to the resignations of some intelligence officials and a shake-up of the national police organization. A voters' referendum called for a change in the way the country was run.

Thanks to the efforts of 150 restorers, custodians, administrators, and volunteers, the Uffizi Gallery reopened only twenty-four days after the bombing. Salvaging of the Academia dei Georgofili began the very same day of the attack. Within five days of the bombing, more than forty thousand priceless books had been retrieved from the destruction and moved to the Sala Magliabechiana,

*Firefighters clear debris after a car bomb damaged the Uffizi Gallery in Florence.* (AP/Wide World Photos)

1993

the historic headquarters of the Teatro Mediceo. Many of Florence's store owners contributed 2 percent of their net receipts to help defray the cleanup costs. The positive response of the Italian citizenry convinced the gallery's administration to complete work on thirty new display rooms, which had been stalled since 1990 because of budgetary and bureaucratic problems. The startlingly rapid turnabout so impressed members of the United Nations Educational, Scientific, and Cultural Organization (UNESCO) that they suggested the Uffizi experience should be used as a model for arts administrations worldwide.

—*William B. Folkestad, revised by Mark Miller*

**FURTHER READING**

Bohlen, Celestine. "Clues in '93 Uffizi Blast Point to Mafia." *The New York Times*, August 7, 1995, p. A2. Discusses the Sicilian Mafia's role in the Uffizi bombing and the difficulty of investigating and prosecuting the Mafia.

Giraldi, Juliet Love. "The Uffizi, a Year Later." *Contemporary Review*, September, 1994, 148. Reassesses the damage done to nearly one hundred priceless artworks and reports on the progress being made toward restoration of the building and its contents. Also includes a detailed discussion of the particular restoration techniques applied to two pieces by Peter Paul Rubens.

Horn, Miriam. "The Impact of Blasts to the Past." *U.S. News & World Report*, September 13, 1993, 20. Briefly discusses the bombing as an attack on Italian heritage. Notes the attempt to break the people's will by destroying the items held most dear and describes a general disbelief that the Mafia, fellow Italians, could be involved.

"Returned and Restored." *ArtNews*, February, 1996, 69. Brief news item describes the ceremony by Uffizi Gallery officials announcing the return of the final artwork restorations to the museum two and a half years after the terrorist attack.

Schneider, Jane C., and Peter T. Schneider. *Reversible Destiny: Mafia, Antimafia, and the Struggle for Palermo.* Berkeley: University of California Press, 2003. Traces the history of the Sicilian Mafia and discusses efforts by the judiciary and citizens' groups to reduce the organization's power.

**SEE ALSO:** Mar. 15, 1972-Dec. 20, 1990: Coppola's *Godfather* Trilogy Explores Organized Crime; Mar. 16-May 9, 1978: Terrorists Kidnap and Murder Former Italian Prime Minister; Mar., 1994: Italy's Voters Move Right; Apr. 19, 1995: Bombing of the Oklahoma City Federal Building.

---

# June 14-25, 1993
# WORLD CONFERENCE ON HUMAN RIGHTS

*The World Conference on Human Rights established the Office of the High Commissioner for Human Rights and highlighted the importance of human rights for women, children, the disabled, and people of all races, ethnicities, and religions. It also led to the adoption of the Vienna Declaration and Program of Action, which emphasized the importance of human rights and equality.*

**ALSO KNOWN AS:** Vienna Declaration and Program of Action

**LOCALE:** Vienna, Austria

**CATEGORIES:** Human rights; indigenous peoples' rights; women's issues

**KEY FIGURES**

*Boutros Boutros-Ghali* (b. 1922), secretary-general of the United Nations, 1992-1996

*José Ayala Lasso* (b. 1932), first U.N. high commissioner for human rights, 1994-1997

*Ibrahima Fall* (b. 1942), secretary-general of the World Conference on Human Rights and director of the Center for Human Rights in Geneva, 1992-1997

**SUMMARY OF EVENT**

In 1948, fifty-eight United Nations member states authored the Universal Declaration of Human Rights, which called on member states to promote civil, human, social, and economic rights. The Universal Declaration was the first international attempt to limit states' behavior, emphasizing each state's duty to its citizens. In 1968, the International Conference on Human Rights was held in Tehran, Iran, marking the twenty-year anniversary of the Universal Declaration. The conference in Tehran led to the adoption of the Proclamation of Tehran, which dealt with the problems of racial discrimination, illiteracy, colonialism, and protection of the family. Along with the 1948 Universal Declaration of Human Rights, the 1966 International Covenant on Civil and Political Rights and the 1966 International Covenant on Economic, Social, and Cultural Rights formed what came to be called the International Bill of Rights.

More than seven thousand representatives from more than 171 countries convened from June 14 to June 25, 1993, to adopt legislation that would protect women's rights, children's rights, and the rights of indigenous peoples and to ensure the equal treatment of all, regardless of religious affiliation, race, ethnic background, or disability. Boutros Boutros-Ghali, secretary-general of the United Nations, opened the conference by indicating how proud he was of the delegates of the World Conference on Human Rights for focusing on the protection and promotion of human rights.

The conference ended with a call for a number of different actions to be taken, with an emphasis on six specific categories of human rights. First, the Vienna Declaration and Program of Action, adopted on the final day of the conference, called for better coordination between different parts of the United Nations and a continual adaptation of the United Nations to deal with present and future needs related to human rights violations. Additionally, the declaration called for equality in the following areas: race, nationality, ethnicity, and religious affiliation. The declaration also called for the protection of the rights of migrant workers, women, children, and the disabled. Furthermore, the declaration endorsed the freedom from torture for all.

The declaration indicated an increased need for national and international cooperation, as well as a need for human rights education and training. The declaration stated the need for enhanced promotion of human rights across the world. The Vienna Declaration and Program of Action called for an annual follow-up to determine if the goals were being met. Finally, the Vienna Declaration established the Office of the High Commissioner for Human Rights. On April 5, 1994, José Ayala Lasso assumed office as the first high commissioner after being nominated for the position by the secretary-general.

The conference took exceptional measures to protect and promote the rights of women, indigenous peoples, and children. With respect to children's rights, the Vienna Declaration called for ratification of the U.N. Convention on the Rights of the Child, which was adopted by the United Nations in November, 1989, and entered into force in 1990. The Convention on the Rights of the Child contains fifty-four articles that focus on a variety of is-

sues pertaining to juveniles, including the right to be treated fairly under the law and the right to appropriate medical and mental care, when needed. The Convention on the Rights of the Child also called for states to do all they could to educate minors about the dangers of drug use and to attempt to prevent such use. Furthermore, the convention outlined the right of the child to rest and play and to take full part in his or her culture.

Not only children's rights but also the rights of indigenous peoples and migrant workers were discussed at the World Conference on Human Rights. Five paragraphs of the Vienna Declaration were devoted to indigenous peoples' rights, which included setting up a fund devoted exclusively to this category and urging all member states to encourage indigenous groups to participate in all aspects of society, particularly those that interested them. Three brief sections were also devoted to migrant workers, asking for greater harmony between migrant workers and the rest of society.

Although not the focus of the conference itself, the idea for centralizing women's rights arose from some previous events, including the World Women's Congress for a Healthy Planet, which took place in Miami, Florida, in 1991, and the International Tribunal on Crimes Against Women, which took place in Brussels, Belgium, in 1976. Women's issues were often subsumed in other categories of official documents; however, nine paragraphs highlighting the rights of women were included in a separate section of the Vienna Declaration. The section on the human rights and equal status of women contained paragraphs devoted to the organization and activities of the United Nations itself, highlighting the reduction of both outward and hidden discrimination against women. The paragraphs also discussed the physical and mental health of women and the elimination of violence against women. A five-year follow-up was submitted at the end of 1997, which indicated either the progress of states or the lack thereof. Overall, significant progress was made, but some discriminatory laws still needed to be altered.

### SIGNIFICANCE

The World Conference on Human Rights led to the Vienna Declaration, which emphasized enhanced coordination on human rights within the United Nations and a focus on the rights of all. These rights included the freedom from torture and the freedom from discrimination on the basis of race, nationality, ethnicity, gender, disability, or one's status as a juvenile. The World Conference on Human Rights reemphasized the importance of state maintenance of fair and equal treatment of people

1993

across the globe. Although more progress remained to be made in regard to equal treatment in the world, this conference was a step in the right direction and was significant in that all members unanimously agreed with the Vienna Declaration and Program of Action.

—*Sheryl L. Van Horne*

**FURTHER READING**

Beetham, David, ed. *Politics and Human Rights*. Cambridge, Mass.: Blackwell, 1995. Demonstrates how human rights debates help shape politics in different regions of the world.

Bunch, Charlotte, and Niamh Reilly. *Demanding Accountability: The Global Campaign and Vienna Tribunal for Women's Human Rights*. New Brunswick, N.J.: Center for Women's Global Leadership, 1994. Provides information about events leading up to the World Conference on Human Rights and the struggle to add women's issues to the discussion.

Donnelly, Jack. *Universal Human Rights in Theory and Practice*. Ithaca, N.Y.: Cornell University Press, 2002. Covers numerous aspects of human rights in a multidisciplinary approach, using international relations, international law, political theory, and sociology.

Evans, Tony. *The Politics of Human Rights: A Global Perspective*. 2d ed. Ann Arbor, Mich.: Pluto Press, 2005. Focuses globally on human rights and examines states' declining role in protecting people due to the political economy and globalization.

Jacobson, Thomas L., and Won Yong Jang. "Rights, Culture, and Cosmopolitan Democracy." *Communication Theory* 11, no. 4 (2001): 434-453. Weighs the costs and benefits of democratization and cultural homogenization using Jürgen Habermas's theory of communicative action.

Nowak, Manfred. *Introduction to the International Human Rights Regime*. Herndon, Va.: Brill Academic, 2003. Contains information about human rights from an interdisciplinary perspective, while defining human rights and providing concrete examples.

Patel, Jayan, ed. *Addressing Discrimination in the Vienna Declaration: A Guide for NGO's and Interested Individuals*. Tokyo: International Movement Against All Forms of Discrimination and Racism, 1995. Briefly discusses numerous publications related to various forms of discrimination.

**SEE ALSO:** Dec. 20, 1971: United Nations Declares Rights for the Mentally Retarded; June 19-July 2, 1975: World Conference on Women Sets an International Agenda; Dec. 9, 1975: United Nations Issues a Declaration Against Torture; Aug.-Dec., 1978: World Conference Condemns Racial Discrimination; Dec. 18, 1979: U.N. Convention Condemns Discrimination Against Women; Nov. 20, 1989: United Nations Adopts the Convention on the Rights of the Child.

## June 25, 1993
# CAMPBELL BECOMES CANADA'S FIRST WOMAN PRIME MINISTER

*When Kim Campbell succeeded Brian Mulroney as the leader of Canada's Progressive Conservative Party, she also became the prime minister of Canada, the first woman ever to hold that post.*

**LOCALE:** Ottawa, Ontario, Canada
**CATEGORIES:** Government and politics; women's issues

**KEY FIGURES**

*Kim Campbell* (b. 1947), prime minister of Canada, June-November, 1993

*Jean Chrétien* (b. 1934), prime minister of Canada, 1993-2003

*Brian Mulroney* (b. 1939), prime minister of Canada, 1984-1993

**SUMMARY OF EVENT**

Three individuals served as Canada's prime minister during 1993, including Kim Campbell, the first woman to hold the office. Born on March 10, 1947, in British Columbia, Campbell studied at the University of British Columbia and the London School of Economics. She earned a law degree in 1983. Between 1983 and 1988, Campbell participated in British Columbia's politics and was elected to the provincial legislative assembly. She was elected to Canada's House of Commons in 1988 to represent a Vancouver district. As a Progressive Conservative Party member, Campbell supported the leadership and program of Prime Minister Brian Mulroney.

Campbell's abilities and reputation eventually led to several cabinet appointments. After working in the Department of Indian and Northern Affairs, she was named Canada's minister of justice in 1990. In January, 1993, she became minister of national defense. After more than eight years in office, Mulroney, in February, 1993, announced his decision to resign as Canada's prime minister and as leader of the Progressive Conservative Party. His decision was made for personal reasons, compounded by public opinion polls indicating his continuing as prime minister would be a serious detriment to his party's chances in the 1993 parliamentary elections. Through the spring of 1993, the Progressive Conservatives considered several candidates as Mulroney's successor. Kim Campbell won the party's top post on June 13 and was sworn in as prime minister on June 25, 1993.

Upon assuming office, the new prime minister energetically began placing her mark on the nation. The new federal cabinet was reduced in size, and several government departments were abolished or consolidated for greater efficiency. Campbell attended the G7 (Group of Seven) conference of major industrialized nations in July in Tokyo and earned praise for the skills she showed there. Trade relations with other nations, especially with the United States on the proposed North American Free Trade Agreement (NAFTA), continued in a positive and cooperative atmosphere. Domestically, the prime minister proposed programs to retrain workers who were losing jobs as a result of plant closings and workforce reductions. She also promised to eliminate the government's deficit within five years without increasing taxes. Most social programs would be continued, but with some consolidation or reduction. In addition, Campbell suggested constitutional reform, especially in the selection and authority of the Canadian Senate.

Public opinion polls in early July showed wide support (40 percent) for the new prime minister, even higher than public support for her party (33 percent). As Canada's national leader, Campbell faced economic challenges. Sizable government deficits inherited from the prior administration had to be tackled, and Campbell was held partly responsible for those problems as a result of her association with the Mulroney administration. Efforts to reduce or eliminate budget deficits required reductions in well-established and heavily funded programs, such as defense, transfer payments to provinces, pensions, and programs for Canada's indigenous peoples. Many groups and constituencies feared they would be affected adversely by such reductions.

During the summer of 1993, the Campbell administration took an active role in foreign policy issues. Canada supported expansion of the number of permanent members of the United Nations Security Council and promised to continue its peacekeeping presence in the Bosnian civil war. On trade issues, negotiations resolved NAFTA "side deals" on labor and environmental questions, and Campbell's administration obtained significant rulings affecting Canada-U.S. trade in softwood lumber, beer, and steel.

Within her own party, the prime minister made news headlines with the expulsion of three Progressive Conservative members from their party after they had been charged with corruption during Campbell's predecessor's tenure. This enhanced the party's image as a clean, reputable political organization, but critics questioned Campbell's decision because the individuals had not yet been found guilty of the allegations in court.

In a major policy speech in August, Campbell criticized the influence of lobbyists, promised to make political appointments based on merit, and indicated a possible change in the pension rules for members of Parliament. She supported openness in providing full information before government decisions were made, in a bid to convince Canadians that her administration was more democratic than its predecessors. Parliamentary committees also would have more authority in shaping proposed legislation. Considering the history of strong party discipline in Canadian politics, Campbell's support for permitting members of Parliament to vote based on their own consciences rather than following the call of their parties was an unusual departure from tradition. Her call for reforms in the educational sector also attracted public support.

By August, Campbell's reputation had grown significantly, raising hopes of a solid Progressive Conservative win in the fall parliamentary election. Public opinion polls showed Campbell with a 51 percent approval rating, the highest for a prime minister in three decades. The polls also indicated that Canadians favored her by a two-to-one margin over Jean Chrétien, the Liberal Party leader. A Gallup poll predicted a close race between the Progressive Conservatives and the Liberals, but this represented a substantial gain for the former party over its low standing in polls earlier in the year.

After the prime minister, in early September, announced the federal election date for October 25, campaigning began in earnest, with an estimated ten million dollars in the Progressive Conservatives' war chest. The five major parties agreed to several television debates in early October to provide the electorate with a view of party agendas, issues, and leaders. The Progressive Conservatives, seeing Campbell as their most popular and ef-

1993

fective advocate, scheduled her to appear throughout the nation in an extensive political campaign. By mid-September, polls showed the Progressive Conservatives taking a slight lead over the Liberals, 36 percent to 33 percent. Other parties lagged behind.

The campaign, in addition to emphasizing the personalities of the party leaders, increasingly focused on economic issues: NAFTA, the federal deficit, and unemployment. On the campaign trail, Prime Minister Campbell promised to eliminate the deficit in five years but not at the expense of social services. By late September, polls began to show erosion of Progressive Conservative strength. Canadians appeared more concerned about jobs than about deficit reduction. The 1.6 million unemployed made job creation a strong campaign issue, and opposition parties hammered the point home to Canadian voters.

As the campaign intensified and the Progressive Conservative momentum began to weaken, Campbell moved away from providing specifics on many controversial issues and vaguely promised to present the government's policies following the election. Her opponents promptly accused the government of hiding possible deep cuts in social services that would adversely affect many Canadians. In addition, Campbell's sharp comments and abrasive manner (some accused her of arrogance) appeared to undercut voter support. Several of her party's television advertisements also offended many viewers.

Following the scheduled television debates in early October, in which Campbell aggressively took the offensive against her opponents, polls showed the Liberals moving ahead of the Progressive Conservatives, 37 percent to 22 percent. By the week before the election, polls revealed an even larger Liberal lead (44 percent), with the Reform Party (19 percent) in second place and Progressive Conservatives in third place (16 percent). An estimated 18.5 million Canadians were eligible to vote in the October 25 general election, and 69 percent cast their ballots. For the first time, thanks to a revision of election laws, Canadians living outside the country on election day were able to submit absentee ballots.

The results were a Liberal landslide and a Progressive Conservative debacle. The Progressive Conservatives received only 16 percent of the popular vote, compared with 50 percent in the 1984 election and 43 percent in the 1988 election. The number of party seats in the new House of Commons actually determined the future of Canadian politics. Jean Chrétien's Liberals won 177 seats, followed by the Bloc Québécois (54), Reform Party (52), and New Democrats (9). Kim Campbell's

Progressive Conservatives won only 2 seats: 1 in Quebec and 1 in New Brunswick. This number, compared with the 154 seats held before the election, shows the extent of the party's disaster. To add to the humiliation, the prime minister lost her own district seat in Vancouver.

The transfer of office occurred on November 4, 1993, when Jean Chrétien took the oath as Canada's twentieth prime minister. Nine years of Progressive Conservative Party rule, including Kim Campbell's 134 days in office as Canada's first woman prime minister, had ended. On December 13, 1993, Campell resigned as head of the Progressive Conservative Party.

## SIGNIFICANCE

Campbell's brief tenure as Canadian prime minister ended with a crushing electoral defeat such as no Canadian party in power had ever before suffered. Campbell's controversial leadership may partly explain the results, but public alienation from the Progressive Conservatives had deeper roots. The unpopularity of Campbell's predecessor was certainly an element in her party's defeat.

Although she was prime minister for only a short time, Campbell made a strong impression on Canadians and others with her irreverence and her individuality. Despite the briefness of her tenure as prime minister, the fact that she rose to such high office in the world's second-largest nation showed that women were increasingly being taken seriously as leaders in Western democracies.

*—Taylor Stults*

## FURTHER READING

Campbell, Kim. *Time and Chance: The Political Memoirs of Canada's First Woman Prime Minister*. Toronto: Doubleday Canada, 1996. Presents Campbell's own perspective on her life in Canadian politics. Includes photographs and index.

Dobbin, Murray. *The Politics of Kim Campbell: From School Trustee to Prime Minister*. Toronto: Lorimer, 1993. Biography focuses on Campbell's life in politics. Includes index.

Fife, Robert. *Kim Campbell: The Making of a Politician*. Toronto: HarperCollins, 1993. Examines Campbell's rise to the office of prime minister. Includes index.

Frizzel, Alan, Jon H. Pammett, and Anthony Westell, eds. *The Canadian General Election of 1993*. Ottawa: Carleton University Press, 1994. Collection of essays provides excellent analysis of the campaign.

McMenemy, John. *The Language of Canadian Politics: A Guide to Important Terms and Concepts*. 3d ed. Waterloo, Ont.: Wilfrid Laurier University Press,

2001. Collection of more than five hundred brief essays on a wide range of topics related to the Canadian system of government, Canadian political history, Canadian laws and legal history, and more.

Martin, Lawrence. *Chrétien*. 2 vols. Toronto: Lester, 1995. Extended biography of the Liberal Party leader includes discussion of the 1993 campaign.

Norris, Pippa, ed. *Women, Media, and Politics*. New York: Oxford University Press, 1997. Collection of essays examines how the mass media cover the cam-

paigns of women politicians as well as the actions of women holding public office. Chapter 8 includes discussion of Kim Campbell.

**SEE ALSO:** May 23, 1979: Clark Is Elected Canada's Prime Minister; Sept. 14, 1984: Mulroney Era Begins in Canada; Oct. 26, 1992: Defeat of the Charlottetown Accord; Nov. 4, 1993: Chrétien Takes Charge in Canada; Nov. 20, 1993: North American Free Trade Agreement.

## July 23-24 and August 29-30, 1993
# BRAZILIAN POLICE MASSACRE SLUM DWELLERS

*When off-duty police massacred street children and slum dwellers in Rio de Janeiro in 1993, they showed the world the extent of Brazilian police brutality and touched off worldwide protests that led to attempted reforms.*

**LOCALE:** Rio de Janeiro, Brazil
**CATEGORIES:** Terrorism, atrocities, and war crimes; civil rights and liberties

**KEY FIGURES**
*Wagner dos Santos* (b. 1971), victim of the Candelária massacre who survived to testify against the police
*Marcus Vinicius Borges Emanuel* (fl. late twentieth century), police officer convicted of murder and other crimes at the Candelária massacre
*Elizabeth Cristina de Oliveira Maia* (1977?-2000), survivor of the Candelária massacre who testified against the police and was later murdered

**SUMMARY OF EVENT**

In mid-1993, Brazilian police inflicted two massacres on the poor of Rio de Janeiro. Eight street children died in a hail of bullets at the Pius X Square near Our Lady of Candelária church during the night of July 23-24, 1993, and a month later, during the night of August 29-30, a squad of masked policemen attacked the Vigário Geral favela (slum) and killed twenty-one residents. These incidents were the most infamous sources for the reputation of the Brazilian police for brutality and corruption. The massacres provoked an outcry within Brazil and international protests by human rights organizations.

At the Candelária church, members of the Ninth Battalion of military police decided to teach a bloody lesson to several dozen children who lived and slept in the public square. The day before, some of the children report-

edly had thrown rocks at a police car. When the police returned the following night, they asked for the children's ringleader, Marco Antonio da Silva. Not suspecting what was about to happen, Marco answered. The policemen forced him and two of his friends into a car and drove away. The police then shot all three youths in the head and discarded their bodies near the Museum of Modern Art before returning to Candelária. The other children screamed and tried to run away, but the police fired on them; in addition to Marco, seven others died, and several were severely wounded.

The Candelária slaughter showed not only the brutality of the police but the problems caused by street children in Brazil. Like other Brazilian cities, Rio de Janeiro included in its population hordes of children who had been abandoned by their families or who had run away from their homes. One estimate placed the number of such children throughout Brazil at eight to ten million. These street children worked at whatever jobs they could find, but many also committed petty crimes to survive. They stole from merchants, robbed tourists, and were generally considered a public nuisance. Some were addicted to drugs. Packs of children such as the one at the Candelária square harassed neighborhoods and undermined public order.

Many Brazilians felt threatened by the street children. At times, merchants reportedly hired off-duty police to attack the children and remove them from the area. Sometimes the police murdered children in such raids, although the Candelária massacre stood out because of the large number of youths killed and because it occurred in downtown Rio, in front of one of the city's most famous churches. Nonetheless, such killings had become commonplace in Brazil. In 1990, an estimated one thou-

*Brazilian police forcibly evict residents of a slum built on the outskirts of São Paulo in 1998.* (AP/Wide World Photos)

sand street children were killed by death squads and other vigilante actions. However, such murders typically occurred in the more remote, slum sections of cities and drew relatively little public attention. In November, 1991, a death squad, perhaps of off-duty policemen, killed six children in Nova Jerusalém, on the periphery of Rio de Janeiro.

With Brazilians still debating what had happened at the Candelária church in late July, late August brought another outrage by the police, this time in the Vigário Geral favela. After four policemen had been killed there two days earlier by drug dealers, thirty-three hooded men, reportedly members of the Ninth Battalion of military police, returned to take revenge on the slum dwellers. They cut telephone wires to prevent anyone from calling for help and then rampaged through the slum in a two-hour spree of killing and destruction.

Eight members of the Gilberto Cardoso dos Santos family died in the massacre, including a fifteen-year-old girl. The slaughter also claimed seven men who had been playing cards in a bar. They died when the police set off a

bomb inside the bar and then shot everyone who tried to escape. At one point, the police were about to shoot a woman but allowed her and her family to flee unscathed when the woman's husband, Edmilson Costa, agreed to die in their place. Spraying machine-gun fire around the Corsican Plaza, the police destroyed carts used by the slum dwellers to sell fruit, juice, soft drinks, and other merchandise. A teenage boy and a man died in the hail of bullets in the plaza. Much of the killing was random violence, designed as angry vengeance on the favela rather than as an attempt to identify and punish the individuals responsible for the deaths of the policemen's comrades.

Like the Candelária slaughter, the massacre in Vigário Geral showed the extreme violence that can result from urban poverty and social tensions, especially when these are heightened by growing problems with drug trafficking and abuse. Brazilian shantytowns such as Vigário Geral were rife with petty criminals and networks of drug dealers. Investigators later discovered evidence that several members of the Ninth Battalion had gone to Vigário Geral to shake down Flávio Pires da Silva, who ran drugs with a network based in the favela. A shootout ensued, and four members of the police were killed.

## SIGNIFICANCE

The massacres in Brazil provoked tremendous public outcry, but attempts to punish and reform the police brought only limited success. Testifying against the police was risky. One of the original three Candelária victims, Wagner dos Santos, survived serious wounds and was able to recognize the police who had carried out the slaughter. He knew that if he identified them, it would put his life in danger again, but he bravely denounced the perpetrators and offered to testify against them in court. For his courage, he suffered two more attempts on his life and was again severely wounded. A children's rights group subsequently hid him in Switzerland until it was time for him to return to Brazil to provide evidence in the trial of Officer Marcos Vinicius Borges Emanuel. Seven other survivors of the Candelária massacre also testified, but only by deposition, as they were too fearful to participate in open court.

Elizabeth Cristina de Oliveira Maia survived the Candelária massacre and then courageously agreed to testify against the policemen-murderers. On July 16, 2000, she appeared before the Inter-American Commission on Human Rights of the Organization of American States to describe her life as a child living in the streets of Rio de Janeiro and what had happened during the bloody night in 1993 at the Candelária church. The governor of Rio de Janeiro State, Anthony Garotinho, attended the proceedings and acknowledged the government's responsibility for the carnage. Garotinho promised to provide pensions for the Candelária survivors and the families of those who had been killed. The government failed to protect Elizabeth Cristina, however. On September 26, 2000, a hooded assassin gunned down the twenty-three-year-old mother of three near her home in the Botafogo district of Rio de Janeiro. She was scheduled to testify in judicial proceedings against some of the accused policemen the following week. The murder not only prevented her testimony but also was meant to intimidate other potential witnesses into silence.

The judicial proceedings that took place as a result of the massacres did not yield completely satisfactory results. In late April, 1996, for example, a jury convicted two military policemen of crimes associated with the Candelária killings, including six cases of murder: the previously mentioned Emanuel and Nelson Oliveira dos Santos Cunha. Emanuel received a sentence of 390 years in prison (Brazil has no death penalty), and Cunha was sentenced to 261 years. However, Emanuel, with no previous convictions, in reality faced only a maximum of 20 years in prison and was eligible for parole after 4 years beyond the 3 he had already served while awaiting trial.

Both Emanuel and Cunha claimed that the real perpetrator of the massacre was Maurício "Friday the Thirteenth" da Conceição, another policeman, who had died two years before the trial. Human rights observers were also troubled by Emanuel and Cunha's protection of their superior, Lieutenant Marcelo Cortés, from prosecution. Emanuel claimed that Cortés had not participated in the massacre but seemed to be taking responsibility to shield higher-ups in the military police command structure. In fact, Wagner dos Santos identified Cortés as a participant in the massacre.

As for the Vigário Geral slaughter, the government eventually accused fifty-two military police of participating in the carnage. By 1998, only two had been convicted, and these again were lower-ranking men.

Brazilians found themselves trapped between a rising wave of criminal violence on one hand and police brutality and corruption on the other. Police publicly boasted of the numbers of people they had killed, although many, perhaps even a majority, of the alleged lawbreakers they executed had no previous criminal records. The police also enjoyed widespread support from a public dismayed and terrified by street crime. Indeed, support for the police was perhaps strongest among the poorest citizens, whose precarious lives in the slums were especially threatened by gangs of thieves, drug dealers, and other criminals. Brazilians did not trust the police, however. Public opinion polls showed that large majorities of Brazilians believed that the police were corrupt, sometimes needlessly violent, and often implicated in the activities of death squads.

The Candelária and Vigário Geral massacres were only the most visible part of a shocking national phenomenon. In 1991, for example, military police from the same Ninth Battalion had kidnapped and eventually murdered ten people from the Acari favela while trying to find several million dollars reported to belong to a truck hijacker. In 1992, military police in São Paulo ended a riot in an overcrowded prison by shooting 111 unarmed prisoners. Because most of their victims were poor and had no political influence, the police were under little pressure to change their behavior.

Others issues related to police violence were also difficult to solve. Street children continued to infest Brazilian cities, and violence against them continued. According to Amnesty International, of the seventy-two people present at the Candelária massacre, forty-four had died violently by mid-2000. Despite public outcry regarding the Candelária slaughter, the killing of street children increased after 1993.

A major obstacle to the elimination of police corruption was low salaries. With pay as low as $300 per month, many police officers succumbed to the temptation to supplement their incomes by conspiring with drug dealers, participating in merchant-funded death squads, and extorting protection money. The government promised to raise police salaries, but financial problems stood in the way. Human rights organizations such as Amnesty International called for Brazil to institute witness protection programs to shield people such as Wagner dos Santos and Elizabeth Cristina de Oliveira Maia from police retaliation, but little was achieved.

The Candelária and Vigário Geral massacres highlighted the terrorist behavior of Brazil's police, and the conviction of Emanuel and a few others did little to eliminate police violence and corruption. The fate of Wagner dos Santos illustrates the ineffectiveness of Brazil's police reforms. On August 27, 1997, military police from the Second Battalion attacked Santos as he was walking to work. According to a report by Amnesty International, police gunshots left him partially paralyzed and brain-damaged. Witnesses also claimed that the attackers planted drugs and a pistol at the scene to frame Santos and then charged him with attacking the police. In 1998,

1993

a Brazilian court began prosecuting him for the apparently trumped-up charges. Santos managed to escape to Switzerland, however, where he was taken in by a Swiss family and given an opportunity to pursue formal education and employment.

—*Kendall W. Brown*

## FURTHER READING

Cavallaro, James. *Police Brutality in Urban Brazil.* New York: Human Rights Watch/Americas, 1997. Analyzes police violence in the cities of Rio de Janeiro, São Paulo, Porto Alegre, Recife, Belo Horizonte, Natal, and Salvador. Discusses attempted reforms by human rights organizations and offers recommendations to curb the violence.

Epstein, Jack. "Reining in the Rogue Cops of Brazil and Its Neighbors." *Christian Science Monitor*, December 10, 1998, 7. Discusses reasons for police brutality and corruption in South America, particularly Brazil, and the uneven attempts to eliminate them.

Michaels, Marguerite. "Rio's Dead End Kids." *Time*, August 9, 1993, 36-37. Mentions the Candelária massacre, but focuses on the conditions that produce Brazil's street children and possible solutions to the problem.

Penglase, Ben. *Final Justice: Police and Death Squad Homicides of Adolescents in Brazil.* New York: Human Rights Watch, 1994. Surveys Brazil's record in the late twentieth century of violence against street children in São Paulo, Rio de Janeiro, and Pernambuco and makes recommendations for curbing the violence.

Schemo, Diana Jean. "Rio Ex-Officer Is Convicted in Massacre of Children." *The New York Times*, May 1, 1996, p. A11. Covers Officer Emanuel's trial and conviction and provides background information on the Candelária massacre.

**SEE ALSO:** 1978-1985: Guatemalan Death Squads Target Indigenous Indians; Mar. 15, 1985: Democracy Returns to Brazil; Jan. 1, 1995-Jan. 1, 2003: Cardoso Brings Prestige to Brazilian Presidency.

---

## August 19, 1993
# MATTEL AND FISHER-PRICE FORM THE WORLD'S BIGGEST TOY COMPANY

*A merger between Mattel and Fisher-Price was an ideal way to produce better sales for both companies and to compete with the number one toy maker at the time, Hasbro. Mattel gained control of the toy market by the end of the decade.*

**LOCALE:** El Segundo, California

**CATEGORIES:** Business and labor; trade and commerce

### KEY FIGURES
*John Amerman* (b. 1932), chairman of the board of Mattel

*Ronald Jackson* (b. 1946), president of Fisher-Price

### SUMMARY OF EVENT

By 1993, Mattel was slumping in sales and sitting at number two in the $17 billion toy industry. Mattel, with a history of mergers of various success, was looking for another way to gain market share by adding companies to its fold. Fisher-Price had hit a ceiling. The company was wasteful in production and did not have the infrastructure to expand globally. The two companies had flirted with the idea of a merger two years earlier, but

Fisher-Price's parent company, Quaker Oats, would not allow the deal to go through. Since that time, Hasbro had surpassed Mattel for the number one spot in the industry and was obtaining more market share because its young-child division was fully developed. Mattel lacked such a division and sought desperately to catch up with its competitor. Hasbro's Playskool line was competing directly with Fisher-Price; however, Fisher-Price did not have the resources to compete with such a large company. Since the last attempt at a merger, Fisher-Price had also gained its independence from Quaker Oats Company and had begun to trade on the New York Stock Exchange. This led to an easier transition and finalization of a merger that would create the world's largest toy company.

The merger that was announced on August 19, 1993, was considered a strong business decision. Mattel would gain a critical share in the market, the zero- to five-year-old bracket. Fisher-Price had been the leading name in this area almost since its incorporation in 1930. The brand name boasted near 100 percent name recognition among American parents, but its activities were limited outside the United States. Mattel had global operations that far surpassed those of Fisher-Price. With factories in Indonesia, Portugal, China, Mexico, Malaysia, Taiwan, Australia, and other parts of the globe, Mattel provided an infrastructure for the distribution of Fisher-Price products globally. Mattel also provided the business sense to restructure Fisher-Price to cut overhead and to build a larger profit margin.

Mattel brought many possibilities to the table for Fisher-Price. Barbie, Mattel's flagship toy line, had been a solid source of income since its conception in 1959, with sales approaching $1 billion by 1993. Mattel's chairman of the board, John Amerman, had spent the last six years rebuilding the Mattel franchise, focusing on its core elements, Barbie and Hot Wheels. Amerman had rescued the company twice after huge financial setbacks. The first disaster was in the fledgling video game industry, where Mattel lost nearly $400 million because of failed efforts at producing a console system; the second came when the market for the popular He-Man action figures suddenly dried up in 1986. Amerman quickly and cautiously turned the company around in 1987 by reducing its output and slashing overhead 40 percent. His experience would benefit the restructuring of Fisher-Price after the merger.

Under Amerman's direction, Mattel successfully negotiated the licensing rights to Walt Disney Company characters in 1989. Because of the enormous popularity of Disney movies during the early 1990's, Disney-licensed toys accounted for half a billion dollars in sales per year. With excess cash flow and new possibilities for licensing, Fisher-Price would be able to grow from what Mattel could offer. Some of Fisher-Price's greatest successes of the past revolved around the licensing of Disney television shows and Sesame Street. The excess capital and experience abroad would secure the future for the Fisher-Price line under Mattel.

Fisher-Price not only would allow Mattel to further penetrate the markets but also would offer more brand recognition. With such recognition, Mattel could build further customer loyalty. Under Ronald Jackson, Fisher-Price's president at the time of the merger, the company had moved to consolidate its holdings and cut overhead. During the mid-1980's, under the direction of its parent company, Fisher-Price had let its attention to its main product lines such as Little People and other educational toys for toddlers dwindle, allowing the company's main competitors gain market share. In return, overproduction and poor marketing led to the leadership change that brought in Jackson. However, it seemed that Fisher-

Price's current global infrastructure would not be able to propel the business forward rapidly in the coming decade—this was one reason a merger was considered.

The merger of Mattel and Fisher-Price was completed by December 1, 1993. The previous merger attempt was ultimately foiled by the lack of successful negotiation by the companies to establish a stock conversion for shareholders, but the successful 1993 merger established a favorable rate. One share in Fisher-Price was exchanged for 1.275 shares of Mattel common stock. Mattel immediately took action to streamline its new Fisher-Price division. Plants were closed in Mexico, and operations were combined in other parts of the world to cut overhead. However, Fisher-Price kept its main offices in East Aurora, New York, rather than moving to the headquarters of its new parent company in El Segundo, California. The merger was a success from the beginning, as Mattel's earnings went up 27 percent in 1993.

The merger led to two more extremely profitable years for Mattel and Fisher-Price. With capital from its parent company, Fisher-Price was able to tap into new markets while focusing on its traditional target age group. It began to distribute board games and video games and raised production on its popular Power Wheels line. The added volume, customer base, and revenue allowed Mattel to consider merger ideas with then number two toy producer Hasbro. While issues about antitrust suits squashed the plan, Mattel did purchase many smaller companies in the years that followed, including the third-largest toy company; Tyco Toys. The acquisition of Tyco eliminated a large chunk of competition for the toddler market, and Fisher-Price was granted total control of Mattel's production in this market. The merger also proved to save Fisher-Price in 1998, when the company had to recall ten million Power Wheels vehicles because of possible flammability. Mattel paid for the $30 million recall.

## SIGNIFICANCE

The merger of Mattel and Fisher-Price was one of many mergers in a growing trend among global companies. It was also the largest merger within the toy industry. The merger was beneficial to both companies: Mattel received increased revenues, improved customer loyalty, an increased consumer base, and quality products to sell for years to come; Fisher-Price could move to a more global strategy that allowed the company to tap the more populated Asian and Latin American markets. Fisher-Price received the capital needed to restructure and reinvent the company, and it received coveted licenses to

1993

broaden its toys' appeal. The merger allowed Fisher-Price to become the dominant force in the preschool toy market and allowed Mattel to become the number one toy company in the world.

—*Daniel R. Vogel*

**FURTHER READING**

Miller, G. Wayne. *Mortal Combat: A True Story of Toys, Big Money, and Brutal Business.* New York: Random House, 1998. Discusses hostile takeover attempts in the toy industry, with a focus on the Mattel-Hasbro rivalry. Information on 1990's toy company mergers.

_____. *Toy Wars: The Epic Struggle Between G.I. Joe,* *Barbie, and the Companies That Make Them.* New York: Times Books, 1998. Details the history of the business and describes how the two giants divided and controlled the toy industry.

Schoenhaus, Ted, and Sydney Ladensohn Stern. *Toyland: The High-Stakes Fame of the Toy Industry.* New York: Contemporary Books, 1991. Looks at the American toy industry, its trends, product creation, boom and bust cycles, the companies that have existed over the last century, and some popular products.

**SEE ALSO:** Nov., 1978: FTC Conducts Hearings on Ads Aimed at Children.

---

# September 16, 1993-May 13, 2004
# *FRASIER* DOMINATES TELEVISION COMEDY

*Frasier was the first television show to win five consecutive Emmy Awards for Outstanding Comedy Series. The situation comedy's popularity demonstrated that the American public welcomed literate writing and highly intelligent characters.*

**LOCALE:** United States
**CATEGORY:** Radio and television

**KEY FIGURES**

*Kelsey Grammer* (b. 1955), actor who played the leading role of Dr. Frasier Crane
*David Hyde Pierce* (1959), actor who played Frasier's brother, Dr. Niles Crane
*John Mahoney* (b. 1940), actor who played Martin Crane, father of Frasier and Niles
*Jane Leeves* (b. 1961), actor who played Martin's physical therapist, Daphne Moon
*Peri Gilpin* (b. 1961), actor who played Roz Doyle, producer of Frasier's radio show

**SUMMARY OF EVENT**

The television show *Frasier* originated with the character Dr. Frasier Crane, who was introduced on September 27, 1984, in the opening episode of the third season of the popular situation comedy (or sitcom) *Cheers* (1982-1993). Frasier, played by actor Kelsey Grammer, was a pompous yet likable psychiatrist and the love interest of Diane Chambers, a major character on *Cheers*. Originally, Grammer was hired for only seven episodes, but the character caught the audience's attention, and Frasier became a regular on the show. The character was so suc-

cessful that in 1989, three years before *Cheers* ended, Grammer was approached by executives at Paramount about doing his own show. Although committed to staying with *Cheers* for its duration, Grammer began planning a new show in 1990, meeting with a number of people, including the writing team of David Angell, Peter Casey, and David Lee, who would also become the show's producers.

The initial idea was that Grammer would play a new character, a bedridden mogul crippled in a motorcycle accident. The script was written, but the consensus was that the concept was not funny. After more discussion, it was decided that the character of Frasier would continue, but in a different place, Seattle, playing a radio talk-show host dispensing psychiatric advice, and with a different group of characters. The show was going to be set at radio station KACL, but Lee, whose father just had a stroke, was inspired to make the show both a workplace- and a home-based comedy, having Frasier taking care of his disabled father.

When *Cheers* concluded in 1993, additional actors for *Frasier* were hired. John Mahoney played Frasier's father, Martin, a retired Seattle policeman whose "blue-collar" habits and mind-set contrast with the professional, elitist attitudes and demeanor Frasier exhibits. Niles, Frasier's brother, also a psychiatrist but in private practice, was not part of the original concept until a casting director showed a picture of David Hyde Pierce to the producers. Pierce, who looked like a younger version of Grammer, was hired and instructed to play the role like Frasier, only "stuffier," to act as Frasier might if he had not relocated to Boston and "become an actual human being." Jane Leeves, an English actor, was hired to play Martin's physical therapist, the occasionally psychic Daphne Moon, whose working-class background combines with Martin's to puncture the pompousness of the Crane brothers. The final principal cast member was Peri Gilpin, who played Roz Doyle, the sexy, savvy producer of Frasier's radio show. Gilpin was not the first actress cast as Roz; the producers had initially hired Lisa Kudrow, but they found that the dynamics between her version of Roz and Frasier did not work. An additional cast member, who received more fan mail than any other character, was a Jack Russell terrier named Eddie.

Angell, Casey, and Lee wrote the pilot script, "The Good Son," in two weeks. The story was simple: Frasier now has the perfect life. He is single, has a fabulous apartment, and is just starting a new job. However, life intrudes when his father needs a place to live while recovering from a gunshot wound sustained in the line of duty. Martin comes with a dog, Eddie, who has a tendency to stare, and Martin's disability requires a live-in health care worker. Frasier's life and his apartment are turned upside down. His peace is shattered by "my father, Mary Poppins, and the hound from hell."

Both the script and the episode's director, James Burrows, won Emmy Awards. The pilot episode was shot on May 4, 1993, two months after *Cheers* ended, before a live studio audience. When the filming concluded, the audience gave the cast a standing ovation. The show first aired on NBC on Thursday, September 16, 1993, at 9:30 P.M., following the popular *Seinfeld*. Reviews were good, praising the writing and applauding the cast. The show was a success and became NBC's "best-performing rookie."

Two major contributions to the success of the show were the writing and directing. The pilot episode introduced Frasier's signature "hello" to those calling in to his radio program: "This is Dr. Frasier Crane. I'm listening." What he heard were bizarre stories. The callers were played by celebrities who recorded their lines over the telephone. They included Linda Hamilton playing a woman with boyfriend problems, Christopher Reeve playing an agoraphobic, and Mel Brooks playing a man who had been traumatized by receiving a dead puppy from Santa. Witty dialogue from the cast included Frasier introducing himself to his radio audience by speaking about his past life in Boston and his wife who had left him, "which was very painful; then she came back, which was excruciating." In another episode, Niles comments: "Oh dear, look at the time. I have a session with

my multiple personality. Well, not to worry. If I'm late, he can just talk amongst himself." The writers also created a character who is never seen—Niles's wife Maris, described by Frasier as "bleached, 100 percent fat free, and best if kept in an airtight container."

On stage and screen, direction is critical in establishing character. James Burrows helped create the cachets that typified the characters in Frasier. For example, in the pilot episode, Niles was to sit down in a chair at the Café Nervosa, a trendy coffee bar, to speak with Frasier; Burrows suggested that before Niles sat down, he should first wipe off the chair, showing his fastidious nature.

Following a successful first season, for which the show won four Emmys, *Frasier* was moved to Tuesday at 9:00 P.M., for the 1994-1998 seasons. It was moved back to Thursday in September of 1998, and in September of 2000, to Tuesday, where it remained until the final hour-long episode that aired May 13, 2004.

## SIGNIFICANCE

In its eleven seasons, *Frasier* won a record thirty-nine Emmy Awards. One of the reasons for the show's success, as Grammer stated, was that it was "not like a sitcom." Grammer and the producers agreed that the show would have neither stupid jokes nor stupid characters. Unlike many sitcoms, *Frasier*'s major character was not played by a comedian. Much of the humor of the show was developed through the contrast of the characters. The conflict between the brothers, a sophisticated version of sibling rivalry, generated humor, as did the opposition of down-to-earth, beer-drinking Martin to his sons' sophistication, love of good wine, and knowledge of opera. While the sons dine at gourmet restaurants, Martin prefers Hoppy's Old Heidelberg, featuring the "steak trolley." The comedy, which Grammer described as minimalist, was also created through situations. Producer Peter Casey's idea was to find "something small" and build an episode around it.

As noted by television critic Joseph Adalian, the show "succeeded by being distinct." Rather than speeding up its pace, as many shows were doing at the time, *Frasier* did the opposite. The show's executive producer, Christopher Lloyd, decided that, rather than having multiple scenes, the stories would be told "in the least number of scenes possible." Settings were restricted to three: Frasier's high-rise apartment, with its panoramic view of the Seattle skyline; the radio studio; and the aptly named Café Nervosa. Scene changes were indicated by catchy subtitles rather than by music. The song that accompanied the closing credits was "Tossed Salads and Scrambled Eggs," by Bruce Miller and Daryl Phinessee, sung by Grammer. Miller said that the title referred to things that were "mixed up," like Frasier's callers.

What set *Frasier* apart from other sitcoms was that there were not always "perfect endings" to the stories. Moreover, as Grammer remarked in a 2004 interview published in *USA Today*, "No show has ever played up to its audience as well as ours did. We respected the idea that everyone in America is probably smarter than television gives them credit for."

*—Marcia B. Dinneen*

**FURTHER READING**

Adalian, Joseph. "The Doctor Is Out." *Daily Variety*, May 13, 2004, p. A1. Detailed commentary of the various elements that contributed to the show's success.

Angell, David, Peter Casey, and David Lee. *The Frasier Scripts*. Introduction by Christopher Lloyd. New York: Newmarket Press, 1999. Fifteen scripts, selected from seasons one through six, include "The Good Son," the pilot script.

Gates, Anita. "Yes, America Has a Class System." *The New York Times*, April 19, 1998, sec. II, p. 35. Lengthy discussion of the class system as explored in *Frasier*. Provides detailed information on what made the show a success.

Graham, Jefferson. *Frasier*. New York: Pocket Books, 1996. Includes material on the origins of the show, discussion of characters, biographical information on the actors, abstracts of episodes one through seventy-two, and a list of awards.

Grammer, Kelsey. *So Far*. New York: Dutton, 1995. Autobiography provides background information on the role of Frasier in *Cheers* and *Frasier*.

O'Connor, John J. "A *Cheers* Spinoff, Set in Seattle." *The New York Times*, October 21, 1993, p. C22. Lengthy, favorable review of the first episode of *Frasier*.

**SEE ALSO:** Jan. 14, 1990: *The Simpsons* Debuts, Anchoring the Fledgling Fox Network; Jan. 23, 1991: *Seinfeld* Takes a Regular Slot on NBC.

## September 24, 1993
# *MYST* ENERGIZES THE COMPUTER GAME MARKET

*The adventure game* Myst *revolutionized the computer game industry when it introduced an entirely new kind of interactive experience in which a single player, immersed in various surreal worlds, had to interpret clues to solve puzzles and complete the game.*

**LOCALE:** Spokane, Washington
**CATEGORIES:** Computers and computer science; trade and commerce; travel and recreation

**KEY FIGURES**
*Rand Miller* (b. 1959), American software developer, artist, and cocreator of *Myst*
*Robyn Miller* (b. 1966), American businessman, artist, and cocreator of *Myst*
*Chuck Carter* (b. 1957), American visual artist, graphic artist, and animator for *Myst*

**SUMMARY OF EVENT**

In 1987, brothers Rand Miller and Robyn Miller founded Cyan Worlds, a computer game development company based in Spokane, Washington. They created a children's game, *The Manhole*, that brought them a publishing deal with Activision. This was the first entertainment

product on the new medium of CD-ROM. Cyan then released *Cosmic Osmo* and *Spelunx and the Caves of Mr. Seudo*, an educational game. These children's games won awards and praise for their whimsical, nonviolent, and nonthreatening exploratory environments.

In 1991, with some funding from Sunsoft of Japan, Cyan began work on *Myst*, its first game aimed at an adult audience. Jules Verne's *The Mysterious Island* (1875; originally published in French as *L'Île mystérieuse*) inspired the game's name and the general dreamlike, lonely, and mysterious qualities of the island setting in *Myst*.

The Miller brothers were the creators and designers of *Myst*; they also did the video and film editing for the game. Robyn Miller and visual artist Chuck Carter created the graphics and animation, and Rand Miller and Rich Watson did the programming. Sound engineer Chris Brandkamp created the audio and sound effects, and Robyn Miller produced the musical score.

The development team used relatively simple tools to create *Myst*. The entire game was created on Apple Macintosh Quadra computers and constructed in Hypercard. Modeling and rendering were done in StrataVision

3D and Macromedia MacroModel. Image editing was done in Photoshop, and Adobe Premiere was used for video editing, compression, and compositing. Quick-Time movies with Cinepak compression constituted the animation.

In creating *Myst*, Rand and Robyn Miller aimed to provide an alternative virtual environment that was not linear, flat, or shallow; they wanted to offer a three-dimensional, interactive world in which a lone player could explore, collect clues, and solve puzzles. They spent hundreds of hours making the preliminary sketches for the worlds in *Myst*.

Unlike other computer games, *Myst* has no set story line, inventory, antagonists to fight or kill, icon-controlled movements, time limits, violence, arbitrary punishments, or threat of death. The player can move around in *Myst* by mouse clicking on the desired locations or areas. To examine, use, or pick up an object, the player can click on it or click and drag it. The player can also move levers and other objects by dragging them.

The game begins with a falling figure and then a linking book titled *Myst*, which opens to show aerial views of a distant island. Touching the image page transports the player into this isolated island world. In exploring the island, the player discovers many objects, buildings, and sounds. For instance, there are levers to manipulate, buttons to push, doors to open, stairs to climb, and wheels to turn. Eventually the player enters a library and discovers books that tell the stories of a mysterious man named Atrus (the owner of Myst Island), who wrote special linking books that could transport readers to other worlds. Atrus is the father of two feuding sons, Sirrus and Achenar, who have disappeared. The books contain drawings of maps, buildings, and other clues to their whereabouts. Red and blue books contain videos of the two sons, who are trapped in the books and beg for help from the player.

The goal of the game is for the player to explore the island, as well as the other worlds and periods of island history called "Ages," and analyze various objects and sounds for clues. The game is completed when the player returns to Myst Island from these mysterious worlds with all the necessary information and pieces of the puzzle to solve the mystery of the vanished people of Myst Island.

Robyn Miller and Carter developed beautiful graphics for the rich, detailed scenes and objects in *Myst*, down to the tiniest nails and screws. They mapped textures onto three-dimensional models and then rendered these to develop the game's landscapes and terrains. Sequences of camera shots were used to give the player the sense of actually being in the game's world. Miller and Carter created more than twenty-five hundred photo-realistic images and more than one hour of video animations. These labor-intensive, time-consuming methods helped to create more depth and reality than had ever been seen before in a computer game.

In 1993, after two years of production, *Myst* was released to much critical acclaim. Broderbund, a software company based in Novato, California, published the CD-ROM. A Microsoft Windows version followed in 1994. The disc also included a fourteen-minute QuickTime movie titled *The Making of Myst*. Word of mouth, enhanced by the speed of communications on the Internet, quickly spread the news about this exciting new game, which was unlike any other computer game available up to that time. The success of *Myst* provides an early example of the use of the Internet as an important communications tool in promoting products. *Myst* became the best-selling computer game throughout most of the 1990's and one of the most commercially successful and popular computer games in history.

### SIGNIFICANCE

*Myst* and its sequels sold more than twelve million copies worldwide, making it one of the best-selling computer games of all time. In 1997, *Riven*, the first sequel to *Myst*, was released. This five-disc game included four thousand photorealistic images, two hours of music and sound effects, and three hours of video animation. *Riven* was followed by a whole series of related games, up through *Myst V: End of Ages*, the final game in the *Myst* saga, released in 2005.

*Myst* was important because it generated an entirely new genre of computer game entertainment: a three-dimensional interactive adventure and mystery game for a single player who could explore, discover clues, and solve puzzles. *Myst* also set new high standards for the CD-ROM medium with the game's simple intuitive interface and realistic, detailed, and rich environment. The incredibly beautiful graphics, intriguing sounds, and dreamlike world had immediate, widespread appeal, and *Myst* soon became a classic game and a lasting part of popular culture. Dark Horse Comics published two comic books in a series called *Myst: The Book of Black Ships*, and *Myst* enthusiasts developed Web sites as well as an annual event called Mysterium, where *Myst* fans from all over the world could gather and share their love of the game.

—*Alice Myers*

1993

**FURTHER READING**

Barba, Rick, and Rusel DeMaria. *"Myst": The Official Strategy Guide*. Rev. ed. Rocklin, Calif.: Prima Games, 1995. Best-selling complete source for information and puzzle solutions. Includes an interview with the Miller brothers. Illustrated.

Kadrey, Richard. *From "Myst" to "Riven": The Creations and Inspirations*. New York: Hyperion, 1997. Provides an in-depth look at the development and design process of the best-selling games, with sketches, maps, and photographs. Includes a foreword by Rand and Robyn Miller, profiles of the games' creators, and behind-the-scenes stories.

Miller, Rand, and Robyn Miller, with David Wingrove. *The "Myst" Reader*. New York: Hyperion, 2004. One-volume literary companion to the game contains all three volumes of the best-selling *Myst* trilogy: *The Book of Atrus, The Book of Ti'ana,* and *The Book of D'ni*. Illustrated.

Ryman, Anne. *"Myst": Strategies and Secrets*. San Francisco: Sybex, 1995. Essential guide provides hints and tips for playing the game, troubleshooting help, and puzzle solutions. Beautifully illustrated.

**SEE ALSO:** Nov. 15, 1971: Intel Introduces the First "Computer on a Chip"; 1980's-1990's: Rise of Video and Computer Games; July 3, 1991: IBM and Apple Agree to Make Compatible Computers; Mar. 22, 1993: Intel Introduces the Pentium Processor; Dec. 15, 1994: Release of Netscape Navigator 1.0; Mid-1990's: Rise of the Internet and the World Wide Web.

---

## September 26, 1993
# CREW OF BIOSPHERE 2 EXITS AFTER TWO YEARS

*The Biosphere 2 project both demonstrated the feasibility of colonizing outer space in self-sustaining artificial environments and publicized scientific efforts to solve existing ecological problems.*

**LOCALE:** Oracle, Arizona
**CATEGORIES:** Health and medicine; environmental issues

**KEY FIGURES**

*Edward Perry Bass* (b. 1949), Texas oil billionaire who financed Biosphere 2 at an estimated cost of $150 million

*Abigail Alling* (fl. late twentieth century), Biosphere 2 crew member who specialized in marine biology

*Linda Leigh* (fl. late twentieth century), Biosphere 2 crew member who specialized in botany

*Taber MacCallum* (fl. late twentieth century), Biosphere 2 crew member who specialized in environmental management

*Jane Poynter* (fl. late twentieth century), Biosphere 2 crew member who specialized in greenhouse management

*Sally Silverstone* (b. 1955), Biosphere 2 crew member who specialized in tropical agriculture management

*Mark Van Thillo* (b. 1961), Biosphere 2 crew member who was responsible for quality control and maintenance

*Roy Walford* (1924-2004), Biosphere 2 crew member who was responsible for medical monitoring, communications, and computer data gathering

*Bernd Zabel* (b. 1949), Biosphere 2 crew member who was responsible for coordination of construction and installation of plant and animal life

**SUMMARY OF EVENT**

On September 26, 1993, four men and four women emerged from two years of isolation in a futuristic ecosystem in the Sonoran Desert in Arizona. The human-made ecosystem was called Biosphere 2; Earth itself was considered to be the prototype, or Biosphere 1. The eight "biospherians" marched out of Biosphere 2, a 3.15-acre terrarium, to an elaborate welcoming ceremony that included impressionistic flute music and what one reporter described as "New Age oratory." The two-year experiment, a combination of science and media hype, was criticized by some scientists but was praised by others for helping to popularize scientific concerns and win public support for further experimentation.

The creation of Biosphere 2 was possible only because of the work conducted by scientists and technologists over the preceding hundreds of years. The crew members—Abigail Alling, Linda Leigh, Taber MacCallum, Jane Poynter, Sally Silverstone, Mark Van Thillo, Roy Walford, and Bernd Zabel—not only had to grow their own food but also had to recycle the water they drank and produce the oxygen they breathed. They were responsible for the health of all the other plant and animal species inside the sealed structure. They had to maintain all the complex apparatus that kept Biosphere 2 functioning. The combined scientific knowledge of these versatile, idealistic biospherians represented much of what humans had learned through centuries of observation and experimentation.

Many U.S. astronauts and Soviet cosmonauts had spent long periods in outer space, but they had always taken their food, water, and air along with them. Consequently, the amount of time that these early space explorers could survive away from Earth was strictly limited. Biosphere 2 was designed to prove that humans could exist indefinitely without access to the resources of the mother planet.

Planned to last for one hundred years, the Biosphere 2 structure looked like a gigantic, futuristic greenhouse. It contained a small ocean complete with machinery to create waves, a twenty-thousand-square-foot agricultural area, a tiny rain forest, a savanna, and a desert. The interior also housed machinery and computers to monitor everything that went on inside Biosphere 2, including the regulation of temperature, humidity, artificial tides, and artificial seasons.

Journalists covering the crew's experiment called the structure a modern Noah's ark because it held so many different animals, birds, fish, insects, and microbes. It also contained numerous species of plant life to provide food, a pleasant ambience, and the oxygen that was vital to human and animal inhabitants. Altogether, the initial experiment included more than thirty-eight hundred species of interdependent plant and animal life.

The $150 million project was conceived by the Institute of Ecotechnics in London and implemented by Space Biospheres Ventures with funding from Texas billionaire Edward Perry Bass. During the two-year experiment, the crew met with problems that would have been disastrous if they had occurred in outer space. The experiment, however, taught scientists many valuable lessons. It also demonstrated that human beings could live comfortably and harmoniously in a human-made, self-sufficient ecosystem.

The biospherians reported the inevitable personality conflicts but agreed that they managed to cooperate be-

---

## A BIOSPHERIAN GIVES HER SIDE OF THE STORY

*In her book* The Human Experiment: Two Years and Twenty Minutes Inside Biosphere 2 *(2006), biospherian Jane Poynter explains what happened after she had to leave Biosphere 2 briefly for emergency surgery on an injured finger:*

After my surgery . . . I wafted into an auditorium to field journalists' questions, my mind afloat in a sea of painkillers. I staggered out to an ambulance, which returned me to the airlock only six-and-a-half hours after exiting it. I had eaten one granola bar, drunk one glass of water, and taken approximately six thousand breaths of air from Biosphere 1.

I didn't even get a Big Mac, let alone a pizza or a margarita.

Unfortunately, as I entered the airlock, Norberto Romo, the head of Mission Control, placed a duffel bag inside the airlock with me, which I obediently took inside. I did not peek, but apparently, it only contained two computer boards, a planting plan of the Wilderness biomes, and a couple of other forgotten spare parts. This was not enough to compromise the Biosphere's material closure, but the media seized upon the surreptitious way in which it was done, causing another needless scandal. The papers erroneously claimed that I clandestinely brought supplies of food back into the Biosphere with me, and further stated that my exit and entrance negated the hermetic seal. "For want of a fingertip, might an experiment be lost?" wrote the *Arizona Republic* newspaper.

It was infuriating because they plainly did not understand that the airlock was intended precisely for such situations. A small and measured amount of air was exchanged with Biosphere 1, which would be included in any scientific calculations.

---

cause of their emotional stake in the success of the mission. They were not entirely isolated from the world: Biosphere 2 became an instant tourist attraction, and many people came to observe the day-to-day operations of the crew through the structure's triangular windows. The crew members also kept in contact with the outside world through telephone calls, e-mail, and closed-circuit television.

The most serious problem involved oxygen. The integrity of the sealed environment had to be broken when it became apparent that the trees and plants were not producing enough oxygen to support the human occupants. By January, 1992, a few months into the crew's planned two-year stay, the oxygen content had diminished to about 15 percent from the desired 21 percent of the interior atmosphere. The oxygen content was equivalent to that of air at an altitude of 13,400 feet, and the biospherians were suffering from fatigue, headaches, and sleep disorders.

As the oxygen content fell, the carbon dioxide content rose to ten times its normal concentration in the out-

1993

side air. This had bizarre effects on the plant life and narcotizing effects on the human crew. It was discovered that the soil inside the biosphere was absorbing more oxygen than had been anticipated, and it became necessary to pump in oxygen to save the experiment.

Another unforeseen event attracted much attention. One crew member had to be taken out of Biosphere 2 because she needed emergency surgery on a wounded finger. When she returned, she brought some supplies with her, and the press speculated that the giant terrarium was not as self-sufficient as had been claimed. Such incidents received wide media coverage, but the project directors reiterated that they had never expected perfection in this first model and that finding the flaws in their design was precisely the purpose of the experiment.

The biospherians produced about 80 percent of the food they needed but suffered crop failures because of unanticipated depredations by mites and other insects. One of the major complaints of the crew members when they emerged from Biosphere 2 was that they had been chronically hungry. Some of them lost as much as 18 percent of their body weight. They reported that their efficiency had been undermined by the fact that they had been obsessed with food that was simply not available in their austere living conditions.

The promoters of Biosphere 2 claimed that overall the experiment had been a great success in spite of its surprises and disappointments. They immediately set to work correcting the problems that had been encountered and recruiting a new crew of biospherians for a second experiment in prolonged isolation; that experiment, however, conducted in 1994, lasted only six months.

## SIGNIFICANCE

Biosphere 2 attracted nationwide attention because of its futuristic design and because the human drama lived by the crew members for two years within the self-sustaining environment fascinated observers. Reporters, scientists, and tourists traveled to southern Arizona from all over the world to see it. The structure's thousands of windows allowed spectators to view almost everything going on inside. All this public exposure made Biosphere 2 an excellent tool for generating interest in ecological concerns as well as in the potential for human space travel.

In spite of the problems encountered by the eight biospherians, their courage, self-sacrifice, and ingenuity led to many important findings. Most significant, they demonstrated that it would be possible, with further study and experimentation, for scientists and engineers

to build space colonies in which human beings could live indefinitely. The crew was made up of both men and women partly to draw attention to the fact that future space voyagers would perhaps be producing, rearing, and educating new generations of humans while in space.

Not only science-fiction writers but also scientists, engineers, architects, psychologists, sociologists, philosophers, and other serious-minded authorities have written about the future colonization of space by humans. The designers of Biosphere 2 had much theoretical material on which to draw when they undertook the daring task of turning fantasy and theory into reality. Biosphere 2 also modeled what cities of the future might be like, not only orbiting in outer space or attached to inhospitable planets but also on Earth itself. The creators of this project demonstrated that humans have the power to create healthier, more beautiful, and more life-supporting environments to replace polluted, congested, overcrowded, and unsightly cities. The Biosphere 2 experiment suggested that investment in space colonization could lead to vast improvements in the quality of life on Earth as well.

Biosphere 2 became a a lucrative tourist attraction in Arizona, an arid state that depends on tourism to support its economy. Men, women, and children who know little about science could see in Biosphere 2 tangible evidence that space colonization is not merely a theme of science fiction; rather, it is on the verge of becoming reality. The educational value of the Biosphere 2 experiment was perhaps its greatest contribution.

The creative men and women involved in the project claimed that they had demonstrated the feasibility of "terraforming" Mars—that is, providing another entire planet with an Earthlike atmosphere. They anticipated the development of island ecosystems all around the world that would be used to study and preserve rare and endangered species of plants while serving as laboratories, educational institutions, and tourist attractions.

The futuristic Biosphere 2 structure standing in the middle of the barren desert like a human outpost on a distant planet was the subject of newspaper and magazine articles as Space Biospheres Ventures continued to improve on the original design. In 1995, management of Biosphere 2 was given to Columbia University, and college classes were held there into the early twenty-first century. The property was put up for sale in 2005 and was purchased in 2006 by Fairfield Homes for the development of a planned community.

*—Bill Delaney*

**FURTHER READING**

Allen, John. *Biosphere 2: The Human Experiment*. New York: Penguin Books, 1991. Provides one of the most thorough descriptions of the Biosphere 2 program available. Copiously illustrated with both color and black-and-white photographs showing the interior and exterior of the structure, the people involved, and major botanical, zoological, and technological features.

Lovelock, James. *Gaia: A New Look at Life on Earth*. 1979. Reprint. New York: Oxford University Press, 2000. Scientific and philosophical work has become a classic in the modern ecology movement. Argues that the earth functions as a single organism that has created humans as an inseparable part of itself.

Maranto, Gina. "Earth's First Visitors to Mars." *Discover* 8 (May, 1987): 28-43. Offers a complete description of the Biosphere 2 project and presents the project as a prelude to the colonization of Mars. Discusses the technical aspects of achieving a balance of plant and animal life within the closed environment. Includes many color illustrations and diagrams.

O'Neill, Gerard K. *The High Frontier: Human Colonies in Space*. 3d ed. Burlington, Ont.: Apogee Books, 2000. Professor of physics at Princeton University and leading space-colony authority presents a detailed account of the feasibility of building space colonies that would have controlled climates and artificial gravity and be fueled by solar power. Features many illustrations.

Poynter, Jane. *The Human Experiment: Two Years and Twenty Minutes Inside Biosphere 2*. New York: Thunder's Mouth Press, 2006. Interesting insider's account by a crew member details what life was like in Biosphere 2. Includes photographs, bibliography, and index.

Walford, Roy L. *Beyond the 120-Year Diet: How to Double Your Vital Years*. Rev. ed. New York: Four Walls Eight Windows, 2000. Senior nutritionist of the Biosphere 2 crew offers his ideas on achieving health and longevity through proper food consumption. Crew members tried many of Walford's ideas during their two-year seclusion.

**SEE ALSO:** Apr. 19, 1971: Russians Launch the Salyut Space Station; 1979: Lovelock Publishes *Gaia: A New Look at Life on Earth*; Feb. 20, 1986: First Permanently Manned Space Station Is Launched; June 29, 1995: Space Shuttle Docks with Mir; Nov. 2, 2000: International Space Station Is Manned.

## October 13, 1993
# BELL ATLANTIC AND TCI ANNOUNCE MERGER PLANS

*The proposed merger of a leading cable operation and a telephone company signaled a new era in the American communications industry.*

**LOCALE:** New York, New York

**CATEGORIES:** Business and labor; communications and media; trade and commerce

**KEY FIGURES**

*John C. Malone* (b. 1941), president and chief executive officer of Tele-Communications Inc.

*Raymond W. Smith* (b. 1937), chairman of the Bell Atlantic Corporation

*James G. Cullen* (b. 1942), president of the Bell Atlantic Corporation

*Bob John Magness* (b. 1924), chairman of Tele-Communications Inc.

**SUMMARY OF EVENT**

The proposed merger of Bell Atlantic Corporation and Tele-Communications Inc. (TCI) in 1993 was one of the largest and most complicated deals of its kind in the history of American business. The deal, announced by James G. Cullen, president of Bell Atlantic, was valued at $26 billion, second only to the buyout of RJR Nabisco by Kohlberg Kravis Roberts in 1989. The merger would have involved two large commercial operations in different areas—telephone communications and cable television—that had been brought closer together by advances in communications technology. The rapid development of digital transmission technology made it possible to send both sound and images along wires and thus to bring a wide range of entertainment and services into the home. Bell Atlantic and TCI positioned themselves to take advantage of this opportunity. Although the plan ultimately fell through, the proposed merger signaled a new era for telecommunications companies.

Bell Atlantic was one of the "Baby Bell" companies formed in the breakup of the nationwide communications system operated by the American Telephone and

Telegraph Company (AT&T). The U.S. Justice Department forced AT&T to relinquish its monopoly on telephone communications in 1982, and the old Bell system was restructured as seven independent companies. Bell Atlantic covered six states along the northeastern seaboard. In 1992, it served approximately thirteen million residential and business customers.

Although telephone services remained profitable business ventures in the 1980's, communications technology was developing rapidly and bringing new challenges to telephone companies. Bell Atlantic earned a reputation as the most innovative of the Baby Bells by moving quickly into cellular phone operation, computer services, and fiber-optic communications. The company was also an innovator in telephone services, introducing features such as caller ID and paging.

The most important development in communications technology in the 1980's was satellite-delivered television programming, which transferred cable television from a niche operation serving inaccessible areas into the dominant form of home entertainment. TCI began as a small cable television venture in 1972 and grew rapidly under the aggressive leadership of John C. Malone and Bob John Magness. It acquired numerous other companies and became the largest cable television operation in the United States. In 1993, it operated in forty-eight states, served about thirteen million subscribers, and had a large stake in several leading cable programmers, including the Discovery Channel, Black Entertainment Television (BET), and the Turner Broadcasting System. TCI formed a separate company, Liberty Media Corporation, to handle this side of the business.

Telephone and cable television companies both ran wires into the homes of their subscribers. During the 1980's, the capabilities of wired communications soared exponentially as fiber-optic cable and digital compres-

*James G. Cullen (right), president of Bell Atlantic, listens as Tele-Communications Inc. (TCI) chief executive officer John C. Malone (via telescreen) announces from New York City that Bell Atlantic has agreed to buy TCI. The deal was valued at $26 billion. (AP/Wide World Photos)*

sion made it possible to transmit many more signals along a wire. The telephone companies' fiber-optic cables carried less than 1 percent of their capacity with the existing level of telephone transmissions. Bell Atlantic began a program to send video images along its fiber-optic wires and introduced a pay television film service to a small number of subscribers on a trial basis. At the same time, TCI experimented with transmitting information along its cables. The broadband wires of the cable companies were capable of carrying large amounts of digitized picture, voice, and data signals. This capacity gave cable companies the means to provide more than images and sound to their subscribers.

With these resources at hand, Malone of TCI and Raymond W. Smith, the chair of Bell Atlantic, were determined to lead the movement into wired interactive communications, but each realized that his company could not go it alone. Bell Atlantic had expertise in operating advanced communications networks but did not have access to programming, which would be essential if the telephone company was to compete with television companies in providing home entertainment. TCI had control of several organizations that produced television programming but lacked the finances to expand into new areas. It also lacked the technical expertise required to deal in a broad range of information and communications services over a wired network.

In 1989, Smith predicted that the telephone companies would diversify into cable services by utilizing their fiber-optic networks and suggested that telephone and cable companies should work together. Smith decided that the only way for Bell Atlantic to move into the next phase of the communications business was to ally with a cable television operator. Malone recognized that he could not push TCI into the field of wired communications without the support of a telephone company. In a deal announced on October 13, 1993, the two companies agreed to merge in an exchange of shares. Bell Atlantic would acquire TCI and its programming arm, Liberty Media, for about $12 billion and would assume more than $9 billion in TCI's debt.

The new Bell Atlantic would have the capability to offer an unprecedented number of services to the home consumer. In addition to normal telephone communications, it could provide video telephone calls and a new type of wireless phone service, called Personal Communications Services, that would employ the cable system of TCI. The fiber-optic cables of Bell Atlantic could carry video games, interactive media contained in entertainment and information computer software, films, mu-

sic, news, and the broad spectrum of cable programming. It could also provide interactive shopping services through TCI's Home Shopping Network.

Bell Atlantic had ambitions to become a source of programming for the new networks of telecommunications. It developed an electronic navigation system called Stargazer to guide television viewers through the host of options provided by cable and fiber-optic networks. Viewers would receive access to banking, education, shopping, and entertainment services. Bell Atlantic also discussed new sources of entertainment with the Walt Disney organization, Paramount Pictures, and Home Box Office. The new Bell Atlantic was conceived as the pioneer multimedia company, bringing together information processing, communications, and entertainment media.

## SIGNIFICANCE

The announcement of the merger came as a shock to the business community. The planning had been carried out in secret, and it was widely believed in the cable industry that John Malone would never concede control of his company. The news caused elation in some quarters and despair in others. A new industrial giant with assets of $60 billion and a stake in two vital technologies was heralded as a breakthrough that would open the way to the new "telecomedia" industry of the twenty-first century. Wall Street was enthusiastic about the merger, and the share prices of both companies rose. In contrast, several members of Congress voiced opposition to what they saw as an excessively large company, pointing out that it would serve one-fourth of all American households and have substantial monopoly power. Many legislators and consumer advocates warned that the electronic "information superhighway" of the future would fall prey to narrow commercial interests.

The proposed merger of Bell Atlantic and TCI was notable for the size of the deal and the ambitions of the new company, but other telephone companies had pursued the strategy of forging links with cable television in the United States and Europe, although on a much smaller scale. Merger plans were made during a flurry of acquisitions by the Baby Bell companies. Nynex Corporation of New York invested more than $1 billion in Viacom, a leading cable television operator; U.S. West paid $2.5 billion for a 25 percent stake in Time Warner, the first media conglomerate and the second-largest cable operator in the United States, after TCI; and BellSouth Corporation bought a 22.5 percent share of Prime Management, a cable operator. BellSouth also had begun

1993

negotiations with the QVC network, a cable home shopping service, to provide financial support for QVC's takeover bid for Paramount Communications.

The struggle for Paramount provided a symbolic image of the new era of electronic entertainment. Paramount Pictures had been one of the old film studio giants that had formed in the 1920's and had dominated visual entertainment until the arrival of television. Although its core business declined, Paramount diversified into television and publishing and maintained a strong holding in old films and television programming, making it attractive to cable companies hungry for programming. Two cable companies, QVC and Viacom, competed to take over Paramount.

TCI became part of this struggle because it owned a large share of QVC. It agreed to invest $500 million in QVC to help finance the acquisition of Paramount. Liberty Media Corporation also owned the Home Shopping Network, which was involved in negotiations with QVC to merge all cable shopping services into one organization. The Bell Atlantic-TCI merger presented some regulatory problems for QVC in its struggle to take over Paramount, and subsequently TCI withdrew its support. This opened the door for BellSouth to become QVC's partner in this venture.

By far the most important barriers to the merger of Bell Atlantic and TCI were regulatory issues that would have to be resolved before the two companies could combine. Several government bodies had jurisdiction over the services that would be affected by the merger, ranging from the Federal Communications Commission to the Justice Department. The proposed merger posed a question of monopoly: An organization reaching into millions of homes, with a presence in fifty-nine of the nation's top one hundred markets, could easily act in restraint of trade. Bell Atlantic and TCI together would control the gateway to more than 40 percent of American homes. Any entrepreneur with plans to set up a new entertainment or news channel would need to acknowledge the company's power.

More complex issues surrounded the activities of cable television operators, which were governed by the 1984 Cable Act, and those of telephone companies, which were framed by the settlement enacted when the national telephone monopoly was broken up. A strict reading of the laws and regulations governing telephone and cable operations and the 1982 AT&T settlement would make the merger of Bell Atlantic and TCI impossible. For example, Bell Atlantic announced plans to use TCI's cables to provide communications nationwide, a clear contradiction of the AT&T settlement, which prohibited a telephone company from offering national service. By law, no single organization can run telephone and cable services in the same area. The new Bell Atlantic would not be allowed to provide cable service where the telephone company was in operation, forcing the company to divest itself of several local cable companies operated by TCI. Bell Atlantic agreed to do this but still planned to provide video programming over all of its network, using a technology different from that employed by TCI, leading inevitably to a conflict of interest.

Regulations concerning communications had not stayed abreast of the technology, and there was widespread belief in both Congress and the business community that regulations would have to be rewritten to suit the new order in information technology. Bell Atlantic achieved an important precedent when a federal court declared a provision of the 1984 Cable Act unconstitutional and allowed Bell Atlantic to offer video programs to its subscribers. Other legal barriers to telephone companies moving into cable were expected to be relaxed as new definitions of what constitutes a telecommunications company emerged.

Virulent opposition to this process from some members of Congress and consumer groups meant that Bell Atlantic and TCI faced a difficult fight. The telephone and cable services were both high-profile monopolies in the eyes of the public, and there was a strong belief that both overcharged for their services. Subscribers of Bell Atlantic and TCI expressed fears that their bills would increase to pay for the merger and that there would be no way to keep accounting for telephone and cable operations separate. Senator Howard Metzenbaum, a Democrat from Ohio, called for hearings in Congress to investigate what he called "megamergermania" and led opposition to the Bell Atlantic-TCI merger.

Advocates of the national "information superhighway" of electronic data were dismayed at the union of telephone and cable interests, which would give those business interests control of telecommunications in the United States. When Vice President Al Gore first described the potential of a nationwide electronic network, it was in terms of bringing together individuals, not companies. The pattern of mergers in the telecommunications industry threatened—or promised, depending on one's point of view—to create even more powerful business organizations with the potential to monopolize wired communications and the airwaves.

The development of digital technology was supposed to encourage competition by giving cable television and telephone companies the means to compete with one another. This capability remained even though the merger of Bell Atlantic and TCI fell through. Bell Atlantic showed that it could use both copper telephone lines and the new fiber-optic cables to transmit television programming and thus compete with cable companies. Several cable operators successfully used their existing networks to provide interactive communications to their subscribers. Time Warner and Viacom planned to develop this technology, with or without the support of telephone companies.

Fiber-optic wiring was not the exclusive preserve of telephone companies and could easily be operated by other users. In addition to media and communications companies, the computer and software industries were eager to enter the world of interactive communications. Microsoft, Apple, and International Business Machines (IBM) soon began to develop systems to provide interactive communications to home users. A number of companies were thus poised to fashion the future of the technology of interactive media.

—*Andre Millard*

## FURTHER READING

Evans, David, ed. *Breaking Up Bell: Essays on Industrial Organization and Regulation*. New York: North-Holland, 1983. Collection of scholarly articles on regulation of the telephone industry describes the legal boundaries governing operation of telephone services.

Kneale, Dennis, Johnnie L. Roberts, and Laura Landro. "Plugging In: Bell Atlantic and TCI Are Poised to Shape New Interactive World." *The Wall Street Journal*, October 14, 1993, p. Al. Discusses the businesses in which the merged new firm would compete.

Landler, Mark, Bart Ziegler, Mark Lewyn, and Leah Nathans Spiro. "Bell-Ringer! How Bell Atlantic and TCI Hooked Up—And What It Means for the Information Age." *BusinessWeek*, October 25, 1993, 32-36. Details the planning of the merger and suggests likely responses by competitors. Informative concerning financial aspects of the merger; presents statistics on the firms involved.

McMaster, Susan E. *The Telecommunications Industry*. Westport, Conn.: Greenwood Press, 2002. Presents a concise history of the industry from the invention of the telephone in 1875 to the beginning of the twenty-first century. Includes discussion of the breakup of the Bell system and the mergers and technology changes that have influenced the industry.

Markoff, John. "Phone-Cable Deal May Offer Vehicle for Data Expressway." *The New York Times*, October 14, 1993, pp. Al, C6. Discusses how TCI and Bell Atlantic could implement the idea of an information superhighway. Includes a map showing areas in which the companies operated as of the date of the merger announcement. A chart shows other major media deals of 1993.

Sugawara, Sandra, and Paul Farhi. "Merger to Create a Media Giant: $26 Billion Bell Atlantic-TCI Deal Is a Vision of TV's Future." *The Washington Post*, October 14, 1993, pp. A1, A8. Discusses basics of the merger deal, focusing on antitrust issues. An accompanying article focuses on Smith and Malone.

Tunstall, W. Brooke. *Disconnecting Parties: Managing the Bell System Break-Up*. New York: McGraw-Hill, 1985. An employee of the Bell system describes the breakup and provides information about the origins and corporate culture of Bell Atlantic.

SEE ALSO: 1977-2000: Fiber-Optics Revolution; May 11, 1977: First Commercial Test of Fiber-Optic Telecommunications; 1980's: Electronic Technology Creates the Possibility of Telecommuting; Jan. 8, 1982: AT&T Undergoes Divestiture; July 19, 1982: Great Britain Announces Plans to Privatize British Telecom; Jan. 3, 1996: U.S. Congress Reforms Law Regulating Telecommunications.

1993

## October 21, 1993
# BURUNDIAN PRESIDENT IS ASSASSINATED

*After becoming the first democratically elected president of Burundi and the nation's first Hutu leader, Melchior Ndadaye was assassinated during a military takeover engineered by Tutsis. The assassination led to the bloody Burundi civil war, in which as many as 300,000 were killed.*

**LOCALE:** Burundi
**CATEGORIES:** Government and politics; crime and scandal; wars, uprisings, and civil unrest

**KEY FIGURES**
*Melchior Ndadaye* (1953-1993), first Hutu president of Burundi, 1993
*Sylvie Kinigi* (b. 1952), first female prime minister of Burundi, July 10, 1993-February 7, 1994
*Cyprien Ntaryamira* (1955-1994), minister of agriculture and president of Burundi, February 5-April 6, 1994
*François Ngeze* (fl. late twentieth century), Burundian head of state, October 21-23, 1993
*Pierre Nkurunziza* (b. 1963), president of Burundi beginning in August, 2005

**SUMMARY OF EVENT**
On October 21, 1993, a group of supposedly loyal soldiers escorted Burundian president Melchior Ndadaye and other high government officials to an army barracks, ostensibly to protect them from mutinying soldiers. There the soldiers executed them, along with several other officials and cabinet members, in a military coup that plunged the country into murderous ethnic chaos that escalated into a ten-year-long civil war.

President Melchior Ndadaye was the first Hutu president in Burundi's long history of political and economic domination by the minority Tutsi population. After the country gained its independence from Belgium in 1962, tensions between the Hutu majority and Tutsi minority had led to frequent violence between the two ethnic groups. After several political upheavals, multiparty rule, established in 1992, brought about a new constitution that opened the way for general elections. As the Hutus were in the majority, it was not surprising that a Hutu would become president in a fair election and overthrow the decades-long domination of the country by the Tutsi.

Although the Hutus made up four-fifths of Burundi's population, they had suffered discrimination from the Tutsis since before the Belgian colonial era (1916-1961).

The Tutsis, a tall, lighter-complexioned people who had been skilled warriors, believed that working with a hoe, as the agrarian Hutus traditionally did, was demeaning. The fact that the Belgian overlords favored the Tutsis with more prestigious positions in the government than the Hutus were given also contributed to the Tutsis' conviction that they were the rightful rulers of the country, that they were the lords and the Hutus were the vassals. So when a Hutu, Melchior Ndadaye, became leader of their newly independent country, the Tutsis had little doubt that things would change in Burundi, and not to their advantage.

President Ndadaye, however, an educated and moderate political activist, had no intention of taking revenge on the Tutsis for their years of mistreatment of the Hutus. He hoped to heal the divisiveness and antagonism between the two groups. His initial step in that direction was appointing a Tutsi woman, Sylvie Kinigi, as prime minister. Then he put members of the Tutsi Union for National Progress into one-third of all cabinet posts and into two regional governorships. He loosened government control of the press so that the workings of government and other important areas of Burundian life could be made known to the general public. To avoid the appearance of showing favoritism to Hutus who had for so long been squeezed out of important and/or lucrative jobs, he moved slowly against the entrenched discrimination against them.

However, when Ndadaye investigated some of the activities of the previous, Tutsi-dominated government, he found serious improprieties. His investigations rattled powerful Tutsi higher-ups and military men who realized that their finances would be affected and threatened when contracts and concessions approved by the Tutsi-led government were examined. Perhaps a large part of the increasing Tutsi dissatisfaction with his administration was his proposed reform of the Burundi military: He reassigned the national police and placed them under a command separate from that of the army, thereby diluting the control and power of certain Tutsi longtime leaders. He modified army recruitment regulations as a way to limit the number of Tutsi soldiers and officers and increase the intake of other ethnic constituents. Another part of their concern perhaps was his efforts to replace many of the Tutsi public servants with deserving but inexperienced Hutus. While this was long overdue, the Hutus had little experience dealing with the myriad problems facing Burundi, including dealing with the large numbers of returning refugees. The difficulties resulting from the Hutus' ineptness were reported by the newly free press, consequently making the entire country aware. Tensions between Hutu and Tutsi increased.

Finally, on October 21, 1993, soldiers in the Tutsi-led army gathered President Ndadaye, the National Assembly president Pontien Karibwami, and its vice president Gilles Bimazubute, under the guise of protecting them from mutinying soldiers advancing on the presidential palace. Beer-drinking soldiers had surrounded the palace, and military tanks had even been used to break into the building. There was clearly a danger, and the president believed the soldiers accompanying him and his colleagues were loyal. He and the other administrators were escorted to an army barracks where several other officials and cabinet members had been assembled. There they were all summarily executed, with President Ndadaye being bayoneted to death.

Once the news of the executions was known, chaos and violence broke out. Hutus sought revenge on Tutsis, and the Tutsi-led army retaliated with force against Hutus. Civilians of both groups were targets. Students were taken from schools and burned alive or chopped to death with machetes. Some people ran for their lives, hiding under water in rivers. To stem the violence, leaders of the coup imposed a curfew. Recognizing the value of keeping the population ignorant of what was transpiring, they also cut telephone service and took over the state-run radio stations. To keep out foreign interlopers, they closed the international airport so no flights could go in or out. As Hutu civilians were clearly getting the worst of the violence, attacked as they were by well-armed soldiers, they were encouraged to flee to Rwanda, which huge numbers did.

François Ngeze, who had been interior minister under a previous president, was called on to become temporary head of state on October 21. After two days, he refused to work with the leaders of the coup and said that Prime Minister Kinigi should be given the authority to take control of the government. Even though she was a Tutsi, Kinigi, fearing for her safety, had taken refuge in the French Embassy. She accepted the responsibility but asked the United Nations for an international force to be deployed in Burundi to protect her and the other officials. She and they were suspicious of the Burundian army's intentions. Although both the U.N. Security Council and the U.N. General Assembly condemned the assassination and coup, and the General Assembly demanded immediate restoration of democracy and the country's constitutional regime, Burundi's army commander refused to allow the deployment of outside forces.

Ultimately, more than 300,000 Hutu and Tutsi civilians were killed as the carnage escalated into a civil war that lasted for a decade. In 1999, five men were tried and found guilty in the assassination of President Ndadaye and sentenced to death.

## SIGNIFICANCE

Burundi has always been one of the poorest countries in Africa and was in even worse straits after decades of internal strife, what with uprooted refugees returning to find their homes gone or in shambles, the country's economy battered, and simmering resentment among the various ethnic and political factions threatening to erupt at the slightest provocation. At the end of the barbaric hostilities ignited by Ndadaye's assassination, Burundians, with the support of the United Nations, agreed to interim alternating rule by, first, a Tutsi administrator and then a Hutu until finally, in 2005, elections were held. In August, 2005, a former teacher and former rebel leader, Pierre Nkurunziza, was elected president with his promise to unite all Burundians and all political parties, to stop the ethnic rivalry, and to begin rebuilding the nation.

—*Jane L. Ball*

## FURTHER READING

Lemarchand, René. *Burundi: Ethnic Conflict and Genocide*. New York: Cambridge University Press, 2004. Includes chapters devoted to the civil war that began in 1994. Focuses on the causes and consequences of the Hutu-Tutsi animosity.

Ould-Abdallah, Ahmedou. *Burundi on the Brink, 1993-95: A UN Special Envoy Reflects on Preventive Diplomacy*. New York: U.S. Institute of Peace Press, 2000. Discusses a U.N. envoy's trip to Burundi to work with ethnic rivals for political progress and to stave off genocide. Difficult reading for the marginally interested reader. Focus is on the United Nations' role in the Burundi situation.

Tuhabonye, Gilbert, with Gary Brozek. *This Voice in My Heart: A Genocide Survivor's Story of Escape, Faith, and Forgiveness*. New York: Amistad, 2006. Autobiographical account by a Tutsi high school student of events in the aftermath of the October assassination of Burundi president Ndadaye.

SEE ALSO: May-Aug., 1972: Burundi Commits Genocide of Hutu Majority; July 5, 1973: Habyarimana Overthrows President Kayibanda; Apr. 6-July, 1994: Rwandan Genocide; Sept., 1998: U.N. Tribunal Convicts Rwandans of Genocide.

1993

## October 26-November 3, 1993
# FIRES DEVASTATE SOUTHERN CALIFORNIA

*Chaparral fires burned seventy-nine thousand hectares of land in six Southern California counties, killed several people, and damaged eleven hundred homes and other buildings, most of them in Malibu.*

**LOCALE:** Southern California
**CATEGORY:** Disasters

**KEY FIGURES**

*Thomas McMaster* (fl. late twentieth century), assistant fire chief of Malibu and commander of the city's firefighting task force

*Richard Riordan* (b. 1930), mayor of Los Angeles, who was heavily involved in directing the firefighting efforts

*Bruce Babbitt* (b. 1938), U.S. secretary of the interior, who advocated measures to reduce the risks and damages caused by wildfire in California

*Pete Wilson* (b. 1933), governor of California, 1991-1999, whose veto of spending on costly mitigation measures was criticized in the wake of the fire

**SUMMARY OF EVENT**

Fires began at the Southern California urban-wildland interface on October 26, 1993, and burned for nearly two weeks across an area that stretched from the Mexican border to the northern fringes of Los Angeles. By the end of October, fourteen major conflagrations had destroyed 731 homes and razed 66,800 hectares in Los Angeles, Orange, Riverside, San Bernardino, San Diego, and Ventura counties. By mid-November, losses had exceeded $1 billion.

The nine major Southern California fires that broke out in early November, 1993, killed 3 people and injured 111, displaced more than 30,000 residents, and destroyed 1,084 homes. The worst conflagration was in Malibu, where the deaths and many of the injuries occurred, 350 homes were destroyed, and damages were valued at $375 million. The Malibu disaster was the most spectacular and instructive of the 1993 fires.

Malibu was founded as a ranch in 1804 and developed after 1938 as a center of surfing and home to wealthy people connected with the entertainment industry. The city of Malibu merges with a corridor of Los Angeles suburbs in which the number of inhabitants tripled over the three decades before the 1993 disaster. During that period, no major fires were recorded in the area, although they remained an ever-present risk.

At 11:45 A.M. on November 2, 1993, smoke and flames appeared at Calabasas in Topanga Canyon, east of Malibu. In only four hours, the fire moved about 12 miles through the brush vegetation of the steep canyons that lead toward the city, causing spot fires along the coastal mountain slopes. At dusk, a line of fire stretched along the canyon ridge and flames were shooting 50 to 65 feet into the air. Hot embers blowing in the wind caused palm trees along the waterfront to burst suddenly and spectacularly into flame.

The progress of the fire was hastened, and its path was made very irregular, by Santa Ana winds gusting erratically at more than 55 miles per hour. A high-pressure cell had developed north of Malibu, and a low-pressure cell had developed to the city's south. These conditions generated strong air flows that warmed up as they descended down the mountains to the coast. Consequently, on arrival at Malibu the winds were hot, dry, and strong, and so they remained until the weather system began to migrate away late on November 3. Ambient temperatures during the period of the fire were 9 to 12 degrees Celsius at night and 26 to 31 degrees Celsius during the day.

Schools and factories, including the Hughes Aircraft Corporation laboratories in Malibu Canyon, were evacuated during the afternoon of November 2. House-to-house evacuation continued after nightfall, and in the early evening some luxury homes burned, after which the flames turned toward the campus of Pepperdine University. The university was eventually spared by a change in wind direction. Traffic on Pacific Coast Highway was at a standstill, and attempts by the police to move the traffic and cordon off the area were thwarted by residents who were anxious about the fire threat to their homes. In fact, more than one-half of the firefighters in the Emerald Bay area were used not to combat the flames but to rescue home owners who had refused to leave.

The authorities had received advance warning about extreme fire conditions, but they could do little to halt the progress of the conflagration. About seven thousand firefighters were deployed, some of whom came from as far away as Nevada and Oregon. Their strategy involved bulldozing firebreaks through the chaparral scrub and using Bell-412 helicopters, which could carry 370 gallons of water, and C-130 airplanes, which could haul 2,900 gallons of fire retardants. Overflights ceased at dusk, but helicopters were able to resume flying before dawn, and the aircraft took off again at first light. Fire-retarding foam was also sprayed at the base of the canyon slopes to inhibit the spread of the flames.

The fire lines were drawn at Tuna Canyon on the northern boundary of Malibu, the Pacific Coast Highway on its ocean side, and Topanga Canyon Boulevard to the south. The intensity and speed with which the blaze moved sent firefighters into retreat, and late on November 2 the first command post, located on Pacific Coast Highway, had to be abandoned and a new one organized further west at Pepperdine University. Many of the 250 fire engines at work in the area, as well as bulldozers and their crews, were assembled at the junction of Pacific Coast Highway and Topanga Canyon Boulevard, but they all had to retreat east as the fire spread relentlessly toward them. Meanwhile, in Tuna Canyon some ground crews were nearly overrun by the advancing flames. The Topanga Canyon Boulevard and Pacific Coast Highway lines were held for most of November 3, but sea breezes late in the day blew the fire across the line of fire trucks on the canyon road. Firefighters fought back, and the front was gradually contained, but not until the majority of buildings in Las Flores Canyon Creek had been destroyed.

Eventually, the Malibu fire killed three people, injured more than one hundred (seven of them seriously), burned 13,500 hectares, and damaged or destroyed 350 homes. The injured suffered variously from large-scale burns, smoke inhalation, and damage to the lungs caused by inhaling superheated air.

Ten days later, more than four centimeters of rain fell in only twenty-four hours, causing heavy erosion of the area damaged by the fires. In Malibu, mud flowed across Pacific Coast Highway, blocking three lanes during the morning rush hour. Mudflows also damaged homes that had escaped the flames.

In an election that took place on the day of the Malibu fire, Californians approved Proposition 172, which maintained the 0.5 percent sales tax used to finance public-safety measures. Two days later, Governor Pete Wilson hastily reversed his decision not to allow $1.8 million to be spent on two Canadian-built CL-215 "Super Scooper" aircraft capable of loading more than 1,500 gallons of water in twelve seconds. In the wake of the fires, the U.S. secretary of the interior, Bruce Babbitt, suggested that Californians should think seriously about whether it is wise to extend urbanization into dry chaparral lands.

## SIGNIFICANCE

A wildfire that is burning out of control endangers people, settlements, or resources. Such a fire is considered to be "confined" if it is limited to a predetermined area using natural or constructed barriers, "contained" if it is surrounded with a control line in order to stop its spreading, and "controlled" if the line around it is completed. If valuable resources must be protected, vigorous direct control is preferable, although policy should be reviewed daily in relation to weather conditions. The Malibu fire was first contained and then controlled as firefighters gradually succeeded in their work.

When the leaves and branches of trees burn, the result is a crown fire, which may depend on the flames at the surface or may run ahead as flames propagate through the vegetation canopy. Most chaparral conflagrations are dependent crown fires or surface fires, and they may give rise to ground fires if leaf litter is deep enough to burn thoroughly and if backburns consume areas that have already been warmed by fire. If winds are high or great drafts are caused by atmospheric heating, then spot fires may break out when burning brands are lobbed into dry material ahead of the main front. The Malibu blaze was predominantly a fast surface fire, with elements of the running crown fire, peripheral spot fires, and periods of backburn. Chaparral fires of this kind tend to be very hot, with maximum temperatures of 540 to 1,100 degrees Celsius, as the fuel consists of highly flammable woody grasses and dry, oleose shrubs. Convection and radiation may stimulate the fire to burn uphill, but chaparral fires are often conditioned by overall wind direction and speed, although irregularities of topography and fuel load tend to cause their spreading fronts to become uneven.

A few large conflagrations are responsible for much of the land burned in California. Thus, in the northern part of the state, 1 percent of fires burn 96 percent of area affected. There, where forests predominate, population densities are low and many of fires are caused by lightning. In contrast, most of the three thousand fires each year in Southern California are started by human activity, and many of them are larger than natural fires would be. Although one fire in 1993 was caused when the fierce Santa Ana winds made power lines arc, the Malibu blaze and most others were believed to have been set deliberately. Arson is usually a compulsive trait, and those who indulge in it often have deep-rooted but concealed psychological ailments. In the United States, less than 20 percent of arsonists are ever caught.

Fire risk is greatest at the urban-wildland interface, which is where more than seven million Californians live and where some of the highest rates of population increase are evident in the state. In Berkeley in 1923, fire

1993

destroyed 584 homes; in Santa Barbara, fire destroyed 234 houses in 1977 and 641 in 1990. The tunnel fire of October, 1991, in the hills above Oakland and Berkeley killed 25 people and destroyed 2,810 homes in one of the fiercest conflagrations that suburban California has known. Hot, dry Santa Ana winds spread the flames over 728 hectares in only ten hours. Such events are exceptionally expensive; hence, damage by California brushfires amounts to more than $100 million per year and firefighting costs average $50 million per year.

The October, 1993, fires had particularly severe impacts on rare birds and their habitats. Fires depleted the U.S. population of gnatcatchers by 330 pairs (15 percent), and about 460 pairs of cactus wrens, or 15 to 20 percent of the U.S. population, died. Interior Secretary Bruce Babbitt had proposed that the Endangered Species Act be used to induce developers to create scientifically defined nature preserves, and in Orange County the largest private landowner, the Irvine Company, had earmarked land to conserve, but 1,500 hectares of it were burned in 1993. Earlier in the year, Stanford wildlife biologist Dennis Murphy had argued that no more than 5 percent of Southern California coastal sage scrub could be developed without permanently hurting the chances of recovery of endangered species. Instead, the fires burned such large areas and left such fragmentary habitat that the survival of the remaining birds was called into question.

There was a clear relationship between the Malibu fire and increased rates of erosion. Elimination of chaparral vegetation can increase the rate of dry particle-by-particle gravitational sliding, or dry ravel. When it rains copiously, denuded watersheds can generate networks of rills and gullies or mudflows. Although studies have shown that fire in chaparral is ten times more frequent than debris flows, burning at temperatures of 175 to 200 degrees Celsius may distill organic chemicals until hydrophobic residues make the soil impermeable, allowing even more runoff, gullies, and mudflows to develop.

Devastating fires in 1970 and 1977 led to the formation of California Firescope, which has a centralized incident command system, a multiagency coordinating system, and an operations coordination center. Some twenty-eight agencies are linked to a fire information management system (FIMS) with a comprehensive database, including weather forecasts and infrared surveillance of potential fire areas. The FIMS can give an immediate status report on suppression resources, the progress and behavior of a fire, and the best tactics for fighting it. Under Firescope and the California Fire Disaster Plan,

officials at the Los Angeles County Fire Department call for mutual assistance from the Ventura and Santa Barbara County Fire Services, the California Office of Emergency Services, the California Department of Forestry (which runs a training academy for firefighters), and the U.S. Forest Service, which administers both the mountain watersheds surrounding the basin and the Riverside Fire Research Laboratory.

Surveys conducted in 1976 in Southern California revealed that 74 percent of respondents thought that naturally ignited forest fires should not be allowed to burn, even in the absence of a threat to life or property (although more than one-half agreed that the occasional forest fire could refresh the land). By the 1980's, 80 percent of respondents supported prescribed burning. Surveys of Southern California residents in 1983 revealed growth of awareness of forest-fire hazard; many residents, however, had done nothing to minimize potential fire losses.

Nevertheless, particular events have stimulated improved preparedness. Inadequate hoses caused the water supply to fail during the 1991 Berkeley fire, and narrow, winding roads hampered the evacuation of residents and the arrival of emergency services. Inadequate communications and poor liaison led the Oakland emergency services to miss a Forest Service red alert; after the disaster Oakland purchased a mobile infrared sensor. The city cleared the vegetation on some hillsides, widened some of its roads, and updated the local building codes. When some sixteen thousand properties were inspected two years later, however, one-fourth lacked the mandatory spark arrestors on chimneys or were surrounded by flammable vegetation.

The 1991 Oakland fires did, however, generate enough public awareness to induce the state of California to legislate in favor of fire-resistant roofing standards and the clearance of flammable material from home lots. In the three years before that legislation came into effect, the level of mitigation varied considerably from place to place. In 1992, a fire damaged or destroyed 636 structures in Shasta County, but residents were allowed to rebuild on the same heavily forested land. Other areas responded to fires by tightening their building requirements. For housing, this often involved fire-safe roofs, enclosed eaves, double-glazed windows, spark-arresting chimneys, and fire-resistant exterior cladding. For subdivisions, firebreaks, widened and straightened access roads, and more hydrants were required. The effects were clearly illustrated by the results of a fire in the Chino Hills, where twelve precode buildings were destroyed and two hundred postcode homes came through relatively unscathed. Rebuilding sometimes takes place so quickly, however, that legislation and the upgrading of municipal capabilities cannot keep pace with it.

The answer to steeply rising disaster losses appears to be insurance. Increasing numbers of California properties are being covered under the California Fair Plan, by which the industry reinsures itself and thus shares the burden of high risk. The insurance industry, however, offers few incentives to reduce the risk of fire damage, and some federal agencies are even less concerned. Researchers have concluded that generous disaster loans and reimbursements in effect subsidize and even reward home owners who rebuild without mitigating the risk of fire damage.

—*David E. Alexander*

## FURTHER READING

Barker, Rocky. *Scorched Earth: How the Fires of Yellowstone Changed America*. Washington, D.C.: Island Press, 2005. An environmental reporter discusses the history of fire management policy in general, with a focus on Yellowstone National Park. Includes map, bibliography, and index.

Barro, S. C., and S. G. Conrad. "Fire Effects on California Chaparral Systems: An Overview." *Environment International* 17 (1991): 135-149. Provides a thorough and comprehensive survey of the ecological effects of chaparral fires.

Cortner, Hanna J., Philip D. Gardner, and Jonathan G. Taylor. "Fire Hazard at the Urban-Wildland Interface: What the Public Expects." *Environmental Management* 14 (1990): 57-62. Presents the results of surveys of how the public perceives the wildfire hazard.

McPhee, John A. *The Control of Nature*. New York: Farrar, Straus and Giroux, 1988. Provides a readable introduction to a range of natural hazards and human vulnerabilities in the Los Angeles basin. Addresses wildfire and its consequences in terms of mudflows and erosion.

Pyne, Steven J., Patricia L. Andrews, and Richard D. Laven. *Introduction to Wildland Fire*. 2d ed. New York: John Wiley & Sons, 1996. Definitive work on fire processes, firefighting techniques, and environmental fire management in the United States. Includes maps, bibliographic references, and index.

Wakimoto, Ronald H. "National Fire Management Policy." *Journal of Forestry* 88 (October, 1990): 22-26. Discusses policies, issues, and approaches to firefighting in the wake of the 1988 Yellowstone forest fires.

**SEE ALSO:** Summer, 1988: Fires Burn Much of Yellowstone National Park; Jan. 17, 1994: Northridge Quake Rocks Los Angeles; June-Oct., 1997: Indonesian Forest Fires Devastate Southeast Asia.

## November 1, 1993
# UNIFICATION OF THE EUROPEAN MARKET

*Members of the European Community began a gradual, often qualified implementation of the Maastricht road map for further unification.*

**ALSO KNOWN AS:** Maastricht Treaty
**LOCALE:** Maastricht, the Netherlands
**CATEGORIES:** Trade and commerce; economics

## KEY FIGURES

*Jacques Delors* (b. 1925), president of the European Community Commission
*Helmut Kohl* (b. 1930), chancellor of Germany, 1990-1998
*John Major* (b. 1943), prime minister of Great Britain, 1990-1997
*François Mitterrand* (1916-1996), president of France, 1981-1995

## SUMMARY OF EVENT

In contrast to the 1950-1958 period, which witnessed the birth of the integration process in Europe and during which strong Europeanists and international civil servants played major roles, the 1984-1992 process of converting the European Community (EC) into a single European Union (EU) was—with one notable exception—largely in the hands of the national leaders in the EC's principal member states. The important exception was Jacques Delors, a French Socialist who was selected as president of the European Community Commission at the end of 1984, a particularly dark moment in the EC's history. For more than a decade following the oil crisis of 1973, the EC had stagnated, sapped of its energy by the stagflation (economic stagnation combined with inflation) gripping Europe's economies and the political tensions dividing

1993

2769

its member states. Delors reenergized the integration process by arguing that the best hope for jump-starting the economies of the member states was to be found in the instrument for rapid economic growth that had been used thirty years before: advances in the process of economic integration on the Continent.

By June, 1985, Delors was circulating a draft proposal for developing a fully integrated internal market within the EC by December 31, 1992. Formal commitment to that goal occurred the following year with the passage of the Single European Act (SEA), which was slated to take effect in July, 1987. The plan called for a Europe without frontiers, including an Economic Union (by January 1, 1993) in which there would be no borders to slow down trade among member states, no obstacles to a lawyer or a doctor in one member state establishing a practice in another, a common currency, and further democratization of the EC's decision-making process.

The single Europe objective continued to gain momentum during the late 1980's, getting a large boost from the Cecchini Report issued by the European Community Commission in 1988. The report forecast substantial increases in economic expansion within the EC, in terms of real growth and job creation, as a result of implementing the SEA. Finally, in 1991, with the negotiation at Maastricht, the Netherlands, of the Treaty on European Union, the goals of the SEA became more detailed and more ambitious.

In ratifying the Maastricht Treaty, member states were to commit themselves to a timetable for not only a Europe without frontiers but also a true monetary union, with a single currency, by 1999. They also committed to developing a European central bank, common foreign and defense policies, enhanced power for EC institutions, common citizenship, and further harmonization of judicial, tax, social, and agricultural policies. In addition, under the Social Chapter attached as a protocol to the treaty, they committed to integration in such areas as health, welfare, and the environment. As the ratification process unfolded, however, obtaining such a union became increasingly difficult, largely for two sets of reasons.

First, the Maastricht Treaty, which emerged only after a long process of haggling among European leaders essentially favorable to the idea of further integration, proved to be far ahead of the political climate in many of the member states. Obtaining popular approval for it required a major effort by the leaders of the larger states, especially Prime Minister John Major in Great Britain, President François Mitterrand in France, and Chancellor

Helmut Kohl in Germany. Had any one of these states failed to ratify the treaty, not only would the treaty have failed but in addition the integration process in Europe would almost certainly have stalled. Moreover, each of these states had its own particular set of objections to the treaty. Great Britain, for example, feared loss of control over immigration and currency matters. Germany, with its powerful central bank, was not committed to the idea of a strong central bank with policy control throughout the EU. French voters feared that further economic integration would weaken the French economy and further increase the foreign element in France.

Ultimately, ratification occurred, but only with difficulty, even with men such as Mitterrand and Major working to secure approval of the treaty. The mechanisms of ratification varied from country to country. France and Denmark held national referendums to approve the treaty, with close outcomes. French voters approved by only a 51 percent majority in September, 1992. Other states, such as Great Britain, relied on parliamentary maneuvers and compromises to secure ratification.

Meanwhile, a second element was working to complicate the ratification process. During the time between the adoption of the SEA and the conference at Maastricht, the world beyond the European Community changed in significant ways with the collapse of the Soviet Union and its Eastern European empire. To the EC's east, new states were suddenly available for future membership. Likewise, given the collapse of East-West rivalries on the Continent, the door was open for traditionally neutral states such as Sweden to reexamine their previous reluctance to join the EC. At the same time, West Germany was faced with the immediate opportunity and task of unifying with East Germany. The option was irresistible, but the costs of unification forced the German government to reconsider its priorities. Rebuilding the East meant an enormous drain on the Federal Republic's resources and left far less monetary support available for the EC in the member country that, prior to its reunification, had been one of the most ardent champions of the European Union scheme.

## SIGNIFICANCE

Given the problems besetting ratification of the Maastricht Treaty, the date for the official birth of the European Union was delayed until November 1, 1993. Furthermore, as a result of the concessions necessary to obtain the treaty's ratification by even that date, the occasion largely passed with little celebration or even public notice on the Continent. Too many of the once-anticipated features of the union had been deleted or compromised for there to be much rejoicing. National passports were still necessary for even citizens of EC countries to cross national borders, no common currency was anticipated in the near future, and several states essentially had opted out of some of the treaty's most important provisions.

The advent of the European Union thus marked a major moment in Europe's evolution toward political, social, and economic union, but it also left Europe very much a continent still in search of its potential. The EC became the world's largest market area, with 340 million people. The gross domestic product of its twelve members at the moment of Maastricht's ratification exceeded $5 trillion. Excluding Greece and Portugal, the standard of living and per-capita incomes of the citizens living in its member states compared favorably with those of Americans. The EC contained several of the world's principal capitals, some of its most solid currencies (as well as two of its weaker ones, the British pound and Italian lira), important financial centers, and two medium-grade nuclear powers. In all except political union, it had the profile of a superpower; that dream, however, was still being chased. The dynamics of further integration indicated that the chase was likely to be a lengthy one.

Two members were well behind the others economically, and future applicants for EC membership from the southern and east-central regions of Europe were cut from their pattern, not the advanced industrialized democracy model of the EC's older members. Even among the twelve nations that ratified the Maastricht Treaty, there were obstacles to further growth not easily overcome, such as the problem of multilingualism, which forced much of the EC's budget to be devoted to translation expenditures. The twelve countries represented nine different languages (ten if Ireland's Gaelic is considered and still more if the official regional tongues of Basque and Catalonian Spain are included). Most of the states that later joined the EU expanded that number.

On the other hand, the reinvigoration of the integration process in Europe resulted in some important short- and long-term consequences. In the short term, the SEA had its intended effect of boosting economic growth in the EC. The very promise of a Europe without frontiers led to a tripling of the investment rate, higher rates of economic growth, and lower unemployment figures for the EC as an entity even before the Maastricht Treaty was drafted.

Progress on the political front was not insubstantial, especially measured across the two generations that had passed since the European Coal and Steel Community (ECSC) was launched in 1951. The ECSC's member states retained a controlling voice in the new EU's affairs through the EU's Council of Ministers, in which voting was weighted by population and the larger states thus had the majority of votes. Even there, progress occurred in the sense that the issue areas requiring unanimous decisions all but disappeared. Meanwhile, the Maastricht process enhanced the status of the Eurocrat element controlling the European Commission, which stood alone in the world as a supranational body with budgetary and decision-making authority beyond the nation-state. The European Parliament continued its own unique experiment in transnational democracy.

Both European democracy and European integration were advanced by the ratification of the Maastricht Treaty. Citizens of any member state could run for local office or vote in elections in other member states. Residency, not national citizenship, became the controlling factor among EC member states. Citizens could similarly practice their professions throughout the EC once they met the professional certification requirements of any member state. When outside the EU, they could get help at the consulate of any EU state, not only at the consulate of their home country.

At the same time, political cultures throughout the new EU's member states continued to focus on the nation, not the supranational community of Europe, and national interests remained the crucial ones to national governments. The United Kingdom opted out of the EU's social policy programs (and the Social Chapter protocol to the Maastricht Treaty) in order to retain control in London over such areas as consumer protection, health, welfare, and the environment. The twelve member nations also failed to evolve a common foreign policy with regard to Yugoslavia's descent into chaos on the EU's southeastern rim.

In short, the SEA and the Maastricht Treaty brought the states of Europe nearer to political integration than ever before. Three new states—Austria, Finland, and Sweden—acceded to the EU in 1995, bringing the membership to fifteen. As the 1990's progressed, the EU gradually moved toward successful monetary union for the twelve members who agreed to adopt the new Euro currency in 2001. In May, 2004, the EU admitted ten new members—Cyprus, the Czech Republic, Estonia, Hungary, Latvia, Lithuania, Malta, Poland, Slovakia, and Slovenia—bringing membership to a total of twenty-five countries. At the same time, member states negotiated a

1993

far-reaching new EU constitution that would have furthered and deepened the integration of member states, but French and Dutch rejection of the constitution in 2005 proved a setback.

—*Joseph R. Rudolph, Jr.*

## FURTHER READING

Archer, Clive, and Fiona Butler. *The European Community: Structure and Process.* New York: St. Martin's Press, 1992. Excellent source of general information on the changing nature of Europe, the institutional framework and policy achievements of the European Community, and the EC's relationship with the outside world.

Britton, Andrew J., and David Mayes. *Achieving Monetary Union in Europe.* Newbury Park, Calif.: Sage, 1992. Provides a brief but detailed authoritative examination of the timetable and conditions for achieving monetary union in Europe and of the obstacles to attaining the policy convergence necessary for it.

Friend, Julius W. *The Linchpin: French-German Relations, 1950-1990.* New York: Praeger, 1991. Presents an excellent brief study of Franco-German relations and how changes in those relations both reflected the growth of the new Europe and became one of the major factors affecting the EC's future.

King, Anthony S. *Britain Says Yes: The 1975 Referendum on the Common Market.* Washington, D.C.: American Enterprise Institute for Public Policy Research, 1977. Succinctly covers Great Britain's second thoughts on entry and the national referendum over whether to join the EC. Many of the most important issues in the EC during the 1970's involved Great Britain—enlargement, the battle over energy policy, and the vitality of the integrative process.

Mazzucelli, Colette. *France and Germany at Maastricht: Politics and Negotiations to Create the European Union.* New York: Garland, 1997. Presents discussion of the political context for the negotiations between France and Germany during the creation of the EU. Includes bibliography and index.

Pinder, John. *The Building of the European Union.* 3d ed. New York: Oxford University Press, 1998. Provides basic information on the background of the European Union. Analyzes the policy development for the supranational machinery to unite Europe.

**SEE ALSO:** Oct. 1, 1982: Kohl Becomes Chancellor of West Germany; Jan. 1, 1986: Portugal and Spain Enter the European Community; Feb. 28, 1986: European Economic Community Adopts the Single European Act; July 1, 1991: Sweden Applies for Membership in the European Community; Jan. 1, 1999: Eleven European Nations Adopt the Euro.

---

## November 4, 1993
# CHRÉTIEN TAKES CHARGE IN CANADA

*Crowning a long political career as a dedicated member of Canada's Liberal Party, Jean Chrétien took over the leadership of the federal government of Canada. His eventful tenure as prime minister lasted ten years.*

**LOCALE:** Canada
**CATEGORY:** Government and politics

**KEY FIGURES**
*Jean Chrétien* (b. 1934), prime minister of Canada, 1993-2003
*Pierre Trudeau* (1919-2000), prime minister of Canada, 1968-1979 and 1980-1984
*Lester B. Pearson* (1897-1972), prime minister of Canada, 1963-1968
*Brian Mulroney* (b. 1939), prime minister of Canada, 1984-1993

*Robert Bourassa* (1933-1996), premier of Quebec, 1970-1976 and 1985-1994

**SUMMARY OF EVENT**
Capping a long career with the Liberal Party in Canadian federal politics, Jean Chrétien, a francophone protégé of former Canadian prime minister Pierre Trudeau, assumed the premiership of Canada. In some respects this was a surprising result (Chrétien, in contrast to his longtime sponsor, Trudeau, lacked charisma and spoke somewhat halting English), but Chrétien's election was a case of the right man at the right place at the right time. As prime minister, Chrétien crafted a solution to the festering issue of Quebec separatism, a solution that only he, or someone like him, could have offered.

Born in Shawinigan, Quebec, a mill town just north of the St. Lawrence River in the center of the province, in 1934, Chrétien was a younger son in a typical French Canadian family. His father was a trade union official, and the workers in the local paper mill were well organized. Jean himself worked as a youth in the mill, but he grew up with greater ambitions. He chose to study law and quickly became involved in politics of a liberal kind—that is, he was a confirmed advocate of Quebec's participation in federal Canadian politics. Commitment to federalism was visceral on Chrétien's part, even though he spoke only French until he entered national politics, and he never, unlike his mentor Trudeau, mastered the art of political speech in English.

Chrétien was first elected to Canada's federal parliament in 1963, from a riding (the Canadian term for electoral constituency) of which Shawinigan was an important part. As a protégé of Pierre Trudeau, one of the Liberal Party's leading politicians, Chrétien quickly earned appointments that gave him governmental experience: In 1965, he became parliamentary secretary to Lester B. Pearson, the Liberal prime minister in the mid-1960's; he was made a junior minister of the Ministry of Finance in 1967; and in 1968, he became minister of national revenue. During Trudeau's long premierships, Chrétien held a number of ministerial posts, including minister of finance in 1977. Throughout his early career he was known as a devoted party man who dedicated much of his energy to preserving Liberal electoral dominance.

Chrétien's most important contribution to Canada, however, concerned the growing campaign within Quebec for independence, or sovereignty. Increasing popular demands within Quebec for at minimum some special status in an otherwise predominantly anglophone Canada had been central to Canadian politics since the 1970's. These demands led to the first Quebec referendum, held May 20, 1980, in which the no votes outnumbered the yes votes by a very slim margin. This vote led in turn to repeated attempts on the part of Canadian politicians to create a Canadian political structure that would respect the demands for a special identity coming from the French-speaking inhabits of Quebec but would still preserve the unity of the confederation of Canada.

Trudeau, trading on his own French Canadian background, supervised the rewriting of the Canadian constitution that bore fruit in the revised British North America Act (the confederation constitution provided by the British parliament in 1867). This revised constitution emphasized the importance of the different provinces and provided that much of the governing of Canada would be done in the eleven provinces, not in the federal

*Jean Chrétien casting his ballot in a 1995 election.* (AP/Wide World Photos)

capital in Ottawa; in this solution Canada seemed to be diverging from the model of the United States, its mighty neighbor to the south, where more and more government seemed to be concentrated at the federal level. Canada remained throughout a parliamentary democracy, where federal leadership came not from national electoral victory but from the possession of a majority in the parliament.

Although it might have seemed that Trudeau had masterminded a genuine compromise between Quebec and its fellow provinces, independence sentiment in Quebec continued to simmer. By the late 1980's, it had again reached a crescendo, and Prime Minister Brian Mulroney, leader of the Progressive Conservative Party, attempted to broker another accommodation. He collected the premiers of all the provinces at Meech Lake in Quebec in 1987 to put together another "compromise," but Canadian voters rejected this compromise (known as the Meech Lake Accord), as they did the attempt by Conservatives to rewrite it in the Charlottetown Accord of 1992.

1993

This made the parliamentary elections of 1993 critical; the task fell to the Liberals, now led by Jean Chrétien, who organized a masterful campaign that led to Liberal victory in the elections.

Although the Liberals won nationally, Quebec remained separatist in feeling, and a new referendum in Quebec itself proved the only viable option. The new referendum was set for October 30, 1995, in the province of Quebec only. Although support was strong in Quebec for the national government run by the Liberals, the proponents of Quebec separatism came close to winning: The no vote (opposing separatism) garnered 50.6 percent, and the yes vote, 49.4 percent. The continuance of the Canadian federation was electorally secured, but only barely. It was up to the Chrétien government to find a solution.

The solution Chrétien offered was a masterful one. He began by appealing the issue of sovereignty to the Canadian Supreme Court, which delivered an ambiguous decision. The court agreed that any province had a right to secede from the Canadian federation if a popular majority of voters in the province approved secession, but it ruled that such a majority had to be decisive—it implied that a majority vote that differed from the minority vote by only a fraction of 1 percent. or, indeed, any marginal fraction, was not sufficient. Chrétien then took the issue to the federal parliament in what was known as the Clarity Act. This legislation specified the exact conditions under which secession could occur, making it clear that a province could secede only when a significant majority of the provincial voters required it. Such a vote would be followed by negotiation with the federal parliament, which would act on behalf of the other provinces of Canada. Only someone as manifestly a "child" of Quebec and French Canada could have so clarified the issue as to render it moot for the immediate—and perhaps the distant—future.

## SIGNIFICANCE

The Chrétien government followed up its resolution of the Quebec issue by taking on a number of other issues that Chrétien had promised voters he would address. The most important of these was the federal deficit, which the government managed to eliminate, partly by cutting the sums devolved to the provinces from the federal government and partly by reaping the benefits of the economic boom that characterized the world economy in the late 1990's. By the early years of the twenty-first century, half of the revenues collected by the Canadian government were returned to the provinces, which in turn were

able to improve health care under the nationalized health care system of Canada and to improve education. Following the elimination of the deficit, the Chrétien government was able to expand the reach of the Canada Child Tax Benefit so that many middle-class families were included.

In addition, although Chrétien's government did not bring about all the changes many had hoped it would concerning the situation of Canada's aboriginal peoples, it did improve their ability to express their political views through constitutional changes affecting their political rights.

Finally, the Chrétien government worked to cement the allegiance of the voters of Quebec (who increasingly supported the Liberals in elections in 1997 and 2000) by instigating numerous development projects in the province. Some of these led in 2002 to the "sponsorship" scandals, when it was shown that advertising contracts had been given to political friends of the Liberal Party. These revelations contributed to Chrétien's decision to resign at the end of 2003.

The Chrétien government oversaw a number of important changes in Canada, but unquestionably Chrétien's most outstanding contribution was his role in crafting a strong and very possibly lasting solution to the "independence" movement of the Quebec populists. All of his other achievements pale in comparison to this great accomplishment.

—*Nancy M. Gordon*

## FURTHER READING

Bothwell, Robert, Ian Drummond, and John English. *Canada Since 1945: Power, Politics and Provincialism.* Rev. ed. Toronto: University of Toronto Press, 1989. First-rate history of Canada provides all the details needed for an understanding of Canadian politics.

Chrétien, Jean. *Straight from the Heart.* Toronto: Key Porter Books, 1994. Memoir provides Chrétien's personal point of view. Lawrence Martin, Chrétien's biographer (see below), has criticized this work as being less than truthful.

Frizzell, Alan, Jon H. Pammett, and Antony Westell. *The Canadian General Election of 1993.* Ottawa: Carleton University Press, 1994. Presents a detailed account of the election tactics that brought Chrétien to the premiership.

Harder, Lois, and Steve Patten, eds. *The Chrétien Legacy: Politics and Public Policy in Canada.* Montreal: McGill-Queen's University Press, 2006. Collection of essays by a variety of authors, all specialists in their fields, discusses the accomplishments and shortcomings of the Chrétien government.

Martin, Lawrence. *Chrétien: The Will to Win*. 2 vols. Toronto: Lester, 1995-1999. Detailed biography makes clear Chrétien's origins in the bosom of Quebec federalism and, in particular, the role his parents played in shaping his life.

**SEE ALSO:** June 27-28, 1976: Canada Joins the G7; May 23, 1979: Clark Is Elected Canada's Prime Minister; Apr. 17, 1982: Canada's Constitution Act; Sept. 14, 1984: Mulroney Era Begins in Canada; June 22, 1990: Meech Lake Accord Dies; Oct. 26, 1992: Defeat of the Charlottetown Accord; June 25, 1993: Campbell Becomes Canada's First Woman Prime Minister.

## November 20, 1993
# NORTH AMERICAN FREE TRADE AGREEMENT

*The North American Free Trade Agreement reduced barriers to the flow of goods, services, and investment among Canada, Mexico, and the United States.*

**LOCALE:** Washington, D.C.
**CATEGORIES:** Trade and commerce; diplomacy and international relations; economics

**KEY FIGURES**
*George H. W. Bush* (b. 1924), president of the United States, 1989-1993
*Bill Clinton* (b. 1946), president of the United States, 1993-2001
*H. Ross Perot* (b. 1930), businessman and candidate for U.S. president in 1992
*Carlos Salinas de Gortari* (b. 1948), president of Mexico, 1988-1994

**SUMMARY OF EVENT**

Approval of the North American Free Trade Agreement (NAFTA) in 1993 was one in a long series of policy actions reflecting a commitment by the United States government to relatively unrestricted international trade and finance. This commitment began in 1934, when, in the depths of the Great Depression, the United States adopted a policy of reciprocal trade agreements. Agreements were negotiated whereby the United States reduced tariffs on the products of other countries that agreed to the do the same for U.S. products. This helped trade to expand and gave each country an opportunity both to sell more exports and to buy more imports. At the end of World War II, this policy was extended by the formation of the General Agreement on Tariffs and Trade (GATT), which involved many countries negotiating at once. GATT negotiations involved a series of "rounds," with the Uruguay round ending in new agreements in 1994.

Policy toward international trade has always been controversial. Most economists argue that relatively free international trade encourages each country to specialize in the products it can produce most efficiently. Advocates claim that competition is intensified and innovation encouraged, allowing consumers to benefit from lower prices and higher productivity. Such benefits were evident in products such as automobiles (after the 1950's) and electronic products (after the 1970's). However, within each country there are industries that believe they would not be able to compete with imports. U.S. companies producing clothing and shoes, for example, have complained that they are undersold by imports from low-wage countries such as China. One reason that wages are low in China, however, is that labor productivity has typically also been low there.

As NAFTA was being developed, many firms and labor unions opposed the liberalization of trade, arguing that competition from imports would reduce job opportunities. These issues were strongly debated in the presidential election of 1992. President George H. W. Bush had initiated and encouraged the formulation of NAFTA, and Democratic candidate Bill Clinton supported it, but independent candidate H. Ross Perot strongly opposed NAFTA. He claimed there would be a "giant sucking sound" as U.S. jobs were transferred to Mexico. Many environmentalists also opposed NAFTA, arguing that Mexican products had another unfair advantage because requirements for environmental protection were lax in Mexico. Some libertarian groups opposed NAFTA on the basis that it did not really provide free trade, because of the substantial bureaucratic involvement required to carry out its many complex provisions.

Supporters of NAFTA argued that many U.S. business firms would gain by improved access to Mexican markets. For example, privatization of the Mexican tele-

1993

phone system in 1991 created profit opportunities for U.S. firms that were among the world leaders in this high-tech sector. U.S. firms producing motion pictures, recorded music, television programs, and computer software received much revenue from sales to other countries and often were damaged by intellectual piracy. NAFTA offered them the prospect of improved protection of their intellectual property rights. Pro-NAFTA forces also argued that the treaty would increase the prosperity of the Mexican economy, increasing wage levels and decreasing the large flow of Mexican immigrants across the southern border of the United States. They also pointed out that the economies of Canada and Mexico were far smaller than that of the United States, and thus were unable to flood U.S. markets with goods.

The treaty was first approved in Canada, where it was supported by the ruling Progressive Conservative Party, completing legislative approval on June 23, 1993. In the U.S. Congress, there was considerable opposition, but strong lobbying by President Clinton secured the treaty's

approval on November 20, 1993. In Mexico, support by the dominant Institutional Revolutionary Party of President Carlos Salinas de Gortari assured relatively easy approval on November 22, 1993.

As finally approved, the agreement was a long and complex document. It had four major types of provisions. First, NAFTA reduced, and promised to eliminate, all tariffs (taxes on imports) and most nontariff barriers (such as quantitative quotas on imports) among the three countries. These liberalizations were to be spread over fifteen years, but two-thirds of Mexican imports to the United States and half of U.S. exports to Mexico were duty-free or became so immediately. Government contracts were to be open to competitive bidding by firms from all three countries.

Second, NAFTA provided rules to protect investment and intellectual property rights. NAFTA expanded Canadian and U.S. companies' ability to set up or buy a business in Mexico and made it easier for them sell out if they wanted to quit. U.S. and Canadian banks were given

*NAFTA initialing ceremony, October, 1992. From left to right (standing): Mexican president Carlos Salinas de Gortari, U.S. president George H. W. Bush, and Canadian prime minister Brian Mulroney. Seated: Jaime Serra Puche, Carla Hills, and Michael Wilson.* (George Bush Presidential Library and Museum)

greater freedom to invest in Mexican banks. Restrictions on bringing profits back were removed. Protection of intellectual property rights involved patents, copyrights, trademarks, and computer software. U.S. firms strongly desired protection against people copying books, records, videotapes and audiotapes, and software without permission or payment of royalties. This had been more of a problem in Mexico than in Canada.

Third, NAFTA reduced barriers to trade in services, such as banking and finance, transportation, telecommunications, and audiovisual activities. Mexico extended temporary work permits to service providers from Canada and the United States.

Finally, NAFTA provided administrative procedures to settle disputes over the way each country applied the rules. Special commissions were created to exert influence over environmental policies and over labor market conditions.

## SIGNIFICANCE

NAFTA did not have a large immediate impact on economic relations between the United States and Canada, since their trade, services, investment, and intellectual property conditions were already on a relatively harmonious basis. For the first year after NAFTA's adoption, both the United States and Mexico appeared to benefit. U.S. export sales to Mexico and imports from Mexico increased substantially. Mexico benefited from substantial capital inflow, increased production capacity, and improved technology. In December, 1994, however, Mexico was hit by a financial crisis that resulted in a devaluation of the Mexican peso by about one-half. The International Monetary Fund attributed the panic to a reaction by Mexican investors to a large government deficit and declining foreign reserves. Inflation in Mexico had been running at a rate of nearly 200 percent per year. Feeling the peso was overvalued, investors sold Mexican securities and used the proceeds to buy dollars and other foreign currency.

Previous NAFTA opponents pointed to the panic as justification for their views, although the panic could not be traced directly to NAFTA. The panic led to severe economic depression in Mexico. As Mexican prices and incomes fell, Mexicans reduced their purchases of imports and U.S. export sales to Mexico fell by 40 percent in the spring of 1995. NAFTA did help cushion the impact of the crisis on the Mexican economy. Export-oriented areas, such as the city of Juarez, found their sales to the United States greatly increased. In 1995, there was a large inflow of direct investment by U.S. firms eager to buy or build factories and take advantage of the momentarily inexpensive Mexican property, labor, and materials.

Controversy over the impact of NAFTA has continued since its inception, with labor and liberal interests generally against the agreement and conservative interests generally for it. In 2001, the Economic Policy Institute, a nonprofit think tank devoted to "the economic condition of low- and middle-income Americans," founded by academicians including economist Lester Thurow and former U.S. secretaries of labor Ray Marshall and Robert Reich, noted that all fifty U.S. states had experienced a net loss of more than 766,000 "actual and potential jobs" under NAFTA as of the year 2000. At the same time, U.S., Canadian, and Mexican government officials continued to hail the agreement as a success in lowering labor costs and increasing returns to companies and their investors. While the long-term effects on the economies of these nations remained to be seen, it appeared at the beginning of the twenty-first century that the agreement placed individual workers at a disadvantage when it came to job security and collective bargaining. The debate over NAFTA's impact formed only part of a much larger discussion that had begun in 1994 at the Summit of the Americas. At that meeting, the heads of state of thirty-four democracies of the Western Hemisphere proposed the Free Trade Area of the Americas, an agreement to unite the economies of the Western Hemisphere into a single free trade zone by progressively removing all barriers to trade and investment.

*—Paul B. Trescott*

## FURTHER READING

Belous, Richard S., and Jonathan Lemco, eds. *NAFTA as a Model of Development.* Washington, D.C.: National Planning Association, 1993. Collection of twenty-one conference papers presents a good variety of viewpoints, including several from the perspective of Canada and Mexico.

Cameron, Maxwell A., and Brian W. Tomlin. *The Making of NAFTA: How the Deal Was Done.* Ithaca, N.Y.: Cornell University Press, 2000. Provides some background on the diplomatic process and then presents a full account of the negotiations that resulted in the agreement. Includes chronology, bibliography, and index.

Deere, Carolyn L., and Daniel C. Esty, eds. *Greening the Americas: NAFTA's Lessons for Hemispheric Trade.* Cambridge, Mass.: MIT Press, 2002. Collection of essays focuses on the environmental impacts of

1993

NAFTA. Includes an appendix that lists the environmental provisions of the agreement.

Grayson, George W. *The North American Free Trade Agreement: Regional Community and the New World Order.* Lanham, Md.: University Press of America, 1995. Presents a narrative history of the debates and negotiations surrounding NAFTA. Ends with the approval of the treaty.

Kingsolver, Ann E. *NAFTA Stories: Fears and Hopes in Mexico and the United States.* Boulder, Colo.: Lynne Rienner, 2001. Presents a wide variety of viewpoints about NAFTA as revealed in stories told by people from many different backgrounds. Includes illustrations, bibliography, and index.

Weintraub, Sidney, ed. *NAFTA's Impact on North America: The First Decade.* Washington, D.C.: Center for Strategic and International Studies, 2004. Collection of essays examines the political, social, and nontrade influences of NAFTA in its first ten years and offers opinions regarding its likely impacts in the future.

**SEE ALSO:** 1971: United States Suffers Its First Trade Deficit Since 1888; Nov. 3, 1992: Clinton Wins the U.S. Presidency; June 25, 1993: Campbell Becomes Canada's First Woman Prime Minister; Dec. 1, 1994: General Agreement on Tariffs and Trade; Nov. 15, 1999: United States and China Sign Trade Deal.

---

## December 2-13, 1993
# ASTRONAUTS REPAIR THE HUBBLE SPACE TELESCOPE

*After space shuttle astronauts undertook repairs of the Hubble Space Telescope in Earth orbit, the telescope produced images of unprecedented detail and clarity.*

**LOCALE:** Earth orbit

**CATEGORIES:** Science and technology; spaceflight and aviation; astronomy

**KEY FIGURES**

*Thomas D. Akers* (b. 1951), American astronaut who assisted in replacing solar panels on the Hubble Space Telescope

*Kathryn C. Thornton* (b. 1952), American astronaut who assisted in replacing solar panels on the Hubble Space Telescope

*Kenneth D. Bowersox* (b. 1956), American astronaut who served as pilot of the space shuttle on its mission to repair the Hubble Space Telescope

*Richard O. Covey* (b. 1946), American astronaut who served as commander of the space shuttle on the repair mission

*Jeffrey A. Hoffman* (b. 1944), American astronaut who assisted in replacing optical instruments on the Hubble Space Telescope

*F. Story Musgrave* (b. 1935), American astronaut who served as payload commander of the space shuttle during the repair mission

*Claude Nicollier* (b. 1944), Swiss astronaut who operated the space shuttle's remote arm during the repair mission

**SUMMARY OF EVENT**

One of the earliest envisioned scientific applications of space exploration was the placement of a large telescope beyond the optical distortions imposed by Earth's atmosphere. The Hubble Space Telescope (HST), the first realization of this dream, experienced many setbacks before finally becoming operational. The launch of the telescope was delayed by two years after the explosion of the space shuttle *Challenger* in 1986. Then, when the telescope was launched in April, 1990, astronomers discovered to their horror that its optics contained a major defect.

Like most large astronomical telescopes, the HST uses a large concave mirror, the primary mirror, to focus incoming light to an image. The primary mirror of the HST is 2.4 meters (94.5 inches) in diameter. Secondary mirrors are used to reflect the image to its final viewing location. The secondary mirrors often are curved to assist in focusing the image. The primary and secondary mirrors must be fabricated to exactly the right shape and their curvatures precisely coordinated. The primary mirror in the HST was ground to the wrong shape, resulting in an optical defect known as spherical aberration. Light reflected off different parts of the primary mirror focused in different locations, making it impossible to focus the telescope perfectly.

Ironically, it was the very magnitude of the error that prevented its detection. Telescope mirrors are given their basic shape through grinding; they are then polished to dimensions accurate to within a small fraction of a wave-

*During STS-61, astronaut Kathryn C. Thornton hovers near equipment used to service the Hubble Space Telescope.* (NASA)

the relative crudeness of the test, not a flaw in the telescope.

Many popular media accounts of the problem created the impression that the telescope was useless. In reality, the effects of the spherical aberration could often be largely removed through computer processing of the images. For bright objects, such as planets in our solar system, the HST returned extremely detailed images, even with flawed optics. The problem was most acute for faint objects. Because spherical aberration spreads light out over a larger area than a perfect image, it took about five times longer to make observations of faint objects than would have been the case with the originally designed system. The original design of the HST called for 70 percent of the light from a star to be concentrated in the central core of the image; the flawed HST achieved only 15 percent. It was impossible to collect enough light to observe the faintest objects, such as galaxies at the edge of the observable universe, and observing such faint objects had been one of the principal reasons for launching the telescope.

Replacing the flawed primary mirror was out of the question, but many of the observing instruments aboard the HST were made to be easily replaced. Mirrors in replacement instruments could be shaped to compensate for the flaw in the primary mirror. However, tests showed that the replacement mirrors had to be aligned with great precision or other optical errors would be introduced, making the HST's images even worse. Two of the imaging cameras on the HST were redesigned to correct the HST's optical problems.

Flawed optics were not the only problem aboard the HST. The telescope's large solar panels vibrated every time they expanded and contracted as the HST passed in and out of Earth's shadow. Ground controllers had developed ways of compensating for the vibration, but the compensations taxed the HST's onboard computer. Also, three of the HST's six gyroscopes had failed, leaving the telescope with the bare minimum needed for operation. If another failed, the telescope would be completely inoperable. Replacement of the gyroscopes was a higher priority than even repair of the optics.

length of light, or within the width of a few hundred atoms. The optical instrument used in testing the primary mirror during grinding had a lens about a millimeter out of position, causing the primary mirror to be slightly too flat. The later optical tests applied to the HST mirror were designed to monitor the perfection of the mirror surface; it never occurred to any of the builders of the telescope that a gross error in the basic shape of the mirror was possible.

Severe as it was, the error in the HST's primary mirror was only 0.002 millimeters (less than 0.00008 inches). Nevertheless, the error was 100,000 times as great as any surface irregularities in the mirror. At the level of accuracy routinely required in the design of astronomical telescopes, a flaw such as that in the Hubble Space Telescope might be likened to building a bridge across the wrong river. Scientist Robert Shannon called it "the single largest mistake that's ever been made in optics." A crude optical test of the telescope did reveal the problem, but the test results initially were thought to be a result of

1993

2779

On December 2, 1993, the space shuttle *Endeavour* lifted off on flight STS-61, one of the most complex space missions undertaken up to that time. The crew, six men and one woman, comprised six U.S. astronauts and a Swiss astronaut from the European Space Agency. Beginning on December 5, shuttle astronauts made six-hour space walks on five successive days to replace two imaging cameras on the HST with corrected optics, replace the solar cell panels, replace the failed gyroscopes and their electronics, and add a processor to the HST's computer. *Endeavour* landed on December 13 after eleven days in orbit. The mission proceeded so flawlessly that author R. T. Fienberg, writing about the mission, referred readers to an article written before the mission that described the planned activities and told them simply to "change all the verbs to past tense."

## SIGNIFICANCE

Images returned by the refurbished HST showed that the telescope's problems were completely fixed and that image quality equaled or exceeded original specifications. In the solar system, the HST succeeded in clearly revealing Pluto and its moon Charon and returning the most detailed images ever of the large asteroid Vesta. It also showed that the atmospheric storm patterns on Neptune had changed greatly in the few years since the Voyager

encounter in 1989. One unsuccessful observation dramatically illustrated the quality of the telescope. Astronomers imaged a globular star cluster, hoping to find large numbers of extremely small faint stars. As seen from earth, globular star clusters are so tightly packed with stars that the images overlap, creating a solid mass of light. Although the HST did not find the hoped-for faint stars, its images were so sharp that they peered through the cluster to reveal faint galaxies far beyond.

Another widely published image showed a distant cluster of galaxies surrounded by thin, sharp arcs of light. These arcs are the distorted images of more remote galaxies, an example of gravitational lensing and dramatic support for Albert Einstein's general theory of relativity. In gravitational lensing, massive objects such as clusters of galaxies bend light much like a crude lens, creating the distorted images that the HST showed with unprecedented clarity. In another confirmation of general relativity, observations with the HST in May, 1994, indicated the presence of a giant black hole at the center of the galaxy M87.

The repair of the HST ended a particularly difficult period for the U.S. space program, which had been plagued by a seemingly endless string of problems and mission failures since the loss of the space shuttle *Challenger* in 1986. The almost perfect execution of an ex-

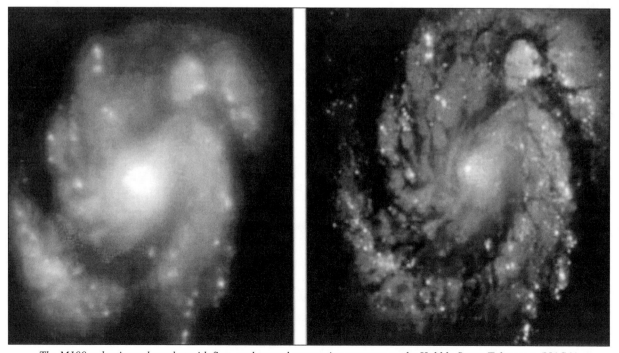

*The M100 galactic nucleus shot with first- and second-generation cameras on the Hubble Space Telescope.* (NASA)

traordinarily complex spaceflight and the equally perfect performance of the repaired Hubble Space Telescope greatly aided in restoring public confidence in the space program.

—*Steven I. Dutch*

**FURTHER READING**

Fienberg, Richard Tresch. "*Endeavour*'s Excellent Adventure." *Sky and Telescope* 87 (April, 1994): 20-23. Presents a photographic history of the repair of the HST in space.

"Gravity's Lens at Work." *Sky and Telescope* 90 (June, 1995): 11. Includes a spectacular image of gravitational lensing caused by distant galaxies.

Hoffman, Jeffrey A. "How We'll Fix the Hubble Space Telescope." *Sky and Telescope* 86 (November, 1993): 23-29. One of the participating astronauts presents a schedule of the repairs to be made to the HST. The mission proceeded almost exactly as projected in this article.

"Hubble's Image Restored." *Sky and Telescope* 87 (April, 1994): 24-27. Article is devoted primarily to a gallery of images made with the repaired Hubble telescope.

"Hubble's Road to Recovery." *Sky and Telescope* 86 (November, 1993): 16-22. Presents a history of the problems with the HST and describes the development of solutions. Aimed at readers who are familiar with telescopes and imaging terminology.

Leverington, David. *New Cosmic Horizons: Space Astronomy from the V2 to the Hubble Space Telescope.* New York: Cambridge University Press, 2000. Presents the history of space-based astronomy since World War II, devoting the final chapter to discussion of the HST. Includes illustrations, glossary, bibliography, and indexes.

Petersen, Carolyn Collins, and John C. Brandt. *Hubble Vision: Further Adventures with the Hubble Space Telescope.* 2d ed. New York: Cambridge University Press, 1998. Comprehensive discussion of the astronomical discoveries made possible by the HST. Includes many illustrations, glossary, bibliography, and index.

Smith, Robert W. *The Space Telescope: A Study of NASA, Science, Technology, and Politics.* New York: Cambridge University Press, 1993. Provides a detailed chronological account of the construction of the HST from its inception to launch preparation. One of the most complete works available on the subject; includes historical background as well as discussion of the involvement of NASA, industry, and the scientific community.

**SEE ALSO:** July 20-Sept. 3, 1976: Viking Spacecraft Send Photographs to Earth from Mars; Aug. 20, 1977-Oct. 2, 1989: Voyagers 1 and 2 Explore the Outer Planets; 1985: Construction of the Keck Telescope Begins in Hawaii; 1986: Kamiokande Neutrino Telescope Begins Operation; Apr. 24, 1990: NASA Launches the Hubble Space Telescope; Dec. 2, 1995: NASA Launches the Solar and Heliospheric Observatory; July 23, 1999: NASA Launches the Chandra X-Ray Observatory.

1993

## December 15, 1993
# ULSTER PEACE ACCORD

*The Ulster Peace Accord made it possible for the peoples of Northern Ireland (Ulster), the Republic of Ireland (Eire), and Great Britain to be involved in determining Northern Ireland's political future.*

**ALSO KNOWN AS:** Joint Declaration of Peace; Downing Street Declaration
**LOCALE:** Ulster, Northern Ireland
**CATEGORY:** Diplomacy and international relations

**KEY FIGURES**

*Gerry Adams* (b. 1948), president of Sinn Féin beginning in 1983
*John Hume* (b. 1937), leader of Northern Ireland's Social Democratic and Labour Party
*John Major* (b. 1943), prime minister of Great Britain, 1990-1997
*Albert Reynolds* (b. 1932), *taoiseach* of the Republic of Ireland, 1992-1994

**SUMMARY OF EVENT**

The Ulster Peace Accord, also known as the Joint Declaration of Peace and the Downing Street Declaration, has deep roots in Anglo-Irish history. It grew from the 1985 Anglo-Irish Agreement, which recognized three interconnections related to Northern Ireland (Ulster): the factions within Ulster itself, the Republic of Ireland and Northern Ireland, and the Irish and British peoples. The next major step was the 1987 bombing in Enniskillen, Northern Ireland, which took place on Remembrance Day (November 8), killing eleven. As a result of that tragedy, John Hume, leader of the Social Democratic and Labour Party, sent a letter to Gerry Adams, president of Sinn Féin, the political wing of the Irish Republican Army (IRA), stating Hume's belief that the terrorist bombings of the IRA were doing more harm than good. Further, Hume contended, the focus needed to be on uniting the people rather than the Republic of Ireland and Ulster. The next major step took place in 1992, when Sinn Féin issued its discussion paper *Toward a Lasting Peace in Ireland*, in which Gerry Adams acknowledged that Northern Ireland Protestants as well as the Irish Republic had legitimate needs and concerns. Adams also cited the importance of the European Union.

The reason for the existence of Northern Ireland, separate and distinct from the Republic, dates to the twelfth and thirteenth centuries, when the English slowly gained control over Ireland, using Dublin as their center of con-

trol. During the Reformation, King Henry VIII converted to Protestantism, making England a Protestant country. Ireland refused to convert, however, and to strengthen its control over Ireland, the English monarchy encouraged large numbers of English and Scottish Protestants to settle in Ulster in the seventeenth century.

Irish resistance to English rule never ended; it rose to a new level of intensity in the late nineteenth century with the Republicans (those seeking independence) centered in Dublin and the Unionists (those favoring England) in Ulster. The Unionists were unable to maintain political control, and the Republicans gained power, forming Sinn Féin in 1905 to promote an independent, united Ireland. Neither side was willing to compromise, and on Easter Monday, 1916, Republicans seized control of the General Post Office in Dublin, holding it for five days until forced out by a superior force of British troops.

The urban, working-class revolutionaries, led by an intellectual elite, did not represent the majority of Irish until the British dealt harshly with the rebel leaders. Fifteen were hanged and hundreds more were deported, resulting in a huge increase in Sinn Féin support. In December of 1918, Sinn Féin refused to participate with the English parliament; it seized control of the Irish government and renamed it the Dáil Éireann of the Irish Republic. When the British government tried to suppress the rebellion, civil war broke out between the IRA and the Irish constabulary, supported by the British army. A brutal and bloody conflict raged for three years, until Prime Minister David Lloyd George of Great Britain persuaded Sinn Féin to negotiate, and on December 6, 1921, the Treaty of Westminster was signed.

Under this agreement, ratified by members of both the British and Irish assemblies, the Republic of Ireland was recognized as a member of the British Commonwealth, with the same rights and privileges as the other member states. Known as Saorstat Eireann (the Irish Free State), it failed to include the six northern counties, known collectively as Ulster. These counties, which included a Protestant majority while the rest of Ireland was predominantly Catholic, were organized under the 1920 Government of Ireland Act, which allowed them to remain a part of the United Kingdom. The Irish Dáil narrowly approved the treaty, despite opposition from Sinn Féin and one-third of the population. Eamon de Valera, president of the Irish Republic, resigned rather than swear allegiance to the English king. Over the next fifteen years, there was limited violence in the Republic, and the ties with the British government were loosened as the Republicans increased control. In 1937, the Republicans severed their remaining ties with the British Commonwealth through a referendum.

Sinn Féin never gave up its goal of a united Ireland. In October of 1968, rioting broke out in Londonderry during a Catholic demonstration, following a clash with police. The next year the British government ordered troops into Ulster. In 1972, a confrontation between demonstrators and the army during a civil rights march resulted in thirteen dead in what became known as Bloody Sunday. Two months later, Prime Minister Edward Hume of Great Britain established direct rule of Northern Ireland from England. From that point until December 15, 1993, when the British and Irish governments issued the Joint Declaration of Peace, the violence continued, with the main combatants being the Catholic IRA and the Protestant Ulster Defense Force (UDF).

A positive step toward peace was taken in 1985 when Prime Minister Margaret Thatcher of Great Britain and Garret FitzGerald, *taoiseach* (prime minister) of the Republic of Ireland, signed the Anglo-Irish Agreement, which granted Ireland some say in the future of Ulster in exchange for the Republic's assistance in helping with the terrorist problem in Northern Ireland. Further steps toward peace came in 1993, when Taoiseach Albert Reynolds recognized the need for the people of Northern Ireland to determine their own fate. Without such self-determination there would be neither stability nor well-being. Reynolds further noted that for Ireland to be unified, all parties must respect one another's civil liberties and religious liberty. Specifically cited in the Joint Declaration, the *taoiseach* referred to free political thought, religious expression, the right to pursue political aspirations through democratic means, the right to seek constitutional change through peaceful means, the right to live where one chooses without intimidation, and the right to equal opportunity without regard to class or creed.

## SIGNIFICANCE

Contained within the Joint Declaration are assurances provided by both Britain's prime minister, John Major, and Albert Reynolds. For his part, Major affirmed that the British would accede to the will of the majority. He noted that the British were willing to work with the Irish Free State because the issue of Ulster's place needs to be resolved by the Irish themselves, "by agreement between the two parts respectively, to exercise their right of self-determination on the basis of consent, freely and concur-

rently given, North and South." Reynolds pledged that Eire would use neither threat nor coercion to achieve its goal of a united Ireland. He acknowledged that the Free State's constitution would need to be amended to recognize the rights of the people of Northern Ireland.

The *taoiseach* recognized the "special links that exist between the peoples of Britain and Ireland" in addition to the new economic links that exist with the rest of Europe. This trend toward unity and acceptance seemed to spring from the growing rapprochement in postnationalist Europe. Both parts of Ireland and the United Kingdom are members of the European Union (EU), and all parties understand the need to establish ways the two principal parties, along with the rest of the EU, can work, trade, and live in peace with one another. The Joint Declaration devoted one of its eleven sections to the issue of these links.

To achieve a lasting peace, both parties needed to recognize the legitimacy of each other's history and tradition. To work toward such a solution, the *taoiseach* recommended the creation of the Forum for Peace and Reconciliation, which would be responsible for finding ways for the people of the Republic and Ulster to accept that both groups have a right to their beliefs and traditions within an environment of unity and peace. Both the prime minister and the *taoiseach* accepted the need to create such an environment and stated that they believed "the framework they have set out offers the people of Ireland, North and South, whatever their tradition, the basis to agree that from now on their differences can be negotiated and resolved exclusively by peaceful political means."

Major progress to this end was achieved by the Good Friday Agreement of April 10, 1998, in which the parties agreed to the release of prisoners, decommissioning of weapons, and civil and criminal justice reforms aimed at establishing a stable and inclusive government. Voters in both Northern Ireland and the Republic of Ireland overwhelmingly supported the agreement when it was put to a vote by referendum in the same year, indicating a wide desire for greater peace. The issue of the timing of decommissioning of IRA weapons remained a major stumbling block in subsequent years, but in 2005, the IRA agreed to the complete decommissioning of all its weapons and recommitted itself exclusively to peaceful political means.

—*Duncan R. Jamieson*

## FURTHER READING

Arthur, Paul. "Anglo-Irish Joint Declaration: Towards a Lasting Peace?" *Government and Opposition* 29

1993

(Spring, 1994): 218-230. Focuses on the possibilities for the success of the declaration.

Bardon, Jonathan. *A History of Ulster*. Belfast: Blackstaff Press, 1992. Presents a comprehensive history of Northern Ireland. Includes maps, bibliography, and index.

Campbell, Flann. *The Dissenting Voice: Protestant Democracy in Ulster from Plantation to Partition*. Belfast: Blackstaff Press, 1991. Gives a Protestant perspective on the history of Northern Ireland from the seventeenth century to the 1990's. Includes bibliography and index.

Farrington, Christopher. *Ulster Unionism and the Peace Process in Northern Ireland*. New York: Palgrave Macmillan, 2006. Focuses on the importance of the politics of Unionism to any peace settlement in Northern Ireland. Includes bibliography and index.

Guelke, Adrian, ed. *New Perspectives on the Northern Ireland Conflict*. Brookfield, Vt.: Avebury, 1994. Collection of essays deals with the wide variety of issues—political, social, economic, and religious—that underlie the violence in Ulster.

McKittrick, David. *Despatches from Belfast*. Belfast: Blackstaff Press, 1989. Collection of essays, many reprinted from newspaper articles, addresses the social conditions of Ulster.

Mitchell, Paul, and Rick Wilford, eds. *Politics in Northern Ireland*. Boulder, Colo.: Westview Press, 1999. Collection of essays covers a wide range of topics concerning the Northern Ireland political arena. Several chapters include discussion of the Joint Declaration of Peace. Includes index.

O'Day, Alan, ed. *Political Violence in Northern Ireland: Conflict and Conflict Resolution*. New York: Praeger, 1997. Collection of essays covers the history of violence in Northern Ireland since the late 1960's and the attempts to end that violence.

**SEE ALSO:** Jan. 30, 1972: "Bloody Sunday" in Northern Ireland; July, 1973: Northern Ireland Witnesses Passage of the Emergency Provisions Act; Dec. 10, 1977: Two Founders of Peace People Receive the Nobel Peace Prize; Mar. 1, 1981: Sands Begins Hunger Strike; Nov. 15, 1985: Anglo-Irish Agreement Is Signed; Dec. 10, 1995: Heaney Receives the Nobel Prize in Literature; Apr. 10, 1998: Good Friday Agreement; Aug. 15, 1998: Omagh Car Bombing.

## January 2, 1994-January 1, 2002
# GIULIANI ADMINISTRATION TRANSFORMS NEW YORK CITY

*During his two terms as New York City mayor, Rudolph Giuliani gained local, national, and international respect for his economic and educational reforms, for reducing crime dramatically, and for unifying the city after the September 11, 2001, terrorist attacks. Although his political agenda and personal style were often polarizing, Giuliani was credited with overcoming crisis conditions to make New York one of the safest and strongest cities in the United States.*

**LOCALE:** New York, New York
**CATEGORIES:** Government and politics; social issues and reform

**KEY FIGURES**
*Rudolph Giuliani* (b. 1944), mayor of New York City, 1994-2002
*David Dinkins* (b. 1927), mayor of New York City, 1990-1993
*Al Sharpton* (b. 1954), American civil rights activist

**SUMMARY OF EVENT**
In the early 1990's, New York City was regarded as a dangerous, deteriorating metropolis. Former U.S. attorney Rudolph Giuliani's vow to restore order and improve quality of life for New Yorkers took him to the mayor's office in 1993 and again in 1997. A Republican in an overwhelmingly Democratic city, Giuliani kept many of his promises and made his share of enemies during his two terms. He cut the city's budgets, taxes, and welfare rolls and increased public education funding. New York's streets became safer and the "Big Apple" became a site tourists wanted to visit rather than a place residents wanted to escape. His successes made Giuliani an almost legendary leader who got results regardless of whether he was loved or loathed. However, Giuliani's popularity declined in his second term as a result of several factors, including a tumultuous private life. The final months of his administration not only restored his reputation but also took him to the height of public esteem when the city's and country's spirits could not have been lower—in the after-

math of the September 11, 2001, terrorist attacks that destroyed the World Trade Center and killed thousands.

Giuliani was elected as New York City's 107th mayor in November, 1993, and took office January 2, 1994. This was Giuliani's second contest with Democrat David Dinkins, who narrowly won a bitter 1989 campaign to become New York's first African American mayor. The 1993 rematch was also hard-fought, with Giuliani on the attack against the incumbent Dinkins, whose restrained governing style received much of the blame for New York's problems. Alarmingly high crime rates driven by the crack cocaine trade, racial and ethnic conflicts, and economic difficulties gave New York a negative national image. With more than twenty years of experience as a U.S. federal government attorney, Giuliani presented himself as the person who could save the city.

Although he clashed with the New York City Police Department (NYPD) leadership, Giuliani forged an effective partnership with the force. Practicing a "broken windows" theory of crime prevention based on a belief that an environment rife with petty crime made felonies more likely, the NYPD pursued and punished what some considered minor offenders—vandals, panhandlers, and even graffiti vandals. "Squeegee people" who plagued motorists with unsolicited windshield cleaning and demands for handouts were perhaps the best-known targets of Giuliani's efforts to improve quality of life. Crime prevention was the NYPD watchword during the Giuliani administration. In addition to increasing the numbers of NYPD officers on the streets, Giuliani oversaw introduction of the CompStat program, a groundbreaking technology that pinpointed criminal activities and facilitated accountability among police precinct commanders. By 2000, the sixth year of Giuliani's mayoralty, the effectiveness of his anticrime methods was indisputable. Violent crimes including assault, murder, rape, robbery, and shootings exhibited remarkable declines, prompting the Federal Bureau of Investigation (FBI) to honor New York City as the safest large U.S. city.

Notable sites of improvement included the Times Square district, once infamous for pornography and prostitution but a pleasant destination for tourists and locals after Giuliani took action. Lower Manhattan's Fulton Fish Market was another Giuliani target, known as much for pervasive organized crime activity as for its seafood. After overcoming stiff resistance from lawbreakers, the NYPD restored legitimacy to this important urban marketplace. However, Giuliani was less successful when his cleanup campaigns seemed to be arbitrary and personally motivated, as shown by his failed 1999 attempt to cut off funding for the Brooklyn Museum of Art because of exhibits he found offensive.

The mayor's museum defeat confirmed that acclaim for "Giuliani time" was not universal. Some observers tried to put Giuliani's results into perspective by stressing that New York's crime rates began dropping during the final two years of the Dinkins administration and that urban crime was declining nationwide in the 1990's. Others criticized Giuliani's penchant for publicity, his lack of civility to colleagues, his refusal to make peace with real or perceived enemies, and the turmoil in his personal life, which included three marriages.

Race tended to play the major role in divisions among Giuliani's adherents and detractors. Relations between New York's African American communities and the mayor were especially strained, starting with his two runs against Dinkins and never recovering during his administration. With few exceptions, Giuliani defended NYPD tactics fiercely, which provoked outrage following the police torture of Haitian immigrant Abner Louima (1997), the brutal shooting death of Guinean immigrant Amadou Diallo (1999), and the killing of Haitian American Patrick Dorismond (2000). These incidents raised questions about overzealous police, racial profiling, and Giuliani's uncritical acceptance of NYPD responses. The uproar over Diallo, an unarmed street vendor who had been shot forty-one times, extended well beyond the African American population and empowered the Reverend Al Sharpton, perhaps the only New Yorker who rivaled Giuliani's intensity and influence. Known for refusing to deal with those he considered enemies, Giuliani found himself on the defensive as Sharpton led demonstrations in Diallo's memory, earning credibility as a civil rights agitator and notoriety as the mayor's chief antagonist.

The last two years of Giuliani's second term brought additional troubles and distractions. Plans to compete against Democrat Hillary Rodham Clinton in the 2000 U.S. Senate race were complicated and eventually dropped because Giuliani was diagnosed with prostate cancer in April, 2000, and his second marriage collapsed one month later. The man who governed New York City confidently and decisively mismanaged his separation from Donna Hanover by telling the media that their marriage was over before informing Hanover herself. Opinion polls showed a steep drop in Giuliani's approval rating prior to the terrorism attacks of September 11, 2001. Ironically, September 11, 2001, was also the date of the primary election to choose candidates who would campaign for the chance to replace Giuliani. The redemption

1994

and reverence that Giuliani found as "America's mayor" in the wake of the terrorist attacks would lead him to attempt an unprecedented extension of his term in office. His inability to achieve that goal was one of the few disappointments in his career.

**SIGNIFICANCE**

New York City's mayors are guaranteed to have some influence beyond the city's limits, given New York's status as the largest and possibly most diverse U.S. city; as a center for international culture, finance, and politics; and as a symbol of the nation's strengths and flaws. Rudy Giuliani became one of the most significant mayors in New York City's history, along with predecessors such as Fiorello Henry La Guardia and Edward I. Koch. Giuliani's two terms as mayor made an imperiled city into a model city, setting high standards for urban communities elsewhere in the United States.

—*Ray Pence*

**FURTHER READING**

Giuliani, Rudolph W. *Leadership*. New York: Hyperion, 2002. The former mayor shares advice on adapting the methods he used for governing New York City to a variety of situations.

Kirtzman, Andrew. *Rudy Giuliani: Emperor of the City*. New York: HarperCollins, 2001. Well-researched, evenhanded, and lively account, with a helpful chronology and updated to address the September 11, 2001, terrorism.

Newfield, Jack. *The Full Rudy: The Man, the Myth, the Mayor*. New York: Thunder's Mouth Press, 2002. Engaging, harsh portrait by a former *Village Voice* reporter seeking to correct what he sees as a distorted post-September 11, 2001, image of Giuliani.

Siegel, Fred, with Harry Siegel. *The Prince of the City: Giuliani, New York, and the Genius of American Life*. San Francisco: Encounter Books, 2005. Admiring analysis of the Giuliani years, written from a politically conservative viewpoint.

Strober, Deborah Hart, and Gerald S. Strober. *Giuliani: Flawed or Flawless? The Oral Biography*. Hoboken, N.J.: John Wiley & Sons, 2007. Panoramic, provocative narrative that relies on conversations with a host of Giuliani friends and foes.

**SEE ALSO:** Dec., 1988: Drexel and Michael Milken Are Charged with Insider Trading; Nov. 7, 2000: Bush Election Stirs Political and Legal Controversy.

## January 17, 1994
# NORTHRIDGE QUAKE ROCKS LOS ANGELES

*The Northridge earthquake, which occurred on a previously unrecognized fault beneath California's San Fernando Valley, demonstrated both the incompleteness of scientists' mapping of the sites of probable earthquakes and the need for improvements in communities' preparations for surviving major earthquakes.*

**LOCALE:** Northridge, Los Angeles, California
**CATEGORIES:** Disasters; earth science

**SUMMARY OF EVENT**

At 4:30:55 A.M. on January 17, 1994, a major earthquake occurred in the vicinity of Los Angeles. The quake measured 6.8 on the Richter scale, and its epicenter was located west-northwest of the city, a mile from the suburb of Northridge. The focus of the earthquake was located about 5 kilometers (a little more than 3 miles) below the Earth's surface, and, luckily, the rupture followed the fault plane upward, away from the area's most densely populated neighborhoods. In the 4,000 square kilometers (roughly 1,500 square miles) where the Earth's crust was severely deformed, the Santa Susana Mountains were reported to have been raised by 40 centimeters (16 inches), to 52 centimeters (20 inches). Although much of its energy was expended in relatively uninhabited areas, the earthquake was felt as far as 400 kilometers (about 250 miles) away, and it affected more than 200,000 square kilometers (more than 77,000 square miles), including the heavily populated areas of Santa Monica, Malibu, Santa Clarita, Simi Valley, and west and central Los Angeles.

Fortunately, the earthquake struck early in the morning on Martin Luther King, Jr., Day, when traffic was light and few people were at work. Had it occurred on a typical weekday morning, the death toll would certainly have been much higher when office buildings collapsed. Still, 57 people died, and between 80,000 and 125,000 lost their apartments or houses. At the Northridge Meadows apartment complex, where sixteen of the twenty-two deaths caused by building failures occurred, the three-story frame building, which had been constructed in 1972 in compliance with antiquated building codes, collapsed under lateral stress, crushing residents on the first floor. Few single-family dwellings caused casualties, but two houses collapsed downhill and killed three people in Sherman Oaks, and one person died in Malibu when a landslide severely damaged several homes that had been built on steep slopes.

In all, more than 60,000 buildings were damaged; of these, 2,076 were red-tagged, meaning that the owners had one month to complete the repairs necessary to pass reinspection before the buildings could be reoccupied or face demolition by contractors paid by the city. All schools in the Los Angeles Unified School District were forced to close for inspection and repair of damages caused by the earthquake. In the area close to the epicenter, the Northridge campus of California State University and the Northridge Fashion Center shopping mall suffered extensive damage, some of which resulted when automatic sprinkler systems were activated by the shock of the quake. Two major stores at the mall—the Robinsons-May department store and the Levitz furniture store—were damaged beyond repair.

The majority of the damage to office and institutional buildings as a result of the earthquake was caused by the collapse of concrete columns and the warping of steel frames. Eight public parking buildings suffered severe damage or collapse, including the four-level parking garage at California State University, Northridge, which had been built in 1991 in accordance with recent building codes. Many buildings in the area that were made of unreinforced masonry had been rehabilitated after the 1971 San Fernando earthquake through the placement of bolts to secure the walls. Although few of them collapsed, major damage was common in such buildings.

The transportation network in the Los Angeles area also suffered from the inadequacy of earlier building codes. Six major bridges collapsed, and 157 more were

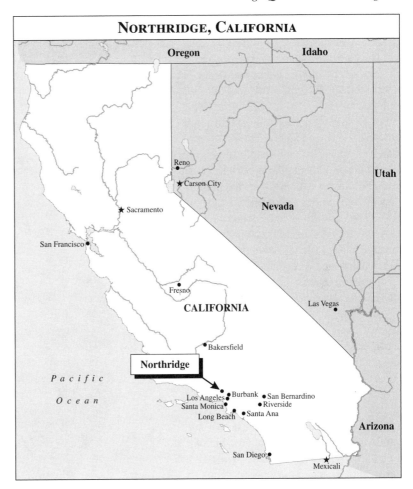

NORTHRIDGE, CALIFORNIA

seriously damaged, resulting in expenditures for repair and replacement reaching $1.5 billion. The Golden State Freeway (Interstates 5 and 405) and the Antelope Valley Freeway (State Routes 2 and 14) were both severely damaged. Five freeway overpasses fell, and the Gavin Canyon Bridge on Interstate 5 collapsed. This bridge collapse was both dramatic (and hence well televised) and instructive; built in 1967 of nonductile concrete, the structure did not have the flexibility to withstand a sharp seismic jolt.

### SIGNIFICANCE

Although the Northridge earthquake was costly in lives and property (at an estimated $20 billion in property damage, it was the most expensive quake the United States had experienced up to that time), it had some positive impacts. Providing a real-world test of the building codes, emergency procedures, and public education that were in place, the quake helped to demonstrate what

1994

worked, what did not, and where more re-search was needed.

The Northridge earthquake occurred in an area where another quake had struck in 1971, and some of the structures that had been destroyed in 1971, such as the Olive View Hospital, had been rebuilt with better materials and techniques. These survived the 1994 quake without much deep structural damage. Other buildings that had only been reinforced with iron rods did not fare so well. Still others, such as the Holiday Inn in Van Nuys, suffered enormous structural damage in 1994 after surviving without much damage in 1971. All of this information contributed to engineers' knowledge of the requirements for building safety in earthquake-prone areas.

Significantly, although the majority of destruction was found in the vicinity of the earthquake's epicenter, pockets of intense destruction were found elsewhere, such as in areas of Santa Monica, West Hollywood, and Sherman Oaks. Geologists ultimately tied these localized centers of destruction to the unconsolidated fill, soft mud, and alluvial sediments on which the structures in these areas stood. When saturated with water, these materials liquefy under the effects of an earthquake, depriving the structures built on them of a solid footing.

In the years following the Northridge earthquake, seismologists identified other

*The Interstate 5 and SR14 freeways collapsed during the Northridge quake.* (National Oceanic and Atmospheric Administration)

blind thrust faults like the one responsible for that event, widening the scope of their ability to predict seismic events and prepare for them. Building codes were improved, and programs for teaching earthquake survival skills were implemented. Over the long term, the Northridge event resulted in improvements in scientists' knowledge of the locations and effects of seismic events that may help to prevent untold loss of lives and property in the future.

*—Denyse Lemaire and David Kasserman*

## FURTHER READING

Bolin, Robert, and Lois Stanford. *The Northridge Earthquake: Vulnerability and Disaster.* New York: Routledge, 1998. Details the Northridge quake and its aftermath. Includes excellent photographic documents.

Coburn, Andrew, and Robin Spence. *Earthquake Protection.* 2d ed. New York: John Wiley & Sons, 2002. An architect and an engineer provide an integrated account of the effects of earthquakes. Emphasizes the relationships among structural damage, human behavior, socioeconomic factors, and casualty patterns.

Hough, Susan Elizabeth. *Earthshaking Science: What We Know (and Don't Know) About Earthquakes.* Princeton, N.J.: Princeton University Press, 2002. Good source of basic information about earthquakes. Includes suggestions for further reading and index.

_____. *Finding Fault in California: An Earthquake Tourist's Guide.* Missoula, Mont.: Mountain Press, 2004. Provides travelers with pertinent information on the locations of earthquake faults. Includes maps, bibliography, and index.

Yeats, Robert S. *Living with Earthquakes in California: A Survivor's Guide*. Corvallis: Oregon State University Press, 2001. Presents a history of quakes in California and offers suggestions for how to live safely in earthquake-prone areas. Includes bibliography and index.

**SEE ALSO:** July 28, 1976: Deadly Earthquake Strikes China; Sept. 19, 1985: Earthquake Devastates Mexico City; Dec. 7, 1988: Armenian Earthquake Leads to Calls for Building Reform; June 21, 1990: Massive Quake Rocks Iran; Jan. 17, 1995: Kōbe Earthquake Kills Thousands.

## January 22, 1994
# *SCHINDLER'S LIST* BEGINS REAPING ACCOLADES

*Beginning with three Golden Globe Awards in January, 1994, director and producer Steven Spielberg's film* Schindler's List *was honored widely for its powerful depiction of factory owner Oskar Schindler's successful efforts to protect twelve hundred Polish Jewish workers from extermination by the Nazis. The worldwide success of* Schindler's List *challenged indifference, ignorance, and denial regarding the historical realities of the Holocaust.*

**LOCALE:** Los Angeles, California
**CATEGORY:** Motion pictures and video

**KEY FIGURES**

*Oskar Schindler* (1908-1974), German Catholic businessman whose negotiations saved twelve hundred Polish Jews during the Holocaust
*Steven Spielberg* (b. 1946), Jewish American director and producer with commercial success across a range of film genres
*Thomas Keneally* (b. 1935), Australian writer whose nonfiction novel *Schindler's Ark* (1982) inspired the Spielberg film
*Leopold Page* (1913-2001), Polish Jew who was saved by Schindler and who introduced the story of Schindler to Keneally
*Janusz Kaminski* (b. 1959), Polish American cinematographer
*Branko Lustig* (b. 1932), Croatian Jewish survivor of Auschwitz who was a producer on *Schindler's List*

**SUMMARY OF EVENT**

In the 1970's and 1980's, Steven Spielberg built an international reputation as a director of amazing skill and vast popular appeal. The success of *Jaws* (1975), Spielberg's first of many blockbusters, reportedly saved Universal Pictures from bankruptcy. In 1982, when Universal bought the film rights to Australian author Thomas Keneally's *Schindler's Ark*, a nonfiction novel about the Holocaust, Spielberg was not an obvious choice to direct. As Spielberg said in numerous interviews, he needed ten years to grow into such a daunting project. During the intervening decade, Spielberg directed two period dramas—*The Color Purple* (1985) and *Empire of the Sun* (1987)—with mixed results while continuing to dazzle audiences with fantasy-adventure entertainment. Keneally tried his hand at writing a screenplay based on his book, but the script was finally passed to veteran script doctor Steven Zaillian, whose screenplay was later revised repeatedly during filming.

Joining Spielberg as producers on *Schindler's List* were frequent associate Gerald R. Molen and Branko Lustig, a television producer and survivor of Auschwitz. The reported budget of $25 million was considered modest, especially in comparison with the $63 million cost of another Spielberg project, *Jurassic Park* (1993). Despite the objections of the studio, Spielberg insisted on black-and-white cinematography for the core narrative in *Schindler's List*, and he was equally adamant about location shooting in Poland. To add to the desired art-film effect, Spielberg cast relatively unknown, non-American actors in the leading roles: Irishman Liam Neeson as the charismatic German entrepreneur Oskar Schindler, Englishman Ralph Fiennes as the cruel Nazi commandant Amon Leopold Goeth, and biracial Englishman Ben Kingsley as the faithful Itzhak Stern, a composite character based on several Polish Jews who assisted Schindler. Polish and Israeli actors—and *Schindlerjuden*, Jewish survivors saved by Schindler, such as Leopold Page (born Leopold Pfefferberg)—played the majority of the more than one hundred speaking parts.

Cinematographer Janusz Kaminski was named director of photography on the film; he headed a predominantly Polish crew. Born and raised in Poland, Kaminski immigrated to the United States when he was twenty-one years old and was educated in American film schools.

1994

2789

Shooting began in Kraków, Poland, on March 1, 1993, and was completed ninety-two days later.

After months of intensive postproduction work, Spielberg premiered the greatly anticipated film in Washington, D.C., on November 30, 1993, several months before the opening of the United States Holocaust Memorial Museum in the nation's capital. Immediate reactions in the popular press were almost uniformly glowing. Frequently mentioned aspects of the film were the riveting, dynamically edited sequence of the liquidation of the Kraków ghetto, the strong performances, and the enigmatic character of Schindler, who transforms from war profiteer to savior. Critics discussed the haunting documentary-like quality of the black-and-white cinematography and the emotional impact of the documentary epilogue, filmed in color in Israel, in which *Schindlerjuden*, along with the actors who portray them in the film, leave remembrances on the actual grave of Schindler, who was buried in a Catholic cemetery on the slopes of Mt. Zion in 1974. Many public officials, including President Bill Clinton, urged Americans to see the film; popular talk-show host Oprah Winfrey claimed she was a "better person" for having seen it.

On January 22, 1994, *Schindler's List* received the first of many official accolades to come: Golden Globe Awards for Best Picture (Drama), Best Director, and Best Screenplay. The film was nominated for twelve Academy Awards and won seven, including Best Picture, Best Director, Best Screenplay (Adaptation), and Best Cinematography. Major awards from Japan and Britain joined scores of other honors from around the world. Spielberg attended eventful premieres of *Schindler's List* in Germany and Israel, spoke about the project in a wide range of venues, and arranged for free educational screenings of the film.

Negative responses to *Schindler's List* took longer to surface, but some were strongly expressed. Several publications—including *The New York Times*, *The New York Review of Books*, and *The New Republic*—printed second, unfavorable reviews of the film in response to earlier praise. Academic writers were especially vociferous in their objections. The most extreme position challenged any photographic representation of the Holocaust, pointing to *Shoah* (1985), the 563-minute, interview-driven documentary by French filmmaker Claude Lanzmann, as an admirable example of such rigorous exclusion.

More often, commentators decried Spielberg's decision to focus on a Holocaust story, albeit a true one, that featured Nazi redemption and Jewish survival. Critics also expressed concern that the tremendous popularity of *Schindler's List* would result in widespread misunderstanding of the overall tragedy of the Holocaust. A related complaint challenged Spielberg's melodramatic focus on a struggle between "a good German" and "a bad German" while experiences of Polish Jews served as mere backdrop to the mythologizing of a heroic Gentile.

On February 23, 1997, *Schindler's List* aired on broadcast television in the United States in an unprecedented format. The National Broadcasting Company (NBC) screened all commercial advertising for the time period before the film began and then broadcast the "director's cut" without interruption. That evening, the docudrama was viewed in sixty-five million American households.

## SIGNIFICANCE

Although the film's influence continued to be debated, *Schindler's List* had an indisputable impact on popular memory. Since its release, the film has served as the master narrative through which many millions have come to know about the Holocaust.

*Schindler's List* was a turning point for Spielberg's directorial career. It earned him the award that had so long eluded him: the Oscar for Best Director. Spielberg would later win a second Academy Award for Best Director for another docudrama, *Saving Private Ryan* (1998), and a nomination for yet another, *Munich* (2005). Long admired for the virtuosity and tremendous commercial appeal of his films, Spielberg was finally recognized for directing serious drama with maturity and dignity.

Spielberg's association with the Schindler project led to the filmmaker's creation of the Shoah Visual History Foundation, an organization that, between 1994 and 1999, collected the testimonies of fifty-two thousand Jewish and Gentile survivors of the Holocaust from fifty-six countries in thirty-two languages. The resulting 120,000 hours of video became the basis for extensive, widely circulated educational resources.

—*Carolyn Anderson*

## FURTHER READING

Brecher, Elinor J. *Schindler's Legacy: True Stories of the List Survivors*. New York: Penguin Books, 1994. Dozens of personal histories and photographs collected from *Schindlerjuden* and their families.

Crowe, David M. *Oskar Schindler: The Untold Account of His Life, Wartime Activities, and the True Story Behind the List*. Boulder, Colo.: Westview Press, 2004. Despite the sensational title, a soundly researched biography with extensive endnotes, bibliography, appendixes, photographs, and index.

Keneally, Thomas. *Schindler's Ark.* London: Hodder & Stoughton, 1982. After interviewing fifty *Schindlerjuden*, Keneally employed novelistic devices to tell a true story of cruelty, heroism, and survival.

Lipkin, Steven N. *Real Emotional Logic: Film and Television Docudrama as Persuasive Practice.* Carbondale: Southern Illinois University Press, 2002. Discusses *Schindler's List* as a prototypical docudrama because it references actual people and events through a melodramatic narrative to make a moral claim.

Loshitzky, Yosefa, ed. *Spielberg's Holocaust: Critical Perspectives on "Schindler's List."* Bloomington: Indiana University Press, 1997. Collection of a dozen scholarly assessments, ranging from celebratory to hostile, of Spielberg's film.

Mintz, Alan. *Popular Culture and the Shaping of Holocaust Memory in America.* Seattle: University of Washington Press, 2001. Provides a comprehensive summary of published praise and criticism of Spielberg's film, in addition to the author's discussion.

Novick, Peter. *The Holocaust in American Life.* Boston: Houghton Mifflin, 1999. Ponders the issue of heightened Holocaust awareness in the United States during the decade of the 1990's.

Palowski, Franciszek. *The Making of "Schindler's List": Behind the Scenes of an Epic Film.* Translated by Anna Ware and Robert G. Ware. Secaucus, N.J.: Carol, 1998. Written by Spielberg's Polish interpreter, this production diary appeared in Poland in 1993, prior to the film's release.

**SEE ALSO:** Sept. 5-6, 1972: Arab Terrorists Murder Israelis at Munich Olympics; June 20, 1975: *Jaws* Prompts a Wave of Special-Effects Films; Apr. 18, 1988: Israel Convicts Demjanjuk of Nazi War Crimes; Apr. 22, 1993: United States Holocaust Memorial Museum Opens.

## March, 1994
# ITALY'S VOTERS MOVE RIGHT

*With their Socialist and Christian Democratic leaders caught in a swirl of corruption and controversy, Italians undertook political reforms and the formation of new political parties.*

**LOCALE:** Italy
**CATEGORIES:** Crime and scandal; government and politics; social issues and reform

### KEY FIGURES
*Bettino Craxi* (1934-2000), first Socialist prime minister of Italy, 1983-1987
*Silvio Berlusconi* (b. 1936), wealthy leader of Forza Italia and prime minister of Italy, 1994-1995 and 2001-2006
*Romano Prodi* (b. 1939), organizer of the Olive Tree coalition and prime minister of Italy, 1996-1998 and again beginning in 2006

### SUMMARY OF EVENT
The Italian government that emerged from the wreckage of Fascist Italy's defeat in World War II was made up of parties ranging from the center to the far left. More conservative voters gravitated to the party that was strongly linked with the Roman Catholic Church—Christian Democracy. At the far left was the large Communist Party with its strong appeal to workers. Between these two was the Italian Socialist Party, which rejected Marxist violence but supported social policies benefiting the lower-middle class and the upper echelons of the working class.

Because the Italian constitution provided that all individuals elected to parliament would be chosen not directly by the voters but by the parties, under a system of proportional representation, party membership was the key to political activity. This form of representation had two effects: It brought into the parliament many small parties that otherwise would have been unable to participate in government, and it meant that the political parties brokered appointment to all government positions. Thus active party membership was not only the key to political participation but also the pathway to a civil service appointment.

As the Cold War developed, Italy's Communist Party was seen as an ally of Soviet Russia. All Italian governments were thus coalitions of the various parties to the right of the Communist Party. Most of these coalitions involved alliances of the Socialists and the Christian Democrats, with some posts reserved for the very small parties that, thanks to proportional representation, had a few seats in parliament. This first Italian Republic, as it came to be known, had both a president and a prime min-

1994

ister; the former selected the latter on the basis of his party leadership and ability to forge a coalition that could win the support of parliament.

As time progressed, however, the larger parties lost popular support for a variety of reasons. The end of the Cold War led to the Italian Communist Party's splitting into two groups: a large group that was more socialist than communist and a small group of hard-line Marxists. With the breakup of the Communist Party, opposition to communism ceased to be a viable justification for supporting either the old-line Socialist Party or, to its right, Christian Democracy.

Moreover, the various Italian governments had for the most part felt that their role was to serve as many Italians as possible. To this end, they had created the Italian "social state," in which the civil service was enlarged to provide jobs for many Italians, and many social services were supplied by government-owned entities—insurance, banking, water supply, and others. These state-owned companies provided secure jobs for many Italians who did not have civil service jobs. However, the companies were relatively inefficient and depended heavily on government subsidies, leading to a large government deficit.

Many activities were supplied by companies on contract to the government, especially construction companies. The contracts, increasingly, came to be awarded with the understanding that part of the money would be "kicked back" to the party of the individual who had awarded the contract; indeed, although the parties enjoyed some state subventions, much of their money arrived by way of these kickbacks. All of this activity, however, occurred out of view of the public—until, in the late 1980's, magistrates in Milan began investigating the network of kickbacks in which all the political parties were involved. The series of bribe scandals, known as Tangentopoli (bribesville), was revealed in 1992.

In 1989, a new criminal code was introduced, replacing that of 1931 with a system more like that in the United States, in which actual prosecution, rather than mere investigation, is key. At the same time, the economy had slowed, and some companies that had hitherto been comfortable paying kickbacks to get government contracts found that these raised the costs to the point that they were no longer profitable. The parties were revealed to be totally dependent on the bribe system, and some of the party leaders were shown to be the personal beneficiaries of the system, notably Bettino Craxi, leader of the Socialist Party, who eventually fled the country (to Tunisia) to avoid prosecution.

As the old parties lost their standing with the public, new parties arose. In the area around Milan, the center of the corruption investigation, disgusted voters migrated to a new party called the Northern League, which grabbed about one-third of the votes in northern Italy in the 1993 municipal elections. Southern Italy, which had been a major beneficiary of the Christian Democracy party, became heavily infiltrated by the Mafia, causing the old party to lose its ability to appeal to large numbers of voters. Thus the old "center" parties, the Socialists who were tainted by the corruption revelations and the Christian Democrats who were shown to be tools of the Mafia, were no longer in a position to put together a governing coalition.

At this point, a group of reformers, among them an Italian economics professor named Romano Prodi, managed to get a package of voting reforms through the Italian parliament. The first of these created a referendum election held in the spring of 1993 that not only abolished the system of government subventions of the parties but also modified the system of proportional representation so that, henceforth, most deputies in parliament would be directly elected to their seats. At first introduced in the 1993 senate elections, this reform was extended to the lower house of parliament in 1994.

By the spring of 1994, in the national elections, the old parties had been replaced by three new large parties: the Northern League, headed by Umberto Bossi; the National Alliance of conservatives from southern Italy; and a brand-new party, Forza Italia, headed by Italy's richest man, Silvio Berlusconi, owner of three of Italy's television networks. Berlusconi formed a government that lasted until December, 1994. By then, under the leadership of Romano Prodi, Italy's center-left had regrouped and formed an alternative to Berlusconi's Forza Italia. For the rest of the decade, various "progressive" groupings provided a succession of cabinets until Berlusconi reclaimed the lead in 2001.

## SIGNIFICANCE

The collapse of the old parties of Italy's first republic, as the vote in the election of 1994 revealed, marked a substantial turning point for Italy. Even though the substantial abandonment of proportional voting in 1993-1994 did not significantly reduce the number of small parties, the political process after 1994 more closely resembled that in other Western democracies, with governments alternating between right- and left-oriented coalitions. The realignment reduced the amount of political corruption as the parties no longer were the sole pathway to a stable career. Although the political reforms were not without difficulties—with pensioners and workers resisting the reforms that decreased the cost of government and that were needed to enable Italy to qualify for membership in the Euro zone—the result may offer greater political stability in the future.

—*Nancy M. Gordon*

## FURTHER READING

Bufacchi, Vittorio, and Simon Burgess. *Italy Since 1989: Events and Interpretations*. New York: Macmillan, 1998. Presents substantial details on the parliamentary voting in the years during which Italian politics were being reconstituted.

Burnett, Stanton H., and Luca Mantovani. *The Italian Guillotine: Operation Clean Hands and the Overthrow of Italy's First Republic*. Lanham, Md.: Rowman & Littlefield, 1998. Presents all the details about the investigation of corruption that brought down the old parties.

Sassoon, Donald. *Contemporary Italy: Economy, Society and Politics Since 1945*. 2d ed. New York: Longman, 1997. Focuses on the evolution of Italian politics since 1945, providing some perspective on the events of the 1990's.

**SEE ALSO:** Mar. 16-May 9, 1978: Terrorists Kidnap and Murder Former Italian Prime Minister; May 22, 1978: Italy Legalizes Abortion; Jan. 1, 1999: Eleven European Nations Adopt the Euro.

---

## March 1, 1994
# U.S. GUN CONTROL LEGISLATION TAKES EFFECT

*The Brady Handgun Violence Prevention Act established a mandatory five-day waiting period and background check before a handgun can be purchased in the United States.*

**ALSO KNOWN AS:** Brady Handgun Violence Prevention Act; U.S. Statutes at Large 107 Stat. 1536; Public Law 103-159; U.S. Code 18 § 921 et seq.; Brady bill

**LOCALE:** Washington, D.C.

**CATEGORIES:** Laws, acts, and legal history; social issues and reform

### KEY FIGURES

*James S. Brady* (b. 1940), press secretary to President Ronald Reagan

*Sarah Brady* (b. 1942), wife of James Brady and chair of Handgun Control, Inc.

*Bill Clinton* (b. 1946), president of the United States, 1993-2001

*Bob Dole* (b. 1923), Republican senator from Kansas and Senate minority leader

*Edward Feighan* (b. 1947), Democratic congressman from Ohio who introduced the bill in the House

*Howard Metzenbaum* (b. 1917), Democratic senator from Ohio who introduced the bill in the Senate

*George Mitchell* (b. 1933), Democratic senator from Maine and Senate majority leader

*Ronald Reagan* (1911-2004), president of the United States, 1981-1989

*Charles Schumer* (b. 1950), Democratic congressman from New York who reintroduced the bill in the House in 1993

### SUMMARY OF EVENT

On November 30, 1993, President Bill Clinton signed the Brady Handgun Violence Prevention Act into law—the first significant federal gun control legislation passed in the United States since 1968. Its passage came after a six-year campaign by James S. Brady, Sarah Brady, and Handgun Control, Inc., which was fiercely opposed by the National Rifle Association (NRA).

James Brady had been active in Republican Party politics from the early 1960's. He had held posts in the administrations of presidents Richard M. Nixon and Gerald R. Ford. In 1980, he joined Ronald Reagan's presidential campaign as director of public affairs. When Reagan became president in January, 1981, Brady was named White House press secretary. On March 30, 1981, a mentally disturbed young man shot at President Reagan and his entourage as they left a Washington, D.C., hotel at which the president had delivered a speech. Reagan was seriously wounded, as were a Washington police officer and a secret service agent. Brady was the most seriously injured, with a gunshot wound to the head. For several days, Brady was near death. His recovery was long and painful. He was not allowed to go home for eight months and did not return to work for almost two years. Even then, he continued to suffer paralysis of the left side, problems with speech, and memory difficulties.

1994

Sarah Kemp was a Republican Party activist when she met James Brady in 1970. They were married in 1973. At the time Brady was shot, they had a two-year-old son, Scott. Sarah Brady helped her husband in his long recovery. In 1984, when Scott was five years of age, Sarah found him playing with a friend's loaded pistol. This event, along with her husband's experience, convinced her to become active in the gun control movement. She called Handgun Control, Inc., the most influential gun control advocacy group then operating in the United States, and offered her help. From that point on, Sarah Brady became a tireless advocate for stricter gun control laws.

A proposed federal gun control law, called the Brady bill because of the activism of Jim and Sarah Brady, was first introduced in Congress by Democratic representative Edward Feighan of Ohio, on February 4, 1987. The main provision of the bill was a seven-day waiting period for the purchase of handguns. Polls at the time showed that the American public favored such a measure, but the bill was strongly opposed by the National Rifle Association. The position of the NRA was that any new gun control legislation violated the Second Amendment to the Constitution.

The Second Amendment is part of the Bill of Rights, which was ratified in 1791. The amendment says simply, "A well regulated Militia, being necessary to the security of a free State, the right of the people to keep and bear Arms, shall not be infringed." Legal interpretations of the amendment have usually concluded that some restrictions on firearms are constitutional. During the 1930's, violence perpetrated by organized crime led to the passage of the first federal gun control laws. These laws banned private ownership of submachine guns and banned the sale of firearms to known criminals. In 1939, in *Miller v. United States*, the Supreme Court found that these restrictions were constitutional, as such weapons had no relationship to the formation of a well-regulated

*Nearly five years after signing the Brady gun control law, President Bill Clinton meets with James Brady to call on Congress to extend the law.* (AP/Wide World Photos)

militia. The next significant piece of federal gun control legislation was passed in 1968, in response to the assassinations of Martin Luther King, Jr., and Robert Kennedy. This law prohibited interstate sales of firearms and required gun dealers to keep records of sales.

The NRA worked throughout the 1970's and 1980's to repeal some provisions of the 1968 Gun Control Act. They had some success in 1986, when Congress voted to repeal the ban on interstate sales of rifles and shotguns. In 1987, the NRA mounted an intense lobbying campaign to defeat the Brady bill and spent approximately two million dollars in the effort. The Brady bill was to be voted on in the House of Representatives in September of 1988. The Bradys and Handgun Control, Inc., lobbied hard for it, and on September 7, a group of 120 uniformed police officers marched on the Capitol in support of the law's passage. The bill was defeated, however, by a vote of 228 to 182.

The Brady bill was reintroduced in Congress in 1990, but it was never brought to a vote at that time because of opposition from powerful members of Congress, including House Speaker Thomas Foley (a Democrat from Washington State). The bill was introduced again in 1991. On May 8, 1991, the House of Representatives passed a bill requiring a seven-day waiting period for gun purchases. The Senate version, passed on June 28, called for a five-day waiting period. The compromise bill, incorporating the Senate requirements, was passed by the House on November 27, but Republican senators launched a filibuster against it and it never came to a vote in the Senate. In 1992, supporters of the Brady bill once again tried to bring it up for a vote in the Senate but were unable to get enough votes to end the filibuster.

By 1993, public support for gun control legislation had increased dramatically. A poll conducted in March of that year showed that 70 percent of all Americans and 57 percent of gun owners felt that there should be more restrictions on the sale of firearms. Passage of the Brady bill was favored by 88 percent of people in the United States. The bill was introduced in the House by Democrat Charles Schumer of New York on February 22, 1993, and in the Senate by Ohio Democrat Howard Metzenbaum on February 24. Both the NRA and Handgun Control, Inc., kept up their intensive lobbying efforts.

## A STEP AGAINST HANDGUN VIOLENCE

*In his remarks on the signing of the Brady Handgun Violence Protection Act on November 30, 1993, President Bill Clinton praised James and Sarah Brady for fighting to get the law through Congress:*

Since Jim and Sarah began this crusade, more than 150,000 Americans, men, women, teenagers, children, even infants, have been killed with handguns. And many more have been wounded—150,000 people from all walks of life who should have been here to share Christmas with us. This couple saw through a fight that really never should have had to occur, because still, when people are confronted with issues of clear common sense and overwhelming evidence, too often we are prevented from doing what we know we ought to do by our collective fears, whatever they may be.

The Brady bill has finally become law in a fundamental sense not because of any of us but because grassroots America changed its mind and demanded that this Congress not leave here without doing something about this. And all the rest of us—even Jim and Sarah—did was to somehow light that spark that swept across the people of this country and proved once again that democracy can work. America won this battle. Americans are finally fed up with violence that cuts down another citizen with gunfire every 20 minutes.

On November 10, 1993, the House passed the bill by a vote of 238 to 182. Ten days later, the Senate passed its bill by a vote of 63 to 36. There were significant differences in the bills passed by the two houses of Congress, and a conference committee negotiated for two days before presenting a conference report to both houses. On November 22, the House of Representatives passed the compromise bill by a vote of 238 to 187. In the Senate, Minority Leader Bob Dole (a Republican from Kansas) threatened to block passage of the bill with a filibuster. Dole negotiated with Senate Majority Leader George Mitchell of Maine and finally agreed not to block passage of the bill if the Senate would consider modifications to it early in the new year. The Senate passed the bill by voice vote on November 24. Jim Brady called it a "Thanksgiving present for the American people." The law went into effect on March 1, 1994.

### SIGNIFICANCE

Assessments of the effectiveness of the Brady bill after its first year of enforcement were mixed. The NRA and other groups opposed to any form of gun control asserted that the law was not only a clear violation of the Second Amendment but also ineffective, because it did not keep criminals from buying guns illegally. They pointed to the fact that the Department of Justice prosecuted only four

1994

cases under the Brady bill in the law's first year. They also pointed out several loopholes that allowed limitations on law-enforcement record keeping and exempted pawnshops from some of the rules. Several judges found some provisions of the law unconstitutional, although it remained in effect pending appeal.

The Bradys and other supporters of the bill maintained that it was a success. They pointed to government figures showing that seventy thousand convicted felons were prevented from buying guns under the law in its first year. They admitted that the bill was weak, but they argued that it was an important first step in stopping handgun violence. Jim Brady called his namesake bill "the end of unchecked madness and the commencement of a heartfelt crusade for a safer and saner country."

*—Deborah D. Wallin*

## FURTHER READING

Cornell, Saul. *A Well-Regulated Militia: The Founding Fathers and the Origins of Gun Control in America*. New York: Oxford University Press, 2006. A constitutional historian presents a historical examination of the gun control issue. Includes bibliography and index.

Cozic, Charles P., ed. *Gun Control*. San Diego, Calif.: Greenhaven Press, 1992. Collection encompasses contributions by authors with varying viewpoints on the issue, including Sarah Brady and representatives of the NRA.

Davidson, Osha Gray. *Under Fire: The NRA and the Battle for Gun Control*. Expanded ed. Iowa City: University of Iowa Press, 1998. Attempts to provide a balanced view of the history of the NRA and its confrontations with gun control advocates in the 1990's.

Jacobs, James B. *Can Gun Control Work?* New York: Oxford University Press, 2002. Examines the practical question of whether gun control can ever actually be an effective policy in the United States. Devotes significant attention to the Brady bill.

LaPierre, Wayne. *Guns, Crime, and Freedom*. Washington, D.C.: Regnery, 1994. A lobbyist for the NRA presents arguments against gun control. Includes extensive bibliography.

Siegel, Mark A., et al. *Gun Control: Restricting Rights or Protecting People?* Wylie, Tex.: Information Plus, 1995. Study guide on the issues provides many tables and charts to help readers interpret the available information on gun control.

**SEE ALSO:** Mar. 30, 1981: Hinckley Attempts to Assassinate President Reagan; 1989: Arnold and Gottlieb Publish *The Wise Use Agenda*; Apr. 20, 1999: Columbine High School Massacre.

## April 6-July, 1994
# RWANDAN GENOCIDE

*Following the death of President Juvénal Habyarimana on April 6, 1994, Rwanda erupted into genocide, with somewhere between 800,000 and 1 million Rwandans, mostly Tutsi, being murdered by their racially motivated Hutu neighbors. The killing lasted until July, and the ensuing refugee crisis was not resolved until 1998.*

**LOCALE:** Rwanda
**CATEGORIES:** Terrorism, atrocities, and war crimes; wars, uprisings, and civil unrest

## KEY FIGURES

*Juvénal Habyarimana* (1937-1994), Rwanda's defense minister who overthrew his cousin to become the country's president, 1973-1994

*Paul Kagame* (b. 1957), leader of the Rwandan Patriotic Front (RPF) who fought against Habyarimana's government and became president of Rwanda in 2000

*Fred Rwigema* (1957-1990), one of the initial leaders of the RPF whose death prompted Kagame to return from military training in the United States and lead the RPF

*Agathe Uwilingiyimana* (1953-1994), Rwanda's final prime minister under Habyarimana, 1993-1994, and one of the first high-profile Interahamwe targets to die in the genocide

## SUMMARY OF EVENT

The racist policies of the Hutu-led Rwandan government from 1962 to 1973 created a Tutsi diaspora, which spurred a revolutionary movement to oust the Rwandan government. The revolutionaries, who were made up of both Tutsis and Hutus, went by the name the Rwandan

*A Rwandan refugee camp in Kimbumba, Zaire, in 1994.* (Centers for Disease Control and Prevention)

Patriotic Front (RPF) and were initially led by Fred Rwigema. It was from Uganda and Tanzania that the RPF launched attacks on Rwanda starting in the 1990's. Rwigema was killed in the first week of fighting. After that, the RPF was led by Paul Kagame.

By the time the RPF began its attacks in the 1990's, hard-line anti-Tutsi forces in the government had already started the country down a murderous path. After the attacks began, the government used the RPF as a scapegoat to encourage ordinary citizens to kill each other. As the RPF strengthened its political position, finally forcing President Juvénal Habyarimana to sign a peace agreement in 1993, in Arusha, Tanzania, the government increased its anti-Tutsi rhetoric. One of the loudest voices in this hue and cry was that of the radio station Radio Télévision Libre des Mille Collines (RTLM), which urged Hutu citizens to take part in the killing of Tutsis. Indeed, the government had for months been training groups of youths into a militia called the Interahamwe, extolling the virtues of Hutu Power and instructing them to murder Tutsis.

Thus, by April 6, 1994, when the airplane carrying President Habyarimana and Burundi's Hutu president Cyprien Ntaryamira was shot down, killing all on board, the country was already primed for violence. The Interahamwe immediately set up roadblocks, making travel difficult within the country. RTLM began announcing the names and locations of Tutsis, so that they could be hunted down and murdered. By the next morning, local militia cells had organized to begin hunting down the country's Tutsis and systematically killing them, using mostly machetes. Hutu moderates were considered as dangerous as the Tutsis, and they were murdered as well. The country's prime minister, Agathe Uwilingiyimana, was pulled from her house and killed on April 7. Foreign arms from a variety of sources, including developed Western nations, continued to be smuggled to Rwanda's Hutu forces throughout the genocide, exacerbating the killing.

The Rwandan genocide remains horrifically remarkable both because so many people were killed in such a short time and because the international community allowed it to happen. The leader of the United Nations Assistance Mission for Rwanda (UNAMIR), Roméo Dal-

1994

laire, pleaded for assistance to prevent the genocide before it began, but his request was turned down. The international community and peacekeeping forces stood aside. After ten Belgian members of the UNAMIR peacekeeping mission were tortured and mutilated before being killed by the Interahamwe, the United Nations cut its presence from 2,500 to 250. Dallaire remained with the small group, and, while he is credited with saving 20,000 lives, his forces had almost nothing to do with ending the genocide. Western nations avoided acknowledging the genocide, and the United States refused to even use the word "genocide," for fear of being required to send aid to the tiny African nation. Having recently suffered a public relations disaster in Somalia, where eighteen U.S. soldiers were killed, Bill Clinton's presidential administration attempted to downplay the genocide as a local conflict that did not require American intervention. In fact, the Rwandan genocide received little mainstream press coverage worldwide, with only a few reporters courageous enough to enter the country, let alone broadcast the horrific events taking place.

Throughout the country, Tutsis fled to places thought safe—hospitals, churches, and schools—but such congregation only made it easier for the Hutus to find and kill them en masse. In fact, ordinary Hutu citizens represented the strongest Hutu killing force in the country. Pressured by the Interahamwe and RTLM, and supported by the country's history of unpunished violence against Tutsis, individuals took up machetes and slaughtered friends and even family members. Tutsis hid in the country's swamps and banana trees, but they were hunted down. Some Hutus were sincerely horrified by the crimes surrounding them and refused to participate in the violence, and some became murder victims themselves. Very few succeeded in staying out of the violence, but some were successful in their rescue efforts. One Hutu man, Paul Rusesabagina, managed to protect more than a thousand people inside the Hôtel des Mille Collines, bartering daily with the Interahamwe and other Hutu Power extremists to save the lives of the hotel's guests for the entirety of the genocide.

Finally, in July, roughly one hundred days after the genocide began, RPF forces captured the country's capital, Kigali, and violence began to taper off. In that time, between 800,000 and 1 million Rwandans, mostly Tutsi, had been murdered.

## PRESIDENT CLINTON APOLOGIZES TO RWANDA

*On March 25, 1998, President Bill Clinton arrived in Rwanda to address the war-ravaged nation, whose genocide was largely ignored by the world community. Clinton, who years later said that his failure to act during the genocide was his greatest regret as president, delivered an apology at Kigali airport:*

I have come today to pay the respects of my Nation to all who suffered and all who perished in the Rwandan genocide. It is my hope that through this trip, in every corner of the world today and tomorrow, their story will be told; that 4 years ago in this beautiful, green, lovely land, a clear and conscious decision was made by those then in power that the peoples of this country would not live side by side in peace. . . .

The international community, together with nations in Africa, must bear its share of responsibility for this tragedy as well. We did not act quickly enough after the killing began. We should not have allowed the refugee camps to become safe haven for the killers. We did not immediately call these crimes by their rightful name: genocide. We cannot change the past. But we can and must do everything in our power to help you build a future without fear and full of hope. . . .

It may seem strange to you here, especially the many of you who lost members of your family, but all over the world there were people like me sitting in offices, day after day after day, who did not fully appreciate the depth and the speed with which you were being engulfed by this unimaginable terror.

## SIGNIFICANCE

The ouster of the Hutu government led to a massive flight from Rwanda by the country's Hutus. Just as the Interahamwe had urged average citizens to murder during the genocide, it encouraged them to panic in their flight, informing them that they would be massacred by the RPF in vengeance for the genocide.

Refugee camps sprang up in Uganda, Tanzania, Burundi, and Zaire. Although the new refugees received an outpouring of humanitarian aid, the camps were, in fact, little more than outposts for the Hutu Power agitators. These extremists used the cover of the French Operation Turquoise, which was supposed to be part of the international response to the genocide, to escape with their arms into neighboring countries. Those who wished to leave the camps and return home to Rwanda were killed, and the Interahamwe exacted a tax from everyone in the camps, in the form of either money or supplies. Raids into Rwanda regularly brought further Tutsi deaths, even as the RPF tried to establish a government of true equality.

As 1994 stretched into 1996, the camps remained a problem. The dictator of Zaire, Mobutu Sese Seko, became involved with the Hutu Power movement, and Zaire began using its government as well as Rwanda's Interahamwe against its own Tutsi population, first trying to expel them to Rwanda, then to kill them outright. The Tutsis formed a defense militia that gained support and troops from both Rwanda and Uganda. The First Congo War erupted, ending only when Mobutu was ousted just before his death from cancer, and Zaire became the Democratic Republic of Congo in 1996.

Rwanda's problems, however, were far from solved. As Hutus from the camps were slowly repatriated, the government began trying to prosecute offenders. Some of the worst faced the U.N. International Criminal Tribunal for Rwanda; this was a source of frustration to the Rwandan government, which wished to prosecute internally. Others remained free, with decreasing likelihood of imprisonment. In order to deal with the huge backlog in overcrowded prisons, many lower-level offenders were mandated to special courts set up beginning in 2001 after the style of old tribal-village councils, called Gacaca. In past times, the Gacaca settled disputes by seeking atonement rather than retribution, but it is difficult to say whether this community-based justice system is truly effective after a genocide.

—*Jessie Bishop Powell*

## FURTHER READING

Adelman, Howard, and Astri Suhrke, eds. *The Path of a Genocide: The Rwandan Crisis from Uganda to Zaire.* New Brunswick, N.J.: Transaction, 1999. Collection of essays discussing the roles of various parties and countries in the Rwandan genocide, including U.S. policies and media coverage and U.N. peacekeeping forces.

Gourevitch, Philip. *We Wish to Inform You That Tomorrow We Will Be Killed with Our Families: Stories from Rwanda.* New York: Farrar, Straus and Giroux, 1998. Several visits to Rwanda in the late 1990's helped Gourevitch develop a strong sense of the forces behind the genocide and the problems facing the country as it recovered.

Rusesabagina, Paul. *An Ordinary Man.* New York: Viking Press, 2006. Autobiography of the man whose story inspired the film *Hotel Rwanda* (2004). Rusesabagina saved one-thousand Tutsis and moderate Hutus from certain death by sheltering them inside the Hôtel des Mille Collines with his family during the genocide.

Waugh, Colin M. *Paul Kagame and Rwanda: Power, Genocide, and the Rwandan Patriotic Front.* Jefferson, N.C.: McFarland, 2004. Discusses the RPF's role, both before, during, and after the Rwandan genocide, in shaping Rwandan policy and fighting the attitudes of Habyarimana's regime.

**SEE ALSO:** May-Aug., 1972: Burundi Commits Genocide of Hutu Majority; July 5, 1973: Habyarimana Overthrows President Kayibanda; Oct. 21, 1993: Burundian President Is Assassinated; Sept., 1998: U.N. Tribunal Convicts Rwandans of Genocide.

1994

## April 14-16, 1994
# ALEXANDER FIGHTS TO SAVE THE NATIONAL ENDOWMENT FOR THE ARTS

*As part of her attempts to save the National Endowment for the Arts, Jane Alexander, the agency's chair, convened a national arts conference, but the event met with criticism from both artists and political conservatives.*

**ALSO KNOWN AS:** "ART-21"
**LOCALE:** Chicago, Illinois
**CATEGORIES:** Organizations and institutions; arts; government and politics

**KEY FIGURE**
*Jane Alexander* (b. 1939), stage and film actor who became chair of the National Endowment for the Arts

**SUMMARY OF EVENT**
In the summer of 1993, President Bill Clinton nominated actor Jane Alexander to become the sixth chairman (the title she preferred) of the National Endowment for the Arts (NEA). An unexpected nominee, Alexander was unanimously confirmed by the U.S. Senate and was sworn into office on October 8, 1993. She thus became the first working artist to head the NEA. In addition to being an accomplished actor, Alexander was a film director and producer and an author. She had been active in the arts for all of her adult life, and as the chair of the NEA she was perceived to be an appealing and effective public advocate for an agency that was embattled.

Between the fall of 1993 and the spring of 1994, Alexander engaged in a series of high-profile barnstorming campaigns to promote the good works of the NEA. The hallmark of those efforts was the convening of the first national arts conference organized by the federal government, "ART-21: Art Reaches into the 21st Century." The event took place in Chicago with funding from the MacArthur Foundation. In a press release, the NEA said that the conference would "address major trends, priorities, and fresh ideas in the arts as changes in resources, demographics, and technologies take our nation in new directions."

Attended by approximately one thousand invited guests, the conference featured four keynote speakers who addressed four major themes: the artist in society, the arts and technology, expanding resources for the arts,

and lifelong learning in the arts. "ART-21" was to provide a big tent for the arts, under which a reconciliation of conflicting aims and visions could be achieved. "ART-21" was central to Alexander's attempt to improve the public image of the NEA and to aid in preserving the agency's very existence in the face of increasing critical scrutiny from Congress.

The stated goals of "ART-21" were in harmony with the foundational principles of the NEA. At its inception on September 29, 1965, the NEA was authorized by an act of Congress to serve as an impartial and unbiased nurturer of the cultural life of America. The act authorized support only for projects that were nonprofit and substantively professional; the projects were to be selected by rotating panels of experts in their fields. These foundational principles relied on the modernist notions of art being loftier than mere commerce, serious, and objectively recognizable to impartial experts in the field. From its inception, the NEA was expected to be apolitical in its granting of support. Implicit to this expectation were the assumptions that art could be recognized and funded apolitically and that, through enlightened tolerance, conflicting visions could be reconciled.

In a press release for "ART-21," Alexander stated: "On the eve of a new millennium, we, as a complex and diverse nation, must ask ourselves where we need to go and how we can get there. We at the Endowment need to ask what role the arts will play in enriching the lives of our citizens, the spirit of our communities, and our character as a nation." Those questions were to be asked, and discussed, under the big tent provided by "ART-21."

These stated goals of "ART-21" evidenced the modernist, or liberal, position that genius makes or recognizes fine art and that tolerance and sensitivity are key to the resolution of conflicts. To the select participants of the "ART-21" conference, Alexander said in her opening remarks: "The tie that unites us is a common love of the arts. And the arts mean different things to different people here in this room. Just as we strive to honor all people in America, so should we strive to honor their art, because that is what tells us who they are, who we are." Those who celebrated the traditional liberal position implicit in the charter of the NEA were soon disappointed. Subsequent events proved politics to be much to the fore and harmony to be elusive.

*Alexander Fights to Save the National Endowment for the Arts*

## SIGNIFICANCE

Despite its hope for achieving harmony, the impact of the big tent offered by "ART-21" was one of increasing political conflict. Opposing critics of the event did, however, find harmony of a sort on one point. They agreed that "ART-21," and Alexander's leadership of the National Endowment for the Arts, was charismatic but superficial and lacking substance. The difficulty was that those outside the tent—for starkly different reasons—were disenchanted with those within the tent. One group outside the big tent offered by "ART-21" were postmodernists, who viewed the event as noninclusive, elitist, and ineffective. Another group outside the "ART-21" tent were political conservatives, who viewed the record of the NEA critically. The former would be heard through various journals and art media. The latter could not be ignored, given that, as a result of the electoral process, they would determine the budget for the agency.

The postmodernist critics of "ART-21" revealed the antagonism between postmodernism and modernism. Postmodernists reject the modernist notions of art being apolitical, serious, and recognizable to impartial experts in the field. They assume that art is necessarily political and often absurd and that experts in the field are anything but impartial. Consequently, they criticized "ART-21" as elitist, not sufficiently inclusive, financially prohibitive to attend, and, consequently, undemocratic and discriminatory. They also viewed the four themes of the conference, noted above, as too traditional and too restrictive. They criticized Alexander's comments at the conference for being too broad in scope, too mainstream, and too evasive of the debates surrounding the difficult questions of defending and promoting controversial art to the public. For postmodernist critics, "ART-21" missed a golden opportunity to advance strategies for resolving, defending, and justifying what they called "difficult art" to the public. There is an irony in that criticism. In clear contradiction to the (modernist) charter of the NEA, authorizing it to serve as an impartial nurturer of the fine arts in the United States, the postmodernist critics of "ART-21" found fault and hypocrisy in its attempt to be impartial and inclusive.

The conservative critics of "ART-21," and of the NEA in general, shared with the postmodernists a skepticism about the possibility and propriety of the NEA's being an impartial nurturer of the fine arts. They did so in three distinct fashions. First, they questioned the idea that the awarding of grants can in fact be impartial. In this respect, they viewed the NEA with the suspicion that it is outside the mainstream of American culture and that it promotes a particular social and political agenda. Second, they argued that the NEA—if it is to exist—should, in fact, be what it must be: partial. It should advocate the preservation and advancement of traditional American culture. Third, they argued that the politicization of culture, which they viewed as inherent to governmentally subsidized art, is inescapably totalitarian.

At the same time postmodernist critics were expressing their displeasure with "ART-21" for being too mainstream and too timid, a number of books were published that argued just the opposite point: that the NEA had lost its cultural moorings. Robert Hughes, a former art critic for *Time* magazine, presented a scathing critique of the contemporary fine arts in two venues: a lecture delivered at the Massachusetts Institute of Technology in 1993, "Making the World Safe for Elitism" (published in *The Washington Post*), and a book titled *Culture of Complaint: The Fraying of America* (1993). This criticism was accompanied by various other works, including Gertrude Himmelfarb's *On Looking into the Abyss: Untimely Thoughts on Culture and Society* (1994).

Those books made Alexander's attempt to save the NEA more difficult, but they were not nearly as damaging as a variety of artistic events funded either directly or indirectly by the NEA itself. In a performance piece by Ron Athey, for example, the back of a person was cut with a knife, the blood was soaked up with a cloth, and the cloth was then sent over the heads of the audience. The resulting controversy made this work and others difficult for Alexander to defend before the public and before Congress.

The "ART-21" conference proved ineffective in Alexander's battle to save the NEA. However, in contrast to the generalities about the importance of the NEA that appeared in Alexander's "1994 Annual Report: Chairman's Statement," her testimony before the Senate Appropriations Committee on May 8, 1996, was more sanguine. Alexander noted that the 1996 budget process resulted in the deepest funding cut in the history of the NEA. She also lamented that the NEA was forced to suspend nearly all grants to individual artists.

The NEA's funding of "difficult art" clearly contributed to the agency's problems in obtaining congressional funding. It is haunting to read Alexander's comment in that same testimony of May 8, 1996: "The phase-out proposal about which we hear so much is a creation of the House leadership, and the fact is, they do not have the votes to pass it." Soon after, the House of Representatives voted to phase out the NEA, and the Senate was poised to do the same. However, Alexander was able to salvage a

1994

budget of $98 million for the NEA for fiscal year 1998. Shortly after, on October 8, 1997, she announced that she was stepping down from her position as chairman of the NEA so that she could resume her acting career.

There were substantive issues at stake that were not addressed by "ART-21." The issue of whether "difficult art" should or should not be funded warranted serious evaluation. Alexander's realization of the complexity of this concern was suggested in her later comments. In testimony she gave on April 24, 1997, to the Senate Subcommittee on Interior and Related Agencies, Alexander spoke not of confidence that the votes to close down the NEA were lacking, but rather of the importance of a modest increase in the NEA's budget "to preserve our heritage and invest in our future. The National Endowment for the Arts remains committed to bringing the most excellent art to the most Americans. Mr. Chairman and members of the subcommittee, I hope I can count on your support." Obtaining that support was linked to the decision to be partial about funding, or not funding, "difficult art." It was also linked to a substantive debate concerning three conflicting paradigms for art and culture: modernist, postmodernist, and conservative.

—*Arthur Pontynen*

**FURTHER READING**
Alexander, Jane. *Command Performance: An Actress in the Theater of Politics.* New York: PublicAffairs, 2000. Entertaining memoir presents Alexander's own viewpoint on her tenure as head of the NEA. Includes index.

Davis, Douglas. "Multicultural Wars." *Art in America* 83 (February, 1995): 35-42. Presents a critical review of the "ART-21" conference from an essentially postmodernist perspective.

Jarvik, Laurence. "Ten Good Reasons to Eliminate Funding for the National Endowment for the Arts." *Heritage Foundation Backgrounder*, April 29, 1997, 1-14. Offers a politically conservative critique of the National Endowment for the Arts.

National Endowment for the Arts. *Six Myths About the National Endowment for the Arts.* Washington, D.C.: U.S. Government Printing Office, 1997. The agency's own brief defense of its work.

Zeigler, Joseph Wesley. *Arts in Crisis: The National Endowment for the Arts Versus America.* Pennington, N.J.: A Cappella Books, 1994. Begins with a history of funding for the arts in the United States and then discusses the role of the NEA and the controversies that have surrounded that agency.

**SEE ALSO:** 1970's: Spanish Art Thrives After Years of Suppression; Sept. 28, 1974: Dalí Museum Opens in Spain; 1980's: Schnabel Emerges as a Celebrity Artist; Sept. 22-Oct. 7, 1985: Christo Wraps the Pont Neuf; May, 1987: National Museum of Women in the Arts Opens Amid Controversy; June 14, 1989: Mapplethorpe's Photographs Provoke Controversy; May 15, 1994: Andy Warhol Museum Opens; June 25, 1998: U.S. Supreme Court Rules That "Decency" Can Be Required for Federal Arts Grants.

## May, 1994
# GENETICALLY ENGINEERED FOOD REACHES SUPERMARKETS

*The field of biotechnology reached a milestone when the Flavr Savr tomato became the first genetically engineered food product available to U.S. consumers.*

**ALSO KNOWN AS:** Flavr Savr tomato
**LOCALE:** United States
**CATEGORIES:** Science and technology; genetics; agriculture; trade and commerce

**KEY FIGURES**
*David A. Kessler* (b. 1951), commissioner of the U.S. Food and Drug Administration
*Roger Salquist* (fl. late twentieth century), chief executive officer of Calgene, Incorporated

*Jeremy Rifkin* (b. 1945), author and social activist who directed resistance against genetically engineered foods through the Pure Food Campaign

**SUMMARY OF EVENT**
In May, 1994, Calgene, Incorporated, marketed the Flavr Savr tomato, the first genetically engineered food made available to consumers in the United States. Development and marketing of the tomato involved eight years of research and testing, $20 million in costs, and nearly four years of review by the U.S. Food and Drug Administration (FDA). The FDA's "safe" ruling on the Flavr Savr, a test case for the agribiotech industry, signaled the feasi-

*In 1991, chief executive officer of Calgene Roger Salquist examines genetically modified tomatoes that are able to ripen on the vine before shipping instead of having to be picked green.* (AP/Wide World Photos)

bility of marketing other genetically engineered foods that had already been developed and field-tested. Fears concerning the effects of genetically engineered foods on consumer health and the environment generated a storm of protest during this period.

The Flavr Savr differed from other tomatoes in that it had been genetically engineered to ripen more slowly. This gave it a significant advantage because the tomato could remain on the vine until it had begun to ripen yet be marketed before it deteriorated. Although picked before fully ripe, it reddened naturally, without exposure to ethylene gas, and developed vine-ripened flavor and texture.

In the Flavr Savr, the production of polygalacturonase (PG), an enzyme that causes the pectin in tomato cell walls to break down, had been inhibited through genetic engineering. Scientists had identified the tomato gene responsible for producing PG and had used antisense ribonucleic acid (RNA) technology, discovered in cancer research, to suppress the gene's expression.

Genetic engineering, also known as recombinant DNA (deoxyribonucleic acid) technology, enables scientists to target the specific gene responsible for a plant characteristic and suppress it or supplement it with a gene from a species with which that plant would traditionally be unable to breed. Genes from animals, bacteria, or other unrelated plant species can thus be inserted into plants.

Genes code for the production of enzymes, proteins that cause cellular reactions, through an intermediary called messenger ribonucleic acid (mRNA). Protein factories called ribosomes attach themselves to the mRNA and read it in order to assemble amino acids into enzymes. To produce the Flavr Savr, researchers determined the sequence of nucleic acids in the mRNA for PG, then reversed and inserted into the plant cells of the Flavr Savr's parent. This reversed sequence adhered to the mRNA for PG and prevented ribosomes from manufacturing it.

The gene for reversed, or antisense, mRNA was inserted into the tomato's DNA through plasmids, circular structures of DNA from a bacterium called *Agrobacterium tumefaciens* (*At*). A marker gene, from another bacterium that confers resistance to the antibiotic kanamycin, was incorporated into the tomato cells along with

1994

2803

the gene for antisense mRNA to flag the tomato cells that had integrated the antisense mRNA gene into their DNA. When the cells were exposed to a medium containing kanamycin, cells without the antisense mRNA and accompanying kanamycin resistance from the marker gene died. The resistant cells survived and generated tomato plants capable of suppressing PG.

The Flavr Savr was controversial because it contained a marker gene from a bacterium that made it resistant to the antibiotics kanamycin and neomycin. Some people feared that eating antibiotic-resistant tomatoes would make them resistant to these antibiotics during illness. Others feared allergic reactions to the protein generated by the marker gene.

Calgene, a biotechnology agribusiness founded in Davis, California, in 1980, saw the potential for substantial profit from the vine-ripened tomato market and began developing the Flavr Savr in 1982. From 1987 to 1992, Calgene conducted premarket testing on the Flavr Savr. To reassure consumers, who were becoming increasingly uneasy about genetically engineered foods, Calgene asked the FDA to examine its test results and rule on the safety of the tomato variety. Agricultural plant products, whether produced by genetic engineering or traditional plant breeding, are regulated by the FDA under the guidelines of the Federal Food, Drug, and Cosmetic Act of 1938 and the 1958 Food Additives Amendment to that act.

In May, 1992, under increasing pressure to clarify its position on the regulation of genetically engineered foods, David A. Kessler, commissioner of food and drugs for the FDA, released a document titled *Statement of Policy: Foods Derived from New Plant Varieties*. In the report, Kessler stated that because the FDA was not aware of any data demonstrating that foods created through genetic engineering present any greater safety concern than traditionally developed foods, the FDA would regulate all food products on the basis of their individual characteristics, not their mode of origin. Furthermore, the producer is legally responsible for ensuring that a food product is safe. The FDA would require premarket testing and labeling of new foods only if they contained lowered concentrations of the important nutrients for which the food was widely consumed, if they had toxicant concentrations above an acceptable range, or if unexpected allergens were present.

The FDA's refusal to regulate or label genetically engineered foods evoked a storm of protest from organizations such as the Environmental Defense Fund (EDF) and the Pure Food Campaign (PFC). The EDF proposed that genetically engineered foods be subject to premarket safety testing, that such products be labeled, and that manufacturers be required to notify the FDA at least ninety days before marketing the new foods. Jeremy Rifkin of the PFC was the Flavr Savr's most vigorous opponent. In 1992, he organized fifteen hundred chefs, numerous independent grocers, and some large grocery chains to boycott genetically engineered foods.

In November, 1990, Calgene requested that the FDA issue an advisory opinion on the use of the marker gene in tomatoes. The FDA ruled it safe. In October, 1991, Calgene requested that the FDA issue a separate advisory opinion on the status of the Flavr Savr tomato as a whole food subject to the same regulation as other tomato varieties. Calgene also made the results of its premarket testing available to the FDA and to the public through the dockets branch of the FDA.

Disturbed by the public outcry following the May, 1992, FDA statement regarding its regulatory policy for genetically engineered foods, and realizing that successful marketing of the Flavr Savr depended on public acceptance, Calgene filed a food additive petition for the selectable marker gene with the FDA on January 4, 1993. This is the most stringent safety test that the FDA applies to a food.

In April, 1994, Calgene published the FDA's review of Calgene's data on the Flavr Savr, which concluded that the tomato had not been significantly altered, that the marker gene could not transfer antibiotic resistance to other organisms, and that the marker did not possess any of the characteristics of allergenic proteins. Also in April, the FDA's Food Advisory Committee undertook a discussion of the safety review of foods produced by new biotechnologies, with the Flavr Savr serving as the discussion's focus. The FDA issued a food additive regulation on the marker gene in May, 1994.

The Flavr Savr was marketed at the end of May, 1994, in the Midwest and in California. Calgene voluntarily labeled the tomato and provided in-store displays explaining its origin. It was reported to have sold out where offered.

## SIGNIFICANCE

The Flavr Savr tomato was the test case for the industry; its successful transit through the regulatory process and subsequent marketing ushered in an era of genetically engineered agricultural products. Marketing of these products was expected to result in enormous profits and growth, over time, for the agribiotech industry. Public pressure on the FDA to increase its regulatory oversight of genetically engineered food products continued, as did the debate between producers of genetically engineered foods and those who feared adverse environmental effects.

By 1994, more than thirty genetically engineered agricultural products had been developed and field-tested and were waiting to be marketed; numerous others were in various stages of development. Products expected to move into the market during the 1990's included crops resistant to specific herbicides, viruses, fungi, drought, frost, salinity, and insects. Also in development were crops with superior food-processing traits such as longer ripening time or higher starch content, grains with the full complement of amino acids required by humans and domestic animals, healthier vegetable oils, and biodegradable plant substitutes for petroleum products such as motor oil.

Surveys indicated that although 70 percent of the American public was not opposed to genetically engineered foods, people favored labeling of these products as well as review of them by the FDA. The presidential administrations of Ronald Reagan and George H. W. Bush had been reluctant to create specific regulations for the biotech industry, which they hoped would dominate international markets. They believed that the industry could be regulated under existing laws created in earlier times for more traditional products.

Bill Clinton's presidential administration adopted a more aggressive stance, not by drafting new laws but by promising to improve coordination of the regulatory efforts of the FDA, the U.S. Department of Agriculture, and the Environmental Protection Agency regarding the industry. As a result of continuing pressure to inspect and label genetically engineered foods, the FDA promised to hold hearings on the issue in 1994 but warned that it would not reverse its position and require a full, premarket review of each new food, nor would it require broad labeling.

Environmental organizations, organic farmers, and scientists outside the biotech industry continued to express various concerns over the ecological effects of genetically engineered plants and urged extreme caution in introducing new plant species. They acknowledged that genetic engineering could be an extremely beneficial technology but pointed to the harm done by other new technologies, such as atomic energy and the insecticide dichloro-diphenyl-trichloroethane (DDT), which were implemented before their full effects were known.

In general, concerns centered on the fact that all elements of the environment exist in sensitive balance with one another. This balance is disrupted and existing elements evolve or are eliminated when a new element is introduced. There is no way to predict all the effects of introducing a new gene into a plant species or of introducing that plant into the environment. Laboratory tests are inconclusive in revealing all possible effects of genetic engineering because the environment cannot be simulated in a laboratory, and field testing poses the danger of releasing organisms into the environment that may affect it negatively and irreversibly.

The agribiotech industry claimed that the new plant species were the basis for a new, more ecologically sound agriculture. Many opponents, however, viewed genetically engineered plants as a temporary solution to serious, long-term environmental mismanagement or as a potential source of continued misuse. Environmentalists were alarmed by the industry's concentration on the development of crops engineered to tolerate herbicides. They believed that they had been betrayed because the new technology had been used to increase dependence on herbicides rather than to develop products and practices that would make herbicides unnecessary.

Insect-resistant crops engineered to contain a gene-producing toxin isolated from *Bacillus thuringiensis* (*Bt*), an environmentally safe pesticide, came under criticism. Insects evolve rapidly to develop resistance to pesticides to which they are repeatedly exposed. There was concern that plants would have to be sprayed with chemical pesticides when insects developed resistance to *Bt*. Organic farmers have used *Bt* as a major weapon in a limited arsenal to control insect damage to their crops, and many were disturbed by the prospect of needing a new weapon.

Gene transfer of engineered characteristics from crops to related weeds was also an issue. The transfer to weeds of resistance to drought, salinity, frost, bacteria, fungi, viruses, herbicides, and pesticides would make them more competitive with both crops and noncrop plants in the environment. Hardier weeds would be more difficult to manage, perhaps requiring stronger herbicides than those currently in use, and might outcompete other species of noncrop plants, diminishing species diversity.

—*Linda Sims Anderson*

## FURTHER READING

Avise, John C. *The Hope, Hype, and Reality of Genetic Engineering: Remarkable Stories from Agriculture, Industry, Medicine, and the Environment.* New York: Oxford University Press, 2004. Examines the potential of genetic engineering and provides examples of

1994

achievements and failures in the field. Includes discussion of the Flavr Savr tomato.

Ellstrand, Norman C., and Carol A. Hoffman. "Hybridization as an Avenue of Escape for Engineered Genes." *BioScience* 40 (June, 1990): 438-442. Presents clear discussion of the threat to plant species diversity and weed control proposed by natural crossbreeding between weeds and related domestic crops genetically engineered to withstand drought, frost, salinity, insects, and herbicides.

Gasser, Charles S., and Robert T. Fraley. "Genetically Engineering Plants for Crop Improvement." *Science* 244 (June 16, 1989): 1293-1296. Discusses issues from the biotechnology industry's standpoint, such as the need for patent protection to offset the cost of developing crops. Authors are employed by Monsanto, a leading agrichemical company.

Hindmarsh, Richard. "The Flawed 'Sustainable' Promise of Genetic Engineering." *Ecologist* 21 (September/October, 1991): 196-205. Presents an articulate, well-supported environmental argument against genetically engineered plants and biopesticides. Discusses the threat to organic farming and the hidden agenda behind the restructuring of the agrichemical industry.

Hubbard, Ruth, and Elijah Wald. "Genes for Sale." In *Exploding the Gene Myth: How Genetic Information Is Produced and Manipulated by Scientists, Physicians, Employers, Insurance Companies, Educators, and Law Enforcers.* Boston: Beacon Press, 1993. Examines the dangers posed by conflicts of interest resulting from the pervasive links between the biotechnology industry and university faculty members and administrators, who often hold patents on biotechnological developments or act as paid consultants to the industry yet testify as government experts on the safety of products and regulatory processes.

Kessler, David A. "Statement of Policy: Foods Derived from New Plant Varieties." *Federal Register* (May 29, 1992): 22964-23005. Provides an excellent, readable overview of the FDA's regulatory policy for genetically engineered foods.

Lee, Thomas F. "Field of Genes." In *Gene Future: The Promise and Perils of the New Biology.* New York: Plenum Press, 1993. Comprehensive discussion of the pros and cons of genetically engineered agricultural products. Presents the positions of the biotechnology industry, government regulatory agencies, and environmental groups with objectivity and balance.

McKelvey, Maureen. *Evolutionary Innovations: The Business of Biotechnology.* New York: Oxford University Press, 1996. Examines the commercial development of biotechnology. Features figures, bibliographic references, and index.

Suzuki, David, and Peter Knudtson. *Genethics: The Clash Between the New Genetics and Human Values.* Rev. ed. Cambridge, Mass.: Harvard University Press, 1990. Addresses the ethical issues that arise from the possibilities presented by DNA technology. Includes discussion of the importance of genetic diversity, recombinant DNA technology, and the use of plasmid for transferring genes from one species to another.

**SEE ALSO:** Apr. 7, 1976: Genentech Is Founded; 1980: Berg, Gilbert, and Sanger Develop Techniques for Genetic Engineering; June 16, 1980: U.S. Supreme Court Grants a Patent for a Living Organism; 1981-1982: Geneticists Create Giant Mice; May 14, 1982: Eli Lilly Releases the First Commercial Genetically Engineered Medication; July, 1986: FDA Approves a Genetically Engineered Vaccine for Hepatitis B; Apr. 24, 1987: Genetically Altered Bacteria Are Released into the Environment; May, 1988: Patent Is Granted for Genetically Engineered Mice; Aug., 1990: Genetically Engineered Rabies Vaccine Is Released.

## May 6, 1994
# OPENING OF THE CHANNEL TUNNEL

*With the opening of the Channel Tunnel, linking England with the Continent, a new age in European rail travel and freight movement began.*

**ALSO KNOWN AS:** The Chunnel
**LOCALE:** Folkestone, Kent, England, to Calais, France
**CATEGORIES:** Transportation; economics; engineering

### KEY FIGURES

*André Bénard* (fl. late twentieth century), French cochair of Eurotunnel
*Alastair Morton* (1938-2004), British cochair of Eurotunnel
*Margaret Thatcher* (b. 1925), prime minister of Great Britain, 1979-1990
*Elizabeth II* (b. 1926), queen of England beginning in 1952
*François Mitterrand* (1916-1996), president of France, 1981-1995

### SUMMARY OF EVENT

A tunnel that would allow people to travel beneath the English Channel between England and France had been considered a technological possibility since the eighteenth century, when scientists and engineers first proposed an underwater tunnel through which horse-drawn vehicles could pass. Progress on such a project was postponed repeatedly, however, because of economic difficulties and political tensions between England and France. Finally, in 1986, an Anglo-French consortium received a concession to construct the Channel Tunnel. The thirty-one-mile-long tunnel, which cost more than $15 billion to construct, was officially opened on May 6, 1994, in a ceremony attended by British and French leaders. Regular train service through the tunnel, however, was deferred to later in the year because of the need to test equipment. The Channel Tunnel, popularly known as the Chunnel, represented a phenomenal feat of engineering and became the most expensive infrastructure project ever financed privately up to that time.

Serious proposals for a tunnel under the English Channel date back more than two centuries. In 1802, Albert Mathieu-Favier, a French mining engineer, suggested to Napoleon that a tunnel "accessible to men, horses, and carriages" be dug in the chalk layer underneath the English Channel. Stagecoaches would travel through the tunnel; transit time was estimated at five hours. Renewed war between France and England killed the project, however. In the 1880's, private companies actually began work on a tunnel using primitive boring machines. More than a mile of tunnel was dug on each side of the Channel before work stopped when a press furor over the alleged threat to Britain's security caused the government to cancel the project in 1883.

In 1966, the French and British governments announced they would plan and build a tunnel under the Channel. Work began in 1974 but stopped the following year. With about a mile and a half of preliminary digging completed on each side of the Channel, the British government had to cancel the publicly financed project because of the cost. In 1978, British Railways and the French National Railways (SNCF) again began planning for a single-track rail tunnel. This later changed to a twin-tunnel plan.

*French president François Mitterrand and British prime minister Margaret Thatcher in Paris, France, where they ratified an agreement in 1987 for the construction of the Channel Tunnel connecting Great Britain and mainland Europe.* (AP/Wide World Photos)

1994

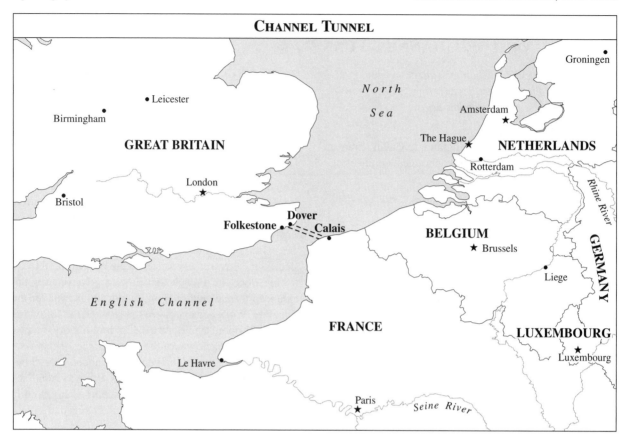

**CHANNEL TUNNEL**

Eventually, improvements in tunneling technology gave impetus to new Channel Tunnel plans. The primary barriers to such a project were now financial rather than technological or political. A new dimension entered the picture when banking studies showed that private financing was feasible.

The plan for a permanent cross-channel link was relaunched at a summit meeting between British prime minister Margaret Thatcher and French president François Mitterrand in September, 1981. This led to a study commission, which selected four plans for further consideration in 1985: a high suspension bridge, a bridge-tunnel road plus a railway tunnel, railway-road tunnels, and railway tunnels.

In January of 1986, a proposal by Eurotunnel (a combination of France Manche and the Channel Tunnel Group), based in London, was announced as the choice of both governments. The option chosen was a railroad system that included railroad trains and special rail shuttle trains (Le Shuttle) carrying road vehicles. Development of the project was agreed upon when Thatcher and Mitterrand signed the Franco-British Treaty of Canter-

bury in February, 1986. In March of 1986, a fifty-five-year concession was signed between the two governments and what would become the Eurotunnel Group, jointly led by André Bénard and Alastair Morton. The treaty and concession agreement were not effective, however, until legislation was passed in both countries in July, 1987.

The Channel Tunnel was to be privately financed (with stock sales and bank loans from several international banks) by a consortium of French and British firms. The project, which would enable high-speed trains to cut surface travel time between Paris and London in half, was considered to be a good investment.

Construction would be done by TransManche Link (*la Manche* is what the French call the English Channel), a consortium of five French and five British firms. Preliminary work began near Calais, France, in late 1986, and construction work began on the tunnel itself in December of 1987 with boring on the British side; boring on the French side began two months later. The Channel Tunnel actually comprises three individual tunnels with entrances near the French and English coasts, in

## June, 1994
# BALD EAGLE IS NO LONGER AN ENDANGERED SPECIES

*The status of the American bald eagle was reduced to "threatened," and the California gray whale was removed from the federal list of endangered species, confirming their comeback from the verge of extinction.*

**LOCALE:** United States
**CATEGORY:** Animals and endangered species

**KEY FIGURES**
*George Frampton* (b. 1944), assistant U.S. secretary of the interior for wildlife who was instrumental in strengthening the Endangered Species Act of 1973
*Mollie Beattie* (1947-1996), director of the U.S. Fish and Wildlife Service who announced plans to reclassify the bald eagle under the Endangered Species Act

**SUMMARY OF EVENT**
The Endangered Species Act of 1973, a cornerstone of federal environmental legislation, was set up to protect plant and animal species in danger of extinction. The act also enabled the protection of endangered local populations of species not generally at risk. Under the act, the U.S. Fish and Wildlife Service in the Department of the Interior and the National Marine Fisheries Service in the Department of Commerce were made responsible for designating a species as either endangered or, if its plight was somewhat less serious, threatened.

In 1994, twenty-one years after they had been officially classified as endangered, the American bald eagle and the California gray whale, both once threatened with extinction, were reclassified, the eagle as threatened and the whale as entirely recovered. Only three other species had until then been moved from the endangered to the threatened category: the American alligator, the Aleutian Canada goose, and the Arctic peregrine falcon.

In 1973, that most majestic of national symbols, the American bald eagle, was listed as endangered in all of the lower forty-eight states except Washington, Oregon, Minnesota, Wisconsin, and Michigan, where it was listed as threatened. (The bald eagle was not considered at risk in Alaska and so was not protected there under the Endangered Species Act.) The June, 1994, decision reclassified the bald eagle as threatened everywhere in the lower forty-eight states except parts of the Southwest (Arizona, New Mexico, western Texas, Oklahoma, and a small part of southeastern California), where it continued

to be listed as endangered. In 1974, shortly after the Endangered Species Act went into effect, only 791 adult nesting pairs of the eagle could be counted in the lower forty-eight states. By 1994, about 4,000 pairs were counted, and more than 9,700 pairs were counted in 2006. In 2007, the decision was made to remove the bald eagle from the endangered species list altogether.

Although the bald eagle had long been by far the most protected American bird—provisions for its protection were included in four previous federal laws—it was undoubtedly its inclusion on the endangered species list that led to the resurgence of its population. Unlike other laws, the Endangered Species Act gives the federal government unprecedented, sweeping powers to control the conditions affecting endangered animals. It is important that the designation "endangered" publicizes the plight of a species and influences wide-ranging policy decisions, but the act also specifies criminal penalties for harassing or killing protected animals. In addition, the act strictly controls construction projects and pollution in areas where such activities could be detrimental to wildlife, and it includes provisions for implementation of captive-breeding programs where necessary.

All of these factors contributed significantly to the success of the effort to save the bald eagle. Most conservationists agree, however, that the key to the bird's dramatic recovery was the Environmental Protection Agency's ban in 1972 on the use in the United States of the pesticide dichloro-diphenyl-trichloroethane (DDT), which was widely sprayed on crops and in suburban gardens in the post-World War II years. Predators such as the eagle were not exposed to the chemical directly; rather, they ingested large amounts of DDT through their diets of contaminated fish and small mammals. The chemical caused the eggs of certain birds, among them the bald eagle, to develop with thin shells that broke easily, leading to devastating effects on natural propagation.

Many of the other threats that had brought the bald eagle to its endangered state were still problematic after 1994. Shootings, disturbance of nests, and contamination continued to be serious threats, exacerbated by the pressures of human population growth and expansion and by the demand for the development of wildlands. Despite concern about the long-range implications of "downlisting" the bald eagle, however, U.S. Fish and Wildlife Service biologists believed that reclassifying the bird as threatened would not lead to relaxation of pro-

1994

*A bald eagle lands on its nest.* (U.S. Fish and Wildlife Service/Dave Menke)

tective measures already in place to protect both the species and its habitats. These measures proved to be strong enough to allow the species to continue to recover, as its removal from the endangered species list in 2007 showed.

The news of the bald eagle's recovery was preceded by the announcement of an even greater success with the California gray whale, which had been considered to be endangered since the early 1970's. On January 7, 1993, the U.S. Fish and Wildlife Service and the National Marine Fisheries determined that the whale, the habitat of which is the eastern North Pacific, had recovered to near its estimated original population. (Its western North Pacific cousin, the Korean gray whale, remained on the endangered list.) The recovery of the California gray whale population resulted in large part from Mexico's efforts to protect the whale's calving and winter habitat. According to the National Oceanic and Atmospheric Administration, there may have been more California gray whales in 1994 than at any time before commercial whaling reached its peak in the mid-1880's. In California waters

alone, the gray whale population doubled between 1974 and 1994.

### SIGNIFICANCE

The Endangered Species Act was scheduled for reauthorization in 1994, soon after the momentous decision was made public to reclassify the American bald eagle from endangered to threatened. That announcement not only publicized the eagle's resurgence but also represented an enormous popular success for environmental legislation. Despite objections from interest groups and a few members of Congress who wanted to weaken the act, a bill to reauthorize and improve the Endangered Species Act was passed by the 103d Congress. A major goal of the reauthorized Endangered Species Act was to prevent species from becoming endangered in the first place. The act therefore included provisions for protecting species that did not qualify for the threatened or endangered designation but whose populations were declining.

The reauthorized act had three other main objectives as well. The first was to plan not only for single species but also for entire ecosystems. One criticism leveled at the 1973 act had been that it attempted to recover species one at a time. The strengthened 1994 bill called for the development of multispecies listings and recovery plans to address the need of all species within a particular ecosystem. A second objective was the improvement of recovery plans for all listed species through participation by state agencies and local communities. Because so much of the critical habitat for endangered species exists on privately owned land, a third objective involved building more effective partnerships with private citizens; it was hoped that economic incentives and technical assistance to landowners would help in the effort to preserve habitats.

News of the eagle's recovery was politically advantageous for the Fish and Wildlife Service in its lobbying for congressional funding, and it certainly helped bring about the strengthened 1994 Endangered Species Act. Most of the money and expertise available under the old act had gone to megavertebrates such as the bald eagle. It was hoped that the 1994 act would promote interest in preserving regional habitats and less glamorous species, such as invertebrates and plants, on which ecosystems and the global equilibrium depend.

*—Elizabeth Brafford and Ruth Bamberger*

**FURTHER READING**

Beans, Bruce E. *Eagle's Plume: Preserving the Life and Habitat of America's Bald Eagle*. New York: Charles Scribner's Sons, 1996. Provides an encouraging look at locations where bald eagles are thriving and relates stories of humans' efforts to assist the birds. Also discusses some human beings' carelessness with the eagle and its habitats.

Dedina, Serge. *Saving the Gray Whale: People, Politics, and Conservation in Baja California*. Tucson: University of Arizona Press, 2000. Describes the gray whale's life cycle, habitats, and history while focusing on a movement in Mexico to protect the whale, whose migratory route includes the waters off Baja California. Features illustrations and maps.

DiSilvestro, Roger L. *The Endangered Kingdom: The Struggle to Save America's Wildlife*. New York: John Wiley & Sons, 1989. Presents a detailed account of American wildlife protected by the Endangered Species Act. Includes a foreword by noted environmentalist and population scholar Paul Ehrlich.

Graham, Frank, Jr. "Winged Victory." *Audubon* (July/August, 1994): 36-41. Relates the history of the bald eagle's plight and the efforts made on its behalf.

Kòhm, Kathryn A., ed. *Balancing on the Brink of Extinction: The Endangered Species Act and Lessons for the Future*. Washington, D.C.: Island Press, 1991. Collection of essays discusses the history, mechanics, and implications of the Endangered Species Act. Provides useful background for understanding the classification and recovery processes.

Peyser, Marc. "Between a Wing and a Prayer." *Newsweek*, September 19, 1994, 58-60. Discusses the conflicting claims of the Eagle Protection Act and the Religious Freedom Restoration Act of 1993, as exemplified in a Yakima Native American's conviction for killing bald eagles, the feathers of which he used for religious purposes.

**SEE ALSO:** Dec. 31, 1972: U.S. Government Bans DDT; Mar. 3, 1973: International Convention Protects Endangered Species; Dec. 28, 1973: U.S. Congress Protects Endangered Species; 1975: Atlantic Salmon Return to the Connecticut River; June 15, 1978: U.S. Supreme Court Protects the Snail Darter; Jan. 1, 1986: International Whaling Ban Goes into Effect; July 23, 1990: Spotted Owl Prompts Old-Growth Timber Controversy; 1991-1992: Captive-Bred Condors and Ferrets Are Reintroduced into the Wild; 1993: Norway Resumes Whaling in Defiance of International Ban.

---

## June 12, 1994
# BOEING'S 777 TAKES TO THE SKIES

*On June 12, 1994, the largest twin-engine plane in operation, the Boeing 777 jumbo jet, ascended on its maiden flight, confirming a new era in airplane design and construction. The three-hour, forty-eight-minute flight proved that Boeing had successfully created a more affordable, customer-oriented aircraft.*

**LOCALE:** Everett, Washington
**CATEGORIES:** Spaceflight and aviation; engineering; science and technology

**KEY FIGURES**
*Richard R. Albrecht* (b. 1945), executive vice president and general manager of Boeing Commercial Airplane Group
*Phil M. Condit* (b. 1941), executive vice president and general manager of the New Airplane Program for Boeing and later president and chief executive officer of Boeing

*James M. Guyette* (b. 1945), executive vice president of operations for United Air Lines
*Alan Roger Mulally* (b. 1945), general manager of the Boeing 777 project and subsequently vice president of engineering for the Boeing Commercial Airplane Group, then president of Boeing
*Stephen M. Wolf* (b. 1941), chairman and chief executive officer of UAL Corporation and United Air Lines, 1987-1994

**SUMMARY OF EVENT**
In 1986, Boeing foresaw a marketing opportunity in creating a new 700 series plane that would replace fleets of aging wide-body commercial aircraft. Preliminary research indicated that a large tri- or twin-engine airplane that fell between Boeing's 767 and 747 series in size, carrying 305-440 passengers, would best suit customer demand. Initial production proposals considered stretching and revamping the 767, but in October, 1988, Boeing's

corporate board recommended the creation of an entirely new plane.

Starting anew allowed Boeing the opportunity to elicit recommendations directly from its customers, the airlines. In January, 1990, eight airlines—All Nippon Airways, American Airlines, British Airways, Cathay Pacific, Delta Air Lines, Japan Airlines, Qantas, and United—the "Gang of Eight," met for the first session of their project, called Working Together. Meetings, discussions, and surveys soon proved that the airlines desired a large, long-range, wide-body, technologically advanced aircraft that was more economical to operate and maintain.

In October, 1990, James M. Guyette, executive vice president of operations at United Air Lines, led a seventy-hour meeting that ended in the airline's selection of the new Boeing 777, with its Pratt & Whitney engine, as its next aircraft purchase. After the meeting, Guyette hand-drafted a one-page objectives agreement between United and Boeing that launched a new phase in aircraft history. The pact, signed by Boeing's executive vice presidents Phil M. Condit and Richard R. Albrecht, was an agreement to work together to create a Boeing 777 that surpassed previous goals. This accord gave United much greater input during the planning and designing stages of the aircraft. In return, Stephen M. Wolf, chairman of United Air Lines, Incorporated, promised Boeing an order for thirty-four aircraft and an option for thirty-four more.

In April, 1991, Boeing signed another liaison agreement, this time with IBM and Dassault Systèmes, a French software company. This simple document created a working relationship that allowed the Boeing 777 to become the first jetliner to be totally digitally designed with three-dimensional graphics known as CATIA (Computer Aided Three-dimensional Interactive Application). Working collectively, these three companies created a system that interconnected thousands of computers and allowed designers, developers, engineers, and manufacturers across the world ready access to important tools and information. This second "working together" agreement was the catalyst that permitted the Boeing 777's project plans to be completed without any paper drawings. Prototypes were designed and assembled online, creating the world's first virtually drafted commercial jetliner.

With networking capabilities in place, the designing and building teams assigned to the project—under the direction of Alan Roger Mulally—could move forward with their various responsibilities and work jointly to assure that the new aircraft would successfully meet their objectives. Among the many goals to be achieved were:

meeting long-range flying requirements, mechanical soundness and dependability, more aerodynamic wings, pleasant and flexible cabin design, appropriate cargo space, and state-of-the-art flying technology. The objectives required the development of new, advanced materials, including titanium alloy and stronger resins critical in reducing weight load while creating a stronger, less corrosive airplane.

New systems and software needed to be created to support two-person operation of this large commercial airliner. Customer demand also necessitated the ability to install jet engines from all three major engine manufacturers: Pratt & Whitney, Rolls-Royce, and General Electric. From across the globe, teams met and worked online to design new parts, enhance existing components from the Boeing 767, and test systems. Customer-training teams worked simultaneously to create effective training manuals and software tools. Efficiency and productivity required online creation to be followed by real-world testing of components in a new, highly refined parts testing lab. Thousands of people from dozens of industries worked to create a new aircraft that not only met all flying requirements on delivery but did so on time.

On June 12, 1994, the initial Boeing 777 left the runway in Everett, Washington, on the first of more than three hundred test flights. Over the next twenty-two months, eight additional test planes, four more with Pratt & Whitney engines for United Air Lines, two with Rolls-Royce engines for Cathay Pacific, and two with General Electric engines for British Airways, joined the test program and logged a total of nearly seven thousand flight hours. Testing was conducted around the world to provide real-life evaluations in various hot, cold, and windy weather scenarios.

On May 15, 1995, after having received certification from both the U.S. Federal Aviation Administration (FAA) and the European Joint Aviation Authorities (JAA), Boeing delivered United Air Lines' first Boeing 777. Fifteen days later, the FAA gave unprecedented 180-minute, extended-range twin-engine operations (ETOPS) certification to the Boeing 777's with Pratt & Whitney engines. In October, 1996, the Rolls-Royce and General Electric engines were also granted ETOPS status. This allowed the plane to be flown up to three hours away from a qualified landing airport. Granting ETOPS certification to an aircraft that had just been brought into service was exceptional; two-engine planes typically required two years of commercial use before being granted this status. The Boeing 777 was permitted to skip this testing process and fly almost anywhere in the world.

On June 7, 1995, the Boeing 777 flew its first commercial flight for United Air Lines. The aircraft, with a Pratt & Whitney engine, left London Heathrow Airport for Dulles International Airport, near Washington, D.C. Years of teamwork, effort, and planning had resulted in the Boeing 777's first revenue-generating flight.

### SIGNIFICANCE

The Boeing 777 was the largest twin-engine aircraft ever built. The designers used state-of-the-art computer systems to create the first computer-designed commercial aircraft. This innovative technology connected thousands of aircraft developers in cyberspace in a timely fashion, and proved to be a more cost-effective method of creating and assembling mock-ups. Global communication systems, strong customer relations, effective design and building teams, advanced resources, digital design, and timely compliance testing were the major dynamics that made the Boeing 777 a remarkable feat of ingenuity and teamwork.

The Boeing 777 received several prestigious awards. On February 15, 1996, the National Aeronautic Association awarded Boeing the Robert J. Collier Trophy for "designing, manufacturing, and placing into service the world's most technologically advanced airline transport." The aircraft also received the Industrial Design Excellence Award in 1992 and 1993 and the 1996 Trophy for Current Achievement from the Smithsonian Institution's National Air and Space Museum. By the early years of the twenty-first century, six Boeing 777 models were in use, and the technology and materials developed in the race to design the Boeing 777 were being used effectively by numerous other industries.

*—Cynthia J. W. Svoboda*

### FURTHER READING

Lynn, Matthew. *Birds of Prey: Boeing vs. Airbus, a Battle for the Skies*. New York: Four Walls Eight Windows, 1997. Reviews the operations and product-idea processes of Boeing and Airbus.

McKinzie, Gordon A. "How United and Boeing Worked Together to Design and Build the 777 Airplane." *National Productivity Review* 16 (Winter, 1996): 7-14. Explains United Air Lines' and Boeing's process in setting up the "work together" design team that was instrumental in creating the Boeing 777.

Norris, Guy, and Mark Wagner. *Boeing 777: The Technical Marvel*. Osceola, Wis.: MBI, 2001. Illustrated guide to the history and production of the Boeing 777.

Petroski, Henry. "The Boeing 777." *American Scientist* 83 (November/December, 1995): 519-522. Discusses the engineering feats inherent in the design of the Boeing 777.

Sabbagh, Karl. *Twenty-First Century Jet: The Making and Marketing of the Boeing 777*. New York: Scribner, 1996. Details the creation process in the design of the Boeing 777.

Sharma, K. J., and B. Bowonder. "The Making of Boeing 777: A Case Study in Concurrent Engineering." *International Journal of Manufacturing Technology and Management* 6, nos. 3-4 (2004): 254-264. Outlines the agreements and coordination processes that went into the creation of a new jet.

Smith, Brian. "The Boeing 777: The Development of the Boeing 777 Was Made Possible by the Development of Breakthrough Materials That Allowed Reductions in Structural Weight While Maintaining Affordability." *Advanced Materials and Processes* 161 (September, 2003): 41-45. Highlights the new materials that made the Boeing 777 possible.

**SEE ALSO:** Jan. 21, 1976: Concorde Flies Passengers at Supersonic Speeds; July 1, 1976: Smithsonian Opens the National Air and Space Museum; Oct. 24, 1978: Deregulation of the U.S. Airline Industry.

1994

## July 8, 1994
# KIM JONG IL SUCCEEDS HIS FATHER IN NORTH KOREA

*Kim Jong Il became North Korea's president following the death of his father, Kim Il Sung, in 1994. This dynastic succession was unprecedented in a communist country and came at a time of domestic and international crisis for the isolated nation. The aftermath of the Soviet Union's collapse tested North Korea's stability and Kim Jong Il's authority. Conditions inside North Korea worsened while its leadership faced the world with a mixture of diplomacy and defiance.*

**LOCALE:** P'yŏngyang, North Korea
**CATEGORY:** Government and politics

**KEY FIGURES**

*Kim Jong Il* (b. 1941), president of North Korea beginning in 1994

*Kim Il Sung* (1912-1994), premier, 1948-1972, and president of North Korea, 1972-1994

*Jimmy Carter* (b. 1924), president of the United States, 1977-1981

*Bill Clinton* (b. 1946), president of the United States, 1993-2001

*Kim Dae Jung* (b. 1924), president of South Korea, 1998-2003

**SUMMARY OF EVENT**

Known officially as the Democratic People's Republic of Korea, North Korea experienced its first and so far only leadership change when Kim Jong Il replaced his father, Kim Il Sung, as the communist nation's president in 1994. Although Kim Jong Il had been identified within North Korea as his father's successor as early as 1980, there was uncertainty about his character and qualifications. Kim Jong Il faced the difficult tasks of living up to the mythical legacy of his father, of preserving North Korea's communist regime after the Soviet Union's collapse, and of dealing with longtime enemies Japan, South Korea, and the United States. Despite severe poverty and famine inside North Korea and an increasingly adversarial relationship with the United States, Kim Jong Il exercises absolute control over his nation more than a decade after Kim Il Sung's death.

The death of Kim Il Sung on July 8, 1994, raised doubts about the survival of North Korea, the nation he had dominated since its founding in 1948. Revered as "supreme leader," Kim Il Sung relied on a cult of personality similar to those of the Soviet Union's Joseph Stalin

and China's Mao Zedong to establish and maintain authoritarian rule. The seeds of Kim Il Sung's self-presentation were sowed prior to World War II when he led guerrilla insurgencies against Japan's brutal colonial occupation and developed ties with the Soviet Union. Contrary to his official biography, Kim Jong Il was born in the Soviet Union during one of his father's sojourns in that nation, not in Korea. The post-World War II division of the Korean peninsula prompted Kim Il Sung to invade its southern half in a reunification bid, triggering the 1950-1953 Korean War as the first major Cold War confrontation. The war ended in a stalemate that left the Koreas divided and Kim Il Sung determined to preserve his notion of Korean sovereignty through totalitarianism.

Whether or not his image as the embodiment of Korean independence and nationalism combined with

*North Korean leader Kim Jong Il waves to P'yŏngyang residents at the fiftieth anniversary of the founding of the ruling Workers' Party of Korea on October 10, 1995.* (AP/Wide World Photos)

elements of Marxism and Leninism was authentic, the power that Kim Il Sung maintained for more than four decades was unquestionably real and total.

Kim Il Sung's death would have been difficult for North Koreans at any point in their history but was especially problematic in the mid-1990's given the nation's domestic and international circumstances. The consequences of the end of Soviet and Eastern European communism put economic and political pressure on North Korea, with reunification of East and West Germany representing a dangerous precedent for the communist regime. Regarding North Korea's relations with the United States, which have been punctuated by crises since the latter's founding in 1948, the aftermath of the Cold War put more rather than less pressure on Kim Il Sung. His nation's nuclear program was the flash point. In 1992, North Korea prevented inspections mandated by an agreement with the International Atomic Energy Agency. The following year brought a report by the Central Intelligence Agency of the United States charging North Korea with possession of one or more nuclear weapons. Concerns arose over whether those weapons threatened Japan, South Korea, or even the United States, which came close to military intervention on the Korean peninsula in late 1993 and early 1994.

At this critical point, Kim Il Sung startled the world with pragmatic actions aimed at decreasing tensions. He made diplomatic moves and welcomed emissaries from the United States, most notably the former president Jimmy Carter. The June, 1994, meeting of Carter and Kim Il Sung in North Korea was a controversial and promising event that made Bill Clinton's presidential administration hopeful yet apprehensive. The talks led to the Agreed Framework, an initiative designed to ease economic sanctions imposed on North Korea, encourage further diplomacy, and curtail North Korea's nuclear program in exchange for oil. Formal talks on the Agreed Framework were set to start July 8, 1994, but Kim Il Sung's sudden death put rapprochement between North Korea and the United States on hold and focused attention on Kim Jong Il, who decreed a long period of national mourning.

North Korea's internal problems and its precarious

---

## TOTALITARIANISM FATIGUE

*In 2006, Andrew Scobell, an associate research professor for the Strategic Studies Institute, published* Kim Jong Il and North Korea: The Leader and the System. *Scobell's introduction considers the nature, and future, of Kim Jong Il's government:*

A variety of labels are given to the North Korean regime. These include likening the regime to an organized crime family and to a corporatist organism. . . . Pyongyang does share some of the attributes of organized crime and certainly engages in criminal activity in a systematic and calculating manner. This pattern of illicit behavior includes the production and distribution of narcotics as well as the counterfeiting of foreign currencies, cigarettes, and pharmaceuticals. But the [Democratic People's Republic of Korea] DPRK is more than a crime family; it possesses a massive conventional military force as well as significant strategic forces. . . .

The most accurate way to characterize North Korea today is as an eroding totalitarian regime. While totalitarianism is a powerful and intimidating system, it places tremendous strain on a state and a society—demanding constant activity and mobilization of personnel and exploitation of resources. The costs of maintaining heightened ideological indoctrination, an ever-vigilant coercive apparatus, and a large national defense organization are high and ultimately debilitating. . . .

An absolute dictator still rules the regime. While the regime continues to hold a monopoly of the instruments of coercion, there has been some slippage or erosion in the defining features of totalitarianism. First of all, Kim Jong Il, although he is virtually an absolute dictator, appears to take into account the opinions of others the way his father did not. And ideology no longer appears to be so focused on transforming the state and society and more on the instrumental goals of economic recovery, development, and firming up regime power. . . . As a result of the shift in ideology and alleviation of the climate of terror, the regime has become corrupted literally as bribery is rampant, and figuratively as the regime seeks to preserve its power and status.

---

global position were daunting challenges facing Kim Jong Il during the power transition from his father. Deprived of Soviet subsidies, the nation's economy was deteriorating and would suffer a 25 to 40 percent gross national product decrease during the 1994-2000 period. Famine broke out in the mid-1990's, persisted throughout the decade, and claimed the lives of hundreds of thousands, perhaps one million North Koreans. Reinforcement and adaptation of his father's personality cult permitted Kim Jong Il to gain control over North Korean military and political institutions he needed to survive these and many more problems, including defections of high government officials. Continuity with Kim Il Sung's *juche* (self-reliance) ideology, which drew from Marxist-Leninist theory on one hand and Korean-

1994

Confucian traditions on the other, was imperative for Kim Jong Il.

During the latter half of the 1990's, Kim Jong Il displayed some of his father's talent for deal-making and diplomacy aimed at crisis management, even if these initiatives bolstered his own power more than the welfare of North Koreans. Starting in 1995, North Korea joined the United Nations World Food Program, which helped it deal with catastrophic famines, floods, and unfavorable agricultural conditions. Surging numbers of North Korean refugees in 1996 and 1997 brought more aid from China. However, the long history of hostility between North Korea and Japan showed no signs of improving, as shown by Japan's concerns over North Korea's weapons development and the kidnapping of Japanese citizens by North Korean agents. Finally, military action by the United States remained a possibility, not only because of North Korea's nuclear program but also in the event of instability on the Korean peninsula should conditions inside North Korea spill over the borders.

Surprisingly, the dawn of the twenty-first century found Kim Jong Il and his South Korean counterparts making diplomatic progress despite the dire state of North Korea and the volatility of its relations with the United States. South Korea's president Kim Dae Jung took a risk with his "sunshine policy," seeking a degree of partnership with the North. Kim Dae Jung's 2000 meeting with Kim Jong Il in P'yŏngyang was dramatic, but some South Koreans questioned its substance. There were negative consequences for Kim Dae Jung when Kim Jong Il failed to visit Seoul. Positive results of the sunshine policy addressed several areas affected by the Korean War, such as reunification of Korean families, trade and transportation between the North and South, and the need to defuse military antagonisms between the Koreas. Without overstating the success of these overtures in the still-divided Korean peninsula, North Korea's subsequent moves to establish relationships with several European countries were notable. Moreover, North Korea's rulers took tentative steps away from their failed centrally planned economy and implemented modest local reforms to alleviate privation.

Of course, none of these developments change the totalitarian nature of Kim Jong Il's power, which continues to have negative consequences for the majority of North Koreans and which U.S. president George W. Bush used as justification for his 2002 inclusion of North Korea in the so-called axis of evil, along with Iran and Iraq.

## SIGNIFICANCE

Despite the common description of North Korea as the world's last Stalinist state, the inheritance by Kim Jong Il of his father's absolute power shows that leadership in North Korea involves more than adherence to communism. Understanding this nation and its ruler are difficult given North Korea's secrecy and the prevalence of depictions (especially in the United States) of Kim Jong Il as a cipher, lunatic, and terrorist. Without excusing any aspect of Kim Jong Il's despotism and its effects on people inside and outside North Korea, the role of cultural, historical, and familial factors in his survival and that of his country must be addressed. A more complex approach to analyzing the persistence of the Kim Jong Il regime in a world where he and North Korea have long been expected to go the way of previous communist leaders and countries is necessary to comprehend, and perhaps to solve, the national, regional, and global problems that Kim Jong Il poses for the twenty-first century.

—*Ray Pence*

## FURTHER READING

Armstrong, Charles K. *The Koreas*. New York: Routledge, 2007. Situates North and South Korea in a contemporary context of globalization and addresses complexities of Korean national and individual identities.

Cumings, Bruce. *North Korea: Another Country*. New York: New Press, 2004. Drawing from his personal experience as a traveler in North Korea, the author offers a provocative portrait of the enigmatic nation.

French, Paul. *North Korea, the Paranoid Peninsula: A Modern History*. London: Zed Books, 2005. Seeks to provide a nuanced history while critiquing North Korea's economic and political rigidity.

Suh, Dae-Sook, and Chae-Jin Lee, eds. *North Korea After Kim il-Sung*. Boulder, Colo.: Lynne Rienner, 1998. Anthology of scholarly essays dealing with the transition from Kim Il Sung to Kim Jong Il and its immediate and future impact on North Korea.

SEE ALSO: Oct. 21, 1994: U.S.-North Korea Pact; 1995-1998: Famine Strikes North Korea.

## July 16-22, 1994
# COMET SHOEMAKER-LEVY 9 COLLIDES WITH JUPITER

*When more than twenty fragments from Comet Shoemaker-Levy 9 collided with the upper atmosphere of Jupiter, the event offered scientists the opportunity to witness the consequences of the collision of extraterrestrial objects and provided insights into the likely effects of asteroid or comet impacts on Earth.*

**ALSO KNOWN AS:** D/1993 F2; SL9
**LOCALE:** Jupiter
**CATEGORIES:** Astronomy; science and technology

### KEY FIGURES

*Eugene Merle Shoemaker* (1928-1997), American geologist and codiscoverer of Comet Shoemaker-Levy 9

*Carolyn Shoemaker* (b. 1929), American astronomer and codiscoverer of Comet Shoemaker-Levy 9

*David H. Levy* (b. 1948), Canadian astronomer, science writer, and codiscoverer of Comet Shoemaker-Levy 9

*Brian G. Marsden* (b. 1937), British astronomer who showed that Shoemaker-Levy 9 was in orbit around Jupiter

### SUMMARY OF EVENT

From July 16 to July 22, 1994, more than twenty fragments of Comet Shoemaker-Levy 9, which had been ripped apart by Jupiter's gravity during an earlier encounter with the planet, collided with the atmosphere of Jupiter. These collisions deposited more energy into the atmosphere of Jupiter than would be produced by all of the nuclear weapons in the military arsenals around the world. These impacts, which were observed from Earth and from spacecraft, provided astronomers with their first opportunity to witness a cosmic collision of a size capable of causing global consequences. The impacts produced bright fireballs in Jupiter's atmosphere and new cloud features visible from Earth.

Comet Shoemaker-Levy 9 was discovered by Eugene Merle Shoemaker, Carolyn Shoemaker, and David H. Levy in photographs taken on March 24, 1993. These photographs were taken using a 0.46-meter diameter Schmidt camera, a low-power telescope with a high light-gathering capability, at the Mount Palomar Observatory in Southern California. A Schmidt camera is designed so that it can see dim objects, and it has a wide field of view, making it an ideal instrument to search a large area of the sky for faint objects such as comets and asteroids. Shoemaker-Levy 9 was the ninth comet discovered by this group of researchers.

The comet was very dim—having a brightness of 13.8, much fainter than the dimmest object that can be seen with the human eye or with binoculars—when it was discovered. Still, it appeared unusual in the photographs, being slightly elongated. Once the position of Shoemaker-Levy 9 was determined, other observers looked at it with telescopes having higher magnification. Photographs taken by John Scotti, an astronomer using the Spacewatch telescope on Kitt Peak, Arizona, showed that Shoemaker-Levy 9 was not a single object but was actually several distinct objects spread out along the same path in space. Astronomers referred to the comet as "a string of pearls" because its bright fragments were distributed in a line along its orbital path. Astronomers wondered what caused Shoemaker-Levy 9 to break into pieces. Other comets had been seen breaking up when they came close to the Sun, but the initial determination of the orbit of Shoemaker-Levy 9 showed that it had not passed close to the Sun.

Within days of its discovery, the comet had been observed by astronomers at the University of Hawaii and the McDonald Observatory in Texas. By April, 1993, these and other observations allowed Brian G. Marsden to determine that Shoemaker-Levy 9, instead of orbiting the Sun as is typical for comets, was actually in orbit around Jupiter.

Other researchers were able to trace the history of the comet's orbit. They determined that the comet passed only 15,500 miles above the clouds of Jupiter, within 1.4 Jupiter radii of the planet's center, on July 7, 1992. They suggested that during this close approach, the difference between the gravitational force Jupiter exerted on the near and far sides of the comet had ripped the weak comet into many pieces.

Shoemaker-Levy 9 had been in a rapidly changing orbit around Jupiter for several decades. The comet did not fragment during earlier encounters with Jupiter because it had approached no closer than about five million miles in its previous orbits. Analysis of high-resolution photographs taken by the National Aeronautics and Space Administration (NASA) Hubble Space Telescope in July, 1993, as well as images taken after the Hubble repair mission, which greatly improved the resolution, showed at least twenty-three discrete fragments, which were assigned letters A through W. The brightness of the Hubble

1994

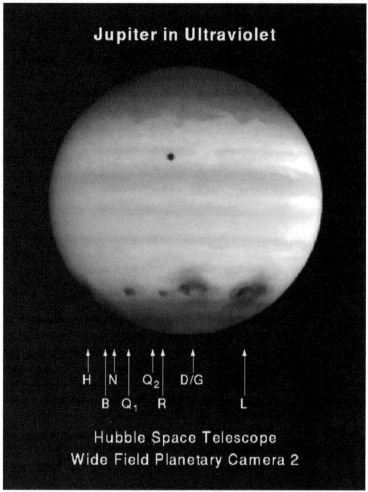

*An ultraviolet image of Jupiter taken by the Hubble Space Telescope on July 21, 1994, shows a number of fragments from Comet Shoemaker-Levy 9 that struck the planet's southern hemisphere. These fragments were embedded in clouds of debris, which appear very dark in the ultraviolet photo, as dust absorbs sunlight. (NASA/JPL)*

explosive effect equivalent to between 6 million and 250 million megatons of TNT.

In the two-year period between the breakup of the comet and the collision with Jupiter, the fragments had spread out along the comet's orbit. The impacts, which took place over a one-week period from July 16 through July 22, 1994, caused enormous fireballs in the atmosphere of Jupiter and produced large, dark storms. Fragments G and H, each about 1.5 miles in diameter, caused the most destruction.

The first two impacts occurred on a part of Jupiter that was facing away from the Earth, so the impacts were not directly observable from Earth. However, astronomers were able to see the bright clouds of debris as they rose over the edge of the planet. An hour later, as Jupiter rotated, the impact sites became visible, and the extent of the damage was clear. The impacts had left dark scars in the atmosphere of Jupiter.

The observation of Shoemaker-Levy 9's impact with Jupiter was a once-in-a-lifetime event for astronomers. The disruption of a comet into many fragments is an unusual event. Capture of a comet into an orbit around Jupiter is even more unusual, and the collision of a large comet with a planet is extremely rare, estimated to occur only once in a thousand years.

### SIGNIFICANCE

Sixty-five million years ago, Earth was struck by a large asteroid, an event which may have brought about the extinction of the dinosaurs. However, exactly what took place as the object passed through Earth's atmosphere has only been modeled, never verified, by experiment. The enormous release of energy into the atmosphere cannot be produced by humans, even with the use of nuclear bombs. Thus the Shoemaker-Levy 9 impacts into the atmosphere of Jupiter provided the first opportunity to observe this type of event and to validate the models, allowing scientists to determine with better accuracy the likely effects of impacts of asteroids or comets on Earth.

Shoemaker-Levy 9's impact on Jupiter provided graphic visual evidence of the destructive power of comet

images suggested that the visible fragments ranged in size from one-half mile to about one mile, with the fragments G and H being the largest. These visible fragments were embedded in a cloud of debris with material ranging from boulder-sized to microscopic particles.

By late May, 1993, it appeared that Shoemaker-Levy 9 was likely to hit Jupiter in 1994, and the fragments would be moving at a speed of about 130,000 miles per hour relative to the planet. At that point, the comet became the subject of intense study by astronomers around the world, since a cosmic collision of that magnitude had never been observed before. Based on the size and speed of each of the fragments, the impacts were expected to produce an and asteroid impacts on a planet. Governments around the world began to recognize the consequences such an event would have if it occurred on Earth. The event resulted in a more ambitious effort to discover and track asteroids and comets that approach Earth.

The impacts also allowed scientists to study Jupiter. The dark spots in the atmosphere were quickly distorted in shape, serving as a tracer to map the winds on Jupiter. Ultraviolet observations from the Hubble Space Telescope showed the debris sinking into Jupiter's atmosphere, providing the third dimension in the motion of Jupiter's winds. Observations also led to the suggestion that linear chains of craters, previously observed on two of Jupiter's moons, Ganymede and Callisto, might have formed by the impact of bodies disrupted in the same way as Shoemaker-Levy 9.

—*George J. Flynn*

**FURTHER READING**

Levy, David H. *Impact Jupiter: The Crash of Shoemaker-Levy 9*. New York: Basic Books, 2003. Well-illustrated, nontechnical account of the impact of Comet Shoemaker-Levy 9 into Jupiter. Discusses how the event changed the understanding of comets and cosmic cataclysms.

_____. *Shoemaker by Levy: The Man Who Made an Impact*. Princeton, N.J.: Princeton University Press, 2000. Account of the life of Eugene Shoemaker, in-

cluding the events that led to the discovery of Shoemaker-Levy 9, and Shoemaker's work on the effects of comet and asteroid collisions with Earth and other heavenly bodies.

Noll, Keith, Harold A. Weaver, and Paul D. Feldman, eds. *The Collision of Comet Shoemaker-Levy 9 and Jupiter*. New York: Cambridge University Press, 2006. A 388-page collection of scientific reports presenting the major scientific results from observation of the impacts.

Shoemaker, Gene, Carolyn Shoemaker, John R. Spencer, and Jacqueline Mitton. *The Great Comet Crash: The Collision of Comet Shoemaker-Levy 9 and Jupiter*. New York: Cambridge University Press, 1995. Collection of images from telescopes around the world showing Comet Shoemaker-Levy 9 and the effects of its collision with Jupiter.

**SEE ALSO:** Feb., 1973-Mar., 1974: Organic Molecules Are Discovered in Comet Kohoutek; Aug. 20, 1977-Oct. 2, 1989: Voyagers 1 and 2 Explore the Outer Planets; June 6, 1980: Scientists Find Evidence of an Asteroid Impact at the End of the Cretaceous Period; Mar. 8, 1986: Space Probes Begin Examination of Comet Halley; Jan. 30, 1996: Comet Hyakutake Is Discovered; Nov. 29, 1996: Asteroid Toutatis Passes Near Earth; Feb. 14, 2000: Near Earth Asteroid Rendezvous Spacecraft Orbits a Small Body.

## July 31, 1994
# UNITED NATIONS AUTHORIZES THE USE OF FORCE IN HAITI

*With the collapse of the Governors Island Agreement, the U.N. Security Council, growing increasingly impatient with the intransigence and human rights abuses of the Raoul Cédras regime in Haiti, authorized the use of force to remove his junta and to restore the legitimately elected government of Jean-Bertrand Aristide.*

**LOCALE:** Haiti
**CATEGORIES:** United Nations; diplomacy and international relations; government and politics

**KEY FIGURES**
*Jean-Bertrand Aristide* (b. 1953), president of Haiti, 1991, 1994-1996, and 2001-2004
*Raoul Cédras* (b. 1949), leader of the military regime that ruled Haiti, 1991-1994

*George H. W. Bush* (b. 1924), president of the United States, 1989-1993
*Bill Clinton* (b. 1946), president of the United States, 1993-2001

**SUMMARY OF EVENT**
On July 31, 1994, the U.N. Security Council authorized the use of force to depose a military junta led by Lieutenant General Raoul Cédras that had been ruling Haiti illegally and to restore Jean-Bertrand Aristide as the democratically elected president. The decision not only had ramifications for the governance of Haiti but also set a precedent in U.N. Security Council policy.

In 1991, Aristide was elected president in Haiti's first truly democratic election. Aristide was a Catholic priest who had been suspended from the Salesian Order for his advocacy of violent revolution and his support for the

1994

liberation theology movement. Through a radio program, he had become a prominent figure in Haitian politics and media. He was highly opposed to U.S. intervention in Haiti.

Shortly after his election, Aristide was overthrown by a military coup d'état and replaced as president by Raoul Cédras. While U.S. president George H. W. Bush condemned the coup and called for a return to democracy, he did not specifically express support for Aristide. He also refused to take any action to intervene in the situation, other than calling for sanctions against the military regime and an embargo on all goods except food and medical supplies coming into Haiti.

During his campaign preceding the 1992 U.S. presidential election, Bill Clinton took a more vocal stance on the Haiti issue. Thousands of Haitian refugees, known as boat people, had been crossing the Gulf of Mexico to Florida, only to be sent back to Haiti. Clinton promised to accept the Haitian boat people into the United States, although it was not until 1994 that he fulfilled this promise. In his first months as president, Clinton sent a special envoy to Haiti to begin putting pressure on the military government, and he began rallying international support. While many of the constituent groups within Clinton's own Democratic Party called for more direct intervention in Haiti, the majority of the American public opposed such intervention.

The U.N. Security Council passed several resolutions

*U.S. troops in Haiti in 1994.* (AP/Wide World Photos)

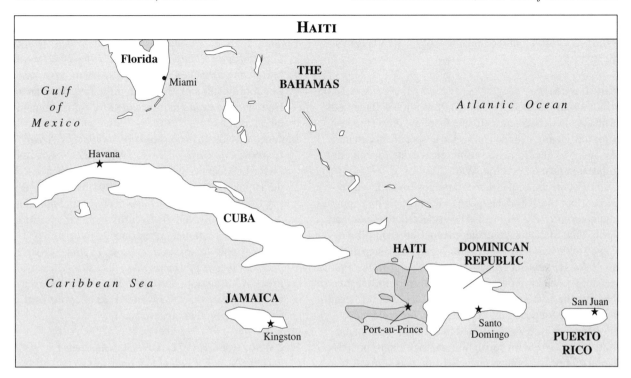

**HAITI**

between June, 1993, and June, 1994, calling for Cédras to step down. The United Nations and the Organization of American States convinced Cédras to sign the Governors Island Agreement on July 3, 1993, and the New York Pact on July 16, 1993, promising him amnesty if he withdrew and Aristide was restored by the end of October, 1993. When no progress was made to implement the accords by October, Clinton sent a naval delegation to help implement them, but the delegation was turned back.

In May, 1994, Clinton took a more active stance, threatening military intervention. The U.N. sanctions were increased to a total embargo except humanitarian aid, and members of the junta were prevented from traveling outside Haiti. Clinton sent naval and marine forces to patrol the waters near Haiti, but he waited for approval from the United Nations to take action. On July 12, 1994, the military regime expelled the International Civilian Mission, whose purpose was to observe the human rights situation in Haiti.

Finally, on July 31, 1994, the U.N. Security Council voted twelve to zero in favor of military intervention in Haiti (Resolution 940). The representatives from Brazil and China opposed the measure but abstained from voting, and the representative from Rwanda was absent. The council authorized the United States to lead a multi-

national force to depose the dictatorship, followed by a six-thousand-member peacekeeping force, the United Nations Mission in Haiti (UNMIH), which would help restore the democratic government after the military regime was deposed.

Even with the U.N. resolution, however, Clinton was reluctant to take military action and made several last-ditch diplomatic efforts. He had the military begin drawing up plans for an invasion, but he refused to set a date. In September, the U.S. Army's Tenth Mountain Division and the Navy's USS *Eisenhower* carrier group mobilized to Haiti.

Despite a great deal of international support, Clinton still needed domestic support, so he held his first live television speech on the issue on September 15. The next day, a delegation led by former U.S. president Jimmy Carter arrived in Haiti as a final diplomatic delegation. Their mission was to convince the Cédras regime to step down peacefully by September 18.

The negotiations were still in progress on the afternoon of September 18 when it was announced that the U.S. had deployed the Army's Eighty-second Airborne Division to Haiti. This announcement was sufficient to convince Cédras to step down. Cédras and the other members of the junta were allowed to leave Haiti with their money. Members of the legislature were given am-

1994

2827

nesty for their involvement in the regime, and Aristide returned to serve out the remainder of his term as president.

## SIGNIFICANCE

United Nations Security Council Resolution 940 marked a change in U.N. Security Council policy. It was the first time the Security Council had acted to specifically change a country's government, setting precedents for, among other things, the 2003 Iraq War.

For Haiti itself, the democratic government was restored, but the social and economic status of its people did not improve. Aristide had been elected to a five-year term, and, after debate about whether he should be allowed to serve out the entire term, he agreed to step down in 1996. He was succeeded by René Préval in the first peaceful transfer of power in Haiti's history. Préval then became the first Haitian president to serve his full term and step down peacefully without seeking reelection.

After Aristide was reelected in 2000, his administration was criticized for corruption and for violent suppression of opposing viewpoints. Aristide was himself deposed by the United States and France in 2004, and, after two years of turmoil, Préval was reelected in 2006.

—*John C. Hathaway*

## FURTHER READING

Ballard, John R. *Upholding Democracy: The United States Military Campaign in Haiti, 1994-1997*. Westport, Conn.: Praeger, 1998. An in-depth analysis of the coordination of the joint military campaign in Haiti and the example it provided for future humanitarian actions.

Malone, David. *Decision-making in the UN Security Council: The Case of Haiti, 1990-1997*. New York: Oxford University Press, 1998. An in-depth study of the United Nation's decision in 1994: how the Security Council came to reach the decision and how that decision has affected the Security Council's position on other international crises since.

Pezzullo, Ralph. *Plunging into Haiti: Clinton, Aristide, and the Defeat of Democracy*. Jackson: University Press of Mississippi, 2006. An account of the events written by the son of Lawrence Pezzullo, one of Bill Clinton's special envoys to Haiti.

SEE ALSO: Apr. 21, 1971: Baby Doc Succeeds Papa Doc in Haiti; Nov. 7, 1973: U.S. Congress Overrides Presidential Veto to Pass the War Powers Act; Dec. 16, 1990: Aristide Wins First Democratic Election in Haiti; Nov. 3, 1992: Clinton Wins the U.S. Presidency.

---

## August 12, 1994-April 2, 1995
# BASEBALL STRIKE FORCES CANCELLATION OF THE WORLD SERIES

*Unresolved issues between Major League Baseball's players' union and the league's team owners led to a lengthy labor strike that did considerable economic and public relations damage to the sport of professional baseball.*

**LOCALE:** United States
**CATEGORIES:** Sports; business and labor

**KEY FIGURES**
*Donald Fehr* (b. 1946), attorney and managing director of the Major League Baseball Players Association
*Bud Selig* (b. 1934), former owner of the Milwaukee Brewers baseball team and acting commissioner of Major League Baseball in 1994

## SUMMARY OF EVENT

One of the most significant events in the history of American professional baseball began on August 12, 1994, when the players' union instituted a labor strike that re-

sulted in the cancellation of the 1994 World Series. From the 1880's onward, there had been a long history of labor distrust between professional baseball players and their teams' owners, who were concerned with the teams' financial business. Players wanted the freedom that other kinds of workers have to negotiate their own wages with their employers, the team ownership. The owners wanted to keep good players on their teams and to keep player salaries low to promote the financial stability and profits of their organizations.

The Major League Baseball strike that began in 1994 occurred specifically because television revenues for the rights to cover league games were fluctuating at the same time player salaries were rising at a significant rate. The owners wanted to stabilize their business income and profits, and they proposed a collective bargaining agreement with the players that included a salary cap (a financial limit on each team's total payroll), elimination of players' rights to salary arbitration (negotiation of salary), and a change in the free agency rules (the rules governing players' freedom to sign with teams of their own choice). The owners' proposal, which was officially revealed on June 14, 1994, would guarantee a record $1 billion in salary and benefits to the players. The owners claimed that their proposal would raise the average player salary from $1.2 million in 1994 to $2.6 million by 2001.

On behalf of the players, attorney Donald Fehr, managing director of the players' union, the Major League Baseball Players Association, rejected the owners' offer on July 18. On July 28, the union's executive board approved August 12, 1994, as the date for a strike. The players refused to play as of that date, and no games were played the entire rest of the season. On September 14, 1994, the acting commissioner of Major League Baseball, Bud Selig, officially called off the season and the 1994 World Series.

For several months after the season was canceled, the owners kept up their pressure on the players by first imposing a salary cap. Lawyers for the players' union objected to this move and formally appealed to the National Labor Relations Board (NLRB), an independent agency of the executive branch of the federal government that administers labor laws and prevents or alleviates unfair labor practices by private employers and unions. The NLRB forced the owners to remove the salary cap provision by threatening the owners with legal action.

In February, 1995, the owners eliminated the players' rights to salary arbitration, free agent bidding, and anticollusion rules (rules that would prevent the owners from agreeing on set salaries for the players). Again, the players' lawyers appealed to the NLRB, and the NLRB filed an injunction, which was granted by a U.S. district court on March 31, 1995. The court ordered the owners to operate on the provisions of the old contract until a new labor agreement could be reached between the players' union and the owners. Given this decision, the union ended the strike promptly, and on April 2, 1995, the owners accepted the players' offer to begin playing without a new agreement and to continue negotiations.

At the beginning of spring training in 1995, the team owners had tried to take action to play the coming season with substitute players, but the settlement of the players' strike ended those plans. Most analysts of baseball agreed that this move would not have been successful for the owners in any case.

## SIGNIFICANCE

The 1994-1995 Major League Baseball strike was the longest players' strike in sports labor history up to that time. Because of the strike, 921 games were canceled, 669 in the 1994 season and 252 in the 1995 season. The financial loss suffered by the league as a result of the games not played, including the World Series, was estimated to be $580 million; it was estimated that the players lost $230 million in salaries.

The cancellation of the 1994 World Series was especially disappointing to a huge number of baseball fans. The strike disgusted a great many fans, who saw it as a case of millionaire owners fighting over money with wealthy athletes who were making ten times or more the salary of the average American worker to play a game in a huge ballpark for television audiences. After the strike ended, baseball stadiums saw a significant reduction in spectator attendance, and the numbers did not recover until the 2000 season.

Some experts have argued that the role of the commissioner of Major League Baseball changed somewhat as a result of the strike. Although the commissioner is chosen by a vote of team owners, after the strike, Bud Selig (officially voted commissioner in 1998, after six years as acting commissioner) seemed to see his role in labor disputes as a more neutral one; in the past, the commissioner had typically sided with the owners in any labor matters.

Experts also believe that athletes and team owners in other sports took notice of the economic and public relations damage caused by the baseball strike and resolved to avoid the same mistake in their own sports. Owners and players alike started to believe that it was not in the best interest of their sports to try to win a labor war. Instead, they began to focus on dividing revenue fairly, especially the hundreds of millions of dollars from television coverage.

*—Alan Prescott Peterson*

## FURTHER READING

Abrams, Roger I. *Legal Bases: Baseball and the Law*. Philadelphia: Temple University Press, 1998. Explains in relatively simple terms the labor and law influences that affect professional baseball.

Helyar, John. *Lords of the Realm: The Real History of Baseball*. New York: Villard, 1994. Discusses player-owner labor relations and the development of baseball as big business.

Korr, Charles P. *The End of Baseball as We Knew It: The Players Union, 1960-1981*. Urbana: University of Illinois Press, 2002. Presents a historical examination of the evolution of the Major League Baseball Players Association from a loose group of players into a pow-

1994

erful and successful labor union that significantly changed the business of professional baseball.

Snyder, Brad. *A Well-Paid Slave: Curt Flood's Fight for Free Agency in Professional Sports.* New York: Viking Press, 2006. Provides an account of baseball player Curt Flood's failed lawsuit against the owners of Major League Baseball.

Zimbalist, Andrew. *May the Best Team Win: Baseball Economics and Public Policy.* Washington, D.C.: Brookings Institution, 2003. An economics professor examines the history and dynamics of the financial prosperity of professional baseball and how the eco-nomics of the game affects its popularity and the prices paid by fans.

**SEE ALSO:** Apr. 1-13, 1972: Professional Baseball Players Go on Strike; Apr. 8, 1974: Aaron Breaks Ruth's Home Run Record; Oct. 2, 1974: Robinson Becomes Baseball's First African American Manager; 1975-1976: Players Challenge Baseball's Reserve Clause; Aug. 3, 1981: Air Traffic Controllers Declare a Strike; Sept. 6, 1995: Ripken Breaks Gehrig's Iron Man Record; Sept. 8, 1998: McGwire Breaks Maris's Home Run Record.

## September 28, 1994
# FERRY SINKS IN THE BALTIC

*The sinking of the ferry M/S* Estonia *while it was en route from Tallinn, Estonia, to Stockholm, Sweden, revealed weaknesses in the region's emergency response systems and raised intense speculation about the chain of events leading up to the catastrophe.*

**LOCALE:** Baltic Sea in Finnish territorial waters
**CATEGORY:** Disasters

**KEY FIGURES**
*Gregg Bemis* (b. 1929), American adventurer whose diving crew filmed the wreckage of the *Estonia* on the sea bottom
*Jutta Rabe* (fl. late twentieth century), German journalist who investigated the sinking of the *Estonia*
*Lars Ångström* (b. 1955), member of the Swedish parliament who accused his government of sponsoring secret military dives to the wreckage of the *Estonia*

**SUMMARY OF EVENT**
The M/S *Estonia*, a German-built luxury ferry, left Tallinn harbor on the evening of September 27, 1994, bound for Stockholm, Sweden, carrying 989 passengers, including 189 Estonian crew members, as well as forty trucks/trailers, twenty-five passenger cars, nine vans, and two buses. The ferry sailed into the stiff winds of a Baltic storm and took waves that reached six feet, but these were not unusual conditions, and there was no compelling reason for concern. As the *Estonia* approached the halfway point of its 350-kilometer (217-mile) journey, sometime around midnight, its fifty-ton bow door, designed to open the ferry to vehicle traffic when in port, broke under the steady

pounding of the waves. As the door broke loose, it broke the locks on the inner door, causing water to pour into the car deck and quickly overwhelm the pumping system. The ferry listed sharply to starboard by 15 degrees.

On the bridge, there was a lack of information about what had happened, and there was confusion among the crew; the panel lights indicated no problems on board, so no alarms were sounded to alert the passengers. Not having full information, the captain and his crew reduced the ship's speed, steered toward port, and made a fatal miscalculation by positioning the listing side of the ship in the direction of the wind and waves. The sea poured into the accommodation decks. By 1:20 A.M., the ship's engines had stopped and the vessel was rolling and jerking starboard, its passengers thrown about, drowning in the cabins and passageways. Passengers and crew had about fifteen minutes in which to save themselves.

The first "Mayday . . . *Estonia*" was sent at 1:22 A.M., about the same time the first alarm was sounded, and within minutes afterward the ferry tilted to nearly 90 degrees, virtually on its side. People met their deaths trapped on the upturned hull or were tossed into the sea when the ship rolled. Passengers struggled to open life rafts and locate life jackets, but there was no systematic launching of rafts, and many jackets were either too large or too small. About 1:50 A.M., the *Estonia* slipped slowly beneath the waves and sunk to the muddy bottom of the Baltic, taking hundreds to their graves.

The first vessel on the scene, the passenger ferry *Mariella*, arrived fifty minutes after the first distress call but was able to pull only a dozen people from the sea. The nations of Finland, Sweden, and Estonia launched a massive emergency response and rescue operation, putting helicopters and patrol boats into operation around the clock. The rescue helicopters were ill equipped and understaffed, however, and as cables broke, some rafts they attempted to lift fell tragically back into the stormy sea. With water temperatures below 50 degrees Fahrenheit, many people succumbed to hypothermia in the sea or in waterlogged rafts while awaiting rescue. Only 137 people survived the catastrophe, and just 94 bodies were recovered by the crews.

The M/S *Estonia* was built in 1979 at the Meyer Werft shipyard in Papenburg, Germany; the SF Line ordered the ferry and later sold it to Rederi Ab Sally, a partner in the Viking Line consortium. Originally named *Viking Sally*, the ferry became *Silja Star* in 1990 when the Silja Line put it into service. Its name was changed to *Wasa King* when it went into service for Wasa Line, and in 1993 it was sold to a long-established Swedish company, Nordström and Thulin, renamed the *Estonia*, and placed in use on the Tallinn-Stockholm route. The ferry was registered in both Estonia and Cyprus and was co-owned by the Estonian state and the Swedish company.

In a report dated December 3, 1997, the Joint Accident Investigation Commission, composed of Swedish, Finnish, and Estonian investigators, placed the blame for the *Estonia* tragedy with the German shipyard, citing failure of the vessel's bow visor locking devices. Another commission, the German Group of Experts, concluded that the vessel was unseaworthy owing to poor maintenance and inspections, including problems with corrosion. The investigations of both groups, however, came under sharp criticism for being inherently flawed in structure and approach.

## SIGNIFICANCE

The sinking of the *Estonia* was the deadliest maritime disaster in Europe since World War II. In addition to the devastating loss of life, it brought to light many deficiencies in the ferry's operation as well as in the region's search-and-rescue procedures. The ferry's alarms did not sound immediately to alert crew and passengers. Many were crushed in narrow doorways, killed by falling equipment, or drowned because life rafts and life jackets were difficult to release and inflate. Life rafts lowered to the water were dangerous and difficult to enter and were easily capsized; some became so heavily waterlogged that the passengers in them died of hypothermia.

There were no video monitors in the vehicle bay, and the vessel's crew members did not act when they heard loud, vibrating noises. Had the extent of the danger been understood, the captain likely would have put the ferry in reverse, thus preventing the swamping and delaying or preventing the sinking. The rescue helicopters sent to help during the disaster were not built to handle the weight of the life rafts, and each was inadequately staffed, with only one rescue worker on board. These were hard lessons that led ultimately to improvements in ferry safety and maritime rescue operations.

The full details of the *Estonia* tragedy remain unknown, and that fact has given rise to abundant speculation, a feature film (*Baltic Storm*, 2003), and numerous books and theories. Within months of the tragedy, the Swedish government announced that there would be no recovery operation. In 1995, the Estonia Agreement was signed by Sweden, Finland, Estonia, Latvia, Denmark, Russia, and the United Kingdom; the treaty recognized the sanctity of the site of the ferry's wreckage and prohibited the citizens of those countries from exploring it. Citizens of nonsignatory countries are not bound by the agreement, however, and in 2000 American adventurer Gregg Bemis led a diving team that explored the wreck and found evidence of an explosion.

German journalist Jutta Rabe investigated the tragedy and pointed the finger of blame at the Russian secret service and the highest levels of the Swedish government. The motion picture *Baltic Storm*, based on Rabe's book, alleges that the Swedish government used the ferry to transport contraband military technologies to the United States, possibly secret space weapons. Suspicion surrounded the Swedish government's decision to encase the wreckage in concrete, an expensive operation and one that many thought suggested a nuclear component. A dozen members of the *Estonia* crew purportedly disappeared after being rescued, and some believe their disappearance was organized by the Swedish government. An investigation by Swedish state television in 2004 led to a documentary film and the revelation that the M/S *Estonia* had transported Soviet military equipment to the West in the weeks prior to its Baltic sinking.

In 2006, Swedish and Estonian family members of the victims requested a suspension of the ban on diving to the wreckage by presenting a letter to the signatories of the Estonia Agreement of 1995. Their intent was to encourage further investigation into the tragedy by allowing the collection of physical evidence from the site. The case of the *Estonia* points up the difficulty of coordinating international investigations of maritime disasters, sorting out fact from fancy, and dealing with highly sensitive intelligence issues on a world stage.

—*Ann M. Legreid*

1994

**FURTHER READING**

Björkman, Anders. *Lies and Truth About the M/V Estonia Accident*. Monaco: Imprime par Multiprint, 1998. Provides details on conspiracy theories concerning the accident, including updates on the findings of international research consortia.

Langewiesche, William. *The Outlaw Sea*. London: Granta Books, 2005. Presents an overview of maritime crimes and criminal investigations, including the problems that arose in the investigation of the *Estonia* tragedy.

Ritchie, David. *Shipwrecks: An Encyclopedia of the World's Worst Disasters at Sea*. New York: Facts On File, 1996. Provides succinct summaries of sea disasters, with basic information on who, what, where, and why.

Wilson, Drew. *The Hole: Another Look at the Sinking of the Estonia Ferry on September 28, 1994*. Liskeard, Cornwall, England: Diggory Press, 2006. Explores alternative explanations for the *Estonia* sinking, with a focus on the Soviet connection.

**SEE ALSO:** Nov. 10, 1975: Sinking of the *Edmund Fitzgerald*; Aug. 25, 1984: Radioactive Cargo Sinks in the North Sea.

---

## October 21, 1994
# U.S.-NORTH KOREA PACT

*The United States and North Korea signed a pact in which North Korea agreed to dismantle its nuclear weapons facilities in exchange for two light-water reactor power plants and other financial aid. The agreement ended an eighteen-month crisis provoked by North Korea's withdrawal from the Nuclear Non-Proliferation Treaty and its refusal to allow its nuclear facilities to be inspected by the International Atomic Energy Agency.*

**ALSO KNOWN AS:** North Korea Pact; Agreed Framework of 1994
**LOCALE:** Geneva, Switzerland
**CATEGORY:** Diplomacy and international relations

**KEY FIGURES**

*Madeleine Albright* (b. 1937), U.S. ambassador to the United Nations, 1993-1997, and U.S. secretary of state, 1997-2001

*Hans Blix* (b. 1928), director-general of the International Atomic Energy Agency, 1981-1997

*Jimmy Carter* (b. 1924), president of the United States, 1977-1981

*Bill Clinton* (b. 1946), president of the United States, 1993-2001

*Kim Il Sung* (1912-1994), premier, 1948-1972, and president of North Korea, 1972-1994

*Kim Jong Il* (b. 1941), successor to Kim Il Sung as leader of North Korea

**SUMMARY OF EVENT**

During 1992, inspectors for the International Atomic Energy Agency (IAEA) reported that North Korea had failed to declare in its inventory of nuclear materials and facilities the existence of two nuclear reactor sites, a plutonium extraction plant, and a stockpile of weapons-usable waste plutonium, near Yongbyon. On March 12, 1993, North Korea announced its intention to withdraw from the Nuclear Non-Proliferation Treaty and refused to admit IAEA inspectors to its nuclear sites. In December, 1993, the IAEA's director-general, Hans Blix, reported to the United Nations Security Council that he could not give assurances that North Korea was not producing nuclear weapons.

In March, 1994, after direct negotiations with the United States, North Korea's president, Kim Il Sung, agreed to permit IAEA inspections, but he again barred the inspectors from taking radioactive samples at the Yongbyon plutonium extraction plant. Consequently, on June 2, 1994, Blix informed the U.N. Security Council that the IAEA was suspending technical assistance to North Korea because that nation had accelerated nuclear operations at Yongbyon and still refused to comply with IAEA safeguards.

On June 15, 1994, Madeleine Albright, U.S. ambassador to the United Nations, went to the Security Council with a proposal for sanctions against North Korea. Albright asked for a worldwide embargo on export of arms to North Korea and, contingent on that nation's reaction, a second phase of sanctions banning all financial dealings with North Korea. North Korea threatened to attack South Korea if such sanctions were imposed. In an attempt to avert war, former U.S. president Jimmy Carter, with approval from President Bill Clinton, went to North Korea for talks with Kim Il Sung. On June 17,

Carter secured Kim's agreement to dismantle the North Korean nuclear weapons program if the United States would engage in high-level talks. Kim's death on July 9, 1994, delayed a formal agreement, but Kim's son and successor, Kim Jong Il, signed an Agreed Statement on August 12, 1994, calling for high-level talks between North Korea and the United States in Geneva, Switzerland.

Between September 23 and October 21, 1994, delegates from the U.S. and North Korean governments reached agreement on the U.S.-North Korea Pact, an Agreed Framework in which North Korea and the United States jointly committed to a nuclear-free Korean Peninsula. The United States gave formal assurances that it would not use nuclear weapons against North Korea, and North Korea agreed to take consistent steps to implement the North-South Joint Declaration on the Denuclearization of the Korean Peninsula. The two parties further committed their governments to move toward normalizing economic and political relations by removing barriers to trade and investment, opening liaison offices, and eventually upgrading relations to an exchange of ambassadors.

The Agreed Framework of 1994 committed North Korea to freezing operation of its 5-megawatt plutonium processing plant at Yongbyon and to halting construction of its 50-megawatt and 200-megawatt graphite-moderated reactors at Yongbyon and Taechon, respectively. All these facilities were to be dismantled prior to completion of two light-water reactor (LWR) power stations to be constructed by the United States in North Korea. Further, North Korea was required to remain a party to the Nuclear Non-Proliferation Treaty and to comply fully with IAEA safeguards. This included allowing inspectors access to all nuclear facilities in the country prior to delivery of key nuclear components for the LWRs. The spent fuel rods from the closed 5-megawatt reactor would be stored in containers—a "canning" process—and removed from North Korea after the first LWR arrived. The four-year canning process, funded by the United States, began April 27, 1996, with a projected completion date of April 1, 2000.

Under the pact, the United States assumed responsibility for organizing a consortium to finance, construct, and supply two 1,000-megawatt LWR power plants in North Korea. On March 9, 1995, the United States, Japan, and South Korea formed the Korean Peninsula Energy Development Organization (KEDO) to design and construct the LWRs. KEDO was later joined by twelve countries and the European Union, which provided fi-

nancial assistance and supplies to help implement the Agreed Framework.

To offset North Korea's loss of electric power in freezing its nuclear reactors, the United States committed to shipments of up to 500,000 tons of heavy oil per year until the first LWR was completed. Deliveries began in January, 1995, with a 50,000-ton shipment from the United States. KEDO assumed responsibility for the oil shipments for the period 1995-1997, at an annual cost of $60 million to $65 million. In mid-1995, when North Korea diverted the oil to the military, KEDO installed meters at the receiving power plants.

KEDO's plans called for South Korean engineers and construction workers to prepare the site and build the LWRs. KEDO members believed that the interaction of South and North Koreans would further peaceful relations on the peninsula. However, North Korea refused to accept South Korea's reactor design and supervision of the project. To resolve this issue, the United States and North Korea agreed on June 13, 1995, that the reactor model would be based on the System 80 model of Combustion Engineering, a U.S. firm. In July, 1995, KEDO selected Duke Engineering & Services, Inc., another U.S. firm, as program coordinator.

A supply agreement between KEDO and North Korea on how the $5.178 billion LWR project would be financed and supplied was concluded on December 15, 1995. South Korea and Japan were given responsibility for financing the project. North Korea would have twenty years following completion of the LWRs to repay the total cost. The supply agreement reaffirmed North Korea's nonproliferation commitments made in the Agreed Framework of 1994. Shipments of fuel oil and construction on the LWRs would cease immediately if North Korea violated any terms of the pact.

Negotiations on protocols continued until September, 1996, when KEDO announced the completion of all basic political agreements needed for construction to begin. Yet another delay was caused by the discovery of a North Korean submarine grounded on South Korea's coast on September 18, 1996. KEDO could not finalize protocols until North Korea apologized for the incident. The apology came on December 29, 1996, after a series of meetings with the United States, and protocols were signed January 8, 1997. In August, 1997, KEDO finally broke ground on the first LWR project.

## SIGNIFICANCE

In 1998, the basic provisions of the Agreed Framework of 1994 seemed to be holding together. The direct rela-

1994

tions established between North and South Korea in negotiating the supply agreement, along with the KEDO-North Korea negotiations to implement the Agreed Framework of 1994, were significant accomplishments. Despite delays caused by North Korea's military incursions and acts of violence against South Korea, the United States, and Japan, KEDO's construction of the LWRs was scheduled to begin in late 1998 and be completed within four years.

Troublesome developments delayed further implementation of the U.S.-North Korea Pact, however. With assistance from Iran, North Korea had been expanding its ballistic missile program throughout the 1990's. It also was producing chemical and biological weapons and had stockpiled large quantities near the Demilitarized Zone between North and South Korea. During meetings with the U.S. envoy, held October 4-6, 2002, North Korea admitted that it had never frozen its nuclear weapons program and had accelerated production, in violation of the 1994 Agreed Framework. North Korea had used the billions of dollars in aid provided by the United States and other nations to expand its production of nuclear weapons and ballistic missiles and had sold missiles and technology to enemies of the United States. The United States linked North Korea with terrorism and imposed sanctions. On January 20, 2003, North Korea announced its withdrawal from the Nuclear Non-Proliferation Treaty, thus abrogating the U.S.-North Korea Pact of 1994.

*—Marguerite R. Plummer*

### FURTHER READING

Albright, David, and Kevin O'Neill, eds. *Solving the North Korean Nuclear Puzzle*. Washington, D.C.: Institute for Science and International Security, 2000. Collection of commentary on North Korea's failure to disclose nuclear weapons programs and the potential effects of that failure.

Lee, Eric Yong-Joong. "The Geneva Framework and the Optimization of DPRK-U.S. Relationship for Nuclear Security: A Legal and Policy Analysis." *Chinese Journal of International Law* 2 (2003): 289-309. Outlines in detail the laws and policies developed to implement the provisions of the U.S.-North Korea Pact.

Mazaar, Michael J. *North Korea and the Bomb: A Case Study in Nonproliferation*. New York: St. Martin's Press, 1995. Provides insights into diplomatic initiatives to stop nuclear proliferation in North Korea and North Korea's failure to comply with the Nuclear Non-Proliferation Treaty and IAEA safeguards.

Sigal, Leon V. *Disarming Strangers: Nuclear Diplomacy with North Korea*. Princeton, N.J.: Princeton University Press, 1998. Presents a comprehensive analysis of North Korea's development of nuclear weapons despite efforts by the United Nations, the United States, and the IAEA to prevent proliferation of such weapons.

**SEE ALSO:** May 18, 1974: India Joins the Nuclear Club; Oct. 16, 1980: China Conducts Atmospheric Nuclear Test; July 8, 1994: Kim Jong Il Succeeds His Father in North Korea; 1995-1998: Famine Strikes North Korea.

**November 8, 1994**
# OREGON VOTERS LEGALIZE PHYSICIAN-ASSISTED SUICIDE

*Oregon's Death with Dignity Act was the first law passed by a U.S. state to legalize the practice of physician-assisted suicide.*

**ALSO KNOWN AS:** Death with Dignity Act
**LOCALE:** Oregon
**CATEGORIES:** Laws, acts, and legal history; health and medicine

**KEY FIGURES**

*Thomas A. Constantine* (b. 1938), administrator of the U.S. Drug Enforcement Administration, 1994-1999
*Robert E. Jones* (1912-1997), U.S. district court judge
*Janet Reno* (b. 1938), U.S. attorney general, 1993-2001
*John Ashcroft* (b. 1942), U.S. attorney general, 2001-2005

**SUMMARY OF EVENT**

On November 8, 1994, Oregon voters narrowly (51 percent) approved a carefully written initiative petition that made physician-assisted suicide legal for terminally ill persons in the state. Implementation of the new law, called the Death with Dignity Act, was delayed by various injunctions, and in 1997, a legislative bill that would have repealed the act was put to the Oregon voters, who turned it down by a large margin (60 percent voted against the measure). Despite repeated efforts by a U.S. attorney general, the U.S. Supreme Court upheld the Death with Dignity Act, and it took effect on October 27, 1997. From 1998 through 2006, a total of 292 Oregon residents took advantage of the provisions of the act and sought physician assistance with their deaths.

The Death with Dignity Act allowed Oregon residents who met certain criteria to request prescriptions for lethal medication from their physicians. To qualify, an individual had to be eighteen years of age or older, had to be found capable of making and communicating health care decisions, and had to have been diagnosed with a terminal illness that would lead to death within six months. The patient had to make two requests for the medication at least fifteen days apart, and the requests had to be confirmed in writing in the presence of two witnesses. The law required a consulting physician to confirm all conditions. In the case of a patient who was found to be incapable of making health care decisions (because of depression or other disorder), the law required that the patient

be referred for counseling. The law also required physicians to inform any patient seeking suicide assistance of alternatives such as comfort or hospice care and pain control measures.

No physician or health care system was required to participate in assisting patient suicide, and the law protected those who did from criminal prosecution. Physicians who refused to participate were required to provide their patients who requested assistance with referrals to doctors who would assist them. In addition, the law stipulated that the choice of physician-assisted suicide could not affect the status of a patient's health or life insurance policies, including Medicare and Medicaid. Physicians had to report all prescriptions for intentionally lethal medications, as well as resulting death certificates, to the Oregon Department of Human Services, which, under the law, was required to issue an annual report on the usage of the act.

Some minor amendments were made to the act in 1999. A requirement was added that physicians must inform pharmacists of any lethal prescription's intended use, and pharmacists were added to the list of those health care-related workers who could refuse to participate. In addition, the law was amended to stipulate that action in accordance with the act does not constitute mercy killing or homicide.

After the 1994 vote, opponents of the new law successfully requested an injunction to prevent its implementation. Following proceedings that included a petition denied by the U.S. Supreme Court, the Ninth Circuit Court of Appeals lifted its injunction just weeks before the voters turned down the 1997 referendum that would have invalidated the act. Immediately thereafter, the U.S. Drug Enforcement Administration (DEA) warned Oregon doctors that they could be arrested or have their licenses revoked for prescribing lethal doses of drugs that DEA administrator Thomas A. Constantine characterized as falling under the restrictions imposed by the Controlled Substances Act. Attorney General Janet Reno overruled Constantine, however.

The U.S. Congress then unsuccessfully considered a law that would have prevented the use of federally controlled drugs for assisted suicide and euthanasia. In 2001, Attorney General John Ashcroft overturned Reno's ruling, and the state of Oregon, supported by the Oregon and Washington State medical associations, filed suit, claiming that Ashcroft was acting unconstitutionally.

1994

The following year, U.S. district court judge Robert E. Jones ruled in favor of the Oregon act. Ashcroft then appealed to the U.S. Court of Appeals. When a three-judge panel denied his appeal in 2004, he requested a review by the full eleven-judge panel, which was declined. In 2006, the U.S. Supreme Court affirmed the lower court's decision.

Aware of, although neutral in, the continued controversy concerning the Death with Dignity Act, the Oregon Department of Human Services from the beginning used control groups of both patients and physicians to compare with those patients and doctors involved in physician-assisted suicide under the act. In its initial report in 1999, the department, acknowledging the small sample with which it had to work, found that there were no appreciable differences in age, race, sex, education, economic status, insurance coverage, or access to hospice care between patients who chose physician-assisted suicide and others who died of similar underlying illnesses. The department did find that divorced or never-married patients were slightly more likely to seek physician assistance with suicide.

The initial report also included the following findings. Of twenty-three persons who received lethal prescriptions, only fifteen used them. All fifteen were white, half were male, and four had psychiatric or psychological consultations but were found capable of making decisions for themselves. Of the fifteen who took lethal prescriptions, none was bedridden at the time. Six had to ask more than one physician before they found one who was willing to prescribe.

Later reports from the Department of Human Services noted some changes in the statistics: Persons who had higher levels of education, those under age eighty-five, and those with amyotrophic lateral sclerosis (Lou Gehrig's disease), acquired immunodeficiency syndrome (AIDS), or cancer were more likely to use physician-assisted suicide than were people in other education and age groups and those with other diseases and conditions. Over the years, the reasons patients have noted for requesting physician assistance with suicide have remained essentially the same: Most have stated that they made their decision not out of a fear of pain, but because they feared a decreasing ability to participate in activities that make life enjoyable, loss of dignity, and loss of autonomy. The Oregon Department of Human Services has concluded that the Death with Dignity Act created an incentive for medical care providers to explore with patients their fears and wishes around end-of-life care and to make patients aware of other options.

## SIGNIFICANCE

Passage of Oregon's Death with Dignity Act stimulated interest across the United States concerning the long-debated issue of an individual's "right to die," and the controversy continued into the twenty-first century. On one side are arguments that each person should have the right to "death with dignity" and that individuals should have the liberty to choose physician-assisted suicide to protect that right. On the other side are arguments regarding the dangers of allowing the establishment of any government-sanctioned right to choose to end a life. Critics of laws allowing physician-assisted suicide assert that such legislation will inevitably lead to abuses and may encourage individuals to seek suicide who might otherwise not consider such a step.

The U.S. Supreme Court has ruled in at least two cases that the right to physician-assisted suicide is not a liberty included in the U.S. Constitution and therefore is not available to persons in states that do not have, as Oregon does, laws expressly permitting it. The Court's upholding of Oregon's Death with Dignity Act thus set an important legal precedent.

*—Erika E. Pilver*

## FURTHER READING

Emanuel, Linda L., ed. *Regulating How We Die: The Ethical, Medical, and Legal Issues Surrounding Physician-Assisted Suicide.* Cambridge, Mass.: Harvard University Press, 1998. Collection of essays provides comprehensive discussion of the topic of physician-assisted suicide. Does not directly address the Oregon law, but deals with a number of well-known specific cases.

Harrison, Maureen, and Steve Gilbert, eds. *Life, Death, and The Law: Landmark Right-to-Die Decisions.* San Diego, Calif.: Excellent Books, 1997. Presents clearly written legal analysis of important court decisions concerning the issue of the right to die.

McKhann, Charles F. *A Time to Die: The Place for Physician Assistance.* New Haven, Conn.: Yale University Press, 1999. Presents a reasoned and dispassionate consideration of physician, patient, legal, and advocacy issues concerning the right to die, expressed in a historical context. Advocates the establishment of state laws that, like Oregon's, allow physician-assisted suicide under controlled conditions.

Smith, Wesley J. *Forced Exit: The Slippery Slope from Assisted Suicide to Legalized Murder.* New York: Times Books, 1997. Argues frankly against assisted suicide. Despite emotional tone and clear bias, nonetheless includes some interesting examples from the campaign for the Oregon act as well as actions in other states.

Weir, Robert F., ed. *Physician-Assisted Suicide*. Bloomington: Indiana University Press, 1997. Collection of essays provides thoughtful discussion of the historical, ethical, and public policy ramifications of physician-assisted suicide.

Wexler, Barbara. *Death and Dying: Who Decides?* Farmington Hills, Mich.: Thomson Gale, 2003. Presents a brief but comprehensive overview of the his-

tory, definitions, ethical and medical considerations, legal status, and opinions on death and dying. Includes two chapters detailing the Oregon experience.

**SEE ALSO:** Jan., 1980-Mar., 1983: Presidential Advisory Commission Studies Medical and Research Ethics; Dec. 18, 1982: United Nations Issues Principles of Medical Ethics; 1989: Oregon Guarantees Basic Health Care for the Uninsured; June 25, 1990: U.S. Supreme Court Upholds the Right to Refuse Medical Treatment.

## November 8, 1994
# REPUBLICANS REGAIN CONTROL OF CONGRESS

*A growing conservative constituency elected a Republican majority to both houses of Congress for the first time in forty years.*

**LOCALE:** United States
**CATEGORY:** Government and politics

**KEY FIGURES**
*Bill Clinton* (b. 1946), president of the United States, 1993-2001
*Newt Gingrich* (b. 1943), Republican U.S. congressman from Georgia

**SUMMARY OF EVENT**
In the fall of 1994, as the midterm congressional elections approached, the U.S. electorate was in volatile mood. People were disillusioned and skeptical about political institutions and political leaders. It seemed to many Americans that government was out of touch and no longer responsive to the needs of ordinary people. Voter anger against the federal establishment made 1994 a difficult year to be an incumbent.

Republicans were optimistic that they would benefit from voter dissatisfaction, pointing to the sharp drop in popularity of President Bill Clinton in public opinion polls. To win control of the House of Representatives, the Republicans needed to win forty new seats. To take the Senate, they needed seven new seats. As the divisive and bitter campaign season drew to a close, the conventional wisdom was that the Republicans would make gains, but they probably would fall short of winning majorities in either house.

Few people expected the political earthquake that followed. Democrats tumbled to defeat all across the coun-

try, and the Republicans seized control of both the House of Representatives and the Senate for the first time since 1954. In the House, Republicans won 230 seats to the Democrats' 204. In the Senate, Republicans secured an advantage of 53 to 47, reversing a preelection situation of 56 to 44 in favor of the Democrats. Some of the most powerful Democratic incumbents were defeated. These included Speaker of the House Thomas Foley and Representative Dan Rostenkowski of Illinois, chair of the House Ways and Means Committee (whose reelection campaign was especially difficult because he had been indicted for misappropriation of funds). Other, younger figures such as Representatives Jim Slattery of Kansas and Jim Cooper of Tennessee, both of whom had been considered future Democratic leaders, also were defeated.

This voting pattern was repeated at the state level, where the Republicans gained twelve governorships, making a total of thirty, including seven of the eight largest states. The Republicans also made big gains in state legislatures across the country. It was the biggest success for the Republican Party since 1946, and it left the Democrats confused and leaderless.

As the Republicans rejoiced, some Democrats were quick to blame President Clinton for the debacle. They pointed out that he had failed to keep his promise of a middle-class tax cut and that he had failed to make the fundamental changes in the way government works that he had promised in his 1992 campaign. Although Clinton had claimed to be a centrist "new Democrat," his policies closely resembled traditional liberalism—which the public had come to associate with high taxes and excessive government spending, the kind of "big government"

1994

2837

that was now being identified as the nation's problem rather than the solution to the nation's ills.

The architect of the Republican victory was Georgia representative Newt Gingrich, formerly the House minority whip; after the election, he was set to become the Speaker of the House. An aggressive, fiercely partisan figure, Gingrich was instrumental in drawing up the Republican platform, the main plank of which was the Contract with America, a ten-point plan that the Republicans promised to bring before Congress in their first hundred days if they were in charge of the new Congress.

The Contract with America called for the enactment of a constitutional amendment that would mandate a balanced federal budget by 2002. The idea was to promote fiscal responsibility by reining in a Congress that was perceived as out of control on spending. The contract also promised a tougher anticrime bill than the one President Clinton had signed the previous September; sharp cuts in welfare programs, including the power to cut

off benefits to unmarried mothers who were less than twenty-one years of age; term limits on members of Congress, which would replace career politicians with "citizen legislators"; legal reforms; a tax cut for the middle class and a 50 percent cut in the capital gains tax; an increase in defense spending; and a reorganization of the way the House does business, involving a cut in the number of congressional committees and a reduction of congressional staff by one-third.

This agenda was so radical that after the Republican victory, commentators predicted that the country was about to undergo the biggest reversal of direction in government policy since President Franklin D. Roosevelt's New Deal programs, which had begun in 1933. Since the New Deal, there had been a consensus that central government should intervene to remedy the social and economic ills of the country. This had culminated in President Lyndon B. Johnson's Great Society social programs of the 1960's. The conservative Republicans who tri-

*Georgia Republican Newt Gingrich became a leading spokesperson for conservativism after he became speaker of the House of Representatives in 1994.* (AP/Wide World Photos)

umphed in 1994 believed this long period of liberal government activism had led to the social problems of the 1990's, such as welfare dependence and an erosion of moral values. They made no secret of their desire to dismantle the welfare state and return many of the accumulated powers of the federal government to the states.

## SIGNIFICANCE

The 1994 elections left President Clinton weakened and returned the nation to another period of divided government, in which the executive branch and the legislature are controlled by different parties. Divided government had been the norm for more than twenty years until Clinton's election in 1992, which coincided with firm Democratic control of Congress. In the days after the 1994 elections, Clinton struggled for a response to the debacle. At first, the White House claimed that voters were merely lashing out at incumbents in a display of antigovernment anger. However, it was clear that the statistics did not support such an interpretation, given that primarily Democratic incumbents were voted out.

A more considered response came in a postelection speech to the Democratic Leadership Council, in which Clinton defended his record. He pointed out he was the first president since Harry Truman to cut the federal budget deficit, which had quadrupled during the presidencies of Ronald Reagan and George H. W. Bush. Clinton also took credit for promoting free trade, which traditionally has been supported by Republicans, and for his anticrime bill, which provided funds for increasing the size of cities' police forces. Clinton pointed out that he had already reduced the size of the federal government by more than a quarter of a million employees. In other speeches, the president said that although he was willing to cooperate with the Republican Congress, he would not compromise on matters of principle. One such matter was the ban on certain kinds of assault weapons, which was enacted as part of the anticrime bill but which many Republicans wanted to repeal.

---

## THE REPUBLICANS' CONTRACT WITH AMERICA

*In their Contract with America, the Republicans promised to take immediate action on ten bills:*

Within the first 100 days of the 104th Congress, we shall bring to the House Floor the following bills, each to be given full and open debate, each to be given a clear and fair vote and each to be immediately available this day for public inspection and scrutiny.

1. THE FISCAL RESPONSIBILITY ACT: A balanced budget/tax limitation amendment and a legislative line-item veto to restore fiscal responsibility to an out-of-control Congress, requiring them to live under the same budget constraints as families and businesses.
2. THE TAKING BACK OUR STREETS ACT: An anti-crime package including stronger truth-in-sentencing, "good faith" exclusionary rule exemptions, effective death penalty provisions, and cuts in social spending from this summer's "crime" bill to fund prison construction and additional law enforcement to keep people secure in their neighborhoods and kids safe in their schools.
3. THE PERSONAL RESPONSIBILITY ACT: Discourage illegitimacy and teen pregnancy by prohibiting welfare to minor mothers and denying increased AFDC for additional children while on welfare, cut spending for welfare programs, and enact a tough two-years-and-out provision with work requirements to promote individual responsibility.
4. THE FAMILY REINFORCEMENT ACT: Child support enforcement, tax incentives for adoption, strengthening rights of parents in their children's education, stronger child pornography laws, and an elderly dependent care tax credit to reinforce the central role of families in American society.
5. THE AMERICAN DREAM RESTORATION ACT: A $500 per child tax credit, begin repeal of the marriage tax penalty, and creation of American Dream Savings Accounts to provide middle-class tax relief.
6. THE NATIONAL SECURITY RESTORATION ACT: No U.S. troops under U.N. command and restoration of the essential parts of our national security funding to strengthen our national defense and maintain our credibility around the world.
7. THE SENIOR CITIZENS FAIRNESS ACT: Raise the Social Security earnings limit which currently forces seniors out of the work force, repeal the 1993 tax hikes on Social Security benefits and provide tax incentives for private long-term care insurance to let Older Americans keep more of what they have earned over the years.
8. THE JOB CREATION and WAGE ENHANCEMENT ACT: Small business incentives, capital gains cut and indexation, neutral cost recovery, risk assessment/cost-benefit analysis, strengthening the Regulatory Flexibility Act and unfunded mandate reform to create jobs and raise worker wages.
9. THE COMMON SENSE LEGAL REFORM ACT: "Loser pays" laws, reasonable limits on punitive damages and reform of product liability laws to stem the endless tide of litigation.
10. THE CITIZEN LEGISLATURE ACT: A first-ever vote on term limits to replace career politicians with citizen legislators.

1994

When the 104th Congress convened in January, 1995, the Republicans delivered on their promise of a dynamic hundred days. They succeeded in bringing all the major points in their Contract with America to a vote in the House of Representatives, and all but one measure passed there. Many Democrats voted with the Republicans. The one failure was the proposal for a constitutional amendment to mandate a federal balanced budget, which failed to secure the two-thirds majority required for a constitutional amendment. Although many of these proposals faced a much tougher fight in the Senate, it was clear that the Republicans had profoundly shifted the focus of political debate for a long time to come.

Bowing to the immediate reality, Clinton, who had campaigned in part on a promise to "end welfare as we know it," cooperated in 1996 with Republican majorities to produce the nation's first major welfare reform law since the inauguration of President Johnson's Great Society in the 1960's. The reform has been largely credited with reducing poverty and encouraging work among the poor. Moreover, the long-anticipated balanced budget became an actual fact within a few years, as government revenues surged with a healthy economy, generating large reductions in federal debt. For this development, both Clinton and the fiscally conservative Republicans claimed some credit. The Republican majority later successfully impeached Clinton, bringing charges of perjury against him in the Monica Lewinsky scandal, but Clinton weathered that storm.

The staying power of the Republican revolution was evidenced by the party's ability to control both houses of Congress in subsequent congressional elections through 2004, even as George W. Bush captured the White House in 2000, ending the era of divided government and ushering in a period of Republican dominance.

—*Bryan Aubrey*

## FURTHER READING

Beschloss, Michael R. "What Took Them So Long?" *Newsweek*, November 21, 1994, 49. Analyzes the resurgence of conservatism in the United States after the 1970's and discusses why that trend took so long to produce Republican majorities in Congress.

Drew, Elizabeth. *Showdown: The Struggle Between the Gingrich Congress and the Clinton White House.* New York: Touchstone, 1996. A journalist's detailed account of the first session of the 104th Congress focuses in large part on Newt Gingrich's difficulties in controlling the new Republican majority and his clashes with Senate Majority Leader Bob Dole. Includes index.

Fineman, Howard. "The Warrior." *Newsweek*, January 9, 1995, 28-34. Discusses House Speaker Newt Gingrich's life and career. Points out the consistency of Gingrich's conservative message from the time of his first run for Congress in 1974, but also describes some contradictions in his personality and philosophy.

Galen, Michele. "How the Election Looks from the Corner Office." *BusinessWeek*, November 21, 1994, 36. Presents interviews with business leaders concerning the Republican victory. Responses were generally positive, but some expressed fears that the bitter election would lead to divisiveness and gridlock.

Jones, Charles O. *Clinton and Congress, 1993-1996: Risk, Restoration, and Reelection.* Norman: University of Oklahoma Press, 1999. Scholarly work examines the changing relations between President Clinton and Congress during Clinton's first term in office. Devotes substantial discussion to the Republicans' return to the majority. Includes tables, figures, and index.

Kaus, Mickey. "They Blew It." *The New Republic*, December 5, 1994, 14-19. Argues that if President Clinton had made welfare reform rather than health care reform his priority, the Democrats would not have suffered such a crushing defeat.

Kelly, Michael. "You Say You Want a Revolution." *The New Yorker*, November 21, 1994, 56-63. Presents detailed analysis of voting patterns, the response of the Clinton administration to the Republican victory, and the difficulty Clinton was expected to have in regaining the political initiative.

**SEE ALSO:** Nov. 8, 1988: Bush Is Elected President; Nov. 3, 1992: Clinton Wins the U.S. Presidency; June 25, 1998: U.S. Supreme Court Strikes Down the Line-Item Veto; Dec. 19, 1998: Clinton Is Impeached; Nov. 7, 2000: Bush Election Stirs Political and Legal Controversy.

## November 16, 1994
# LAW OF THE SEA TREATY ENTERS INTO FORCE

*As technological and political developments in the twentieth century led ocean-bordering nations to claim as their territory increasing areas of the waters extending from their shores, the Law of the Sea Treaty was developed to balance the need for international access to the world's oceans with individual states' needs to control the areas contiguous to their shorelines.*

**LOCALE:** New York, New York
**CATEGORIES:** Natural resources; United Nations

**KEY FIGURES**
*Arvid Pardo* (1914-1999), ambassador from Malta to the United Nations
*Javier Pérez de Cuéllar* (b. 1920), secretary-general of the United Nations, 1982-1991
*Ronald Reagan* (1911-2004), president of the United States, 1981-1989

**SUMMARY OF EVENT**
As the twentieth century opened, virtually all nations recognized that an ocean-bordered country's territory extended three nautical miles out from the shoreline into the ocean. Outside this narrow band of water, freedom of the seas (including free use of natural resources) was a doctrine extending back for centuries. This began to change in 1945, however, when the United States claimed all the natural resources on its continental shelf and in the waters above the shelf. Shortly after, some countries began claiming that their national boundaries extended twelve miles from shore rather than three.

Although the economic and territorial push into the oceans proceeded slowly, as technology increased the economic value of the resources in the water and seabed contiguous to landmasses, greater and greater claims were put forward. Some countries were content just to expand their zones of economic control. Others made territorial claims of up to two hundred miles from their shorelines. In addition to the possible shipping problems caused by these developments, island nations began claiming all the water between their islands, which included many strategic routes. Minor conflicts arose between traditionally friendly countries, and international tensions increased when more than one country claimed particular mineral-rich areas. In 1958, when the United Nations held its first conference on the sea, 65 percent of the world's ocean resources were considered to be in in-

ternational waters. By the time the third U.N. conference on the sea started in 1973, the proportion had decreased to 35 percent.

In the midst of these developments, Arvid Pardo, ambassador to the United Nations from the government of Malta, gave a speech in which he asked that all countries come together to establish a new international agreement to solve the growing problem. Pardo's speech led not only to movement in this area but also to environmental conferences and multinational treaties such as the one that outlawed the placement of nuclear weapons on the seabed. On November, 16, 1973, the General Assembly of the United Nations voted to establish the Third United Nations Conference on the Law of the Sea. U.N. secretary-general Kurt Waldheim convened the first session of the conference in New York City on December 3, 1973. Waldheim left office just prior to the eleventh and final session, which ended on December 10, 1982. At the final session, the vote to accept the results of the nine-year conference was 130 to 4, with the United States voting in the negative.

President Ronald Reagan announced that he would not sign the resulting Law of the Sea Treaty or submit it to the U.S. Senate for ratification. His concerns about the treaty had to do with both national security and economics. Reagan objected to the treaty's provisions regarding submarine travel, which required submarines to surface when traveling through certain straits. He also believed that the treaty restricted free enterprise because it provided for keeping deep ocean minerals as a trust for everyone regulated by an international body; Reagan believed that any nation that could develop the technology to mine such minerals should be able to do so unhindered. Reagan did announce, however, that the United States would abide by the principal provisions of the treaty.

The treaty was to go into effect one year after the sixtieth country had ratified it. The ratification process moved slowly, however. Javier Pérez de Cuéllar, who became secretary-general of the United Nations shortly before the treaty was signed in 1982, called together a study group to develop standard interpretations of some controversial provisions of the treaty as a means to speed up the ratification process. With a statement from that group in 1992, the ratification process picked up speed, and in 1993 the sixtieth country ratified it. The Law of the Sea Treaty thus entered into force on November 16,

1994

1994. Additional countries ratified the treaty after a 1998 agreement on deep-sea mining was added. The United States, however, continued to have disagreements with certain provisions; by the early years of the twenty-first century, it was the only one of the world's major economic powers that had not ratified the treaty.

The Law of the Sea Treaty is an extensive document that attempts to resolve many issues. The principal provisions deal with territorial limits, economic zones, use of the continental shelf, navigation, deep-sea mining, protection of the environment, and mechanisms for settling disputes. The framers of the treaty often had to work out compromises between the developed and the developing countries.

The part of the treaty that deals with territorial limits is both very simple and very complex. The simple definition of "territorial waters" that suffices for most discussions is all waters within twelve nautical miles of the shore. Determining where the shore lies, however, can be quite complicated. The treaty defines how every conceivable type of shoreline affects territorial waters. For example, the land that is exposed at low tide is the point from which the twelve miles is measured, and the line for measurement extends straight across the mouth of a river. The treaty also defines how other types of inlets and islands affect territorial waters, as well as what happens when the open water between two countries measures less than twenty-four miles.

In addition, the treaty defines an area extending up to two hundred nautical miles from shore as a country's "exclusive economic zone." As the name implies, within this area the controlling state has exclusive rights to all economic resources as well as scientific research. The state is also charged with the protection of the environment within this area.

Further, the Law of the Sea Treaty includes provisions for landlocked and geographically disadvantaged states to share in excess economic resources of other states. Coastal states, however, have not proclaimed any of their economic resources to be surplus. The economic resources of a continental shelf belong to the coastal state up to 350 miles from the shore, if the shelf extends that far.

The treaty specifies that traditional navigation routes are to remain open to civilian ships even when these go through territorial waters. Certain straits are defined in such a way that military vessels, in addition to civilian ships, may pass through them unhindered by the countries that claim the waters in the straits. This falls under the doctrine of the "right of innocent passage." The coun-

tries that control the territorial waters in these areas may enforce what are essentially traffic laws to ensure the safe and orderly passage of all ships.

On what are called the "high seas," all nations have rights of navigation and the right to fish and otherwise exploit the natural resources. They also share the responsibility of protecting the environment. The treaty specifically states that all nations should work together to conserve and manage the living resources of the world's oceans. In many areas of deep ocean, fairly pure mineral nodules lie on the bottom under miles of water. Annex III of the treaty outlines in great detail how minerals taken from the high seas should be used to benefit all nations. Even though no nation had found an economically feasible way to mine these resources by the beginning of the twenty-first century, this is one of the provisions of the treaty to which the United States objected.

In terms of international law, the diverse dispute-resolution mechanisms written into the treaty are often seen as innovative. If the parties to a dispute over provisions of the treaty cannot resolve their differences, the treaty specifies four methods by which they can reach a peaceful resolution. Most treaties include just one recognized method to resolve a conflict if a dialogue does not solve the problem.

## SIGNIFICANCE

In the midst of the Cold War and increasing disputes between the developed and developing countries, the Law of the Sea Treaty created a foundation for peaceful conflict resolution and use of the ocean's resources. At a time when many nations were announcing extensive new economic and territorial claims, there was a fear that the concept of international waters might soon disappear, and free trade with it. Efforts in 1958 and 1960 to create an agreement to address these issues did not come close to success; thus, although nine years were required to negotiate it, the Law of the Sea Treaty was a tremendous step forward. Although not all countries have ratified the treaty, its provisions dealing with territorial waters, economic zones, and navigation have become the recognized norms for all. The treaty has thus contributed to a decrease in international tensions and has allowed the orderly development of the ocean's economic resources.

*—Donald A. Watt*

## FURTHER READING

Churchill, R. R., and A. V. Lowe. *The Law of the Sea*. 3d ed. Yonkers, N.Y.: Juris, 1999. Covers the basic legal concepts across the breadth of the international treaty.

Freestone, David, Richard Barnes, and David Ong, eds. *The Law of the Sea: Progress and Prospects.* New York: Oxford University Press, 2006. Collection of essays provides an overview of how the implementation of the treaty has worked and where problems have arisen in adapting it to a changing world.

Strati, Anastasia, Maria Gavouneli, and Nikolaos Skourtos, eds. *Unresolved Issues and New Challenges to the Law of the Sea: Time Before and Time After.* Boston: Martinus Nijhoff, 2006. Collection of essays focuses on potential weaknesses in the treaty and examines how the treaty might be used to cover such areas as migrating fish populations.

**SEE ALSO:** Sept. 1, 1972-June 2, 1976: Cod Wars; Jan. 1, 1986: International Whaling Ban Goes into Effect; Dec. 29, 1987: U.S. Congress Prohibits Marine Plastics Dumping; Dec. 31, 1992: United Nations Bans the Use of Drift Nets; 1993: Norway Resumes Whaling in Defiance of International Ban.

---

## December 1, 1994
# GENERAL AGREEMENT ON TARIFFS AND TRADE

*The ambitious General Agreement on Tariffs and Trade was designed to facilitate free trade and increase exports worldwide. The agreement led to the creation of the World Trade Organization and contributed to the growing globalization of the international economy.*

**LOCALE:** Washington, D.C.
**CATEGORIES:** Trade and commerce; business and labor; diplomacy and international relations; economics

**KEY FIGURES**
*Bill Clinton* (b. 1946), president of the United States, 1993-2001
*Bob Dole* (b. 1923), U.S. senator from Kansas

**SUMMARY OF EVENT**
On December 1, 1994, the U.S. Senate joined the House of Representatives in voting overwhelmingly in favor of what was widely considered to be the most far-reaching trade agreement reached up to that time. The General Agreement on Tariffs and Trade (GATT) slashed tariffs (taxes on imports) by an average of 40 percent in the 124 participating countries. Cuts in tariffs were expected to bring a boom in U.S. exports, leading to more jobs. In addition, American consumers would have access to cheaper imported goods. GATT, which had taken eight years to negotiate, represented a huge leap toward free trade worldwide.

A version of GATT had governed most international trade since 1948, but negotiations to expand the agreement began only in 1986. The new GATT was governed by a new organization, the World Trade Organization, located in Geneva. This organization had more power over signatory nations than its predecessor, the GATT Secretariat, and had the authority to enforce agreements through the imposition of trade penalties.

The votes of the U.S. Senate and House of Representatives in favor of GATT sounded a rare note of unity between Democrats and Republicans. They were brought together by their confidence that the agreement would revitalize the economy. President Bill Clinton's administration estimated that the agreement would create half a million new jobs. The administration also predicted an annual increase of $150 billion in U.S. economic growth when the agreement was fully implemented, after ten years. The Organization for Economic Cooperation and Growth estimated that, worldwide, GATT's lower tariffs and higher import quotas (limits on amounts of goods permitted to be imported) would increase world income by $270 billion per year.

Tariffs have long been used by almost all nations in the world to protect their own farmers and native industries against competition from cheaper foreign goods. Increasingly, however, many economists have come to oppose such self-protectionist measures. They believe that free trade, without the barriers of tariffs, is the key to worldwide economic growth. The principles of free trade that inspired GATT hold that a country that is good at producing a given product will profit from exporting it to countries that are less efficient at producing that product. In return, a country can use the wealth it gains from exports to buy goods and services that are produced more efficiently elsewhere. It is theorized that, when each country focuses on what it does best, market forces of supply and demand organize distribution for maximum economic growth and consumers benefit from lower prices. However, governments have interfered with these market forces by imposing tariffs and strict quotas limit-

1994

ing the amounts of a product that can be imported, giving the product a false scarcity value that pushes up its price.

Not all economists are convinced that promoting free trade through initiatives such as GATT is the answer to the world's economic problems. Some argue that free trade benefits developed nations more than developing nations, since the richer nations can import goods from countries where labor and materials are cheaper. Critics of this view cite the Asian nations as proof of the benefits of free trade for developing nations. During the early 1960's, these countries were in serious economic trouble. Those that favored free trade (Hong Kong, Taiwan, South Korea, and Singapore) experienced more growth than countries that did not (India, North Korea, and Vietnam). Manufacturing did tend to flow toward sources of cheap labor, but this tendency helped develop the local economy and raise the standard of living.

Concerns over the possible negative effects of GATT are not restricted to economics. Cultural conflicts have arisen from the agreement, such as a disagreement between the United States and Japan over rice. The Japanese have always banned the import of rice to protect their own rice crop, which occupies a central position in their culture and religion, but under GATT the Japanese agreed to allow the import of some rice. Although the

conflict was resolved, the episode presented an important challenge to advocates of free trade: How far should a country's cultural traditions be compromised to facilitate world trade?

Resistance to GATT also came from within the United States. Critics expressed fears that the World Trade Organization could attack U.S. consumer protection laws (such as the labeling of food product ingredients), worker protection laws, and environmental regulations as trade barriers. Among those who raised questions about the power of the World Trade Organization were Republican senator Bob Dole, consumer advocate and 2000 presidential candidate Ralph Nader, and various environmental lobby groups. Critics have presented many scenarios to back up their arguments. For example, if the United States decided on ethical grounds to ban the import of South Asian rugs made using child labor, countries that suffered from the decision could take their case to a panel of three World Trade Organization judges. If the judges ruled against the United States, then Congress or the state whose regulation was under challenge would have to decide whether to change that regulation. If the lawmakers refused, trade sanctions could be imposed against U.S. exports. As another example, environmentalists have expressed concern that under GATT, the

*After the Senate overwhelmingly passed legislation supporting the General Agreement on Tariffs and Trade's plan to cut tariffs in December, 1994, President Bill Clinton addressed top leaders of Congress outside the White House.* (AP/Wide World Photos)

United States could not impose its own stringent environmental laws on other nations. In 1991, under existing GATT rules whose enforcement provisions were far weaker than those ratified in 1994, the United States lost a case brought against one of its federal laws banning the importation of tuna caught in nets that also trapped dolphins. A GATT panel ruled that the United States could not impose its environmental restrictions on the rest of the world. Otherwise, the panel said, the United States could use those restrictions to keep out foreign competitors. In an attempt to allay fears about the World Trade Organization and its possible threat to U.S. sovereignty, President Clinton reached an agreement with Senator Dole to create a commission in the United States to review judgments that the organization makes against the United States.

## SIGNIFICANCE

The main areas of trade affected by GATT and its stipulations are as follows. In agriculture, U.S. GATT negotiators were at odds for years with the European Community over agricultural issues. The Europeans wanted to maintain subsidies to their farmers, but the United States wanted subsidies eliminated because they gave an unfair advantage in the marketplace at high cost to consumers. GATT produced a compromise that stipulates that agricultural tariffs be reduced by 36 percent in industrial nations and 24 percent in developing nations.

Regarding intellectual property, GATT required all member countries to respect patents, trademarks, and copyrights. This requirement was expected to eradicate the pirated computer programs, records, videocassettes, and prescription drugs rampant in developing nations.

Regarding automobiles, restrictions on auto exports, such as those that the United States imposed on Japan, were eliminated. The agreement also banned the widespread practice of requiring high local content in some products, such as cars, a practice that protects local jobs but discourages imports. The agreement also limited the ability of countries to favor domestically owned factories at the expense of foreign-owned ones.

Finally, richer nations were required to phase out quotas on clothing imports over a ten-year period. Quotas were to be replaced by less restrictive tariffs. Some of the strongest opposition to GATT in the United States had come from textile states such as North Carolina and South Carolina, which feared that their industries would suffer as a result of cheap foreign imports.

It seemed inevitable that GATT would continue to provoke conflicts of nationalistic self-interest, but there is also hope that its ratification marked the beginning of a new era of increased global cooperation and trust between its signatory nations.

—*Claire J. Robinson*

## FURTHER READING

Barton, John H., Judith L. Goldstein, Timothy E. Josling, and Richard H. Steinberg. *The Evolution of the Trade Regime: Politics, Law, and Economics of the GATT and the WTO*. Princeton, N.J.: Princeton University Press, 2006. Presents a political economic history of the development of GATT and the World Trade Organization. Includes illustrations, tables, bibliography, and index.

Boskin, Michael J. "Pass GATT Now." *Fortune*, December 12, 1994, 137-138. A Republican economist states the reasons he believes members of his party in Congress should put politics aside and approve the trade agreement.

Dentzer, Susan. "A New Tapestry of Protectionism." *U.S. News & World Report*, December 5, 1994, 83. Points out the protectionist potholes built into GATT by some of the agreement's signatory nations.

Harbrecht, Douglas. "GATT: Tales from the Dark Side." *BusinessWeek*, December 19, 1994, 52. Cautions that global trade promoted by GATT may cause protectionist backlash in some nations as a result of trade moving to pools of cheap labor elsewhere in the world.

Mavroidis, Petros C. *The General Agreement on Tariffs and Trade: A Commentary*. New York: Oxford University Press, 2005. Explains how GATT works in the context of international law and clarifies what nations gain and lose by joining the World Trade Organization.

Nader, Ralph. "Drop the GATT." *The Nation*, October 10, 1994, 368-369. Consumer advocate Nader warns against the power of the World Trade Organization, which he believes is undemocratic and a threat to U.S. sovereignty.

Thomas, Rich. "Tempest over Trade." *Newsweek*, December 5, 1994, 50. Presents answers to various objections to GATT, including the issue of U.S. sovereignty and the power of the World Trade Organization.

**SEE ALSO:** 1971: United States Suffers Its First Trade Deficit Since 1888; Nov. 3, 1992: Clinton Wins the U.S. Presidency; June 25, 1993: Campbell Becomes Canada's First Woman Prime Minister; Nov. 20, 1993: North American Free Trade Agreement; Nov. 15, 1999: United States and China Sign Trade Deal.

## December 10, 1994
# ŌE RECEIVES THE NOBEL PRIZE IN LITERATURE

*The awarding of the Nobel Prize to leftist, antiwar activist Japanese writer Kenzaburō Ōe brought worldwide attention to the author's views and to the radical developments in postwar Japanese literature.*

**LOCALE:** Stockholm, Sweden
**CATEGORY:** Literature

**KEY FIGURES**

*Kenzaburō Ōe* (b. 1935), Japanese existentialist writer of novels, short stories, and essays
*Hikari Ōe* (b. 1963), developmentally disabled son of Kenzaburō Ōe who figures in much of the author's fiction
*Jean-Paul Sartre* (1905-1980), French existentialist philosopher who had a powerful influence on Ōe's thought and work

**SUMMARY OF EVENT**

The announcement that Kenzaburō Ōe, one of Japan's most popular writers, had won the Nobel Prize in Literature came on October 13, 1994. Because this prize represents such a great achievement, Ōe became an overnight celebrity. Photographs of the author and stories about his life appeared in newspapers around the world. Reporters stormed his home to question him about his reaction and what significance the prize would have for him and his family.

The award of the prestigious Nobel Prize to the fifty-nine-year-old Ōe came as a surprise to the literary world. In spite of his popularity in his own country, Ōe had not been widely published in English or in other languages. His last book to be published in English was *Nan to moshirenai mirai ni* (1985; *The Crazy Iris, and Other Stories of the Atomic Aftermath*, 1985), a decade before; the English translation had sold only modestly. According to an article in *The New York Times*, the writers who were considered most likely to receive the Nobel Prize in 1994 had been the German novelist and playwright Peter Handke, the Dutch novelist Cees Nooteboom, the Swedish poet Tomas Tranströmer, the Japanese novelist Shusaku Endo, the Irish poet Seamus Heaney, and Hugo Claus, a Belgian poet, playwright, and novelist who writes in Flemish.

Little was known of Ōe outside Japan, and foreign journalists had difficulty writing their first articles about him. All the media reported that he was best known for his gripping accounts of the atomic bombing of Hiro-

shima during World War II and for his many works in which he describes his struggle to come to terms with the birth of a son who was deformed and mentally disabled. These two factors, which have had such prominence in Ōe's published fiction and essays, are closely related. Ōe was deeply concerned about the genetic effects of atomic radiation and suspected that his son's deformity might have been one of them.

The Nobel Prizes are traditionally presented in Stockholm on December 10, the anniversary of the death of Alfred Nobel, who established the awards in 1901. Nobel Week in Sweden is a spectacular event, bringing together notables from all over the world. The king of Sweden and the royal family officiate, and many banquets, balls, cocktail parties, dinners, and press conferences are held before and after the presentation of the awards. Each winner has a chauffeur-driven limousine and a room at the elegant Grand Hotel, and each receives a monetary award of 7.2 million Swedish kronor (equal to about $936,000 at 1994 exchange rates).

Kenzaburō Ōe was accompanied to Stockholm by his wife. His Nobel Prize lecture, presented to the assembled international dignitaries and their guests, was characteristically modest and succinct. As a sort of homage to Yasunari Kawabata, Japan's only previous Nobel laureate in literature, Ōe titled his lecture "Japan, the Ambiguous, and Myself" (Kawabata's Nobel lecture was titled "Japan, the Beautiful, and Myself"). He told the audience that Japan was divided between past and present, old customs and new innovations, between the influence of the East and the West. "The modernization of Japan," he said, "has been oriented toward learning from and imitating the West. Yet the country is situated in Asia and has firmly maintained its traditional culture." Always especially concerned about the folly of war, he cautioned that Japan was moving away from its official policy of pacifism, which was adopted as part of its constitution after its disastrous defeat in World War II and subsequent occupation by American military forces under General Douglas MacArthur.

Ōe took advantage of the occasion to pay tribute in his lecture to some of the Western thinkers who had influenced his thought and work. One of the writers he mentioned was Mark Twain, whose novel *Adventures of Huckleberry Finn* (1884) was one of his all-time favorites. He was particularly impressed by the young Huck Finn's rejection of established conventions and his search for truth. Ōe also paid tribute to William Blake, William Butler Yeats, George Orwell, and François Rabelais, as well as Korean writer Kim Chi Ha and Chinese writers Chon I and Mu Jen. He spoke of the "brotherhood of world literature" to which he belonged.

Ōe's speech exemplified the broadened worldview of modern Japanese writers and intellectuals in general. He alluded to Japanese aggression during the 1930's and 1940's. He did not go so far as to apologize for his country's actions, but he indicated that Japanese imperialism had been only one aspect of the effect of "inhuman technology" (of which the atomic bomb was the supreme obscenity). He reminded his audience that the Japanese constitution had specifically underwritten the principle of permanent peace as the moral basis for the nation's rebirth. He neither blamed nor forgave the Americans for dropping atomic bombs on Hiroshima and Nagasaki in 1945, but he implied that the horrible events and their aftermath were also aspects of the same moral blindness that had led Japan into war.

Ōe concluded his speech as follows: "As one with a peripheral, marginal, and off-center existence in the world, I would like to seek how—with what I hope is a modest, decent, and humanist contribution—I can be of some use in a cure and reconciliation of mankind."

## SIGNIFICANCE

"Oh, East is East, and West is West, and never the twain shall meet," wrote British poet Rudyard Kipling in his "Ballad of East and West" in 1889. Only a little more than one hundred years later, the awarding of the Nobel Prize in Literature to Kenzaburō Ōe symbolized to the entire world that East and West had indeed met and were continuing to form an important part of the intercultural integration and cross-fertilization taking place all around the globe. This phenomenon of the twentieth century was the result of fantastic developments in transportation and communication that Kipling could not have foreseen. It was also in part the result of two great world wars that shattered empires and had an even more shattering effect on traditional beliefs of the peoples of the East and West.

Ōe was only ten years old when a U.S. bomber dropped the first atomic bomb on Hiroshima, one of the most dramatic and far-reaching events in world history. The atomic standoff between the Soviet Union and the United States was to become the centerpiece of the Cold War, which lasted for almost half a century and created what another Nobel Prize winner, William Faulkner, was to call "a general and universal physical fear." The Japanese realized that it was impossible to sustain a

war against such an awesome weapon. Japan's Emperor Hirohito announced the surrender, and Japan was occupied by American military forces under the command of General Douglas MacArthur. Tokyo and many other Japanese cities already lay in ruins. This disastrous period in Japanese history had a powerful impact on the Japanese people, including the young Ōe. It was to have lifelong effects on his thought and writing.

Ōe lost faith in the divinity of the Japanese emperor and in most traditional Japanese beliefs. As a student majoring in French literature at the University of Tokyo, he was profoundly influenced by Western writers. Perhaps the most important influence in his intellectual life was French philosopher Jean-Paul Sartre, who is best known as the father of existentialism. This highly influential post-World War II philosophy holds that life has no meaning or purpose beyond the goals the individual sets for him or herself. Ōe adopted from Sartre the passionate belief that literature must take sides in political issues.

The most important aspect of Ōe's being honored with the Nobel Prize was that it brought worldwide attention to modern Japanese literature. Ōe himself acknowl-

*Kenzaburō Ōe.* (The Nobel Foundation)

edged in his Nobel lecture that he was only one of a new wave of Japanese writers who had made a radical departure from the themes and styles of the traditional literature of their native land. Ōe took advantage of that momentous occasion to call attention to many other writers who shared his values.

Japan has a literary tradition unsurpassed by that of any other nation. The roots of Japanese literature may be traced directly to the even older literature of China. Japanese art has had a powerful influence on Western art, as can be seen in the work of artists such as Vincent van Gogh and Claude Monet. In modern times, Japanese motion pictures, such as Akira Kurosawa's *Rashomon* (1950), have had a potent influence on international cinematography. Japan's literature, however, has not received the attention from the rest of the world accorded to the literatures of Western nations. Ōe's recognition as a Noble laureate helped to change that by encouraging the translation of his and other Japanese writers' works into other languages.

Right after the announcement of Ōe's Nobel Prize, American publisher Grove/Atlantic announced plans to print an additional twenty thousand copies of English translations of each of three Ōe books: *The Crazy Iris, and Other Stories of the Atomic Aftermath, Warera no kyōki o ikinobiru michi o oshieyo* (1969, 1975; *Teach Us to Outgrow Our Madness: Four Short Novels*, 1977), and *Kojinteki na taiken* (1964; *A Personal Matter*, 1968). The American subsidiary of the Japanese publishing firm Kodansha promised ten thousand new copies in English of Ōe's *Man'en gan'nen no futtoboru* (1967; *The Silent Cry*, 1974), and M. E. Sharpe, a publisher in Armonk, New York, made immediate plans to print several thousand additional copies of the English translation of Ōe's novel *Pinchi rannā chōsho* (1976; *The Pinch Runner Memorandum*, 1994). Marion Boyars Publishers quickly brought out an English-language translation of Ōe's first novel, *Memushiri kouchi* (1958; *Nip the Buds, Shoot the Kids*, 1995). Such is the prestige of the Nobel Prize in Literature that practically overnight, Kenzaburō Ōe became a household name and Japanese literature gained worldwide attention.

—*Bill Delaney*

## FURTHER READING

Cameron, Lindsley. *The Music of Light: The Extraordinary Story of Hikari and Kenzaburo Oe*. New York: Free Press, 1998. Biographical work focuses on the relationship between Kenzaburō Ōe and his mentally disabled son, Hikari, who is a musical savant. Discusses the creative interdependence between father and son.

Napier, Susan J. *Escape from the Wasteland: Romanticism and Realism in the Fiction of Mishima Yukio and Ōe Kenzaburō*. Cambridge, Mass.: Harvard University Press, 1991. Compares and contrasts two of the most popular and influential writers of postwar Japan. Presents detailed discussion of many of Ōe's stories and novels. Includes bibliography.

Ōe, Kenzaburō. *An Echo of Heaven*. Translated by Margaret Mitisutani. New York: Kodansha International, 1996. Novel has an international theme, suggesting the broadening of Ōe's interests and influence after he won the Nobel Prize. The story concerns a Japanese woman whose search for religious meaning takes her on a pilgrimage from Japan to a California commune, then to Mexico, where she comes to be venerated as a saint by superstitious peasants.

_____. *A Healing Family*. Translated by Stephen Snyder. New York: Kodansha International, 1996. Collection of personal essays about Ōe and the people closest to him, especially his mentally disabled son, Hikari. The theme throughout is the healing power of family love. Includes delicate sketches and watercolors by Ōe's wife, Yukari, who also contributed an afterword.

_____. *Hiroshima Notes*. Translated by David L. Swain and Toshi Yonezawa. London: Marion Boyars, 1995. Describes a series of visits the author made in the period 1963-1965 to Hiroshima, the city that was obliterated by a U.S. atomic bomb in the closing days of World War II.

_____. Interview by Sanroku Yoshida. *World Literature Today* 62 (Summer, 1988): 369-374. Relaxed, informal interview covers a wide range of topics, including politics, Japanese literature, foreign literature, recent historical events, and relations between the sexes. Includes discussion of many of Ōe's literary works. Serves as a good introduction to the author as a modest, concerned, inquisitive, widely read, and likable human being.

_____. *Japan, the Ambiguous, and Myself: The Nobel Prize Speech and Other Lectures*. New York: Kodansha International, 1995. Slim volume contains English translations of speeches Ōe made to foreign audiences in the period 1990-1994. Provides an excellent introduction to Ōe's political, philosophical, and artistic views.

_____. *Nip the Buds, Shoot the Kids*. Translated by Paul St. John Mackintosh and Maki Sugiyama. London: Marion Boyars, 1995. Novel is representative of Ōe's work. Displays his bitterness, his evocation of myth and archetype, and a prose style heavily influenced by Western writers, which breaks away from Japanese tradition. Describes the adventures of fifteen delinquent teenagers during the dark days of World War II, when Japan was facing defeat.

Wilson, Michiko N. *The Marginal World of Oe Kenzaburo: A Study in Themes and Techniques.* 1986. Reprint. Armonk, N.Y.: M. E. Sharpe, 1997. Presents a close analysis of Ōe's narrative techniques using tools of European literary criticism. Helpful for an understanding of the powerful influence of Western literature on Ōe's work.

Yoshida, Sanroku. "The Burning Tree: The Spatialized World of Kenzaburo Oe." *World Literature Today* 69 (Winter, 1995): 10-16. Brief article provides an excellent overview of Ōe's life, work, artistic objectives, and philosophy.

**SEE ALSO:** Dec. 10, 1978: Singer Is Awarded the Nobel Prize in Literature; Dec. 10, 1986: Soyinka Receives the Nobel Prize in Literature; Dec. 10, 1988: Mahfouz Receives the Nobel Prize in Literature; Dec. 10, 1991: Gordimer Receives the Nobel Prize in Literature; Dec. 10, 1995: Heaney Receives the Nobel Prize in Literature; Dec. 10, 1996: Szymborska Receives the Nobel Prize in Literature.

# December 11, 1994
# RUSSIAN TROOPS INVADE CHECHNYA

*Russian troops invaded Chechnya in an attempt to prevent the province's secession, but the invasion failed to end the independence movement and further eroded the popularity of Russian president Boris Yeltsin.*

**ALSO KNOWN AS:** First Chechen War
**LOCALE:** Chechnya, Russia
**CATEGORIES:** Wars, uprisings, and civil unrest; military history

**KEY FIGURES**
*Viktor Chernomyrdin* (b. 1938), prime minister of Russia, 1992-1998
*Dzhokhar M. Dudayev* (1944-1996), president of Chechnya, 1991-1996
*Pavel S. Grachev* (b. 1948), Russian minister of defense
*Boris Yeltsin* (1931-2007), president of the Russian Soviet Federated Socialist Republic, 1991-1999

**SUMMARY OF EVENT**
On December 11, 1994, Russian president Boris Yeltsin ordered Russian forces to invade the province of Chechnya, in the Caucasus region of southern Russia, in order to end the separatist movement led by Dzhokhar M. Dudayev. Dudayev, a major general in the Soviet air force, had taken advantage of the turmoil that followed the failed coup attempt against Soviet leader Mikhail Gorbachev in August of 1991 to seize power in Chechnya and assert its independence.

The invasion of 1994 was a dramatic episode in a long and troubled relationship between the Chechens and the Russians. During this prolonged struggle, the Chechens and the related Ingush, between the seventeenth and early nineteenth centuries, converted to Islam. Islam, in its Sunni form with militant Sufi brotherhoods, subsequently became a central component of Chechen identity. In 1783, a Chechen named Mansur led the first unified Caucasian resistance against the Russians. After Mansur, the Chechens were rallied by Shamil, an Avar from Dagestan.

Although Chechnya was formally subdued in 1859, the region experienced periodic uprisings and resistance to Russian rule. During World War II, the Chechens and other Caucasian peoples were charged with collaboration with the Nazis and were subjected to a genocidal deportation to Kazakhstan and Kyrgyzstan. Some estimates of the number of Chechens who died during the brutal process of forced movement run as high as 300,000. Grozny, the principal Chechen city, already largely Russian, was settled with Russians, and Russians and Dagestani were settled elsewhere in Chechnya.

The Chechens were not rehabilitated until 1956, during Soviet leader Nikita S. Khrushchev's campaign of de-Stalinization, when they were allowed to return to the reestablished Chechen-Ingush Autonomous Soviet Socialist Republic in 1957. The republic was one of the least developed in Russia. Industry and the service sector provided employment for only 40 percent of the population. Despite one of the highest rates of infant mortality

1994

CHECHNYA, RUSSIA

in the Soviet Union and one of the lowest life expectancies, the Chechen population grew. Subjected to derision by Russians, who considered Chechens to be culturally backward and socially inferior, the Chechens nevertheless controlled access to oil reserves that were of strategic interest to the Soviet Union.

Even after Joseph Stalin's death, Chechens were not often chosen to serve as administrators in the republic. The legacy of the deportations and the desire of the Chechens to control their future and to profit from new opportunities converged in the chaos of the disintegration of the Soviet Union. On September 15, 1991, the self-styled Executive Committee of the All National Congress of the Chechen People, headed by Dudayev, forced the disbanding of the Supreme Soviet of the Chechen-Ingush Autonomous Republic, claiming that the Supreme Soviet had supported the attempted August coup in the Soviet Union.

On October 27, Dudayev was elected president of Chechnya by 84 percent of the electorate. Although the Ingush refused to join the Chechens, Dudayev declared Chechnya to be a sovereign state on November 1, 1991. Yeltsin declared a state of emergency on November 8 and sent troops to Grozny. The Russians, however, completely underestimated their opponents and bungled the execution of their effort to crush Chechen separatism.

Dudayev, who dissolved the Chechen parliament on July 4, 1993, and assumed dictatorial powers, had numerous opponents in Chechnya. As Yeltsin's popularity plummeted in the wake of his October, 1993, attack on the Russian parliament, Yeltsin sought to use Dudayev's opponents as his proxies. If Yeltsin could reassert Russian authority in Chechnya, Russia would control the crucial pipeline connecting the oil of Azerbaijan and Kazakhstan to the Black Sea. Success against the Chechens would bolster Yeltsin against his nationalist opponents in the Russian parliament, which was elected in December of 1993. Despite Dudayev's willingness to accept a degree of local control short of secession, Yeltsin decided to move because of his own interests. The Russian Interior Ministry forces and their Chechen collaborators, however, were humiliatingly defeated in a raid held on November 28, 1994, the fifth failed Russian attempt to oust Dudayev.

Pavel S. Grachev, the Russian defense minister, now decided that the honor of Russia's military was at stake. As Yeltsin retreated to the cover of a hospital, Russian forces launched their invasion on December 11, 1994. Three columns were to converge on Grozny. The plan was to allow Dudayev and his followers to withdraw to the mountains in the south, where they would be cut off and eventually forced to submit. The attack went awry from the start, however. The invasion united the Chechens and won them the sympathy of other Caucasian Muslims.

Faced with additional humiliation, Grachev assumed personal control of the campaign and ordered one of the most difficult military tasks, the taking of a city street by street. He had earlier predicted that Chechnya would be pacified in forty-eight hours. He now asserted that Grozny would be taken in two hours. The result was disaster. Isolated Russian units were decimated, and the Chechens, who were able to resupply their units at night, resisted for a month. The presidential palace, from which Dudayev directed resistance, held until January 19. The Russians were eventually forced to use their artillery and airpower to level much of the city. By the end of the month, some twenty-five thousand civilians had been killed. Russia had lost at least eighteen hundred soldiers and perhaps as many as five thousand, according to some sources, and the Chechens had lost eight thousand fighters. The Chechens finally pulled out, but they continued their stubborn resistance from the countryside. Prime Minister Viktor Chernomyrdin's desire for peace talks and Dudayev's willingness to negotiate were thwarted by the war party surrounding Yeltsin.

Russian attacks on Chechen villages continued through the spring. Then, on the eve of the June 14 summit of the G7 (Group of Seven) nations in Halifax, Nova Scotia, Shamil Basayev led an attack on Budyonnovsk, located two hundred miles inside Russia. Basayev, whose eleven female cousins had been raped and murdered by Russians, assumed the role of the Chechen *abreg*, or bandit of honor, who pursued the Chechen clan tradition of vendetta to the seventh generation. The Chechens, who had bribed their way past Russian security forces, killed twenty Russian policemen and held two thousand people hostage in a hospital. After an inept Russian assault that led to more Russian deaths, Chernomyrdin negotiated on live television for release of the hostages. The Chechens were allowed free passage back to Chechnya, and a cease-fire was negotiated. Yeltsin, who had left the country during the crisis, saw his popularity further eroded and suffered a heart attack.

The cease-fire quickly broke down. Despite the fact that Russia committed fifty-eight thousand troops—forty thousand from the regular army and eighteen thousand from the Interior Ministry—it was not able to pacify or secure Chechnya. In September, Oleg Lobov, Yeltsin's personal representative, barely escaped assassination. General Anatoly Romanov, the Russian commander, was critically wounded in an attack on October 6. On November 20, Doku Zavgayev, the Russia-appointed Chechen administrator, was injured in an assassination attempt.

In January of 1996, Salman Raduyev led a Chechen assault on Kizlyar, in Dagestan, and took two thousand hostages. After negotiations, Raduyev's force was promised safe passage back to Chechnya, but they were stopped and surrounded at Pervomayskoye. The incompetence of the Russian forces and the lack of credibility of the Yeltsin administration were obvious in the fiasco that followed. Raduyev and a number of his band, with hostages, eluded the "impenetrable" Russian circle and made it back to Chechnya.

Yeltsin's desperation was palpable. Following the Communist victory in the parliamentary elections held in December of 1995, Yeltsin said that if he was to win the June presidential election, the struggle in Chechnya had to be brought to an end. He simultaneously called for the execution of Dudayev (who was eventually killed during a missile attack in April, 1996). Yeltsin and Chechen president Aslan Maskhadov signed a peace treaty on May 12, 1997, although the independence of Chechnya remained unresolved.

## SIGNIFICANCE

The Chechnya question remained an open sore for both Russia and the world that watched. The crisis was punctuated by another war in 1999, when the Russians undertook a brutal effort to crush a Chechen rebellion in Dagestan. The Russians succeeded in debilitating the rebels but created some 250,000 refugees who fled the fighting.

Having failed in conventional war, some Chechnyans sought peace, whereas others took part in terrorist acts. The latter included such atrocities as the seizure of nearly eight hundred patrons of a Moscow theater in October, 2002; suspected involvement in plane crashes that killed ninety in August, 2004; and the seizure of a school at Beslan, where eleven hundred schoolchildren and adults were held hostage and more than three hundred people ultimately died. Even as progress was made toward political stabilization, passions clearly continued to run high among militants for whom compromise was unthinkable.

—*Bernard A. Cook*

## FURTHER READING

Avtorkhanov, Abdurahman. "The Chechens and the Ingush During the Soviet Period." In *The North Caucasus Barrier*, edited by Marie Broxup. New York:

1994

St. Martin's Press, 1992. Presents an account of the Chechens under Soviet rule, including the deportations of 1943.

Gall, Carlotta, and Thomas de Waal. *Chechnya: Calamity in the Caucasus.* New York: New York University Press, 1998. Account by two journalists who covered the conflict for the *Moscow Times* provides a historical overview as well as detailed discussion of the events of the war. Includes maps, bibliographic notes, and index.

Goldenberg, Suzanne. *Pride of Small Nations: The Caucasus and Post-Soviet Disorder.* London: Zed Books, 1994. Provides background material and a history of the Chechen declaration of independence and the Russian reaction.

Mesbahi, Mohiaddin, ed. *Central Asia and the Caucasus After the Soviet Union: Domestic and International Dynamics.* Gainesville: University Press of Florida, 1994. Collection of essays covers various facets of the state of the Caucasus after the breakup of the Soviet Union. Chapter by Marie Bennigsen Broxup provides information on the history and culture of Chechnya and the independence movement up to November of 1991.

Nichols, Johanna. "Who Are the Chechens?" *IREX News in Brief*, January/February, 1995, 3-4. A professor of linguistics presents ethnographic and historical information on the Chechens.

Smith, Sebastian. *Allah's Mountains: The Battle for Chechnya.* New York: I. B. Tauris, 1998. Journalistic work describes the conflict between Russians and Chechens and also provides historical background on the people and cultures of the Caucasus. Includes maps, bibliography, and index.

**See also:** May 27, 1997: NATO and Russia Sign Cooperation Pact; Aug. 7, 1999: Second Chechen War Erupts; Aug. 16, 1999: Putin Becomes Russian Prime Minister.

## December 14, 1994
# Premier Li Peng Announces the Three Gorges Dam Project

*The Chang (Yangtze) River in China provides water and rich silt to the farmlands through which it runs, but it has also caused floods that have devastated villages and cities, killing millions. The proposed Three Gorges Dam would not only provide water for a vast segment of the Chinese population but would also save lives, generate electricity, and be a source of enormous national pride. The project, however, could also cause the demise of countless species of wildlife, pollute the Chang, wipe out cultural landmarks, and force the relocation of some 1.4 million people.*

**Locale:** Chang River, Sandouping, near Yichang, Hubei Province, China

**Categories:** Engineering; environmental issues

**Key Figures**

*Li Peng* (Li P'eng; b. 1928), vice minister and minister of the Ministry of Water Conservancy and Power of the People's Republic of China, 1979-1983

*Mao Zedong* (Mao Tse-tung; 1893-1976), chairman of the Communist Party of China, 1935-1976

*Deng Xiaoping* (Teng Hsiao-p'ing; 1904-1997), chairman of the Central Military Commission of the Chinese Communist Party, 1981-1989

*Jiang Zemin* (Chiang Tse-min; b. 1926), general secretary of the Chinese Communist Party, 1989-2002, and president of the People's Republic of China, 1993-2003

*Hu Jintao* (Hu Chin-t'ao; b. 1942), vice president of the People's Republic of China, 1998-2003, general secretary of the Chinese Communist Party beginning in 2002, and president of the People's Republic of China beginning in 2003

**Summary of Event**

In 1919, China's first provisional president, Sun Yat-sen, proposed that the Chang River, also known as the Yangtze River, be tamed by the construction of a dam that would not only halt its flooding but also provide the nation with an abundant source of electrical energy. Political and social upheaval during the ensuing two decades effectively ended planning, yet in 1932, the National Defense Planning Commission of the Guomindang took up the plan again, this time beginning a survey of the Three Gorges site.

Again, tumultuous political conditions interfered with the work, and it was not until 1954, when severe flooding devastated the countryside, that Communist officials resumed plans for the building of one or more

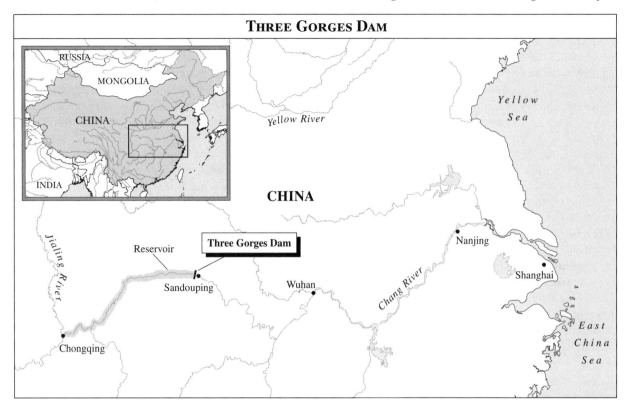

THREE GORGES DAM

dams along the river. Vice minister for electric power Li Rui later determined that the project would be too costly and would wreak too much devastation on the countryside to be undertaken in the early years of the People's Republic of China.

The plan for construction of one or more dams was favored by Chairman Mao Zedong, and in 1958, he urged construction on what he hoped would be the largest hydroelectric plant in the world, a symbol of technological innovation in "New China." Yet this was also the time of the disastrous Great Leap Forward, which crippled the nation and led some thirty-five to fifty million people to starvation and death. Any construction of dams was once again ruled out.

With the intensification of the Cold War, and particularly Chairman Mao's fear of nuclear attack from the United States, the hope of subduing the Chang was seen as part of a comprehensive plan for national defense. In what was termed the Third Front Defense Initiative, in 1964 Mao ordered the dispersal of military bases, armaments, and industries from the vulnerable coastline and northeastern lands (the "First Line") to the less accessible interior regions of the southwest. Military armaments and bases were to be hidden in seemingly impregnable

mountainous areas, and defense industries were to be scattered throughout the territory.

During the Japanese invasion of 1937-1945, China's capital had been moved to Chongqing and consequently was never captured by foreign intruders. Mao believed that the same military strategy would be effective against American incursions, now that the United States military was becoming more deeply involved in the conflict in Vietnam. Relations with the Soviet Union were worsening, and China's natural resources in the areas between the first and third fronts (what was termed the Second Front) seemed vulnerable to attack.

In Mao's initiative, new sources of energy production would be exploited along the Third Front. Suddenly, Sun's plan for the construction of a massive hydroelectric plant along the Chang seemed more important than ever, but even these highly compelling reasons did not lead to implementation of the dam project. China simply did not have the finances or the requisite technology to bring the plans to completion.

In 1994, Li Peng, who had been trained in engineering in the Soviet Union, proclaimed the official commencement of the Three Gorges Dam Project. The Three Gorges Project Committee of the state council was formed,

1994

as was the Power Grid Development Company, which would be responsible for the dam's electrical output. The project was to be financed by institutions worldwide, including many of the preeminent investment firms of the West.

Eleven nations joined in underwriting the Chinese project: Australia, New Zealand, Brazil, Canada, France, Germany, Italy, Japan, Sweden, Switzerland, and the United States. Various international entities, including the World Bank and the Asian Development Bank, supplied many of the funds, as did Chinese financial institutions, among them the Three Gorges Dam Construction Fund, the Gezhouba Power Plant, and the China Development Bank (established in 1994 to finance large infrastructure projects). Among the principal American investment corporations to commit themselves to the project were Goldman Sachs, Merrill Lynch, J. P. Morgan & Company, the U.S. Three Gorges Working Group, Lehman Brothers, Credit Suisse First Boston, BancAmerica Securities, and Morgan Stanley & Company.

In 1992, the People's Congress approved the building of a dam that would span 1.24 miles across the Chang River, at a height of almost 600 feet. The dam, to be constructed of concrete, would create a reservoir of between 350 and 400 miles behind it and would have a capacity of approximately 1.39 trillion cubic feet. The site would also have enormous locks for the moving of heavy shipping vessels up to the level of the reservoir, for travel to Chongqing.

At the dam site, a hydroelectric plant containing twenty-six generators was also being constructed; it would produce some 18,000 megawatts of electrical energy, almost one-ninth of China's total power. The dam, four times the size of the Hoover Dam in the United States, would be the largest on Earth and would probably be visible from space. Approximately twenty thousand workers labored on the project around the clock, and although the original plan called for the dam's completion by 2009, officials were predicting that work would be finished near the end of 2008.

Water started rising on June 1, 2003, and later that year, the first group of generators began operating. By May 20,

*Xiling Gorge, the third of the Three Gorges, just upstream from the Three Gorges Dam site. The dam would create a reservoir that would partially submerge upstream gorges, damage the environment, and displace approximately 1.4 million people.* (Robert S. Carmichael)

2006, structural work had been completed—nine months ahead of schedule—and on June 6, 2006, the temporary construction barrier behind the dam was destroyed. Total cost of the project was estimated at $100 billion.

## SIGNIFICANCE

Opposition to the project, both domestic and international, was intense. Critics warned of impending environmental disasters, such as the elimination of countless species of animals, the creation of breeding grounds for disease-bearing insects, and the concentration of pollutants and garbage in the reservoir that would create a giant, deadly swamp. Just as controversial were the issues surrounding the destruction of ancient temples and the annihilation of the cultural sites of the ancient Ba ethnic group as well as the eradication of hundreds of villages, towns, and cities. Fishing in the East China Sea would also be irreparably damaged as a result of the altering of the water flow and silt patterns of the Chang. The most egregious negative projection, however, was the forced relocation of almost 1.4 million people from the region.

—*Mark DeStephano, S.J.*

## FURTHER READING

Chetham, Deidre. *Before the Deluge: The Vanishing World of the Yangtze's Three Gorges*. New York: Palgrave Macmillan, 2002. Contains data, historical analysis, and an overview of political figures who were instrumental in the development and implementation of the project.

Dai Qing, John G. Thibodeau, and Philip B. Williams, eds. *The River Dragon Has Come! The Three Gorges Dam and the Fate of China's Yangtze River and Its People*. Armonk, N.Y.: M. E. Sharpe, 1998. Collection of essays by Chinese and international scholars examines population displacement, environmental hazards, loss of cultural sites, and military considerations of the project. Includes data and appendixes on all aspects of the initiative.

Heggelund, Gørild, ed. *Environment and Resettlement Politics in China: The Three Gorges Project*. Burlington, Vt.: Ashgate, 2004. Looks at Chinese policy making regarding resettlement and other impacts of the project, and concludes that the Chinese government has not adequately acknowledged the social costs of such a phenomenon.

Hessler, Peter. *River Town: Two Years on the Yangtze*. New York: Perennial/HarperCollins, 2002. Includes a chapter titled "The Dam" that provides a personal account of the effects of the Three Gorges Dam Project on those who live on the banks of the Chang River.

**SEE ALSO:** Jan. 15, 1971: Dedication of Egypt's Aswān High Dam; June 5, 1976: Teton Dam Collapses.

---

## December 15, 1994
# RELEASE OF NETSCAPE NAVIGATOR 1.0

*The release of the first commercial Web browser, Netscape Navigator 1.0, helped to shape the future of the Internet and drove the technologies that became commonplace on the World Wide Web.*

**LOCALE:** Mountain View, California
**CATEGORIES:** Communications and media; computers and computer science; science and technology

## KEY FIGURES

*James H. Clark* (b. 1944), founder of Silicon Graphics and cofounder of Netscape Communications Corporation

*Marc Andreessen* (b. 1971), programmer and cofounder of Netscape Communications Corporation

*Jim Barksdale* (b. 1943), chief executive officer of Netscape Communications Corporation

## SUMMARY OF EVENT

In the early 1990's, the Internet was mainly a place where computer experts, government agencies, and academics shared information. Most of the searching and data transfer tools were text-based and were not user friendly. NCSA Telnet, developed by the National Center for Supercomputing Applications (NCSA), was one of the main tools for users to access information on the Internet. Programmers at the NCSA wished to create a program that would take advantage of the newly developed World Wide Web and allow themselves to access information more easily. The program they developed was called Mosaic. Some of the programmers saw the potential of the Internet and wanted to develop the program so that the average person could use it as well. NCSA and its programmers had differing views on how Mosaic should develop, and they soon parted ways.

1994

On December 15, 1994, the Netscape Navigator browser was released after months of development by the Netscape Communications Corporation. Some of the coders, many of them hired outside of the NCSA's Mosaic team, worked 120-hour weeks in order to finish Netscape Navigator and its accompanying server software. The browser was hugely successful, and within four months, 75 percent of the people on the Internet were using Netscape.

Netscape helped to define the modern browser by rendering Web pages with formatted text, pictures, and hyperlinks that connected to other data on the Internet. It introduced on-the-fly Web page browsing, in which the text would load before the pictures—a beneficial feature for users who did not have the transfer rates offered by modern Internet connections. The Mosaic browser, on which Netscape was based, required an entire Web page to load before it would be displayed. Netscape was also developed so that it worked on the major platforms of the time: UNIX, Apple, and Windows operating systems.

The founders of Netscape Communications Corporation were James H. Clark and Marc Andreessen. Clark founded the successful company Silicon Graphics, Inc., and Andreessen was the lead UNIX coder from the original Mosaic team. Andreessen was responsible for the main split from NCSA, envisioning an Internet that was not dependent on the proprietary networks of the time: America Online (AOL), Prodigy, and CompuServe. He thought that the ability of the casual computer user to access the Internet would be driven by an easily usable browser. Initially, Netscape offered its browser free of charge, with users agreeing to pay for it after ninety days had passed. Some users opted to use the software without paying, but there were enough paying customers that Netscape collected $365,000 for the product within two weeks of its release.

Netscape Navigator was released solely over the Internet and became the first software successfully distributed over the Internet. Netscape demonstrated to the business world that the Internet was a viable place for commercial ventures. It used its success to promote its own encrypted business transaction server. Realizing that their success in the business of the Internet would eventually create competition from Microsoft, Andreessen and Clark moved to try to keep ahead of Microsoft technologically. Netscape sought to saturate the market quickly and pushed speed in product development and company growth.

Netscape hired a public relations person to promote Andreessen's image as an up-and-coming whiz kid and Clark as the business-savvy expert. Netscape hired Jim Barksdale, who was the chief executive officer (CEO) of McCaw Cellular before joining Netscape as CEO in January of 1995 to help steer the company's development. Andreessen and Clark ultimately wanted Netscape to be seen as more than just a browser company and were having trouble defining Netscape's market, even though the second quarter showed a $12 million income. The challenge Netscape defined for itself was to anticipate market needs and to address those needs before Microsoft could.

Netscape made its initial public offering (IPO) on November 8, 1995. It was considered an early offering in the business world; most companies wait at least five years, whereas Netscape had waited eighteen months. Netscape had yet to make a profit but chose to open at $28 per share. It closed the day at $71 per share and became the largest opening day for a company to date, with the company's worth jumping to $4.4 billion. Wall Street saw Netscape as the company that would promote the idea of the Internet to the public. The astounding success of Netscape's IPO helped to fuel the technology boom in Silicon Valley.

Version 2.0 introduced frames, Java, and JavaScript to the browser. Netscape also added file transfer, newsgroup, and e-mail capabilities to make it a business-class product. Netscape also introduced cookies, which were highly controversial at the time. Cookies are packets of text sent to a browser from a server and then sent back when that browser returns to the site. They are used to track and authenticate users and to save user preferences. Online privacy advocates were leery of the use of cookies, but ultimately cookies became commonplace on the Internet.

Version 3.0 of Netscape Navigator, which was released in the fall of 1996, introduced column layout for Web pages and plug-ins for the browser. A gold version of the browser was also released that bundled an e-mail program, a newsgroup reader, and a Web page editor. The bundle was not well integrated and caused some instabilities that made it crash periodically on some machines. Many critics cite this version as the point where Microsoft's Internet Explorer (IE) browser, also at version 3.0, caught up technologically with Navigator.

Microsoft and Netscape became embroiled in what are known as the "browser wars." Netscape renamed version 4.0 of its browser, released in mid-1997, to "Communicator" in an effort to shift the product's focus to the emerging intranet market. Netscape added cascading style sheets (CSS) support and the LAYER element for precise positioning in Web pages. Netscape offered the suite of applications instead of the browser only. Unfortunately, the renaming of the browser diluted its name recognition with the public, and version 4.0 turned out to be the least stable of the versions thus far. As a result of aggressive marketing and the fact that its browser was free, Microsoft's IE market share jumped to 35 percent. Version 5.0 of Netscape was never released since it was viewed internally as too buggy. In January of 1998, Netscape announced that its product would be open source and that it would no longer charge for its product.

Netscape laid off twenty-four hundred employees in early 1998, and its stock dropped to $18 per share. March of 1998 saw the official release of the source code. AOL acquired Netscape in November, 2000. Netscape 6.0 was released at that time but was far from stable and only served to drive customers further from the product.

## SIGNIFICANCE

Despite its browser's demise, Netscape brought about profound changes in the public perception and development of the Internet. By initially offering its browser for free, developing for multiple platforms, and creating an easy-to-use program, Netscape made the Internet accessible to the casual computer user and helped to popularize it. The company also broke the trend of the creation of proprietary networks. Once users had a means to access the Internet, they no longer had to pay subscription fees to access data.

Many of the features that Netscape Navigator was criticized for incorporating, such as frames, cookies, and JavaScript, eventually became widely accepted standards for browsers. Netscape's success demonstrated that the Internet is a viable place for commercial ventures. The company developed the precursor technologies that allowed companies to transact business on the Web safely and efficiently. Netscape helped to fuel the Silicon Valley technological boom and closely mirrored the rise and fall of the dot-com bubble.

*—James J. Heiney*

## FURTHER READING

Quittner, Joshua, and Michelle Slatalla. *Speeding the Net: The Inside Story of Netscape and How It Challenged Microsoft.* New York: Atlantic Monthly Press, 1998. Story of the rise and fall of Netscape through its development, growth, and subsequent rivalry with Microsoft, ending with the releasing of Netscape's source code.

Sherman, Josepha. *The History of the Internet.* New York: Franklin Watts, 2003. History of the development of the Internet from its beginnings as a military computer network to its present uses. Covers the people involved with its development and includes time lines.

Wallace, James. *Overdrive: Bill Gates and the Race to Control Cyberspace.* New York: John Wiley & Sons, 1997. Microsoft's race to catch up to Netscape, its battles over antitrust with the government, and its eventual success with the Internet.

SEE ALSO: Sept., 1988: Prodigy Introduces Dial-Up Service; Mid-1990's: Rise of the Internet and the World Wide Web; May 23, 1995: Sun Microsystems Introduces Java; July, 1995: Amazon.com Sells Its First Book Online; Dec. 31, 1997: Microsoft Acquires Hotmail.

1994

## Mid-1990's
# CABLE TELEVISION CHALLENGES NETWORK TELEVISION

*During the 1990's, the cable television industry dramatically increased its market share of television viewers and brought about a revolution in program options.*

**LOCALE:** United States
**CATEGORIES:** Business and labor; radio and television

**KEY FIGURES**

*Jeffrey L. Bewkes* (fl. late twentieth century), president, chairman, and chief executive officer of Home Box Office (HBO)

*George Bodenheimer* (b. 1958), president of Entertainment and Sports Programming Network (ESPN)

*David Chase* (b. 1945), creator of HBO's critically acclaimed series *The Sopranos*

*Joseph Collins* (b. 1944), chairman of Time Warner Cable

*Ted Turner* (b. 1938), founder of the Turner Broadcasting System

**SUMMARY OF EVENT**

Cable television was first offered during the late 1940's to provide television signals to people who lived in remote areas where it was difficult or impossible to receive regular television broadcast signals. At that time, no one could have imagined the phenomenal growth that the cable industry would undergo during the 1990's. By 1999, almost 75 million American households subscribed to cable television. With more than 99 million American households owning television sets, the proportion of households that had decided to pay for cable service had reached 75 percent. The cable television industry had first shown signs of growth during the 1950's and 1960's. At that time, cable service was offered to many small cities and towns across the country. Subscribers paid for the signals of television network affiliates, educational television stations, and possibly a number of independent stations. Compared to what became available to cable subscribers during the 1990's, these early offerings were extremely modest.

In the early 1960's, there were only 850,000 cable subscribers in the United States. During this period, local television stations began to think of cable television as a competitor to be feared, and the Federal Communications Commission (FCC) stepped in and placed restrictions on the cable industry. It was not until the early 1970's that federal deregulation made it easier for the cable industry to grow. The first pay-television network, Home Box Office (HBO), was started by Charles Dolan and Gerald Levin of Sterling Manhattan Cable in 1972. Out of this venture, a national satellite distribution system was created.

The new satellite system paved the way for an increase in cable program networks. Ted Turner, the owner of a local television station in Atlanta, Georgia, changed his station over to satellite distribution and in so doing created the first "superstation"—TBS, the Turner Broadcasting System. By the end of the twentieth century, Turner's superstation was available to almost every cable subscriber in the country.

In 1980, the number of cable television subscribers had grown to 15 million households. With the passage of the federal Cable Act of 1984, the cable television industry became almost entirely deregulated. Because of deregulation, the cable industry boldly invested vast sums of money to wire the country and to develop new programming. The industry spent more than $15 billion on wiring alone.

In 1992, 82 national cable networks were operating in the United States. By 1998, more than 10,000 cable systems were in operation; 174 national cable networks were in business, and the industry employed more than 127,000 people. In a span of six years, the number of national cable networks had increased by more than 100 percent.

In August, 1998, the Cablevision Bureau (CAB) gathered data that confirmed that "basic cable attracted a larger monthly viewing audience than the combined broadcast networks." This was the first time in the history of television that cable television had accomplished this feat. During the 1997-1998 television season, basic cable programming was watched by an average of 21.9 million households (a 38.5 share of the total audience). This constituted a 2.6 million household increase and a 4.2 share increase over the previous television season. During the same period, the broadcast networks lost 1.4 million viewing households and a 3.2 share of the audience.

In 1999, cable television continued to gain viewers. During the second week of the new television season (September 27-October 3, 1999), basic cable rose 7.6 percent in average prime-time ratings according to CAB's analysis of A. C. Nielsen ratings data. In this time period, some of the basic cable programming that did extremely well included coverage of professional football on ESPN (Entertainment and Sports Programming Network), the USA network's World Wrestling Federation program *Monday Night Raw*, and original films on Turner Network Television (TNT). By the late 1990's, the average cable subscriber could choose from a wide selection of programming options. More than half of all cable subscribers could choose from among at least fifty-four channels in 1998, up from forty-seven in 1996. As the cable television industry grew, the public demanded more diverse programming and programming of higher quality.

In 1996, the U.S. Congress enacted the first major new federal communications law since 1934. The Telecommunications Act of 1996 offered regulatory relief and flexibility that spurred the cable industry to expand. Whereas the growth experienced by the cable industry during the early 1990's was tied primarily to the wiring of previously unserved or underserved areas, it appeared likely that growth in the twenty-first century would be tied more closely to new housing starts.

American cable subscribers were able to watch a number of high-quality programs produced by cable networks during the 1990's. The premium cable network HBO produced the critically acclaimed and popular programs *The Sopranos*, *Sex and the City*, and *Oz*.

### SIGNIFICANCE

With the growth of cable television and public clamor for greater variety and high-quality programming, it seemed almost inevitable that "change" and "innovation" would become cable industry buzzwords going into the twenty-first century. In addition to cable's ever-increasing role in television, the cable industry was poised to become a major force in offering online services, data delivery, and high-speed access to the Internet. Through the use of fiber optics and coaxial cable, cable systems were able to offer Internet access that was hundreds of times faster than that provided over telephone lines. One of the most promising growth areas for the cable industry was digital-package sales, in which companies batched together services to create special packages that customers would find hard to resist. Whether they offered digital packages, premium-channel packages, or pay-per-view packages, cable companies looked to hook new subscribers with innovative and attractive sales offers.

Deregulation further encouraged cable companies to venture into telephony and made it possible for telephone companies to distribute cable television programming.

Cable providers were also emboldened to try their hands at video compression, digital transmission, and high-definition television (HDTV). Some cable operators experimented with two-way channel capability, which allows subscribers to interact with programming facilities or the system's information headquarters, so they can reply to public-opinion polls or have access to written or graphic materials.

Meanwhile, however, the industry began to face strong competition from direct broadcast satellite (DBS) technology. By the end of 1998, more than twelve million customers were getting their programming from noncable multichannel video providers. As the Department of Justice stated, "While programming services are delivered via different technologies, consumers view the [DBS and cable] services as similar and to a large degree substitutable." During the 1990's, the top ten cable multiple systems operators (MSOs) grew extremely large. In 2000, 75 percent of the nation's cable subscribers looked to the top ten MSOs for their programming. With more than sixteen million subscribers, the largest MSO in the country was AT&T Broadband. Time Warner Cable ranked second with roughly thirteen million subscribers. None of the other top ten MSOs had more than six million subscribers.

Cable television altered the way the American public watches television. Through cable, viewers have access to channels that are completely devoted to specific kinds of programming; they can watch twenty-four-hour all-news networks, specialty film channels, Spanish-language programs, programs aimed at women, religious programs, music videos, cooking shows, travel programs, children's programs, science programs, and many more. It has been argued that with all these choices, the public audience has become fragmented. Whereas in decades past the majority of American viewers typically tuned in to the same small group of popular programs, since the 1990's the audience has tended to be spread among many more increasingly different programs.

Throughout the 1990's, the old broadcast television networks were unable to curtail the erosion of their market share as cable stations gained viewers. The broadcast networks had to work harder to maintain viewership, and they fought back in the late 1990's by increasing the numbers of game shows and investigative-reporting programs they aired. Cheaper to produce than situation comedies, drama shows, and other kinds of programming, these shows were popular with a large segment of the viewing public that still watched regular network television.

1995

Some have argued that since the 1990's both basic cable channels and premium cable channels have produced more high-quality programming than has been found on the broadcast networks. Although basic cable channels still have to be concerned about censorship issues with their programming, premium cable channels do not have such worries, so their programming can include graphic violence, nudity, and coarse language, just as theatrical films can. Original premium cable series such as *The Sopranos* and *Sex and the City* made the most of this freedom, and audiences responded.

While the variety of cable television's programming has been criticized as being nothing more than "a map of our most noble and base instincts," the cable television industry rightly can point to how far it has come in a relatively short period of time. American viewers have shown that they are willing to pay for the expanded choices offered to them by cable operators. The days when just a few networks could monopolize news and entertainment audiences ended as Americans opted for freedom of choice and as other voices found outlets to wider audiences that had not previously been available.

—*Jeffry Jensen*

**FURTHER READING**

Aufderheide, Patricia. "Cable Television and the Public Interest." *Journal of Communication* 42 (Winter, 1992): 52-65. Presents a solid overview of how the public interest can best be served by the growth of cable television.

Baldwin, Thomas F., and D. Stevens McVoy. *Cable Communication*. 2d ed. Englewood Cliffs, N.J.: Prentice Hall, 1988. Examines in detail every aspect of the cable industry, from the technical to public policy. Although somewhat dated, remains essential reading for those interested in how the cable industry evolved.

Blanchard, Margaret A., ed. *History of the Mass Media in the United States*. Chicago: Fitzroy Dearborn, 1998. History in encyclopedia format provides several insightful overviews of the rise of cable television programming in the entries "Cable Networks," "Cable News," and "Cable Television." Includes useful bibliographies.

Brenner, Daniel L., and Monroe E. Price. *Cable Television and Other Nonbroadcast Video: Law and Policy*. New York: Clark Boardman, 1986. Discusses how the Cable Communications Act of 1984 as well as various judicial rulings and decisions affected the cable industry.

Hodes, Daniel, Kiran Duwadi, and Andrew Wise. "Cable's Expanding Role in Telecommunications." *Business Economics* 34 (April, 1999): 46-51. Argues that as the cable industry takes on a larger role in the "telecommunications arena" it should make sure that it reduces its debt and improves customer service to hold on to subscribers.

Sterling, Christopher H., and John Michael Kittross. *Stay Tuned: A History of American Broadcasting*. 3d ed. Mahwah, N.J.: Lawrence Erlbaum, 2001. Comprehensive one-volume history of radio and television in the United States. Includes discussion of how the advent of cable television affected the networks, both economically and in their programming.

**SEE ALSO:** Jan. 12, 1971: Relevance Programs Change Entertainment Standards; 1975-1978: Silverman Rescues ABC Television's Ratings; 1980's: Decline of the Big Three Networks; June 1, 1980: Cable News Network Debuts; Aug. 1, 1981: MTV Revolutionizes American Popular Culture; Aug. 15, 1981: EWTN Begins Religious Broadcasting; July 1, 1985: Home Shopping Service Is Offered on Cable Television; Oct. 9, 1986: Fox Television Network Goes on the Air.

## Mid-1990's
# RISE OF THE INTERNET AND THE WORLD WIDE WEB

*As low-cost personal computers, software, and network services began to flood the mass market, a revolutionary communications network mushroomed.*

**LOCALE:** Worldwide

**CATEGORIES:** Communications and media; computers and computer science; science and technology; trade and commerce

**KEY FIGURES**

*Vinton Cerf* (b. 1943), Stanford University researcher who developed the protocols used by computers on the Internet

*Al Gore* (b. 1948), U.S. senator from Tennessee

*Tim Berners-Lee* (b. 1955), creator of the World Wide Web

*Vannevar Bush* (1890-1974), early computer pioneer

**SUMMARY OF EVENT**

The Internet is a loose collection of interconnecting commercial and noncommercial computer networks, including online information services, that use standard protocols (or rules) to exchange information. The Internet began as the ARPANET, an electronic messaging and research tool put together in the late 1960's by the U.S. Defense Department's Advanced Research Projects Agency (ARPA). The ARPANET linked together computers at universities that were doing military-funded research and other research facilities around the world. The ARPANET was designed to allow uninterrupted data routing in the event of a nuclear war bypassing failed connections.

Although the people using the ARPANET at these institutions discovered the enormous utility of a network that linked them with their peers around the world, the network did not have a major effect outside this sphere because few businesses and individuals had computers. When the first commercial online service, CompuServe, started in 1969, few computer users existed to participate.

The ARPANET scheme depended on being able to send messages by any available path, so protocols had to be devised to control and monitor data delivery. Use of Transmission Control Protocol/Internet Protocol (TCP/IP), developed by Vinton Cerf at Stanford University, was important in creating compatibility among a variety of computer equipment. By the early 1980's, a number of networks had developed, with interconnections following. These interconnections led to the term "Internet." In

1986, the National Science Foundation (NSF) created NSFNET to connect supercomputer sites around the United States. It also connected computers at schools and research sites, and soon NSFNET absorbed the ARPANET.

In 1991, Al Gore, then a U.S. senator from Tennessee, promoted federal legislation that expanded NSFNET, renamed it NREN (National Research and Education Network), and brought it into more schools and colleges. The legislation also allowed businesses to purchase part of the network for commercial uses. Mass commercialization followed. Gore proposed creating a "national information infrastructure" consisting of a telecommunications network, "information appliances" connected to the network, and information stored in digital libraries and databases filled with text images and videos. He argued that rapid advances in telecommunications and computer technology were causing the information and telecommunications industries to converge.

Rapid growth of the Internet required the presence of several elements: readily available terminal devices, networks to link them, user-friendly software, and substantial content. These elements came together in the 1990's. Although such development could have happened with a telephone or cable television add-on, the key factor was the growth of personal computer (PC) ownership and the connection of PCs to online services. Many students were introduced to Internet service through their schools' computer networks. As it became easier for nonexperts to navigate this information stream, more new users were attracted each year.

Bill Gates, the founder of Microsoft Corporation, a key computer software provider, has called the Internet's popularity the single most important development in the computing world since IBM introduced the PC in 1981. In the early days of the Internet, Gates predicted that it would continue to evolve into an increasingly powerful information highway that would forever change the way people buy, work, learn, and communicate.

The Internet is not owned or funded by any one institution, organization, or government; rather, this "organized anarchy" is directed by the Internet Society, which works out such issues as standards, resources, and addresses. The computers, routers, and communication links are owned by many parties. By the mid-1990's, the Internet had evolved into a network composed of millions of host computers, all but a few of them privately maintained. Tens of millions of PC users could roam the "information superhighway" and tap into the vast amounts of data found there, thanks to its ease of use.

The many alternative routing possibilities made it almost impossible to block certain types of information selectively. At the same time, the Internet empowered many groups, because use of the Internet is possible at low cost and users can send messages through various Internet communication services to other users anywhere in the world.

Very quickly, the Internet came to be used for four basic processes: communication (through electronic mail, or e-mail), document or file transfer, interactive browsing, and reading and posting to topic-specific bulletin boards. E-mail became the cornerstone of the Internet; the ability to communicate with others in this unobtrusive but effective and comprehensive way was widely embraced because of the tremendous advantages it provides for both senders and receivers.

## SIGNIFICANCE

In addition to its usefulness for e-mail communication, the Internet came to provide access to large amounts of data on subjects ranging from the trivial to the serious. The Internet became a sort of global bulletin board with the initiation of thousands of topical newsgroups established by users to discuss various issues; messages posted to newsgroups were read, forwarded, and responded to by users all over the world.

Use of the Internet expanded rapidly. One 1995 survey found that 9.5 million people in the United States were using the Internet, including 1.1 million children less than eighteen years of age. Half of these 9.5 million had first begun using the Internet that year. Other estimates indicated even higher numbers, and some suggested that 20 to 30 million computers around the world were connected to the Internet in the mid-1990's. The Columbia Broadcasting System (CBS) radio network recognized the importance of the rise of the Internet when it began providing a regular program feature called "Internet Minute."

Companies and individuals found that the ease with which they could place information on the Internet changed the whole idea of what it means to publish. As Internet access became important to businesses, Internet addresses appeared on business cards, in catalogs, and in advertisements. Increasingly, the commercial uses of the Internet became more heavily exploited, and e-commerce of all kinds exploded in importance. Many state governments began to make documents available online, and

many political candidates and elected officials began to use e-mail to disseminate voter education materials and for constituent communication.

The World Wide Web, or Web, is a user-friendly "front end" to the information already on the Internet. Tim Berners-Lee, an expert in communications and text-handling programs, wrote the basic Web software while working at the CERN physics laboratory in Geneva, Switzerland, in 1990, and placed it on the Internet the next year. He developed the standards for addressing, linking language, and transferring multimedia documents on the Web. This software provided a protocol for requesting readable information (including text, graphics, figures, and databases) stored on remote computer systems, using networks.

The key to the Web's success is hypertext, which is information that can be stored and retrieved in a non-hierarchical structure. The concept of hypertext had been suggested by computer pioneer Vannevar Bush in 1945. Every hypertext item has an address of its own, meaning one can move from one file to the next through a series of links. The next file accessed through "point-and-click" connections could be halfway around the world. All the technical aspects of moving from one computer to the other are transparent to the user, who can simply explore without interference by using appropriate "browsers," software that helps the user to find the topic of interest.

Soon after the World Wide Web was developed, many institutions and individuals established Web sites. In late 1995, even the Vatican opened a Web site, with the ultimate intent of making papal messages and Church documents available for downloading by scholars, clerics, and laity around the world. More than one million people visited the Vatican's Web site during the first two weeks of its existence. When the Internal Revenue Service opened its Web site in early 1996, some 220,000 people visited it during the first twenty-four hours, and more than one million visited in its first week—even before the site's debut was officially announced.

The protocols that control information transmission on the Internet and the Web have worked exceptionally well, despite rapid growth of usage. The Web has experienced tremendous growth and diversification, becoming a library, marketplace, stage, and funhouse. By 1995, it was the Internet's center of activity, as thousands of companies, organizations, and individuals set up sites. In two years, the Web grew from 100 to 100,000 sites. By 2000, the number of Web sites had grown to more than 7 million registered domains, and by 2005 to about 46.5 million, although it is impossible to know how many are active at any given time. Tremendous energy and creativity continue to be channeled into the Web, and new kinds of sites appear almost daily. The Internet's vast possibilities—social, economic, and scientific—promise to continue to revolutionize human society during the twenty-first century.

—*Stephen B. Dobrow*

**FURTHER READING**

Cavalier, Robert J., ed. *The Impact of the Internet on Our Moral Lives*. Albany: State University of New York Press, 2005. Collection of essays examines how various aspects of the Internet and the use of online technology may be affecting cultural and social standards of morality as well as the personal lives of individuals.

Diamond, Edwin, et al. "The Ancient History of the Internet." *American Heritage* 46, no. 6 (October, 1995): 34-41. Discusses the background of the Internet.

Gates, Bill. *The Road Ahead*. 2d ed. New York: Penguin Books, 1996. The founder of Microsoft discusses his vision of the changes that computer usage can potentially bring to everyday life.

Goodman, Danny. *Living at Light Speed: Your Survival Guide to Life on the Information Superhighway*. New York: Random House, 1994. Explains the operation of the Internet in terms understandable to general readers and discusses potential problems such as fraud and invasion of privacy.

Kleinman, Daniel Lee. *Science and Technology in Society: From Biotechnology to the Internet*. Malden, Mass.: Blackwell, 2005. Scholarly work addresses the impacts on society of various forms of technological innovation. Chapter 3 is devoted to discussion of the Internet and the World Wide Web.

**SEE ALSO:** Nov.-Dec., 1971: Tomlinson Sends the First E-Mail; Aug. 12, 1981: IBM Introduces Its Personal Computer; Sept., 1988: Prodigy Introduces Dial-Up Service; Feb. 16, 1990: Cisco Systems Goes Public; July 3, 1991: IBM and Apple Agree to Make Compatible Computers; Dec. 15, 1994: Release of Netscape Navigator 1.0; Feb. 15, 1995: Arrest of Hacker Kevin Mitnick; May 4, 2000: ILOVEYOU Virus Attacks Computers.

## 1995
# SOUTH AFRICA ESTABLISHES A TRUTH AND RECONCILIATION COMMISSION

*South Africa's Truth and Reconciliation Commission served as an archetypal statutory government body that defined the path of a peaceful transition from the apartheid past to a multiracial and multicultural democratic future. It produced a rare example of nonviolent conflict resolution in its efforts to address human rights violations by both the apartheid regime and those who had engaged in the struggles to end that regime.*

**LOCALE:** South Africa
**CATEGORIES:** Human rights; government and politics; social issues and reform

**KEY FIGURES**
*Nelson Mandela* (b. 1918), president of South Africa, 1994-1999
*Desmond Tutu* (b. 1931), Anglican archbishop and chairman of the Truth and Reconciliation Commission
*F. W. de Klerk* (b. 1936), president of South Africa, 1989-1994

**SUMMARY OF EVENT**

South Africa experienced a seminal year in 1994. Nelson Mandela became the first democratically elected majority president of South Africa, replacing the last president elected under the apartheid system, F. W. de Klerk. The change in leadership formally proclaimed the end of apartheid, the system of structural racism that had deprived black South Africans of their basic human rights since 1948. To pave the way for a new united and democratic South Africa and to prevent possible large-scale and violent race-based retribution, the newly elected Mandela took proactive steps to establish a transitional justice system. The Truth and Reconciliation Commission (TRC) was created under the provisions of the Promotion of National Unity and Reconciliation Act of 1995. The purpose of the TRC was to assess the human rights violations committed both by the apartheid regime and by those who engaged in struggles to overthrow that regime from March 1, 1961, to October 8, 1990.

Until 1994, South Africa's apartheid regime disfranchised nonwhites politically, socially, and economically.

Deprived of voting rights, blacks in South Africa had been subjugated by whites since the colonial era, but complete institutional racism was not solidified in South Africa until 1948, when Daniel François Malan of the National Party defeated Jan Christian Smuts of the United Party to become South Africa's president in a whites-only general election. In the ensuing years, apartheid became the chief political apparatus deployed by the administration to disfranchise black South Africans systematically. An array of apartheid legislation was promulgated and enacted to strip black South Africans (as well as Asian Indians and people of mixed race) of their basic rights to share in the wealth and resources of South Africa.

Two landscapes were constructed, one white and one black. Racial segregation was realized in every geographic, social, and political space in South Africa. More than 80 percent of black South Africans were confined to less than 20 percent of the land. "Homelands" were designated for large ethnic groups of black South Africans,

*President Nelson Mandela and Archbishop Desmond Tutu in October, 1998, after Mandela accepted the latter's delivery of the report of the Truth and Reconciliation Commission.* (AP/Wide World Photos)

and urban black South Africans were relocated involuntarily to "townships" on the outskirts of cities. The Bantu Education Act of 1953 denied black South Africans access to education equal to that available to whites. Miscegenation was banned, and public amenities—including the most basic, such as buses, restrooms, telephone booths, and entrances to public services—were racially segregated. Whites were free to cross any geographic and social spaces, but blacks had to carry passes and were subjected to inspection at any time anywhere. Those without passes were arrested. These and other racist laws completed the structural disfranchisement of black South Africans.

As the apartheid regime accelerated its institutional deprivation and political suppression of black South Africans, black political organizations, although banned by law, grew in strength. Mobilized by two of the most prominent black political organizations, the African National Congress (ANC) and the Pan-Africanist Congress, black liberation struggles escalated from passive resistance to armed struggles after the Sharpeville incident of March 21, 1960, when the police opened fire on a crowd of unarmed blacks during a demonstration against the pass laws, killing more than sixty. It was during this time that the most prominent activists of the ANC, including Nelson Mandela, were arrested and sentenced to life imprisonment for treason. Armed resistance continued to spread in the aftermath of the regime's armed crackdown on the Soweto student rebellion of June, 1976 (also known as Children's Uprising), which started as a demonstration against the regime's mandate that English be the only language of instruction in the segregated black South African schools.

By the 1980's, mass defiance campaigns and substantial international sanctions began to weaken the foundation of the apartheid regime. In 1989, F. W. de Klerk became the last apartheid state president of South Africa and initiated negotiations with the ANC leaders, Mandela in particular, on power transfer. On February 11, 1990, Mandela was released after twenty-seven years of imprisonment. Because the apartheid regime was not defeated, the transition had to be brokered. Political elites from the old regime made amnesty for the crimes of apartheid administration a nonnegotiable demand during the negotiations, thus amnesty legislation was a necessary precondition for a successful transition to majority rule.

Laid out in the Interim Constitution of 1993, the TRC was enacted by the new parliament in 1995 under the Promotion of National Unity and Reconciliation Act with the power to grant amnesty. Mandela, the first democratically elected president of South Africa in 1994, appointed Archbishop Desmond Tutu as chairman of the TRC; Alex Boraine was appointed deputy chairman. The statute called for three separate committees under the TRC: The Human Rights Violations Committee (HRVC) was to hear and investigate accounts by victims and survivors of human rights violations through public hearings, the Reparations and Rehabilitations Committee was to formulate policies to be adopted into the law that would assist victims and facilitate reconciliation, and the Amnesty Committee was to hear amnesty applications.

By December, 1995, seventeen commissioners had been appointed to the TRC from lists of candidates suggested by various religious, civil, and political organizations. The work of the TRC commenced shortly thereafter. Ten more committee members were appointed in 1997. The HRVC held its first public hearing in April, 1996.

Throughout the rest of 1996 and early 1997, the committee heard more than twenty thousand cases in about fifty public hearings in town halls, hospitals, and churches around the country. In October, 1998, the TRC published its initial report of findings on most of the cases that had been brought forth. In June, 2001, the TRC was dissolved following the conclusion of the amnesty portion of the process; a final report was published in 2003.

## SIGNIFICANCE

The negotiation of power transfer from the old South African regime to majority rule and the challenging transition from apartheid to a new democracy necessitated an unconventional political process. The TRC, as the archetypal statutory government body during the transition, was legitimated by its mission to address human rights violations committed by both the apartheid regime and those engaged in violent struggles to overthrow that regime; therefore, it was largely effective. Acceptance of

---

### TUTU'S TRUTHS

*Anglican archbishop and human rights activist Desmond Tutu was the chair of the South African Truth and Reconciliation Commission after the fall of apartheid. As head of the commission, Tutu witnessed humanity's extraordinary capacity for evil. In a June 12, 2004, interview with the Academy of Achievement, he expressed how he is more amazed at people's immense capacity for good:*

People who suffered untold misery, people who should have been riddled with bitterness, resentment and anger come to the Commission and exhibit an extraordinary magnanimity and nobility of spirit in their willingness to forgive, and to say, "Hah! Human beings actually are fundamentally good." Human beings are fundamentally good. The aberration, in fact, is the evil one, for God created us ultimately for God, for goodness, for laughter, for joy, for compassion, for caring.

*In a 2004 interview with Peter Biles of the British Broadcasting Corporation, Tutu asserted that without the Truth and Reconciliation Commission, turmoil would have erupted in South Africa:*

We lanced a boil which, had we not done, would have meant that our country would have gone down the tubes. Almost everybody agrees that we certainly avoided the bloodbath that most people had been predicting.

*In a January 29, 2006, interview on National Public Radio's* All Things Considered*, Tutu expressed the need to face old wounds:*

People almost always will say . . . "Don't bring up the past. Let bygones be bygones." Unfortunately, you see, they don't get to be bygones. They have an incredible capacity to return and haunt us.

---

the principle of amnesty for politically motivated crimes under apartheid was probably a worthy sacrifice and a necessary path taken by the ANC leadership in pursuit of national unity and peace during the difficult political transformation. Reconciliation in place of social justice certainly did not serve the interests of those South Africans who had endured decades of institutional racism, but reconciliation appeared to provide the best option for a peaceful transition that preempted the potential for explosive retributive bloodshed.

The construction of and the dedicated pursuit of reconciliation by the TRC created a possible channel for the largely nonviolent transition of South Africa from an apartheid state to a new multicultural, multiracial, and democratic state. The TRC took more truth-telling statements than any previous such commission in history. Although the TRC's process was imperfect and what the commission accomplished was quite limited in addressing social justice, South Africa's experience set the stage for a test of alternatives to violence in realizing social and political transformation. The TRC proved to the world that nonviolent solutions could be effective in mediating the most violent racial conflicts, even those deeply rooted in long-term and intense oppression legitimated by political institutions.

—*Linda Q. Wang*

## FURTHER READING

Edelstein, Jillian. *Truth and Lies: Stories from the Truth and Reconciliation Commission in South Africa*. New York: New Press, 2001. Presents many of the heart-wrenching stories recounted at the TRC hearings. Includes photographs.

Gibson, James L. *Overcoming Apartheid: Can Truth Reconcile a Divided Nation?* New York: Russell Sage Foundation, 2004. Uses survey data to assess the correlation and the limitations between truth and reconciliation. Points out the discrepancies in reconciliation among different racial groups.

_____. "Truth, Justice, and Reconciliation: Judging the Fairness of Amnesty in South Africa." *American Journal of Political Science* 46 (July, 2002): 540-556. Examines the different forms of justice and the ramifications of granting amnesty to those who committed gross human rights violations.

Malan, Rian. *My Traitor's Heart: A South African Exile Returns to Face His Country, His Tribe, and His Conscience*. New York: Atlantic Monthly Press, 1990. Autobiography of a white South African journalist describes the brutality of apartheid and the author's feelings about his powerlessness as an individual against the regime.

Mathabane, Mark. *Kaffir Boy: The True Story of a Black Youth's Coming of Age in Apartheid South Africa*. New York: Macmillan, 1986. Autobiography recounts the experiences of a black youth growing up in a South African township.

Wilson, Richard A. *The Politics of Truth and Reconciliation in South Africa: Legitimizing the Post-apartheid State*. New York: Cambridge University Press, 2001. Presents an anthropological examination of the limitations of the TRC in affecting popular ideas concerning justice and retribution in the Johannesburg area.

**SEE ALSO:** Nov. 30, 1973: United Nations Sanctions South Africa for Apartheid; May, 1979: U.N. Declaration Condemns Apartheid; Dec. 10, 1984: Tutu Receives the Nobel Peace Prize; 1987: South African Black Workers Strike; Feb. 11, 1990: Mandela Is Freed; Feb. 1, 1991: De Klerk Promises to Topple Apartheid Legislation.

## 1995-1998
# FAMINE STRIKES NORTH KOREA

*Rigid government control intensified by a series of catastrophic calamities brought on a famine of epic proportions in North Korea during the mid-1990's. Despite worldwide response, Premier Kim Jong Il failed to implement necessary structural changes to prevent future crises from occurring in his country.*

**LOCALE:** North Korea

**CATEGORIES:** Disasters; environmental issues; agriculture

## KEY FIGURES

*Kim Jong Il* (b. 1941), leader of the Democratic People's Republic of Korea beginning in 1994

*Kim Il Sung* (1912-1994), premier, 1948-1972, and president of the Democratic People's Republic of Korea, 1972-1994

*Kim Young Sam* (b. 1927), president of the Republic of Korea, 1993-1998

## SUMMARY OF EVENT

The emergence of Kim Jong Il as premier of North Korea after the death of his father, Kim Il Sung, in July of 1994, marked the first time a change in leadership occurred in the country since the promulgation of the Democratic People's Republic of Korea (DPRK) in 1948. Unfortunately, however, the effects of the sixty-year dictatorship of father and then son had precipitated negative economic growth since 1989. In 1995, severe flooding weakened an already vulnerable economy and hastened a devastating famine that killed between 900,000 and 2.4 million people, threatening to topple the socialist state.

Although flooding was the immediate catalyst of famine in North Korea in the mid-1990's, it was not the sole cause of the crisis. The state's traditional isolation from the world's healthiest economies resulted in its limited economic base, ultimately rendering it vulnerable to internal and external forces.

In keeping with his party's adoption of economic self-reliance, the elder Kim had encouraged his country to grow subsistence crops such as maize, potatoes, rice, and other essentials to discourage exporting from the global economy. (North Korea, however, never attained complete financial independence, as it relied heavily on the Soviet Union and Communist China.) Ironically, rampant malnutrition followed after Kim Il Sung's relentless drive to achieve self-sufficiency, which resulted in the overuse of North Korea's prime land (only 1.85 million hectares of arable land exists, with a short growing season that lasts from June to October). Additionally, farmers utilized chemical fertilizers, which further depleted the already taxed soil. The net result yielded worrisome food shortages even before the flooding of 1995.

Appealing to the national will, Kim Il Sung in 1991 announced that his people should consume two meals a day in the name of patriotic self-reliance. Despite his call for solidarity, food riots resulted two years later. North Korea's state distribution system, in operation prior to the crisis, had been required to provide 600-700 grams of food for the average citizen. The military and state officials were allotted additional grams because of their status. Nonetheless, as the 1990's progressed, food quotas were rarely, if ever, met, and many trekked to China, desperately searching for food.

Compounding an already unstable economic situation, China, North Korea's primary trade partner after the fall of the Soviet Union in 1991, severely limited its foreign exchange and further demanded hard cash for its exports. With a weak economic base and a falling food supply, North Korea could not meet China's demands and faced almost certain economic ruin.

In July, 1995, severe flooding rocked the already precarious economic environment in North Korea when twenty-three inches of rain flooded premium North Korean soil; the northwest provinces of North P'yŏngan and Chagang were especially affected. An estimated 15 percent of all land destroyed was considered to be of the highest quality. Not only were people malnourished, but also major power outages caused a sharp dip in industrial and agricultural output and adversely affected medical supplies.

In response, individual farmers began to fend for themselves by hoarding grain and concentrating on subsistence rather than communal farming, thereby defeating the ultimate purpose of a socialist economy. In an unprecedented move that summer, the former Hermit Kingdom sought global resources by petitioning individual countries and U.N. agencies.

Even before the floods hit, North Korea had petitioned Japan and South Korea (the Republic of Korea, ROK) for food. Within a year, however, ROK's leader Kim Young Sam, who promised to contribute 150 tons of rice, appeared to have a change of heart after his party suffered defeat at the polls on June 27. After his initial delivery of rice, Kim Young Sam not only refused further aid but also discouraged other countries from doing the same. Hoping to unite Korea under his republic, he sought to accelerate the demise of his enemy to the north. The ROK's policy toward North Korea would change in 1998 when Kim Young Sam was ousted from office.

In part, general reluctance to assist the DPRK was a response to the erratic rule of Kim Jong Il, who since his rise to power in 1994 had insulated himself from the citizenry by focusing on a buildup of military forces on one hand and the harnessing of nuclear power for alternate sources of energy on the other—both costly ventures that diverted funds from the needy citizenry. Kim Jong Il's insistence on developing a nuclear reactor in Yŏngbyŏn (north of P'yŏngyang), under construction since 1982, alarmed the international community, which feared that the reactor would place nuclear weaponry in the hands of this unpredictable leader.

Flooding again plagued North Korea in 1996, followed by a drought in 1997, which had severe negative impacts on the resource-rich areas of North P'yŏngan, South P'yŏngan, North Hwanghae, and Kangwŏn—much of whose land had already been adversely affected by two previous years of flooding. By 1997, North Korea was at the center of a grave crisis, and major donors felt compelled to deliver emergency food despite North Korea's belligerent behavior.

The World Food Program and the United States supplied the beleaguered country with much of the aid. (According to Senate hearings conducted before the Foreign Relations Committee in 2003, the United States contributed close to 1.9 million tons of food to North Korea.) However, the North Korean government committed grave injustices by failing to oversee the distribution of aid to its citizenry and in refusing to accept responsibility for famine-related deaths. In many cases, goods were diverted and sold illegally at prohibitive prices or redirected to the military; unnamed sources estimate that only 10 percent of products donated were given to their rightful recipients.

## SIGNIFICANCE

The onset of famine in North Korea brought the once-isolated kingdom into the global arena. Although Kim

Jong Il broke with tradition by petitioning the United Nations and individual countries to provide assistance to his people, he failed to ensure the equitable delivery of these materials to those in need. Additionally, Kim Jong Il's emphasis on military preparedness at the expense of his nation's collective health revealed to the international community of nations the character of this despotic ruler who failed to meet the needs of his people.

The historically closed nature of society in North Korea precludes an accurate tally of the fatalities related to the famine. Analysts have concluded, however, that the North Korean government resisted recommended structural changes despite the evidence of inequities that emerged following the famine. It has been reported that North Korea faced more than a decade of steady economic decline. Although the famine officially ended in 1998, the presence of malnutrition in that nation was still widespread in the early years of the twenty-first century.

—*Debra A. Mulligan*

**FURTHER READING**

Cumings, Bruce. *Korea's Place in the Sun: A Modern History.* New York: W. W. Norton, 1997. A solid study of the development of Korean statecraft, spotlighting the unique history and culture that informed its modernity. Cumings convincingly contends that North Korea forged its own brand of communism separate from that of the Soviet Union. Photo inserts and maps.

Goodkind, Daniel, and Loraine West. "The North Korean Famine and Its Demographic Impact." *Population and Development Review* 27, no. 2 (June, 2001): 219-238. Attempts to present a reliable estimate of the effects of the North Korean famine on the country's population. Charts and graphs.

Noland, Marcus, Sherman Robinson, and Tao Wang. "Famine in North Korea: Causes and Cures." *Economic Development and Cultural Change* 49, no. 4 (July, 2001): 741-746. Through close analysis of available, albeit unreliable statistics, the authors contend that positive change can come about through a transformation of North Korea's infrastructure rather than through foreign aid.

Oberdorfer, Don. *The Two Koreas: A Contemporary History.* Rev. ed. New York: Basic Books, 2001. Journalist Oberdorfer presents a thoughtful analysis of the two Koreas, artificially divided at the end of World War II, which battled internal and external forces that threatened their place in an interdependent world. Photo inserts.

U.S. Congress. Senate. *World Hunger from Africa to North Korea: Hearing Before the Committee on Foreign Relations, United States Senate.* 108th Congress, 1st session, 2003. Evaluates the global hunger crisis and recommends further assistance from the United States for areas most in need, such as Afghanistan, Africa, and North Korea.

**SEE ALSO:** July 8, 1994: Kim Jong Il Succeeds His Father in North Korea; Oct. 21, 1994: U.S.-North Korea Pact.

---

## January 1, 1995-January 1, 2003
# CARDOSO BRINGS PRESTIGE TO BRAZILIAN PRESIDENCY

*As Brazil's president, Fernando Henrique Cardoso pledged to bring fiscal responsibility, social reforms, and financial stability and prosperity to his nation. Despite persistent congressional and judicial resistance, he achieved many of his goals, passing on to his successor a more stable economy and government.*

**LOCALE:** Brazil

**CATEGORIES:** Government and politics; economics; social issues and reform

**KEY FIGURES**

*Fernando Henrique Cardoso* (b. 1931), president of Brazil, 1995-2003

*Sérgio Roberto Vieira da Motta* (1940-1998), principal political ally of Cardoso, friend, and business partner

*Antônio Carlos Magalhães* (b. 1927), political ally of Cardoso who eventually turned against him

*Itamar Franco* (b. 1930), president of Brazil, 1992-1995, who became a critic of Cardoso's government

**SUMMARY OF EVENT**

When he took office in 1995, Fernando Henrique Cardoso inherited the largest economy in Latin America, one that for most of the twentieth century had suffered through a series of corrupt democracies or military rule. Brazil also had one of the world's most unequal distributions of income. Cardoso set out to turn the country toward a new and positive future.

In 1993, having been appointed finance minister by then president Itamar Franco, who had replaced a president impeached for corruption, Cardoso implemented a program designed to curb the country's crippling inflation. The plan included a new currency, the real, and constitutional reform that would redistribute federal funds in a way that would help balance the budget. Cardoso's plan reduced inflation from 40 to 2.5 percent a month by the end of 1994, and on the strength of his economic successes, he was elected president. He immediately set further goals: land reform, privatizing state-owned companies to give the government needed income, creating more jobs, improving health care and education, and reducing poverty. To many Brazilians, Cardoso offered a corruption-free government, improved civil rights, and a stable economy.

Brazil's economic problems stemmed largely from an inflated bureaucracy, a burdensome pension system, inefficient tax collecting, and inadequate social security contributions. The 1988 constitution had shifted presidential power and federal revenue from the central government to the states, municipalities, and courts, leaving no funds for social programs. In addition, thirty-two million Brazilians lived in poverty, and nearly a third of Brazil's labor force could not afford adequate food and housing for their families. Addressing these problems, Cardoso encountered strong resistance from the Brazilian congress, whose members served powerful groups benefiting financially from the status quo. In urgent need to reorganize public finances and allow faster economic growth, Cardoso turned to other sources of revenue, including privatization of state-owned businesses, raising taxes, and improving tax collection.

Cardoso had powerful and savvy political allies in his struggle to balance the budget and implement social reforms. One of his strongest aides was Sérgio Roberto Vieira da Motta, Cardoso's friend and business partner who cofounded the Social Democratic Party. Perhaps Motta's greatest contribution to Cardoso's government was the sale of Telebras, Brazil's giant telecommunications company. Despite criticism from Itamar Franco, who had turned against Cardoso after leaving the central government, the sale continued, taking two years to complete. The final settlement included the establishment of a governmental regulatory authority, embodied in a new telecommunications law. The sale gave a boost to Cardoso's campaign for a second term, which required an amendment to the constitution. At the last moment,

however, Cardoso's reputation for personal honesty was tarnished, and his hopes for reelection were jeopardized, when Motta was accused of paying several congressmen to vote for the constitutional amendment that would allow the president and other politicians to seek a second term.

Cardoso won reelection and continued to push for reforms to avoid a prolonged economic crisis, all the while trying to maintain financial stability. He pressed for fiscal austerity to curb inflation and to restore confidence in Brazil's economy to encourage foreign investments. In a show of support for Cardoso's budgetary concerns, many states trimmed bloated payrolls, but in early 1999, Brazilians were again facing an economic crisis, exacerbated by Itamar Franco, who had become governor of Minas Gerais, one of Brazil's southern states. Franco stopped payment on his state's huge federal debt, causing a devaluation of the real and heightening the crisis. A few months later, he joined other governors and labor leaders in denouncing the Cardoso government. Cardoso's troubles increased when the Brazilian Supreme Court blocked a proposed increase of pension contributions meant to save the government $1.2 billion.

By January, 2000, the economy had begun to recover, but Brazil's congress continued to resist pension reform. At issue was a new formula that determined pensions according to age, previous contributions, and life expectancy after retirement. Eventually, the Supreme Court ruled against the opposition.

Cardoso made efforts to improve other areas of government as well. He allocated $3.5 billion to modernize Brazil's air force and another $1.7 billion to combat the increase in violent crime. The police force was also to be enlarged and given further training, and command of the country's drug war was shifted from the ineffectual police forces to the federal Justice Ministry.

By 2000, government agencies throughout Brazil began to rid themselves of corrupt politicians, replacing incumbents with candidates who promised to clean up the government. Cardoso saw these changes as a desire among leaders and voters alike to bring higher standards into public service. Additionally, the new era included the establishment of anticorruption courts. Ironically, just as voters were ejecting corrupt politicians from office, Cardoso faced accusations of corruption in his government by Antônio Carlos Magalhães, who had been one of Cardoso's strongest political allies. Cardoso had alienated Magalhães by backing a rival of Magalhães in the race for speaker of the senate. Magalhães sought revenge by trying to obtain secret voting results from federal prosecutors, and when the attempt was exposed, he was disgraced and forced to resign his office.

In the remaining months of his presidency, Cardoso also helped to reform the civil service and establish a bureaucracy needed to carry out social programs. For eight years, Cardoso's policies and practices enabled the government to function positively without disruption. He established a more open and stable system of government. His administration privatized $91 billion worth of government-owned enterprises, including industrial and mineral businesses, telecommunications, and most of the government-owned banks. His measures resulted in the Fiscal Responsibility Law of 2000, requiring states and municipalities to improve accounting practices.

Cardoso brought fiscal discipline to the political realm while maintaining economic growth. Serious social problems remained at the end of his presidency, such as increased crime and deficits in the social security system, but he had made genuine gains in Brazil's economic and social realms.

## SIGNIFICANCE

Brazil suffered a wide array of problems, both internally and externally, before Cardoso took office as president. In the eight years preceding 1994, the government had revalued the currency five times, and by 1995, thirty-two million Brazilians were classified as destitute. Congress comprised nineteen distinct and disorganized political parties whose members were dedicated to aggrandizing themselves and to protecting the interests of those who elected them. The government's pension system was a ruinous drain on the federal budget, and foreign debt had risen to $52 billion. The country's budget had not been balanced in two decades.

Cardoso brought credibility to the federal government and made a sincere effort to institute political, financial, and social reforms. He stabilized the country's finances and brought a degree of unity to a government widely known for corruption. Perhaps the most significant contribution Cardoso made was bringing integrity to Brazil's political offices. His prestige as finance minister, his strong political skills and commitment to fiscal restraint, his knowledge of economics, and his dedication to solving the country's major economic and social

problems raised Brazil's standing as a member of the world's financial institutions and gave hope to Brazilians that their country was stable and prosperous.

—*Bernard E. Morris*

## FURTHER READING

Goertzel, Ted George. *Fernando Henrique Cardoso: Reinventing Democracy in Brazil*. Boulder, Colo.: Lynne Rienner, 1999. Traces Cardoso's transition from a leftist intellectual to a leader of Brazil's democratic party, assessing Cardoso's political achievements to the end of his presidency.

Mainwaring, Scott. *Rethinking Party Systems in the Third Wave of Democratization: The Case of Brazil*. Stanford, Calif.: Stanford University Press, 1999. Examines Brazil's political system, showing the weaknesses responsible for corruption and the ineffective leadership that obstructed Cardoso's efforts toward reform.

Nylen, William R. *Participatory Democracy Versus Elitist Democracy: Lessons from Brazil*. New York: Palgrave Macmillan, 2003. A study of Brazil's Workers' Party shows how citizen participation in the political system can strengthen democracy, even in the United States.

Smith, William C., and Nizar Messari. *Democracy and Reform in Cardoso's Brazil: Caught Between Clientelism and Global Markets?* Paper 33. Coral Gables, Fla.: University of Miami, North-South Center Press, 1998. Discusses Cardoso's attempts to make Brazil's economy competitive in the global market and the conflicts between Cardoso's efforts at social reforms and entrenched social and political interests.

Weyland, Kurt Gerhard. *Democracy Without Equity: Failures of Reform in Brazil*. Pittsburgh: University of Pittsburgh Press, 1996. Examines efforts to redistribute wealth and power through the democratic process, citing initiatives to reform Brazil's taxation laws, social security system, and health care program.

**SEE ALSO:** Mar. 15, 1985: Democracy Returns to Brazil; Oct. 12, 1988: Brazilian President Announces Plans to Protect Rain Forests; July 23-24 and Aug. 29-30, 1993: Brazilian Police Massacre Slum Dwellers.

## January 17, 1995
# KŌBE EARTHQUAKE KILLS THOUSANDS

*The major earthquake that struck Kōbe, Japan, in 1995 showed that, despite a long and generally successful tradition of earthquake preparedness, the Japanese were not as well prepared to handle a quake of such magnitude as they had believed.*

**ALSO KNOWN AS:** Great Hanshin-Awaji earthquake; Hyōgo-ken Nanbu earthquake
**LOCALE:** Kōbe, Japan
**CATEGORIES:** Disasters; earth science; urban planning

### SUMMARY OF EVENT

Kōbe, Japan's sixth-largest city and third-largest seaport, is located along Ōsaka Bay on the nation's main island of Honshū. At 5:46 A.M. on January 17, 1995, an earthquake measuring 7.2 on the Richter scale occurred on Awaji Island, 20 kilometers (a little more than 12 miles) south of the city. The focus of the earthquake was located about 16 kilometers (roughly 10 miles) beneath the epicenter, near the Nojima fault.

When the earthquake struck, the strong seismic motion followed the Nojima fault and the neighboring Suma and Suwayama faults, which dip to a depth of 20 kilometers underneath the city of Kōbe in the direction of the Rokko Mountains to the north. These faults are part of a very active and complex system produced because Japan lies at the intersection of the Pacific, Philippine, and Eurasian tectonic plates. At this triple junction, the Philippine Sea plate is sliding beneath the Eurasian plate at a rate of 4 centimeters (about 1.6 inches) per year in a process called subduction.

The effects of the earthquake were dramatic. Changes of elevation took place that reached 1.3 meters (about 4.3 feet), lateral displacements of 3 meters (9.8 feet) occurred, ground subsidence reached 3 meters in the Kōbe harbor, and average ground elevation increased by 26 centimeters (10 inches) over a rupture of 6 kilometers (3.7 miles). The shaking lasted only about twenty seconds, but it resulted in the deaths of at least 5,000 people (estimates range from 5,378 to 6,433) and injuries to approximately 30,000 more.

The area that surrounds Ōsaka Bay is covered by young, unconsolidated alluvial sediment and soft mud. These sediments do not stand up well to ground motion triggered by an earthquake. Fill was also used to extend Kōbe's urban areas and its harbor along the shore ringing Ōsaka Bay. Unconsolidated fill, soft mud, and alluvial deposits, particularly when saturated with water, amplify an earthquake's shaking and can produce severe ground failure in a geologic process called liquefaction. During liquefaction, the strength of the soils decreases and the ability of these materials to support bridge and building foundations is so diminished that buildings constructed on it lose their support, with catastrophic results. Most of the loss of life in Kōbe was associated with the failure of human-made structures. In the prefecture of Hyōgo, more than 100,000 buildings were damaged. Many buildings were tilted and collapsed in the streets, interrupting traffic. Altogether, some 1.3 million people were left homeless by the quake.

Although the Ōsaka Gas Company stopped the de-

*Part of the Hanshin Expressway in Nishinomiya lies on its side after the powerful Kōbe earthquake.* (AP/Wide World Photos)

1995

livery of gas immediately when the quake began, the rupture of gas mains started fires, the deadliest of which took place in a shoe factory in a very densely populated neighborhood. With the streets gridlocked and many of the underground water storage tanks empty, the fire spread quickly to the fragile wooden homes in the low-income area nearby. Many people fleeing the fires were killed when heavy roof tiles—used to protect traditional houses from typhoons—fell on them.

Eight commuter trains were derailed by the earthquake because of damage to the metallic and concrete frames of viaducts and the collapse of electric poles on the railroad tracks. No one was killed in these derailments, but many injuries were reported. A great deal of damage was concentrated along Kōbe's Hanshin Expressway, where 20-meter (66-foot) supporting piers broke and 500 meters (1,640 feet) of the elevated road fell on its side, catapulting cars and trucks to the ground. Many other viaducts and bridges collapsed in the area as well.

In addition, most of the piers, storehouses, and cranes in Kōbe harbor were destroyed. Out of 186 harbor berths, only 9 were operational after the earthquake; the rest were so badly damaged that it took twenty-six months and $5 billion to restore them. In all, property damage from the quake was estimated to be in excess of $100 billion.

### SIGNIFICANCE

The damage and deaths caused by the Kōbe earthquake, which occurred almost five decades after the previous major earthquake in Japan, shook the confidence of Japanese authorities, who had believed that their broad experience with earthquakes had led to efficient and dependable preparations for such events. Because of their location in a tectonically active area of the world, the Japanese had developed many proven methods of minimizing earthquake damage—including yearly earthquake preparedness drills and strict building codes—but the 1995 event demonstrated the need for improvement. When the Kōbe quake struck, emergency response efforts were impeded by traffic gridlock caused by the collapse of bridges, expressways, and buildings. Many of the emergency food and medical supplies that had been stored at key points around the city were inaccessible. In addition, the underground water reservoirs that had been built to fight fires in the event of breaks in water mains were too small and quickly depleted.

Given these shortcomings, after the Kōbe earthquake Japan modified the required specifications for the seismic design of new buildings, highway bridges, overpasses, and railroad tracks. In addition to enhancing overall construction quality, prefecture and local governments examined the problems that occurred in rescue and relief efforts in the hours following the seismic disaster: traffic congestion, water shortages, and deficiencies in preparedness and response systems. To enable quick response to the basic needs of the population in the event of an earthquake, all Japanese schools began storing food and other emergency supplies. Before the Kōbe earthquake, Japan had no system in place for the military to respond to nonmilitary emergencies; such a system was created after the quake, and an emergency communication system and a response plan were also put in place. In addition, bureaucratic regulations that might hamper relief efforts (such as the quarantine laws that kept European search-and-rescue dogs caged at customs buildings following the Kōbe quake instead of deployed around the city) were examined and revised.

—*Denyse Lemaire and David Kasserman*

**FURTHER READING**

Clancy, Gregory. *Earthquake Nation: The Cultural Politics of Japanese Seismicity, 1868-1939.* Berkeley: University of California Press, 2006. Discusses the Nobi and Tokyo earthquakes and their consequences for Japan.

Coburn, Andrew, and Robin Spence. *Earthquake Protection.* 2d ed. New York: John Wiley & Sons, 2002. An architect and an engineer provide an integrated account of the effects of earthquakes. Emphasizes the relationships among structural damage, human behavior, socioeconomic factors, and casualty patterns.

Hough, Susan Elizabeth. *Earthshaking Science: What We Know (and Don't Know) About Earthquakes.* Princeton, N.J.: Princeton University Press, 2002. Good source of basic information about earthquakes. Includes suggestions for further reading.

Özerdem, Alpaslan, and Tim Jacoby. *Disaster Management and Civil Society: Earthquake Relief in Japan, Turkey, and India.* New York: I. B. Tauris, 2006. Focuses on the rescue efforts made in the critical first few hours after a quake in the three earthquake-plagued nations discussed.

Stein, Seth, and Michael Wysession. *An Introduction to Seismology, Earthquakes, and Earth Structure.* Malden, Mass.: Blackwell, 2003. Textbook aimed at advanced college undergraduates and beginning graduate students presents comprehensive information about earthquakes and plate tectonics. Includes many illustrations.

**SEE ALSO:** July 28, 1976: Deadly Earthquake Strikes China; Sept. 19, 1985: Earthquake Devastates Mexico City; Dec. 7, 1988: Armenian Earthquake Leads to Calls for Building Reform; June 21, 1990: Massive Quake Rocks Iran; Jan. 17, 1994: Northridge Quake Rocks Los Angeles.

## January 24-October 3, 1995
# O. J. SIMPSON TRIAL

*O. J. Simpson was one of America's most famous celebrities when he went on trial for the murder of his former wife and one of her acquaintances. The trial featured virtually uninterrupted news coverage and analysis, frequent melodrama, and strong racial undercurrents, and raised far-reaching questions about violence against women and the role of racism in the American legal system.*

**ALSO KNOWN AS:** Trial of the Century
**LOCALE:** Los Angeles, California
**CATEGORY:** Crime and scandal

**KEY FIGURES**

*O. J. Simpson* (b. 1947), former professional football player and popular actor
*Nicole Brown Simpson* (1959-1994), former wife of O. J. Simpson

*Ronald Goldman* (1968-1994), acquaintance of Nicole Brown Simpson
*Johnnie Cochran* (1937-2005), prominent California defense attorney
*Marcia Clark* (b. 1953), Los Angeles assistant district attorney
*Mark Fuhrman* (b. 1952), Los Angeles police detective
*Lance Ito* (b. 1950), Los Angeles Superior Court judge
*Kato Kaelin* (b. 1959), resident at O. J. Simpson's guest house

**SUMMARY OF EVENT**

O. J. Simpson, a former athlete who had won the Heisman Trophy as a college football player and had been a National Football League all-pro running back, had made a successful transition to film acting by the mid-1990's. On the night of June 12, 1994, Simpson's former wife, Nicole Brown Simpson, was murdered outside her home, along with an acquaintance, Ronald Goldman. Goldman had stopped by to return a pair of glasses that Nicole Brown Simpson had left that evening at the restaurant where he worked. Two years earlier, Brown Simpson and Simpson had ended their seven-year marriage after numerous allegations of domestic violence, although they still shared custody of their two children and occasionally spent time together.

Evidence discovered at the scene of the murders and later at O. J. Simpson's home quickly implicated Simpson, and five days later, a warrant was issued for his arrest. He fled in a Ford Bronco driven by his friend Al Cowlings and led police on a slow sixty-mile chase through Los Angeles, threatening suicide before returning home and eventually surrendering.

On January 24, 1995, Simpson went on trial in Los Angeles for two counts of murder. His personal attorney, Robert Shapiro, assembled a team of prominent attorneys from across the nation, including F. Lee Bailey, a personal friend of Shapiro and at the time perhaps the most famous attorney in the United States; outspoken

Harvard professor Alan Dershowitz; Barry Scheck, DNA expert and codirector of the Innocence Project; and Johnnie Cochran, a flamboyant and highly respected personal injury lawyer whose charisma would give the trial its most memorable moments. After opening statements, prosecutors Marcia Clark and Christopher Darden began building a long and complex case against Simpson based on a time line of the murders and Simpson's movements during that period, DNA evidence left at the crime scene, and a pair of leather gloves that appeared to tie Simpson to the murders.

The time line was established largely through the testimonies of Rosa Lopez, a domestic worker for a Simpson neighbor who at one point in the trial fled the country to avoid testifying; Allan Park, a limousine driver who arrived to take Simpson to the airport at about the time of the crime and could get no answer on the home's intercom; and Kato Kaelin, a guest in Simpson's guesthouse who had hamburgers with Simpson early in the evening and later heard a strange noise outside his window close to where a bloody glove was found. In early March, Los

*O. J. Simpson and attorneys discuss strategy for cross-examining a forensic scientist during Simpson's 1995 murder trial.* (AP/Wide World Photos)

Angeles police detective Mark Fuhrman testified that he had found the glove behind Simpson's home and that it matched another found at the crime scene, but Bailey's cross-examination of Fuhrman focused instead on Fuhrman's frequent use of a racial epithet. Fuhrman denied having used the word in the previous ten years. Two months later, on June 15, prosecutor Darden suddenly asked Simpson to try on the gloves, a move that backfired when Simpson struggled to pull the gloves on before finally announcing that they did not fit.

DNA evidence discovered in blood samples placed Simpson at the scene of the murders and indicated that Goldman's blood had somehow found its way into Simpson's car. In late July, however, a forensic toxicologist working for the defense testified to finding a preservative in the blood samples, suggesting that the samples had not actually been collected at the scene and allowing the defense to argue that police had planted Simpson's blood at the scene and on the gloves. Earlier in the trial, Scheck had forced a prosecution witness from the Los Angeles Police Department to admit that procedural errors had indeed been made, so when, in late August and early September, the defense presented a series of witnesses testifying that Fuhrman had in fact used racial epithets several times in the previous ten years, the defense argument that police had planted evidence against Simpson seemed to become more convincing. During his closing argument, Cochran drove home the theory with the jury by repeatedly using the refrain, "If it doesn't fit, you must acquit."

Complicating the Fuhrman episode, several audiotapes Fuhrman had made with a pair of authors who had interviewed him as background for a book revealed that Fuhrman had insulted Judge Lance Ito's wife, a police captain in the Los Angeles Police Department. The prosecution attempted unsuccessfully to remove Ito from the bench, but by that point, the trial had become so infused with petty issues—jury strikes, bickering among the at-

---

## IF IT DOESN'T FIT . . .

*In his closing statement at the criminal trial of O. J. Simpson, lead defense attorney Johnnie Cochran appealed to the jury's sense of racial injustice and distrust of the police investigation:*

The Defendant, Mr. Orenthal James Simpson, is now afforded an opportunity to argue the case, if you will, but I'm not going to argue with you, ladies and gentlemen. What I'm going to do is to try and discuss the reasonable inferences which I feel can be drawn from this evidence. . . .

From the very first orders issued by the LAPD so-called brass, they were more concerned with their own images, the publicity that might be generated from this case than they were in doing professional police work. . . . Because of their bungling, they ignored the obvious clues. . . . We think if they had done their job as we have done, Mr. Simpson would have been eliminated early on. . . .

And so as we look then at the time line and the importance of this time line, I want you to remember these words. Like the defining moment in this trial, the day Mr. Darden asked Mr. Simpson to try on those gloves and the gloves didn't fit, remember these words; if it doesn't fit, you must acquit. . . .

And when you are back there deliberating on this case, you're never going to be ever able to reconcile this time line and the fact there's no blood back there. . . . They don't have any mountain or ocean of evidence. It's not so because they say so. That's just rhetoric. We this afternoon are talking about the facts. And so it doesn't make any sense. It just doesn't fit. If it doesn't fit, you must acquit. . . .

Then we come, before we end the day, to Detective Mark Fuhrman. This man is an unspeakable disgrace. He's been unmasked for the whole world for what he is. . . . And they put him on the stand and you saw it. You saw it. It was sickening. . . . Then Bailey says: "Have you used that word, referring to the 'n' word, in the past ten years? . . . I want you to assume that perhaps at some time since 1985 or '86, you addressed a member of the African American race as a Nigger. Is it possible that you have forgotten that act on your part?" . . .

Let's remember this man. . . . Why did they then all try to cover for this man Fuhrman? . . . This man could have been off the force long ago if they had done their job, but they didn't do their job. People looked the other way. People didn't have the courage. One of the things that has made this country so great is people's willingness to stand up and say that is wrong. I'm not going to be part of it. I'm not going to be part of the cover-up. That is what I'm asking you to do. Stop this cover-up. Stop this cover-up. If you don't stop it, then who? Do you think the police department is going to stop it? Do you think the D.A.'s office is going to stop it? Do you think we can stop it by ourselves? It has to be stopped by you.

---

torneys, Fuhrman's disappearance from the trial after pleading the Fifth Amendment—that the motion to remove Ito quickly passed.

The jury began deliberating on the morning of October 3 and soon called for a review of Park's testimony. Then suddenly, less than four hours after they had begun deliberations, they announced that they had reached a verdict. The next day, with as many as 100 million people watching on television or listening on radio, Simpson was declared "not guilty."

## SIGNIFICANCE

In the wake of the media frenzy and the trial's frequent melodrama, the trial not only posed serious questions about justice in America but also appeared at times to be a parody of a trial. The jury went on strike when three deputies who had accompanied them on trips were reassigned, the parade of eccentric witnesses and grandstanding attorneys blurred the lines between entertainment and news, and the gavel-to-gavel television coverage made celebrities of many of the participants, several of whom made millions of dollars from books and media appearances. Throughout the trial and after, Simpson's own celebrity status prompted accusations that he was, according to some, receiving preferential treatment or, for others, being subjected to overly aggressive prosecution.

Perceptions of Simpson's guilt or innocence differed dramatically between white Americans and black Americans, both during the trial as well as after the verdict. Whites considered the evidence convincing and overwhelming, but blacks generally dismissed both physical evidence and witness testimony as tainted by investigative error or police misconduct. The fact that Simpson was black and his victims were white only magnified the racial overtones, and with memories still fresh of the videotaped beating of Rodney King four years earlier by Los Angeles police officers who were later exonerated, the issue of race would emerge again and again throughout the trial.

Just over a year after he was found not guilty in the criminal trial, Simpson was sued in civil court by Gold-man's family for Goldman's wrongful death. On February 4, 1997, after only a four-month trial, the jury brought back a $33.5 million judgment against Simpson. Soon afterward, Simpson moved to Florida, where the laws protected many of his assets. For years following the judgment, he avoided paying the award.

—*Devon Boan*

## FURTHER READING

Dershowitz, Alan M. *Reasonable Doubts: The Criminal Justice System and the O. J. Simpson Case*. New York: Touchstone, 1996. Inside perspective on the Simpson trial by one of the members of Simpson's legal defense team, including an analysis of the jury's decision in the context of the American legal system.

Fuhrman, Mark. *Murder in Brentwood*. New York: Zebra Books, 1997. Account of the Brown-Goldman murders, including a detailed description of the crime scene and a critique of the investigation, by the detective whose earlier use of racial epithets proved devastating for the Simpson prosecution team.

Hunt, Darnell M. *O. J. Simpson Facts and Fictions: News Rituals in the Construction of Reality*. New York: Cambridge University Press, 1999. Examination of the news coverage of the Simpson trial, including differences of perception across racial lines and the manner in which the media used these perceptions to shape its coverage of the trial.

Toobin, Jeffrey. *The Run of His Life: The People Versus O. J. Simpson*. New York: Random House, 1996. Examination of the social and legal strategies used by Simpson's defense team and the reasons for their success, by a former prosecutor and writer for *The New Yorker* magazine.

**SEE ALSO:** Apr. 29-May 1, 1992: Los Angeles Riots.

## January 31, 1995
# UNITED STATES BAILS OUT MEXICO

*When the Mexican economy threatened to collapse and send shock waves throughout the world economy, the United States joined with the International Monetary Fund to create a multilateral financial package to bail out Mexico and prevent a global economic crisis.*

**ALSO KNOWN AS:** Mexican peso crisis
**LOCALE:** Mexico
**CATEGORIES:** Diplomacy and international relations; banking and finance; economics; trade and commerce

### KEY FIGURES
*Ernesto Zedillo* (b. 1951), president of Mexico, 1994-2000
*Jaime Serra Puche* (b. 1955), Mexican secretary of finance, December, 1994-January, 1995
*Carlos Salinas de Gortari* (b. 1948), president of Mexico, 1988-1994
*Michel Camdessus* (b. 1933), managing director of the International Monetary Fund, 1987-2000

### SUMMARY OF EVENT
December 1, 1994, marked the inauguration of Ernesto Zedillo as the newest president of Mexico. The inauguration ceremony signaled the beginning of a promising presidential term and was a crowning event for outgoing president Carlos Salinas de Gortari, who was praised for his economic policies, which included the signing of the North American Free Trade Agreement (NAFTA) on January 1, 1994, and a set of economic reforms that helped Mexico achieve outstanding economic growth during the early 1990's. The euphoria experienced by Mexicans and the Mexican government was not just a local feeling; other major world economic players such as the United States and the International Monetary Fund (IMF) were also praising Mexico's economic performance in the 1990's.

The feeling of confidence experienced during Zedillo's inauguration festivities lasted less than a month, however. While Mexico was praised as a growing economy, it was far from a strong one, and after a few months of unexpected financial shocks within the country and worldwide, the government had to take action. On December 19, 1994, as a consequence of growing problems experienced by the Mexican economy, President Zedillo's administration decided to change the value of the peso against the dollar, devaluing the Mexican currency by 15 percent, from 3.7 pesos to a dollar to 4 pesos

to a dollar. At the time of the crisis, the Mexican economy was using what is known as a pegged currency—that is, the Mexican peso was worth a certain amount of dollars and it could not be worth more or less than that amount. The Mexican government's move went against prescribed policy, and it led to a speculative run against the peso that forced the government to let the peso float freely against the dollar.

In a matter of days, the peso was highly devalued (at approximately 7.2 pesos to the dollar), and widespread panic started to hit not only the Mexican government but also investors. By late January, 1995, the newly installed Mexican secretary of finance, Jaime Serra Puche—a former secretary of commerce in the Salinas administration and an important player in the negotiation and creation of NAFTA—had resigned amid pressures from investors and the government. The quick devaluation of the peso led foreign investors to see the Mexican economy as unstable and unfit for investment, leading to a massive capital flight from the country.

Many see the beginning of the Mexican crisis as a self-fulfilling prophecy. Investors had worried in 1994 that the Mexican economy was not strong enough to sustain internal and external pressures, and this concern, together with a few dubious policies implemented by the Mexican government, led to the beginning of capital flight from the country. As the foreign reserves were slowly depleted, the government had no option but to let the peso float against the dollar, and as the peso floated, investors became worried that the peso would devalue dramatically against the dollar, leading to a dumping of pesos in the market and consequently leading to the dramatic devaluation of the peso. In other words, the fear of devaluation led investors to take their investments elsewhere, and this exodus of capital led to the devaluation of the peso.

As a consequence of the dramatic devaluation of the peso and the subsequent market panic, the Mexican economy was pushed to its limit, leaving the government on the edge of default. The possibility that Mexico could default on its debt payments was a dire prospect that the United States could not afford. Not only had Mexico become a more important economic partner with the United States since the creation of NAFTA, but also many of the Mexican government's creditors were American companies that could not afford to have their biggest debtor fail to pay what it owed.

## MEXICO'S BAILOUT

*In declaring that the United States would lend $20 billion to Mexico, President Bill Clinton expressed that it was in the interest of both countries that Mexico's economy remains stable. His brief statement was delivered on January 31, 1995:*

We agree that, in order to ensure orderly exchange arrangements and a stable system of exchange rates, the United States should immediately use the Exchange Stabilization Fund (ESF) to provide appropriate financial assistance for Mexico. We further agree that under Title 31 of the United States Code, Section 5302, the President has full authority to provide this assistance. Because the situation in Mexico raises unique and emergency circumstances, the required assistance to be extended will be available for a period of more than 6 months in any 12-month period.

　　The United States will impose strict conditions on the assistance it provides with the goal of ensuring that this package imposes no cost on U.S. taxpayers. We are pleased that other nations have agreed to increase their support. Specifically, the International Monetary Fund today agreed to increase its participation by $10 billion for a total of $17.8 billion. In addition, central banks of a number of industrial countries through the Bank for International Settlements have increased their participation by $5 billion for a total of $10 billion.

　　We must act now in order to protect American jobs, prevent an increased flow of illegal immigrants across our borders, ensure stability in this hemisphere, and encourage reform in emerging markets around the world.

　　This is an important undertaking, and we believe that the risks of inaction vastly exceed any risks associated with this action. We fully support this effort, and we will work to ensure that its purposes are met. We have agreed to act today.

In addition to the direct interest the United States had in seeing Mexico's economy stay afloat, other countries had a considerable amount of vested interest in the health of the Mexican economy. The developing nations especially were paying close attention to what was happening in Mexico in 1995. Many countries feared that the kind of economic crisis taking place in Mexico could spread to other developing nations and even developed nations.

On January 31, 1995, with Mexico on the brink of default and investors all over the world worried about the global economic environment, the U.S. government, together with the IMF, announced a financial support package for Mexico totaling $52 billion. Of this amount, $20 billion would come directly from the United States (through the U.S. Treasury's Exchange Stabilization Fund), $17.8 billion would come from the IMF, and the remainder would come from other creditors. The main objectives of the United States and the IMF in offering this "bailout" package were to prevent the feared Mexican default and to increase confidence in the Mexican economy. The United States also helped Mexico in other ways during the crisis, such as by purchasing pesos in the market to help stabilize the country's foreign reserves and consequently increasing the value of the peso against the dollar.

### SIGNIFICANCE

For the most part, the U.S.-IMF loan package did what it was intended to do. It prevented Mexico from defaulting on its debts, and it encouraged some much-needed confidence in the Mexican economy. After a bad year in 1995, the Mexican economy was able to bounce back in 1996, and its strong recovery continued through the end of the twentieth century.

　　The Mexican peso crisis was the first major economic crisis since the end of the Cold War, making it the first crisis of the "new world economic order." The loan package offered by the United States and the IMF, the first of its kind, set a precedent for future bailouts, such as the one the IMF and the World Bank offered during the Russian financial crisis of 1998.

　　The Mexican crisis showed the world's nations how dangerous economic crises can be in the new economic order and how reliant countries are on one another to create a stable global economic system. The assertiveness of the United States in providing the financial help that Mexico needed in its period of crisis was a very important moment in U.S. foreign policy, showing the direction of the American economy and American policy making not only in regard to Mexico and NAFTA but also in regard to the position of the United States in the world economy in the 1990's.

*—Pedro dos Santos*

### FURTHER READING

Boughton, James M. "From Suez to Tequila: The IMF as Crisis Manager." *Economic Journal* 110 (January, 2000): 273-291. Explains the role played by the IMF in the handling of the Mexican crisis.

Claessens, Stijin, and Kristin J. Forbes, eds. *Interna-*

*tional Financial Contagion*. Norwell, Mass.: Kluwer Academic, 2001. Collection of essays discusses not only the Mexican crisis but other financial crises of the late twentieth century, explaining the reasons and consequences of theses crises.

Edwards, Sebastian, and Moises Naim, eds. *Mexico, 1994: Anatomy of an Emerging Market Crash*. Washington, D.C.: Carnegie Endowment for International Peace, 1997. Collection of essays discusses different approaches to understanding the market crash.

Naim, Moises. "Mexico's Larger Story." *Foreign Policy* 99 (Summer, 1995): 112-130. Presents a detailed ex-

planation of the factors (internal and external) that played a role in creating the Mexican crisis.

Sachs, Jeffrey, et al. "The Collapse of the Mexican Peso: What Have We Learned?" *Economic Policy* 11 (April, 1996): 13-63. Detailed economics essay describes the reasons for the Mexican crisis and the policies implemented afterward.

**See also:** July 23, 1989: Mexico Renegotiates Debt to U.S. Banks; Nov. 20, 1993: North American Free Trade Agreement; July 2, 2000: PRI Rule Ends in Mexico.

1995

## February 13, 1995
# Serbs Face Charges at the International Criminal Tribunal for Yugoslavia

*One year after the U.N. Security Council created an international criminal tribunal in 1994 to try war criminals in the former Yugoslavia, the tribunal charged twenty-one Serbs for war crimes.*

**Locale:** The Hague, the Netherlands
**Categories:** Laws, acts, and legal history; terrorism, atrocities, and war crimes

### Key Figures
*Richard Goldstone* (b. 1938), chief prosecutor for the International Criminal Tribunal for the former Yugoslavia, 1994-1996
*Slobodan Milošević* (1941-2006), president of Serbia, 1989-1997, and president of the Federal Republic of Yugoslavia, 1997-2000
*Radovan Karadžić* (b. 1945), president of the Republika Srpska, 1992-1995
*Ratko Mladić* (b. 1943), chief of staff of the army of the Republika Srpska, 1992-1995
*Dušan Tadić* (b. 1955), first person indicted by the International Criminal Tribunal for Yugoslavia

### Summary of Event
After World War I, the Kingdom of the Serbs, Croats, and Slovenes was established with Belgrade as the capital, recognizing the dominance of the former Serbia within a multiethnic state with several provinces. In 1929, the country was renamed the Kingdom of Yugoslavia. During World War II, some of the ethnic provinces fought on opposite sides of the war, but afterward the country was held together by the charismatic Tito (Josip Broz).

The new Serbian leadership was unable to cope with separatist tendencies in the provinces after Tito died in 1980, and in 1991 Slovenia declared independence. When Croatia followed suit later that year, Belgrade ordered the Yugoslav army to stop the secession, but a peace agreement allowing independence for Croatia was obtained through mediation by the United Nations. When a referendum in Bosnia and Herzegovina agreed to independence in 1992, the Serbian population in the country began to carve a new state inside Bosnia and Herzegovina, the Republika Srpska (or Serb Republic), with military support from Serbia. In 1993, Bosnia and Herzegovina charged Serbia with war crimes at the International Court of Justice in The Hague; although the court twice ordered provisional measures, requiring Belgrade to stop supporting genocidal actions, Serbia did not comply.

Massive violations of international human rights law associated with "ethnic cleansing," a euphemism for genocide, during the wars in the former Yugoslavia led the U.N. Security Council to try conciliation in 1991, condemnation in 1992, and then adoption of a statute in 1994 for the International Criminal Tribunal for the Prosecution of Persons Responsible for Serious Violations of International Humanitarian Law Committed in the Territory of the Former Yugoslavia Since 1991, commonly known as the International Criminal Tribunal for the former Yugoslavia (ICTY).

In 1995, in defiance of the United Nations, Republika Srpska troops engaged in ethnic cleansing of Bosniaks (Bosnian Muslims) in Srebrenica, one of the cities that the U.N. Security Council had designated as a "safe haven." Some eight-thousand men were slaughtered, and twelve-thousand women and children were expelled from the town.

In response, Richard Goldstone, chief ICTY prosecutor, indicted twenty-one Serbs for war crimes. The first ICTY indictment was against Dušan Tadić for his role in rounding up and killing Croats and Muslims in the Omarska concentration camp in 1992. After his arrest in Germany, he was tried and found guilty in 1997 of most of the thirty-four counts in the indictment. Despite various appeals, he was sentenced to a twenty-year prison term within Germany.

The most famous cases involve Republika Srpska leaders of the war in Bosnia and Herzegovina, Radovan Karadžić and Ratko Mladić, who were indicted in 1995 for their roles in the Srebrenica massacre that year. Both remained at large, along with eight others who were indicted; the rest were placed in the custody of the court, which is located at The Hague, pending the outcome of their trials. Most charges in the indictments involved violations of the Geneva Conventions, which were reiterated in the ICTY statute. In particular, the charges were cruel and inhuman treatment, deportation, forcible sexual intercourse and mutilation, injury to body and health, murder, persecution on ethnic or religious grounds, torture, and unlawful confinement.

However, more war crimes resumed in 1995, when the Serbian army entered the province of Kosovo to subdue another independence movement. As violence escalated in 1998, North Atlantic Treaty Organization (NATO) airplanes bombed Serbia, which then agreed to an armistice. After the Kosovo independence movement broke the cease-fire in 1999, Serbian troops went into Kosovo with the apparent intention of killing as many Kosovars (ethnic Albanians) as possible, or so it seemed, when forty-five Kosovars were massacred in Račak. As a result, the European Union imposed economic sanctions, and the United States demanded another armistice. In 1999, Serbia rejected terms of a proposed peace agreement, which would give NATO unlimited access within Kosovo as well as Serbia. NATO forces then bombed Serbia into suing for peace. The United Nations then took over the civilian administration of Kosovo, so the ICTY had more war criminals to pursue. In 2000, Slobodan Milošević was voted out as president of Serbia in an election marred by irregularities, leading to street protests and Milošević's resignation. He was handed over to the ICTY in 2001 as a condition of having multilateral sanctions lifted from Serbia.

In 2005, the court indicted four Croatian journalists for contempt of court after they published testimony of two protected witnesses in an ongoing trial. Other Croats have been charged with war crimes, and the Kosovo War has resulted in charges against Kosovars.

By the end of 2006, the ICTY had found fifty-three persons guilty; they were serving sentences from three years to life. By that date, five had been found not guilty; one had committed suicide. Some appeals caused reductions in the years of the sentences. Also in 2006, Milošević died while in custody at The Hague in the midst of his trial.

## SIGNIFICANCE

In 1994, the U.N. Security Council also drafted a statute for the International Criminal Tribunal for Rwanda, and in 1998 the International Criminal Court was established to provide a common tribunal for war crimes worldwide. Special national war crimes tribunals were established with U.N. assistance in East Timor (2000), Sierra Leone (2002), Cambodia (2003), and Iraq (2004).

The ICTY has developed important legal principles in the field of international criminal law. For example, to find a commander guilty of crimes committed by subordinates, a prosecutor must demonstrate not only vicarious liability but also subjective awareness (or aiding and abetting). After the war in Bosnia and Herzegovina, the tribunal, for the first time in history, chose to prosecute rape as a war crime in 1997.

The ICTY has forced those in the former Yugoslavia to rethink the past. The tribunal has aided in reconciliation by enabling victims to come forward to share their stories and by disqualifying from political life those who committed heinous acts. In early 2004, the U.N. Security Council asked the ICTY to finish investigations by the end of the year, trials by 2008, and appeals by 2010.

*—Michael Haas*

## FURTHER READING

Bass, Gary Jonathan. *Stay the Hand of Justice: The Politics of War Crimes Tribunals*. Princeton, N.J.: Princeton University Press, 2001. Review of war crimes trials to determine whether true justice can emerge from tribunals that have been created within a highly political context.

Cigar, Norman, Paul Williams, and Banac Ivo. *Indictment at the Hague: The Milošević Regime and Crimes of the Balkan Wars*. New York: New York University Press, 2002. Assembles documentary evidence to demonstrate the culpability of Milošević for war crimes.

Honig, Jan Willem, and Norbert Both. *Srebrenica: Record of a War Crime.* New York: Penguin Books, 1996. Presents detailed descriptions of the atrocities that led to the formation of the ICTY.

Human Rights Watch. *Genocide, War Crimes, and Crimes Against Humanity: A Topical Digest of the Case Law of the International Criminal Tribunal for the Former Yugoslavia.* New York: Author, 2006. Provides a comprehensive guide to the proceedings before the ICTY.

Rieff, David. *Slaughterhouse: Bosnia and the Failure of the West.* New York: Simon & Schuster, 1995. Points out that efforts to stop war crimes in Bosnia came too late.

SEE ALSO: July-Nov., 1988: Ethnic Violence Erupts in Yugoslavian Provinces; June 25, 1991: Civil War Begins in Yugoslavia; Feb. 21, 1992: United Nations Authorizes Troop Deployment to the Balkans; Nov. 21, 1995: Dayton Negotiations Produce Bosnian Peace Accord; Feb. 28, 1998-June 9, 1999: Kosovo Conflict Escalates; Jan. 14, 2000: Hague Court Convicts Bosnian Croats of 1993 Massacre.

## February 15, 1995
# ARREST OF HACKER KEVIN MITNICK

*The FBI's arrest of Kevin Mitnick brought widespread attention to the crime of computer hacking.*

**LOCALE:** Raleigh, North Carolina

**CATEGORIES:** Computers and computer science; crime and scandal

### KEY FIGURES

*Kevin Mitnick* (b. 1963), American con artist and computer hacker

*Tsutomu Shimomura* (fl. late twentieth century), American computer security expert

### SUMMARY OF EVENT

By the end of the 1980's, advances in technology had led to the use of computers in nearly every home and business in the United States. Computers had become common tools for personal and business use around the world as well, and as the 1990's progressed, more and more of these computers were connected to the Internet. Any computer that is connected to the Internet opens a line of communication that can be accessed by computer hackers anywhere in the world. Such hackers have been responsible for threats to national security, financial fraud and identity theft, software piracy, theft of trade secrets and other information, and wanton destruction of data, software, and hardware, as well as other malicious behaviors.

The term "hacker" originally applied to anyone who gained entry to a computer without the consent of the computer's owner. In the early days of computers, the typical hacker simply sought knowledge about how computers worked and how they communicated with each other. Companies that used computers eventually hired many of these hackers to test computer security systems and to fix any holes they found; these hackers became known as "white hats." Malicious computer hackers, known as "black hats," seek access primarily for the purpose of committing vandalism and theft.

The first time the U.S. government prosecuted an individual for computer hacking, computer usage was still in its infancy. In 1966, a computer programmer under contract to a Minneapolis bank experienced what he considered to be a temporary shortage of funds in his own bank account. He then manipulated the data on his account so that no overdrafts were reported. The programmer committed this fraud so easily that he kept at it, and eventually he had hidden $14,000 in overdrafts within a computer program that only he understood. Unfortunately for the programmer, the bank's computer system crashed, forcing bank employees to record account activity manually; at that point, he was found out and arrested.

Kevin Mitnick, who used the handle "Condor," was the first computer hacker to become widely known. He was first arrested for hacking in 1980, when he was seventeen years old. He spent the next fifteen years marauding through the computers of the world's largest technology corporations. Mitnick typically gained access to computer systems through what he called "social engineering"—that is, he employed his knowledge of human nature to trick people into giving him computer passwords and other secure data. He repeatedly burrowed into the computer systems of corporations such as Motorola and Digital Equipment Corporation (DEC) to pilfer their source codes, the electronic blueprints of their systems' operations. In 1989, Mitnick went to jail for the theft of one million dollars' worth of software from DEC. He was released on probation in 1990, but he violated the terms of his probation when he stopped attending treatment for computer addiction.

At one point, Mitnick stole more than twenty thousand credit card numbers from the files of an Internet service provider; some of the numbers belonged to the best-known millionaires in Silicon Valley. Additionally, Mitnick used computer space belonging to a lobbying group called Computers, Freedom and Privacy to store stolen programs for controlling cellular phones. Altogether, it is estimated that Mitnick's hacking activities cost his victims some $300,000.

Mitnick's crimes brought him to the attention of the Federal Bureau of Investigation (FBI), which instituted a nationwide search for the hacker. His downfall came after he teased a computer security expert in San Diego, Tsutomu Shimomura, by breaking into Shimomura's home computer on Christmas Day in 1994, using a technique called protocol spoofing. Shimomura's computer was linked to a network, which allowed Mitnick to steal files related to computer security. He then left mocking, distorted messages on Shimomura's voice mail. Shimomura monitored the intrusions and was able to trace Mitnick to a cellular telephone site near Raleigh, North Carolina, where the FBI captured him on February 15, 1995.

In 1996, the U.S. Justice Department indicted Mitnick on twenty-six counts of computer, telephone, and wire fraud. Convicted of cellular telephone fraud, Mitnick served more than five years in prison before being released on probation. When his probation ended in 2003, Mitnick returned to the Internet to start a security consulting company, Defensive Thinking. Mitnick aimed to block the same holes that he had once exploited.

Mitnick was very successful in using social engineering to gain access to computer systems, but this method is employed by relatively few hackers. Viruses, worms, and logic bombs are far more common means of hacking into systems. Viruses are intended to infect computers; they can do anything from launching denial-of-service attacks to sending junk e-mail (spam) to thousands of recipients. Worms copy themselves and exploit weaknesses in computer systems. They are not usually criminal in intent, but viruses and worms can be enormously damaging and thus expensive for their targets. To remove such code, victims have to reformat hard disk drives and thereby lose all data they have not backed up. The costs in time and lost productivity can run into millions of dollars when many victims are involved. For example, the Melissa worm, first identified in 1999, caused an estimated $80 million in damages as it spread from network to network. In 2003, the SQL Slammer worm shut down thirteen thousand Bank of America automated teller machines (ATMs) and slowed worldwide Internet traffic to a crawl. By the early twenty-first century, more than fifty thousand computer viruses and worms were being identified annually.

The proliferation of malicious hackers led to a new descriptive word, "malware." This term is applied to software that is intended to plant a program on a computer, without the owner's knowledge, that will cause damage to the computer's software. Malware programs are also known as Trojan horses. Hackers may use malware to install programs that allow them to listen in on conversations around the target computers or, more commonly, to record computer users' keystrokes and thus transmit information back to the hackers. Through such methods, hackers can ob-

---

## BIRTH OF A SOCIAL ENGINEER

*In his 2002 book* The Art of Deception: Controlling the Human Element of Security *(coauthored with William L. Simon), Kevin Mitnick describes how he got his start on the road to computer hacking:*

My first encounter with what I would eventually learn to call *social engineering* came about during my high school years when I met another student who was caught up in a hobby called *phone phreaking*. Phone phreaking is a type of hacking that allows you to explore the telephone network by exploiting the phone systems and phone company employees. He showed me neat tricks he could do with a telephone, like obtaining any information the phone company had on any customer, and using a secret test number to make long-distance calls for free. (Actually it was free only to us. I found out much later that it wasn't a secret test number at all. The calls were, in fact, being billed to some poor company's MCI account.)

That was my introduction to social engineering—my kindergarten, so to speak. My friend and another phone phreaker I met shortly thereafter let me listen in as they each made *pretext* calls to the phone company. I heard the things they said that made them sound believable; I learned about different phone company offices, lingo, and procedures. But that "training" didn't last long; it didn't have to. Soon I was doing it all on my own, learning as I went, doing it even better than my first teachers.

The course my life would follow for the next fifteen years had been set.

tain bank information and other private data that can be used for criminal purposes.

Some criminals use computer hacking to commit crimes that would have required physically breaking and entering businesses in the past. In 1997, an FBI sting at the San Francisco International Airport netted a criminal who was trying to sell a compact disc containing 100,000 credit cards numbers for $260,000. The list had been compiled through the hacking of a number of different organizations' computers.

## SIGNIFICANCE

The U.S. government has taken some steps to halt the spread of hacking. The Computer Fraud and Abuse Act of 1986 made it a federal crime for an individual to access a computer intentionally without authority or by exceeding authority to obtain information to which that person is not entitled. Congress has since amended the act a number of times to keep it responsive to changes in technology. The Economic Espionage Act of 1996 was a response to the growing network of professional spies and saboteurs who earn money by hacking the computers of rival businesses or governments. The legislation made it a federal offense to profit in any way from the misappropriation of another person's trade secrets, including through computer downloads and uploads as well as electronic mail. Individual U.S. states have also developed laws to make hacking a criminal offense.

Although the legislation passed to fight hacking has been beneficial to the business sector, a number of basic tools are more effective at providing protection from hackers. The most commonly used protective tool is the password—that is, requiring an authorized user to enter a password that is a mix of letters and numbers to gain access to particular systems, services, or programs. A more sophisticated method of protection is the encryption of information so that hackers cannot easily read it. Firewalls, a common element of security software, are often used to block unauthorized access to individual computers or networks.

By the early twenty-first century, both U.S. government agencies and private companies began to pour significant funding into computer security in response to

intelligence experts' fears that terrorists could use the Internet or other computer technology to attack the United States. The Department of Homeland Security was specifically concerned that terrorist groups could launch cyberattacks and physical attacks simultaneously, perhaps disabling safety systems at nuclear plants or air traffic control systems. However, the human element that Mitnick so successfully exploited continued to be the main security risk and the one most difficult to guard against. Despite widespread knowledge about computer crimes, people continued to be careless with passwords and other data that hackers could use to gain access to computer systems.

*—Caryn E. Neumann*

## FURTHER READING

Mitnick, Kevin D., and William L. Simon. *The Art of Deception: Controlling the Human Element of Security.* New York: John Wiley & Sons, 2002. Mitnick provides an interesting look into his use of social engineering to get around security systems.

Power, Richard. *Tangled Web: Tales of Digital Crime from the Shadows of Cyberspace.* Indianapolis: Que, 2000. Entertaining volume examines all varieties of cybercrime. Chapter 5 discusses Mitnick. Includes glossary and index.

Shimomura, Tsutomu, with John Markoff. *Takedown: The Pursuit and Capture of Kevin Mitnick, America's Most Wanted Computer Outlaw—by the Man Who Did It.* New York: Hyperion, 1996. Account of the efforts to find Mitnick and the hacker's capture by a computer security expert who was instrumental in tracking him down. Includes index.

SEE ALSO: 1980's: Electronic Technology Creates the Possibility of Telecommuting; Aug. 12, 1981: IBM Introduces Its Personal Computer; Nov. 20, 1985: Microsoft Releases the Windows Operating System; July 3, 1991: IBM and Apple Agree to Make Compatible Computers; Dec. 15, 1994: Release of Netscape Navigator 1.0; Mid-1990's: Rise of the Internet and the World Wide Web; May 4, 2000: ILOVEYOU Virus Attacks Computers.

## March 20, 1995
# TERRORISTS USE SARIN GAS IN TOKYO SUBWAY ATTACK

*When the religious movement Aum Shinrikyo released sarin gas on three major Tokyo subway lines in 1995, killing twelve and injuring thousands, the event led nations around the world to examine the possibility that marginal religious groups with beliefs rooted in apocalyptic thought might bring real destruction to the larger world.*

**LOCALE:** Tokyo, Japan
**CATEGORY:** Terrorism, atrocities, and war crimes

**KEY FIGURES**

*Shoko Asahara* (Chizuo Matsumoto; b. 1955), founder and leader of the Aum Shinrikyo religious movement

*Masami Tsuchiya* (b. 1965), Aum Shinrikyo member who spearheaded sarin production for the Tokyo subway attacks

*Ikuo Hayashi* (b. 1947), chief medical official of Aum Shinrikyo

**SUMMARY OF EVENT**

In early 1995, the Aum Shinrikyo religious movement had fewer than ten thousand members in Japan, thirty thousand members in Russia, and a scattering of followers in the United States. Aum Shinrikyo was established primarily on peaceful Buddhist principles, but it also drew heavily from Hinduism, the apocalyptic ideas in the book of Revelation in the Christian Bible, the ideas of Adolf Hitler, and the writings of sixteenth century Christian monk Nostradamus, and the group held strong beliefs in a nearing Armageddon, or cosmic war. Fanatical Aum Shinrikyo leader Chizuo Matsumoto, known to his followers and the world by the holy name of Shoko Asahara, forecast that this Armageddon would come very soon, and as he and his followers saw increasing evil in the world, they began to pursue the notion that their group would be instrumental in forcing this Armageddon into being.

On March 20, 1995, Aum Shinrikyo believers attempted to set in motion the early steps of this Armageddon. During the morning rush hour, they attacked three major subway lines that intersected at Tokyo's Kasu-

migaseki station, located near the city's center for top governmental offices and police. The terrorists quietly boarded subway trains wearing protective gas masks and carrying six-inch bags concealed by newspapers. The bags contained sarin, a destructive nerve gas originally developed by the Nazis for use in World War II. The Aum Shinrikyo members released the gas from their bags at a predetermined time and then quickly exited the trains. Once the nerve gas was fully released into the air, the subway passengers exposed to it suffered from severe coughing and choking attacks, vomiting, violent convulsions, foaming at the mouth, and fainting. Twelve people died as a result of their exposure to the gas.

During the investigation that took place in the days following the Tokyo subway attack, Aum Shinrikyo denied any responsibility for or connection to the incident. In reality, the group had perpetrated the attack in large part in reaction to rumors that police were planning to

*Shoko Asahara (left) with one of his disciples.* (AP/Wide World Photos)

stage raids on the Aum Shinrikyo headquarters; it then used the event to portray Aum Shinrikyo members as victims of social and political injustice.
The group had publicized reports in
the months prior to the attack asserting
that members had become ill from exposure to sarin gas (most likely leaked
from their own supplies) and blaming
this exposure on attacks by American
and Japanese aircraft. Asahara also
aired several messages on radio and
television after the attack in which he
proclaimed his innocence. Aum Shinrikyo had struggled to be accepted as
an official Japanese religion since its
founding in 1987, and group members
claimed they were being persecuted
and framed for the subway attack in an
act of religious discrimination.

Before the Tokyo subway attack,
Aum Shinrikyo members had been
suspected, but never convicted, of several dubious activities, including the
1989 murder of Tsutsumi Sakamoto, a
lawyer who had been acting on behalf
of a missing person connected to Aum
Shinrikyo, and the disappearance of
his wife and daughter. In addition, the
group had been suspected in a small
release of sarin nerve gas aimed at
judges who opposed Aum Shinrikyo
activities in the village of Matsumoto
and the testing of sarin gas on Austra-
lian sheep. The ambiguous nature of the crimes and their
circumstances often made it difficult for police to pinpoint Aum Shinrikyo members as the culprits.

During the investigation of the subway attack, Tokyo
metropolitan police officers raided twenty-five Aum
Shinrikyo centers on March 22, 1995, under the official
guise of investigating the group's involvement in the
disappearance of a sixty-eight-year-old notary public.
The police discovered significant amounts of cash and
other valuables, massive amounts of dangerous chemicals and medications, and several Aum Shinrikyo members in a state of debilitation. Following these discoveries, several doctors who were members of the group
were arrested, Asahara was officially summoned for
questioning, and an official investigation was launched
into the organization. Among other crimes, members

## AUM SHINRIKYO

Variously translated as "Om Supreme Truth Religion" and "Aum Divine
Wizard Association," Aum Shinrikyo began as a doomsday cult, but Shoko
Asahara, unlike most end-of-the-world prophets, was unwilling simply to
wait for doomsday—he wanted to speed it along. After his spiritual revelation in the Himalayas in 1989, he returned to Japan with a plan. He introduced
group religious training for his disciplines, preparing them for Armageddon.
Asahara taught that nuclear war would inevitably break out in 1999 as a punishment for the evil of the world. Still, there remained one hope for humanity:
If he could lead thirty thousand people to spiritual awakening, their holy energy would stave off the worst effects of the nuclear holocaust.

Proclaiming himself the reincarnation of the Hindu god Shiva, Asahara
taught a mixture of Hindu, Buddhist, and yogic doctrines but took his basic
doomsday scenario from the Bible's book of Revelation and the teachings of
the sixteenth century Christian monk Nostradamus. His training focused on
four areas: the doctrine assembled from these sources, meditation, asceti-
cism, and initiation to spiritual awakening. These his students practiced in
three courses: a Tantric yoga course, a bodha course, and a siddhi course.
They could quicken their progress to spiritual awakening, salvation from Armageddon, and eternal happiness by drinking Asahara's bathwater or blood,
for a small fee. As for their connections to society and their wealth, they did
not need them. They were to give themselves and all their worldly goods to
the Aum Shinrikyo.

To ensure that Armageddon happened according to schedule, sect members attempted to synthesize chemical weapons (the nerve agent sarin among
them) and to acquire nuclear weapons. Even though their two nerve gas attacks in Japan failed to jump-start the war, even though the prophesied
doomsday date of 1999 has come and gone, and even though their leader is in
prison and eleven members have been sentenced to death, Aum Shinrikyo
lives on. It has been renamed Aleph and retains well over one thousand members. However, Aleph has split into two groups, one still attached to Asahara
and the other following one of his former lieutenants.

were suspected of attempting to assassinate Japanese
police chief Takaji Kunimatsu and of perpetrating a second attempt at biological terrorism with cyanide at the
Shinjuku subway station. Aum Shinrikyo members were
also suspected of sending a parcel bomb to the Tokyo
city hall on May 16, 1995, in an attempt to kill the city's
governor.

Asahara was captured on May 16, 1995, after authorities followed up on the murder of Hideo Murai, a top
Aum Shinrikyo scientist. A confession was solicited
from Masami Tsuchiya, another scientist with the group,
who admitted to having produced sarin nerve gas several
days prior to the Tokyo subway attack. Ikuo Hayashi,
Aum Shinrikyo's top medical official, then admitted to
police that he was among the ten members of the group
who had carried the sarin gas onto the subway trains; he

2885

stated that he had done so under Asahara's command, thus directly implicating Asahara in the incident.

The purposes of Aum Shinrikyo's Tokyo subway attack and other destructive activities were primarily twofold: to get rid of journalists, politicians, and legal professionals who appeared to be against Aum Shinrikyo and to ignite the start of a global Armageddon that would eliminate the human race. Members believed that humankind had become so drenched in political and religious bad karma that worldwide destruction was inevitable and that promoting such destruction was a social responsibility. In the days leading up to the Tokyo subway attack, Aum Shinrikyo was also facing the possibility of its own death as a result of mounting legal charges, complaints from parents of members, and the fears of Aum Shinrikyo members. Asahara thus viewed the subway attack as both an act of destruction and an act of survival.

## SIGNIFICANCE

The sarin attack on the Tokyo subway had ramifications that echoed throughout Japan and the world. The attack marked the first time a marginal religious group whose members believed in the inevitable nearness of the end times had the means to carry out a version of the apocalypse, using chemical weapons that were relatively easy to obtain. Asahara's dependence on and passion for biologically destructive materials allowed Aum Shinrikyo to make the transition between apocalyptic thought and apocalyptic action, and for the first time the world saw the power of religious apocalyptic thought carried out in a destructive physical manner.

Aum Shinrikyo had kept a low profile for much of its existence, and the subway attack on March 20, 1995, prompted many to question why the group had not been stopped prior to the attacks, given the warning signs of questionable activities at its headquarters. The attack thus heightened awareness of new religious groups around the world, especially those that encourage or support theories of an apocalypse in the near future and have possible access to biological or chemical weapons.

The Tokyo subway attack had an especially great impact on Japan. Following the attack, many Japanese suffered anxiety related to the sudden onset of disorder in their society, which had long prided itself on its lack of chaos.

—*Jennifer L. Amel*

## FURTHER READING

Lifton, Robert Jay. *Destroying the World to Save It: Aum Shinrikyo, Apocalyptic Violence, and the New Global Terrorism*. New York: Henry Holt, 1999. Investigates the rise of Shoko Asahara, his psychological background and intellectual makeup, and the roots of the Aum Shinrikyo belief systems. Compares the Tokyo subway incident with other incidents of religious terrorism and mass suicide in the United States and investigates the connection between the Tokyo subway attacks and the larger Japanese culture.

Robbins, Thomas, and Susan J. Palmer, eds. *Millennium, Messiahs, and Mayhem: Contemporary Apocalyptic Movements*. New York: Routledge, 1997. Collection of thought-provoking essays discusses in detail relatively recent religious movements that use the fear of a nearing apocalypse as a keystone to their dogma. Essays explore the relationship between such movements and apocalyptic thought. Chapter 16 deals specifically with Aum Shinrikyo.

Tharp, Mike. "Death in the Subway." *U.S. News & World Report*, April 3, 1995. Newsmagazine report describes the Tokyo subway attacks immediately after they occurred.

Van Biema, David. "Prophet of Poison." *Time*, April 3, 1995. Investigates the aftermath of the subway attack. Includes photographs and quotations from interviews with people who were involved.

SEE ALSO: Nov. 18, 1978: People's Temple Members Commit Mass Suicide; Feb. 26, 1993: World Trade Center Bombing; Apr. 19, 1995: Bombing of the Oklahoma City Federal Building; Mar. 23-25, 1997: Heaven's Gate Cult Members Commit Mass Suicide.

# March 30, 1995
# NATIONAL LIBRARY OF FRANCE OPENS

*The new Bibliothèque Nationale de France continued the traditional research orientation and legal deposit function of the old Bibliothèque Nationale while increasing access for nonresearch visitors and embracing new information technologies.*

**ALSO KNOWN AS:** Bibliothèque Nationale de France
**LOCALE:** Paris, France
**CATEGORY:** Organizations and institutions

**KEY FIGURES**

*François Mitterrand* (1916-1996), president of France, 1981-1995
*Charles V* (1337-1380), king of France, r. 1364-1380
*Francis I* (1494-1547), king of France, r. 1515-1547
*Dominique Perrault* (b. 1953), French architect

**SUMMARY OF EVENT**

The origins of the Bibliothèque Nationale de France (National Library of France) go back to 1368, when King Charles V established a royal library in the Louvre Palace. In 1537, King Francis I established the *dépôt légal* (legal deposit), which required publishers to provide the royal library with a copy of every work printed. The terms of the *dépôt légal* ensured that every facet of French culture was preserved, not just great works of art or literature deemed appropriate by a government bureaucracy. In the seventeenth century, Jean-Baptiste Colbert, one of King Louis XIV's ministers, moved the royal library to the rue de Richelieu palace of Cardinal Jules Mazarin, the site at which it remained for more than three hundred years. During the French Revolution, the royal library became the Bibliothèque Nationale and was greatly expanded by the confiscation of collections from princes, emigrants, and the clergy.

Despite some twentieth century predictions that computers would create "paperless offices" and make the printed page obsolete, the growth of printed documents continued explosively. By the late twentieth century, the Bibliothèque Nationale was running out of space for the expanding numbers of books, periodicals, audio and visual materials, computer software, and esoteric collections of every type housed there. It was also being overwhelmed by increased demands from students and scholarly researchers.

On April 13, 1988, Minister of Culture François Léotard announced that the Bibliothèque Nationale would be reorganized and a second library would be built to house all documents and other covered materials published after 1990 (this was later changed to materials published after 1945). In his annual television interview on July 14, 1988, French president François Mitterrand disclosed his plan to build one of the world's largest and most modern libraries. The charter of the new library, as defined and articulated later, was to create a library "to encompass every field of knowledge, to be accessible to one and all, to make use of the very latest data transmission technologies, to afford long-distance consultation, and to be linked with other European libraries." Because the old Bibliothèque Nationale is located in a prime area in Paris's fourth arrondissement, where it would be too expensive to add the new buildings required, it was decided that the new library would be built a few miles away on the Left Bank of the Seine at the Quai de Tolbiac, in Paris's thirteenth arrondissement.

In 1989, the plan to divide the libraries' holdings chronologically between the two buildings was changed in favor of making the two libraries a single entity. The rue de Richelieu site would continue to house the specialized collections, such as manuscripts, coins, maps, and medals, while all books, periodicals, and audiovisual materials would be transferred to the new Tolbiac site, which would also host a bibliographic research department. The Bibliothèque Nationale de France was officially established in January, 1994.

An open architectural design competition, chaired by I. M. Pei (designer of the controversial Louvre pyramid), selected architect Dominique Perrault to design the building. Perrault's design is stunning, but it has engendered controversy: It comprises four twenty-two-story glass and concrete towers situated at the corners of a rectangular site and facing in toward a central garden area; each building is L-shaped, to represent an open book. Stark and modern on the outside, the interiors of the towers are softened by rich hardwoods and carpets. After book conservationists raised concerns that light and fluctuations in temperature and humidity would damage books, an innovative system of shutters was designed for the floors on which books are stored. Many of the books are stored underground at a temperature of 64 degrees Fahrenheit and a humidity of 50 percent. The new buildings also house administrative and support staff and provide exhibition space, lecture halls, restaurants, bookshops, and other services.

The printed materials collection relocated to the

Tolbiac site includes not only books and periodicals but also government publications, booksellers' and publishers' catalogs, flyers and posters, and pamphlets and leaflets. The rare book collection contains not only antiquities but also books that were condemned as obscene in the nineteenth century and underground newspapers and other publications from World Wars I and II.

The periodicals in the printed materials collection include all journals and newspapers published in France, along with more than eighty-five hundred other periodicals from about 150 countries. The collection comprises tens of millions of issues dating back more than three centuries, providing intimate and detailed insights into the full strata of politics, society, and public opinion in France over the course of the period.

The audiovisual collection began with the creation of France's first sound library, Archives de la Parole, in 1911. Under the direction of Ferdinand Brunot, the voices of many famous persons were recorded, and ethnographic recordings were made. In 1938, the Phonothèque Nationale (National Sound Library) was established as the *dépôt légal* for records, tapes, and other sound recordings. In 1975, this was expanded to be the legal deposit for video recordings and multimedia products; in 1977, it became the Sound Archives and Audiovisual Department of the National Library. The department also oversees a collection of four hundred listening devices dating back to the late nineteenth century.

President Mitterrand officially inaugurated the Bibliothèque Nationale de France on March 30, 1995, although only a small number of documents had actually been moved at that time, and the final disposition of the collections was still a few years away.

## SIGNIFICANCE

With the opening of the Bibliothèque Nationale de France, the French government took a major step toward several goals: reorganizing a massive national collection that ranges from priceless antique books to oddities such as a phonograph that plays chocolate records, making information more accessible to researchers and the general public, expanding its holdings to create a truly interdisciplinary collection, and preparing for

the technological changes in information delivery of the twenty-first century.

One major flaw of the old Bibliothèque Nationale was its separate and uncoordinated series of catalogs. Holdings were spread among twenty-nine individual and confusing catalogs, some devised in the seventeenth century. The reorganization of the library's holdings provided an opportunity to create a comprehensive, computerized catalog that can be accessed remotely. The Bibliothèque Nationale de France is the core of the nation's bibliographic and documentary network and is connected to similar networks throughout the world. The library's electronic catalog contains more than seven million entries covering the library's entire collection, including the French Union Catalog, a comprehensive listing of all documents in French libraries—the Bibliothèque Nationale, thirty-one university libraries, and fifty-four municipal libraries.

By 1997, two French bibliographic databases (BN-OPALE and BN-OPALINE) were accessible to cooperating libraries through the Internet, and the collections of other major libraries were available similarly to persons in France. The BN-OPALE database is also available to the general public through the Internet and on CD-ROM, tape, and computer disks.

Part of the library's charter is to provide information in every field of knowledge. The Bibliothèque Nationale had a preeminent collection in the humanities, particu-

*The Bibliothèque Nationale de France.* (Tim Pritlove/GDFL)

larly literature and history; to complete the new library's charter, it increased its acquisitions in law, economics, political science, the sciences, and technology. The library also implemented an active policy of acquiring foreign publications, audio materials, and multimedia sources in these areas. The reading rooms and collections were reorganized from the twenty-nine old catalogs into four departments: philosophy, history, and human sciences; political, economic, and legal sciences; science and technology; and art and literature. The rare books section incorporates applicable volumes from the four departments.

Greater accessibility of the collections to a wider audience was another goal of the new library. The old Bibliothèque Nationale generally was available only to researchers and students, who not only had to prove their credentials but also had to prove that they could not find the materials they wanted to use elsewhere. The resources of the new library are more available to visitors and tourists. The new facility has two sections: a general-access library and reading rooms on the upper floors, and a research library at garden level. The general library has about seventeen hundred desks and is open to anyone eighteen years old or older.

Like all research libraries, the Bibliothèque Nationale de France faces the challenge of simultaneously conserving the heritage and scholarship of the past, taking advantage of the scholarship and technology of the present and future, and advancing distribution of both. While high-tech specialists maintain the electronic catalog, establish computerized links to the rest of the world, and digitize documents, other specialists work to restore and preserve the fragile paper documents of the past.

It has been argued that in the twenty-first century, the processing and distribution of information will be the basis of wealth and power. The Bibliothèque Nationale de France is preserving its vast collection of documents both in their original form and digitally, ensuring that they will remain available to both the national community of France and the rest of the world.

*—Irene Struthers*

## FURTHER READING

Favier, Jean. "The History of the French National Library." *Daedalus* 125 (Fall, 1996): 283-291. The library's president gives his insights into the political issues and technological challenges accompanying the library's transition into the new millennium.

Jamet, Dominique, and Hélène Waysbord. "History, Philosophy, and Ambitions of the Bibliothèque de France." In *Future Libraries*, edited by R. Howard Bloch and Carla Hesse. Berkeley: University of California Press, 1995. Provides a useful overview of the history of the Bibliothèque Nationale de France, followed by a brief discussion of its place among the world's major libraries in the twenty-first century. Jamet was the chair of the library's planning group established in 1989.

Reynolds, Catharine. "Volumes of Controversy: Bibliothèque Nationale de France." *Gourmet* 57 (January, 1997): 26, 28. Presents a brief but comprehensive discussion of the library's design and the controversy it engendered.

Tesnière, Marie-Hélène, and Prosser Gifford, eds. *Creating French Culture: Treasures from the Bibliothèque Nationale de France*. New Haven, Conn.: Yale University Press, 1995. Beautifully illustrated catalog for an exhibition held at the Library of Congress presents a variety of materials from the Bibliothèque Nationale along with essays and commentary by both French and American authors.

Wernick, Robert. "A Treasure House That Holds One Nation's Memory." *Smithsonian* 21 (September, 1990): 114-125. Beautifully illustrated article on the Bibliothèque Nationale on the rue de Richelieu before the dispersion of the main collections to the Tolbiac site. Helpful for understanding the scope of the print and other collections.

**SEE ALSO:** Sept. 28, 1974: Dalí Museum Opens in Spain; Jan. 31, 1977: Pompidou Center Opens in Paris; Dec. 9, 1986: Opening of the Musée d'Orsay; Mar. 4, 1988: Pei Creates a New Entrance to the Louvre.

1995

## April 19, 1995
# BOMBING OF THE OKLAHOMA CITY FEDERAL BUILDING

*One of the worst terrorist incidents in U.S. history demonstrated that Americans were vulnerable to attack by rogue ideologues.*

**ALSO KNOWN AS:** Murrah Building bombing; Alfred
　P. Murrah Federal Office Building bombing
**LOCALE:** Oklahoma City, Oklahoma
**CATEGORY:** Terrorism, atrocities, and war crimes

### KEY FIGURES
*Timothy McVeigh* (1968-2001), American terrorist
　convicted and executed for his role in the bombing
*Terry Lynn Nichols* (b. 1955), American terrorist
　convicted of being an accomplice to McVeigh
*Frank Keating* (b. 1944), governor of Oklahoma,
　1995-2003

### SUMMARY OF EVENT
On April 19, 1995, a truck bomb parked in front of the Alfred P. Murrah Federal Office Building in downtown Oklahoma City exploded, shattering the foundation and lower floors of the nine-story concrete edifice. The building housed fifteen federal agencies employing more than 500 people; it also was the site of a day-care center for employees' children. Direct casualties included 168 dead as a result of the blast and more than 600 injured. These numbers made the bombing the worst incident of terrorism in U.S. history up to that time, but they do not fully recount the level of the damage done. The blast claimed many more indirect victims, stretching from the more than 250 children who lost a parent in the blast to the tens of thousands in the Oklahoma City community who counted among their friends and loved ones those killed or wounded by the explosion and to citizens across the country who suddenly needed to adjust to the reality of their vulnerability to terrorism, wherever they might work or live.

Rescue workers from as far away as Virginia traveled to Oklahoma City to help seek survivors amid the rubble while state, local, and federal law-enforcement agencies joined in what was reportedly the largest criminal investigation undertaken up to that time in U.S. history. Initial news stories suggested a Middle Eastern connection with the bombing, and Arab Americans were subjected to intense scrutiny in airports across the country. Lobbyist groups would later protest that the early news releases stereotyped Middle Easterners as terrorists and exposed them to abuse by an outraged U.S. public; however, cir-

cumstantial evidence did point in that direction. The explosive, a mixture of fuel oil and an ammonium nitrate fertilizer, was the same compound that Arab terrorists had employed in the February 26, 1993, bombing of the World Trade Center in New York, which killed six and injured one thousand. The mode of delivery was also the same—a parked rental van.

Moreover, because of Oklahoma's links with the international oil community, people from the Middle East had long been familiar sights on Oklahoma City streets. Even the initial leads developed in the same way as those that resulted in the apprehension of the Arabs involved in the World Trade Center bombing: The vehicle that had contained the explosives was identified and tracked to the agency that rented it. The day following the blast, however, to the shock of many, the Federal Bureau of Investigation (FBI) released composite sketches of the men who had rented the van—two white Americans.

Although violence is not unusual in the United States, political violence is relatively rare. Assassinations of political leaders have been infrequent, and those that have occurred have invariably been the work of alienated and often psychotic individuals. Similarly, although U.S. history is replete with the names of legendary villains, they have tended to be criminals such as bank robbers (for example, Jesse James). Criminals acting for political reasons, such as John Brown, have been few, and even such violent political organizations as the Ku Klux Klan and the Minutemen, and more recent groups such as antiabortion organizations that resort to violent acts, overwhelmingly have had as their targets either individuals or corporate America, not the federal government.

The 1970 bombing of the Army Math Research Center at the University of Wisconsin by antiwar protesters thus stood as the major postwar instance of political violence by U.S. citizens against an arm of the federal government prior to the Oklahoma City explosion, and statistics still indicate that of the more than three thousand bombs detonated in anger in the United States each year, virtually all are set off by individuals with personal grievances, with the overwhelming majority finding their targets at the municipal level. For most people in the United States, the idea that U.S. citizens could have conspired to have killed so many federal workers in Oklahoma City was nearly as hard to absorb as the fact of the bombing itself.

With sketches of the prime suspects, designated John Doe 1 and John Doe 2, in hand, investigators moved swiftly. John Doe 2 was eventually cleared of involvement in the terrorist attack; John Doe 1, identified as Timothy McVeigh, was quickly captured and charged with the bombing. As authorities reconstructed events, the planning of the attack had begun as early as the previous December, when McVeigh and an Army buddy, Michael Fortier, cased the nine floors of the federal building. During the following weeks, Fortier assisted McVeigh in raising the money needed to buy the tons of fertilizer used in the blast by selling guns (possibly stolen) at a series of gun shows, while another Army friend, Terry Lynn Nichols, allegedly assisted McVeigh in constructing the bomb. The momentarily popular theory that the blast was the work of the Michigan Militia, an ultra-right-wing anti-Washington group that counted Nichols among its devoted members, remained unsubstantiated.

## SIGNIFICANCE

As the investigation proceeded from arrest to the indictment of McVeigh, Fortier, and Nichols, the national political process mobilized for action against domestic and foreign terrorist threats to the United States. The destruction in Oklahoma City testified grimly to the vulnerability of democratic societies to terrorism, given the freedom to travel and associate that they accord to those within their borders, the ease with which the ingredients for bombs such as that used in Oklahoma City can be ob-

tained, and the modern revolutions in transportation and communications that enable transnational terrorists to operate ever more easily and even to network with one another.

Within the same week as the bombing in Oklahoma City, a gas attack in a Tokyo subway attributed to a Japanese Buddhist cult hospitalized four hundred people, and in Canada, the bombing of the historic provincial legislative building in Charlottetown on Prince Edward Island killed one person in an incident feared to be a copycat act inspired by the Oklahoma City tragedy. Most ominously, by the end of April, a U.S. State Department report titled *Patterns of Terrorism: 1994* noted the increasing tendency of international terrorists to develop ties with domestic groups, including the Mafia and drug gangs in the United States. The future, intelligence analysts concluded, is apt to be one of more, not less, terrorism, with terrorists placing greater emphasis on mass casualties than had been the case historically. This prediction was borne out by a number of later terrorist attacks, including the September 11, 2001, attacks in New York City and Washington, D.C., which killed more than 3,000; the March 11, 2004, Madrid train bombings, which killed 191; and the London subway bombings of July 7, 2005, which killed 52.

The Omnibus Counterterrorism Act of 1995, previously placed before Congress by Bill Clinton's presiden-

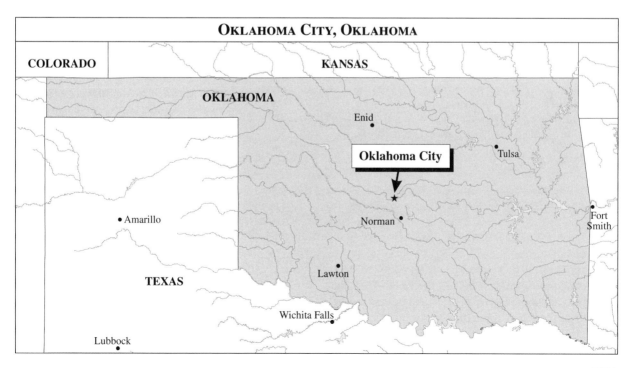

OKLAHOMA CITY, OKLAHOMA

## MCVEIGH'S REASONS

*On April 27, 2001, Timothy McVeigh wrote a letter of explanation to several media figures and news outlets that read in part:*

MCVEIGH: I chose to bomb a federal building because such an action served more purposes than other options. Foremost, the bombing was a retaliatory strike; a counter attack, for the cumulative raids (and subsequent violence and damage) that federal agents had participated in over the preceding years (including, but not limited to, Waco). From the formation of such units as the FBI's "Hostage Rescue" and other assault teams amongst federal agencies during the '80's; culminating in the Waco incident, federal actions grew increasingly militaristic and violent, to the point where at Waco, our government—like the Chinese—was deploying tanks against its own citizens.

Knowledge of these multiple and ever-more aggressive raids across the country constituted an identifiable pattern of conduct within and by the federal government and amongst its various agencies. For all intents and purposes, federal agents had become "soldiers" . . . and they were escalating their behavior. Therefore, this bombing was also meant as a preemptive (or pro-active) strike against these forces and their command and control centers within the federal building. When an aggressor force continually launches attacks from a particular base of operation, it is sound military strategy to take the fight to the enemy.

Bombing the Murrah Federal Building was morally and strategically equivalent to the U.S. hitting a government building in Serbia, Iraq, or other nations. . . . From this perspective, what occurred in Oklahoma City was no different than what Americans rain on the heads of others all the time, and subsequently, my mindset was and is one of clinical detachment.

Fox News *reporter Rita Cosby interviewed McVeigh regarding his motives; here are his replies to two of her questions:*

COSBY: What were some other options considered besides bombing?
MCVEIGH: I waited two years from "Waco" for nonviolent "checks and balances" built into our system to correct the abuse of power we were seeing in federal actions against citizens. . . . When violent action thus became an option, I considered, among other things, a campaign of individual assassination, with "eligible" targets to include: Federal Judge Walter Smith (Waco trial), Lon Horiuchi (FBI sniper at Ruby Ridge), and Janet Reno (making her accept "full responsibility" in deed, not just word).
COSBY: Lessons?
MCVEIGH: Many foreign nations and peoples hate Americans for the very reasons most Americans loathe me. Think about that.

---

billion bill would be enacted by the end of May. The wheels of the U.S. political system, however, like those of justice, grind very sluggishly. Slowed by opposition from domestic Muslim American and militia lobbyists, who attacked the bill as an unconstitutional restraint on individual freedoms, the bill came to a halt in May, 1995, when the Senate rejected the president's proposal to permit emergency roving wiretaps in cases involving terrorism or potential terrorism, and Republicans saddled the bill with the capital punishment debate by including in it exceedingly stringent curbs on death penalty appeals.

As a consequence, nearly a year after the Oklahoma City bombing, with the suspects still awaiting trial, the political process had not produced a single piece of counterterrorism legislation. The wheels of justice do turn, however, if slowly. McVeigh was eventually convicted on eleven federal charges and was sentenced to death on June 13, 1997; he was executed on June 11, 2001. Terry Nichols was convicted of manslaughter and of conspiracy to use a weapon of mass destruction, although he was found innocent on the count of the use of such a weapon. He was sentenced to life in prison on June 4, 1998. In 2004, Nichols was also found guilty on 160 counts of murder in Oklahoma state court, but he was spared the death sentence owing to a deadlocked jury. In a plea bargain, Fortier testified against both McVeigh and Nichols at their trials, and in 1998 he was sentenced to twelve years in prison and a fine of $200,000 for failing to alert authorities to the impending attack. He served only part of his sentence, however; he was released from prison in January, 2006.

*—Joseph R. Rudolph, Jr.*

tial administration as a response to the growing menace of international terrorism, initially benefited from the events in Oklahoma City. Congressional leaders vowed to join with the White House in a bipartisan effort to pass the measure, and provisions were added to give the bill a wider reach. Boasts were made that the enlarged, $1.5

### FURTHER READING

Crenshaw, Martha, ed. *Terrorism in Context*. University Park: Pennsylvania State University Press, 1995. Outstanding collection of essays provides informative background on many aspects of terrorism around the world. Includes bibliographic references and index.

Hansen, Jon. *Oklahoma Rescue*. New York: Ballantine, 1995. Human-interest account by one of Oklahoma's City's pivotal rescue workers, an assistant fire chief. Includes photographs.

Irving, Clive, ed. *In Their Name: Dedicated to the Brave and the Innocent, Oklahoma City, April, 1995*. New York: Random House, 1995. Official commemorative volume presents recollections of survivors, rescue workers, medical personnel, and others who experienced the events in Oklahoma City as well as essays concerning the bombing and its aftermath. Includes photographs.

Linenthal, Edward T. *The Unfinished Bombing: Oklahoma City in American Memory*. New York: Oxford University Press, 2001. Examines the psychic impacts of the bombing for Americans in general as well as for the family members and friends of those lost in the event.

Riley, Kevin Jack, and Bruce Hoffman. *Domestic Terrorism: A National Assessment of State and Local Preparedness*. Santa Monica, Calif.: RAND, 1995. Sixty-six pages of chilling reading prepared for the Department of Justice.

Serrano, Richard A. *One of Ours: Timothy McVeigh and the Oklahoma City Bombing*. New York: W. W. Norton, 1998. Journalist's account focuses on McVeigh's background and role in the bombing.

**SEE ALSO:** Feb. 26, 1993: World Trade Center Bombing; Mar. 20, 1995: Terrorists Use Sarin Gas in Tokyo Subway Attack; Aug. 7, 1998: Terrorists Bomb U.S. Embassies in East Africa; Oct. 12, 2000: Terrorists Attack USS *Cole*.

---

## May 14-December 8, 1995
# NEW PANCHEN LAMA IS NAMED

*In 1995, in response to the Dalai Lama's choice of Gendun Choekyi Nyima as the Eleventh Panchen Lama, the Chinese government abducted the child and his family and made a replacement choice of another child, Gyaincain Norbu. The event was interpreted as an attempt by Beijing to control religious freedom and further suppress human rights in an apparent return to the Cultural Revolution goal of eliminating the so-called four olds in Tibet.*

**LOCALE:** Xigazê, Tibet; Dharmsala, India
**CATEGORIES:** Religion, theology, and ethics; government and politics

**KEY FIGURES**
*Gendun Choekyi Nyima* (b. 1989), Tibetan child recognized by the Dalai Lama as the Eleventh Panchen Lama
*Dalai Lama* (Tenzin Gyatso; b. 1935), exiled spiritual and political leader of Tibet
*Gyaincain Norbu* (Qoigyijabu; b. 1990), Tibetan child chosen by Beijing as the Eleventh Panchen Lama

**SUMMARY OF EVENT**
From the seventeenth century until the Chinese invasion in 1950, the Dalai Lama and the Panchen Lama of the Dge-lugs-pa, or Yellow Hat Sect, lineage of Tibetan Buddhism were at the top of the lama, or monk, hierarchy in old Tibet. The Dalai Lama is considered to be the physical incarnation of Chenrezi, the bodhisattva of compassion. There have been fourteen Dalai Lamas; each one is considered to be the reincarnation of the former. The Panchen Lama, the second-highest-ranking lama after the Dalai Lama and abbot of the Tashi Lhunpo Monastery in Tibet, is esteemed as the physical manifestation of Amitayus, the Buddha of Infinite Light. There have been eleven Panchen Lamas, and, like the Dalai Lama, each one is considered to be the reincarnation of the former.

One duty entrusted to the Dalai Lama and the Panchen Lama is the recognition of each other's successor. Tenzin Gyatso, the Fourteenth Dalai Lama, was recognized by the Ninth Panchen Lama in 1940. The Tenth Panchen Lama was recognized by the Fourteenth Dalai Lama in 1952. After the Tenth Panchen Lama's death in 1989, the Dalai Lama recognized the Eleventh Panchen Lama in 1995. However, the Chinese government did not accept the Dalai Lama's candidate and subsequently named another one. Therefore, two Eleventh Panchen Lamas were chosen in 1995.

After an aborted anti-Chinese uprising in 1959, the Fourteenth Dalai Lama and his followers fled to India and settled in Dharmsala; however, the Tenth Panchen

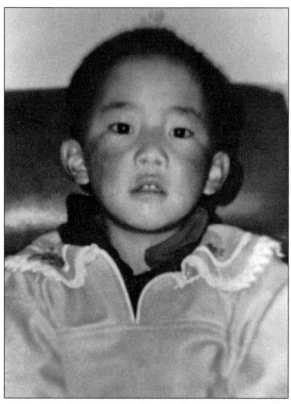

*Gendun Choekyi Nyima, seen here in an undated photo, was kidnapped in 1995 at the age of six by Chinese authorities, days after the Dalai Lama named him the Eleventh Panchen Lama. The lama's whereabouts are unknown to this day.* (AP/Wide World Photos)

Lama stayed in Tibet. His outspoken comments about Chinese policies in Tibet led to his imprisonment in China for nearly ten years. He died in 1989. Since the Dalai Lama was living outside Tibet, the first steps in identifying the reincarnation of the Panchen Lama were assumed by the senior lamas in exile. The lamas compiled a list of about thirty names of potential candidates from both Tibet and India. The lamas then tested the best ones by asking them to identify personal objects owned by the Tenth Panchen Lama. The Dalai Lama utilized oracles and divinations to confirm the final four candidates. The divination performed in 1991 revealed that the reincarnation happened in Tibet. In 1993, the lamas conducted their search east of Tashi Lhunpo, searching among children born in the Tibetan years of the snake, horse, and sheep. Divinations revealed Gendun Choekyi Nyima to be the best candidate. Finally, on May 14, 1995, the Dalai Lama recognized Gendun as the true reincarnation of the Tenth Panchen Lama. Gendun, whose

father was Konchok Phuntsog and whose mother was Dechen Chodon, was born in Lhari County in Nagchu, Tibet, on April 25, 1989, in the year of the snake.

During these years, the Dalai Lama contacted the Chinese authorities in Tibet regarding the search for the new Panchen Lama. In 1991, he asked permission to send a delegation of senior lamas to Lhamo Lhatso, a sacred lake near Lhasa, to observe prophetic visions. Seven months later, the Chinese government said it did not need outside interference in the matter. In 1993, the Dalai Lama invited Beijing's Panchen Lama search committee to India for a discussion. There was no response from the Chinese authorities.

A couple days after the Dalai Lama announced his recognition of Gendun, the child and his family disappeared. It was rumored that they had been abducted by the Chinese authorities and kept on a military base near Beijing. Immediately after Gendun's disappearance, the Chinese authorities in Tibet forced monks and senior lamas of Tashi Lhunpo to denounce the Dalai Lama's candidate. One monk refused to and committed suicide. On November 5, 1995, a number of lamas and Tibetan Communist Party members were summoned to Beijing to choose an alternate Panchen Lama. These representatives were told that three candidates had already been chosen and that the Dalai Lama's choice was illegal because he no longer lived in Tibet. The Chinese attempted to discredit the Dalai Lama's choice. Gendun was described as a sinner and his parents were labeled deceitful, avaricious, and overly ambitious. On November 29, Chinese officials presided over a ceremony in which the Eleventh Panchen Lama was selected through the drawing of lots from a golden urn. Gyaincain Norbu—who was born on February 13, 1990, in Lhari—was the child selected. His parents were local officials and Communist Party members. Gyaincain was enthroned at Tashi Lhunpo on December 8. The next day, he was flown to Beijing and kept under close guard. He did not return to Tibet until 1999. Nine lamas from Tashi Lhunpo were given prison sentences of up to thirty months for protesting against the new Panchen Lama's enthronement; seven others were expelled.

Beijing's choice of Gyaincain met with protest from Tibetans at home and abroad. About four hundred Tibetans in New Delhi demonstrated in protest, and the Tibetans in Dharmsala went on a token hunger strike for twenty-four hours. The Dalai Lama rejected Beijing's choice and perceived it as a politically motivated attempt to tighten control over Tibet. As a result, Chinese authorities issued a ban on assembly of more than three persons in Tibet and imposed curfew in Xigazê, Lhasa, and Qamdo.

## SIGNIFICANCE

The whereabouts and welfare of Gendun and his family remained unknown. In May, 1996, the Chinese government revealed that they had been holding Gendun in custody since 1995. The continued detention of, and denial of access to, Gendun was interpreted as China's attempt to control religious expression and suppress human rights in Tibet. China's ceremony to choose the Panchen Lama was condemned as contrary to the religious beliefs and practices of the Tibetan people. The golden urn system was suggested by a Manchu emperor to the Eighth Dalai Lama. However, it had been used in Tibet in the recognition of only three Dalai Lamas and two Panchen Lamas. Since the tradition of mutual recognition between the Dalai Lama and the Panchen Lama was ignored, it was feared that the choice of the next Dalai Lama would be controlled by Beijing. Moreover, China's selection of the new Panchen Lama seemed to be a justification of its occupation of Tibet. Furthermore, China's actions signaled a return to some of the practices undertaken by the Chinese government during the Cultural Revolution in which it tried to abolish the "four olds"—old tradition, old thoughts, old cultures, and old customs. To the Tibetans, especially those in exile, the Fourteenth Dalai Lama represented possibly the last religious leader of old Tibet. The new Panchen Lama, to avoid the previous Panchen Lama's fate, could do nothing but serve as Beijing's puppet.

—*Anh Tran*

## FURTHER READING

Dalai Lama. *Freedom in Exile: The Autobiography of the Dalai Lama*. New York: HarperCollins, 1990. Autobiography begins with the Dalai Lama's childhood and concludes with his acceptance of the Nobel Peace Prize in 1989. Includes testimony of Tibet's suffering under Chinese rule.

Goldstein, Melvyn C. *The Snow Lion and the Dragon: China, Tibet, and the Dalai Lama*. Berkeley: University of California Press, 1997. Provides a historical outline of Tibet-China relations and the problems surrounding modern-day Tibet.

Hilton, Isabel. *The Search for the Panchen Lama*. New York: W. W. Norton, 2000. Explains the political intricacies surrounding the search for the Eleventh Panchen Lama, while offering an extensive history of Tibetan Buddhism's struggle with China.

Sautman, Barry, and June Teufel Dreyer, eds. *Contemporary Tibet: Politics, Development, and Society in a Disputed Region*. Armonk, N.Y.: M. E. Sharpe, 2006. Collection of essays provides historical background and a general framework to examine Tibet's present situation in world politics, China's relationship with the West, and Tibet's prospects for the future.

**SEE ALSO:** Spring, 1978: China Promises to Correct Human Rights Abuses; June 4, 1989: China Crushes Prodemocracy Demonstration in Tiananmen Square; Dec. 10, 1989: Tibet's Dalai Lama Receives the Nobel Peace Prize; July 20, 1999: China Suppresses Falun Gong Religious Group.

1995

## May 17, 1995
# CHIRAC TAKES OFFICE AS PRESIDENT OF FRANCE

*The election of Jacques Chirac as president of France brought about a significant change in the political climate in that country. The office of president was once again occupied by an adherent of the French right wing after the fourteen year (1981-1995) presidency of the left-wing Socialist François Mitterrand.*

**LOCALE:** Paris, France
**CATEGORY:** Government and politics

**KEY FIGURES**

*Jacques Chirac* (b. 1932), prime minister of France, 1974-1976 and 1986-1988, mayor of Paris, 1977-1995, and president of France, 1995-2007

*Charles de Gaulle* (1890-1970), French general and freedom fighter during World War II instrumental in the creation of the Fifth Republic, and president of France, 1959-1969

*François Mitterrand* (1916-1996), president of France, 1981-1995

*Édouard Balladur* (b. 1929), French minister of economy, finance and privatization, 1986-1988, and prime minister of France, 1993-1995

*Lionel Jospin* (b. 1937), French minister of national education, 1988-1992, and prime minister of France, 1997-2002

**SUMMARY OF EVENT**

In 1958, General Charles de Gaulle returned to political power in France because of the crisis caused by the Algerian War of Independence (1954-1962). As a result of his influence, France adopted a new constitution. The French Fourth Republic (1946-1958) ended, and the Fifth Republic was born. De Gaulle inspired many young Frenchmen of the time to seek careers in civil service and politics. Jacques Chirac was among them.

In 1957, Chirac gained admission to the École Nationale d'Administration (ENA), the French college from which all of France's high-level civil servants graduate. Chirac completed his studies and received his degree in 1959. He was immediately employed in the civil service, and by April, 1962, Prime Minister Georges Pompidou appointed him head of his personal staff. Pompidou was impressed with Chirac's no-nonsense, straight-to-the-point approach to getting things done and took a special interest in his political career. At his suggestion, in 1967 Chirac ran for and won a seat in the National Assembly

as a Gaullist candidate. In May, 1968, he played an instrumental role in bringing student and worker strikes to an end.

Chirac's political career continued to develop favorably. He held several positions as minister during Pompidou's presidency, including minister of agriculture and rural development and minister of the interior. In these posts, Chirac began to establish a popularity with the French farmers, opposing policies of the European Commission as well as those of the United States and of West Germany, which were detrimental to the farming community in France. He was appointed to the office of prime minister when Valéry Giscard d'Estaing, with whom he had worked in the Ministry of Economy and Finance under Pompidou, became president in 1974.

However, dissatisfied by the lack of authority granted to him, Chirac resigned as prime minister in 1976. He immediately began efforts to acquire the leadership of the political right wing in France as a way to the presidency. In order to achieve this goal, he brought about the formation of the Rally for the Republic Party (RPR), a neo-Gaullist organization. At this time, Giscard d'Estaing decided to re-create the office of mayor of Paris. That office, which dates back to 1789, had been abolished for the second time in 1871.

In 1977, Chirac ran for the office of mayor of Paris against Michel d'Ornano, a friend of Giscard d'Estaing. Ironically, this office became the platform from which Chirac was able to build his political power and eventually become president of France. He remained in this position until he was elected to the presidency in 1995. While there remains a certain amount of controversy over Chirac's performance as mayor, he is credited with creating programs to aid single mothers, the disabled, and the elderly and with encouraging businesses to remain in Paris through an incentives program.

In 1981, Chirac launched his first candidacy for the presidency. His opponent was Giscard d'Estaing, also a candidate from the right, thus splitting the vote. Chirac received only 18 percent of the vote in the first round. In the second round, he threw his support behind Giscard d'Estaing but did not instruct his RPR party members to vote for his fellow right-wing candidate. Giscard d'Estaing lost the election to the Socialist François Mitterrand. This loss eliminated Giscard d'Estaing as a significant figure in the French political right wing and left the way clear for Chirac, who still held his politically significant office as mayor of Paris, to assume leadership of the Right.

In 1986, the candidates representing a right-wing coalition of Chirac's RPR party and of Giscard d'Estaing's Union for French Democracy (UDF) party gained a slight majority in the National Assembly. This situation forced the government into "cohabitation," a situation in which the president appoints a prime minister from outside his own party. The constitution that created the Fifth Republic assured both a powerful executive in the office of president and a strong parliament under the leadership of a prime minister. The president was given the power to appoint the prime minister, but the legislative branch, the National Assembly, was given the power of approval of the appointment. Presidential elections were set at every seven years, while the elections of the members of the National Assembly were to occur every five years. This formula of elections could and did result in a president facing a National Assembly in which his party did not have the majority. In this scenario, a prime minister chosen from his own party was not likely to receive approval. In view of the right-wing majority in the National Assembly, Mitterrand had little choice but to appoint a prime minister from among the leaders of the Right.

Thus Chirac became prime minister for a second time.

In 1988, Chirac was once again a candidate for president. He made a good showing in the first round with 20 percent of the vote but was defeated by Mitterrand in the second round. Once again, Chirac resigned from the post of prime minister.

When the 1993 legislative election again resulted in a right-wing majority and placed Mitterrand's presidency in a situation of cohabitation, Chirac stated that he did not wish to be prime minister again and proposed Édouard Balladur for the office. Chirac intended to be a candidate in the 1995 presidential election and had been assured that Balladur would not run. Encouraged by his popularity as indicated by the polls, Balladur had a change of heart and became a presidential candidate. Chirac severely criticized the political philosophies of Balladur and promised that as president, he would reduce the inequality, particularly economic, that existed among the social classes. This decision created a splinter RPR party and split the RPR vote in the first round of voting. In spite of Balladur's seeming popularity, Chirac received a greater number of votes in the first round. In the second round, running on a platform of lowering taxes and implementing programs to ease the shortage of em-

*Jacques Chirac (right) in 1999 with U.S. president Bill Clinton.* (NARA/David Scull)

ployment opportunities, Chirac defeated Lionel Jospin, the Socialist candidate. Chirac received 52.6 percent of the vote. On May 17, 1995, Chirac began his first term as president of France.

## SIGNIFICANCE

The election of Jacques Chirac as president of France provides insight into how the French political system works, presenting an opportunity to trace the career of a French civil servant from the École Nationale d'Administration to the presidency of France. The election of Chirac represented the return of the French executive branch to France's conservative, traditional right-wing political party, which traces its roots to Charles de Gaulle and the creation of the Fifth Republic.

—*Shawncey Webb*

## FURTHER READING

Ardagh, John. *France in the New Century: Portrait of a Changing Society.* 1999. Rev. ed. London: Penguin Books, 2001. Broad overview of French culture and society. Chapters on Mitterrand's and Chirac's presidencies, privatization, and corruption charges against Chirac.

Bell, David S. *Presidential Power in Fifth Republic France.* New York: Berg, 2000. Includes chapters on De Gaulle's presidency and on Chirac and his political policies. Bibliography, index.

King, Anthony, ed. *Leaders' Personalities and the Outcomes of Democratic Elections.* New York: Oxford University Press, 2002. Chapter 4 examines the issue of candidates' personalities in French elections. Bibliography, index.

Lewis-Beck, Marshall S. *How France Votes.* New York: Chatham House, 1999. Compares French voters to American voters and discusses French political views and cohabitation in government. Lists of additional readings, index.

Thody, Philip. *The Fifth Republic: Presidents, Politics and Personalities.* London: Routledge, 1999. Chapters on each of the presidents of the Fifth Republic. Annotated bibliography, three appendixes (one on the French civil service), index.

**SEE ALSO:** May 10, 1981: Mitterrand Is Elected to the French Presidency; Mar. 30, 1995: National Library of France Opens; Sept. 5, 1995-Jan. 27, 1996: France Resumes Nuclear Testing.

## May 23, 1995
# SUN MICROSYSTEMS INTRODUCES JAVA

*In 1995, Sun Microsystems announced the development of the object-oriented Java programming language and its incorporation into the popular Web browser Netscape Navigator. Released on January 23, 1996, Java allowed the convergence of digitally controlled consumer devices and computers.*

**LOCALE:** Santa Clara, California
**CATEGORIES:** Communications and media; computers and computer science; science and technology

## KEY FIGURES

*James Gosling* (b. 1955), creator of the Java programming language
*Patrick Naughton* (b. c. 1965), computer programmer who helped to create Java
*Mike Sheridan* (fl. late twentieth century), computer programmer who helped to create Java
*Andy Bechtolsheim* (b. 1956), computer scientist and cofounder of Sun Microsystems

*Bill Joy* (b. 1954), computer scientist and cofounder of Sun Microsystems
*Vinod Khosla* (b. 1955), computer scientist and cofounder of Sun Microsystems
*Scott McNealy* (b. 1954), computer scientist and cofounder of Sun Microsystems
*John Gage* (b. 1942), director of the Science Office for Sun Microsystems

## SUMMARY OF EVENT

Sun Microsystems was founded in 1982 by Stanford graduate students Andy Bechtolsheim, Vinod Khosla, and Bill Joy, who named the company using the initials of their communications project: Stanford University Network. The company established a name for innovation, and in 1992, Sun Microsystems introduced the concept of the Java platform and the accompanying programming language. The Java platform was designed to create programs that could run on a number of devices, from personal computers to cell phones. The slogan was Write Once, Run Anywhere.

The project was started in June, 1991, by James Gosling, who gave it the name "Oak," in honor of the tree that stood outside the door of the Sun Microsystems office. Oak, which soon involved programmers Patrick Naughton and Mike Sheridan, became known as the Green Project as it swelled to a team of thirteen people. The team had been chartered by Sun to anticipate the next wave in computing, which they concluded was the convergence of digitally controlled consumer devices and computers.

Gosling intended to create a virtual machine and an operating language that would use the familiar C/C++ notation that programmers were accustomed to and allow programmers to target any device or platform, whether personal computer or consumer device. Goals for the language included the following: It should employ an object-oriented programming methodology; it should allow the same program to be executed on different platforms; it should support using computer networks; it should be able to execute code from remote sources securely; and it should be easy to use, employing the best of other programming languages.

The first demo employed an interactive, hand-held home entertainment device controller with a touch screen to serve as user interface. The Java technology mascot, Duke, waved at the user and did cartwheels across the screen. The device was called StarSeven (*7)—named for a telephone feature that allowed a team member to answer a phone from any extension in the office. The demo featured an "agent," a software entity that performed tasks as directed by the user.

As others in the company saw the potential of the new project, the team grew and became known as First-Person. While the team was trying to enter the television and video-on-demand markets, they suffered from being several years ahead of their time: The other industries, still trying to figure out their business models, failed to realize the opportunity that the technology offered. A group from FirstPerson realized that perhaps the Internet, which was becoming an increasingly popular way to convey media content to users, might be the right industry for their platform. The team created a Java-technology-based clone of the Web browser Mosaic that they named WebRunner (in tribute to the 1982 film *Blade Runner*). The unique application would eventually become the HotJava browser, allowing browsers to hold animated, moving objects and dynamic, executable content.

WebRunner was made available over the Internet to beta testers. Soon after, the team released the Java source code on the Internet, available for anyone to download. 1Downloads surged into the thousands as word of it spread across the computing world. When it was announced that the Java team would partner with Netscape Communications Corporation, maker of Netscape Navigator, the Java language became established as a leader in object-oriented languages aimed at programming for the Internet.

The Java platform is the name for a bundle of related programs that allow Java programs to be developed and to run. The platform is not specific to any one processor or operating system—rather, it is an execution engine called the Java Virtual Machine (JVM), packaged with a compiler and set of libraries implemented for a variety of hardware and operating systems. Initially, the Java platform was promoted as a platform for client-side applets (small programs) running inside Web browsers, but coming at a time of rising security concerns, this approach never became popular. The platform has been significantly more successful for server-side programs, running on main computers rather than on the machines of individual users.

The Java programming language, which was created specifically for the project, borrowed many of the features from the programming language C++, which had become the industry standard, while removing many of the older language's more arcane and difficult concepts, such as memory pointers and overloading operators. Java includes a massive class library that provides extensive functionality for its programmers, including file IO, GUIs, encryption, and so on. For Java-language programs to run on a variety of devices, the programs are compiled to bytecode, which can be executed by any JVM. JavaScript, a low-level scripting language, is sometimes mistaken for Java because of similarities of name and syntax, but the two are not directly related.

In the second version, Sun released multiple configurations built for different platform types. Java 2 Platform, Enterprise Edition (J2EE), for example, was designed for large enterprise applications. Sun's license for Java insisted that all implementations be compatible—wording that would lead Sun to file a complaint against Microsoft in 1997 for distributing a version of Java that was incompatible with Sun's.

**SIGNIFICANCE**

The Java language was one of the first object-oriented languages designed to enable developers to produce flexible but scalable applications. It rapidly became one of the world's most popular programming languages. At the same time, the idea of the "virtual machine" introduced by Java would serve as a design metaphor for other programming languages, including Microsoft's C#.

The use of bytecode as an intermediate language permits Java programs to run on any platform for which a virtual machine is available. Using a JIT (just-in-time) compiler means that after a short loading delay, most Java programs run with a speed indistinguishable from native programs. For programmers, not having to know the intricacies of a particular platform they are designing for, particularly if it is one very different from the one for which they usually program, is a valuable source of productivity.

Most important, the introduction of the concept of the Java platform and its ability to run programs not just on personal computers but on a variety of devices signaled a growing acceptance and acknowledgment of the importance of the Internet to the world at large and its growing importance not only for computers but also for user devices.

—*Cat Rambo*

**FURTHER READING**

Eckel, Bruce. *Thinking in Java.* 4th ed. New York: Prentice Hall, 2006. Computer programming classic provides a thorough overview of the basic concepts of the language.

Lindsey, Clark S. *JavaTech: An Introduction to Scientific and Technical Computing.* New York: Cambridge University Press, 2005. Practical introduction to the Java programming language that discusses how Java interacts with hardware.

Spolsky, Joel. *Joel on Software.* New York: Apress, 2004. These essays, selected from the author's Web site, discuss a variety of topics related to software programming.

Sun Microsystems. *Hello World(s): From Code to Culture, a Ten Year Celebration of Java Technology.* New York: Prentice Hall, 2005. The history of Java is discussed in this volume produced to mark the ten-year anniversary of the language.

Watt, David, and Deryck Brown. *Programming Language Processors in Java: Compilers and Interpreters.* New York: Prentice Hall, 2000. Shows how to write a compiler in pure Java and points out useful Java programming techniques.

**SEE ALSO:** July 3, 1991: IBM and Apple Agree to Make Compatible Computers; Dec. 15, 1994: Release of Netscape Navigator 1.0; Mid-1990's: Rise of the Internet and the World Wide Web; May 18, 1998: United States Sues Microsoft; Sept. 7, 1998: Google Is Founded.

## May 30, 1995
# POPULAR FICTION ADDRESSES THE END TIMES

*The best-selling Left Behind series grew to include sixteen novels, revolutionized Christian propaganda in print markets, and led to an increased concern in American evangelical churches and popular American culture about the biblical Apocalypse.*

**LOCALE:** United States
**CATEGORIES:** Literature; publishing and journalism; religion, theology, and ethics

**KEY FIGURES**

*Tim LaHaye* (b. 1926), coauthor of the Left Behind series
*Jerry B. Jenkins* (b. 1949), coauthor of the Left Behind series
*Peter Lalonde* (b. 1960), executive producer of *Left Behind: The Movie* (2000)

**SUMMARY OF EVENT**
In the tradition of Hal Lindsey's *The Late Great Planet Earth* (1970), a novel that predicted the coming end of the world, and with the year 2000 approaching, Jerry B. Jenkins and Tim LaHaye coauthored *Left Behind: A Novel of the Earth's Last Days* (1995). The first in a series of novels that aim to interpret the Bible's book of Revelation of John the Divine, *Left Behind* details the events on Earth after God's Rapture has delivered the "innocents" to Heaven and has left the "heathens" behind to fight on God's behalf or to join the Antichrist. The series follows a core group of nonbelievers, later converted, who are left behind at the Rapture to suffer through the seven-year tribulation, the tyrannical rule of the Antichrist, and the battle of Armageddon, until the ultimate reappearance of Jesus. After *Left Behind*, the series chronicles this saga through fifteen other novels:

*Tribulation Force: The Continuing Drama of Those Left Behind* (1996), *Nicolae: The Rise of Antichrist* (1997), *Soul Harvest: The World Takes Sides* (1998), *Apollyon: The Destroyer Is Unleashed* (1999), *Assassins: Assignment—Jerusalem, Target—Antichrist* (1999), *The Indwelling: The Beast Takes Possession* (2000), *The Mark: The Beast Rules the World* (2000), *Desecration: Antichrist Takes the Throne* (2001), *The Remnant: On the Brink of Armageddon* (2002), *Armageddon: The Cosmic Battle of the Ages* (2003), *Glorious Appearing: The End of Days* (2004), *The Rising: Antichrist Is Born* (2005), *The Regime: Evil Advances* (2005), *The Rapture: In the Twinkling of an Eye—Countdown to the Earth's Last Days* (2006), and *Kingdom Come: The Final Victory* (2007).

Both the writers of the series and Tyndale House, the publisher, noted that these books served a dual purpose: to entertain and to speak to the American people about the state of their spiritual lives. The novels in the series had a substantial run from a publishing standpoint. Not including sales from Christian booksellers, print runs of *Left Behind* ran between 150,000 and 200,000 copies in its early days, reaching nearly 5 million copies at the debut of the eighth novel in the series. The seventh book in the series, *The Indwelling*, reached the top of several national publishing lists in 2000. *Desecration*, the tenth novel in the series, claimed the title of best-selling fiction book of 2001, and an additional Left Behind children's series sold more than 60 million copies. By July of 2001, the series had collectively sold more than 25 million copies.

Left Behind is the first series of novels defined by popular opinion as "Christian" to have broken these previously "secular" publishing milestones. The mainstream success is in part due to the fact that many Left Behind readers purchased these books at large retail stores like Wal-Mart and Target, not strictly religious booksellers. The Left Behind series prescribed to no specifically designated religious order or group, although its events are clearly based on biblical references, and its broad audience reflected that ambiguity: Despite obvious religious overtones, the books' readers were not exclusively Christian. Although the largest readership is evangelical Protestant, Left Behind also affected, and sometimes even converted, mainstream Americans. Numbers indicate that near the production of the eighth book, in 2000, at least a quarter of Americans were aware of the Left Behind phenomenon, and one of ten adults in the United States was reading one of the books.

Left Behind was not only a publishing phenomenon;

the series also launched the production of clothing accessories, a dramatic radio show, books on tape, board games, and other merchandise. *Left Behind: The Movie* (2000) was brought to the big screen by producer Peter Lalonde. Lalonde was also responsible for the production of a video titled *Have You Been Left Behind?* that was released concurrently with the first Left Behind book. The video detailed what a non-Christian should do if he or she is left behind when the Rapture occurs.

At the time of its production, *Left Behind: The Movie* was the most expensive Christian-funded film ever produced. Despite the significant public reaction to the Left Behind fiction, the film had a poor response at the box office and did not bring in the non-Christian audience that had responded to the literature. Although the film ultimately did not succeed as directors hoped it would, the revenue invested by Lalonde, Christian booksellers, and other parties who handled the promotion demonstrates the importance of the implication that Left Behind reached beyond the boundaries of Christian merchandising to a secular public.

Left Behind spawned heated debate in both secular and religious circles about the specifics of the "end times," and readers were forced to reconsider issues within their own religions and their own lifestyles. Even within evangelical Christian groups, there was dissent about whether or not the books followed the chronology of the biblical book of Revelation closely enough to be taken as truth. Reading groups, church study sessions, and online chat rooms revealed that themes in the Left Behind novels caused readers to question not only faith but also the concepts of good versus evil, the place of religion in world politics, and the roles of gender and race in society. The September 11, 2001, attacks on the World Trade Center—which caused many Americans to reevaluate the world for signs of a coming apocalypse and to reexamine their individual lifestyles—coincided with an increased interest in apocalyptic fiction, as reflected in increased sales.

## SIGNIFICANCE

The success of the Left Behind series, and its related merchandise, indicates a breach in the separation of religion and secular culture in America. These "Christian" novels marked a new period in twentieth century popular culture, wherein products with overtly religious themes were marketed not only to their niche audiences but also to the mainstream. The distribution of these books by major retailers also reflects U.S. consumers, who were becoming more diverse and less defined by religion and background. The ambiguous identity of Left Behind's religious market also illustrates that typically evangelical publishers had begun to tailor their message to appeal to a wider audience.

The popularity of the Left Behind books and other so-called Christian or spiritual fiction speaks to both an American need and an American fear: the need to understand events like the World Trade Center bombing, and the fear that the world is headed for disaster. *Left Behind*'s barely veiled comparison of its Antichrist-led, seemingly benevolent world government with institutions such as the United Nations, and the support the series received from the Bush administration all had a part in making this series a significant cultural landmark. Although the novels are set in an undefined future, the benchmarks that bring the plot to fruition are events that can arguably be seen in the world in which it was published.

*—Jennifer L. Amel*

**FURTHER READING**

Forbes, Bruce David, and Jeanne Halgren Kilde, eds. *Rapture, Revelation, and the End Times: Exploring the Left Behind Series*. New York: Palgrave Macmillan, 2004. Six essays by six different authorities on the Left Behind books. Investigates the success of the Left Behind series; the history of its apocalyptic

thought in American culture; the language of the biblical Revelation; social, political, and religious commentary found in the Left Behind series; and the Christian faith and apocalyptic thought.

Frykholm, Amy. *Rapture Culture: Left Behind in Evangelical America*. New York: Oxford University Press, 2004. Offers interviews, case studies, and broad-based research that demonstrates the powerful effects—both positive and negative—of Left Behind on American culture. Research investigates both Christian and non-Christian reactions to Left Behind and investigates consequential changes in American approaches to religion.

Hendershot, Heather. *Shaking the World for Jesus*. Chicago: University of Chicago Press, 2004. An investigation into how American media handled the influx of Christian marketing and products in the preceding ten to fifteen years. Dissects the evangelical media and refers to products like the Left Behind novels to explore how the evangelical Christian message changed in order to fit the nature of contemporary media. Includes illustrations.

**SEE ALSO:** Aug. 15, 1981: EWTN Begins Religious Broadcasting; 1989: Robertson Founds the Christian Coalition; Mar. 20, 1990: McCartney Conceives Promise Keepers.

## June 12, 1995
# U.S. SUPREME COURT LIMITS RACIAL PREFERENCES IN AWARDING GOVERNMENT CONTRACTS

*In the case of* Adarand Constructors v. Peña, *the U.S. Supreme Court ruled that all racial preferences in government-financed programs were inherently suspect and must be assessed using the standard of "strict scrutiny," which meant that they were unconstitutional unless narrowly tailored to promote a compelling governmental interest.*

**ALSO KNOWN AS:** *Adarand Constructors v. Peña*, 515 U.S. 200

**LOCALE:** Washington, D.C.

**CATEGORIES:** Laws, acts, and legal history; social issues and reform

**KEY FIGURES**

*Randy Pech* (b. 1954), owner of Adarand Constructors in Colorado Springs, Colorado

*Sandra Day O'Connor* (b. 1930), associate justice of the United States, 1981-2006

*John Paul Stevens* (b. 1920), associate justice of the United States beginning in 1975

*Ruth Bader Ginsburg* (b. 1933), associate justice of the United States beginning in 1993

*Antonin Scalia* (b. 1936), associate justice of the United States beginning in 1986

*Clarence Thomas* (b. 1948), associate justice of the United States beginning in 1991

**SUMMARY OF EVENT**

The U.S. Supreme Court's landmark decision in the 1995 case of *Adarand Constructors v. Peña* is one in a long series of Court decisions relating to affirmative action— that is, policies designed to increase the participation of underrepresented minorities and women in business, employment, and education. Although the Civil Rights Act of 1964 explicitly disallowed the use of racial and ethnic preferences in hiring, the agencies of the federal government soon began to enforce the statute by requiring that employers and schools achieve particular statistical outcomes. In the Public Employment Act of 1977, the U.S. Congress for the first time utilized the quantitative approach, mandating that contracts for public works projects include, whenever feasible, a 10 percent "set-aside" for minority business enterprises (MBEs).

An angry group of nonminority contractors went to federal court to challenge the set-asides as a form of unconstitutional "reverse discrimination" against white males. Referring to the precedent of *Bolling v. Sharpe* (1954), the plaintiffs argued that the due process clause of the Fifth Amendment to the U.S. Constitution contains an implicit "equal protection component" that protects all persons equally. Their hopes were dashed, however, when the Supreme Court, in *Fullilove v. Klutznick* (1980), voted six to three to uphold MBE set-asides as a "reasonable necessary means of furthering the compelling governmental interest" in redressing the discrimination that had long affected minority contractors. This ruling encouraged substantial expansion of minority set-aside provisions by the federal government as well as at the state and local levels.

Randy Pech, the white owner of Adarand Constructors in Colorado Springs, Colorado, was one of many entrepreneurs who was disappointed by the *Fullilove* decision. Pech's company, which specialized in building guardrails on public highways and bridges, had been founded in 1976 by Pech and Tom Adams (the name Adarand was a combination of the founders' names). By the mid-1980's, Adarand Constructors had grown to become the most successful guardrail company in Colorado, but Pech was infuriated to observe that because of minority-owner preferences, his company was losing 10 to 15 percent of the jobs for which it was the low bidder. Testifying at hearings, Pech emerged as a vociferous opponent of racial preferences. He even considered transferring ownership of Adarand to his wife, Val Pech, so that the company would qualify as a disadvantaged enterprise, but he eventually concluded that such a maneuver, even if commonly practiced, would be fraudulent.

Because of the conservative judicial appointments of President Ronald Reagan, the Supreme Court was gradually taking a more skeptical view of government requirements for remedial preferences. In the case of *Richmond v. J. A. Croson Co.* (1989), a five-to-four majority of the Court overturned a city council's plan mandating that at least 30 percent of the value of city contracts be awarded to MBEs. Justice Sandra Day O'Connor, the swing vote in the case, wrote in the majority opinion that set-aside plans by state and local governments must be based on a showing of past discrimination, not simply reliance on general societal discrimination, and she insisted that they be assessed by the demanding standard of "strict scrutiny." The *Croson* ruling, however, applied only to state and local programs under the Fourteenth Amendment, and thus it was uncertain whether the Court would evaluate the constitutionality of federal programs by the same standards.

In 1989, Adarand Constructors submitted the lowest bid to subcontract the guardrail work for a large project in the San Juan National Forest—a project sponsored by the Federal Highway Administration, which was part of the Department of Transportation (DOT). Instead of accepting the low bid, the prime contractor selected a minority-owned company, the Gonzales Construction Company. In federal court, Pech sued the DOT and its head, Federico Peña, arguing that the *Croson* principles should apply to the federal government under the Fifth Amendment. As the case was being argued in lower federal courts, however, the Supreme Court decided the similar case of *Metro Broadcasting v. F.C.C.* (1990), with the justices voting five to four to uphold federal preferences designed to increase black ownership of broadcast licenses. The ruling appeared to endow Congress with almost unlimited discretion to authorize race-based preferences. Applying this precedent, two lower federal courts ruled against Pech.

When the case reached the Supreme Court, however, in *Adarand Constructors v. Peña*, the justices decided, in a five-to-four vote, that federally financed set-asides were in the same constitutional category as state and local mandates, thereby overturning the *Metro Broadcasting* ruling. The impact of this decision was to apply the demanding test of strict scrutiny to federal programs that disadvantaged nonminority applicants because of race. This meant, according to Justice O'Connor's opinion for the Court, that all governmental race-conscious classifications must be "subjected to detailed judicial inquiry to ensure that the personal right to equal protection of the laws has not been infringed." The two most conservative justices, Antonin Scalia and Clarence Thomas, wrote concurring opinions that condemned all race preferences as unconstitutional. Scalia declared: "In the eyes of the government we are just one race here. It is American." Thomas argued that set-asides and other preferences are

1995

patronizing and reinforce the perception that blacks are incapable of success based on the principle of equal opportunity.

The four dissenters, led by Justices John Paul Stevens and Ruth Bader Ginsburg, argued that the history of racial discrimination in the United States provided a constitutional rationale for the federal government to take remedial action. Stevens argued that when Congress authorizes benign race-conscious measures, the appropriate test of review is the less demanding "important governmental objective test." Similarly, Ginsburg argued that the DOT program was carefully designed to achieve a valid objective and was therefore consistent with the equal protection clause of the Fourteenth Amendment. Noting that the Court's conservative justices claimed to be opposed to judicial activism, she chided the majority for failing to allow legislatures appropriate discretion in deciding how to apply the amendment.

## SIGNIFICANCE

The Supreme Court's ruling in *Adarand Constructors v. Peña* did not automatically overturn the DOT program challenged by Pech. Instead, the ruling sent the case back to the lower courts for a decision concerning whether the program was unconstitutional according to the strict scrutiny standard, which required that the program be justified by a compelling reason and be narrowly tailored to eliminate discrimination that could be proven (not just generalized bias). At the time of the ruling, nevertheless, the courts had struck down almost all policies that had been evaluated according to the rigorous test, to the extent that most law books characterized it as "strict in theory but fatal in practice." As expected, the lower courts soon determined that the program violated the constitutional rights of nonminority contractors such as Adarand.

Eight years later, however, in the case of *Grutter v. Bollinger* (2003), the Supreme Court for the first time approved a less demanding application of the strict scrutiny test. The case involved the admissions policy of the University of Michigan Law School, which included preferences for members of underrepresented groups in order to enhance the "diversity" of the school's student body. Although claiming to utilize the strict scrutiny test, the Court ruled that the admissions policy was constitutional. Writing for the five-to-four majority, Justice O'Connor argued that diversity was a compelling goal and that the policy, which guaranteed individualized consideration, was narrowly tailored. Although the *Grutter* decision did not directly affect public works contracts, it did suggest that the Court would likely approve of prefer-

ential programs that are not inflexible or grossly discriminatory.

*—Thomas Tandy Lewis*

## FURTHER READING

Anderson, Terry H. *The Pursuit of Fairness: A History of Affirmative Action*. New York: Oxford University Press, 2004. Presents an excellent and balanced historical account of affirmative action from the beginning of racial and gender preferences to the early twenty-first century.

Bean, Jonathan J. *Big Government and Affirmative Action: The Scandalous History of the Small Business Administration*. Lexington: University Press of Kentucky, 2001. Critical evaluation of the Small Business Administration argues that many of its scandals have resulted from the agency's use of gender and racial preferences, to the detriment of meritocracy.

Eastman, Terry. *Ending Affirmative Action: The Case for Colorblind Justice*. New York: Basic Books, 1996. Provides a historical summary of affirmative action and presents a case for ending all preferences based on race or gender, arguing for a policy of equal opportunity.

Kranz, Rachel. *Affirmative Action*. New York: Facts On File, 2002. Introductory research guide for students summarizes the political debate and includes a historical overview as well as a summary of important legal cases.

Leiter, Samuel. *Affirmative Action in Antidiscrimination Law and Policy: An Overview and Synthesis*. Albany: State University of New York Press, 2002. Examines various affirmative action programs, including their origins, growth, impacts, and future prospects.

Spann, Girardeau. *Law of Affirmative Action: Twenty Five Years of Supreme Court Decisions on Race and Remedies*. New York: New York University Press, 2000. Comprehensive work chronicles the Court's rulings from *DeFunis v. Odegaard* (1974) to the end of the twentieth century.

Wise, Tim J. *Affirmative Action: Racial Preference in Black and White*. New York: Routledge, 2005. Presents a one-sided defense of racial preferences as necessary remedies for historical discrimination against minorities.

SEE ALSO: Mar. 8, 1971: U.S. Supreme Court Bans Discrimination in Hiring; June 28, 1978: U.S. Supreme Court Bans Racial Quotas in College Admissions; June 27, 1979: U.S. Supreme Court Rules on Affirmative Action Programs; June 12, 1984: U.S. Supreme Court Upholds Seniority Systems; 1986: U.S. Supreme Court Upholds Goals, Not Quotas, to Remedy Discrimination; Mar. 22, 1988: U.S. Congress Mandates Nondiscriminatory Practices by Recipients of Public Funds; June 28, 2000: U.S. Supreme Court Protects Restrictions on Membership in Private Groups.

## June 26, 1995

# U.S. SUPREME COURT RULES ON RANDOM DRUG TESTING IN SCHOOLS

*The U.S. Supreme Court ruled that public schools may require student athletes to submit to random drug tests as a condition of their participation in interscholastic sports.*

**ALSO KNOWN AS:** *Vernonia School District 47J v. Acton*, 515 U.S. 646
**LOCALE:** Washington, D.C.
**CATEGORIES:** Civil rights and liberties; laws, acts, and legal history; education

**KEY FIGURES**
*Antonin Scalia* (b. 1936), associate justice of the United States beginning in 1986
*Sandra Day O'Connor* (b. 1930), associate justice of the United States, 1981-2006
*James Acton* (b. c. 1979), seventh-grade student whose parents challenged the constitutionality of his school's drug-testing policy

**SUMMARY OF EVENT**
In the mid-1980's, teachers and administrators in the public schools in Vernonia, Oregon, began noticing a sharp and progressive increase in drug and alcohol abuse among students, as well as disciplinary problems. Of particular concern were the deleterious effects of alcohol and drug abuse on student athletes, who were not only more susceptible to physical injury than students generally but also believed to be the leaders of the schools' drug culture.

In 1989, after making unsuccessful efforts to deter students' drug and alcohol use through education, the local school board, with parental approval, instituted a compulsory drug-testing policy for all student athletes. Every student wishing to participate in interscholastic athletics was required to sign a form consenting to the drug testing and to obtain a parent's written consent as well. At the beginning of each season of competition, every student athlete was tested; then, throughout the season, 10 percent of the student athletes were tested at ran-

dom. James Acton, a seventh-grade student, signed up to play district-supported football, but his parents refused to consent to the drug testing. The parents of James Acton then sued the school district.

After the trial court dismissed the lawsuit, the Actons appealed. The U.S. Court of Appeals for the Ninth Circuit struck down the school district's policy, saying that it violated the Fourth Amendment to the U.S. Constitution. The Fourth Amendment guarantees citizens freedom from unreasonable searches and seizures; it reads, "The right of the people to be secure in their persons, houses, papers, and effects, against unreasonable searches and seizures, shall not be violated, and no Warrants shall issue, but upon probable cause, supported by Oath of affirmation, and particularly describing the place to be searched, and the persons or things to be seized." The school district then requested review of the decision from the U.S. Supreme Court.

In *Vernonia School District 47J v. Acton* (1995), the U.S. Supreme Court, by a vote of six to three, reversed the decision of the Ninth Circuit, declaring that the school district's policy did not amount to unreasonable search and seizure under the Fourth Amendment. The Court's opinion was written by Associate Justice Antonin Scalia; he was joined by Chief Justice William H. Rehnquist and Associate Justices Anthony Kennedy, Clarence Thomas, Ruth Bader Ginsburg, and Stephen G. Breyer. Although the justices acknowledged that state-compelled drug testing constitutes a search subject to the demands of the Fourth Amendment, they determined that the school district's testing scheme fit squarely within the "special needs" exception to the Fourth Amendment. This exception holds that an administrative search—a search that is not executed as a pretext for obtaining evidence of criminal activity—does not require either a warrant or individualized suspicion so long as the search is a reasonable one.

To determine reasonableness, the Court balanced the strength of the student's privacy interest guaranteed by the Fourth Amendment against any legitimate governmental interest in conducting the search. First considering the individual privacy interest of the student, the opinion noted that unemancipated minors and public school students, because they are in the temporary custody of the state as "schoolmaster," have a lesser expectation of privacy than do adults. Moreover, those expectations are even less for student athletes, who voluntarily subject themselves to a degree of regulation higher than that imposed on students generally. "Public school locker rooms . . . are not notable for the privacy they afford," Justice Scalia wrote.

Finally, because the drug-testing procedures presented conditions of collection that were "nearly identical" to the conditions typically encountered in public restrooms, the Court noted, the nature of the intrusion was negligible. (For the testing, each student athlete entered an empty locker room accompanied by an adult monitor of the same sex. Each male produced a urine sample while remaining fully clothed and with his back to the monitor. Each female produced a sample in an enclosed bathroom stall. The monitor listened for normal sounds of urination, checked the sample for temperature and tampering, and then transferred the sample to a vial.)

The Court then assessed the strength of the government's interest in the drug testing by considering the nature and the immediacy of the government's concern. The nature of the concern, the opinion held, was "important—indeed perhaps compelling." The majority, as had the district court, agreed that drug use in schools has negative effects not only on the actual users but also on the entire student body and the faculty because of disruptions to the educative process. Additionally, the justices agreed that drug use presents substantial physical risks—reduction in the oxygen-carrying capacity of the blood and increased body temperature, for example—to student athletes in particular. Finally, the immediacy of the concern was heightened by the school district's findings that drug use was increasing among the student body in large part because other students looked up to student athletes who were drug abusers themselves.

Given the decreased expectation of privacy among student athletes, the unobtrusive nature of the search, and the severity of the need met by the search, the Court held the policy to be reasonable and, therefore, constitutional.

Three justices—John Paul Stevens, David Souter, and Sandra Day O'Connor—disagreed. In an opinion written by Justice O'Connor, the dissenters found the policy unreasonable, and thus unconstitutional, for four primary reasons: First, the school board policy dispensed with the standard requirement of individualized suspicion; second, there was a strong basis for concluding that vigorous suspicion-based testing would have "gone a long way" toward solving the drug problem; third, there was no evidence at all of a drug problem at the actual grade school attended by James Acton; and fourth, the choice of student athletes as the class to subject to suspicionless testing was unreasonable. If the school district was really concerned about the rise in drug-related disorders and disruptions of the educative process, the dissenters noted, a far more reasonable course of action would have been to test those students who had violated published school rules against severe disruptions in class and around campus. In sum, the dissenters asserted, no justifiable reason existed to drug test every student athlete in the entire school district.

## SIGNIFICANCE

*Vernonia School District 47J v. Acton* marked the first time the U.S. Supreme Court had sustained the use of random, suspicionless drug testing outside the public employment context. It did so with some apprehension, however, cautioning against the assumption that suspicionless drug testing would readily pass "constitutional muster." Even so, the Court extended the holding in *Vernonia* seven years later in the case of *Board of Education of Independent School District No. 92 of Pottawatomie County v. Earls* (2002), in which it upheld a public school policy that required suspicionless drug testing of all students who participated in any extracurricular activity. Central to the Court's position in both cases was the fact that the policies at hand dealt with minors temporarily entrusted to the care of the state. It is, therefore, highly questionable whether a similar policy would be upheld outside of the public school context. For example, government would probably not be allowed to drug test all persons entering or leaving a known drug-ridden neighborhood, even though the need to fight the scourge of drugs may provide a compelling governmental interest.

*—Richard A. Glenn*

## FURTHER READING

Alexander, Kern, and M. David Alexander. *American Public School Law*. 6th ed. Belmont, Calif.: Thomson/West, 2005. Textbook aimed at graduate students provides a comprehensive analysis of legal cases involving a multitude of issues that affect public schools, including student privacy rights against unreasonable searches and seizures.

Gold, Susan Dudley. *Vernonia School District v. Acton: Drug Testing in the Schools*. Tarrytown, N.Y.: Marshall Cavendish Benchmark Books, 2006. Volume intended for young readers presents discussion of the *Vernonia* case and of subsequent Supreme Court decisions involving the Fourth Amendment and mandatory drug testing of public school students.

Hudson, David L. *Rights of Students*. Philadelphia: Chelsea House, 2004. Uses a point-counterpoint format to examine various topics related to civil liberties in U.S. public schools.

Persico, Deborah A. *Vernonia School District v. Acton: Drug Testing in Schools*. Springfield, N.J.: Enslow, 1999. Volume intended for young adult readers discusses the facts, issue, holding, rationale, and significance of the 1995 Supreme Court decision.

Raskin, Jamin B. *We the Students: Supreme Court Cases for and About Students*. 2d ed. Washington, D.C.: Congressional Quarterly Press, 2003. Designed to help students achieve literacy on their constitutional rights as students. Includes learning exercises, case excerpts, and discussion prompts.

Stephens, Otis H., and Richard A. Glenn. *Unreasonable Searches and Seizures: Rights and Liberties Under the Law*. Santa Barbara, Calif.: ABC-CLIO, 2006. Examines the Fourth Amendment from its historical origins through controversies of the early twentieth century. Analyzes the Supreme Court's efforts to reconcile the constitutional rights of public school students with the government's interest in promoting a safe learning environment. Includes chronology of relevant Fourth Amendment decisions and annotated bibliography.

**SEE ALSO:** Apr. 20, 1971: U.S. Supreme Court Endorses Busing to End School Segregation; May 15, 1972: U.S. Supreme Court Protects Home Schooling; Jan. 21, 1974: U.S. Supreme Court Mandates Bilingual Education.

## June 29, 1995
# SPACE SHUTTLE DOCKS WITH MIR

*When NASA's space shuttle* Atlantis *docked with the Russian space station Mir, the event marked the beginning of an era of cooperation in human spaceflight between the two nations.*

**LOCALE:** Low Earth orbit

**CATEGORIES:** Spaceflight and aviation; science and technology

**KEY FIGURES**

*Robert Gibson* (b. 1946), NASA astronaut who served as mission commander of the space shuttle on the first docking mission with Mir

*Charlie Precourt* (b. 1955), NASA astronaut who served as pilot of the space shuttle on the first docking mission with Mir

*Norm Thagard* (b. 1943), NASA astronaut who, after spending more than three months on Mir, returned to Earth on *Atlantis*

**SUMMARY OF EVENT**

In the late 1960's, the United States was searching for a space project to follow its successful Apollo lunar landing program. The National Aeronautics and Space Administration (NASA) developed a plan for an Earth-orbiting space station and a reusable launch vehicle, the space shuttle, which would transport crews and supplies back and forth from Earth to the space station. However, in an era when the United States was funding a war in Vietnam, the combined cost of the space station and the space shuttle was deemed excessive. NASA had to downsize its plan, proposing to build only the space shuttle, the cargo bay of which was expanded to allow it to carry much larger payloads into orbit. The original NASA plan to use the space shuttle to transport crews and supplies to a space station was finally realized on June 29, 1995, when the space shuttle *Atlantis* docked with the Russian space station Mir. Aside from its crew of NASA astronauts, *Atlantis* brought two Russian cosmonauts—Anatoly Solovyev, who had flown on three previous Russian space missions, and Nikolai Budarin, a novice on his first mission—to Mir. They replaced Vladimir Dezhurov, Gennady Strekalov, and Norm Thagard, who returned to Earth on *Atlantis*.

The Soviet Union launched Mir in 1986. It was the first space station to be built using the modular concept, in which individual, pressurized sections are built on Earth and launched into orbit, where they are joined together. After the collapse of the Soviet Union in 1991, Russia took over operation of Mir, but as the space sta-

*Orbiting over Lake Baikal in southern Siberia,* Atlantis *and Mir are docked to Mir's Kristall module, which joins the orbiter to the space station.* (NASA)

tion aged, it became increasingly unreliable. Russia announced plans to replace it with Mir 2 and began developing a reusable launch vehicle, *Barun*, which was very similar to the American space shuttle. At the same time, having completed the development of the space shuttle, NASA had resurrected its plan for a space station, to be called Freedom. As the cost of both projects escalated, the United States decided to open its project to international participation, and Russia abandoned its plan for Mir 2, deciding instead to participate in the international project, renamed the International Space Station.

In 1993, the United States and Russia signed an agreement making Russia a partner in the International Space Station. As part of that agreement, Russia was to train NASA astronauts and allow them to gain experience working on Mir. In addition, NASA's space shuttles would dock with Mir, providing the crews with experience in the docking maneuvers. *Atlantis* was the first of NASA's space shuttles to be modified to carry the "docking adapter," a pressurized tube connecting the hatch on

the space shuttle to a hatch on Mir, so *Atlantis* could mate with the Mir and the crew could move back and forth without wearing space suits.

*Atlantis* had to be launched in a ten-minute, nineteen-second time window in order to be placed in an orbit that would allow it to rendezvous with Mir. After two postponements, on June 23 and 24, because of thunderstorms in the launch area, *Atlantis* was launched at 3:32 P.M. on June 27, 1995, the sixty-ninth flight of a space shuttle and the one hundredth manned space mission by the United States. U.S. Navy captain Robert Gibson commanded the space shuttle, and Air Force lieutenant colonel Charlie Precourt served as pilot. Serving as mission specialists were Dr. Ellen Baker, a physician; Greg Harbaugh, a former NASA manager; and Dr. Bonnie Dunbar, a biomedical engineer.

Initially, *Atlantis* was placed in an orbit with a high point of 158 nautical miles and a low point of 85 nautical miles. This was the lowest orbital altitude ever flown by a space shuttle, picked to allow *Atlantis* to rapidly catch up with Mir, closing the gap of 7,000 nautical miles by about 880 nautical miles on each orbit. Three hours and thirty-nine minutes after launch, *Atlantis* fired its orbital maneuvering system for two minutes, raising its orbit to an altitude of 210 by 158 nautical miles, slowing the rate of closure with Mir.

As practice for this mission, the space shuttle *Discovery* had approached to within thirty-seven feet of Mir in February, 1995. That effort provided astronauts and ground controllers with experience trying to bring the two large spacecraft, orbiting the Earth at more than 17,000 miles per hour, together.

Ground controllers woke up the *Atlantis* crew at 1:30 A.M. central time on June 29 to begin preparations for the rendezvous. Shortly before 3:00 A.M., *Atlantis* fired its orbital maneuvering system for forty-five seconds, raising the low point of its orbit and placing the shuttle about eight nautical miles behind Mir, with a slow closing rate.

NASA flight director Bob Castle and Russian flight director Viktor Blagov decided to have Gibson proceed with the docking. By 7:40 A.M., *Atlantis* approached within thirty feet of Mir. For the docking, Commander Gibson positioned *Atlantis* directly below Mir, allowing Earth's gravity to slow the shuttle and bring it up to the space station. To avoid any collision with Mir, Gibson had the *Atlantis* creep toward the space station at a closing rate of about an inch per minute. As the spacecraft passed over Lake Baikal, Russia, at a height of 216 nautical miles, the gentle docking was accomplished at 8:00 A.M. central time.

When the 122-foot-long *Atlantis* docked with the 112-foot-long Mir, the orbital assembly became the largest spacecraft ever to orbit the Earth, having a combined weight of almost a half a million pounds. Once the docking was accomplished, the cosmonauts on Mir greeted the astronauts on *Atlantis*, and the two crews exchanged gifts. The Americans brought flowers, candy, and fruit to Mir. Following a Russian tradition, the cosmonauts presented gifts of bread and salt to the shuttle crew. The combined crew of ten cosmonauts and astronauts then began five days of research projects.

On July 4, *Atlantis* undocked, carrying astronaut Thagard and cosmonauts Dezhurov and Strekalov home to Earth. Thagard, a NASA astronaut and physician, had been launched into orbit on a Russian rocket from the Baykonur Cosmodrome in Kazakhstan on March 14, 1995. His mission was planned to be ninety days, but delays in launching *Atlantis* extended his spaceflight, and Thagard broke the previous American spaceflight endurance record of eighty-four days.

*Atlantis* continued in orbit until July 7, when Gibson fired its engine at 9:45 A.M. eastern standard time to begin its return to Earth. The space shuttle landed at the Kennedy Space Center in Florida at 10:54 A.M., completing its historic mission to Mir. This was the first time a shuttle returned to Earth with a larger crew than it departed with, having left two crew members on Mir but bringing three crew members home.

## SIGNIFICANCE

NASA and the Russian Federal Space Agency began a new era in international space cooperation when the space shuttle *Atlantis* docked with the Russian space station Mir. Two decades had elapsed since the two nations' previous space exploration effort, the Apollo-Soyuz Test Project, in which an Apollo spacecraft docked with a Soyuz capsule in 1975. Just after the *Atlantis* launch, NASA administrator Daniel S. Goldin said, "You can't

make this unbelievable transition from pointing weapons at one another to working together without bumps in the road . . . but . . . this proves that if you put your mind to something and search for common interests, you can build bridges." The event marked the beginning of an era of cooperation on the construction of the International Space Station, where the role of Russia proved critical when the U.S. space shuttle *Columbia* disintegrated during reentry in 2003, requiring the use of Russian Progress resupply vehicles and Soyuz capsules for crew transport while the U.S. shuttle fleet was being redesigned.

*—George J. Flynn*

## FURTHER READING

Harland, David. *The Story of the Mir Space Station*. New York: Springer, 2005. Comprehensive history of Mir, including an account of how it was assembled and operated, the visits of the *Atlantis* space shuttle to Mir, and how the technology that was developed for Mir was incorporated into the International Space Station.

Jenkins, Dennis R. *Space Shuttle: The History of the National Space Transportation System—The First Hundred Missions*. Cape Canaveral, Fla.: D. R. Jenkins, 2001. Describes the space shuttle, including the modifications required to dock with Mir, and provides an account of the first one hundred flights, including the first flight to Mir.

Reichhardt, Tony. *Space Shuttle: The First Twenty Years—The Astronauts' Experiences in Their Own Words*. London: Dorling Kindersley, 2002. A series of personal accounts, written in conjunction with *Air & Space* magazine, describing the first two decades of space shuttle flights.

SEE ALSO: Apr. 19, 1971: Russians Launch the Salyut Space Station; July 31, 1973: European Space Agency Is Formed; July 15-24, 1975: Apollo-Soyuz Test Project; Feb. 20, 1986: First Permanently Manned Space Station Is Launched; Nov. 2, 2000: International Space Station Is Manned.

## July, 1995
# AMAZON.COM SELLS ITS FIRST BOOK ONLINE

*After incorporating in 1994, Amazon.com sold its first online book in 1995. The company soon emerged as a leading Internet commerce site for the purchase of books and eventually many other products, initiating a new era of e-business.*

**LOCALE:** Seattle, Washington
**CATEGORIES:** Marketing and advertising; publishing and journalism

**KEY FIGURE**
*Jeffrey Preston Bezos* (b. 1964), founder and chief executive officer of Amazon.com

**SUMMARY OF EVENT**

In 1999, at the age of thirty-four, Jeffrey Preston Bezos became the fourth-youngest person ever to be named *Time* magazine's person of the year. It was not Bezos's age, however, that made his selection a surprise to most readers. *Time* magazine usually reserves the distinction of person of the year for newsmakers and celebrities, and, although known as the king of cyberbusiness, Bezos was not a national figure. His creation, Amazon.com, had become a household name, however—credited, in fact, with starting and defining the rapidly expanding field of electronic commerce (e-commerce) through the Internet and the World Wide Web. Through the honor to Bezos, therefore, *Time* also recognized a novel, powerful cultural force. Although only four years old, the new form of marketplace had not only transformed how companies sell products and services to each other and to consumers but had affected social behavior and politics as well.

Bezos founded Amazon in 1995 to sell books to consumers over the Internet. Many business commentators predicted failure, but the company's sales skyrocketed. In 1998, its book sales grew 275 percent, followed by another 82 percent the following year, and by then books accounted for only about one-half of Amazon's total sales. Amazon had expanded to offer so many other retail goods that its Web site amounted to an online mall. Investors, initially skeptical, took note. When Amazon began trading its stock publicly in 1997, shares sold for $1.50 each; by the end of 1999, a share cost $80. In part, Amazon was successful because it was the first company of its kind in cyberspace, but its success also owed a great deal to the emphasis placed on customer service to ensure speed of delivery and customer satisfaction. In addi-

tion, Amazon provided browsers with handy consumer information, such as reviews, product ratings, and technical data.

Other innovators soon capitalized on the Internet, too, and some enjoyed success that was nearly as spectacular as Amazon's. For instance, Ebay, the first business to offer online auctions to general customers, started in late 1995 and had more than four million listings in 4,320 categories by early 2000. Beginning in 1997, Handyman Online offered to match home owners with craftspeople and contractors in their local areas for construction projects. In 1998, Ticketmaster began selling tickets online for events nationwide.

A host of other electronic retailers (e-tailers) joined Amazon, many of them start-up companies that copied Amazon's sales and customer service methods. The number of small American and Canadian businesses operating on the Internet increased 40 percent between 1996 and 1998. At first large corporations, such as Sears and Whirlpool, shied away from Internet business, worried that it was just a fad. By 2000, so many had joined the trend and opened Web sites that the term "dot-com" (".com") was firmly embedded in world business culture and Americans' vocabulary. Even advertisements in other media included firms' e-mail and Web site addresses as a matter of course. During the 2000 Super Bowl, more than a dozen "dot-com" companies bought television advertising spots. Meanwhile, other strictly Internet companies, such as Yahoo! and Excite, opened virtual malls of their own in direct competition with Amazon.

Goods offered on the Internet spanned nearly the entire range of the traditional "bricks-and-mortar" retail business stock: books, prescription drugs, toys, electronic equipment and computers, airline tickets, tools and instruments, clothes, and even cars. The convenience, speed, and wealth of information directly accessible online appealed to technologically sophisticated consumers—so much so that e-commerce firms stole customers away from other venues. Bookstores claimed that they were being driven out of business by Amazon and Barnes and Noble, which opened its own Web site. Car dealers began to worry as well when it was found that 5 percent of car purchases in the United States were being conducted over the Internet. Travel agents lost much of their reservation-making business to online self-enrollment reservation services, such as Netscape's

Travelocity, and to Web sites maintained by individual airlines, hotels, and car rental agencies.

Companies also sold services online. Infoseek and AltaVista, for example, conducted information searches, and other Web sites offered professional consultations in such fields as law and insurance, arranged contacts among single men and women, or posted advertisements for job seekers. Banks administered accounts through the Internet, and investment firms sold stocks and bonds. Charles Schwab, in fact, eventually conducted two-thirds of its business on the Web. Auction Web sites became popular almost overnight because they appealed to the American craving for bargains and antiques. Through Ebay and others, private owners could sell new and used items—from books and clothes to automobiles and speedboats—to the highest bidders, no matter their location.

Even though online companies specializing in dealing directly with customers earned $14.9 million in 1999, nearly double the amount of 1998, theirs was the smallest portion of e-commerce profits. Businesses selling to other businesses earned $109 billion during the same period. In fact, business-to-business e-commerce grew so important that it spurred a revolution in American supply and manufacturing procedures. Online catalogs allowed large manufacturers to order parts from suppliers more quickly, and the records of online sales let companies respond to demand more efficiently, saving time and reducing errors. The reduction in overhead expenses, estimated at between 10 and 50 percent, and the reduced waste increased profits. Governments also realized the benefits of e-commerce; they began to distribute benefits and information online and allowed citizens and businesses to file tax returns electronically.

Some fundamental problems with e-commerce emerged during this period of dramatic success, however. Security systems had to be installed to protect Web sites from the vandalism of hackers, and new laws were passed to punish offenders. More important, because credit cards were the usual means of payment for consumer orders, encryption systems had to be devised to ensure that thieves could not intercept credit card numbers.

Some companies found that their supply and shipping systems could not keep up with the rapidly accumulating orders posted on their Web sites. In order to support expansion, Amazon itself had to borrow $1.25 billion in bonds to pay for new warehouses, a distribution system, acquisition costs, and operating expenses in 1999, which gave it a $611 million net loss. Nevertheless, Bezos believed that the company would soon become profitable again, and he was proved right.

Most inhibiting of all, however, was the scarcity of workers with the technical skills for e-commerce. An estimated 360,000 jobs in this field were waiting to be filled in the United States and Canada alone in the year 2000.

## SIGNIFICANCE

Bezos's recognition by *Time* magazine symbolized the sudden emergence of e-commerce as a significant part of American life. With approximately 2.2 million Web sites available to the public, and 300 million pages of information, the Internet presented a vast commercial potential. Increasing numbers of Americans took advantage of it through the late 1990's, and industry experts confidently expected large upswings in holiday sales in 1999. They were not disappointed: Between Thanksgiving and New Year's Day, 26.4 million shoppers spent more than $5 billion online, a threefold increase from 1998.

The successes of 1999 attracted ever more firms to e-commerce, especially after studies found that online small businesses brought in an average of nearly one-third more revenue than traditional companies. Moreover, companies often modified their corporate structures to accommodate the new type of market. Many found that they had to expand customer service depart-

---

### A BET ON BEZOS

*In an interview with the Academy of Achievement on May 4, 2001, Amazon.com founder Jeffrey Preston Bezos spoke about his parents and their generous contribution to his new enterprise:*

The first initial start-up capital for Amazon.com came primarily from my parents, and they invested a large fraction of their life savings in what became Amazon.com. And you know, that was a very bold and trusting thing for them to do, because they didn't know. My dad's first question was, "What's the Internet?" Okay. So he wasn't making a bet on this company or this concept. He was making a bet on his son, as was my mother. So I told them that I thought there was a 70 percent chance that they would lose their whole investment, which was a few hundred thousand dollars, and they did it anyway. And, you know, I thought I was giving myself triple the normal odds, because really, if you look at the odds of a start-up company succeeding at all, it's only about ten percent. Here I was, giving myself a 30 percent chance.

ments because customers contacted retailers directly more frequently by phone or e-mail to ask questions or arrange for replacements or refunds. Companies doing substantial business online could eliminate "middleman" distributors and offer differential pricing for small items as well as for such big items as cars. Even small businesses found that they suddenly could sell products worldwide. At the same time, e-companies saw some expenses rise, especially in training to keep workers abreast of evolving Internet capabilities and in purchases of sophisticated hardware and software.

Meanwhile, e-commerce became deeply involved in other sectors of the economy. For example, the increase in direct shipping of goods to customers multiplied the demand on commercial shippers, such as the U.S. Postal Service, United Parcel Service, and Federal Express.

The implications of e-commerce for society, first studied in the late 1990's, promised to be profound. Stanford University researchers found that Internet use in general tended to isolate people, even from other family members, an antisocial trend abetted by e-commerce: Most online shoppers said that they resorted to the Web to avoid crowded shopping malls and traffic. There was also concern that the ease of shopping online would tempt people to overspend, which could lead to a risky general increase in personal debt and bankruptcies.

A clear relation existed in 2000 between income and online shopping. The likelihood of a household having a computer that was connected to the Internet rose with income level. Because the level of education also rose with income, the wealthy and well educated were the people who used the Internet most often. This phenomenon threatened to intensify divisions between rich and poor, and social observers called for more public-financed Internet facilities at such places as libraries and schools. Public schools were urged to increase instruction devoted to computers and information technology.

Concerns arose also over issues of nationalism. The Internet could internationalize commerce in a way that was difficult for local governments to control, opening traditionally closed markets to global products and affecting nations' economies and their autonomy. Countries with extensive technological infrastructure and research and development would certainly dominate developing countries online, increasing global economic stratification. Moreover, global connectiveness through the Internet created an autonomous behavioral milieu, which could erode cultural differences—a possibility as disturbing to nationalists as it was pleasing to e-commerce companies.

Proponents and critics alike predicted that e-commerce could to some degree reconstruct society in the twenty-first century. Accordingly, politicians anticipated that local and federal government policies would require reshaping as well, but exactly how remained controversial as the century began. Business leaders resisted any regulation of e-commerce, fearing it would cripple their operations; they wanted governmental involvement only in the form of support for developing new technology. Starting in 2000, the U.S. Census Bureau began collecting data on e-commerce to help the government address related policy issues.

The collapse of the NASDAQ and technical sector that occurred in the spring of 2000 took a little of the bloom off the rose of e-commerce, and many companies took a financial bath during that year. Such a shakeout of the less successful companies was inevitable after the first blush of success, however; despite the setbacks that some experienced, the concept of e-commerce was here to stay.

*—Roger Smith*

## FURTHER READING

Burnham, Bill. *How to Invest in E-Commerce Stocks.* New York: McGraw-Hill, 1999. Presents a concise introduction to e-commerce as well as a practical guide to the advantages and dangers of investing through the Internet.

Fellenstein, Craig, and Ron Wood. *Exploring E-Commerce, Global E-Business, and E-Society.* Upper Saddle River, N.J.: Prentice Hall, 2000. Explains e-commerce for business owners and considers the future influence of e-commerce on government, medicine, and education.

Ramo, Joshua Cooper. "Why the Founder of Amazon .com Is Our Choice for 1999." *Time,* December 27, 1999, 50-51. Article announcing the choice of Bezos as person of the year is accompanied by articles about e-retailing and prominent cybermerchants.

Schiller, Dan. *Digital Capitalism: Networking the Global Marketing System.* Cambridge, Mass.: MIT Press, 1999. Analyzes market-driven policies, economic potentiality, and influence on the educational and social policy of cyberspace. Warns that powerful corporations could misuse it.

Tiernan, Bernadette. *E-Tailing.* Chicago: Dearborn, 2000. Provides a guide to the basics of e-commerce structure and procedures, Internet psychology, online merchants, and likely products and technology of the future.

**SEE ALSO:** July 1, 1985: Home Shopping Service Is Offered on Cable Television; Sept., 1988: Prodigy Introduces Dial-Up Service; 1990's: Libraries Transform into Information Technology Centers; Dec. 15, 1994: Release of Netscape Navigator 1.0; Mid-1990's: Rise of the Internet and the World Wide Web; Sept. 7, 1998: Google Is Founded; Mar. 14, 2000: King Releases the First E-Novel.

## July, 1995
# VENONA CABLES ARE DECLASSIFIED

*Venona was the code name used for an American project for decrypting Soviet diplomatic messages sent between the Soviet consulate in the United States and Moscow. The decrypted messages identified numerous Soviet spies and provided insight into the workings of Soviet espionage in the United States. The release of these decryptions in the mid-1990's revised historians' understanding of the early years of the Cold War.*

**LOCALE:** Arlington, Virginia
**CATEGORIES:** Cold War; diplomacy and international relations

**KEY FIGURES**
*Meredith Gardner* (1912-2002), skilled linguist and veteran code breaker assigned to the Venona project
*Robert Lamphere* (1919-2002), Federal Bureau of Investigation chief agent of the Venona project
*Pavel Fitin* (1907-1971), head of spy recruiting for Soviet intelligence
*Julius Rosenberg* (1918-1953), American Communist whose identity was confirmed by the Venona cables
*Ethel Rosenberg* (1915-1953), Julius Rosenberg's wife, who was found to have known of her husband's work
*Alger Hiss* (1904-1996), American accused of being a Soviet spy

**SUMMARY OF EVENT**
In July, 1995, the National Security Agency (NSA) began to release transcripts of Soviet consular messages that had been intercepted and decoded during the Cold War. This top secret decryption effort was code-named Venona, a randomly assigned word with no meaning. In addition to exposing the methods of Soviet spy craft throughout the 1930's-1950's, the Venona transcripts helped to confirm the identities of numerous Cold War spies whose complicity with the Soviets had been debated by many historians in the 1970's and 1980's. Among the most prominent of these were Alger Hiss and Julius and Ethel Rosenberg.

The Venona project began in 1943. The head of the U.S. Army's Signal Intelligence Service (SIS), fearing secret German and Soviet peace negotiations, ordered that intercepted Soviet consular messages be decrypted to validate this expectation. These telegraph and radio messages between the Soviet ambassadorial staffs in the United States and their superiors in Moscow were encrypted using a "one-time pad system." This method replaces words and letters with numeric sequences from a page filled with random number sequences; both sender and receiver have identical copies of this page, and, after one use, the page is destroyed. The strength of this system is that every message's code would differ from that

*Meredith Gardner (left) works as a code breaker for the Venona project.* (U.S. Department of Energy)

## JULIUS ROSENBERG, SOVIET SPY

*The Venona Cables, decrypted World War II Soviet messages between KGB offices in Moscow and the United States, were released by the National Security Agency in 1995. A key transcript from 1944 offers strong evidence identifying Julius Rosenberg as a spy in the atomic bomb project. His wife, Ethel Rosenberg, is identified as being aware of her husband's (code name LIBERAL) work:*

From: NEW YORK

To: MOSCOW

No: 1657

27 November 1944

To VIKTOR[i].

Your no. 5356[a]. Information on LIBERAL's[ii] wife[iii]. Surname that of her husband, first name ETHEL, 29 years old. Married five years. Finished secondary school. A FELLOWCOUNTRYMAN [ZEMLYaK][iv] since 1938. Sufficiently well developed politically. Knows about her husband's work and the role of METR[v] and NIL[vi]. In view of delicate health does not work. Is characterized positively and as a devoted person.

No. 922

Advise on the possibility of using in our work the engineer MAZURIN Vladimir N.[vii]. He worked as deputy to the constructor of Plant 155. He graduated from MAI[viii] in 1936. Is now working at ARSENIJ's[ix] plant[x]. [2 groups unrecovered] [D% I request your decision on the question].

No. 923

ANTON[xi]

---

Notes:    [a]    Not available.

Comments:

     [i]      VIKTOR: Lt. Gen. P. M. FITIN.

     [ii]      LIBERAL: Julius ROSENBERG.

     [iii]      Ethel ROSENBERG, nee GREENGLASS.

     [iv]      ZEMLYaK: Member of the Communist Party.

     [v]      METR: Probably Joel BARR or Alfred SARANT.

     [vi]      NIL: Unidentified.

     [vii]      Vladimir Nikolaevich MAZURIN.

     [viii]      MAI: i.e. MOSKOVSKIJ AVIATSIONNYJ INSTITUT, Moscow Aviation Institute.

     [ix]      ARSENIJ: Andrej Ivanovich ShEVChENKO.

     [x]      Bell Aircraft Plant, NIAGARA FALLS, N.Y.

     [xi]      ANTON: Leonis Romanovich KVASNIKOV.

---

Unfortunately for Russia, the first few months after the German invasion in 1941 resulted in confusion as the Germans advanced on Moscow. It appears that during this chaotic period, the Soviets reprinted and issued a number of duplicate one-time pads so that during the war a number of the sequences were repeated, thus making the code vulnerable. America's first efforts to crack these codes failed, but in 1943 the SIS began to recognize that some sequences were being reused. After much work, some messages could be partially decoded. This discovery was made in the SIS facility at the Arlington Hall Station, so throughout World War II Venona efforts were ascribed to Arlington Hall. In 1946, Meredith Gardner was assigned to Venona. A skilled linguist and veteran of the successful breaking of Japan's diplomatic codes, Gardner became a key player in the project.

Deciphering the numeric codes was made more difficult by the Soviets' use of cover names. Every person mentioned—whether target or agent—was to be referenced with a cover name (for example, President Franklin D. Roosevelt was "KAPITAN"). To make sense of intercepted cables, Gardner first had to break the codes so that letters could be discerned, combine the letters into probable words, and then link the cover names to individuals. In December, 1947, Gardner transcribed a cable that listed the cover names of Soviet agents who were supplying information on America's atomic weapons program. After this, it was decided to combine the SIS efforts with the expertise of the Federal Bureau of Investigation (FBI), and for the first time since the 1920's, when the FBI began investigating Russian spies, it had access to secret Soviet instructions. Prior FBI efforts had been based on surveillance, wiretaps, and the confessions of a small number of Soviet spies who had defected for reasons of fear or greed.

on the next page, so it is nearly "unbreakable." To facilitate several messages, books of these one-time pads were printed in Moscow and sent to the embassies in diplomatic pouches that by treaty could not be opened or inspected by the host countries. All nations' ambassadors communicate by coded transmissions, but Soviet use of the one-time pad system made their communications seem very secure.

In 1947, the FBI assigned Robert Lamphere to Venona as the agency's chief agent. By linking the insights offered by confessions with his knowledge of Soviet operations, Lamphere was able to help Gardner by giving context to the decoded messages and thus identify cover names. Further assistance was provided by British code breakers in Cheltenham, England, at the Government Communications Headquarters (GCHQ), who had been trying to crack Soviet codes on their own. This assistance proved significant, as did that of Canadian officers who debriefed a defected Soviet cipher clerk in 1945.

These combined efforts were aided by the Soviets' centralized operational style of strict control over subordinates. Foreign espionage was controlled by the first directorate of the KGB (the best-known name of the Committee for State Security, the Soviet Union's apparatus for collecting foreign and internal intelligence). Each embassy's intelligence officers sent frequent reports to the KGB and in return received detailed instructions. During World War II, the commander of the first directorate was Lieutenant General Pavel Fitin, code-named VIKTOR. Under Fitin, Soviet intelligence officers recruited Americans to spy on government programs, industrial developments, and weapons developments. A great number of these spies were recruited from members of the Communist Party of the United States. Venona decryptions, when added to Lamphere's understanding of the Soviet organization, were pivotal in the identification of several Soviet operatives.

This effort was time-consuming, as each successful decryption provided clues that were used to break earlier unread cables. Venona operations continued into 1980, although the bulk of the cables were broken between 1947 and 1952. Ultimately, only a small portion of the several thousand intercepted cables were ever broken—less than 3,000—and those were messages sent between 1942 and 1945, with a few sent as late as 1948. It appears that the duplicate one-time pads were used up during the war and replacement pads were not breakable by the Venona staff.

Regardless, Venona proved very useful. Decrypts corroborated the claims of the Soviet defectors such as Whittaker Chambers who had described Soviet methods, successes, and agents. The link between their confessions and decrypts provided nearly certain identification of some agents. For example, the identification of Julius Rosenberg as a spy in the atomic bomb project was immeasurably strengthened by decrypt number 1657 of November 27, 1944. Similarly, the Soviet agent ALES was identified by Lamphere as Alger Hiss based on details found in Venona transcripts. The reports to Moscow also indicated that Soviet agents were operating in the Department of the Treasury, the Office of Strategic Services, the War Department, the Department of State, and the Justice Department.

## SIGNIFICANCE

The release of the Venona cables is an important part of ongoing efforts to understand the Cold War. In the aftermath of the Vietnam War and the Watergate scandal, many historians claimed that government prosecutions of American spies were based on hysteria, shoddy FBI procedures, and perhaps perjured testimony. The trial of the Rosenbergs, for example, relied on evidence given by Ethel Rosenberg's brother, David Greenglass, who had been a courier for a Soviet espionage ring. Although some of his testimony can be described as perjured, the decision was made to use it rather than expose the Venona project to public view. The revisionist writings of the 1970's have been compromised by the Venona releases and the opening of some KGB archives in the first years after the fall of the Soviet government. The result is a more nuanced and thorough understanding of the espionage conflict between the United States and the Soviet Union.

While Venona certainly provided evidence of Soviet spies in many agencies of the U.S. government, this evidence was fragmentary and tentative until the mid-1990's, when some Soviet archives were opened to historians. While these two sources certainly make it clear that many Americans did spy for Moscow, their impact is easily overstated. For example, the U.S. atomic bomb effort, the Manhattan Project, was a huge undertaking. Perhaps 100,000 people worked on it—most unknowingly. The Soviet spies identified by Venona number perhaps a few dozen, and only one was placed significantly. Thus, although Venona confirmed the presence of Americans operating as spies for the Soviets, it did not prove that their efforts greatly compromised U.S. security.

The 1995 release of the Venona decoded top secret transcripts of Soviet consular messages helped to rewrite the history of the Cold War. Venona provided the United States with insight into the personnel and methods of operations of Soviet espionage throughout the 1930's-1950's and helped confirm the identities of numerous individuals accused of spying for the Soviets. Among the most prominent of these were Alger Hiss and Julius and Ethel Rosenberg.

*—Kevin B. Reid*

**FURTHER READING**

Benson, Robert Louis, and Michael Warner. *Venona: Soviet Espionage and the American Response, 1939-1957*. Washington, D.C.: National Security Agency, 1996. The official description and analysis of the project. Provides 450 pages of transcripts of reports and analyzed cables.

Romerstein, Herbert, and Eric Breindel. *The Venona Secrets: Exposing Soviet Espionage and America's Traitors*. Washington, D.C.: Regnery, 2000. Written by two former American intelligence agents, the book, however biased, provides an in-depth description of the many Soviet activities exposed and confirmed by Venona.

West, Nigel. *Venona: The Greatest Secret of the Cold War*. London: HarperCollins, 1999. Focuses primarily on British efforts, but provides a well-balanced and insightful description of the Venona operations.

**SEE ALSO:** May 26, 1973-Dec. 26, 1991: Détente with the Soviet Union; Dec., 1991: Dissolution of the Soviet Union.

## July 11, 1995
# UNITED STATES RECOGNIZES VIETNAM

*U.S. diplomatic recognition of Vietnam marked an end to the traumatic and divisive Vietnam War era.*

**LOCALE:** Washington, D.C.
**CATEGORY:** Diplomacy and international relations

**KEY FIGURES**

*Bill Clinton* (b. 1946), president of the United States, 1993-2001
*Jimmy Carter* (b. 1924), president of the United States, 1977-1981
*George H. W. Bush* (b. 1924), president of the United States, 1989-1993
*Bob Kerrey* (b. 1943), U.S. senator from Nebraska
*John McCain* (b. 1936), U.S. senator from Arizona
*Vo Van Kiet* (b. 1922), prime minister of Vietnam, 1991-1997

**SUMMARY OF EVENT**

On July 11, 1995, President Bill Clinton announced the diplomatic recognition of the Socialist Republic of Vietnam by the United States. Recognition of Vietnam brought to a close a war that officially had ended more than twenty years before. In announcing his decision, Clinton said, "We can now move on to common ground. Whatever divided us before, let us consign to the past."

Concerning Vietnam, moving away from the past had proved a long and agonizing process for the United States. The Vietnam War took the lives of more than fifty-eight thousand U.S. personnel between 1961 and the fall of Saigon on April 30, 1975. The United States had hoped that the peace agreement of January, 1973, which provided for a cease-fire, withdrawal of foreign troops, return of prisoners of war, and a peaceful reunifi-

cation of Vietnam, might prevent a communist takeover of all of Vietnam.

North Vietnamese forces, however, remained in South Vietnam after the agreement and, after consolidating their areas of control, launched an offensive in March, 1975, that would lead, by the end of April, to complete victory and establishment of one Vietnam, with Hanoi as its capital. The final resolution of the war intensified United States resentment toward Vietnam and made reconciliation with the former enemy even more difficult. An embargo on trade with North Vietnam, imposed in 1964, was extended to all of Vietnam. Nevertheless, President Jimmy Carter, elected in 1976, took some first steps toward a rapprochement by lifting the prohibition on travel to Vietnam, beginning discussions with the Vietnamese government, and accepting Vietnam as a member of the United Nations.

These initial steps were halted by the Vietnamese demand in 1978 for reconstruction aid promised in the 1973 Peace Accords. Hostility between Vietnam and the United States was increased in the same year by a Vietnamese friendship treaty with the Soviet Union, recognition of the People's Republic of China (Vietnam's historic enemy) by the United States, and Vietnam's invasion of Cambodia. From the perspective of the United States, improved relations with Vietnam henceforth were dependent on that nation's withdrawal from Cambodia, its recognition of an independent Cambodian government, commitment to basic human rights for its own citizens, and, most important, a strict accounting of all U.S. servicemen missing in action or taken prisoner in Vietnam.

The Vietnamese agreement in 1989 to withdraw from Cambodia opened the way for a sequence of steps that ultimately would lead to normalization of relations. In 1991, President George H. W. Bush defined the incremental steps, known as the "road map," that Vietnam would have to take before the United States would grant diplomatic recognition. One of these steps, a peace agreement between Vietnam and Cambodia, was completed in October, 1991.

The United States reciprocated in 1992 by permitting U.S. companies to open offices in Vietnam. With the trade embargo still in effect, however, there was little incentive for companies to do so. The next significant development was Clinton's decision in 1993 to end U.S. opposition to international institutions and other nations making money available to Vietnam. Soon afterward, U.S. businesses were declared free to bid on projects funded by international financial institutions, so that they would not be shut out of business opportunities partially financed by U.S. dollars.

Throughout the early 1990's, the Vietnamese had been increasingly helpful in locating the remains of missing U.S. servicemen. Teams from the United States were permitted to search the Vietnamese countryside; and war records, including the archives of the war museum in Hanoi, were turned over to the United States.

One major step short of diplomatic recognition remained: lifting the trade embargo. Debate centered on several issues, including the economic implications of maintaining the trade embargo. The U.S. business community recognized Vietnam's resources, including oil reserves estimated to be the fourth largest in the world and a labor force with one of the highest literacy rates in Southeast Asia. It also was obvious that other nations were gaining significant investment advantages in the country. Impediments to foreign investments also were recognized, among them inadequate distribution capabilities, state control of businesses, and both a market philosophy and legal system still in flux.

The continuing communist nature of the government and restrictions on individual rights raised concerns among many persons in the United States, but others noted that the United States had long done business with a variety of repressive regimes, including China. From a geopolitical perspective, it was argued that an economi-

*U.S. president Bill Clinton (left) and Vietnamese president Tran Duc Luong sit in front of a bust of Ho Chi Minh in Hanoi in 2000. Clinton's visit marked the first time a U.S. president had visited Vietnam since 1969.* (AP/Wide World Photos)

cally strengthened Vietnam would be a counterbalance to Chinese domination in the region.

The most emotional issue surrounding the trade embargo and diplomatic recognition of Vietnam was continuing uncertainty over the fate of U.S. troops still listed as missing in action or known to have been taken prisoner. Many viewed the trade embargo as a means to pressure the Vietnamese government into cooperating on the issue of prisoners of war (POWs) and those missing in action (MIAs). On the other hand, many argued that improving relations with Hanoi would both reward the country for past cooperation and encourage future efforts.

On February 3, 1994, President Clinton announced an end to the U.S. trade embargo against Vietnam. This decision, Clinton stated, had been based on only one criterion: "gaining the fullest possible accounting for our

2917

prisoners of war and our missing in action." He continued, "Today I am lifting the trade embargo against Vietnam because I am absolutely convinced it offers the best way to resolve the fate of those who remain missing and about whom we are not sure." Lifting the embargo did not involve granting Vietnam most favored nation trade status, so tariffs on Vietnamese goods imported into the United States remained high. In addition, U.S. businesses operating in Vietnam would not have the support afforded by a U.S. embassy.

Diplomatic recognition was the next logical step, but it also excited controversy. The arguments for and against lifting the trade embargo, especially regarding POW/MIA issues, were also applied to normalization of relations. President Clinton's announcement on July 11, 1995, was boycotted by the American Legion and by several family groups, including the National League of Families of American Prisoners and Missing in Southeast Asia. Members of Congress were divided, arguing either that recognition acknowledged Vietnam's cooperation and would further the effort to reach as final an accounting as possible, or that it would remove the final incentive for Vietnamese cooperation.

As Clinton spoke, he was accompanied by politicians from both parties, including Republican senator John McCain, a former prisoner of war, and Democratic senator Bob Kerrey, who had lost part of a leg in combat during his tour of duty. "Never before in the history of warfare has such an extensive effort been made to resolve the fate of soldiers who did not return," the president said. He promised that "normalization of our relations with Vietnam is not the end of [that] effort."

## SIGNIFICANCE
Prime Minister Vo Van Kiet of Vietnam greeted the resumption of diplomatic relations with an expression of gratitude to President Clinton and a promise that Vietnam would continue to help the United States resolve questions concerning the fate of the missing U.S. servicemen. The U.S. business community generally welcomed the president's decision but called

for additional steps, such as granting most favored nation status to reduce tariffs and making insurance available from the Overseas Private Investment Corporation in order to protect U.S. investments.

*—Edward J. Rielly*

## FURTHER READING
Castelli, Beth. "The Lifting of the Trade Embargo Between the United States and Vietnam: The Loss of a Potential Bargaining Tool or a Means of Fostering Cooperation?" *Dickinson Journal of International Law* 13 (Winter, 1995): 297-328. Provides a reasoned

---

### RECOGNIZING VIETNAM AND HEALING OLD WOUNDS

*When President Bill Clinton announced the normalization of diplomatic relations between the United States and Vietnam on July 11, 1995, he concluded by speaking of healing:*

I believe normalization and increased contact between Americans and Vietnamese will advance the cause of freedom in Vietnam, just as it did in Eastern Europe and the former Soviet Union. I strongly believe that engaging the Vietnamese on the broad economic front of economic reform and the broad front of democratic reform will help to honor the sacrifice of those who fought for freedom's sake in Vietnam.

I am proud to be joined in this view by distinguished veterans of the Vietnam war. They served their country bravely. They are of different parties. A generation ago they had different judgments about the war which divided us so deeply. But today they are of a single mind. They agree that the time has come for America to move forward on Vietnam. All Americans should be grateful especially that Senators John McCain, John Kerry, Bob Kerrey, Chuck Robb and Representative Pete Peterson, along with other Vietnam veterans in the Congress . . . have kept up their passionate interest in Vietnam but were able to move beyond the haunting and painful past toward finding common ground for the future. Today, they and many other veterans support the normalization of relations, giving the opportunity to Vietnam to fully join the community of nations and being true to what they fought for so many years ago.

Whatever we may think about the political decisions of the Vietnam era, the brave Americans who fought and died there had noble motives. They fought for the freedom and the independence of the Vietnamese people. Today the Vietnamese are independent, and we believe this step will help to extend the reach of freedom in Vietnam and, in so doing, to enable these fine veterans of Vietnam to keep working for that freedom.

This step will also help our own country to move forward on an issue that has separated Americans from one another for too long now. Let the future be our destination. We have so much work ahead of us. This moment offers us the opportunity to bind up our own wounds. They have resisted time for too long. We can now move on to common ground. Whatever divided us before let us consign to the past. Let this moment, in the words of the Scripture, be a time to heal and a time to build.

discussion of background, considerations involved in lifting the trade embargo, and projections for the future.

Chang, Tim Tien-Chun. "Joint Ventures in Vietnam." *Commercial Law Bulletin* 9 (July 1, 1994): 17-19. Offers succinct, clear explanations of types of investments and of challenges facing foreign investors in Vietnam.

Howes, Craig. *Voices of the Vietnam POWs.* New York: Oxford University Press, 1993. Provides important context for understanding the continuing importance of the POW/MIA issue.

Moss, George Donelson. *Vietnam: An American Ordeal.* 5th ed. Upper Saddle River, N.J.: Prentice Hall, 2006. Although no single book can adequately cover the story of American involvement in the Vietnam War, this work is among the most thorough available. Includes maps, bibliographic references, and index.

Solomon, Richard H. *Exiting Indochina: U.S. Leader-ship of the Cambodia Settlement and Normalization with Vietnam.* Washington, D.C.: United States Institute of Peace, 2000. Brief volume describes the diplomatic negotiations that led to U.S. recognition of Vietnam. Includes bibliographic references and index.

Sutter, Robert G. *Vietnam-U.S. Relations: The Debate over Normalization.* Washington, D.C.: Library of Congress, 1992. Presents a detailed view of the political debate regarding normalization of relations with Vietnam.

**SEE ALSO:** Jan. 27, 1973: Vietnam Releases U.S. Prisoners of War; Mar., 1973: U.S. Troops Leave Vietnam; Aug. 19, 1974: United States Grants Amnesty to Vietnam War Draft Evaders; Nov., 1974: *Dog Soldiers* Portrays Vietnam in Fiction; May, 1975: Indo-Chinese Boat People Begin Fleeing Vietnam; Aug. 15, 1979: *Apocalypse Now* Expresses Antiwar Cynicism; Dec. 24, 1986: *Platoon* Explores the Vietnam Experience.

## July 21, 1995-March 23, 1996
# THIRD TAIWAN STRAIT CRISIS

*The People's Republic of China conducted a series of missile tests and military maneuvers in the vicinity of Taiwan to force the island to end its quest for independence and to stop apparent American support for Taiwan. American response was measured: The Taiwanese reelected their independence-minded president, but the United States reassured mainland China that it did not support Taiwanese independence. A major deterioration of Sino-American relationships, or even war, was averted.*

**LOCALE:** Taiwan Strait
**CATEGORIES:** Government and politics; diplomacy and international relations

**KEY FIGURES**
*Lee Teng-hui* (Li Denghui; b. 1923), president of Taiwan, 1988-2000
*Jiang Zemin* (Chiang Tse-min; b. 1926), president of the People's Republic of China, 1993-2003
*Bill Clinton* (b. 1946), president of the United States, 1993-2001
*Qian Qichen* (Ch'ien Ch'i-ch'en; b. 1928), foreign minister of the People's Republic of China, 1988-1998

*Warren Christopher* (b. 1925), U.S. secretary of state, 1993-1997
*William Perry* (b. 1927), U.S. secretary of defense, 1994-1997

**SUMMARY OF EVENT**
Both the communist People's Republic of China (PRC), on the mainland, and the rival nationalist Republic of China (ROC), on the island of Taiwan, claimed to be the one and only seat of the Chinese government. Taiwan was an ally of the United States, but as U.S.-PRC relations warmed in the 1970's, the United States downgraded its diplomatic relations with the nationalist government.

Taiwan sought an internationally recognized independence. Mainland China fiercely opposed Taiwanese independence, insisting on the "one China" policy, which the United States also supported. The visit of Taiwanese president Lee Teng-hui to Cornell University, his alma mater, on June 9-10, 1995, deeply angered mainland China. It perceived the visit as an attempt to win support for an independent Taiwan.

To teach both Taiwan and the United States a lesson, from July 21 to 26, 1995, Beijing triggered what became known as the Third Taiwan Strait Crisis. China performed missile tests and joint sea and air military exercises in the Taiwan Strait, the waterway that separates the Chinese mainland from Taiwan. There were two previous, Cold War crises—in 1954-1955 and 1958—in the strait, involving the PRC and Taiwan. In the third crisis, the PRC test-fired four surface-to-surface short-range missiles and two medium-range missiles, all capable of carrying a nuclear warhead. The targets were just thirty-eight miles off the Taiwanese island of Pengchiayu and one hundred miles north of Taiwan.

In late July, the ROC launched its own retaliatory missile tests and military exercises. The United States pursued a conciliatory approach. At a meeting on August 1, U.S. secretary of state Warren Christopher told PRC foreign minister Qian Qichen that U.S. president Bill Clinton was committed to the one China policy, opposed Taiwanese independence, and did not support a U.N. seat for Taiwan. Clinton insisted that Lee's U.S. visit should not be overestimated. However, Qian was not satisfied and declared that Washington must act on its policy.

Beijing heightened the pressure by performing a second round of missile tests and joint sea and air and artillery exercises from August 15 to August 25. Guided missiles landed in the sea eighty miles north of Taiwan. The PRC declared that Lee must be punished for his stubbornness and the United States was warned against intervention.

While Taiwan countered with missile tests in September and military defense exercises in October, the United States remained restrained. Washington tried to reassure the PRC of its commitment to the one China policy and its rejection of Taiwanese independence. The PRC countered that it wanted to see concrete U.S. measures.

In spite of the crisis in the Taiwan Strait, a summit meeting between Clinton and PRC president Jiang Zemin was held in New York City on October 24, 1995. However, at the end of October, Jiang attended major military exercises off southern China, facing Taiwan. On November 15, the PRC launched massive military maneuvers, involving land, sea, and air forces, that were publicly announced as directed against Taiwan.

Beijing's threatening moves appeared to pay off during the December 2, 1995, Taiwanese parliamentary elections. Having just suffered a stock market decline of 33 percent and witnessed the transfer of US$10 million in capital from Taiwan, voters gave Lee's Kuomintang Party fewer seats and increased the mandate of the pro-mainland Chinese New Party (CNP) to twenty-one seats.

Even though Washington remained conciliatory, the PRC was not satisfied. On December 19, the U.S. aircraft

carrier USS *Nimitz* crossed the Taiwan Strait. According to U.S. sources, this happened because of bad weather elsewhere. In January, 1996, however, Taiwan proclaimed this event to be a sign of U.S. support.

Beijing decided on further provocations. Between January and February 1996, it gathered more than one hundred thousand soldiers in Fujian Province, which is opposite Taiwan. Early in March, Jiang and Qian told mainland Communist delegates that Taiwanese independence moves were a recipe for military conflict.

The crisis escalated just prior to Taiwan's presidential elections in March, 1996. On March 4, the PRC announced that it would hold surface-to-surface missile tests very close to Taiwan from March 8 to March 18. Despite intense U.S. diplomatic efforts to prevent it, on March 7, the PRC fired three missiles into target areas twenty-three miles off the northern Taiwanese harbor of Keelung and thirty-three miles off the southern Taiwanese port of Kaohsiung.

There is debate as to whether these missiles affected Taiwanese shipping and delayed air traffic to Japan, but the threatening nature of the exercise was understood. In the evening of March 7, Christopher and Secretary of Defense William Perry met with PRC vice foreign minister Liu Huaqiu in Washington and stressed American disapproval of the military exercises.

On March 8, Perry acted to prove Washington's commitment to the protection of Taiwan but decided on the least confrontational show of force. He ordered the battle group of the aircraft carrier USS *Independence* to sail to Taiwan. Significantly, the *Independence* was not ordered into the Taiwan Strait but to the other side of Taiwan, facing the Philippine Sea. The *Nimitz* was ordered to join the *Independence*, but it was told to sail leisurely, a fact that was conveyed to the PRC.

While the PRC seemed to escalate the crisis on March 9, by announcing live ammunition air and sea exercises in the Taiwan Strait from March 12 to March 20, the American naval response caused a de-escalation. On March 13, Beijing fired its last test missile, supposedly laden with a dummy warhead only. Two further announced firings were canceled.

Even though, on March 15, the PRC declared that further military exercises were to take place from March 18 to March 25, no more missiles were fired. On March 23, the Taiwanese reelected Lee as president, with a surprising 54 percent majority. Although the stock market was still down by 17 percent from precrisis days, the people of Taiwan showed their anger toward Beijing and refusal to be intimidated. After the election, the crisis ended.

## SIGNIFICANCE

The Third Taiwan Strait Crisis had the potential to seriously strain Sino-American relations. However, while the United States demonstrated that it would defend Taiwan and gained international support for its stance, the Clinton administration realized that it had risked a conflict over formal Taiwanese independence, an issue that it did not consider relevant. Soon after the crisis, the United States renewed its diplomatic efforts to show the PRC that it was committed to the one China policy.

The PRC gained from the postcrisis attempt at conciliation made by the United States. When Clinton and Jiang met in Manila in November, 1996, they agreed on mutual state visits to highlight the quality of Sino-American relations. During President Jiang's visit to Washington, D.C., in October, 1997, he obtained the crucial public declaration that the United States was opposed to Taiwanese independence and the island's desire for a U.N. seat. In turn, Clinton was warmly welcomed in Beijing in June, 1998.

In the future, whenever Lee pressed the issue of independence, the Clinton administration would call on Taiwan to rein in its rhetoric. Having been on the brink of conflict, the PRC and the U.S. moved closer to a common policy of rejecting Taiwanese independence because of its threat to regional stability.

—*R. C. Lutz*

## FURTHER READING

Copper, John F. *Playing with Fire: The Looming War with China over Taiwan*. Westport, Conn.: Praeger Security International, 2006. Argues that Taiwan's desire for independence will tangle the United States in war with the PRC. Places event in context of Sino-American relationships up to 2004.

Ross, Robert. "The 1995-1996 Taiwan Strait Confrontation: Coercion, Credibility, and Use of Force." *International Security* 25 (Autumn, 2000): 87-123. Detailed analysis of event; argues that both mainland China and the United States benefited from the crisis, albeit at a price.

Sutter, Robert. "Domestic Politics and U.S.-China-Taiwan Triangle: The 1995-1996 Taiwan Strait Conflict and Its Aftermath." In *After the Cold War: Domestic Factors and U.S.-China Relations*, edited by Robert Ross. Armonk, N.Y.: M. E. Sharpe, 1998. Analyzes U.S. public opinion of the issue.

Swaine, Michael. "Chinese Decision-Making Regarding Taiwan, 1978-2000." In *The Making of Chinese Foreign and Security Policy in the Era of Reform: 1978-2000*, edited by David Lampton. Stanford, Calif.: Stanford University Press, 2001. Focuses on mainland Chinese hard-liners and their affect on policy making during event.

Zhao, Suisheng, ed. *Across the Taiwan Strait: Mainland China, Taiwan, and the 1995-1996 Crisis*. New York: Routledge, 1999. Collection of essays providing further insight into the PRC's view of the event and its decision making during the crisis.

**SEE ALSO:** Oct. 25, 1971: People's Republic of China Is Seated at the United Nations; Sept. 9, 1976: Death of Mao Zedong Leads to Reforms in China; Oct. 16, 1980: China Conducts Atmospheric Nuclear Test; July 28, 1989: Chinese Top Leadership Changes as Jiang Zemin Takes the Party Chair; Nov. 15, 1999: United States and China Sign Trade Deal.

## September 5, 1995-January 27, 1996
# FRANCE RESUMES NUCLEAR TESTING

*French president Jacques Chirac shocked the world with his announcement that, after a three-year moratorium, France would undertake a series of eight underground nuclear weapons tests in the South Pacific. Massive criticism, protests, and boycotts forced Chirac to end the series at six tests early in 1996, when he made it clear that France was willing to join other nations in the Comprehensive Nuclear-Test-Ban Treaty.*

**LOCALE:** Mururoa and Fangataufa, French Polynesia
**CATEGORIES:** Government and politics; diplomacy and international relations; science and technology

**KEY FIGURES**
*Jacques Chirac* (b. 1932), president of France, 1995-2007
*Alain Juppé* (b. 1945), prime minister of France, 1995-1997
*François Mitterrand* (1916-1996), president of France, 1981-1995
*John Major* (b. 1943), prime minister of the United Kingdom, 1990-1997
*Paul Keating* (b. 1944), prime minister of Australia, 1991-1996

**SUMMARY OF EVENT**
In the decades after World War II, nuclear weapons, their proliferation, testing, and deployment, had profound political and environmental effects. France, a nuclear power since 1960, had conducted thirty-one nuclear tests in the 1960's, sixty-nine in the 1970's, and ninety-two in the 1980's, many of them in the Mururoa Atoll in the Tuamotu Archipelago east of Tahiti. Protests against these tests occurred in the Pacific islands most directly affected by them as well in such Pacific Rim countries as Japan, Australia, and New Zealand. So seriously did French officials take these protests that, when Greenpeace sent its boat the *Rainbow Warrior* to New Zealand prior to its travel into the test area, French secret service agents, acting under authorization of President François Mitterrand, destroyed the vessel with two bombs, killing one person aboard. Some scholars claim that the nuclear tests and the *Rainbow Warrior* incident led to a deterioration in French international relations, whereas others assert that, through apologies and financial assistance, French politicians were able to mitigate the region's antinuclear sentiments.

During the Cold War, the French government, whether it was conservative, centrist, or socialist, had a consistent nuclear weapons policy. Apart from any alliances, the French insisted on maintaining an independent nuclear force capable of inflicting unacceptable damage to any potential nuclear aggression, but in the 1990's, when the newly non-Communist Russia no longer posed a threat to European nations, many politicians, military leaders, and scientists urged France to change its nuclear policy. Mitterrand, however, fearing nuclear attacks from terrorists or unstable nuclear nations, reconfirmed France's traditional nuclear doctrine, though he did institute a moratorium on nuclear tests. However, this moratorium ended when, shortly after becoming president, Jacques Chirac stunned the international community by announcing, on June 13, 1995, that France would conduct a series of eight nuclear tests in the Mururoa and Fangataufa atolls.

Because of intense national and international criticism, Chirac had to defend his decision. He argued that the security and reliability of France's nuclear deterrent was at stake, and that, as president, he had the duty to protect the French people. France was also in the process of reducing and modernizing its nuclear arsenal. For example, the French were developing a new submarine-launched ballistic missile system and a powerful computer system that would enable scientists to simulate how their new weapons would perform. When critics countered that France could acquire this technology and knowledge from the United States, Chirac reiterated his nation's customary position of nuclear independence from the East and West, though some saw his arguments as influenced by his political need to appease right-wing Gaullists, who viewed nuclear weapons as a way of showing the world that France was still a major power.

Even before the tests began, national and international pressure intensified on French officials to revoke their decision. A poll in August of 1995 revealed that 63 percent of French citizens opposed the tests. These negative opinions were undoubtedly influenced by the worldwide criticism of French actions in the previous month when commandos stormed, teargassed, and forcibly removed Greenpeace's *Rainbow Warrior II* from waters near the nuclear test sites. Protests against the tests broke out in Tahiti, where officials called the French government "arrogant" and "out of touch" with the rest of the world. Both houses of the Japanese parliament went on record as strongly demanding that France abrogate its decision to reopen testing. When Prime Minister Paul Keating of Australia voiced his country's strong opposition, a French diplomat stated that France could live without being liked by the Australians.

In responding to these protests, French officials emphasized that the tests posed no danger to people of the Pacific region, because Mururoa was seventy-five miles from the nearest inhabited island. Furthermore, only twenty-five hundred people lived within a three-hundred-mile radius of the test sites, compared to several million people who lived within a similar radius of the American Nevada test sites. In attempting to blunt European criticism, French prime minister Alain Juppé put forward the idea of "concerted deterrence," in which he tried to formulate a model of nuclear deterrence for the countries of the European Union. However, leaders in these countries were skeptical that the French tests were being carried out to buttress European security, because their countries were not consulted before the announce-

ment of the tests. Furthermore, they feared that France was setting a bad example for such new nuclear countries as India and others that would follow.

Ignoring criticisms, diplomatic objections, and threats of boycotts or sanctions, the French tested a twenty-kiloton nuclear device on September 5, 1995, deep beneath the Mururoa Atoll. Riots broke out in Tahiti, and by the time that the French Foreign Legion had restored order, many people had been injured, and millions of dollars in property damage had resulted. Several Pacific island nations sundered relations with France. In Berlin, twelve thousand protesters stormed a French cultural center, although the German government, hoping to continue amicable Franco-German relations, refrained from expressing disapproval such as the Chilean government's recalling its ambassador from Paris. Public protests also occurred in Japan, Australia, and the Philippines.

Although the political cost was mounting, France continued with its tests, and on October 1, 1995, French scientists detonated under the Fangataufa Atoll a gigan-

*A French tugboat (right) approaches the Greenpeace ship* Rainbow Warrior II *to prevent it from reaching the South Pacific atoll of Mururoa, where France planned to resume nuclear testing. Navy commandos stormed, teargassed, and forcibly removed the ship from waters near the nuclear test sites on July 9, 1995.* (AP/Wide World Photos)

tic nuclear bomb whose yield was estimated at 110 kilotons. Countries of the Pacific region reiterated their condemnation, but on October 27 a third, smaller nuclear device was detonated underneath the Mururoa Atoll. The furor over these tests continued as British prime minister John Major met with French leaders, during which he expressed his country's support for the French tests. (Like the French, the British were developing a new class of nuclear-armed ballistic missile submarines.)

Despite an intensive letter-writing campaign instigated by Greenpeace, and despite objections by such influential organizations as the United Nations, the French tests proceeded as planned in November and December. On December 15, ten Southeast Asian countries signed a treaty in which each country agreed not to develop or acquire nuclear weapons and also not to test, transport, or station such weapons in their territories. On January 27, 1996, France conducted the sixth nuclear test in the series and its 197th since the country acquired the atomic bomb in 1960. By this time, scientists who were critical of the tests had discovered evidence that radioactive material had leaked away from the test sites, but French officials responded that the amounts were ecologically insignificant. Boycotts of French products, especially wines, continued in some Pacific Rim countries, and a French airplane manufacturer lost a $370 million contract with Australia.

Finally, on February 22, 1996, French officials, asserting that their goals had been achieved, abandoned the last two tests, and announced the end of France's nuclear underground testing program. In September, several nuclear weapons states, including the United States, Russia, France, and the United Kingdom, signed the Comprehensive Nuclear-Test-Ban Treaty, which required the ratification of forty-four nuclear-capable states to make it legally binding. However, this treaty was dealt a serious blow when, in 1999, the U.S. Senate voted to reject the treaty because it was unverifiable and because it compromised the reliability and safety of the American nuclear arsenal. Furthermore, despite French ratification of this treaty, the French continued to modernize their nuclear arsenal.

## SIGNIFICANCE

The French nuclear tests in 1995-1996 raised a number of issues, national and international, political and legal, ethical and environmental. Under the treaty of the European Atomic Energy Community (Euratom), France had to provide data confirming that its tests met safety guidelines, but it only partially complied with this require-

ment. Nevertheless, the commission overseeing compliance concluded that the French tests did not create serious risks for technical personnel or the public.

After the tests, the French government claimed that their workers had returned the cleaned and restored atolls to civilian authorities, but independent scientists provided evidence that the test sites would be dangerously contaminated for many years. Greenpeace, drawing on data from previous tests and the work of such scientists as Jacques Cousteau, argued that every French test had produced environmental contamination. In fact, French scientists documented an increase in thyroid cancers in the populations inhabiting islands around the test sites. In the years after the tests, the French signed treaties on nuclear tests, nonproliferation, and the reduction in nuclear arms, but, like other nuclear nations, France's policies continued to exhibit inconsistencies, most notably its recognition of the horrendous evil that the use of nuclear weapons would cause, while it retained and improved its nuclear weapons.

—*Robert J. Paradowski*

## FURTHER READING

Diehl, Sarah J., and James Clay Moltz. *Nuclear Weapons and Nonproliferation.* Santa Barbara, Calif.: ABC-CLIO, 2002. Provides a historical introduction on nuclear weapons, chronology, biographies, relevant documents, and material on organizations. Excellent annotated bibliography on selected print and nonprint sources, glossary, and index.

Goldstein, Avery. *Deterrence and Security in the Twenty-First Century: China, Britain, France, and the Enduring Legacy of the Nuclear Revolution.* Stanford, Calif.: Stanford University Press, 2000. Analyzes the nuclear strategies of China, Britain, and France during the Cold War. Presents the controversial thesis that a totally denuclearized world would be more unstable than a selectively nuclearized one.

Heuser, Beatrice. *NATO, Britain, France, and the FRG: Nuclear Strategies and Forces for Europe, 1949-2000.* New York: St. Martin's Press, 1997. Uses newly declassified documents as well as interviews to trace the development of nuclear weapons and strategies in Europe by focusing on the United Kingdom, France, and Germany. Includes extensive bibliographic notes and index.

Larkin, Bruce. *Nuclear Designs: Great Britain, France, and China in the Global Governance of Nuclear Arms.* New Brunswick, N.J.: Transaction, 1996. Written in the midst of France's modernization of its nuclear forces, this book emphasizes that, in a post-Cold War world, the nuclear nations face an important choice among alternative nuclear futures. Includes glossary, bibliography, and index.

**See also:** 1971: Canadian Activists Found Greenpeace; Jan., 1973: Cousteau Society Is Founded; Oct. 16,

1980: China Conducts Atmospheric Nuclear Test; 1981: Activists Oppose Deployment of the MX Missile; Oct., 1983: Europeans Demonstrate Against Nuclear Weapons; Feb. 4, 1985: New Zealand Closes Ports to U.S. Nuclear Warships; July 10, 1985: French Agents Sink the *Rainbow Warrior*; May 11 and 13, 1998: India Conducts Nuclear Tests.

## September 6, 1995
# Ripken Breaks Gehrig's Iron Man Record

*Baltimore Orioles third baseman Cal Ripken, Jr., broke Lou Gehrig's "Iron Man" record for consecutive games played in baseball. When the game became official in the bottom of the fifth inning, fans interrupted the game and applauded his achievement for more than twenty minutes.*

**Locale:** Baltimore, Maryland
**Category:** Sports

**Key Figures**

*Cal Ripken, Jr.* (b. 1960), nineteen-time Major League Baseball all-star shortstop who played his major-league career for the Baltimore Orioles, 1981-2001

*Lou Gehrig* (1903-1941), first baseman for the New York Yankees, 1923-1939, who played 2,130 consecutive games from 1925 to 1935

*Cal Ripken, Sr.* (1935-1999), father of Cal Ripken, Jr., who served his thirty-six-year baseball career in the Baltimore Oriole system as a player, manager, coach, and scout

**Summary of Event**

Cal Ripken, Jr., was a Major League Baseball player from 1981 to 2001. He played his entire career in the majors with the Baltimore Orioles and is best known for his streak of 2,632 consecutive games. On September 5, 1995, Ripken tied Lou Gehrig's streak by playing in his 2,130th consecutive game. Before this time, it was widely believed that Gehrig's record was one of two major-league records that would never be broken. The other is the record held by Joe DiMaggio, who had at least one base hit for fifty-six consecutive games.

Gehrig had played for the New York Yankees and was known as the Iron Horse. His consecutive game streak started in 1925 and lasted until his health failed in 1939. He had symptoms of weakness and was diagnosed with amyotrophic lateral sclerosis, today often referred to as Lou Gehrig's disease. Gehrig's streak ended on

April 30. Knowing that he was dying, he gave his famous "luckiest man" speech on July 4, 1939, at Yankee Stadium. Waiving existing rules, the National Baseball Hall of Fame inducted him in 1939, but he was unable to attend the ceremony because of his disease. He died on June 2, 1941, at the age of thirty-seven.

Ripken was born on August 24, 1960, in Havre de Grace, Maryland, the oldest of three boys and a girl. From 1987 to 1988, he and his brother Billy played on the same Orioles team that Cal Ripken, Sr., managed. Cal, Jr., approached baseball with a blue-collar work ethic learned from his father. Once given the chance to be a starter in 1982, he worked every day thereafter for seventeen years until September 20, 1998, when he voluntarily decided to step down from playing to help his team avoid the distraction of the streak during the 1999 season.

Ripken viewed the streak as an approach to the game rather than a quest to break Gehrig's record. He worked and played hard every game in the major leagues and often risked the record to make a diving catch of a line drive or take a hard base-runner slide into second base as the runner tried to break up a double play. He also credited teammate Eddie Murray for teaching him how to be a major leaguer and how to play hard and win.

On September 5, when he tied Gehrig's record of 2,130 consecutively played games, Ripken's baseball magic illuminated the evening even further when he hit a home run in the bottom of the sixth inning. The Orioles won the game 8-0, and the stage was set for the record-breaking game on September 6 against the California Angels.

Mike Mussina was the starting pitcher for the Orioles. The stands were packed with 46,272 jubilant fans, including President Bill Clinton. Ripken's two children, five-year-old Rachel and two-year-old Ryan, threw out the first pitch. In the fourth inning, Ripken launched a 3-0

*Cal Ripken, Jr., waves to fans after breaking Lou Gehrig's record of 2,130 consecutive games on September 6, 1995.* (AP/Wide World Photos)

pitch from Angels pitcher Shawn Boskie over the left field fence for a home run. At 9:20 P.M., at the start of the bottom of the fifth inning, the game became official. Illuminated numbers on the B&O Warehouse in right field had been tracking the length of Cal's streak for the previous few weeks. As the game became official, the number changed from 2,130 to 2,131, and baseball had a new Iron Man.

Fireworks erupted and everyone celebrated. Cal went to his wife Kelly and his kids to hug them. Always humble, he was pushed out of the dugout eight times by teammates to receive the fans' accolades. As the applause continued, teammates Rafael Palmeiro and Bobby Bonilla told him to take a lap of the field or the game would not get restarted. Cal was reluctant to do so but was pushed into a lap of the field by teammates. During this emotional circuit, Ripken shook hands with fans, Angels players, and even the umpires. The acknowledgment was not only for the streak but also for the outstanding character he had demonstrated throughout his career. While Ripken was taking the lap, he looked up at his father in

the stands. The stern taskmaster was giving his son the thumbs-up sign to acknowledge how proud he was. The celebration interrupted the game for twenty-two minutes and fifteen seconds, and the Orioles won the game 4-2.

The game was followed by a celebration to mark the event. Teammates spoke and presented Cal with gifts. Ripken thanked his family and teammates and concluded by honoring Gehrig and their shared commitment to playing the best they could at the highest level. His teammates also presented Cal with a rock that weighed 2,131 pounds and had the number 2,131 chiseled on it. The Iron Horse's record had given way to that of the Iron Man.

## SIGNIFICANCE

When Cal Ripken, Jr., broke Lou Gehrig's record for consecutive games played, he reminded fans of the importance of fundamental life values: humility, hard work, doing your best, and showing up every day. In the era where steroid use was beginning, Ripken was a throwback to earlier generations of ballplayers who played the game hard and according to the rules. When asked about the streak, Cal once responded: "I never wanted to break Lou Gehrig's record. I never wanted to break any record. I just wanted to play baseball every day. . . . I don't want people to remember me as a guy who played in 2,131 games, but just a guy who wanted to play baseball every day."

Ripken's legacy goes beyond his consecutive-games streak. He was the first big man, at six feet, four inches, to excel at shortstop, which paved the way for other tall players at the position. He also is believed to hold the record for consecutive innings played, with 8,243. Among his other honors are American League Rookie of the Year (1982), the league's Most Valuable Player (1983, 1991, 2001), American League All-Star (annually, 1983-2001), and the game's Most Valuable Player (1991, 2001). He won Gold Gloves for fielding in 1991-1992 and finished his career with 431 home runs and 3,184 hits. He retired from baseball on October 6, 2001, and in July, 2007, he was inducted into the Baseball Hall of Fame.

*—Douglas A. Phillips*

## FURTHER READING

Beckett, James. *Nine Innings with Cal Ripken, Jr.* Dallas: Beckett, 1998. Includes chapters written by people who knew Cal Ripken: his parents, Alex Rodriguez, Earl Weaver, Harold Reynolds, and others.

Chadwick, Bruce. *The Baltimore Orioles: Memories and Memorabilia of the Lords of Baltimore*. New York: Abbeville Press, 1995. Includes stories and pictures of the Baltimore Orioles, with a section on the consecutive-games streak.

Ripken, Cal, Jr. *Ripken: Cal on Cal*. Arlington, Tex.: Summit, 1995. Ripken's life story in his own words.

Ripken, Cal, Jr., and Mike Bryan. *The Only Way I Know*. New York: Penguin Books, 1997. Authorized biography of Ripken that includes a detailed account of his career and the consecutive-games streak.

Will, George F. *Bunts: Curt Flood, Camden Yards, Pete Rose, and Other Reflections on Baseball*. New York: Scribner's Sons, 1998. Provides an account of Ripken and puts the consecutive-games streak into a larger context.

**SEE ALSO:** Apr. 1-13, 1972: Professional Baseball Players Go on Strike; Apr. 8, 1974: Aaron Breaks Ruth's Home Run Record; Oct. 2, 1974: Robinson Becomes Baseball's First African American Manager; Aug. 12, 1994-Apr. 2, 1995: Baseball Strike Forces Cancellation of the World Series; Sept. 8, 1998: McGwire Breaks Maris's Home Run Record.

## September 15, 1995
# DVD TECHNOLOGY IS ANNOUNCED

*After a period of intense competition and the emergence of divergent formats for optical disc storage capacity far greater than that of the digital compact disc, a large international consortium of technology and media companies agreed to merge their concepts and designs to create a shared, standard format for the digital video disc, also known as the digital versatile disc, or DVD.*

**LOCALE:** United States
**CATEGORIES:** Communications and media; computers and computer science; inventions; science and technology

### KEY FIGURES
*Kees A. Schouhamer Immink* (b. 1946), scientist who helped the Philips-Sony partnership perfect the CD and the DVD
*Toshitada Doi* (b. 1942), engineer who established the Sony Computer Science Lab and promoted the merger of audiovisual with data storage and retrieval technologies
*Hiroshi Ogawa* (b. 1948), scientist who helped the Philips-Sony partnership perfect the CD and the DVD
*Louis V. Gerstner, Jr.* (b. 1942), chairman and chief executive officer of IBM
*David Paul Gregg* (1923-2001), inventor of the laser optical disc
*James Russell* (b. 1931), physicist who invented the prototype of the laser-readable digital compact disc in 1965

### SUMMARY OF EVENT
Although the analog optical disc (later marketed by Pioneer as the laser disc) had been developed by David Paul Gregg in the late 1950's, and its digital counterpart by James Russell in 1965, it took well over a decade for these products to enter the consumer market: the optical disc in 1978, and the digital compact disc (CD) in 1980. The analog optical disc was designed for the playback of movies, and its entry into the consumer market was somewhat overshadowed by the popularity of videotapes, which had been introduced just two years earlier.

For many years, the dominant format for music playback had been the vinyl disk. A needle contacted grooves on a spinning disk, where an impression of the audio vibrations had been stored. With repeated play, the friction of the needle eventually caused the degradation of the audio information on the vinyl.

The use of digital compact discs for audio was an attractive alternative because there was no friction between the light beam reading the signal and the surface where the data were stored. The mechanisms and codes were perfected by scientists such as Hiroshi Ogawa at Sony Corporation and Kees A. Schouhamer Immink at Philips. Sony and Philips collaborated on these and other technologies, and both owned patents on various components. After CD players became widely available and record companies embraced the standard, audio CDs quickly replaced analog vinyl disks in popularity.

Another important application of the digital compact disc was computer data storage. The medium was much less fragile than the floppy disks in use at the time and could hold exponentially more data. The situation for video was quite different, however, because video formats had remained analog, primarily using videocassette tapes.

An additional complication was the fact that these videocassettes, although fundamentally based on the same technology, had been issued commercially in two competing and totally incompatible formats, Betamax and VHS. The Betamax format, which had been introduced by Sony in 1976, was supported by Sony, Toshiba, Pioneer, and other companies. The VHS format, introduced by JVC the same year, was supported by Matsushita, Hitachi, Mitsubishi, and others. This had resulted in an unproductive and costly international struggle for dominance of a single standard, popularly known as a "format war."

Although digital audio CDs were highly successful, almost completely supplanting analog vinyl disks by the mid-1990's, a two-hour digitized movie at full-screen resolution required too much data storage space to fit onto a compact disc, which holds much less than a single gigabyte of data. Toshitada Doi, who established the Sony Computer Science Lab, could see that the expansion of data storage and retrieval capabilities would eventually encompass video, and he worked toward that goal.

Three primary user groups were set to benefit from the new format; not just consumers in the music and computer industries—which had been using the audio and CD-ROM compact disc formats—but also the movie industry. When proposals were made to increase the capacity of digital compact discs to encompass video, many in the industry wanted to avoid repeating the videocassette format war by agreeing on a uniform standard. New alliances were formed, and old collaborations, such as the one between Sony and Philips, continued. Many of the same engineers and computer scientists who had worked to develop the CD—such as Ogawa and Immink— worked to establish the technical foundation for the next generation of mass-produced digital optical discs.

By 1995, two major groups had formed, and it appeared that a new international format war was imminent, between the MultiMedia Compact Disc (MMCD)—a product of the Philips-Sony alliance—and the Super Density Disc (SD), promoted by a consortium including Time Warner, Toshiba, Pioneer, JVC, Matsushita, Mitsubishi, Thomson, and Hitachi.

As with videocassettes in previous decades, the technologies were very similar, but the two formats were totally incompatible. Fortunately, a third consortium, made up of major computer companies, had also emerged. These companies had a significant stake in the conver-

gence of audiovisual media and data and wanted to ensure the profitability of their own contributions to the new technology.

The computer companies, including IBM, Apple, Microsoft, Compaq, and Hewlett-Packard, formed the Technical Working Group, led by Dr. Alan Bell, an expert in data storage. This group had enough technological background and economic clout to mediate among the scientists and engineers of the consumer electronics and media consortia.

Louis V. Gerstner, Jr., chairman of IBM, encouraged this mediation, and most parties were convinced that it was in everyone's best interests to agree on standards. As a compromise, the Sony-Philips group agreed to the Super Density format but contributed two important components to the standard: Immink's coding system, which was slightly less capacious but also less fragile than the competing format's code, and adaptations in the tracking mechanism. In addition, backward compatibility with the digital compact disc allowed the Sony-Philips group to continue receiving licensing fees from earlier patents.

On September 15, 1995, a press release was issued jointly by both sides that announced the agreed-upon format for the DVD (a shared acronym for both "digital video disc" and "digital versatile disc"), which was capable of holding up to 4.7 gigabytes of data. Ten companies that had contributed to the standard established the DVD Consortium.

With the involvement of the motion-picture industry, however, there was increased concern about issues of intellectual property rights. The possibility of making digital copies of full-length movies increased the risk of piracy. The Walt Disney Company, which had previously sued Sony over the ability of video recorders to tape television broadcasts, was especially concerned, and contacted Alan Bell soon after the DVD format was announced. After further negotiations and additional written agreements, copy-protection codes were added to the standard to discourage illegal copying. In May, 1997, the DVD Consortium opened its membership to more companies, changing its name to the DVD Forum. By October, 2006, its membership had expanded to include more than 220 companies.

## SIGNIFICANCE

The unprecedented level of cooperation proved both lucrative for the corporate participants and beneficial to consumers. By 2003, the rental and sale of movies on DVD exceeded the VHS-tape format, which was soon dropped by major retailers. Soon afterward, DVD authoring tools reached the consumer market and began to generate additional sales for computer companies.

The introduction of DVD led to new possibilities for archivists and librarians, who wanted to keep up with the emerging technologies and assess their viability in terms of product longevity and other factors. Congress appropriated $100 million in December, 2000, for the Library of Congress to lead a national collaborative effort in digitizing and archiving media. Engineers at the National Institute of Standards and Technology developed and published testing procedures to determine the durability of various kinds of optical discs.

By the fall of 2006, new competing extensions of digital compact disc technologies with even greater storage capacities were being developed, and new concerns arose over potential format wars. But the successes of the DVD Consortium and the Technical Working Group in 1995—a collaboration in which competing entities shared technical expertise to develop a product adhering to a mutually beneficial industry standard—have been studied as a business model for the rapidly changing but interconnected technology companies of the twenty-first century.

—*John Myers*

## FURTHER READING

Brinkley, Joel. "On New DVD Formats, the Sound of Good Things to Come." *The New York Times*, December 9, 1999. Concise overview of emerging audio-DVD formats.

Shapiro, Carl, and Hal Varian. *Information Rules: A Strategic Guide to the Network Economy*. Boston: Harvard Business School Press, 1999. Includes an analysis of the collaboration over standards which proved to be a profitable business model. Illustrated, with index and bibliography.

Taylor, Jim. *DVD Demystified*. New York: McGraw-Hill Professional, 2006. Includes sections on the history of the technology, technical summaries, information on production, and criticism of features. Illustrated, with index.

**SEE ALSO:** 1977-2000: Fiber-Optics Revolution; July 1, 1979: Sony Introduces the Walkman; 1980's-1990's: Rise of Video and Computer Games; 1982-1983: Compact Disc Players Are Introduced; 1984: Introduction of Optical Discs for Data Storage.

---

## October 16, 1995
# FARRAKHAN LEADS THE MILLION MAN MARCH

*Nation of Islam leader Louis Farrakhan organized and led a massive march of African American men in Washington, D.C., with the aim of changing public and private perceptions of African American males. The event resulted in critical discussions within the African American community and placed Farrakhan in a prominent and powerful leadership role.*

**LOCALE:** Washington, D.C.
**CATEGORIES:** Religion, theology, and ethics; social issues and reform

**KEY FIGURES**
*Louis Farrakhan* (b. 1933), leader of the Nation of Islam
*Benjamin Chavis* (b. 1948), former executive director of the National Association for the Advancement of Colored People

**SUMMARY OF EVENT**
In 1995, more than 50 percent of the individuals incarcerated in the United States were African American men, yet African Americans made up only 12 percent of the nation's population. There were more African American men unemployed and underemployed than attending college, and the numbers registered to vote were even lower. Moreover, the black and white races in the United States were more divided than unified. Feelings in the African American community were still raw after the acquittal of Los Angeles police officers who were videotaped beating black motorist Rodney King a few years earlier. The subsequent riots in Los Angeles in 1992 and the acquittal of former professional football player O. J. Simpson for the murder of his ex-wife, Nicole Brown Simpson, and her friend Ronald Goldman gave evidence of a serious racial divide in the country. In addition, popular culture was feeding negative perceptions of African Americans, particularly males, through films, television programs, and music that highlighted violence and illegal drug activity among members of this group.

Minister Louis Farrakhan, the impassioned leader of the Nation of Islam religious organization, used the unrest of African Americans and negative images of African American males specifically as an impetus to call for one million African American men to join in a march to the Lincoln Memorial in Washington, D.C., on October 16, 1995. Farrakhan called the event a holy day for African American men to reconnect with themselves, their families, one another, and the African American community. The Million Man March would encourage African American men to take their rightful place in their communities as fathers, leaders, and providers. The event, which Farrakhan organized in cooperation with the Reverend Benjamin Chavis, former executive director of the National Association for the Advancement of Colored People (NAACP), and approximately three hundred local community organizations, became the stimulus for public and private discussion of many issues related to the African American community and race relations in the United States.

The mission statement of the Million Man March required African American men to repent or atone for their "sins" against themselves and humanity. The purpose of the march was to emphasize the need for African American men to be accountable and responsible while taking primary steps toward self-sufficiency in their personal, social, political, and economic lives. The march brought together young and old, rich and poor, professionals and unemployed.

Speakers at the event included a number of popular and politically prominent African American men, among them Kweisi Mfume, former U.S. congressman from Maryland and president of the NAACP; the Reverend Jesse Jackson, founder of the Rainbow/PUSH Coalition; actor and entertainer Bill Cosby; former professional baseball player Reggie Jackson; and scholar Cornel West. Farrakhan spoke for more than two hours, during which he asked participants to recite a long pledge to engage in civic, social, political, cultural, and religious activities.

Famed poet Maya Angelou also participated in the official program, although the Million Man March was exclusively for African American men—women and

*In October, 1995, hundreds of thousands of African Americans converged on Washington, D.C., heeding the call of Nation of Islam leader Louis Farrakhan (visible on television screen) for a million men to demonstrate the commitment of black men to building strong families and communities. (AP/Wide World Photos)*

men of other races were not invited. Several women spoke at the event, but African American women in general were encouraged to participate only in supporting, background roles. It was suggested that African American women should stay home and support the men by making the day a "holy day." In addition, all African Americans who did not attend the march were asked to avoid spending any money that day, to demonstrate the economic power of African Americans as a group. Many African American women did attend the event to show their support, but others adamantly objected to the gender divide it imposed.

The organizers intended the march to be nondenominational and nonpolitical; nevertheless, debates quickly arose concerning the reception, treatment, role, and participation in the march of Christians, Jews, and others who were not adherents of the Nation of Islam, as well as homosexuals and women, who were excluded. Moreover, the participation of Farrakhan, a man known for rhetoric that was often considered sexist and racist, added to the debates surrounding the event. Before, during, and after the Million Man March, observers pointed out the need in the African American community for further discussion and action concerning the gender divide, religious differences and mutual respect, economic self-empowerment, and political and social involvement and advancement.

In regard to Farrakhan's participation, many found it difficult to separate the message from the messenger. The often politically incendiary and radical rhetoric of the Nation of Islam leader tended to separate him and others from the idealistic and positive goals of the march. Another widespread sentiment, however, was that although the controversial Farrakhan originated the idea for the march, the event's goals superseded his personality and rhetoric. Still, many condemned the march as a separatist event that served what they believed were sexist, patriarchal, and even racist motives on the part of Farrakhan.

Another controversy that followed the march concerned the numbers of people in attendance. The National Park Service originally estimated the crowd gathered in the nation's capital at 400,000, whereas the Nation of Islam's estimate was closer to 2 million. Some charged that the low "official" estimates of the size of the

---

## FARRAKHAN'S MILLION MAN SPEECH

*On October 16, 1995, Louis Farrakhan addressed his audience at the Million Man March, held in Washington, D.C. Farrakhan urged blacks to join organizations that seek to uplift the people:*

So, my beloved brothers and sisters, here's what we would like you to do. Everyone of you, my dear brothers, when you go home, here's what I want you to do. We must belong to some organization that is working for, and in the interests of, the uplift and the liberation of our people. Go back, join the NAACP if you want to, join the Urban League, join the All African People's Revolutionary Party, join us, join the Nation of Islam, join PUSH, join the Congress of Racial Equality, join SCLC, the Southern Christian Leadership Conference. But we must become a totally organized people and the only way we can do that is to become a part of some organization that is working for the uplift of our people. . . .

I know that the NAACP did not officially endorse this march. Neither did the Urban League. But, so what? So what? Many of the members are here anyway. . . . These are our brothers and we're not going to stop reaching out for them simply because we feel there was a misunderstanding. We still want to talk to our brothers because we cannot let artificial barriers divide us. . . .

No, we must continue to reach out for those that have condemned this, and make them to see that this was not evil, it was not intended for evil, it intended for good. Now, brothers, moral and spiritual renewal is a necessity. Every one of you must go back home and join some church, synagogue or temple or mosque that is teaching spiritual and moral uplift. I want you, brothers, there's no men in the church, in the mosque. The men are in the streets, and we got to get back to the houses of God.

---

crowd reflected attempts by the political establishment to minimize the event's importance. Later review of panoramic photographs of the event led to some consensus that the number was actually around 835,000. This was not the only area where there was a lack of agreement, as responses to the Million Man March varied widely within and outside the African American community.

### SIGNIFICANCE

It is believed that one result of the Million Man March was that thousands of African American men registered to vote and participated in the 1996 elections. Also, according to the National Association of Black Social Workers, adoption rates of African American children by African Americans increased after the march. Membership in national African American organizations such as the NAACP, the Southern Christian Leadership Conference, and the Nation of Islam grew significantly after the march as well. Many individuals who had been concerned about the march or even opposed to it because of the often controversial and heated rhetoric of Louis Farrakhan later saw the overall impact of the event as positive, representing a welcome renewal for African Americans.

The organization and implementation of the Million Man March demonstrated the political and social impact that one person can have on the United States and within the African American community. Farrakhan gained additional public prominence from his role in organizing the march, and his success in creating an event aimed at encouraging the empowerment, self-determination, and self-sufficiency of African American men demonstrated the Nation of Islam leader's influence and power.

The march clearly highlighted the state of race relations in the United States in the 1990's, showing the divisions that existed within the African American community as well as the division between white and African Americans. The event renewed debates surrounding questions that had been asked for years in the United States: What is the nature of the roles of African American women and African American men? Is there a composite leader for the African American community? Among African Americans, whose voices are heard most and whose are heard least? Who is responsible for racism in the United States? Will African Americans and white Americans ever truly be treated as equals?

The Million Man March demonstrated to all Americans that a large group of African American men can congregate together in a peaceful manner for a positive purpose. Although the ultimate goals of the march were not met in the decade following—given that the numbers of African American men incarcerated, unemployed, underemployed, and without housing did not decrease significantly—the event did encourage discussion around the country on the many issues that Farrakhan pro-posed to address concerning the empowerment of African Americans.

—*Khadijah O. Miller*

## FURTHER READING

Dyson, Michael Eric. "Words Unsaid: African American Women and the Million Man March." *Christian Century*, November 22, 1995, 1100. A march participant addresses the need to focus on both men and women in the African American community. Sets some distance between Farrakhan and the issues important to African Americans.

Karenga, Maulana. "The Million Man March/Day of Absence Mission Statement." *Black Scholar* 25 (Fall, 1995): 2. Mission statement for the event highlights the social, economic, and spiritual focus of the day. The author, a participant in the march, focuses on key behaviors, principles, and responsibilities of African American men.

Walton, Hanes, Jr. "Public Policy Responses to the Million Man March." *Black Scholar* 25 (Fall, 1995): 17-22. Focuses on the political and social ramifications of the march.

West, Cornel. "The Million Man March." *Dissent* 43 (Winter, 1996): 97-98. Distinguished African American scholar focuses on his own participation and input in the march. Discusses how the march spoke to the greater good of African Americans and the possibilities for African American men in a democratic U.S. society.

**SEE ALSO:** Apr. 20, 1971: U.S. Supreme Court Endorses Busing to End School Segregation; Oct. 14, 1979: Gay Rights March in Washington; Nov. 3, 1983: Jackson Becomes the First Major Black Candidate for U.S. President; Apr. 9, 1989: NOW Sponsors a March for Abortion Rights; Mar. 20, 1990: McCartney Conceives Promise Keepers.

## November 4, 1995
# RABIN IS ASSASSINATED

*The assassination of Israeli prime minister Yitzhak Rabin underscored not only the instability in the Middle East but also the political differences dividing Jews in Israel.*

**LOCALE:** Tel Aviv, Israel

**CATEGORIES:** Crime and scandal; government and politics

### KEY FIGURES

*Yitzhak Rabin* (1922-1995), prime minister of Israel, 1974-1977 and 1992-1995

*Shimon Peres* (b. 1923), Israeli Labor Party leader and prime minister of Israel, 1984-1985 and 1995-1996

*Yigal Amir* (b. 1970), Rabin's assassin

*Yasir Arafat* (1929-2004), head of the Palestine Liberation Organization

### SUMMARY OF EVENT

Yitzhak Rabin, born in Jerusalem in 1922, spent most of his life in the service of his country. Shortly after his graduation from Kadourie Agricultural School in 1941, Rabin joined the Palmach, the commando unit of the Haganah, a Jewish paramilitary defense force. This experience prepared him well for his role as chief of staff of the Israel Defense Forces during Israel's Six-Day War in 1967.

Rabin left the army in 1968 and became Israel's ambassador to the United States, serving in that capacity until March, 1973, when he returned to Israel and was elected to the Knesset, the Israeli parliament, as a Labor Party representative. In March, 1974, Israeli prime minister Golda Meir appointed Rabin minister of labor. When Meir retired in June of that year, Rabin became leader of his party and the first Israeli prime minister born in Israel. He served as prime minister until May, 1977, when he was replaced by Shimon Peres. Rabin went on to serve as defense minister from 1984 until 1990. In February, 1992, he was elected leader of the Labor Party and, in June, 1992, again became prime minister.

Rabin gained international recognition in 1993 when he took part in talks with the leader of the Palestine Liberation Organization (PLO), Yasir Arafat, that led to the Oslo Accords, in which Israel agreed to extend limited self-rule to Palestinians on the West Bank and in the Gaza Strip. Rabin's efforts in the negotiations for the

Oslo Accords resulted in his sharing the Nobel Peace Prize with Peres and Arafat in 1994. Two months before Rabin claimed that prize, he negotiated secretly with King Hussein I of Jordan and signed a peace treaty between Jordan and Israel. Israeli hard-liners viewed such efforts toward peace as intolerable concessions to Israel's enemies by a dangerous political maverick.

On the evening of Saturday, November 4, 1995, a peace rally was scheduled to be held in the huge public area outside Tel Aviv's city hall, the Kikar Malchei Yisrael, or Kings of Israel Square. Rabin was somewhat reluctant to attend the rally, fearing it would be sparsely attended, but he finally assented to joining the other Israeli dignitaries who would grace the speakers' platform, including his political rival, Shimon Peres. Rabin's fears that the rally would attract few people turned out to be groundless; attendance was conservatively estimated at more than 100,000.

Aliza Goren, who organized the rally, urged Rabin and Peres to acknowledge each other on the platform. At her urging, the two embraced before the cheering crowd and, also at her urging, joined with the crowd in singing the "Song of Peace." When the singing ended, Rabin prepared to leave the square to be driven to a scheduled reception. As he left the podium, agents of the Israel Security Agency (known as the Shabak) guarded Rabin's front and back, and two guards flanked his left and right sides. For unknown reasons, the agent walking behind Rabin fell back, leaving the prime minister vulnerable to attack. Shots rang out, but they did not sound like actual gunshots, and people in the audience shouted out that they were blanks.

The agents pushed Rabin into his waiting armored Cadillac. An agent asked him if he had been hurt, to which Rabin responded that he had been shot, saying that he had pain in his back but that it was not terrible. Those were his final words before he lapsed into an unconsciousness from which he would not awaken. Rabin was driven to Ichilov Hospital, which had not been alerted to the prime minister's imminent arrival and need for immediate urgent treatment, a questionable oversight given that the prime minister's car had a telephone in working order.

Rabin had been struck by two bullets, one of which ruptured his aorta; the other penetrated his spleen and lodged in his spine. Hospital physicians performed emergency surgery to remove his spleen, and they massaged

*Israeli prime minister Yitzhak Rabin (left) shakes hands with PLO chairman Yasir Arafat on the White House lawn at the signing of the Oslo Accords on September 13, 1993. President Bill Clinton stands behind them. Rabin was assassinated two years later.* (AP/Wide World Photos)

Rabin's heart for a full hour in a futile attempt to save him, but all their efforts failed. Rabin's death was announced on Israeli television at 11:00 P.M. on November 4, 1995.

Rabin's assassin, Yigal Amir, an Israeli political and religious extremist of Yemeni extraction, was apprehended. Before the shooting, he had been lurking in a restricted area near the stage on which Rabin appeared. It was eventually revealed that Amir, with the complicity of his brother, Hagai Amir, and a close friend, Dror Adani, had earlier planned three different attacks on Rabin but had been thwarted in their efforts. Shabak agent Avishai Raviv had heard Amir discuss ways of assassinating Rabin, but he had not taken such threats seriously and had not reported them, causing some people to speculate that the Israeli Security Agency might have been complicit in the murder.

Yigal Amir was brought to trial, where he served as his own attorney. On September 11, 1996, he was found guilty of conspiracy and of murdering the prime minister. He received a sentence of life imprisonment plus six years; this was later increased to life plus fourteen years.

### SIGNIFICANCE

The Rabin assassination immediately resulted in heightened attention to security in Israel and moved the Knesset to enact legislation forbidding the commutation of a sentence imposed on anyone who assassinates a prime minister. This legislation served to assure the public that Amir would never again be free.

Rabin's assassination emphasized that Jews, who had been fellow sufferers in many situations, were capable of turning on their fellow Jews. Extremists such as Amir believed that Rabin's efforts to bring about peace with the

PLO were destructive to the state of Israel. The assassination, therefore, highlighted not only the violence between Arabs and Israelis but also the political differences within Israel.

Ironically, at the time of Rabin's death, Israel was approaching its fiftieth anniversary as a sovereign state, and the nation's citizens had cause for optimism. Israel had established diplomatic relations with ten Arab states and had embassies in 150 other countries. The tourism industry had grown dramatically, from 1.5 million visitors in 1992 to 2.5 million by 1995, and per-capita income had increased from eight thousand dollars per year in 1985 to fifteen thousand dollars per year in 1995. Foreign investment in Israel had grown from fifty million dollars in the early 1990's to two billion dollars in 1995. Rabin was instrumental in bringing about these improvements in his country's financial stability.

—*R. Baird Shuman*

**FURTHER READING**

Karpin, Michael, and Ina Friedman. *Murder in the Name of God: The Plot to Kill Yitzhak Rabin.* New York: Henry Holt, 1998. Presents material suggesting that Rabin's assassination was the result of a plot by members of right-wing religious groups in Israel who deplored the prime minister's attempts to bring about peace between Israel and Palestine.

Kirkham, James F., Sheldon G. Levy, and William J. Crotty. *Assassination and Political Violence.* New York: Praeger, 1970. Presents a thorough theoretical analysis of the roots of assassination in societies under significant political stress. This discussion is directly applicable to the political situation that beset Israel during the 1980's and 1990's.

Morrison, David. *Lies: Israel's Secret Service and the Rabin Murder.* Hewlett, N.Y.: Gefen Books, 2000. Presents compelling evidence that Rabin's assassination was part of a well-orchestrated conspiracy involving the Shabak.

Peri, Yoram, ed. *The Assassination of Yitzhak Rabin.* Stanford, Calif.: Stanford University Press, 2000. Collection of essays by an impressive group of Hebrew scholars presents a balanced account of Rabin's murder and of the events that led up to it.

Rabin, Leah. *Rabin: Our Life and His Legacy.* New York: G. P. Putnam's Sons, 1997. Memoir by Rabin's wife presents a heartfelt account of his life as a statesman.

**SEE ALSO:** Nov. 19-21, 1977: Sadat Becomes the First Arab Leader to Visit Israel; Sept. 5-17, 1978: Camp David Accords; Dec., 1987: Palestinian Intifada Begins; Oct. 15-23, 1998: Wye River Accords; May 17, 1999: Barak Takes Charge in Israel.

---

## November 10, 1995
# NIGERIA HANGS SARO-WIWA AND OTHER RIGHTS ADVOCATES

*In violation of internationally accepted standards of due process and in the face of worldwide protest, Nigeria's military government executed prominent writer Ken Saro-Wiwa and eight other human rights activists.*

**LOCALE:** Port Harcourt, Nigeria
**CATEGORIES:** Indigenous peoples' rights; human rights; terrorism, atrocities, and war crimes

**KEY FIGURES**

*Ken Saro-Wiwa* (1941-1995), playwright, Nobel Peace Prize nominee, and environmental/human rights activist

*Sani Abacha* (1943-1998), military dictator and president of Nigeria, 1993-1998

*Brian Anderson* (b. 1943?), chairman and managing director of Shell Nigeria

**SUMMARY OF EVENT**

Ken Saro-Wiwa and the other activists who were executed with him in 1995 belonged to the Ogoni tribe, a relatively small community within Nigeria's ethnically diverse population. The Ogoni live in a 350-square-mile area of the Niger Delta, where most of Nigeria's oil is produced. The region has been identified by the United Nations as the most endangered river delta in the world. Traditionally, the Ogoni were farmers and fishermen who prospered in the region's fertile wetlands, coastal rain forest, and mangrove habitats. However, in 1958, Shell Oil, which later became the Royal Dutch/Shell Company, began oil drilling and removal operations in the region, contaminating the fragile ecosystem. Over time, the fish and crop harvests dwindled, but the oil operations continued to expand after Nigerian independence in 1960. In the years following independence,

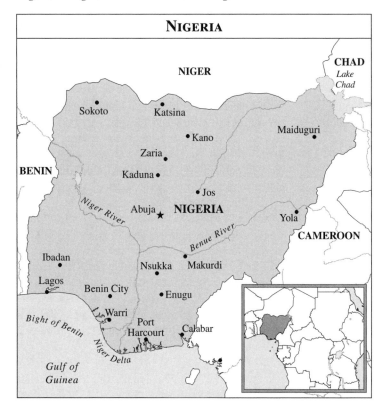

## NIGERIA

1980's. His internationally acclaimed literary works reflected his views about the complexity of postcolonial identity and the continued manipulation of ethnic tensions by politicians and their corporate allies.

In 1987, President Ibrahim Babangida enlisted Saro-Wiwa to help the government in its efforts to restore civilian rule. Saro-Wiwa became suspicious of the government's intent, however, and resigned to devote himself to the plight of the Ogoni people and the restoration of their environmental and political rights. By writing in English, he could communicate with Nigerians from other ethnic backgrounds as well as with a sympathetic international audience. When Ogoni tribal leaders formed the Movement for the Survival of the Ogoni People (MOSOP) in 1990, they appointed Saro-Wiwa as spokesman. In addition to demands for improved environmental and economic policies, the group advocated political autonomy for the Ogoni region. Group members committed themselves to the nonviolent pursuit of MOSOP's goals.

MOSOP's Ogoni Bill of Rights stated that thirty billion dollars of revenue had been taken from Ogoni lands, with no compensation for the people living there, and identified both Shell and the Nigerian government as being responsible for the situation. The ecological damage continued at an increased pace, and more than 6.4 million liters of oil were spilled in Nigeria between 1982 and 1992.

Saro-Wiwa was highly effective in his role as a spokesman, and his activities included the use of film and other media, which were distributed internationally. He began to advocate sabotage of the Shell Oil operations, although not all of the Ogoni people agreed with this policy. Saro-Wiwa also continued to be an articulate and effective critic of Nigeria's military government, and he became a target of Nigeria's military ruler, Sani Abacha, who seized power in 1993. Although his personal wealth would have permitted Saro-Wiwa to extricate himself from an increasingly dangerous situation, he remained in Nigeria as tensions escalated. He sought support from international groups such as Greenpeace, and in 1992 he went to Geneva to address the United Nations Working Group on Indigenous Populations and to the United States, where he spoke to a committee of delegates to the United Nations in New York.

young intellectuals such as Ken Saro-Wiwa became concerned that the international corporations were wielding too much power and influence.

Like several other famous Nigerian writers, such as Chinua Achebe, Saro-Wiwa was educated in English at the Government College in Umuahia. After finishing his studies at Ibadan University in 1965, he worked as a teaching assistant at the University of Nigeria at Nsukka and later lectured at Lagos University. Although Saro-Wiwa had served as a high-level administrator for the federal side during the disastrous Nigerian Civil War (1967-1970), he was committed to nonviolence. In terms of political philosophy, he argued for cultural decentralization and against the dominance of ethnic majorities.

In 1973, Saro-Wiwa left the public sector and became a successful business owner. Financially independent, he focused on his writing career and published works in many genres, including novels, short stories, poems, folklore, plays, children's books, and essays. Saro-Wiwa ridiculed Nigeria's corrupt military government and the dehumanizing effects of war in his most famous novel, *Sozaboy: A Novel in Rotten English* (1985). His satirical television soap opera *Basi and Company* ran for five years and was popular throughout the country during the

Meanwhile, conditions in Nigeria deteriorated rapidly. Shell Oil ordered Nigeria's military government to protect Shell's operations from activists, and the military conducted a brutal offensive in Ogoniland, massacring entire villages and displacing thousands of Ogoni. Saro-Wiwa was first arrested on June 21, 1993, and was imprisoned until July 22, 1993. He was then rearrested on May 22, 1994, along with fourteen others who were all accused by the government of conspiracy in the murders of several moderate Ogoni leaders who had been killed by a mob. The mob's victims included Chief Edward Kobani, who had been a deputy president of MOSOP.

After the arrests, the Rivers State Internal Security Task Force, under the command of Lieutenant Colonel Paul Okuntimo, conducted more raids in Ogoni territory and engaged in atrocities that Okuntimo described as "psychological warfare." International concern over these events mounted, and the fate of Saro-Wiwa and the other detainees was uncertain. Meanwhile, Saro-Wiwa was beaten, deprived of food, and manacled to the wall of his cell. He and his colleagues were held for eight months before they were charged.

In November, 1994, under the auspices of the Special Tribunal Edict (Offenses Relating to Civil Disturbances), the government appointed a special three-member tribunal to handle the matter. This edict permitted the death penalty for "capital offenses committed in connection with civil disturbances, as well as previously noncapital crimes including attempted murder." Because the tribunal was not part of the normal judicial system, its rulings could not be appealed; they merely required confirmation by the military rulers.

In 1995, while in prison awaiting trial, Saro-Wiwa was awarded the Goldman Environmental Prize, a prestigious award given annually to one environmental activist on each continent. On November 2, 1995, his trial began, but it was widely regarded as a farce, and two of the prosecution's witnesses later signed affidavits saying that they and several other witnesses had been bribed, claiming that they had been offered money, government jobs, and contracts from Shell. One of the presiding tribunal members was an active officer in the armed forces, and defense lawyers were often threatened or denied access to the defendants.

Saro-Wiwa and eight others were executed on November 10, 1995, despite the frantic efforts of Saro-Wiwa's son, Ken Wiwa, who lobbied Commonwealth leaders meeting in Auckland, New Zealand, and despite last-minute pleas for clemency from international leaders. The executions, which were filmed, were carried out in such a way that the deaths were prolonged; many felt that the executions were filmed for the sadistic enjoyment of the military leaders.

### SIGNIFICANCE

World reaction to the executions of Saro-Wiwa and his colleagues was almost immediate, fueled by the embarrassment of governments who had assumed that their efforts at "quiet diplomacy" with the Nigerian rulers were being taken seriously. A coalition of members of Trans-Africa, Greenpeace, labor organizations, and many other groups formed to organize an international boycott of Royal Dutch/Shell. British prime minister John Major called the hangings "judicial murder," and South African president Nelson Mandela called them "a heinous act." The World Bank canceled its support for a $100 million gas development loan to Nigeria, and many powerful

*A protester hangs himself in a mock execution from a Shell station sign on November 8, 1995, in San Francisco, in protest of the impending execution of Nigerian environmental activist Ken Saro-Wiwa, who led a campaign against Royal Dutch Shell's presence in the Niger Delta. (AP/Wide World Photos)*

countries, including the United States, withdrew their ambassadors in protest. Nigeria was eventually suspended from the Commonwealth of Nations.

The Nigerian dictatorship was nonrepentant, however; the government banned mourning for the executed prisoners and continued its repressive policies at home while conducting a public relations campaign abroad, claiming that Saro-Wiwa and the other activists were indeed guilty of murder. Royal Dutch/Shell also insisted that the allegations about its role in the deaths were false.

A year after the executions, Ken Wiwa took advantage of a U.S. law that allows aliens to bring suits in the United States for alleged violations of customary international law. In a petition to a New York court, he accused Royal Dutch/Shell of colluding with Nigeria's military government and of polluting and destroying the Ogoniland ecosystem. Shell requested that Judge Kimba Wood declare the petition illegal, but in February, 2002, the U.S. district court for the Southern District of New York held that most of the allegations were substantial enough to allow attorneys to interview the defendants, including Brian Anderson, who was managing director of the Nigerian branch of the oil company during the time of the persecutions and hangings, and to review documents in the case.

While these legal proceedings continued, Saro-Wiwa and his companions became international heroes for the global environmental movement, and foundations were established in Saro-Wiwa's name. In Nigeria, a more reasonable government assumed power and the dialogue continued, while a new generation discovered and treasured Saro-Wiwa's writings. Many people noticed that the plight of the Ogoni closely paralleled situations in other countries. "Globalization" became identified as an insidious worldwide phenomenon that threatened the well-being of indigenous peoples, environments, and local economies all over the world.

—*Alice Myers*

## FURTHER READING

McLuckie, Craig W., and Aubrey McPhail, eds. *Ken Saro-Wiwa: Writer and Political Activist*. Boulder, Colo.: Lynne Rienner, 2000. Collection of essays is an excellent resource providing diverse information about and perspectives on Saro-Wiwa and his writings. Includes comprehensive bibliography.

Maja-Pearce, Adewale. *Remembering Ken Saro-Wiwa, and Other Essays*. Surulere, Lagos, Nigeria: New Gong, 2005. Delves into the myths surrounding Saro-Wiwa and critically examines his life.

Na'Allah, Abdul-Rasheed, ed. *Ogoni's Agonies: Ken Saro-Wiwa and the Crisis in Nigeria*. Trenton, N.J.: Africa World Press, 1998. Explores Saro-Wiwa's work as an author, activist, and politician, and examines the context of that work. Includes literary criticism and political perspectives from a diverse group of prominent authors.

Ojo-Ade, Femi. *Ken Saro-Wiwa: A Bio-critical Study*. Brooklyn, N.Y.: Africana Legacy Press, 1999. Work by a Nigerian exile focuses on national politics, specifically Saro-Wiwa's part in the Nigerian Civil War. Proposes that Saro-Wiwa's former northern Nigerian federalist allies were responsible for his death.

Okome, Onookome, ed. *Before I Am Hanged: Ken Saro-Wiwa—Literature, Politics, and Dissent*. Trenton, N.J.: Africa World Press, 1999. Collection of essays interprets the sociopolitical dimensions of Saro-Wiwa's writings. Includes discussions of Nigerian nationhood, power politics, dissent, and the new political literature.

Saro-Wiwa, Ken. *A Month and a Day: A Detention Diary*. New York: Penguin Books, 1995. The diary Saro-Wiwa began during his first imprisonment, from June 21 to July 22, 1993, and revised during his second imprisonment. Although his own imprisonment is the starting point for the work, it focuses on the political, economic, and environmental abuses that led to the conflict.

_____. *Sozaboy: A Novel in Rotten English*. New York: Longman, 1994. First-person narrative of a young villager who goes to be a "sozaboy" (soldier boy) but does not understand why he is fighting. Poignant antiwar story is written in a form of speaking popular among semieducated West Africans: a beautiful mixture of Nigerian pidgin English, broken English, and formal English.

Wiwa, Ken. *In the Shadow of a Saint: A Son's Journey to Understand His Father's Legacy*. South Royalton, Vt.: Steerforth Press, 2001. Personal memoir by Saro-Wiwa's eldest son, who candidly describes his childhood and difficult relationship with his famous and controversial father as well as his efforts to save his father from execution. Also explores the conflicts among traditional Nigerian life, politics, and foreign corporate interests.

**SEE ALSO:** Jan., 1983: Nigeria Expels West African Migrant Workers; Dec. 31, 1983: Nigerian Military Topples President Shagari; May 29, 1999: Democracy Returns to Nigeria.

## November 21, 1995
# DAYTON NEGOTIATIONS PRODUCE BOSNIAN PEACE ACCORD

*More than three years after Bosnia and Herzegovina proclaimed its independence from Yugoslavia, NATO military intervention ended the bloody fighting there and set the stage for the war's negotiated settlement. Shortly thereafter, the presidents of Bosnia, Croatia, and the former Yugoslavia met near Dayton, Ohio, to work out the details of that settlement.*

**ALSO KNOWN AS:** Dayton Accords; Dayton Agreement; Dayton-Paris Agreement; Paris Protocol
**LOCALE:** Dayton, Ohio
**CATEGORY:** Diplomacy and international relations

**KEY FIGURES**
*Slobodan Milošević* (1941-2006), president of Serbia, 1989-1997, and president of Yugoslavia, 1997-2000
*Franjo Tudjman* (1922-1999), president of Croatia, 1990-1999
*Alija Izetbegović* (1925-2003), president of Bosnia and Herzegovina, 1990-1996
*Richard Holbrooke* (b. 1941), President Clinton's special envoy during the Yugoslav civil wars and chair of the Dayton Peace Conference

**SUMMARY OF EVENT**
Although the fighting in Bosnia was neither the first nor the last round of the civil wars that tore Yugoslavia apart, from the time Bosnia and Herzegovina proclaimed its independence in February, 1992, over the strenuous objection of its approximately one-third Serbian minority, the fighting there was the worst—a multicornered fight involving regular and irregular military units that sometimes pitted Croats and Bosnian Muslims against one another and sometimes allied them against the Serbs. Before the fighting ended, members of all three communities had committed war crimes so horrific that the United Nations was moved to create a permanent criminal court to try crimes arising from conflicts such as the ethnic warfare that destroyed Yugoslavia.

Particularly outrageous was the Serbian massacre of at least eight thousand unarmed civilians in the U.N.-designated "safe haven" of Srebrenica in July, 1995. Combined with the Serbian attack on Sarajevo, another supposedly safe haven, the ferociousness and arrogance of the attack on Srebrenica convinced the North Atlantic Treaty Organization (NATO) of the need for aggressive military intervention. Soon thereafter, NATO action against Serbian artillery installations and other hard tar-

gets essentially ended the fighting, and three months later the presidents of Croatia, Bosnia, and what remained of Yugoslavia gathered in Dayton, Ohio, to negotiate a durable peace. By then, the Yugoslav civil wars had claimed approximately 200,000 lives and left a million either refugees abroad or internally displaced in the former Yugoslavia.

Given the wartime dislocation of the various communities and the multinational (Croat, Serbian, and Bosnian Muslim) composition of the republic of Bosnia and Herzegovina, whose independence had been recognized by Western governments and the United Nations in 1992, the peace negotiations at Dayton were both sensitive and necessarily multifaceted. Wright-Patterson Air Force Base near Dayton was specifically chosen as the site for the conference so that the participants could be sequestered in a location where their opportunities for public posturing in the mass media would be minimal. Nonetheless, achieving agreement to the compromises necessary to settle the conflict in Bosnia and Herzegovina and establish a functioning democracy there remained extremely difficult, especially with respect to the issues of refugee resettlement and the future of the Republika Srpska, or Serb Republic.

The repatriation of those dislocated in wartime embodied the basic issue of who would eventually control local governments in the new state. The wartime flight of hundreds of thousands of Serbs, Croats, and Bosnian Muslims had left large portions of Bosnia and parts of Croatia ethnically homogeneous, or very nearly so. Guaranteeing the displaced the right to return securely to their homes meant that Serbs would be allowed to return to essentially Serb-free tracts in Croatia and that Bosnian Muslims would be permitted back into their homes in Serbian Bosnia. Consequently, both the president of Croatia, Franjo Tudjman, and Yugoslavia's president, Slobodan Milošević, strongly opposed the repatriation of displaced persons. In the end, however, international pressure prevailed, and the final text of the Dayton Accords recognized both the right of the wartime dislocated to return to their homelands and the rights of minorities throughout Bosnia.

The disposition of the question of the Serb Republic was something of a trade-off to the Serbs for consenting to these repatriation and human rights provisions. When the Serb-dominated Federal Republic of Yugoslavia began to disintegrate with the secession of Slovenia and

Croatia in June, 1991, Bosnia's Serbs read the writing on the wall. Bosnia and Herzegovina was likely to follow, and they would be under Croatian and Bosnian Muslim rule. Accordingly, on October 24, 1991, their leaders created a separate assembly for the Serbs of Bosnia and Herzegovina. Moreover, by the end of the year—as war was raging in Croatia—Bosnia's Serbs had overwhelmingly voted in favor of separating from Bosnia to become a part of Serbia and Montenegro. The following January, the rump Serb Assembly established the Republic of the Serbs in Bosnia and Herzegovina, with Radovan Karadžić as its president and Banja Luka as its capital.

One of the first acts of the internationally recognized government of Bosnia and Herzegovina following the republic's secession was to declare the Serbian referendum and resultant Serb Republic null and void. Any remaining doubts concerning the Serb Republic's legal status disappeared after the war when Milošević, representing the Bosnian Serbs in place of Karadžić (who was being sought as a war criminal), accepted Bosnia and Herzegovina's independence. Still, the reintegration of the Serb Republic into the rest of the country under a unitary structure was unthinkable. In addition, the country's predominantly Croat areas did not look forward to governance by Sarajevo, where the state's Muslim community, more than 40 percent of the population, would be in the plurality. Croats, too, had fought Bosnian Muslims during the war. Hence, instead of a unitary design, the Dayton Accords provided for the establishment of a complex federal state in Bosnia and Herzegovina composed of two federal "entities." One was to be the Serb Republic, and the other was to be a federation of the predominantly Croat or Bosnian Muslim regions.

## SIGNIFICANCE

As completed on November 21, 1995, and formally signed in Paris on December 14, the Dayton Accords committed the guarantors to a long-term process of institution building and political tutelage and to maintaining the peace necessary to establish a stable democracy in a country whose multinational communities had recently and often brutally been killing one another. The agreement's implementation thus required an unprecedented coordination of international machinery, including U.N. officials to oversee the country's transition to full self-government, personnel from the Organization for Security and Cooperation in Europe (OSCE) to ensure fair elections, and the initial deployment of approximately eighty thousand NATO peacekeeping troops.

The difficulty of their tasks became clear almost immediately. Protests in the Serb Republic frequently challenged the ability of the NATO forces to maintain order, and not infrequently they and the unarmed members of the International Police Task Force became the targets of rock-throwing, car-burning demonstrators. Refugees, fearing for their safety, refused to return to their homes. When elections were held, they most often placed in office the hard-line nationalist leaders of the country's three communities, not politicians committed to sharing power. Indeed, three years after the Dayton Accords were signed, teenage Muslim girls serving as translators for the OSCE's poll supervisors were still being taunted over the radios assigned to them by Serbs threatening to return to rape them, their mothers, and their grandmothers before torching their homes.

Nevertheless, peace slowly began to take root. It gradually became possible for NATO to scale down its presence and, approximately a decade after Dayton, to turn its peacekeeping operations over to a small, lightly armed European Union contingent. Elections continued to institutionalize the nationalist leaders of the Muslim, Croat, and Serbian communities within the country's federal assemblies; however, the battles increasingly became political fights over such matters as water rights rather than firefights employing mines, mortars, and automatic weapons.

Perhaps most significant, in the early years of the twenty-first century, refugees began to return to Bosnia and Herzegovina—a process that eventually required NATO to use force to evict from their confiscated houses the Muslim fighters from abroad who had been drawn to the country to support its Muslims during the war and had taken up residence there afterward. Still, more than a decade after Dayton, the multinational communities of Bosnia and Herzegovina remained as unintegrated into a multicultural society as the citizens of the country's capital city, Sarajevo, whose Serbian inhabitants gradually returned to live well apart from the Muslim majority.

—*Joseph R. Rudolph, Jr.*

## FURTHER READING

Biermann, Wolfgang, and Martin Vadset, eds. *U.N. Peacekeeping in Trouble: Lessons Learned from the Former Yugoslavia*. Brookfield, Vt.: Ashgate, 1998. Presents a critical analysis of the U.N. peacekeeping operations in Croatia and Bosnia during and after the Yugoslav civil wars.

Bose, Sumantra. *Bosnia After Dayton: Nationalist Partition and International Intervention*. New York: Oxford University Press, 2002. Provides a solid, scholarly discussion of the early years of state building in Bosnia and Herzegovina.

Chollet, Derek H. *The Road to the Dayton Accords: A Study of American Statecraft*. New York: Palgrave Macmillan, 2005. Offers a well-documented account of American initiatives to end the conflicts in the former Yugoslavia, from the earliest attempts to the peace accord attained in Dayton.

Innes, Michael A., ed. *Bosnian Security After Dayton: New Perspectives*. New York: Routledge, 2006. Valuable collection of essays on the efforts to build multinational governing institutions in a country recently emerged from bloody communal warfare.

Ramet, Sabrina P. *Balkan Babel: The Disintegration of Yugoslavia from the Death of Tito to the Fall of Milošević*. 4th ed. Boulder, Colo.: Westview Press, 2002. Outstanding resource for understanding the violent unraveling of Yugoslavia during the 1990's.

**SEE ALSO:** July-Nov., 1988: Ethnic Violence Erupts in Yugoslavian Provinces; June 25, 1991: Civil War Begins in Yugoslavia; Feb. 21, 1992: United Nations Authorizes Troop Deployment to the Balkans; Feb. 13, 1995: Serbs Face Charges at the International Criminal Tribunal for Yugoslavia; Jan. 14, 2000: Hague Court Convicts Bosnian Croats of 1993 Massacre.

---

## December 2, 1995
# NASA LAUNCHES THE SOLAR AND HELIOSPHERIC OBSERVATORY

*The Solar and Heliospheric Observatory, the product of a joint effort by the U.S. National Aeronautics and Space Administration and the European Space Agency, was the first spacecraft to provide uninterrupted observations of the Sun, with scientific instruments monitored by more than fifteen hundred scientists around the world.*

**ALSO KNOWN AS:** SOHO
**LOCALE:** Cape Canaveral, Florida
**CATEGORIES:** Astronomy; spaceflight and aviation; science and technology

**KEY FIGURES**
*Roger Bonnet* (b. 1938), director of science at the European Space Agency, 1983-2001
*Vicente Domingo* (fl. late twentieth century), SOHO project scientist at the European Space Agency
*Bernhard Fleck* (fl. late twentieth century), SOHO project scientist for the European Space Agency at NASA's Goddard Space Flight Center
*Michel Verdant* (fl. late twentieth century), SOHO program manager for the European Space Agency

**SUMMARY OF EVENT**
The Sun is only one of uncountable billions of stars scattered through space. It is an average star in size, temperature, and other factors. It is mostly hydrogen, and it is estimated to be 4.5 billion years old; at 860,000 miles in diameter, it would take 110 Earths lined up side by side to

span it. Life on Earth depends on the Sun's light and heat, which originate in nuclear reactions deep inside its core. As stable as it is, the Sun can affect radio communications on Earth with sunspot activities, and its plasma eruptions can cause geomagnetic storms that disrupt the communications of human-made satellites in orbit around Earth, radio communications, and power systems.

On December 2, 1995, the Solar and Heliospheric Observatory (SOHO) was launched on an Atlas II-AS rocket from Cape Canaveral, Florida. The purpose of the billion-dollar mission was to provide scientists with their first uninterrupted observations of the Sun. The SOHO spacecraft was built in Europe under the management of the European Space Agency. The twelve instruments it carried were developed by scientists in both Europe and the United States; nine were the work of European scientists, and three were created by teams led by U.S. scientists. The National Aeronautics and Space Administration (NASA) handled the launch and then took charge of SOHO's operations from Goddard Space Flight Center in Greenbelt, Maryland.

SOHO was designed to send data on the Sun back to Earth at the rate of one thousand images a day, beamed to the radio dishes of NASA's Deep Space Network around the world. In all, more than fifteen hundred scientists have been involved with monitoring the data gathered by SOHO.

The SOHO spacecraft has two parts: a service module that houses the power, communication, and navigation systems; and a payload module that contains the scientific instruments. Previous Sun-observing instrument packages had been placed on spacecraft that orbited Earth and therefore experienced data interruptions when the planet came between them and the Sun. SOHO, in contrast, moves around the Sun at the same pace the Earth does. It orbits Earth at a distance about four times that between Earth and the Moon, at a point where the gravities of the Earth and the Sun keep SOHO locked into a constant position relative to the Sun.

Because life on Earth is in many ways directly dependent on the Sun, it is important for scientists to know as much as possible about our solar system's star. The instruments aboard SOHO constantly monitor phenomena as wide-ranging as the interior heat of the Sun, its visible surface and stormy atmosphere, and the solar wind in sectors of outer space distant from the Sun, where incoming atoms from more distant stars are encountered. SOHO also sends data back to Earth on the complex flow of gases formerly hidden beneath the Sun's visible surface and on changes in the patterns of the Sun's magnetic fields.

*The Solar and Heliospheric Observatory assembled in the Spacecraft Encapsulation Facility 2 at Kennedy Space Center. Note the solar arrays stowed at the base, ready for launch.* (NASA)

Discoveries that scientists have made based on data provided by SOHO include the existence of forces that affect the solar wind in various directions and possible ways to predict the occurrence of the Sun's plasma eruptions, which react with Earth's magnetic field to affect radio communications, television and telephone signals, air and sea navigation systems, satellites in space, and power sources on Earth. Gradually, data gathered by SOHO have clarified the complexities of the seemingly constant Sun.

When SOHO was launched, the craft's expected life span was two to three years, and in June, 1998, transmissions from SOHO ceased. Engineers in Europe and the United States went to work on the problem and, after weeks of effort, were able to restore communication with the satellite. Then, however, the last gyroscope on the craft that had been working went bad. This made it hard to orient SOHO correctly, and precious fuel was wasted in attempts to get it pointed in the right direction again.

Eventually, the engineers and controllers were able to

perform the equivalent of a computer upgrade, even though the computer in question was about a million miles away. The accomplishment left SOHO performing better than it had originally, because it was able to reorient itself in a different way, no longer relying on the guide star it had needed to locate to orient itself correctly. With the new software, SOHO could be oriented through measurements of changes in the speed of its momentum wheels, devices used to provide the force necessary to position the craft. In effect, this procedure turned the entire spacecraft into a gyroscope, and SOHO became the first spacecraft to function without the original gyroscopes with which it was launched.

The procedure also fixed a related problem. One of SOHO's telescopes, used to observe phenomena such as the Sun's corona and plumes, had been experiencing problems with blurred images caused by frozen water vapor, hydrocarbon residue, and other contaminants. When SOHO was spinning out of control, the mission's ground personnel worried that the alternating heat and cold it was experiencing while spinning would harm the sensitive instrumentation on board. That did not happen; rather, the heat burned off the contaminants that had plagued the telescope, improving its sensitivity from before the loss of control by some 60 percent. When SOHO experienced additional problems in 2003, project scientists found that they could continue to receive data from the satellite by using radio dishes that were more powerful than those used previously.

Far exceeding its initial expected life span, SOHO continued operating into the early years of the twenty-first century, allowing scientists to observe some solar phenomena in more long-term fashion than they had originally hoped. One example is the information SOHO provided on sunspots, including how they behave and how their behavior affects the Sun. In 1996, soon after SOHO was launched, the Sun had relatively few sunspots. By 2000, sunspots were at their peak in terms of numbers. SOHO was able to provide more long-term data on sunspot phenomena than originally anticipated.

## SIGNIFICANCE

SOHO gave physicists their first uninterrupted look at the Sun and then went on to exceed its projected three-year life span by more than a decade. The full significance of the data gathered by SOHO may not be known for many years, until all the analyses are done and scientific papers are published that bring together the findings from scientists' examinations of the data from all twelve of its instruments. SOHO's data have provided hints of what forces lie behind the solar wind as well as information on the relationship between magnetic changes in the Sun and solar flares that affect telecommunications and power grids on Earth, so that scientists can predict these changes and preparations can be made for the problems they cause. SOHO made it possible for scientists to see what lies within the Sun through the detection and measurement of sound waves at its surface. An unanticipated extra came when SOHO sent back to Earth outstanding images of Comet Hyakutake, providing data for another field of space study.

As the product of two space agencies operating on different continents, SOHO demonstrated how cooperative space projects can turn out. When SOHO began to fail in 1998, the project staff provided a textbook study on how new programming can be uploaded into a spacecraft as far away from Earth as a million miles. More than ten years after its launch, SOHO continued to provide a window on the Sun that was expected to lead to nothing less than a revolution in solar science.

*—Paul Dellinger*

## FURTHER READING

Birney, D. Scott, Guillermo Gonzalez, and David Oesper. *Observational Astronomy*. 2d ed. New York: Cambridge University Press, 2006. Textbook provides an introduction to observational astronomy, covering telescopes, types of stars, and solar observations, including SOHO.

Fleck, Bernhard, and Zdenek Svestka, eds. *The First Results from SOHO*. New York: Springer, 1998. Presents detailed descriptions of SOHO's twelve scientific instruments as well as reports on the first results from SOHO.

Hanslmeier, Arnold, Astrid Veronig, and Mauro Messerotti, eds. *Solar Magnetic Phenomena: Proceedings of the Third Summer School and Workshop Held at the Solar Observatory Kanzelhöhe, Kärnten, Austria*. New York: Springer, 2005. Collection of documents about magnetic phenomena in the atmosphere of the Sun, including the physics of solar flares, coronal mass ejections, and high-energy solar radiation. Presents highlights from the SOHO findings.

Wimmer-Schweingruber, Robert F., ed. *Solar and Galactic Composition: A Joint SOHO/ACE Workshop*. Melville, N.Y.: American Institute of Physics, 2001. Collection of papers from a workshop that involved representatives of SOHO and the Advanced Composition Explorer. Both projects focus on the composition of the Sun and its immediate environment.

SEE ALSO: Feb., 1973-Mar., 1974: Organic Molecules Are Discovered in Comet Kohoutek; Jan. 26, 1978: International Ultraviolet Explorer Is Launched; June, 1981: Cassinelli and Associates Discover the Most Massive Star Known; Mar. 8, 1986: Space Probes Begin Examination of Comet Halley; Feb. 23, 1987: Supernova 1987A Corroborates Theories of Star Formation; Apr. 24, 1990: NASA Launches the Hubble Space Telescope; Dec. 7, 1995: Galileo Achieves Orbit Around Jupiter; Jan. 6, 1998-July 31, 1999: Lunar Prospector Mission; July 23, 1999: NASA Launches the Chandra X-Ray Observatory.

## December 7, 1995
# GALILEO ACHIEVES ORBIT AROUND JUPITER

*The Galileo spacecraft was the first to enter orbit around Jupiter. It carried a suite of instruments to investigate the giant planet's atmosphere, ring structure, moons, and radiation and plasma environments.*

**LOCALE:** Jupiter
**CATEGORIES:** Astronomy; science and technology; spaceflight and aviation

**KEY FIGURES**
*William J. O'Neil* (fl. late twentieth century), Galileo project manager at the Jet Propulsion Laboratory
*Torrence V. Johnson* (fl. late twentieth century), Galileo project scientist at the Jet Propulsion Laboratory
*Neal E. Ausman, Jr.* (fl. late twentieth century), Galileo mission director at the Jet Propulsion Laboratory
*Marcia S. Smith* (b. 1951), Galileo probe manager

**SUMMARY OF EVENT**
One of the first interplanetary missions scheduled to be launched from an American space shuttle, Galileo was approved to be an orbiter and atmospheric probe to study the Jovian system (the system of the planet Jupiter) up close and in depth. Galileo suffered a tortured developmental phase. Originally, it was meant to be propelled directly to Jupiter using a Centaur liquid-fueled upper-stage space vehicle. However, program delays and the *Challenger* space shuttle accident on January 28, 1986, forced the National Aeronautics and Space Administration (NASA) to change Galileo's trajectory, scheduling, and spacecraft structure.

Liquid-fueled boosters such as the high-performance Centaur were banned from the shuttle after the *Challenger* accident for safety reasons. This meant that Galileo would have to use lower-performance solid-fueled upper stages to escape Earth orbit, and these did not have sufficient performance to take such a large spacecraft as Galileo directly to the Jovian system. As a result, Galileo would have to first take advantage of multiple gravity assists while flying about the inner solar system. Thermal protection for certain components had to be added to the spacecraft as a result of having to spend many months close to the Sun. A sunshade was added atop the orbiter's umbrella-like high-gain antenna, a structure that was folded up at launch and would be deployed after Galileo's first gravitational boost from Earth. This particular

aspect of the spacecraft's redesign would lead to a serious problem with data transmission rates from Galileo.

The Galileo spacecraft consisted of two major parts, one maintained in stable attitude using thrusters and another that was spin-stabilized at a rotation rate of three revolutions per minute. An atmospheric probe was mounted at the base of the towering spacecraft beneath the 400-Newton main engine. Operating too far from the Sun to conveniently use solar power, Galileo was outfitted with two radioisotope thermoelectric generators filled with plutonium. Galileo's sixteen instruments, weighing 118 kilograms (260 pounds), were distributed around the spacecraft structure according to function, or in the atmospheric probe. Those mounted in the despun section included a solid-state imager, a near-infrared mapping spectrometer, an ultraviolet/extreme ultraviolet spectrometer, and a photopolarimeter/radiometer. Those mounted on the spun section included a magnetometer boom, a heavy ion counter, a plasma subsystem, an energetic particle detector, a dust detection subsystem, and a plasma wave subsystem. The 339-kilogram (747-pound) probe incorporated an atmospheric structure instrument group, a neutral mass spectrometer, a helium-abundance interferometer, a nephelometer, a net flux radiometer, and a lightning/radio-emission instrument.

Galileo was deployed from the space shuttle *Atlantis* on mission STS-34 on October 18, 1989. The spacecraft's two-stage inertial upper state sent it inward toward Venus for the first of several gravity assists. After flying by Venus on February 10, 1990, and Earth in December, 1990, and December, 1992, the spacecraft gained 11.1 kilometers (6.9 miles) per second in speed, enough to head outward toward Jupiter. These gravity assists took thirty-eight months to complete but negated the need for more than five metric tons of propellant had Galileo been sent on a simpler 2.5-year trajectory toward Jupiter.

Months after Galileo flew past Earth for the first time, in April, 1991, it was time to unfurl the spacecraft's 4.8-meter-diameter high-gain antenna. The antenna was designed to handle transmission rates as high as 134 kilobits per second, much faster than previous spacecraft imaging the outer solar system. Unfortunately, at least three of the ribs on the antenna remained stuck to a restraint attached to the thermal shield structure; despite numerous approaches to deploy the antenna, it remained only partially opened and as such unable to transmit usefully. Data would have to be transmitted at the snail's pace of 8 to 16 bits per second available through use of the low-gain antenna. With data compression techniques, the transmission rate was eventually ramped up to 160 bits per second. Obviously, that would greatly increase the time it would take to send the information contained in each image. Data had to be recorded and then played back slowly when observations were not being made.

Galileo next passed through the asteroid belt, coming close enough to a pair of asteroids to train its cameras and instruments on them. On October 29, 1991, the spacecraft passed within 1,600 kilometers (994 miles) of Gaspra, and on August 28, 1993, Galileo passed within 2,400 kilometers (1,491 miles) of Ida, discovering that it had a small moon, which was given the name Dactyl. In 1994, the spacecraft was in an advantageous position to observe the unique celestial collision of pieces of Comet Shoemaker-Levy 9 into Jupiter. Those pieces created holes in the outer atmosphere that were of the order of the size of Earth, providing temporarily a window into the lower levels of Jupiter's atmosphere.

After years of coasting along the Venus-Earth-Earth-Gravity-Assist (VEEGA) trajectory with only intermittent scientific observations, Galileo experienced a very active year in 1995. As Galileo neared the Jovian system, spacecraft controllers dealt with slipping tape within the onboard data recorder, the high-gain antenna issue, and a leaky valve in the main propulsion system. None of these problems precluded independent deployment of the atmospheric probe on July 13 or the orbital insertion maneuver of the orbiter in December coupled with the coordination of the orbiter with the probe for the probe's atmospheric plunge. The probe was spun up to ten revolutions per minute prior to its release in order to provide a stable attitude for its independent motion. Then the probe flew on its own trajectory for five months, powering up at the precise moment to begin collecting data as it descended through the upper atmosphere of Jupiter on December 7. Hitting the outer fringes at 170,000 kilometers per hour (106,000 miles per hour), the probe experienced an initial deceleration period sufficient to allow deployment of a large Dacron parachute; the probe continued to descend in the thick atmosphere for an hour before being crushed by the tremendous pressure.

Meanwhile, Galileo made its closest planned approach to Io, the innermost Galilean moon, an active volcanic body covered with various forms of sulfur and sulfur dioxide deposits emitted by the volcanoes, giving it the look of an unappetizing pizza. Galileo passed within some of the most intense radiation zones surrounding Jupiter—the reason the flyby had originally been planned to be the only time Galileo flew so close to that moon. Because of a tape recorder anomaly, data from this highly anticipated Io encounter and a set of high-resolution photographs were lost. However, Galileo did record the atmospheric probe's data. Two days later, using the low transmission rate, Galileo began the slow process of sending probe data back to Earth; when Jupiter achieved superior conjunction, data reception was interrupted for two weeks until January, 1996.

*This composite of the Jovian system includes the edge of Jupiter, with its Great Red Spot, and the planet's four largest moons, known as the Galilean satellites. From top to bottom, they are Io, Europa, Ganymede, and Callisto.* (NASA/JPL)

## SIGNIFICANCE

In early 1610, the Italian physicist, mathematician, and astronomer Galileo, using a crude, homemade telescope, became the first to observe the orbital movement of moons around Jupiter. In his honor, these four large moons are now referred to as the Galilean moons. In the twentieth century, the United States dispatched a spacecraft to Jupiter bearing the name of this great thinker.

Some of the spacecraft Galileo's major observations included determining that Io has a hundred times as much volcanic activity as Earth, providing circumstantial evidence of liquid water beneath Europa's icy surface, finding that Ganymede has a magnetic field, determining that Jupiter's ring is created from dust ejected by meteorite impacts on four small inner moons, measuring the dynamics of Jupiter's magnetosphere, and finding a liquid-saltwater layer on Europa, Ganymede, and Callisto.

Galileo's primary mission in the Jovian system concluded after two years, but the spacecraft remained in excellent condition. Several mission extensions were approved, each focusing on Europa and Io, and taking greater risks as time proceeded. Going deeper and deeper into the Jovian radiation environment, Galileo's camera eventually suffered irreparable radiation damage and was deactivated on January 17, 2002. Then, on September 21, 2003, during its thirty-fifth orbit, Galileo executed a destructive entry into Jupiter's atmosphere, thereby precluding a potential impact on and plutonium or bacteriological contamination of either Europa or Ganymede.

Galileo data and observations rewrote planetary science textbooks, answering many of the questions raised by Voyager data, and raised new questions that could only be answered by more direct observations from perhaps an orbiter around or a lander on Europa. Galileo observations led to a host of proposals for next-generation missions to investigate icy Europa and perhaps even plumb the depths of the ocean believed to be under that thick ice.

—*David G. Fisher*

## FURTHER READING

Bagenai, Fran, et al. *Jupiter: The Planet, Satellite, and Magnetosphere*. New York: Cambridge University Press, 2004. A series of papers cover all aspects of our understanding of Jupiter, including telescope observations and spacecraft data. Includes a CD with color images.

Harland, David M. *Jupiter Odyssey: The Story of NASA's Galileo Mission*. New York: Springer, 2000. Relates the entire history of the Galileo project and explains its scientific results.

Hartmann, William K. *Moons and Planets*. 5th ed. Belmont, Calif.: Brooks/Cole, 2005. Accessible textbook on planetary science for high school and college undergraduates; includes Galileo data and imagery.

SEE ALSO: Mar. 2, 1972-Jan. 22, 2003: Pioneer 10 Explores Jupiter and the Outer Planets; Aug. 20, 1977-Oct. 2, 1989: Voyagers 1 and 2 Explore the Outer Planets; Mar. 4-7, 1979: First Ring Around Jupiter Is Discovered; July 16-22, 1994: Comet Shoemaker-Levy 9 Collides with Jupiter.

## December 10, 1995
# HEANEY RECEIVES THE NOBEL PRIZE IN LITERATURE

*Following a cease-fire between the Irish Republican Army and Great Britain, the awarding of the Nobel Prize in Literature to an Irishman for the fourth time brought the world's attention to both the tensions between Northern Ireland and the Republic of Ireland and those between politics and aesthetics in poetry.*

**LOCALE:** Stockholm, Sweden
**CATEGORY:** Literature

**KEY FIGURE**
*Seamus Heaney* (b. 1939), Irish poet, critic, essayist, translator, and university professor

**SUMMARY OF EVENT**

Although each of his books of poetry earned him critical acclaim and an ever-larger audience of readers, few could have foreseen Seamus Heaney's growth from a skillful bard of provincial Irish life to a Nobel laureate who deservingly commands the attention of the world. The fourth Irishman—after William Butler Yeats, George Bernard Shaw, and Samuel Beckett—to be awarded the Nobel Prize in Literature, Heaney is a man whose subtle facility with the art of poetry has led him to make politically important aesthetic judgments.

Heaney was vacationing in Greece on October 5, 1995, when he and the world learned that he had been awarded the Nobel Prize in Literature. Citing his "works of lyrical beauty and ethical depth," the Swedish Academy, which confers the prize, also noted that Heaney's writings analyze the violence in Northern Ireland in insightful terms. Although no one who was well acquainted with his accomplishments in poetry objected to the award, some of Heaney's staunchest friends grumbled that, in hinting at the political significance of awarding the prize to an Irishman in the midst of the ongoing peace process between England and the Irish Republican Army, the Swedish Academy had called attention away from Heaney's poetic accomplishments. While the Irish prime minister John Bruton praised Heaney as a literary symbol of the peace effort, the Roman Catholic political leader John Hume noted that Heaney deserved the recognition for his poetry, not for politics. Derek Walcott, the 1992 Nobel laureate in literature, put the close connection between aesthetics and politics into perspective when, in a statement congratulating Heaney for receiving "just recognition," he called the poet "the guardian spirit of Irish poetry."

Born a Roman Catholic in predominantly Protestant Northern Ireland (Ulster) in 1939, Heaney left home to begin his advanced studies at age eleven at St. Columb's College in Londonderry. In 1957 he attended Queen's University in Belfast, where he studied the works of Ted Hughes and Robert Frost and submitted poems to the university literary magazine using the pen name Incertus. He took a position as a lecturer in English at St. Joseph's College of Education in Belfast in 1963, and in 1965 he married Marie Devlin and published *Eleven Poems*. In 1966 he published his first commercially distributed book of poems, *Death of a Naturalist*, which, in the next two years, would earn him the E. C. Gregory Award, the Cholmondeley Award, the Somerset Maugham Award, and the Geoffrey Faber Memorial Prize.

*Death of a Naturalist*, like his second book of poems, *Door into the Dark* (1969), focuses on the provincial life he knew growing up on a farm in Northern Ireland. Its use of autobiographical themes shows the influence of Ted Hughes and Robert Frost, and Heaney's lyrical use of nature imagery makes the comparison to Frost especially apt. The first poem, "Digging," in which Heaney remembers his father digging "down and down/ for the good turf," and which ends with him deciding to dig with "the squat pen" that rests between his thumb and forefinger, introduces the theme of poetry as an excavation of what lies hidden in the earth. Heaney continued to develop this theme throughout his career. Similarly, in "Personal Helicon," he compares the effort of writing poetry, which he does "to see myself, to set the darkness echoing," to looking down into a well as a child.

Beginning with "Bogland," in *Door into the Dark*, Heaney began to develop an interest in writing about the preserved bodies of people who had been ritually killed during the Iron Age that had been found in Irish peat bogs. Although "Bogland" does not develop this interest in any overtly political way, lines such as "Our unfenced country/ Is bog that keeps crusting" hint at the political directions he would use to develop this theme in later volumes. In "Tollund Man," "Bog Queen," and "Punishment," among other poems from *Wintering Out* (1972) and *North* (1975), he develops his "bog poems" by focusing on the dead people found in the boglands. He sees in these victims of the tribal practices from an earlier age a mirror for the victims of the tribal split between Protestants and Catholics. Perhaps the most remarkable of

1995

these is "Punishment," in which, contemplating a woman who was apparently killed for adultery, he writes:

> I almost love you
> but would have cast, I know,
> the stones of silence.
> I am the artful voyeur . . .
> I who have stood dumb
> when your betraying sisters
> cauled in tar,
> wept by the railings,
> who would connive
> in civilized outrage
> yet understand the exact
> and tribal, intimate revenge.

Here he makes explicit the comparison that has been growing through the bog poems: These dead bodies from the bogs are like the dead killed by the ongoing war between Irish Catholics and Irish Protestants. The bog people now seem to be demanding that Heaney speak out against such violence.

*Seamus Heaney in 1993.* (AP/Wide World Photos)

Concurrently with this new emphasis on the effects of political division, Heaney left Belfast to resettle in Dublin, in part because of threats he had received as a Catholic living in a Protestant area. Nonetheless, although the political violence tearing up Northern Ireland provided the unifying moment for the insights of *North*, he remained unconcerned with fostering political jingoism or with indicting one side or the other. His concern was with marking the costs of war, and in *North* he used not only the bog people but also images from mythology (such as in "Hercules and Antaeus") to make this vivid.

The increasing political content of Heaney's poetry, as well as its increasingly conversational tone, made the comparison to Yeats inevitable and increasingly valid. However, whereas Yeats seemed only intermittently to accept W. H. Auden's claim, in "In Memory of W. B. Yeats," that poetry changes nothing, Heaney seemed to proceed from this assumption. Looking at the shape of his career, it would be inaccurate to say that politics moved him to poetry. Rather, the aesthetic realm existed for him as a rich realm through which the world could be understood and through which truth could be found in language. However, the world that had to be understood also included the world of politics. In "Casualty," from his 1979 book *Field Work*, he contemplates the death of a friend who was killed because he violated a curfew to get a drink. "How culpable was he," the poet asks, "That last night when he broke/ Our tribe's complicity?" It is as if he is asking why his friend deserved to die. The poem offers no answers, but ends with the poet saying to the rain, "Ask me again," as if to admit the insolubility of such questions for the poet. Here as elsewhere Heaney uses his own inability to answer such questions as a way of raising them.

As Yeats turned to Irish legends for inspiration early in his career, so Heaney used the medieval Gaelic poem *Buile Suibhne* as the basis for his freely translated version, *Sweeney Astray* (1984), which Henry Hart has suggested offers Heaney another mask through which to express dissatisfaction with his own inability to face the Irish problem resolutely. Heaney returned to Sweeney as a character in "Station Island" (in *Station Island*, 1984) which imagines a Dantesque journey through hell and purgatory. In it, Heaney encounters figures from the past and from mythology who take him to task for his obeisance to masochistic, life-denying rituals.

Some of Heaney's most affecting poetry comes in *The Haw Lantern* (1987), in which he memorializes his deceased mother in a sequence of linked sonnets. In the third of this series, he remembers peeling potatoes with his mother while the rest of his family is away at Mass, an image to which he returns at the end of the poem, after she has died, to tell readers that they were "Never closer the whole rest of our lives."

Fundamentally, Heaney has an elegiac imagination. Memorializing the dead is the most dominant theme in his poetry. If his courage to face a political landscape that has given him so much to elegize has set him apart, it has not removed any of the power of his elegies.

## SIGNIFICANCE

If Heaney had been less well known before he won the Nobel Prize in Literature, the impact of the award certainly would have been more dramatic. As it was, the Nobel Committee chose to recognize one of the most widely appreciated poets working in the English language. Therefore, although the prize had the effect of commanding world attention to the literary shores of Ireland for a few weeks, the subtle effects of an increased attention to the poetry of Heaney—along with greater sales of his work and more invitations for the poet to visit colleges and universities—developed only slowly.

In his Nobel lecture, titled "Crediting Poetry," delivered a few days before the awards ceremony held on December 10, 1995, Heaney did not hesitate to link his award with the need for peace in Ireland. He told the story of a minibus carrying laborers that was stopped by armed guerrillas who demanded that the Catholics in the group step forward, presumably to be killed. Heaney focused his story on the protective gesture of one worker who, with a squeeze of the hand, assured the only Catholic in the group that he did not have to step forward. The man did anyway and he, rather than his Protestant fellows, was the only person saved from the ensuing slaughter. Poetry, Heaney said, "knows that the massacre will happen again," but it also memorializes "the squeeze of the hand," the sympathy between human beings.

Heaney freely embraced the comparison between himself and Yeats that much of the world had already made. Heaney noted that by the end of his life Yeats claimed that Ireland had changed phenomenally, that it was not the "dead Ireland of my youth, but an Ireland/ The poets have imagined." Similarly, the Ireland that Heaney inhabits is not the Ireland he was born into, but one that his Irish coworkers have helped to imagine. That Ireland remains a place where roadside slaughters may still happen

### BOOKS OF POETRY BY SEAMUS HEANEY, 1966-2006

| Published | Title |
|---|---|
| 1966 | *Death of a Naturalist* |
| 1969 | *Door into the Dark* |
| 1972 | *Wintering Out* |
| 1975 | *North* |
| 1975 | *Stations* |
| 1979 | *Field Work* |
| 1980 | *Poems, 1965-1975* |
| 1984 | *Sweeney Astray: A Version from the Irish* (revised as *Sweeney's Flight*, 1992) |
| 1984 | *Station Island* |
| 1987 | *The Haw Lantern* |
| 1990 | *New Selected Poems, 1966-1987* |
| 1991 | *Seeing Things* |
| 1996 | *The Spirit Level* |
| 1998 | *Opened Ground: Selected Poems, 1966-1996* |
| 1998 | *Audenesque* |
| 1999 | *The Light of the Leaves* |
| 2001 | *Electric Light* |
| 2006 | *District and Circle* |

underscores the need for a poetry that can be hard and retributive but, on the other hand, not so hard that it forgets the importance of trust.

In a time of violence not only in Belfast and Dublin but also, Heaney says, in Israel, Bosnia, and Rwanda, there is a tendency to discredit not only human nature but also the aestheticization of the work of art. Nonetheless, by crediting the inevitability of hope and compassion, poetry can keep alive the spirit that inspires, for example, the downfall of the Iron Curtain in Europe and the beginning of reconciliation between African and Afrikaner in South Africa. Poetry has the power to persuade the vulnerable part of ourselves that tries to gather lasting values that it is right, despite the evidence of wrongness all around.

It is surely coincidental that Heaney received the Nobel Prize as his collection of essays *The Redress of Poetry* (1995) was nearing publication, but that work makes at greater length the argument he made expressively in his Nobel lecture. Writing in a time when English literature is often attacked by those who have lived in countries that have known the sharp edge of British bayonets, Heaney chooses not to dismiss British literature monolithically but to praise it selectively. Poetry, he argues, has the power to redress the profound spiritual imbalances of its age, a power lost somewhat when it enters the political realm as a combatant.

By the time Heaney won the Nobel Prize in Literature, criticism that destabilized the certainties of literature and that looked at the political cost of spiritual ideals had come to define what was considered to be critical sophistication. By giving Heaney a worldwide audience to express a more idealistic view, the Swedish Academy allowed him to broadcast a message of hope and healing to the readers of the world.

—*Thomas Cassidy*

## FURTHER READING

Allen, Michael, ed. *Seamus Heaney: New Casebooks*. New York: St. Martin's Press, 1997. Collection of essays is designed largely for those who are interested in understanding the place of Heaney's work as regarded from a variety of late twentieth century critical views.

Burris, Sidney. *The Poetry of Resistance: Seamus Heaney and the Pastoral Tradition*. Athens: Ohio University Press, 1990. Attempts to resolve the apparent contradiction between Heaney's predominant orientation toward nature in his writing and his growing social concerns as a poet. Argues that the tradition of nature writing into which Heaney falls is one of outward concern with pastoral themes but an inward concern with many social and philosophical ideas.

Durkan, Michael J., and Rand Brandes, comps. *Seamus Heaney: A Reference Guide*. New York: G. K. Hall, 1996. Extensive bibliography gathers together information on numerous secondary works about Heaney.

Garratt, Robert, ed. *Critical Essays on Seamus Heaney*. New York: G. K. Hall, 1995. Collection of essays focuses primarily on Heaney's place within the sweep of Irish literature. Contributors consider his work from remarkably diverse viewpoints.

Hart, Henry. *Seamus Heaney: Poet of Contrary Progressions*. Syracuse, N.Y.: Syracuse University Press, 1992. Extensive, well-informed study of Heaney's poetry examines Heaney's development as a poet, focusing not only on his position within Ireland's literary history but also on how his reactions to it and to Ireland's political history have shaped his work.

Heaney, Seamus. *The Redress of Poetry*. New York: Farrar, Straus and Giroux, 1995. Collection of essays based on lectures Heaney delivered as a professor of poetry at Oxford gives a full airing to his belief in the power of poetry to provide a spiritual balance to hostile social forces. Includes essays on Oscar Wilde, Dylan Thomas, Yeats, and Christopher Marlowe.

_____. *Selected Poems: 1966-1987*. New York: Farrar, Straus and Giroux, 1991. Probably the best collection of Heaney's poems to introduce a reader to his work. Includes an extensive selection from Heaney's most important works of poetry and a brief sampling of prose poems from his 1975 pamphlet, *Stations*.

O'Brien, Eugene. *Seamus Heaney: Searches for Answers*. Sterling, Va.: Pluto Press, 2003. Examines the evolution of the themes found in all of Heaney's writings over the course of his career, including his prose works and translations as well as his poetry. Includes bibliographic references.

Tyler, Meg. *A Singing Contest: Conventions of Sound in the Poetry of Seamus Heaney*. New York: Routledge, 2005. Presents close readings of selected Heaney poems, with an emphasis on structural analysis of diction, meter, and form.

SEE ALSO: Dec. 10, 1978: Singer Is Awarded the Nobel Prize in Literature; Dec. 10, 1986: Soyinka Receives the Nobel Prize in Literature; Dec. 10, 1988: Mahfouz Receives the Nobel Prize in Literature; Dec. 10, 1991: Gordimer Receives the Nobel Prize in Literature; Dec. 10, 1994: Ōe Receives the Nobel Prize in Literature; Dec. 10, 1996: Szymborska Receives the Nobel Prize in Literature.

# 1996
# HOPES FOR DEMOCRACY IN BANGLADESH RISE

*Sheikh Hasina's Awami League party took over the beleaguered nation from Nationalist Party leadership. Despite instability following Hasina's tenure that continued long after her rule, her victorious 1996 election is regarded as one of the most important in the nation's history.*

**LOCALE:** Bangladesh
**CATEGORY:** Government and politics

## KEY FIGURES

*Sheikh Hasina* (b. 1947), prime minister of
    Bangladesh, 1996-2001
*Mujibur Rahman* (1920-1975), president of
    Bangladesh, 1972 and 1975, and prime minister,
    1972-1975
*Ziaur Rahman* (1936-1981), president of Bangladesh,
    1977-1981
*Abdus Sattar* (1906-1985), president of Bangladesh,
    1981-1982, who was deposed by Ershad
*Hossain Mohammad Ershad* (b. 1930), president of
    Bangladesh, 1983-1990
*Begum Khaleda Zia* (b. 1945), prime minister of
    Bangladesh, 1991-1996 and 2001-2006

## SUMMARY OF EVENT

Democracy in Bangladesh was not on firm footing following the country's liberation from Pakistan in 1971. However, movements led by the Bangladeshi people reshaped the nation's history and resisted political instability. Sheikh Mujibur Rahman (popularly known as Mujib), Bangladesh's founding leader, was at the helm in the years immediately following independence, but his assassination in 1975 threw the nation into uncertainty. It was not until two decades after his death that Bangladesh elected a stable government, this time led by Mujib's eldest daughter, Sheikh Hasina.

The 1971 Liberation War saw the rise of Mujib as the nation's new doyen of freedom and liberty. He was installed as the nation's first president and promised to guide the nation from the tumultuous years as a territory of Pakistan. Mujib's biggest contribution was the establishment of the Awami League party, which won an overwhelming majority in the Pakistan elections of 1970. The party's concentration in then East Pakistan and its securing of 167 of 169 seats in the National Assembly led to Mujib's elevation as the liberator of Bengali people in the region. The following year, East Pakistan became

independent and was renamed Bangladesh; thus a new Muslim nation with a unique Bengali ethnic group emerged. The demands of the six-point movement, which sought independence from West Pakistan, was seen as a guiding document by Mujib and served as a framework for Bangladesh to formalize the nation's constitution.

The years immediately following independence were anything but hope-filled or progressive. Severe financial losses following the war left Bangladesh as one of the most impoverished nations in the world. In one 1972 United Nations estimate, the national per-capita income was pegged at eighty-seven U.S. dollars, one of the lowest in the world. In 1974, as a result of drought and refusal of international food aid by Western nations, Bangladesh suffered a famine that wiped out more than twenty-six thousand people by official Bangladesh government estimates. In 1975, with the assassination of Mujib, the nation succumbed to instability and depression.

In 1977, General Ziaur Rahman emerged as the nation's president. Ziaur Rahman was intimately associated with Bangladesh's independence. As an army leader, he was Mujib's chief of army staff during the nation's formative years. His tenure as president, which lasted until 1981, witnessed improvements in the nation's economic and regional cooperation. His efforts to improve the police force and restore security to this once-troubled nation were some of his greatest contributions. In 1981, an army coup assassinated Ziaur Rahman, throwing Bangladesh into yet another period of instability. Abdus Sattar stepped in as acting president and was later elected, but another coup, conducted by Army Chief of Staff Hossain Mohammad Ershad, removed him from power. For the next nine years, the nation was put under martial law. With amendments made to the constitution, unprecedented power was given to the martial law rulers, making those years some of the most anxious in the nation's history.

With Ershad's resignation in 1990, fresh elections were called in 1991 that witnessed the emergence of Begum Khaleda Zia, widow of slain Bangladeshi president Ziaur Rahman, as the nation's first female prime minister. Zia's Bangladesh Nationalist Party (BNP) was also the arch-opponent of the Awami League party, now led by Mujibur Rahman's eldest daughter, Sheikh Hasina.

Zia's leadership lasted one complete term, during which her administration changed the national constitution to convert Bangladesh into a parliamentary democ-

*Bangladeshi women march in Dhaka during a general strike called in October, 1995, to bring down the government of Prime Minister Begum Khaleda Zia.* (AP/Wide World Photos)

racy. This gave the prime minister the absolute power in national decision making. Instability emerged toward the end of her term. In the first of the two 1996 elections, there was discordance among the BNP, and accusations of election rigging were made by the Awami League. Zia claimed a landslide victory. However, within a few months, another election was called, and Sheikh Hasina was elected. To prevent any civil unrest, more than forty thousand armed soldiers and more than a quarter million police personnel manned the streets of the nation, with maximum security in Dhaka and Chittagong, the largest cities. The 1996 elections were some of the most successful in terms of voter turnout—at 74 percent. Thus, 1996 witnessed the change of power between two administrations, and for the first time since Mujib's death in 1975 the Awami League assumed leadership.

With Sheikh Hasina as prime minister, Bangladesh witnessed unprecedented growth. For the first time, a national political coalition emerged. Because Hasina's Awami League barely secured a majority with 37 percent

of the votes, Ershad's Jatiya Party, winning 32 seats from the northern regions, supported Hasina's plans to form a government. Ershad's encouragement, together with Mujib's legacy, enabled Hasina to promote peace and security in the region. Her resolution of water disputes with India and her negotiating agreements with minority tribal groups are some of the key highlights of her administration. Her tenure lasted until the close of the century, and the rivalry between the BNP and the Awami League only continued with more vigor and determination.

## SIGNIFICANCE

The dawn of the twenty-first century witnessed the continuation of changes in the power structure of Bangladesh. The 2001 elections resulted in Begum Khaleda Zia's assuming a second term as prime minister, but this time with a four-party coalition government. The 1996 caretaker clause in the constitution allowing for the formation of an interim government during civil unrest was used several times in the years following. Since 1972, the constitution has been amended more than fourteen times, creating a volatile government structure. In 2007, the nation plunged into its worst-ever civil unrest with BNP and Awami League party workers clashing in the streets of Dhaka and other cities, bringing the nation into a state of emergency. The army calmed the crisis, but the nation was still under a caretaker government.

—*Aswin Subanthore*

## FURTHER READING

Ahameda, Sirajuddina, and Sirajuddin Ahmed. *Sheikh Hasina, Prime Minister of Bangladesh*. New Delhi: UBS, 1998. Documents Bangladesh's formative years between 1975 and 1998 and Sheikh Hasina's emergence in 1996.

Chowdhury, Ghulam A. *Politics of Bangladesh and the Role of Awami League*. Calcutta, India: Ratna Prakashan, 1999. Examines Sheikh Mujibur Rahman's Awami League and its role in the nation's political history.

Umar, Badruddin. *The Emergence of Bangladesh: Class Struggles in East Pakistan, 1947-1958*. New York: Oxford University Press, 2004. Documents early movements following India's independence up to the emergence of East Pakistan.

**SEE ALSO:** Mar. 26-Dec. 16, 1971: Bangladesh Secedes from Pakistan; 1972-1973: Worldwide Droughts Bring Famine.

*1996*

## January-May, 1996
# MENINGITIS OUTBREAK PROVES DEADLY IN WEST AFRICA

*The largest meningococcal epidemic to date struck sub-Saharan Africa, affecting hundreds of thousands and killing tens of thousands. Local governments with the help of international aid organizations attempted to contain the epidemic, while preparing for future outbreaks.*

**LOCALE:** Meningitis Belt, from Senegal to Ethiopia
**CATEGORY:** Health and medicine

## KEY FIGURES

*Gaspard Vieusseux* (1746-1814), Swiss physician
*Anton Weichselbaum* (1845-1920), Austrian pathologist and bacteriologist
*Léon Lapeyssonnie* (1915-2001), French physician, teacher, and scientist

## SUMMARY OF EVENT

Meningitis, or cerebrospinal meningitis (CSM), is an infection of the membranes that cover both the brain and spinal cord. Several bacteria cause CSM, but only *Neisseria meningitidis* (*N. meningitidis*, also known as meningococcus) gives rise to widespread epidemics. In the spring of 1805, Gaspard Vieusseux described the first meningococcal outbreak in Geneva, Switzerland. Meningococcal disease occurs worldwide, but Africa has been the continent most affected by recurrent, severe epidemics of meningitis.

Since the early twentieth century, numerous meningococcal epidemics have devastated sub-Saharan Africa

and have recurred in a specific geographic location—a semiarid savanna between the fourth and sixteenth degrees north latitude. The area is characterized by minimal rainfall and by the harmattan—a dry, dusty wind originating in the Sahara. In 1963, Léon Lapeyssonnie appropriately named the area the African "Meningitis Belt." The largest recorded meningitis outbreak struck this region in 1996-1997. It killed tens of thousands of people and affected hundreds of thousands of others.

Anton Weichselbaum cultured the meningococcus in 1887. Since then, twelve serogroups have been identified, of which A, B, C, and W135 have caused outbreaks of epidemic CSM. Characterization of the 1996-1997 bacterium has shown that *N. meningitidis* serogroup A clonal subgroup III-1 was at the origin of Africa's largest epidemic. This strain first surfaced in Nepal in 1983-1984. It made its appearance again in India and Pakistan in 1985 and caused an epidemic during the 1987 pilgrimage to Mecca; returning pilgrims likely brought the strain to Africa.

In the two years preceding the 1996 epidemic, large meningococcal outbreaks occurred in Niger. In October of 1995, Nigeria saw a rise in meningococcal disease, and in the subsequent month the town of Jibia reached epidemic threshold, reporting more than 15 cases per 100,000 inhabitants during two consecutive weeks.

Sahelian epidemics typically occur during the dry season, which begins in December and continues through June, and come to an abrupt end at the start of the rain season. True to this trend, the 1996 epidemic began in January of that year. CSM cases were on the rise in early February and peaked between mid-March and mid-April when temperatures soared to 42 degrees Celsius (about 107 degrees Fahrenheit), and relative humidity dropped to 10 percent. The disease struck the poor, who lived in overcrowded, poorly ventilated housing. The population most affected comprised children from five to fifteen years of age, but the disease did not spare other age groups. Mortality was high: 22 percent of those affected died during the first ten weeks of the epidemic, about 15 percent during the second ten weeks, and close to 5 percent toward the end of the epidemic. Hearing loss, paralysis, mental retardation, and loss of limbs occurred in probably 10 to 20 percent of the survivors. In 1996, nearly 95 percent of all cases and fatalities occurred in Mali, Burkina Faso, Niger, and Nigeria.

The countries most affected by the epidemic organized a massive response with the help of the World Health Organization (WHO), the United Nations Children's Fund (UNICEF), Doctors Without Borders, and the International Federation of Red Cross and Red Crescent Societies. The first treatment centers opened in early March. They were operated by minimally trained health care personnel and were commonly located at the outskirts of villages. The constructions were simple, and patients frequently received treatment while lying on bare floors. Only health centers in large cities had access to skilled nursing care, and there was a paucity of physicians.

The treatment of choice during West African epidemics has been the antimicrobial oily chloramphenicol. A single injection of the drug effectively treats the disease. Even though international aid organizations donated vast amounts of oily chloramphenicol during the 1996 outbreak, not enough was available, and many patients received ampicillin or penicillin, antibiotics that require frequent dosing over several days.

A massive immunization effort was launched in mid-March. After a minimal amount of training, health care workers were sent from village to village on horseback, bicycle, or motorcycle. Because of a limited supply of needles and syringes, vaccinators had to resort to the use of jet injectors. Incorrect use of the jet injector may also have led to the transmission of hepatitis and HIV between individuals. The impact of treatment and mass immunization became apparent by the second half of April, as fewer cases and fatalities were reported. The rain season started in early May and by the beginning of June, the 1996 outbreak ended.

The large-scale immunization efforts of 1996—Nigeria alone vaccinated 13.4 million people—had led to global depletion of meningococcal vaccine. It was feared that the epidemic would resurge in 1997, and this caused concern about the timely availability of sufficient quantities of vaccines and antibiotics. Under the auspices of the WHO, sixteen African nations met in October of 1996 in Ouagadougou, Burkina Faso, to discuss their anticipated needs. As a result of this meeting, the International Coordinating Group on Vaccine Provision for Epidemic Meningitis Control (ICG) was formed in January of 1997. The group's primary mission was to assess the needs of affected countries and to gather and distribute necessary supplies.

As anticipated, the epidemic resurged in 1997. With the help of the ICG, there was timely delivery of vaccines, antibiotics, and so-called autodestruct injection materials. In 1997, no cases were reported in Nigeria, but the disease was rampant in Burkina Faso, Ghana, and Mali. Eritrea, Gambia, Mauritania, and Senegal saw no cases of CSM in 1996 but noted the presence of the disease in their countries the following year. The total number of cases reported to the WHO in 1996 reached 152,693 and included 16,213 deaths; in 1997, 60,861 people fell ill and 6,027 died. There was likely substantial underreporting of cases. Some patients succumbed to the disease before reaching a treatment center; others were never taken to health centers out of fear or ignorance. Health officials discovered graves where people had secretly buried their dead. The true number of affected and killed people can therefore only be estimated.

## SIGNIFICANCE

In the early years of the twenty-first century, meningococcal disease remained a significant public health problem in West Africa. A surveillance system for early detection of burgeoning epidemics had been put in place, however. Countries within the Meningitis Belt began to report their cases to the WHO weekly during the high-risk season and every other week during the remainder of the year. The enhanced epidemic surveillance system identified the emerging meningococcal serotypes and monitored the development of antibiotic resistance. Meningococcal polysaccharide vaccines have proven effective against *N. meningitidis* A and C. They do not provoke a protective immune response in children under the age of two, and the protection in older children lasts approximately three to five years. Mass immunization thus came to be used only when evidence arises of an impending epidemic.

The solution to recurring meningococcal epidemics in West Africa lies in preventive immunization of the at-risk population with a meningococcal vaccine that provides long-lasting protection in all age groups. Conjugate meningococcal vaccines have this ability. The Meningitis Vaccine Program (MVP), supported by the Bill and Melinda Gates Foundation, anticipates having a group A conjugate vaccine available for the Meningitis Belt by 2009. Mass vaccination of the high-risk population may soon bring an end to the feared sub-Saharan epidemics of meningococcal meningitis.

*—Elisabeth Faase*

### FURTHER READING

"Enhanced Surveillance of Epidemic Meningococcal Meningitis in Africa: A Three-Year Experience." *Weekly Epidemiological Record* (September, 2005): 313-320. Describes the efforts of the ICG for early detection and containment of emerging meningococcal epidemics.

Greenwood, Brian."100 Years of Epidemic Meningitis in West Africa: Has Anything Changed?" *Tropical Medicine and International Health* (June, 2006): 773-780. Contains detailed information about past African epidemics, the different meningococcal serotypes, and the immunization approach for the management of epidemic meningitis.

Mohammed, Idris. "A Severe Epidemic of Meningo-coccal Meningitis in Nigeria, 1996." *Transactions of the Royal Society of Tropical Medicine and Hygiene* (May/June, 2000): 265-270. Describes in great detail the extent of the 1996 epidemic in Nigeria and the efforts of both the Nigerian government and international aid organizations to contain it.

Molesworth, Anna. "Where Is the Meningitis Belt? Defining an Area at Risk of Epidemic Meningitis in Africa." *Transactions of the Royal Society of Tropical Medicine and Hygiene* (May/June, 2002): 242-249. Documents the southward extension of the Meningitis Belt initially described by Lapeyssonnie.

"Response to the Epidemic Meningitis in Africa, 1997." *Weekly Epidemiologic Record* (October, 1997): 313-318. Discusses the response of the ICG during the second year of the epidemic and the results of its interventions.

Tikhomirov, Eugene. "Meningococcal Disease: Public Health Burden and Control." *World Health Statistics Quarterly* (May, 1997): 170-177. Gives the number of meningococcal cases and deaths for each affected sub-Saharan country during the 1996-1997 epidemic.

**SEE ALSO:** Sept. 8, 1976: Ebola Epidemic Kills First of Many in Africa; Mar. 20, 1996: Britain Announces Human Cases of Mad Cow Disease; Dec. 16, 1997: First Cases of Avian Flu Are Reported; 1998: AIDS Devastates Africa.

1996

---

## January 3, 1996
# U.S. CONGRESS REFORMS LAW REGULATING TELECOMMUNICATIONS

*The Telecommunications Act of 1996, the first overhaul of U.S. communications law in sixty years, was overdue in the face of new technologies, but even so, it may have been implemented too soon to account fully for the technological innovations that swept the globe within the next decade.*

**ALSO KNOWN AS:** Telecommunications Act of 1996; Public Law 104-104; U.S. Statutes at Large 110 Stat. 56

**LOCALE:** Washington, D.C.

**CATEGORIES:** Communications and media; laws, acts, and legal history; radio and television

### KEY FIGURES

*Bill Clinton* (b. 1946), president of the United States, 1993-2001

*Newt Gingrich* (b. 1943), Speaker of the U.S. House of Representatives, 1995-1999

### SUMMARY OF EVENT

Because the United States left its telecommunications development to private industry, rather than nationalizing it as European countries had done, creating a balance between market forces and public interest has always been challenging. This conflict became apparent in the nineteenth century with the establishment of nationwide telephone service. At the end of the century, the Bell Company's monopoly-producing patents lapsed, just as phone service was rapidly expanding throughout the country. The competition between Bell and some six thousand new independent telephone companies served as a catalyst for expansion but also threatened the effectiveness of the system. People using different telephone companies frequently could not call each other, because Bell, wanting to maintain its monopoly, refused to allow independents to interconnect with its lines. Rural and poor areas were not getting service because they did not have the potential to generate enough profits to cover the large capital investment required to bring lines to them.

In the first decades of the twentieth century, business and government leaders concluded that it was beneficial for one company (Bell, by then part of a larger corporation that included the American Telephone and Telegraph Company, or AT&T) to monopolize the telephone business in order to achieve complete interconnection and affordable service. With the Willis-Graham Act of 1921, the U.S. government granted AT&T exemption from antitrust laws as long as it agreed to government regulation. Federal regulation of telecommunications was legislated in the 1934 Communications Act, which set up the Federal Communications Commission (FCC), an independent government agency that oversees all wired and broadcast communications. AT&T held on to its monopoly over U.S. telephone service for decades, until a 1984 court-ordered divestiture created the "Baby Bells," or regional Bell Operating Companies, and opened long-distance service to competition.

By the 1990's, telecommunications corporations were lobbying hard for relaxation of government regulation. President Bill Clinton was initially skeptical of deregulation, but he was captivated with the idea of using market competition to hasten the deployment of technological advances, particularly connecting all American classrooms to the Internet. Clinton worked with deregulation promoters in order to see some of his "information superhighway" goals achieved. The Telecommunications Act of 1996 was thus created with the stated intention of letting competition, rather than regulated monopoly, drive U.S. telecommunications systems. The two-hundred-page bill was put before the U.S. Congress in January, where it was passed with little debate by an overwhelming bipartisan majority.

The act encompassed a wide range of communications industries, including radio and television broadcasting, cable television, wireless systems, local and long-distance telephone, and the Internet. In most cases, the act attempted to allow competition, rather than regulation, to rule the industry. In order to create the greatest amount of competition, the act provided for easy entry into industry networks for new companies by ensuring that networks remain open to one another. Industry leaders, pleased with the act, pledged to compete fairly and to

open their networks to competitors as the government relaxed its regulations. The act also opened the way for mergers between companies in different areas of telecommunications, which had been prohibited prior to the 1996 act. The limits on how much television and radio air could be owned by one corporate entity were greatly extended.

To observers in 1996, the act appeared be in the public interest. Its promoters promised that it would result in consumer savings of as much as $550 billion in telephone and cable television charges, create millions of new jobs, and vastly increase the nation's gross national product. They predicted that the bill would prevent concentrations of ownership of television and radio stations, thus leading to more diversity in radio and television programming and offering consumers more choices in their cable, Internet, and local telephone service providers. The act was lauded for facilitating a new era of readily accessible education opportunities through the Internet. To ensure fairness, the act included a "universal service" clause that provided for substantial subsidies to enable the extension of telecommunications systems to rural and poor communities as well as the connection of all schools and libraries to the Internet within five years.

The only major controversy at the time arose from the act's "decency" section, an attempt to prevent the transmission of pornography and offensive speech over the Internet and to provide a filter that parents could use to protect their children. That section of the bill was overturned as a violation of First Amendment rights.

After the Telecommunications Act went into effect, dominant companies in the industry took advantage of deregulation and joined in a fevered rush to merge with or acquire their competition—despite their pledges to compete fairly. The Democrats in Congress took steps to try to halt the growth of industry conglomerates, but Republicans had gained control of Congress in 1996. Under House Speaker Newt Gingrich, reforms to the 1996 act were geared more toward deregulation than toward slowing down consolidation trends. In 2003, the FCC further deregulated media ownership laws.

## SIGNIFICANCE

Within five years, it was clear that the 1996 act had drastically shrunk competition in telecommunications. Radio was transformed dramatically and quickly. By 2005, two companies, Clear Channel Communications and Viacom (owner of Infinity Broadcasting) owned from one-third to one-half of the entire radio industry, and their constant efforts to economize significantly decreased the number of local stations. This resulted in the loss of tens of thousands of jobs in radio, a widespread loss of local news programs, and a dramatic decrease in the diversity of radio programming. On the other hand, before the mergers radio had been failing financially; after 1996, it became quite profitable. In television, deregulation allowed broadcast networks to purchase cable networks and to own more stations. Ten years after the Telecommunications Act, five companies—the National Broadcasting Company (NBC), Viacom, Disney, News Corporation, and Time Warner—controlled about three-quarters of prime-time television.

The distribution of media and communications changed dramatically after passage of the Telecommunications Act in 1996. Video, voice, and data were increasingly sent over the same networks. The giant telephone companies began to compete with the giant cable companies in offering television, Internet delivery, and mobile phone service. The media corporations that controlled the wires and cable lines, such as Comcast, Verizon, AT&T, Google, Time Warner, Viacom, and Microsoft— gained control within the industry, along with untold political influence. They lobbied continually to eliminate local oversight of wireless networks and to reduce FCC oversight of the industry.

These industry leaders also promoted plans under which consumers would pay on a sliding scale for different levels of network service: Individuals would pay less, while corporations would pay more. Critics of these proposals called for "network neutrality," regulations that would prevent an environment in which wealthy corporations gain even more space and influence in the media while nonprofit organizations, individuals, and minority groups are eclipsed.

Observers on all sides of the political spectrum have acknowledged that the Telecommunications Act of 1996 was flawed; while striving to create open competition, the act opened the door for the concentration of ownership and power in the industry. With only a handful of companies controlling the nation's networks, the public did not receive the promised diversified programming, cost reductions, or options. On the other hand, deregulation probably played a role in speeding up the nationwide launch of the Internet, which drastically changed the playing field. Advancing technology and independent innovation brought new platforms to compete with the

giant corporations. For example, traditional television faced unexpected competition from extremely popular nontraditional video platforms on the Internet, such as YouTube, that provide diversity and independent views.

—*Sonia G. Benson*

**FURTHER READING**

Crandall, Robert W. *Competition and Chaos: U.S. Telecommunications Since the 1996 Telecom Act.* Washington, D.C.: Brookings Institution, 2005. Examines the economic impacts of the 1996 act.

Furchtgott-Roth, Harold W. *A Tough Act to Follow? The Telecommunications Act of 1996 and the Separation of Powers Failure.* Washington, D.C.: AEI Press, 2006. A former FCC commissioner analyzes the failure of the 1996 act in terms of the design and practices of the FCC.

McChesney, Robert W. *The Problem of the Media: U.S. Communication Politics in the Twenty-First Century.* New York: Monthly Review Press, 2004. Describes the media crisis that led to suppression of viewpoints, declining standards of journalism, and a system that favors corporations over the needs of the population.

Mueller, Milton L. *Universal Service: Interconnection, Competition, and Monopoly in the Making of the American Telephone System.* Cambridge, Mass.: MIT Press, 1997. Chronicles the history of the development of the American telephone system.

Sterling, Christopher H., Phyllis W. Bernt, and Martin B. H. Weiss. *Shaping American Telecommunications: A History of Technology, Policy, and Economics.* Mahwah, N.J.: Lawrence Erlbaum, 2005. Presents a multidisciplinary examination of telecommunications technology and the way it shapes, and is shaped by, economics and government policy.

**SEE ALSO:** 1971: Direct Transoceanic Dialing Begins; Apr. 3, 1973: First Cellular Phone Call; 1977-2000: Fiber-Optics Revolution; May 11, 1977: First Commercial Test of Fiber-Optic Telecommunications; 1980's: Decline of the Big Three Networks; 1980's: Electronic Technology Creates the Possibility of Telecommuting; Jan. 8, 1982: AT&T Undergoes Divestiture; Mid-1990's: Rise of the Internet and the World Wide Web.

1996

## January 30, 1996
# COMET HYAKUTAKE IS DISCOVERED

*The discovery of Comet Hyakutake, a comet of great brightness that passed very close to Earth, thrilled many and renewed discussions of the likelihood of a large body colliding with Earth at some point in the future.*

**ALSO KNOWN AS:** C/1996 B2; Great Comet of 1996
**LOCALE:** Kagoshima, Japan
**CATEGORIES:** Astronomy; science and technology

**KEY FIGURE**
*Yuji Hyakutake* (1950-2002), Japanese amateur
    astronomer

**SUMMARY OF EVENT**
Human beings have taken note of comets since ancient times. A comet is a celestial body that moves around the Sun; it consists of a central mass surrounded by a misty envelope that often forms a tail that streams away from the Sun. Comets vary considerably in the size of their central masses, and most comets are too small to be observed from Earth. Through the centuries, a few comets, such as Comet Halley, have attracted fame; these comets have been easily seen with the naked eye as they made repeated close passes by Earth.

In the twentieth century, improvements in technology led to the discovery of a number of comets, including Comet Hyakutake, which was discovered by Japanese amateur astronomer Yuji Hyakutake (comets are typically named for their discoverers). As a fifteen-year-old in Fukuoka, Japan, in 1965, Hyakutake saw Comet Ikeya-Seki in the night sky, and the experience led him to a lifelong interest in astronomy. As an adult, Hyakutake, who worked as a photoengraver, moved to Kagoshima, Japan, because the area's isolation meant that light pollution was low, allowing for relatively clear astronomical observations.

Hyakutake sought to discover a comet with a far orbit. To do so, he traveled to a rural mountaintop about ten miles from his home to get a better view of the night sky. For four nights a month beginning in July, 1995, Hyakutake scanned the sky from 2:00 A.M. to 5:00 A.M. using only high-powered field binoculars with six-inch lenses. On December 26, he stayed a bit longer than usual and discovered a comet (later designated C/1995 Y1) at 5:40 A.M. This comet, which was not especially bright, attracted little attention outside the astronomy community. It could not be seen with the naked eye, but it was

bright enough to be seen well with the use of a small telescope.

At 4:50 A.M. on January 30, 1996, Hyakutake discovered his second comet. He had returned to the mountain to take photographs of the first comet, but clouds in the comet's path foiled his plan. As he scanned the sky to find a clear spot, he saw a comet, but logic dictated that it could not be the same one he had seen in December because it was in almost the same location as the earlier sighting. Hyakutake realized that he had found a second body. He took photographs of the comet with a telephoto lens, developed the pictures, and, at 11:00 A.M., notified the National Astronomical Observatory in Tokyo of his discovery. Independent observations confirmed Hyakutake's find later that day. On February 27, 1996, Terry Lovejoy of Australia made the first naked-eye sighting of the comet, which had been designated C/1996 B2 or Comet Hyakutake.

With the discovery of Comet Hyakutake, sky watchers hoped for a truly big and active comet, but another spectacular comet along the lines of Comet Halley seemed unlikely. However, Hyakutake soon appeared to be brighter than even the original optimistic forecast. It produced roughly as much water vapor as Halley does at a comparable distance from the Sun as it approached Earth. To many experienced observers, Hyakutake qualified as a monster of a comet.

Comet Hyakutake remained visible with the naked eye for about one hundred days after February 27. On March 23, 1996, luminous knots of material—possibly small pieces of the comet's nucleus—were first observed moving back from its golden, starlike center. The head of the comet had an aquamarine hue. The apparent proportions of the comet's features were unlike anything the late twentieth century generation of observers had ever experienced, so they often found it difficult to interpret what they saw.

On March 23, the comet passed directly overhead the United States as seen from near 40 degrees north latitude. The comet passed perigee (the point at which it was closest to Earth) on March 25 at a distance of 9.3 million miles. Radar signals that bounced off Hyakutake's nucleus on that date indicated that the comet was surprisingly small, only about 0.6 to 1.9 miles in diameter. Ions disconnected from the tail from March 24 to March 26, and between April 8 and April 16 great tail lengths were again seen. The tail was detected out to about 60 degrees and possibly even 80 degrees or more. (A gas tail of 20 degrees is considered long.) Gas tails are more difficult to observe than dust tails because the eye is much less sensitive to the wavelengths of light emitted by gas tails than to the light reflected by dust tails. The greatest angular lengths of Hyakutake's tail were equivalent to about 20 million miles of gas tail.

By April 16, the comet's nucleus became less active and less bright, as noted in both the light curve and spectrographic observations. Perihelion passage (the point at which the comet was closest to the Sun) took place on May 1, 1997, at which time there was a distance of 21.4 million miles between the comet and the Sun. Lovejoy made the last naked-eye sighting of Comet Hyakutake in late June, 1996. It is not expected to be visible with the naked eye from Earth again for at least 72,000 years.

Yuji Hyakutake spent the remainder of his life searching fruitlessly for another comet. He died of an aneurysm at the age of fifty-one. In addition to the comet he discovered, Asteroid 7291 Hyakutake was named in his honor.

## SIGNIFICANCE

In 1996, Comet Hyakutake became the brightest comet to pass near Earth in more than four hundred years. Before it appeared, perhaps only thousands of living people in all the world had managed to get a good look at a great comet (that is, a comet of particularly great brightness). Hyakutake did not come as close to Earth as 1983's Comet IRAS-Araki-Alcock, but it captured a far greater amount of public attention. Part of this attention came from increasing fears that a close pass or collision with a comet could have disastrous consequences for the planet. A number of prominent scientists had speculated that a comet strike was responsible for environmental changes that led to the extinction of the dinosaurs, and many people had become concerned that such an event in the future would have similar consequences for humankind.

Although Comet Hyakutake thrilled many people who were interested in comets, the discovery had comparatively little significance within the scientific com-munity. Part of the reason that most recent discoveries of comets had been made by amateur astronomers was that professional astronomers were focusing their attention on other subjects, such as greater understanding of the other planets in our solar system. It is likely, however, that just as Yuji Hyakutake was inspired to study the skies by Comet Ikeya-Seki in 1965, future astronomers were inspired by Comet Hyakutake.

*—Caryn E. Neumann*

## FURTHER READING

Burnham, Robert. *Great Comets*. New York: Cambridge University Press, 2000. Lavishly illustrated volume provides a brief introduction to the history, nature, and beauty of comets. Includes index.

Crovisier, Jacques, and Thérèse Encrenaz. *Comet Science: The Study of Remnants from the Birth of the Solar System*. Translated by Stephen Lyle. New York: Cambridge University Press, 2000. Presents an overview of the forces and processes involved in the origin and evolution of comets. Intended for readers with strong background in science. Includes glossary, bibliography, and index.

Schaaf, Fred. *Comet of the Century: From Halley to Hale-Bopp*. New York: Copernicus Springer-Verlag, 1997. Combines solid history on comets and discussion of comet science with a personal account of the author's fascination with comets. Includes maps, photographs, and index.

SEE ALSO: Feb., 1973-Mar., 1974: Organic Molecules Are Discovered in Comet Kohoutek; Mar. 10-11, 1977: Astronomers Discover the Rings of Uranus; Mar. 4-7, 1979: First Ring Around Jupiter Is Discovered; 1982-1989: Astronomers Discover an Unusual Ring System of Planet Neptune; Mar. 8, 1986: Space Probes Begin Examination of Comet Halley; July 16-22, 1994: Comet Shoemaker-Levy 9 Collides with Jupiter; Nov. 29, 1996: Asteroid Toutatis Passes Near Earth.

1996

## February 10, 1996
# DEEP BLUE BEATS KASPAROV IN CHESS

*Deep Blue, an IBM computer designed to play chess at the highest competitive level, stunned the chess world by defeating World Chess Champion Garry Kasparov in the first game of their 1996 match. Kasparov swept the rest of the match without losing another game. However, in their 1997 rematch, the computer triumphed.*

**LOCALE:** Philadelphia, Pennsylvania; New York, New York

**CATEGORIES:** Computers and computer science; science and technology

**KEY FIGURES**

*Garry Kasparov* (b. 1963), world chess champion, hailed by some as the greatest player in chess history

*Feng-hsiung Hsu* (b. 1959), principal designer and team leader in the development of Deep Blue

*Murray Campbell* (b. 1967), expert chess player and computer scientist active in the development of Deep Blue

*A. Joseph Hoane, Jr.* (b. 1962), software engineer who joined the Deep Blue team when it moved to IBM

*Joel Benjamin* (b. 1964), international chess grand master who helped expand Deep Blue's chess knowledge

**SUMMARY OF EVENT**

Building a chess machine that could compete with the best human players had been a goal of computer scientists interested in artificial intelligence since the 1950's. Mastering chess seemed an ideal task for computers, since the game involves a limited number of physical objects governed by simple, clearly defined rules that can be quantified. A properly programmed computer can methodically consider various continuations of a given

*Garry Kasparov thinks over his moves during his third game with IBM's supercomputer Deep Blue on February 13, 1996, in Philadelphia. Kasparov was defeated in his first game against Deep Blue, but he came back to win the series. (AP/Wide World Photos)*

## REFLECTIONS FROM THE FATHER OF DEEP BLUE

*In the introduction to* Behind Deep Blue: Building the Computer That Defeated the World Chess Champion *(2002), the principal designer of Deep Blue, Feng-hsiung Hsu, sets the scene for the historic chess match between Deep Blue and Garry Kasparov:*

Off the street, in the basement of the Equitable Building, I was staring at the blank screens in an empty auditorium. In a few days, the auditorium would be filled with an overflowing crowd; TV cameras would be entrenched at vantage locations and the three huge projection screens at the front would come to life. The left screen would be showing a live image from a TV studio on the 35th floor of the building, serving as the game room. . . .

It had taken me almost twelve years to reach this point. When I started, Garry was not the World Champion; it was a few months yet before he was crowned. For the past eleven years, since 1986, my partners and I had been building successively more powerful chess computers. Our eventual goal was to beat the World Chess Champion, whoever he or she was. . . .

. . . We, or at least I, viewed the [Computer Chess Problem] as a purely engineering one. Since the late 1970s, it had been established that chess computers became stronger as their hardware speed increased. By 1985, when I started my small project that eventually became Deep Blue, the extrapolation from the experimental data indicated that a one thousandfold increase in hardware speed might be sufficient to produce a World Champion-class chess machine. Our project began with a simple goal, namely, to find out whether a massive increase in hardware speed would be sufficient to "solve" the Computer Chess Problem. Building this "Mother of all Chess Machines" was an interesting problem by itself. Of course, it would be an added bonus if our machine could indeed defeat the World Champion.

position and assign numerical values to every possible move, identifying the best next move. By 1980, several chess machines could defeat all but the most expert human players. That year, computer chess proponents established the $100,000 Fredkin Prize, which would be awarded to the creator of the first computer to defeat the world chess champion under standard tournament conditions.

Deep Blue began as chess-playing chips designed by Feng-hsiung Hsu as his doctoral dissertation in the computer science program at Carnegie Mellon University. Once he started designing chess machines, Hsu set out to win the Fredkin Prize. When Hsu graduated in 1989, International Business Machines (IBM), aware of the publicity value to the company if he succeeded, hired Hsu and his associate, Murray Campbell.

In 1991, IBM changed the name of the machine to

Deep Blue (previous versions had been called Deep Thought), echoing IBM's "Big Blue" nickname. Hsu developed a more powerful move-generating computer chip. Assisted by Campbell and IBM engineer A. Joseph Hoane, Jr., he embedded more than two hundred chips in IBM's newest supercomputer, the RS/6000 SP2. Harnessing the power of thirty-two computers working together through parallel processing, the machine could examine over 100 million moves per second.

When Deep Blue defeated World Chess Champion Garry Kasparov on February 10 in the first game of their 1996 match, chess aficionados reacted with shock. No chess machine had ever won against Kasparov before. However, the champion swept the Philadelphia match, tying two and winning three of the next five games. Deep Blue's team went back to their lab to improve their machine for a planned rematch.

For IBM, Deep Blue's first victory against Kasparov more than justified its sponsorship of the chess machine. News of the triumph was on the front page of major American newspapers. A flood of favorable worldwide newspaper, magazine, and TV coverage greeted the win and continued even as Kasparov dominated the rest of the match. IBM willingly agreed to a rematch, supported its computer chess team in developing an even more powerful version of Deep Blue, and offered a $1.1 million purse, $700,000 of which would go the victor.

Hsu worked hundred-hour weeks designing another new chess chip with improved position-evaluation functions, while Campbell and Hoane modified the software to take advantage of the new chip. Grand master Joel Benjamin played test games against the machine, uncovering gaps in its chess knowledge that the engineers corrected, thereby increasing the acuity of Deep Blue's positional analysis. Commentators pointed out that IBM provided a new supercomputer that was twice as fast as its 1996 predecessor, able to consider 200 million positions per second. However, most commentators undervalued Hsu's improved chip, as well as the increased chess knowledge added to Deep Blue's evaluation procedures by its chess instructor and engineers.

More than two hundred reporters representing every

1996

major news organization, along with television crews from around the world, arrived in New York to cover the 1997 rematch. Expert chess commentators unanimously predicted an easy win for Kasparov; one even asserted that Kasparov would win every game, since his victories in the final two games the previous year proved that he had learned to take Deep Blue's measure. When Deep Blue resigned at the forty-fifth move of their opening encounter on May 7, Kasparov had won three games in a row; expectations of an easy triumph for the world champion appeared validated.

The second game upset that assumption. This time, Kasparov resigned on the forty-fifth move, believing the computer had a clear path to victory. However, to Kasparov's dismay, chess aficionados who had been following the match over the Internet discovered a move he had overlooked that would have forced Deep Blue to concede a draw. News of his slip shook Kasparov's confidence and may have affected his play during the succeeding games.

Games three, four, and five ended in draws, leaving the match tied. The sixth and final game would be decisive. The audience at the press conference following the fifth game demonstrated their bias, applauding Kasparov and booing Deep Blue's operators. The incident deeply upset Hsu, whose account published five years later showed that his hurt feelings still smarted.

Unlike the previous lengthy, heavily fought contests, game six on May 11 lasted less than one hour. Some commentators termed Kasparov's surprising seventh move a blunder, but others considered it a bold attempt to present the computer with an unexpected situation it was not programmed to counter effectively. The move failed to confuse Deep Blue, which relentlessly pressed Kasparov into an untenable position, forcing him to resign after nineteen moves.

## SIGNIFICANCE

For IBM, the outcome of the chess matches was an unalloyed success; once again the company appeared to lead the way in computer technology and innovation. Sales of supercomputers boomed. Favorable publicity sent the price of IBM stock upward, adding billions to the value of the company and to the net worth of stockholders. Aware they could not better their position, IBM retired Deep Blue, shifted Hsu and his team members to other duties, and assigned the computer to research problems. On July 29, 1997, Hsu, Hoane, and Campbell received the Fredkin Prize, splitting the $100,000 award. IBM kept Deep Blue's $700,000 winner's share for its research funds.

Kasparov accused IBM of setting up a hostile environment that damaged his thinking, and he angered Deep Blue engineers by hinting that a hidden human, rather than the computer, selected the computer's most damaging moves. Chess fans who had cheered Kasparov's triumph in the first 1997 game turned negative, criticizing him for not exhibiting his normal level of skill. They condemned the quality of chess displayed by both champion and computer, saying the games lacked interest.

A few computer analysts claimed that Deep Blue had demonstrated true artificial intelligence in defeating Kasparov, but most commentators, including Hsu, disagreed. Hsu insisted that the only intelligence displayed at the chess table was Kasparov's; the computer simply followed rules laid down by its designers. The engineer also rejected the idea that the matches were a contest of man versus machine. The real contest, Hsu asserted, was between one outstanding man and the men who programmed the machine. To his satisfaction, the programmers triumphed.

*—Milton Berman*

## FURTHER READING

Hsu, Feng-hsiung. *Behind Deep Blue: Building the Computer That Defeated the World Chess Champion.* Princeton, N.J.: Princeton University Press, 2002. The primary designer of Deep Blue narrates its development from a doctoral dissertation topic to its triumph over the world chess champion.

Newborn, Monroe. *Kasparov Versus Deep Blue: Computer Chess Comes of Age.* New York: Springer-Verlag, 2003. Easily understandable narrative of the two matches by a computer-chess proponent.

Pandolfini, Bruce. *Kasparov and Deep Blue: The Historic Chess Match Between Man and Machine.* New York: Simon & Schuster, 1997. Chess instructor Pandolfini provides move-by-move analysis of all six games of the 1997 match.

SEE ALSO: Nov. 15, 1971: Intel Introduces the First "Computer on a Chip"; 1976: Speech Recognition Machines Master One Thousand Words; Mar. 4, 1976: First Cray-1 Supercomputer Is Shipped to the Los Alamos National Laboratory; Aug. 12, 1981: IBM Introduces Its Personal Computer.

## March 20, 1996
# BRITAIN ANNOUNCES HUMAN CASES OF MAD COW DISEASE

*During the mid-1990's, unusual forms of Creutzfeldt-Jakob disease, a type of spongiform encephalopathy, began to appear among young persons in England. The outbreak of what was later termed "mad cow disease" was traced to beef contaminated with a bovine form of the disease-causing agent.*

**ALSO KNOWN AS:** Bovine spongiform encephalopathy
**LOCALE:** England
**CATEGORIES:** Biology; health and medicine; science and technology

**KEY FIGURES**

*D. Carleton Gajdusek* (b. 1923), American physician and medical researcher who demonstrated the infectious nature of the prion disease kuru

*Stanley B. Prusiner* (b. 1942), American neurologist and biochemist who determined the protein makeup of prions

**SUMMARY OF EVENT**

The first recognition of what is now known to be a prion disease was in the eighteenth century, when British farmers observed a degenerative disease among sheep in which the animals would scrape their wool off, rubbing themselves raw on fence posts. The disease, dubbed "scrapie" by the English, was demonstrated in the 1930's to be transmissible among the animals.

Initially thought to be a "slow virus disease" of animals, scrapie was not at first associated with human forms of disease. In the 1950's, D. Carleton Gajdusek, a visiting investigator working at the Walter and Eliza Hall Institute of Medical Research in Australia, began an investigation of a neurological disorder/dementia known as kuru among the Fore tribe on the island of New Guinea (the Fore word *kuru* means "shaking"). Gajdusek determined that the disease, found primarily among the women and children of the tribe, was passed by the Fore practice of cannibalism. Transmission of the disease to nonhuman primates by inoculation of brain tissue from victims demonstrated the infectious nature of the etiological agent. In subsequent years, a number of similar human dementias, most notably Creutzfeldt-Jakob disease (CJD), were found to be associated with a similar agent.

Microscopic analysis of brain tissue obtained from both humans and other animals stricken by similar illnesses demonstrated a "spongy" appearance resulting from extreme vacuolation (the formation of small spaces

in the tissue containing air or fluid). The diseases were termed transmissible spongiform encephalopathies (TSEs). Certain forms of these diseases were shown to be inherited, but most commonly they appeared sporadically among persons in their sixties or older.

In the 1970's, Stanley B. Prusiner at the University of California, San Francisco, began a series of studies on the agent associated with scrapie in animals. At the same time, a similar agent associated with CJD in humans was likewise undergoing study. Prusiner's data increasingly suggested that the infectious agents lacked any evidence for genetic material composed of nucleic acid. In 1982, Prusiner termed the agent a "prion" (PrP), or "proteinaceous infectious substance." Prusiner's hypothesis that the agent lacked nucleic acid went against the core of geneticists' belief, that only deoxyribonucleic acid (DNA) or ribonucleic acid (RNA) would allow transmission and replication of an infectious agent.

Although Prusiner's suggestion did not achieve universal acceptance, the overwhelming consensus has been that he was correct. Indeed, for their work in prion research, Gajdusek and Prusiner both received the Nobel Prize in Physiology or Medicine, Gajdusek in 1976 and Prusiner in 1997.

Prusiner and Charles Weissman later collaborated on cloning the cell gene that encodes the prion. The normal function of the cell prion, dubbed $PrP^c$, is unknown. The agent itself is made entirely of protein, a chain of some 231 amino acids prepared from a larger precursor. Mutations in the amino acid sequence alter the shape of the protein, which is key to its ability to cause disease. When the mutated agent enters a cell, it twists or transforms the shape of the normal $PrP^c$, resulting in degeneration and death of the infected cells and, eventually, the organism. The particular site of the mutation determines the form of disease the TSE will exhibit.

The presence of a prion disease in cattle, termed bovine spongiform encephalopathy (BSE), was observed in Europe in the 1980's. This development was probably the result of changes in the ways feed for animals was produced. It had long been common practice to use ground-up animal carcasses in cattle bonemeal, but prior to the mid-1980's, the bonemeal had been subjected to solvent extraction followed by heating at 70 degrees Centigrade for eight hours, a practice that destroyed the scrapie ($PrP^{sc}$) agent. Changes in the process allowed the scrapie agent to survive and resulted in infection of the

1996

*A cow afflicted with bovine spongiform encephalopathy, or "mad cow disease," which causes progressive degeneration of the nervous system.* (USDA/APHIS/Art Davis)

cattle that ate the bonemeal. The actual source of the BSE outbreak was never determined. Whether it originated from a spontaneous case of BSE, an admittedly rare phenomenon, or from the ingestion of material from scrapie-infected sheep is unknown.

BSE, which became known as "mad cow disease" in the popular press, was first recognized in Great Britain in 1986. Approximately one hundred animals were known to be involved at that time. The extent of the disease within the cattle industry was unknown, but the evidence even then was that the disease was more widespread in cattle than was initially apparent. As a result, the use of protein obtained from sheep or other animals in cattle feed was banned. The outbreak of BSE was a serious blow to the British cattle industry, as consumption of beef dropped steeply in what had always been a beef-eating population.

The first evidence that BSE might pass from cattle to humans appeared in 1994 and 1995 with an increase and change in the demographics of CJD. CJD typically appears in older persons; it rarely develops in persons under age sixty-five. In 1994 and 1995, however, a variant of CJD was observed in ten younger persons, nine of whom were under age thirty-five. The brains of those who subsequently died from the variant CJD demonstrated large protein deposits typical of TSEs but not commonly found in classical CJD. On March 20, 1996, the British government released a report that conceded that the variant form of CJD was likely the result of the victims' having eaten contaminated meat.

Confirmation of the link between the variant CJD in humans and BSE in cattle was provided in October of 1996. John Collinge of the Prion Disease Group at Saint Mary's Medical School in London reported the results of a "fingerprint" analysis comparing the proteins of BSE and variant CJD in which the proteins were shown to be effectively identical. The infectious nature of the human agent was also shown the following year, when scientists used infected human brain tissues to transmit the disease to mice. The lesions that developed in the brains of the infected mice were identical to those in the human brains, confirming the likely source of the variant disease.

Although the number of new cases of variant CJD continued to increase in subsequent years, the rate of increase leveled off. By 2006, approximately 150 cases of variant CJD had been diagnosed in Great Britain. Not surprisingly, the average age of the victims had increased, with some cases developing in persons in their mid-fifties.

## SIGNIFICANCE

Recognition that the BSE agent could pass from cattle to humans resulted in a ban on the use of bonemeal from diseased animals in animal feed. Further, diseased cattle could no longer enter the human food chain. Strict enforcement of these rules was successful in preventing transmission of CJD from cattle to humans in the United States. Vigilance, of course, remains necessary, and occasionally meat from a "mad cow" has managed to enter the food chain. There has been no evidence for any human disease associated with these animals, however.

Long-term effects of the BSE outbreak in Great Britain may remain unknown for some time. The total number of persons exposed to the agent was probably in the hundreds of thousands. Given that the incubation period for the CJD agent can be measured in decades, by the early twenty-first century it was not known whether the approximately 150 persons diagnosed with variant CJD by that time would represent the likely total or merely the tip of a disease iceberg.

The ability of the agent to be transmitted through ingestion also raised concerns about similar diseases in other animals. For example, a prion-associated illness known as chronic wasting disease has been observed in deer and elk in the western United States. Although there has been no evidence that the agent has been passed to humans who have eaten animals with this disease that have been killed by hunters, there is still concern that transmission is possible.

*—Richard Adler*

## FURTHER READING

Ansell, Christopher, and David Vogel, eds. *What's the Beef? The Contested Governance of European Food Safety.* Cambridge, Mass.: MIT Press, 2006. Collection of essays by leading advocates on particular issues addresses the politics behind food regulation in (primarily) England, France, and Germany.

Becker, Geoffrey, ed. *Mad Cow Disease: Are We Safe?* Hauppauge, N.Y.: Novinka Books, 2004. Collection discusses the means by which prion diseases may enter the human food chain as well as how realistic the actual threat may be.

Prusiner, Stanley B. "Prion Diseases and the BSE Crisis." *Science* 278 (October 10, 1997): 245-251. Scholarly article presents a review of prion structures as well as a synopsis of the outbreak of CJD in Great Britain that resulted from bovine-human transmission.

Schwartz, Maxime. *How the Cows Turned Mad: Unlocking the Mysteries of Mad Cow Disease.* Berkeley: University of California Press, 2004. Provides a history of prion diseases, from the description of scrapie in the eighteenth century to modern transmission among animals and humans.

Strauss, James H., and Ellen G. Strauss. *Viruses and Human Disease.* New York: Academic Press, 2002. College-level textbook includes a section about the history of prion research.

**SEE ALSO:** Sept. 8, 1976: Ebola Epidemic Kills First of Many in Africa; June 5, 1981: U.S. Centers for Disease Control Recognizes AIDS; Mar., 1991: Medical Researchers Test Promising Drugs for the Treatment of AIDS; Jan.-May, 1996: Meningitis Outbreak Proves Deadly in West Africa; Dec. 16, 1997: First Cases of Avian Flu Are Reported; 1998: AIDS Devastates Africa.

1996

## May, 1996
# SUDAN EXPELS OSAMA BIN LADEN

*Under pressure from the United States, Egypt, and Saudi Arabia, the Sudanese government expelled Osama Bin Laden, who then shifted the operations of his al-Qaeda terrorist organization to Afghanistan, where al-Qaeda was able to expand its membership, training, and funding.*

**LOCALE:** Sudan
**CATEGORIES:** Diplomacy and international relations; terrorism, atrocities, and war crimes

**KEY FIGURES**

*Osama Bin Laden* (b. 1957), leader of al-Qaeda
*Omar Hassan Ahmad al-Bashir* (b. 1944), chief of state of Sudan, 1989-1993, and president of Sudan beginning in 1993
*Hassan al-Turabi* (b. 1932), leader of the National Islamic Front in Sudan
*Mohammad Omar* (b. 1959/1962), leader of the Taliban in Afghanistan, 1996-2001
*Abdul Rasul Sayyaf* (b. 1946), leader of the Islamic Union for the Liberation of Afghanistan and a member of the Afghan Northern Alliance
*Hosnī Mubārak* (b. 1928), president of Egypt beginning in 1981

**SUMMARY OF EVENT**

In early 1991, Osama Bin Laden, who was born in Saudi Arabia, relocated from Afghanistan to Sudan. At that time, the United States considered Bin Laden a member of the mujahideen, or Islamic guerrilla fighters. Bin Laden spent the next five years in Sudan, where he poured millions of dollars into thirty businesses, beginning with some initial investments in heavy machinery. Wadi al-Aqiq, the first business that Bin Laden created, is believed to have been the main source of financial backing for the terrorist organization al-Qaeda while Bin Laden was in Sudan. Under Wadi al-Aqiq, Laden International was established as an import-export company, allowing al-Qaeda to import goods without paying taxes or undergoing inspections.

Taba Investment, a money-exchange business, was also created under Wadi al-Aqiq, as was al-Hajira, a construction company that helped to build roads in Sudan. Bin Laden built more than 300 miles of roads under contract with the Sudanese government before Sudan reneged on the deal. A large part of Bin Laden's Sudanese business profits were obtained through the export of gum arabic, which is used to make carbonated beverages, among many other things. It is believed that many of these businesses either directly or indirectly aided efforts to expand the power of al-Qaeda, although there is debate about the extent of the profits made by these and other Bin Laden companies.

Eventually, Bin Laden owned companies dealing in agriculture and manufacturing. Outside the city of Ad-Damazin, al-Qaeda members grew sesame, peanuts, and white corn, which were processed and sold by al-Themar al-Mubaraka, another of Bin Laden's companies. The farm was also used as a location for training al-Qaeda members in the use of weapons. In late 1991, local residents complained about explosions at the farm, and the Sudanese police arrested a few al-Qaeda members. Sudanese intelligence officials released them, however. Bin Laden had been providing funds to the Sudanese government, and, in return, the National Islamic Front (NIF) provided Bin Laden with land for training camps.

Prior to the time he spent in Sudan, Bin Laden had been relatively lenient in his opposition to the Saudi Arabian government, but in Sudan he shifted to a very outspoken view, calling for serious reforms in Saudi Arabia, criticizing the government and its religious institutions, which he asserted were hypocritical. One important reason for this significant shift was Bin Laden's feeling of betrayal when the Saudi royal family allowed U.S. troops to enter Saudi Arabia after the 1990 confrontation between Iraq and Kuwait. Saudi Arabia also played a role in the ousting of Bin Laden from Sudan. In March of 1994, the Saudi government stripped Bin Laden of his citizenship, denounced his behavior, and froze his Saudi bank accounts.

In June of 1995, an assassination attempt was made against Egypt's president, Hosnī Mubārak, who was on his way to attend a diplomatic summit in Ethiopia. Egypt, a major ally of the United States, believed that Sudanese NIF agents helped orchestrate the attempt. Hassan al-Turabi, leader of the NIF in Sudan, had often clashed with Bin Laden, and behind Bin Laden's back, Turabi convinced the NIF to eject Bin Laden from Sudan. Turabi believed this would help improve the global view of Sudan, get Sudan back into the good graces of the United States, and eliminate the world's suspicions that Sudan was supporting terrorists. Since August of 1993, Sudan had been on the U.S. State Department's list of states that sponsor terrorism (along with Iran, Iraq, Libya, Syria, North Korea, and Cuba).

In 1994, Turabi had aided France in the capture of the international terrorist Illich Ramírez Sánchez (known as Carlos the Jackal), so there was little doubt of Turabi's potential success with respect to handing over Bin Laden, but the United States did not have enough evidence of Bin Laden's involvement in specific crimes to present in court and thus justify his extradition. The United States believed, however, that if Bin Laden could be removed from his vast wealth in Sudan, his influence on terrorist organizations would be reduced.

In May, 1996, Sudanese president Omar Hassan Ahmad al-Bashir responded to political pressure from the United States, Egypt, and Saudi Arabia and ordered the expulsion of Bin Laden from Sudan. According to some, Bin Laden helped negotiate the terms on which he left. Earlier that year, he had threatened to leave Sudan and take all his money and businesses with him, and because this removal of significant revenues and important businesses would have crushed Sudan's economy, he was allowed to transport various assets to Pakistan, then to Afghanistan, over a period of weeks with the aid of Sudanese intelligence operatives.

When he was ordered to leave, Bin Laden chartered a plane and flew from Sudan to Kabul, Afghanistan, then settled in Jalālābād, having been invited there by Abdul Rasul Sayyaf, the leader of the Islamic Union for the Liberation of Afghanistan and a member of the Afghan Northern Alliance. Bin Laden then developed close relationships with leaders of the Taliban, the ruling government in Afghanistan, especially Mullah Mohammad Omar. While in Afghanistan, Bin Laden supported the Taliban financially and through paramilitary aid.

### SIGNIFICANCE

It is believed that Bin Laden's years in Sudan were crucial to the expansion of al-Qaeda because they provided the terrorist organization with numerous opportunities to increase its wealth, strengthen its network, and import the goods needed to carry out its activities. Experts have also argued that the expulsion from Sudan increased Bin Laden's hatred of the United States, because the United States was influential in bringing about his exile. Because he could not return to Saudi Arabia, Bin Laden traveled to Afghanistan, where he was able to build up al-Qaeda even further with the aid, direct and indirect, of Afghan leaders. While in Afghanistan, Bin Laden had complete freedom to train individuals to fight his jihad, or holy war. Within two years after he was expelled

from Sudan, Bin Laden became one of America's most wanted men following al-Qaeda's attacks on the U.S. embassies in Dar es Salaam, Tanzania, and Nairobi, Kenya.

*—Sheryl L. Van Horne*

### FURTHER READING

Andersen, Lars Erslev, and Jan Aagaard. *In the Name of God: The Afghan Connection and the U.S. War Against Terrorism*. Odense, Denmark: University Press of Southern Denmark, 2005. Describes the evolution of global terrorism and how terrorism can flourish in weak states.

Bergen, Peter L. *Holy War, Inc.: Inside the Secret World of Osama Bin Laden*. New York: Free Press, 2001. Draws parallels between the corporation and the jihad al-Qaeda has waged. Presents detailed information in a journalistic style.

_____. *The Osama Bin Laden I Know: An Oral History of al-Qaeda's Leader*. New York: Free Press, 2006. Compilation of transcripts of court proceedings, newspaper articles, and interviews tells the story of the creation of al-Qaeda and documents the actions of Bin Laden.

Bin Laden, Osama. *Messages to the World: The Statements of Osama Bin Laden*. Edited by Bruce Lawrence and translated by James Howarth. New York: Verso, 2005. Contains translations of twenty-four public statements made by Bin Laden from 1994 to 2004.

Bodansky, Yossef. *Bin Laden: The Man Who Declared War on America*. New York: Random House, 2001. Chronicles Bin Laden's rise to power and discusses some of the possible reasons Bin Laden turned his anger against the United States.

Gunaratna, Rohan. *Inside al-Qaeda: Global Network of Terror*. New York: Columbia University Press, 2002. Presents detailed descriptions of numerous al-Qaeda operations and documents related court proceedings. Focuses much attention on Bin Laden.

Hamud, Randall B. *Osama Bin Laden: America's Enemy in His Own Words*. San Diego, Calif.: Nadeem, 2005. Provides translations of statements made by Bin Laden, presented in chronological order and accompanied by a discussion of the context of each statement.

Randal, Jonathan. *Osama: The Making of a Terrorist*. New York: Alfred A. Knopf, 2004. Details the events of Bin Laden's life and the numerous failed attempts made by the United States to capture him.

1996

SEE ALSO: 1988: Osama Bin Laden Forms al-Qaeda; 1989: Soviet Troops Leave Afghanistan; 1990's: Algeria and Egypt Crack Down on Islamic Militants; Feb. 26, 1993: World Trade Center Bombing; Sept. 27, 1996: Taliban Begins Suppression of Human Rights in Afghanistan; Aug. 7, 1998: Terrorists Bomb U.S. Embassies in East Africa; Oct. 12, 2000: Terrorists Attack USS *Cole*.

## May 10, 1996
# VIETNAMESE REFUGEES RIOT IN HONG KONG

*Vietnamese refugees, known popularly as "boat people," had lived in Hong Kong refugee camps since their arrival from Vietnam in the 1970's. Escaping political and social turmoil in their own country, they found an uneasy refuge in Hong Kong. In 1996, Vietnamese refugees, never considered full citizens, rioted in the Whitehead Refugee Camp in anticipation of Hong Kong's transfer of sovereignty from Britain to China.*

**LOCALE:** Hong Kong
**CATEGORIES:** Wars, uprisings, and civil unrest; immigration, emigration, and relocation

**KEY FIGURES**
*Christopher Patten* (b. 1944), head of the Hong Kong government, 1992-1997
*Anson Chan* (b. 1940), chief secretary of Hong Kong, 1993-1997

**SUMMARY OF EVENT**

Hong Kong experienced a flood of immigration during the late twentieth century. Its population was due, in large part, to refugee movements. Beginning in the late 1950's and continuing through the 1960's, mainland China implemented various campaigns of social control, such as the Hundred Flowers Campaign, the Great Leap Forward, and the Cultural Revolution. These campaigns caused hundreds of thousands of refugees to immigrate to Hong Kong. The emigration from mainland China represented an escape from economic hardship and an arrival to greater freedom and safety.

During the 1970's, Hong Kong experienced an upsurge in its economy and, subsequently, liberalized its immigration policies. Social support policies were enacted to aid and rehabilitate refugees in Hong Kong. However, by the 1980's, Hong Kong reported a strain on government services. Hong Kong politicians pushed for the repatriation of all illegal immigrants. A national immigration dialogue ensued; the debate addressed the difference in definition between immigrant and refugee, and questioned who could stay in the country and who must leave. After 1980, the Hong Kong government created an immigration tribunal that accepted appeals from political refugees and those seeking political asylum.

Responding to social and political pressures from Southeast Asian regimes, the Hong Kong government adopted the definition of "refugee" used by the United Nations. According to the U.N. Convention Relating to the Status of Refugees (1951), a refugee is a person who, "owing to well-founded fear of being persecuted for reasons of race, religion, nationality, membership of a particular social group or political opinion, is outside the country of his nationality and is unable, or owing to such fear, is unwilling to avail himself of the protection of that country; or who, not having a nationality and being outside the country of his former habitual residence as a result of such events, is unable or, owing to such fear, is unwilling to return to it."

Having adopted this definition, the Hong Kong government considered all other newcomers to be illegal immigrants. A distinct difference was established between those who fled a politically repressive regime and those who sought an economically better situation.

The brutality of, and the great suffering caused by, the Vietnam War served as the impetus for hundreds of thousands of Vietnamese to flee their homeland and seek refuge in other countries around Southeast Asia and elsewhere in the world. Because of its proximity to Vietnam and its economic stability, Hong Kong was a country that thousands of Vietnamese saw as a potential refuge.

In April, 1975, the government in Saigon announced its unconditional surrender to North Vietnamese forces. The new communist-controlled government imprisoned people who were thought to support the old regime. Thousands of citizens were also sent to reeducation camps. This was done without the benefit of formal trials. Masses of Vietnamese were desperate to flee their war-torn homeland and to escape the newly unified Vietnam. In 1980 alone, one hundred thousand Vietnamese refugees sought asylum in Hong Kong; many of the refugees traveled in small boats, thus earning the name "boat people."

Throughout 1970's and 1980's, Hong Kong was one of the many Southeast Asian countries—including Thailand, Singapore, Malaysia, and Indonesia—to absorb thousands of refugees. Hong Kong experienced a huge surge in population growth throughout this period, due to large numbers of immigrants coming from Vietnam and mainland China.

To deal with this massive influx of population, there were three refugee conferences held in July, 1979, in Geneva, Switzerland. Each conference was convened by a different international body: the International Council of Voluntary Agencies Consultation on the Indo-China Refugee Problem, the United Nations Meeting on Refugees and Displaced Persons in Southeast Asia, and the World Council of Churches Consultation on Indochinese Refugees. The outcome of these international conferences was the establishment of many refugee camps throughout Southeast Asia—including several in Hong Kong—to house Vietnamese and ethnic Chinese refugees.

Under the Office of the United Nations High Commissioner for Refugees (UNHCR), a system of camps was established that housed thousands of Vietnamese in Hong Kong. At the height of immigration, about 224,000 refugees arrived in Hong Kong. Many refugee camps became overcrowded quickly.

From 1975 to 1985, Vietnam embarked on an economic campaign to nationalize business and collectivize agriculture. These measures were disastrous for Vietnam and its citizens—particularly as the country had disappointing harvests and food deficits. In addition to suffering a repressive political regime, Vietnamese citizens languished under a failing economy. Thus a second wave of economic refugees—as opposed to political refugees—predominantly from northern Vietnam, began to arrive in Hong Kong in the 1980's. Hong Kong, because of its increasingly limited resources, wanted to stop this sort of immigration.

A surge in Vietnamese boat arrivals to Hong Kong began in 1987. In response, in 1989, the government of Hong Kong began to separate economic immigrants from political refugees. The U.N. Steering Committee of the International Conference on Indo-Chinese Refugees met in Geneva in June, 1989, and created the Comprehensive Plan of Action (CPA) that sought to stem the influx of Vietnamese refugees.

Through the CPA, the United Nations High Commission on Refugees began to systematically interview all

1996

*Vietnamese refugees protest on the rooftops at the Whitehead Refugee Camp in Hong Kong in May, 1996, in anticipation of the territory's transfer of sovereignty from Britain to China.* (AP/Wide World Photos)

camp residents to discern if they were refugees or if they were economic immigrants. Economic immigrants were sent back to Vietnam for repatriation.

The CPA was a seven-year plan scheduled to end on March 6, 1996. By that time, all the refugee camps for Vietnamese immigrants throughout Southeast Asia were to be closed. The United Nations agreed to finance all refugee camps until June of 1996. Hong Kong camps had to be closed before the country reverted to Chinese rule on July 1, 1997; China insisted that the Vietnamese immigrants be returned to Vietnam by this time. Vietnam agreed to cooperate with Hong Kong to speed up the repatriation. The United Nations chartered more than three hundred flights back to Vietnam, returning more than 57,500 people who agreed to make the trip. The government of Hong Kong repatriated an additional 94,700 people to Vietnam.

Hong Kong's efforts to complete this process were sidetracked when, in April, 1996, a Hong Kong high court ruled that some refugees were illegally detained. In May, the Vietnamese living in the Whitehead Refugee Camp exploded in violence. The refugees threw fire balls off the roof of the camp's residential barracks. An estimated two hundred Whitehead residents escaped the camp. Escapees torched the camp's administration building. Sixteen other buildings and more than forty vehicles were destroyed by fire.

Police clad in riot gear fought residents of the camp with tear gas. The Vietnamese fought back with improvised weapons, including clubs and knives. By the late afternoon, sixty-one Vietnamese had been recaptured, and twenty-two Hong Kong police, firefighters, and camp workers had been injured.

At the time of the 1996 uprising, Whitehead had 8,600 remaining Vietnamese. The government sought to liberalize its refugee policies after the 1996 Whitehead Refugee Camp uprising. It changed its policy of enclosed camps to encourage refugees to find employment outside the camps. Finally, Hong Kong imposed a deadline of May 31, 2000, for the remaining, approximately one thousand, refugees of Pillar Point, the last operational Vietnamese refugee camp, to move out. Pillar Point Camp closed in June of that year.

## SIGNIFICANCE

The conditions of the Vietnamese refugee camps in Hong Kong were deplorable. The refugees in the camps were victims of human rights violations. In reaction to these conditions and in anticipation of the Sino-British Joint Declaration—the transfer of sovereignty from British rule to the People's Republic of China in 1997—Vietnamese refugees rioted in the Whitehead Refugee Camp in May of 1996. There was extensive damage to the camp's property, and two hundred refugees escaped into Hong Kong's northern New Territories. While there were no reported deaths, a number of people on both sides were injured.

—*Alison Harper Stankrauff*

## FURTHER READING

Erlanger, Steven. "U.S. and Hanoi Agree to Give Boat People One Last Chance." *The New York Times*, May 15, 1996, p. A13. Describes how thousands of Vietnamese were allowed to move from Hong Kong to the United States.

Freeman, James M. *Voices from the Camps: Vietnamese Children Seeking Asylum*. Seattle: University of Washington Press, 2003. Accounts by Vietnamese refugee children detailing their experiences in Hong Kong refugee camps.

Gargan, Edward A. "Two Hundred Vietnamese Refugees Flee Detention Camp in Hong Kong; Barracks Are Set Afire in the Chaos of an Uprising." *The New York Times*, May 11, 1996, p. 4. A contemporaneous report of the refugee conflict in Hong Kong.

Hein, Jeremy. *From Vietnam, Laos, and Cambodia: A Refugee Experience in the United States*. New York: Twayne, 1995. Looks at the refugee experience in the United States and the sociological impact of the displacement of Indochinese.

**SEE ALSO:** Mar., 1973: U.S. Troops Leave Vietnam; May, 1975: Indo-Chinese Boat People Begin Fleeing Vietnam; June, 1989: Helsinki Watch Proposes Reform of Refugee Laws; Sept., 1989: Vietnamese Troops Withdraw from Cambodia.

## May 20, 1996
# U.S. SUPREME COURT STRIKES DOWN COLORADO ANTIGAY LAW

*In 1992, Colorado citizens voted in favor of a state constitutional amendment that would have imposed a statewide prohibition against protection from discrimination based on sexual orientation. The U.S. Supreme Court declared the amendment unconstitutional, setting the stage for later decisions that would find laws prohibiting consensual homosexual sodomy to be unconstitutional.*

**ALSO KNOWN AS:** *Romer v. Evans*, 517 U.S. 620
**LOCALE:** Colorado
**CATEGORIES:** Civil rights and liberties; laws, acts, and legal history

**KEY FIGURES**

*Richard G. Evans* (fl. late twentieth century), employee of Denver municipal government
*Roy Romer* (b. 1928), governor of Colorado, 1987-1999
*Anthony Kennedy* (b. 1936), associate justice of the United States beginning in 1988

**SUMMARY OF EVENT**

After the gay and lesbian revolution of the 1970's faded, antigay backlash swept across the United States in the form of the Christian Right in the 1980's, with conservative politicians supporting the trend. By the 1990's, debates about individual issues, most related to some specific questions, began to dominate the news. Some of the most prominent issues addressed questions of employment, marriage, and sexual privacy. Many political battles were fought at the local level, not a few of which were swept into the national debate. Gay, lesbian, bisexual, and transgender (GLBT) rights activists argued that sexual orientation should not affect a person's ability to marry or to secure housing and employment. Opponents advanced arguments against GLBT rights: that only a heterosexual orientation is moral and that supporting GLBT goals promotes immoral behavior; that sexual orientation should be kept private, and that those who choose to publicize a GLBT orientation do not deserve special treatment because of it; and that the rights the GLBT community expects go beyond the protections offered to other citizens, and it is unfair to protect one group more than others.

In the early 1990's in Colorado, voters, by a narrow margin (53.4 percent), accepted an anti-gay rights amendment to the state constitution, designed to rebuff laws in Aspen, Denver, and Boulder that already existed to protect gay rights. Amendment 2 to the Colorado state constitution was designed to prevent anyone from claiming minority status based on sexual orientation and to prevent government (state or local) from offering protections based on sexual orientation.

GLBT groups throughout the state immediately protested that the amendment would bring Colorado's constitution into conflict with the U.S. Constitution and filed suit to prevent the amendment from being enacted. Colorado governor Roy Romer was named as the primary defendant. The fight against Amendment 2 was led by eight individuals, including Richard G. Evans, in addition to the Boulder Valley School District, the city and county of Denver, the cities of Boulder and Aspen, and Aspen's city council. These groups opposed the Colorado amendment based on several factors in the First and Fourteenth Amendments to the U.S. Constitution. The largest part of their argument came from the Fourteenth Amendment, which requires governments to provide all citizens equal protection under the law. They believed that, in addition to lacking rational governmental interest, the amendment placed an unfair burden on the GLBT community to gain protection from discrimination.

They also believed that Amendment 2, because it was directed at all levels of government, hampered the ability of gays, lesbians, and bisexuals (transgender individuals were not named specifically in the amendment) to seek redress from the government, a violation of the First Amendment to the U.S. Constitution. Finally, because it would have prevented governments from enforcing policies prohibiting discrimination based on sexual orientation, the plaintiffs argued the law violated the due process clauses of both the U.S. and Colorado constitutions.

On January 15, 1993, Colorado district court judge Jeffrey Bayless issued an injunction against Amendment 2's becoming part of the Colorado constitution. The state immediately appealed Bayless's injunction to Colorado's supreme court, which, on July 19, 1993, upheld the injunction. The opinion, authored by Colorado's chief justice, Luis Rovera, found that Amendment 2 denied gays, lesbians, and bisexuals equal protection under the law—specifically, equal access to the normal political process. He stated that Amendment 2 would prevent gays, lesbians, and bisexuals from seeking protection from discrimination without entering into the process of seeking a constitutional amendment.

Rovera thus required the amendment to face the "strict scrutiny" test. Under this test, a law must advance a compelling state interest in order to be allowable. He returned the case to the district court, where Judge Bayless ruled on December 14, 1994, that the law did not advance any such compelling state interest and that it was therefore unconstitutional. When the state appealed once more to the state supreme court, that group upheld the district court ruling, declaring Amendment 2 unconstitutional on October 11, 1994. The state of Colorado, therefore, had no further option but to appeal the case to the U.S. Supreme Court.

The oral arguments were presented to the Court on October 10, 1995, nearly a year to the day after the Colorado state supreme court ruling. During the questioning of the state's counsel, the justices asked some very pointed questions about the amendment's vague language and its singling out a specific group of people and preventing them from having redress from prejudice except through constitutional amendment. The verdict was rendered on May 20, 1996, with the court voting 6-3 to strike the amendment. In the Supreme Court's decision, Justice Anthony Kennedy took a slightly different tack from that of Colorado. Whereas Colorado's supreme court had required the amendment to meet the strict scrutiny test, Justice Kennedy declared that the amendment failed to demonstrate a rational relationship to a genuine government interest. Kennedy stated that the amendment did indeed single out homosexuals and denied them the same protections of law enjoyed by other persons. Although Justice Antonin Scalia wrote a dissent, he was joined by only a minority of the Court, and Amendment 2 was prohibited from being enacted.

## SIGNIFICANCE

The *Romer* case is significant for both legal and social reasons. Legally, it set a precedent that Cincinnati activists attempted to use to overturn a similar ordinance. However, because the Cincinnati ordinance was local, the Sixth Circuit Court of Appeals ruled it to be unaffected by the *Romer* decision, and the Supreme Court refused to hear the case. Nationally, *Romer* set a precedent discussed in a later Supreme Court decision. In his dissent, Scalia observed that the decision in *Romer* was entirely contrary to the Court's decision in the 1986 *Bowers v. Hardwick* (478 U.S. 186) case, which had upheld a Georgia law prohibiting consensual sodomy. Thus when the 2003 case of *Lawrence and Garner v. Texas* (539 U.S. 558) came before the Supreme Court some seven years after the *Romer* decision, *Romer* was again dis-

cussed. *Lawrence and Garner v. Texas* overturned the *Bowers* decision, forbidding states to make laws that render consensual homosexual sodomy illegal. The precedent the Court set in *Romer* by going against *Bowers* thus helped fuel the arguments in *Lawrence and Garner*.

At the social level, *Romer v. Evans* was significant for entirely different reasons. The language of both Kennedy's majority opinion and Scalia's dissent demonstrated that the real argument over Amendment 2 was over the perceived morality of homosexuality. Although the state framed its case in terms of preventing homosexuals from having what it dubbed special rights, Kennedy bluntly stated that the amendment would have effectively singled out homosexuals for discrimination. Moreover, Scalia supported the amendment not on the grounds that it allowed the state to prevent itself from giving special rights to one group but because he felt it was acceptable for Colorado voters to use legal means to protect what he deemed traditional sexual social behavior. Thus the Supreme Court's decision, even the dissent, affirmed the activists' position that the amendment was aimed at allowing antigay discrimination.

*—Jessie Bishop Powell*

## FURTHER READING

Chauncey, George. *Why Marriage? The History Shaping Today's Debate over Gay Equality*. New York: Basic Books, 2004. Examines the reasons for the GLBT rights debate to center on gay marriage, from the perspective of a gay rights activist.

Gallagher, John, and Chris Bull. *Perfect Enemies: The Religious Right, the Gay Movement, and the Politics of the 1990's*. New York: Crown, 1996. Examines the contrasting perspectives in conservative religious movements and the GLBT rights movements in the context of the unique political situation of the 1990's.

Keen, Lisa, and Suzanne B. Goldberg. *Strangers to the Law: Gay People on Trial*. Ann Arbor: University of Michigan Press, 1998. Discusses the politics behind gay rights struggles, with a focus on the law. Includes a section regarding the debate comparing legal rights against "special" rights as well as the *Romer v. Evans* case.

**SEE ALSO:** Dec. 15, 1973: American Psychiatric Association Delists Homosexuality as a Psychiatric Disorder; July 3, 1975: Civil Service Decides That Gays Are Fit for Public Service; Oct. 14, 1979: Gay Rights March in Washington; Aug. 17, 1984: U.S. Court of

Appeals Upholds the Navy's Ban on Homosexuality; Apr. 23, 1990: U.S. Government Authorizes Collection of Data on Crime Against Gays; June 28, 2000:

U.S. Supreme Court Protects Restrictions on Membership in Private Groups; July 1, 2000: Vermont's Civil Union Law Takes Effect.

## June 10, 1996
# CENTER-RIGHT GOVERNMENT TAKES OVER IN SPAIN

*The victory of José María Aznar's Popular Party in 1996 ended the fourteen-year rule of Spain's Socialist Party, under the leadership of Felipe González. In spite of the scandals and corruption that plagued the Socialist government, the Popular Party failed to win an absolute majority in the Congress of Deputies, reflecting the electorate's deep mistrust of a political party with roots in Spain's fascist past.*

**LOCALE:** Madrid, Spain
**CATEGORY:** Government and politics

**KEY FIGURES**
*José María Aznar* (b. 1953), prime minister of Spain, 1996-2004, and general secretary of the Partido Popular, 1990-2003
*Manuel Fraga Iribarne* (b. 1922), minister of information and tourism in Francisco Franco's dictatorship, 1962-1969, founder of the Alianza Popular in 1976, and mentor to José María Aznar
*Felipe González* (b. 1942), prime minister of Spain, 1982-1996, and general secretary of the Partido Socialista Obrero Español, 1974-1997

**SUMMARY OF EVENT**
Spain successfully transitioned to democratic rule following the death of its fascist dictator, Francisco Franco, in 1975. After an initial period in which Spain was governed by the center-right Unión de Centro Democrático (Centrist Democratic Union), the center-left Partido Socialista Obrero Español (Spanish Socialist Workers' Party), or PSOE, a party that had been illegal during Franco's rule, won the election of 1982 by a wide margin and ruled Spain for fourteen years under Felipe González as prime minister (1982-1996).

The PSOE governed with an absolute majority from 1982 until 1993. The party sought to modernize Spain, consolidate its democracy, and integrate it into Europe. It brought Spain into the North Atlantic Treaty Organization (NATO) in 1986. It lowered Spain's external debt and reduced inflation through painful economic adjustments that brought labor unrest. A series of political

scandals associated with senior PSOE leaders that began in the 1980's also undermined support for the Socialist government.

Although support for the PSOE progressively weakened, the Alianza Popular, renamed Partido Popular (PP) in 1989, failed to increase its support among the electorate. Most of its leadership is made up of the children and grandchildren of leading figures of Francisco Franco's dictatorship (1939-1975). In part because the Spanish electorate feared putting in power a party with such roots, the PP performed dismally in the 1980's.

The PP came to be the ruling party in Spain in 1996 by casting itself as the true political center and by taking measures to quell the electorate's fears of its fascist roots. Manuel Fraga Iribarne relinquished the presidency of the Partido Popular and designated the uncharismatic but skillful José María Aznar to take his place, thus making someone who never held office in Franco's government the public face of the party. The PP's move to redefine itself as centrist did have the desired result of improving its standing with the electorate. Its share of the vote rose to almost 35 percent in the 1993 election, while in the three previous elections it had gained an average of 25 percent of the vote.

Due to the PP's improved performance in the 1993 election, the PSOE was forced to form a minority government with the support of the Basque and Catalan nationalist parties. When those parties withdrew their support in late 1995, the PSOE had to call an election. The scandal of the Grupos Antiterroristas de Liberación (antiterrorist liberation groups), or GAL, was an important factor in their decision. The GAL were individuals secretly hired by the Ministry of Interior to kill Basque separatists with ties to Euskadi Ta Askatasuna (Basque homeland and freedom), or ETA, a secret organization that sought Basque independence from Spain through violent means. The GAL scandal damaged the PSOE the most and dominated public attention for the last two years of the party's rule.

The 1996 election campaign pitted the PP, led by José María Aznar, against the PSOE, led by the Prime Minis-

1996

ter Felipe González. Since both parties were trying to claim the center of the political spectrum, their platform proposals did not greatly differ. Political observers predicted that González and the PSOE would lose the election badly because of the numerous scandals associated with them and because they had alienated their working-class base.

The PSOE argued that it had modernized Spain and brought it prosperity. The economy was growing, and unemployment and inflation were down. The PP claimed it was in a better position to lead Spain forward and would continue many of the PSOE's policies, but would execute them with greater success. It campaigned on the need for a change of government and presented itself as the party of the center that would end the corruption and abuse of power perpetrated by the PSOE.

The PP did not make an issue of the corruption allegations that plagued the PSOE because a partisan press kept the corruption investigations and allegations in the electorate's awareness. Most notably, the newspaper *El Mundo* aggressively investigated and reported on charges of corruption against members of the PSOE government. Especially explosive were the investigations of the links between the GAL scandal and the government of Felipe González.

The defeat of the PSOE was a foregone conclusion. To try to avoid what looked to be inevitable, the PSOE mounted a defensive and highly negative campaign that included ads that linked the PP with the dictatorship of Francisco Franco. It argued that the social welfare benefits established by the Socialist government would be dismantled by the PP. González told voters to the left of the PSOE that a vote for a leftist party that had no chance of governing, such as the Communist Party, would be in effect a vote for the PP. However, the PSOE misstepped when it made the minister of interior, José Barrionuevo, a PSOE candidate while he was being prosecuted for having set up the GAL to fight a dirty war against Basque separatists.

In the end, the PP won the election, but not with the wide margins that most political pundits predicted. The PP did not win enough seats in the Congress of Deputies to govern with an absolute majority. Felipe González actually looked happier than José María Aznar on election night, since the PSOE lost by a much narrower margin than anticipated. Aznar and the PP were faced with the need to form a coalition government with the same Catalan nationalist party (Convergència i Unió) that had been a coalition partner of the PSOE. This made the victory of the PP almost sweet for the PSOE, since the PP was espe-

cially opposed to the nationalist aspirations of Catalonia and the other regional nationalities of Spain, such as the Basque Country and Galicia. While Aznar and the PP negotiated with Convergència i Unió and other minor nationalist parties, González led an interim government from March, 1995, until Aznar was able to install his government in June.

## SIGNIFICANCE

The election results of 1996 confirm trends in political attitudes and behavior characteristic of the Spanish electorate since Spain became a constitutional monarchy in 1978. Most of the Spanish electorate favors the political center. In order to govern successfully for fourteen years, the PSOE had to move to the center. In order to achieve electoral success for the first time, the PP had to position itself in the center. The strength of the vote for the PSOE, in spite of the scandals associated with its rule, attests to the persistent distrust of the right in a significant portion of the Spanish electorate. The PP's move to the political center turned out to be more apparent than real. Aznar's first guest after he assumed control of the government was his mentor Manuel Fraga Iribarne, who had been a minister in Franco's dictatorship. Although the PP did enact many moderate policies in its first term (1996-2000), its policies became much more conservative when it was able to govern with an absolute majority (2000-2004).

—*Evelyn Toft*

## FURTHER READING

Amodia, José. "Spain at the Polls: The General Election of 3 March 1996." *West European Politics* 19 (April, 1996): 813-819. Discusses the campaign themes of the Popular and Socialist parties in the 1996 election and the election results. Includes tables.

Balfour, Sebastian, ed. *The Politics of Contemporary Spain.* New York: Routledge, 2005. Collection of articles on Spanish politics since Spain's embrace of democratic government in 1977 on such topics as corruption, terrorism, the Popular Party, the Socialist Party, and the monarchy. Analyzes electoral politics. Extensive endnotes.

Gibbons, John. *Spanish Politics Today.* New York: Manchester University Press, 1999. Features a chapter on political parties and elections and on the structure and inner workings of the branches of government. Lists references after each chapter.

Gies, David T. "Spain Today: Is the Party Over?" *Virginia Quarterly Review* 72 (March, 1996): 392-407.

Overview of the history of Spain's democracy from 1977 to 1996, with emphasis on the lead-up to the 1996 election.

Hopkin, Jonathan. "An Incomplete Alternation: The Spanish Elections of March 1996." *International Journal of Iberian Studies* 9 (February, 1996): 110-116. Gives background and analysis on why the Popular Party did not realize a more decisive victory against the Socialists in the 1996 election. Includes tables.

Montero, José Ramón. "Stabilising the Democratic Order: Electoral Behavior in Spain." *West European*

*Politics* 21 (April, 1998): 53-79. Examines Spanish elections from 1977 through 1996, including party performance over time, the effects of election laws on election outcomes, and characteristics of the electorate. Includes many tables.

**SEE ALSO:** Nov. 20, 1975: Death of Franco; June 15, 1977: Spain Holds Its First Free Elections Since the Civil War; 1980: Basques Are Granted Home Rule but Continue to Fight for Independence.

## July 5, 1996
# WILMUT CLONES THE FIRST LARGE MAMMAL FROM AN ADULT CELL

*A team of scientists working in Scotland achieved their goal of creating an exact copy of an adult mammal.*

**ALSO KNOWN AS:** Dolly the sheep
**LOCALE:** Roslin Institute, near Edinburgh, Scotland
**CATEGORIES:** Science and technology; biology

**KEY FIGURES**
*Ian Wilmut* (b. 1944), embryologist with the Roslin Institute
*Keith H. S. Campbell* (fl. late twentieth century), experiment supervisor with the Roslin Institute
*J. McWhir* (fl. late twentieth century), researcher with the Roslin Institute
*W. A. Ritchie* (fl. late twentieth century), researcher with the Roslin Institute

**SUMMARY OF EVENT**
On February 22, 1997, officials of the Roslin Institute, a biological research institution near Edinburgh, Scotland, held a press conference to announce startling news: They had succeeded in creating a clone—a biologically identical copy—from cells taken from an adult sheep. Although cloning had been performed previously with simpler organisms, the Roslin Institute's experiment marked the first time that a large, complex mammal had been successfully cloned.

Cloning, or the production of genetically identical individuals, has long been a staple of science fiction and other popular literature. Clones do exist naturally, as in the example of identical twins. Scientists have long understood the process by which identical twins are created, and agricultural researchers dreamed of a method by

which cheap identical copies of superior livestock could be created. The discovery of the double helix structure of deoxyribonucleic acid (DNA), or the genetic code in the 1950's led to extensive research into cloning and genetic engineering. Using the discoveries of James D. Watson, Francis Crick, and other geneticists, scientists were soon able to develop techniques to clone laboratory mice.

However, the cloning of complex, valuable animals such as livestock proved to be hard going. Early versions of livestock cloning were technical attempts at duplicating the natural process of fertilized egg splitting that leads to the birth of identical twins. Artificially inseminated eggs were removed, split, and then reinserted into surrogate mothers. This method proved to be overly costly for commercial purposes, a situation aggravated by a low success rate.

Researchers at the Roslin Institute found these earlier attempts to be fundamentally flawed. Even if the success rate could be improved, the number of clones created (of sheep, in this case) would still be limited. The Scots, led by embryologist Ian Wilmut and experiment supervisor Keith H. S. Campbell, decided to take an entirely different approach. The result was the first live birth of a mammal produced through a process known as nuclear transfer.

Nuclear transfer involves the replacement of the nucleus of an immature egg with a nucleus taken from another cell. Previous attempts at nuclear transfer had cells from a single embryo divided up and implanted into an egg. Because a sheep embryo has only about forty usable cells, this method also proved limiting. The Roslin team therefore decided to grow their own cells in a laboratory culture. They took more mature embryonic cells than those previously used, and they experimented with the use of a nutrient mixture. One of their breakthroughs occurred when they discovered that these "cell lines" grew much more quickly when certain nutrients were absent. Using this technique, the Scots were able to produce a theoretically unlimited number of genetically identical cell lines.

The next step was to transfer the cell lines of the sheep into the nucleus of unfertilized sheep eggs. First, 277 nuclei with a full set of chromosomes were transferred to the unfertilized eggs. An electric shock was then used to cause the eggs to begin development, the shock performing the duty of fertilization. Of these eggs, twenty-nine developed enough to be inserted into surrogate mothers. All the embryos died before birth except one: a ewe the scientists named Dolly. Her birth on July 5, 1996, was witnessed by only a veterinarian and a few researchers. Not until the clone had survived the critical earliest stages of life was the success of the experiment disclosed; Dolly was more than seven months old by the time her birth was announced to a startled world.

## SIGNIFICANCE

The news that the cloning of sophisticated organisms had left the realm of science fiction and become a matter of accomplished scientific fact set off an immediate uproar. Ethicists and media commentators quickly began to debate the moral consequences of the use—and potential misuse—of the technology. Politicians in numerous countries responded to the news by calling for legal restrictions on cloning research. Scientists, meanwhile, speculated about the possible benefits and practical limitations of the process.

The issue that stirred the imagination of the broader public and sparked the most spirited debate was the possibility that similar experiments might soon be performed using human embryos. Although most commentators seemed to agree that such efforts would be profoundly immoral, many experts observed that they would be virtually impossible to prevent. "Could someone do this tomorrow morning on a human embryo?" Arthur L. Caplan, the director of the University of Pennsylvania's bioethics center, asked reporters. "Yes. It would not even take too much science. The embryos are out

*Dolly the sheep, the first animal to be cloned from adult cells.* (AP/Wide World Photos)

## DOLLY THE SHEEP

In 1997, the world was taken aback when a group of scientists headed by embryologist Ian Wilmut at the Roslin Institute in Scotland announced the successful cloning of a sheep named Dolly. Scientists had already cloned cows and sheep, but they had used embryo cells. Dolly was the first vertebrate cloned from the cell of an adult vertebrate.

Although environmental factors would make Dolly individual, genetically she would never have the individuality that an organism produced by usual reproductive means would possess. Over the next six years, she gave birth to several apparently healthy offspring. In 2002, at the age of six, Dolly became lame in her left hind leg, a victim of arthritis. Although sheep commonly suffer arthritis, a veterinarian noted that both the location and the age of onset were uncommon. Then, in February, 2003, Dolly was euthanized after the discovery that she had a progressive lung disease, ovine pulmonary adenocarcinoma.

Dolly's health problems led to speculation about premature aging in clones, but her problems were complicated by her unique situation as well. As Wilmut noted, in the early years following the announcement of Dolly's cloning she became something of a celebrity, which led to overfeeding by visitors and in turn a period of obesity, later corrected. More significant were the discovery of her arthritis and then her lung disease, conditions not uncommon in sheep but that tend to emerge later—sheep typically live to be eleven or twelve years old.

Theories of premature aging in clones are supported by the fact that Dolly's telomeres were shorter than normal. These cell structures function as "caps" that prevent "fraying" at the ends of DNA cells. As a cell ages, its telomeres become progressively shorter, until finally they disappear altogether and are no longer able to protect the cell, which then dies.

Was Dolly older genetically than she was chronologically? The answer remains unclear, and experimentation with the cloning of complex large mammals continues in the hope that one day it will be possible to breed animals that are resistant to foot-and-mouth disease, bovine spongiform encephalopathy (mad cow disease), brucellosis, tuberculosis, and other diseases. Nevertheless, the widespread cloning of mammals—and especially the implications this would have for human cloning—remains both distant and controversial as researchers work through the painstakingly slow process of experimentation and the public debate over bioethics continues.

steadfastly proclaimed their own opposition to human experimentation. Moreover, most scientists were quick to point out that such scenarios were far from realization, noting the extremely high failure rate involved in the creation of even a single sheep.

Most experts emphasized more practical possible uses of the technology: improving agricultural stock by cloning productive and disease-resistant animals, for example, or regenerating endangered or even extinct species. Even such apparently benign schemes had their detractors, however, as other observers remarked on the potential dangers of thus narrowing a species' genetic pool.

Ten days after the announcement of Dolly's birth, U.S. president Bill Clinton issued an executive order that banned the use of federal money for human cloning research, and he called on researchers in the private sector to refrain from such experiments voluntarily.

Dolly was euthanized in 2003 after it was found she had developed the lung disease ovine pulmonary adenocarcinoma. Death from lung disease is not uncommon in sheep, although Dolly was relatively young. Questions about whether her death was speeded by her genetic makeup remain, as do the ethical debates surrounding her symbolic significance. Since Dolly's death, many other large animals—including horses, bulls, dogs, and cats—have been cloned in an attempt to create animals for a variety of both noble and mercenary reasons: to develop disease resistance, to save endangered species, and even to reproduce beloved pets. The ethical and public debate continues not only about cloning of large animals but also about the use of genetic material from stem cells for medical research. Few observers, however, would debate the fact that Dolly's birth marked only the beginning of a promising, and morally complex, chapter in the history of science.

*—Jeff Cupp*

1996

there." Such observations conjured visions of a future that seemed marvelous to some, nightmarish to others. Optimists suggested that the best and brightest of humanity could be forever perpetuated, creating an endless supply of Albert Einsteins and Wolfgang Amadeus Mozarts. Pessimists warned of a world overrun by clones of self-serving narcissists and petty despots, or of the creation of a secondary class of humans to serve as organ donors for their progenitors. The Roslin Institute's researchers

## FURTHER READING

Drlica, Karl. *Understanding DNA and Gene Cloning: A Guide for the Curious.* 4th ed. New York: John Wiley & Sons, 2003. Offers clear and accessible explanations of the techniques of cloning. Includes extensive glossary and bibliography.

Kolata, Gina Bari. *Clone: The Road to Dolly, and the Path Ahead.* New York: HarperCollins, 1998. The science journalist who broke the story of Dolly's birth analyzes Dolly's story in the social and cultural context of the public fear of and fascination with cloning for almost a century.

McGee, Glenn, and Arthur Caplan, eds. *The Human Cloning Debate.* 4th ed. Berkeley, Calif.: Berkeley Hills Books, 2006. Collection of essays addresses the history and techniques of cloning as well as the ethics involved in using the techniques on humans. Includes bibliographic references.

Wilmut, Ian, Keith Campbell, and Colin Tudge. *The Second Creation: The Age of Biological Control by the Scientists That Cloned Dolly.* London: Headline, 2000. Describes the research that led to Dolly's birth and early evaluations of cloning techniques.

Wilmut, Ian, and Roger Highfield. *After Dolly: The Uses and Misuses of Human Cloning.* New York: W. W. Norton, 2006. Focuses on the social and policy implications of cloning in the wake of Wilmut's research with Dolly. Delineates fact from fiction to dispel fears about cloning, advocating the place of cloning technology in the fight against disease yet at the same time reasserting Wilmut's long-held views against attempts at human cloning.

**SEE ALSO:** 1980: Berg, Gilbert, and Sanger Develop Techniques for Genetic Engineering; Sept., 1983: Murray and Szostak Create the First Artificial Chromosome; Mar. 10, 1984: Willadsen Clones the First Farm Animal by Nuclear Transfer; May, 1988: Patent Is Granted for Genetically Engineered Mice; Mar. 4, 1997: Clinton Rejects Federal Support for Human Cloning.

## July 27, 1996
# CENTENNIAL OLYMPIC PARK BOMBING

*The first attack on an Olympic Games since the murders of Israeli athletes at Munich in 1972, the Centennial Olympic Park bombing resulted in two deaths, dozens of injuries, and criticism of the handling of the incident by officials and police. The event also increased security concerns at subsequent Olympic Games.*

**LOCALE:** Atlanta, Georgia
**CATEGORIES:** Crime and scandal; terrorism, atrocities, and war crimes

**KEY FIGURES**
*Eric Robert Rudolph* (b. 1966), former U.S. Army private who was convicted of the Centennial Olympic Park bombing
*Richard Jewell* (1962-2007), security guard who became a person of interest in the bombing
*Alice Hawthorne* (1952-1996), Georgia resident who was killed in the bombing
*Melih Uzunyol* (1959-1996), Turkish cameraman who died in the aftermath of the bombing

**SUMMARY OF EVENT**
The atmosphere was festive in Centennial Olympic Park in downtown Atlanta, Georgia, in the early morning hours of July 27, 1996. The second week of the 1996

Olympic Games had just begun, and thousands of celebrants had gathered in the park for a concert by the Georgia rock band Jack Mack and the Heart Attack. Suddenly, at 1:21 A.M., the revelry was broken as a bomb blast shook the Olympic complex and sprayed shrapnel into the crowd. The games of the Twenty-sixth Olympiad, held on the hundred-year anniversary of the first modern games, had become the scene of a premeditated act of mass violence.

Forty-four-year-old Alice Hawthorne was dead of a shrapnel wound to the head, and thirty-seven-year-old Turkish cameraman Melih Uzunyol, rushing to film the immediate aftermath of the bombing, suffered a heart attack and died. The blast wounded 111 other spectators and put a temporary halt to the festivities surrounding the Olympic Games. The Games would continue the following day under increased security, but although the 1996 Olympics were considered a general success—both financially and athletically—the bombing cast a pall over the event that prompted International Olympic Committee chairman Juan Antonio Samaranch to forgo the customary closing-ceremonies declaration that the most recent Olympics were the best ever.

Although U.S. president Bill Clinton immediately pledged to use the full resources of the federal govern-

*Centennial Olympic Park in Atlanta, Georgia, after an explosion hit a tower near the stage at a concert during the 1996 Olympics.* (AP/Wide World Photos)

ment to bring the perpetrators of the attack to justice, authorities were left with little evidence and few plausible leads in the immediate aftermath of the bombing. Investigation of the scene and interviews with witnesses indicated that the bomb, fashioned from pipe and packed with nails, had been planted underneath a park bench inside a military-style backpack. Its design and placement were intended to inflict large-scale damage by firing shrapnel directly toward the crowd gathered in front of the stage where the musical act was to perform; the bomb had tipped over prior to the blast, however, alleviating the likelihood of increased casualties.

Richard Jewell, a private security guard working at the event, had discovered the backpack just minutes prior to the blast and reported its presence to police. Shortly after Jewell and other security guards began evacuating the area, the bomb exploded. At first, Jewell was commended for his vigilance in discovering the bomb and for his courage while attempting to clear spectators from the

scene. Suspicions quickly began to turn to Jewell, however, as agents of the Federal Bureau of Investigation (FBI) questioned him intensively, conducted searches of the apartment he shared with his mother, and placed him under twenty-four-hour surveillance.

Media reports that Jewell had exhibited overzealous and erratic behavior in his previous employment as a police officer, along with photographs showing Jewell dressed in camouflage and posing with firearms, fueled public suspicion that Jewell had perpetrated the bombing. Although Jewell was never charged with a crime or officially named as a suspect, in the days and weeks following the bombing the news media routinely identified him as the primary suspect in the investigation. After months of investigation yielded no evidence against Jewell, federal authorities formally cleared him of all suspicion in October, 1996. In July, 1997, U.S. attorney general Janet Reno apologized to Jewell on behalf of the federal government.

Having failed to yield any formal suspects, the FBI investigation of the Olympic Park bombing appeared to be at a standstill by the end of 1996. In January and February, 1997, two more bombings in the Atlanta area—one at an abortion clinic and the other at a nightclub frequented by lesbians—revived the investigation as authorities explored possible connections between the Olympic Park bombing and the more recent attacks. The bombs used in all three cases were similarly designed, and letters received by local newspapers attributing the bombings to a mysterious organization called the "Army of God" suggested that the attacks were the work of political extremists. Witnesses to a bombing of an abortion clinic in Birmingham, Alabama, on January 29, 1998, under similar circumstances provided a description of a white pickup truck leaving the scene and a partial license plate number, and this information led authorities to identify North Carolina resident Eric Robert Rudolph as a suspect in the Birmingham bombing in February, 1998.

Rudolph, a former U.S. Army private with ties to the white supremacist Christian Identity organization, subsequently fled to the mountains of western North Carolina to evade capture. Federal authorities searching for Rudolph in the area found themselves hindered both by the rugged terrain and by the resistance of some local residents, who either sympathized with Rudolph or believed him innocent. Surviving on stolen and scavenged food (and, allegedly, on the assistance of supporters), Rudolph remained a fugitive until May 31, 2003, when he was arrested in Murphy, North Carolina, by an officer on routine patrol who spotted him searching for food in a garbage bin. Rudolph subsequently pleaded guilty to the Olympic Park bombing and the other attacks and received four consecutive life sentences. He was incarcerated at a federal "supermax" (highest level of security) prison in Florence, Colorado, on August 22, 2005.

Richard Jewell subsequently became a symbol in American popular culture for persons wrongfully accused of crimes and vilified in the media. Following his exoneration, Jewell filed lawsuits against various media outlets, including the National Broadcasting Company (NBC) television network and the *Atlanta Journal-Constitution* newspaper. By 2005, all of these cases except the suit against the *Journal-Constitution* had been settled out of court. On August 1, 2006, more than

---

### RUDOLPH'S ARREST

*In 2003, five years after he was first listed on the FBI's Ten Most Wanted Fugitives list, Eric Robert Rudolph was arrested and charged with bombing attacks that killed 2 people and injured more than 150 others. He was sentenced to life without parole in 2005. On May 31, 2003, Attorney General John Ashcroft released the following statement regarding Rudolph's capture:*

Today, Eric Robert Rudolph, the most notorious American fugitive on the FBI's "Most Wanted" list has been captured and will face American justice. American law enforcement's unyielding efforts to capture Eric Robert Rudolph have been rewarded. Working with law enforcement nationwide, the FBI always gets their man. This sends a clear message that we will never cease in our efforts to hunt down all terrorists, foreign or domestic, and stop them from harming the innocent.

I want to especially congratulate the local authorities in Murphy, North Carolina, who with the FBI and other local and state law enforcement throughout the country were able to apprehend this suspect. While it has been a long struggle, they never stopped, never yielded and never gave up. The American people, most importantly the victims of these terrorist attacks, can rest easier knowing that another alleged killer is no longer a threat.

Eric Robert Rudolph is charged in connection with the bombing of a health clinic in Birmingham, Alabama, in which a police officer was killed and a nurse critically wounded. He is also charged in connection with the fatal bombings at Centennial Olympic Park in downtown Atlanta, Georgia, the double bombings at the Sandy Springs Professional Office Building north of Atlanta, and the double bombings at the Otherside Lounge in midtown Atlanta. These bomb blasts injured more than 150 people.

---

ten years after the bombings, Georgia governor Sonny Perdue formally honored Jewell for his heroism during the Centennial Olympic Park bombing. In August, 2007, Jewell died from complications of diabetes.

### SIGNIFICANCE

The Centennial Olympic Park bombing was the first act of violence to occur at the site of the Olympic Games since the murder of eleven Israeli athletes and one police officer by religious extremists during the 1972 Games in Munich, West Germany. The perpetrator of the Olympic Park bombing was unsuccessful in his stated objective to create a major disruption of the Games, given that all subsequent events were held as scheduled under heightened security. The attack did, however, contribute to a general air of negativity surrounding the Atlanta Games, which had already been marred by traffic problems and technological failures. Olympic officials drew criticism for what some perceived to be a lack of responsiveness to the bombing, including the decision to hold the events of the following day as scheduled.

In addition, the attack proved embarrassing to the United States, which had urged other nations to crack down on extremist activity during the Olympics, and to federal authorities as a result of their treatment of Jewell and the difficulties they encountered in identifying and apprehending the perpetrator. The bombing inspired the use of increased security measures at subsequent Olympic Games—a trend that would be further heightened following the terrorist attacks on New York City and Washington, D.C., of September 11, 2001.

The Olympic Park bombing and the subsequent attacks for which Rudolph claimed responsibility were part of a wave of activity by right-wing political groups in the United States in the 1990's that led to numerous acts of violence and confrontations with police, including the FBI siege of the Branch Davidian compound in Waco, Texas, in 1993; the bombing of the Alfred P. Murrah Federal Office Building in Oklahoma City, Oklahoma, in 1995; the standoff between police and the Montana Freemen in 1996; and the murder of Dr. Bernard Slepian by an antiabortion activist in 1998.

Media coverage of the Olympic Park attack and the subsequent investigation, particularly concerning the handling of the Richard Jewell story, inspired popular debate concerning the ethical responsibility of broadcasters and journalists to ensure the credibility and objectivity of news content; yet the fallout over the Jewell incident did not result in significant change in the treatment of criminal suspects in the media.

—*Michael H. Burchett*

## FURTHER READING

Martin, Gus. "The American Case: Terrorism in the United States." In *Understanding Terrorism: Challenges, Perspectives, and Issues*. Thousand Oaks, Calif.: Sage, 2006. Places the Olympic Park bombing within the larger context of domestic terrorism in the United States.

Shepard, Alicia C. "Going to Extremes (Olympic Bombing Suspect Richard A. Jewell)." *American Journalism Review* 18 (October, 1996): 38-53. Presents a critical analysis of the news media coverage of the bombing and the subsequent investigation.

Vollers, Maryanne. *Lone Wolf: Eric Rudolph—Murder, Myth, and the Pursuit of an American Outlaw*. New York: HarperCollins, 2006. Journalistic narrative of Eric Rudolph's life and criminal activities includes a detailed account of the Centennial Park bombing.

Yarbrough, C. Richard. *And They Call Them Games: An Inside View of the 1996 Olympics*. Macon, Ga.: Mercer University Press, 2000. Account of the Atlanta Olympics by a member of the Atlanta Committee for the Olympic Games. Discusses the bombing and its aftermath from the perspective of an insider.

SEE ALSO: Sept. 5-6, 1972: Arab Terrorists Murder Israelis at Munich Olympics; Feb. 26, 1993: World Trade Center Bombing; Apr. 19, 1995: Bombing of the Oklahoma City Federal Building.

1996

## July 28, 1996
# KENNEWICK MAN IS DISCOVERED

*The 1996 discovery of ancient human remains on the bank of the Columbia River near Kennewick, Washington, on public land under control of the U.S. Army Corps of Engineers, triggered a decade-long controversy that pitted forensic and cultural anthropologists against Native Americans who fought for the right to bury their "Ancient One" with dignity and respect.*

**ALSO KNOWN AS:** Ancient One

**LOCALE:** Columbia River near Kennewick, Washington

**CATEGORIES:** Anthropology; archaeology; indigenous peoples' rights; prehistory and early cultures and civilizations

**KEY FIGURES**

*Floyd Johnson* (b. 1939), coroner of Benton County, Washington, 1989-2007

*Will Thomas* (b. 1975), college student who discovered Kennewick man

*Dave Deacy* (b. 1977), college student who accompanied Will Thomas

*James C. Chatters* (b. 1949), forensic anthropologist, archaeologist, and state crime lab analyst for Washington's Benton and Franklin counties

*John Jelderks* (b. 1938), U.S. magistrate judge of the U.S. District Court, Oregon

*Douglas Owsley* (b. 1951), forensic osteologist, researcher, and anthropologist with the National Museum of Natural History

*Robson Bonnichsen* (1940-2004), director of the Center for the Study of the First Americans

*Doc Hastings* (b. 1941), U.S. congressman from Washington beginning in 1995

**SUMMARY OF EVENT**

On July 28, 1996, two college students, Will Thomas and Dave Deacy, happened upon a human skull that was sitting in Lake Wallula, a reservoir along the Columbia River near Kennewick, Washington. The two friends notified local police officers, who contacted the Benton County coroner, Floyd Johnson. Based on the condition of the bones, Johnson decided it would be most prudent to call forensic anthropologist James C. Chatters in to investigate. Chatters's preliminary findings suggested that the skull's long, thin face and protruding jaw appeared to be most closely aligned with Caucasoid characteristics,

but the wear pattern of the teeth indicated that the remains were ancient. The fact that the bone configuration did not look Native American and yet the skull appeared to be exceedingly old created great intrigue. Scientists wondered who this man was, where he came from, and what he could reveal about the earliest inhabitants of North America.

During the month following the skull's discovery, Chatters worked, under a permit granted under a provision of the Archaeological Resources Protection Act of 1979, to uncover the skull's accompanying well-preserved skeletal remains. The skeleton was found to be that of a forty- to fifty-five-year-old male, approximately 5 feet, 9 inches tall, who showed evidence of having suffered from multiple life traumas. The injuries included a gray area in the right pelvis that computed tomography (CT) scans showed to be a leaf-shaped projectile (arrow) dating from 4,500 to 9,000 years ago. Because this object caused more perplexity in determining the age of the remains, Chatters received authorization from the coroner to conduct DNA and radiocarbon analysis. These tests, conducted on the skeleton's finger, indicated that the individual, who came to be called Kennewick man, was a fish eater who lived some 9,000 years ago, sometime in the period 7300 to 7600 B.C.E.

On August 30, 1996, four days after the test results were disclosed, the U.S. Army Corps of Engineers (USACE) declared that because the remains were ancient and found on federal land, the Native American Graves Protection and Repatriation Act (NAGPRA) of 1990 applied. Under NAGPRA, federal officials must notify Native American tribes who have inhabited the geographic areas near such discoveries, provide the tribes with the opportunity to show cultural affiliation with the discovered remains, and then return the remains to the tribes if affiliation is shown. The USACE seized the Kennewick man remains, required all scientific studies on the remains to halt, and declared its intention to return the remains to the five federated tribes of the Umatilla Indian Reservation (Umatilla, Yakama, Nez Perce, Colville, and Wanapum). The news that the remains would likely be returned to the Umatilla for sacred reburial horrified many scientists who saw the well-preserved remains as priceless clues in the mystery of the population of the Americas. In addition, the USACE's action triggered other ethnic groups to stake their own claims.

In October, eight well-known archaeologists and anthropologists, including Robson Bonnichsen, director of the Center for the Study of the First Americans, and Douglas Owsley of the Smithsonian Institution's National Museum of Natural History, sued the federal government to gain the right to conduct further scientific investigation on Kennewick man. They asserted that there was a lack of due process in the seizure of the remains and that NAGPRA did not pertain in the case because no direct cultural link between Kennewick man and the Native American tribes had been proven. Other groups, including a European religious group, the Asatru Folk Assembly, also filed suits, claiming the right to investigate whether the remains belonged to their ancestors. The claimants understood that the Umatilla planned a quiet hidden burial where the remains of the man they called the Ancient One would be lost to any future research. The scientists contended that further research was vital to learning about Kennewick man's life and thus gaining information about North America's past.

In August, 2002, the case *Bonnichsen et al. v. United States et al.* was heard in the U.S. District Court in Portland, Oregon. Judge John Jelderks concluded that NAGPRA did not apply to Kennewick man because the government had failed to prove that the skeleton was di-

rectly linked to modern Native Americans. Because that burden of proof had not been met, Jelderks decided, scientists had the right to access and continue to study the remains under the provisions of the Archaeological Resources Protection Act. In 2004, after an appeal that again temporarily blocked further scientific studies of Kennewick man, Judge Jelderks's decision was upheld by in the Ninth U.S. Circuit Court of Appeals.

With access to the remains, which were held for study at the University of Washington's Burke Museum, an eleven-person team of scientists, led by Douglas Owsley, gained new information. The researchers learned that Kennewick man had suffered several traumas, that his projectile injury came from the front, and that he had been buried with respect. Scientists continued to examine the remains into the twenty-first century, hoping that further testing will reveal more in-depth information on Kennewick man's origin. Some research has indicated that he may be genetically most similar to Polynesians or to the Ainu people, who are native to the Japanese islands.

Since the Ninth Circuit Court's decision, a number of attempts have been made to reverse its effects through legislation. In 2006, for example, Congressman Doc Hastings of Washington State introduced a bill in the

1996

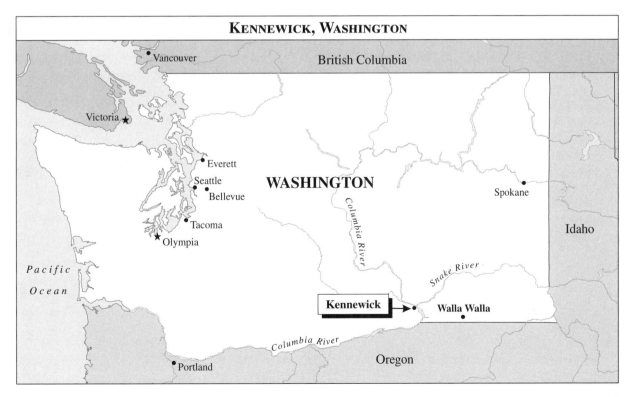

# KENNEWICK, WASHINGTON

Vancouver

British Columbia

Victoria ★

Everett

Seattle
Bellevue

WASHINGTON

Spokane

Tacoma

Olympia

*Pacific*

*Ocean*

*Columbia River*

*Snake River*

Idaho

Kennewick → Walla Walla

*Columbia River*

Portland

Oregon

U.S. House of Representatives to clarify NAGPRA. The bill was designed to protect scientists' right to research ancient remains while respecting Native Americans' tribal rights to their direct ancestors.

## SIGNIFICANCE

The discovery of the ancient human skeleton dubbed Kennewick man by scientists and Ancient One by Native Americans stirred debate as to the legal, ethical, moral, and cultural rights of scientists and indigenous peoples. Scientists argued that the remains could possibly shed light on the peopling of the Americas, while Native Americans were primarily concerned with respecting their ancestor's right to a proper reburial. The decision to permit scientific research on Kennewick man was finally settled in court, but the battle exposed a major rift regarding the best approach to handling the remnants of ancient inhabitants. Attempts to modify federal legislation affecting archaeological findings have been ongoing. Many Native Americans adhere to the belief that all remains of ancient people found on their traditional lands are the remains of their ancestors. Scientists remain protective of their rights to study skeletons that are not genetically proven to be Native American. Further attempts to clarify the legislation that affects the finding of human remains on federal lands that were once populated by Native Americans have been proposed to help prevent additional ambiguity regarding future vestiges of the legacy of early human beings.

*—Cynthia J. W. Svoboda*

## FURTHER READING

Barkan, Elazar, and Ronald Bus, eds. *Claiming the Stones, Naming the Bones: Cultural Property and the Negotiation of National and Ethnic Identity*. Los Angeles: Getty Publications, 2002. Collection of essays explores the concept of cultural property from multiple perspectives, including those of law, archaeology, physical anthropology, ethnobiology, and ethnomusicology.

Benedict, Jeff. *No Bone Unturned: The Adventures of a Top Smithsonian Forensic Scientist and the Legal Battle for America's Oldest Skeleton*. New York: HarperCollins Publishers, 2003. Reviews the significant work of Douglas Owsley of the Smithsonian Institution and discusses Owsley's part in the case of Kennewick man. Includes index.

Bruning, Susan B. "Complex Legal Legacies: The Native American Graves Protection and Repatriation Act, Scientific Study, and Kennewick Man." *American Antiquity* 71 (July, 2006): 501-522. Discusses the legal aspects of NAGPRA and the provisions of the law concerning scientific study.

Chatters, James C. *Ancient Encounters: Kennewick Man and the First Americans*. New York: Simon & Schuster, 2001. Readable account by the first forensic anthropologist to examine the bones. Includes bibliographic notes and index.

Dewar, Elaine. *Bones: Discovering the First Americans*. New York: Carroll & Graf, 2001. Journalistic work investigates the politics and history in the battle of the remains. Includes bibliography and index.

Downey, Roger. *Riddle of the Bones: Politics, Science, Race, and the Story of Kennewick Man*. New York: Copernicus, 2000. Discusses the major concerns and parties involved in the controversial issues surrounding Kennewick man. Includes index.

Thomas, David Hurst. *Skull Wars: Kennewick Man, Archaeology, and the Battle for Native American Identity*. New York: Basic Books, 2000. Covers the historical background in the disagreement between Native Americans and archaeologists in handling ancient American remains. Includes bibliography and index.

SEE ALSO: Nov., 1974: Anthropologists Discover the Early Hominid "Lucy"; Aug. 11, 1978: U.S. Congress Protects Native American Religious Practices; Aug., 1979: Ancient Sanctuary Is Discovered in El Juyo Cave; June, 1980: Radar Reveals Canals at Mayan Agricultural Centers.

**August 19, 1996**

# GREEN PARTY NOMINATES NADER FOR PRESIDENT

*In 1996, Ralph Nader made his first of three unsuccessful bids to become president of the United States. Backed by the Green Party, Nader overcame a number of barriers to garner 685,128 popular votes, or 0.71 percent of the popular vote.*

**LOCALE:** United States
**CATEGORY:** Government and politics

**KEY FIGURES**
*Ralph Nader* (b. 1934), attorney, political activist, and U.S. presidential candidate in 1996, 2000, and 2004
*Winona LaDuke* (b. 1959), Native American activist and U.S. vice presidential candidate in 1996 and 2000

**SUMMARY OF EVENT**

Throughout American history, a number of presidential candidates have run on third-party tickets, but one of the most controversial in the twentieth century was the candidacy of Ralph Nader. On August 19, 1996, Nader gave a speech in which he criticized the major political parties. Nader noted that it had become impossible to tell Democrats from Republicans in America, as both were beholden to corporate America. This speech was highly significant: It showed the important role that third parties can play in presidential elections. Nader's idealism garnered support for his cause, although voters also had many pragmatic concerns about him.

Nader had long been known as a consumer activist and political idealist. Born on February 27, 1934, in Winsted, Connecticut, he attended Princeton University, graduating in 1955, and studied law at Harvard University. In 1959, he served in the U.S. Army for six months and then started practicing law in Hartford, Connecticut. In 1964, Nader began working for Daniel Patrick Moynihan, the assistant secretary of labor. In 1965, Nader published the book that secured his reputation as a consumer activist, *Unsafe at Any Speed: The Designed-In Dangers of the American Automobile*.

Nader continued his consumer activism throughout the 1970's and 1980's, founding the nongovernmental organization Public Citizen and publishing numerous other books. Other Nader-inspired organizations include the Center for Study of Responsive Law, the Aviation Consumer Action Project, the Public Interest Research Group, the Center for Auto Safety, the Clean Water Action Project, and the Congressional Accountability Proj-

ect. Nader was also largely responsible for a number of major federal consumer protection laws, such as the Freedom of Information Act (1967) and the Safe Drinking Water Act (1974). By the 1996 election, Nader was well established as a consumer advocate and citizen activist. His idealism and his high levels of public recognition attracted the eye of the Green Party, beginning a long relationship.

The United States Green Party is technically a federation of state Green parties that has existed since the mid-1990's. The strongest support for the party has been on the West Coast, in the Northeast, and in the states surrounding the Great Lakes. During the 1980's and early 1990's, the party was active mainly at the local level. With the nomination of Nader as its candidate for president of the United States and Winona LaDuke as candidate for vice president, the Greens made a bid for power at the national level. This first bid garnered less than 1 percent of the national vote, but a subsequent 2000 presidential bid, in which Nader received almost 2.9 million votes (2.74 percent), figured in the outcome of that year's presidential election.

**SIGNIFICANCE**

Nader adopted many planks of the United States Green Party platform and offered a liberal and largely idealistic alternative at the voting booth. Nader supported the idea of gay marriage, yet most gay voters gave their support to the Democratic candidate, Al Gore. In his campaign, Nader continued to support consumer advocacy. True to Green Party values, he sought more funding for the National Park Service, decreased reliance on foreign energy sources, and limits on the commercial logging industry. Furthermore, Nader opposed the death penalty and was in favor of maintaining *Roe v. Wade* (1973). Nader supported the legalization of marijuana and supported rehabilitation over incarceration for drug addicts. Of paramount concern to Nader before and during his campaign was a focus on empowering citizens to create a government that is responsive to their needs.

When running for the presidency, Nader was aware that he had no chance of winning. Third-party candidates face tremendous challenges and find it difficult to draw voters away from the traditional Democratic and Republican parties. The institutional obstacles that limit third-party candidates include ballot access laws, filing fees, campaign finances, and the adoption of issues by the ma-

1996

*Consumer advocate Ralph Nader speaks at a news conference after the Green Party formally nominated him for president in 1996. Nader made two more unsuccessful bids for the presidency in 2000 and 2004.* (AP/Wide World Photos)

jor parties. Nevertheless, in 1996 Nader and the Green Party were able to appear on the ballot in twenty-two states and acquired 685,128 popular votes, or 0.71 percent of the popular vote. Initially this appears to be a dismal failure, but Nader and the Green Party were very successful in a number of ways.

The first area in which the Greens were successful was in challenging the traditional two-party system. This system is practically ingrained in American culture, but the Greens offered an alternative voice to those who felt their needs and interests were ignored by the mainstream parties. Although a mere fraction of the total population of the United States, the Greens were able to overcome a cultural bias and appear on ballots across the nation. In general, this can be a significant sign that there are voices unrepresented by the major parties and thus voters who are willing to turn to third parties. In this particular case, Nader emphasized the similarities between the Republi-

cans and the Democrats and their connections to corporate America.

In many cases, Nader and the Greens were also able to overcome the barrier of ballot access laws. Each state has its own bureaucratic hurdles that a minor party must leap to be listed on the ballot. The procedures to do so vary from state to state, but even by 2007 only fifteen states had granted full ballot access to the Green Party. Nader's presence on the 1996 ballot made political strategists for both Bob Dole and Bill Clinton worry that Nader would siphon away enough votes that the opposition would win.

A second barrier that third parties have to overcome is the fear on the part of voters that casting a nontraditional vote is a waste of a vote. Third parties have little chance of being elected to high office; thus the voter is disinclined to vote for third-party candidates. However, it can be argued that citizens who vote for third-party candidates use their vote to register their disagreement with the major candidates and thus to send a message to the winning candidate—although a counterargument makes the case that it is impossible to determine what, exactly, third-party support indicates. Regardless, the more support a third party receives, the more attention is paid to it, both by the media and by the major parties. In 1892, for example, the Populist Party received 8.6 percent of the popular vote; after the election, the Democratic Party adopted a number of Populist positions, in effect incorporating the Populist Party into its fold.

After running for president in 1996, Nader remained willing to run for public office. He ran in 2000 as a Green with LaDuke as his running mate and received 2.74 percent of the popular vote. In 2004, Nader ran as an Independent with Peter Miguel Camejo and garnered only 0.4 percent of the popular vote. Although Nader never won, he left his mark on American politics. Along with other third-party presidential candidates such as business tycoon Ross Perot, Nader helped to revitalize the acknowledgment of third parties in the United States. Furthermore, Nader's candidacy in 1996 paved the way for his 2000 campaign, an unforgettable race that had an impact on the major parties and arguably decided the electoral college vote in favor of George W. Bush.

*—Kathryn A. Cochran*

### FURTHER READING

Bibby, John F., and L. Sandy Maisel. *Two Parties or More? The American Party System.* 2d ed. Boulder, Colo.: Westview Press, 2003. Presents an overview of third parties, surveying the impact they have had. Includes an appendix of third parties as well as a glossary of terms related to party politics.

Collet, Christian, and Jerrold Hansen. "The Declining Significance of Ralph." In *The State of the Parties: The Changing Role of Contemporary American Politics*, edited by John C. Green and Daniel J. Coffey. 5th ed. Lanham, Md.: Rowman & Littlefield, 2007. A thorough overview of the changing role of American political parties. A chapter by the editors explores Nader's three campaigns for president and assesses the efficiency of his endeavors.

Herrnson, Paul S., and John C. Green, eds. *Multiparty Politics in America*. Lanham, Md.: Rowman & Littlefield, 1997. Collection of articles that examine the possibilities for a multiparty system in America, the

performance of third-party campaigns, and prospects for third parties.

Sabato, Larry J., and Howard R. Ernst. *Encyclopedia of American Political Parties and Elections*. New York: Facts On File, 2006. Along with an article discussing the United States Green Party, this reference work offers entries on terms, candidates, and parties throughout American political history.

**SEE ALSO:** Feb., 1973: Ecology Party Is Founded in Great Britain; Mar., 1983: West German Green Party Gains Seats in Parliament; Feb. 20, 1992: Perot Mounts a Third-Party Bid for the U.S. Presidency; Nov. 7, 2000: Bush Election Stirs Political and Legal Controversy.

1996

## August 29, 1996
# DAM BURST CONTAMINATES THE PILCOMAYO RIVER

*The rupture of a large commercial mine impoundment released tons of sludge into a headwater tributary of the Pilcomayo River southwest of Sucre, Bolivia, adding more sediment to an already seriously degraded watershed and focusing international attention on the laissez-fare attitude of the Bolivian mining industry to safety and environmental standards.*

**LOCALE:** Potisí, Bolivia
**CATEGORIES:** Disasters; environmental issues; manufacturing and industry

**KEY FIGURE**
*Gonzalo Sánchez de Lozada* (b. 1930), president of Bolivia, 1993-1997

**SUMMARY OF EVENT**
Tectonic activity has significantly concentrated metals of economic value within the crustal terranes of western South America, including Bolivia. Consequently, mining within the Pilcomayo River watershed is concentrated in the high altitudes of the folded, mountainous belt of the Bolivian cordilleras, especially near Potisí, southwest of Sucre. Reportedly, in 1996 forty-two mining operations were directly discharging wastes into the streams of the Pilcomayo watershed, continuing a long-standing tradition of no physical or chemical treatment prior to discharge of wastewater from ore-processing facilities.

Bolivia, a sparsely populated nation of approximately nine million people of mixed ancestry, is one and one-half times the size of Texas. It paid a heavy price at the

end of the twentieth century for its unbridled pursuit of metals. Tarnished in reputation, mining for precious and base metals in Bolivia lost some of its luster. On August 29, 1996, an inadequately engineered holding pit for mining wastes, which was adjacent to a headwaters of the upper Pilcomayo River, ruptured near Potisí. This disaster would end four centuries of mining laissez-faire in Bolivia. Previously, mining operations had been heavily subsidized by cheap, indigenous labor and natural infrastructures such as the Pilcomayo River. After the rupture, Bolivian and international mine operators could no longer disregard local and national safety and environmental issues.

Like Bolivia itself, the Pilcomayo River is a lesson in stark physical contrasts. Volumetrically variable, the lengthy waterway is fed by rains and snows from the highest Andean peaks of the Cordillera Real and the Cordillera Oriental, on the eastern edge of the Altiplano, or Bolivian Plateau, and flows southeasterly across the Tropic of Capricorn. Tracing a course of approximately 900 kilometers (about 600 miles), the Pilcomayo merges with the larger Paraguay River opposite Asunción, the capital of neighboring Paraguay. Crossing the folded granitic ridges and valleys of the higher, cooler, Bolivian Andes, the river flows onto and meanders across the Gran Chaco, a flat, torrid, subtropical savanna between northern Argentina and southwestern Paraguay that harbors diverse plant and animal life. Culturally, the Pilcomayo arises within the Bolivian departments of Oruro

2987

and Potisí and passes through Chuquisaca and Tarija departments, forming a winding frontier between the lowland Argentine and Paraguayan provinces of Formosa, Boquerón, and Presidente Hayes.

As of the early 2000's, approximately one million people lived within the river's upper watershed, with Sucre, the national judiciary center of Bolivia, the largest city relying on its limited resources. Reportedly, no communities had wastewater treatment facilities; untreated wastes were thus directly discharged into the Pilcomayo's Bolivian reaches. Because of limited rainfall within its evaporative, poorly vegetated upper watershed, the river had a minimal base flow and could be seasonally ephemeral, making it susceptible to irrigation demands, erosion, sedimentation, and pollutants from municipal and industrial sources. Volumetrically, a substantial portion of the river's perennial base flow within the cordilleran provinces was made up of untreated wastewaters from Bolivian mines and municipalities.

Coupled with similarly laissez-faire governmental policies toward municipal wastes, the Bolivian government's lack of regulations regarding river dumping resulted in a severe negative impact on the freshwater aquatic ecosystem of the upper Pilcomayo River: It had been severely degraded and was devoid of any commercially exploitable fisheries. Consequently, the 1996 levee failure at the tailings impoundment of the El Porco mine near Potisí only added insult to injury, releasing approximately 350,000 tons of metallic tailings and sludge into the Pilcomayo River in highlands Bolivia, upstream from its border with Argentina and Paraguay. Solids from all human sources, particularly agriculture and mining, only contributed to the large loads of sediments from natural erosional processes within the entire, water-limited basin. Downstream, within the Gran Chaco, metals-laced loadings from mine wastes also clogged the sediment-choked river, making it undependable as a fishery for local residents.

In 1997, Bolivian and Dutch biologists assayed the metals concentrations in fish harvested from the river within Bolivia's southernmost department, Tarija. Supplied by additional mountain streams, the Tarijan reaches of the Pilcomayo were less impacted by the disastrous discharge. Although the filtering livers of the dissected animals contained higher than normal concentrations of zinc and copper, the edible muscle tissues had not been seriously affected. Fatty tissues and skeletal components, however, had anomalously elevated metals concentrations. Regardless, fear of contaminated fish had a negative impact on the local fishing economy, particularly for ethnic Guaranis, who sold shad to commercial markets in larger communities like Sucre.

Financially, the El Porco metals mine was a joint venture between Compania Minera del Sur (COMSUR, founded in 1962) and Rio Tinto, an international, Australian-based mining corporation. Former two-time Bolivian president Gonzalo Sánchez de Lozada was one of the active partners of COMSUR. Educated in the United States at the University of Chicago, President Lozada engineered extreme economic reforms for the Bolivian economy during his first term (1993-1997). Significantly, he decentralized national government and partially privatized Bolivia's hydrocarbon industry. Ironically, the El Porco levee break occurred while Lozada was in office.

During the latter half of the twentieth century, COMSUR largely mined lead, gold, silver, tin, and zinc in cordilleran Bolivia and Argentina. The company was wholly owned by Panamanian-registered Minera, S.A., and 11 percent of its equity was held by the International Finance Corporation, a private-sector investment section of the World Bank Group. In 2005, COMSUR was sold to a Swiss financial conglomerate that hoped to improve mining operations and recover wasted metals from tailings at COMSUR's various Bolivian operations. Rio Tinto controlled 33 percent of the El Porco mine's holdings.

### SIGNIFICANCE

At the time of the disaster in 1996, uncontrolled water diversions and human-sponsored sedimentation had significantly affected the shad fishery, the most important commercial species within the Pilcomayo watershed. However, the El Porco mine discharge into the Pilcomayo River had a silver lining. National and international diligence were shifted from indifference to concern for local communities and the precious, vital resource of clean water within this water-limited region of Bolivia.

Attention was focused on comprehensive, international watershed management of the Pilcomayo basin between Bolivia, Argentina, and Paraguay, with significant financial and technical assistance from the European Union. A tri-national commission, the National Commission of the Pilcomayo and Bermejo Rivers, undertook significant scientific and engineering studies of the entire tri-national basin to manage its natural and cultural resources with greater regard for environmental impact. In addition, Bolivian authorities forced the closure of nineteen ore-processing operations that had directly discharged metallic wastes into the Pilcomayo River. In 2001, the Bolivian government also promulgated a policy of requiring foreign operators with more than three violations of environmental regulations to forfeit their metals concessions.

—*Hayes K. Galitski*

**FURTHER READING**

Alcázar, José Luis. "Pilcomayo River to Be Saved from Ruin." *Tierramerica*, May 24, 2005. A news account of efforts to overcome the neglect and abuse of the Pilcomayo watershed in west-central South America. Available in Spanish, Portuguese, and English, the news journal is published by the Inter Press Service News Agency with financial support from the United Nations Development and Environment Programs.

Cesar, Mike. "Solutions Elusive for Dead Pilcomayo River." *World Rivers Review* 14, no. 3 (1999): 10. A journalistic account focusing on the cultural repercussions of the El Porco levee break and attempts to alleviate pollution in the upper watershed of highland Bolivia.

Smolders, A. J. P., R. A. C. Lock, G. van der Velde, R. I. Medina Hoyos, and J. G. M. Roelofs. "Effects of Mining Activities on Heavy Metal Concentrations in Water, Sediment, and Macroinvertebrates in Different Reaches of the Pilcomayo River, South America." *Archives of Environmental Contamination and Toxicology* 44, no. 3 (2003): 314-323. A scientific paper summarizing a biological and heavy metal toxicological assay of the Pilcomayo River between 1997 and 1999 after the El Porco levee failure.

Velasco, Pablo. "The Mineral Industry of Bolivia." *The United States Geological Survey Minerals Yearbook.* Denver, Colo.: U.S. Geological Survey, 2001. A brief section providing an economic summary of the mineral resources of Bolivia at the close of 2001.

**SEE ALSO:** Aug. 18, 1971: Bánzer Seizes Power in Bolivian Coup; Sept. 21-Oct. 1, 1987: Radioactive Powder Injures Hundreds of Brazilians; Oct. 12, 1988: Brazilian President Announces Plans to Protect Rain Forests; June 3-14, 1992: Earth Summit Convenes in Rio de Janeiro; Jan. 1, 1995-Jan. 1, 2003: Cardoso Brings Prestige to Brazilian Presidency.

1996

## September 18, 1996
# GRAND STAIRCASE-ESCALANTE IS DECLARED A NATIONAL MONUMENT

*Amid conflicting pressures to preserve or exploit a 1.7-million-acre expanse of rugged land in southern Utah, U.S. president Bill Clinton protected its unique natural features by establishing it as a national monument.*

**LOCALE:** Southern Utah
**CATEGORIES:** Environmental issues; government and politics; monuments

**KEY FIGURES**
*Bill Clinton* (b. 1946), president of the United States, 1993-2001
*Bruce Babbitt* (b. 1938), U.S. secretary of the interior, 1993-2001
*Joe Judd* (b. 1930?), commissioner of Kane County, Utah
*Orrin G. Hatch* (b. 1934), U.S. senator from Utah

**SUMMARY OF EVENT**
The mountainous American West has long been shaped by its huge tracts of public lands and their abundant resources. In the past, these lands supported a diverse mix-

ture of economic activities: cattle grazing, forest industries, mining, and other extractive processes. There has long been a recognition that these lands are a public trust, to be maintained for the benefit of Americans and for future generations. The rise of the environmental movement brought a nationwide constituency to the preservation of unique natural resources, often coming into conflict with local interests.

U.S. president Bill Clinton was well aware of the conflict between local and national interests when, on September 18, 1996, on the South Rim of the Grand Canyon, he signed a document preserving the Grand Staircase, the Escalante Canyons, and the Kaiparowits Plateau areas by designating the three areas as the Grand Staircase-Escalante National Monument. Under the Antiquities Act of 1906, presidents were given the power to establish national monuments without additional enabling legislation. By the end of the twentieth century, presidents had proclaimed more than one hundred national monuments. In many cases, setting the land aside was a first step before an area was granted national park status, but Clinton and Secretary of the Interior Bruce Babbitt had a different plan in mind for Grand Staircase-Escalante.

Their plan was to keep the 1.7 million acres of land as a national monument, under the jurisdiction of the Bureau of Land Management (BLM), but with emphasis on guarding the monument's natural and archaeological treasures. The BLM had long had a reputation as the "Bureau of Livestock and Mining," concerned mainly with the interests of these two industries, but there were many people in the agency who took a wider view of its responsibilities. Babbitt, known for his interest in environmental issues, wanted to give the bureau a chance to address such issues in a protected-lands setting. Unlike national parks, which exclude uses other than recreation and preservation, the BLM rules call for managing for multiple uses. Sustained yields and environmental protection are among the BLM's guiding principles. The presidential

proclamation stated that all valid existing leases, rights, and uses would continue to be honored. State-owned lands within the monument area would remain under the state's authority regarding their use. It seemed that an effort had been made to honor all interests insofar as could reasonably be done.

Those most affected by Clinton's maneuver—most residents of southern Utah—viewed the issue much differently. There was a widespread belief that Clinton created the monument solely to ensure the votes of environmentalists in the upcoming 1996 presidential election. The lack of prior discussion with local and state officials before a new national monument was created in their midst outraged Utahans. The fact that the signing ceremony was held off-site in Arizona was cited as evidence of underhanded motives. Utah held parcels of school trust lands within the monument, so local politicians

*Grosvenor Arch, Grand Staircase-Escalante National Monument, Utah.* (Bureau of Land Management)

claimed that the state's schoolchildren were being cheated (although an amicable trade of these parcels for outside lands was soon worked out).

Clinton's proclamation also prevented a potential mining operation, the Andalex coal mine, from being developed on the Kaiparowits Plateau. In a sparsely developed county where high-paying employers had closed down and left, the mining prospect offered hope for a turnaround. Kane County commissioner Joe Judd bitterly criticized the Clinton administration for ruining the last hope for decent wages for the ten thousand people living in his county. Judd, with the other commissioners, then sent county-owned bulldozers to carve rough roads through some areas of the monument's pristine wilderness in a show of asserting local rights. Even Senator Orrin G. Hatch of Utah joined the outcry against the designation, calling the new monument "the mother of all land grabs."

In his 2004 memoir *My Life*, Clinton himself says that his action was necessary to prevent a large coal mine from going in and altering the nature of the land. In actuality, both sides' assertions overstate their cases somewhat. The Andalex coal mine had remained only a rumor for some years. Although high-grade coal definitely was present on the Kaiparowits Plateau, its isolation and the cost of transporting it out had made its mining unfeasible. Also, the new national monument is located among spectacular existing parklands. Bryce Canyon, Grand Canyon, and Lake Powell form a rough triangle around it. It seems likely that in the long run, tourism could bring in at least as many new jobs as would the coal mine.

## SIGNIFICANCE

The proclamation itself portrays Grand Staircase-Escalante as a trove of natural resources and historic human artifacts. The national monument's geology includes sedimentary rock layers that rise in ascending cliffs and plateaus, showing processes in the earth's formation. The monument's biological riches include five life zones, with warm and cold desert areas and a stand of piñon and juniper trees up to fourteen hundred years old. Signs of human habitation go back to the Anasazi and Fremont cultures, and the area was also important in early Mormon colonization. The area was the last place to be explored and mapped in the continental United States, and its landscape is dotted with unique, rugged natural rock formations and twisting canyons.

Previous monument designations had been met with much opposition from local citizens, but as time went on, the anger was largely replaced by pride, and residents adjusted to the new status by creating new economic ventures based on it. Grand Staircase-Escalante seems poised to follow the same pattern. Even Judd, after his bitter resistance to the federal government, accepted $200,000 in federal money for the county to begin planning its new relationship to the monument lands.

The declaration also pointed the way to other Clinton-era endeavors to protect natural resources. During the administration's first term, Secretary Babbitt had worked tirelessly to limit the impact of mining and grazing on fragile public lands. Meeting angry opposition from both congressmen and their outspoken constituents, he was often frustrated in his efforts. Thanks to the Antiquities Act, public land can be set aside in national monuments while bypassing congressional oversight. After Grand Staircase-Escalante, Clinton went on to establish fifteen other national monuments in the West.

The Republican administration that took office in 2001 had a much different set of priorities. Regarding public lands, it promulgated a policy that favored energy over environmental concerns. However, this policy had some unexpected side effects, including pitting cattle ranchers against mining and oil production companies in fights over land use. As with previous administrations, other policy areas took precedence over that of public lands use, so that the actual impact on resource conservation was somewhat limited.

National monument status is difficult to undo. Many efforts have been made to reverse such declarations in the past, but almost all have failed. Grand Staircase-Escalante continues to protect the grandeur and treasures of its wild, rugged scenery and expanses of wilderness.

—*Emily Alward*

## FURTHER READING

Harmon, David, et al., eds. *The Antiquities Act: A Century of American Archaeology, Historic Preservation, and Nature Conservation*. Tucson: University of Arizona Press, 2006. Inclusive survey of the act's results. The Clinton-era monuments are examined as a study in the exercise of presidential power.

Keiter, Robert B., et al., eds. *Visions of the Grand Staircase-Escalante: Examining Utah's Newest National Monument*. Salt Lake City: Utah Museum of Natural History and Wallace Stegner Center, 1998. Symposium with essays on the physical setting, historical and economic background, legal and political considerations, and planning for the future. A Hopi view speaks of the sacred nature of the land. Useful appendixes list national monuments and include the proclamation's text.

1996

Larmer, Paul, ed. *Give and Take: How the Clinton Administration's Public Lands Offensive Transformed the American West.* Paonia, Colo.: High Country News Books, 2004. Articles with on-the-spot reportage of stages, people, and issues in the monument's establishment, plus some parallel controversies.

Soden, Dennis L., ed. *The Environmental Presidency.* Albany: State University of New York Press, 1999. A look at twentieth century presidents' handling of environmental concerns. Concludes that all the presidents treated environmental problems cautiously, as "sec-
ond-tier issues," but still managed some lasting accomplishments.

**SEE ALSO:** Jan. 3, 1975: U.S. Congress Expands Eastern Wilderness; Dec. 31, 1975: Hells Canyon Is Preserved as a National Recreation Area; Dec. 2, 1980: U.S. Congress Protects Alaskan Lands and Wildlife; Apr. 3, 1993: Clinton Convenes the Forest Summit; Dec. 11, 2000: U.S. Government Funds Everglades Restoration.

## September 27, 1996
# TALIBAN BEGINS SUPPRESSION OF HUMAN RIGHTS IN AFGHANISTAN

*With their capture of Afghanistan's capital city, Kabul, the Taliban completed their conquest of the country and inaugurated a regime characterized by a severe suppression of human rights.*

**LOCALE:** Kabul, Afghanistan

**CATEGORIES:** Terrorism, atrocities, and war crimes; civil rights and liberties; human rights

**KEY FIGURE**
*Mohammad Omar* (b. 1959/1962), leader of the Taliban

**SUMMARY OF EVENT**

In 1989, after a ten-year occupation of Afghanistan, the Soviet Union withdrew its military from the country. Three years later, the Soviet-backed Afghan government collapsed, and Afghanistan lapsed into lawlessness and civil war. A new regime may be said to have been established four years later, when, on September 27, 1996, a fundamentalist Islamic organization known as the Taliban captured the nation's capital, Kabul. The Taliban had already taken the important eastern city of Jalālābād earlier in the month; by the following June, the Taliban controlled two-thirds of Afghanistan.

Islamic fundamentalist former students (*talib*) had founded the Taliban Islamic Movement of Afghanistan in 1994 in Qandahār, in the southern part of the country. The group of founders, graduates of Pakistani Islamic schools known as madrassas, was led by a one-eyed cleric, Mullah Mohammad Omar, then in his early thirties. The Taliban sought an Islamic revolution based on strict adherence to the traditional Islamic legal code known as sharia. The group's stated aim was the creation of a "pure and clean Islamic state."

The Taliban's founding leadership had attended fundamentalist Islamic schools while living in the refugee camps that sprang up along the Pakistan border during the Soviet occupation. The organization was backed by armed forces whose soldiers were mostly the same "holy warriors" who had vanquished the Soviets with Western (mostly American) military assistance. From the beginning, the Taliban went about the task of instituting a fundamentalist version of a proper Islamic social order, especially through enforcement of sharia. In doing so, the regime cast aside the entire extensive range of individual rights and human treatment long regarded as human rights and enclosed the nation in a long reign of cruel and barbaric theocratic rule. In September, 1999, the director of the Voice of America wrote that "Afghanistan has become [a] land of terror, torture, and injustice," including "war crimes, crimes against humanity, genocide, and cultural genocide."

As the Taliban understood the requirements of the Islamic faith, many of the liberties that Afghans had long taken for granted had to be outlawed. The Taliban thus decreed that Islamic law forbade music; any representations of living things, including photographs and toys such as stuffed animals; and most forms of entertainment, including games, television, and radio, with the exception of its own station.

Among the regime's most flagrant, extreme, and widespread abuses of human rights were those directed against women. These abuses so shocked Western norms and sensibilities that the Taliban were soon accused of waging a "war against women." Not long after the Taliban took power, girls in Afghanistan were no longer allowed to be educated in the schools. The ban on education for girls was later partially rescinded, but to little effect. Girls were allowed schooling until the age of eight, but they were allowed to learn only about Islam.

With few exceptions, women were also barred from all employment and were forced to remain at home. They were banned from all public gatherings and were permitted to leave their homes only in the company of male relatives; even then, they were allowed out only for religiously sanctioned purposes and were required to be dressed in the burka, a garment that covers the whole of the body, with only a mesh area at the eyes for sight. Because the burka restricts vision, many women were hit by vehicles they could not see approaching. Outside the home, women's shoes were to make no noise; inside the home, windows through which women might be seen were to be blacked out, ensuring their nonvisibility. Women could not be photographed or filmed. For the women of Afghanistan, these policies resulted in a regime of brutalization and systematic neglect enforced by beating, rape, arbitrary imprisonment, and execution.

Western journalists were able to document the beatings of Afghan women by smuggling video cameras into the country and filming the beatings in the streets. Women found attempting to escape the country with men other than their husbands or male relatives were stoned to death for presumed adultery. In addition, there was trafficking of women and girls, who were forced into prostitution and marriage. Knowledgeable Western sources reported that Afghan women were voiceless, invisible, nonbeings with no right to an independent existence.

Among the worst human rights abuses of women concerned health care. In September, 1997, the Taliban announced that health care was segregated by sex into separate hospitals. This rule became strictly enforced during the following September. In Kabul, health care for 500,000 women was confined to a single poorly equipped hospital that had only thirty-five beds. After a concerted international outcry, the Taliban leadership partially relented, permitting the limited opening of wom-

en's wards in a few selected hospitals. However, this dispensation did not resolve the Afghan women's health care crisis, which continued throughout the Taliban's five-year reign of terror. Many women died in childbirth or from infectious diseases left untreated by Taliban edict. The situation was made worse by the restrictions forbidding women to move around freely. In one case, a woman rushing a sick child to a hospital failed to stop when challenged by a teenage enforcer of the Taliban's "Virtue and Vice" codes, and the boy shot the woman several times.

Few women doctors were allowed to work, and male doctors were permitted to treat women only with proper chaperons, if at all. Even then they could not adequately examine these patients, as they were prohibited from touching or viewing women's bodies. One dentist reported to Western researchers that he dared examine a woman's teeth only with a lookout posted when her veil was lifted. Dentists and their patients risked beatings, and dentists also risked jailing and closure of their practices.

The Taliban's elimination of the ordinary liberties considered basic to human rights applied to men and boys as well as to women and girls. Like women, men were subject to beatings, arbitrary imprisonment, and execution for a long list of infractions of religious law. Homosexuals were executed, although homosexual acts between men and adolescents continued to be widely practiced. Child labor was widespread, and boys as young as ten were coerced into military service.

To enforce its rules and policies, the Taliban regime created the Department for the Promotion of Virtue and Prevention of Vice. Members of this section of the Taliban government, some in their early teens, roamed city streets wielding implements to use as whips, searching for those disobeying rules. These enforcers were videotaped beating women for such petty offenses as wearing burkas of insufficient length or wearing shoes that made noise. Men might be arrested for having insufficient facial hair and jailed until their beards grew to the

prescribed length. Due process of law and proper defense of the accused were nonexistent; arbitrary detention was commonplace. While in jail, men might be subjected to numerous human rights violations, such as beatings, torture, and gang rape. Others who were arrested might simply disappear, never to be seen again.

In addition to public beatings, torture, and executions, among the draconian punishments meted out by the Taliban was the amputation of limbs—a practice that recurred throughout the regime's rule. It was possible for the wealthy, however, to bribe their way out of this punishment, leaving the innocent to pay the price. In one documented instance, after a wealthy man paid a bribe to escape punishment, a man imprisoned on a minor charge was chosen at random as a replacement, driven to the Kabul sports stadium, and subjected to amputation of his hand before a jeering crowd.

Finally, reliable sources documented many massacres of innocent civilians by the Taliban. In September,

*Taliban fighters around the presidential palace on September 27, 1996, in Kabul. The rebels captured the capital, inaugurating a new era of human rights violations.* (AP/Wide World Photos)

1997, Taliban fighters massacred civilian villagers near Mazār-e Sharīf after failing to capture the city. When the Taliban succeeded in overrunning the city nearly a year later, between 2,000 and 5,000 men, women, and children were slaughtered over a period of several days. Among other similar events, some 600 civilians were reported massacred in Faryab Province in late 1997. The total number of massacre victims of the Taliban is unknown, but it is believed to amount to many thousands.

## SIGNIFICANCE

The opening of the Taliban era had a multitude of serious consequences, both within Afghanistan and beyond that country's borders. The inauguration of Taliban rule led to innumerable human rights violations of the most serious nature, including exclusion from the economic, social, and political life of the nation of half its population, as women were confined to their homes except under limited defined circumstances. The regime's policies led to the widespread suffering of millions of men, women, and children through execution, poor nutrition and resulting ill health, outright starvation, and lack of medical treatment. In addition, the population was visited with a wide range of severe, chronic human rights abuses such as mutilation through judicially sanctioned amputations, beatings, rape of men as well as women, arbitrary detention, denial of due process of law, denial of elementary freedoms of social and personal activity, and denial of education. The Taliban was also responsible for the deliberate destruction of irreplaceable cultural artifacts, including the gigantic sixth century C.E. Buddhist statues blown up in 2001 despite urgent international calls for restraint and offers to buy the offending objects.

The reign of terror and human rights abuse by the Taliban regime led to a worldwide outcry, replete with expressions of dismay and disgust. In Europe and the United States, knowledge of the Taliban's abuses helped to increase the cultural and political distance between Islam and the West, even though most Muslims do not practice fundamentalism on the Taliban model. In the early twenty-first century, cultural tension between the Islamic world and the West appeared to be moving toward a deepening chasm of alienation and distrust. Public confrontation between Muslim and Western countries gave new weight to claims that the two sides are engaged in a "clash of civilizations"—a conflict capable of eventuating in international violence of the most serious order.

At the opening of the twenty-first century, the poten-

tial for such violence was already realized after the installation of the Taliban led to the migration to Afghanistan of terrorist leader Osama Bin Laden and his many lieutenants and followers. Once established in the country, Bin Laden used its territory to train and further organize thousands of members of his formidable terrorist organization, al-Qaeda. Operations of the organization led first to a series of terrorist attacks on American targets in the Middle East and Africa. These operations culminated in the September 11, 2001, attacks on the World Trade Center in New York City and the Pentagon near Washington, D.C. The export of terrorism thus must be accounted among the consequences of Taliban rule.

The September, 2001, attacks led directly to a military assault on Afghanistan by the United States and its allies that began in October of the same year, resulting in the destruction of the Taliban regime. The American action, aided by a number of other nations, in turn inflamed numerous Muslims in the Middle East, Africa, and Southeast Asia.

—*Charles F. Bahmueller*

## FURTHER READING

Amanpour, Christiane. "Tyranny of the Taliban: A Visit to the Capital of Afghanistan's Extremist Regime Reveals a Harsh World of Suppression and Despair." *Time*, October 13, 1997. Well-known journalist's account of her visit to the Afghan capital a year after its occupation by the Taliban. Provides brief but informative description of dealings with the Taliban and the fate of basic rights, especially those of women, under Taliban rule.

Marsden, Peter. *The Taliban: War and Religion in Afghanistan*. London: Zed Books, 2001. Account by the information coordinator of the British Agencies Afghanistan Group discusses the origins and development of the Taliban and the circumstances that led to the Taliban takeover of Afghanistan. Describes what should be done to relieve the enormous burden of human suffering visited on the Afghan people during the Taliban period.

Palmer, Caitriona. "The Taliban's War Against Women." *The Lancet* (London), August 29, 1998, 734. Informative article focuses on women's health, both psychological as well as physical, under Taliban rule. Presents considerable detail in a clear, concise style.

Skaine, Rosemarie. *The Women of Afghanistan Under the Taliban*. Jefferson, N.C.: McFarland, 2001. Comprehensive account of the treatment of women under Taliban rule. Contrasts how Afghan women lived

1996

prior to the Taliban takeover, when they worked in a variety of professions and occupations, with their transformation under the Taliban into virtual ghosts. Features interviews with Afghan women that provide detailed insights into their fate and human rights generally under Mullah Omar and his followers.

**SEE ALSO:** Dec. 24-27, 1979: Soviet Union Invades Afghanistan; 1988: Osama Bin Laden Forms al-Qaeda; 1989: Soviet Troops Leave Afghanistan; May, 1996: Sudan Expels Osama Bin Laden; Feb. 23, 1998: Osama Bin Laden Declares Jihad Against "Jews and Crusaders."

## October 12, 1996
# CLINTON SIGNS LEGISLATION TO HELP RESTORE THE EVERGLADES

*The Water Resources Development Act of 1996 specified the development of a comprehensive ecosystem restoration plan for the damaged Florida Everglades and provided for funding of habitat enhancement and ecosystem repair at dozens of water resource projects in the United States.*

**ALSO KNOWN AS:** Water Resources Development Act of 1996; Public Law 104-303
**LOCALE:** Washington, D.C.
**CATEGORIES:** Laws, acts, and legal history; environmental issues

**KEY FIGURES**
*Bill Clinton* (b. 1946), president of the United States, 1993-2001
*Al Gore* (b. 1948), vice president of the United States, 1993-2001
*Bruce Babbitt* (b. 1938), U.S. secretary of the interior, 1993-2001
*Marjory Stoneman Douglas* (1890-1998), author and environmental activist

**SUMMARY OF EVENT**
In 1996, the environmental condition of the Florida Everglades had become a national concern because a century of development pressures and controversial environmental management had resulted in serious ecological damage in the area. The efforts of Vice President Al Gore, Secretary of the Interior Bruce Babbitt, and activists such as Marjory Stoneman Douglas helped President Bill Clinton's administration make restoration of the Everglades an environmental priority. On October 12, 1996, President Clinton signed the Water Resources Development Act of 1996 (WRDA-96) into law. WRDA-96 authorized numerous water resources development projects and programs to be carried out by the U.S. Army Corps of Engineers.

The Water Resources Development Act is typically reauthorized by Congress every two years to provide for maintenance and improvements of the nation's waterways and coastal areas. The 1996 reauthorization of WRDA included a mechanism to address escalating problems with the ecology of the Florida Everglades. Although restoration of the Everglades was just a part of the thirty-one new water resources projects and sixty-one preexisting projects approved in the legislation for areas around the United States, the act's provisions addressing the Everglades drew attention because ongoing damage to the amazingly diverse Everglades ecosystem was the subject of great controversy.

The Everglades ecosystem essentially consists of a very shallow river that is about 50 miles (80 kilometers) wide and extremely slow moving. In the main channel, the river is only about 1 to 3 feet (30-90 centimeters) deep, and for most of its width, it is only around 6 inches (15 centimeters) deep. Historically, it has been one of the most productive and diverse ecosystems in the world. Plants native to the Everglades include live oak, mangrove, cypress, bay, willow, pond apple, wild lemon, wild orange, cucumber, orchids, bromeliads (epiphytes in the pineapple family), ferns, sedges, and vast regions of saw grass. Maidencane, white water lily, bladderwort, and spatterdock float in undisturbed areas. Periphyton algae anchor the base of the Everglades food web.

Of the many freshwater and saltwater fish, amphibians, reptiles, mammals, and birds native to the Everglades, approximately 68 species are on the federal threatened and endangered lists, and even more appear on state lists. More than 350 bird species are native to the area, including the roseate spoonbill, ibises, storks, herons, and egrets. In the late twentieth century, the Cape Sable seaside sparrow population began a decline as a result of changes in Everglades ecology and moves toward proposed development, leading to a dispute among the Miccosukee Indians, the state of Florida, and federal agencies. Other unusual species, such as the snail kite—

which feeds exclusively on the apple snail—are examples of those endangered by habitat destruction. The alligator is a keystone species, important in habitat maintenance. The West Indian manatee and bottlenose dolphin inhabit saltwater bays and coastal areas as part of the Everglades ecosystem. Of all the rare, endangered, and threatened animal species in the Everglades, perhaps the Florida panther is the most symbolic, with only about thirty remaining by the end of the twentieth century.

The dense, pervasive saw grass, standing water, climate, and other environmental conditions discouraged early human exploration or settlement in or adjacent to the Everglades. In the nineteenth century, military forces entered the area to attack the Seminole Indians, who managed to survive as practically the only human inhabitants. When Philadelphia millionaire Hamilton Disston bought four million acres of Everglades land in 1881, it was still a robust ecosystem with a fairly pristine environment. By 1900, however, land in the Everglades was being drained for development, and wading birds were being exterminated for their feathers, which were in high demand for use in the millinery trade.

In the early twentieth century, an Everglades invasion began as Melaleuca trees (*Melaleuca quinquenervia* and an Australian native commonly known as the punk tree or paperbark tea tree) began forming dense stands, outcompeting native wetlands plants in marshes and helping to draining the wetlands. By far, however, the greatest sources of damage to the Everglades ecosystem were the levees, canals, and drainage systems built for agriculture. In 1912, a railroad was cut through the Everglades to Key West. Floridians appealed to the federal government for flood control as the surrounding areas were developed.

Along with increased population and increased regulation, however, came appreciation of the natural quality of the Everglades; this appreciation eventually led to the U.S. Congress's authorization of the area as a national park in 1934. Meanwhile, Lake Okeechobee was disconnected from the Everglades by the Herbert Hoover

1996

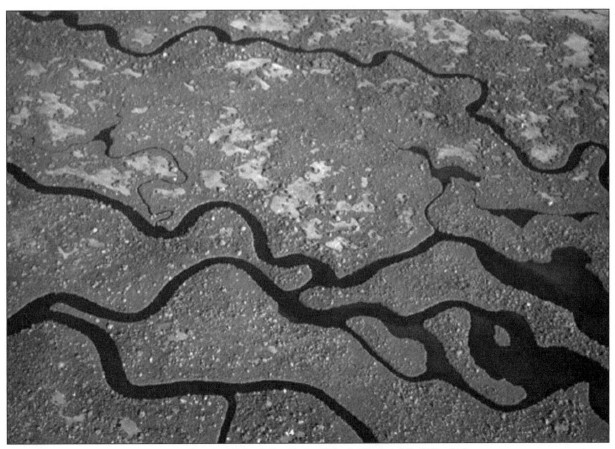

*An aerial view of Everglades National Park.* (National Park Service)

Dike, a seven-year project completed in 1937. In the mid-twentieth century, increased droughts and fires associated with changes in the land further deteriorated the ecosystem, which was finally dedicated in 1947 as the 1.3-million-acre Everglades National Park.

By 1959, canals, levees, dams, and other water-control devices separated the northern Everglades from the rest of the ecosystem. Throughout the twentieth century, millions of people moved into adjacent areas, and increased farm runoff, storm-water overflow, and waste-water discharge further damaged the Everglades ecosystem's water quality and habitat. Congress responded to public concern in 1970 by setting minimum flows into Everglades National Park—an unusual move of direct intervention. However, the minimum-flow program was not comprehensive enough to result in significant improvement in the environmental quality of the complex ecosystem. Further, in 1979, the South Florida Water Management District began pumping untreated water into the central Everglades.

In the early 1990's, environmental activists, inspired by Marjory Stoneman Douglas and others, agitated for increased environmental responsibility for the Everglades by the agricultural sector, the state of Florida, and the federal government. Vice President Al Gore and Secretary of the Interior Bruce Babbitt made the Everglades into one of the top environmental issues of the Clinton administration.

WRDA-1996 authorized the U.S. Army Corps of Engineers to develop a comprehensive restoration plan for the Everglades and submit it for congressional approval. The act also authorized the Critical Projects Program at a maximum federal cost of $75 million. The U.S. Army Corps of Engineers and the South Florida Water Management District were to unite in restoring the Everglades ecosystem. A major task in this collaboration was the crafting of the Comprehensive Everglades Restoration Plan (CERP), a plan for restoring and preserving South Florida's natural ecosystems while enhancing water supplies and maintaining flood control. Other resources were also committed to Everglades restoration; the Farm Bill of 1996, signed just weeks before the Water Resources Development Act, earmarked $200 million for land acquisition and augmentation of water storage capacity in the Everglades. Much more restoration work remained, but CERP was a notable beginning.

## SIGNIFICANCE

By the mid-1980's, the Army Corps of Engineers was shifting toward a more open, public form of management

and environmental accountability, including environmental restoration, in contrast with its history of "conquering" the environment. In Florida after the passage of WRDA-96, Corps district engineer Colonel Terry Rice encouraged and challenged a citizens' group to work toward a new plan. The creation of the comprehensive plan for the Everglades was an opportunity for the Corps to apply ecosystem management and use open, public processes in planning.

The case of the Everglades showed the importance of environmental activists in helping U.S. states and the federal government to be more accountable for environmental management. WRDA-96 and its resultant restoration plans exemplify a trend at the end of the twentieth century toward coordination among state, federal, and local agencies and organizations in attempts to reverse negative ecological impacts in regions of international biological significance.

*—Robert M. Sanford*

## FURTHER READING

Cech, Thomas V. *Principles of Water Resources: History, Development, Management, and Policy.* 2d ed. New York: John Wiley & Sons, 2005. Presents a broad-based look at almost all aspects of water resources and related issues. Includes a brief history of U.S. Army Corps actions and major policies.

Douglas, Marjory Stoneman. *The Everglades: River of Grass.* 50th anniversary ed. Sarasota, Fla.: Pineapple Press, 1997. Commemorative reprint edition of a classic work (first published in 1947) that was among the first to galvanize public awareness about the Everglades.

_____. *Florida: The Long Frontier.* New York: Harper & Row, 1967. Provides historical perspective on the long fight to save the Everglades. This work helped spark renewed public attention to the area.

Grunwald, Michael. *The Swamp: The Everglades, Florida, and the Politics of Paradise.* New York: Simon & Schuster, 2006. Dissects the political wars that have surrounded the issues related to the Everglades.

Kelly, Mary Sidney, and Gretel Schueller. "The 104th Congress." *Audubon* 99 (January/February, 1997): 94. Summarizes the environmentally important legislation passed by the 104th Congress. Includes discussion of how WRDA-96 benefited restoration of the Florida Everglades.

Lodge, Thomas E. *The Everglades Handbook: Understanding the Ecosystem.* 2d ed. Boca Raton, Fla.: CRC Press, 2005. One of the most efficient and usable guides available concerning the biogeography and ecosystem functions of the Everglades.

Panel to Review the Critical Ecosystems Studies Initiative. *Science and the Greater Ecosystem Restoration: An Assessment of the Critical Ecosystems Studies Initiative.* Washington, D.C.: National Academies Press, 2003. Presents a technical and policy examination of the new methods being used in repairing the Everglades.

**SEE ALSO:** Mar. 1, 1972: U.S. Congress Updates Water Pollution Law; Apr. 15, 1972: Great Lakes Water Quality Agreement Is Signed; Dec. 16, 1974: U.S. Congress Requires Safe Drinking Water; June 29, 1987: Florida Passes the Surface Water Improvement and Management Act; Nov. 28, 1990: Environmentalists Defeat the Cross-Florida Barge Canal; Dec. 11, 2000: U.S. Government Funds Everglades Restoration.

## November 29, 1996
# ASTEROID TOUTATIS PASSES NEAR EARTH

*Discovered and named in 1989, the asteroid Toutatis, which passes near Earth roughly every four years, not only promises astronomers unprecedented access to data concerning asteroid formation but also has generated frank discussions concerning possible scenarios should an object of that magnitude ever collide with Earth.*

**LOCALE:** Orbit between Earth and the main asteroid belt between Mars and Jupiter

**CATEGORIES:** Astronomy; science and technology

**KEY FIGURE**

*Christian Pollas* (fl. late twentieth century), French astronomer

**SUMMARY OF EVENT**

On January 4, 1989, asteroid 4179 was discovered by French astronomer Christian Pollas while he was working at the Observatoire de la Côte d'Azur at Caussols, in southern France. Pollas, a veteran astronomer credited with discovering numerous asteroids, happened to spot the bright, fast-moving object on photographic plates that had been taken in an effort to measure the telemetry of Jupiter's obscure satellites. Pollas named the asteroid Toutatis after a powerful, protective god of fertility, war, and prosperity common to both Gallic and Celtic mythologies. As Pollas found out, however, Toutatis was also a deity figure in Les Aventures d'Asterix, a hugely successful, long-running French comic book series set in medieval Europe; ironically, in the series, the tribe that worships Toutatis is convinced the sky is soon to fall. Once the new asteroid was identified, its approach was tracked by the scientific community, which confirmed its Earth-crossing orbit, its speed (roughly 67,112 miles per hour), and its dimensions (2.9 miles long, 1.5 miles wide, 1.2 miles thick, considerable for asteroids).

Apart from the usual scientific buzz that inevitably accompanies the identification of any new heavenly body, particularly a near-Earth object, the discovery of Toutatis brought additional excitement because, given the asteroid's location—just inside the Earth's orbit out to the main asteroid belt between Mars and Jupiter—it would return to the Earth's observation roughly every four years. Further, its particularly low orbit would bring the asteroid close to the Earth—relative to space measurement. In 1992, for instance, the asteroid came within 2.5 million miles; in November, 1996, 3.3 million miles; and in September, 2004, just over 1 million miles, the closest approach of any known object until 2060. Such regular "close" brushes have enabled astronomers unprecedented access to the asteroid using only Doppler ground radar without having to launch satellites to obtain the data. Following the 1996 pass, for instance, the NASA Jet Propulsion Laboratory in Pasadena, California, released startlingly vivid delay-Doppler radar images of the asteroid's pocked surface. Indeed, in its 2004 flyby, Toutatis was visible for backyard sky watchers with only binoculars.

Thus, within the relatively brief time Toutatis has been known, scientists have been able to study it. They have found that it is quite an unusual object, which led, in turn, to alarmist concerns. The images of Toutatis revealed that it did not possess an asteroid's usual spherical shape; rather, it is oblong with a peanut-shell shape, with one lobe substantially smaller than the other. Astronomers conjecture that, given the asteroid's heavily cratered face, Toutatis was once two asteroids that slammed together in a violent fusion.

*A computer-generated view of Earth as seen from Asteroid Toutatis.* (NASA)

Further intriguing astronomers was Toutatis's irregular rotation: Asteroids spin in a tight and predictable spiral, like a child's top, along a single axis of rotation; but Toutatis spins in a wobbly, tumbling motion—the result, astronomers theorize, of numerous collisions with other floating debris. Consequently, Toutatis does not have a fixed pole of rotation; rather, it follows what is termed non-principal axis rotation—quite a rare occurrence. Toutatis maintains two entirely different rotation motions, which means that if a person could actually stand on the asteroid, he or she would see the Sun rise and set along a different path each day. Thus the asteroid does not maintain a fixed "day"; rather, it completes its spin sometimes in 5.4 days and sometimes in 7.3 days, a period that in either case is far slower than those of most asteroids.

The implications for scientific investigation were promising: Given the asteroid's irregular rotation, its

quadrennial flybys, and its slow tumbling movement, Toutatis would expose virtually its entire circumference at one time or another for Earth observation. The scientific community came to view the regular approach of Toutatis as an opportunity to advance theoretical explanations for the beginnings of the universe, as asteroids are widely believed to be debris left over from initial cosmic eruptions that first forged the planets and the stars. Asteroids' mineral contents are particularly helpful in directing such theories. Given Toutatis's relatively close orbit, the scientific community has raised the possibility of launching a robotic exploratory vehicle to engage the asteroid and to determine its exact mineral makeup during one of three approaches in the 2020's.

The very characteristics of Toutatis's orbit that have so intrigued scientists, however, have caused alarm in the lay community. Such alarm was perhaps inevitable when, because of its orbit, Toutatis was pro forma designated early on as a "potentially hazardous asteroid" (PHA). Asteroids have been known to collide with the Earth's surface. Most recently, a devastating strike took place in 1908 in Tunguska, Russia, in which an asteroid much smaller than Toutatis leveled more than 700 square miles of Siberian wilderness. An asteroid roughly twice the size of Toutatis is believed to have caused the extinction of the dinosaurs more than sixty million years ago. Astronomers have conjectured that asteroids regularly collided with the Earth during its earliest eons of formation and that the cratered face of the Moon verifies the impacts of such collisions. Given the traffic of asteroids currently in the solar system (conservative estimates suggest more than 300,000 such objects of at least 300 feet long), scientists have long held that collisions with the Earth are inevitable, although they predict such collisions would occur only every thousand years or so.

The topsy-turvy orbital patterning of Toutatis, however, means that scientists cannot confidently predict the exact path of Toutatis's approaches beyond several centuries. In fact, given the asteroid's unusually low inclination—less than half a degree from Earth's—in several computer scenarios played out six centuries into the future, Toutatis is tracked to actually collide with the Earth, encouraging lay speculation to dub the mountainous asteroid the "Doomsday Rock." Such speculation routinely describes Toutatis's eccentric orbit as "unpredictable," although scientists quickly point out the significant difference between an "unpredictable" orbit and Toutatis's "irregular" orbit, which is unique but definitely patterned.

Nevertheless, within the nonscientific community (fed by Internet hype), each approach of Toutatis triggers a considerable volume of alarmist misinformation suggesting that the asteroid's close pass confirms anxieties about an apocalyptic collision with the Earth, although astronomers are quick to point out that "close" still assures millions of miles between the Earth and the asteroid. The asteroid's 1996 flyby, however, inspired two disaster movies: the 1998 blockbuster *Armageddon*, in which a emergency space mission must detonate an approaching asteroid, and, that same year, the less successful *Deep Impact*, in which a chunk of a rogue comet actually strikes the Earth and triggers monumental destruction on the East Coast of the United States.

## SIGNIFICANCE

Although Toutatis offers a rare opportunity for astronomical observation, it has also occasioned a concerted effort by an international cartel of scientists, astronauts, diplomats, insurance executives, lawyers, and astrophysicists to petition the United Nations to draft a specific protocol for addressing the threat of a collision. Despite the mathematical certainty that an asteroid of considerable dimension will collide with the Earth, no framework exists setting out a concrete course of response.

In 2007, a U.N. blue-ribbon committee submitted a draft of just such a global policy, including recommendations for determining which governments would be charged with directing attempts to deflect any incoming objects and a proposed structure for international relief operations should a catastrophic collision occur. Debate on the protocol is set to conclude by 2009. Given the enormous reach into the visible universe afforded by computer-enhanced observation technologies and the detection over the last decade of many new PHAs—as many as 20,000 of which have yet to be exactly identified—the National Aeronautics and Space Administration was charged by Congress in 2005 to increase its efforts agressively both to identify asteroids that could pose a threat to the Earth (only one hundred such objects had been cataloged by 2007) and to investigate feasible strategies of preparation should the planet face such a threat.

*—Joseph Dewey*

## FURTHER READING

Bobrowsky, Peter T., and Hans Rickman, eds. *Comet/Asteroid Impacts and Human Society: An Interdisciplinary Approach*. New York: Springer, 2007. Measured analyses that project the immense cultural and social alterations in the event of an impact.

Hallam, Tony. *Catastrophes and Lesser Catastrophes: The Causes of Mass Extinction*. New York: Oxford University Press, 2005. From a distinguished geologist, a look at historic evidence of catastrophes including asteroid impacts. Closes with a review of current international efforts—scientific, technological, and political—to confront such collisions.

Palmer, Trevor. *Perilous Earth: Catastrophe and Catastrophism Through the Ages*. New York: Cambridge University Press, 2003. Written for a general audience but grounded in meticulous research, the book explores the differences between preparation and panic.

Spangenburg, Ray, and Kit Moser. *If an Asteroid Hit the Earth*. New York: Franklin Watts, 2000. Sobering analysis of the effects of an asteroid hit. Includes helpful context concerning past collisions.

Verschuur, Gerrit L. *Impact! The Threat of Comets and*

1996

*Asteroids.* New York: Oxford University Press, 1997. Landmark investigation into historic collisions and their impact, particularly the Tunguska catastrophe.

**SEE ALSO:** Feb., 1973-Mar., 1974: Organic Molecules Are Discovered in Comet Kohoutek; June 6, 1980: Scientists Find Evidence of an Asteroid Impact at the End of the Cretaceous Period; Mar. 8, 1986: Space Probes Begin Examination of Comet Halley; July 16-22, 1994: Comet Shoemaker-Levy 9 Collides with Jupiter; Jan. 30, 1996: Comet Hyakutake Is Discovered; Mar. 23-25, 1997: Heaven's Gate Cult Members Commit Mass Suicide; Feb. 14, 2000: Near Earth Asteroid Rendezvous Spacecraft Orbits a Small Body.

## December 8, 1996
# RAWLINGS WINS REELECTION TO GHANA'S PRESIDENCY

*After taking power in 1979 by military coup, Jerry John Rawlings saved Ghana from government corruption and from the devastating conflicts experienced in neighboring countries. In 1992, he stood for election, and although fraud was claimed, he won the presidency and was reelected in 1996.*

**LOCALE:** Ghana
**CATEGORY:** Government and politics

**KEY FIGURES**

*Jerry John Rawlings* (b. 1947), head of state of Ghana, June-September, 1979, and 1981-1993 and president of Ghana, 1993-2001
*Hilla Limann* (1934-1998), president of Ghana, 1979-1981
*Kofi Abrefa Busia* (1913-1978), prime minister of Ghana, 1969-1972
*Frederick Akuffo* (1937-1979), head of the Supreme Military Council in Ghana, 1978-1979, who was executed by Rawlings
*John Atta-Mills* (b. 1944), Rawlings's vice president and handpicked successor who was defeated by Kufuor in both the 2000 and 2004 presidential elections
*John Kufuor* (b. 1938), president of Ghana beginning in 2001
*Kwame Nkrumah* (1909-1972), leader of the mass movement for independence and first president of Ghana, 1960-1966

**SUMMARY OF EVENT**

As the first sub-Saharan African state to receive independence (1957), Ghana was intended to be a model for African political stability. Its independence leader, Kwame Nkrumah, won a landslide victory for the presidency. Persistent economic problems, however, led him in 1964 to declare Ghana a one-party state with himself as president for life. By the beginning of 1966, a military coup, allegedly staged to end abusive and corrupt government, ousted Nkrumah from power. A caretaker regime composed of four army officers and four police officers took control until August, 1969. Its elected head, Kofi Abrefa Busia of the Progress Party (PP), maintained power for twenty-seven months until economic difficulties—high foreign debts, inflation, and tax increases coupled with wage freezes—undercut his support. Busia's austerity policies alienated the army officers. Lieutenant Colonel Ignatius Kutu Acheampong, temporarily commanding the first brigade around Accra, led a bloodless coup that ended the Second Republic in 1972.

To justify their takeover, coup leaders leveled charges of corruption against Busia and his ministers. In its first years, the National Redemption Council (NRC) drew support from a public pleased by the reversal of Busia's austerity measures. Acheampong's popularity continued into 1974 as the government successfully negotiated international loan agreements and rescheduled Ghana's debts. However, as world oil prices continued their steep climb in 1974, demonstrations against the NRC mounted. The military broke up student demonstrations and repeatedly closed the universities, which had become centers of opposition to NRC policies.

In July, 1978, in a sudden move, the other Supreme Military Council (SMC) officers forced Acheampong to resign, replacing him with Lieutenant General Frederick Akuffo. The SMC apparently acted in response to continuing pressure to find a solution to the country's economic dilemma. Inflation was estimated to be as high as 300 percent that year. The decree lifting the ban on party politics went into effect on January 1, 1979, as planned. The constitutional assembly that had been working on a new constitution presented an approved draft and adjourned in May. All appeared set for a new attempt at constitutional government in July, when a group of young army officers overthrew the SMC government in June,

1979. The leader of the coup was a little known flight lieutenant named Jerry John Rawlings, who had earned his commission the year before.

Rawlings was born in 1947 to a Ghanaian mother and a Scottish father. Disciplinary problems prevented him from receiving a high school diploma, and he enlisted in 1967 as a flight cadet in the Ghanaian air force. Increasingly alienated from the SMC, Rawlings led a mutiny of junior officers on May 15, 1979. He was arrested two weeks later and appeared before a court-martial. Instead of defending himself, Rawlings used the trial to denounce the shortcomings of the SMC that caused him to seek its overthrow. As he sat in jail waiting for another court appearance on June 4, 1979, a large group of military and civilians freed him from prison and proceeded to overthrow the SMC, which was replaced by the Armed Forces Revolutionary Council (AFRC) with Rawlings at its head.

Rawlings wasted no time in ridding Ghana of its former power structure. The three former military dictators were executed, along with five other generals, and most senior officers were dismissed. Having completed the purge, Rawlings organized free elections. On September 24, 1979, Hilla Limann of the People's National Party was elected president. Two years later, Rawlings removed Limann for incompetence and corruption. Rawlings ruled as chairman through a mixed civilian and military board of seven members, termed the Provisional National Defense Council (PNDC). He justified his action through a self-declared role as guardian of the revolution. Supporters quipped that Rawlings's initials stood for "Junior Jesus."

From 1980 to 1990, Rawlings ruled Ghana through the PNDC without a constitution and with little tolerance for criticism. He experimented with using production and price controls, workers' councils to achieve the goals of economic self-sufficiency, and a higher living standard for the poor. As the economy began to stabilize, and with assistance for economic recovery given by the International Monetary Fund and World Bank, Rawlings began instituting more conservative fiscal policies. He also created 110 districts that elected officials with policy-making powers in areas such as health, education, and general public welfare. He then decided that multiparty national elections had long been overdue. He resigned his military commission to shed the image of military dictator.

When elections were held in 1992, Rawlings ran as a candidate from the National Defense Council (NDC), the successor party to the PNDC. Rawlings won with more than 58 percent of the vote, and NDC candidates won nearly 95 percent of the parliamentary seats in an election judged free and fair by foreign observers but denounced as fraught with irregularities by opposition candidates. Running for a second term in 1996, Rawlings instituted fairer registration processes. When the election was held in December, about 7 out of 9.3 million eligible voters went to the polls.

Rawlings's victory in the 1996 election was partly the result of opposition coalition parties failing to select joint candidates in a timely manner. The coalition parties were certain that a runoff election would have to be held; however, Rawlings was able to negate this by winning a simple majority of the vote. His victory was also the product of solid support in rural areas where heavy investments were made in improving the infrastructure and delivering basic services such as potable water and electricity.

1996

*Ghanaian president Jerry John Rawlings addresses a crowd in Accra in December, 1996, days before national elections.* (AP/Wide World Photos)

## SIGNIFICANCE

Rawlings's victory was a clear democratic mandate to govern and a clear sign that military dictatorship had no place in Ghana's future. His stated goal was simply to produce a democratic system free from corruption and backed by a sustainable economy. As the year 2000 approached, Rawlings made no effort to change the two-year term limit set by the 1992 constitution. Instead, he named John Atta-Mills as his party's successor. In the election, the victor was John Kufuor, candidate of the New Patriotic Party, who was the main opponent of Rawlings in the 1996 election. Kufuor was reelected in a first ballot victory in December, 2004, when he again faced Atta-Mills.

With the exception of Kwame Nkrumah, no political leader has had a greater impact on Ghana as Jerry John Rawlings. In a region permeated with incessant civil wars, rampant corruption, brutal dictatorship, and continued economic deterioration, he used a mild form of military dictatorship to reduce civil unrest and produce economic stability. At the right time, though perhaps in a two-step movement, he presided over the transition to democratic government. Fifty years after gaining independence, Ghana serves as a model for other African states, for stability and democratic government.

—*Irwin Halfond*

## FURTHER READING

Amoah, Michael. *Reconstructing the Nation in Africa: The Politics of Nationalism in Ghana.* New York: Palgrave Macmillan, 2007. Deals with the behavior of groups within the Ghanaian political system to un-cover national problems rooted neither in modernity nor in Western concepts of the nation. Bibliography and index.

Gocking, Roger. *History of Ghana.* Westport, Conn.: Greenwood Press, 2005. Concise history of Ghana by a specialist in the subject describing its turbulent history and clearly delineating major developmental themes. Contains time line, photographs, maps, and an appendix of biographies of notable figures.

Nugent, Paul. *Big Men, Small Boys, and Politics in Ghana, 1982-1994.* New York: Pinter, 1995. Analysis of Ghanaian politics within both the national and regional context. Contains bibliographic references and index.

Shillington, Kevin. *Ghana and the Rawlings Factor.* New York: St. Martin's Press, 1992. Interpretive study by a noted historian of Africa on Rawlings's impact on Ghanaian development. Bibliography and index.

Yeebo, Zaya. *Ghana: The Struggle for Popular Power—Rawlings, Savior or Demagogue.* London: New Beacon Books, 1991. Political and economic analysis of Rawlings's policies as well as his charismatic appeal to the Ghanaian masses. Provides and insider's view. Bibliography and index.

**SEE ALSO:** May 28, 1975: Formation of the Economic Community of West African States; Jan., 1983: Nigeria Expels West African Migrant Workers; Aug., 1991: African Countries Begin to Revive Democratization.

---

## December 10, 1996
# SZYMBORSKA RECEIVES THE NOBEL PRIZE IN LITERATURE

*The award of the Nobel Prize to Wisława Szymborska acknowledged the increasing prominence of women writers worldwide as well as the growing international prestige of Poland and Polish literature.*

**LOCALE:** Stockholm, Sweden
**CATEGORY:** Literature

## KEY FIGURES

*Wisława Szymborska* (b. 1923), Polish poet
*Czesław Miłosz* (1911-2004), Polish poet whose translations helped popularize Szymborska's work among English-speaking readers

## SUMMARY OF EVENT

On October 23, 1996, the Swedish Academy in Stockholm announced that the winner of the Nobel Prize in Literature was a seventy-three-year-old poet named Wisława Szymborska. Because this shy, self-effacing woman was not widely known outside her native Poland, there was an immediate scramble among the news media of the world to find out more about her life, her work, and her reaction to winning such a great honor, which carried with it a monetary award worth approximately $1.2 million.

It was learned that Szymborska had retreated to Zakopane, a small town in the mountains, to escape the onslaught of reporters, well-wishers, and celebrity hounds. She stated that she wanted to think about what she was going to say to the world in her Nobel acceptance speech, to be delivered a few days before the award presentation ceremony in Stockholm on December 10, 1996. In Zakopane, the small, chain-smoking author received a flurry of telephone calls from friends, admirers, and assorted dignitaries, including a congratulatory call from her friend and mentor Czesław Miłosz, the Polish-born poet who won the Nobel Prize in Literature in 1980 and had emigrated to France and later to the United States after becoming disillusioned with communism. "I'm a private person," she told Miłosz in their telephone conversation. "The most difficult thing will be to write a speech. I will be writing it for a month. I don't know what I will be talking about, but I will talk about you."

*Wisława Szymborska.* (AP/Wide World Photos)

1996

The world soon learned the essential facts about Szymborska. She was born in Bnin (now part of Kornick), Poland, near the western city of Poznań, and moved to Kraków with her parents at the age of eight. She had attended Jagellonian University. She endured the occupation of Poland by Nazi Germany during World War II and the subsequent domination of her country by Poland's other aggressive neighbor, the Soviet Union. She had been married twice and had been a widow since the early 1990's. She lived in a very modest fifth-floor walkup apartment in the center of Kraków. She had a handful of close friends and was personally acquainted with many of Poland's best poets, but she hated crowds and avoided literary gatherings and conferences.

Szymborska had been writing poetry since 1945. Her early work was communist-inspired, dealing with the threat of Western imperialism and the sufferings of the working people under capitalism. She was following the party line under pressure; poets were not permitted to write freely under the domination of the Polish communist government. Like many Poles, Szymborska became disillusioned with communism as a result of the regime's bad management of the economy as well as the oppression and exploitation endured under Soviet domination. Her later work was more personal and apolitical. In a telephone interview she stated, "Of course, life crosses politics, but my poems are strictly not political. They are more about people and life."

Szymborska was the fifth Polish writer to win the Nobel Prize in Literature. Novelist Henryk Sienkiewicz won the prize in 1905 for his very popular novel *Quo vadis* (1896; *Quo Vadis: A Narrative of the Time of Nero*, 1896). Władysław Reymont won in 1924 for his stories and novels about rural life, particularly his four-volume work *Chłopi* (1904-1909; *The Peasants*, 1924-1925). Isaac Bashevis Singer, who had moved to New York City, was awarded the prize in 1978 for his stories and novels about pre-Holocaust Polish-Jewish life, and Czesław Miłosz, who had translated many of Szymborska's poems and helped to make her better known to English-speaking readers, won the Nobel Prize in Literature in 1980.

Szymborska was the first Polish woman to receive the prize and one of the few women ever to be awarded a Nobel Prize of any kind since the prizes were inaugurated in 1901. An article in *The New York Times* announcing the award to Szymborska quoted the poet as saying, "I think that dividing literature or poetry into women's and men's poetry is starting to sound absurd. Perhaps there was a time when a woman's world did exist, separated from certain issues and problems, but at present there are no things that would not concern women and men at the same time. We do not live in the boudoir anymore."

## SIGNIFICANCE

Sweden is a relatively small country, with a population of fewer than ten million, but the annual awarding of the Nobel Prizes by the Swedish Academy has come to be an event of great international importance. The prizes honor not only individuals but also the countries those men and women represent. The Nobel Prize in Literature is the highest honor a writer can achieve. It often represents an entire lifetime of work and a large body of published writing. When the American novelist William Faulkner accepted the Nobel Prize in Literature in 1949, he said that it represented "a life's work in the agony and sweat of the human spirit," and this description could apply to most of the other recipients of the prize, including Wisława Szymborska.

Throughout the long years of the Cold War, which began in the late 1940's and lasted until the early 1990's, the Nobel Prizes had political overtones. The Swedish Academy favored spokespersons for democracy and individualism as opposed to collectivism and tyranny. By awarding the Nobel Prize in Literature to a Polish poet in 1996, the academy in effect recognized the transformation of Poland from a Soviet satellite to a valued member of the democratic West and the North Atlantic Treaty Organization (NATO). It also paid tribute to the indomitable spirit of the Polish people, who had survived the tyranny of Nazism as well as the tyranny of Soviet communism.

The choice of Szymborska, an author of deceptively simple, apolitical poetry about ordinary things, seemed to symbolize the healing of a world divided by political ideologies and a return, after a century of turmoil, to something resembling peace and normalcy. Szymborska had lived through Nazi occupation and Soviet domination, and she was thoroughly disgusted with uncompromising ideologies. As she wrote in her poem "No Title Required": "I'm no longer sure/ that what's important/ is more important than what's not."

Wisława Szymborska is one of the very few women ever to receive the Nobel Prize in Literature. Awarding the coveted prize to a woman was evidence of a recognition by the Swedish Academy of the growing importance of women in world literature. It is a fact that many more women than men now read short stories, novels, and poetry. This has inevitably led to an increasing prominence of women as writers and to a corresponding increase in the number of women involved in the world of publishing. Because of the prestige of the Nobel Prizes, Szymborska's receipt of the award helped to bring greater worldwide attention to women poets and women writers in general. It seems likely that in future years, women writers from around the world will be receiving a much more equitable share of the Nobel Prizes in Literature, along with a comparably greater share of other Nobel Prizes.

It is also likely that Szymborska's achievement will help to inspire young women all over the world to choose careers in literature, a situation that could have a major impact on reshaping the form and content of poetry and every other literary genre. Many years ago, the great English novelist Virginia Woolf predicted what she called a "feminization" of literature—that is, a greater tendency to deal with issues of importance to women, reflecting feminine intuition and sensitivity. Time has proven Woolf to have been correct. Szymborska's achievement symbolizes, among other things, the ongoing progress of women throughout the world in literature and every other field of human endeavor.

Awarding the Nobel Prize in Literature to a Polish writer also had the effect of focusing greater worldwide attention on Polish poetry and Polish literature in general. Polish writers have been handicapped in comparison with writers in countries such as England, the United States, France, and Germany, because Polish is a language not widely studied in other countries. Most foreign readers probably become acquainted with Polish literature in translation, but some are sufficiently moved by the powerful writing they discover to study the Polish language and Polish history.

—*Bill Delaney*

---

### SZYMBORSKA ON INSPIRATION

*In her Nobel lecture, delivered in Stockholm before an audience of international dignitaries on December 7, 1996, Wisława Szymborska spoke about the nature of inspiration:*

Inspiration is not the exclusive privilege of poets or artists generally. There is, has been, and will always be a certain group of people whom inspiration visits. It's made up of all those who've consciously chosen their calling and do their job with love and imagination. It may include doctors, teachers, gardeners—and I could list a hundred more professions. . . . Their work becomes one continuous adventure as long as they manage to keep discovering new challenges in it. Difficulties and setbacks never quell their curiosity. A swarm of new questions emerges from every problem they solve. Whatever inspiration is, it's born from a continuous "I don't know."

## FURTHER READING

Aaron, Jonathan. "In the Absence of Witnesses: The Po-etry of Wisława Szymborska." *Parnassus: Poetry in Review* 11 (Fall/Winter, 1983): 254-264. Describes Szymborska's poetry as penetrating and exploring an astonishing variety of subjects. Includes many quota-tions in translation. Clear, intelligent discussion helps the reader understand Szymborska's difficult position as a truth seeker in Soviet-dominated Poland before the Cold War ended.

Carpenter, Bogdana. "Wisława Szymborska and the Im-portance of the Unimportant." *World Literature To-day: A Literary Quarterly of the University of Okla-homa* 71 (Winter, 1997): 8-12. Insightful analysis of Szymborska's poetry by a professor of Polish and comparative literature. Provides many excerpts from the poet's work in English translation. Focuses on finding the deeper, hidden meanings in Szymborska's "deceptively transparent poems."

Krzysztov, Karasek. "Mozartian Joy: The Poetry of Wisława Szymborska." In *The Mature Laurel: Es-says on Modern Polish Poetry*, edited by Adam Czerniawski. Chester Springs, Pa.: Dufour Editions, 1991. Argues that Szymborska's poetry "radiates au-thentic joy, as does the music of Mozart," and notes that this joy "issues from the sensation of a game of in-tellect and imagination" and "from the unaffectedness of her language." Answers critics who complain that Szymborska's work does not offer "cognitive revela-tions."

Szymborska, Wisława. "I Don't Know: The 1996 Nobel Lecture." Translated by Stanislaw Baranczak and Clare Cavanagh. *World Literature Today: A Literary Quarterly of the University of Oklahoma* 71 (Winter, 1997): 5-7. Presents the complete text of Szymbor-ska's Nobel lecture. Also includes an English transla-tion of "No Title Required," one of Szymborska's most representative poems.

_____. *Monologue of a Dog*. Translated by Stanislaw Baranczak and Clare Cavanagh. Orlando, Fla.: Har-court, 2005. Slim volume of the poet's work at the be-ginning of the twenty-first century. Includes both the original Polish and an English translation of each poem.

_____. *People on a Bridge*. Translated by Adam Czerniawski. London: Forest Books, 1990. Includes an interesting and informative introduction by the translator, one of the best-known translators of Polish poetry in Great Britain. Includes the original Polish of some poems on facing pages.

_____. *Sounds, Feelings, Thoughts: Seventy Poems*. Translated by Magnus J. Krynski and Robert A. Maguire. Princeton, N.J.: Princeton University Press, 1981. One of the best collections of Szymborska's poetry available in English. Contains poems written between 1957 and 1979, with Polish originals and English translations on facing pages. "Comments" section contains interesting explications, anecdotes, and references.

Vendler, Helen. "Unfathomable Life." *The New Repub-lic*, January 1, 1996, 36-39. Interesting discussion of Szymborska's life and work focuses on *View with a Grain of Sand: Selected Poems* (1995), translated by Stanislaw Baranczak and Clare Cavanagh. Includes excerpts from Szymborska's poems in English trans-lation.

**SEE ALSO:** Dec. 10, 1978: Singer Is Awarded the Nobel Prize in Literature; Dec. 10, 1986: Soyinka Receives the Nobel Prize in Literature; Dec. 10, 1988: Mahfouz Receives the Nobel Prize in Literature; Dec. 10, 1991: Gordimer Receives the Nobel Prize in Literature; Dec. 10, 1994: Ōe Receives the Nobel Prize in Litera-ture; Dec. 10, 1995: Heaney Receives the Nobel Prize in Literature.

1996

## December 29, 1996
# FARC OFFENSIVE INTENSIFIES THE GUERRILLA WAR IN COLOMBIA

*An attack on a military base in Guaviare, Colombia, by the Colombian Revolutionary Armed Forces initiated a three-week guerrilla offensive that resulted in at least 130 casualties.*

**LOCALE:** Guaviare, Colombia
**CATEGORY:** Wars, uprisings, and civil unrest

**KEY FIGURES**

*Pedro Antonio Marín* (Manuel Marulanda Vélez; b. 1930), commander in chief of the Colombian Revolutionary Armed Forces

*Ernesto Samper* (b. 1950), Liberal Party activist and president of Colombia, 1994-1998

*César Gaviria Trujillo* (b. 1947), Liberal Party activist and president of Colombia, 1990-1994

*Andrés Pastrana* (b. 1954), Conservative Party activist and president of Colombia, 1998-2002

*Luis Carlos Galán* (1943-1989), Liberal Party activist and presidential precandidate

**SUMMARY OF EVENT**

Colombia's long history of political violence is legendary. For a time, a political power-sharing arrangement known as the National Front (1958-1974) managed to calm the traditionally violent rivalries between the Liberal and Conservative parties. However, it left little room for organizations that more directly advocated for peasants, workers, and other politically excluded sectors. This situation led to the formation of radical underground movements, including the Colombian Revolutionary Armed Forces (FARC), led by Pedro Antonio Marín, also known as Manuel Marulanda Vélez and nicknamed "Tirofijo" (Sureshot).

Marulanda was a veteran peasant activist of earlier struggles who espoused a Marxist-Leninist vision of revolutionary socialist struggle. Convinced that the only viable strategy for revolution would be to create a military structure capable of capturing state power, FARC guerrillas proceeded to exert their control over areas in the countryside where governmental presence was weak or nonexistent. By the end of the 1970's, the guerrillas were able to sustain nine active fronts. Five of these strongholds were concentrated in the southern departments of Caquetá, Putumayo, Huila, Cauca, and Tolima, which included areas engaged in illegal coca cultivation.

During the 1980's, the FARC continued to steadily grow in the face of severe government repression of legal leftist opposition groups. By 1983, it had expanded to eighteen active fronts. President Belisario Betancur (1982-1986) responded to its growing strength by negotiating a cease-fire, in the hopes of a peaceful way out of the conflict. The FARC responded by participating in the creation of the Patriotic Union (UP), a legal political organization in which its close ally, the Communist Party of Colombia, would play a central role. However, Betancur was widely criticized for seeking these negotiations, and his successor, Virgilio Barco Vargas (1986-1990), withdrew the initiatives. What ensued was a "dirty war" that killed thousands of UP members over the following decade. This mass murder of practically an entire generation of militants would contribute to a lasting reticence on the part of Colombia's armed groups to participate in peace talks with the government.

The 1990's was a politically turbulent period in Colombia with the continuation of high rates of violence, registering more than twenty-five thousand political killings a year between 1991 and 1996. In March, 1990, the UP's presidential candidate, Bernardo Jaramillo, was assassinated at the international airport in Bogotá, becoming yet another victim of rightist forces that by then had killed at least three thousand members of his organization. A month later, the presidential candidate of the radical 19th of April Movement (M-19), Carlos Pizarro Leongómez, was also killed. In May, 1990, César Gaviria Trujillo of the Liberal Party was elected president, but only after his party's original candidate, Luis Carlos Galán, had been murdered at the onset of the campaign in August, 1989. Gaviria put forward a series of initiatives to negotiate with armed guerrillas, echoing what he called the "positive intentions" of Betancur. While pursuing neoliberal economic policies and fighting the Medellín drug cartel, Gaviria managed to negotiate the disarmament of several major guerrilla groups by agreeing to a Constituent Assembly, which drafted a new constitution for the country in 1991.

However, in December, 1990, President Gaviria launched a major military offensive against the FARC. He claimed that such actions would be necessary to pressure the organization into joining the disarmament negotiations. In May, 1992, a military operation targeted the FARC base at La Uribe, Meta, in hopes of taking out the entire FARC leadership. The attempt at a knockout blow failed, and the violence continued unabated. In December, 1992, a report issued by School of the Americas

Watch declared that 40 percent of political assassinations were carried out by government agents, another 30 percent by paramilitary groups, 27.5 percent by armed guerrillas, and only 2.5 percent by drug mafias.

In January, 1994, the government made the controversial announcement that 120 U.S. military advisers had joined the Colombian military offensive against the illegal narcotics trade. Ernesto Samper was narrowly elected president in June, although he was accused by his Conservative opponent of having accepted drug money in his campaign. To counter these accusations and to improve its deteriorating relations with Washington, the Samper administration ordered expansive aerial spraying of coca crops. Between 1994 and 1999, about 240,000 hectares of coca were fumigated with more than two million liters of glyphosate, a powerful and ecologically destructive herbicide. The result was a gradual displacement of coca cultivation into Putumayo, leading to a tripling of total production and embarrassing the government, who insisted that the supply of coca was being eradicated.

By July, 1996, thousands of farmers and members of surrounding indigenous communities in the department of Guaviare were protesting the government's crop eradication policies and increasing political repression. These unprecedented peasant mobilizations numbered to around 300,000 strong at their peak. The resulting militarization of the area by the government and the attempt to criminalize all legal protest conspired to make the FARC an obvious political option for peasants under fire. The protests soon spread to Putumayo, where confrontations with the government also intensified.

On August 29, the FARC mounted a dramatic and unprecedented show of strength by directly attacking the military base in Las Delicias, Putumayo, killing fifty-four members of the government forces, wounding seventeen, and taking sixty soldiers captive. On September 9, FARC forces attacked the military base of La Carpa, Guaviare, killing twenty-two soldiers. The combined actions there and elsewhere amounted to a major FARC offensive and a stinging setback for the government.

A U.S. Department of State document released in 2002 revealed that a representative of the U.S. congressional staff had arrived in Guaviare just in time to see the bodies of the twenty-two Colombian soldiers being loaded onto helicopters following the FARC attack. The report indicated that Guaviare was by that time one of the largest coca-growing regions in the country and that the FARC offensive amounted to "retaliation for destroying the coca fields." These and similar reports were signifi-

cant because they showed that, contrary to U.S. congressional insistence, arms being provided to Colombia for the "war on drugs" were in fact being used to fight the FARC insurgency.

## SIGNIFICANCE

The 1996 FARC offensive in Guaviare and adjacent areas paved the way to similar actions in the following years, all of which convincingly demonstrated the accumulated military capacity of the FARC. President Samper's successor, Andrés Pastrana, would later decide to meet directly with Marulanda and the FARC leadership to negotiate the withdrawal of government troops from five municipalities, creating a demilitarized zone about the size of Switzerland that would serve as a base for comprehensive peace talks in 1999. In so doing, the government granted political recognition to the FARC.

Also significant was the persistent agility of the FARC in positioning itself among those sectors most affected by the agrarian crisis, especially in zones traditionally abandoned by the Colombian state. In the 1990's, this was reinforced by the FARC's expansion into territories where coca and poppy cultivation was widespread, booming on account of the ever-expanding drug trade. The FARC was able to consolidate an impressive financial base via the "taxes" it levied in agricultural zones under its control in exchange for armed protection. For its part, the Colombian government remained single-mindedly focused on the FARC's military capacity while blinded to the resilient social base being built up in these departments. In the case of coca and poppy production, the incessant demands of Washington to expand illicit crop eradication programs effectively placed the Colombian government at odds with thousands of communities where the continued presence of the FARC constituted the sole form of protection of their livelihood.

—*Richard A. Dello Buono*

## FURTHER READING

Bergquist, Charles, Ricardo Peñaranda, and Gonzalo Sánchez G., eds. *Violence in Colombia, 1990-2000: Waging War and Negotiating Peace.* Wilmington, Del.: Scholarly Resources, 2001. Collection of essays by prominent Colombian intellectuals that discuss various aspects of the Colombian conflict.

Dudley, Steven. *Walking Ghosts: Murder and Guerrilla Politics in Colombia.* New York: Routledge, 2004. Analysis of the Colombian leftist organization Patriotic Union based on the author's firsthand experience.

1996

Kirk, Robin. *More Terrible than Death: Massacres, Drugs, and America's War in Colombia*. New York: PublicAffairs, 2003. Account of Colombia's political violence from a human rights perspective.

Murillo, Mario, and Jesus Rey Avirama. *Colombia and the United States: War, Terrorism, and Destabilization*. New York: Seven Stories Press, 2003. Analyzes the effects of U.S. policies on the Colombian conflict.

Ramírez Cuellar, Francisco. *The Profits of Extermination: How U.S. Corporate Power Is Destroying Colombia*. Monroe, Maine: Common Courage Press, 2005. Analysis of political repression in Colombia that focuses on the link with U.S.-based multinational corporations.

Safford, Frank, and Marco Palacios. *Colombia: Fragmented Land, Divided Society*. New York: Oxford University Press, 2001. Provides a broad, historical overview, including a detailed analysis of contemporary political violence.

**SEE ALSO:** 1976: Colombian Guerrilla War Begins; 1989-1990: Colombian Presidential Candidates Are Killed.

## December 29, 1996
# GUATEMALAN PEACE ACCORDS END CIVIL WAR

*A wide-ranging set of peace accords were signed by the Guatemalan government and the Guatemalan National Revolutionary Unity, putting an end to more than three and a half decades of civil conflict that claimed at least 200,000 lives. The final installment of the accords, signed in late December, 1996, culminated a six-year peace process in which international pressure and an active U.N. presence played a key role in reaching a definitive agreement.*

**LOCALE:** Guatemala City, Guatemala

**CATEGORIES:** Diplomacy and international relations; wars, uprisings, and civil unrest

### KEY FIGURES

*Rigoberta Menchú* (b. 1959), indigenous activist of the Mayan Quiché ethnic group

*Efraín Ríos Montt* (b. 1926), president of Guatemalan military government, 1982-1983

*Jorge Serrano Elías* (b. 1945), president of Guatemala, 1991-1993

*Álvaro Arzú* (b. 1946), president of Guatemala, 1996-2000

*Juan José Gerardi Conedera* (1922-1998), Guatemalan auxiliary archbishop and director of the Human Rights Office of the Archdiocese of Guatemala

*Mirna Mack* (1949-1990), Guatemalan anthropologist and human rights activist

### SUMMARY OF EVENT

Guatemala experienced a brief period of democratic, progressive governance beginning in the mid-1940's until it was abruptly halted by a military coup in 1954.

The military takeover enjoyed tactical support from the United States Central Intelligence Agency (CIA) as part of its Cold War strategy to prevent communist penetration in the Americas. Washington was also responding to complaints of the U.S.-based United Fruit Company, whose banana investments in Guatemala were being challenged with demands for agrarian reform and higher wages. In the years following the 1954 coup, military rule sought to repress all forms of legal dissent, but this repression eventually resulted in the formation of underground, armed guerrilla groups that eventually united to form the Guatemalan National Revolutionary Unity (URNG).

More than half the population of Guatemala is made up of linguistically distinct Mayan descendants. These communities are by far the country's poorest and have been subjected to considerable discrimination. By 1960, a significant number of indigenous Guatemalans had joined with other peasants and organized sectors of urban laborers to initiate a decades-long guerrilla struggle against poverty, social exclusion, and authoritarian military rule. As the armed rebellion spread, so too did the violent counterinsurgency activities of the military-led government. With various members of her immediate family killed by government forces during the 1979-1983 period, indigenous activist Rigoberta Menchú wrote that the violent repression of successive military regimes essentially left few alternatives for those Guatemalans who sought access to land and better living conditions. Menchú received the Nobel Peace Prize in 1992 for her efforts on behalf of the indigenous peoples of Guatemala.

There is little room to doubt the U.S. support given to the Guatemalan military throughout the war. In 1966-1968, President Lyndon B. Johnson sent U.S. Army Special Forces (Green Berets) to Guatemala to provide training and strategic aid for counterinsurgency. This support continued until the mounting human rights violations led President Jimmy Carter's administration to cut off all official U.S. military aid to Guatemala in 1977. In early 1982, Efraín Ríos Montt took power in a military shake-up with the blessing of Ronald Reagan's presidential administration, which reversed Carter's policy and worked to reestablish official U.S. military assistance. Reagan himself visited Guatemala and declared that Ríos Montt had personally given firm assurances of his democratic intentions.

With Washington on his side, Ríos Montt applied a "scorched earth" policy throughout the countryside designed to repel important advances made by guerrilla forces. Authorities of the Roman Catholic Church in Guatemala bitterly denounced the extreme violence, but Ríos Montt made little secret of his disdain for human rights criticism. A self-declared born-again Christian, he publicly stated that his policy was simply one of "scorched Communists." By the time Ríos Montt could be forced out of office by another group of military officers in 1983, international condemnation of Guatemalan military rule had considerably intensified. The generals that replaced him, however, showed little or no improvement and by 1990, official U.S. aid was once again cut off by the George H. W. Bush administration.

Precise figures on the victims of the bloody internal conflict that spanned thirty-six years in Guatemala were slow to emerge. Mirna Mack, a Guatemalan anthropologist, attempted to conduct an in-depth study of the military's genocide and forced displacement of indigenous communities. Before she could finish her work, however, she was brutally assassinated in 1990 outside her office in Guatemala City. In 1998, an influential report on the war coordinated by Catholic bishop Juan José Gerardi Conedera with support by the United Nations revealed that about 200,000 Guatemalan civilians had lost their lives by that time, including the nearly complete destruction of about four hundred indigenous villages. In addition, it reported that the war had forcibly displaced at least one million Guatemalans from their homes, with more than 100,000 refugees fleeing abroad. The four-volume report concluded that the Guatemalan army or its affiliated paramilitary groups were responsible for at least 80 percent of deaths or disappearances while only about 9 percent were clearly attributable to the guerrillas, with the remainder too difficult to determine. Two nights after the report was released, Bishop Gerardi himself was brutally murdered at his home in Guatemala City, apparently in government reprisal. Many experts believe that additional archaeological-forensic work will be necessary to uncover the full extent of atrocities that took place in the Guatemalan countryside during the worst years of the conflict.

By 1990, the counterinsurgency effort had effectively contained the guerrilla forces, and the government showed little interest in negotiating a truce, demanding instead that insurgents unilaterally disarm in unconditional defeat. When the civilian government of Jorge Serrano Elías came to power in early 1991, he ordered the military to begin participation in a dialogue aimed at setting up direct peace talks. The process was temporarily derailed in 1993 when Serrano fell from power. By January, 1994, the combination of international pressure and domestic calls from the Catholic Church and others resulted in government acceptance of a U.N. role in peace talks. This marked a turning point for negotiations, setting regular deadlines and establishing an overall

*Efraín Ríos Montt.* (AP/Wide World Photos)

framework for the process. A broad role was established for civil society organizations, effectively deprived of any public participation since the 1950's, and this fueled a sense that real negotiations could now take place in Guatemala.

In March, 1994, a human rights accord framework was agreed to by the contending parties, mandating the U.N. Verification Mission in Guatemala (MINUGUA), which arrived in November. In the 1995 general elections, the URNG abided by its agreement not to disrupt them and even called upon its supporters to participate. The electoral victory of Álvaro Arzú yielded a civilian president publicly committed to reaching a comprehensive peace agreement. A series of confidence-building measures by the Arzú administration included assent to the Accord on Identity and Rights of Indigenous Peoples in 1995, establishing a mandate for substantial social reforms toward the establishment of a multiethnic and multicultural nation. This paved the way for the URNG leadership to announce an indefinite suspension of armed actions on March 19, 1996. The Guatemalan government reciprocated the following day by announcing a suspension of its counterinsurgency operations.

In May, 1996, the Accord on Socioeconomic and Agrarian Issues offered some economic reforms, though it was widely protested by civil society organizations as insufficient to address the magnitude of economic problems underlying the conflict. In September, 1996, the demilitarization accord stipulated substantial reforms to curtail the power of the Guatemalan military and to reestablish its subordination to civilian state control. It also provided for judicial reforms and the abolition of government-sponsored paramilitary civilian patrols. Finally, a culminating accord established a timetable for implementation of all agreements, legal reinsertion of URNG combatants into Guatemalan society, and amnesty for the military. This allowed the URNG leadership to return legally from Mexico to an emotional reception in Guatemala City on December 28, 1996, where the signing of the Accord for a Firm and Lasting Peace took place on the following day.

## SIGNIFICANCE

The Guatemalan peace accords are testimony to the influence and limitations of the United Nations in helping to broker an end to long-standing hostilities. It was international outcry over the atrocious human rights violations of successive military governments that resulted in

the United Nations' taking a role in the peace process. Because there is no statute of limitations applicable to crimes against humanity and genocide under international law, the peace accords that provided amnesty for the military left Guatemala in an ambiguous situation with regard to human rights violators. While the deeply rooted ethnic and social-class inequalities that drove the country to war were essentially left unresolved by the peace process, the accords remain an important point of reference in Guatemalan national politics. The new space opened by a negotiated end to the conflict made it possible for opposition figures such as Rigoberta Menchú to participate in civilian government and work for additional reforms.

*—Richard A. Dello Buono*

## FURTHER READING

Chase-Dunn, Christopher, Susanne Jonas, and Nelson Amaro, eds. *Globalization on the Ground: Postbellum Guatemalan Democracy and Development.* Lanham, Md.: Rowman & Littlefield, 2001. Scholarly essays on development and the struggle for democracy in post-civil war Guatemala. Includes work by prominent Guatemalan experts. Subject index, bibliography, notes.

Jonas, Susanne. *Of Centaurs and Doves: Guatemala's Peace Process.* Boulder, Colo.: Westview Press, 2000. Sober analysis of postconflict Guatemala that raises serious questions about the sustainability of the democratization process envisioned by the 1996 peace accords.

Schirmer, Jennifer G. *The Guatemalan Military Project: A Violence Called Democracy.* Philadelphia: University of Pennsylvania Press, 1999. Revealing study of the mentality of Guatemalan authoritarian rulers as presented in their own words.

Wilkinson, Daniel. *Silence on the Mountain: Stories of Terror, Betrayal, and Forgetting in Guatemala.* Durham, N.C.: Duke University Press, 2002. A human rights worker in Guatemala during the 1990's, the author describes how a frustrated struggle for land reform later evolved into a full-scale armed rebellion.

SEE ALSO: 1977-1981: Carter Makes Human Rights a Central Theme of Foreign Policy; 1978-1985: Guatemalan Death Squads Target Indigenous Indians; Dec. 10, 1987: Arias Sánchez Receives the Nobel Peace Prize.

**January, 1997**

# ARCHAEOLOGISTS ANNOUNCE THE DISCOVERY OF ARISTOTLE'S LYCEUM

*During excavation for the construction of a new gallery for modern art, workers uncovered parts of what is believed to be the site of the original Lyceum, the school founded by the philosopher Aristotle in 335 B.C.E.*

**LOCALE:** Athens, Greece
**CATEGORY:** Archaeology

**KEY FIGURES**

*Effi Lygouri* (fl. late twentieth century), archaeologist who led the rescue dig that uncovered the palaestra of the Lyceum

*Evangelos Venizelos* (b. 1957), Greek minister of culture, 1996-1999 and 2000-2004

*Basil P. Goulandris* (1913-1994), philanthropist and art collector

*Elise B. Goulandris* (1917-2000), philanthropist and art collector

**SUMMARY OF EVENT**

Most of the known works of the Greek philosopher Aristotle were produced during his twelve years as head of the Lyceum in Athens, Greece. Continuing and extending the tradition of Plato's Academy, where Aristotle himself had studied, the Lyceum formed the prototype for schools and libraries throughout the Greco-Roman area of influence. Although many of Aristotle's writings were lost, some of them, including those that probably began as lecture notes for his talks at the Lyceum, were preserved for more than twenty-three hundred years and were seminal in the development of Western science, philosophy, logic, and other disciplines. The term "lyceum" itself was eventually applied not only to schools but also to learned societies, libraries, museums, and even theaters around the world.

More than two millennia later, citizens of the modern city of Athens, now the capital of Greece, found themselves having to balance the care, preservation, and systematic study of their many archaeological sites with the needs of a bustling metropolis. The general vicinity of the original Lyceum had become a prestigious urban area filled with museums and embassies. Because of the proximity to other museums, the area was selected by Basil P. Goulandris and Elise B. Goulandris, two philanthropists who were avid collectors of modern European art, for the location of a new museum to display their collection and

share it with the public. At first they were interested in another site in the neighborhood, but this would have entailed the destruction of an older building. After this plan was rejected, they chose a relatively empty parcel of land near the juncture of Rigillis Street and Vasilissis Sofias Avenue near Syntagma Square. World-famous architect I. M. Pei was chosen to design the building.

After the Greek government granted the site to the Goulandris Foundation, excavation for the Museum of Modern Art began in May, 1996. Part of the location was being used as an unpaved parking lot. In accordance with the policies of protecting any hidden antiquities that might be inadvertently damaged or remain lost, the first step in preparing the construction site was for archaeologists to complete a "rescue" excavation. With its long history and layers of culture, any kind of construction within the city would almost inevitably unearth artifacts from previous eras.

The preconstruction project was conducted by the Third Ephorate of Prehistoric and Classical Antiquities and was led by Effi Lygouri. After about half of the excavation was completed, workers discovered the foundations of a large structure, forty-eight meters wide, with its northern, eastern, and western sides inside the new construction site, and extending south past the boundaries of the excavation toward the former bed of the Ilissos River. It was noted that many aspects of the structure's form, including the very symmetrical arrangement of the rooms, its north-south orientation, its earthen floors, and its central court surrounded by stoas, were consistent with the palaestrae of the Academy, Delphi, Delos, and Olympia. The structure included a room in which wrestlers were oiled, tanks for bathing in both hot and cool water, and a drain leading to the river.

By studying coins, pottery shards, and other objects found on the same level, archaeologists identified the last quarter of the fourth century B.C.E. as the time of the building's original construction. Because its foundations were on bedrock, no older layers were discovered. They determined that the building had been in use for a very long period and that it had gone through at least two cycles of reconstruction during the Roman period, the first after the destruction of Athens by Roman general Lucius Cornelius Sulla in 86 B.C.E. and another after the Herulian invasion in 267 C.E. After this, it was rebuilt and

3013

used once again until its final destruction near the end of the fourth century C.E.

For centuries, the general location of the original Lyceum had been known from literary sources, but little evidence had remained of any physical structure. In the smaller Athens of classical times, its location would have been in a park-like suburban area outside the city walls and near the Ilissos River, with groves of trees, springs, and temples on the banks of the river. According to the classical literature, Aristotle had liked to teach while walking the grounds with his students. The name "Ly-

*An aerial photograph shows ruins discovered in Athens in 1997 that are thought to be the remains of the Lyceum, the school founded by the Greek philosopher Aristotle in 335 B.C.E. (AP/Wide World Photos)*

ceum" comes from the protective wolf-slayer or wolf-related form of Apollo Lykeios, to whom a shrine was dedicated at that location, even before the days of the great philosophers. Like many places of worship and learning at this time, the Lyceum had been a place for physical cultivation as well and included a palaestra, a structure for wrestling matches as well as meetings and discussions. This very palaestra was the setting for one of Plato's dialogues. Troops had been mustered at the Lyceum to defend the city-state in times of emergency. However, in spite of many references in literature, the exact location had been lost for centuries.

The discovery of a building of such large dimensions, with these particular qualities, and so consistent with the ancient literary descriptions, made it clear to scholars that the newly discovered palaestra belonged to the original Lyceum of Aristotle. Excitement built very quickly, and formal announcements were made in January, 1997, by Minister of Culture Evangelos Venizelos. While there has been some skepticism, most scholars have accepted the validity of the claim. Having the precise location of this part of the Lyceum has also proven useful in determining the overall placement of other ancient structures described in the classics.

**SIGNIFICANCE**

At first, it was thought that the new Museum of Modern Art and the Lyceum site could somehow coexist, which was suggested by Evangelos Venizelos in his initial announcements. The generosity of Basil and Elise Goulandris had presented the city with a great opportunity, and the proximity of the site to other museums, especially the nearby Byzantine and Christian Museum and the Museum of Cycladic Art, suggested the potential for the new museum to become a popular location for visitors. Eventually, however, the Goulandris Foundation started to explore other locations for the modern art museum. Meanwhile, the rediscovered palaestra of the Lyceum was in need of care. In response to concerns about rain causing damage to the sensitive archaeological site, it was agreed in 2003 that a light protective roof would be constructed, and plans were also made to integrate the site with an archaeological park adjacent to the expanded Byzantine and Christian Museum. The concept of a park, with its open space, was more consistent with the area's appearance in classical times. The idea that one could walk in Aristotle's footsteps was now more than just a metaphor.

—*John Myers*

## FURTHER READING

Blackman, David. "Archaeology in Greece, 1996-97." *Archaeological Reports* 43 (1996-1997): 1-125. Detailed description of the site just after it was unearthed, including the layout of the building and the rationale for identifying it as part of Aristotle's Lyceum. Illustrations.

Haworth, Karla. "Greek Archaeologists Say They Have Found the Lyceum." *Chronicle of Higher Education*, January 24, 1997, p. A14. Summary of initial announcements of the discovery, including the issue of whether or not the Byzantine and Christian Museum would still be built at the site.

Isle, Mick. *Aristotle: Pioneering Philosopher and Founder of the Lyceum.* New York: Rosen Publishing Group, 2006. Primarily for precollege readers, this is a comprehensive introduction to Aristotle, with biographical material as well as discussion of ideas and impact. Illustrations.

Lynch, John Patrick. *Aristotle's School: A Study of a Greek Educational Institution* Berkeley: University of California Press, 1972. Begins with detailed discussion of the Lyceum's physical setting, including its role as a gymnasium and its even more ancient role as a shrine. Indexes, appendixes, extensive notes.

**SEE ALSO:** Mar., 1974: Clay Soldiers Are Discovered in China; Aug., 1979: Ancient Sanctuary Is Discovered in El Juyo Cave; June, 1980: Radar Reveals Canals at Mayan Agricultural Centers.

1997

## January-March, 1997
# KAREN REFUGEE CRISIS

*Karen peoples fleeing persecution in Burma met with a hostile reception in Thailand, where the military stopped some from crossing the border and forced the repatriation of some five thousand others. Because the Karen were subjected to extensive human rights abuses in their homeland, humanitarian organizations protested the Thai policy.*

**LOCALE:** Northwestern Thailand-Myanmar border; Shan, Karenni, and Karen, Myanmar

**CATEGORIES:** Immigration, emigration, and relocation; indigenous peoples' rights

## KEY FIGURES

*Chettha Thanajaro* (b. 1938), Thai army commander and defense minister

*Than Shwe* (b. 1933), commanding military officer of the dictatorial Myanmar government

*Bo Mya* (1927-2006), chairman, 1976-2000, of the Karen National Union and commander, 1966-2005, of the Karen National Liberation Army

*Chavalit Yongchaiyudh* (b. 1932), prime minister of Thailand, 1996-1997

## SUMMARY OF EVENT

In January and February of 1997, Thai soldiers under the command of General Chettha Thanajaro forcibly repatriated some five thousand Karen refugees who had fled to the Thai border from Myanmar (formerly known as Burma). The Karen people have been subjected to brutally repressive policies in Myanmar, but Chettha asserted that the refugees in question either were illegal migrants who were not fleeing immediate conflict or were not civilians but members of the revolutionary Karen National Liberation Army.

For political, economic, and military reasons, the Myanmar capital, Yangon (formerly Rangoon), marginalized hundreds of thousands of indigenous peoples, either displacing them internally—forcing many into the jungle—or causing them to flee to neighboring Thailand. The forced repatriations by the Thai Ninth Infantry Division, known as *refoulements* under international law, raised protests from international humanitarian organizations. The Thai military temporarily ceased repatriation of the Karen, although a policy hostile to refugees remained in place.

3015

After World War II, the Karen were frustrated by the failure of the Allies to recognize the role they had played in fighting the Japanese. At the same time, they were being forced from their villages because of aggressive assimilation policies on the part of the Myanmar government or for reasons of economic development. The Karen National Union (KNU) therefore sought to establish an autonomous state in Myanmar, which it would call Kawthoolei, understood to mean "land without evil." The KNLA, under the rigid leadership of General Bo Mya, began guerrilla action against Myanmar government targets.

In 1962, a military junta led by General Ne Win and known as the State Law and Order Restoration Council (SLORC) seized power in Yangon and launched a campaign of ethnic cleansing against the Karen and other indigenous peoples, including the Shan, Mon, and Karenni.

*Soldiers of the rebel Karen National Union march at their headquarters near the Thai border on January 31, 1997—a date they celebrate as Revolution Day. Two weeks after this picture was taken, Myanmar government troops attacked the camp and scattered the rebels.* (AP/Wide World Photos)

SLORC also forced relocation on some villages. In 1969, the military regime began the "Four Cuts" (Pya Ley Pya) offensive, attempting to eliminate all contact between civilian communities and the KNLA.

Villagers suspected of aiding the guerrillas were punished severely, and the financing and recruitment of new guerrillas was therefore interrupted. When General Than Shwe became commander in 1992, counterinsurgency measures were intensified to intimidate noncombatants: These included rape, looting, arbitrary executions, the burning of crops and homes, and other atrocities. The Myanmar military forced Karen villagers to clear mines and serve as porters against the nationalist guerrillas. If a village was suspected of harboring Karen insurgents, official policy was to burn it to the ground. Accusations of many human rights violations were leveled against a special paramilitary unit known as the Sa Sa Sa.

Although most Karen are Buddhists/animists, a significant number were converted to Christianity during the nineteenth century and particularly during World War II, when they fought with the British against the Japanese. The leadership of the KNU was primarily Christian, a phenomenon which led to a political-religious division among the Karen.

In 1995, the Democratic Karen Buddhist Army (DKBA), formed by monk U Thu Zana and led militarily by former KNLA sergeant Maung Chit Htoo, broke away from the KNU and sought accommodation with the Myanmar junta. Having inside knowledge, the DKBA was soon able to capture KNLA headquarters at Manerplaw on the Salween River, forcing a massive exodus of refugees into Thailand. The situation was also worsened by the building of the Yadana gas pipeline in the Tenasserim district of Myanmar, as several villages were forced to relocate to make way for the development. At the same time, an offensive against the KNLA by the Myanmar government declared the Duplaya district of the central Karen state a free-fire zone and targeted villagers who did not relocate. Thousands sought asylum across the border, where they were still at risk because of regular cross-border raids by Myanmar troops and the DKBA.

Thailand's reception of asylum seekers has always been restricted. Bangkok did not sign the 1951 United Nations accord on refugees and has maintained a narrow policy that extends refuge to civilians in immediate flight from conflict, but not to victims of forced relocation, forced labor, or other forms of ethnic harassment.

In 1995, the Thai National Security Council decided that the situation in Myanmar had returned to normal and repatriation should begin when SLORC agreed to accept returnees. In 1996, on the eve of the East Asian financial crisis, Thailand's economy was extremely sluggish, a situation that could have been exacerbated by border conflict or by the burden of thousands of additional displaced persons from Myanmar. Furthermore, a rampant drug trade flowing into Thailand was made more difficult to police by the number of refugees. The Thai government was also aware that its refugee camps, which housed leaders of the KNU and KNLA, were potential sources of support for the Karen insurgency. Thailand enjoyed commercial ties with Myanmar, and its government was reluctant to jeopardize those connections.

Under these circumstances, the Thai Ninth Army refused entry to some refugees from Myanmar and repatriated others, with assurances from SLORC that they would not be harmed. The Thai military claimed that the villagers, including many women and children—some suffering from malaria and diarrhea—had voluntarily returned to their homes under promise of reconciliation from Yangon. However, on hearing reports from aid groups about the forced repatriations, the United States, the European Union, and the Office of the United Nations High Commissioner for Refugees (UNHCR) formally deplored the actions and urged Thailand to grant asylum to unarmed refugees according to international humanitarian principles.

International criticism led General Chettha and Ninth Division commander Lieutenant General Taweep Suwannasingh to halt the repatriation policy momentarily. However, interior minister Snoh Thienthong denounced the aid organizations' reporting of the deportations and vowed to continue the ministry's long-standing plan to send home all illegal Karen migrants on grounds that Thailand had to ensure the well-being and safety of its own people. In spite of further forced repatriation, by the end of 1997, nearly one million refugees from Myanmar, including 200,000 Karen—some 91,000 of them in refugee camps—were thought to be in Thailand.

## SIGNIFICANCE

At the beginning of 2007, despite the threat of sanctions from the U.N. Security Council, the military government of Myanmar (now called the State Peace and Development Council) was still in power and exercising repres-sive policies against its peoples, including some seven million Karen. In addition, proposals that the UNHCR administer refugee camps in Thailand were rejected, and Thai authorities tightened circulation into and out of camps, including Mae La and Mae Sot. At the same time, the DKBA, having ingratiated itself with Yangon, continued military attacks on the KNU and on villages and camps thought to shelter the KNLA.

In 2000, Thai public opinion against the Karen was further hardened when a group called God's Army, under the leadership of twins Johnny and Luther Htoo (who were only about twelve years old at the time), took some seven hundred people hostage at the Ratchaburi hospital in Thailand. Following the death of long-term Karen leader Bo on December 24, 2006, resistance seemed increasingly futile. Still facing policies of ethnic cleansing, hundreds of thousands of displaced Karen continued to struggle to survive as a people.

—*Bland Addison*

## FURTHER READING

Burma Ethics Research Group and Friedrich Naumann Foundation. *Forgotten Victims of a Hidden War: Internally Displaced Karen in Burma.* Chaingmai, Thailand: Nopburee Press, 1998. A study of the living conditions of Karen peoples and the circumstances leading to their expulsion from their villages.

Delang, Claudio O. *Suffering in Silence: The Human Rights Nightmare of the Karen People of Burma.* Boca Raton, Fla.: Universal, 2001. A report on the rape, torture, execution, forced labor, and other abuses committed against Karen villagers by the military of Myanmar.

Human Rights Watch. *Burma/Thailand: No Safety in Burma, No Sanctuary in Thailand.* New York: Author, 1997. Presents an indictment of the treatment of indigenous peoples by the government of Myanmar.

Thornton, Phil. *Rebels, Refugees, Medics and Misfits on the Thai-Burma Border.* Bangkok: Asia Books, 2006. A journalist's account, including pictures of life among the Karen refugees and guerrillas.

**SEE ALSO:** May, 1975: Indo-Chinese Boat People Begin Fleeing Vietnam; Jan., 1983: Nigeria Expels West African Migrant Workers; Oct., 1984: Ethiopia Resettles Famine Victims from the North to Southern Ethiopia; Dec., 1991-1992: Muslim Refugees Flee Persecution in Myanmar.

1997

## March 4, 1997
# CLINTON REJECTS FEDERAL SUPPORT FOR HUMAN CLONING

*Given the moral and ethical issues raised by the prospect of human cloning, President Bill Clinton issued a directive banning the use of federal funds for research into the cloning of human beings and referred the issue to the National Bioethics Advisory Commission for study.*

LOCALE: Washington, D.C.

CATEGORIES: Government and politics; religion, theology, and ethics; science and technology

### KEY FIGURES

*Bill Clinton* (b. 1946), president of the United States, 1993-2001

*Bill Frist* (b. 1952), U.S. senator from Tennessee

*Ted Kennedy* (b. 1932), U.S. senator from Massachusetts

*Richard Seed* (b. 1928?), physicist and supporter of human cloning

### SUMMARY OF EVENT

In July, 1996, the first successfully cloned mammal, a sheep called Dolly, was created by scientists through the method of somatic cell nuclear transfer (SCNT). Immediately, interest in using the method to replicate human beings intensified among scientists and researchers around the world. President Bill Clinton moved quickly to stem the rush toward such experimentation in the United States by proposing the Cloning Prohibition Act, which would ban human cloning for a period of five years. The intent was to give the scientific community and others time to evaluate the implications of such experimentation.

Scientists had been experimenting with cloning for many years before the amazing creation of Dolly. The potential benefits of such research were many; they included the possibility of producing replacement skin, cartilage, bone, and nerve tissues to treat people with burn, accident, and spinal cord injuries. Cloning had already increased agricultural production and led to advances in the treatment of cancer, diabetes, and other medical disorders. The exciting possibilities of SCNT stimulated considerable interest in the scientific community.

However, when human cloning appeared to become a distinct possibility after the successful experiment that resulted in Dolly, enough opponents denounced such interference with the "natural order" of things that President Clinton believed the issue was too troubling to ignore. He moved to ban the use of federal funds for such research until the government, along with scientists and other interested parties, could consider the issue of human cloning from all standpoints, including the ethical and moral implications. Saying that any discovery touching on human creation is a matter of morality and spirituality as well as scientific inquiry, he turned the matter over to the National Bioethics Advisory Commission (NBAC) for study. President Clinton had created the NBAC in 1995 to give advice and recommendations to government entities on bioethical issues and clinical applications. The commission was composed of law professors, doctors, psychologists, and other scientists.

In May, 1997, the NBAC reported on its findings concerning cloning. It noted that although the cloning of a sheep was an impressive breakthrough, 277 failed attempts had preceded the creation of Dolly, a healthy cloned sheep. The cloning of a human being would be far more complicated and risky. There was no way of knowing, for example, whether a cloned baby would have chromosomes that matched the donor's in terms of age. In other words, it was unknown whether a cloned human would age more rapidly than normal, to match the age of the donor, or whether he or she would be quickly afflicted with heart disease or some other debilitating, age-related disease.

The NBAC thus recommended continuing the moratorium on human cloning, although it noted that it did not wish to interfere with other scientific research. It suggested that cloning experiments aimed at creating specific tissues—such as muscle, nerve, and skin—should probably be allowed. The commission stated that both privately funded and federally funded sectors of the scientific community should abide by the ban on human cloning until such time as all aspects of the debate could be examined and understood.

The decision to ban human cloning became the subject of debate among politicians, scientists, and religious leaders, many of whom believed the cloning of a human being to be the "ultimate blasphemy." Some scientists in the private sector felt hamstrung by the ban and even threatened to leave the United States to pursue their work in more welcoming countries. Richard Seed, a Chicago physicist and longtime proponent of alternative methods of procreation, vowed to clone a human before a federal law could be passed to prohibit it. Seed, one of the first to perform a successful transplant of a human embryo from one healthy female to a surrogate, had been practicing the technique of embryo transfer since the early 1980's on prize cows. He believed that cloning humans would be the next step in helping infertile couples to have children, and he calculated that about 15 percent of women who could not conceive by alternative methods would be willing to try human cloning.

Members of the U.S. Congress were largely supportive of the ban on human cloning. Several senators, including Bill Frist, a Republican from Tennessee, sponsored a bill to prohibit "implanting the nucleus of a cell of a body other than the eggs or sperm . . . into an egg from which the nucleus has been removed" (the SCNT technique). Frist, who was himself a surgeon, believed this bill would not interfere with ongoing in vitro and embryo research, and would thus allow scientists and researchers to continue to do cloning research that did not involve human cloning.

Others members of Congress, however, opposed the ban on human cloning, believing that many Americans suffering from fatal diseases might benefit from cloning research. Democratic senator Ted Kennedy was one who proposed legislation that would allow cloning experimentation to create muscle, skin, and nerve tissue that could contribute to the study, treatment, and possible cure of certain diseases. Similar to what President Clinton proposed, this legislation would allow the cloning of molecules, deoxyribonucleic acid (DNA), cells, tissue, and animals, just not humans.

Early in 1998, many countries throughout the world—including Sweden, Finland, France, Greece, and Italy—signed an agreement to prohibit any kind of technique that would attempt to create a human being identical to another human being, living or dead. The United Kingdom, however, declared itself "open" to the new cloning technology and did not sign on to the international agreement.

## SIGNIFICANCE

The creation of Dolly the sheep through cloning opened up debate concerning the vast possibilities of cloning technology. Scientists noted the promise of cloning for medical research, in the search for cures for diseases and infertility, while the idea

---

## CLINTON ON CLONING

*On March 4, 1997, President Bill Clinton explained his reasons for imposing a prohibition on federal funding for human cloning:*

The recent breakthrough in animal cloning is one that could yield enormous benefits, enabling us to reproduce the most productive strains of crops and livestock, holding out the promise of revolutionary new medical treatments and cures, helping to unlock the greatest secrets of the genetic code. But like the splitting of the atom, this is a discovery that carries burdens as well as benefits.

Science often moves faster than our ability to understand its implications. That is why we have a responsibility to move with caution and care to harness the powerful forces of science and technology so that we can reap the benefit while minimizing the potential danger.

This new discovery raises the troubling prospect that it might someday be possible to clone human beings from our own genetic material. There is much about cloning that we still do not know. But this much we do know: Any discovery that touches upon human creation is not simply a matter of scientific inquiry; it is a matter of morality and spirituality as well.

My own view is that human cloning would have to raise deep concerns, given our most cherished concepts of faith and humanity. Each human life is unique, born of a miracle that reaches beyond laboratory science. I believe we must respect this profound gift and resist the temptation to replicate ourselves.

At the very least, however, we should all agree that we need a better understanding of the scope and implications of this most recent breakthrough. Last week, I asked our National Bioethics Advisory Commission, headed by President Harold Shapiro of Princeton, to conduct a thorough review of the legal and the ethical issues raised by this new cloning discovery and to recommend possible actions to prevent its abuse, reporting back to me by the end of May.

In the meantime, I am taking further steps to prevent human cloning. The Federal Government currently restricts the use of Federal funds for research involving human embryos. After reviewing these restrictions, our administration believes that there are loopholes that could allow the cloning of human beings if the technology were developed. Therefore, today I am issuing a directive that bans the use of any Federal funds for any cloning of human beings.

Effective immediately, no Federal agency may support, fund, or undertake such activity. . . .

As we gain a fuller understanding of this technology, we must proceed not just with caution but also with a conscience. By insisting that not a single taxpayer dollar supports human cloning, and by urging a moratorium on all private research in this area, we can ensure that as we move forward on this issue, we weigh the concerns of faith and family and philosophy and values, not merely of science alone.

1997

*Ian Wilmut, who cloned an adult sheep named Dolly, in his laboratory. The Scottish scientist believes that it would be inhumane to experiment with cloning humans.* (AP/Wide World Photos)

that scientists might soon be able to replicate the DNA and genetic makeup of a person raised many questions about the moral and ethical ramifications of doing so. Images of a modern Frankenstein's monster or of reproducing the genius of an Albert Einstein or a William Shakespeare undoubtedly occurred to many, as did concerns about the actual consequences of such an undertaking.

Debates on human cloning continued into the twenty-first century, and in the United States, the two sides remained entrenched in their positions. Many American scientists moved abroad to continue experimentation for which U.S. federal funding was denied, and others found private funding to allow them to continue their work.

*—Jane L. Ball*

## FURTHER READING

Andrews, Lori B. *The Clone Age: Adventures in the New World of Reproductive Technology*. New York: Henry Holt, 1999. Discusses the wide-ranging concerns regarding genetic manipulation and some of the possible results of human cloning, including legal issues.

Hoge, Warren. "U.S. Drops Effort for Treaty Banning Cloning." *The New York Times*, November 20, 2004. Relates how, after trying to convince other members of the United Nations to ban human cloning worldwide, the United States gave up when the members could not agree whether to limit therapeutic and reproductive cloning or ban it outright.

Kolata, Gina. *Clone: The Road to Dolly and the Path Ahead*. New York: William Morrow, 1998. A science journalist provides a clearly written history of cloning as well as discussion of the implications of the technique for humankind.

Pence, Gregory E. *Who's Afraid of Human Cloning?* Lanham, Md.: Rowman & Littlefield, 1998. Offers explanations of arguments both for and against human cloning and examines the philosophical issues involved, which are similar to those offered for and against in vitro fertilization.

Stolberg, Sheryl G. "House Backs Ban on Human Cloning for Any Objective." *The New York Times*, August 1, 2001. Discusses the human cloning ban, which made no distinction between reproductive and therapeutic research, and notes the religious and moral issues that obstructed the medical considerations.

**SEE ALSO:** 1980: Berg, Gilbert, and Sanger Develop Techniques for Genetic Engineering; Mar. 10, 1984: Willadsen Clones the First Farm Animal by Nuclear Transfer; May, 1994: Genetically Engineered Food Reaches Supermarkets; July 5, 1996: Wilmut Clones the First Large Mammal from an Adult Cell; Nov. 6, 1998: First Embryonic Stem Cell Line Is Derived; June 26, 2000: Completion of the Sequencing of the Human Genome Is Announced.

## March 23-25, 1997
# HEAVEN'S GATE CULT MEMBERS COMMIT MASS SUICIDE

*As Comet Hale-Bopp approached Earth, thirty-nine members of the Heaven's Gate cult, led by Marshall Applewhite, committed suicide, believing they would be transported into the cosmos to reunite with a "mother ship" traveling behind the comet from "the level beyond human."*

**ALSO KNOWN AS:** UFO suicides
**LOCALE:** Rancho Santa Fe, California
**CATEGORY:** Religion, theology, and ethics

**KEY FIGURES**
*Marshall Applewhite* (1931-1997), coleader of the Heaven's Gate cult
*Bonnie Nettles* (1924-1985), coleader of the Heaven's Gate cult
*Charles Humphrey* (1943-1998), Heaven's Gate cult member and spokesman

**SUMMARY OF EVENT**
Marshall Applewhite and Bonnie Nettles met at a hospital in Houston, Texas, in March, 1972, on the propitious day of the spring equinox. Applewhite had recently lost his position as music director at the University of St. Thomas, and his wife had earlier left him because of his several homosexual affairs. The loss of his job and ambivalence over his sexuality made him depressed. According to his account, however, he was not a patient but a visitor at the hospital, where Nettles worked as a nurse. She wrote an astrological column for a Houston newspaper; information that she used for her column came from a nineteenth century Franciscan friar, "Brother Francis," whom she believed she was channeling. She was also active in the Theosophical Society. Her group in Houston held weekly séances. When Nettles met Applewhite, her marriage was also dissolving.

Applewhite and Nettles became inseparable, although their relationship was described as strictly platonic. She introduced him to Theosophy, spiritualism, and channeling. They founded the Christian Art Center in a Houston church and taught astrology, Theosophy, and spiritualism. Lack of funds and rumors that they held séances in the church caused the center's closing within six months. Both of them had been hearing voices from unidentified flying objects (UFOs), which persuaded them that they had a destiny that required leaving behind their ordinary lives.

The two abruptly left Houston in January, 1973, on a "trip into the wilderness" to find their calling and headed westward. They eventually reached the Oregon coast, where after a month of meditation they learned their destiny from their UFO voices: Like the two witnesses described in the biblical book of Revelation, they would be martyred, resurrected, and then taken in a spaceship to heaven on another planet. Those who wished to join them in that journey would have to undergo a metamorphosis, which required giving up property and human attachments and being celibate, since sex took energy away from "the Process," as they called that metamorphosis. The Process would be completed when they and their followers boarded the UFO. Meanwhile, their lack of money and hostility to convention led them to defraud motel keepers and credit card companies. They were arrested in August, 1974, for failing to return a rental car; both spent time in jail in St. Louis, Missouri.

Once Applewhite was released from jail in early 1975, he and Nettles went to Los Angeles, where they began to win followers. When they left the city two weeks later, twenty-four people went with them. The believers were told that they could transform their human bodies into eternal, genderless, extraterrestrial beings, at which time UFOs would pick them up to take them home. The two traveled widely, speaking in forty states and two Canadian provinces over the next two years. Their audiences were made up mostly of college students, and soon

1997

3021

they had some two hundred followers. They began to call themselves "Bo" and "Peep," shepherds of their flock. Peep received a revelation that a UFO would pick them up in Colorado; and when it failed to appear, most members left the group, reducing it to about twenty people.

After being heckled at a meeting in Kansas in April, 1976, "Do" and "Ti," as they now called themselves (referring to notes in the musical scale), became secretive and stopped proselytizing. Little is known about their lives over the next years except that they dashed from place to place across the western states expecting to board a UFO. In 1983, Ti was diagnosed with cancer, and she died in Dallas, in June, 1985. In Do's words, she had left her "earthly vessel" and gone to the next level. He declared that she had come from another planet to teach him the Process, and she had returned to the "level beyond human," as Jesus had done two thousand years earlier.

Do and his followers reappeared in public in 1993, making a video, advertising in magazines, and creating a Web site to win converts. The site was called "Heaven's Gate," which became the popular name for the group. They formed a successful business called Higher Source for creating Web sites. Members took new names for use within the group. Their time was tightly regulated when they left the group to conduct business, which they always did as male and female pairs, and they had to phone in regularly. After two members were arrested for vagrancy because they had no money, members carried five-dollar bills and several quarters for making the required phone calls. The group ate out frequently, ordering exactly the same menu items, and they were described as dressing identically and having the same haircuts, making it difficult to tell the women from the men. Also in 1993, eight men in the group, including Do, were castrated to remove their sexual drive.

By then, Do was suffering from coronary arteriosclerosis, and his message became more urgent. In 1996, the group moved from a ranch in New Mexico and rented a mansion in Rancho Santa Fe, an affluent community near San Diego, with money they had made from their Web site business. They rose before dawn every morning to scan the sky for a sign that they would soon be taken from Earth. When Comet Hale-Bopp came into view in 1997, Internet reports that a UFO had been sighted behind it led the Heaven's Gate members to conclude that Ti was coming to take them home.

Because they believed that it was necessary to leave their "earthly containers" behind, Do and thirty-eight followers (twenty-one women and seventeen men) committed suicide in a meticulous fashion over a three-day period beginning on March 23. Initially the dead were identified as men, since the police found them dressed alike in black clothing and black athletic shoes with close-cropped hair, making it difficult to determine their gender at first glance. Their faces and chests were covered with purple shrouds, and those who wore glasses had them carefully placed at their sides. The dead had five-dollar bills and quarters in their pockets. Their bags had been packed neatly in the dormitory-style rooms. They had taken phenobarbital mixed in pudding and drank vodka before lying down in bed. The last two cleaned up the house and sent farewell videos and a letter to a former member before committing suicide themselves. That former member went to the mansion on March 26 and then alerted police.

Charles Humphrey, who had joined the group in 1975 and whose group name was "Rkkody," was not present at the mass suicide. He served as a spokesman for the "Away Team" in the months following the incident. Following a botched suicide attempt in May, 1997, that left another member dead, he killed himself in Arizona in February, 1998, dressed identically to the thirty-nine members who had died the previous year.

*Marshall Applewhite.* (AP/Wide World Photos)

## SIGNIFICANCE

News of the mass suicide and the castrations of six of the cult members astounded the nation. Two sociologists, Robert Balch and David Taylor, studied the cult in the 1970's and the 1980's; their research provided important insights into the process of creating the sort of group coherence that could lead to mass suicide. The pathos of those expecting the imminent end of the world and their ressurrection from it is revealed in a comment of one cult member, reported by the sociologists, who said that she always bought a small tube of toothpaste, expecting that she would not need more, but she always wound up buying another.

The belief system promulgated by Heaven's Gate has baffled civil authorities and ordinary people, seeming poignant to some and ridiculous to many. Such beliefs, however, hold a strong appeal for those who have difficulty in finding meaning in their lives. One message of the suicides at Rancho Santa Fe, therefore, is the degree to which such personalities may be willing to subject themselves to the visions and wills of others.

*—Frederic J. Baumgartner*

## FURTHER READING

Balch, Robert. "Bo and Peep: A Case Study of the Origins of Messianic Leadership." In *Millennialism and Charisma*, edited by Roy Wallis. Belfast, Northern Ireland: Queen's University, 1982. Balch and David Taylor joined Bo and Peep's group as observer-participants for two months in 1975. This article provides information on the cult's background and early beliefs, drawing on letters and interviews before the events of 1997 distorted perceptions.

_____. "The Evolution of a New Age Cult: From Total Overcomers Anonymous to Death at Heaven's

---

### STILL CRAZY AFTER ALL THESE YEARS

*In 2007, the Heaven's Gate Web site was still accessible, spreading its dangerous message and glorifying the tragic suicides that occurred in conjunction with the sighting of the Hale-Bopp comet in 1997:*

Whether Hale-Bopp has a "companion" or not is irrelevant from our perspective. However, its arrival is joyously very significant to us at "Heaven's Gate." The joy is that our Older Member in the Evolutionary Level Above Human (the "Kingdom of Heaven") has made it clear to us that Hale-Bopp's approach is the "marker" we've been waiting for—the time for the arrival of the spacecraft from the Level Above Human to take us home to "Their World"—in the literal Heavens. Our 22 years of classroom here on planet Earth is finally coming to conclusion—"graduation" from the Human Evolutionary Level. We are happily prepared to leave "this world" and go with Ti's crew. If you study the material on this website you will hopefully understand our joy and what our purpose here on Earth has been. You may even find your "boarding pass" to leave with us during this brief "window." We are so very thankful that we have been recipients of this opportunity to prepare for membership in Their Kingdom, and to experience Their boundless Caring and Nurturing.

1997

---

Gate." In *Sects, Cults, and Spiritual Communities*, edited by William Zellner. Westport, Conn.: Praeger, 1998. Follows the story of Heaven's Gate from 1975 to the suicides of 1997. Emphasizes the type of small-group cohesion that in this case led to group suicide.

Wessinger, Catherine. *How the Millennium Comes Violently: From Jonestown to Heaven's Gate*. New York: Seven Bridges Press, 2000. Contains a lengthy section on Heaven's Gate with details about Applewhite's and Nettles's lives and the founding of Heaven's Gate. Offers valuable insights into how a group can be motivated into committing mass suicide.

SEE ALSO: Nov. 18, 1978: People's Temple Members Commit Mass Suicide; Apr. 19, 1993: Branch Davidians' Compound Burns.

## May 1, 1997

# LABOR PARTY WINS MAJORITY IN BRITISH NATIONAL ELECTIONS

*The Labor Party under Tony Blair regained power after eighteen years in opposition, defeating the Conservatives, led by Prime Minister John Major. The new government retained many of the Conservatives' policies, so that the transition went smoothly and without controversy.*

**LOCALE:** London, England
**CATEGORY:** Government and politics

**KEY FIGURES**

*Tony Blair* (b. 1953), leader of the Labor Party beginning in 1994 and prime minister of the United Kingdom, 1997-2007

*John Major* (b. 1943), prime minister of the United Kingdom, 1990-1997, who succeeded Margaret Thatcher as leader of the Conservative Party

*Gordon Brown* (b. 1951), Blair's rival in the 1994 Labor leadership election who was appointed Chancellor of the Exchequer in the New Labor government

*John Smith* (1938-1994), previous leader of the Labor Party who had begun the process of modernization

*Peter Mandelson* (b. 1953), member of Parliament who ran Blair's successful bid to become party leader and became one of his trusted advisers

*Alastair Campbell* (b. 1957), one of the architects of New Labor and Blair's press officer who had much influence in the 1997 elections and thereafter

**SUMMARY OF EVENT**

Elections to the House of Commons, the lower legislative branch of the British parliament, are held every five years, or sooner. The Conservative Party, under Margaret Thatcher, and then John Major, had won four straight elections from 1979 onward. They had expected to lose the 1992 elections, but by dropping the right-wing Thatcher and appointing the moderate Major, the party had succeeded again.

After their fourth straight loss, many in the Labor Party saw themselves as unelectable with the socialist policies that had been traditional to them. Under their leaders Neil Kinnock, and then John Smith, they began a program of modernization, especially to curb the influence of the trade unions on Labor Party policy and at its annual conference. At Smith's untimely death, the young Tony Blair put himself forward for leadership on a platform of a far more radical modernization program than

before, in order to win back the trust of the British electorate, with so-called New Labor policies. On winning the leadership contest against Gordon Brown, his main rival, Blair spent the next two years as leader of the opposition developing Labor's program for community, direct democracy, and social responsibility. His main success was getting the party to renounce "Clause IV," its policy of nationalization, or government ownership of certain industries, and instead to embrace a mixed economy.

In the 1997 elections, held on May 1, Labor campaigned on a platform of moderation, promising to keep many of the reforms the Conservative Party had made in economic policy, promising entry into the European Union, and promising trade union legislation. The country as a whole turned against the Conservatives, feeling that they had been in office too long and that there was too much corruption and too many divisions within their party, especially over Europe. Labor campaigning, orchestrated by Alastair Campbell, highlighted the youthfulness of Blair and concentrated on the marginal constituencies that Labor would have to win to form a government.

The result was a complete landslide victory for the Labor Party, which won with a majority of 179 over all other parties in a House of some 636 seats. At age forty-three, Tony Blair became the youngest British prime minister since 1812, having won the largest majority ever for a Labor government. However, rather than using the large majority to make sweeping changes, Blair and his advisers, including Campbell and Peter Mandelson, decided to hold to their centrist position, keep many of the Conservative policies that had restored the economy to a sound footing after years of inflationary turmoil, and remain cautious regarding the European Union, apart from signing the social chapter, a sort of bill of rights for workers.

Blair gained further popularity in September, with the death of Princess Diana. He sensed the public mood of deep devotion to the princess, while the royal family remained aloof. His advice to the queen to take an active part in the mourning saved the monarchy from huge unpopularity and gave Blair the reputation for being in touch with the nation.

Gordon Brown was appointed Chancellor of the Exchequer, or finance minister, and remained in that position through the subsequent two elections, both won fairly easily by Labor. Brown gave the Bank of England its independence in deciding interest rates and refused to raise income tax, thus fulfilling Labor's election pledge. The economy did well, and the government began to enjoy a reputation for efficiency and moderation. The Conservative Party, having lost the center ground of British politics to New Labor, suffered further divisions and proved a very poor opposition. In fact, most of Blair's opposition came from "Old Labor" members of Parliament who disliked his abandoning of socialist policies. However, Blair's insistence on education and the building up of the National Health Service proved popular, and fears that Britain's failure to join the European single currency would isolate the country proved groundless.

Although Blair failed to deliver on undoing the Conservatives' botched privatization of the railroad system, in most other areas he made good on election promises. In one area, he gained great prestige in building on one of John Major's achievements: the Northern Ireland peace process. This had faltered badly in Major's final years, when the Irish Republican Army had resumed its bombing campaign. Blair managed to restart the process, which culminated in the Good Friday Agreement in April, 1998, with a commitment by the Republican movement to lay down the armed struggle. Although the issue of the decommissioning of weapons was to remain a thorny issue for many years, a de facto peace was obtained in the province.

*Newly elected British prime minister Tony Blair, with his wife Cherie, at a victory rally in London on May 2, 1997. Blair's Labor Party regained power after eighteen years of Conservative rule. (AP/Wide World Photos)*

1997

### SIGNIFICANCE

The election of Tony Blair as prime minister and his continuing success in subsequent general elections meant a long period of stable government for the United Kingdom. The old economic seesaw between right- and left-wing governments that had hindered Britain's economic progress in the second half of the twentieth century halted, as Labor continued with basically centrist economic policies first laid down by the Conservatives. Trade unions were prevented from resuming their old militancy, and an era of industrial peace ensued, with both inflation and wages rising very slowly.

In foreign relationships, also, Blair continued the close Anglo-American entente begun in the years when Ronald Reagan was the U.S. president and Margaret Thatcher was British prime minister. Blair's politics were close to those of President Bill Clinton, and the two leaders met frequently, as both sought for a "third way" in politics between right and left. Clinton gave Blair support in Northern Ireland and Europe, and Blair supported Clinton in Kosovo

3025

and Iraq. On George W. Bush's election, Blair managed to maintain the same entente, especially after the September 11, 2001, terrorist attacks on the United States. Blair endorsed Bush's "war on terror" and supported him fully in the invasion of Iraq in 2003, committing British troops to the invasion, a move that caused deep divisions within the party. Blair's stance on Europe brought a much better relationship with the European Union than under the Conservatives.

There were continuing criticisms of Blair's style as premier, however. The charge of "spin" was substituted for the "sleaze" charges made of the Major government, and Mandelson and Campbell were deeply suspected and even disliked. Blair was suspected of being a lightweight, although he preferred Thatcher's more presidential style to Major's cabinet style of government. Charges that the democratically elected Commons was being sidelined were also persistent.

Against the charge of spin, however, there was plenty of evidence that Blair was a politician of convictions. He made no secret of his Christian faith and principles, and his support of the Iraq invasion was purely on the conviction that it was the right thing to do. Blair forestalled the negative attacks on him over the latter by announcing in 2005 that he would not stand again as prime minister in the next election.

—*David Barratt*

**FURTHER READING**

Rentoul, John. *Tony Blair: Prime Minister.* London: Warner Books, 2001. Concentrates on Blair's performance as prime minister, giving a detailed, contemporary assessment of his early performance, but written before the controversial decision to invade Iraq.

Riddell, Peter. *The Unfulfilled Prime Minister: Tony Blair's Quest for a Legacy.* London: Politico's Publishing, 2005. Riddell is a shrewd political commentator who attempts to assess Blair's successes and failures in achieving a permanent place in British politics.

Seldon, Anthony. *Blair.* London: Free Press, 2004. Full, semiofficial biography of Blair based on six hundred interviews. Deals fully with the 1997 and 2001 elections and Blair's subsequent relationship with Clinton and Bush.

Sopel, Jon. *Tony Blair: The Moderniser.* London: Bantam Books, 1995. Written soon after Blair had become leader of the Labor Party on a platform of modernizing it, especially its unpopular policies of nationalization.

**SEE ALSO:** May 4, 1979: Thatcher Becomes First Woman to Serve as British Prime Minister; Nov. 28, 1990: Major Succeeds Thatcher as British Prime Minister; Nov. 3, 1992: Clinton Wins the U.S. Presidency.

## May 22-June 12, 1997
# GLOBE THEATRE OPENS IN LONDON

*The opening of the rebuilt Globe Theatre marked the first time that a modern audience was able to watch one of William Shakespeare's plays in the same type of theater in which the play was first performed.*

**LOCALE:** London, England
**CATEGORIES:** Theater; architecture

**KEY FIGURES**
*Sam Wanamaker* (1919-1993), actor, director, producer, and executive director of the Globe Playhouse Trust
*Mark Rylance* (b. 1960), actor and artistic director of the Globe Theatre Company

**SUMMARY OF EVENT**
The opening of the rebuilt Globe Theatre on the South Bank of the Thames River, opposite St. Paul's Cathedral,

represented the fulfillment of a centuries-old dream and a long practical campaign that began in the 1950's. The original Globe, which was burned to the ground in 1613, was central to the work of playwright William Shakespeare. Many of Shakespeare's greatest plays were written for and first performed at the Globe.

The rebuilt Globe officially opened on May 22, 1997, as construction workers hurried to get the job finished. The following week, on May 27, the theater opened its doors to the public for the first preview of Shakespeare's *Henry V.* Tickets for five hundred "groundlings" (spectators who stand in a space in front of the stage) were sold for a penny apiece, as in Shakespeare's day, and people waited in long lines hoping to purchase them. Mark Rylance, an actor and artistic director of the Globe, concluded the preview evening with an homage to the late Sam Wanamaker, the "founding father" of the project. Shakespeare's *The Winter's Tale* was presented on May 28.

The theater's gala opening was held on June 12, 1997. It featured a special performance titled "Triumphes and Mirth" and was graced by the presence of Her Majesty Queen Elizabeth II and His Royal Highness Prince Philip. The queen arrived by barge, following the example of Elizabethan playgoers, who would have crossed the Thames by boat to attend a play on Bankside.

Actor Zoë Wanamaker, daughter of Sam Wanamaker, spoke the famous words of the prologue of *Henry V* that refer directly to the Globe Theatre: "Can this cockpit hold/ The vasty fields of France? Or may we cram/ Within this wooden O the very casques/ That did affright the air at Agincourt?" The Globe Company then performed act 4 of *Henry V*, directed by Richard Olivier. An international cast of actors who had long been supporters of the Globe project then joined forces to present "The Triumph of Hope," an homage to the founders of the original Globe and to Wanamaker, with a special appearance by actor Jane Lapotaire on horseback as Queen Elizabeth I. This was followed by the final scenes of *The Winter's Tale*.

The idea of rebuilding Shakespeare's Globe began in earnest in the nineteenth century, and in the early twentieth century three separate plans were proposed to accomplish this goal, including a project of the Globe-Memorial Association of England and America, which wanted to build a Shakespeare complex on the Bankside. World War II put an end to all these plans.

The origins of the plan that succeeded date back to 1949, when Sam Wanamaker, an American actor, visited London and was disappointed to find only an obscure bronze tablet on the side of a brewery to commemorate the Globe. When in the 1950's Wanamaker took up residence in Southwark, England, he began a campaign to rebuild the Globe in its original location. The founding of the Globe Playhouse Trust in the early 1970's marked the formal beginning of the project. Wanamaker launched an international fund-raising effort, gaining much of his support in the United States, and steadily picked his way through innumerable bureaucratic obstacles such as indifference, opposition from local groups, and legal disputes. After a court battle was resolved in the 1980's—Southwark Council attempted to revoke the grant of land it had made to the Globe Playhouse Trust—actor Dame Judi Dench appeared at a ceremony to break ground on the site on April 23, 1988, and the construction work began.

Raising the money was only one obstacle to the project, however. The design of the rebuilt Globe presented many challenges, as only fragmentary knowledge exists of what the original Globe was like. For example, although much is known of other Elizabethan theaters, no building contract for the Globe survives, and no contemporary information about the interior of the theater is available. Hundreds of scholars struggled with questions such as whether the original Globe was round or polygonal. Evidence from the period is ambiguous, but the conclusion was that the structure could not have been circular because Elizabethans did not have the technology to bend oak. In the end, a convention of scholars voted, fourteen to six, for a twenty-sided structure. Other questions concerned the stage: Was it square? How far did it jut out? Which direction did it face? It was decided to place the stage of the rebuilt Globe in the northwest, facing southeast, which meant that some spectators would have the sun in their eyes for parts of the afternoon performances.

The rebuilt Globe was constructed out of solid oak, using methods of craftsmanship from the Tudor (1485-1603) era. The plaster was made out of limestone and goat's hair (cow hair would have been more authentic, but none could be found of the requisite length). The thatched roof, which left the center of the theater open to the elements, made the rebuilt Globe the first thatched-roof building to be constructed in London since the Great Fire in 1666.

The builders made some necessary concessions to modernity, but as few as possible. In addition to the placing of fire sprinklers, the roof was coated with a fire-retardant liquid. Door frames were lengthened by six inches from the height likely in the original Globe because modern people are taller than the Elizabethans were, and seats were widened considerably from the mere eighteen inches, both sideways and front to back, that the original Globe spectator was probably granted. A bank of overhead lights was added to re-create daylight, allowing performances at night (in Shakespeare's time, all performances of his plays started at 2:00 P.M.).

In spite of the most meticulous efforts, however, scholars conceded that the rebuilt Globe represented only an approximation of the original. In this regard, controversy erupted only months before the official opening when, in March, 1997, the British government refused to order an archaeological dig on the site where the original Globe stood, a few hundred feet from the present site. On the site now stands a Georgian property, the owners of which received planning permission to convert it into luxury apartments. This made it impossible for researchers to test the assumptions that were made in rebuilding the Globe against archaeological evidence. Protesters

1997

held a rally at the site, pledging to launch a campaign similar to the battle that saved the site of another Elizabethan theater, the Rose, in 1989. However, the protest had no effect and the remains of Shakespeare's Globe were probably lost forever.

## SIGNIFICANCE

Critics' responses to the opening performances at the rebuilt Globe were mixed. John Gross wrote in the *Telegraph* (June 14, 1997) of *Henry V*, "Shakespeare's Globe Theatre comes thrillingly back to life with this fine production of Britain's greatest patriotic epic," a verdict echoed by John Peter in *The Sunday Times* (June 15, 1997), who reported that a torrential downpour during act 2 sent all but about fifty of the groundlings scurrying for shelter under the eaves but did not stop the performance. Peter pointed out that in all of Elizabethan literature, there is not a single instance of a performance being

rained out, and commented that "perhaps the Globe will make us rethink our priorities between theatrical excitement and physical comfort."

In contrast, the other opening production, *The Winter's Tale*, provoked some censure. Gross commented that some of it was "poorly spoken," concluding that "first-rate verse-speaking from the entire company needs to become an urgent priority at this marvelous, challenging theatre." Peter pointed out that two aspects of the production were the complete opposite of Elizabethan practice: There was elaborate scenery, whereas the Elizabethans used almost none, and the costumes were drab, in contrast to the finery often displayed on the stage of Shakespeare's Globe. In contrast, a number of Elizabethan practices were observed in *Henry V*: Men played all the roles (women had prominent parts in the opening season's other plays), the actors wore Elizabethan clothing, and some performances had no intermissions.

*The interior of London's Globe Theatre, which opened in 1997.* (Tohma/CC-BY-SA2.5)

Questions of authenticity aside, actors at the Globe soon learned that the Globe is a unique theater, an unfamiliar acting environment that demands a new approach to their craft. The most successful productions have been those that have made use of the Globe's peculiarities, and so have been unlike any performances elsewhere. Powerful acting is needed to cope with open-air acoustics, and the lack of spotlights and a darkened auditorium means that actors need to summon all their resources to command the audience's attention. Some scholars have predicted that over the years a new tradition of ensemble playing will arise at the Globe, depending more for its success on the actors than on the staging or production. So-called director's theater is less relevant in the Globe than it is elsewhere.

For both actors and audiences, the intimacy of the Globe is a revelation, quite unlike anything found in an ordinary theater. The seats in the three galleries curve around the stage: No spectator is more than fifty feet from the action, and groundlings are so close that those in the front can rest their arms on the stage. Some even join in the performances with shouted comments. One early performer at the rebuilt Globe, Patrick Godfrey, said, "Performing here feels like being a pip inside an orange. You have faces at your ankles, people packed in the galleries and the eyes are all so close you are entirely enclosed."

The closeness of the audience and the fact that playgoers report feeling almost a part of the play itself is an effect that the builders of the new Globe earnestly hoped to achieve. The theater was not constructed to serve as an antiquarian museum or Shakespearean theme park, of interest only as a tourist attraction. Rather, it was hoped that performances would generate the kind of excitement and sense of immediacy that were undoubtedly experienced by the original Globe audiences. It is often pointed out that Shakespeare's Globe drew audiences from all corners of English society, the illiterate as well as the educated and the nobility. Such a heterogeneous crowd—raucous, uninhibited, and attuned to the sounds of words and the power of images—is a far cry from the sedate, largely middle-class audience that passively observes performances in a modern theater with darkened auditorium and "picture frame" proscenium. The original Globe both created and reflected a social unity and classlessness that the new Globe Theatre Company strives to emulate. The aim is to restore theater as an exhilarating expression of the varieties of human experience for the entire community.

Another long-term effect of the rebuilt Globe has been a reinforcement of the position of Shakespeare's

works as a great training ground for aspiring actors. There are few great actors who have not honed their skills on Shakespeare's plays, and the Globe keeps those plays alive for new generations of actors as they learn new skills not available to their predecessors. The existence of the Globe gives actors the opportunity to draw on a growing body of knowledge concerning exactly how Shakespeare's plays worked in their original stagings, for their original audiences, during that remarkable period of approximately seventy years (from 1574 to 1642) when English drama flowered in its fullness as never before and never since.

Beyond Shakespeare, many scholars and actors also hope that the Globe will eventually stimulate new playwrights to accept the challenge of writing plays for a company with relationships among actors, stage, and audience that are different from those of any other company. Such new plays, it is suggested, would depend for their effects less on the sophisticated mechanisms of theater that technicians devise and more on the acting itself, and so perhaps convey the dramatist's intention in a simpler, more human way.

*—Bryan Aubrey*

## FURTHER READING

Day, Barry. *This Wooden "O": Shakespeare's Globe Reborn—Achieving an American's Dream.* London: Oberon Books, 1996. Entertaining account of Wanamaker's efforts to get the Globe built. Includes illustrations, bibliography, and index.

Gurr, Andrew. *Playgoing in Shakespeare's London.* 3d ed. New York: Cambridge University Press, 2004. Focuses on the audiences for Shakespeare's plays during the author's lifetime, including the physical conditions under which playgoers viewed the works. Includes illustrations, bibliography, and index.

_____. *The Shakespearean Stage, 1574-1642.* 3d ed. New York: Cambridge University Press, 1992. One of the best one-volume guides to all aspects of the Shakespearean stage. Discusses the acting companies of the period, the staging of the plays, the playhouses (including an evaluation of various interpretations of contemporary sketches and accounts), and the audiences. Includes bibliography and illustrations.

Gurr, Andrew, and John Orrell. *Rebuilding Shakespeare's Globe.* New York: Routledge, 1989. Gurr was one of the principal academic advisers to the Globe project. Discusses the growth of the idea to rebuild the Globe, the scholarly disputes about the structure of the original playhouse, the company that performed there, and

1997

the types of audience. Describes the complete Globe Theatre complex. Includes numerous illustrations.

Hodges, C. Walter. *Enter the Whole Army: A Pictorial Study of Shakespearean Staging, 1576-1616.* New York: Cambridge University Press, 1999. Well-illustrated volume explains how various challenging Shakespearean scenes were staged at the Globe and other theaters.

Orrell, John. *The Quest for Shakespeare's Globe.* New York: Cambridge University Press, 1983. Provides abundant material on the size, shape, and orientation of the second Globe Theatre, which was built after the original burned down and which survived until it was closed in 1642. Focuses more on what the two Globes had in common than on their differences.

**SEE ALSO:** Feb. 10, 1971: Guare's *The House of Blue Leaves* Joins Naturalistic and Nonrepresentational Theater; Aug. 4, 1971: Audiences Embrace Mortimer's *A Voyage Round My Father*; June 27, 1978-1979: Shepard's *Buried Child* Promotes Off-Broadway Theater.

## May 27, 1997
# NATO AND RUSSIA SIGN COOPERATION PACT

*The signing of a cooperation pact between NATO and Russia cleared the way for eastward expansion of NATO. Hungary, Poland, and the Czech Republic would join NATO in July.*

**ALSO KNOWN AS:** NATO-Russia Founding Act
**LOCALE:** Paris, France
**CATEGORIES:** Diplomacy and international relations; organizations and institutions

**KEY FIGURES**

*Tony Blair* (b. 1953), prime minister of the United Kingdom, 1997-2007

*Jacques Chirac* (b. 1932), president of France, 1995-2007

*Bill Clinton* (b. 1946), president of the United States, 1993-2001

*Helmut Kohl* (b. 1930), chancellor of the Federal Republic of Germany, 1982-1990, and chancellor of unified Germany, 1990-1998

*Boris Yeltsin* (1931-2007), president of the Russian Soviet Federated Socialist Republic, 1991-1999

**SUMMARY OF EVENT**

On May 27, 1997, leaders of the sixteen member countries of the North Atlantic Treaty Organization (NATO) and Russian president Boris Yeltsin signed an agreement that institutionalized a consultative role for Russia in NATO deliberations. The agreement was widely understood to be the source of political cover that Yeltsin required to allow him to accede to NATO's expansion into Eastern European countries that once were Soviet satellites.

The North Atlantic Treaty Organization was established in 1949 as a military alliance linking the United States, Canada, and Western Europe. The organization's founding was prompted by the rapidly escalating Cold War and by increasing tensions between the United States and the Soviet Union over Germany. In the same year, Germany was divided into democratic West Germany, which was allied with (and to a large extent controlled by) the United States, Britain, and France, and communist East Germany, which was dominated by the Soviet Union. West Germany was admitted to NATO in 1955; East Germany was included in the newly formed Warsaw Treaty Organization (usually called the Warsaw Pact) several weeks later.

The North Atlantic Treaty placed on NATO members obligations of mutual defense; an attack on any one country would be considered an attack on all. This binding of American security interests to Europe was the military centerpiece of U.S. containment policy. For four decades, NATO would be credited with preventing the spread of Soviet communism beyond the Soviet Union's eastern sphere of influence and with permitting the rearmament of West Germany to be accomplished with sufficient international safeguards. In the words of Lord Ismay, NATO's purpose in Europe was to keep the Americans in, the Russians out, and the Germans down.

Eventually NATO expanded to sixteen member countries, including most of Western Europe. The Warsaw Pact included the Soviet Union and six Eastern European countries: Bulgaria, Czechoslovakia, East Germany, Hungary, Poland, and Romania. The European political order thus was bipolar, centered on Washington and Moscow. The two blocs were separated by an imaginary "Iron Curtain" that ran between East and West Germany. In many respects, the existence of the two alliances ensured a "balance of power" that had eluded Europe for centuries. As a result, the Great Powers of Europe (and North America) did not directly fight one another for the next half century and beyond.

In the late 1980's, however, the Soviet bloc began to fall apart. In 1989, all of the Warsaw Pact countries overthrew their Soviet-imposed Communist governments and adopted varying degrees of democratic reforms. Perhaps even more dramatically, German unification seemed increasingly likely once East Germany's Communist government was eliminated. Because East Germany was arguably the most strategic country of the Warsaw Pact, German unification could well destroy what little was left of the European balance of power. Based on that logic, the Soviets insisted that any plan for the unification of Germany could not cede the territory of eastern Germany to NATO. The question of German unification thus came to hinge on the matter of NATO expansion.

By the fall of 1990, Germany did unify wholly within NATO. A few months later, the Warsaw Pact was officially dissolved. These previously unimaginable events were facilitated largely by Western assurances to the Soviets that NATO would not use its geographically expanded and now unchecked strength against legitimate Soviet interests. Those assurances could not protect the Soviet Union from nationalist movements within the country, however, and the Soviet Union dissolved into its fifteen constituent republics before the end of 1991.

Under President Boris Yeltsin, post-Soviet Russia sought to reestablish itself as an influential European power. The continued existence of NATO, however, served as a constant reminder that the West had "won" the Cold War. Constantly chafing at this geopolitical reminder of Russia's marginalization in post-Cold War Europe, Moscow alternately called for the elimination of NATO, for its conversion from a military alliance to a political one, and for Russian membership in the organization. Meanwhile, the former Warsaw Pact countries publicly expressed a desire to join NATO, as did many of the former Soviet republics. Those countries presumably wanted to institutionalize their long-sought escape from

---

## YELTSIN ON THE NATO-RUSSIA FOUNDING ACT

*At the signing ceremony for the NATO-Russia Founding Act, held in Paris, France, on May 27, 1997, Russian president Boris Yeltsin spoke about the importance of the agreement and the difficulty of the negotiations that led to it:*

Europe is undergoing a time of deep transitions. What is being created is a foundation for a new type of relations among states. We are determining the face of the future European environment, and the decisions being taken at this time will determine which way and how our continent will enter the twenty-first century. . . .

What we're going to do now, ladies and gentlemen, is to put our signatures to a historic, in my view, document. . . . We will do that jointly and this will determine the new quality in the relations between Russia and NATO. It will protect Europe and the world from a new confrontation and will become the foundation for a new, fair and stable partnership, a partnership which takes into account the security interests of each and every signatory to this document. . . .

What we're going to do today was preceded by very difficult negotiations, maybe the most difficult negotiations throughout the whole period which followed the end of the Cold War. I'll be absolutely frank and candid with you and tell you that for the Russian leadership the decision to prepare a document with NATO was far from easy. We had to make sure we protected the security of our country; but at the same time we also had to, of course, create the basis, the foundation for a constructive cooperation between Russia and NATO.

Russia still views negatively the expansion plans of NATO. At the same time, however, we recognize—we pay tribute to the readiness exhibited by NATO countries, despite those difficulties, to reach an agreement with Russia and take into account our interests. And that is precisely the rationale of the situation we're experiencing now, the difficulty of negotiations between Russia and NATO and also the essence, the thrust, of the Founding Act itself.

Through joint efforts in that document we try to answer very difficult questions. And those very difficult issues deal, first of all, with nondeployment of nuclear weapons and also making sure that such a deployment is not something that we will be preparing for. . . . All of this means that we have agreed not to harm the security interests of each other. And I think it is the most important accomplishment for us all.

1997

---

Soviet military pressure and political domination. There was significant sympathy in Western Europe and the United States for expanding NATO to those countries. In the eyes of Moscow, however, NATO's further expansion into Eastern Europe (beyond eastern Germany) without a suitably influential Russian voice in NATO would be a violation of the spirit of NATO's promise not to take undue advantage of Moscow's weakened condition.

By the mid-1990's, an unofficial short list had emerged of countries likely to be considered for membership in an expanded NATO. That list included Poland, the Czech Republic, and Hungary, all of which were eventually admitted into NATO on March 12, 1999. Russia vociferously opposed such proposals, arguing that expanding NATO in such a way would simply redivide Europe, which had so recently managed to draw back the Iron Curtain. Although the Russian public did not consider NATO expansion a particularly salient issue, Russian politicians—particularly those in the Communist and nationalist parties—made it a rallying cry. Yeltsin came under increasing pressure by various opposition groups in the parliament to halt the expansion, but it was unclear exactly what Moscow could do about it.

The issue reached a climax as a July, 1997, meeting of NATO leaders neared. NATO was expected to announce at the Madrid meeting the specific countries to which an invitation to join the alliance would be extended. The NATO leaders clearly hoped to secure Yeltsin's acquiescence, however grudging, in order to prevent a major diplomatic row with Moscow. Toward that purpose, a NATO-Russia agreement was negotiated in the months leading up to the Madrid summit. The NATO-Russia "Founding Act" was signed in Paris on May 27, only weeks before the Madrid summit.

## SIGNIFICANCE

The Founding Act generally committed Russia and the NATO countries to cooperate in building "a stable, peaceful and undivided Europe, whole and free, to the benefit of all its peoples." More specifically, the agreement provided for the establishment of the Russia-NATO Permanent Joint Council, based in Brussels, to facilitate Russia's participation in NATO's policy discussions. (It did not, however, provide Moscow with either a vote or a veto in NATO's decision making. Yeltsin had repeatedly sought this.) The Permanent Joint Council would meet monthly to discuss matters of concern to any of the countries.

The agreement also committed the countries to negotiate new national limits on the 1991 Conventional Forces in Europe Treaty. Although not specified in formal treaty commitments, NATO did reassure Russia that the alliance had neither the intention of nor interest in deploying nuclear weapons on the territory of new member countries. For his part, Yeltsin promised that Russian nuclear weapons previously targeted at NATO countries would be dismantled.

After its signing, the Founding Act was to be considered for ratification by the legislatures of the signatory countries. The agreement was expected to encounter especially strong opposition in the Russian parliament, where Russian nationalist and Communist parties held sway. At the time of the Founding Act's signing, the Russian parliament still had not ratified the 1993 START II agreement, which would cut American and Russian strategic nuclear arsenals. Indeed, the possibility of NATO expansion was one of the main issues that held up Russian ratification of START II.

In any event, the Founding Act was less important as a legal instrument than as a symbolic expression of NATO's assurances to Russia and Russia's acquiescence to NATO expansion. To be sure, Yeltsin continued to insist that NATO expansion was "a grave mistake," but he seemed to accept that it was inevitable. In that sense, the signing ceremony was a post-Cold War catharsis.

In 2004, NATO added seven new members, all from the former Soviet bloc—Bulgaria, Estonia, Latvia, Lithuania, Romania, Slovakia, and Slovenia—bringing membership to twenty-six. In 2002, the NATO-Russian Council was established to foster the cooperation between the expanded alliance and Russia that had begun with the signing of the cooperation pact in 1997.

—*Steve D. Boilard*

## FURTHER READING

Brenner, Michael, ed. *NATO and Collective Security.* New York: St. Martin's Press, 1997. Offers useful background information on NATO and its role in ensuring international security. Includes a bibliography.

Clemens, Clay, ed. *NATO and the Quest for Post-Cold War Security.* New York: St. Martin's Press, 1997. Collection of essays focuses primarily on NATO's complex role in furthering collective security in Western Europe without offending the national interests of individual members.

Gann, L. H., and Peter Duignan. *Contemporary Europe and the Atlantic Alliance: A Political History.* Malden, Mass.: Blackwell, 1997. Provides an excellent overview of how NATO shaped and was shaped by postwar European political developments.

Rupp, Richard E. *NATO After 9/11: An Alliance in Continuing Decline.* New York: Palgrave Macmillan, 2006. Discusses the state of NATO since the terrorist attacks on the United States on September 11, 2001. Argues that threats to Western security have failed to unify the organization's member nations.

Whitney, Craig R. "Russia and NATO Sign Cooperation Pact." *The New York Times*, May 28, 1997, A1. Describes the terms of the Founding Act and the signing ceremony itself.

Wijk, Rob de. *NATO on the Brink of a New Millennium: The Battle for Consensus*. Washington, D.C.: Brassey's, 1997. Focuses on organizational changes within NATO that occurred after the late 1980's and how these changes shifted the balance of power among its member nations.

**SEE ALSO:** Mar. 11, 1985: Gorbachev Initiates a Policy of Glasnost; July 16, 1990: Gorbachev Agrees to Membership of a United Germany in NATO; July 1, 1991: Dissolution of the Warsaw Pact; Dec., 1991: Dissolution of the Soviet Union.

## June-October, 1997
# INDONESIAN FOREST FIRES DEVASTATE SOUTHEAST ASIA

*In Indonesia, subsistence and industrial agriculturists set fires to expand land available to cultivate food crops and palm oil trees. Because drought conditions existed, fires blazed out of control, burning millions of acres, including rain forests. The large amounts of smoke caused by the fires covered Indonesia and other Southeast Asian countries for several months. Pollutants harmed both humans and animals exposed to the smoke and interfered with trade and travel in the region.*

**LOCALE:** Indonesia; Malaysia; Singapore; Thailand; Vietnam; Philippines
**CATEGORIES:** Disasters; environmental issues

### KEY FIGURES

*Suharto* (1921-2008), president of Indonesia, 1967-1998
*Djamaludin Suryohadikusumo* (b. 1934), Indonesian forestry minister, 1993-1998
*Sarwono Kusumaatmadja* (b. 1943), Indonesian environment minister, 1993-1998
*Syarifuddin Baharsyah* (b. 1933), Indonesian agriculture minister, 1993-1998
*Datuk Seri Mahathir bin Mohamad* (b. 1925), prime minister of Malaysia, 1981-2003
*Emmy Hafild* (b. 1958), director of the Indonesian Forum for the Environment
*Bob Hasan* (b. 1931), Indonesian timber plantation investor

### SUMMARY OF EVENT

In 1997, Indonesia suffered its worst drought in a half century. The problem was exacerbated by El Niño conditions that altered normal precipitation and weather. During 1997, these conditions delayed the September monsoon season for two months. Subsistence farmers welcomed the abnormal weather pattern and burned additional land to clear it for crops. This practice was a well-established tradition for survival within Indonesian culture; however, in 1995, national leaders had banned extensive burning because previous fires had interfered with diplomacy and shipping. In 1997, commercial farmers and investors viewed the extra phase of dryness as an opportunity to earn more profits. As a result, beginning in June, immense human-caused forest fires swept through the country.

During the drought, private companies harvested hardwood timber to export. After workers cleared the harvested land by burning brush, landowners planted oil palms—creating plantations tens of thousands of acres in size—to produce oil from palm fruit to be used for a variety of goods. Several thousand acres burned weekly and rain forests in Indonesia became depleted quickly as a result of the agricultural developments. The fires raged uncontrolled—emitting toxins and pollutants in the air—in order for agribusinesses to attain larger plantations to grow more palm oil trees.

Indonesian president Suharto, hoping to profit from the increase in agribusiness, approved burning licenses for business investors whom he knew. Emmy Hafild, director of the Indonesian Forum for the Environment, strived to stop the excessive burning. She realized the majority of Indonesian politicians were corrupt and eager to accept bribes from land investors. Hafild noted that political conditions provided minimal means to enforce the 1995 burning ban or gain control over land-hungry businesspeople.

Some officials, though, particularly Environment Minister Sarwono Kusumaatmadja, attempted to stop unlawful burning, providing information for the forestry ministry to strip companies of licenses. Publicly stating the fires were an overwhelming disaster, Kusumaatmadja established a group to use satellite images to watch the fires and vowed that anyone setting fires would be penalized. Despite those efforts, palm oil companies continued burning land, realizing Suharto and his supporters would not interfere.

In addition to blaming drought conditions for the fires, Indonesian officials encouraged the media to ac-

1997

*Pollution caused by forest fires covers Indonesia and the Indian Ocean in 1997.* (NASA)

cuse subsistence farmers and foreigners—specifically Malaysians—for setting the fires and allowing them to expand unchecked. The amount of damage to the rain forest and air, however, was too great and swift for small farmers to have caused. Such rapid, fiery destruction seemed most likely attributable to industrial agribusinesses and influential plantation owners such as Bob Hasan, who owned millions of acres in Indonesia and was a close friend of Suharto. Until smoke obscured the view, satellites verified that companies were burning large areas.

Hasan spoke publicly in support of Suharto. Citing statistics, he emphasized that 49 million hectares of Indonesia's 143 million hectares of forest were located in national park and protected areas. Hasan also stated that 64 million hectares had stipulations that controlled harvesting to a maximum of ten trees on each hectare. He stressed that only 30 million hectares were available for agricultural usage.

Hasan emphasized that forest-related businesses employed four million workers, which aided economic stability. As a result of the fires, Indonesia established the world's largest palm oil orchards; Hassan argued the orchards were industrial resources for workers and communities that eased impoverished conditions. Hasan stated that he encouraged reforesting land and wanted the Indonesian government to sue anyone who burned forests. Despite Hasan's assertions, environmentalists detected that large percentages of money designated for reforestation were diverted to unrelated projects pursued by Suharto's cronies, including Hasan.

Smoke from the Indonesian fires floated above the South China Sea to Kuala Lumpur, Malaysia, staining the sky gray and yellow and polluting it with noxious odors. Similar problems were not experienced in Jakarta, Indonesia's capital, where air currents diverted smoke elsewhere. Suharto's advisers, in order not to alarm the president, did not report foreign complaints immediately. By September 9, Suharto asked the military to assist in enforcement of the 1995 laws; however, no fines were levied against those who continued to burn land after the October 3 deadline. After Suharto became aware of problems in nearby countries caused by the smoke, he extended a halfhearted apology in mid-September, 1997, passively saying God had created the haze.

Investors worried licenses to clear additional land might be denied and approved the immediate burning of land. Instead of handling the problem decisively, Suharto concentrated on other problems plaguing Indonesia, such as the disintegrating economy and currency devaluation. Syarifuddin Baharsyah, agriculture minister of Indonesia, stated that 173 plantations with palm oil and rubber trees were ablaze. Forestry minister Djamaludin Suryohadikusumo stripped nine businesses of their licenses, claiming they had not provided evidence they no longer burned land. Suryohadikusumo stopped renewal of sixty licenses, but those businesses kept clearing land.

After demonstrators protested the fires, Malaysian prime minister Datuk Seri Mahathir bin Mohamad shifted his attention from economic concerns in late September, 1997, to the deployment of firefighters to Indonesia. In some urban areas, people hosed the smoke from the tops of tall buildings. Some foreign firefighters were used to fight the blazes on the ground, while others dropped water from aircraft.

In November and December, rainfall interrupted most fires, although some peat fires smoldered underneath the surface. Indonesian leaders finally created legislation in late 1997, which outlawed people from burning land from July through October. Although almost two hundred companies violated the law, none were held legally accountable. Fires resumed and expanded in February, 1998, and occurred in 1999, also. Laws against burning were ineffective partly because influential businesses emphasized that commercial agricultural money helped Indonesia's weak economy.

## SIGNIFICANCE

Approximately 25 million acres in Indonesian forests burned in 1997. Damages related to the fires totaled $9 billion. Smoke reached several Southeast Asian countries, complicating diplomatic relations. Malaysian leaders stated that the smoke reduced that country's tourism by 13 percent.

Approximately seventy-five million people, including forty-eight million Indonesians, were affected. Chemical toxins, especially carbons and sulfurs, entered the atmosphere and caused the air pollution index to reach dangerous levels. People suffered from fire-related ailments, included breathing and cardiovascular disorders, and wore masks and carried respirators. Many people could not work and had large medical costs because of the smoke. Wildlife—including endangered species— was significantly affected. Orangutans could not survive in burned habitats.

Ironically, despite investors' ambitions, smoke hindered growth of trees, interrupted palm oil exportation, and depleted food supplies. The lack of sunlight impeded vegetable growth and reduced bee pollination. Soil erosion affected coral reefs and fish populations. Upset about the destruction of tropical rain forests, environmentalists worried about the fires' long-term damage to the ecosystem, affect on weather, and contribution to global warming.

In 1997, the Association of Southeast Asian Nations (ASEAN) discussed ways to prevent fires in Indonesia. The financial impact of the fires provoked dissension in Indonesia, and Suharto resigned in May, 1998. At the 1999 ASEAN meeting, Indonesian leaders proposed seeding clouds from airplanes to create rain. Scientific studies utilized satellites, radiometry, and remote sensors to consider ways to stop disastrous practices. Traditional farming culture in Indonesia, entrenched political response, and recurrent droughts resulted in most critics realizing obvious solutions could not be easily implemented.

*—Elizabeth D. Schafer*

## FURTHER READING

Aiken, S. Robert. "Runaway Fires, Smoke-Haze Pollution, and Unnatural Disasters in Indonesia." *Geographical Review* 94 (January, 2004): 55-79. Examines history of twentieth century Indonesian fires and their causes, blaming humans, not drought.

Brauer, Michael, and Jamal Hisham-Hashim. "Fires in Indonesia: Crisis and Reaction." *Environmental Science and Technology* 32 (September 1, 1998): 404A-407A. Health professionals discuss hazardous particles in air from the fires, providing graphs and satellite images.

Eaton, Peter, and Miroslav Radojević, eds. *Forest Fires and Regional Haze in Southeast Asia*. Huntington, N.Y.: Nova Science, 2001. Exploration of the fires' economic, medical, climatic, and political factors by authors located in Asia who experienced the Indonesian fires' impacts.

Jim, C. Y. "The Forest Fires in Indonesia 1997-98: Possible Causes and Pervasive Consequences." *Geography* 84 (July, 1999): 251-260. A Hong Kong scholar focuses on biodiversity, emphasizing the protection of wildlife from fires.

Simons, Lewis M., and Michael Yamashita. "Indonesia's Plague of Fire." *National Geographic*, August, 1998, 100-119. Author and photographer document their experiences with the 1997 fires, discussing the

perspectives of subsistence farmers, laborers, tycoons, politicians, and environmentalists.

**SEE ALSO:** Summer, 1988: Fires Burn Much of Yellowstone National Park; Oct. 26-Nov. 3, 1993: Fires Devastate Southern California; May 21, 1998: Suharto Resigns, Making Way for Habibie; Aug. 30, 1999: Voters in East Timor Vote for Independence.

## June 15, 1997
# TIGER WOODS BECOMES WORLD'S TOP-RATED GOLFER

*After turning professional in 1996, Tiger Woods quickly came to dominate the sport of golf. In 1997, he won the Masters Tournament, his first major tournament as a professional, and became the youngest player up to that time to achieve the top spot in the Official World Golf Ranking.*

**LOCALE:** United States
**CATEGORY:** Sports

**KEY FIGURES**
*Tiger Woods* (b. 1975), American professional golfer
*Earl Woods* (1932-2006), father of Tiger Woods

**SUMMARY OF EVENT**
When Tiger Woods exploded onto the professional golf scene in 1996 he had already experienced notable successes in golf. He won his first golf tournament at the age of eight, and at fifteen he became the youngest golfer up to that time to win the U.S. Junior National Championship. He went on to become the first African American and the youngest golfer to win the U.S. Amateur Golf Championship, a tournament he then won three years in a row. In 1996, he became the first African American to earn a PGA (Professional Golfers' Association) Tour card since Adrian Stills in 1985.

On his way to winning his first major professional tournament, the Masters, in April, 1997, at twenty-one years of age, Woods shattered several PGA records. His score of 270 over four rounds was the lowest in the history of the Masters, and his twelve-stroke victory over the second-place finisher was the greatest winning margin since 1862. Not long after his Masters win, on June 15, 1997, Tiger Woods became the youngest professional golfer ever to take the number one spot in the Official World Golf Ranking.

Woods's phenomenal success drew a great deal of media attention. In 1997, television coverage of the Mas-

ters included sixty-six of his sixty-nine final-round shots and earned the Columbia Broadcasting System (CBS) record television ratings for a Masters final. After Woods joined the PGA Tour in 1996, hundreds of millions of new dollars began to flow into the sport of professional golf, including increases in television contracts. Prize money on the PGA Tour in 1996, the year Woods turned pro, added up to a little more than $69 million. In contrast, by 2001 the total purse had escalated to $180 million. As the most recognized athlete in the world, Woods brought more people out to the tournaments and created more media coverage.

In addition to raising the financial status of professional golf, Woods transformed the public image of the sport, taking golf's long history as a decadent pastime for white people and turning it inside out. As Tim Finchem, commissioner of the PGA Tour, noted, Woods's impact came not only from his skill but also from his persona and the dignified way he carried himself.

In December, 1996, several months after Woods left Stanford University to become a professional golfer, an article in *Sports Illustrated* quoted his father, Earl Woods, as claiming that his son was qualified through his ethnicity to do more than any other man in history to change the course of humanity. According to the elder Woods, Tiger's heritage—which includes Thai, Chinese, American Indian, and European as well as African forebears—placed him in a position to stimulate new interest in the concept of the United States as a melting pot. Building on the interest in Tiger Woods, stories about mixed-race children and racially mixed marriages proliferated in the mass media. Woods, however, was somewhat reluctant to make public statements about issues of race and ethnicity. He frowned on being referred to as African American because he felt that such categorization neglected his Asian mother. For the most part, he

*Tiger Woods.* (PaddyBriggs)

seemed inclined to concentrate on golf and let others speak on behalf of race relations. He did, however, always find time to devote to helping disadvantaged youth, both on and off the golf course. To that end, he and his father established the Tiger Woods Foundation in 1996.

## SIGNIFICANCE

Tiger Woods's success and popularity had major impacts on the sport of golf, which had long stood as a potent symbol of exclusion and racial intolerance. Although golf is still overwhelmingly a sport played and watched by white people, surveys have shown that from 1996 to 2003, the number of African Americans who identified themselves as avid fans of professional golf rose 380 percent. In the same period, the percentage of African American golfers doubled. By 2003, approximately five hundred golf programs were operating in urban, inner-city areas in the United States, compared with just eighty-five such programs in 1994.

Woods attracted interest to the sport of golf in the United States and around the world, among adults and children of all ethnic groups who previously had no interest in the sport. The country-club mystique of golf began to disappear as the sport became democratized and more affordable, with an increasing proportion of new courses open to the public (in 2003, 90 percent of new golf courses built in the United States were public courses).

In addition, Woods's example of commitment to a relentless work ethic in the gym and on the practice range brought a new level of physical fitness and dedication to the realm of professional golf. The game's equipment revolution around the end of the twentieth century was also fueled in part by the desire among lesser players to catch up to Woods. His mile-long drives were a major contributor to an obsession with distance off the tee, which led many golf courses, including Augusta National, to redesign golf holes to allow for greater length.

Woods's influence and success continued into the twenty-first century. In 2000, his fifteen-stroke victory at the U.S. Open at Pebble Beach made Woods the first golfer since Ben Hogan in 1953 to win three major tournaments in a year. In April, 2001, Woods became the first golfer to hold all four majors titles at once, although not in the same year, when he again captured the Masters title. This feat became known as the "Tiger slam."

—*Mary McElroy*

1997

## FURTHER READING

Londino, Lawrence. *Tiger Woods: A Biography*. Westport, Conn.: Greenwood Press, 2006. Describes the life and career of the golf prodigy. Includes information on Woods's early life, the influence of his parents, and how he handles celebrity and the media.

Owen, David. *The Chosen One: Tiger Woods and the Dilemma of Greatness*. New York: Simon & Schuster, 2001. Examines Woods's impacts on the sport of golf and on American society in general since he came to public attention as a golf phenomenon.

Sampson, Curt. *Chasing Tiger*. New York: Atria Books, 2002. Describes how Woods's success transformed the PGA Tour and the game of professional golf.

Sounes, Howard. *The Wicked Game: Arnold Palmer, Jack Nicklaus, Tiger Woods, and the Story of Modern Golf*. New York: HarperCollins, 2004. Presents an interesting comparison of three golf superstars of different eras and how they affected the sport of golf in different ways.

**SEE ALSO:** Spring, 1972: Nike Produces Its First Running Shoe; Oct. 2, 1974: Robinson Becomes Baseball's First African American Manager; Sept. 15, 1985: Europe Takes the Ryder Cup; Mar. 28, 1999: Williams Sisters Meet in Historic Tennis Final.

## June 30, 1997
# *HARRY POTTER* RESUSCITATES READING

*The publication of the children's book* Harry Potter and the Philosopher's Stone *marked the beginning of an unprecedented cultural phenomenon. The Harry Potter series is credited with rekindling interest in reading among upper elementary and middle school children.*

**ALSO KNOWN AS:** *Harry Potter and the Sorcerer's Stone*
**LOCALE:** United States; United Kingdom
**CATEGORIES:** Literature; publishing and journalism

**KEY FIGURES**

*J. K. Rowling* (b. 1965), author of the Harry Potter series
*Arthur A. Levine* (b. 1962), head of Arthur A. Levine Books, a subsidiary of Scholastic, Inc.

**SUMMARY OF EVENT**

On June 30, 1997, Bloomsbury in London published *Harry Potter and the Philosopher's Stone*, by J. K. Rowling. The final manuscript, having taken the author six years to complete, was accepted for representation by the Christopher Little Literary Agency. After an additional year of searching and multiple rejections, Bloomsbury accepted it for publication. Because of the book's immediate popularity, Arthur A. Levine Books/Scholastic secured the American publishing rights and in September of 1998 published the book under the title *Harry Potter and the Sorcerer's Stone*. Rowling then completed additional books in the series, and an industry of Harry Potter-related movies and products was born.

The idea for Harry Potter came to Rowling while riding the train from Manchester to London in 1990. For the next six years, Rowling spent considerable time developing the richly detailed magical world and complex stories of good versus evil that form the basis for all seven of the books of the Harry Potter series. While working on the first book, Rowling also developed outlines for the entire series. This was a tumultuous period in the author's life, as she experienced the death of her beloved mother, moved to Portugal and taught English, married a Portuguese journalist, gave birth to her first child, was divorced from her husband, and moved to Scotland to be near her sister. Despite these events, Rowling completed the manuscript in 1996, much of it written on paper in local cafés, and began the hunt for a literary agent.

The first agent to whom she submitted her book rejected it, but the next, the Christopher Little Literary

Agency, expressed interest and became Rowling's representative. The agency spent the next year submitting the manuscript to a variety of publishers. Eight publishers rejected the manuscript, but the ninth, Bloomsbury, accepted it and offered Rowling a financial advance for its publication. The publisher suggested that while Rowling had written the novel without a particular age group in mind, they would target it toward nine- to eleven-year-old children. In addition, because boys in this age group were believed to perceive books written by women as books for girls only, the publisher suggested that Rowling adopt a more gender-neutral name. Rowling adopted the

*Author J. K. Rowling reads from her Harry Potter series at a children's literacy party hosted by Queen Elizabeth II to celebrate her eightieth birthday at Buckingham Palace in London in 2006.* (AP/Wide World Photos)

name of her grandmother, Kathleen, as her middle name, and coined her famous pen name.

*Harry Potter and the Philosopher's Stone* was greeted with many positive literary reviews, and these and word of mouth from readers catapulted the book to best-seller status. In particular, the book appealed to young boys, who traditionally spent more time with video games. The book's success was noted by publishers in the United States, and Arthur A. Levine Books/Scholastic secured the American publishing rights with an offer to Rowling of approximately $105,000. This extraordinary sum allowed Rowling to quit her teaching job and work full-time on writing the subsequent books in the series. For the American edition, Scholastic changed some of the language, as well as the title, to reflect American English. The philosopher's stone, for example, is associated with alchemy and magic, but the publisher was concerned that the American audience would not be familiar with the term. For this reason, the title of the American version is *Harry Potter and the Sorcerer's Stone*, and British slang was rendered for an American audience.

The series captured both children's and adults' imaginations. The stories follow the protagonist, Harry Potter, and his friends Hermione Granger and Ron Weasley as they experience adventures, challenges, and dilemmas at their school of wizardry, Hogwarts. Their magical world is threatened throughout the series by the evil wizard Voldemort, a satanic figure who killed Harry's parents but, astonishingly, failed to kill the infant Harry, leaving him only with a zig-zag scar on his forehead that throbs painfully in the presence of Voldemort's evil. Harry's fame since infancy as the one who survived "You-Know-Who" precedes him, plagues him as he grows up during the course of the seven novels' events, and ultimately shapes (but does not define) his destiny. The combined themes of good versus evil and Harry's coming-of-age story made the novels compelling to young readers, accounting for much of their success.

## HARRY POTTER AND THE OCCULT CONTROVERSY

*Despite the huge success of the Harry Potter series, the books are not universally applauded. A number of fundamentalist Christian religious groups, and even Pope Benedict XVI, have expressed concern that the books promote the occult. Here are some criticisms:*

On March 7, 2003, Cardinal Joseph Ratzinger (later Pope Benedict XVI) wrote a letter congratulating German writer Gabriele Kuby on her book *Harry Potter: Gut oder böse?* (Harry Potter: good or evil?). The cardinal wrote, "It is good that you enlighten people about Harry Potter, because those are subtle seductions, which act unnoticed and by this deeply distort Christianity in the soul, before it can grow properly."

In her article "Bewitched by Harry Potter" (1999), Berit Kjos wrote, "The witchcraft and wizardry in Harry Potter books may be fantasy, but they familiarize children with a very real and increasingly popular religion—one that few really understand. Far removed from the terrors of tribal witchcraft and shamanism, Americans are oblivious to the bondages that normally follow occult favors."

*In a BBC special, "Harry Potter and Me," which aired December 28, 2001, J. K. Rowling responded to the general occult controversy surrounding her books:*

"Not once has a child come up to me and said, 'Due to you I've decided to devote my life to the occult.' People underestimate children so hugely. They know it's fiction. When people are arguing from that kind of standpoint, I don't think reason works tremendously well. But I would be surprised if some of them had read the books at all."

*Some Christians have praised the Harry Potter series and have interpreted the books in a Christian light. In an interview with Belinda Elliott, Gina Burkart said that Christianity and Harry Potter share an important universal theme:*

"The biggest parallel is that love saves Harry. It was the love of his mother that leaves the mark that saved him from Voldemort, and that is a parallel to Christ. Christ died for us and it was His love that saved us. And God is love."

1997

The continuing saga of Harry Potter became wildly successful. The first three books of the series, *Harry Potter and the Sorcerer's Stone*, *Harry Potter and the Chamber of Secrets* (1998), and *Harry Potter and the Prisoner of Azkaban* (1999), occupied the top three slots on the *New York Times* best-seller list for more than one year. When the fourth book of the series, *Harry Potter and the Goblet of Fire*, debuted in 2000, *The New York Times* instituted a new best-seller list specifically for children's literature. The first six books together sold more than 300 million copies worldwide and were translated into forty-two languages. The books also spawned a film franchise, each film corresponding to a novel in the series.

The Harry Potter series has been credited with recharging interest in reading among late elementary and early middle school children. In July, 2006, Yankelovich, Inc., with Scholastic, released "The Kids and Family Reading Report," which supports this claim. The survey included five hundred children ages five to seventeen and one parent or guardian per child. Fifty-one percent of the Harry Potter readers said that they did not read for fun before beginning to read the Harry Potter series, but that they do now; 89 percent of parents said that Harry Potter has helped their children enjoy reading more; and 76 percent said that reading Harry Potter has helped their child do better in school. Half of all the surveyed parents indicated that they too were Harry Potter readers, confirming the cross-generational appeal of the books.

The books were not universally applauded, however. Many predominantly fundamentalist Christian religious groups expressed concern that the novels promote paganism and witchcraft, and that children could be influenced to adopt such beliefs and practices if allowed to read the books. Since 1999, the Harry Potter books have been consistently at the top of the American Library Association's list of the most protested books, and some communities have banned them.

## SIGNIFICANCE

The Harry Potter books, films, and merchandise earned a fortune for J. K. Rowling and publishers Bloomsbury and Scholastic and have been critically acclaimed with numerous literary awards and honors. Harry Potter be-

came more than a series of books—it became a cultural phenomenon. The highly readable and engaging stories grew a huge and devoted following, with their universal themes of friendship, family, hard work, and the struggle of good against evil. The series as a whole, moreover, is among the best-selling series of all time.

—*Karen E. Kalumuck*

## FURTHER READING

Anatol, Giselle Liza, ed. *Reading Harry Potter: Critical Essays*. Westport, Conn.: Praeger, 2003. Essays analyze the novels from the perspectives of child development, literary, and historical theories, as well as moral and social values. Anthology covers the first four novels.

Heilman, Elizabeth E., ed. *Critical Perspectives on Harry Potter*. New York: Falmer Press, 2002. Scholars from a variety of academic disciplines provide literary, cultural, sociological, and psychological examinations of the Harry Potter books as a cultural phenomenon. Especially useful for teachers and those interested in cultural studies, this book is geared to an adult reader.

Sexton, Colleen. *J. K. Rowling*. Minneapolis, Minn.: Lerner, 2005. Highly readable biography of J. K. Rowling provides a glimpse into her life as a writer and mother; written for children ages nine to eleven.

**SEE ALSO:** Dec. 10, 1978: Singer Is Awarded the Nobel Prize in Literature; May 30, 1995: Popular Fiction Addresses the End Times.

**July 1, 1997**

# HONG KONG BECOMES PART OF THE PEOPLE'S REPUBLIC OF CHINA

*Great Britain's return of Hong Kong to China in 1997 ended more than 150 years of colonial rule in a territory that had grown to be a world-class financial and economic center. A long-standing issue between two of the world's leading powers was resolved peacefully.*

**LOCALE:** Hong Kong, China

**CATEGORIES:** Diplomacy and international relations; government and politics; expansion and land acquisition

**KEY FIGURES**

*Deng Xiaoping* (Teng Hsiao-p'ing; 1904-1997), leader of the People's Republic of China in a variety of top positions, 1977-1989

*Margaret Thatcher* (b. 1925), prime minister of the United Kingdom, 1979-1990

*Christopher Patten* (b. 1944), governor of Hong Kong, 1992-1997

*Tung Chee-hwa* (Dong Jianhua; b. 1937), chief executive of Hong Kong, 1997-2005

**SUMMARY OF EVENT**

In its entirety, Hong Kong the British colony comprised three territories that Great Britain acquired at different times. Hong Kong Island was ceded to Britain by China in 1842, after China's loss of the First Opium War. In 1860, having been defeated in the Second Opium War, China ceded to Britain the part of the Kowloon Peninsula that is south of the present-day Boundary Street, including Stonecutter's Island. In 1898, Britain leased from China what is known as the New Territories for a period of ninety-nine years.

After the founding of the People's Republic of China in 1949, China's new government, under the leadership of the Chinese Communist Party, refused to recognize the validity of the treaties by which Britain secured the control of Hong Kong. The Chinese government, however, did not actively seek the return of Hong Kong in the three decades that followed. In the late 1970's, as the expiration date for the lease on the New Territories drew closer, uncertainty about the future of Hong Kong began to affect the economic stability of the British colony. Around the same time, following the death of Chinese leader Mao Zedong in 1976, China began to experiment with reformist policies, one component of which was a greater degree of openness to the outside world. The British and Chinese governments approached each other and launched negotiations on the Hong Kong question.

In the initial stage of the negotiations, British officials explored the possibility of resolving the issue through the exchange of administrative rights for sovereignty—Britain would restore sovereignty over Hong Kong to China, and China, in return, would recognize a continued British role in the administration of Hong Kong beyond 1997. On her visit to Beijing in September, 1982, British prime minister Margaret Thatcher held talks with China's paramount leader Deng Xiaoping in which she stressed the benefits of continued British involvement in Hong Kong's administration beyond 1997. The Chinese government, however, was not receptive to the idea, insisting that sovereignty was not negotiable. Subsequent talks then proceeded on the assumption that the return of Hong Kong would apply to both sovereignty and administration and would include Hong Kong Island, Kowloon Peninsula, and the New Territories. For its part, the Chinese government promised to apply to Hong Kong the policy of "one country, two systems," under which Hong Kong would become part of the People's Republic of China but would enjoy a high degree of autonomy.

On December 19, 1984, the Chinese and British governments signed the Joint Declaration of the Government of the United Kingdom of Great Britain and Northern Ireland and the Government of the People's Republic of China on the Question of Hong Kong, commonly known as the Sino-British Joint Declaration. The British government announced that it would "restore Hong Kong to the People's Republic of China with effect from 1 July 1997." The Chinese government proclaimed its decision "to establish a Hong Kong Special Administrative Region upon resuming the exercise of sovereignty over Hong Kong." The Hong Kong Special Administrative Region (SAR) is "to enjoy a high degree of autonomy, except for foreign and defence affairs." It would be "vested with executive, legislative and independent judicial power, including that of final adjudication." Hong Kong would also retain its existing social and economic systems as well as lifestyle. These policies, the Chinese government pledged, would remain unchanged for fifty years after the return of Hong Kong. In April, 1990, the National People's Congress (NPC) of China passed the Basic Law of the Hong Kong Special Administrative Region of the People's Republic of China, which would serve as Hong Kong's constitution after 1997.

1997

With the 1984 Joint Declaration and the 1990 Basic Law, Britain and China laid the path to the 1997 handover. Still, wrangling over Hong Kong's future continued, in particular with regard to political issues and especially after the Chinese government's violent suppression of popular protests in Beijing's Tiananmen Square in 1989. Many residents in the colony were skeptical of Chinese leaders' intentions toward Hong Kong and called for democratic reforms of the governmental system in Hong Kong before the Chinese takeover. Christopher Patten, the last British governor of Hong Kong, proposed and implemented policies to that effect. Hong Kong's Legislative Council, which hereto had been largely an appointed body, was strengthened, with twenty of its sixty members to be produced through direct elections.

The Chinese government denounced such reform efforts as hypocritical in nature since they took place at the last minute before Britain's return of Hong Kong to China, and it viewed the changes as violations of the Joint Declaration. The NPC accordingly declared that the Legislative Council of Hong Kong would not survive beyond July 1, 1997. The Chinese government vowed to follow the gradual approach to political reforms outlined in the Basic Law, which provides that approximately seven years after Hong Kong's return, thirty of the sixty members of the Legislative Council shall be produced through direct elections, and that eventually all members of the Legislative Council will be returned by universal suffrage.

In December, 1996, an electoral college of four hundred Hong Kong voters selected sixty members of a Provisional Legislative Council, which was to hold office until a new election, scheduled for May, 1998, to produce a new legislature. The electoral college also named Tung Chee-hwa, a fifty-nine-year-old businessman, as the first chief executive of the Hong Kong SAR; the central government formally appointed Tung shortly afterward.

The transfer of the sovereignty over Hong Kong from Britain to China officially took place through a spectacular but solemn ceremony held on June 30-July 1, 1997, in the Hong Kong Convention and Exhibition Center. Representing the United Kingdom at the ceremony were Prince Charles, Prime Minister Tony Blair, Governor Christopher Patten, Foreign Secretary Robin Cook, and Chief of the Defense Staff Charles Guthrie. Appearing on behalf of China were President Jiang Zemin, Premier Li Peng, Foreign Minister Qian Qichen, Vice Chairman of the Central Military Commission Zhang Wannian, and Chief Executive Tung Chee-hwa. Among the dignitaries witnessing the transfer were former British prime minister Margaret Thatcher and U.S. secretary of state Madeleine Albright.

Shortly before midnight, Prince Charles delivered a farewell speech on behalf of Queen Elizabeth II to Hong Kong residents in which he praised the Hong Kong people and wished them good fortune in the years to come. British national flag and the Hong Kong colonial flag were then lowered, accompanied by the U.K. anthem, "God Save the Queen." At midnight, China's national flag and the flag of the Hong Kong SAR were raised, accompanied by the Chinese anthem, "March of the Volunteers." President Zemin then delivered a speech in which he promised the faithful implementation of the "one country, two systems" policy and expressed his confidence in the future of Hong Kong.

## SIGNIFICANCE

In the years immediately following its return to China, Hong Kong experienced various challenges but generally weathered the difficulties well. Politically, concerns remain over the pace of democratic reforms and the protection of people's liberties, but the much-feared collapse and chaos did not materialize. Economically, in spite of the ill effects of the Asian financial crisis in 1997-1998 and the global downturn in 2001-2002, Hong Kong achieved an average annual gross domestic product growth rate of 4.3 percent from 2000 to 2005.

Hong Kong's return in 1997 is a matter of great national pride to the Chinese people. The loss of Hong Kong Island in 1842 marked the beginning of a historical period full of defeats and humiliation for China. With the recovery of Hong Kong, many Chinese could finally bring closure to that ignominious chapter in their history. The reversion of Hong Kong also testifies to the ability of countries in the world to settle their disagreements peacefully and to bring about results generally acceptable to all the parties involved. Furthermore, the return of Hong Kong based on the principle of "one country, two systems" provides China with an opportunity to confront issues such as pluralism, freedom, and democratic changes as the country pursues modernization in the twenty-first century.

*—Jing Li*

## FURTHER READING

Ash, Robert, et al., eds. *Hong Kong in Transition: One Country, Two Systems*. London: RoutledgeCurzon, 2003. Articles covering the economic, political, legal, and cultural life of Hong Kong since 1997.

Brown, Judith M., and Rosemary Foot, eds. *Hong Kong's Transitions, 1842-1997.* New York: St. Martin's Press, 1997. History of Hong Kong.

Buckley, Roger. *Hong Kong: The Road to 1997.* New York: Cambridge University Press, 1997. History of Hong Kong from 1945 to the events leading up to the handover.

Chung, Sze-yuen. *Hong Kong's Journey to Reunification: Memoirs of Sze-yuen Chung.* Hong Kong: Chinese University Press, 2001. Recollections and reflections of a Hong Kong industrialist and politician.

Dimbleby, Jonathan. *The Last Governor: Chris Patten and the Handover of Hong Kong.* London: Little, Brown, 1999. Biography of the British official who oversaw Hong Kong's return to China.

Patten, Chris. *East and West: The Last Governor of Hong Kong on Power, Freedom, and the Future.* New York: Times Books, 1998. The last British governor of Hong Kong reflects on issues related to Hong Kong and China.

**SEE ALSO:** Oct. 25, 1971: People's Republic of China Is Seated at the United Nations; Sept. 9, 1976: Death of Mao Zedong Leads to Reforms in China; Spring, 1978: China Promises to Correct Human Rights Abuses; Late 1984: Hong Kong's Citizens Prepare for Chinese Takeover; June 4, 1989: China Crushes Prodemocracy Demonstration in Tiananmen Square; July 28, 1989: Chinese Top Leadership Changes as Jiang Zemin Takes the Party Chair; 1990: Avon Begins Operations in China; May 10, 1996: Vietnamese Refugees Riot in Hong Kong.

## July 1, 1997
# JAPAN ENACTS A LAW TO PROTECT THE AINU PEOPLE

*After a long history of legislation ostensibly enacted to meet Ainu demands for human rights, political participation, and self-reliance as a recognized people, Japan passed a new law that appeared to shift the emphasis to the promotion of the Ainu culture and dissemination of knowledge about Ainu traditions.*

**ALSO KNOWN AS:** Cultural Promotion Act; Act for the Promotion of Ainu Culture and the Dissemination of Knowledge Regarding Ainu Traditions

**LOCALE:** Sapporo, Hokkaidō, Japan

**CATEGORIES:** Indigenous peoples' rights; laws, acts, and legal history

### KEY FIGURES
*Giichi Nomura* (b. 1914), leader of the Ainu Association of Hokkaidō
*Tomiichi Murayama* (b. 1924), leader of the Japan Socialist Party and prime minister of Japan, 1994-1996
*Shigeru Kayano* (1926-2006), first Ainu to be elected to the Japanese Diet
*Kozo Igarashi* (b. 1926), Japanese chief cabinet secretary, 1994-1995

### SUMMARY OF EVENT
The Ainu people were the original inhabitants of Japan's northern island of Hokkaidō. They had a distinct hunting, fishing, and gathering culture, and the Ainu lifestyle was closely tied to the natural and spiritual environment. This situation changed in the fifteenth century, when Japanese from the large island of Honshū crossed over into Ainu territory and began trading with the local people. The Japanese exploited the Ainu economically and ignored their social customs. The Ainu often resisted these inroads into their culture and well-being, but their efforts were not successful. Nevertheless, many Ainu remained determined to maintain connections to their people's heritage.

Gradually, the Japanese government took over administration of the Ainu, banned the traditional Ainu lifestyle, and required the Ainu to use the Japanese language and to adopt Japanese culture. In 1899, the Japanese government passed the Hokkaidō Kyūdojin Protection Act (*kyūdojin* translates as "former aborigines"). Although the government publicized the act as protective, it proved to be an indirect way for Japan to legalize its policies of colonization and assimilation. No further action was taken to change the status of the Ainu for almost another half century.

In 1946, a number of concerned Ainu formed the Ainu Association of Hokkaidō for the purpose of finding ways to eliminate discrimination against the Ainu people, to improve their employment prospects and education, and to initiate needed welfare services. It became evident, however, that the association's efforts were not sufficient to bring about changes in the long-standing pattern of discrimination. Real progress would be made only if

3043

the group could break down the basic structure of Japan's one-hundred-year-old assimilation policies.

By 1984, the Ainu Association of Hokkaidō, then under the leadership of Giichi Nomura, had grown considerably. During that year, the group drafted a proposal for a new law that would require the government to take responsibility for having forced assimilation policy on the Ainu and to grant the Ainu rights as an indigenous people. The governor and the prefectural parliament of Hokkaidō voted in favor of enacting the law in 1988, but when it was sent to the central government, an interministerial committee was formed to consider new legislation in 1989, and the matter was never taken up.

It appeared in 1993 that change might be coming. First, the United Nations designated 1993 the International Year for the World's Indigenous People. Then, for the first time in forty years, the Liberal Democratic Party lost its power in the Japanese government, replaced by the Japan Socialist Party, led by Tomiichi Murayama. The following year, in 1994, Shigeru Kayano became the first Ainu to be elected to the national Diet (Japan's parliament). Kayano was an activist in the Ainu ethnic movement; he had been one of the parties to a lawsuit in the Sapporo District Court that sought to reverse a decision of the Hokkaidō Land Expropriation Commission to allow the government's taking of land that Kayano owned for a dam project on the Saru River.

Japan's chief cabinet secretary at the time, Kozo Igarashi, a politician from the Hokkaidō city of Asahikawa, was a friend of Kayano, and Igarashi lost no time in establishing the Ruling Parties Project Team for Consideration of the New Ainu Law, although there was considerable opposition to this move by a number of bureaucrats. The team then set up the Council of Experts on Implementation of Countermeasures for the Ainu People, an ad hoc consultative group, in 1995. The Council of Experts met eleven times and held hearings with prominent experts on the Ainu issue; members also visited Hokkaidō for further fact gathering before submitting the council's report on April 1, 1996. This report became the basis for the Act for the Promotion of Ainu Culture and the Dissemination of Knowledge Regarding Ainu Traditions, also known as the Cultural Promotion Act.

By the end of January, 1997, a draft of the Cultural Promotion Act was ready for presentation and explanation by the officials of the Hokkaidō Development Agency. A special meeting of the directors of the Council of Experts was held for this purpose, and the council gave its qualified approval. The cabinet accepted the draft in March, followed by the unanimous approval of the Cabinet Committee of the House of Councillors in April and of the Cabinet Committee of the House of Representatives in May. The act became effective on July 1, 1997.

The act stated that Japan will respect the Ainu's pride in being Ainu and support the Ainu people by disseminating knowledge about Ainu traditions and culture. The act defined "Ainu culture" as the Ainu language, music, dance, crafts, and other "cultural derivatives" that the Ainu have perpetuated or will in the future. It mandated that national and regional government bodies respect the will and ethnic pride of the Ainu in promoting their culture, but it gave the prime minister the power to establish fundamental policy, the tenets of which were general ones about prescribing ways to promote Ainu culture. The law also addressed the restoration of communal properties to their owners and designated the process for doing so.

The act allowed the secretary of the Hokkaidō Development Bureau and the Japanese minister of education to appoint one Japanese juridical person to promote awareness of Ainu traditions and to monitor those who participate in such promotion. The law further provided for reports, inspections, and monitoring by the appointed juridical person as well as for revocation of the appointment and the levying of fines against that person for failure to make required reports or making false reports. Supplemental provisions of the Cultural Promotion Act repealed the 1899 Hokkaidō Kyūdojin Protection Act and the 1934 Act for the Protection of Land Disposition of the Indigenous People of Asahikawa (the location of a major concentration of Ainu in Hokkaidō).

## SIGNIFICANCE

The 1997 Cultural Promotion Act had both positive and negative impacts. When the law was enacted, it was hailed as a genuine effort to redress past injustices. It appeared to grant the Ainu recognition as an indigenous people of Japan and to promise respect for their distinct culture. In addition to repealing "protection" laws passed in 1899 and 1934, the Cultural Promotion Act partially amended the 1947 District Government Act, the 1949 Ministry of Education Enabling Act, and the 1950 Hokkaidō Development Act—all necessary to clear the way for the provisions of the new act. Rulings were made that recognized the Ainu people as an indigenous people, as that term is defined by the United Nations.

As time passed, however, it became clear that the Japanese government in fact recognized the Ainu only as an ethnic minority, not as an indigenous people with inherent rights. The Ainu people continued to struggle for substantive rights and for true recognition as an indigenous people.

— *Victoria Price*

**FURTHER READING**
Kayano, Shigeru. *Our Land Was a Forest: An Ainu Memoir*. Boulder, Colo.: Westview Press, 1994. Memoir outlines the author's substantial role as a leader in the Ainu's struggle for appropriate recognition.
Nettle, Daniel, and Suzanne Romaine. *Vanishing Voices: The Extinction of the World's Languages*. New York: Oxford University Press, 2000. Discussion of dead and dying languages around the world includes a recounting of the premodern history of the Ainu and their struggle to retain language, culture, and ethnic identity.
Siddle, Richard. "An Epoch-Making Event? The 1997 Ainu Cultural Promotion Act and Its Impact." *Japan Forum* 14, no. 3 (2002): 405-423. Outlines the history leading up to the act and discusses the act's impacts on all areas of Ainu life. Concludes that although passage of the act appeared to signal a new attitude toward the Ainu, the act may in fact have had negative effects on Ainu identity.

**SEE ALSO:** Dec. 18, 1971: Native Alaskans Are Compensated for Their Land; Feb. 27-May 8, 1973: Native Americans Occupy Wounded Knee; Feb. 27, 1976: Inuit File Claim to a Section of Canadian Territory; Aug. 11, 1978: U.S. Congress Protects Native American Religious Practices; Jan. 13, 1992: Japan Admits to Sex Slavery During World War II.

1997

## July 3, 1997
# MISSISSIPPI SETTLES LAWSUIT WITH CIGARETTE MAKERS

*When Mississippi became the first state to settle a lawsuit with tobacco manufacturers, the settlement provided the state with reimbursement for past health care expenditures on smoking-related illnesses paid for by state-funded medical programs. The lawsuit was the catalyst for a $246 billion settlement between state attorneys general and the tobacco industry.*

**LOCALE:** Mississippi
**CATEGORIES:** Government and politics; health and medicine

**KEY FIGURES**
*Kirk Fordice* (1934-2004), governor of Mississippi, 1992-2000
*Mike Moore* (b. 1952), attorney general of Mississippi, 1988-2004
*Richard F. Scruggs* (b. 1946), trial lawyer from Mississippi

**SUMMARY OF EVENT**
Throughout most of the last half of the twentieth century, tobacco companies successfully fought legal battles related to smoking-related illnesses and deaths. Their success was predicated on a three-pronged strategy. They refused to admit any negative health effects from cigarettes, including the addictiveness of nicotine or that smoking causes cancer. They instead focused on smoking as a personal decision by individuals who should be held responsible for their own actions. These arguments, combined with virtually unlimited spending on legal defense, helped tobacco companies to either win jury trials or have negative verdicts overturned on appeal.

Tobacco suits had traditionally been filed by individual smokers or as class-action suits on behalf of smokers suffering from the effects of tobacco. However, on May 23, 1994, the state of Mississippi filed an innovative suit against thirteen tobacco companies in its court system. Mississippi attorney general Mike Moore argued that regardless of individual culpability in smoking cases, the state had been forced to pick up millions of dollars worth of Medicaid and other medical bills on behalf of elderly and poor smokers and public employees covered by the state health plan. The lawsuit alleged that tobacco companies were aware of the health consequences of smoking but continued to claim otherwise. The Mississippi lawsuit was the first time that a government had sued the tobacco companies to recoup tax money spent on treating smoking-related illnesses. Attorney General Moore filed the suit in the state chancery court to ensure that the case would be decided by a judge rather than a jury of citizens, because juries had been unwilling to rule against tobacco companies in past suits.

The lawsuit was opposed by Mississippi's Republican governor Kirk Fordice, who argued that it was a pub-

*Mississippi attorney general Mike Moore speaks at a news conference in Jackson, Mississippi, on July 3, 1997, after the tobacco industry agreed to pay $3.6 billion to the state over twenty-five years.* (AP/Wide World Photos)

lic relations gimmick by the Democratic attorney general to shake down tobacco companies. Fordice filed suit to dismiss Moore's case, arguing that the governor, not the attorney general, was responsible for the operation of the state's Medicaid program. Fordice's suit was dismissed, but the governor actively opposed Moore's suit and even filed a friend of the court brief supporting the tobacco companies.

Mississippi's lawsuit used a unique blend of government and private resources in order to confront the tobacco companies. Personal injury attorney Michael T. Lewis conceptualized the innovative concept of suing tobacco companies on behalf of state taxpayers in May, 1993. He took the idea to Attorney General Moore, who enlisted the help of a friend from law school, Richard F. Scruggs. Moore did not have the monetary resources to fight a protracted court battle with the well-endowed

tobacco companies. Consequently, he signed Scruggs, Lewis, and other private lawyers to contingency contracts with the state. The private lawyers used their own resources during the court case in hopes of reaping a potential windfall of millions of dollars if the case was settled. This contingency model was used by all of the other states that followed Mississippi in suing the tobacco companies. The arrangement was praised by supporters of the lawsuits, who claimed that it gave more resources to the antitobacco effort. However, opponents of the contingency model claimed that politically connected lawyers were often used by attorneys general and that private lawyers were more interested in settling for large sums of money than in preventing smoking deaths.

Moore and Scruggs became the leaders of a national movement among state attorneys general to sue the tobacco companies on behalf of taxpayers. The two men actively lobbied states to join their lawsuits and then served as the primary negotiators between the tobacco companies and the state attorneys general that led to a monetary settlement. The states' lawsuits, in addition to Scruggs's tenacity, were effective in getting former tobacco industry employees to testify against the companies and to turn over documents showing the companies' knowledge of the addictiveness of cigarettes.

Mississippi and four other states received their first victory on March 13, 1995, when cigarette producer Liggett Group settled out of court for $41 million in payments over twenty-five years. This brought the larger tobacco companies to the table, and negotiations on a nationwide settlement to the states' suits continued over the next year. During this time, more state attorneys general joined Moore in suing the industry. The major tobacco companies were finally convinced to enter into an agreement after twenty-two states reached a new settlement in March, 1997, with Liggett that required the company to declare that smoking causes lung cancer and that the firm marketed to youths. The tobacco industry settled out of court on June 20, 1997, for $368.5 billion in payments to forty states over twenty-five years. They also agreed to numerous provisions designed to reduce youth smoking and to be regulated by the federal Food and Drug Administration. In exchange for the settlement, the tobacco companies would have limited their liability in future suits. These regulatory and liability issues required that the federal government consent to the agreement before it could go into effect.

The provisional nature of the national agreement led Mississippi to settle its lawsuits with cigarette companies on July 3, 1997, just days before the case would have started in court. The state agreed to drop their suit in exchange for $3.6 billion over twenty-five years and $136 million annually in the following years. The agreement was purely monetary; the tobacco companies did not agree to any of the marketing or public health provisions contained in the national settlement. Further, the pact ensured that Mississippi would be entitled to more funds if any other states reached more advantageous terms in settlements with the tobacco companies. The agreement guaranteed that Mississippi would receive restitution even if the national pact was not ratified by Congress.

The June 20, 1997, settlement between the state attorneys general and the tobacco industry required the consent of Congress before it could go into effect. Throughout the fall of 1997 and the spring of 1998, President Bill Clinton and Congress debated alternative settlements that would have resulted in harsher penalties for the tobacco companies. Any hope of federal action died in mid-1998 when a bill sponsored by Arizona senator John McCain was defeated on the floor of the Senate by tobacco supporters. The states were forced to renegotiate with the tobacco companies. Forty-six states (including Mississippi) reached a final agreement with the tobacco companies on November 23, 1998. The settlement guaranteed $246 billion to the states over a twenty-five-year period. It also contained stringent requirements to limit youth access to tobacco, to cut cigarette advertising, and to fund antismoking initiatives. The absence of federal regulatory and liability provisions in the final agreement resulted in a smaller monetary payout to the states.

## SIGNIFICANCE

Mississippi's successful lawsuit against the tobacco companies was the beginning of a landmark triumph for public health advocates against the tobacco industry in the United States. Tobacco companies had been successful at defeating lawsuits in the past. However, Mississippi's innovative approach of suing on behalf of taxpayers instead of individual smokers finally brought tobacco interests to the negotiating table. Mississippi built a large coalition of states who were collectively able to pressure the tobacco companies into a $246 billion settlement. The tobacco companies ultimately capitulated rather than face numerous protracted court cases against the states with uncertain outcomes.

The multibillion-dollar settlement helped the states recoup past expenditures on smoking-related illnesses and funded antismoking campaigns across the country. However, from the vantage point of public health ex-

perts, the most important components of the settlement related to the end of cigarette marketing toward youth. The tobacco companies agreed to stop sponsoring events attended by young people, to do away with popular images such as Joe Camel, and to cease the distribution of merchandise with tobacco logos. This triumph for public health advocates and the states was somewhat offset by the fact that the original June, 1997, settlement giving the U.S. Food and Drug Administration the power to regulate tobacco was never ratified by Congress.

—*J. Wesley Leckrone*

## FURTHER READING

Brandt, Allan M. *The Cigarette Century: The Rise, Fall, and Deadly Persistence of the Product That Defined America.* New York: Basic Books, 2007. Comprehensive "biography" of the cigarette covers all aspects of the topic of smoking. Sections address the culture, science, politics, law, and globalization of tobacco products.

Derthick, Martha. "Federalism and the Politics of Tobacco." *Publius: The Journal of Federalism* 31 (Winter, 2001): 47-63. Overview of the factors that brought states together in their tobacco suits. Derthick also discusses the ramifications of the settlement for tobacco politics in the United States.

Mollenkamp, Carrick, Adam Levy, Joseph Menn, and Jeffrey Rothfeder. *The People vs. Big Tobacco: How the States Took on the Cigarette Giants.* Princeton, N.J.: Bloomberg Press, 1998. Journalistic reconstruction of the events that led to the tobacco companies' huge settlement with the states.

Pertschuk, Michael. *Smoke in Their Eyes: Lessons in Movement Leadership from the Tobacco Wars.* Nashville: Vanderbilt University Press, 2001. Insider's account of the day-to-day negotiations leading up to the tobacco settlement with the states.

Snell, Clete. *Peddling Poison: The Tobacco Industry and Kids.* Westport, Conn.: Praeger, 2005. Provides a historical overview of tobacco control and a chapter examining the phases of the states' 1998 settlement with the tobacco companies.

SEE ALSO: June, 1988: Canada Passes the Tobacco Products Control Act; June 13, 1988: First Monetary Damages Are Awarded to the Estate of a Cigarette Smoker; 1989: U.S. Surgeon General Reports on Tobacco and Health; June, 1991: CDC Publicizes the Dangers of Secondhand Smoke.

1997

## July 4, 1997
# PATHFINDER LANDS ON MARS

*The Mars Pathfinder mission achieved its primary goal of validating the new technologies on the Pathfinder lander and rover, which were successful in transmitting data on the Martian atmosphere and on the planet's surface geology and geochemistry, contributing to knowledge concerning whether Mars had been warmer and wetter in its past.*

**LOCALE:** Ares Vallis region of Mars
**CATEGORIES:** Spaceflight and aviation; science and technology; astronomy

**KEY FIGURE**
*Daniel S. Goldin* (b. 1940), administrator of the National Aeronautics and Space Administration

**SUMMARY OF EVENT**
For the first several years of the 1990's, the exploration of Mars encountered serious setbacks with the loss of the American Mars Observer mission in 1992 and, in 1996, the losses of the Russian Mars 96 mission and three American spacecraft either on the way to Mars or in orbit around it. Many countries had participated in these projects, and the hopes of scientists seeking knowledge of the Red Planet had been dashed. Around this time, National Aeronautics and Space Administration (NASA) administrator Daniel S. Goldin helped develop a new approach to Mars reconnaissance and research that would be "faster, better, and cheaper" than previous missions. Scientists and technicians designed the Mars Pathfinder, which was publicized as costing "only one dollar per American," to test several new ideas, including a direct touchdown on Mars by means of air-bag-protected lander and rover vehicles. Unlike its failed predecessors, Mars Pathfinder proved to be a phenomenal success.

During the early phase of its three-year planning and development, Mars Pathfinder was known as the Mars Environmental Survey. Its basic idea of a stationary lander and a surface rover was the focus of scientific and technical personnel at the Jet Propulsion Laboratory (JPL) of the California Institute of Technology, the institution primarily responsible for NASA's Mars Exploration Program. A Delta II rocket launched the Mars Pathfinder from the Cape Canaveral Air Station on December 4, 1996. Because of a favorable configuration between Mars and Earth, the spacecraft reached its destination in only seven months, during which time four trajectory maneuvers directed from the Deep Space Network on

Earth adjusted the flight path. (The Deep Space Network is a system of communications complexes that provides Earth-based radio links to all of NASA's uncrewed interplanetary spacecraft.)

Without orbiting Mars, the spacecraft entered the planet's atmosphere directly on July 4, 1997. During descent, the lander's scientific instruments took atmospheric measurements. Pathfinder's ablative heat shield slowed its rate of descent to about 830 miles per hour (370 meters per second), and a parachute slowed it even further, to about 160 miles per hour (68 meters per second). Twenty seconds later, the heat shield was released, and the lander and rover were prepared for initial contact with the surface when protective air bags surrounding them were inflated. At an altitude of 322 feet (98 meters), three solid rockets fired to slow the descent speed. The air-bag-encased lander and rover, traveling at 40 miles per hour (18 meters per second), hit the surface at nearly 3:00 in the morning Mars local solar time (a few minutes before 1:00 P.M. EDT on Earth). The first bounce of about 40 feet was followed by another fifteen bounces before the spacecraft rolled to rest, right side up, about two and one-half minutes after impact and about 1 kilometer (0.6 miles) from the initial impact point. It landed in the planet's Ares Vallis region at 19.3 degrees north latitude and 33.53 degrees west longitude, at the mouth of a flood channel near Chryse Planitia.

A little more than an hour after the landing, the air bags deflated and retracted, and the Pathfinder spacecraft opened its three triangular solar panels. After sunrise, the imaging system went into operation, taking pictures of the rover and the nearby Martian surface as well as a panoramic view of the location. Pathfinder then began transmitting to Earth the atmospheric and engineering data collected during entry and landing as well as the images it had collected. Scientists on Earth then received the information that the landing site was well within the planned landing site ellipse, which was near enough to the planet's equator to provide sufficient sunlight for the solar panels. The landing site, which was named Carl Sagan Memorial Station in honor of the recently deceased planetary astronomer, had been chosen for the opportunities it provided for the study of an ancient water channel, which was populated not only with many local rocks, but also, it was hoped, with rocks that had been carried from hundreds of kilometers upstream.

During Sol 1, Pathfinder's first Martian day, JPL engineers recognized that one of the partially deflated air bags posed a problem for the upcoming deployment of the rover. They were able to use various commands to flatten the impeding air bag, and on Sol 2, the rover, which had been nicknamed Sojourner, exited the lander via a lowered ramp. Over the next several weeks, while the lander took pictures of the rover and the surrounding landscape, Sojourner, the first self-propelled vehicle to study a planet's surface, made measurements of Martian rocks and soil.

Barnacle Bill was the first rock to be examined on Sol 3 (JPL scientists named prominent rocks for cartoon characters). It took the rover's X-ray spectrometer about ten hours to complete a scan of this rock, which turned out to be similar to terrestrial andesite, a very common volcanic rock (its name derives from the Andes mountain range, where this silicate mineral is found). The rock called Yogi, the form and texture of which indicated former deposition by floodwater, was a basalt and more primitive than Barnacle Bill. The rock named Scooby

Doo had white deposits, probably left by evaporating water. Several other rocks were studied, and most exhibited a high silicon content. In addition to volcanic rocks, Pathfinder discovered rocks similar to terrestrial sedimentary rocks, such as conglomerates, which may have formed in a watery matrix of sand, silt, and clay. In general, these rock analyses gave evidence of an ancient Mars that was more Earth-like than its highly arid present state.

The soils near the landing site, which contained rock fragments and meteoritic material, varied in color from red to dark gray. Chemically these soils, which were rich in silicon, sulfur, iron, and magnesium, were similar to the compositions found at the Viking 1 and Viking 2 sites, but, unlike the soils at the Viking sites, the Pathfinder soils provided evidence that water and wind erosion contributed to the current appearance of this section of the Martian surface. Pathfinder's scientific instruments also studied the dust in the atmosphere by observing its deposition on magnetic targets on the spacecraft.

1997

*The Pathfinder landed using a system of air bags that inflated about 100 meters above the planet's surface and protected the rover upon impact.* (NASA)

This dust was highly magnetic, perhaps owing to the presence of maghemite, an iron oxide mineral.

Among the images captured by Pathfinder's camera were vistas of distant hills. For example, Twin Peaks, a gentle ridge southwest of the lander, may have been deposited by the ancient flood that provided the "rock garden" explored by Sojourner. Further evidence of this ancient flood was provided by shallow grooves running parallel to the direction of the ancient water flow and the way that certain rocks were now piled against each other. However, bright patches on the flanks of these hills were most likely the result of drifting dust caused by recent windstorms.

During their activity on the planet, the Pathfinder's instruments also made important meteorological observations. In general, the collected data revealed an extremely dry and dusty atmosphere, with patterns of pressure and temperature fluctuations. The pressure averaged about 6 millibars, about $1/170$th of Earth's value. The temperature varied from a maximum of 14 degrees Fahrenheit (−10 degrees Celsius) in the early afternoon to a minimum of −105 degrees Fahrenheit (−76 degrees Celsius) just before sunrise. Pressures and temperatures also varied with the height above the surface; for example, the air just a few feet above the ground was several degrees colder than the air at ground level. Dust devils, swirling columns of dust, were also a frequent occurrence, often caused by morning turbulence in the atmosphere.

These and other observations came to an end on September 27, 1997 (Sol 83), when flight operators at JPL failed to establish communications with the spacecraft, although they did not announce the end of the mission until November 4. The lander's battery had been recharged many times, but after 40 Sols, the battery kept losing the capacity to keep the lander warm through the very cold Martian nights. After the public announcement, NASA's flight team tried contacting Pathfinder through its main and its secondary transmitters, but all attempts failed. Nevertheless, the lander and rover had performed for much longer than the expected one month, and far more successfully.

## SIGNIFICANCE

Pathfinder was the most important mission to Mars since the Viking landings in 1976. Pathfinder cost only one-fifteenth of NASA's expenditures for Viking, and it demonstrated that a relatively small and inexpensive planetary project could be completed successfully, even one that involved such new techniques as air-bag-protected touchdown of the spacecraft and automated obstacle avoidance by the rover. Pathfinder returned to Earth more than 2.5 billion bits of information, including more than 16,000 images from the lander and 550 images from the rover. By comparing the data from the Viking mission with those from Pathfinder, scientists were able to determine precisely how Mars wobbled as it rotated. In addition to the detailed information the mission provided on surface morphology, petrology, geology, geochemistry, and meteorology, Pathfinder helped to buttress the theories of planetary astronomers that, in its past, Mars had been warm and wet, with substantial liquid water existing on its surface beneath a thicker atmosphere than at present.

The Pathfinder mission was also very popular with the public. During the first month of the mission's Martian explorations, the Pathfinder Web site generated 566 million hits. Some NASA officials were displeased by all the publicity surrounding Pathfinder, however, because they felt it diminished the prestige of the expensive space shuttle program. Indeed, scientists such as physicist Robert Park urged the abandonment of the shuttle in favor of more Pathfinder-like missions. Despite such disagreements over the future of the manned space program, most scientists agreed that Pathfinder had advanced knowledge of Mars in many significant ways and had set the standard for twenty-first century planetary explorations.

—*Robert J. Paradowski*

## FURTHER READING

Croswell, Ken. *Magnificent Mars*. New York: Free Press, 2003. Provides an accessible and beautifully illustrated synthesis of the new knowledge acquired of Mars by various missions, including Pathfinder. Structured around the four ancient elements of earth, air, fire, and water. Includes glossary, suggestions for further reading, and index.

Goldsmith, Donald. *The Hunt for Life on Mars*. New York: E. P. Dutton, 1997. Written before the Pathfinder mission, this work only anticipates what might be found to settle the centuries-old debate about whether life now exists or has ever existed on Mars. Includes glossary, suggestions for further reading, and index.

Hartmann, William K. *A Traveler's Guide to Mars: The Mysterious Landscapes of the Red Planet*. New York: Workman, 2003. Survey of the "new Mars" supplies for general readers an accurate, attractively illustrated, and comprehensive account of Mars as seen through the data collected by vicarious visitors such as Pathfinder. Includes glossary, bibliography, and index.

Tokano, Tetsuya, ed. *Water on Mars and Life*. New York: Springer-Verlag, 2005. Collection of essays by experts in their respective fields surveys advances in research concerning water on Mars. Some authors explore the astrobiological implications of new data and discoveries. Includes maps, individual chapter bibliographies, and index.

**SEE ALSO:** Apr. 19, 1971: Russians Launch the Salyut Space Station; May 19, 1971-Mar., 1972: Mars 2 Is the First Spacecraft to Impact Mars; May 30, 1971-Oct. 27, 1972: Mariner 9 Is the First Spacecraft to Or-

bit Another Planet; Mar. 2, 1972-Jan. 22, 2003: Pioneer 10 Explores Jupiter and the Outer Planets; May 14, 1973-Feb. 8, 1974: Skylab Inaugurates a New Era of Space Research; Nov. 3, 1973-Mar. 24, 1975: Mariner 10 Uses the Gravitational Pull of One Planet to Reach Another; Oct. 22, 1975: Soviet Venera Spacecraft Transmit the First Pictures from the Surface of Venus; July 20-Sept. 3, 1976: Viking Spacecraft Send Photographs to Earth from Mars; Aug. 20, 1977-Oct. 2, 1989: Voyagers 1 and 2 Explore the Outer Planets; Mar. 4-7, 1979: First Ring Around Jupiter Is Discovered; 1982-1989: Astronomers Discover an Unusual Ring System of Planet Neptune; Mar. 8, 1986: Space Probes Begin Examination of Comet Halley.

## July 15, 1997
# MURDER OF GIANNI VERSACE

*When designer Gianni Versace was murdered in front of his Miami Beach mansion, many in the general public as well as celebrities and those in the fashion world reacted emotionally to the senseless crime.*

**LOCALE:** Miami Beach, Florida
**CATEGORY:** Crime and scandal

**KEY FIGURES**
*Gianni Versace* (1946-1997), Italian fashion designer and founder of an international fashion empire
*Andrew Cunanan* (1969-1997), young Californian who committed several murders, including Versace's

**SUMMARY OF EVENT**
Gianni Versace had reached the pinnacle of success as a couturier and lived a life that bordered on the fantastic. In contrast, Andrew Cunanan survived by deceit in a pathetic world of fantasy that he had invented. These opposite forces collided on July 15, 1997, when Cunanan shot Versace twice in the back of the head and left him to die on the steps of his palatial home Casa Casuarina in Miami, Florida. The killer escaped, setting off a massive manhunt, then committed suicide when cornered on July 23. Whether the two men had ever met before that violent morning remained a mystery. Some said they knew each other, but Versace's friends and family denied it.

When the news of Versace's death flashed around the world, it was as though a king or a president, someone with great power and influence over the fate of millions, had been assassinated. In fact, the press employed such metaphors: One Italian newspaper called Versace a

"prince," and other reports referred to him as "king of couture," "emperor of dreams," and "fashion czar." The events received widespread television coverage, with cameras repeatedly focusing on the bloodstained steps of what grim-faced reporters called a "palazzo," where mourners gathered to pay respects and to leave flowers. One admirer dipped a Versace advertisement into the designer's blood for a keepsake.

Images of the man crowned the "king of fashion" standing beside celebrities ranging from Elton John to Madonna to Princess Diana to Sylvester Stallone were recycled for print and television. Shoppers the world over snatched up merchandise with the Versace name on it. Ten minutes after the story of Versace's murder broke, Christopher Mason completed negotiations for a contract with Little, Brown & Co. to write the designer's biography. Many people had likely never heard of Versace before, and most had never donned one of his gowns or worn the underwear he designed, or slept on his sheets or dried off on his towels, but in the days after the murder he became a household name, a ubiquitous presence through death.

Being a celebrity has its downside, and immediately rumors spread. Reviving earlier, unsustained accusations that the Versace empire had connections with organized crime, those given to belief in conspiracy saw his death as a Mafia hit. After treatment for a rare ear cancer in 1996, Versace had not fully recovered his vitality, which led some to speculate he suffered from acquired immunodeficiency syndrome (AIDS). Others questioned the financial well-being of Versace's billion-dollar company, which was expected to go public in 1998 after being placed on an austerity budget. That Versace had never hidden his homosexuality gave rise to suspicions about what role his personal relations had played in the murder.

Then the police discovered in a nearby parking garage a stolen pickup truck, which led to the assumed identity of the killer, Andrew Cunanan. The truck, which contained Cunanan's passport and other personal items, was owned by William Reese, who had been murdered on May 9 in Pennsville, New Jersey. As the story unfolded, a curious world learned that Cunanan was already wanted by the Federal Bureau of Investigation (FBI) for a string of murders, including those of two acquaintances, Jeffrey Trail on April 29 and David Madson on May 3, both in Minnesota.

In Chicago, on May 4, Cunanan murdered a wealthy seventy-two-year-old real estate developer, Lee Miglin, whom he apparently had not known beforehand. He stole his victim's Lexus, which was found in New Jersey near the dead Reese, a cemetery caretaker and another apparent stranger to Cunanan. Deserting the Lexus and setting off in Reese's pickup, Cunanan, according to the FBI, spent a few days in New York City's Greenwich Village before heading south in the pickup, stealing license plates in South Carolina along the way. In Miami Beach, he moved into an inexpensive hotel, the Normandy, on May 12, and spent the days unnoticed until he visited

Casa Casuarina with gun in hand. From the time he shot Versace until he committed suicide, Cunanan hid on a houseboat, where the police found him on July 23.

Ironically, in the days following the revelations about Cunanan, the media and public found him more intriguing than Versace himself, who had been buried quietly in Italy. Versace's life represented the classic success story: a boy from a middle-class family and a South Italy dressmaking shop rising to international fame. In contrast, Cunanan's life spelled failure. Described by his estranged mother as "a high-classed male prostitute," he did not even deserve that dubious title. He had reinvented himself at will, sometimes claiming to be the heir to a plantation fortune, always the sophisticate, the wealthy, eccentric party boy, the flagrant homosexual—an orientation he had proudly displayed even in high school. In truth, he came from a dysfunctional family, lived off older homosexual men, and, when this source of income failed, sold drugs.

Contradictory stories about Cunanan's life surfaced from friends and enemies. Some stressed his charm, whereas others revealed his darker side. A theory that he had AIDS and had set out on a mission of revenge against the homosexual community proved to be false once an autopsy was conducted.

Other issues arose. Law-enforcement agencies met with criticism from representatives of the gay and lesbian community, who said that officials had been lax in searching for Cunanan as long as he was murdering average gay men, but when he killed a celebrity they mobilized. The same critics took the press to task for its emphasis on Cunanan's sexuality. All the while, the general public relished the media's revelations about the exclusive and wealthy international gay community. During this period, one gay columnist pointedly observed that only a tiny segment of gays and lesbians lived such dashing lives; the rest were hardworking, ordinary, and often dull.

### SIGNIFICANCE

When considering a creative form as ephemeral as design, it is difficult to determine the impact of Versace's death on the fashion industry and the commerce that profits from it. Major couture magazines such as *Vogue* and *Elle* brought out their fall, 1997, issues, several hundred pages in

*Italian fashion designer Gianni Versace at his show in Paris in 1996.* (AP/Wide World Photos)

length, to introduce the new lines and to reveal what colors, cuts, lengths, and fabrics would be absolutely right for the months ahead. Tucked away amid page after page of glossy advertisements, some featuring Versace designs completed before his death, were tributes to the fallen "fashion czar." The writers knew him as a friend and praised him as much for his personal vitality and charm as for his contribution to the industry.

Beyond the tributes, these magazines affirmed that life goes on in the realms of high fashion. Versace's fascination with and dependence on popular culture, which he is credited with wedding to the fashion industry more so than any other designer, might have been his downfall as well. The adjective "popular" reflects what is generally accepted at the time, but along with changing times the icons of popular culture shift and vanish, sometimes forever, at other times to be revived. Versace was said to be proudest of his costume designs for the theater, and perhaps that work will be his most lasting.

Many speculated about the future of Versace's empire at the time of his death. Always a family affair, the business was shared by Gianni's brother Santo and his sister Donatella. Santo, a trained accountant and the company's chief executive officer, handled the business side efficiently, while Donatella, who was especially close to Gianni, served as vice president. Donatella emerged as a capable designer in her own right, and during her brother's illness and afterward she played a fuller role in the fashion matters of the business. Her American-born husband, Paul Beck, managed the company's advertising. Even Donatella's two young children, whom Gianni adored and considered his heirs, appeared in company advertising.

The general opinion about the business's future was that it would not be the same without the founder's rare genius but that it would remain solid. After all, world sales of Versace products and those manufactured under the Versace brand by licensed companies were expected to exceed $1 billion in 1997. The merchandise ranged from evening gowns to bath towels, each with the company's Medusa-head logo. Although most Versace products were sold at established, prestigious stores, the Versaces had also opened more than three hundred of their own elegant boutiques around the world.

Fashion experts as well as those outside the field who discussed the Versace murder tended to address two issues: the reasons so many people reacted to the designer's death as though Versace were a major world figure and the contribution that Versace made to society. Pundits explained endlessly that the age of celebrity, per-

sonality, and superstars, prompted in large part by mass-media coverage, keeps people from Indiana to Indonesia informed on the daily lives of the so-called rich and famous. Sometimes the reporting is intrusive, unfair, untrue, insensitive, and vulgar, but it nevertheless finds an audience, made up apparently of people chafing at their own limitations and wanting, at least vicariously, to know those who seemingly live fulfilled dreams. Some must imagine themselves wearing one-of-a-kind gowns and attending theatrical openings, charity balls, fashion shows like the ones Versace staged—the famed "frock and rock" concerts, and all such chic gatherings.

Even Versace's open homosexuality and appreciation of handsome young men added to the mystique. After all, his work was layered with sexuality in its multiple forms and yearnings. Versace understood the longings of ordinary folk and, at least in the public's eye, constructed his private life to border on the fantastic. At the same time, he managed to attach his personal glamour to the merchandise he was selling, so that the designer and the designed became one and the same.

Versace knew that sex intrigues and fascinates—and he understood that sex sells. In a *New Yorker* article titled "The Emperor of Dreams," based on interviews with Versace and published shortly after his death, Andrea Lee quoted the curator of the Costume Institute at the Metropolitan Museum of Art, Richard Martin, who summed up the way Versace brought together what Lee called "the raw energy of street culture and the sumptuous tradition of high fashion":

> The street was in a sense plundered by fashion in the second half of the twentieth century, but there is one isolated figure standing on the street corner, and that, of course, is the prostitute. That's the person Versace made fashion. He looked at prostitute style and made it high style in the eighties. I think of him as the great post-Freudian designer—one who had no guilt whatsoever. He created things about sensuality and sexuality. It was all unabashed.

What Versace gave to the world and what it lost through his death cannot be defined in concrete terms. He left no memorable works of art behind, but for a while he helped people set inhibitions aside, embrace life to its fullest, and appreciate elegance—if only in their imaginations. Versace was not just "the emperor of dreams" but also the merchant of dreams. A grim world can always use such a merchant to sell glamour.

*—Robert L. Ross*

1997

## FURTHER READING

"Facing Death." *Newsweek*, July 28, 1997, 20-30. Provides a brief biography of Cunanan, who is called "a great and gaudy pretender," charts his murderous cross-country spree, and theorizes on what motivated him. A sideline sketch within the main text, "Glamour After Dark" by Richard Alleman, examines the South Beach elite homosexual scene, what he calls the "A-gays"— a group that Cunanan aspired, but failed, to join.

Lee, Andrea. "The Emperor of Dreams." *The New Yorker*, July 28, 1997, 42-53. Article based on a series of interviews with Versace conducted in various parts of the world was adjusted to reflect his death two weeks before it was published. Offers an insightful look into Versace's personality as well as his work and provides extensive information on the his company/family operation.

Martin, Richard. *Gianni Versace*. New York: Harry N. Abrams, 1998. Richly illustrated catalog published in conjunction with an exhibition of the designer's work at New York's Metropolitan Museum of Art. Includes historical and analytic discussion of Versace's place in fashion.

Orth, Maureen. *Vulgar Favors: Andrew Cunanan, Gianni Versace, and the Largest Failed Manhunt in U.S. History*. New York: Dell, 1999. Focuses on Versace's killer and his life leading up to the crime. Sheds light on how the designer's celebrity status influenced the investigation of his murder.

Wintour, Anna. "Gianni Versace: A Remembrance." *Vogue*, September, 1997, 628-629. Editor of *Vogue* recalls her friendship with the designer and explains how he turned fashion into entertainment. Provides another look at Versace, both personal and professional, from the viewpoint of a friend and colleague.

**SEE ALSO:** 1974-1976: Punk's Antifashion Style First Appears; 1980's: Madonna Revolutionizes Popular Fashion; Dec. 8, 1980: Assassination of John Lennon; Aug. 31, 1997: Princess Diana Dies in a Car Crash.

## August 31, 1997
# PRINCESS DIANA DIES IN A CAR CRASH

*Princess Diana, former wife of Great Britain's Prince Charles, was fatally injured when the car she was riding in crashed as the driver attempted to outrun pursuing press photographers. Her sudden death brought about a remarkable public outpouring of grief.*

**LOCALE:** Paris, France
**CATEGORY:** Crime and scandal

**KEY FIGURES**

*Diana, Princess of Wales* (1961-1997), Princess of Wales and former wife of Charles, Prince of Wales

*Charles, Prince of Wales* (b. 1948), Prince of Wales and Diana's former husband

*Elizabeth II* (b. 1926), Charles's mother and queen of England, r. beginning in 1952

*Tony Blair* (b. 1953), prime minister of the United Kingdom, 1997-2007

*Mohamed al-Fayed* (b. 1929), owner of Harrods department store in London and the Ritz Hotel in Paris

*Dodi al-Fayed* (1955-1997), Mohamed's son and Diana's fiancé

**SUMMARY OF EVENT**

On July 29, 1981, Lady Diana Spencer, who had celebrated her twentieth birthday less than a month earlier, married Charles, Prince of Wales and heir presumptive to the British throne, in a lavish ceremony at Saint Paul's Cathedral that was televised and viewed by an estimated 750 million people around the world. From then on, she was known formally as Diana, Princess of Wales, and informally as Princess Diana.

On July 21, 1982, Diana gave birth to Prince William, and two years later, on September 15, 1984, to Prince Harry. The princes are second and third in the line of succession to the British throne, respectively, after their father, Prince Charles.

Diana, having discovered that Charles was engaged in an extramarital affair with Camilla Parker Bowles, and suffering from the constant and extreme lack of privacy associated with her status as the glamorous wife of the heir to Britain's throne, spoke publicly about her marriage problems. On August 28, 1996, Diana and Charles divorced. Queen Elizabeth II reluctantly ruled that Diana could retain her titles, including that of Princess of Wales, but that she could no longer be referred to as Her Royal Highness.

*The coffin of Diana, Princess of Wales, is carried inside London's Westminster Abbey on September 6, 1997.* (AP/Wide World Photos)

In the year following her divorce, Diana immersed herself in humanitarian causes and was often in the public eye. She was constantly pursued by hordes of press photographers, or paparazzi, who could make hundreds of thousands of dollars by selling pictures of the princess to the local and international media. Diana found refuge from such pressures aboard the private yachts where she spent much of her last summer, first cruising the Mediterranean with Rosa Monckton and a crew of three aboard the *Della Grazia*, then aboard business mogul Mohamed al-Fayed's 195-foot yacht, *Jonikal*, with its crew of sixteen. With her on the *Jonikal* was Fayed's playboy son, Dodi al-Fayed. Dodi had planned to marry model Kelly Fisher on August 9, 1997, but Diana and Dodi apparently fell in love.

When the cruise ended, the pair flew from southern France to Paris. Pursued by paparazzi, they were driven away from Le Bourget Airport at such a high speed that Diana warned that someone might get hurt. The couple's driver, Philippe Dourneau, finally evaded the paparazzi and drove Dodi and Diana to Villa Windsor, the former home of Queen Elizabeth's uncle, King Edward VIII, a property now owned by Mohamed al-Fayed.

After forty minutes at Villa Windsor, the couple continued to the Ritz, where Diana occupied the Imperial Suite. Dodi had purchased a $205,000 diamond ring, which he intended to give to Diana later in the evening at his ten-room apartment on the rue Arsène-Houssaye. They now retired to that apartment, where Diana dressed for dinner at Chez Benoît. They left Dodi's apartment at 9:30. They intended to return and spend the night there, and Dodi was expected to propose marriage to Diana at that time.

The flood of paparazzi that awaited them at Chez Benoît discouraged the pair from dining there, so they retreated to the Ritz for dinner. When the stares of other diners unnerved them, they decided to head to Diana's suite for a private meal. Making every effort to avoid the waiting paparazzi, Diana and Dodi left the Ritz through a back entrance, but some photographers were already there.

At precisely 12:20 on the morning of August 31, 1997, the couple left the Ritz in a black Mercedes driven by Henri Paul, who was later determined to have been intoxicated. Trevor Rees-Jones, Dodi's longtime bodyguard, occupied the front passenger seat.

The Mercedes, pursued by photographers in automobiles and on motorcycles, set off hurriedly. Paul stopped for a traffic light, but, presumably at Dodi's urging, he then shot through it, heading for Dodi's apartment. It has been estimated that when the car emerged from the first of two tunnels, its speed was eighty miles per hour. It then entered the Alma Tunnel, going so fast that one witness described the Mercedes as almost flying. At this point, Rees-Jones reportedly buckled his seat belt.

The car, now exceeding one hundred miles per hour, crashed into the tunnel's thirteenth pillar. The hood crumpled, and Henri Paul and Dodi perished almost instantly. Rees-Jones was badly injured, his face virtually torn away and his tongue severed. Diana, thrown forward, lay on the car's floor, semiconscious and moaning. It took six minutes for an ambulance to arrive, whereupon Diana was given emergency treatment by paramedics for forty minutes before being transported to Pitié-Salpêtrière Hospital for immediate surgery. Bleeding internally, she could not be saved and was declared dead at four o'clock in the morning.

## SIGNIFICANCE

Diana's death marked a turning point for Great Britain's royals, who had already incurred the public's disdain for the aloofness they displayed toward the British people. Queen Elizabeth was wakened from sleep and informed of Diana's death. She was said to have wanted a small, private funeral for Diana on the grounds that she was not a royal by blood. She also reportedly did not want Charles to travel to Paris. Charles apparently persuaded the queen that there would be a public outcry if he did not make that trip. The queen relented, granting Charles permission to fly to France in a royal plane. He arrived there at five in the evening, and, accompanied by Diana's two sisters, went immediately to Pitié-Salpêtrière.

By contrast, Mohamed al-Fayed, who was informed at about one o'clock on the morning of August 31 of Dodi's death, flew to Paris immediately in his private jet, arriving there before Diana's death at four. He arranged for Dodi's body to be flown to England, along with Dodi and Diana's personal effects.

The queen initially refused to allow the flag at Balmoral, her residence at the time, to be flown at half-mast. (The flag over Buckingham Palace flies only when the reigning monarch is in residence. When Elizabeth returned to London for Diana's funeral, she had apparently instructed that the flag over Buckingham Palace fly at full mast. She also declined to make a formal statement immediately after Diana's death.)

A public that loved Diana greatly would not permit her funeral to be the private event that the queen had envisioned. Hundreds of thousands of mourners lined the streets outside Kensington Palace, Diana's London residence. Thousands of bouquets amassed outside the gates of both Kensington Palace and Buckingham Palace in the days that followed Diana's death. Conspiracy theories were expressed that labeled Diana's death an assassination, and as late as December, 2006, a survey in Britain concluded that one-third of those interviewed still believed such theories.

Tony Blair, who had become British prime minister shortly before Diana's death, convinced Queen Elizabeth to make herself more visible to the mourners, and to eulogize Diana publicly. Mourners who had assembled in public gave many signs expressing their displeasure with the queen—and with the royals in general. Yielding to public pressure, Elizabeth finally delivered a statement praising Diana, and stating that her priority at the time of her death had been to comfort her grieving grandsons. Many would argue that Diana's death and its aftermath served to soften the public demeanor of Britain's queen, who now seems more likely to register her concern for the public than was the case before the princess was killed.

—*R. Baird Shuman*

## FURTHER READING

Andersen, Christopher. *The Day Diana Died.* New York: William Morrow, 1998. Provides a detailed account of the events leading up to and following Diana's death.

King, Jon, and John Beveridge. *Princess Diana: The Hidden Evidence.* New York: S. P. I. Books, 2002. Presents material suggesting that Diana's death was not accidental but an assassination linked to a complex international conspiracy.

Simmons, Simone, with Ingrid Seward. *Diana: The Last Word.* New York: St. Martin's Press, 2005. An account by a clairvoyant who worked closely with Diana during the last five years of her life.

Smith, Sally Bedell. *Diana in Search of Herself: Portrait of a Troubled Princess.* New York: Times Books, 1999. Detailed work discusses Diana's life as Princess of Wales and paints Diana as insecure and lonely.

SEE ALSO: Mar. 25, 1976: Assassination of King Faisal; Dec. 8, 1980: Assassination of John Lennon; July 15, 1997: Murder of Gianni Versace.

## October 15, 1997
# CASSINI-HUYGENS PROBE IS LAUNCHED

*The Cassini-Huygens mission was designed to investigate Saturn's dynamic atmosphere as well as the planet's complex ring system, varied and numerous moons and moonlets, and gravity and magnetic fields. Particular attention was focused on Saturn's largest moon, Titan, a moon with a thick atmosphere and suspected lakes of cryogenic hydrocarbons; some scientists believed Titan to be representative of conditions on a primordial Earth.*

**LOCALE:** Cape Canaveral, Florida
**CATEGORIES:** Astronomy; spaceflight and aviation; science and technology

**KEY FIGURES**
*Robert Mitchell* (fl. late twentieth century), Jet Propulsion Laboratory program manager for the Cassini project
*Dennis L. Matson* (fl. late twentieth century), Jet Propulsion Laboratory Cassini project scientist
*Mark Dahl* (fl. late twentieth century), NASA headquarters Cassini program executive
*Jean-Pierre Lebreton* (b. 1949), Huygens mission manager and project scientist for the European Space Agency
*David Southwood* (b. 1945), science director for the European Space Agency

**SUMMARY OF EVENT**
The Pioneer 11, Voyager 1, and Voyager 2 flybys of Saturn in the late 1970's and early 1980's revealed a rich and diverse Saturnian system and sparked far more questions than the tantalizing data they provided could answer. The next step in understanding Saturn would be to place a spacecraft in orbit around the planet for a prolonged time and to make numerous close approaches to its moons, particularly Titan, while training a diverse suite of instruments on targets of interest. The proposal included a large orbiter called Cassini and a detachable probe called Huygens that would descend through Titan's atmosphere.

The orbiter was named for Giovanni Cassini, who in 1675 discovered a large gap in Saturn's rings that now bears his name. The probe was named after Christiaan Huygens, who in 1655 discovered Titan, thus furthering the understanding of the nature of Saturn's rings.

Cooperation and cost sharing were necessary in an era guided by the "faster, better, cheaper" philosophy of Daniel S. Goldin, the National Aeronautics and Space

Administration (NASA) administrator who promoted more space missions for less money. Cassini was too ambitious a mission to be completed any faster. It was more like the Galileo and Voyager projects than the Mars missions of the 1990's, a number of which failed miserably.

NASA collaborated with partners in the European Space Agency (ESA) and the Italian Space Agency (ISA). NASA provided the orbiter and launch services, ESA the Huygens probe, and ISA the spacecraft's high-gain antenna communications system.

The orbiter's mass was 2,150 kilograms, and the probe's was 350 kilograms; 3,120 kilograms of propellant were required for maneuvering and insertion into planetary orbit. Fully assembled, Cassini was 6.8 meters tall and 4 meters wide; it was outfitted with twelve scientific instruments: a plasma spectrometer, a cosmic dust analyzer, a composite infrared spectrometer, an ion and neutral mass spectrometer, an imaging science subsystem, a dual-technique magnetometer, a magnetospheric imaging instrument, a radio detection and ranging instrument, a radio and plasma wave science instrument, a radio science subsystem, an ultraviolet imaging spectrograph, and a visible and infrared mapping spectrometer. Electrical power to these and other essential spacecraft systems was provided by plutonium-fueled radioisotope thermoelectric generators capable of generating 628 watts.

The Huygens probe was outfitted with the Huygens Atmospheric Structure Instrument, a Doppler wind experiment, a descent imager/spectral radiometer, a gas chromatograph mass spectrometer, an aerosol collection and pyrolyser, and a surface-science package. These were powered by batteries with limited life once they were activated for descent through Titan's clouds.

Among primary Cassini objectives were analysis of the structure and behavior of Saturn's rings; determination of the geological history and composition of satellite surfaces; identification of the differences between extremely dark and light surface materials on Iapetus, one of Saturn's moons; investigation of the structure and dynamics of Saturn's magnetosphere; study of cloud-layer dynamics; observation of clouds and hazes on Titan; and characterization of Titan's surface.

Cassini was launched on October 15, 1997, from Cape Canaveral Air Force Station's Complex 40 atop a Titan IV-B/Centaur booster. Despite its boost from the Titan's Centaur, Cassini did not have enough energy to

1997

3057

*Artist's image of the Cassini-Huygens spacecraft orbiting Saturn.* (NASA)

head directly toward Saturn. Instead, the mission made use of gravitational encounters with Venus on April 26, 1998, and again on June 24, 1999, and with Earth on August 18, 1999, before heading toward the outer solar system. The spacecraft flew past the asteroid Masursky on January 23, 2000, and received a gravitational boost by flying close to Jupiter on December 30, 2000. The Jovian encounter phase produced twenty-six thousand images and generated a high-resolution global atlas of Jupiter superior to that of the Galileo spacecraft that spent years orbiting Jupiter.

A six-minute burn of Cassini's main engine on May 27, 2004, positioned the spacecraft for an encounter with the unusual moon Phoebe on June 11, and insertion into Saturn's orbit nineteen days later. Cassini images revealed a primordial world composed of a mixture of ices, rocky materials, and carbon compounds; this terrain reminded planetary scientists of Pluto and Neptune's moon Triton.

After the Cassini passed through the gap between Saturn's F and G rings on June 30, it changed its attitude so that the high-gain antenna pointed away from Earth and the main engine pointed along the velocity vector. Early after midnight on July 1, following a 96.4-minute retrograde propulsion burn, Cassini achieved orbit, having flown within 20,000 kilometers of Saturn's cloud tops. The next day, the orbiter at a distance of 339,000 kilometers, an initial encounter provided better views of Titan than were previously acquired.

On Christmas Day, 2004, the Huygens probe separated from the side of Cassini. It continued flying independently and intercepted Titan's upper atmosphere on January 14, 2005. Descent through the atmosphere to the surface took roughly 150 minutes. Data were collected on two spacecraft channels; however, a software error resulted in the loss of roughly half of the images collected by this unique probe. Cassini recorded the data coming from the probe and was meant to be collecting data from both of Huygens's data channels; it only listened to channel B. Huygens's data was picked up directly on a weak signal coming from Saturn by the Green Bank Telescope, helping to retrieve some of the information that might otherwise have been lost; also, there was a great deal of redundancy between channel A and channel B. Wind-speed data, however, were transmitted to Cassini only on channel A and were therefore lost. Huygens landed in Titan's Xanadu region near what was first believed to be a shoreline, and it survived briefly while sitting on the extremely cold surface. Counter to expectations, initial analysis of early Cassini data failed to locate any liquid hydrocarbons on Titan, puzzling the planetary scientists involved with the Cassini program.

This marked the end of perhaps the most dramatic portions of the Cassini mission, but over the next few years the orbiter performed numerous flybys of Titan at close range. For example, in 2007, Cassini would use its radar to map the surface of this mysterious and intriguing moon during seventeen separate close encounters.

## SIGNIFICANCE

The planet Saturn was first explored at close range by flyby spacecraft that collected data and photographs during close approach, encounter, and postencounter periods. The Pioneer 11 spacecraft was targeted to encounter Jupiter in late 1974 in such a way that it would come into close proximity of Saturn in 1979. Voyager 1 and Voyager 2, carrying far more sophisticated instruments and camera systems, flew through Saturn's complex family of rings and moons in 1980 and 1981, respectively. These early looks at Saturn's rich diversity of rings, moons, and atmospheric dynamics led to the approval in 1982 of an orbiting spacecraft dedicated to prolonged investigations. Given the name Cassini, this spacecraft became the most complex and expensive ($3.26 billion) interplanetary probe developed by the time of its launch; indeed, in light of NASA's shift toward the "faster, better, cheaper" philosophy, Cassini was the last American tour de force interplanetary probe of its kind in the twentieth century.

The Cassini mission was approved for four years of operation within the Saturn system, with the possibility for mission extensions. In 2006, Cassini data and imagery provided strong evidence that Saturn's moon Enceladus may possess water reservoirs that erupt in geyserlike fashion through the icy surface. A hurricane-like storm was detected near Saturn's south polar region. In the January, 2007, issue of *Nature*, radar imaging data were presented that for the first time definitively proved the existence of bodies of liquid methane on Titan's surface. Lake features—some dry, others partially filled, some showing evidence of having once been full in the past but currently displaying partial evaporation, and some full—ranged in scale from 3 to 70 kilometers across. More lakes were found in the northern hemisphere than the southern one, but a twenty-nine-year seasonal cycle was expected to alter the lakes as they fill with methane precipitation or obtain liquid methane from a saturated subsurface layer.

—*David G. Fisher*

## FURTHER READING

Harland, David M. *Cassini at Saturn: Huygens Results.* New York: Springer-Praxis, 2007. Provides a thorough examination of data returned from the Huygens probe's encounter with Titan's atmosphere and surface.

_____. *Mission to Saturn: Cassini and the Huygens Probe.* New York: Springer-Praxis, 2002. Written prior to the arrival of Cassini at Saturn, this previews the spacecraft's mission.

Hartmann, William K. *Moons and Planets.* 5th ed. Belmont, Calif.: Brooks/Cole, 2005. A planetary-science textbook suitable for high school and college students; includes Cassini data and imagery. Also suitable for the general reader.

SEE ALSO: Jan. 6, 1998-July 31, 1999: Lunar Prospector Mission; Oct. 24, 1998: Deep Space 1 Is Launched; Dec. 11, 1998-Jan. 3, 1999: Mars Climate Orbiter and Mars Polar Lander Are Launched and Lost; July 23, 1999: NASA Launches the Chandra X-Ray Observatory; Feb. 14, 2000: Near Earth Asteroid Rendezvous Spacecraft Orbits a Small Body; June 20, 2000: Scientists Release Evidence of Water on Mars.

1997

## November 17, 1997
# TEMPLE OF HATSHEPSUT MASSACRE

*Egypt's tourism industry, an important source of income for the nation, was severely affected after sixty-two people were killed by Islamic militants outside the Temple of Hatshepsut, a popular tourist destination located in Luxor.*

**ALSO KNOWN AS:** Luxor Temple Massacre
**LOCALE:** Luxor, Egypt
**CATEGORY:** Terrorism, atrocities, and war crimes

**KEY FIGURES**

*Hatshepsut* (c. 1525 B.C.E.-c. 1482 B.C.E.), sixth pharaoh of the Eighteenth Dynasty, r. c. 1503-1482 B.C.E.
*Midhat Muhammad Abd al-Rahman* (d. 1997), one of the Islamic militants who participated in the attacks
*Hosnī Mubārak* (b. 1928), president of Egypt beginning in 1981

**SUMMARY OF EVENT**

On the morning of November 17, 1997, terrorists armed with knifes and automatic weapons massacred sixty-two visitors who stood on the terrace of one of Egypt's top tourist attractions, the mortuary temple of Hatshepsut. The spectacular temple is located at the archaeological site of Deir el-Bahri, near Luxor in the Valley of the Kings. Hatshepsut was the sixth pharaoh of the Eighteenth Dynasty and was one of only six women to rule ancient Egypt. Hatshepsut commissioned several large-scale building projects to celebrate her rule, and Hatshepsut's mortuary temple, partly carved into a limestone cliff, is considered the finest of them all. The temple draws visitors from around the globe. The attack captured international headlines because of its savage nature and the large number of foreign visitors that were involved. The assailants, all of whom were killed in the aftermath, were members of the terrorist group known as Gamaat Islamiya (the Islamic Group).

The attackers entered the temple complex after shooting the police guards stationed at the ticket booth. Eyewitnesses recounted how the armed men, wearing clothing similar to the winter uniforms of Egyptian police and security forces, descended on the Temple of Hatshepsut with no warning and sprayed the area with automatic gunfire. Most of the victims were trapped in the middle of the courtyard and fell instantly. The attackers then slit the throats of those who had fallen and continued to hunt down the tourists who tried to escape by hiding behind the large colonnades that line the back of the courtyard. The massacre was particularly gruesome and included disfigurement, disembowelment, and beheading.

The victims included three Egyptian police officers and one Egyptian tour guide; thirty-five Swiss citizens and a foreign resident of Switzerland; nine Japanese, including four couples on their honeymoons; six residents of Great Britain, including a mother and young child; four Germans; a Bulgarian; a Colombian; and a Frenchman. Several other tourists and employees of the site were wounded in the attack.

After a gun battle with Egyptian police, in which one of the terrorists was killed, the surviving assailants hijacked a tour bus that had dropped off Swiss visitors the previous hour at the base of the site. The terrorists forced the driver to take them to another place where they could continue their killing spree. In an effort to save lives, the driver, Hagag Nahas, drove around for almost an hour before being forced to stop at another tourist attraction. Nahas stopped near the entrance to the Valley of the Queens, near the Temple of Hatshepsut. Police caught up with the tourist bus and a gun battle ensued; one of the terrorists was killed. The remainder of the attackers fled into the mountains near the Valley of the Queens. Another exchange of gunfire took place between the terrorists and Egyptian police and military forces. It is unclear whether the remaining terrorists were killed in this battle or committed suicide; however, they were found dead at the scene. One of the dead was identified as Midhat Muhammad Abd al-Rahman, who had left Egypt in 1993 for military training in Pakistan and Sudan, where he became involved with Islamic Group leaders.

The militant fundamentalist organization al-Gama'a al-Islamiya claimed responsibility for the attack, and some pamphlets of this organization were found at the scene of the massacre. The group claimed that its representatives planned only to kidnap the tourists in order to secure the release of one of their spiritual leaders, Omar Abdel Rahman, who was serving a life sentence in the United States for masterminding the 1993 bombing of New York City's World Trade Center. However, eyewitnesses claim that the attackers showed no intentions of anything other than a wholesale slaughter. The terrorists did not attempt to take hostages; rather, they chased the victims, made them get down on their knees, and systematically executed them.

Luxor, approximately 310 miles south of Cairo, had been spared attacks from Islamic militants until this point. Tourist sites had often been targets in Egypt since Islamic extremist groups took up arms in 1992 in an effort to topple the government and create an Islamic state.

## SIGNIFICANCE

While visiting the Temple of Hatshepsut the day following the massacre, Egyptian President Hosnī Mubārak announced that stronger measures would be taken to protect foreign tourists. Security was increased at sites throughout Egypt. The country provided more armed police and soldiers to guard tourists, and there were more frequent helicopter patrols of the Nile River. For several months following the attacks, a curfew was imposed on Luxor; tour buses were not allowed south of Aswan. Those wanting to visit the famous Temple of Ramses II at Abu Simbel were forced to reach it by air. Mubārak called for an immediate crackdown on terrorism and fundamentalist Islamic groups operating within the country and fired Interior Minister General Hassan al-Alfi, replacing him with Major General Habib al-Adly. The Egyptian president also fired the police chief of Luxor and several other security officials on the grounds that they had failed to protect the tourist site and had ignored security warnings that sites in Luxor were potential terrorist targets.

The Temple of Hatshepsut Massacre severely damaged Egypt's tourist industry. The attack came at the start of the winter tourism season in Luxor, an area that is economically dependent on the tourist industry. Approximately two million visitors pass through Luxor each year. Immediately after the attack, governments and travel agencies issued travel warnings and began bringing back tourists from Egypt. Great Britain's largest travel company, Thomson Holidays, recalled thirteen hundred clients and canceled trips to the country for the remainder of November. Egypt's tourism industry, an integral revenue source for the country, had a long road to recovery.

—*Amanda J. Bahr-Evola*

## FURTHER READING

Anderson, Sean K., and Stephen Sloan, eds. *Historical Dictionary of Terrorism*. Lanham, Md.: Scarecrow Press, 2002. Includes a concise recap of the events of the Luxor Temple Massacre along with a discussion of the actions taken by Egypt following the attack.

Hawass, Zahi. *The Temple of Queen Hatshepsut at Deir El Bahari*. Cairo: American University in Cairo Press, 2003. Provides a history of the archaeology of the site and its role in international tourism. Filled with illustrations of the area.

Kushner, Harvey W. *Encyclopedia of Terrorism*. Thousand Oaks, Calif.: Sage, 2003. Particularly useful for information on the Islamic Group in Egypt and Omar Abdel Rahman. Does not include a specific entry on the Luxor Temple Massacre, but does include a thorough discussion of Egypt.

Mickolus, Edward F., and Susan L. Simmons. *Terrorism, 1996-2001: A Chronology*. Westport, Conn.: Greenwood Press, 2002. Detailed discussion of the at-

1997

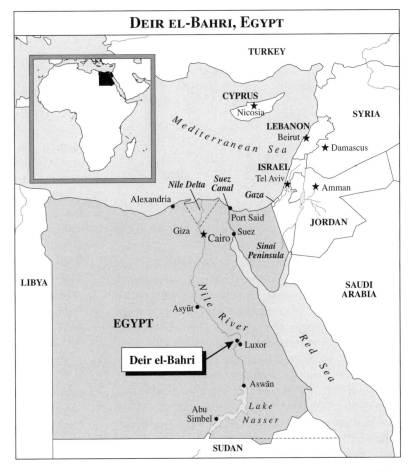

DEIR EL-BAHRI, EGYPT

tack. Includes eyewitness accounts and a follow-up of the trials and arrests relating to the attack.

Shanty, Frank, and Raymond Picquet, eds. *Encyclopedia of World Terrorism, 1962-2002.* Armonk, N.Y.: M. E. Sharpe, 2003. Provides comprehensive information on terrorism in Egypt. Includes a breakdown of the relationships among, and the history of, the three main Egyptian-led terrorist groups: the Islamic Group, Islamic Jihad, and al-Takfir w'al-Hijra. Also contains a chronology of terrorist incidents related to Egypt since 1995.

Stock, Raymond. "The Dust Devils of Luxor." *Massachusetts Review* 42 (Winter, 2001/2002): 689-695.

Interesting personal account of a visit to the site just after the attacks. Includes a history of the violence in Egypt and a discussion of the country's tourist industry. Also includes accounts by eyewitnesses and current residents of Luxor.

Tyldesley, Joyce A. *Hatchepsut: The Female Pharaoh.* New York: Penguin Books, 1998. Provides a detailed biography of the female pharaoh whose mortuary temple was the scene of the attack.

**SEE ALSO:** Feb. 26, 1993: World Trade Center Bombing; Aug. 7, 1998: Terrorists Bomb U.S. Embassies in East Africa.

## December 1-11, 1997
# KYOTO CONFERENCE ON GREENHOUSE GASES

*Representatives of more than 150 nations gathered in Kyoto, Japan, to negotiate a protocol committing signatory nations to reducing their production of greenhouse gases over the next fifteen years.*

**ALSO KNOWN AS:** Kyoto Protocol
**LOCALE:** Kyoto, Japan
**CATEGORIES:** Diplomacy and international relations; environmental issues; United Nations

**KEY FIGURES**

*Al Gore* (b. 1948), vice president of the United States, 1993-2001

*Stuart Eizenstat* (b. 1943), U.S. undersecretary of state, 1997-1999, and head of the U.S. delegation to the Kyoto conference

*George H. W. Bush* (b. 1924), president of the United States, 1989-1993

**SUMMARY OF EVENT**

Global warming, or climate change, became a major international issue in the last two decades of the twentieth century. There were several developments in the period since World War II that contributed to the emergence of global warming onto the world scene. Perhaps the most important of these was the development of mathematical modeling by scientists, which, by charting the changes in the global climate, particularly within recent decades, enabled climatologists to predict likely trends. Utilizing an ever-widening meteorological record, which through new techniques such as ice cores could be projected back millennia, scientists were able to establish patterns of climate change at least since the last major glacial period.

These scientific developments led, in 1988, to the establishment of the Intergovernmental Panel on Climate Change (IPCC), under the sponsorship of the United Nations and the World Meteorological Organization. The IPCC's mission was to bring together all scientific research that bore on the question of climate change. By 1990, the IPCC had come up with its first "assessment report" on the scientific research, embracing the work of some two thousand scientists by the end of the twentieth century. Reports began to come in of warming temperatures everywhere, increases in sea temperatures, and melting glaciers throughout the world—all data that seemed to confirm the hypothesis that the Earth was growing warmer than it had been for several centuries.

By 1992, many people who were dedicated to the health and welfare of the environment were expressing deep concern about the significance of the findings on climate change. Under the sponsorship of the United Nations, a meeting attended by representatives of 172 countries met in Rio de Janeiro, Brazil, in June of 1992, to express their concerns about the environment. Some 108 heads of state, including U.S. president George H. W. Bush, attended; Bush addressed the delegates and promised that the United States would continue to lead in developing policies that would protect the environment.

In 1995, the leading nations of the developed world agreed that a further international meeting was needed. The IPCC had produced a second assessment report on the scientific data that confirmed all the dire predictions of the first report. The Framework Convention on Climate Change, adopted by the United Nations in 1992,

*Signatories to the Kyoto Protocol of 1997 agreed to reduce emissions of six greenhouse gases from all sources, including industry.* (Jim West)

had been signed by the major developed nations, including those belonging to the European Union. This agreement, which entered into force in 1994, did not establish binding targets of reduced emissions of greenhouse gases, however. By 1997, there was general agreement that these targets were needed.

Meanwhile, most scientists had come to agree that the greenhouse gases produced by industrial activity in the developed world were largely responsible for the changes that were occurring in the Earth's climate. Accordingly, efforts were directed at ways to reduce greenhouse gas emissions, particularly carbon dioxide. In particular, the goal was the reduction of greenhouse gases to the level prevailing in 1990, and the question became primarily one of how to meet that goal. Most authorities agreed that the burning of fossil fuels (coal, oil, natural gas) was the chief cause of the rising temperatures that, if not somehow controlled, could result in disastrous environmental changes. Besides rising temperatures that could affect the way the environment was exploited by humankind, melting glaciers could result in a major rise in sea level. This, in turn, could inundate many coastal communities.

There were two major disagreements at the Kyoto Conference. The first was over the specific targets for greenhouse gas reductions that each nation would agree to adopt. The European nations advocated higher targets than did the United States, which was prepared to accept the emissions level of 1990 as a goal, while the Europeans wanted to reduce emissions up to 15 percent below that level. Further, the United States argued that unless the developing nations were included (chiefly China, India, and Brazil), industrial activity would simply move from the developed to the developing nations and do nothing to cut emissions worldwide. These disagreements to some extent reflected the different circumstances of Europe, where the collapse of the Soviet Union and the closing of many of its outmoded plants had already sharply cut emissions, as compared with the United States. Moreover, the developing nations argued that cutting emissions all over the world would merely prevent the economic development that Europe, Japan, and the United States had already achieved, making the developing nations bear the brunt of the movement to control emissions.

The United States stuck by its position, sending Vice President Al Gore to the meeting to support the argument. Further, the Americans supported a trading system under which those who had achieved substantial reductions would be given a credit that could be used by those who, for whatever reason, were unable to bring down their emissions. The disagreements led to breaking up the negotiations into small groups in which individual nations worked for their own advantage. Nevertheless, in the end, a measure of agreement was achieved when the protocol had been ratified by fifty-five countries that had been responsible for 55 percent of the emissions produced in 1990. Since the United States had produced more than 25 percent of all greenhouse gas emissions in 1990, its participation was highly important.

In the end, an agreement was reached in which various reduction targets (mostly around 5 percent below 1990 levels) were assigned to different countries. The U.S. proposal to allow trading reduction credits among different countries was adopted. However, the future of the agreement remained uncertain, because even though it had been signed, it still had to be ratified by the signatories. A U.S. senator who attended the meetings indicated that its prospects in the Senate were remote.

The agreement was subject to heavy criticism, especially by representatives of big industry. In the United States, these had grouped together in the Global Climate Coalition to oppose actions to reduce greenhouse gases. The coalition argued that the scientific evidence of global warming was not as overwhelming as the IPCC maintained, particularly because a portion of global warming is caused not by carbon dioxide but rather by water vapor in the upper atmosphere, so reducing carbon dioxide emissions would not avoid that climate-changing effect; and that the cost of any changes to control greenhouse gas emissions would have a decidedly negative effect on the economies of the developed world. By contrast, environmental organizations strongly supported the goals set by the protocol.

## SIGNIFICANCE

As it happened, further negotiations were required until enough nations had ratified the Kyoto Protocol, an especially arduous task when the change of political leadership in the United States in late 2000 led to its withdrawal from the agreement. However, tense negotiations in the early years of the twenty-first century led to its ratification by the requisite 55 percent of producers of greenhouse gas emissions in 1990.

The Kyoto Conference represented the full emergence of environmental issues on the international stage. Although the agreement was less than perfect, and although the United States refused to participate, it signaled widespread recognition that economic development has its dark side, one that could in the long run overwhelm its beneficiaries.

*—Nancy M. Gordon*

## FURTHER READING

Fisher, Dana. *National Governance and the Global Climate Change Regime*. Lanham, Md.: Rowman & Littlefield, 2004. Useful and compact summary of some aspects of the Kyoto process.

Gore, Al. *An Inconvenient Truth: The Planetary Emergency of Global Warming and What We Can Do About It*. Emmaus, Pa.: Rodale Press, 2006. Gore makes the science of global warming accessible. Includes graphs.

Ierland, Ekko C. van, Joyeeta Gupta, and Marcel T. J. Kok, eds. *Issues in International Climate Policy*. Northampton, Mass.: Edward Elgar, 2003. Collection of essays on the topic of climate policy from a large number of specialists. Valuable for readers interested in the details of international approaches to global warming.

Intergovernmental Panel on Climate Change. *Climate Change 1995*. New York: Cambridge University Press, 1996. A large volume, particularly focused on the economic and social effects of climate change.

Organization for Economic Cooperation and Development. *Global Warming: Economic Dimensions and Policy Responses*. Paris: Author, 1995. Compact and neat summary of the major issues affecting the Kyoto Protocol.

**SEE ALSO:** June 5-16, 1972: United Nations Holds an Environmental Conference in Stockholm; 1975: U.N. Global Environment Monitoring System Is Inaugurated; May 3, 1978: Sun Day Celebration Promotes Solar Energy; Oct. 12, 1988: Global ReLeaf Program Is Initiated; Nov., 1988: United Nations Creates a Panel to Study Climate Change; June 29, 1990: U.N. Agreement Protects Ozone Layer; June 3-14, 1992: Earth Summit Convenes in Rio de Janeiro.

## December 10, 1997
# LAND MINE ACTIVIST RECEIVES NOBEL PEACE PRIZE

*Jody Williams and the International Campaign to Ban Landmines received the Nobel Peace Prize in recognition of their efforts to remove antipersonnel land mines from around the world, destroy supplies of the land mines not yet deployed, and prevent additional production and distribution of that weapon. The recognition encouraged many reluctant world leaders to sign the 1997 Ottawa Treaty.*

**LOCALE:** Oslo, Norway
**CATEGORY:** Human rights

**KEY FIGURES**

*Jody Williams* (b. 1950), chief spokesperson for the International Campaign to Ban Landmines

*Robert Muller* (b. 1945), president of the Vietnam Veterans of America Foundation and peace activist

*Rae McGrath* (fl. late twentieth century), founder of the Mines Advisory Group and representative of the International Campaign to Ban Landmines

*Tun Channareth* (b. 1960), Cambodian anti-land mine activist and representative of the International Campaign to Ban Landmines

*Francis Sejersted* (b. 1936), chairman of the Nobel Prize Committee

*Patrick Leahy* (b. 1940), U.S. senator from Vermont

*Lloyd Axworthy* (b. 1939), Canadian foreign minister

*James P. McGovern* (b. 1959), U.S. representative from Massachusetts

**SUMMARY OF EVENT**

Throughout the world, military forces have defended their borders by using antitank and antipersonnel land mines, most of which are planted in Asian, African, Central American, Middle Eastern, and Eastern European countries. After conflicts ended, troops abandoned land mines, which were concealed by dirt, foliage, or water. Designed to injure enemy combatants, antipersonnel land mines often kill or maim innocent civilians, many of them children or farmers who accidentally trigger them.

Early efforts to clear land mines included the work of Mines Advisory Group, established by former British military officer Rae McGrath, and the Vietnam Veterans of America Foundation (VVAF), founded by Robert Muller, who traveled to Cambodia in 1991 to assist civilian land mine survivors in need of artificial limbs. In November, 1991, Muller consulted his friend Thomas Gebauer, who represented Medico International, a Frank-

furt, Germany, humanitarian organization, regarding aid for land mine survivors. They discussed seeking a worldwide land mine ban and decided to hire Jody Williams, who had experience with land mine relief work in El Salvador, to coordinate a campaign to secure global government support.

By October, 1992, the International Campaign to Ban Landmines (ICBL), established as a network of diverse nongovernmental organizations (NGOs), mostly humanitarian groups, formally initiated plans to secure a global treaty controlling land mine use. Meeting in New York City, the ICBL's first steering committee included members of the VVAF, Medico International, Mines Advisory Group, Human Rights Watch, Physicians for Human Rights, and Handicap International. Some representatives believed that the ban would not be achieved for at least three decades.

Supporters of the worldwide ban included U.S. senator Patrick Leahy, who encouraged Congress to pass a 1992 bill banning the export of U.S. land mines for one year. The bill became law, signed by President George H. W. Bush, and was extended in 1993 for three additional years. In 1995, Belgium and Norway became two of the first countries to ban the use of land mines. After meetings to discuss amending the 1980 Convention on Certain Conventional Weapons to include the regulation of land mines proved unsuccessful, Canadian foreign minister Lloyd Axworthy encouraged delegates to meet in Oslo, Norway, and Ottawa, Canada, in 1997 to draft and sign the Convention on the Prohibition of the Use, Stockpiling, Production and Transfer of Anti-Personnel Mines and on Their Destruction (also known as the Ottawa Treaty, or Mine Ban Treaty). U.S. president Bill Clinton, stating that Pentagon officials insisted that land mines were essential for military needs, refused to sign the treaty.

The ICBL expanded to include approximately 1,100 NGOs in sixty countries by 1997. Williams distributed information to members and governmental authorities and traveled to meet with world leaders. The ICBL benefited from the endorsement of its work by Britain's Princess Diana during trips to Angola and Bosnia. At that time, approximately 100 million land mines existed in sixty-eight countries, and an estimated 26,000 people died annually or were severely injured from exploding land mines.

In December, 1996, the ICBL Steering Committee

1997

3065

met in Brussels, Belgium, to determine that Williams should be named in any Nobel Peace Prize nominations of the ICBL, to receive the prize for its campaign. Massachusetts Democratic representative James P. McGovern, whom Williams had known in El Salvador, sent a letter to the Nobel Committee recommending the ICBL and Williams for the prize. Senator Leahy submitted a letter nominating the ICBL and Axworthy.

On October 10, 1997, the Norwegian Nobel Committee in Oslo stated that it would present the Nobel Peace Prize and $1 million jointly to Williams and the ICBL. Francis Sejersted, chairman of the Nobel Committee, stated that the committee hoped that honoring the anti-land mine activists would encourage countries to sign the Ottawa Treaty. He praised the activists for transforming the idea for banning land mines into effective results within several years. By forming a coalition, Williams and the ICBL represented how people could seek political change independently of the United Nations and other powerful bodies. World leaders congratulated Williams, who criticized President Clinton for not contacting her and for refusing to sign the treaty.

Williams joined ICBL representatives, Axworthy, and U.N. secretary-general Kofi Annan on December 3, 1997, for the Ottawa Treaty signing. Although forty signers needed for ratification were obtained, significant non-signers included the United States, Russia, India, China, Pakistan, Iran, and Iraq. Seven days later, Williams attended the Nobel Prize ceremony at Oslo City Hall. King Harald and Queen Sonja of Norway greeted Williams and ICBL representatives McGrath and Tun Channareth, a Cambodian who had lost both his legs in a land mine injury.

Eleven ICBL Steering Committee members observed the ceremony, including Muller. In his speech, Sejersted compared nuclear devices to land mines, emphasizing that land mines restricted movement and posed constant threats to harm people. He noted the irony that dynamite, invented by Alfred Nobel, is the explosive component of land mines.

Williams presented her Nobel lecture, describing the historical use of land mines and various stages of humanitarian work and conventions addressing problems related to that weapon. Discussing her experiences, she stressed the importance of governments assisting civilians. Williams expressed gratitude for the Nobel Prize but said that the land mine treaty was the ultimate prize.

Delivering the ICBL's Nobel lecture, McGrath described injuries his colleague Channareth had suffered and the dangers posed to land mine clearers. He asked that countries that had signed the Ottawa Convention rat-

*Nobel Peace Prize winners Jody Williams (left) and Tun Channareth pose with their awards at Oslo City Hall in December, 1997. Williams shared the honor with the International Campaign to Ban Landmines, represented by Channareth, a Cambodian who had lost both legs to a land mine injury. The recognition encouraged many world leaders to sign the Ottawa Treaty.* (AP/Wide World Photos)

ify it and that they destroy stockpiles. Concluding, he declared that the ICBL's Nobel Prize represented all land mine victims and relatives, mined communities, and clearers.

Accepting the Nobel Prize for the ICBL, Channareth did not speak in Oslo because the committee had been unable to arrange a Khmer translation. While he attended the Oslo ceremony, a representative at Phnom Penh read his speech, urging land mine bans and removal. Buddhist monks and land mine survivors lit candles and walked to that city's Independence Monument to honor the ICBL.

## SIGNIFICANCE

When the 1997 Nobel Peace Prize winners achieved worldwide cooperation to ban antipersonnel land mines, it was the first time since the post-World War I global agreement to restrict poison gas that a controversial weapon was banned. Williams and the ICBL emphasized how activists and organizations could unite to convince political leaders to endorse international accords.

Using money she was awarded with the Nobel Peace Prize, Williams ceased focusing on ICBL administration work in order to travel, pursuing international cooperation for antipersonnel land mine removal. Her primary goal was to convince leaders to commit legally to a land mine ban by accepting and ratifying the Ottawa Treaty. Williams's Nobel Prize spurred Japanese foreign minister Keizo Obuchi to sign the treaty. Williams also served as senior editor of *Landmine Monitor Report*.

The ICBL and Williams demonstrated how communications technology proved valuable in connecting activists expeditiously. Their efforts had a socioeconomic impact on agricultural yields from cleared fields in addition to business profits, as routes to markets were made safer. Their work influenced some manufacturers, including Motorola and Thiokol Corporation, to stop contributing to the production of antipersonnel land mines. By 1998, nineteen of forty-seven U.S. companies involved in the manufacture of antipersonnel mines agreed to renounce any involvement in their production. Manufacturers in China, Russia, and North Korea continued to produce and distribute mines. By 2007, 155 countries had signed the Ottawa Treaty, with 153 ratifying it.

—*Elizabeth D. Schafer*

## FURTHER READING

Cameron, Maxwell A., Robert J. Lawson, and Brian W. Tomlin, eds. *To Walk Without Fear: The Global Movement to Ban Landmines*. New York: Oxford University Press, 1998. Chapters written by Williams, Axworthy, and other notable anti-land mine activists. Photographs.

DeChaine, D. Robert. *Global Humanitarianism: NGOs and the Crafting of Community*. Lanham, Md.: Lexington Books, 2005. Sections featuring the ICBL and Doctors Without Borders evaluate international approaches for developing programs to assist civilians affected by war.

Hopkins, Jeffrey, ed. *The Art of Peace: Nobel Laureates Discuss Human Rights, Conflict and Reconciliation*. Ithaca, N.Y.: Snow Lion Publications, 2000. Chapters feature Williams and Muller, whose commentaries at a 1998 conference on humanitarian work are also included in other laureates' sections.

Matthew, Richard A., Bryan McDonald, and Kenneth R. Rutherford, eds. *Landmines and Human Security: International Politics and War's Hidden Legacy*. Albany: State University of New York Press, 2004. Collection on land mines features forewords by Queen Noor, Lloyd Axworthy, Heather Mills McCartney and Paul McCartney, and Senator Patrick Leahy. Includes a chapter by Williams that describes her efforts to achieve effective global coooperation for humanitarian goals and offers practical advice.

Roberts, Shawn, and Jody Williams. *After the Guns Fall Silent: The Enduring Legacy of Landmines*. Washington, D.C.: Vietnam Veterans of America Foundation, 1995. Comprehensive guide to areas where land mines were concentrated during the ICBL's initial work. Appendixes, figures, bibliography.

SEE ALSO: Dec. 10, 1975: Sakharov Is Awarded the Nobel Peace Prize; Dec. 10, 1977: Amnesty International Is Awarded the Nobel Peace Prize; Oct., 1983: Europeans Demonstrate Against Nuclear Weapons; Dec. 10, 1987: Arias Sánchez Receives the Nobel Peace Prize; Sept., 1989: Vietnamese Troops Withdraw from Cambodia; Feb. 26, 1990: Soviet Troops Withdraw from Czechoslovakia; Dec. 16, 1992: U.N. Security Council Brokers Peace in Mozambique.

1997

## December 16, 1997
# FIRST CASES OF AVIAN FLU ARE REPORTED

*The avian influenza A (H5N1) strain was isolated from birds in South Africa in 1961, but in May, 1997, it directly passed from birds to humans for the first time when a three-year-old boy died of respiratory failure in Hong Kong. The strain has the potential to mutate into a form more readily passed among humans, which could lead to a devastating human pandemic.*

**ALSO KNOWN AS:** Avian influenza; bird flu
**LOCALE:** Hong Kong, China
**CATEGORY:** Health and medicine

**KEY FIGURES**

*Yi Guan* (b. 1962), director of the State Key Laboratory of Emerging Infectious Diseases at the University of Hong Kong
*Keiji Fukuda* (b. 1955), medical epidemiologist for the World Health Organization's Global Influenza Program
*Kennedy F. Shortridge* (b. 1942), microbiologist and professor emeritus at the University of Hong Kong
*Robert G. Webster* (b. 1932), microbiologist at St. Jude Children's Research Hospital

**SUMMARY OF EVENT**

Influenza pandemics occur when a new strain quickly appears, sickening and killing large numbers of people worldwide over several years. There have likely been ten to twenty human influenza pandemics that have traveled the globe in the last couple of centuries, but the 1918 pandemic was the most devastating, killing as many as fifty million people worldwide, most of whom were young adults (unlike seasonal influenza, which typically kills only the very young and elderly). The 1997 influenza outbreak in Hong Kong resulted in the hospitalization of eighteen people and the deaths of six individuals. Kennedy Shortridge, a microbiologist at the University of Hong Kong, advocated the prompt culling of all of Hong Kong's poultry in an effort to stop the virus from spreading, and no new cases were identified for six years.

Most new influenza strains originate in Asia, where millions live in close quarters with domestic animals. Wild birds harbor the virus and migrate to other places, and can spread the virus. Efforts to identify and study the new H5N1 strain were coordinated between Shortridge's team at the University of Hong Kong and Robert G. Webster and colleagues at St. Jude Children's Research Hospital.

In 2003, the strain appeared again when two family members visiting Hong Kong became ill, and one of them died. H5N1 was later identified in two tigers and leopards in a Thai zoo, where the animals had eaten infected chickens. Between December, 2003, and February, 2004, there were outbreaks of H5N1 in Vietnam, Thailand, Korea, Japan, Cambodia, Laos, Indonesia, and China. More than 100 million chickens either died or were destroyed. The World Health Organization (WHO) called these incidents the first stage of the outbreak.

The second stage was preceded in April, 2005, by the deaths of 6,345 wild fowl at Qinghai Lake in northwest China. Unlike domestic fowl, wild birds are not usually made ill by influenza strains. Concerns increased because migrating wild fowl can spread the disease by fecal-oral transmission through the water supply. By May, H5N1 was discovered in Indonesian pigs, and later, Chinese pigs—animals that facilitate gene exchange between avian and human influenza strains—raising concerns that there was an increased possibility of a mutant strain rapidly spreading to humans. By August, three people in Vietnam were infected and died, and birds in Siberia, Tibet, and Kazakhstan were infected. More humans died in Indonesia and Cambodia in September, in addition to outbreaks in birds and poultry in Mongolia, Romania, Turkey, Croatia, and the Greek island of Chios in October.

The WHO issued a stage 3 pandemic alert, applied when there are human infections with a new subtype but no human-to-human transmission (stages 4-6). Local governments and the WHO took measures to lower the risk of a pandemic by implementing active surveillance, immunizing healthy domestic birds, killing infected and exposed birds, and developing vaccinations and antiviral medications for people—difficult tasks, considering that influenza strains are constantly changing, as exemplified by the new strain identified in 1997.

Viruses consist of genetic material that is packaged into a protein shell called the capsid, or coat. Proteins also project from the virus and usually target the host's immune system. These proteins help the virus to enter the host cell and change more often than other viral components. Once inside the cell, the virus replicates itself with the host's machinery. Subtypes A, B, and C characterize the capsid types, and only influenza A and B can kill humans. Viral subtypes are also identified on the basis of the two proteins on the surface of the virus: hemagglutinin (HA) and neuraminidase (NA). There are sixteen known HA subtypes and nine known NA subtypes, and many combinations are possible. The H5N1 virus has an HA 5 protein and an NA 1 protein. All known subtypes of A infect birds, but not all subtypes infect birds and people.

Influenza is a challenging disease to anticipate because the virus is constantly changing. An accumulation of small mutations, known as antigenic drift, occurs in the influenza virus and is not likely to cause problems. By contrast, antigenic shift creates new strains to which individuals may not be resistant. The director of the State Key Laboratory of Emerging Infectious Diseases at the University of Hong Kong, Yi Guan, and colleagues noted that from July, 2005, to June, 2006, the proportion of infected ducks, geese, and chickens increased from 0.9 to 2.4 percent, indicating that influenza would be hard to eradicate in domestic birds. They also discovered a new dominant strain called the Fujian strain, responsible for 95 percent of samples examined from April to June, 2006. The hemagglutinin strain from some human cases in China also belonged to this strain, and similar strains were found in Hong Kong, Laos, and Malaysia. Chicken vaccines were ineffective against the Fujian strain.

## SIGNIFICANCE

Constant surveillance and, following outbreaks, quarantine of farms and destruction of exposed birds are the primary means of stopping the spread of the virus in birds. However, complete elimination of the virus is unlikely, given the crowded and unsanitary conditions of commercially raised, genetically identical chickens. In the United States, many species of live birds are slaughtered in metropolitan areas, but the U.S. Department of Agriculture (USDA) does not regulate these activities. Wild birds are monitored by the U.S. Geological Survey, the U.S. Fish and Wildlife Service, and the National Park Service, but many illegally imported wild birds still make it into the country. Domestic birds are tested by the Animal and Plant Health Inspection Service division of the USDA. The department made efforts to educate large poultry producers and urged farmers to report sick birds.

1997

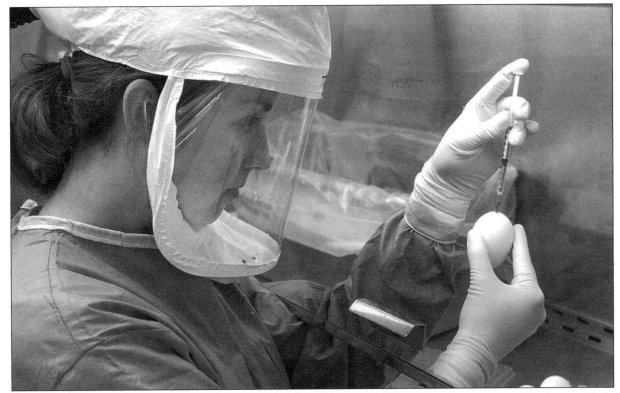

*A microbiologist at the U.S. Centers for Disease Control and Prevention inoculates ten-day-old embryonated hens' eggs with the H5N1 avian influenza virus as part of a study to investigate the pathogenicity and transmissibility of newly emerging bird flu viruses.* (Centers for Disease Control and Prevention)

The best protection against an avian influenza pandemic is vaccination. However, given the high mutation rate of the virus, vaccines stockpiled today are unlikely to protect against future pandemic strains. In addition, it may take many months to manufacture a new vaccine and to distribute it to billions of people worldwide. The United States established the National Strategy for Pandemic Influenza, and the government continued to work closely with the WHO—efforts coordinated by Keiji Fukuda, formerly of the Centers for Disease Control in Atlanta, Georgia. The WHO advocated countries to draft national pandemic preparedness plans and to hold drills.

By 2006, nine years after its discovery, the H5N1 strain of avian influenza had been identified in birds in almost fifty countries, with twenty-eight countries reporting since 2006. The WHO confirmed about two hundred human cases, with more than half of those leading to death. The general consensus in the scientific community is that the world is due for another pandemic. The H5N1 virus looks very similar to the 1918 virus, but the outbreaks of the H5N1 avian influenza that originated in Southeast Asia in mid-2003 and spread to other parts of the world were the largest and most virulent cases of influenza disease on record. The expense and global threat led to coordinated efforts worldwide, including the formation of the International Partnership on Avian and Pandemic Influenza during the U.N. General Assembly in September, 2005. The U.S. Department of State hosted the first meeting in October of that year; included were representatives from eighty-eight countries and organizations such as the WHO, the Food and Agricultural Organization, and the World Organization for Animal Health.

*—Joan C. Stevenson*

**FURTHER READING**

Davis, Mike. *The Monster at Our Door: The Global Threat of Avian Flu*. New York: Henry Holt, 2006. Gives the political context for why avian influenza may lead to a pandemic.

Greene, Jeffrey, with Karen Moline. *The Bird Flu Pandemic: Can It Happen? Will It Happen? How to Protect Yourself and Your Family If It Does*. New York: Thomas Dunne Books, 2006. Basic information on the virus and related pandemics, how the virus may spread to the United States, and practical tips for reducing one's risk before and during a pandemic. Excellent list of Web resources.

Normile, Dennis. "New H5N1 Strain Emerges in Southern China." *Science* 314 (November, 2006): 742. The latest information on avian flu is consistently reported in this journal and in *Nature*.

Sfakianos, Jeffrey N. *Avian Flu*. New York: Chelsea House, 2006. The biology of avian flu is explained clearly with an excellent glossary.

Siegel, Marc. *Bird Flu: Everything You Need to Know About the Next Pandemic*. Hoboken, N.J.: John Wiley & Sons, 2006. Argues that there is a lot of alarmist rhetoric about the virus that can be confronted with commonsense precautions. Good bibliography.

**SEE ALSO:** Sept. 8, 1976: Ebola Epidemic Kills First of Many in Africa; May, 1977: World Health Organization Sets a Goal of Health for All; Oct., 1977: Last Natural Case of Smallpox Occurs; Jan.-May, 1996: Meningitis Outbreak Proves Deadly in West Africa; Mar. 20, 1996: Britain Announces Human Cases of Mad Cow Disease; 1998: AIDS Devastates Africa.

## December 16, 1997
# MANDELA MAKES WAY FOR MBEKI

*When Thabo Mbeki took the role of head of the African National Congress, he and the party leadership continued the process of correcting the legacy of apartheid in South Africa.*

**LOCALE:** South Africa
**CATEGORIES:** Government and politics; social issues and reform

### KEY FIGURES

*Nelson Mandela* (b. 1918), president of the African National Congress and president of South Africa, 1994-1999
*Thabo Mbeki* (b. 1942), president of the African National Congress and president of South Africa beginning in 1999
*Oliver Tambo* (1917-1993), former secretary-general and former president of the African National Congress

### SUMMARY OF EVENT

On December 16, 1997, Nelson Mandela resigned as president of the African National Congress (ANC), choosing deputy president Thabo Mbeki as his successor. Later, during South Africa's 1999 national elections, the ANC won a landslide victory, earning itself a second term in a postapartheid country and Mbeki the role of South Africa's second multiracially elected leader. Noted for a less compromising attitude than Mandela's, Mbeki consolidated and expanded the ANC's control of the South African parliament. He faced challenges including those concerned with balancing new social and political ideas with social, political, and economic equity for the previously oppressed black underclass. As Mandela's chosen successor, Mbeki's political history and experience arguably made him an appropriate candidate to contend with South Africa's political challenges.

Mbeki's political interests began in his youth. Born into a politically active family, he was involved with the ANC Youth League, a wing of the African National Congress, and later saw his father jailed in 1964 along with Nelson Mandela for their political involvement with the ANC against the apartheid regime. The ANC was founded in 1912 as one of the first black political associations in South Africa. It represented a voice for black political union in the decades after the Boer Wars when white political powers were establishing their authority in the region. Later, the ANC became known for its ac-

tive opposition to the apartheid government that established itself during a 1948 national election in which only whites were allowed to vote. The elected apartheid government instituted a policy of racial segregation, which led to the economic, social, and political marginalization of nonwhites, particularly blacks, in South Africa.

In postapartheid South Africa, during Mandela's rule, the African National Congress faced the challenge of balancing South Africa's new democratic ideals with issues of economic, social, and political transformation for segments of the population previously marginalized. In 1997, when Mbeki took the role as head of the ANC, he and the party leadership were to continue the stabilization process in a bid to correct apartheid's impact. In 1999, after the ANC won its second term, Mbeki set out to achieve this transformation.

President Mbeki shifted the government's focus to economic growth, viewing this as key to South Africa's overall transformation. His intent was to bring increased economic power to the black majority in South Africa and to provide overall economic support to those who had difficulties accessing education, health care, housing, and a host of other needs. If these challenges were met, it was hoped that other socioeconomic problems—problems such as poverty and crime—would also be eliminated.

During the 1990's, high crime rates became a concern for the ruling government. In a postapartheid South Africa, it was necessary to address the key catalysts for criminal activity such as a lack of educational and economic opportunities. The end of apartheid saw the further marginalization of certain segments of society, including young people, some of whom shifted their activities from political violence against the previously oppressive regime to crime for profit. While these individuals no longer had an apartheid regime against which to fight, they were still left with the legacy of poverty and the vestiges of the oppressed.

Notwithstanding the link between poverty and crime, crime for profit was considered disruptive and criminal by a new government grappling with massive, necessary reforms and an international community eager to see the success of the postapartheid system. However, criminal activity continued to rise throughout Mbeki's rule, prompting the government to acknowledge that there was an immediate need for some basic services. In this vein, an affirmative action plan was put in place to provide basic services such as housing, health care, educa-

1997

tion, and even financial compensation for some families and victims of past injustices. Thus, Mbeki's government carried out concrete changes to improve conditions for the majority of the population who previously lacked such services. However, even with the provision of basic services, crime continued to increase, and concerns arose regarding police enforcement. For instance, as early as 1997, reports of abuse of suspects in police custody prompted the establishment of the Independent Complaints Directorate to investigate allegations of physical abuse and deaths of prisoners in custody.

In addition to rising crime, the government has dealt with other areas in need of reform. Mbeki faces a health care crisis as the rates of acquired immunodeficiency syndrome (AIDS) and human immunodeficiency virus (HIV) have reached epidemic proportions. The high rate of HIV/AIDS has resulted in a high mortality rate among adults, resulting in an increased number of orphaned children. The government must also contend with the fact that a South African woman of childbearing age is more likely to die from AIDS than from any other disease. HIV/AIDS has ravaged South Africa in terms of both economic and human costs.

Mbeki has faced criticism in the way he has approached the issue of HIV/AIDS. In assessing the severity of the situation, he has questioned whether the number of infected are in fact on the rise and whether there is indeed a link between HIV and AIDS. He has also suggested that the rise of AIDS in South Africa has been exaggerated by profit-motivated drug companies who sell antiviral medications. Mbeki's doubts about AIDS and his reluctance to declare a state of emergency points to what his critics describe as an uncompromising attitude. However, notwithstanding the challenges, Mbeki and the ANC continued to experience popularity at home. In April, 2004, the ANC won 70 percent of the popular vote during South Africa's third postapartheid elections. As reelected leader, Mbeki continues to focus on the changes he believes will bring real transformation to the country.

## SIGNIFICANCE

In focusing on economic reform, Thabo Mbeki has sought to transform South Africa from a fragile democracy and create political and social stability for the people. He is determined in particular to give power to the black majority, who were denied economic opportunities under apartheid. However, critics wonder whether his focus on economic growth has pushed aside numerous other issues in need of direct reform, such as policing and health care, particularly the infrastructure to deal with the HIV/AIDS crisis, which could have a significant effect on the nation's gross domestic product.

—*Esmorie Miller*

## FURTHER READING

Arnold, Guy. *The New South Africa*. New York: St. Martin's Press, 2000. Examines the postapartheid transformation and discusses the tasks facing the South African government. Includes bibliographic references and index.

Jacobs, Sean. *Thabo Mbeki's World: The Politics and Ideology of the South African President*. London: Zed Books, 2002. Offers an insightful glimpse into the South African leader's thinking. Includes bibliography and index.

Reynolds, Andrew, ed. *Election '99 South Africa: From Mandela to Mbeki*. New York: St. Martin's Press, 1999. Collection of essays highlights the continued success of the ANC as a political party. Includes bibliography.

Spence, J. E., ed. *After Mandela: The 1999 South African Elections*. London: Royal Institute of International Affairs, 1999. Collection of essays addresses Mandela's final handover of leadership of both the ANC and South Africa.

**SEE ALSO:** Feb. 11, 1990: Mandela Is Freed; 1995: South Africa Establishes a Truth and Reconciliation Commission; 1998: AIDS Devastates Africa.

**December 24, 1997**

# JAPANESE MAGNETIC TRAIN REACHES RECORD SPEED

*After a magnetically levitating train in Japan set a world record speed of 550 kilometers per hour, the Chinese and Germans followed up with trains that continued to break speed records.*

**ALSO KNOWN AS:** Maglev train

**LOCALE:** Japan

**CATEGORIES:** Engineering; transportation; science and technology

## SUMMARY OF EVENT

Trains that are propelled by electromagnetic force are called maglev trains (for magnetic levitation). With no wheels and no engine, these trains "float" on a magnetic field and can travel at astonishing rates of speed. As early as 1941, German engineers had devised the first patent for a train run by magnetic levitation.

On December 24, 1997, a land speed record was broken by a Japanese magnetic train that clocked 550 kilometers per hour (342 miles per hour) on an experimental track. The three-car train was unmanned, but an earlier sprint on December 12 achieved a record speed of 531 kilometers per hour (330 miles per hour) with passengers. The experimental track—the Yamanashi Maglev Test Line—became famous. The developers included Central Japan Railway Company (JR Central) and the Railway Technical Research Institute, whose scientists had been studying the technology at Yamanashi with intensity since 1962 and rapidly applied the idea to operational passenger lines. The project was nationally funded.

Maglev trains are usually propelled by a linear induction motor. Whereas normal trains are propelled by an engine, maglev trains are moved forward by the track itself, pulled, section by section, by the track's changing magnetic fields. The trains hover only 10 millimeters (about 0.4 inch) above the track. A significant advantage of maglev trains, aside from their astounding speed (even uphill), is that they are not in contact with a rail and thus do not generate friction. Regular trains touch the tracks, which causes wear on the trains' moving parts. Maglev trains, in contrast, do not require maintenance for such wear. One downside of maglev trains, however, is that they can run only on very costly magnetic tracks; because of this expense, there are few such trains in the world. Compared with regular trains, maglevs take more money to build but less money to maintain. They also start up very quickly: Shanghai's maglev train smoothly achieves 350 kilometers per hour (220 miles per hour) in two minutes. Passengers say the ride is very comfortable; it is also quiet, owing to specially designed windows.

Luggage on a maglev train is stowed in racks above the seats and between cabins. The Shanghai train can carry almost a thousand people at once and has nine compartments. Maglev trains meant to carry cargo can have all-cargo sections or can mix cargo with passenger sections. The trains are not slowed by their length or the weight of their load.

Because of wind resistance, maglev trains use as much energy as regular trains. Although they emit less air pollution directly, the energy to run them must still be created at another location that then incurs the pollution. Nevertheless, a maglev train consumes 25 percent of the energy that an aircraft would need for the same speed and capacity. In fact, the train's levitation uses less energy than its air conditioning. Further, while traveling, the train's batteries recharge themselves.

These unique trains rely on the track to get them to their destinations. Each train has superconducting magnets, and the sides of the track have coils. The track develops an electromagnetic propelling force. A substation provides an alternating current to the coils, thereby shifting the track's magnetic field. The train pulls forward when its magnets are attracted by the changing magnetic field. The coils repel the magnets on the train, and the train is pulled forward. The train stops by using aerodynamic brake panels. The Chinese experimented with making the trains more efficient by using high-temperature superconducting magnets, cooled by inexpensive liquid nitrogen. The Japanese maglev trains used low-temperature superconductors.

In developing a maglev train, there are a number of engineering issues to resolve. For instance, researchers must take into account the sharpest curve and the steepest hill on the route. They must consider how much space to put between the tracks, so that maglev trains can charge past each other without affecting each other. In addition, there are concerns over building and maintenance costs as well as noise-control features.

The building of the guideway for the Shanghai maglev train, which began in 2001, took on the discipline of a military project. Despite the tons of steel required and the intricate calculations and fittings, the project was finished in just over one and a half years. The Germans built the train, and the Chinese built the track. However, the two countries hoped to transfer the train technology to

China, forging a bond between the two countries.

## SIGNIFICANCE

A maglev train is a symbol that a country has "arrived" as a major technological contender in the world. Although the Shanghai train was initially unprofitable, it was a strong statement of China's wish to be a modern leader, and it demonstrated the manufacturing ingenuity of the Germans.

In the 1970's, the Japanese studied levitation, testing maglev vehicles in 1972 and 1975. By the late 1970's, inverted guideway and tunnel tests began at an early track called the Miyazaki Maglev Test Track in Miyazaki Prefecture. A U-shaped guideway was tested there in 1980, and later a two-car maglev was tested with passengers. By the end of that decade, the Japanese had experimented with substation crossovers, inverters, braking systems, and a traverser turnout. They ran three-car trains, and, in 1987, a manned two-car train reached a speed just over 400 kilometers per hour (about 250 miles per hour). In 1990, the Japanese began building the Yamanashi track, culminating in the record-breaking ride in 1997. Efforts evolved to focus on testing for maximum speeds.

In the fall of 2003 in China, Shanghai's maglev train, made in Germany, reached a top speed of 501 kilometers per hour (311 miles per hour), taking travelers from downtown to the airport—a distance of 30 kilometers (19 miles)—in about seven minutes. When the train made its debut, reporters referred to its first trip as a "flight," as if it were comparable to a supersonic jet plane. Japanese maglev trains, which are run remotely, have run as fast as 581 kilometers per hour (361 miles per hour)—a record speed set in 2003. Millions of Japanese each year travel between cities on these trains.

*—Jan Hall*

*The JR-Maglev train in Yamanashi, Japan, that clocked 550 kilometers per hour on December 24, 1997.* (Yosemite/CC-BY-SA2.5)

## FURTHER READING

Brennan, Richard P. *Levitating Trains and Kamikaze Genes*. Hoboken, N.J.: John Wiley & Sons, 1994. Explores future technology, from medical to weapons to engineering.

Hood, Christopher. *Shinkansen: From Bullet Train to Symbol of Modern Japan*. New York: Routledge, 2006. Although the Japanese *shinkansen* (bullet train) is not a maglev, it is a high-speed train. Hood shows why the Japanese are attached to their fast trains.

Lynch, Thomas, ed. *High Speed Rail in the U.S.* New York: Gordon & Breach, 1998. Shows the process of linking high-speed rail to other means of transportation and investigates whether high-speed rail in the United States is feasible.

Strohl, Mitchell P. *Europe's High Speed Trains*. Westport, Conn.: Praeger, 1993. Examination of Europe's train systems in the context of geography and economics.

Vranich, Joseph. *Derailed: What Went Wrong and What to Do About America's Passenger Trains*. New York: St. Martin's Press, 1997. Discussion of ways to improve the U.S. rail system by a former Amtrak official.

_____. *Supertrains: Solutions to American's Transportation Gridlock*. New York: St. Martin's Press, 1993. Makes the case for high-speed trains such as maglevs in the United States.

**SEE ALSO:** Jan. 21, 1976: Concorde Flies Passengers at Supersonic Speeds; May 6, 1994: Opening of the Channel Tunnel; Apr. 5, 1998: Opening of the World's Largest Suspension Bridge.

**December 31, 1997**
# MICROSOFT ACQUIRES HOTMAIL

*With Hotmail established as a popular, free e-mail service with almost nine million members, Microsoft moved to acquire the company and add it to its range of online services.*

**LOCALE:** Mountain View, California

**CATEGORIES:** Business and labor; trade and commerce; computers and computer science

## KEY FIGURES

*Sabeer Bhatia* (b. 1969), entrepreneur and cofounder of Hotmail who became its president and chief executive officer

*Bill Gates* (b. 1955), entrepreneur and cofounder of Microsoft Corporation

*Jack Smith* (b. 1968), entrepreneur and cofounder of Hotmail

*Steve Jurvetson* (b. 1967), partner in venture capitalist firm Draper Fisher Jurvetson, which financed Hotmail

## SUMMARY OF EVENT

One of the most successful start-up companies of the Internet boom, Hotmail was launched in Mountain View, California, on July 4, 1996, a date chosen to represent the product's ability to free its users from reliance on Internet service providers (ISPs). Hotmail was a free e-mail service that could be accessed through a Web browser. The rapidly expanding company was acquired at the end of 1997 by Microsoft Corporation in Microsoft's largest acquisition of the year.

Hotmail—originally HoTMaiL, to reference the Web markup language HTML—was established by entrepreneurs Sabeer Bhatia and Jack Smith, who were funded by the venture capital firm Draper Fisher Jurvetson. The firm's Steve Jurvetson was one of the strongest supporters of the enterprise. The firm also funded Four11, another free e-mail service that was purchased by Yahoo! for $94 million in the same three-month period as the Microsoft acquisition.

In their meeting with Jurvetson (their twenty-first meeting with venture capitalists), Bhatia and Smith had pitched an idea for Internet-based database software. Jurvetson was unimpressed by the overall idea. As the two entrepreneurs packed up the rest of the presentation, however, he asked what other ideas they had. They mentioned another idea involving a free, advertising-supported e-mail service that would be available over the World Wide Web. One week later, Jurvetson gave them $300,000, despite the lack of a business plan, and would continue to remain a major influence on the company.

The result of that collaboration was Hotmail, which Jurvetson would lead through five rounds of financing to become one of the Internet's first "killer applications," a program whose usefulness soon made it ubiquitous and capable of driving competing "apps" from the market rapidly and efficiently. It was originally run on the FreeBSD, a free operating system.

Hotmail expanded its user base with amazing speed, in part due to its viral marketing strategy. The company appended an advertisement for Hotmail to every outgoing e-mail sent through its service, thereby selling itself every time a person read a message from a Hotmail user. At the time, the major source of e-mail was the offerings supplied by the various ISPs, which were often unreliable, limited, or subject to other difficulties. By the end of 1997, the Hotmail service had acquired more than 8.5 million subscribers.

In the mid-1990's, Microsoft had come to realize that it needed to find new territory in which it could expand. The Internet, a place of rapidly evolving technology and flux, seemed the perfect new space in which to profit, and Microsoft began exploring the Web services and software already in place, with an aim to acquiring the companies and thus getting a preestablished Internet presence. In 1995, it launched a major online service provider, Microsoft Network (MSN), which was intended to be a direct competitor to the leader in the field, America Online. MSN rapidly became the umbrella under which the majority of Microsoft's Internet ventures were launched.

In its campaign to claim the Internet, Microsoft purchased WebTV for $425 million in 1997. Microsoft tacticians soon realized that Hotmail would form another vital part of their online offerings. Acquisition of the service would allow Microsoft to capture Hotmail's lead position by rebranding the product as its own. Later, in a similar strategy, Microsoft would introduce an instant messaging service.

The initial acquisition offer made to Hotmail's owners was $120 million in cash. However, the partners were advised not to take the offer but to hold onto their valuable and rapidly growing company. It was not until intense negotiations had taken place over a period of several weeks that the partners ended up settling for $400 million in Microsoft shares.

1997

Within one year after its acquisition and rebranding as MSN Hotmail, the Hotmail service had tripled in size; within another year, the company reported more than thirty million active members and supported seventeen languages, establishing Microsoft as a major presence in this segment of the online market.

In October, 1998, the U.S. Department of Justice filed a motion charging that Microsoft had forced computer makers to include its Internet Explorer with its popular Windows operating system. William Harris pointed to Microsoft's acquisition of Hotmail as an example of the corporation's monopolistic tendencies, testifying that the e-mail service had become "the default electronic mail system."

## SIGNIFICANCE

The acquisition of Hotmail signaled an important shift in Microsoft's strategy. In its early days, the company had worked to establish dominance over the desktop; by the mid-1990's, it had nearly unshakable control of the market as well as the emerging Internet. The technological innovations introduced by entrepreneurs eager to take advantage of the Internet represented a pool of income and talent that Microsoft wanted to co-opt as quickly and efficiently as possible. Rather than beginning from scratch and trying to catch up with advances in the field, the company looked for the leaders in this new arena and moved to acquire them as quickly as possible.

The acquisition of Hotmail demonstrated that a "trade sale" could be almost as lucrative as an initial public offering and started a trend in which many entrepreneurs and investors worked on building companies with an eye to selling them as quickly and as lucratively as possible. The acquisition also demonstrated how much Microsoft's innovation depends on competition. It was not until the appearance of Google's Gmail service almost a decade later that Microsoft began expanding Hotmail's features and storage space.

*—Cat Rambo*

## FURTHER READING

Auletta, Ken. *World War 3.0: Microsoft vs. the U.S. Government, and the Battle to Rule the Digital Age*. New York: Broadway Books, 2002. This discussion of the case against Microsoft uses Hotmail as an example of the company's monopolistic practices.

Cusumano, Michael. *Microsoft Secrets: How the World's Most Powerful Software Company Creates Technology, Shapes Markets, and Manages People*. New York: Free Press, 1998. Discussion of Microsoft business practices that uses Hotmail as an example of building the company through acquisitions.

Microsoft Corporation. *Inside Out: Microsoft—In Our Own Words*. New York: Warner Business Books, 2000. This commemoration of Microsoft's twenty-fifth anniversary looks at numerous aspects of the company from the viewpoint of its employees and includes several notes on Hotmail's acquisition and development.

Slater, Robert. *Microsoft Rebooted: How Bill Gates and Steve Ballmer Reinvented Their Company*. New York: Portfolio Hardcover, 2004. Discussion of how Gates and Ballmer reshaped their business strategy in order to take advantage of and establish control over the Internet.

Wallace, James. *Hard Drive: Bill Gates and the Making of the Microsoft Empire*. New York: Collins, 1993. Discusses Microsoft and its evolution in the years before the move to the Internet.

SEE ALSO: Aug. 12, 1981: IBM Introduces Its Personal Computer; Nov. 20, 1985: Microsoft Releases the Windows Operating System; Dec. 15, 1994: Release of Netscape Navigator 1.0; Mid-1990's: Rise of the Internet and the World Wide Web; May 18, 1998: United States Sues Microsoft; Sept. 7, 1998: Google Is Founded.